Counterterrorism Law

ASPEN CASEBOOK SERIES

Counterterrorism Law

Second Edition

Stephen Dycus
Professor of Law
Vermont Law School

William C. Banks
Director, Institute for National Security and Counterterrorism (INSCT)
Board of Advisors Distinguished Professor
Syracuse University

Peter Raven-Hansen
Glen Earl Weston Research Professor of Law
Co-director, National Security and U.S. Foreign Relations Law Program
George Washington University Law School

Wolters Kluwer
Law & Business

Printed in the United States of America.

1 2 3 4 5 6 7 8 9 0

ISBN 978-0-7355-9863-8

Library of Congress Cataloging-in-Publication Data

Dycus, Stephen.
    Counterterrorism law / Stephen Dycus, William C. Banks, Peter Raven-Hansen. — 2nd ed.
        p. cm.
    Includes bibliographical references and index.
    ISBN 978-0-7355-9863-8
1. Terrorism — United States. 2. Terrorism — United States — Prevention. 3. National security — Law and legislation — United States. 4. Intelligence service — Law and legislation — United States. 5. Terrorism — Prevention — International cooperation. 6. Terrorists.
7. Data mining. I. Banks, William C. II. Raven-Hansen, Peter, 1946- III. Title.
    KF9430.D93 2012
    345.73'02317 — dc23

                                                                          2011047635

SUSTAINABLE FORESTRY INITIATIVE

Certified Sourcing
www.sfiprogram.org
SFI-01234

SFI label applies to the text stock

About Wolters Kluwer Law & Business

Wolters Kluwer Law & Business is a leading global provider of intelligent information and digital solutions for legal and business professionals in key specialty areas, and respected educational resources for professors and law students. Wolters Kluwer Law & Business connects legal and business professionals as well as those in the education market with timely, specialized authoritative content and information-enabled solutions to support success through productivity, accuracy and mobility.

Serving customers worldwide, Wolters Kluwer Law & Business products include those under the Aspen Publishers, CCH, Kluwer Law International, Loislaw, Best Case, ftwilliam.com and MediRegs family of products.

CCH products have been a trusted resource since 1913, and are highly regarded resources for legal, securities, antitrust and trade regulation, government contracting, banking, pension, payroll, employment and labor, and healthcare reimbursement and compliance professionals.

Aspen Publishers products provide essential information to attorneys, business professionals and law students. Written by preeminent authorities, the product line offers analytical and practical information in a range of specialty practice areas from securities law and intellectual property to mergers and acquisitions and pension/benefits. Aspen's trusted legal education resources provide professors and students with high-quality, up-to-date and effective resources for successful instruction and study in all areas of the law.

Kluwer Law International products provide the global business community with reliable international legal information in English. Legal practitioners, corporate counsel and business executives around the world rely on Kluwer Law journals, looseleafs, books, and electronic products for comprehensive information in many areas of international legal practice.

Loislaw is a comprehensive online legal research product providing legal content to law firm practitioners of various specializations. Loislaw provides attorneys with the ability to quickly and efficiently find the necessary legal information they need, when and where they need it, by facilitating access to primary law as well as state-specific law, records, forms and treatises.

Best Case Solutions is the leading bankruptcy software product to the bankruptcy industry. It provides software and workflow tools to flawlessly streamline petition preparation and the electronic filing process, while timely incorporating ever-changing court requirements.

ftwilliam.com offers employee benefits professionals the highest quality plan documents (retirement, welfare and non-qualified) and government forms (5500/PBGC, 1099 and IRS) software at highly competitive prices.

MediRegs products provide integrated health care compliance content and software solutions for professionals in healthcare, higher education and life sciences, including professionals in accounting, law and consulting.

Wolters Kluwer Law & Business, a division of Wolters Kluwer, is headquartered in New York. Wolters Kluwer is a market-leading global information services company focused on professionals.

To our teachers

Summary of Contents

Contents

Preface

Throughout our history this nation has faced a variety of serious threats to its security. Terrorism — both homegrown and international — is only the latest. This book addresses the relatively recent development of law and policy concerning counter-terrorism, part of the larger field of national security law.

The law of counterterrorism actually began to take shape long before 9/11. The League of Nations adopted a convention for the prevention and punishment of terrorism in 1937, although it never came into force. Domestic terrorist attacks became a serious concern in states around the world — from Northern Ireland to Algeria to Sri Lanka and elsewhere — after World War II. The United Nations General Assembly approved the first of many conventions addressing a variety of international terrorist threats in 1963, and the Security Council adopted the first of a succession of resolutions targeting terrorists and terrorist activities in 1989. The United States launched a military retaliation against Libya for the terrorist bombing of a Berlin night club in 1986. The bombings of the World Trade Center in 1993 and of the Alfred P. Murrah Building in Oklahoma City in 1995 led to revisions in FBI Guidelines for investigation and helped spur enactment of the Anti-Terrorism Act and Effective Death Penalty Act of 1996, Pub. L. No. 104-132, 110 Stat. 1214. Terrorist attacks on U.S. embassies in East Africa in 1998 and on the U.S.S. *Cole* in Yemen in 2000 focused even greater attention from lawyers and policy makers on this growing threat.

By revealing the vulnerability of the American homeland, the attacks by Al Qaeda on the World Trade Center and the Pentagon on September 11, 2001, created a new sense of fear and urgency that have led in turn to a number of extraordinary legal measures designed to counter terrorism. These have included military detention of terrorist suspects who earlier might have been charged under the criminal laws, dramatically increased foreign intelligence surveillance, coercive interrogation of terrorist suspects, a revival of military commissions, and an expanded use of classified evidence in criminal cases, among many other initiatives. These developments have been accompanied by presidential orders, legislation, and numerous court challenges.

In this book we provide both content and an analytical framework to give teachers and students a good grounding in this still-maturing field. Here we can identify several basic themes. The most important is the continuing primacy of checks and balances in our government. We see persistent evidence of the distinction Justice Jackson drew in *The Steel Seizure Case* between "the President's power to act without congressional authority [and to] ... act contrary to an Act of Congress." *Youngstown Sheet & Tube Co. v. Sawyer,* 343 U.S. 579, 635 n.2 (1952) (Jackson, J., concurring). After a period of hesitancy, the courts have reasserted their role in interpreting the law, increasingly affording access to the judicial process, insisting on due process, and recognizing the primacy of statutory law — even in this field so closely tied to national security. Congress has also awakened to a more aggressive role in overseeing and regulating counterterrorism efforts. The shifting balance of executive "law" and execution, statutory law and oversight, and judicial gatekeeping and interpretation offers deep insights into the way law can work to protect us from terrorists without sacrificing the very values of liberty and democracy that terrorists seek to destroy. Users of the casebook will find these broad themes reflected in every chapter.

This study of counterterrorism law is both comprehensive and self-contained. We have organized the materials in this book into functional categories in order to facilitate study and to help put new developments in the field into perspective. This is not a "how-to-do-it" course, however. Rather, it is a collection of resources to help bright students and citizens reflect intensively on how to protect national security under the rule of law; whether civil rights and liberties must be traded for security, and, if so, how much; and what roles each of the three branches of government should play in making these decisions and trade-offs. A key to using this casebook successfully is therefore not mastery of the nuances of each functional subject but recognition of the themes they share.

Another key to success is active incorporation of new materials as they are reported in the media and a growing number of online sources that monitor the field. Given the dynamic quality of counterterrorism law, it is virtually certain that breaking news will supply opportunities to rehearse and apply principles addressed in the book. To aid in this effort the authors will provide significant new teaching materials — judicial opinions, statutes, executive orders, and the like — on a Web site maintained by Aspen Publishers.

We remind readers that counterterrorism law is only a subset of the larger and equally dynamic field of national security law. That broader field includes war, foreign affairs, covert operations, emergency powers, and the protection of state secrets. While this book focuses strictly on counterterrorism law, we hope that you will explore the larger and, in many ways, even richer subject of national security law as well.

Our most important goal here is to encourage you to help create new ways to make this nation both secure and free under law. We hope you find these materials interesting and provocative, and we welcome your comments.

Stephen Dycus
William C. Banks
Peter Raven-Hansen

November 2011

Acknowledgments

This book builds on work the authors began together in the late 1980s with Arthur L. Berney, now Professor Emeritus at Boston College Law School. It owes a great debt to friends, colleagues, and professionals in the national security field who have shared their ideas and experience in the years since. This is also a better book because of the contributions of several generations of law students who, in and out of the classroom, have taught us a lot about teaching.

Stephen Dycus is especially grateful to the late Reverend William Sloane Coffin Jr., whose stubborn patriotism and generosity inspired so many. Special thanks are due as well to my wife Elizabeth for her unflagging patience and support. I appreciate the encouragement of my Dean, Geoffrey B. Shields, and my other colleagues at Vermont Law School. I also want to recognize the contributions of a long succession of bright, energetic research assistants. Those involved most recently in the completion of this book are Daniel Burke, Kimberly Chehardy, Michael Cretella, Eric Goldwarg, Eric Hutchens, Michael Kennedy, Caitlin Morgenstern, Alexander Mullee, Taylor Neff, and Alexandra Sherertz. Finally, I am grateful for the opportunity to undertake this work with two wonderful coauthors, whose brilliance, dedication, and sense of humor have made it all possible.

William Banks continues to recognize the memory of Brady Howell, a former National Security Law student and victim of the September 11 attack on the Pentagon. I also thank the Syracuse University law and graduate students who wrestled with and helped improve these materials from early drafts through the new edition. I am grateful to Deans Hannah Arterian and Mitchell Wallerstein for their generous support of this project, and to Cheryl Ficarra for her patience and support through many seven-day work weeks. My most recent research assistants, Elizabeth Platt, Benjamin Snyder, Jessica Trombetta, and Ryan Cole, were immensely helpful and supportive along the way. Finally, I want to thank my friends Steve Dycus and Peter Raven-Hansen for their commitment to excellence, dedication, and good humor through this remarkable project. Their intelligence and persistence in exploring this evolving new field continue to be an invaluable source of inspiration to me.

Peter Raven-Hansen expresses his thanks to current and former George Washington University Law School students Kyle Jones, who provided timely assistance with last-minute tasks in getting this book ready for publication, and Lisa Fuller, Jennifer Healy, Evan R. Minsberg, Zlatomira Simeonova, and Joshua A. Weiss, who helped with the underlying research and editing. Thanks once again to my co-authors for life, Bill Banks and Steve Dycus, for their hard work, inspiration, and sense of humor, and to Steve Dycus also for again leading the march through drafts, page proofs, and publication with unflagging and patient insistence on accuracy and consistency. Finally, but most importantly, thanks to my wife Winnie for putting up with back-to-back-to-back book projects.

Together, the authors wish to express their gratitude for the continuing support and encouragement of the staff at Aspen, especially Carol McGeehan, John Devins, Jay Harward, Barbara Roth, and Michael Gregory.

The authors also gratefully acknowledge permission to reprint images or excerpts from the following:

Abraham Lincoln Presidential Library and Museum. *President Lincoln in Spring 1861.* Photographer unknown.

Carroll Publishing. Chart on organization of the intelligence community (2005). Reprinted by permission of Carroll Publishing.

Curator, Supreme Court of the United States. Image of Justice O'Connor.

Ken Heinen. *Associate Justice Lewis F. Powell Jr.* Copyright © 1986 by Ken Heinen.

Inglesby, Thomas, Rita Grossman & Tara O'Toole, *A Plague on Your City: Observations from TOPOFF,* 32 Clinical Infectious Diseases 436 (2001). Copyright © 2001 by The University of Chicago Press. Reprinted by permission of the authors and Oxford University Press.

Lowenthal, Mark M., Intelligence: *From Secrets to Policy* (4th ed. 2009). Reprinted by permission of the publisher, CQ Press. Copyright © 2009 CQ Press, a division of Congressional Quarterly Inc.

National Archives and Records Administration. *Japanese-American heads of families line up for relocation, San Francisco, 1942.*

Editors' Note

In general we have adhered to the rules for citation of authority followed by most lawyers and courts. They are set out in *The Bluebook: A Uniform System of Citation* (19th ed. 2010). For reasons of economy we have omitted without notation many citations within excerpted materials, and we have removed almost all parallel citations. We have, on the other hand, sought to provide citations that will enable readers to locate and review original sources. We have included URLs for many materials available online, but not for those easily located by a Google search.

To make it easier to refer back to materials where they were originally published, we have preserved original footnote numbers in all excerpted materials. Editors' footnotes are numbered consecutively throughout each chapter. Additions to quoted or excerpted materials are enclosed in brackets.

Counterterrorism Law

I
Introduction

Defining Terrorism and Counterterrorism 1

Terrorism is a phenomenon that is easier to describe than to define. It is the unlawful use or threat of violence against persons or property to further political or social objectives. It is generally intended to intimidate or coerce a government, individuals, or groups to modify their behavior or policies.

Some experts see terrorism as the lower end of the warfare spectrum, a form of low-intensity, unconventional aggression....

...Americans...realize that terrorism needs an audience; that it is propaganda designed to shock and stun them; that it is behavior that is uncivilized and lacks respect for human life. They also believe that terrorism constitutes a growing danger to our system, beliefs, and policies worldwide. [*Public Report of the Vice President's Task Force on Combating Terrorism* 1, 21 (1986).]

Unlike war, terrorism often deliberately targets noncombatants. Unlike the ordinary murderer or mugger, who directs his violence against the victim alone without wanting to alert others, a terrorist uses violence "to instill fear in the targeted population ... [in a] deliberate evocation of dread." Jessica Stern, *The Ultimate Terrorists* 11 (1999).

This chapter introduces the book and our study of the role of law in countering terrorism. In Part A we provide a short survey of terrorism in the United States — its history and our approaches to defining what it is. Among the thorny questions introduced here is whether terrorism should be treated as a crime, as a species of war, as some combination of the two, or as a unique phenomenon meriting separate legal controls. The answer to this question matters in sorting out the legal bases for responding to terrorism. In Part B we offer two compelling and contrasting judicial decisions that question the existence of a consensus in the international community that terrorism violates international law.

A.   SEEKING A DEFINITION OF TERRORISM: A BRIEF SKETCH

Terrorism has ancient roots. For more than 2,000 years, terrorists have wrought destruction in furtherance of religious or secular ends. Sometimes by assassinating individual targets, at other times by fomenting mass uprisings or forming marauding bands of roving thugs, early terrorists probably inflicted more harm than any equivalent modern group. *See* Stern, *supra*, at 15. In the United States, where terrorism is generally considered a modern phenomenon, terrorist acts have in fact occurred throughout our history. From presidential and other political assassinations, to Civil

War–related terrorist violence, to anarchist and other radical group actions, our nation has experienced its share of lethal and usually politically motivated terrorism. *Id.* at 17.

Still, terrorism has emerged as a central national security concern in the United States only since the end of the Cold War. At first, the vulnerability of U.S. interests abroad dominated the policy agenda. Not long after terrorist Abu Nidal killed 19 tourists at airports in Rome and Vienna in December 1985, however, President Reagan issued NSDD-207, establishing a comprehensive counterterrorism policy for the United States and noting that terrorists use or threaten violence against innocents "to achieve a political objective through coercion or intimidation of an audience beyond the immediate victims." NSDD-207 (Jan. 20, 1986) (partly classified), *reprinted in* Christopher Simpson, *National Security Directives of the Reagan & Bush Administrations* 656 (1995). The bombings of the World Trade Center in 1993 and the Oklahoma City federal building in 1995, along with the 1995 Aum Shinrikyo nerve gas attack in Tokyo, shifted attention toward homeland security and domestic terrorist threats. In 1994, President Clinton found "that the proliferation of nuclear, biological, and chemical weapons ('weapons of mass destruction'), and of the means for delivering such weapons, constitutes an unusual and extraordinary threat to the national security," and he declared "a national emergency to deal with that threat." Exec. Order No. 12,938, 59 Fed. Reg. 58,099 (Nov. 14, 1994). After the September 11, 2001, attacks on the World Trade Center and the Pentagon, President George W. Bush also declared a national emergency, citing "the continuing and immediate threat of further attacks on the United States." Proclamation No. 7463, 66 Fed. Reg. 48,199 (Sept. 14, 2001.)

Beginning in the 1990s, terrorism changed in important ways:

> As the 1990s began, the conventional wisdom that terrorists employed violence in discriminate and proportionate ways was called into question. A new, more ruthless breed of terrorists began to leave its mark on the world. The first sharp departure from their predecessors was that many terrorists who became active in this time period did not necessarily espouse political causes or aim to take power. The second distinguishing feature was that a fair share of 1990s terrorists were intent on harming a maximum number of people. Instead of kidnaping an ambassador, the 1990s-vintage terrorists took a whole embassy hostage. Rather than hijack an aircraft, terrorists plotted to blow planes out of the sky. Terrorists upped the ante from pipe bombs to truck bombs capable of blowing up entire buildings, peppering the decade with headlines about the World Trade Center in 1993, the Murrah Federal Building in Oklahoma City in 1995, the Khobar Towers barracks in Saudi Arabia in 1997, and U.S. embassies in Kenya and Tanzania in 1998. [Amy E. Smithson, *Grounding the Threat in Reality*, in *Ataxia: The Chemical and Biological Terrorism Threat and the U.S. Response* 15 (Amy E. Smithson & Leslie-Anne Levy eds., Henry L. Stimson Center 2000).]

The September 11 attacks vividly displayed these terrorism trends and catapulted the United States into what the Bush administration called a "global war on terror." After ten years of sustained efforts to combat Al Qaeda, including the successful May 2011 operation that killed Osama bin Laden, "[Al Qaeda] remains the preeminent terrorist threat to the United States. Though the AQ core has become weaker...the affiliates have grown stronger...[including Al Qaeda] in the Arabian Peninsula (AQAP)...al Shabaab in east Africa...[and Al Qaeda] in the Islamic Maghreb

(AQIM)." U.S. Dep't of State, *Country Reports on Terrorism 2010,* at 6-7 (2011). Trends in terrorism show that "English-speaking militants increasingly connected to each other through online discussion venues like militant discussion forums and video sharing platforms...encouraged violent behavior and individual action." *Id.* at 6. At the same time, "the wave of non-violent democratic demonstrations that began to sweep the Arab world at the end of 2010...raised the possibility that terrorist groups would exploit the new openness, and in some cases, disarray, to carry out conspiracies, a possibility with significant and worrisome implications for states undergoing democratic transitions." *Id.* at 7.

Exactly what is terrorism? Before we can be confident of the scope of our subject—counterterrorism law—we need to know what it is that we are countering. Although everyone who uses the term today agrees that terrorism is bad, the inevitable politicization of terrorism renders any search for a consensus definition futile. Because polemicists have used the term in a variety of self-serving ways over the years, "terrorism" might be applied today to describe any disfavored action taken in response to another's policies.

Inspired by international political implications, the United Nations General Assembly devoted considerable energy during the 1970s to avoiding application of the term "terrorists" to groups that might instead be called "national liberation movements," "urban guerrillas," or "freedom fighters." In the summer of 2005, after ten years of negotiations, it appeared that the United Nations might reach agreement on a definition of terrorism, in anticipation of the adoption of a Comprehensive Convention on International Terrorism. A draft of the Convention contained this statement: "The targeting and deliberate killing of civilians and non-combatants cannot be justified or legitimized by any cause or grievance." *See Advanced Unedited Version,* Aug. 5, 2005, *at* http://www.un.org/ga/59/hlpm_rev.2.pdf. The United States ambassador urged that the words "by terrorists" be inserted between "killing" and "of." *See* Letter from John R. Bolton (n.d.), *at* http://www.un.int/usa/reform-un-jrb-ltr-terror-8-05.pdf. Some governments, however, sought to exclude from the definition of terrorism actions taken in "resistance to occupation," and to add language that would reach collateral damage caused by military action. When government leaders gathered in September, they approved an agenda-setting document in anticipation of the 60th session of the General Assembly that avoided these controversies by simply deleting all of the definitional language. *See Draft Outcome Document,* Sept. 13, 2005, *at* http://www.un.org/summit2005/ Draft_Outcome130905.pdf. One year later, a General Assembly resolution aimed at promoting adoption of a comprehensive convention still lacked a definition of the contentious term. Instead, it declared that member states "consistently, unequivocally and strongly condemn terrorism in all its forms and manifestations, committed by whomever, wherever and for whatever purposes, as it constitutes one of the most serious threats to international peace and security." *United Nations Global Counter-Terrorism Strategy,* G.A. Res. 60/288, U.N. Doc. A/RES/60/288 (Sept. 20, 2006). See *infra* p. 794. In 2011, a U.N. committee continued to work on the draft Comprehensive Convention and a definition of terrorism. *See* Report of the Ad Hoc Committee established by General Assembly resolution 51/210 of 17 December 1996, 15th Sess., Apr. 11-15, 2011, U.N. Doc. A/66/37, GAOR, 66th Sess., Supp. No. 37 (2011).

Despite the ongoing U.N. debate over a general definition, at least 13 U.N. conventions have designated specific acts as terrorism. *See* Upendra D. Acharya, *War on Terror or Terror Wars: The Problem in Defining Terrorism,* 37 Denv. J. Int'l L. 653 (2009); *infra* pp. 793-805. Typically these treaties and protocols require states to criminalize the prescribed acts and set penalties for them, and commit to arrest and prosecute or extradite the suspects. *See* Antonio Cassese, *Terrorism as an International Crime*, in *Enforcing International Law Norms Against Terrorism* 213-214 (Andrea Bianchi ed., 2004). Thus, in the international sphere, it is fair to say that "[d]espite the . . . grey areas, the word 'terrorism' is now part of both the legal and public discourse, and cannot be avoided." Karima Bennoune, *Terror/Torture*, 26 Berkeley J. Int'l L. 1, 27 (2008).

One federal statute directing the State Department to compile annual Country Reports on Terrorism defines "terrorism" as "premeditated, politically motivated violence perpetrated against noncombatant targets by subnational groups or clandestine agents." 22 U.S.C. §2656f(d)(2) (2006). Another provides criminal sanctions for "international terrorism," defined as activities that—

> (A) involve violent acts or acts dangerous to human life that are a violation of the criminal laws of the United States or of any State, or that would be a criminal violation if committed within the jurisdiction of the United States or of any State;
>   (B) appear to be intended—
>   (i) to intimidate or coerce a civilian population;
>   (ii) to influence the policy of a government by intimidation or coercion; or
>   (iii) to affect the conduct of a government by mass destruction, assassination or kidnaping; and
>   (C) occur primarily outside the territorial jurisdiction of the United States, or transcend national boundaries in terms of the means by which they are accomplished, the persons they appear intended to intimidate or coerce, or the locale in which their perpetrators operate or seek asylum. [18 U.S.C. §2331(1) (2006).]

See also 18 U.S.C. §2332b(g)(5) (2006 & Supp. IV 2010) (defining "Federal crime of terrorism"). The USA Patriot Act, passed in response to the September 11 attacks, borrows from the foregoing definition of "international terrorism" to define as "domestic terrorism" such acts that occur primarily *within* the jurisdiction of the United States. Pub. L. No. 107-56, §802(5), 115 Stat. 560 (2001) (codified at 18 U.S.C. §2331(5) (2006)). The same definition is used (with one change) to identify permissible targets of electronic surveillance or surreptitious physical searches under the Foreign Intelligence Surveillance Act. 50 U.S.C. §1801(c) (2006). See Chapter 7. There are, however, hundreds of federal statutes and regulations that address terrorism in some way, ranging from the Justice Department's "Victims of Crime Act Compensation Grant Program," to Commerce Department export controls, to FBI requirements that banks disclose financial information on terrorists to the Bureau, to a law waiving limits on the liability of government and nonprofit volunteers who have committed terrorist acts. *See* Elizabeth Martin, *"Terrorism" and Related Terms in Statute and Regulation: Selected Language* 1 (Cong. Res. Serv. RS21021), Dec. 5, 2006; Nicholas J. Perry, *The Numerous Federal Legal Definitions of Terrorism: The Problem of Too Many Grails*, 30 J. Legis. 249 (2004).

NOTES AND QUESTIONS

1. *One Definition?* How would you rate the chances of arriving at a single definition of terrorism on which everyone could agree? Bearing in mind our desire to be clear about our subject matter in this book, is it wise even to attempt a single consensus definition?

   2. *Terrorism as Crime?* Is terrorism a crime, and therefore best viewed as a matter to be addressed by law enforcement agencies? What are the legal and practical implications of characterizing terrorism as part of the criminal law? Consider this observation:

> Since 1986, presidents have taken international terrorism, drug-trafficking, and international organized crime out of the law enforcement closet of ordinary crimes and relabeled them as "national security threats." "Threats" must be prevented, not just detected and prosecuted like ordinary crimes. To prevent them, law enforcement must conduct the open-ended collection of intelligence, instead of just the more focused and close-ended assembly of criminal evidence. Furthermore, law enforcement cannot do it alone. Both the intelligence community and the military are therefore now tasked to participate, breaching the walls that society (and, some would have said, our Constitution) has traditionally maintained between civilian law enforcement and military or intelligence operations.
>   In short, under the twin banners of the war on terrorism and international crime...federal *law enforcement* is metamorphosing into *security enforcement* in the new national security state. [Peter Raven-Hansen, *Security's Conquest of Law Enforcement,* in *In Democracy's Shadow* 217 (Marcus G. Raskin & A. Carl Levin eds., 2005).]

   What considerations prompt government to lump international terrorism together with other, more traditional law enforcement problems? Can you see the value in doing so? What legal issues are likely to arise with a policy of security enforcement that includes international terrorism? *See also* Tyler Raimo, *Winning at the Expense of Law: The Ramifications of Expanding Counter-Terrorism Law Enforcement Jurisdiction Overseas,* 14 Am. U. Int'l L. Rev. 1473, 1481-1485 (1999).
   A definition provided by Congress to guide the Secretary of State in preparing annual Country Reports on Terrorism describes terrorism as "premeditated, politically motivated violence perpetrated against noncombatant targets by subnational groups or clandestine agents." 22 U.S.C. §2656f(d)(2) (2006). The first two qualifiers — premeditation and political motivation — are well-suited to the evidentiary intent requirements of criminal law. What is there about the intent to commit terrorist violence that distinguishes it from the *mens rea* in other violent crimes? If political motivation is central to terrorism, and if it includes some deep grievance against a government and its policies, is it possible that terrorism is not appropriately understood as a crime?

   3. *Terrorism and Spreading the Message of Fear.* Recall Jessica Stern's evocation, *supra* p. 3, of the terrorist's aim to instill fear in the target population. In this respect, the threat of terrorism can be terrorism. Do criminal laws offer a good remedy to counter the threat of terrorism?
   In order to instill the desired fear, terrorists seek to exploit available media to communicate news of the actual or threatened violence to the widest possible audience. Whether through traditional broadcast or cable services or through their own television, radio, and Internet media outlets, as one observer noted more than 30 years ago, "terrorism is theater." Brian M. Jenkins, *International Terrorism: A New Mode of Conflict,* in *International Terrorism and World Security* 16 (David Carlton & Carlo Schaerf eds., 1975).
   What legal mechanisms are capable of countering this aspect of terrorism? How should they be employed?

   4. *Terrorism as War?* In an October 31, 2003, speech, then-National Security Adviser Condoleezza Rice stated that "Iraq is the central front in the war on Terror."

Condoleezza Rice, Remarks at the National Legal Center for the Public Interest, *available at* http://www.whitehouse.gov/news/releases/2003/10/20031031-5.html. In the same week, former National Security Adviser Zbigniew Brzezinski argued that the "war on terrorism" is a misleading phrase, because its abstractness obscures the nature of the enemy: "[T]errorism is a technique for killing people. That doesn't tell us who the enemy is. It's as if we said that World War II was not against the Nazis but against the blitzkrieg." Zbigniew Brzezinski, Remarks at the New American Strategies for Security and Peace Conference (Oct. 28, 2003), *available at* http://www.prospect.org/webfeatures/2003/10/brzezinski-z-10-31.html.

The Obama administration dropped the "war on terror" label. Instead, the President stated in 2009 that "we are indeed at war with al Qaeda and its affiliates." President Barack Obama, Protecting Our Security and Our Values, Address at the National ArchivesMay 21, 2009). Does this change in labels have any significance? If so, what is it?

What harm could there be in fixing the "war" label to terrorism? The statutory definitions quoted above point out that terrorists deliberately attack those who cannot shoot back. Does this fact — distinguishing terrorism from traditional military operations — suggest a limit to the terrorism/war metaphor? Does the reference to "subnational groups or clandestine agents" distinguish terrorism from war?

Do you see any downside to defining terrorism as a crime for law enforcement purposes, as war where a military response is desirable, and so on?

5. *Guerrilla War vs. Insurgency vs. Terrorism.* Insurgents and guerrillas may share goals with terrorists, such as changing a government or political system. They also may use the same tactics, such as assassinations or bombings in public places, for similar purposes — to cause fear that leads to a change in government. The similarities do not end there. The three types of violent individuals also do not wear uniforms or other insignia that would distinguish them from noncombatant civilians. *See* Bruce Hoffman, *Inside Terrorism* 35 (rev. ed. 2006).

While it may be accurate in some colloquial sense to lump the three together as "irregulars," their differences may be more important for our purposes. NATO defines "insurgency" as "an organized movement aimed at the overthrow of a constituted government through the use of subversion and armed conflict," while "guerrilla warfare" is "military and paramilitary operations conducted in enemy-held or hostile territory by irregular, predominantly indigenous forces." U.S. Army Training & Doctrine Command, *A Military Guide to Terrorism in the Twenty-First Century (Version 3.0)* 1-7 (Aug. 15, 2005). Can you see how terrorism may differ from the other activities described here?

Some terrorist groups, such as Hezbollah, FARC (Revolutionary Armed Forces of Colombia), and the LTTE (Liberation Tigers of Tamil Eelam), are sometimes called guerrilla movements because they control territory and its people, and they are large movements. Hoffman, *supra*, at 35. Hoffman estimates that about one-third of the groups designated as "foreign terrorist organizations" by the State Department could be described as guerrilla movements. *Id.* at 35-36.

One study of suicide terrorism reaches this conclusion:

> What all suicide terrorist campaigns have in common is a specific secular and strategic goal: to compel democracies to withdraw military forces from the terrorists' homeland. Religion is rarely the root cause, although it is often used as a tool by terrorist organizations in recruiting and in other efforts in service of the broader strategic objective. [Robert A. Pape, *Dying to Win* 38 (2005).]

The study cites Hezbollah's campaign to oust the United States and Israel from Lebanon, LTTE's fight to make Sri Lanka recognize a Tamil state, Hamas's effort to force Israel out of the West Bank, the PKK's (Kurdistan Workers' Party's) struggle to make Turkey grant Kurd autonomy, Al Qaeda's campaign to compel the United States to withdraw from various Arab states, and the Afghan Taliban's efforts to expel the United States from Afghanistan. If this assessment is true, does it make sense to distinguish "guerilla" campaigns from terrorist campaigns?

Does the fuzziness of these distinctions present any legal difficulties that you can see in countering the terrorism that such groups practice?

6. *Defining Terrorism by What It Does.* Most of the definitions offered by scholars follow the State Department determination to focus on the premeditated political motivation of the violence or threat of violence as central to the act of terrorism. In view of the seemingly futile quest for a consensus definition, would it be prudent to focus on the nature of the terrorist act, rather than its purpose? Consider this view:

> The early American experience with terrorism — the post-Civil War phenomenon of the Ku Klux Klan — indicates that the most salient defining characteristic of terrorism is not the purpose of the terrorist but the threat level represented by the terrorist. It is the level of threat, and the organized nature of the perpetrators, rather than their political motive, that should drive the distinction between terrorism and more common violence. [Wayne McCormack & Jeffrey Breinholt, *Defining Terrorism: Perfection as Enemy of the Possible* (Int'l Assessment & Strategy Ctr. Jan. 17, 2007), *available at* http://www.strategycenter.net/printVersion/print_pub.asp?pubID=141.]

If political motivation is eliminated from the definition of terrorism, what would be included? What would be left out? Would national armed forces potentially become terrorists under such a definition? What factors distinguish the violence produced by regular national armies from that caused by terrorists?

7. *Differences in Definitions.* How do the statutory definitions of terrorism excerpted above differ? Why do you think they are different? One possibility is that the definitions reflect the emphases or concerns of the institutions they represent. Is there any harm in the State Department's adopting regulations that define terrorism to suit its purposes, while the Defense Department and Department of Justice do the same?

8. *Domestic Terrorism.* Note that by adapting the definition of international terrorism to acts that occur primarily inside the United States, the USA Patriot Act defines as "domestic terrorism" some acts attributed to Operation Rescue (an anti-abortion group), the Environmental Liberation Front, Greenpeace, and PETA (People for the Ethical Treatment of Animals). Should members of these groups be defined as terrorists? What legal issues would arise if a member of one of those groups were charged with "domestic terrorism"?

9. *The Politics of Labeling.* Do any of the definitions of terrorism set out above permit us to distinguish among the following: the attack on the World Trade Center on September 11, 2001; the attack on the Pentagon on the same day; the 1995 bombing of the federal building in Oklahoma City; acts of violence by Nelson Mandela and the ANC — carried out for the political purpose of fighting apartheid; the 1946

bombing for political purposes of the King David Hotel, housing civilian as well as military guests, by Menachem Begin (later Prime Minister of Israel); and the 2001 Palestinian suicide bombing that killed more than a dozen Israeli teenagers at a discotheque to avenge Israeli attacks on other Palestinians who allegedly had participated in bombings?

Could you argue that some of these acts were not terrorism? Which ones, and why not? Note that our courts have sometimes refused to extradite members of the IRA who have killed British troops in Northern Ireland, on grounds that they were engaged in "political" acts. Does it matter that Mandela and Begin succeeded in their political purposes, while the Palestinians have not? *See Symposium, Post-Cold War International Security Threats: Terrorism, Drugs, and Organized Crime*, 21 Mich. J. Int'l L. 527, 569 (2000) (so suggesting).

10. *State Sponsorship of Terrorism.* How do the lawful options for countering terrorism change when governments provide support to non-state terrorist organizations? In mid-2011, the State Department listed Cuba, Iran, Sudan, and Syria as state sponsors of terrorism. U.S. Dep't of State, *State Sponsors of Terrorism* (n.d.), *at* http://www.state.gov/s/ct/c14151.htm. Legal responses to state-sponsored terrorism are assessed in Chapters 25 and 26.

B.   DEFINING TERRORISM IN INTERNATIONAL LAW

Almog v. Arab Bank

United States District Court, Eastern District of New York, 2007
471 F. Supp. 2d 257

GERSHON, J. . . . [More than 1,600 United States and foreign national plaintiffs alleged that the defendant Arab Bank was part of a formalized system of financing that the Islamic Resistance Movement (HAMAS), the Palestinian Jihad (PIJ), the Al Aqsa Martyrs' Brigade (AAMB), and the Popular Front for the Liberation of Palestine (PFLP) used to sponsor suicide bombings and other murderous attacks on innocent civilians in Israel. The foreign nationals asserted violations of the law of nations, basing jurisdiction on the Alien Tort Claims Act (or Alien Tort Statute (ATS)), 28 U.S.C. §1350 (2006). The Bank moved to dismiss the amended complaints for lack of subject matter jurisdiction and for failure to state a claim.]

III.   ALIEN TORT CLAIMS ACT CLAIMS

The ATS provides that "[t]he district courts shall have original jurisdiction of any civil action by an alien for a tort only, committed in violation of the law of nations or a treaty of the United States." 28 U.S.C. §1350. On its face, the statute requires that plaintiffs must 1) be aliens, 2) claiming damages for a tort only, 3) resulting from a violation of the law of nations or a treaty of the United States. Arab Bank moves to dismiss the claims of the foreign nationals brought under the ATS, arguing that this court lacks jurisdiction and that plaintiffs have failed to state a claim because plaintiffs have failed to plead a violation of the law of nations. Neither the Almog nor the Afriat-Kurtzer plaintiffs assert that the torts they allege are in violation of a treaty of the United States; rather, they assert a violation of the law of nations. The essential issues

in contention are therefore whether plaintiffs have pled a violation of the law of *Issue*
nations that should be recognized by this court under the ATS, and whether Arab
Bank can be liable for aiding and abetting those violations.

Any discussion of the ATS must begin with the Supreme Court's recent decision
in *Sosa v. Alvarez-Machain,* 542 U.S. 692 (2004). Humberto Alvarez-Machain, the
plaintiff in *Sosa,* was a Mexican national who had been indicted for the torture and
murder of an agent of the United States Drug Enforcement Agency (the "DEA"). *Id.*
at 697-98. The DEA authorized a plan whereby a group of Mexican nationals, including Jose Francisco Sosa, seized Alvarez-Machain and brought him back to the United
States for trial. *Id.* Alvarez-Machain brought a civil action against Sosa, among others,
seeking damages under the ATS for a violation of the law of nations, namely, arbitrary
arrest and detention. *Id.* at 699. The defendant argued that the ATS provides courts
only with subject matter jurisdiction and neither creates nor authorizes a court to
recognize a cause of action for an alleged violation of the law of nations. *Id.* at 712.

The Supreme Court, in *Sosa,* stated that, "although the ATS is a jurisdictional statute
creating no new causes of action . . . [t]he jurisdictional grant is best read as having been
enacted on the understanding that the common law would provide a cause of action for
the modest number of international law violations with a potential for personal liability at
the time" the ATS was enacted. *Id.* at 724. Thus, under the ATS, courts can hear a limited
category of claims "defined by the law of nations and recognized at common law." *Sosa,*
542 U.S. at 712. . . . The Court assumed that the "First Congress understood that the
district courts would recognize private causes of action for certain torts in violation of the
law of nations. . . ." *Id.* at 724. In particular, the Court stated, "[i]t would take some
explaining to say now that federal courts must avert their gaze entirely from any international norm intended to protect individuals." *Id.* at 730. . . .

Having held that, under the ATS's jurisdictional grant, federal courts can recognize a cause of action that arose after enactment of the ATS, the *Sosa* Court set out the
standard for doing so: "federal courts should not recognize private claims under
federal common law for violations of any international law norm with less definite
content and acceptance among civilized nations than the historical paradigms familiar when §1350 was enacted." 542 U.S. at 732. The norm of international law may not
be merely aspirational; rather, it must be specific and well-defined. *Id.* at 738. . . .

Sosa instructs that courts consider the *current* state of the law of nations in deciding whether to recognize a claim under the ATS. *Id.* at 733. . . .

. . . First, then, in order for a rule to become a norm of international law, States must ①
universally abide by or accede to it. *Flores* [*v. Southern Peru Copper Corp.,* 414 F.3d 233, 248
(2d Cir. 2003)]; *Filartiga* [*v. Pena-Irala,* 630 F.2d 876, 881 (2d Cir. 1980)] ("The requirement that a rule command the 'general assent of civilized nations' to become binding
upon them all is a stringent one."). The question is not one of whether the rule is often
violated, but whether virtually all States recognize its validity. *Filartiga,* 630 F.2d at 884
(citing the Department of State, Country Reports on Human Rights for 1979, published
as Joint Comm. Print, House Comm. on Foreign Affairs, and Senate Comm. on Foreign
Relations, 96th Cong.2d Sess. (Feb. 4, 1980), Introduction at 1.). Thus, that a norm of
international law is honored in the breach does not diminish its binding effect as a norm
of international law. *Filartiga,* 630 F.2d at 884 n.15; *cf. Sosa,* 542 U.S. at 738 n.29.

Second, States must abide by or accede to the rule from a sense of *legal obligation* ②
and not for moral or political reasons. *Flores,* 414 F.3d at 248. Whether States abide by
or accede to a rule out of a sense of legal obligation is shown by, among other things,
state practice.

Third, "[i]t is only where the nations of the world have demonstrated that the wrong is of *mutual,* and not merely *several,* concern, by means of express international accords, that a wrong generally recognized becomes an international law violation within the meaning of the statute." *Filartiga,* 630 F.2d at 888 (emphasis added). Matters of "mutual" concern are those involving States' actions performed with regard to each other. *Flores,* 414 F.3d at 249. Matters of "several" concern are "matters in which States are separately and independently interested." *Id.* "[O]ffenses that may be purely intra-national in their execution, such as official torture, extrajudicial killings, and genocide, do violate customary international law because the nations of the world have demonstrated that such wrongs are of mutual concern and capable of impairing international peace and security." *Id.* (internal quotation marks, citations, and alterations omitted)....

Finally, under *Sosa,* in deciding whether to recognize a claim under the ATS, a court must consider the practical consequences of making the claim available to litigants in the federal courts. 542 U.S. at 732-33. For instance, there may be collateral consequences, such as implications on foreign relations, that advise against recognizing a claim. *Id.* at 727. The Court in *Sosa* also cautioned courts to tread lightly in exercising their discretion because courts generally have to look for "legislative guidance before exercising innovative authority over substantive law" and because the "decision to create a private right of action is one better left to legislative judgment in the great majority of cases." *Id.* at 726, 727.

It is against this backdrop and mindful of *Sosa*'s direction that the court's "judicial power should be exercised on the understanding that the door is still ajar subject to vigilant doorkeeping, and thus open to a narrow class of international norms today," *Sosa,* 542 U.S. at 729, that I address the motion to dismiss the ATS claims....

A. Violation of the Law of Nations

1. Genocide and Crimes Against Humanity

Acts of genocide and crimes against humanity violate the law of nations and these norms are of sufficient specificity and definiteness to be recognized under the ATS. *See Flores,* 414 F.3d at 244 n.18 ("Customary international law rules proscribing crimes against humanity, including genocide, and war crimes, have been enforceable against individuals since World War II."); *Kadic v. Karadzic,* 70 F.3d 232, 241-42 (2d Cir.1995) ("In 1946, the General Assembly of the United Nations declared that genocide is a crime under international law that is condemned by the civilized world, whether the perpetrators are private individuals, public officials or statesmen." (internal quotation marks omitted)).

Δ argues Defendant does not contest the availability of genocide or crimes against humanity claims under the ATS but argues that plaintiffs have not sufficiently pled a claim for genocide and crimes against humanity. The Convention on the Prevention and Punishment of the Crime of Genocide ("Genocide Convention") defines genocide as:

> any of the following acts committed with intent to destroy, in whole or in part, a national, ethnical, racial or religious group, as such:
> (a) Killing members of the group;
> (b) Causing serious bodily or mental harm to members of the group;

(c) Deliberately inflicting on the group conditions of life calculated to bring about its physical destruction in whole or in part;

(d) Imposing measures intended to prevent births within the group;

(e) Forcibly transferring children of the group to another group.

Genocide Convention, art. 2, Dec. 9, 1948, 78 U.N.T.S. 227, *implemented in* Genocide Convention Implementation Act of 1987 (the Proxmire Act), 18 U.S.C. §1091 (2000). The Second Circuit has found a violation of the international norm proscribing genocide where the plaintiffs alleged that the defendant "personally planned and ordered a campaign of murder, rape, forced impregnation, and other forms of torture designed to destroy the religious and ethnic groups of Bosnian Muslims and Bosnian Croats." *Kadic*, 70 F.3d at 242.

Article 7 of the Rome Statute of the International Criminal Court (the "Rome Statute"), defines crimes against humanity:

1. For the purpose of this Statute, "crime against humanity" means any of the following acts when committed as part of a *widespread or systematic attack directed against any civilian population*, with knowledge of the attack:

(a) Murder;

(b) Extermination; . . .

(h) Persecution against any identifiable group or collectivity on political, racial, national, ethnic, cultural, religious, gender . . . or other grounds that are universally recognized as impermissible under international law, in connection with any act referred to in this paragraph or any crime within the jurisdiction of the Court; . . .

(k) Other inhumane acts of a similar character intentionally causing great suffering, or serious injury to body or to mental or physical health.

2. For the purpose of paragraph 1:

(a) "Attack directed against any civilian population" means a course of conduct involving the multiple commission of acts referred to in paragraph 1 against any civilian population, pursuant to or in furtherance of a State or organizational policy to commit such attack;

(b) "Extermination" includes the intentional infliction of conditions of life, inter alia the deprivation of access to food and medicine, calculated to bring about the destruction of part of a population. . . .

July 17, 1998, 37 I.L.M. 999, 1004-05 (emphasis added).

"Customary international law defines 'widespread' as 'massive, frequent, large scale action, carried out collectively with considerable seriousness and directed against a multiplicity of victims,' and 'systematic' as 'thoroughly organised action, following a regular pattern on the basis of a common policy and involving substantial public or private resources.'" *Wiwa* [*v. Royal Dutch Petroleum Co.*, No. 96-CIV-8386, 2002 WL 319887, at *10 (S.D.N.Y. Feb. 28, 2002)] (quoting *Prosecutor v. Rutaganda*, Case No. ICTR-96-3-T, 69 (Dec. 6, 1999)). To be a crime against humanity, the emphasis must not be on the individual but rather on the collective — the individual is victimized not because of his or her individual attributes but because of membership in a targeted civilian population. *Id.* Although the requirement of widespread or systematic action ensures that a plaintiff must allege not just one act but, instead, a course of conduct, "a single act by a perpetrator, taken within the context of a widespread or systematic attack against a civilian population entails individual criminal responsibility and an individual perpetrator need not commit numerous offences to be held liable." *Id.*

Applying the standards provided in the Genocide Convention and the Rome Statute to the facts alleged here, plaintiffs have successfully stated claims for genocide and crimes against humanity. The amended complaints allege that HAMAS, the PIJ, the AAMB, and the PFLP act with the united purpose and shared mission to eradicate the State of Israel, murder or throw out the Jews, and liberate the area by replacing it with an Islamic or Palestinian State through the use of suicide bombings and other shockingly egregious violent acts. These goals reflect an intent to target people based on criteria prohibited by both the Genocide Convention and the Rome Statute.

Plaintiffs allege that the terrorist organizations seek to accomplish their shared goal by cooperating in the planning and commission of suicide bombings and other murderous attacks using explosives, incendiary weapons, and lethal devices in public places, which has resulted in the systematic and continuous killing and injury of thousands of unarmed innocent civilians in Israel, the West Bank, and the Gaza Strip. These are precisely the sorts of acts proscribed in both the Genocide Convention and the Rome [S]tatute.

Plaintiffs also allege that the terrorist organizations have developed and implemented a sophisticated financial structure through which they seek to accomplish their goals. The amended complaints describe dozens upon dozens of instances in which hundreds of innocent civilians were killed, and countless others injured, in attacks caused by individuals sponsored by the terrorist organizations. The acts as alleged constitute the "widespread" and "systematic" action necessary for claims of genocide and crimes against humanity. Even the acts other than suicide bombings, specifically those that defendant contends are nothing more than street crimes, may be sufficient for liability if plaintiffs can prove they were committed as part of a genocidal scheme or crimes against humanity.

2. Suicide Bombings and Other Murderous Attacks on Innocent Civilians Intended to Intimidate or Coerce a Civilian Population

The third international norm which plaintiffs allege Arab Bank has violated is the financing of suicide bombings and other murderous attacks on innocent civilians which are intended to intimidate or coerce a civilian population. The underlying norm thus differs from the genocide norm with respect to the purpose of the perpetrators, and it differs from the more general crimes against humanity norm in that it specifically condemns bombings and other attacks intended to coerce or intimidate a civilian population....

In 1997, the United Nations General Assembly adopted the International Convention for the Suppression of Terrorist Bombings ("Bombing Convention"). G.A. Res. 52/164, 1, U.N. Doc A/RES/52/164 (Dec. 15, 1997). The Bombing Convention states in pertinent part:

Article 2

1. Any person commits an offence within the meaning of this Convention if that person unlawfully and intentionally delivers, places, discharges or detonates an explosive or other lethal device in, into or against a place of public use, a State or government facility, a public transportation system or an infrastructure facility:

(a) With the intent to cause death or serious bodily injury; or

(b) With the intent to cause extensive destruction of such a place, facility or system, where such destruction results in or is likely to result in major economic loss....

Article 5

Each State Party shall adopt such measures as may be necessary, including, where appropriate, domestic legislation, to ensure that criminal acts within the scope of this Convention, in particular where they are intended or calculated to provoke a state of terror in the general public or in a group of persons or particular persons, are under no circumstances justifiable by considerations of a political, philosophical, ideological, racial, ethnic, religious or other similar nature and are punished by penalties consistent with their grave nature.

Dec. 15, 1997, S. Treaty Doc. No. 106-6 (1998), *implemented in* 18 U.S.C. §2332f, Pub. L. No. 107-197, 116 Stat. 721 (2002). This Convention focuses on the principal method of attacking civilians alleged in the amended complaints in that it specifically makes it an offense to bomb public places or public transportation systems with the intent to cause death or serious bodily harm. The Bombing Convention particularly condemns such acts when they are, as alleged here, intended to provoke a state of terror in the general public or a group of persons. It specifies that such acts are not justifiable by any racial, ethnic, religious, political, or other similar considerations. In terms of its evidentiary weight, the Bombing Convention is significant. It has been ratified by over 120 United Nations Member States, including the United States (June 26, 2002). *Cf. Kadic*, 70 F.3d at 241 (noting that the Genocide Convention "has been ratified by more than 120 nations, including the United States. . . ."). In addition, the United States has implemented the Bombing Convention in the Terrorist Bombings Convention Implementation Act of 2002. *See* Pub. L. No. 107-197, 116 Stat. 721 (2002), *enacting* 18 U.S.C. §2332f.

Two years after the Bombing Convention was adopted by the General Assembly, the International Convention for the Suppression of the Financing of Terrorism ("Financing Convention") was also adopted by the General Assembly of the United Nations. G.A. Res. 54/109, U.N. Doc. A/RES/54/109 (Dec. 9, 1999). It has been ratified by over 130 countries, including the United States (June 26, 2002). The United States implemented the Financing Convention via the Suppression of the Financing of Terrorism Convention Implementation Act of 2002. *See* 18 U.S.C. §2339C. The Convention makes it an offense to finance certain acts, including those proscribed in the Bombing Convention. Article 2 of the Financing Convention states:

1. Any person commits an offence within the meaning of this Convention if that person by any means, directly or indirectly, unlawfully and wilfully, provides or collects funds with the intention that they should be used or in the knowledge that they are to be used, in full or in part, in order to carry out:
    (a) An act which constitutes an offence within the scope of and as defined in [the Bombing Convention]; or
    (b) Any other act intended to cause death or serious bodily injury to a civilian, or to any other person not taking an active part in the hostilities in a situation of armed conflict, when the purpose of such act, by its nature or context, is to intimidate a population, or to compel a Government or an international organization to do or to abstain from doing any act.

Dec. 9, 1999, S. Treaty Doc. No. 106-49 (2000). Thus, the Financing Convention, along with the Bombing Convention, specifically condemns suicide bombings and other murderous attacks against innocent civilians intended to intimidate or coerce a population. Once again, this Convention provides that such acts "are under no circumstances justifiable by considerations of a political, philosophical, ideological, racial, ethnic, religious or other similar nature." Financing Convention, art. 6.

The prohibition against attacks on innocent civilians that is reflected in both of these Conventions is not a new one. The three-century-old "principle of distinction," which requires parties to a conflict to at all times distinguish between civilians and combatants, forbids the deliberate attacking of civilians. State practice establishes the principle of distinction as a long-established norm of the customary law of armed conflict. This principle is also reflected in Common Article 3 of the Geneva Conventions of 1949 (the "Geneva Conventions"), which provides in pertinent part:

> In the case of armed conflict not of an international character occurring in the territory of one of the High Contracting Parties, each Party to the conflict shall be bound to apply, as a minimum, the following provisions:
>
> (1) *Persons taking no active part in the hostilities,* including members of armed forces who have laid down their arms and those placed *hors de combat* by sickness, wounds, detention, or any other cause, *shall in all circumstances be treated humanely, without any adverse distinction founded on race, colour, religion or faith, sex, birth or wealth, or any other similar criteria.*
>
> To this end the following acts are and shall remain prohibited at any time and in any place whatsoever with respect to the above-mentioned persons:
>
> (a) violence to life and person, in particular murder of all kinds, mutilation, cruel treatment and torture; . . . .

Geneva Convention for the Amelioration of the Condition of the Wounded and Sick in Armed Forces in the Field, Aug. 12, 1949, 6 U.S.T. 3316; Geneva Convention for the Amelioration of the Condition of Wounded, Sick and Shipwrecked Members of Armed Forces at Sea, Aug. 12, 1949, 6 U.S.T. 3316; Geneva Convention Relative to the Treatment of Prisoners of War, Aug. 12, 1949, 6 U.S.T. 3316; Geneva Convention Relative to the Protection of Civilian Persons in Time of War, art. III, Aug. 12, 1949, 6 U.S.T. 3316 (emphasis added).

Under the customary law of armed conflict, as reflected in the Geneva Conventions, all "parties" to a conflict, including insurgent military groups, must adhere to these most fundamental requirements. *Kadic,* 70 F.3d at 243. While the principle of distinction and the Geneva Conventions apply expressly only in situations of armed conflict, their long-standing existence supports the conclusion, made explicit in the Bombing and Financing Conventions, that attacks against innocent civilians of the type alleged here are condemned by international law.

United Nations Security Council Resolution 1566 also supports this conclusion. It states, in pertinent part, that the Security Council:

> 3. *Recalls* that criminal acts, including against civilians, committed with the intent to cause death or serious bodily injury, or taking of hostages, with the purpose to provoke a state of terror in the general public or in a group of persons or particular persons, intimidate a population or compel a government or an international organization to do or to abstain from doing any act, which constitute offences within the scope of and as defined in the international conventions and protocols relating to terrorism, are under no circumstances justifiable by considerations of a political, philosophical, ideological, racial, ethnic, religious or other similar nature, and *calls upon* all States to prevent such acts and, if not prevented, to ensure that such acts are punished by penalties consistent with their grave nature.

S.C. Res. 1566, ¶3, U.N. Doc. S/RES/1373 (Oct. 8, 2004). Resolution 1566 specifically condemns attacks against civilians intended to intimidate a civilian population, regardless of who commits the attacks or what the motivation behind such attacks may be. While such resolutions cannot be relied on as a sole source of international law, they are informative as to what the current state of international law is. *See Filartiga*, 630 F.2d at 882 n.9 (observing that non-self-executing agreements serve as evidence of binding principles of international law and relying on several United Nations General Assembly Resolutions).

In the face of all these sources evidencing universal condemnation of the types of acts alleged here, Arab Bank does not address the actual conduct condemned by these sources. Rather, it argues that the underlying suicide bombings and other Δ arg. murderous acts alleged in Count Three, which it says are "commonly referred to as terrorism," cannot be a violation of the law of nations because there is no consensus on the meaning of "terrorism." In support of its argument, Arab Bank relies on *United States v. Yousef*, a pre-*Sosa* case, in which the court stated that "customary international law currently does not provide for the prosecution of 'terrorist' acts under the universality principle, in part due to the failure of States to achieve anything like consensus on the definition of terrorism." 327 F.3d 56, 97 (2d Cir. 2003) (per curiam).

Arab Bank's reliance on *Yousef* is misplaced. First, the court in *Yousef* was reviewing whether the district court had criminal jurisdiction under the universality principle[1] and not whether the district court should recognize a claim under the civil jurisdictional grant of the ATS. The *Yousef* Court held that "the universality principle permits jurisdiction over only a limited set of crimes that *cannot be expanded judicially*" whereas *Sosa* held, with regard to the ATS, that federal courts *can* recognize new causes of action, albeit with restraint, under the ATS. *Compare Yousef*, 327 F.3d at 103 (emphasis added), *with Sosa*, 542 U.S. at 725.

Second, the court in *Yousef*, in addressing the issue as framed by the parties, whether "terrorism" was a violation of the law of nations, criticized the lower court's reliance on the Restatement (Third) of the Foreign Relations Law of the United States, a non-authoritative source, for the finding that "terrorism" violates international law. 327 F.3d at 98-103 n.37. The parties in *Yousef* had not addressed specific international law sources, and the district court relied, not on such sources, but on the Restatement. The appellate briefs also did not address accepted sources of international law. The court in *Yousef* emphasized that the proper sources for determining international law are the sources described in *Kadic* and *Filartiga*, that is, the sources this court relies on here. *See id.*

Defendant also errs in relying on the following language in *Yousef*: "nor have we shaken ourselves free of the cliché that 'one man's terrorist is another man's freedom fighter.'" *Id.* at 107. This court does not accept that the Court of Appeals, in referring to this cliché, was accepting . . . this . . . principle. On the contrary, if anything, the Court of Appeals seemed concerned that defining terrorism in a way that would receive international agreement could exclude outrageous conduct that should properly be condemned. *See, e.g., id.* at 108 n.42 ("This attempt to distinguish 'terrorists' from 'freedom fighters' potentially could legitimate as non-terrorist certain groups nearly universally recognized as terrorist, including the Irish Republican Army, Hezbollah, and Hamas.").

[1. Customary international law imposes an obligation on states to detain, extradite, or prosecute those within its territory or control who are reasonably accused of committing war crimes, genocide, or other acts that violate peremptory norms, wherever they are committed. *See* Jordan Paust, *International Law as Law of the United States* 405 (1996).]

[handwritten margin note: no need to define terrorism for this case]

In any event, in this case, there is no need to resolve any definitional disputes as to the scope of the word "terrorism," for the Conventions expressing the international norm provide their own specific descriptions of the conduct condemned. Although the Conventions refer to such acts as "terrorism," the pertinent issue here is only whether the acts as alleged by plaintiffs violate a norm of international law, however labeled. *See Sosa*, 542 U.S. at 738 (examining whether the specific conduct alleged by plaintiff violated a norm of international law). In exploring that question, this court has examined the very sources of international law found to be valid by the Second Circuit in *Kadic, Filartiga* and *Yousef,* and by the Supreme Court in *Sosa*. These authoritative sources establish that the specific conduct alleged — organized, systematic suicide bombings and other murderous attacks on innocent civilians intended to intimidate or coerce a civilian population — are universally condemned.

In a similar way, the *Yousef* court, after holding that there was no jurisdiction under the universality principle, held that there was jurisdiction in the district court to try the defendant for bombing a Philippines Airlines flight under the Montreal Convention, which expressly addresses offenses against aircraft. 327 F.3d at 108-110. It did so because it found that the conduct charged, "whether it is termed 'terrorist' — constitutes the core conduct proscribed by the Montreal Convention and its implementing legislation." *Id.* at 97-98. In sum, regardless of whether there is universal agreement as to the precise scope of the word "terrorism," the conduct involved here is specifically condemned in the Conventions upon which this court relies.

[handwritten margin note: Δ arg]

Arab Bank attempts to undermine the weight of the international sources discussed above by arguing that state practice does not support the existence of a universal norm. The basis for this argument is that "some 80 nations in Africa, in the Arab world and elsewhere expressly exempt from the definition of terrorism conduct that they believe furthers the rights of self-determination of a people." To begin with, Arab Bank ignores that the international sources relied upon here themselves evidence state practice. As stated in *Flores*, 414 F.3d at 256, treaties evidence the "customs and practices" of the States that ratify them. This is so because ratification of a treaty that embodies specific norms of conduct evidences a State's acceptance of the norms as legal obligations. Here, the international sources specifically articulate a universal standard that condemns the conduct alleged.

In addition, Arab Bank's state practice argument is based upon a flawed premise and is devoid of factual support. As for the premise, Arab Bank's argument is that the acts alleged here — organized, systematic suicide bombings and other murderous acts intended to intimidate a civilian population — are viewed by some States as acceptable acts in furtherance of the right to self-determination. However, Arab Bank offers no authority for the proposition that the right to self-determination can be effectuated in violation of the law of nations. . . . Indeed, the Bombing Convention, the Financing Convention and Resolution 1566 all expressly acknowledge that violation of the principles embodied in those documents are under no circumstances justifiable by political, philosophical, ideological, racial, ethnic, or religious considerations. Moreover, there have been no formal reservations to either of the Conventions purporting to assert that a right to self-determination justifies committing otherwise condemned acts. On the contrary, even the statements relied upon, which are made by officials of varying official stature, never expressly state that the type of conduct alleged here is a legitimate means of asserting the right to self-determination.

Turning to the lack of factual support for defendant's state practice argument, it is significant that the United States prohibits the specific conduct alleged in the cases at hand. *See* 18 U.S.C. §2332f (implementing the Bombing Convention); 18 U.S.C. §2339C (implementing the Financing Convention); *see also* 18 U.S.C. §§2331 *et seq.* (setting forth the criminal penalties and civil remedies for enforcement of these laws); *cf. Flores*, 414 F.3d at 257 n.33 (citing *Yousef*, 327 F.3d at 92 n.25 ("While it is not possible to claim that the practice or policies of any one country, including the United States, [have] such authority that the contours of customary international law may be determined by reference only to that country, it is highly unlikely that a purported principle of customary international law in direct conflict with the recognized practices and customs of the United States and/or other prominent players in the community of States could be deemed to qualify as a *bona fide* customary international principle.")). Arab Bank has offered no evidence that it is lawful in any State to engage in organized, systematic murderous attacks on civilians for the purpose of coercing or intimidating the civilian population. *Cf. Filartiga*, 630 F.2d at 884 ("We have been directed to no assertion by any contemporary state of a right to torture its own or another nation's citizens."). Both sides to this litigation note that the Palestinian Authority has explicitly condemned suicide bombings and that it "arrests, convicts, and sentences to imprisonment terrorists who kill Israeli citizens in the occupied territories." The international sources cited above, coupled with the fact that no State has expressly stated that such conduct would be legal in its country, provide further support for the conclusion that the alleged conduct violates a norm of international law. *Cf. Filartiga*, 630 F.2d at 880 ("In light of the universal condemnation of torture in numerous international agreements, and the renunciation of torture as an instrument of official policy by virtually all of the nations of the world (in principle if not in practice), we find that an act of torture committed by a state official against one held in detention violates established norms of the international law of human rights, and hence the law of nations.").

The next issue to be addressed is whether the international norm is of mutual, and not merely several, concern. [The court held that the suicide bombings are of mutual concern.] . . .

Finally, the collateral consequences about which the *Sosa* Court expressed concern seem limited here. . . . Based upon all of the factors set forth above, organized, systematic suicide bombings and other murderous attacks against innocent civilians for the purpose of intimidating a civilian population are a violation of the law of nations for which this court can and does recognize a cause of action under the ATS.

[The court also found that similar principles of the law of nations extend secondary liability under the ATS to Arab Bank for its conduct aiding and abetting the suicide bombings and other attacks.] . . .

Saperstein v. The Palestinian Authority

United States District Court, Southern District of Florida, 2006
2006 WL 3804718

SEITZ, J. . . . [Foreign national plaintiffs alleged that the Palestinian Authority (PA) and Palestine Liberation Organization (PLO), as the *de jure* and *de facto* rulers of territories in the Gaza Strip and West Bank, sponsored and executed acts of violence and terrorism against Jewish civilians in Israel, Gaza, and the West Bank, and granted financial support to the families of members of the Al Aqsa Brigade who had been captured or killed while carrying out acts of terrorist violence. The court sought *Issue* to determine whether the Alien Tort Claims Act (or Alien Tort Statute ("ATS")), 28 U.S.C. §1350 (2006), provides subject matter jurisdiction over claims based on the non-state, private actions of the PA and PLO, and, if so, whether the claims described constitute violations of the law of nations.]

2.   Tel-Oren v. Libyan Arab Republic

In *Tel Oren v. Libyan Arab Republic*, 726 F.2d 774 (D.C. Cir. 1984), *cert. denied*, 470 U.S. 1003 (1985), victims of a 1978 terrorist attack in Israel sued a number of parties, including several private organizations, for violations of the law of nations under the ATS. The terrorists seized a civilian bus, a taxi, a passing car, and subsequently a second civilian bus and took the passengers hostage. *Id.* at 776. The terrorists tortured, shot, wounded and murdered many of the hostages. *Id.* A three-judge panel unanimously dismissed the case with three separate opinions. Judge Edwards gave the ATS the broadest reach, generally agreeing with the decision in *Filartiga* that acts of official torture violate the law of nations. *Id.* at 791. Judge Edwards, however, found no consensus that private actors are bound by the law of nations with regard to torture. *Id.* at 791-95. Only a year later, the court of appeals addressed the issue again in *Sanchez-Espinoza v. Reagan*, 770 F.2d 202 (D.C. Cir. 1985), a case involving allegations of "execution, murder, abduction, torture, rape, [and] wounding" by the Nicaraguan Contras. In *Sanchez-Espinoza*, the appellate court stated quite clearly that the law of nations "does not reach private, non-state conduct of this sort" for the reasons stated by Judge Edwards and Judge Bork in *Tel-Oren*. *Id.* at 205-207.

In *Tel Oren*, Judge Edwards undertook an in-depth analysis of whether to stretch *Filartiga's* reasoning to incorporate torture perpetuated by a party other than a recognized state or one of its officials. *Tel Oren*, 726 F.2d at 792-95. Judge Edwards observed that the extension would necessarily require the court to venture out of the realm of established international law in which states are the actors and would mandate an assessment of the extent to which international law imposes not only rights but also obligations on individuals.[9] *Id.* at 792. He concluded his analysis saying that he "was not prepared to extend the definition of the 'law of nations' absent direction from the Supreme Court." *Id.*

Judge Edwards also examined the question of whether terrorism in and of itself was a law of nations violation, regardless of whether it is conducted by a state or private actor. *Id.* at 795-96. In finding that condemnation of terrorism was not universal, he stated that "the nations of the world are so divisively split on the legitimacy of such

9. Judge Edwards highlighted some of the ramifications of extending the *Filartiga* reasoning to the actions of private entities, stating: "[i]t would require a determination of where to draw a line between persons or groups who are or are not bound by dictates of international law, and what the groups look like. Would the terrorists be liable, because numerous international documents recognize their existence and proscribe their acts?" He further asked, "would all organized political entities be obliged to abide by the law of nations? Would everybody be liable? As firmly established as is the core principle binding states to customary international obligations, these fringe areas are only gradually emerging and offer, as of now, no obvious stopping point." *Tel Oren*, 726 F.2d 59.

aggression as to make it impossible to pinpoint an area of harmony or consensus."[10] *Id.* Thus, he concluded that the law of nations, defined as the principles and rules that states feel themselves bound to observe, did not outlaw politically motivated terrorism. *Id.*

3. Kadic v. Karadzic

The 1995 *Kadic v. Karadzic* decision is the most recent circuit court opinion thoroughly analyzing those actions for which international law imposes individual liability. 70 F.3d 232 (2nd Cir. 1995). In *Kadic*, the plaintiffs, Croat and Muslim citizens of Bosnia-Herzegovina, sued the president of the self-proclaimed Bosnian-Serb republic within Bosnia-Herzegovina. 70 F.3d at 237. Plaintiffs asserted causes of action for various atrocities at the hands of the Bosnian-Serb republic including, genocide, rape, forced prostitution and impregnation, torture, and other cruel, inhuman and degrading treatment such as assault and battery, sex and ethnic inequality, summary execution and wrongful death. *Id.* The district court dismissed the case finding that defendant was not a state actor for purposes of the ATS but the court of appeals reversed. *Id.* at 239. In so doing, the Second Circuit found that the law of nations, as understood in the modern era, did not confine its reach to state action. *Id.* The court of appeals held that "certain forms of conduct violate the laws of nations whether undertaken by those acting under the auspices of a state or only as [ ] private individuals, such as piracy, slave-trading, aircraft hijacking, genocide, and war crimes." *Id.* at 240-43. The Second Circuit, however, held that torture and summary execution, when not perpetrated in the course of genocide or war crimes, are proscribed by international law only when committed by state officials under color of law. *Id.* at 243.

These cases reflect the trend toward finding that certain conduct violates the law of nations whether committed by a state or a private actor, however, which conduct falls into this realm has not been completely defined. Plaintiffs contend that a violation of the "law of war" now called "international humanitarian law" is recognized as a breach of the law of nations and the actions alleged in the TAC [third amended complaint] constitute such violations. . . .

With this legal landscape in mind and noting the Supreme Court's cautionary advice regarding the creation of new offenses in the law of nations in *Sosa* [*v. Alvarez-Machain*, 542 U.S. 692 (2004)], the Court turns to the Plaintiffs' allegations.

C.   Plaintiffs Fail to Plead a Violation of the Law of Nations Sufficient to Invoke the Court's Subject Matter Jurisdiction.

To resolve Defendants' motion, it is necessary to determine if the Plaintiffs' TAC allegations fit the categories of conduct that prior courts have found constitute a violation of the law of nations, even when carried out by a private actor. The conduct

---

10. As support for the proposition that terrorism is not a violation of the law of nations, Judge Edwards referenced documents of the United Nations. He contends that they demonstrate that to some states acts of terrorism, in particular those with political motives, are legitimate acts of aggression and are therefore immune from condemnation. As an example, Judge Edwards points to a resolution entitled "Basic principles of the legal status of the combatants struggling against colonial and alien domination an racist regimes," G.A. Res. 3103, 28 U.N. GAOR at 512, U.N. Doc. A/9102 (1973), which declared, "The struggle of peoples under colonial and alien domination and racist regimes for the implementation of their right to self-determination and independence is legitimate and in full accordance with principles of international law."

in *Tel Oren* is substantially similar to the conduct in the present case. Judge Edwards, in *Tel Oren*, made it abundantly clear that politically motivated terrorism has not reached the status of a violation of the law of nations. In their own words, Plaintiffs describe Defendants' conduct as terrorism. Beginning with their introduction, Plaintiffs state that they bring this action for damages caused by Defendants' "acts of terrorism as defined in federal law, and by reason of related tortious terrorist behavior." Further, Plaintiffs specifically allege that the PA and PLO failed to "denounce and condemn acts of terror, apprehend, prosecute and imprison persons involved directly, and/or indirectly in acts of terrorism and outlaw and dismantle the infrastructure of terrorist organizations." Thus, if the conduct of the Defendants is construed as terrorism, then Plaintiffs have not alleged a violation of the law of nations.

Plaintiffs attempt to get around such facts in their response to Defendants' motion to dismiss by characterizing the allegations in the TAC as a "murder of [a] civilian[ ] in the course of an armed conflict," or a war crime. In doing this, Plaintiffs are grasping at the *Kadic* decision and attempting to bring the alleged conduct within the language of Common Article 3. Plaintiffs' strategy in this regard is certainly obvious, as the Second Circuit in *Kadic* based much of its analysis of the definition of "war crimes" on Common Article 3. *Kadic*, 70 F.3d at 242-43. However, Plaintiffs then make the overreaching leap by stating that if the conduct falls within Common Article 3 and is prohibited thereby, then they have sufficiently alleged a violation of the law of nations for purposes of the ATS. Essentially, Plaintiffs are saying that if they allege a murder of an innocent person during an armed conflict, then they have alleged a per se violation of the law of nations and federal courts have subject matter jurisdiction over the dispute under the ATS. No court has so held. In fact, as discussed above, international customary law is not taken from one source but rather is "discerned from [a] myriad of decisions made in numerous and varied international and domestic arenas." *See Flores*, 343 F.3d at 154.

Further, while Plaintiffs' reliance on the *Kadic* decision's references to Common Article 3 is understandable, the severe and horrendous conduct alleged in that case, including "brutal acts of rape, forced prostitution, forced impregnation, torture and summary execution" against an entire class of citizens, differentiate[s] it from this case. Unlike the conduct alleged here, the abominate actions the Croat and Muslim plaintiffs asserted in *Kadic* did not require the same extent of canvassing of international law to determine if the prohibition of such conduct was "universally recognized." Thus, the Second Circuit's reliance on Common Article 3 was sufficient to ascertain a consensus in customary international law. In fact, the appellate court specifically directed their decision to the particular horrendous allegations by stating that the "offenses alleged by the [plaintiffs], if proved, would violate the most fundamental norms of the law of war embodied in common article 3." *See Kadic*, 73 F.2d at 243. The court of appeals did not make a blanket holding that any alleged violation of Common Article 3 would be sufficient for the purposes of the ATS.

Further, two practical considerations highlight the flaws in Plaintiffs' desired expansion of the law of nations. First, if it were accepted that any alleged violation of Common Article 3 was sufficient for subject matter jurisdiction under the ATS, then a violation of any provision in the Article would yield the same result. This includes such unspecific conduct as "violence to life," "cruel treatment" and "outrages upon personal dignity." For federal courts to interpret such ambiguous standards to assess [their] own subject matter jurisdiction would pose problems for federal courts and would not meet the defined standards of specificity that *Sosa* requires. Second, if Plaintiffs' specific allegation, i.e., the murder of an innocent civilian during an armed conflict, was sufficient for the purposes of the ATS, then whenever an innocent person was murdered during an "armed conflict" anywhere in the world, whether it be Bosnia, the Middle East or Darfur, Sudan, the federal courts would have subject matter jurisdiction over the dispute. Clearly, such an interpretation would not only make district courts international courts of civil justice, it would be in direct contravention of the Supreme Court's specific prudential guidance admonishing lower courts to be cautious in creating new offenses under the law of nations. *See Sosa*, 542 U.S. 725. For the foregoing reasons, Plaintiffs do not sufficiently allege a violation of the law of nations and, thus, this Court lacks subject matter jurisdiction. . . .

NOTES AND QUESTIONS

1. *Reconciling the Cases.* In light of the factually similar bases for the claims in *Almog* and *Saperstein,* what best explains their different outcomes in finding a law of nations violation? Is it that the *Almog* plaintiffs argue genocide, while the *Saperstein* plaintiffs make claims for victims of terrorism? Are you persuaded, based on the sources discussed in the cases, that genocide but not terrorism violates the law of nations? If there is another basis for explaining the different outcomes of the cases, what is it?

Do you agree that the differences between the ethnic cleansing chronicled in the *Kadic* decision and the suicide attacks and bombings complained of in *Saperstein* justify a finding that there was no violation of the law of nations in the latter? What is the utility of Common Article 3 of the Geneva Conventions in this regard? Should Judge Seitz's worry that district courts might become "international courts of civil justice" stand in the way of a finding that the terrorism complained of in *Saperstein* violates the law of nations?

2. *Genocide and Crimes Against Humanity.* Consider the terms of the Genocide Convention and Rome Statute quoted in *Almog.* Are you satisfied that the attacks alleged to have been carried out or supported by the Palestinian defendants meet the requirements of these instruments? Do they also constitute terrorism? If so, what is the value of the labels?

3. *The Financing Convention, the Bombing Convention, and United Nations Resolutions.* Compare the terms of the United Nations Conventions and Resolutions with the Genocide Convention and the Rome Statute, and then with the U.S. statutory definitions set out earlier in the chapter. What are the common and distinct elements of each? How do you explain the different approaches taken by the United Nations in General Assembly Resolution 3103 and Security Council Resolution 1566? How much weight should these various instruments have in determining the current state of international law?

4. *Consensus on the Meaning of "Terrorism"?* Are you persuaded by Judge Gershon's response to the defendants' argument in *Almog* that the actions alleged cannot be a violation of the law of nations because there is no consensus on the meaning of the term "terrorism"? Do you agree with Judge Gershon that the reasoning in *Yousef,*

upon which the *Almog* defendants rely, was distinguishable as a criminal prosecution in which the government sought jurisdiction under the universality principle? Was Judge Seitz on firmer ground in *Saperstein* in finding that the 1985 *Tel Oren* decision shows a lack of consensus about the illegality of terrorism?

More recently, another Florida judge followed *Saperstein* in holding that terrorism allegations are not actionable under the ATS. In *In re Chiquita Brands International Litigation*, No. 08-01916-MD, 2011 WL 2163973 (S.D. Fla. June 3, 2011), estates, survivors, and heirs of U.S. citizens who were kidnapped, held hostage, and murdered by terrorists in Colombia sued the banana producer based on allegations that Chiquita made payments to a Colombian terrorist organization and provided terrorists with weapons, ammunition, and other supplies. Relying on *Saperstein* and *Tel Oren*, the court found that the allegations were "not limited to any specific, narrow category of conduct, such as hijacking civilian aircraft or suicide bombing civilian targets. Rather, Plaintiffs allege a broad range of alleged terrorist acts, linked only by the facts that the victims are civilians and the intent is to intimidate." *Id.* at *12.

The cliché "one man's terrorist is another man's freedom fighter" lives on. In *Cheema v. Ashcroft*, 383 F.3d 848 (9th Cir. 2004), the court reversed a Board of Immigration Appeals order denying asylum and directing deportation of an Indian Sikh alien. The court rejected the Board's determination that "a person engaged in extra-territorial or resistance activities — even militant activities — is necessarily a security threat to the United States. One country's terrorist can often be another country's freedom fighter." *Id.* at 858. The court recounted the terrorist tactics employed by Contras in Nicaragua in an attempt to overthrow the Sandinista government during a period when the United States was providing financial and other support to the Contras. *Id.* It also offered the heroic example of Nelson Mandela, whose paramilitary branch of the African National Congress conducted guerrilla warfare against the ruling white government in South Africa. *Id.* at 859. Do these examples add support to the cliché? Do they describe terrorism as we understand it today?

Does consensus on one or more definitions matter if treaties provide sufficient descriptions of the conduct condemned to permit claims to go forward? Are you persuaded by Judge Gershon's conclusion that Arab Bank's state practice argument is based on a flawed premise and lacks factual support? Upon what basis does Judge Seitz come to a different conclusion?

II
Authorities and Limits in the War on Terrorists

Terrorism and International Humanitarian Law (*jus in bello*)

2

The international law concerning the right to wage war, or *jus ad bellum*, is aimed at deterring the use of armed force by states against each other. It is also supposed to regulate states' uses of force against terrorists and other non-state actors. The main structural elements of the modern *jus ad bellum* are spelled out in the U.N. Charter. A related, parallel body of law, *jus in bello*, is concerned with the conduct of war once it has begun. Also referred to as international humanitarian law (IHL) or the law of armed conflict (LOAC),[1] its purpose is to limit the suffering of combatants and non-combatants alike to what is necessary to achieve the legitimate political goals of a conflict.

Several framework principles constitute IHL, including requirements that any use of military force be based on *distinction* (distinguishing carefully between military targets and civilians in order to protect the latter), and *proportionality* (forbidding any use of force that causes incidental civilian casualties that are disproportionate to the military advantage from the operation). IHL has been extensively codified, most prominently in a series of Hague Conventions, which address permissible targets and weaponry, and Geneva Conventions, which are concerned with the treatment of prisoners and other noncombatants and the conduct of occupying forces. Other such conventions deal with poison gas, anti-personnel land mines, blinding lasers, the protection of cultural objects, and other matters relating to the effects of war. Humanitarian law principles are also found in a robust, rapidly evolving body of customary international law. In addition, some IHL violations are criminalized by the Rome Statute of the International Court, July 17, 1998, 2187 U.N.T.S. 90, an international agreement to which the United States is not yet a party. *See generally The International Criminal Court: Challenges to Achieving Justice and Accountability in the 21st Century* (Mark S. Ellis & Richard J. Goldstone eds., 2008).

IHL is a subset of international law, partially incorporated as U.S. law. Another subset of international law, international human rights law (HRL), applies in peacetime and, some would say, during armed conflicts as well. The view of the United States is that, during armed conflicts, HRL gives way to IHL and its *jus in bello* principles. *Operational Law Handbook* 40 (Marie Anderson & Emily Zukauskas eds., 2008). (The relationship between IHL and HRL is considered in Chapter 4.)

---

1. We use the term international humanitarian law (IHL) because of its international currency and its growing use in academic discourse. The terms law of armed conflict and laws of war are synonymous.

For reasons of national interests, as well as military strategy and tactics, limits on what soldiers may do in war have existed throughout history. From religious precepts to chivalry to customs and then rules, nations and their armies eventually developed military codes for conflict that included penalties for their violation. In the United States in 1862, Professor Francis Lieber persuaded the Union War Department to assign him to write a compilation of the customary rules of warfare — the Lieber Code. Then came the Hague and the 1949 Geneva Conventions and, eventually, 1977 Protocols that have expanded the reach and protections of the basic instruments.

The extensive provisions of the Geneva Conventions of 1949 apply only to armed conflicts of an international (inter-state) character, not to non-international armed conflicts (most other armed conflicts, including at least some insurrections), except for baseline, general humanitarian protections for victims of all armed conflicts found in Common Article 3. The Protocols, adopted 28 years later, sought to extend the basic Geneva principles to a wider range of conflicts, especially to national liberation movements then battling colonial powers, and to describe emerging customs and new principles. Additional Protocol I (AP I) is concerned with international armed conflicts, while Additional Protocol II (AP II) is applicable to non-international armed conflicts, but neither has been ratified by the United States. Still, as explained below, the United States follows some of their principles as customary international law.

The resulting law leaves much to be desired. Because armed conflicts today frequently involve violent clashes between states and non-state actors — terrorists, insurgents, guerrilla groups, even pirates — the Geneva Conventions and their Protocols often fail to provide clear guidance for belligerents. *See* John B. Bellinger III & Vijay M. Padmanabhan, *Detention Operations in Contemporary Conflicts: Four Challenges for the Geneva Conventions and Other Existing Law*, 105 Am. J. Int'l L. 201, 205-213 (2011). Even when the Conventions apply to such conflicts, they may not adapt easily to the weaponry, tactics, and personnel employed in modern irregular warfare.

Some argue that HRL, supplemented by domestic laws, can govern all such conflicts. But the relationship of these laws to IHL is complex, and the patchwork of rules that would result from this approach might be more bewildering than helpful. *Id.* at 209-212. As things now stand, states and lawyers struggle to apply IHL to these conflicts, and state militaries may in practice simply treat all armed conflicts the same. *See* Michael N. Schmitt, *Targeting and International Humanitarian Law in Afghanistan*, 39 Israel Y.B. on Hum. Rts. 307, 308 (2009) (IHL norms in international and non-international armed conflicts "have become nearly indistinguishable.")

This chapter offers an introduction to IHL — just enough to understand the basics and the significance of *jus in bello* for counterterrorism law. Three sets of materials provide the framework. In Part A, we review excerpts of the Geneva Conventions, one of their two Protocols, and the Rome Statute of the International Criminal Court (ICC), focusing chiefly on provisions intended to protect the victims of war. In Part B, we consider IHL rules for selecting targets and protecting civilians during armed conflict, applying them to the 2011 U.S. and NATO military operation against Libya. Finally, in Part C, we examine a judicial decision arising from the conflict in the Balkans in the 1990s to examine the *in bello* rules for detention and treatment of prisoners in war. Our broader objective here is to lay the foundation for a more extensive application of these principles when we consider targeted killings, detention and interrogation of terrorist suspects, and military commissions in later chapters.

A. AUTHORITIES FOR *JUS IN BELLO*

1. IHL for the Victims of War—The 1949 Geneva Conventions

The 1863 Lieber Code and a first Geneva Convention adopted at a meeting of the International Committee of the Red Cross (ICRC) in 1864 established the practice of codifying customary law for the conduct of armed conflicts. Despite continuing efforts to institutionalize humane wartime practices before and after World War I, the horrific casualties and brutal atrocities of World War II brought renewed determination to protect the victims of war. Meanwhile, regulation of the means of waging war was partly addressed by Hague treaties and partly left to customary law. The 1949 Geneva Conventions continued to deal with the victims of war, leaving regulation of battlefield conduct to the earlier Hague rules and custom. Additional Protocols to the Geneva Conventions in 1977 combined elements of the earlier conventions and customs to create a more nearly comprehensive set of *in bello* rules.

There are four separate 1949 Geneva Conventions. The Convention for the Amelioration of the Condition of the Wounded and Sick in Armed Forces in the Field (Geneva I) and the Convention for the Amelioration of the Condition of Wounded, Sick and Shipwrecked Members of the Armed Forces at Sea (Geneva II) provide similar protections for, respectively, land and seaborne forces. Several provisions of Geneva III and Geneva IV, excerpted next, contain central components of contemporary *in bello* safeguards. Note that Common Articles 1-3 are identical throughout the four Conventions. Provisions of Geneva III and IV and Additional Protocol I set out below fall roughly into three categories: (1) those stating broad ideals or describing procedural requirements, (2) those regulating the means for waging warfare, and (3) those dealing in greater detail with the treatment of prisoners. See if you can place each provision into one of these categories, recognizing that there may be some overlap in a few instances. The Rome Statute subsequently drew on IHL in listing prosecutable war crimes.

Geneva Convention Relative to the Treatment of Prisoners of War, August 12, 1949 (Geneva III)
T.I.A.S. 3362, 75 U.N.T.S. 135

Article 1

The High Contracting Parties undertake to respect and to ensure respect for the present Convention in all circumstances.

Article 2

In addition to the provisions which shall be implemented in peace time, the present Convention shall apply to all cases of declared war or of any other armed conflict which may arise between two or more of the High Contracting Parties, even if the state of war is not recognized by one of them.

The Convention shall also apply to all cases of partial or total occupation of the territory of a High Contracting Party, even if the said occupation meets with no armed resistance.

Although one of the Powers in conflict may not be a party to the present Convention, the Powers who are parties thereto shall remain bound by it in their mutual relations. They shall furthermore be bound by the Convention in relation to the said Power, if the latter accepts and applies the provisions thereof.

Article 3

Hamdan

In the case of armed conflict not of an international character occurring in the territory of one of the High Contracting Parties, each party to the conflict shall be bound to apply, as a minimum, the following provisions:

1. Persons taking no active part in the hostilities, including members of armed forces who have laid down their arms and those placed hors de combat by sickness, wounds, detention, or any other cause, shall in all circumstances be treated humanely, without any adverse distinction founded on race, colour, religión or faith, sex, birth or wealth, or any other similar criteria.

To this end the following acts are and shall remain prohibited at any time and in any place whatsoever with respect to the above-mentioned persons:

(a) Violence to life and person, in particular murder of all kinds, mutilation, cruel treatment and torture;

(b) Taking of hostages;

(c) Outrages upon personal dignity, in particular, humiliating and degrading treatment;

(d) The passing of sentences and the carrying out of executions without previous judgment pronounced by a regularly constituted court affording all the judicial guarantees which are recognized as indispensable by civilized peoples. . . .

Article 4

POW

A. Prisoners of war, in the sense of the present Convention, are persons belonging to one of the following categories, who have fallen into the power of the enemy:

1. Members of the armed forces of a Party to the conflict as well as members of militias or volunteer corps forming part of such armed forces.

2. Members of other militias and members of other volunteer corps, including those of organized resistance movements, belonging to a Party to the conflict and operating in or outside their own territory, even if this territory is occupied, provided that such militias or volunteer corps, including such organized resistance movements, fulfil the following conditions:

(a) That of being commanded by a person responsible for his subordinates;

(b) That of having a fixed distinctive sign recognizable at a distance;

(c) That of carrying arms openly;

(d) That of conducting their operations in accordance with the laws and customs of war.

3. Members of regular armed forces who profess allegiance to a government or an authority not recognized by the Detaining Power.

4. Persons who accompany the armed forces without actually being members thereof, such as civilian members of military aircraft crews, war correspondents,

supply contractors, members of labour units or of services responsible for the welfare of the armed forces, provided that they have received authorization from the armed forces which they accompany, who shall provide them for that purpose with an identity card similar to the annexed model.

5. Members of crews, including masters, pilots and apprentices, of the merchant marine and the crews of civil aircraft of the Parties to the conflict, who do not benefit by more favourable treatment under any other provisions of international law.

6. Inhabitants of a non-occupied territory, who on the approach of the enemy spontaneously take up arms to resist the invading forces, without having had time to form themselves into regular armed units, provided they carry arms openly and respect the laws and customs of war. . . .

Article 5

The present Convention shall apply to the persons referred to in Article 4 from the time they fall into the power of the enemy and until their final release and repatriation.   *Application to POW*

Should any doubt arise as to whether persons, having committed a belligerent act and having fallen into the hands of the enemy, belong to any of the categories enumerated in Article 4, such persons shall enjoy the protection of the present Convention until such time as their status has been determined by a competent tribunal. . . .

Article 17

Every prisoner of war, when questioned on the subject, is bound to give only his surname, first names and rank, date of birth, and army, regimental, personal or serial number, or failing this, equivalent information.

If he wilfully infringes this rule, he may render himself liable to a restriction of the privileges accorded to his rank or status. . . . [Most of the remaining provisions of this Convention spell out conditions of confinement of prisoners of war, including rights to health care, exercise, mail, food, etc.] . . .

Article 87

Prisoners of war may not be sentenced by the military authorities and courts of the Detaining Power to any penalties except those provided for in respect of members of the armed forces of the said Power who have committed the same acts.

When fixing the penalty, the courts or authorities of the Detaining Power shall take into consideration, to the widest extent possible, the fact that the accused, not being a national of the Detaining Power, is not bound to it by any duty of allegiance, and that he is in its power as the result of circumstances independent of his own will. . . .

Collective punishment for individual acts, corporal punishments, imprisonment in premises without daylight and, in general, any form of torture or cruelty, are forbidden. . . .

Geneva Convention Relative to the Protection of Civilian Persons in Time of War, August 12, 1949 (Geneva IV)

T.I.A.S. 3362, 75 U.N.T.S. 287

Article 1 [see Geneva Convention III] ...

Article 2 [see Geneva Convention III] ...

Article 3 [see Geneva Convention III] ...

Article 4

Persons Protected

Persons protected by the Convention are those who, at a given moment and in any manner whatsoever, find themselves, in case of a conflict or occupation, in the hands of a Party to the conflict or Occupying Power of which they are not nationals.

Nationals of a State which is not bound by the Convention are not protected by it. Nationals of a neutral State who find themselves in the territory of a belligerent State, and nationals of a co-belligerent State, shall not be regarded as protected persons while the State of which they are nationals has normal diplomatic representation in the State in whose hands they are.

The provisions of Part II are, however, wider in application, as defined in Article 13. . . .

Article 5

Where, in the territory of a Party to the conflict, the latter is satisfied that an individual protected person is definitely suspected of or engaged in activities hostile to the security of the State, such individual person shall not be entitled to claim such rights and privileges under the present Convention as would, if exercised in the favour of such individual person, be prejudicial to the security of such State.

Where in occupied territory an individual protected person is detained as a spy or saboteur, or as a person under definite suspicion of activity hostile to the security of the Occupying Power, such person shall, in those cases where absolute military security so requires, be regarded as having forfeited rights of communication under the present Convention.

In each case, such persons shall nevertheless be treated with humanity, and in case of trial, shall not be deprived of the rights of fair and regular trial prescribed by the present Convention. They shall also be granted the full rights and privileges of a protected person under the present Convention at the earliest date consistent with the security of the State or Occupying Power, as the case may be. . . .

Article 31

No physical or moral coercion shall be exercised against protected persons, in particular to obtain information from them or from third parties. . . .

Article 49

Individual or mass forcible transfers, as well as deportations of protected persons from occupied territory to the territory of the Occupying Power or to that of any other country, occupied or not, are prohibited, regardless of their motive.

Nevertheless, the Occupying Power may undertake total or partial evacuation of a given area if the security of the population or imperative military reasons do demand. Such evacuations may not involve the displacement of protected persons outside the bounds of the occupied territory except when for material reasons it is impossible to avoid such displacement. Persons thus evacuated shall be transferred back to their homes as soon as hostilities in the area in question have ceased. . . .

[margin note: Forcible Transfers Prohibited]

Article 146

The High Contracting Parties undertake to enact any legislation necessary to provide effective penal sanctions for persons committing, or ordering to be committed, any of the grave breaches of the present Convention defined in the following Article.

Each High Contracting Party shall be under the obligation to search for persons alleged to have committed, or to have ordered to be committed, such grave breaches, and shall bring such persons, regardless of their nationality, before its own courts. It may also, if it prefers, and in accordance with the provisions of its own legislation, hand such persons over for trial to another

High Contracting Party concerned, provided such High Contracting Party has made out a *prima facie* case.

Each High Contracting Party shall take measures necessary for the suppression of all acts contrary to the provisions of the present Convention other than the grave breaches defined in the following Article.

In all circumstances, the accused persons shall benefit by safeguards of proper trial and defence, which shall not be less favourable than those provided by Article 105 and those following of the Geneva Convention relative to the Treatment of Prisoners of War of August 12, 1949.

Article 147

Grave breaches to which the preceding Article relates shall be those involving any of the following acts, if committed against persons or property protected by the present Convention: wilful killing, torture or inhuman treatment, including biological experiments, wilfully causing great suffering or serious injury to body or health, unlawful deportation or transfer or unlawful confinement of a protected person, compelling a protected person to serve in the forces of a hostile Power, or wilfully depriving a protected person of the rights of fair and regular trial prescribed in the present Convention, taking of hostages and extensive destruction and appropriation of property, not justified by military necessity and carried out unlawfully and wantonly.

[margin note: Grave Breaches defined]

2. IHL Revised: The Protocols Additional and the Rome Statute

After the Korean War, the world's wars began to evolve from large, state-against-state conflicts involving competing armies into smaller, more episodic conflicts, often involving states fighting non-state entities, such as insurgents, guerrillas, revolutionaries, or terrorists. At the same time, a growing body of HRL called into question certain IHL assumptions. In 1977, with the encouragement of national liberation groups, and despite strong opposition from the United States and some of its allies, delegates from a majority of states approved significant amendments to the Geneva Conventions. The Protocols supplement rather than replace the Conventions. Protocol I, excerpted below, covers international armed conflicts — defined more broadly than before — and it effectively codifies the *in bello* regulation of the battlefield. Protocol II, not excerpted here, expands upon the protections in Common Article 3 for individuals in armed conflicts that are not of an international (interstate) character.

A continuing determination to provide a forum for international criminal prosecution of the worst offenders of *in bello* rules came to fruition in 1998, with adoption of the Rome Statute and creation of the International Criminal Court. Its central provision conferring jurisdiction over war crimes is also excerpted below.

The United States has not ratified Protocol I or Protocol II to the Geneva Conventions. In AP I, the United States particularly objected to detailed rules about discrimination during attacks, a prohibition on reprisals that could deter IHL violations, modifications to prisoner-of-war (POW) categories, and changes in the definition of international armed conflicts to include indigenous armed struggles against colonial or racist regimes. However, in 1987 the Deputy Legal Adviser to the Department of State indicated that the United States recognizes nearly two-thirds of the articles in Protocol I as customary international law. Michael J. Matheson, *Additional Protocol I as Expressions of Customary International Law*, 2 Am. U. J. Int'l L. & Pol'y 415 (1987). Such recognition is indicated by annotations to some of the provisions below. Almost 20 years later, Matheson affirmed his earlier position. Michael J. Matheson, *Continuity and Change in the Law of War: 1975-2005: Detainees and POWs*, 38 Geo. Wash. Int'l L. Rev. 543 (2006). Some have asserted that the Matheson statement is not authoritative, *see* W. Hays Parks, *"Special Forces" Wear of Non-Standard Uniforms*, 4 Chi. J. Int'l L. 519 n.55 (2003), but no office of the U.S. government has disavowed his statement. In March 2011, President Obama announced that he would urge the Senate to ratify AP II, and that the United States would apply Article 75 of AP I (below) to individuals detained in international armed conflicts. Office of the Press Secretary, The White House, *Fact Sheet: New Actions on Guantanamo and Detainee Policy*, Mar. 7, 2011.

Protocol Additional to the Geneva Conventions of August 12, 1949, and Relating to the Protection of Victims of International Armed Conflicts, June 8, 1977 (Protocol I)

1125 U.N.T.S. 3, 16 I.L.M. 1391

PART I — GENERAL PROVISIONS

Article 1 — General principles and scope of application

1. The High Contracting Parties undertake to respect and to ensure respect for this Protocol in all circumstances.

2. In cases not covered by this Protocol or by other international agreements, civilians and combatants remain under the protection and authority of the principles of international law derived from established custom, from the principles of humanity and from dictates of public conscience.

3. This Protocol, which supplements the Geneva Conventions of 12 August 1949 for the protection of war victims, shall apply in the situations referred to in Article 2 common to those Conventions.

4. The situations referred to in the preceding paragraph include armed conflicts in which peoples are fighting against colonial domination and alien occupation and against racist regimes in the exercise of their right of self-determination, as enshrined in the Charter of the United Nations and the Declaration on Principles of International Law concerning Friendly Relations and Co-operation among States in accordance with the Charter of the United Nations. . . .

PART III — METHODS AND MEANS OF WARFARE, COMBATANT AND PRISONER-OF-WAR STATUS

Article 35 — Basic rules[2]

1. In any armed conflict, the right of the Parties to the conflict to choose methods or means of warfare is not unlimited.

2. It is prohibited to employ weapons, projectiles and material and methods of warfare of a nature to cause superfluous injury or unnecessary suffering.

3. It is prohibited to employ methods or means of warfare which are intended, or may be expected, to cause widespread, long-term and severe damage to the natural environment. . . .

Article 41 — Safeguard of an enemy hors de combat

1. A person who is recognized or who, in the circumstances should be recognized to be *hors de combat* shall not be made the object of attack.

2. A person is *hors de combat* if:
    (a) he is in the power of an adverse Party;
    (b) he clearly expresses an intention to surrender; or
    (c) he has been rendered unconscious or is otherwise incapacitated by wounds or sickness, and therefore is incapable of defending himself;
provided that in any of these cases he abstains from any hostile act and does not attempt to escape.

3. When persons entitled to protection as prisoners of war have fallen into the power of an adverse Party under unusual conditions of combat which prevent their evacuation as provided for in Part III, Section I, of the Third Convention, they shall be released and all feasible precautions shall be taken to ensure their safety. . . .

Article 43 — Armed forces

1. The armed forces of a Party to a conflict consist of all organized armed forces, groups and units which are under a command responsible to that Party for the

[2. Recognized as customary international law by the United States. — Eds.]

conduct of its subordinates, even if that Party is represented by a government or an authority not recognized by an adverse Party. Such armed forces shall be subject to an internal disciplinary system which, inter alia, shall enforce compliance with the rules of international law applicable in armed conflict.

2. Members of the armed forces of a Party to a conflict (other than medical personnel and chaplains covered by Article 33 of the Third Convention) are combatants, that is to say, they have the right to participate directly in hostilities.

3. Whenever a Party to a conflict incorporates a paramilitary or armed law enforcement agency into its armed forces it shall so notify the other Parties to the conflict.

Article 44 — Combatants and prisoners of war

1. Any combatant, as defined in Article 43, who falls into the power of an adverse Party shall be a prisoner of war.

2. While all combatants are obliged to comply with the rules of international law applicable in armed conflict, violations of these rules shall not deprive a combatant of his right to be a combatant or, if he falls into the power of an adverse Party, of his right to be a prisoner of war, except as provided in paragraphs 3 and 4.

3. In order to promote the protection of the civilian population from the effects of hostilities, combatants are obliged to distinguish themselves from the civilian population while they are engaged in an attack or in a military operation preparatory to an attack. Recognizing, however, that there are situations in armed conflicts where, owing to the nature of the hostilities an armed combatant cannot so distinguish himself, he shall retain his status as a combatant, provided that, in such situations, he carries his arms openly:

(a) during each military engagement, and

(b) during such time as he is visible to the adversary while he is engaged in a military deployment preceding the launching of an attack in which he is to participate. Acts which comply with the requirements of this paragraph shall not be considered as perfidious within the meaning of Article 37, paragraph 1 (c).

4. A combatant who falls into the power of an adverse Party while failing to meet the requirements set forth in the second sentence of paragraph 3 shall forfeit his right to be a prisoner of war, but he shall, nevertheless, be given protections equivalent in all respects to those accorded to prisoners of war by the Third Convention and by this Protocol. This protection includes protections equivalent to those accorded to prisoners of war by the Third Convention in the case where such a person is tried and punished for any offences he has committed.

5. Any combatant who falls into the power of an adverse Party while not engaged in an attack or in a military operation preparatory to an attack shall not forfeit his rights to be a combatant and a prisoner of war by virtue of his prior activities.

6. This Article is without prejudice to the right of any person to be a prisoner of war pursuant to Article 4 of the Third Convention.

7. This Article is not intended to change the generally accepted practice of States with respect to the wearing of the uniform by combatants assigned to the regular, uniformed armed units of a Party to the conflict. . . .

Article 45 — Protection of persons who have taken part in hostilities

1. A person who takes part in hostilities and falls into the power of an adverse Party shall be presumed to be a prisoner of war, and therefore shall be protected by

the Third Convention, if he claims the status of prisoner of war, or if he appears to be entitled to such status, or if the Party on which he depends claims such status on his behalf by notification to the detaining Power or to the Protecting Power. Should any doubt arise as to whether any such person is entitled to the status of prisoner of war, he shall continue to have such status and, therefore, to be protected by the Third Convention and this Protocol until such time as his status has been determined by a competent tribunal.

2. If a person who has fallen into the power of an adverse Party is not held as a prisoner of war and is to be tried by that Party for an offence arising out of the hostilities, he shall have the right to assert his entitlement to prisoner-of-war status before a judicial tribunal and to have that question adjudicated. Whenever possible under the applicable procedure, this adjudication shall occur before the trial for the offence. The representatives of the Protecting Power shall be entitled to attend the proceedings in which that question is adjudicated, unless, exceptionally, the proceedings are held in camera in the interest of State security. In such a case the detaining Power shall advise the Protecting Power accordingly.

3. Any person who has taken part in hostilities, who is not entitled to prisoner-of-war status and who does not benefit from more favourable treatment in accordance with the Fourth Convention shall have the right at all times to the protection of Article 75 of this Protocol. In occupied territory, any such person, unless he is held as a spy, shall also be entitled, notwithstanding Article 5 of the Fourth Convention, to his rights of communication under that Convention. . . .

PART IV — CIVILIAN POPULATION

Article 48 — Basic rule

In order to ensure respect for and protection of the civilian population and civilian objects, the Parties to the conflict shall at all times distinguish between the civilian population and combatants and between civilian objects and military objectives and accordingly shall direct their operations only against military objectives.

Article 49 — Definition of attacks and scope of application

1. "Attacks" means acts of violence against the adversary, whether in offence or in defence.

2. The provisions of this Protocol with respect to attacks apply to all attacks in whatever territory conducted, including the national territory belonging to a Party to the conflict but under the control of an adverse Party.

3. The provisions of this section apply to any land, air or sea warfare which may affect the civilian population, individual civilians or civilian objects on land. They further apply to all attacks from the sea or from the air against objectives on land but do not otherwise affect the rules of international law applicable in armed conflict at sea or in the air.

4. The provisions of this section are additional to the rules concerning humanitarian protection contained in the Fourth Convention, particularly in part II thereof, and in other international agreements binding upon the High Contracting Parties, as well as to other rules of international law relating to the protection of civilians and civilian objects on land, at sea or in the air against the effects of hostilities.

Article 50 — Definition of civilians and civilian population

Defines Civilians

1. A civilian is any person who does not belong to one of the categories of persons referred to in Article 4 (A) (1), (2), (3) and (6) of the Third Convention and in Article 43 of this Protocol. In case of doubt whether a person is a civilian, that person shall be considered to be a civilian.

2. The civilian population comprises all persons who are civilians.

3. The presence within the civilian population of individuals who do not come within the definition of civilians does not deprive the population of its civilian character.

Article 51 — Protection of the civilian population[3]

Protections of Civilians

1. The civilian population and individual civilians shall enjoy general protection against dangers arising from military operations. To give effect to this protection, the following rules, which are additional to other applicable rules of international law, shall be observed in all circumstances.

2. The civilian population as such, as well as individual civilians, shall not be the object of attack. Acts or threats of violence the primary purpose of which is to spread terror among the civilian population are prohibited.

3. Civilians shall enjoy the protection afforded by this section, unless and for such time as they take a direct part in hostilities.

4. Indiscriminate attacks are prohibited. Indiscriminate attacks are:

(a) those which are not directed at a specific military objective;

(b) those which employ a method or means of combat which cannot be directed at a specific military objective; or

(c) those which employ a method or means of combat the effects of which cannot be limited as required by this Protocol;

and consequently, in each such case, are of a nature to strike military objectives and civilians or civilian objects without distinction.

5. Among others, the following types of attacks are to be considered as indiscriminate:

(a) an attack by bombardment by any methods or means which treats as a single military objective a number of clearly separated and distinct military objectives located in a city, town, village or other area containing a similar concentration of civilians or civilian objects; and

(b) an attack which may be expected to cause incidental loss of civilian life, injury to civilians, damage to civilian objects, or a combination thereof, which would be excessive in relation to the concrete and direct military advantage anticipated.

6. Attacks against the civilian population or civilians by way of reprisals are prohibited.

7. The presence or movements of the civilian population or individual civilians shall not be used to render certain points or areas immune from military operations, in particular in attempts to shield military objectives from attacks or to shield, favour or impede military operations. The Parties to the conflict shall not direct the

[3. Recognized in part as customary law by the United States. — Eds.]

movement of the civilian population or individual civilians in order to attempt to shield military objectives from attacks or to shield military operations.

8. Any violation of these prohibitions shall not release the Parties to the conflict from their legal obligations with respect to the civilian population and civilians, including the obligation to take the precautionary measures provided for in Article 57....

Article 57 — Precautions in attack[4]

1. In the conduct of military operations, constant care shall be taken to spare the civilian population, civilians and civilian objects.

2. With respect to attacks, the following precautions shall be taken:

(a) those who plan or decide upon an attack shall:

(i) do everything feasible to verify that the objectives to be attacked are neither civilians nor civilian objects and are not subject to special protection but are military objectives within the meaning of paragraph 2 of Article 52 and that it is not prohibited by the provisions of this Protocol to attack them;

(ii) take all feasible precautions in the choice of means and methods of attack with a view to avoiding, and in any event to minimizing, incidental loss of civilian life, injury to civilians and damage to civilian objects;

(iii) refrain from deciding to launch any attack which may be expected to cause incidental loss of civilian life, injury to civilians, damage to civilian objects, or a combination thereof, which would be excessive in relation to the concrete and direct military advantage anticipated;

(b) an attack shall be cancelled or suspended if it becomes apparent that the objective is not a military one or is subject to special protection or that the attack may be expected to cause incidental loss of civilian life, injury to civilians, damage to civilian objects, or a combination thereof, which would be excessive in relation to the concrete and direct military advantage anticipated;

(c) effective advance warning shall be given of attacks which may affect the civilian population, unless circumstances do not permit.

3. When a choice is possible between several military objectives for obtaining a similar military advantage, the objective to be selected shall be that the attack on which may be expected to cause the least danger to civilian lives and to civilian objects.

4. In the conduct of military operations at sea or in the air, each Party to the conflict shall, in conformity with its rights and duties under the rules of international law applicable in armed conflict, take all reasonable precautions to avoid losses of civilian lives and damage to civilian objects.

5. No provision of this article may be construed as authorizing any attacks against the civilian population, civilians or civilian objects....

Article 72 — Field of application

The provisions of this Section are additional to the rules concerning humanitarian protection of civilians and civilian objects in the power of a Party to the conflict contained in the Fourth Convention, particularly Parts I and III thereof, as well as to

[4. Recognized as customary law by the United States. — Eds.]

other applicable rules of international law relating to the protection of fundamental human rights during international armed conflict....

Article 75 — Fundamental guarantees[5]

1. In so far as they are affected by a situation referred to in Article 1 of this Protocol, persons who are in the power of a Party to the conflict and who do not benefit from more favourable treatment under the Conventions or under this Protocol shall be treated humanely in all circumstances and shall enjoy, as a minimum, the protection provided by this Article without any adverse distinction based upon race, colour, sex, language, religion or belief, political or other opinion, national or social origin, wealth, birth or other status, or on any other similar criteria. Each Party shall respect the person, honour, convictions and religious practices of all such persons.

2. The following acts are and shall remain prohibited at any time and in any place whatsoever, whether committed by civilian or by military agents:

(a) violence to the life, health, or physical or mental well-being of persons, in particular:

    (i) murder;

    (ii) torture of all kinds, whether physical or mental;

    (iii) corporal punishment; and

    (iv) mutilation;

(b) outrages upon personal dignity, in particular humiliating and degrading treatment, enforced prostitution and any form of indecent assault;

(c) the taking of hostages;

(d) collective punishments; and

(e) threats to commit any of the foregoing acts.

3. Any person arrested, detained or interned for actions related to the armed conflict shall be informed promptly, in a language he understands, of the reasons why these measures have been taken. Except in cases of arrest or detention for penal offences, such persons shall be released with the minimum delay possible and in any event as soon as the circumstances justifying the arrest, detention or internment have ceased to exist.

4. No sentence may be passed and no penalty may be executed on a person found guilty of a penal offence related to the armed conflict except pursuant to a conviction pronounced by an impartial and regularly constituted court respecting the generally recognized principles of regular judicial procedure, which include the following:

(a) the procedure shall provide for an accused to be informed without delay of the particulars of the offence alleged against him and shall afford the accused before and during his trial all necessary rights and means of defence;

(b) no one shall be convicted of an offence except on the basis of individual penal responsibility;

(c) no one shall be accused or convicted of a criminal offence on account of any act or omission which did not constitute a criminal offence under the national or international law to which he was subject at the time when it was committed; nor shall a heavier penalty be imposed than that which was applicable at the time when the criminal offence was committed; if, after the commission of the offence,

[5. Recognized as customary law by the United States. — Eds.]

provision is made by law for the imposition of a lighter penalty, the offender shall benefit thereby;

(d) anyone charged with an offence is presumed innocent until proved guilty according to law;

(e) anyone charged with an offence shall have the right to be tried in his presence;

(f) no one shall be compelled to testify against himself or to confess guilt;

(g) anyone charged with an offence shall have the right to examine, or have examined, the witnesses against him and to obtain the attendance and examination of witnesses on his behalf under the same conditions as witnesses against him;

(h) no one shall be prosecuted or punished by the same Party for an offence in respect of which a final judgement acquitting or convicting that person has been previously pronounced under the same law and judicial procedure;

(i) anyone prosecuted for an offence shall have the right to have the judgement pronounced publicly; and

(j) a convicted person shall be advised on conviction of his judicial and other remedies and of the time-limits within which they may be exercised....

6. Persons who are arrested, detained or interned for reasons related to the armed conflict shall enjoy the protection provided by this Article until their final release, repatriation or re-establishment, even after the end of the armed conflict.

7. In order to avoid any doubt concerning the prosecution and trial of persons accused of war crimes or crimes against humanity, the following principles shall apply:

(a) persons who are accused of such crimes should be submitted for the purpose of prosecution and trial in accordance with the applicable rules of international law; and

(b) any such persons who do not benefit from more favourable treatment under the Conventions or this Protocol shall be accorded the treatment provided by this Article, whether or not the crimes of which they are accused constitute grave breaches of the Conventions or of this Protocol.

8. No provision of this Article may be construed as limiting or infringing any other more favourable provision granting greater protection, under any applicable rules of international law, to persons covered by paragraph 1....

Article 85 — Repression of breaches of this Protocol[6]

1. The provisions of the Conventions relating to the repression of breaches and grave breaches, supplemented by this Section, shall apply to the repression of breaches and grave breaches of this Protocol.

2. Acts described as grave breaches in the Conventions are grave breaches of this Protocol if committed against persons in the power of an adverse Party protected by Articles 44, 45 and 73 of this Protocol, or against the wounded, sick and shipwrecked of the adverse Party who are protected by this Protocol, or against those medical or religious personnel, medical units or medical transports which are under the control of the adverse Party and are protected by this Protocol.

3. In addition to the grave breaches defined in Article 11, the following acts shall be regarded as grave breaches of this Protocol, when committed wilfully, in violation

[6. Recognized as customary law by the United States. — Eds.]

of the relevant provisions of this Protocol, and causing death or serious injury to body or health:

(a) making the civilian population or individual civilians the object of attack;

(b) launching an indiscriminate attack affecting the civilian population or civilian objects in the knowledge that such attack will cause excessive loss of life, injury to civilians or damage to civilian objects, as defined in Article 57, paragraph 2 (a) (iii);

(c) launching an attack against works or installations containing dangerous forces in the knowledge that such attack will cause excessive loss of life, injury to civilians or damage to civilian objects, as defined in Article 57, paragraph 2 (a) (iii);

(d) making non-defended localities and demilitarized zones the object of attack;

(e) making a person the object of attack in the knowledge that he is hors de combat;

(f) the perfidious use, in violation of Article 37, of the distinctive emblem of the red cross, red crescent or red lion and sun or of other protective signs recognized by the Conventions or this Protocol.

4. In addition to the grave breaches defined in the preceding paragraphs and in the Conventions, the following shall be regarded as grave breaches of this Protocol, when committed wilfully and in violation of the Conventions or the Protocol:

(a) the transfer by the occupying Power of parts of its own civilian population into the territory it occupies, or the deportation or transfer of all or parts of the population of the occupied territory within or outside this territory, in violation of Article 49 of the Fourth Convention;

(b) unjustifiable delay in the repatriation of prisoners of war or civilians;

(c) practices of apartheid and other inhuman and degrading practices involving outrages upon personal dignity, based on racial discrimination;

(d) making the clearly-recognized historic monuments, works of art or places of worship which constitute the cultural or spiritual heritage of peoples and to which special protection has been given by special arrangement, for example, within the framework of a competent international organization, the object of attack, causing as a result extensive destruction thereof, where there is no evidence of the violation by the adverse Party of Article 53, subparagraph (b), and when such historic monuments, works of art and places of worship are not located in the immediate proximity of military objectives;

(e) depriving a person protected by the Conventions or referred to in paragraph 2 of this Article of the rights of fair and regular trial.

5. Without prejudice to the application of the Conventions and of this Protocol, grave breaches of these instruments shall be regarded as war crimes.

Article 86 — Failure to act[7]

1. The High Contracting Parties and the Parties to the conflict shall repress grave breaches, and take measures necessary to suppress all other breaches, of the Conventions or of this Protocol which result from a failure to act when under a duty to do so.

[7. Recognized as customary law by the United States. — Eds.]

2. The fact that a breach of the Conventions or of this Protocol was committed by a subordinate does not absolve his superiors from penal disciplinary responsibility, as the case may be, if they knew, or had information which should have enabled them to conclude in the circumstances at the time, that he was committing or was going to commit such a breach and if they did not take all feasible measures within their power to prevent or repress the breach. . . .

Rome Statute of the International Criminal Court

2187 U.N.T.S. 90, July 17, 1998

Article 8: War crimes

1. The Court shall have jurisdiction in respect of war crimes in particular when committed as part of a plan or policy or as part of a large-scale commission of such crimes.

War Crimes Defined

2. For the purpose of this Statute, "war crimes" means:

(a) Grave breaches of the Geneva Conventions of 12 August 1949, namely, any of the following acts against persons or property protected under the provisions of the relevant Geneva Convention:

(i) Wilful killing;

(ii) Torture or inhuman treatment, including biological experiments;

(iii) Wilfully causing great suffering, or serious injury to body or health;

(iv) Extensive destruction and appropriation of property, not justified by military necessity and carried out unlawfully and wantonly;

(v) Compelling a prisoner of war or other protected person to serve in the forces of a hostile Power;

(vi) Wilfully depriving a prisoner of war or other protected person of the rights of fair and regular trial;

(vii) Unlawful deportation or transfer or unlawful confinement;

(viii) Taking of hostages.

(b) Other serious violations of the laws and customs applicable in international armed conflict, within the established framework of international law, namely, any of the following acts:

(i) Intentionally directing attacks against the civilian population as such or against individual civilians not taking direct part in hostilities;

(ii) Intentionally directing attacks against civilian objects, that is, objects which are not military objectives;

(iii) Intentionally directing attacks against personnel, installations, material, units or vehicles involved in a humanitarian assistance or peacekeeping mission in accordance with the Charter of the United Nations, as long as they are entitled to the protection given to civilians or civilian objects under the international law of armed conflict;

(iv) Intentionally launching an attack in the knowledge that such attack will cause incidental loss of life or injury to civilians or damage to civilian objects or widespread, long-term and severe damage to the natural environment which would be clearly excessive in relation to the concrete and direct overall military advantage anticipated;

(v) Attacking or bombarding, by whatever means, towns, villages, dwellings or buildings which are undefended and which are not military objectives; ...

(xiv) Declaring abolished, suspended or inadmissible in a court of law the rights and actions of the nationals of the hostile party; ...

(xxi) Committing outrages upon personal dignity, in particular humiliating and degrading treatment; ....

(c) In the case of an armed conflict not of an international character, serious violations of article 3 common to the four Geneva Conventions of 12 August 1949, namely, any of the following acts committed against persons taking no active part in the hostilities, including members of armed forces who have laid down their arms and those placed hors de combat by sickness, wounds, detention or any other cause:

(i) Violence to life and person, in particular murder of all kinds, mutilation, cruel treatment and torture;

(ii) Committing outrages upon personal dignity, in particular humiliating and degrading treatment;

(iii) Taking of hostages;

(iv) The passing of sentences and the carrying out of executions without previous judgement pronounced by a regularly constituted court, affording all judicial guarantees which are generally recognized as indispensable.

(d) Paragraph 2 (c) applies to armed conflicts not of an international character and thus does not apply to situations of internal disturbances and tensions, such as riots, isolated and sporadic acts of violence or other acts of a similar nature.

(e) Other serious violations of the laws and customs applicable in armed conflicts not of an international character, within the established framework of international law, namely, any of the following acts:

(i) Intentionally directing attacks against the civilian population as such or against individual civilians not taking direct part in hostilities; ...

(f) Paragraph 2 (e) applies to armed conflicts not of an international character and thus does not apply to situations of internal disturbances and tensions, such as riots, isolated and sporadic acts of violence or other acts of a similar nature. It applies to armed conflicts that take place in the territory of a State when there is protracted armed conflict between governmental authorities and organized armed groups or between such groups.

3. Nothing in paragraph 2 (c) and (e) shall affect the responsibility of a Government to maintain or re-establish law and order in the State or to defend the unity and territorial integrity of the State, by all legitimate means.

NOTES AND QUESTIONS

1. *Architecture and Stature of the Conventions.* Every nation in the world has ratified the four 1949 Geneva Conventions. Like the earlier Geneva Conventions, the overarching purpose of the 1949 Conventions is to protect the victims of armed conflict, including the wounded, prisoners of war, and civilians. Accordingly, the regulation of battlefield tactics is left to other treaties, such as the 1907 Hague Regulation IV, and to customary law. Can you see the basic orientation of the Conventions toward victim protection in the provisions of Geneva III and IV excerpted above?

Articles 1-3 are "Common Articles," in that they are repeated verbatim in all four Conventions. Other common articles deal with execution of the Conventions or with procedural matters. What are the cornerstone protections of Articles 1-3? What is their likely practical effect?

2. *Grave Breaches.* Each of the four Geneva Conventions requires the enactment of domestic legislation to punish grave breaches. *See, e.g.,* Geneva IV, art. 146. Exactly what constitutes a "grave breach"? What is the difference between a grave breach and a war crime, and where would you expect to find a list of war crimes? What are the scope and content of each state's obligation to seek redress for grave breaches? *See id.* art. 147.

What domestic criminal provisions would you expect to find in U.S. laws that reflect the obligations of Geneva IV? Consider, for example, the Torture Act, 18 U.S.C. §§2340-2340B (2006), assessed in Chapter 17. What do you suppose is the measure of compliance with Article 146? In the United States, the Uniform Code of Military Justice (UCMJ) has since 1951 provided the mechanism for trying our own soldiers for alleged grave breaches. Civilians may now also be tried for grave breaches pursuant to the War Crimes Act of 1996, 18 U.S.C. §2441 (2006), and the Military Extraterritorial Jurisdiction Act, 18 U.S.C. §§3261-3267 (2006). Historically, enemy soldiers have been tried for grave breaches before military commissions, "juries" of military officers. See Chapter 22.

What is the jurisdiction of the International Criminal Court (ICC)? Could it try alleged grave breaches? What about war crimes? Genocide? Crimes against humanity?

3. *International and Non-International Armed Conflicts.* A wholly indigenous rebellion within a single state is one kind of non-international armed conflict. Before 9/11, the Taliban were the de facto government of parts of Afghanistan, in armed conflict with the Northern Alliance, an indigenous group of war lords. Was that conflict of a non-international character? Did its character change when the United States deployed forces in Afghanistan against the Taliban and Al Qaeda after 9/11? Which type is the U.S. conflict with Al Qaeda and the Taliban today? With reference to the Geneva Conventions, what is the legal and practical significance of the distinction?

Apart from the difficulty in distinguishing international from non-international armed conflicts, how would you distinguish an internal armed conflict from a domestic riot or rebellion? AP II states that it does not apply to "situations of internal disturbances and tensions, such as riots, isolated and sporadic acts of violence and other acts of a similar nature, as not being armed conflicts." AP II art. 2. What is the dividing line? *See Commentary, Convention (I) for the Amelioration of the Condition of the Wounded and Sick in Armed Forces in the Field. Geneva, 12 August 1949* (Jean S. Pictet ed., 1952), at 49, *available at* http://www.icrc.org/ihl.nsf/com/365-570006?opendocument (suggesting criteria, including "an organized military force, an authority responsible for its acts...having the means of respecting...the Convention...[and a] *de jure* Government [that] has recognized the insurgents as belligerents."). Who decides, and what legal difference, if any, does it make?

4. *Common Article 3.* Until Additional Protocol II was adopted in 1977, Common Article 3 was the only provision in the Geneva Conventions dealing explicitly with

conflicts "not of an international character." What protections are provided in Common Article 3, and which persons are entitled to them? What is the measure of "humane treatment"? Are these protections different from those afforded to victims of an international conflict?

5. *Jus in Bello as Custom and the Protocols.* As indicated above, the 1949 Geneva Conventions did not address issues of targeting, including the core principles of distinction, military necessity, unnecessary suffering, and proportionality. Yet those principles were part of customary law and were, to some extent, codified separately in the Hague and other treaties. What difference does it make whether IHL is customary or enshrined in a treaty provision? Can you figure out why the United States has recognized some of the AP I provisions as customary law but not others? Why not sign on, lock, stock, and barrel?

Reviewing the excerpted provisions of AP I, which ones articulate the principles of distinction, necessity, unnecessary suffering, and proportionality? See if you can extract from those articles a workable set of rules to guide soldiers in the field.

6. *Are the Geneva Conventions Obsolete?* Fresh from the horrors of World War II, the delegates to the 1949 conference in Geneva were determined to codify an extensive set of protections for the victims of state-on-state wars. They were not thinking about terrorism, insurgencies, guerrilla movements, or armed revolutions. The 1977 Protocols made only modest progress toward explicitly addressing such asymmetric warfare.

Even before the September 11 attacks, however, it was clear that conflicts between states and non-state entities were becoming increasingly common. In 2002, then-White House Counsel Alberto Gonzales wrote that the war on terrorism "renders obsolete Geneva's strict limitations on questioning of enemy prisoners and renders quaint some of its provisions." Alberto R. Gonzales, *Memorandum to the President, Decision re Application of the Geneva Convention on Prisoners of War to the Conflict with Al Qaeda and the Taliban,* Jan. 25, 2002. Do you agree?

Do the Geneva Conventions and their Protocols apply to an armed conflict between a state and a terrorist organization? Between a state and an insurgent group? Soldiers in an armed conflict of an international character are entitled to "combatant immunity" for uses of force that otherwise comply with IHL. They can be detained as POWs, but not tried for shooting at enemy soldiers, which is lawful combat. Could individuals fighting for a terrorist group or an insurgency be similarly entitled to combatant immunity? Are they be entitled to *any* of the protections of the Conventions or Protocols? *See* Common Article 3. If not, should the Conventions be amended? What specific amendments would you recommend?

There may soon be greater clarity about IHL, at least from the perspective of the United States. The Pentagon's Law of War Working Group has worked off and on for 14 years on a new *Department of Defense Law of War Manual,* the first comprehensive compilation of U.S. understandings of the treaties and state practice that make up IHL. The new *Manual* was expected to be released in 2011. *See* W. Hays Parks, *National Security Law in Practice: The Department of Defense Law of War Manual* (Nov. 8, 2010), *available at* http://www.americanbar.org/content/dam/aba/migrated/natsecurity/hays_parks_speech11082010.authcheckdam.pdf.

B. TARGETING AND PROTECTING CIVILIANS IN ARMED CONFLICT

Authority to Use Military Force in Libya

U.S. Department of Justice, Office of Legal Counsel, Apr. 1, 2011
35 Op. O.L.C. ___

Memorandum opinion for: The Attorney General

From: Caroline D. Krass, Prin. Dep. Asst. Att'y General

. . . In mid-February 2011, amid widespread popular demonstrations seeking governmental reform in the neighboring countries of Tunisia and Egypt, as well as elsewhere in the Middle East and North Africa, protests began in Libya against the autocratic government of Colonel Muammar Qadhafi, who has ruled Libya since taking power in a 1969 coup. Qadhafi moved swiftly in an attempt to end the protests using military force. Some Libyan government officials and elements of the Libyan military left the Qadhafi regime, and by early March, Qadhafi had lost control over much of the eastern part of the country, including the city of Benghazi. The Libyan government's operations against its opponents reportedly included strafing of protesters and shelling, bombing, and other violence deliberately targeting civilians. Many refugees fled to Egypt and other neighboring countries to escape the violence, creating a serious crisis in the region.

On February 26, 2011, the United Nations Security Council ("UNSC") unanimously adopted Resolution 1970, which "[e]xpress[ed] grave concern at the situation in the Libyan Arab Jamahiriya," "condemn[ed] the violence and use of force against civilians," and "[d]eplor[ed] the gross and systematic violation of human rights" in Libya. S.C. Res. 1970, U.N. Doc. S/RES/1970 (Feb. 26, 2011); Press Release, Security Council, In Swift, Decisive Action, Security Council Imposes Tough Measures on Libyan Regime, Adopting Resolution 1970 in Wake of Crackdown on Protesters, U.N. Press Release SC/10187/Rev. 1 (Feb. 26, 2011). The resolution called upon member states, among other things, to take "the necessary measures" to prevent arms transfers "from or through their territories or by their nationals, or using their flag vessels or aircraft"; to freeze the assets of Qadhafi and certain other close associates of the regime; and to "facilitate and support the return of humanitarian agencies and make available humanitarian and related assistance" in Libya. S.C. Res. 1970, ¶¶9, 17, 26. The resolution did not, however, authorize members of the United Nations to use military force in Libya.

The Libyan government's violence against civilians continued, and even escalated, despite condemnation by the UNSC and strong expressions of disapproval from other regional and international bodies. See, e.g., African Union, Communique of the 265th Meeting of the Peace and Security Council, PSC/PR/COMM.2(CCLXV) (Mar. 10, 2011) (describing the "prevailing situation in Libya" as "pos[ing] a serious threat to peace and security in that country and in the region as a whole" and "[r]eiterat[ing] AU's strong and unequivocal condemnation of the indiscriminate use of force and lethal weapons"); News Release, Organization of the Islamic Conference, OIC General Secretariat Condemns Strongly the Excessive Use of Force

Against Civilians in the Libyan Jamahiriya (Feb. 22, 2011), *available at* http://www.oic-oci .org/topic_detail.asp?t_id=4947&x_key= (reporting that "the General Secretariat of the Organization of the Islamic Conference (OIC) voiced its strong condemnation of the excessive use of force against civilians in the Arab Libyan Jamahiriya")....

By March 17, 2011, Qadhafi's forces were preparing to retake the city of Benghazi. Pledging that his forces would begin an assault on the city that night and show "no mercy and no pity" to those who would not give up resistance, Qadhafi stated in a radio address: "We will come house by house, room by room. It's over. The issue has been decided." See Dan Bilefsky & Mark Landler, *Military Action Against Qaddafi Is Backed by U.N.*, N.Y. Times, Mar. 18, 2011, at A1. Qadhafi, President Obama later noted, "compared [his people] to rats, and threatened to go door to door to inflict punishment.... We knew that if we ... waited one more day, Benghazi, a city nearly the size of Charlotte, could suffer a massacre that would have reverberated across the region and stained the conscience of the world." Press Release, Office of the Press Secretary, The White House, Remarks by the President in Address to the Nation on Libya (Mar. 28, 2011) ("Obama March 28, 2011 Address"), *available at* http://www. whitehouse.gov/the-press-office/2011/03/28/remarks-president-address-nation-libya.

Later the same day, the UNSC addressed the situation in Libya again by adopting, by a vote of 10-0 (with five members abstaining), Resolution 1973, which imposed a no-fly zone and authorized the use of military force to protect civilians. See S.C. Res. 1973, U.N. Doc. S/RES/1973 (Mar. 17, 2011); Press Release, Security Council, Security Council Approves 'No-Fly Zone' Over Libya, Authorizing 'All Necessary Measures' to Protect Civilians, by Vote of 10 in Favour with 5 Abstentions, U.N. Press Release SC/10200 (Mar. 17, 2011). In this resolution, the UNSC determined that the "situation" in Libya "continues to constitute a threat to international peace and security" and "demand[ed] the immediate establishment of a cease-fire and a complete end to violence and all attacks against, and abuses of, civilians." S.C. Res. 1973. Resolution 1973 authorized member states, acting individually or through regional organizations, "to take all necessary measures ... to protect civilians and civilian populated areas under threat of attack in the Libyan Arab Jamahiriya, including Benghazi, while excluding a foreign occupation force of any form on any part of Libyan territory." *Id.* ¶4. The resolution also specifically authorized member states to enforce "a ban on all [unauthorized] flights in the airspace of the Libyan Arab Jamahiriya in order to help protect civilians" and to take "all measures commensurate to the specific circumstances" to inspect vessels on the high seas suspected of violating the arms embargo imposed on Libya by Resolution 1970. *Id.* ¶¶6-8, 13.

In remarks on March 18, 2011, President Obama stated that, to avoid military intervention to enforce Resolution 1973, Qadhafi needed to: implement an immediate ceasefire, including by ending all attacks on civilians; halt his troops' advance on Benghazi; pull his troops back from three other cities; and establish water, electricity, and gas supplies to all areas. Press Release, Office of the Press Secretary, The White House, Remarks by the President on the Situation in Libya (Mar. 18, 2011) ("Obama March 18, 2011 Remarks"), *available at* http://www.whitehouse.gov/the-press-office/ 2011/03/18/remarks-president-situation-libya.... Despite a statement from Libya's Foreign Minister that Libya would honor the requested ceasefire, the Libyan government continued to conduct offensive operations, including attacks on civilians and civilian-populated areas. See Press Release, Office of the Press Secretary, The White House, Letter from the President Regarding Commencement of Operations in Libya:

Text of a Letter from the President to the Speaker of the House of Representatives and the President Pro Tempore of the Senate (Mar. 21, 2011) ("Obama March 21, 2011 Report to Congress"), *available at* http://www.whitehouse.gov/the-press-office/2011/03/21/letter-president-regardingcommencement-operations-libya. In response, on March 19, 2011, the United States, with the support of a number of its coalition partners, launched airstrikes against Libyan targets to enforce Resolution 1973. Consistent with the reporting provisions of the War Powers Resolution, 50 U.S.C. §1543(a) (2006), President Obama provided a report to Congress less than forty-eight hours later, on March 21, 2011. The President explained:

> At approximately 3:00 p.m. Eastern Daylight Time, on March 19, 2011, at my direction, U.S. military forces commenced operations to assist an international effort authorized by the United Nations (U.N.) Security Council and undertaken with the support of European allies and Arab partners, to prevent a humanitarian catastrophe and address the threat posed to international peace and security by the crisis in Libya. As part of the multilateral response authorized under U.N. Security Council Resolution 1973, U.S. military forces, under the command of Commander, U.S. Africa Command, began a series of strikes against air defense systems and military airfields for the purposes of preparing a no-fly zone. These strikes will be limited in their nature, duration, and scope. Their purpose is to support an international coalition as it takes all necessary measures to enforce the terms of U.N. Security Council Resolution 1973. These limited U.S. actions will set the stage for further action by other coalition partners.

Obama March 21, 2011 Report to Congress....

... [T]he President explained that "United States forces are conducting a limited and well-defined mission in support of international efforts to protect civilians and prevent a humanitarian disaster" and thus had targeted only "the Qadhafi regime's air defense systems, command and control structures, and other capabilities of Qadhafi's armed forces used to attack civilians and civilian populated areas." *Id.* The President also indicated that "[w]e will seek a rapid, but responsible, transition of operations to coalition, regional, or international organizations that are postured to continue activities as may be necessary to realize the objectives of U.N. Security Council Resolutions 1970 and 1973." *Id.* As authority for the military operations in Libya, President Obama invoked his "constitutional authority to conduct U.S. foreign relations" and his authority "as Commander in Chief and Chief Executive." *Id.*...

On March 28, 2011, President Obama addressed the nation regarding the situation in Libya. The President stated that the coalition had succeeded in averting a massacre in Libya and that the United States was now transferring "the lead in enforcing the no-fly zone and protecting civilians on the ground... to our allies and partners." Obama March 28, 2011 Address. In future coalition operations in Libya, the President continued, "the United States will play a supporting role — including intelligence, logistical support, search and rescue assistance, and capabilities to jam regime communications." *Id.* The President also reiterated the national interests supporting military action by the United States. "[G]iven the costs and risks of intervention," he explained, "we must always measure our interests against the need for action." *Id.* But, "[i]n this particular country — Libya — at this particular moment, we were faced with the prospect of violence on a horrific scale," and "[w]e had a unique ability to stop that violence." *Id.* Failure to prevent a slaughter would have disregarded

America's "important strategic interest in preventing Qaddafi from overrunning those who oppose him":

> A massacre would have driven thousands of additional refugees across Libya's borders, putting enormous strains on the peaceful—yet fragile—transitions in Egypt and Tunisia. The democratic impulses that are dawning across the region would be eclipsed by the darkest form of dictatorship, as repressive leaders concluded that violence is the best strategy to cling to power. The writ of the United Nations Security Council would have been shown to be little more than empty words, crippling that institution's future credibility to uphold global peace and security. So while I will never minimize the costs involved in military action, I am convinced that a failure to act in Libya would have carried a far greater price for America.

Id. As of March 31, 2011, the United States had transferred responsibility for all ongoing coalition military operations in Libya to the North Atlantic Treaty Alliance ("NATO")....

NOTES AND QUESTIONS

1. *Status of the Conflict.* What defines an "armed" conflict? Is it the level of violence? Number of casualties? Duration of the fighting? Nature of the warfare? Do the Conventions provide a clear definition? *See* Common Articles 2 and 3; AP I art. 1. Is there any doubt that the fighting in Libya in early 2011 was an armed conflict?

There is, as we have seen, more than one kind of armed conflict. A declared war between two or more states is easy to characterize: it is an international armed conflict, and all of the protections of the Geneva Conventions are applicable. By contrast, the uprising in Libya that began in early 2011 was, at least initially, a wholly indigenous armed insurrection bordering on civil war, giving it the appearance of a conflict not of an international character. Did that character change when NATO, the United States, and other states became involved militarily?

Who is entitled to label an armed conflict as international or non-international? How did the label or labels affect the rules for conducting military operations in Libya?

2. *Effect of the Security Council Resolutions on Jus in Bello.* Do you think the Security Council's establishment of a no-fly zone over Libya affected the applicability of IHL there? Did Security Council Resolution 1973 authorize military action beyond the maintenance of a no-fly zone? If it did, what was the scope of the authorization? How much discretion was conferred on NATO to protect civilians and civilian "populated areas"? Could NATO forces have undertaken ground or naval operations against Libyan armed forces? Could they have attacked members of the Libyan security forces who were not directly engaged in attacks on civilians but were supporting those attacks in some way, far from the field of battle? *See* Michael N. Schmitt, *Wings Over Libya: The No-Fly Zone in Legal Perspective,* 36 Yale J. Int'l L. Online 45 (2011) (arguing that the resolution creates broad authority to attack Libyan air and ground forces that is nevertheless limited by IHL).

A Secretary-General Bulletin and an International Committee of the Red Cross (ICRC) commentary agree that IHL applies in enforcing a Security Council action. *See* U.N. Secretariat, *Secretary-General's Bulletin: Observance by United Nations Forces of International Humanitarian Law,* U.N. Doc. ST/SGB/1999/13 (Aug. 6, 1999), *reprinted in* 38 I.L.M. 1656; International Comm. of the Red Cross, *Commentary to the Third*

Geneva Convention Relative to the Treatment of Prisoners of War 23 (Jean S. Pictet ed., 1960). *See also* Schmitt, *supra*, at 50-51, 54.

3. *Individual Battlefield Status.* One important qualifier to the principle noted just above is that IHL rules are "tempered by the scope of the authorization." Schmitt, *supra*, at 54. Review the Geneva Convention provisions on individual status alongside Security Council Resolution 1973. What is the geographic extent of the zone that may be targeted? Who may be attacked while enforcing the no-fly zone? Must the targets be inside the zone? If Qaddafi forces are captured by NATO personnel enforcing the no-fly zone, what provisions govern their detention and return? Do the same provisions apply to any NATO troops captured by the Libyan armed forces?

Can you describe the categories of persons who may be found on a battlefield? Why do you suppose it has become so hard to reliably distinguish combatants from civilians? We explore more fully the post–September 11 problems of labeling prisoners as combatants, unlawful combatants, or something else, *infra* p. 444.

In the Libya conflict, as in many other contemporary armed conflicts both international and not of an international character, government forces did not always wear uniforms or otherwise distinguish themselves as members of the state's military. How can we determine whether an apparently protected civilian is taking a "direct part in hostilities"? *See* AP I art. 51.3. What does it mean to end civilian protection from attack "for such time" as they directly participate? Must there be specific hostile acts, or would hostile intent suffice? Is a bomb maker or military accountant taking "direct part"? A driver? A chef? Does the civilian who takes direct part regain his immunity when he goes home at night?

What was the battlefield status of persons fighting for the Libyan rebels against Libyan government forces? Did the rebels constitute "armed forces" as understood in Common Article 3? Did the status of an individual rebel fighter turn on whether she was taking a "direct part in hostilities," or were members of such non-state armed groups equivalent to state soldiers? According to an influential 2009 study by the ICRC, membership in an organized armed group depends on the individual's function. A member is a combatant if he engages in a "continuous combat function . . . rather than a spontaneous, sporadic, or temporary role." ICRC, *Interpretive Guidance on the Notion of Direct Participation in Hostilities under International Humanitarian Law* 1007-1008, *reprinted in* 872 Int'l Rev. Red Cross 991 (Dec. 2008). Does the "continuous combat function" criterion make it easier to determine who directly participates in hostilities?

Today, Common Article 3 is customary international law applicable to all armed conflicts. What is the measure of the humane treatment required by that article? See Chapter 17. What other *jus in bello* protections are due captured persons in any kind of conflict? What additional protections are required for detainees in an international armed conflict?

4. *Distinction.* Many feel that the principle of distinction is the most important *jus in bello* rule. An ICRC study begins its list of customary norms this way: "Rule 1. The parties to the conflict must at all times distinguish between civilians and combatants. . . . Attacks must not be directed against civilians." Jean-Marie Henckaerts, *Study on Customary International Humanitarian Law: A Contribution to the Understanding and Respect for the Rule of Law in Armed Conflict*, 87 Int'l Rev. Red Cross 175, 198 (Mar. 2005). Civilian objects are subject to the same principle. *Id.*; AP I art. 52.

Distinction was not mentioned as such in the Conventions until the Additional Protocols were adopted in 1977. If you advised the NATO forces enforcing the Security Council resolution, how would you translate AP I art. 48 into operational rules? If Libyan armed forces purposefully wore civilian clothing, with no insignias or other identifying features, how would U.S. and NATO commanders and pilots in the air know who their lawful targets were?

Applying the principle of distinction, civilian aircraft should not be attacked. But Security Council Resolution 1973 established a ban on all flights in Libyan air space. Did that mean a civilian aircraft entering the no-fly zone forfeited its civilian status and became a lawful target? *See* AP I art. 50(1), *supra*; art. 52(2) (Military objectives are objects "which by their nature, location, purpose or use make an effective contribution to military action and whose total or partial destruction, capture or neutralization, in the circumstances ruling at the time, offers a definite military advantage."). *See also* Schmitt, *supra*, at 51 (concluding that the resolution and the AP I provisions permit targeting of civilian aircraft).

5. *Necessity.* If distinction is the most humanitarian principle in IHL, the principle of necessity permits only "those measures which are indispensable for securing the ends of war, and which are lawful." U.S. War Dep't, *Instructions for the Government of Armies of the United States in the Field* (*General Orders No. 100: The Lieber Code*) art. 14 (Apr. 24, 1863). Which GC provisions reflect the principle of necessity? How should legal advisers give the concept practical meaning?

6. *Unnecessary Suffering.* The AP I provision in Article 35 makes it clear that the principle of unnecessary suffering limits the means for waging war. How would you define the key terms "of a nature," "superfluous injury," and "unnecessary suffering"? Does the U.S. use of cruise missiles fail the test? How about the use of cluster bombs in residential neighborhoods by Libyan armed forces? How is the principle of unnecessary suffering different from the principle of distinction?

7. *Proportionality.* Review AP I arts. 51.5(b) and 57.2(b), *supra*. The focus is clearly on civilians, not combatants. How do the two sets of protections differ? What do you suppose is the measure of "excessive" harm to civilians? Could you draft a more precise rule? Why do you think the drafters employed such open-ended terms? Is the 1956 U.S. Army field manual provision better: "[L]oss of life and damage to property incidental to attacks must not be excessive in relation to the concrete and direct military advantage expected to be gained"? Department of the Army, *The Law of Land Warfare* (FM 27-10) ¶41 (1956). Under the Army rule, could a military operation that is anticipated to cause extensive civilian casualties ever be lawful?

Do proportionality requirements apply in non-international armed conflicts? If attacks on civilian aircraft violating the Libyan no-fly zone would not violate the principle of distinction and related AP I articles (see Note 5, *supra*), might they nonetheless have violated the principle of proportionality? Does the answer depend on whether those aircraft were determined to be directly participating in hostilities at the time of targeting? *See* Schmitt, *supra*, at 52 (yes to both questions). Would the presence of clearly innocent civilians on the civilian aircraft in such circumstances alter the calculus and preclude an attack? *See id.* (maybe).

How does the principle of proportionality differ from the principles of distinction and unnecessary suffering?

8. *War Crimes.* What, according to the Rome Statute of the International Criminal Court, must be shown to prove a war crime? How do the requirements differ in international and non-international armed conflicts? What is the differences between war crimes and grave breaches?

Because no definition can capture all possible violations of IHL, there is no fixed catalog of offenses. May civilians commit war crimes? How about members of organized armed groups? Taliban or Al Qaeda members? Where would prosecutions against such persons be brought? Should a greater effort be made to try to define all war crimes?

C.   TREATMENT OF PRISONERS IN WAR

In 1992, during the conflict in the Balkans that accompanied the breakup of Yugoslavia, Bosnian Muslim and Croat forces took control of villages with mostly Bosnian Serb populations in and around Konjic in central Bosnia and Herzegovina. Persons detained in a prison camp in the village of Celebici were tortured, sexually assaulted, subjected to cruel and inhuman treatment, and killed by camp guards and their commanders. In 1993, following mass atrocities in Croatia and Bosnia and Herzegovina, the United Nations Security Council created its first international criminal tribunal, the International Criminal Tribunal for the former Yugoslavia (ICTY). *See* Statute of the International Criminal Tribunal for the Former Yugoslavia (ICTY), as amended, *available at* http://www.un.org/icty/legaldoc-e/index.htm, established by S.C. Res. 827, U.N. Doc. S/RES/827 (May 25, 1993). Later that same year three Bosnian Muslims and one Bosnian Croat connected to the abuses at Celebici were indicted. They were arrested in 1996 and brought to the Hague in 1997 for a trial before the ICTY. The judgment of the trial chamber in *Prosecutor v. Delalic,* IT-96-T (ICTY Nov. 1998), found three of the four defendants guilty of multiple grave breaches of the Geneva Conventions for acts of willful killing, torture, sexual abuse, and inhuman treatment of detainees at the Celebici prison camp. In the Appeals Chamber of the ICTY, the four defendants and the prosecution challenged the Trial Chamber's legal standard for determining what constitutes the unlawful confinement of civilians, and its decision that some of the civilians in the camp were unlawfully detained. Excerpts from the Appeals Chamber decision follow:

Prosecutor v. Delalic (Celebici Case)

International Criminal Tribunal for the Former Yugoslavia, 2001
Appeals Chamber, Case No. IT-96-21-A
http://www.icty.org/x/cases/mucic/acjug/en/cel-aj010220.pdf

V.   UNLAWFUL CONFINEMENT OF CIVILIANS...

(i)   The unlawful confinement of civilians

320. The offence of unlawful confinement of a civilian ... [is] a grave breach of the Geneva Conventions.... The Trial Chamber found that the confinement of civilians during armed conflict may be permissible in limited cases, but will be unlawful if the detaining party does not comply with the provisions of Article 42 of Geneva Convention IV, which states:

> The internment or placing in assigned residence of protected persons may be ordered only if the security of the Detaining Power makes it absolutely necessary.
> If any person, acting through the representatives of the Protecting Power, voluntarily demands internment, and if his situation renders this step necessary, he shall be interned by the Power in whose hands he may be.

Thus the involuntary confinement of a civilian where the security of the Detaining Power does not make this absolutely necessary will be unlawful. Further, an initially lawful internment clearly becomes unlawful if the detaining party does not respect the basic procedural rights of the detained persons and does not establish an appropriate court or administrative board as prescribed in Article 43 of Geneva Convention IV. That article provides:

> Any protected person who has been interned or placed in assigned residence shall be entitled to have such action reconsidered as soon as possible by an appropriate court or administrative board designated by the Detaining Power for that purpose. If the internment or placing in assigned residence is maintained, the court or administrative board shall periodically, and at least twice yearly, give consideration to his or her case, with a view to the favourable amendment of the initial decision, if circumstances permit.
> Unless the protected persons concerned object, the Detaining Power shall, as rapidly as possible, give the Protecting Power the names of any protected persons who have been interned or subjected to assigned residence, or have been released from internment or assigned residence. The decisions of the courts or boards mentioned in the first paragraph of the present Article shall also, subject to the same conditions, be notified as rapidly as possible to the Protecting Power.

321. In its consideration of the law relating to the offence of unlawful confinement, the Trial Chamber also referred to Article 5 of Geneva Convention IV [*supra* p. 32].... This provision reinforces the principle behind Article 42, that restrictions on the rights of civilian protected persons, such as deprivation of their liberty by confinement, are permissible only where there are reasonable grounds to believe that the security of the State is at risk.

322. The Appeals Chamber agrees with the Trial Chamber that the exceptional measure of confinement of a civilian will be lawful only in the conditions prescribed by Article 42, and where the provisions of Article 43 are complied with. Thus the detention or confinement of civilians will be unlawful in the following two circumstances:

> (i) when a civilian or civilians have been detained in contravention of Article 42 of Geneva Convention IV, i.e., they are detained without reasonable grounds to believe that the security of the Detaining Power makes it absolutely necessary; and
> (ii) where the procedural safeguards required by Article 43 of Geneva Convention IV are not complied with in respect of detained civilians, even where their initial detention may have been justified.

(ii)   Was the confinement of the Celebici camp detainees unlawful?

323. As stated above, the Trial Chamber found that the persons detained in the Celebici camp were civilian protected persons for the purposes of Article 4 of Geneva Convention IV [*supra* p. 32]. The Trial Chamber accepted evidence that indicated that a number of the civilians in the camp were in possession of weapons at the time of their capture, but refrained from making any finding as to whether the detaining power could legitimately have formed the view that the detention of this category of persons was necessary for the security of that power. However, the Trial Chamber also found that the confinement of a significant number of civilians in the camp could not be justified by any means. Even taking into account the measure of discretion which should be afforded to the detaining power in assessing what may be detrimental to its own security, several of the detained civilians could not reasonably have been considered to pose any sufficiently serious danger as to warrant their detention. The Trial Chamber specifically accepted the evidence of a number of witnesses who had testified that they had not participated in any military activity or even been politically active, including a 42-year old mother of two children. It concluded that at least this category of people were detained in the camp although there existed no serious and legitimate reason to conclude that they seriously prejudiced the security of the detaining party, which indicated that the detention was a collective measure aimed at a specific group of persons, based mainly on their ethnic background. . . .

326. [One of the defendants] contends that since "the Trial Chamber, in determining that they [the civilians] were protected persons, found that they were not loyal to [. . .] Bosnia and Herzegovina, then they are virtually ipso facto security risks to the Government in that they are supporting the rebel forces." He explains the detention of persons who may not have borne arms on the basis that "if not engaged in actual fighting, then they are certainly in a position to provide food, clothing, shelter and information to those who are."

327. In the Appeals Chamber's view, there is no necessary inconsistency between the Trial Chamber's finding that the Bosnian Serbs were regarded by the Bosnian authorities as belonging to the opposing party in an armed conflict and the finding that some of them could not reasonably be regarded as presenting a threat to the detaining power's security. To hold the contrary would suggest that, whenever the armed forces of a State are engaged in armed conflict, the entire civilian population of that State is necessarily a threat to security and therefore may be detained. It is perfectly clear from the provisions of Geneva Convention IV referred to above that there is no such blanket power to detain the entire civilian population of a party to the conflict in such circumstances, but that there must be an assessment that each civilian taken into detention poses a particular risk to the security of the State. This is reflected in the ICRC Commentary to Article 42 of Geneva Convention IV:

> [. . .] the mere fact that a person is a subject of an enemy Power cannot be considered as threatening the security of the country where he is living; it is not therefore a valid reason for interning him or placing him in assigned residence.

Thus the Appeals Chamber agrees with the conclusion reached by the Trial Chamber that "the mere fact that a person is a national of, or aligned with, an enemy party cannot be considered as threatening the security of the opposing party where he is living, and is not, therefore, a valid reason for interning him."

328. It was contended by [one defendant] that detention in the present case was justified under international law because "[t]he government is clearly entitled to some reasonable time to determine which of the detainees is a danger to the State's security." Although the Appeals Chamber accepts this proposition, it does not share the view apparently taken by [this defendant] as to what is a "reasonable time" for this purpose. The reasonableness of this period is not a matter solely to be assessed by the detaining power. The Appeals Chamber recalls that Article 43 of Geneva Convention IV provides that the decision to take measures of detention against civilians must be "reconsidered as soon as possible by an appropriate court or administrative board." Read in this light, the reasonable time which is to be afforded to a detaining power to ascertain whether detained civilians pose a security risk must be the minimum time necessary to make enquiries to determine whether a view that they pose a security risk has any objective foundation such that it would found a "definite suspicion" of the nature referred to in Article 5 of Geneva Convention IV. Although the Trial Chamber made no express finding upon this issue, the Appeals Chamber is satisfied that the only reasonable finding upon the evidence is that the civilians detained in the Celebici camp had been detained for longer than such a minimum time.

329. The Trial Chamber found that a Military Investigative Commission for the crimes allegedly committed by the persons confined in the Celebici camp was established, but that this Commission did not meet the requirements of Article 43 of Geneva Convention IV as it did not have the necessary power to decide finally on the release of prisoners whose detention could not be considered as justified for any serious reason. There is therefore nothing in the activities of the Commission which could justify the continued detention of detainees in respect of whom there was no reason to categorise as a security risk. Indeed, it appears to have recommended the release of several of the Celebici camp detainees, albeit without result. Delic submits that "the government had the right to continue the confinement until it determined that the State's security would not be harmed by release of the detainees." This submission, which carries the implication that civilian detainees may be considered a risk to security which makes their detention absolutely necessary until proved otherwise, completely reverses the onus of justifying detention of civilians. It is upon the detaining power to establish that the particular civilian does pose such a risk to its security that he must be detained, and the obligation lies on it to release the civilian if there is inadequate foundation for such a view.

330. The Trial Chamber, as the trier of facts, is in the best position to assess and weigh the evidence before it, and the Appeals Chamber gives a margin of deference to a Trial Chamber's evaluation of the evidence and findings of facts. Nothing put to the Appeals Chamber indicates that there is anything unreasonable in the relevant sense in the Trial Chamber's findings as to the unlawful nature of the confinement of a number of civilians in the Celebici camp. As observed in the ICRC Commentary, the measure of confinement of civilians is an "exceptionally severe" measure, and it is for that reason that the threshold for its imposition is high — it must, on the express terms of Article 42, be "absolutely necessary." It was open to the Trial Chamber to accept the evidence of a number of witnesses that they had not borne arms, nor been active in political or any other activity which would give rise to a legitimate concern that they posed a security risk. The Appeals Chamber is also not satisfied that the Trial Chamber erred in its conclusion that, even if it were to accept that the initial confinement of the individuals detained in the Celebici prison-camp was lawful, the continuing confinement of these civilians was in violation of international humanitarian law, as the detainees were not granted the procedural rights required by article 43 of Geneva Convention IV.

NOTES AND QUESTIONS

1. *Confining Civilians.* Under what circumstances are civilians *not* protected persons according to the Geneva Conventions? When would it be permissible to confine civilians during an armed conflict? Reading Articles 5, 42, and 43 of Geneva Convention IV together, what grounds would justify civilian detention? What procedures must attend such confinement?

2. *Loyalty to the Host State as a Measure of Who May Be Detained?* If some of the civilians detained were not loyal to Bosnia and Herzegovina, why wasn't it lawful for the Bosnian authorities to presume that they were not protected? Do you think the requirement that the detaining authority have a "reasonable time" to determine whether detainees are a danger to the state strikes the right balance between liberty and security? Did the Appeals Chamber correctly weigh the competing interests? Could the Military Investigative Commission have made definitive judgments about loyalty if it had met the requirements of Article 43?

3. *Other Protections for Protected Persons.* The excerpt of the *Delalic* case provided here concerns the unlawful confinement of civilians. Reviewing the provisions of Geneva Conventions II and IV and AP I set out above, can you say what other protections exist for persons *while* they are confined? How and why do these protections differ from those considered in Part B of this chapter, which are designed to protect persons *before* they are taken into custody?

4. *Redress for Violations of IHL?* The ICTY is an extraordinary court, one created by the U.N. Security Council after worldwide condemnation of the atrocities in the Balkans. If there were no ICTY, how could the victims of Celebici gain redress? What courts would conceivably hear their cases? *See generally* Mark S. Ellis, *Combating Impunity and Enforcing Accountability as a Way to Promote Peace and Stability — The Role of International War Crimes Tribunals*, 2 J. Nat'l Security L. & Pol'y 111 (2006).

5. *POWs and Combatants.* Who qualifies as a POW in an armed conflict? How would you apply the Geneva Convention criteria for POW status to insurgents? To members of terrorist groups? To rebels fighting to liberate a nation from colonial rule? What is the significance, in each instance, of the fact that a person did or did not take a direct part in hostilities?

Whatever the status of detainees, can the detaining authority employ torture or cruel and inhuman methods to obtain information from them? We address this question in connection with the interrogation of Taliban and Al Qaeda prisoners after 9/11, in Chapters 17-18.

6. *Custom and Human Rights Law.* In addition to the protections embedded in the Geneva Conventions, there is a large and growing body of related customary law and HRL. Where would you look to find these supplemental norms? How would they be interpreted alongside the Geneva provisions?

Waging War on Terrorists 3

Shortly after the terrorist bombings of U.S. embassies in East Africa in 1998, and again following the September 11, 2001, attacks on the World Trade Center and the Pentagon, U.S. authorities determined that Al Qaeda was responsible for planning and carrying out the attacks. Did the United States have the right under international law to strike back against Al Qaeda camps in Afghanistan or against Al Qaeda's allies in Pakistan? Was the President authorized to order a military response against Al Qaeda — and possible other terrorist groups — without the approval of Congress? If Congress had a role to play, how extensive was that role, and what form should its approval have taken?

The United Nations Charter forbids the use of force against the territorial integrity or political independence of any state, but also preserves an "inherent right of individual and collective self-defense if an armed attack occurs." U.N. Charter arts. 2(4) & 51. The United States thus has an "inherent" right of self-defense under international law, as well as the right to seek United Nations action with respect to attacks on the United States.

At the Constitutional Convention, the delegates substituted "declare" for "make" in the Declare War Clause of Article I, section 8, "leaving to the Executive the power to repel sudden attacks," according to Madison's notes. 2 Max Farrand, *The Records of the Federal Convention of 1787*, at 318-319 (rev. ed. 1937). The implication is that the President has some inherent constitutional power to respond to a terrorist attack without prior statutory authorization — what we will call his defensive war power. Alternatively, he could ask Congress to declare war, or, as we shall see, to give him a more limited statutory authorization for the use of military force.

In Part A of this chapter, we look briefly at the international law regarding aggression — *jus ad bellum* — and related portions of the U.N. Charter. In Part B, we explore the origins and scope of the President's defensive war power. In Part C, we consider express and implied statutory authorizations for the use of military force, and we ask whether other forms of congressional action can supply whatever authority is necessary. In Part D, we apply the foregoing law to the use of military force against Al Qaeda, both before and after the 9/11 attacks.

A. INTERNATIONAL LAW REGARDING
THE RIGHT TO WAGE WAR
(*JUS AD BELLUM*)

On June 26, 1945, world leaders gathered in San Francisco to sign the Charter of the United Nations. The agony of the world's greatest armed conflict was fresh in their minds. The fighting in Europe had just ended, but the U.S. atomic bombings of Hiroshima and Nagasaki, as well as a peace treaty with Japan, still lay in the future. This searing experience inspired a declaration that the first purpose of the newly formed organization was

> [t]o maintain international peace and security, and to that end: to take effective control measures for the prevention and removal of threats to the peace, and for the suppression of acts of aggression or other breaches of the peace, and to bring about by peaceful means, and in conformity with the principles of justice and international law, adjustment or settlement of international disputes or situations which might lead to a breach of the peace. [U.N. Charter art. 1, para. 1.]

The core principle for implementation of this resolution was set forth in Article 2, paragraph 4, of the Charter, which declares: "All Members shall refrain in their international relations from the threat or use of force against the territorial integrity or political independence of any state, or in any other manner inconsistent with the Purposes of the United Nations." It is mirrored in Article 2(3) by a commitment that "[a]ll Members shall settle their international disputes by peaceful means in such a manner that international peace and security, and justice, are not endangered."

But the signers of the Charter were students of history, and they understood that despite such high-minded declarations conflicts would erupt into violence in the future. They therefore adopted two carefully tailored, narrow exceptions to this foundational prohibition. These exceptions are designed to ward off breaches of the peace or to restore peace if fighting breaks out.

One exception concerns the Security Council, to which the Charter gives "primary responsibility for the maintenance of international peace and security." Art. 42(1). The Security Council is a political body with five permanent members, each of which has veto power (China, France, Russia, the United Kingdom, and the United States), and ten non-permanent, elected members. Acting entirely on its own initiative, the Security Council may approve the use of force when it determines the existence of a threat to the peace, a breach of the peace, or an act of aggression. Member states have agreed in Article 25 to "accept and carry out the decisions of the Security Council."

The other recognized exception to the Article 2(4) ban on the use of force allows one nation to defend itself from an armed attack by another, or to come to the aid of another state that is attacked — at least for a time. But the Security Council also has an important role to play in the exercise of this "inherent right of individual or collective self-defense." Both exceptions are outlined in the Charter provisions set forth below, and the latter is discussed in the following opinion by the International Court of Justice.

Charter of the United Nations

June 26, 1945, 59 Stat. 1031, T.S. No. 993

CHAPTER VII. ACTION WITH RESPECT TO THREATS TO THE PEACE, BREACHES OF THE PEACE, AND ACTS OF AGGRESSION

Article 39

The Security Council shall determine the existence of any threat to the peace, breach of the peace, or act of aggression and shall make recommendations, or decide what measures shall be taken in accordance with Articles 41 and 42, to maintain and restore international peace and security.

Article 40

In order to prevent an aggravation of the situation, the Security Council may, before making the recommendations or deciding upon the measures provided for in Article 39, call upon the parties concerned to comply with such provisional measures as it deems necessary or desirable. Such provisional measures shall be without prejudice to the rights, claims, or position of the parties concerned. The Security Council shall duly take account of failure to comply with such provisional measures.

Article 41

The Security Council may decide what measures not involving the use of armed force are to be employed to give effect to its decisions, and it may call upon the Members of the United Nations to apply such measures. These may include complete or partial interruption of economic relations and of rail, sea, air, postal, telegraphic, radio, and other means of communication, and the severance of diplomatic relations.

Article 42

Should the Security Council consider that measures provided for in Article 41 would be inadequate or have proved to be inadequate, it may take such action by air, sea, or land forces as may be necessary to maintain or restore international peace and security. Such actions may include demonstrations, blockade, and other operations by air, sea, or land forces of Members of the United Nations.

Article 51

Nothing in the present charter shall impair the inherent right of individual and collective self-defense if an armed attack occurs against a Member of the United Nations, until the Security Council has taken measures necessary to maintain international peace and security. Measures taken by Members in the exercise of this right of self-defense shall be immediately reported to the Security Council and shall not in any way affect the authority and responsibility of the Security Council under the present Charter to take at any time such action as it deems necessary in order to maintain or restore international peace and security.

Case Concerning Military and Paramilitary Activities In and Against Nicaragua (Nicaragua v. United States of America)

International Court of Justice, 1986
1986 I.C.J. 14

[In 1984 Nicaragua filed an application with the Court asserting that the United States was engaged in aggression against it, in violation of Article 2(4) of the United Nations Charter, other treaty obligations, and customary international norms. Specifically, it alleged (1) that U.S. forces had carried out direct armed attacks against Nicaragua by air, land, and sea; and (2) that the United States had recruited, trained, armed, equipped, financed, and directed paramilitary actions in and against Nicaragua by a group known as Contras. Nicaragua sought an order from the Court to stop the aggression and pay compensation.

The dispute between Nicaragua and the United States began with the fall of President Anastasio Somoza Debayle in Nicaragua in July 1979. A junta led by the Frente Sandinista de Liberacion Nacional (Sandinistas) took over the government. Opponents of the new regime, mainly former supporters of Somoza, in particular ex-members of the National Guard, formed themselves into irregular military forces and began an armed opposition.

In 1981, partly in response to reports that the Sandinistas were supplying arms and other logistical support to guerrillas in El Salvador, the Reagan administration began covert aid to the Contras. This aid was later publicly acknowledged in official statements by the President and high U.S. officials, and in a 1983 budget resolution Congress provided funds for U.S. intelligence agencies to support "directly or indirectly, military or paramilitary operations in Nicaragua." The United States also laid mines in Nicaraguan waters.

Because the United States had expressly withheld consent to the International Court's jurisdiction over "disputes arising under a multilateral treaty" absent conditions not met in the principal case, the Court relied on the customary international law of armed conflict instead of the Charter in the following opinion.]

MERITS...

[I.   APPLICABLE LAW]

[A.   U.N. Charter vs. Customary International Law]

176. ... [The U.N. Charter] itself refers to pre-existing customary international law; this reference to customary law is contained in the actual text of Article 51, which mentions the "inherent right" (in the French text the "droit naturel") of individual or collective self-defence, which "nothing in the present Charter shall impair" and which applies in the event of an armed attack. The Court therefore finds that Article 51 of the Charter is only meaningful on the basis that there is a "natural" or "inherent" right of self-defence, and it is hard to see how this can be other than of a customary nature, even if its present content has been confirmed and influenced by the Charter. Moreover the Charter, having itself recognized the existence of this right, does not go on to regulate directly all aspects of its content. For example, it does not contain any specific rule whereby self-defence would warrant only measures which are proportional to the armed attack and necessary to respond to it, a rule well established in customary international law. Moreover, a definition of the "armed attack" which, if found to exist, authorizes the exercise of the "inherent right" of self-defence, is not provided in the Charter, and is not part of treaty law. It cannot therefore be held that Article 51 is a provision which "subsumes and supervenes" customary international law. It rather demonstrates that in the field in question, the importance of which for the present dispute need hardly be stressed, customary international law continues to exist alongside treaty law. . . .

181. . . . The essential consideration is that both the Charter and the customary international law flow from a common fundamental principle outlawing the use of force in international relations. . . .

[B. Content of Customary International Law]

[1. Prohibition on the Threat or Use of Force]

183. In view of this conclusion, the Court has next to consider what are the rules of customary international law applicable to the present dispute. For this purpose, it has to direct its attention to the practice and opinio juris of States; as the Court recently observed,

> It is of course axiomatic that the material of customary international law is to be looked for primarily in the actual practice and opinio juris of States, even though multilateral conventions may have an important role to play in recording and defining rules deriving from custom, or indeed in developing them. (*Continental Shelf (Libyan Arab Jamahiriya/ Malta)*, I.C.J. Reports 1985, pp. 29-30, para. 27.)

. . .

188. . . . The Parties . . . both take the view that the fundamental principle in this area is expressed in the terms employed in Article 2, paragraph 4, of the United Nations Charter. They therefore accept a treaty-law obligation to refrain in their international relations from the threat or use of force against the territorial integrity or political independence of any State, or in any other manner inconsistent with the purposes of the United Nations. . . . The . . . attitude referred to expresses an opinio juris respecting such rule (or set of rules), to be thenceforth treated separately from the provisions . . . of the Charter. . . .

190. . . . The United States, in its Counter-Memorial on the questions of jurisdiction and admissibility, found it material to quote the views of scholars that this principle is a "universal norm," a "universal international law," a "universally recognized principle of international law," and a "principle of jus cogens." . . .

[2. Exception to the Prohibition for Self-Defense]

193. The general rule prohibiting force allows for certain exceptions. . . . [I]n the language of Article 51 of the United Nations Charter, the inherent right (or "droit naturel") which any State possesses in the event of an armed attack, covers both collective and individual self-defence. Thus, the Charter itself testifies to the existence of the right of collective self-defence in customary international law. . . .

194. With regard to the characteristics governing the right of self-defence, since the Parties consider the existence of this right to be established as a matter of customary international law, they have concentrated on the conditions governing its use. . . . The Parties also agree in holding that whether the response to the attack is lawful depends on observance of the criteria of the necessity and the proportionality of the measures taken in self-defence. . . .

195. In the case of individual self-defence, the exercise of this right is subject to the State concerned having been the victim of an armed attack. Reliance on collective self-defence of course does not remove the need for this. There appears now to be general agreement on the nature of the acts which can be treated as constituting armed attacks. . . . [I]n customary law, the prohibition of armed attacks may apply to the sending by a State of armed bands to the territory of another State, if such an operation, because of its scale and effects, would have been classified as an armed attack rather than as a mere frontier incident had it been carried out by regular armed forces. But the Court does not believe that the concept of "armed attack" includes not only acts by armed bands where such acts occur on a significant scale but also assistance to rebels in the form of the provision of weapons or logistical or other support. Such assistance may be regarded as a threat or use of force, or amount to intervention in the internal or external affairs of other States. It is also clear that it is the State which is the victim of an armed attack which must form and declare the view that it has been so attacked. There is no rule in customary international law permitting another State to exercise the right of collective self-defence on the basis of its own assessment of the situation. Where collective self-defence is invoked, it is to be expected that the State for whose benefit this right is used will have declared itself to be the victim of an armed attack. . . .

200. . . . Article 51 of the United Nations Charter requires that measures taken by States in exercise of this right of self-defence must be "immediately reported" to the Security Council. . . . Whatever influence the Charter may have had on customary international law in these matters, it is clear that in customary international law it is not a condition of the lawfulness of the use of force in self-defence that a procedure so closely dependent on the content of a treaty commitment and of the institutions established by it, should have been followed. On the other hand, if self-defence is advanced as a justification for measures which would otherwise be in breach both of the principle of customary international law and of that contained in the Charter, it is to be expected that the conditions of the Charter should be respected. Thus for the purpose of enquiry into the customary law position, the absence of a report may be one of the factors indicating whether the State in question was itself convinced that it was acting in self-defence. . . .

[II.   APPLICATION OF LAW TO THE FACTS]

227. . . . For the most part, the complaints by Nicaragua are of the actual use of force against it by the United States. Of the acts which the Court has found imputable to the Government of the United States, the following are relevant in this respect:

— the laying of mines in Nicaraguan internal or territorial waters in early 1984;

— certain attacks on Nicaraguan ports, oil installations and a naval base.

These activities constitute infringements of the principle of the prohibition of the use of force, defined earlier, unless they are justified by circumstances which exclude their unlawfulness....

228.... As to the claim that United States activities in relation to the contras constitute a breach of the customary international law principle of the non-use of force, the Court finds that, subject to the question whether the action of the United States might be justified as an exercise of the right of self-defence, the United States has committed a prima facie violation of that principle by its assistance to the contras in Nicaragua, by "organizing or encouraging the organization of irregular forces or armed bands . . . for incursion into the territory of another State," and "participating in acts of civil strife . . . in another State," in the terms of General Assembly resolution 2625 (XXV). According to that resolution, participation of this kind is contrary to the principle of the prohibition of the use of force when the acts of civil strife referred to "involve a threat or use of force." In the view of the Court, while the arming and training of the contras can certainly be said to involve the threat or use of force against Nicaragua, this is not necessarily so in respect of all the assistance given by the United States Government. In particular, the Court considers that the mere supply of funds to the contras, while undoubtedly an act of intervention in the internal affairs of Nicaragua, . . . does not in itself amount to a use of force.

229. The Court must thus consider whether, as the Respondent claims, the acts in question of the United States are justified by the exercise of its right of collective self-defence against an armed attack....

[The Court then reviewed the facts surrounding Nicaragua's actions toward El Salvador in relation to the use of force by the United States against Nicaragua.]

238.... [T]he Court concludes that the plea of collective self-defence against an alleged armed attack on El Salvador . . . advanced by the United States to justify its conduct toward Nicaragua, cannot be upheld; and accordingly that the United States has violated the principle prohibiting recourse to the threat or use of force by the acts listed in paragraph 227 above, and by its assistance to the contras to the extent that this assistance "involve[s] a threat or use of force" (paragraph 228 above)....

NOTES AND QUESTIONS

1. *The Need for Security Council Approval.* Recognizing the provisions of Chapter VII of the U.N. Charter as exceptional, can you describe the sequence of events that might provoke the invocation of each respective article, from Article 39 to Article 42, leading to eventual authorization for the use of military force? Do you think an individual state or group of states might find it extremely inconvenient, even dangerous, to have to persuade a majority of the U.N. Security Council members to authorize such use (and to persuade all of the permanent members not to veto it)? Can you imagine why every member state agreed to abide by these provisions?

2. *Article 42: Actions "It May Take."* The United Nations has no military force of its own to deploy. The Security Council relies instead on voluntary contributions of

forces by member states in response to "recommendations" or "authorizations" under Article 39 — or more generally under Chapter VII. *See* Yoram Dinstein, *War, Aggression, and Self-Defense* 310 (4th ed. 2005).

3. *Formation of Customary International Law.* In the view of one authority, the formation of customary international law "results from a general and consistent practice of states followed by them from a sense of legal obligation." *Restatement (Third) of Foreign Relations Law of the United States* §102(2) (1987). Regarding the consistent practice of states, in another case the Court remarked, "State practice . . . should have been both extensive and virtually uniform in the sense of the provision invoked." *The North Sea Continental Shelf Case* (Judgment), 1969 I.C.J. 12, 43. Unfortunately, history is replete with examples, many of them very recent, of states resorting to violence without the approval of the U.N. Security Council and for reasons having nothing to do with self-defense. Nevertheless, the *Nicaragua* Court found evidence that the practice of states was, in general, sufficiently consistent to form a customary norm prohibiting the use of force. Inconsistent state practice was to be treated as a breach of the norm, "not as indications of the recognition of a new rule." ¶186.

The development of customary international law also requires state practice to be based on a sense of legal obligation, or *opinio juris.* Where does the Court find the requisite sense of legal obligation? What, if any, was the effect of characterizing the prohibition on the use of force as peremptory law — *jus cogens*? *See* Dinstein, *supra,* at 99-104.

4. *Scope of the Customary Prohibition on the Threat or Use of Force.* A substantial, direct, armed attack by one state against another violates the customary prohibition on the use of force, unless it is excused by some recognized exception to the prohibition. The Court found that the United States committed such an attack when U.S. personnel mined Nicaraguan harbors and carried out aerial strikes against ports, a military base, and oil installations in that country. But the United States also engaged in various lesser, indirect uses of force. The Court determined that some of these lesser actions, such as arming and training the Contras, violated the prohibition, while the mere supply of funds to the Contras did not. Do you think the distinction was based on the instrumentalities employed in the actions — training of rebel forces versus financial support? The severity of the effects of those actions? Can you distinguish for this purpose between (a) a mercenary force paid for by a state engaged in unlawful aggression, and (b) funding by a state for a group with which it shares an interest in the overthrow of another state's government?

A definition of aggression was adopted by the U.N. General Assembly in Resolution 3314, G.A. Res. 3314 (XXIX), U.N. Doc. A/3314 (Dec. 14, 1974). In addition to acts condemned by the Court in the *Nicaragua Case,* it includes blockades and permission by a state for use of its territory to attack other states. It also describes the *first* use of force in contravention of the Charter as prima facie evidence of aggression.

5. *Self-Defense.* Because of the U.S. multilateral treaty reservation, the Court was asked to identify not only a customary general ban on the use of force in international relations, but also customary exceptions to that ban. Where did it find a customary exception for self-defense?

The threat or use of force in self-defense can only be justified, under either Article 51 or customary law, by the existence of an "armed attack." What, according to the Court, constitutes an armed attack, and what does not? Why do you suppose the Court drew the line where it did?

The right of self-defense is also generally agreed to be qualified by a requirement that it be based on "a necessity of self-defense, instant, overwhelming, leaving no choice of means, no moment for deliberation." Secretary of State Daniel Webster penned this formula in connection with an 1837 dispute between the United States and Great Britain — the *Caroline* affair. 6 *The Works of Daniel Webster* 261 (1851). What purpose is served by each of these criteria?

In another case the Court declared that the burden of proving facts showing the existence of an armed attack rests on the state claiming to act in self-defense. *Case Concerning Oil Platforms (Iran v. United States)*, 2003 I.C.J. 161, 189 (Nov. 6). Why place the burden there?

Article 51 also provides that any exercise of the inherent right of self-defense "shall be immediately reported to the Security Council." What is the purpose of this requirement? How does it bear on the outcome of the *Nicaragua Case*?

6. *Collective Self-Defense.* Why does the Court insist that before one state comes to the aid of another as an act of collective self-defense, the second state must (a) declare that it has come under attack and (b) request assistance? Even with these safeguards, of course, one can see a potential for collusion between assisting and assisted states to create a pretext for aggression against a third state. How could this potential be reduced?

7. *Necessity and Proportionality.* The Court declares that if the use of force is ever justified as a matter of customary international law, it must satisfy the criteria of necessity and proportionality. In its 1996 Advisory Opinion on the *Legality of the Threat or Use of Nuclear Weapons*, 1996 I.C.J. 226, 245 (July 8), the Court indicated that the same requirements exist under Article 51. By "proportionality," the Court meant something different from proportionality of an attack under the law of armed conduct or international humanitarian law. See *supra* p. 52. One scholar has explained,

> Necessity comes to the fore when a war is begun following an isolated armed attack. Before the defending State opens the floodgates to full-scale hostilities, it is obligated to verify that a reasonable settlement of the conflict in an amicable way is not attainable....
>
> ... When on-the-spot reaction or defensive armed reprisals are involved, proportionality points at a symmetry or an approximation in "scale and effects" between the unlawful force and the lawful counter-force....
>
> ... Once war is raging, the exercise of self-defence may bring about "the destruction of the enemy's army," regardless of the condition of proportionality.... By its nature, war (as a comprehensive use of force) [and in distinction to "an isolated armed attack"] is virtually bound to be disproportionate to any measure "short of war." [Dinstein, *supra*, at 237-238.]

What policy is served by these requirements?

B.   THE PRESIDENT'S DEFENSIVE WAR POWER

At the Constitutional Convention, the Committee on Detail prepared a draft Constitution vesting "The Executive Power of the United States . . . in a . . . President," who would be "Commander in Chief of the Army and Navy of the United States, and of the Militia of the several States." Farrand, *supra* p. 59, at 171-172. It gave Congress the power to "make war," to appropriate funds, and "to call for the aid of the militia, in order to execute the laws of the Union, enforce treaties, suppress insurrections, and repel invasions." *Id.* at 168.

In the ensuing debates on the draft, Charles Pinckney of South Carolina complained that requiring the whole Congress to declare war would be cumbersome:

> Mr. Pinckney. . . . Its proceedings were too slow. It wd. meet but once a year. The Hs. of Reps. would be too numerous for such deliberations. The Senate would be the best depositary, being more acquainted with foreign affairs, and most capable of proper resolutions. If the States are equally represented in Senate, so as to give no advantage to large States, the power will notwithstanding be safe, as the small have their all at stake in such cases as well as the large States. It would be singular for one authority to make war, and another peace.
>
> Mr. Butler. The Objections agst the Legislature lie in a great degree agst the Senate. He was for vesting the power in the President, who will have all the requisite qualities, and will not make war but when the Nation will support it.
>
> Mr. M(adison) and Mr. Gerry moved to insert "*declare*," striking out "*make*" war; leaving to the Executive the power to repel sudden attacks.
>
> Mr. Sharman thought it stood very well. The Executive shd. be able to repel and not to commence war. "Make" better than "declare" the latter narrowing the power too much.
>
> Mr. Gerry never expected to hear in a republic a motion to empower the Executive alone to declare war.
>
> Mr. Elseworth. there is a material difference between the cases of making *war*, and making *peace*. It shd. be more easy to get out of war, than into it. War also is a simple and overt declaration. peace attended with intricate & secret negociations.
>
> Mr. Mason was agst giving the power of war to the Executive, because not (safely) to be trusted with it; or to the Senate, because not so constructed as to be entitled to it. He was for clogging rather than facilitating war; but for facilitating peace. He preferred "*declare*" to "*make*." [*Id.* at 318-319.]

In support of Madison's motion, Rufus King of Massachusetts argued "that 'make' war might be understood to 'conduct' it which was an Executive function." *Id.* at 319.

Eventually, Pinckney's motion to vest the war power solely in the Senate was overwhelmingly rejected and Madison's motion was approved. As for military action short of declared war, the Committee on Detail did not include in the list of powers given to the new legislature the power to issue letters of marque and reprisal, which the old Congress enjoyed under the Articles. Such letters had traditionally been used as public commissions for privateers to raid and capture merchant vessels of an enemy state — typically in response to the unlawful acts of the enemy state — but gradually had come to "signify any intermediate or low-intensity hostility short of declared war that utilized public *or* private forces, although the emphasis on the use of private forces remained." Jules Lobel, *Covert War and Congressional Authority: Hidden War and Forgotten Power*, 134 U. Pa. L. Rev. 1035, 1045 (1986) (emphasis in original). At Pinckney's request the Marque and Reprisal language was added and approved without discussion. *Id.* at 324, 326.

It was not until the Civil War that the federal courts had occasion to consider the President's implied power to repel attack. Then, of course, the "attack" was the insurrection of the Confederate states commenced by the bombing of Fort Sumter.

President Lincoln responded by imposing an armed blockade on the Confederacy, prompting the following challenge.

The Prize Cases

United States Supreme Court, 1863
67 U.S. (2 Black) 635

Mr. Justice GRIER. . . . [At the beginning of the Civil War, during a congressional recess, President Lincoln issued a proclamation by which he "deemed it advisable to set on foot a blockade of the ports within [certain of the Confederate states], in pursuance of the laws of the United States and of the law of nations. . . . If, therefore, with a view to violate such blockade, a vessel shall approach or shall attempt to leave either of said ports, she will be duly warned by the commander of one of the blockading vessels, who will endorse on her register the fact and date of such warning, and if the same vessel shall again attempt to enter or leave the blockaded port, she will be captured and sent to the nearest convenient port for such proceedings against her and her cargo, as prize, as may be deemed advisable." The owners of vessels that were captured as prizes during the blockade brought this action challenging the legality of the President's proclamation.]

Had the President a right to institute a blockade of ports in possession of persons in armed rebellion against the Government, on the principles of international law, as known and acknowledged among civilized States? . . .

The right of prize and capture has its origin in the "*jus belli*," and is governed and adjudged under the law of nations. To legitimate the capture of a neutral vessel or property on the high seas, a war must exist *de facto*, and the neutral must have a knowledge or notice of the intention of one of the parties belligerent to use this mode of coercion against a port, city, or territory, in possession of the other.

Let us enquire whether, at the time this blockade was instituted, a state of war existed which would justify a resort to these means of subduing the hostile force.

War has been well defined to be, "That state in which a nation prosecutes its right by force." . . .

By the Constitution, Congress alone has the power to declare a national or foreign war. It cannot declare war against a State, or any number of States, by virtue of any clause in the Constitution. The Constitution confers on the President the whole Executive power. He is bound to take care that the laws be faithfully executed. He is Commander-in-Chief of the Army and Navy of the United States, and of the militia of the several States when called into the actual service of the United States. He has no power to initiate or declare a war either against a foreign nation or a domestic State. But by the Acts of Congress of February 28th, 1795, and 3d of March, 1807, he is authorized to call out the militia and use the military and naval forces of the United States in case of invasion by foreign nations, and to suppress insurrection against the government of a State or of the United States.

If a war be made by invasion of a foreign nation, the President is not only authorized but bound to resist force by force. He does not initiate the war, but is bound to accept the challenge without waiting for any special legislative authority. And whether the hostile party be a foreign invader, or States organized in rebellion, it is none the less a war, although the declaration of it be "*unilateral*." Lord Stowell (1 Dodson, 247) observes, "It is not the less a war on *that account*, for war may exist without a declaration on either side. It is so laid down by the best writers on the law of nations. A declaration of war by one country only, is not a mere challenge to be accepted or refused at pleasure by the other." ...

This greatest of civil wars was not gradually developed by popular commotion, tumultuous assemblies, or local unorganized insurrections. However long may have been its previous conception, it nevertheless sprung forth suddenly from the parent brain, a Minerva in the full panoply of *war*. The President was bound to meet it in the shape it presented itself, without waiting for Congress to baptize it with a name; and no name given to it by him or them could change the fact. . . .

Whether the President in fulfilling his duties, as Commander-in-Chief, in suppressing an insurrection, has met with such armed hostile resistance, and a civil war of such alarming proportions as will compel him to accord to them the character of belligerents, is a question to be decided *by him*, and this Court must be governed by the decisions and acts of the political department of the Government to which this power was entrusted. "He must determine what degree of force the crisis demands." The proclamation of blockade is itself official and conclusive evidence to the Court that a state of war existed which demanded and authorized a recourse to such a measure, under the circumstances peculiar to the case. . . .

If it were necessary to the technical existence of a war, that it should have a legislative sanction, we find it in almost every act passed at the extraordinary session of the Legislature of 1861, which was wholly employed in enacting laws to enable the Government to prosecute the war with vigor and efficiency. And finally, in 1861, we find Congress "*ex majore cautela*" [out of caution] and in anticipation of such astute objections, passing an act "approving, legalizing, and making valid all the acts, proclamations, and orders of the President, &c., as if they had been *issued and done under the previous express authority* and direction of the Congress of the United States."

Without admitting that such an act was necessary under the circumstances, it is plain that if the President had in any manner assumed powers which it was necessary should have the authority or sanction of Congress, that on the well known principle of law, "*omnis ratihabitio retrotrahitur et mandato equiparatur*" [ratifications relate back and are the equivalent of prior authority], this ratification has operated to perfectly cure the defect. . . .

The objection made to this act of ratification, that it is *ex post facto*, and therefore unconstitutional and void, might possibly have some weight on the trial of an indictment in a criminal Court. But precedents from that source cannot be received as authoritative in a tribunal administering public and international law.

On this first question therefore we are of the opinion that the President had a right, *jure belli*, to institute a blockade of ports in possession of the States in rebellion, which neutrals are bound to regard. . . .

Mr. Justice NELSON, dissenting [in an opinion in which Chief Justice TANEY and Justices CATRON and CLIFFORD concurred]. . . . It is not to be denied . . . that if a civil war existed between that portion of the people in organized insurrection to overthrow this Government at the time this vessel and cargo were seized, and if she was guilty of a violation of the blockade, she would be lawful prize of war. But before this insurrection against the established Government can be dealt with on the footing of a civil war, within the meaning of the law of nations and the Constitution of the United States, and which will draw after it belligerent rights, it must be recognized or declared by the war-making power of the Government. No power short of this can change the legal status of the Government or the relations of its citizens from that of peace to a state of war, or bring into existence all those duties and obligations of neutral third parties growing out of a state of war. The war power of the Government must be exercised before this changed condition of the Government and people and of neutral third parties can be admitted....

... [W]e find ... that to constitute a civil war in the sense in which we are speaking, before it can exist, in contemplation of law, it must be recognized or declared by the sovereign power of the State, and which sovereign power by our Constitution is lodged in the Congress of the United States — civil war, therefore, under our system of government, can exist only by an act of Congress, which requires the assent of two of the great departments of the Government, the Executive and Legislative....

... But we are asked, what would become of the peace and integrity of the Union in case of an insurrection at home or invasion from abroad if this power could not be exercised by the President in the recess of Congress, and until that body could be assembled?

The framers of the Constitution fully comprehended this question, and provided for the contingency. Indeed, it would have been surprising if they had not, as a rebellion had occurred in the State of Massachusetts while the Convention was in session, and which had become so general that it was quelled only by calling upon the military power of the State. The Constitution declares that Congress shall have power "to provide for calling forth the militia to execute the laws of the Union, suppress insurrections, and repel invasions." Another clause, "that the President shall be Commander-in-chief of the Army and Navy of the United States, and of the Militia of the several States when called into the actual service of the United States;" and, again: "He shall take care that the laws shall be faithfully executed." Congress passed laws on this subject in 1792 and 1795. 1 United States Laws, pp. 264, 424. [It also passed a law on the subject in 1807. Act of Mar. 3, 1807, ch. 39, 2 Stat. 443.] ...

The Acts of 1795 and 1807 did not, and could not under the Constitution, confer on the President the power of declaring war against a State of this Union, or of deciding that war existed, and upon that ground authorize the capture and confiscation of the property of every citizen of the State whenever it was found on the waters. The laws of war, whether the war be civil or *inter gentes*, as we have seen, convert every citizen of the hostile State into a public enemy, and treat him accordingly, whatever may have been his previous conduct. This great power over the business and property of the citizen is reserved to the legislative department by the express words of the Constitution. It cannot be delegated or surrendered to the Executive. Congress alone can determine whether war exists or should be declared; and until they have acted, no citizen of the State can be punished in his person or property, unless he has committed some offence against a law of Congress passed before the act was committed, which made it a crime, and defined the punishment. The penalty of confiscation for the acts of others with which he had no concern cannot lawfully be inflicted....

... [C]onsequently, ... the President had no power to set on foot a blockade under the law of nations, and ... the capture of the vessel and cargo in this case, and in all cases before us in which the capture occurred before the 13th of July, 1861 [the date on which Congress first authorized a naval blockade of the Confederacy], for breach of blockade, or as enemies' property, are illegal and void, and ... the decrees of condemnation should be reversed and the vessel and cargo restored.

NOTES AND QUESTIONS

1. *Inherent Defensive War Power.* The legal challenge to the naval blockade of the South in *The Prize Cases* presented the Supreme Court for the first time with the question whether the President has the inherent power to repel attacks — to conduct defensive war — without prior congressional authorization.

The threshold question was whether the United States was lawfully at "war." To what source of law did the Court look to find an answer? What answer did the Court give? What answer would the International Court of Justice have given based on the *Nicaragua Case?*

On September 12, 2001, President George W. Bush declared that the terrorist attacks on the World Trade Center and the Pentagon were "acts of war." *Remarks by the President in Photo Opportunity with the National Security Team,* Sept. 12, 2001, *at* http://georgewbush-whitehouse.archives.gov/news/releases/2001/09/20010912-4.html. Did the circumstances that day or since fit the Supreme Court's definition of "war"?

Is there any danger that a President might *create* the conditions said to warrant a military response? Consider Lincoln's warning in 1846 about the President's invocation of the repel attack authority to fight the undeclared Mexican War:

> Allow the President to invade a neighboring nation, whenever he shall deem it necessary to repel an invasion and you allow him to do so, whenever he may choose to say he deems it necessary for such purpose, and you allow him to make war at pleasure. Study to see if you can fix any limit to his power in this respect, after you have given him so much as you propose. [2 Abraham Lincoln, *The Writings of Abraham Lincoln* 51 (Arthur Brooks Lapsley ed., 1906).]

2. *A Narrower Holding?* Could the Court in *The Prize Cases* have upheld the President's actions on any narrower ground? Can you argue that it did so? *See generally* Ludwell H. Johnson III, *Abraham Lincoln and the Development of Presidential War-Making Powers: Prize Cases (1863) Revisited,* 35 Civil War Hist. 208 (1989).

The dissenters in *The Prize Cases* did not contest the proposition that a civil war places the nation *in extremis.* Why then did they find the blockade unlawful? Did they conclude that the President's actions were forbidden by Congress? That they exceeded a congressional grant of authority? That the President lacked any inherent authority to order the blockade?

3. *Defensive War or Just Defense?* The *Prize Cases* involved the President's authority to respond to force with force in a war. Does it support the same authority to respond immediately to attack, even when the attack is not part of a larger conflict? By the logic of the Court, is the President constitutionally empowered to meet *any* violent threat with as much force as he determines, without awaiting congressional authorization? What answer does the "sudden attack" language in Madison's notes of the framing of the Declaration Clause suggest? How important is "sudden"? How far can he go beyond immediate self-defense?

In deciding whether a President's use of military force is justified as a matter of domestic law, should a court apply the customary international law principles of necessity and proportionality?

4. *Executive Practice and Congressional Acquiescence.* In *Youngstown Sheet & Tube Co. v. Sawyer*, 343 U.S. 579, 610-611 (1952), Justice Felix Frankfurter wrote:

The Constitution is a framework for Government. Therefore the way the framework has consistently operated fairly establishes that it has operated according to its true nature. Deeply embedded traditional ways of conducting government cannot supplant the Constitution or legislation, but they give meaning to the words of a text or supply them. It is an inadmissibly narrow conception of American constitutional law to confine it to the words of the Constitution and to disregard the gloss which life has written upon them. In short, a systematic, unbroken, executive practice, long pursued to the knowledge of the Congress and never before questioned, engaged in by presidents who have also sworn to uphold the Constitution, making as it were such exercise of power part of the structure of our Government, may be treated as a gloss on "executive Power" vested in the President by §1 of Art. II. . . .

In other words, Congress may by its *inaction* (or by collateral legislation) *acquiesce* in a long-standing executive practice or policy of which it is aware, and thus suggest a kind of customary legal authority in the executive to engage in the practice.

Although we have formally declared war only 11 times in our history, we have used armed force abroad on more than 300 occasions, most of them well-known to Congress. *See* Richard F. Grimmett, *Instances of Use of United States Armed Forces Abroad, 1798-2004* (Cong. Res. Serv. RL30172), Jan. 27, 2010. Does this history indicate that the President can use armed force whenever he thinks it necessary to protect national security? That argument was made to support the legality of American participation in the Vietnam War. The Legal Adviser to the State Department inferred from 125 prior congressionally unauthorized uses of armed force abroad that the President had the "power to deploy American forces abroad and commit them to military operations when . . . [he] deems such action necessary to maintain the security and defense of the United States. . . ." Leonard C. Meeker, *The Legality of United States Participation in the Defense of Viet-Nam*, 75 Yale L.J. 1085, 1100-1101 (1966); *see also* J. Terry Emerson, *War Powers Resolution*, 74 W. Va. L. Rev. 53 app. A (1971) (citing usage for the same proposition). Is this inference supported by the theory of customary law suggested by Justice Frankfurter?

Or does history suggest a narrower claim of presidential war power: that the President has acquired *particular* customary war powers with congressional acquiescence? For example, he has occasionally ordered military force to protect or rescue American nationals and their property from foreign threats of violence. *See* Francis D. Wormuth & Edwin B. Firmage, *To Chain the Dog of War* 145-151 (2d ed. 1989) (listing some uses of force for rescue and protection). Not only was Congress generally aware of such uses of force, but it has given strong evidence of acquiescing in them. *See* Peter Raven-Hansen, *Constitutional Constraints: The War Clause*, in *The U.S. Constitution and the Power to Go to War* 38-39 (1994). On the other hand, one of us has argued that any resulting customary

rescue/protection authority . . . must be confined to cases of actual or reasonably imminent risk to Americans. In addition, its logical limit is its immediate object: rescue and protection. Once American nationals are evacuated out of harm's way or otherwise secured, the authority is exhausted. Neither customary law demarcated by the practice that Congress understood and acquiesced to, nor international law . . . permits the President to order reprisals on his own initiative. [*Id.* at 40-41.]

The constitutional assignment of the power to "grant letters of Marque and Reprisal" to Congress may suggest that the Framers meant for Congress, not the President alone, to decide on reprisals taken in response to unlawful acts against us, at least when there is time to choose among responses.

A mid-nineteenth century opinion by a Supreme Court Justice riding circuit asserted in dictum that the President has customary authority to use force to rescue American nationals taken hostage by terrorists. *See Durand v. Hollins*, 8 F. Cas. 111, 112 (No. 4186) (S.D.N.Y. 1860) ("...as it respects the interposition of the executive abroad, for the protection of the lives and property of the citizen, the duty must, of necessity, rest in the discretion of the president."). Do you think that authority extends to counterterrorist military operations?

5. *Anticipatory Self-Defense?* Does the President's defensive war power also include the power to use military force against the threat of terrorism? Consider again Secretary of State Daniel Webster's classic statement that under the law of nations, a valid plea of anticipatory self-defense must rest on a showing of "a necessity of self-defense, instant, overwhelming, leaving no choice of means, no moment for deliberation." 6 *The Works of Daniel Webster* 261 (1851).

If so, has the advent of suicide terrorism, with surprise attacks in which the terrorists intentionally perish, changed the meaning of "no moment for deliberation"? An immediate response to a terrorist attack is often impossible. Terrorist targets are unpredictable and therefore difficult to protect, and attribution of responsibility is typically problematic and time-consuming. *See* David Turndorf, *The U.S. Raid on Libya: A Forceful Response to Terrorism*, 14 Brook. J. Int'l L. 187, 216 (1988). Consequently, as a practical matter, the best defense against terrorist attack may be to attack the terrorists first. *See Durand, supra*, at 112 ("Acts of lawless violence, or of threatened violence to the citizen or his property, cannot be anticipated and provided for; and the protection, to be effectual or of any avail, may, not infrequently, require the most prompt and decided action.").

In other words, does the President's defensive war power include "anticipatory self-defense"? If so, what is the scope of anticipatory self-defense? How, if at all, can you distinguish between anticipatory self-defense and reprisal, assuming that reprisal requires congressional authorization?

6. *The Evidentiary Standard for Anticipatory Self-Defense.* When a state defends itself against ongoing attack, "the factual predicate for self-defense is clear and observable." Jules Lobel, *The Use of Force to Respond to Terrorist Attacks: The Bombing of Sudan and Afghanistan*, 24 Yale J. Int'l L. 537, 543 (1999). But when a state uses force in anticipatory self-defense against a stateless terrorist group operating abroad or against a state that gives such a group sanctuary, the factual predicate is more ambiguous. If unsubstantiated, self-serving claims by the counterterrorist state are not deemed sufficient justification, what sort of proof must be supplied, and to whom?

Some scholars have argued that, because death may ensue from such attacks, the appropriate evidentiary standard is a criminal one — beyond a reasonable doubt. *See id.* at 551; Sara N. Scheideman, *Standards of Proof in Forcible Responses to Terrorism*, 50 Syracuse L. Rev. 249 (2000). That is, the preemptively attacking state must make public for international scrutiny evidence that shows beyond a reasonable doubt that the terrorist group was responsible for terrorist attacks or that the state attacked knowingly harbored the group. Another scholar suggests instead that responsible decision makers must consider a host of "prudential considerations," including

> whether [the use of force] will make a martyr of the leader of the target organization, or deeply offend good relations with affected countries, or waste military assets that are not limitless . . . , whether the use of force will save the lives of victims and prevent future attacks; whether the only realistic way to achieve deterrence is to signal that the responsible country will strike back hard; and whether a leader who has come to power by brutal means is likely to scoff at words and remonstrations that are not backed by force. [Ruth Wedgwood, *Responding to Terrorism: The Strikes Against bin Laden*, 24 Yale J. Int'l L. 559, 563 (1999).]

She notes that the counterterrorist state will often be unable to disclose its evidence in public without compromising its intelligence sources, but that sometimes it may take this risk in order to influence world opinion or obtain foreign support. *Id.* at 574.

Which of these standards is more appropriate?

C.   STATUTORY AUTHORIZATION AND LIMITS

The Framers assigned Congress both the power to "declare War" and the power to "grant letters of Marque and Reprisal." U.S. Const. art. I, §8, cl. 11. Although the constitutional debates shed little light on the meaning of "declare," contemporaneous writings indicate that a nation could "declare war" "not only by formal announcement, but also by an act of hostility." Michael D. Ramsey, *Textualism and War Powers*, 69 U. Chi. L. Rev. 1543, 1590 (2002). As John Locke wrote, a "state of War" could be "declar[ed] by Word or Action. . . ." *Two Treatises of Government* 278 (Peter Laslett ed., 1967). While in our system of divided powers Congress may not itself act by engaging in an act of hostility, it may pass a law to authorize the President to act. That is precisely what Congress did in the so-called Quasi-War with France, as the following case points out.

Bas v. Tingy

United States Supreme Court, 1800
4 U.S. (4 Dall.) 37

[As relations between France and the United States deteriorated between 1798-1800, Congress enacted a succession of measures approving naval actions against France. Initially, it authorized U.S. armed vessels of the recently established navy to capture French vessels that had "committed depredations" on U.S.-owned vessels or that were "found hovering" off U.S. coasts for that purpose. Act of May 28, 1798, ch. 48, 1 Stat. 561. When this measure did not adequately protect U.S. merchants on the high seas, Congress next authorized such merchants to defend themselves against "any search, restraint or seizure" by vessels operating under French colors. Act of June 25, 1798, ch. 60, 1 Stat. 572. This act also provided for the recapture of U.S.-owned vessels from the French and their restoration to their former owners upon payment of salvage value. Three days later Congress passed another act that provided for the judicial condemnation of captured vessels, and for the return of recaptured vessels to their owners for a salvage payment of one-eighth the full value. Act of June 28, 1798, ch. 62, 1 Stat. 574. Eventually, Congress authorized U.S. public and private armed vessels to take any French armed vessels found on the high seas. Act of July 9, 1798, ch. 68, 1 Stat. 578.

The next year Congress passed a set of rules and regulations for its infant navy. This act provided:

> That for the ships or goods belonging to the citizens of the United States, or to the citizens or subjects of any nation, in amity with the United States, if retaken from the enemy within twenty-four hours, the owners are to allow one eighth part of the whole value for salvage, if after twenty-four hours, and under forty-eight, one fifth thereof, if above that and under ninety-six hours, one third part thereof, and if above that, one half, all of which is to be paid without any deduction whatsoever. . . . [Act of March 2, 1799, ch. 24, §7, 1 Stat. 709, 716.]

On April 21, 1799, Captain Tingy, commander of the public armed ship *Ganges*, recaptured the *Eliza*, which belonged to John Bas and had been captured by a French privateer on the high seas on March 31, 1799. After he returned the vessel to Bas, Tingy brought an action in libel for salvage. The question in the case was whether Tingy was entitled to one-eighth the value of the *Eliza*, as provided by the 1798 act, or one-half as provided by the 1799 act. The lower courts ruled that Tingy was entitled to half the value. On appeal to the Supreme Court, the Justices delivered their opinions seriatim. The opinion of Justice Moore in favor of affirmance is omitted.]

WASHINGTON, Justice. . . . 1st. [The 1798 Act] relates to re-captures from *the French*, and [the 1799 Act] relates to re-captures from *the enemy;* and, it is said, that "the enemy" is not descriptive of France, or of her armed vessels, according to the correct and technical understanding of the word.

The decision of this question must depend upon another; which is, whether, at the time of passing the act of congress of the 2d of March 1799, there subsisted a state of war between the two nations? It may, I believe, be safely laid down, that every contention by force between two nations, in external matters, under the authority of their respective governments, is not only war, but public war. If it be declared in form, it is called *solemn*, and is of the perfect kind; because one whole nation is at war with another whole nation; and *all* the members of the nation declaring war, are authorised to commit hostilities against all the members of the other, in every place, and under every circumstance. In such a war all the members act under a general authority, and all the rights and consequences of war attach to their condition.

But hostilities may subsist between two nations more confined in its nature and extent; being limited as to places, persons, and things; and this is more properly termed *imperfect war*, because not solemn, and because those who are authorised to commit hostilities, act under special authority, and can go no farther than to the extent of their commission. Still, however, it is *public war*, because it is an external contention by force, between some of the members of the two nations, authorised by the legitimate powers. It is a war between the two nations, though all the members are not authorised to commit hostilities such as in a solemn war, where the government restrain the general power.

Now, if this be the true definition of war, let us see what was the situation of the United States in relation to France. In March 1799, congress had raised an army; stopped all intercourse with France; dissolved our treaty; built and equipt ships of war; and commissioned private armed ships; enjoining the former, and authorising the latter, to defend themselves against the armed ships of France, to attack them on the high seas, to subdue and take them as prize, and to re-capture armed vessels found in their possession. Here, then, let me ask, what were the technical characters of an American and French armed vessel, combating on the high seas, with a view the one to subdue the other, and to make prize of his property? They certainly were not friends, because there was a contention by force; nor were they private enemies, because the contention was external, and authorised by the legitimate authority of the two governments. If they were not our enemies, I know not what constitutes an enemy.

2d. But, secondly, it is said, that a war of the imperfect kind, is more properly called acts of hostility, or reprizal, and that congress did not mean to consider the hostility subsisting between France and the United States, as constituting a state of war.

In support of this position, it has been observed, that in no law prior to March 1799, is France styled our enemy, nor are we said to be at war. This is true; but neither of these things were necessary to be done: because as to France, she was sufficiently described by the title of the French republic; and as to America, the degree of hostility meant to be carried on, was sufficiently described without declaring war, or declaring that we were at war. Such a declaration by congress, might have constituted a perfect state of war, which was not intended by the government. . . .

. . . [T]herefore, in my opinion, the decree of the Circuit Court ought to be affirmed.

CHASE, Justice. . . . Congress is empowered to declare a general war, or congress may wage a limited war; limited in place, in objects, and in time. If a general war is declared, its extent and operations are only restricted and regulated by the *jus belli*, forming a part of the law of nations; but if a partial war is waged, its extent and operation depend on our municipal laws.

What, then, is the nature of the contest subsisting between America and France? In my judgment, it is a limited, partial, war. Congress has not declared war in general terms; but congress has authorized hostilities on the high seas by certain persons in certain cases. There is no authority given to commit hostilities on land; to capture unarmed French vessels, nor even to capture French armed vessels lying in a French port; and the authority is not given, indiscriminately, to every citizen of America, against every citizen of France; but only to citizens appointed by commissions, or exposed to immediate outrage and violence. So far it is, unquestionably, a partial war; but, nevertheless, it is a public war, on account of the public authority from which it emanates.

There are four acts, authorised by our government, that are demonstrative of a state of war. A belligerent power has a right, by the law of nations, to search a neutral vessel; and, upon suspicion of a violation of her neutral obligations, to seize and carry her into port for further examination. But by the acts of congress, an American vessel is authorised: 1st. To resist the search of a French public vessel: 2d. To capture any vessel that should attempt, by force, to compel submission to a search: 3d. To re-capture any American vessel seized by a French vessel; and 4th. To capture any French armed vessel wherever found on the high seas. This suspension of the law of nations, this right of capture and re-capture, can only be authorized by an act of the government, which is, in itself, an act of hostility. But still it is a restrained, or limited, hostility; and there are, undoubtedly, many rights attached to a general war, which do not attach to this modification of the powers of defence and aggression. . . .

The acts of congress have been analyzed to show, that a war is not openly denounced against France, and that France is no where expressly called the enemy of America: but this only proves the circumspection and prudence of the legislature. Considering our national prepossessions in favour of the French republic, congress had an arduous task to perform, even in preparing for necessary defence, and just retaliation. As the temper of the people rose, however, in resentment of accumulated wrongs, the language and the measures of the government became more and more energetic and indignant; though hitherto the popular feeling may not have been *ripe* for a solemn declaration of war; and an active and powerful opposition in our public councils, has postponed, if not prevented that decisive event, which many thought would have best suited the interest, as well as the honour of the United States. The progress of our contest with France, indeed, resembles much the progress of our revolutionary contest; in which, watching the current of public sentiment, the patriots of that day proceeded, step by step, from the supplicatory language of petitions for a redress of grievances, to the bold and noble declaration of national independence.

Having, then, no hesitation in pronouncing, that a partial war exists between America and France, and that France was an enemy, within the meaning of the act of March 1799, my voice must be given for affirming the decree of the Circuit Court.

PATERSON, Justice. As the case appears on the record, and has been accurately stated by the counsel, and by the judges, who have delivered their opinions, it is not necessary to recapitulate the facts. My opinion shall be expressed in a few words. The United States and the French republic are in a qualified state of hostility. An imperfect war, or a war, as to certain objects, and to a certain extent, exists between the two nations; and this modified warfare is authorized by the constitutional authority of our country. It is a war *quoad hoc* [to this extent]. As far as congress tolerated and authorized the war on our part, so far may we proceed in hostile operations. It is a maritime war; a war at sea as to certain purposes. The national armed vessels of France attack and capture the national armed vessels of the United States; and the national armed vessels of the United States are expressly authorized and directed to attack, subdue, and take, the national armed vessels of France, and also to re-capture American vessels. It is therefore a public war between the two nations, qualified, on our part, in the manner prescribed by the constitutional organ of our country. In such a state of things, it is scarcely necessary to add, that the term "enemy," applies; it is the appropriate expression, to be limited in its signification, import, and use, by the qualified nature and operation of the war on our part. The word enemy proceeds the full length of the war, and no farther. . . .

By the COURT: Let the decree of the Circuit Court be affirmed.

NOTES AND QUESTIONS

1. *The Obsolescent Declaration of War?* Increasing state sensitivity to public diplomacy and world opinion, as well as the decline of opportunities for the lawful use of

force occasioned by the proliferation of treaties and the evolution of customary international law, have long made declarations of war impolitic. As a consequence, "[a]lthough conflicts between and among states continue, no state has issued a formal declaration of war [since the 1948 Arab-Israeli War]. Indeed, some argue that a declaration of war today would constitute prima facie evidence of illegal aggression." Robert F. Turner, *The War Powers Resolution: Its Implementation in Theory and Practice* 25 (1983).

In fact, there is evidence that the declaration of war was already obsolete in 1789, by which date the concept of "defensive war" had taken such firm root in the law of nations that it was widely understood that war could be started without the formality of a declaration. *See, e.g., The Federalist No. 25,* at 165 (Alexander Hamilton) (Clinton Rossiter ed., 1961); Turner, *supra,* at 16 nn.45-57 (citing sources). In this light, is it likely that the Framers intended to vest Congress with only the increasingly anachronistic formal declaration power, *see* J. Gregory Sidak, *To Declare War,* 41 Duke L.J. 27 (1991) (supplying reasons for such an intent), and no other constitutional means to choose war? What answer did the members of the Court give in *Bas*? Regardless of the framing history or current geopolitical realities, does the advent of non-state enemies, such as non-state-sponsored terrorists, now make formal declarations of war obsolete?

2. *Expressly Authorizing War Without Declaring It.* How did Congress express its decision to make war on France at the end of the eighteenth century? How broad was the resulting authority in the President as Commander in Chief? Could he have deployed land forces to invade France or French possessions? Could he have deployed the Navy to take the war to French ports? *See Little v. Barreme,* 6 U.S. (2 Cranch) 170 (1804) (finding that when Congress had specified by statute that U.S. ships could intercept vessels heading *to* French ports, a presidential order was ineffective to legalize interception of vessels coming *from* French ports).

Less than a year after *Bas,* the Court was again called upon to decide rights of salvage during the naval war with France. Writing for the Court, Chief Justice Marshall concluded that "[t]he whole powers of war being, by the constitution of the United States, vested in congress, the acts of that body can alone be resorted to as our guides in this enquiry." *Talbot v. Seeman,* 5 U.S. (1 Cranch) 1, 28 (1801). The Court unanimously found that Congress had authorized "partial hostilities" against France.

Do the Quasi-War cases (*Bas, Talbot, Little*) tell us anything about whether the President could have ordered similar hostilities without any congressional authorization at all? *Compare* J. Gregory Sidak, *The Quasi-War Cases — and Their Relevance to Whether "Letters of Marque and Reprisal" Constrain Presidential War Powers,* 28 Harv. J.L. & Pub. Pol'y 465, 482, 486 (2005) (asserting that the answer is no, because the cases do not address "how the Constitution divides between Congress and the President the power to commit the nation to waging a limited war"), *with Campbell v. Clinton,* 203 F.3d 19, 30 n.7 (D.C. Cir. 2000) (Randolph, J., concurring) (citing *Little* for the proposition that executive power in war "was constrained by an absence of legislation"), *and with id.* at 38 (Tatel, J., concurring) (citing *Talbot* for the proposition that Congress possesses the "whole powers of war").

3. *Impliedly Authorizing War by Statute.* Must Congress *expressly* authorize the use of force? In *Orlando v. Laird,* 443 F.2d 1039 (2d Cir. 1971), the court found congressional authorization for the Vietnam War in, *inter alia,* military appropriations and selective service statutes. It did not cite *Bas.* Is there a difference between the form of authorization found in *Bas* and authorization by appropriation for counterterrorist strike

forces or selective service legislation? If Congress can indirectly authorize war by appropriating money for it, is there any constitutional or practical limit on the form of war authorization?

4. *Impliedly Authorizing War Without a Statute?* Does Congress even need to use a statute? Could it authorize war by separate and substantively different actions in each House? Single-chamber resolutions ("simple resolutions") do not have bicameral approval and are not presented to the President for his signature. Conceding that such separate actions by each House lack the force and effect of statutes, Charles Tiefer nonetheless argues that

> [a]ctions by Congress short of enactment may elucidate the intent of congressional appropriations.... Formal and express presidential requests for congressional approval [to use military force] ... may [also] bestow or confirm the legal significance of the corresponding congressional "partial" approval actions. Finally, Congress may take legally significant positions, even apart from a presidential request. [Charles Tiefer, *War Decisions in the Late 1990s by Partial Congressional Declaration*, 36 San Diego L. Rev. 1, 105 (1999).]

Is this theory of "partial congressional declaration" supported by any constitutional text or framing history? If you are skeptical, is the theory strengthened if we require that *each* House pass a "partial declaration," voting to support military action, even though the resulting simple resolutions do not match?

Finally, does either House need to do anything at all to approve war? Can Congress authorize war silently by acquiescence in a conflict started by the Executive?

5. *The Legal Domino Effects of War.* A formal declaration of war by Congress gives notice to neutrals of the existence of hostilities and of the identity of the belligerents, and it activates certain rights and obligations of neutrals and belligerents alike under international law. It also triggers approximately 30 standby statutory authorities that would not otherwise be available to the President. For example, under the Alien Enemy Act, 50 U.S.C. §21 (2006), "[w]henever there is a declared war between the United States and any foreign nation or government," citizens of "the hostile nation or government" who are not naturalized are subject to summary arrest, internment, and deportation when the President so proclaims.

More than 170 other standby authorities are triggered "in time of war" or "when war is imminent," without requiring a declaration of war. *See generally* David M. Ackerman & Richard F. Grimmett, *Declarations of War and Authorizations for the Use of Military Force: Historical Background and Legal Implications* (Cong. Res. Serv. RL31133), Mar. 17, 2011; J. Gregory Sidak, *War, Liberty, and Enemy Aliens*, 67 N.Y.U. L. Rev. 1402, 1430 & nn.138-145 (1992). These authorize the President to take land for military purposes; commandeer private production lines for war manufacturing; take control of private transportation for war transport; and sequester, hold, and dispose of enemy property, among other powers.

Do these differences between declarations of war and non-declaratory statutory authorizations help explain why Congress did not declare war on France during the Quasi-War? What explanation did Justice Chase give? Do they provide any guidance for whether the United States *should* declare war on terrorists today?

If you have concluded that Congress can impliedly authorize the use of force, what, if any, domino effects does an implied authorization have? It is partly the domino effects, as well as the need for accountability for war decisions, that have caused some scholars to insist on the formality of a declaration as a predicate for war. *See* Sidak, *supra* Note 1. Tiefer, in response, notes that the interaction between a President who requests approval for the use of force and the Houses of Congress that respond separately but approvingly "cranks up an elaborate machinery for the democratic inclusion of the nation in the military commitment decision," including "[h]earings, news coverage, briefings, disputes over conditions or demands for assurances, and floor debate." Tiefer, *supra* Note 4, at 125. Does this machinery satisfy the need for accountability?

6. *Area and Use Limitations in War.* The congressional authorizations for the Quasi-War with France established limitations on both the area of hostilities and the types of forces that could be used. In *Little v. Barreme*, 6 U.S. (2 Cranch) 170 (1804), the Court effectively enforced a use limitation (permitting naval vessels to intercept vessels going to, but not coming from, French ports) over a presidential order to the contrary.

On the other hand, most scholars agree that Congress could not under the guise of a statutory use limitation direct Platoon Alpha to seize the third house from the corner on Baghdad Boulevard during an authorized war. The Framers vested such real-time tactical decisions in the Commander in Chief, partly because they remembered the unhappy experience of command by committee during the Revolutionary War. The Commander in Chief Clause assured not only civilian control of the military and unity of command, but also efficiency in such decisions. "As commander in chief," the Court has emphasized, "[the President] is authorized to direct the movements of the naval and military forces placed by law at his command, and to employ them in the manner he may deem most effectual to harass and conquer and subdue the enemy." *Fleming v. Page*, 50 U.S. (9 How.) 603, 614-615 (1851).

Could Congress authorize counterterrorist operations subject to area and use limitations: "no attacks in civilian areas using unmanned Predator aircraft," or "no more than 5,000 active-duty troops in counterterrorist operations in Afghanistan"? Would it make any difference that a limitation is framed as an appropriations rider ("No funds authorized or appropriated pursuant to this [appropriation] or any other Act may be used to finance the use of the U.S. armed forces for....")? *See* U.S. Const. art. I, §9, cl. 7. Or would such a limitation amount to unconstitutional micromanaging of hostilities in violation of the Commander in Chief Clause? Recognizing that there is no bright-line test, one scholar has suggested that the constitutionality of a congressional area or use limitation depends, in part, on its "intrusiveness as to the monopoly of command itself" (i.e., its impact on civilian control and unity of command), and the "generality" of the limitation (i.e., whether it lays down a "general rule" addressing "overall structure and relations of the components of the armed forces" or operates instead as an order "direct[ed]... toward a particular operation or mission"). *See* Charles Tiefer, *Can Appropriations Riders Speed Our Exit From Iraq?*, 42 Stan. J. Int'l L. 291, 320-323 (2006). How would the proposed counterterrorist limitations fare by this analysis?

7. *Command Authority Revisited.* Consider this summary of the President's powers as Commander in Chief in time of war:

> The President, not Congress, makes all day-to-day tactical decisions in the combat deployment of armed forces. Indeed, even when it ends a use of force by cutting off

funds, Congress cannot constitutionally interfere with the Commander in Chief's tactical decisions for the safe withdrawal of the armed forces. But as powerful as the command authority is, the framers still intended that the Commander in Chief "would amount to nothing more than the supreme command and direction of the military and naval forces, as first General and Admiral of the Confederacy...," as Alexander Hamilton explained in the *Federalist Papers*. By making the President the Commander in Chief in Article II, the framers addressed what they recognized as a defect in the conduct of the Revolutionary War. They did not compromise their insistence in Article I on collective judgment in the decision for war.

Nor did they give the Commander in Chief any constitutional right to ignore the terms of a congressional authorization for the use of force. When Congress gives the President the authority to conduct war, he or she must conduct it within that authority, just as the President must follow any law that is constitutionally made. [*Deciding to Use Force Abroad: War Powers in a System of Checks and Balances* 15 (The Constitution Project) (Peter Raven-Hansen rptr., 2005).]

Do you think congressional constraints have the same force when the President is fighting a war thrust upon us by attack as when he is fighting one authorized by Congress? Put another way, are you clear about precisely which Commander-in-Chief powers are exclusive? *See generally* Louis Fisher, *Presidential War Power* (2d rev. ed. 2004).

D.   DEFENDING AGAINST AL QAEDA

1.   Terrorist Attacks on U.S. Embassies in East Africa — 1998[1]

On August 7, 1998, truck bombs exploded at the U.S. embassies in Kenya and Tanzania, killing nearly 300 people, including 12 Americans. Two weeks later, on August 20, the United States launched 79 Tomahawk cruise missiles against terrorist training camps in Afghanistan and a Sudanese pharmaceutical plant that the United States alleged to be a chemical weapons facility. President Clinton explained that he ordered the attacks because "we have convincing evidence that [Islamic terrorist groups, including that of Osama bin Laden]...played the key role in the Embassy bombings...and compelling information that they were planning additional terrorist attacks against our citizens...." He had notified certain congressional leaders on August 19 that the attacks were coming and sent Congress a letter the day after the attacks reporting that

[t]he United States acted in exercise of our inherent right of self-defense consistent with Article 51 of the United Nations Charter. These strikes were a necessary and proportionate response to the imminent threat of further terrorist attacks against U.S. personnel and facilities. These strikes were intended to prevent and deter additional attacks by a clearly identified terrorist threat. [Letter to Congressional Leaders Reporting on Military

---

1. Except as otherwise noted, background information on the 1998 Al Qaeda attacks and U.S. strikes in response on Sudan and Afghanistan is drawn from Scheideman, *supra* p. 74; Sean Murphy, *Contemporary Practice of the United States Relating to International Law*, 93 Am. J. Int'l L. 161-166 (1999); Lobel, *supra* p. 74; Wedgwood, *supra* p. 75; William C. Banks, *To "Prevent and Deter" International Terrorism: The U.S. Response to the Kenya and Tanzania Embassy Bombings* (National Security Studies CS 0699-12, 1999).

Action Against Terrorist Sites in Afghanistan and Sudan, 34 Weekly Comp. Pres. Doc. 1650 (Aug. 21, 1998).]

The President's National Security Adviser explained that it was "appropriate" not only under Article 51, but also "under a 1996 statute in Congress, for us to try to disrupt and destroy those kinds of military terrorist targets." The statute referred to apparently was the Antiterrorism and Effective Death Penalty Act of 1996 (AEDPA), Pub. L. No. 104-132, 110 Stat. 1214. In the AEDPA, Congress prohibited various kinds of assistance to countries that sponsor or harbor terrorists. In the preamble to these prohibitions, Congress made the following "finding," among others: "the President should use all necessary means, including covert action and military force, to disrupt, dismantle, and destroy international infrastructure used by international terrorists, including overseas terrorist training facilities and safe havens." *Id.* §324(4). The finding was not codified, but it appears instead in the annotations to a codified prohibition on assistance to countries that aid terrorist states. 22 U.S.C. §2377 note (2006).

Reports on the results of the attacks varied. A spokesman for bin Laden reported that 28 people were killed in the attacks on the camps. Sudan reported that ten were injured in the attack on the pharmaceutical plant. The U.S. government subsequently asserted that a soil sample from the plant revealed the presence of a precursor chemical for the production of VX, a nerve agent. Other evidence suggested that the plant was an unguarded pharmaceutical factory that had often been visited by foreign dignitaries, and that the soil sample contained a chemical structure resembling an agricultural insecticide. It was subsequently reported that the Defense Intelligence Agency had reviewed the evidence and concluded that the attack was based on bad intelligence and bad science. *See Last Summer's Attack in the Sudan, Was It Based on Faulty Evidence?*, ABC World News Tonight, Feb. 10, 1999, *available at* 1999 WL 6800665. *But see* Daniel Benjamin & Steven Simon, *A Failure of Intelligence?*, N.Y. Rev. Books, Dec. 20, 2001, at 7 (asserting that the attack was correctly based on classified evidence).

NOTES AND QUESTIONS

1. *Express(?) Congressional Authorization for the 1998 Attacks.* Did either law cited by the Clinton administration supply authority for the 1998 attacks? Would either one support the invasion of Afghanistan? A continuing campaign against Al Qaeda camps and host regimes in Sudan, Somalia, Afghanistan, and Iraq? Did either law authorize an attack against bin Laden himself?

2. *Congressional Acquiescence in Counterterrorism Strikes?* In April 1986, the United States conducted an air strike against Libya in response to its alleged involvement in a terrorist bombing in Berlin that took the life of an American soldier. Does this earlier attack suggest any other source of authority for the 1998 strikes? Consider this testimony by the Legal Adviser to the State Department in support of the 1986 air strike:

> It is also important to note, in this regard, that the President is not simply acting alone, under this inherent constitutional authority, when taking the types of actions we are discussing today. The Congress has, over the years, learned of, considered, and effectively endorsed in principle the use of U.S. forces for a variety of purposes through its adoption of laws and other actions. Most significantly, Congress has authorized and

appropriated money for creation of forces specifically designed for anti-terrorist tasks. For example, Section 1453 of the 1986 Department of Defense Authorization Act specifically states that it is the duty of the government to safeguard the safety and security of U.S. citizens against a rapidly increasing terrorist threat, and that U.S. special operations forces provide the immediate and primary capability to respond to such terrorism; and the Congress has appropriated funds for the specific purpose of improving U.S. capabilities to carry out such operations.... In this sense, Congress has participated in the creation and maintenance of the forces whose function, at least in part, is to defend Americans from terrorism through the measured use of force. The President has openly discussed and explained the need for and propriety of these uses of force, which he has correctly assumed are widely supported by Congress and the American people. All of the actions undertaken were clearly signaled well in advance, and therefore posed no threat to the role of Congress under the Constitution in military and foreign affairs.... [*War Powers, Libya, and State-Sponsored Terrorism: Hearing Before the Subcomm. on Arms Control, Int'l Sec. & Sci. of the H. Comm. on Foreign Affairs*, 99th Cong. 26-31 (1986) (hereinafter *Libya Hearings*) (statement of Abraham D. Sofaer, Legal Adviser to the Department of State).]

What theory of legal authority was the Legal Adviser invoking? Was he right?

3. *Striking First or Striking Back: Does It Make a Legal Difference?* The 1998 attacks can be characterized either as striking first (in anticipatory self-defense) or striking back (in reprisal). Assuming that there was no prior congressional authorization for the attacks, does the proper characterization of them make any difference to their legality? *See* U.S. Const. art. I, §8, cl. 11.

Professor Bowett has argued that, "coming after the event and when the harm has already been inflicted, reprisals cannot be characterized as a means of protection." D. Bowett, *Reprisals Involving Recourse to Armed Force*, 66 Am. J. Int'l L. 1, 3 (1972). Recall also Daniel Webster's statement of the conditions for anticipatory self-defense. See *supra* p. 67. If you conclude that the attacks were not self-defense under international law, does that conclusion affect their legality under U.S. law?

4. *Anticipatory Self-Defense.* Recall the proposed evidentiary standards for anticipatory self-defense. How would the conflicting standards apply to the 1998 attacks on Sudan and Afghanistan? Bin Laden and several of his associates were eventually indicted for the embassy bombings. The indictment alleged that these defendants, "together with other members and associates of al Qaeda and others known and unknown to the Grand Jury, unlawfully, willfully, and knowingly combined, conspired, confederated and agreed to kill nationals of the United States," including those who served in the U.S. embassies in Tanzania and Kenya. *See* Murphy, *supra* p. 82, at 166. Although bin Laden was not apprehended for trial, the defendants who were tried were all convicted of various crimes and sentenced to life in prison without the possibility of parole. The convictions came, however, after lengthy trials and almost three years after the embassy bombings.

5. *Applicability of the War Powers Resolution to Counterterrorist Operations.* The War Powers Resolution (WPR), 50 U.S.C. §§1541-1548 (2006), was enacted over President Richard Nixon's veto in 1973 in response to the Vietnam War. By it Congress required the President to report to Congress within 48 hours after introducing "United States armed forces into hostilities or into situations where imminent involvement in

hostilities is clearly indicated by the circumstances"; "into the territory, airspace, or waters of a foreign nation, while equipped for combat, except for deployments which relate solely to supply, replacement, repair, or training of such forces"; or "in numbers which substantially enlarge United States Armed Forces equipped for combat already located in a foreign nation." *Id.* §1543(a). Within 60 days after a report of a "hostilities" deployment is made or required to be made, the President must terminate the deployment unless he obtains a declaration of war or specific statutory authorization for the deployment. *Id.* §1544(b). Was the 1998 attack on bin Laden's terrorist training camps in Afghanistan subject to the WPR?

Professor Cox has suggested that the WPR does not apply to military action to "directly repel immediate acts of terrorists and promptly capture terrorists without encounter with the armed forces of a *de jure* [or] *de facto* government." *See Libya Hearings, supra,* at 247. According to the Legal Adviser to the State Department:

> We have substantial doubt that the Resolution should, in general, be construed to apply to the deployment of . . . antiterrorist units, where operations of a traditional military character are not contemplated and where no confrontation is expected between our units and forces of another state. To be sure, the language of the resolution makes no explicit exception for activities of this kind, but such units can reasonably be distinguished from "forces equipped for combat" and their actions against terrorists differ greatly from the "hostilities" contemplated by the Resolution. *[language]*
>
> Nothing in the legislative history indicated, moreover, that the Congress intended the Resolution to cover deployments of such antiterrorist units. These units are not conventional military forces. A rescue effort or an effort to capture or otherwise deal with terrorists, where the forces of a foreign nation are not involved, is not a typical military mission, and our *antiterrorist forces are not equipped to conduct sustained combat with foreign armed forces.* Rather, these units operate in secrecy to carry out precise and limited tasks designed to liberate U.S. citizens from captivity or to attack terrorist kidnappers and killers. *When used, these units are not expected to confront the military forces of a sovereign state.* In a real sense, therefore, action by an antiterrorist unit constitutes a use of force that is more analogous to law enforcement activity by police in the domestic context than it is to the "hostilities" between states contemplated by the War Powers Resolution. [*Id.* at 20-21 (statement of Abraham D. Sofaer, Legal Adviser to the Department of State) (emphasis in original).] *[legislative intent]*

Do you agree? Can you find these distinctions in the Constitution? In the quoted language of the WPR? Suppose bin Laden and his network were intertwined with the Taliban (which ruled most of Afghanistan before the September 11 attacks), sharing resources and engaging in joint planning and defense. On this supposition, were the attackers stateless or state-sponsored? Should the President's legal authority for attacks in anticipatory self-defense turn on nice distinctions about the sponsorship of the terrorists?

2.   Terrorist Attacks on the World Trade Center and the Pentagon — 2001

Three years after the 1998 Embassy bombings, hijackers flew commercial airliners into the World Trade Center towers and the Pentagon on September 11, 2001. The next day, the U.N. Security Council passed the following resolution.

United Nations Security Council, Resolution 1368

U.N. Doc. S/RES/1368 (Sept. 12, 2001)

The Security Council,
   Reaffirming the principles and purposes of the Charter of the United Nations, Determined to combat by all means threats to international peace and security caused by terrorist acts,
   Recognizing the inherent right of individual or collective self-defence in accordance with the Charter,
   1. Unequivocally condemns in the strongest terms the horrifying terrorist attacks which took place on 11 September 2001 in New York, Washington, D.C. and Pennsylvania and regards such acts, like any act of international terrorism, as a threat to international peace and security;
   2. Expresses its deepest sympathy and condolences to the victims and their families and to the people and Government of the United States of America;
   3. Calls on all States to work together urgently to bring to justice the perpetrators, organizers and sponsors of these terrorist attacks and stresses that those responsible for aiding, supporting or harbouring the perpetrators, organizers and sponsors of these acts will be held accountable;
   4. Calls also on the international community to redouble their efforts to prevent and suppress terrorist acts including by increased cooperation and full implementation of the relevant international anti-terrorist conventions and Security Council resolutions, in particular resolution 1269 (1999) of 19 October 1999;
   5. Expresses its readiness to take all necessary steps to respond to the terrorist attacks of 11 September 2001, and to combat all forms of terrorism, in accordance with its responsibilities under the Charter of the United Nations;
   6. Decides to remain seized of the matter.

Congress quickly took up bills to authorize military force against those who were involved in the September 11, 2001, attacks or who gave support or sanctuary to those involved. The White House reportedly first proposed a joint resolution that would have authorized force against those involved in the attacks "*and* to deter and pre-empt any future acts of terrorism and aggression against the United States." David Abramowitz, *The President, the Congress and Use of Force: Legal and Political Considerations in Authorizing Use of Force Against International Terrorism,* 43 Harv. Int'l L.J. 71, 73 (2002) (emphasis added). Instead, Congress passed the following resolution, and the President signed it into law on September 18, 2001.

Authorization for Use of Military Force

Pub. L. No. 107-40, 115 Stat. 224 (2001)

Joint Resolution To authorize the use of United States Armed Forces against those responsible for the recent attacks launched against the United States.
   Whereas, on September 11, 2001, acts of treacherous violence were committed against the United States and its citizens; and
   Whereas, such acts render it both necessary and appropriate that the United States exercise its rights to self-defense and to protect United States citizens both at home and abroad; and

Whereas, in light of the threat to the national security and foreign policy of the United States posed by these grave acts of violence; and

Whereas, such acts continue to pose an unusual and extraordinary threat to the national security and foreign policy of the United States; and

Whereas, the President has authority under the Constitution to take action to deter and prevent acts of international terrorism against the United States:

Now, therefore, be it resolved by the Senate and House of Representatives of the United States of America in Congress assembled,

SECTION 1. SHORT TITLE

This joint resolution may be cited as the "Authorization for Use of Military Force."

SECTION 2. AUTHORIZATION FOR USE OF UNITED STATES ARMED FORCES

(a) **In General**. — That the President is authorized to use all necessary and appropriate force against those nations, organizations, or persons he determines planned, authorized, committed, or aided the terrorist attacks that occurred on September 11, 2001, or harbored such organizations or persons, in order to prevent any future acts of international terrorism against the United States by such nations, organizations or persons.

(b) **War Powers Resolution Requirements** —

(1) **Specific Statutory Authorization**. — Consistent with section 8(a)(1) of the War Powers Resolution, the Congress declares that this section is intended to constitute specific statutory authorization within the meaning of section 5(b) of the War Powers Resolution.

(2) **Applicability of Other Requirements**. — Nothing in this resolution supercedes any requirement of the War Powers Resolution.

NOTES AND QUESTIONS

1. *9/11: Armed Attack and Self-Defense?* The United States wrote to the Security Council on October 7, 2001, to say that it had clear and compelling evidence that Al Qaeda played a central role in the 9/11 attacks. Furthermore, it said, in the exercise of its Article 51 right of self-defense to prevent and deter further attacks, it was initiating military action — Operation Enduring Freedom (OEF) — against Al Qaeda terrorist training camps and Taliban military bases in Afghanistan. Letter from the Permanent Representative of the United States of America to the President of the Security Council (Oct. 7, 2001), 40 I.L.M. 1281 (2001). The letter presumably satisfied Article 51's requirement to immediately report to the Security Council any resort to self-defense.

Were the 9/11 attacks "armed attacks" that justified the use of force in self-defense within the meaning of international law? *Compare* Louis Henkin, *International Law: Politics and Values* 126 (1995) ("It is difficult to make an 'armed attack' out of a limited, isolated terrorist attack or even a few sporadic ones."), *with* Adam Roberts, *Afghanistan and International Security*, in *The War in Afghanistan: A Legal Analysis* 4, 15 (Michael N. Schmitt ed., 2009) (arguing that in Resolution 1368 "the Council accepted that a right of self-defense could apply to a State when it was attacked by a non-State entity"), *and* Dinstein, *supra* p. 66, at 208 ("terrorist attacks qualify as armed attacks"). *See also* Mary Ellen O'Connell, *Lawful Self-Defense to Terrorism*,

63 U. Pitt. L. Rev. 889, 890-893 (2002) (arguing that a forceful response was justified, based on the scale and gravity of the attacks). Can you argue that the Security Council recognized them as such? That the Council approved U.S. military action in self-defense? If so, what actions?

2. *Attacking the Terrorists Where They Live.* Did the United States violate Article 2(4) of the U.N. Charter when it launched an attack on Al Qaeda and the Taliban inside the territory of another sovereign state, Afghanistan? According to one observer, if the host state cannot or will not deal with its resident terrorist threat, the victim state may use force to do what the host state should have done. Dinstein, *supra*, at 244-245.

How much responsibility is borne by a state that, willingly or unwillingly, hosts terrorists? In a 1949 decision, the World Court declared that it is "every State's obligation not to allow knowingly its territory to be used for acts contrary to the rights of other States." *Corfu Channel (U.K. v. Alb.),* 1949 I.C.J. 4, 22 (Apr. 9). Were U.S. forces justified by a breach of this obligation in attacking the state of Afghanistan and its Taliban government? According to one observer, "the Taliban, Afghanistan's de facto government, developed such close links to the known terrorist organization al Qaeda that it became responsible for the acts of al Qaeda." O'Connell, *supra*, 63 U. Pitt. L. Rev. at 901. *See also* Sean D. Murphy, *Terrorism and the Concept of "Armed Attack" in Article 51 of the U.N. Charter,* 43 Harv. Int'l L.J. 41, 50 (2002) (suggesting that the incidents of September 11 might be imputable to the de facto Taliban government of Afghanistan).

In December 2001, the U.N. Security Council eliminated any doubt about its approval of the use of force in Afghanistan when it authorized the creation of an International Security Assistance Force (ISAF) in Afghanistan, with responsibility for supporting an interim Afghan government and disarming Taliban insurgents, among other concerns. S.C. Res. 1386, U.N. Doc. S/RES 1386 (Dec. 20, 2001). By early 2011, ISAF included more than 130,000 troops from 48 countries, including the United States. *See* NATO/OTAN, *Afghanistan: International Security Assistance Force* (updated regularly), *at* http://www.nato.int/isaf/.

Is the United States justified under Article 51 in attacking Al Qaeda and Taliban targets inside Pakistan? *See generally* Sean D. Murphy, *The International Legality of US Cross-Border Operations from Afghanistan into Pakistan,* in *The War in Afghanistan: A Legal Analysis, supra,* at 109, and sources cited therein. What about U.S. military attacks on suspected terrorist targets in Yemen? Targeted killing of terrorist suspects is addressed in Chapter 4.

3. *Declaring War on Al Qaeda?* Formal declarations of war have always named belligerents that were sovereign states. Following the September 2001 terrorist attacks on the World Trade Center and the Pentagon, however, a newspaper columnist wrote and some members of Congress reportedly agreed that "Congress . . . should immediately declare war. It does not have to name a country. It can declare war against those who carried out [the] attack. . . ." Robert Kagan, *We Must Fight This War,* Wash. Post, Sept. 12, 2001. May Congress declare war on a group of people? May it declare war without naming any enemy at all? Should Congress have declared war on Al Qaeda or on international terrorists after September 11?

4. *The September 18, 2001 AUMF.* How is the September 18 Authorization for Use of Military Force (generally referred to as AUMF) different from the bill the White

House proposed? Four days after the attacks of 9/11, President Bush declared that victory against terrorism would require "a series of decisive actions against terrorist organizations and those who harbor and support them." Radio Address of the President to the Nation (Sept. 15, 2001), *at* http://georgewbush-whitehouse.archives. gov/news/releases/2001/09/20010915.html. Does the scope of the AUMF match the Administration's rhetorical commitment to combating terrorists wherever they can be found, as well as the states that give them support? Does the last clause of the measure, relating to the War Powers Resolution, serve as a limitation on the authority otherwise bestowed by the AUMF?

Is there any important difference between this law and a formal declaration of war against Al Qaeda? Do these two different forms of legislative authority affect U.S. relations with other nations differently? Or the domestic powers of the President? Or the legal "dominos" discussed *supra?*

5. *Necessity and Proportionality.* Pursuant to the September 18, 2001, AUMF, U.S. armed forces eventually deployed to Afghanistan and, in coordination with indigenous anti-Taliban forces, not only drove Al Qaeda leadership out of the country, but ousted the Taliban from power, using both ground forces and air power. Did this response meet the international law requirements of necessity and proportionality? U.S. ground forces have stayed in Afghanistan ever since, and in 2011 they are still battling returning Taliban elements. Does this continuing use of armed force meet the same requirements?

6. *The AUMF and the Invasion of Iraq.* President George W. Bush and members of his administration asserted, or at least strongly suggested, that there was a link between Saddam Hussein and Al Qaeda, and even that Saddam bore some responsibility for the 9/11 attacks. *See, e.g.,* State of the Union Address (Jan. 28, 2003) ("Saddam Hussein aids and protects terrorists, including members of al Qaeda"); Remarks of National Security Adviser Condoleeza Rice, on Morning Show, CBS (Nov. 28, 2003) ("Oh, indeed there is a tie between Iraq and what happened on 9/11."). These claims were later shown to be false. *See Report on Whether Public Statements Regarding Iraq by U.S. Government Officials Were Substantiated by Intelligence Information*, S. Rep. No. 110-345, at 59-72 (2008), *available at* http://intelligence.senate.gov/pdfs/ 110345.pdf. Examining the 2001 AUMF, can you see how such claims might nevertheless be used to build a legal case for the invasion of Iraq, even without the passage of a later resolution specifically naming Iraq? How would you rebut that case?

Targeting Terrorists

4

"Targeted killing" was not a term of art in human rights law or international humanitarian law prior to the 9/11 attacks. It has been used with increasing frequency since then to refer to U.S. attacks by unmanned aerial vehicles (UAVs) or "drones" on alleged Al Qaeda or Taliban targets. The U.N. Special Rapporteur for Human Rights asserts:

> The common element in all these contexts is that lethal force is intentionally and deliberately used, with a degree of pre-meditation, against an individual or individuals specifically identified in advance by the perpetrator. In a targeted killing, the specific goal of the operation is to use lethal force. This distinguishes targeted killings from unintentional, accidental, or reckless killings, or killings made without conscious choice. It also distinguishes them from law enforcement operations, e.g., against a suspected suicide bomber. Under such circumstances, it may be legal for law enforcement personnel to shoot to kill based on the imminence of the threat, but the goal of the operation, from its inception, should not be to kill. [Special Rapporteur on Extrajudicial, Summary or Arbitrary Executions, *Addendum: Study on Targeted Killings* at 5, U.N. Doc. A/HRC/14/24/Add.6 (May 28, 2010) (by Philip Alston).]

In Part A of this chapter, we begin with several brief accounts of U.S. targeted killing operations. The legality of each operation depends in part on the legal paradigm under which it is analyzed and in part on how it is conducted. In Part B, we apply the paradigm of international human rights law. In Part C, we shift to the paradigm of international humanitarian law. Finally, in Part D, we consider the effects of domestic law and an executive ban on "assassination."

A. TARGETED KILLING BY THE UNITED STATES AFTER 9/11[1]

In October 2001, on the first night of the campaign against Al Qaeda and the Taliban authorized by Congress after the September 11 attacks, a 27-foot-long,

---

1. This report is drawn from William C. Banks, *The Predator* (Maxwell Sch. of Citizenship & Pub. Affairs, Syracuse Univ., CS 0603-32, 2003); Kristen Eichensehr, *On the Offensive: Assassination Policy Under International Law*, 25 Harv. Int'l Rev. 1 (Fall 2003), *available at* http://hir.harvard.edu/articles/1149/3/; Seymour Hersh, *Manhunt*, New Yorker, Dec. 23, 2002, at 66, 74; Eblen Kaplan, *Targeted Killings* (Council on Foreign Rel. Mar. 2, 2006); Scott Shane, Mark Mazzetti & Robert F. Worth, *Secret Assault on Terrorism*

unmanned aerial vehicle (or drone) with a 49-foot wingspan called the Predator deployed over southern Afghanistan apparently identified Taliban leader Mullah Mohammed Omar in a convoy of cars fleeing Kabul. Following its agreement with military commanders, the CIA operators sought approval from the United States Central Command in Tampa to launch a Hellfire missile at Omar, who by then had sought cover in a building with an estimated 100 guards. General Tommy Franks reportedly declined to give approval based upon on-the-spot advice of his military lawyer. Other reports suggest that, in light of the number of possible casualties, he sought approval from the President, who personally approved the strike. But the resulting delay apparently allowed Omar to escape.

In February 2002, another Predator filmed a very tall man being greeted effusively by villagers. Osama bin Laden was said to be about six feet five inches tall. The order was quickly given to fire, but by that time the group had disbanded, and the Predator captured another image of a tall man and two others emerging from a wooded area. The Hellfire was launched, killing all three. Journalists later reported that they were locals who had been scavenging for wood. Bin Laden was not among them.

On November 3, 2002, video feeds from television cameras on a Predator, flying slowly 10,000-15,000 feet above Marib Province in Yemen, showed an RV speeding through the desert. A joint Yemeni and American intelligence team had for days been tracing cell phone calls by an Al Qaeda leader named Qaed Salim Sinan al-Harethi, and it determined that he was in the car. Al-Harethi was a prime suspect in the 2000 suicide bombing of the USS *Cole*, which had killed 17 U.S. sailors. Using a joystick to control the Predator remotely, a U.S. operator fired a Hellfire missile from the plane, striking the RV dead center and killing all five of its passengers. Yemeni security officials later took the bodies to a hospital in Yemen's capital, where U.S. officials obtained DNA samples. They confirmed that the Predator attack had "taken out" al-Harethi. They also identified one of the other victims as Kamal Derwish, a U.S. citizen who grew up near Buffalo and who reportedly recruited American Muslims for training in Al Qaeda camps.

MQ-1 Predator (armed with an AGM-114 Hellfire missile).

U.S. Air Force photo.

The United States employed drones in the Iraq war, but the pace of their use quickened and the geographic expanse of their deployment widened after 2006 intelligence findings by President Bush and revisions of them by President Obama in 2009 and 2010 authorized targeting Osama bin Laden and other top terrorist targets. Rather than "the hammer," according to White House counterterrorism adviser John O. Brennan, the United States would use "the scalpel." Indeed, in the first year of the Obama administration, more drone strikes were carried out than in the entire Bush presidency.

Widens on Two Continents, N.Y. Times, Aug. 14, 2010; Mark Mazzetti, Helene Cooper & Peter Baker, *Behind the Hunt for Bin Laden*, N.Y. Times, May 2, 2011; Michael D. Shear, *White House Corrects Bin Laden Narrative*, N.Y. Times, May 3, 2011.

Taliban and Al Qaeda insurgents in Afghanistan took advantage of the porous border and difficult terrain to maintain encampments in Pakistan as staging areas for cross-border raids on U.S. and NATO forces in Afghanistan. Drone strikes were, to some, an effective counter to these tactics. In an August 2009 strike, Hellfire missiles fired from a drone killed Baitullah Mehsud, head of the Pakistan Taliban. Mehsud had been a thorn in the side of the government of Pakistan for years, while he ordered abductions and killings on the streets of Pakistan, sabotaged Pakistani government officials and installations, and likely masterminded the assassination of former Prime Minister Benazir Bhutto. When he was killed, Mehsud was in Pakistan, either resting or receiving medical care on the roof of his father-in-law's house. To U.S. officials, killing Mehsud was an important tactical victory in the war against Taliban and Al Qaeda terrorists and insurgents. Yet Mehsud had commanded his extremists inside Pakistan, not Afghanistan, and the missile strike killed family members, bodyguards, and bystanders as well as Mehsud.

On May 25, 2010, another drone strike in remote Marib Province in Yemen targeted a small group of Al Qaeda operatives meeting in a desert location. The missile killed its targets, but it also killed the Deputy Governor of Marib Province who, unknown to U.S. officials, was meeting the Al Qaeda operatives to persuade them to lay down their arms (according to Yemen government sources). The Yemen strikes were neither confirmed nor denied by U.S. officials. Later the same year, the United States reportedly approved the targeting in Yemen of U.S. citizen Anwar al-Aulaqi on grounds that he was taking an active part in planning terrorist activities directed at the United States. He was killed by a drone strike on September 30, 2011, alongside another U.S. citizen who was traveling with him.

Finally, after months of careful intelligence gathering and extensive planning, on May 1, 2011, 79 American special forces personnel in 4 helicopters descended on a walled compound in Abbottabad, Pakistan, and, near the end of a 40-minute firefight, shot and killed Osama bin Laden. President Obama settled on a commando raid rather than a drone strike to avoid collateral damage (incidental civilian casualties) in a residential area and to permit verification of bin Laden's identity once he was captured or killed. When the Navy Seals located bin Laden on the top floor of the dwelling, he reportedly resisted arrest and was shot in the head. Bin Laden was not armed at the time, however. Several couriers and a woman were killed, but others in the compound (reportedly including one of bin Laden's wives) were uninjured, and apparently no damage was caused outside the compound.

Since September 11, 2001, Predators and other drones have reportedly been used hundreds of times to fire on targets in Afghanistan, Pakistan, Yemen, Iraq, and elsewhere. Apart from Osama bin Laden, a number of senior Taliban and Al Qaeda operatives have been killed in these attacks, including Al Qaeda's reputed chief of military operations, Mohammed Atef. But some number of innocent civilians have also been killed, sometimes deliberately as unavoidable collateral damage and sometimes simply by mistake.

B.   TARGETED KILLING AND HUMAN RIGHTS LAW

Human rights law — international law that constrains governments in their treatment of civilians during peacetime — generally requires some kind of judicial procedure before anyone is executed (hence, the oft-stated concern about "*extra-judicial* killing or imprisonment"). The law enforcement model under human rights law rests on a presumption of innocence, a preference for arrest and detention by due process, and an insistence on credible evidence and fair trial before judicial punishment. *See generally* David Kretzmer, *Targeted Killing of Suspected Terrorists: Extra-Judicial Executions or Legitimate Means of Defence?*, 16 Eur. J. Int'l L. 171 (2005).

The International Covenant on Civil and Political Rights art. 6, Mar. 23, 1976, 999 U.N.T.S. 171, provides: "Every human being has the inherent right to life. This right shall be protected by law. No one shall be arbitrarily deprived of his life." This language resembles the text of the Fifth Amendment to the United States Constitution, which states: "No person shall . . . be deprived of life, liberty, or property, without due process of law. . . ."

The European Convention on Human Rights is similar:

Convention for the Protection of Human Rights and Fundamental Freedoms
Nov. 4, 1950, 213 U.N.T.S. 222

ARTICLE 2 – RIGHT TO LIFE

1. Everyone's right to life shall be protected by law. No one shall be deprived of his life intentionally save in the execution of a sentence of a court following his conviction of a crime for which this penalty is provided by law.
2. Deprivation of life shall not be regarded as inflicted in contravention of this Article when it results from the use of force which is no more than absolutely necessary:
   (a) in defence of any person from unlawful violence;
   (b) in order to effect a lawful arrest or to prevent the escape of a person lawfully detained;
   (c) in action lawfully taken for the purpose of quelling a riot or insurrection.

The United Nations Basic Principles on the Use of Force and Firearms by Law Enforcement Officials (Sept. 7, 1990), *available at* http://www2.ohchr.org/english/law/pdf/firearms.pdf, address the subject in detail. Article 9 provides that "intentional lethal use of firearms may only be made when strictly unavoidable in order to protect life." Article 10 further provides that

> law enforcement officials shall identify themselves as such and shall give a clear warning of their intent to use firearms, with sufficient time for the warnings to be observed, unless to do so would unduly place the law enforcement officials at risk or would create a risk of death or serious harm to other persons, or would be clearly inappropriate or pointless in the circumstances of the incident.

In effect, the imminence of the threat provides the evidence needed to justify the use of lethal force and obviates any need to prove the target's intention. Kretzmer, *supra*, at 182. But unless the strict requirements of imminence and necessity through unavailability of other means are satisfied, the use of lethal force by law enforcement officers or, except in combat, military personnel would deny a suspected terrorist basic due process, "preventing the target from contesting the determination that he or she is a terrorist, and imposing a unilateral death penalty." Vincent-Joel Proulx, *If the Hat Fits, Wear it, If the Turban Fits, Run for Your Life: Reflections on the Indefinite Detention and Targeted Killing of Suspected Terrorists*, 56 Hastings L.J. 801, 889 (2005). Thus, "the very purpose of international human rights is defeated, whether through the violation of the right to a fair trial, the absolute circumvention of the right to liberty, or the disregard of the inherent right to life." *Id.* at 889-890.

Human rights law (HRL) is to be contrasted with international humanitarian law (IHL), addressed at length in Chapter 2, which governs the conduct of states in the midst of an armed conflict. There is overlap between the two sets of principles, and some resulting confusion. Indeed, as we see below, there is a growing tendency to apply HRL in armed conflicts, expanding the protections otherwise available to civilians and disarmed combatants. *See* Theodor Meron, *The Humanization of Humanitarian Law*, 94 Am. J. Int'l L. 239 (2000).

McCann v. United Kingdom

European Court of Human Rights, 1996
21 E.H.R.R. 97

[Authorities in the United Kingdom learned that Daniel McCann, Sean Savage, and Mairead Farrell of the Provisional IRA were planning to detonate a car bomb at a changing of the guard ceremony in Gibraltar on March 8, 1988. The authorities believed that the suspects would use a radio controlled detonation device. On March 6, 1988, the suspects were allowed to enter Gibraltar and were clandestinely followed by soldiers in the Special Air Service (SAS). The soldiers were wearing plain clothes and carrying concealed weapons.

The suspects parked a car and began to walk away. McCann appeared to notice Soldier A and then both McCann and Farrell made sudden movements. Fearing that they were going to detonate a bomb, Soldiers A and B shot and killed both McCann and Farrell. Soldier C ordered Savage to stop. Savage turned around and reached toward his hip. Soldier C, also fearing that Savage was going to detonate a bomb, shot and killed Savage. McCann, Savage, and Farrell were unarmed and did not have any detonating devices. Authorities later found keys to the parked car in Farrell's handbag. A subsequent search of the parked car turned up keys to a second car. The second car contained 64 kilograms of Semtex explosives, around which were packed 200 rounds of ammunition.

A coroner's inquest determined that the killings were lawful and justified. Relatives of the deceased disagreed. They first sued the United Kingdom's Ministry of Defence in Northern Ireland, but their suits were dismissed on grounds of sovereign immunity. They then complained to the European Commission on Human Rights, asserting that the killings violated Article 2 of the European Convention on Human Rights. The Commission concluded by a vote of 11 to 6 that no violation had occurred. The European Court of Human Rights reviewed the Commission's report, and issued the following judgment, adopted by a vote of 10 to 9.] . . .

200. The Court accepts that the soldiers honestly believed, in the light of the information that they had been given, as set out above, that it was necessary to shoot the suspects in order to prevent them from detonating a bomb and causing serious loss of life. The actions which they took, in obedience to superior orders, were thus perceived by them as absolutely necessary in order to safeguard innocent lives.

It considers that the use of force by agents of the State in pursuit of one of the aims delineated in Article 2(2) of the Convention may be justified under this provision where it is based on an honest belief which is perceived, for good reasons, to be valid at the time but which subsequently turns out to be mistaken. To hold otherwise would be to impose an unrealistic burden on the State and its law enforcement personnel in the execution of their duty, perhaps to the detriment of their lives and those of others.

It follows that, having regard to the dilemma confronting the authorities in the circumstances of the case, the actions of the soldiers do not, in themselves, give rise to a violation of this provision.

201. The question arises, however, whether the anti-terrorist operation as a whole was controlled and organised in a manner which respected the requirements of Article 2 and whether the information and instructions given to the soldiers which, in effect, rendered inevitable the use of lethal force, took adequately into consideration the right to life of the three suspects.

CONTROL AND ORGANISATION OF THE OPERATION

202. The Court first observes that, as appears from the Operational Order of the Commissioner, it had been the intention of the authorities to arrest the suspects at an appropriate stage. Indeed evidence was given at the Inquest that arrest procedures had been practised by the soldiers before 6 March and that efforts had been made to find a suitable place in Gibraltar to detain the suspects after their arrest.

203. It may be questioned why the three suspects were not arrested at the border immediately on their arrival in Gibraltar and why, as emerged from the evidence given by Inspector Ullger, the decision was taken not to prevent them from entering Gibraltar if they were believed to be on a bombing mission. Having had advance warning of the terrorists' intentions it would certainly have been possible for the authorities to have mounted an arrest operation. Although surprised at the early arrival of the three suspects, they had a surveillance team at the border and an arrest group nearby. In addition, the security services and the Spanish authorities had photographs of the three suspects, knew their names as well as their aliases and would have known what passports to look for.

204. On this issue, the Government submitted that at that moment there might not have been sufficient evidence to warrant the detention and trial of the suspects. Moreover, to release them, having alerted them to the authorities' state of awareness but leaving them or others free to try again, would obviously increase the risks. Nor could the authorities be sure that those three were the only terrorists they had to deal with or of the manner in which it was proposed to carry out the bombing.

205. The Court confines itself to observing in this respect that the danger to the population of Gibraltar — which is at the heart of the Government's submissions in the case — in not preventing their entry must be considered to outweigh the possible consequences of having insufficient evidence to warrant their detention and trial.

In its view, either the authorities knew that there was no bomb in the car — which the Court has already discounted — or there was a serious miscalculation by those responsible for controlling the operation. As a result, the scene was set in which the fatal shooting, given the intelligence assessments which had been made, was a foreseeable possibility if not a likelihood.

The decision not to stop the three terrorists from entering Gibraltar is thus a relevant factor to take into account under this head.

206. The Court notes that at the briefing on 5 March attended by Soldiers A, B, C and D it was considered likely that the attack would be by way of a large car bomb. A number of key assessments were made. In particular, it was thought that the terrorists would not use a blocking car; that the bomb would be detonated by a radio-control device; that the detonation could be effected by the pressing of a button; that it was likely that the suspects would detonate the bomb if challenged; that they would be armed and would be likely to use their arms if confronted.

207. In the event, all of these crucial assumptions, apart from the terrorists' intentions to carry out an attack, turned out to be erroneous. Nevertheless, as has been demonstrated by the Government, on the basis of their experience in dealing with the IRA, they were all possible hypotheses in a situation where the true facts were unknown and where the authorities operated on the basis of limited intelligence information.

208. In fact, insufficient allowances appear to have been made for other assumptions. For example, since the bombing was not expected until 8 March when the changing of the guard ceremony was to take place, there was equally the possibility that the three terrorists were on a reconnaissance mission. While this was a factor which was briefly considered, it does not appear to have been regarded as a serious possibility.

In addition, at the briefings or after the suspects had been spotted, it might have been thought unlikely that they would have been prepared to explode the bomb, thereby killing many civilians, as Mr McCann and Ms Farrell strolled towards the border area since this would have increased the risk of detection and capture. It might also have been thought improbable that at that point they would set up the transmitter in anticipation to enable them to detonate the supposed bomb immediately if confronted.

Moreover, even if allowances are made for the technological skills of the IRA, the description of the detonation device as a "button job" without the qualifications subsequently described by the experts at the Inquest, of which the competent authorities must have been aware, over-simplifies the true nature of these devices.

209. It is further disquieting in this context that the assessment made by Soldier G, after a cursory external examination of the car, that there was a "suspect car bomb" was conveyed to the soldiers, according to their own testimony, as a definite identification that there was such a bomb. It is recalled that while Soldier G had experience in car bombs, it transpired that he was not an expert in radio communications or explosives; and that his assessment that there was a suspect car bomb, based on his observation that the car aerial was out of place, was more in the nature of a report that a bomb could not be ruled out.

210. In the absence of sufficient allowances being made for alternative possibilities, and the definite reporting of the existence of a car bomb which, according to the assessments that had been made, could be detonated at the press of a button, a series of working hypotheses were conveyed to Soldiers A, B, C and D as certainties, thereby making the use of lethal force almost unavoidable.

211. However, the failure to make provision for a margin of error must also be considered in combination with the training of the soldiers to continue shooting once they opened fire until the suspect was dead. As noted by the Coroner in his summing up to the jury at the Inquest, all four soldiers shot to kill the suspects. Soldier E testified that it had been discussed with the soldiers that there was an increased chance that they would have to shoot to kill since there would be less time where there was a "button" device. Against this background, the authorities were bound by their obligation to respect the right to life of the suspects to exercise the greatest of care in evaluating the information at their disposal before transmitting it to soldiers whose use of firearms automatically involved shooting to kill.

212. Although detailed investigation at the Inquest into the training received by the soldiers was prevented by the public interest certificates which had been used, it is not clear whether they had been trained or instructed to assess whether the use of firearms to wound their targets may have been warranted by the specific circumstances that confronted them at the moment of arrest.

Their reflex action in this vital respect lacks the degree of caution in the use of firearms to be expected from law enforcement personnel in a democratic society, even when dealing with dangerous terrorist suspects, and stands in marked contrast to the standard of care reflected in the instructions in the use of firearms by the police which had been drawn to their attention and which emphasised the legal responsibilities of the individual officer in the light of conditions prevailing at the moment of engagement.

This failure by the authorities also suggests a lack of appropriate care in the control and organisation of the arrest operation.

213. In sum, having regard to the decision not to prevent the suspects from travelling into Gibraltar, to the failure of the authorities to make sufficient allowances for the possibility that their intelligence assessments might, in some respects at least, be erroneous and to the automatic recourse to lethal force when the soldiers opened fire, the Court is not persuaded that the killing of the three terrorists constituted the use of force which was no more than absolutely necessary in defence of persons from unlawful violence within the meaning of Article 2(2)(a) of the Convention.

214. Accordingly, it finds that there has been a breach of Article 2 of the Convention. . . .

Joint Dissenting Opinion of Judges RYSSDAL, BERNHARDT, THÓR VILHJÁLMSSON, GÖLCÜKLÜ, PALM, PEKKANEN, FREELAND, BAKA and JAMBREK.

1. We are unable to subscribe to the opinion of a majority of our colleagues that there has been a violation of Article 2 of the Convention in this case. . . .

8. First, in undertaking any evaluation of the way in which the operation was organised and controlled, the Court should studiously resist the temptations offered by the benefit of hindsight. The authorities had at the time to plan and make decisions on the basis of incomplete information. Only the suspects knew at all precisely what they intended; and it was part of the purpose, as it had no doubt been part of their training, to ensure that as little as possible of their intentions was revealed. It would be wrong to conclude in retrospect that a particular course would, as things later transpired, have been better than one adopted at the time under the pressures of an ongoing anti-terrorist operation and that the latter course must therefore be regarded as culpably mistaken. It should not be so regarded unless it is established that in the circumstances as they were known at the time another course should have been preferred.

9. Secondly, the need for the authorities to act within the constraints of the law, while the suspects were operating in a state of mind in which members of the security forces were regarded as legitimate targets and incidental death or injury to civilians as of little consequence, would inevitably give the suspects a tactical advantage which should not be allowed to prevail. The consequences of the explosion of a large bomb in the centre of Gibraltar might well be so devastating that the authorities could not responsibly risk giving the suspects the opportunity to set in train the detonation of such a bomb. Of course the obligation of the United Kingdom under Article 2(1) of the Convention extended to the lives of the suspects as well as to the lives of all the many others, civilian and military, who were present in Gibraltar at the time. But, quite unlike those others, the purpose of the presence of the suspects in Gibraltar was the furtherance of a criminal enterprise which could be expected to have resulted in the loss of many innocent lives if it had been successful. They had chosen to place themselves in a situation where there was a grave danger that an irreconcilable conflict between the two duties might arise.

10. Thirdly, the Court's evaluation of the conduct of the authorities should throughout take full account of (a) the information which had been received earlier about IRA intentions to mount a major terrorist attack in Gibraltar by an active service unit of three individuals; and (b) the discovery which (according to evidence given to the Inquest by Witness O) had been made in Brussels on 21 January 1988 of a car containing a large amount of Semtex explosive and four detonators, with a radio-controlled system — equipment which, taken together, constituted a device familiar in Northern Ireland.

In the light of (a), the decision that members of the SAS should be sent to take part in the operation in response of the request of the Gibraltar Commissioner of Police for military assistance was wholly justifiable. Troops trained in a counter-terrorist role and to operate successfully in small groups would clearly be a suitable choice to meet the threat of an IRA active service unit at large in a densely populated area such as Gibraltar, where there would be an imperative need to limit as far as possible the risk of accidental harm to passers-by.

The detailed operational briefing on 5 March 1988 shows the reasonableness, in the circumstances as known at the time, of the assessments then made. The Operational Order of the Gibraltar Commissioner of Police, which was drawn up on the same day, expressly proscribed the use of more force than necessary and required any recourse to firearms to be had with care for the safety of persons in the vicinity. It described the intention of the operation as being to protect life; to foil the attempt; to arrest the offenders; and the securing and safe custody of the prisoners.

All of this is indicative of appropriate care on the part of the authorities. So, too, is the cautious approach to the eventual passing of control to the military on 6 March 1988.

11. As regards the particular criticisms of the conduct of the operation which are made in the judgment, foremost among them is the questioning of the decision not to prevent the three suspects from entering Gibraltar. It is pointed out in paragraph 203 that, with the advance information which the authorities possessed and with the resources of personnel at their disposal, it would have been possible for them "to have mounted an arrest operation" at the border.

The judgment does not, however, go on to say that it would have been practicable for the authorities to have arrested and detained the suspects at that stage. Rightly so, in our view, because at that stage there might not be sufficient evidence to warrant their detention and trial. To release them, after having alerted them to the state of readiness of the authorities, would be to increase the risk that they or other IRA members could successfully mount a renewed terrorist attack on Gibraltar. In the circumstances as then known, it was accordingly not "a serious miscalculation" for the authorities to defer the arrest rather than merely stop the suspects at the border and turn them back into Spain. . . .

25. The accusation of a breach by a State of its obligation under Article 2 of the Convention to protect the right to life is of the utmost seriousness. For the reasons given above, the evaluation in paragraphs 203 to 213 of the judgment seems to us to fall well short of substantiating the finding that there has been a breach of the Article in this case. We would ourselves follow the reasoning and conclusion of the Commission in its comprehensive, painstaking and notably realistic report. Like the Commission, we are satisfied that no failings have been shown in the organisation and control of the operation by the authorities which could justify a conclusion that force was used against the suspects disproportionately to the purpose of defending innocent persons from unlawful violence. We consider that the use of lethal force in this case, however regrettable the need to resort to such force may be, did not exceed what was, in the circumstances as known as the time, "absolutely necessary" for that purpose and did not amount to a breach by the United Kingdom of its obligations under the Convention.

NOTES AND QUESTIONS

1. *Weighing the Alternative Outcomes in McCann.* The European Court of Human Rights sits like a court of appeals in cases like *McCann*, reviewing the fact and law conclusions of the European Commission on Human Rights. In this closely divided decision, on what basis did the majority of the Court reject the findings of the Commission? Was it failure of the UK security forces in not stopping the suspects from traveling into Gibraltar, or in using lethal force against them once there? Which opinion more faithfully applies Article 2 of the European Convention?

2. *Were the Predator Attacks in Pakistan and Yemen Extrajudicial Killings?* Applying HRL, the U.N. Special Rapporteur to the Commission on Human Rights expressed the opinion that the 2002 U.S. "attack in Yemen constitutes a clear case of extrajudicial killing." U.N. Econ. & Soc. Council, *Civil and Political Rights, Including the Questions of Disappearances and Summary Executions, Submitted to Comm'n on Human Rights,* U.N. Doc. E/CN.4/2003/3 (Jan. 13, 2003). The Swedish Foreign Minister reached a similar conclusion, calling the attack "a summary execution that violates human rights. Terrorists must be treated according to international law. Otherwise, any country can start executing those whom they consider terrorists." *Quoted in* Hersh, *supra* p. 90 n.1, at 4.

Do you agree? Does it matter legally whether the targeted killing is in the border region of Pakistan, in remote provinces of Yemen, in Somalia — or in Germany? Note that although Yemeni officials apparently cooperated in the targeted killing of al-Harethi, they had previously failed to apprehend him and may have been reluctant to do so because of a perceived debt owed to Osama bin Laden, who had assisted the Yemeni president in putting down a separatist movement in 1994. Should the availability of "normal judicial channels" make a difference in the law enforcement analysis? Should it matter legally that one of the persons traveling with al-Harethi in 2002 in Yemen was an American? Was the 2011 drone strike in Yemen that killed U.S. citizens Anwar al-Aulaqi and Samir Khan lawful under HRL? Aulaqi was a propagandist for Al Qaeda in the Arabian Peninsula with reported links to several terrorists, including two of the 9/11 hijackers, while Khan was editor of Al Qaeda's online jihadist magazine, *Inspire. See Anwar al-Awlaki*, N.Y. Times, Oct. 15, 2011, *at* http://topics.nytimes.com/topics/reference/timestopics/people/a/anwar_al_awlaki/index.html.

3. *Human Rights Law in Times of War or Armed Conflict?* If the incident that gave rise to the *McCann* litigation had occurred in Northern Ireland in the 1970s, or in Afghanistan in 2010, with the UK personnel deployed as part of the NATO force there, would HRL apply? The view of the United States is that, during armed conflicts, HRL gives way to IHL and its *jus in bello* principles. *Operational Law Handbook* 40 (Marie Anderson & Emily Zukauskas eds., 2008). Yet the ICJ and other international courts have applied HRL in armed-conflict settings. *See Legality of the Threat or Use of Nuclear Weapons, Advisory Opinion*, 1996 I.C.J. 226 (July 8). In the event of a conflict between HRL and IHL on the battlefield, the traditional U.S. view has been that the *in bello* rules are *lex specialis*, trumping HRL. Anderson & Zukauskas, *supra*, at 40. The European view is that HRL always applies, even alongside IHL on the battlefield. Marco Sassoli & Laura M. Olson, *The Relationship Between Human Rights and Humanitarian Law Where It Matters: Admissible Killing and Internment of Fighters in Non-International Armed Conflicts*, 90 Int'l Rev. Red Cross 599, 603 (Sept. 2008).

Can you think of situations in which the choice of law makes a practical difference? In an international armed conflict, a member of an armed group may be attacked so long as he has not surrendered or been rendered *hors de combat* (disabled from continuing to fight) by injury. But does the same presumption of lawful targeting apply in a non-international armed conflict? *See id.*

4. *Killing bin Laden.* Was the killing of Osama bin Laden by U.S. special forces lawful? Applying HRL, was the killing a permitted law enforcement operation or an extrajudicial killing? *See* Nils Melzer, *Targeted Killing in International Law* 423 (2008) (targeted killing must have a legal basis in domestic law, be preventative rather than punitive, have protection of human life from unlawful attack by the target as its exclusive purpose, "be absolutely necessary in qualitative, quantitative and temporal terms for the achievement of this purpose," and be the "undesired outcome of an operation planned and conducted to minimize resource to lethal force"). Apparently, bin Laden was not armed when he was shot. Would that fact make the operation unlawful from an HRL perspective? Is it important that the Navy Seals feared that bin Laden might have prepared for the threat of capture by rigging himself as a "human IED" (improvised explosive device)?

C. TARGETED KILLING AND INTERNATIONAL HUMANITARIAN LAW

In the following case, the Israeli Supreme Court applies IHL to Israel's targeted killing of Hamas operatives on the West Bank and in Gaza. But IHL does not make these areas free-fire zones. What are its requirements? For references to that law in Protocol I to the Geneva Convention, see *supra* p. 38.

Public Committee Against Torture in Israel v. Israel

Supreme Court of Israel, sitting as the High Court of Justice, 2006
46 I.L.M 375

President (Emeritus) A. BARAK: The Government of Israel employs a policy of preventative strikes which cause the death of terrorists in Judea, Samaria, or the Gaza Strip. It fatally strikes these terrorists, who plan, launch, or commit terrorist attacks in Israel and in the area of Judea, Samaria, and the Gaza Strip, against both civilians and soldiers. These strikes at times also harm innocent civilians. Does the State thus act illegally? That is the question posed before us.

1. FACTUAL BACKGROUND

In February 2000, the second intifada began. A massive assault of terrorism was directed against the State of Israel, and against Israelis, merely because they are Israelis. This assault of terrorism differentiates neither between combatants and civilians, nor between women, men, and children. The terrorist attacks take place both in the territory of Judea, Samaria, and the Gaza Strip, and within the borders of the State of Israel. They are directed against civilian centers, shopping centers and markets, coffee houses and restaurants. Over the last five years, thousands of acts of terrorism have been committed against Israel. In the attacks, more than one thousand Israeli citizens have been killed. Thousands of Israeli citizens have been wounded. Thousands of Palestinians have been killed and wounded during this period as well.

2. In its war against terrorism, the State of Israel employs various means. As part of the security activity intended to confront the terrorist attacks, the State employs what it calls "the policy of targeted frustration" of terrorism. Under this policy, the security forces act in order to kill members of terrorist organizations involved in the planning, launching, or execution of terrorist attacks against Israel. During the second intifada, such preventative strikes have been performed across Judea, Samaria, and the Gaza Strip. According to the data relayed by petitioners, since the commencement of these acts, and up until the end of 2005, close to three hundred members of terrorist organizations have been killed by them. More than thirty targeted killing attempts have failed. Approximately one hundred and fifty civilians who were proximate to the location of the targeted persons have been killed during those acts. Hundreds of others have been wounded. The policy of targeted killings is the focus of this petition. . . .

5.   THE GENERAL NORMATIVE FRAMEWORK

A.   International Armed Conflict

16. The general, principled starting point is that between Israel and the various terrorist organizations active in Judea, Samaria, and the Gaza Strip (hereinafter "the area") a continuous situation of armed conflict has existed since the first intifada. . . . [T]he situation was described in the supplement to the summary on behalf of the State Attorney (on January 26 2004):

> For more than three years now, the State of Israel is under a constant, continual, and murderous wave of terrorist attacks, directed at Israelis — because they are Israelis — without any discrimination between combatants and civilians or between men, women, and children. In the framework of the current campaign of terrorism, more than 900 Israelis have been killed, and thousands of other Israelis have been wounded to date, since late September 2000. In addition, thousands of Palestinians have been killed and wounded during that period. For the sake of comparison we note that the number of Israeli casualties in proportion to the population of the State of Israel, is a number of times greater than the percentage of casualties in the US in the events of September 11 in proportion to the US population. As is well known, and as we have already noted, the events of 9/11 were defined by the states of the world and by international organizations, with no hesitation whatsoever, as an "armed conflict" justifying the use of counterforce. . . .

23. . . . Are terrorist organizations and their members combatants, in regard[] to their rights in the armed conflict? Are they civilians taking an active part in the armed conflict? Are they possibly neither combatants nor civilians? What, then, is the status of those terrorists?

B.   Combatants

24. What makes a person a combatant? This category includes, of course, the armed forces. It also includes people who fulfill the following conditions: [see Geneva Convention III, art. 4, *supra* p. 30] . . . In one case, I wrote:

> "The Lebanese detainees are not to be seen as prisoners of war. It is sufficient, in order to reach that conclusion, that they do not fulfill the provisions of article 4a(2)(d) of The Third Geneva Convention, which provides that one of the conditions which must be fulfilled in order to fit the definition of 'a prisoner of war' is 'that of conducting their operations in accordance with the laws and customs of war.' The organizations to which the Lebanese detainees belonged are terrorist organizations acting contrary to the laws and customs of war. Thus, for example, these organizations intentionally harm civilians, and shoot from within the civilian population, which serves them as a shield. Each of these is an act contrary to international law. Indeed, Israel's constant stance throughout the years has been to view the various organizations, like the Hizbollah, as organizations to which The Third Geneva Convention does not apply. We found no cause to intervene in that stance."

25. The terrorists and their organizations, with which the State of Israel has an armed conflict of international character, do not fall into the category of combatants.

They do not belong to the armed forces, and they do not belong to units to which international law grants status similar to that of combatants. Indeed, the terrorists and the organizations which send them to carry out attacks are unlawful combatants. They do not enjoy the status of prisoners of war. They can be tried for their participation in hostilities, judged, and punished. The Chief Justice of the Supreme Court of the United States, Stone C.J. discussed that, writing:

> "By universal agreement and practice, the law of war draws a distinction between the armed forces and the peaceful population of belligerent nations and also between those who are lawful and unlawful combatants. Lawful combatants are subject to capture and detention as prisoners of war by opposing military forces. Unlawful combatant are likewise subject to capture and detention, but in addition they are subject to trial and punishment by military tribunals for acts which render their belligerency unlawful" (*Ex Parte Quirin* 317 U.S. 1, 30 (1942); see also *Hamdi v. Rumsfeld*, 542 U.S. 507 (2004)).

... Needless to say, unlawful combatants are not beyond the law. They are not "outlaws." God created them as well in his image; their human dignity as well is to be honored; they as well enjoy and are entitled to protection, even if most minimal, by customary international law. That is certainly the case when they are in detention or brought to justice (see §75 of The First Protocol [Additional Protocol I, *supra* p. 40], which reflects customary international law). Does it follow that in Israel's conduct of combat against the terrorist organizations, Israel is not entitled to harm them, and Israel is not entitled to kill them even if they are planning, launching, or committing terrorist attacks? If they were seen as (legal) combatants, the answer would of course be that Israel is entitled to harm them. Just as it is permissible to harm a soldier of an enemy country, so can terrorists be harmed. Accordingly, they would also enjoy the status of prisoners of war, and the rest of the protections granted to legal combatants. However, as we have seen, the terrorists acting against Israel are not combatants according to the definition of that term in international law; they are not entitled to the status of prisoners of war; they can be put on trial for their membership in terrorist organizations and for their operations against the army. Are they seen as civilians under the law? It is to the examination of that question which we now turn.

C. Civilians

26. Customary international law regarding armed conflicts protects "civilians" from harm as a result of the hostilities. . . . From that follows also the duty to do everything possible to minimize collateral damage to the civilian population during the attacks on "combatants." Against the background of that protection granted to "civilians," the question what constitutes a "civilian" for the purposes of that law arises. The approach of customary international law is that "civilians" are those who are not "combatants" (see §50(1) of The First Protocol). In the *Blaskic* case, the International Criminal Tribunal for the former Yugoslavia ruled that civilians are —

> "Persons who are not, or no longer, members of the armed forces."

That definition is "negative" in nature. It defines the concept of "civilian" as the opposite of "combatant." It thus views unlawful combatants — who, as we have seen, are not "combatants" — as civilians. Does that mean that the unlawful combatants are entitled to the same protection to which civilians who are not unlawful combatants are entitled? The answer is, no. Customary international law regarding armed conflicts determines that a civilian taking a direct part in the hostilities does not, at such time, enjoy the protection granted to a civilian who is not taking a direct part in the hostilities (see §51(3) of The First Protocol). The result is that an unlawful combatant is not a combatant, rather a "civilian." However, he is a civilian who is not protected from attack as long as he is taking a direct part in the hostilities. . . .

D. A Third Category: Unlawful combatants?

27. In the oral and written arguments before us, the State asked us to recognize a third category of persons, that of unlawful combatants. These are people who take active and continuous part in an armed conflict, and therefore should be treated as combatants, in the sense that they are legitimate targets of attack, and they do not enjoy the protections granted to civilians. However, they are not entitled to the rights and privileges of combatants, since they do not differentiate themselves from the civilian population, and since they do not obey the laws of war. Thus, for example, they are not entitled to the status of prisoners of war. The State's position is that the terrorists who participate in the armed conflict between Israel and the terrorist organizations fall under this category of unlawful combatants.

28. . . . We shall take no stance regarding the question whether it is desirable to recognize this third category. The question before us is not one of desirable law, rather one of existing law. In our opinion, as far as existing law goes, the data before us are not sufficient to recognize this third category. . . .

6. CIVILIANS WHO ARE UNLAWFUL COMBATANTS

A. The Basic Principle: Civilians Taking a Direct Part in Hostilities are not Protected at Such Time they are Doing So

29. Civilians enjoy comprehensive protection of their lives, liberty, and property. "The protection of the lives of the civilian population is a central value in humanitarian law." "The right to life and bodily integrity is the basic right standing at the center of the humanitarian law intended to protect the local population." As opposed to combatants, whom one can harm due to their status as combatants, civilians are not to be harmed, due to their status as civilians. A provision in this spirit is determined in article 51(2) of The First Protocol, which constitutes customary international law:

> "The civilian population as such, as well as individual civilians, shall not be the object of attack. . . ."

Article 8(2)(b)(i)-(ii) of the Rome Statute of the International Criminal Court determines, in the same spirit, in defining a war crime, that if an order to attack civilians is given intentionally, that is a crime. That crime applies to those civilians who are "not taking direct part in hostilities." In addition, civilians are not to be harmed in an indiscriminate attack; in other words, in an attack which, inter alia, is not directed against a particular military objective (see §51(4) of The First Protocol, which constitutes customary international law). That protection is granted to all civilians, excepting those civilians taking a direct part in hostilities. . . .

B.   The Source of the Basic Principle and its Customary Character

30. The basic principle is that the civilians taking a direct part in hostilities are not protected from attack upon them at such time as they are doing so. This principle is manifest in §51(3) of The First Protocol, which determines:

> "Civilians shall enjoy the protection afforded by this section, unless and for such time as they take a direct part in hostilities."

As is well known, Israel is not party to The First Protocol. Thus, it clearly was not enacted in domestic Israeli legislation. Does the basic principle express customary international law? The position of The Red Cross is that it is a principle of customary international law. That position is acceptable to us. . . . In military manuals of many states, including England, France, Holland, Australia, Italy, Canada, Germany, the United States (Air Force), and New Zealand, the provision has been copied verbatim, or by adopting its essence, according to which civilians are not to be attacked, unless they are taking a (direct) part in the hostilities. The legal literature sees that provision as an expression of customary international law. . . .

[handwritten margin note: looks to other nations]

C.   The Essence of the Basic Principle . . .

32. . . . [T]he basic principle is that the civilian population, and single civilians, are protected from the dangers of military activity and are not targets for attack. That protection is granted to civilians ['unless and for such time as they take a direct part in hostilities"] (§51(3) of The First Protocol). That provision is composed of three main parts. The first part is the requirement that civilians take part in "hostilities"; the second part is the requirement that civilians take a "direct" part in hostilities; the third part is the provision by which civilians are not protected from attack "for such time" as they take a direct part in hostilities. We shall discuss each of those parts separately.

D.   The First Part: "Taking . . . part in hostilities"

33. Civilians lose the protection of customary international law dealing with hostilities of international character if they "take . . . part in hostilities." What is the meaning of that provision? The accepted view is that "hostilities" are acts which by nature and objective are intended to cause damage to the army. Thus determines *Commentary on the Additional Protocols*, published by the Red Cross in 1987:

> "Hostile acts should be understood to be acts which by their nature and purpose are intended to cause actual harm to the personnel and equipment of the armed forces."

. . . It seems that acts which by nature and objective are intended to cause damage to civilians should be added to that definition. According to the accepted definition, a civilian is taking part in hostilities when using weapons in an armed conflict, while gathering intelligence, or while preparing himself for the hostilities. Regarding taking part in hostilities, there is no condition that the civilian use his weapon, nor is [there] a condition that he bear arms (openly or concealed). It is possible to take part in hostilities without using weapons at all. *Commentary on the Additional Protocols* discussed that issue:

"It seems that the word 'hostilities' covers not only the time that the civilian actually makes use of a weapon, but also, for example, the time that he is carrying it, as well as situations in which he undertakes hostile acts without using a weapon."

As we have seen, that approach is not limited merely to the issue of "hostilities" toward the army or the state. It applies also to hostilities against the civilian population of the state.

E.   Second Part: "Takes a Direct Part"

34. Civilians lose the protection against military attack, granted to them by customary international law dealing with international armed conflict (as adopted in The First Protocol, §51(3)), if "they take a direct part in hostilities." That provision differentiates between civilians taking a direct part in hostilities (from whom the protection from attack is removed) and civilians taking an indirect part in hostilities (who continue to enjoy protection from attack). What is that differentiation? A similar provision appears in Common Article 3 of The Geneva Conventions, which uses the wording "active part in hostilities." The judgment of the International Criminal Tribunal for Rwanda determined that these two terms are of identical content. What is that content? It seems accepted in the international literature that an agreed upon definition of the term "direct" in the context under discussion does not exist.

In that state of affairs, and without a comprehensive and agreed upon customary standard, there is no escaping going case by case, while narrowing the area of disagreement. . . . On this issue, the following passage from *Commentary on the Additional Protocols* is worth quoting:

> "Undoubtedly there is room here for some margin of judgment: to restrict this concept to combat and active military operations would be too narrow, while extending it to the entire war effort would be too broad, as in modern warfare the whole population participates in the war effort to some extent, albeit indirectly."

Indeed, a civilian bearing arms (openly or concealed) who is on his way to the place where he will use them against the army, at such place, or on his way back from it, is a civilian taking "an active part" in the hostilities. However, a civilian who generally supports the hostilities against the army is not taking a direct part in the hostilities. Similarly, a civilian who sells food or medicine to unlawful combatants is also taking an indirect part in the hostilities. The third report of the Inter-American Commission on Human Rights states:

> "Civilians whose activities merely support the adverse party's war or military effort or otherwise only indirectly participate in hostilities cannot on these grounds alone be considered combatants. This is because indirect participation, such as selling goods to one or more of the armed parties, expressing sympathy for the cause of one of the parties or, even more clearly, failing to act to prevent an incursion by one of the armed parties, does not involve acts of violence which pose an immediate threat of actual harm to the adverse party."

And what is the law in the space between these two extremes? On the one hand, the desire to protect innocent civilians leads, in the hard cases, to a narrow interpretation of the term "direct" part in hostilities. Professor Cassese writes:

"The rationale behind the prohibition against targeting a civilian who does not take a direct part in hostilities, despite his possible (previous or future) involvement in fighting, is linked to the need to avoid killing innocent civilians."

On the other hand, it can be said that the desire to protect combatants and the desire to protect innocent civilians leads, in the hard cases, to a wide interpretation of the "direct" character of the hostilities, as thus civilians are encouraged to stay away from the hostilities to the extent possible. Schmitt writes:

"Gray areas should be interpreted liberally, i.e., in favor of finding direct participation. One of the seminal purposes of the law is to make possible a clear distinction between civilians and combatants. Suggesting that civilians retain their immunity even when they are intricately involved in a conflict is to engender disrespect for the law by combatants endangered by their activities. Moreover, a liberal approach creates an incentive for civilians to remain as distant from the conflict as possible — in doing so they can better avoid being charged with participation in the conflict and are less liable to being directly targeted."

35. Against the background of these considerations, the following cases should also be included in the definition of taking a "direct part" in hostilities: a person who collects intelligence on the army, whether on issues regarding the hostilities or beyond those issues; a person who transports unlawful combatants to or from the place where the hostilities are taking place; a person who operates weapons which unlawful combatants use, or supervises their operation, or provides service to them, be the distance from the battlefield as it may. All those persons are performing the function of combatants. The function determines the directness of the part taken in the hostilities. However, a person who sells food or medicine to an unlawful combatant is not taking a direct part, rather an indirect part in the hostilities. The same is the case regarding a person who aids the unlawful combatants by general strategic analysis, and grants them logistical, general support, including monetary aid. The same is the case regarding a person who distributes propaganda supporting those unlawful combatants. If such persons are injured, the State is likely not to be liable for it, if it falls into the framework of collateral or incidental damage....

36. What is the law regarding civilians serving as a "human shield" for terrorists taking a direct part in the hostilities? Certainly, if they are doing so because they were forced to do so by terrorists, those innocent civilians are not to be seen as taking a direct part in the hostilities. They themselves are victims of terrorism. However, if they do so of their own free will, out of support for the terrorist organization, they should be seen as persons taking a direct part in the hostilities.

37. We have seen that a civilian causing harm to the army is taking "a direct part" in hostilities. What says the law about those who enlist him to take a direct part in the hostilities, and those who send him to commit hostilities? Is there a difference between his direct commanders and those responsible for them? Is the "direct" part taken only by the last terrorist in the chain of command, or by the entire chain? In our opinion, the "direct" character of the part taken should not be narrowed merely to the person committing the physical act of attack. Those who have sent him, as well, take "a direct part." The same goes for the person who decided upon the act, and the person who planned it. It is not to be said about them that they are taking an indirect part in the hostilities. Their contribution is direct (and active).

F.   The Third Part: "For Such Time"

38. Article 51(3) of The First Protocol states that civilians enjoy protection from the dangers stemming from military acts, and that they are not targets for attack, unless "and for such time" as they are taking a direct part in hostilities. The provisions of article 51(3) of The First Protocol present a time requirement. A civilian taking a part in hostilities loses the protection from attack "for such time" as he is taking part in those hostilities. If "such time" has passed — the protection granted to the civilian returns....

39. As regarding the scope of the wording "takes a direct part" in hostilities, so too regarding the scope of the wording "and for such time" there is no consensus in the international literature. Indeed, both these concepts are close to each other. However, they are not identical. With no consensus regarding the interpretation of the wording "for such time," there is no choice but to proceed from case to case. Again, it is helpful to examine the extreme cases. On the one hand, a civilian taking a direct part in hostilities one single time, or sporadically, who later detaches himself from that activity, is a civilian who, starting from the time he detached himself from that activity, is entitled to protection from attack. He is not to be attacked for the hostilities which he committed in the past. On the other hand, a civilian who has joined a terrorist organization which has become his "home," and in the framework of his role in that organization he commits a chain of hostilities, with short periods of rest between them, loses his immunity from attack "for such time" as he is committing the chain of acts. Indeed, regarding such a civilian, the rest between hostilities is nothing other than preparation for the next hostility.

40. These examples point out the dilemma which the "for such time" requirement presents before us. On the one hand, a civilian who took a direct part in hostilities once, or sporadically, but detached himself from them (entirely, or for a long period) is not to be harmed. On the other hand, the "revolving door" phenomenon, by which each terrorist has "horns of the alter" (1 Kings 1:50) to grasp or a "city of refuge" (Numbers 35:11) to flee to, to which he turns in order to rest and prepare while they grant him immunity from attack, is to be avoided. In the wide area between those two possibilities, one finds the "gray" cases, about which customary international law has not yet crystallized. There is thus no escaping examination of each and every case. In that context, the following four things should be said: first, well based information is needed before categorizing a civilian as falling into one of the discussed categories. Innocent civilians are not to be harmed. Information which has been most thoroughly verified is needed regarding the identity and activity of the civilian who is allegedly taking part in the hostilities. Cassese rightly stated that —

> "[I]f a belligerent were allowed to fire at enemy civilians simply suspected of somehow planning or conspiring to plan military attacks, or of having planned or directed hostile actions, the basic foundations of international humanitarian law would be seriously undermined. The basic distinction between civilians and combatants would be called into question and the whole body of law relating to armed conflict would eventually be eroded."

The burden of proof on the attacking army is heavy. In the case of doubt, careful verification is needed before an attack is made. Henckaerts & Doswald-Beck made this point:

"[W]hen there is a situation of doubt, a careful assessment has to be made under the conditions and restraints governing a particular situation as to whether there are sufficient indications to warrant an attack. One cannot automatically attack anyone who might appear dubious."

Second, a civilian taking a direct part in hostilities cannot be attacked at such time as he is doing so, if a less harmful means can be employed. In our domestic law, that rule is called for by the principle of proportionality. Indeed, among the military means, one must choose the means whose harm to the human rights of the harmed person is smallest. Thus, if a terrorist taking a direct part in hostilities can be arrested, interrogated, and tried, those are the means which should be employed. Trial is preferable to use of force. A rule-of-law state employs, to the extent possible, procedures of law and not procedures of force. That question arose in *McCann v. United Kingdom*, 21 E.H.R.R. 97 (1995).... In that state of affairs, [lethal force] should not be used. Third, after an attack on a civilian suspected of taking an active part, at such time, in hostilities, a thorough investigation regarding the precision of the identification of the target and the circumstances of the attack upon him is to be performed (retroactively). That investigation must be independent. In appropriate cases it is appropriate to pay compensation as a result of harm caused to an innocent civilian (see §3 of The Hague Regulations; §91 of The First Protocol). Last, if the harm is not only to a civilian directly participating in the hostilities, rather also to innocent civilians nearby, the harm to them is collateral damage. That damage must withstand the proportionality test. We shall now proceed to the examination of that question.

7. PROPORTIONALITY...

B. Proportionality in an International Armed Conflict

42. The principle of proportionality is a substantial part of international law regarding armed conflict (compare §51(5)(b) and 57 of The First Protocol). That law is of customary character. The principle of proportionality arises when the military operation is directed toward combatants and military objectives, or against civilians at such time as they are taking a direct part in hostilities, yet civilians are also harmed. The rule is that the harm to innocent civilians caused by collateral damage during combat operations must be proportionate. Civilians might be harmed due to their presence inside of a military target, such as civilians working in an army base; civilians might be harmed when they live or work in, or pass by, military targets; at times, due to a mistake, civilians are harmed even if they are far from military targets; at times civilians are forced to serve as "human shields" from attack upon a military target, and they are harmed as a result. In all those situations, and in other similar ones, the rule is that the harm to the innocent civilians must fulfill, inter alia, the requirements of the principle of proportionality....

44. The requirement of proportionality in the laws of armed conflict focuses primarily upon what our constitutional law calls proportionality "stricto senso," that is, the requirement that there be a proper proportionate relationship between the military objective and the civilian damage. However, the laws of armed conflict include additional components....

C. Proper Proportion between Benefit and Damage

45. The proportionality test determines that attack upon innocent civilians is not permitted if the collateral damage caused to them is not proportionate to the military advantage (in protecting combatants and civilians). In other words, attack is proportionate if the benefit stemming from the attainment of the proper military objective is proportionate to the damage caused to innocent civilians harmed by it. That is a values based test. It is based upon a balancing between conflicting values and interests. It is accepted in the national law of various countries. It constitutes a central normative test for examining the activity of the government in general, and of the military specifically, in Israel. In one case I stated:

> "Basically, this subtest carries on its shoulders the constitutional view that the ends do not justify the means. It is a manifestation of the idea that there is a barrier of values which democracy cannot surpass, even if the purpose whose attainment is being attempted is worthy."...

46. That aspect of proportionality is not required regarding harm to a combatant, or to a civilian taking a direct part in the hostilities at such time as the harm is caused. Indeed, a civilian taking part in hostilities is endangering his life, and he might — like a combatant — be the objective of a fatal attack. That killing is permitted. However, that proportionality is required in any case in which an innocent civilian is harmed. Thus, the requirements of proportionality stricto senso must be fulfilled in a case in which the harm to the terrorist carries with it collateral damage caused to nearby innocent civilians. The proportionality rule applies in regards to harm to those innocent civilians (see §51(5)(b) of The First Protocol). The rule is that combatants and terrorists are not to be harmed if the damage expected to be caused to nearby innocent civilians is not proportionate to the military advantage in harming the combatants and terrorists. Performing that balance is difficult. Here as well, one must proceed case by case, while narrowing the area of disagreement. Take the usual case of a combatant, or of a terrorist sniper shooting at soldiers or civilians from his porch. Shooting at him is proportionate even if as a result, an innocent civilian neighbor or passerby is harmed. That is not the case if the building is bombed from the air and scores of its residents and passersby are harmed. The hard cases are those which are in the space between the extreme examples. There, a meticulous examination of every case is required; it is required that the military advantage be direct and anticipated (see §57(2)(iii) of The First Protocol). Indeed, in international law, as in internal law, the ends do not justify the means....

IMPLEMENTATION OF THE GENERAL PRINCIPLES IN THIS CASE

60. ...The examination of the "targeted killing" — and in our terms, the preventative strike causing the deaths of terrorists, and at times also of innocent civilians — has shown that the question of the legality of the preventative strike according to customary international law is complex. The result of that examination is not that such strikes are always permissible or that they are always forbidden. The approach of customary international law applying to armed conflicts of an international nature is that civilians are protected from attacks by the army. However, that protection does not exist regarding those civilians "for such time as they take a direct part in hostilities" (§51(3) of The First Protocol). Harming such civilians, even if the result is death, is permitted, on the condition that there is no other less harmful means, and on the condition that innocent civilians nearby are not harmed. Harm to the latter must be proportionate. That proportionality is determined according to a values based test, intended to balance between the military advantage and the civilian damage. As we have seen, we cannot determine that a preventative strike is always legal, just as we cannot determine that it is always illegal. All depends upon the question whether the standards of customary international law regarding international armed conflict allow that preventative strike or not.

CONCLUSION

61. The State of Israel is fighting against severe terrorism, which plagues it from the area. The means at Israel's disposal are limited. The State determined that preventative strikes upon terrorists in the area which cause their deaths are a necessary means from the military standpoint. These strikes at times cause harm and even death to innocent civilians. These preventative strikes, with all the military importance they entail, must be made within the framework of the law. The saying "when the cannons roar, the muses are silent" is well known. A similar idea was expressed by Cicero, who said: "during war, the laws are silent" (silent enim legis inter arma). Those sayings are regrettable. They reflect neither the existing law nor the desirable law. It is when the cannons roar that we especially need the laws. Every struggle of the state — against terrorism or any other enemy — is conducted according to rules and law. There is always law which the state must comply with. There are no "black holes." In this case, the law was determined by customary international law regarding conflicts of an international character. Indeed, the State's struggle against terrorism is not conducted "outside" of the law. It is conducted "inside" the law, with tools that the law places at the disposal of democratic states. . . .

Harold Koh, The Obama Administration and International Law

Remarks to the Annual Meeting of the American Society of International Law, Mar. 25, 2010
transcript available at http://www.state.gov/s/l/releases/remarks/139119.htm

B. USE OF FORCE

. . . [I]n all of our operations involving the use of force, including those in the armed conflict with al-Qaeda, the Taliban and associated forces, the Obama Administration is committed by word and deed to conducting ourselves in accordance with all applicable law. With respect to the subject of targeting, which has been much commented upon in the media and international legal circles, there are obviously limits to what I can say publicly. What I can say is that it is the considered view of this Administration — and it has certainly been my experience during my time as Legal Adviser — that U.S. targeting practices, including lethal operations conducted with the use of unmanned aerial vehicles, comply with all applicable law, including the laws of war.

The United States agrees that it must conform its actions to all applicable law. As I have explained, as a matter of international law, the United States is in an armed conflict with al-Qaeda, as well as the Taliban and associated forces, in response to the horrific 9/11 attacks, and may use force consistent with its inherent right to self-defense under international law. As a matter of domestic law, Congress author-ized the use of all necessary and appropriate force through the 2001 Authorization for Use of Military Force (AUMF). These domestic and international legal authorities continue to this day.

As recent events have shown, al-Qaeda has not abandoned its intent to attack the United States, and indeed continues to attack us. Thus, in this ongoing armed con-flict, the United States has the authority under international law, and the responsi-bility to its citizens, to use force, including lethal force, to defend itself, including by targeting persons such as high-level al-Qaeda leaders who are planning attacks. As you know, this is a conflict with an organized terrorist enemy that does not have conven-tional forces, but that plans and executes its attacks against us and our allies while hiding among civilian populations. That behavior simultaneously makes the applica-tion of international law more difficult and more critical for the protection of inno-cent civilians. Of course, whether a particular individual will be targeted in a particular location will depend upon considerations specific to each case, including those related to the imminence of the threat, the sovereignty of the other states involved, and the willingness and ability of those states to suppress the threat the target poses. In particular, this Administration has carefully reviewed the rules gov-erning targeting operations to ensure that these operations are conducted consis-tently with law of war principles, including:

- First, the principle of distinction, which requires that attacks be limited to military objectives and that civilians or civilian objects shall not be the object of the attack; and

- Second, the principle of proportionality, which prohibits attacks that may be expected to cause incidental loss of civilian life, injury to civilians, damage to civilian objects, or a combination thereof, that would be excessive in relation to the concrete and direct military advantage anticipated.

In U.S. operations against al-Qaeda and its associated forces — including lethal operations conducted with the use of unmanned aerial vehicles — great care is taken to adhere to these principles in both planning and execution, to ensure that only legitimate objectives are targeted and that collateral damage is kept to a minimum.

Recently, a number of legal objections have been raised against U.S. targeting practices. While today is obviously not the occasion for a detailed legal opinion responding to each of these objections, let me briefly address four:

First, some have suggested that the very act of targeting a particular leader of an enemy force in an armed conflict must violate the laws of war. But individuals who are part of such an armed group are belligerents and, therefore, lawful targets under international law. During World War II, for example, American aviators tracked and shot down the airplane carrying the architect of the Japanese attack on Pearl Harbor, who was also the leader of enemy forces in the Battle of Midway. This was a lawful operation then, and would be if conducted today. Indeed, targeting particular indi-viduals serves to narrow the focus when force is employed and to avoid broader harm to civilians and civilian objects.

Second, some have challenged the very use of advanced weapons systems, such as unmanned aerial vehicles, for lethal operations. But the rules that govern targeting do not turn on the type of weapon system used, and there is no prohibition under the laws of war on the use of technologically advanced weapons systems in armed conflict — such as pilotless aircraft or so-called smart bombs — so long as they are employed in conformity with applicable laws of war. Indeed, using such advanced technologies can ensure both that the best intelligence is available for planning operations, and that civilian casualties are minimized in carrying out such operations.

Third, some have argued that the use of lethal force against specific individuals fails to provide adequate process and thus constitutes unlawful extrajudicial killing. But a state that is engaged in an armed conflict or in legitimate self-defense is not required to provide targets with legal process before the state may use lethal force. Our procedures and practices for identifying lawful targets are extremely robust, and advanced technologies have helped to make our targeting even more precise. In my experience, the principles of distinction and proportionality that the United States applies are not just recited at meetings. They are implemented rigorously throughout the planning and execution of lethal operations to ensure that such operations are conducted in accordance with all applicable law....

In sum, let me repeat: as in the area of detention operations, this Administration is committed to ensuring that the targeting practices that I have described are lawful.

NOTES AND QUESTIONS

1. *Interpreting IHL.* Based on your understanding of the basic principles of IHL reviewed in Chapter 2, is the Israeli government policy of preventative strikes lawful? Why didn't the Court say whether the policy of preventative strikes is always lawful or always unlawful?

2. *Classifying the Conflict.* Was the Second Intifada an international armed conflict? If the Geneva Conventions do not clearly answer the classification question in Israel, what other sources of law should be consulted? Of what legal and practical importance is the answer to the classification question?

The Special Rapporteur for the Human Rights Committee of the United Nations provided this assessment of what constitutes a non-international armed conflict:

The tests for the existence of a non-international armed conflict are not as categorical as those for international armed conflict. This recognizes the fact that there may be various types of non-international armed conflicts. The applicable test may also depend on whether a State is party to Additional Protocol II to the Geneva Conventions. [Recall from Chapter 2 that the United States is not a party to AP II.] Under treaty and customary international law, the elements which would point to the existence of a non-international armed conflict against a non-state armed group are:

(i)   The non-state armed group must be identifiable as such, based on criteria that are objective and verifiable. This is necessary for IHL to apply meaningfully, and so that States may comply with their obligation to distinguish between lawful targets and civilians. The criteria include:
   • Minimal level of organization
   • Capability of the group to apply the Geneva Conventions (i.e., adequate command structure, and separation of military and political command)
   • Engagement of the group in collective, armed, anti-government action
   • For a conflict involving a State, the State uses its regular military forces against the group

- Admission of the conflict against the group to the agenda of the UN Security Council or the General Assembly
(ii) There must be a minimal threshold of intensity and duration. The threshold of violence is higher than required for the existence of an international armed conflict. To meet the minimum threshold, violence must be:
  - "Beyond the level of intensity of internal disturbances and tensions, such as riots, isolated and sporadic acts of violence and other acts of a similar nature" (AP II).
  - "[P]rotracted armed violence" among non-state armed groups or between a non-state armed group and a State;
  - If an isolated incident, the incident itself should be of a high degree of intensity, with a high level of organization on the part of the non-state armed group;
(iii) The territorial confines can be:
  - Restricted to the territory of a State and between the State's own armed forces and the non-state group (AP II); or
  - A transnational conflict, i.e., one that crosses State borders (GC Art. 3). This does not mean, however, that there is no territorial nexus requirement.

Addendum: Study on Targeted Killings, supra p. 90.

Applying the Special Rapporteur's analysis, is the United States engaged in an armed conflict with Al Qaeda, the Taliban, and associated forces outside Iraq and Afghanistan? How important are the duration and intensity of the attacks, the closeness of ties among the attackers? Does this analysis account for changing conditions, say, in Pakistan or Yemen? If the United States is not engaged in an armed conflict in those places, is the only lawful means for countering those groups the use of law enforcement methods? What legal theories might then support the U.S. targeting operations? *See* Michael N. Schmitt, *21st Century Conflict: Can the Law Survive?*, 8 Melbourne J. Int'l L. 443, 458-468 (2007) (asymmetric warfare with non-state actors stresses IHL *in bello* rules); Eyal Benvinisti, *The Legal Battle to Define the Law on Transnational Asymmetric Warfare*, 20 Duke J. Comp. & Int'l L. 339 (2010) (same).

In what respects does State Department Legal Adviser Harold Koh disagree with the Special Rapporteur concerning the nature of the conflict the United States is fighting? Do his "considerations specific to each case," along with commitments to follow IHL principles of distinction and proportionality, satisfactorily respond to the Special Rapporteur's concerns? Are his historical examples on point? If not, what more is needed?

3. *Self-Defense?* The international law right of self-defense that Koh relies on to support U.S. actions is described in Chapter 3. Is the self-defense argument persuasive in relation to the terrorist and insurgent groups? How does the international law of self-defense fit, if at all, alongside IHL? (Domestic law authorities are considered in the next part of this chapter.)

4. *Status of Individuals Involved in the Conflict.* On what basis did the Israeli Supreme Court determine the status of the terrorist organizations and their members? Does Article 4 of the Third Geneva Convention answer the question? Is the netherworld between combatants and civilians unregulated by IHL? Are you persuaded that IHL should not regulate the third category of unlawful combatants? If so, is it because the IHL principle that permits targeting civilians taking direct part in hostilities provides the necessary authority? Taking into account the Court's

opinion in *Committee Against Torture* and the materials in Chapter 2, can you offer guidance to Israeli Defense Force (IDF) officials on when civilians may be targeted?

Is HRL clearer? Should it apply in this context? Did the Israeli Court apply HRL? Do you think the *McCann* precedent and the principle of proportionality require the IDF to try to arrest and detain rather than target the suspect individuals? Or does proportionality justify targeting individuals so long as the harm to innocent civilians is proportionate to the military gains? What is meant by what the Court called the "central normative test" for proportionality?

The U.N. Special Rapporteur offered the following perspective on targeting civilians who directly participate in hostilities:

> There are three key controversies over DPH [direct participation in hostilities]. First, there is dispute over the kind of conduct that constitutes "direct participation" and makes an individual subject to attack. Second, there is disagreement over the extent to which "membership" in an organized armed group may be used as a factor in determining whether a person is directly participating in hostilities. Third, there is controversy over how long direct participation lasts.
>
> It is not easy to arrive at a definition of direct participation that protects civilians and at the same time does not "reward" an enemy that may fail to distinguish between civilians and lawful military targets, that may deliberately hide among civilian populations and put them at risk, or that may force civilians to engage in hostilities. The key, however, is to recognize that regardless of the enemy's tactics, in order to protect the vast majority of civilians, direct participation may only include conduct close to that of a fighter, or conduct that directly supports combat. More attenuated acts, such as providing financial support, advocacy, or other non-combat aid, does not constitute direct participation.
>
> Some types of conduct have long been understood to constitute direct participation, such as civilians who shoot at State forces or commit acts of violence in the context of hostilities that would cause death or injury to civilians. Other conduct has traditionally been excluded from direct participation, even if it supports the general war effort; such conduct includes political advocacy, supplying food or shelter, or economic support and propaganda (all also protected under other human rights standards). Even if these activities ultimately impact hostilities, they are not considered "direct participation." But there is a middle ground, such as for the proverbial "farmer by day, fighter by night," that has remained unclear and subject to uncertainty.
>
> In 2009, the ICRC issued its Interpretive Guidance on DPH, which provides a useful starting point for discussion. In non-international armed conflict, according to the ICRC Guidance, civilians who participate directly in hostilities and are members of an armed group who have a "continuous combat function" may be targeted at all times and in all places. With respect to the temporal duration of DPH for all other civilians, the ICRC Guidance takes the view that direct participation for civilians is limited to each single act: the earliest point of direct participation would be the concrete preparatory measures for that specific act (e.g., loading bombs onto a plane), and participation terminates when the activity ends.
>
> Under the ICRC's Guidance, each specific act by the civilian must meet three cumulative requirements to constitute DPH:
>
> (i) There must be a "threshold of harm" that is objectively likely to result from the act, either by adversely impacting the military operations or capacity of the opposing

party, or by causing the loss of life or property of protected civilian persons or objects; and

(ii)   The act must cause the expected harm directly, in one step, for example, as an integral part of a specific and coordinated combat operation (as opposed to harm caused in unspecified future operations); and

(iii)   The act must have a "belligerent nexus" — i.e., it must be specifically designed to support the military operations of one party to the detriment of another.

Addendum: Study on Targeted Killings, supra. How do the criteria suggested by the Special Rapporteur and the ICRC differ from those employed by the Israeli Supreme Court? From the approach of the United States explained by Legal Adviser Koh? If the direct participation test is not met, what legal authorities govern targeting? Does the "continuous combat function" designator provide needed flexibility or unbridled discretion for the targeting personnel?

If U.S. military personnel determine that a U.S. citizen is taking a direct part in hostilities in Afghanistan or Yemen against the United States, do you see any IHL principles that would stand in the way of carrying out the operation?

5.   *Who May Conduct a Targeted Killing?* Assuming the existence of an armed conflict, may targeted killings lawfully be committed by agents of a state who are not members of its armed forces? Consider the views of the Special Rapporteur:

Under IHL, civilians, including intelligence agents, are not prohibited from participating in hostilities. Rather, the consequence of participation is two-fold. First, because they are "directly participating in hostilities" by conducting targeted killings, intelligence personnel may themselves be targeted and killed. Second, intelligence personnel do not have immunity from prosecution under domestic law for their conduct. They are thus unlike State armed forces which would generally be immune from prosecution for the same conduct (assuming they complied with IHL requirements). Thus, CIA personnel could be prosecuted for murder under the domestic law of any country in which they conduct targeted drone killings, and could also be prosecuted for violations of applicable US law.

It is important to note that if a targeted killing violates IHL (by, for example, targeting civilians who were not "directly participating in hostilities"), then regardless of who conducts it — intelligence personnel or State armed forces — the author, as well as those who authorized it, can be prosecuted for war crimes.

Additionally, unlike a State's armed forces, its intelligence agents do not generally operate within a framework which places appropriate emphasis upon ensuring compliance with IHL, rendering violations more likely and causing a higher risk of prosecution both for war crimes and for violations of the laws of the State in which any killing occurs. To the extent a State uses intelligence agents for targeted killing to shield its operations from IHL and human rights law transparency and accountability requirements, it could also incur State responsibility for violating those requirements....

Addendum: Study on Targeted Killings, supra. Does it make sense legally to authorize the CIA to engage in targeted killings but not to immunize them from prosecution? In the ongoing counterterrorism campaign against Al Qaeda, the Taliban, and associated groups, who would prosecute CIA or contract personnel for war crimes? Do you think that the CIA could earn immunity from prosecution by demonstrating that its agents are trained in IHL? That they or contract personnel are subject to accountability mechanisms that approximate a chain of command?

6. *Targeting bin Laden Redux.* Was the killing of Osama bin Laden by U.S. Navy Seals in Abbottabad, Pakistan, on May 1, 2011, lawful under IHL and other parts of international law? Review the *in bello* rules applied by the Israeli Supreme Court. *See also* Melzer, *supra* p. 100, at 426-427 (during armed conflict, a targeted killing must be "likely to contribute effectively to the achievement of a concrete and direct military advantage without there being an equivalent non-lethal alternative," and abide by principles of distinction and proportionality and any other precautionary measures required by IHL). If there was no armed conflict in Abbottabad, is there *any* legal justification at international law for using lethal force against bin Laden? If so, what is it? *Compare* Koh, *supra* p. 111, *with* Thomas Darnstadt, *Was Bin Laden's Killing Legal?*, Spiegel Online, May 3, 2011, *at* http://www.spiegel.de/international/world/0,1518,druck-760358,00.html (suggesting that it is not clear that, at the time of his death, bin Laden commanded an organization that was conducting an armed conflict in or from Pakistan).

7. *Targeting Qaddafi.* If U.S. or NATO forces executed a similar operation to kill Colonel Muammar el-Qaddafi in Libya as part of operations to implement U.N. Security Council Resolution 1973, *supra* p. 48, how would the legal analysis of the targeting differ from the legal framework that applied to killing bin Laden?

D.   U.S. LAW AND EXECUTIVE ORDER NO. 12,333

In 1976, a congressional committee found evidence of CIA involvement in assassination plots against foreign leaders (including President Ngo Dinh Diem of South Vietnam, who was murdered in a coup, and General René Schneider of Chile, who died in a kidnapping attempt), but it was unable to determine whether such involvement had been approved by senior officials. *See* Select Comm. to Study Governmental Operations with Respect to Intelligence Activities (Church Comm.), *Alleged Assassination Plots Involving Foreign Leaders*, S. Rep. No. 94-465 (1975) (*Church Comm. Report*). The CIA acknowledged, however, that it subsequently made payments to the Schneider kidnappers. *See* Central Intelligence Agency, *CIA Activities in Chile*, Sept. 18, 2000, *at* https://www.cia.gov/cia/reports/chile/index.html#15. When the Church Committee proposed legislation to forbid political assassination, the Ford administration preemptively promulgated its own prohibition by executive order. The prohibition was carried forward, with slight modifications, in Executive Order No. 12,333, 46 Fed. Reg. 59,941 (Dec. 4, 1981), which remains in effect at this writing:

> 2.11 Prohibition on Assassination. No person employed by or acting on behalf of the United States Government shall engage in, or conspire to engage in, assassination.
> 2.12 Indirect Participation. No agency of the Intelligence Community shall participate in or request any person to undertake activities forbidden by this Order....

Partly owing to this prohibition, military actions against terrorists or their supporters have usually been planned so as to avoid any appearance of targeting specific persons.

W. Hays Parks, Memorandum of Law:
Executive Order 12333 and Assassination

Dep't of the Army Pamphlet 27-50-204, *reprinted in* Army Law. 4 (Dec. 1989)

1. *Summary.* Executive Order 12333 prohibits assassination as a matter of national policy, but does not expound on its meaning or application. This memorandum explores the term and analyzes application of the ban to military operations at three levels: (a) conventional military operations; (b) counterinsurgency operations; and (c) peacetime counterterrorist operations. It concludes that the clandestine, low visibility, or overt use of military force against legitimate targets in time of war, or against similar targets in time of peace where such individuals or groups pose an immediate threat to United States citizens or the national security of the United States, as determined by competent authority, does not constitute assassination or conspiracy to engage in assassination, and would not be prohibited by the proscription in EO 12333 or by international law....

3. a. *Assassination in General.* ... While assassination generally is regarded as an act of murder for political reasons, its victims are not necessarily limited to persons of public office or prominence. The murder of a private person, if carried out for political purposes, may constitute an act of assassination. For example, the 1978 "poisoned-tip umbrella" killing of Bulgarian defector Georgi Markov by Bulgarian State Security agents on the streets of London falls into the category of an act of murder carried out for political purposes, and constitutes an assassination. In contrast, the murder of Leon Klinghoffer, a private citizen, by the terrorist Abu el Abbas during the 1985 hijacking of the Italian cruise ship *Achille Lauro*, though an act of murder for political purposes, would not constitute an assassination. The distinction lies not merely in the purpose of the act and/or its intended victim, but also under certain circumstances in its covert nature.[1] Finally, the killings of Martin Luther King and Presidents Abraham Lincoln, James A. Garfield, William McKinley and John F. Kennedy generally are regarded as assassination because each involved the murder of a public figure or national leader for political purposes accomplished through a surprise attack.

b. *Assassination in Peacetime.* In peacetime, the citizens of a nation — whether private individuals or public figures — are entitled to immunity from intentional acts of violence by citizens, agents, or military forces of another nation....

Peacetime assassination, then, would seem to encompass the murder of a private individual or public figure for political purposes, and in some cases also require that the act constitute a covert activity, particularly when the individual is a private citizen. Assassination is unlawful killing, and would be prohibited by international law even if there were no executive order proscribing it.

c. *Assassination in Wartime.* ... In wartime the role of the military includes the legalized killing (as opposed to murder) of the enemy, whether lawful combatants

---

1. *Covert operations* are defined as "operations which are planned and executed so as to conceal the identity of or permit plausible denial by the sponsor. They differ from clandestine operations in that emphasis is placed on concealment of identity of [the] sponsor rather than on concealment of the operation." In contrast, low visibility operations are ... undertaken with the knowledge that the action and or sponsorship of the operation may preclude plausible denial by the initiating power. JCS Pub. 1, *Dictionary of Military and Associated Terms* (1 June 1987).

or unprivileged belligerents, and may include in either category civilians who take part in the hostilities.

The term *assassination* when applied to wartime military activities against enemy combatants or military objectives does not preclude acts of violence involving the element of surprise. Combatants are liable to attack at any time or place, regardless of their activity when attacked. . . . An individual combatant's vulnerability to lawful targeting (as opposed to assassination) is not dependent upon his or her military duties, or proximity to combat as such. Nor does the prohibition on assassination limit means that otherwise would be lawful; no distinction is made between an attack accomplished by aircraft, missile, naval gunfire, artillery, mortar, infantry assault, ambush, land mine or boobytrap, a single shot by a sniper, a commando attack, or other, similar means. All are lawful means for attacking the enemy and the choice of one vis-a-vis another has no bearing on the legality of the attack. If the person attacked is a combatant, the use of a particular lawful means for attack (as opposed to another) cannot make an otherwise lawful attack either unlawful or an assassination.

Likewise, the death of noncombatants ancillary to the lawful attack of a military objective is neither assassination nor otherwise unlawful. Civilians and other noncombatants who are within or in close proximity to a military objective assume a certain risk through their presence in or in proximity to such targets. . . .

The scope of assassination in the U.S. military was first outlined in U.S. Army General Orders No. 100 (1863). Paragraph 148 states

> *Assassination.* The law of war does not allow proclaiming either an individual belonging to the hostile army, or a citizen, or a subject of the hostile government, an outlaw, who may be slain without trial by any captor, any more than the modern law of peace allows such international outlawry; on the contrary, it abhors such outrage. . . .

This provision, consistent with the earlier writings of Hugo Grotius (Cf. Bk, III, Sec. XXXVIII(4)), has been continued in U.S. Army Field Manual 27-10, *The Law of Land Warfare* (1956), which provides (paragraph 31):

> Article 23b, Annex to Hague Convention IV, 1907) is construed as prohibiting assassination, proscription, or outlawry of an enemy, or putting a price upon an enemy's head, as well as offering reward for an enemy "dead or alive." . . .

[4]. *Conventional War.* . . . [An] unresolved issue concerns which civilians may be regarded as combatants, and therefore subject to lawful attack. While there is general agreement among the law of war experts that civilians who participate in hostilities may be regarded as combatants, there is no agreement as to the degree of participation necessary to make an individual civilian a combatant. . . . There is a lack of agreement on this matter, and no existing law of war treaty provides clarification or assistance. Historically, however, the decision as to the level at which civilians may be regarded as combatants or "quasi-combatants" and thereby subject to attack generally has been a policy rather than legal matter. . . .

[5]. *Counterinsurgency.* Guerrilla warfare is particularly difficult to address because a guerrilla organization generally is divided into political and guerrilla (military) cadre, each garbed in civilian attire in order to conceal their presence or movement from the enemy. . . .

Just as members of conventional military units have an obligation to wear uniforms in order to distinguish themselves from the civilian population, civilians have an obligation to refrain from actions that might place the civilian population at risk. A civilian who undertakes military activities assumes a risk of attack, and efforts by military forces to capture or kill that individual would not constitute assassination.

The wearing of civilian attire does not make a guerrilla immune from lawful attack, and does not make a lawful attack on a guerrilla an act of assassination. As with the attack of civilians who have combatant responsibilities in conventional war, the difficulty lies in determining where the line should be drawn between guerrillas/combatants and the civilian population in order to provide maximum protection from intentional attack to innocent civilians. The law provides no precise answer to this problem, and one of the most heated debates arising during and after the U.S. war in Vietnam surrounded this issue. As with conventional war, however, ultimately the issue is settled along policy rather than legal lines. If a member of a guerrilla organization falls above the line established by competent authority for combatants, a military operation to capture or kill an individual designated as a combatant would not be assassination.

[6]. *Peacetime operations.* The use of force in peacetime is limited by . . . article 2(4) of the Charter of the United Nations. However, article 51 of the Charter of the United Nations recognizes the inherent right of self defense of nations. Historically the United States has resorted to the use of military force in peacetime where another nation has failed to discharge its international responsibilities in protecting U.S. citizens from acts of violence originating in or launched from its sovereign territory, or has been culpable in aiding and abetting international criminal activities. For example:

— 1804-1805: Marine First Lieutenant Presley O'Bannon led an expedition into Libya to capture or kill[6] the Barbary pirates.

— 1916: General "Blackjack" Pershing led a year-long campaign into Mexico to capture or kill the Mexican bandit Pancho Villa following Villa's attack on Columbus, New Mexico.

— 1928-1932: U.S. Marines conducted a successful campaign to capture or kill the Nicaraguan bandit leader Augusto Cesar Sandino.

— 1967: U.S. Army personnel assisted the Bolovian Army in its campaign to capture or kill Ernesto "Che" Guevara.

— 1985: U.S. naval forces were used to force an Egypt Air airliner to land at Sigonella, Sicily, in an attempt to prevent the escape of the *Achille Lauro* hijackers.

— 1986: U.S. naval and air forces attacked terrorist-related targets in Libya in response to the Libyan government's continued employment of terrorism as a foreign policy means.

---

6. In the employment of military force, the phrase "capture or kill" carries the same meaning or connotation in peacetime as it does in wartime. There is no obligation to capture rather than attack an enemy. In some cases, it may be preferable to utilize ground forces to capture (*e.g.*) a known terrorist. However, where the risk to U.S. forces is deemed too great, if the President has determined that the individual(s) pose such a threat to U.S. citizens as to require the use of military force, it would be legally permissible to employ (*e.g.*) an air strike against that individual or group rather than attempt his, her, or their capture, and would not constitute assassination.

Hence there is historical precedent for the use of military force to capture or kill individuals whose peacetime actions constitute a direct threat to U.S. citizens or national security.

The Charter of the United Nations recognizes the inherent right of self defense and does not preclude unilateral action against an immediate threat.

In general terms, the United States recognizes three forms of self defense:

a.   Against an actual use of force, or hostile act.

b.   Preemptive self defense against an imminent use of force.

c.   Self defense against a continuing threat.[8]

A national decision to employ military force in self defense against a legitimate terrorist or related threat would not be unlike the employment of force in response to a threat by conventional forces; only the nature of the threat has changed, rather than the international legal right of self defense. The terrorist organizations envisaged as appropriate to necessitate or warrant an armed response by U.S. military forces are well-financed, highly-organized paramilitary structures engaged in the illegal use of force.[9] . . .

NOTES AND QUESTIONS

1. *The Origins of the Executive Order Ban on Assassination.* As noted above, in 1976 the Church Committee proposed to criminalize the assassination or attempted assassination of "any foreign official because of such official's political views, actions, or statements, while such official is outside the United States." *Church Committee Report, supra* p. 117, at App. A. "Foreign official" was defined as "Chief of State or the political equivalent . . . of a foreign government . . . or of a foreign political group, party, military force, movement or other association with which the United States is not at war pursuant to a declaration of war or against which the United States Armed Forces have not been introduced into hostilities or situations pursuant to the provisions of the War Powers Resolution." *Id.*

However, President Ford headed off such legislation by adopting Executive Order No. 11,905, 41 Fed. Reg. 7703 (Feb. 19, 1976), prohibiting U.S. employees from engaging in "political assassination." In 1978, President Carter replaced this order with Executive Order No. 12,036, 43 Fed. Reg. 3674 (Jan. 26, 1978), which expanded the prohibition to include agents of the United States, and which dropped, without explanation, the modifier "political." President Reagan retained Carter's language as sections 2.11 and 2.12 in the still-current Executive Order No. 12,333, set out above. *See generally* William C. Banks & Peter Raven-Hansen, *Targeted Killing and*

---

8. . . . This right of self defense would be appropriate to the attack of terrorist leaders where their actions pose a continuing threat to U.S. citizens or the national security of the United States. As with an attack on a guerrilla infrastructure, the level to which attacks could be carried out against individuals within a terrorist infrastructure would be a policy rather than a legal decision.

9. In a conventional armed conflict, such individuals would be regarded as unprivileged belligerents, subject to attack, but not entitled to prisoner of war protection or exemption from prosecution for their crimes. Employment of military force against terrorists does not bestow prisoner of war protection upon members of the terrorist organization.

Assassination: The U.S. Legal Framework, 37 U. Rich. L. Rev. 667, 717-726 (2003); Jonathan M. Fredman, *Covert Action, Loss of Life, and the Prohibition on Assassination*, 1 Stud. Intelligence 15 (1997 unclassified ed.).

The Legal Adviser to the Department of State has argued that "the use of lawful weapons systems — consistent with the applicable laws of war — for precision targeting of specific high-level belligerent leaders when acting in self-defense or during an armed conflict is not unlawful, and hence does not constitute 'assassination'" under the executive order. Koh, *supra* p. 111. Is that argument consistent with the history of the order?

 2. *Who May Be Targeted?*

 a. *Saddam Hussein?* Would the executive order have barred the killing of Saddam Hussein, leader of Iraq, in 1991 during the first Gulf War, or in 2003, during the invasion of Iraq? *See* Stuart Taylor Jr., *Should We Just Kill Saddam?*, Legal Times, Feb. 4, 1991.

 b. *Manuel Noriega?* Would the prohibition have applied to General Manuel Antonio Noriega, leader of Panama? In 1989 the CIA was approached for help by Panamanian military officers who proposed a coup against Noriega after he nullified a national election that he had lost. The officers sought nonlethal assistance in the form of money and equipment, but they admitted that Noriega might be killed in the coup. Could the U.S. have legally furnished assistance? *See* David B. Ottaway & Don Oberdorfer, *Administration Alters Assassination Ban*, Wash. Post, Nov. 4, 1989; David B. Ottaway, *CIA Aides Call Hill Rules No Hindrance*, Wash. Post, Oct. 18, 1989.

 c. *Pablo Escobar?* How about targeting Colombian drug trafficker Pablo Escobar, who reportedly conducted a campaign of narco-terror and assassination against the government of Colombia, and who was indicted in the United States for drug trafficking and multiple drug-related murders? *See* Mark Bowden, *Killing Pablo* (2001) (asserting that U.S. Special Forces were actively involved in his death).

 d. *The "Gucci Guys" Who Finance Terror?* After the September 11 terrorist attacks, some argued that the United States should go beyond targeting terrorist leaders. Consider the following recommendation:

> The United States should adopt a[n assassination] program aimed not only at the heads of the [terrorist] networks, but also at the arms and the fingers. It should locate and assassinate the killers, the planners, and the trainers. It should go beyond the organizations to target those who finance them and those who tend to communications and logistics. The program should target officials of the governments that give terrorists shelter. None should feel safe who knowingly aid these organizations — whether they launder their money or their clothes. [Lawrence J. Siskind, *Our Killer Instinct*, Legal Times, Oct. 8, 2001.]

Would such a program be lawful under the executive order? Would it be wise, now that we have learned that the "arms and fingers" of the group that executed the September 11 attacks apparently made significant preparations in Germany and that they had financing from institutions in Switzerland and Saudi Arabia? *See* Barton Gellman, *CIA Weighs "Targeted Killing" Missions*, Wash. Post, Oct. 28, 2001 (reporting that senior managers in CIA's Directorate of Operations urged targeting not just Al Qaeda's commanders, but also its financiers — "the Gucci guys, the guys who write the checks," because they are easier to find and because "it would have a tremendously chilling effect"). *See* Daniel Byman, *Do Targeted Killings Work?* 85 For. Aff. 95 (2006).

3. *Force and Effect of the Executive Order Ban.* How do you think the legal force of the executive order ban was affected by President Reagan's 1984 secret intelligence findings authorizing lethal operations against Libyan leader Muammar el-Qaddafi (*see* Bob Woodward & Walter Pincus, *1984 Order Gave CIA Latitude; Reagan's Secret Move to Counter Terrorists Called "License to Kill,"* Wash. Post, Oct. 5, 1988)? How about orders to kill bin Laden from President Clinton (*see* James Risen, *Bin Laden Was Target of Afghan Raid, U.S. Confirms,* N.Y. Times, Nov. 14, 1998), President George W. Bush, and President Obama? How would you assess President Obama's order for lethal operations against Anwar al-Aulaqi? *See* David Johnston & David E. Sanger, *Fatal Strike in Yemen Was Based on Rules Set Out by Bush,* N.Y. Times, Nov. 6, 2002; Scott Shane, *U.S. Approves Targeted Killing of American Cleric,* N.Y. Times, Apr. 6, 2010. *See* Memorandum from Acting Asst. Attorney General Randolph D. Moss to the President, *Legal Effectiveness of a Presidential Directive as Compared to an Executive Order,* Jan. 29, 2000 (concluding that presidential directives — and, by implication, findings — can have the same substantive legal effect as an executive order, and that any such presidential decision, however it is memorialized, remains effective upon a change in administration and until subsequent presidential action is taken). *See also* Banks & Raven-Hansen, *supra,* 37 U. Rich. L. Rev. at 725-726.

In the wake of the September 11 attacks, Rep. Bob Barr introduced the Terrorist Elimination Act of 2001, which provided that sections 2.11 and 2.12 of Executive Order No. 12,333 "shall have no further force or effect." H.R. 19, 107th Cong. (2001). Is such a law necessary to permit the military to use military strikes to remove a terrorist leader, as the bill's proposed findings indicate? Would it be constitutional? *See* Banks & Raven-Hansen, *supra,* 37 U. Rich. L. Rev. at 745-747.

4. *Targeted Killing at Home?* All the discussions about the executive order contemplate targeted killings or assassinations of foreign persons *abroad.* But is the order so restricted geographically?

A variety of domestic laws, in addition to ordinary criminal laws, seemingly prohibit the use of such tools against any person in the United States. *See, e.g.,* U.S. Const. amend. V (providing that "no person" shall be deprived of life "without due process of law"); Posse Comitatus Act, 18 U.S.C. §1385 (2006), *infra* p. 761 (prohibiting the Army or Air Force from executing the laws without express constitutional or statutory authority); National Security Act of 1947, 50 U.S.C. §403-4a(d)(1) (2006) (prohibiting the CIA from performing "internal security functions"); *Idaho v. Horiuchi,* 253 F.3d 359, 377 (9th Cir.) (asserting, in a suit growing out of the Ruby Ridge killing by an FBI sharpshooter, that "wartime rules" of engagement permitting the targeting of suspects who pose no "immediate threat... [are] patently unconstitutional for a police action"), *vacated as moot,* 266 F.3d 986 (9th Cir. 2001).

Even assuming that the President could disregard these authorities, would a targeted killing of Ayman al-Zawahiri, the presumptive head of Al Qaeda after bin Laden's death, as he stepped off a civilian airline flight at O'Hare Airport in Chicago meet *any* of the other standards discussed in these notes?

5. *Costs and Benefits of Targeted Killing.* In 2009, CIA Director Leon Panetta claimed that drone strikes have been very effective because they have been very

precise in their targeting and involved a minimum amount of collateral damage. Charles Cooper, *No Longer a Debate About Targeted Killing*, CBSnews.com, July 21, 2010, http://www.cbsnews.com/stories/2009/07/21/opinion/main5176876.shtml. Targeted killing of the leaders of a terrorist group can change the group's organizational behavior. Elimination of its leaders may cause confusion and disarray; successors may become paranoid and secretive, impeding their ability to communicate with members; and members may become fearful about communicating even with one another. The terrorists may spend more and more of their time protecting themselves, with correspondingly less time to attack others. *See, e.g.,* Byman, *supra* p. 123, at 102-104 (reporting significant drop-off in Israeli civilian deaths from terrorist attacks "partly because Israel's targeted killings have shattered Palestinian terrorist groups and made it difficult for them to conduct effective operations"); Gal Luft, *The Logic of Israel's Targeted Killing*, 10 Middle East Q. 1 (Winter 2003). Lives are saved by attacks averted. In addition, the targeted killing of a suspected terrorist may cause fewer casualties (and lower costs) among counterterrorist forces than seeking to arrest him in hostile territory, let alone invading to destroy his group. Eichensehr, *supra* p. 90 n.1, at 4. Furthermore, extradition and prosecution may not be viable alternatives to the use of force when the terrorists take refuge in failed or sympathetic states. Finally, targeted killing satisfies domestic demands for the government to "do something" after a society has suffered terrorist attacks. *See* Byman, *supra*, at 102. Can you identify other benefits from targeted killing?

On the other hand, targeted killings carry significant costs as well. Terrorist groups adjust to decapitation; their decentralization largely negates the disruptive effect by creating many, or no, leaders. Successful targeted killing requires a heavy investment in real-time continuing intelligence and surveillance, as well as rapid response capability. Byman, *supra*, at 100 (quoting a former Israeli intelligence director as saying, "When a Palestinian child draws a picture of the sky, he doesn't draw it without a helicopter."). Even a successful killing may create a martyr for the terrorists, and perversely help them to recruit others, and it will often prompt retaliation. Finally, as the discussion of international law should suggest and the tense relationship between the United States and Pakistan after U.S. targeted killings inside Pakistani territory proves, targeted killing carries serious diplomatic costs, not just for negotiations to end the terrorism or to coordinate allies in the counterterrorist effort, but also for diplomatic efforts to condemn targeted killing by other states. Can you think of other costs of targeted killing? Should we include a moral cost in the calculus?

How would you balance costs and benefits of targeted killings by the United States in Afghanistan? In Northern Pakistan? In Yemen?

III
Detecting Terrorist Threats

5

Organizing for Intelligence Collection

In this chapter we lay the foundation for a systematic consideration of the rules governing intelligence collection. How does the United States organize its intelligence collection missions? Which agencies are in charge of collection? What are the permissible collection techniques? How is surveillance, a critical subset of intelligence collection, managed and overseen? What legal arrangements facilitate the sharing of intelligence information, and which ones help ensure that the collection and dissemination of that information do not threaten personal freedoms?

The chart on the next page, depicting the organization of the intelligence community, serves as an important reminder that we have no single "Department of National Security." Instead, intelligence collection is overseen by the Office of the Director of National Intelligence and collected by several component agencies within the Department of Defense, the Department of State, the Department of Homeland Security, the Department of Justice (the FBI), the CIA, and other entities in scattered parts of our federal bureaucracy.

In Part A, we first introduce the intelligence cycle. In Part B, we survey briefly the range of intelligence collection disciplines and their evolution from 1947 to the present. In Part C, we examine the legal bases for intelligence collection and particular collection techniques, although we explore those techniques further in subsequent chapters. Finally, in Part D, we consider problems of information sharing and reform of the governance of intelligence collection.

A. THE INTELLIGENCE CYCLE

Select Committee to Study Governmental Operations with Respect to Intelligence Activities (Church Committee), Foreign and Military Intelligence
S. Rep. No. 94-755, bk. I, at 17-19 (1976)

In theory at least [intelligence] operations can be described in simple terms by the following cycle:

— Those who use intelligence, the "consumers," indicate the kind of information needed.

127

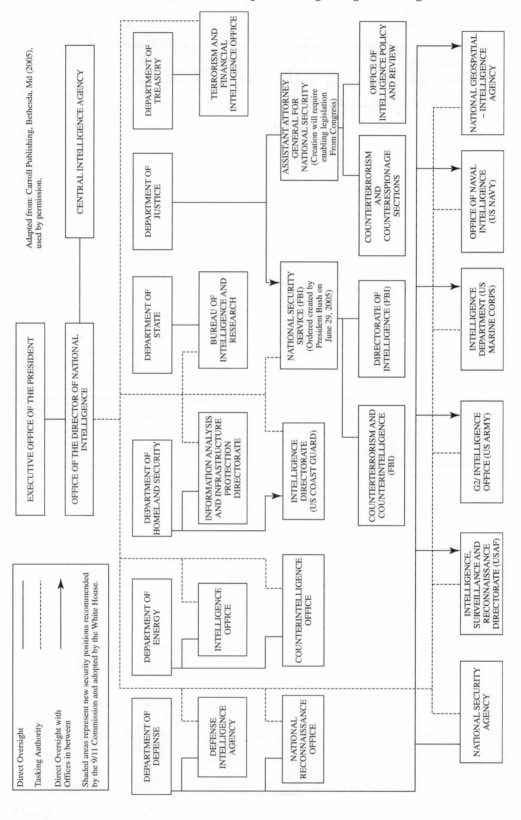

— These needs are translated into concrete "requirements" by senior intelligence managers.

— The requirements are used to allocate resources to the "collectors" and serve to guide their efforts.

— The collectors obtain the required information or "raw intelligence."

— The "raw intelligence" is collated and turned into "finished intelligence" by the "analysts."

— The finished intelligence is distributed to the consumer and the intelligence managers who state new needs, define new requirements, and make necessary adjustments in the intelligence programs to improve effectiveness and efficiency.

In reality this pattern is barely recognizable.

There are many different consumers, from the President to the weapons designer. Their needs can conflict. Consumers rarely take the time to define their intelligence needs and even if they do so there is no effective and systematic mechanism for translating them into intelligence requirements.

Therefore, intelligence requirements reflect what intelligence managers think the consumers need, and equally important, what they think their organizations can produce. Since there are many managers and little central control, each is relatively free to set his own requirements.

Resources therefore tend to be allocated according to the priorities and concerns of the various intelligence bureaucracies. Most intelligence collection operations are part of other organizations — the Department of Defense, the Department of State — and so their requirements and their consumers are often the first to be served.

Collecting intelligence is not an automatic process. There are many different kinds of intelligence, from a radar return to an indiscreet remark, and the problems in acquiring it vary greatly. Information that is wanted may not be available, or years may be required to develop an agency or a technical device to get it. Meanwhile intelligence agencies collect what they can.

In the world of bureaucracy, budgets, programs, procurement, and managers, the needs of the analyst can be lost in the shuffle. There has been an explosion in the volume and quality of raw intelligence but no equivalent increase in the capacity of analytical capabilities. As a result, "raw" intelligence increasingly dominates "finished" intelligence; analysts find themselves on a treadmill where it is difficult to do more than summarize and put in context the intelligence flowing in. There is little time or reward for the task of providing insight.

In the end the consumer, particularly at the highest levels of the government, finds that his most important questions are not only unanswered, but sometimes not even addressed.

To some extent, all this is in the nature of things. Many questions cannot be answered. The world of intelligence is dominated by uncertainty and chance, and those in the intelligence bureaucracy, as elsewhere in the Government, try to defend themselves against uncertainties in ways which militate against efficient management and accountability.

Beyond this is the fact that the organizations of the intelligence community must operate in peace but be prepared for war. This has an enormous impact on the kind of intelligence that is sought, the way resources are allocated, and the way the intelligence community is organized and managed.

The Idealized Intelligence Cycle

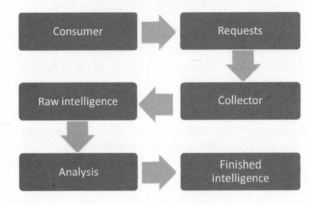

NOTES AND QUESTIONS

1. *Setting Requirements.* Intelligence serves policymakers and helps to shape policy. That policy in turn determines the need for additional intelligence and guides intelligence operations. There is, however, no formal mechanism for translating policy into intelligence requirements. Who should set intelligence objectives? How should those objectives be communicated to intelligence officials, following what kind of process?

2. *Collection.* Technical means offer tremendous advantages in collecting large volumes of information. Technical collection is, however, very expensive. Human intelligence is cheaper and may be more narrowly focused. How should these collection trade-offs be made, and by whom? If the mass of data collected through technical means cannot realistically be processed and analyzed, how should collection priorities be modified?

3. *Analysis, Delivery, and Consumption.* Some intelligence products are widely known — the President's Daily Briefings (PDBs), for example, and National Intelligence Estimates (NIEs). Analysis of intelligence and other, less well-known products are discussed in this and the next two chapters. How do you suppose it is decided which material collected is important enough to report, in whatever form? Who should receive intelligence reports — in the executive branch and in Congress? How rapidly should the information be provided, in how much detail, and in what form?

4. *Changing Requirements.* The Cold War and a preoccupation with the Soviet Union dominated the intelligence agenda until the fall of the Berlin Wall in 1989. From 1989 until the September 11 terrorist attacks in 2001, there was no comparably focused intelligence mission. September 11 provided a mission. The dominant role and most important legal questions concerning intelligence collection now revolve around countering the ongoing threat of terrorism.

B.   HOW IS INTELLIGENCE COLLECTED? — THE "INTs"

Intelligence collection is engaged in by people — human intelligence or espionage (HUMINT) — and by machines — geospatial intelligence (GEOINT), signals intelligence (SIGINT), and measurement and signatures intelligence (MASINT). Except for open-source intelligence (OSINT), each of the INTs has a self-contained process, from collection to delivery. This tendency toward "stovepipes" is exacerbated by an intentional redundancy among the separate INTs. By deploying different collection systems in pursuit of the same intelligence we hope to learn from the shared perspectives they offer — "all-source intelligence." We also compensate in one INT for a shortcoming in another.

Mark M. Lowenthal, Intelligence: From Secrets to Policy
pp. 82-105 (4th ed. 2009)

GEOINT

. . . is a direct descendant of the brief practice of sending soldiers up in balloons during the U.S. Civil War. In World War I and World War II, both sides used airplanes to obtain photos. Airplanes are still employed, but several nations now utilize imagery satellites. In the United States, the National Reconnaissance Office (NRO) develops these satellites. The National Geospatial-Intelligence Agency (which was the National Imagery and Mapping Agency, NIMA, until 2003) is responsible for processing and exploiting imagery. Some imagery also comes via the Defense Department's airborne systems, such as unmanned aerial vehicles (UAVs), or drones. . . .

Imagery offers a number of advantages over other collection means. First, it is sometimes graphic and compelling. When shown to policymakers, an easily interpreted image can be worth a thousand words. Second, imagery is easily understood much of the time by policymakers. Even though few of them, if any, are trained imagery analysts, all are accustomed to seeing and interpreting images. . . .

Imagery also suffers from a number of problems. The very graphic quality that is an advantage is also a disadvantage. An image can be too compelling, leading to hasty or ill-formed decisions or to the exclusion of other, more subtle intelligence that is contradictory. Also, the intelligence on an image may not be self-evident; it may require interpretation by trained photo interpreters who can see things that the untrained person cannot. At times, the policymakers must take on faith that the skilled analysts are correct.

Another disadvantage of imagery is that it is a snapshot, a picture of a particular place at a particular time. . . . Imagery is a static piece of intelligence, revealing something about where and when it was taken but nothing about what happened before or after. . . .

SIGNALS INTELLIGENCE

SIGINT is a twentieth-century phenomenon. British intelligence pioneered the field during World War I, successfully intercepting German communications by tapping underwater cables. The most famous product of this work was the Zimmermann Telegram, a German offer to Mexico of an anti-U.S. alliance that Britain made available to the United States without revealing how it was obtained. With the advent of radio communications, cable taps were augmented by the ability to pluck signals from the air. The United States also developed a successful signals intercept capability that survived World War I. Prior to World War II the United States broke Japan's Purple code; Britain, via ULTRA, read German codes.

Today signals intelligence can be gathered by Earth-based collectors — ships, planes, ground sites or satellites. Again, U.S. SIGINT satellites are built by the NRO. The National Security Agency is responsible for both carrying out U.S. signals intelligence activities and protecting the United States against hostile SIGINT....

SIGINT consists of several different types of intercepts. The term is often used to refer to the interception of communications between two parties, which is also known as communications intelligence (COMINT). SIGINT can also refer to the pickup of data relayed by weapons during tests which is sometimes called telemetry intelligence (TELINT). Finally, SIGINT can refer to the pickup of electronic emissions from modern weapons and tracking systems (military and civil), which are useful means of gauging their capabilities, such as range and frequencies on which systems operate. This is sometimes referred to as electronic intelligence (ELINT)....

The ability to intercept communications is highly important, since it gives insight into what is being said, planned, and considered. It comes as close as one can, from a distance, to reading the other side's mind, a goal that cannot be achieved by imagery. Reading the actual messages and analyzing what they mean is called *content analysis*. Tracking communications also gives a good *indication and warning*....

COMINT has some weaknesses. First and foremost, it depends on the presence of communications that can be intercepted. If the target goes silent or opts to communicate via secure landlines instead of through the air, then the ability to undertake COMINT ceases to exist. Perhaps the landlines can be tapped, but doing so is a more difficult task than remote interception from a ground site or satellite. The target can also begin to *encrypt* — or code — its communications. Within the offensive/defensive struggle over SIGINT is a second struggle, that between encoders and codebreakers, or *cryptographers*. ... Computers greatly increase the ability to construct complex, one-time use codes. Meanwhile, computers also make it more possible to attack these codes. Finally, the target can use false transmissions as a means of creating less compromising patterns or of subsuming important communications amid a flood of meaningless ones — in effect, increasing the ratio of noise to signals.

Another issue is the vast quantity of communications now available: telephones of all sorts, faxes, e-mails, and so on. ... Even a focused collection plan collects more COMINT than can be processed and exploited. One means of coping with this is the *key-word search*, in which the collected data are fed into computers that look out for specific words or phrases. The words are used as indicators of the likely value of an intercept. ... The war against terrorism has underscored a growing concern for SIGINT. As with the other collection disciplines, SIGINT was developed to collect intelligence on the Soviet Union and other nations. Terrorist cells offer much smaller signatures, which may not be susceptible to interception by remote SIGINT sensors. Therefore, a growing view is that future SIGINT will have to rely on sensors that have been physically placed close to the target by humans. In effect, HUMINT will become the enabler for SIGINT. ...

HUMAN INTELLIGENCE

HUMINT is espionage — spying — and is sometimes referred to as the world's second-oldest profession. It is as old as the Bible. Joshua sent two spies into Canaan before leading the Jewish people across the Jordan River. Spying is what most people think about when they hear the word "intelligence," whether they conjure up famous spies from history such as Nathan Hale or Mata Hari (both failures) or the many fictional spies such as James Bond. In the United States HUMINT is largely the responsibility of the CIA, through its Directorate of Operations (DO). DIA [Defense Intelligence Agency] also has a HUMINT capability with the Defense Humint Service, which it has sought to expand since the war in Afghanistan....

HUMINT largely involves sending agents to foreign countries, where they attempt to recruit foreign nationals to spy.... [Agents must] identif[y] individuals who have access to the information that the United States may desire... gain[] their confidence and assess[] their weaknesses and susceptibility to being recruited... [and] mak[e] a *pitch* to them, suggesting a relationship. A source may accept a pitch for a variety of reasons: money, disaffection with their own government, blackmail, or thrills. Once the pitch has been accepted, the agent must meet with his sources [assets] regularly to receive information, holding meetings in a manner and in places that will reduce the risk of being caught and then transmitting the information back home....

In addition to gaining the skills required for this activity, agents have to maintain their cover stories — the overt lives that give them a plausible reason for being in that foreign nation....

In addition to recruiting foreign nationals, HUMINT agents may undertake more direct spying, such as stealing documents or planting sensors. Some of their information may come through direct observation of activity....

An important adjunct to one's own HUMINT capabilities are those of allied or friendly services. Known as foreign liaison relationships, they offer several important advantages. First, the friendly service has greater familiarity with its own region. Second, its government may maintain a different pattern of relations with other states, more friendly in some cases or even having diplomatic relations where one's own government does not. These HUMINT-to-HUMINT relationships are somewhat formal in nature and tend to be symbiotic. They also entail risks, as one can never be entirely sure of the liaison partner's security procedures.... Furthermore, some liaison relationships may be with intelligence services that do not have the same standards in terms of operational limits, acceptable activities, and other criteria. A choice therefore has to be made between the value of the information being sought or exchanged and the larger question of the propriety of a relationship with this service....

Espionage provides a very small part of the intelligence that is collected. IMINT [imagery intelligence] and SIGINT produce a greater volume of intelligence. But HUMINT, like SIGINT, has the major advantage of affording access to what is being said, planned, and thought. Moreover, clandestine human access to another government also may offer opportunities to influence that government by feeding it false or deceptive information. For intelligence targets where the technical infrastructure may be irrelevant as a fruitful target — such as terrorism, narcotics, or international crime, where the "signature" of activities is rather small — HUMINT may be the only available source.

HUMINT also has disadvantages. First, it cannot be done remotely, as is the case with various types of technical collection. It requires proximity and access and therefore must contend with the counterintelligence capabilities of the other side. It is also far riskier, as it jeopardizes individuals, and, if they are caught, could have political ramifications that are less likely to occur with technical collectors....

Like all the other collection INTs, HUMINT is susceptible to deception....

OPEN-SOURCE INTELLIGENCE

To some, OSINT may seem like a contradiction in terms. How can information that is openly available be considered intelligence? . . . OSINT includes a wide variety of information and sources:

- Media: newspapers, magazines, radio, television, and computer-based information.

- Public data: government reports, official data such as budgets, demographics, hearings, legislative debates, press conference speeches.

- Professional and academic: conferences, symposia, professional associations, academic papers, and experts. . . .

The major advantage of OSINT is its accessibility, although it still requires collection. . . .

The main disadvantage of OSINT is its volume. In many ways, it represents the worst wheat and chaff problem. Some argue that the so-called information revolution has made OSINT more difficult without a corresponding increase in usable intelligence. Computers have increased the ability to manipulate information; however, the amount of derived intelligence has not increased apace. . . .

NOTES AND QUESTIONS

1. *The Players.* An intelligence community organization chart showing the various member agencies as they existed in late 2011 is set forth *supra* p. 128. You may find it helpful in relating the INTs to the agencies that conduct them and in understanding the relationships among the agencies.

2. *Redundancy.* Recall that one aim of intelligence collection is redundancy: send as many INTs as possible to pursue the same issue, resulting in all-source intelligence. Can you see the value in this purposeful overkill? Do you see particular strengths or weaknesses in any of the INTs that would cause you to emphasize or reduce its role in collection?

3. *Wheat vs. Chaff.* Technical collection systems are like vacuum cleaners. They sweep up lots of information, some of which may be useful for intelligence purposes. The National Security Agency (NSA) records 650 million events each day, and produces ten thousand daily reports. Lowenthal, *supra*, at 73. Can you see downside risks in relying on these technical systems? How may the risks be ameliorated?

4. *Diplomats as Spies?* Following the Wikileaks dissemination of State Department diplomatic cables in November 2010, attention was drawn to a few cables from 2008 and 2009 that instruct State Department personnel about how to fulfill the demands of a CIA National HUMINT Collection Directive. One such cable asked embassy staff abroad to gather information about foreign officials, including telephone numbers, e-mail addresses, credit card account numbers, frequent flier account numbers, work schedules, and other biographical and biometric information. Mark Mazzetti, *U.S.*

Expands Role of Diplomats in Spying, N.Y. Times, Nov. 28, 2010. Do you see any legal or practical objections to using diplomats to gather intelligence information? *See* Executive Order No. 12,333 §§1.4, 3.4(f), below.

C. WHO DOES THE COLLECTING?

Following creation of the Office of the Director of National Intelligence (ODNI) in 2004, the Director of National Intelligence (DNI) sits at the top of the 16 agencies considered part of the Intelligence Community. Here we focus on the agencies whose collection activities are at once most central to the intelligence mission and most controversial legally.

Executive Order No. 12,333
United States Intelligence Activities

(as amended by Executive Order Nos. 13,284 (2003),
13,355 (2004), and 13,470 (2008))
73 Fed. Reg. 45,325 (July 30, 2008)

Timely, accurate, and insightful information about the activities, capabilities, plans, and intentions of foreign powers, organizations, and persons and their agents, is essential to the national security of the United States. All reasonable and lawful means must be used to ensure that the United States will receive the best intelligence possible. For that purpose, by virtue of the authority vested in me by the Constitution and the laws of the United States of America, including the National Security Act of 1947 (Act), as amended, and as President of the United States of America, in order to provide for the effective conduct of United States intelligence activities and the protection of constitutional rights, it is hereby ordered as follows:

PART 1. *GOALS, DIRECTIONS, DUTIES, AND RESPONSIBILITIES WITH RESPECT TO UNITED STATES INTELLIGENCE EFFORTS*

1.1 *Goals.* The United States intelligence effort shall provide the President, the National Security Council, and the Homeland Security Council with the necessary information on which to base decisions concerning the development and conduct of foreign, defense, and economic policies, and the protection of United States national interests from foreign security threats. All departments and agencies shall cooperate fully to fulfill this goal.

(a) All means, consistent with applicable Federal law and this order, and with full consideration of the rights of United States persons, shall be used to obtain reliable intelligence information to protect the United States and its interests....

(g) All departments and agencies have a responsibility to prepare and to provide intelligence in a manner that allows the full and free exchange of information, consistent with applicable law and presidential guidance.

1.2 *The National Security Council.*

(a) *Purpose.* The National Security Council (NSC) shall act as the highest ranking executive branch entity that provides support to the President for review of, guidance for, and direction to the conduct of all foreign intelligence, counter-intelligence, and covert action, and attendant policies and programs.

(b) *Covert Action and Other Sensitive Intelligence Operations.* The NSC shall consider and submit to the President a policy recommendation, including all dissents, on each proposed covert action and conduct a periodic review of ongoing covert action activities, including an evaluation of the effectiveness and consistency with current national policy of such activities and consistency with applicable legal requirements. The NSC shall perform such other functions related to covert action as the President may direct, but shall not undertake the conduct of covert actions. The NSC shall also review proposals for other sensitive intelligence operations.

1.3 *Director of National Intelligence.* Subject to the authority, direction, and control of the President, the Director of National Intelligence (Director) shall serve as the head of the Intelligence Community, act as the principal adviser to the President, to the NSC, and to the Homeland Security Council for intelligence matters related to national security, and shall oversee and direct the implementation of the National Intelligence Program and execution of the National Intelligence Program budget. The Director will lead a unified, coordinated, and effective intelligence effort. In addition, the Director shall, in carrying out the duties and responsibilities under this section, take into account the views of the heads of departments containing an element of the Intelligence Community and of the Director of the Central Intelligence Agency.

(a) Except as otherwise directed by the President or prohibited by law, the Director shall have access to all information and intelligence described in section 1.5(a) of this order. For the purpose of access to and sharing of information and intelligence, the Director: . . .

(2) Shall develop guidelines for how information or intelligence is provided to or accessed by the Intelligence Community in accordance with section 1.5(a) of this order, and for how the information or intelligence may be used and shared by the Intelligence Community. All guidelines developed in accordance with this section shall be approved by the Attorney General and, where applicable, shall be consistent with guidelines issued pursuant to section 1016 of the Intelligence Reform and Terrorism Protection Act of 2004 (Public Law 108-458) (IRTPA) [*infra* p. 152].

(b) In addition to fulfilling the obligations and responsibilities prescribed by the Act, the Director:

(1) Shall establish objectives, priorities, and guidance for the Intelligence Community to ensure timely and effective collection, processing, analysis, and dissemination of intelligence, of whatever nature and from whatever source derived; . . .

(3) Shall oversee and provide advice to the President and the NSC with respect to all ongoing and proposed covert action programs;

(4) In regard to the establishment and conduct of intelligence arrangements and agreements with foreign governments and international organizations:

(A) May enter into intelligence and counterintelligence arrangements and agreements with foreign governments and international organizations;

(B) Shall formulate policies concerning intelligence and counterintelligence arrangements and agreements with foreign governments and international organizations; and

(C) Shall align and synchronize intelligence and counterintelligence foreign relationships among the elements of the Intelligence Community to further United States national security, policy, and intelligence objectives; . . .

(6) Shall establish common security and access standards for managing and handling intelligence systems, information, and products, with special emphasis on facilitating:

(A) The fullest and most prompt access to and dissemination of information and intelligence practicable, assigning the highest priority to detecting, preventing, preempting, and disrupting terrorist threats and activities against the United States, its interests, and allies; and

(B) The establishment of standards for an interoperable information sharing enterprise that facilitates the sharing of intelligence information among elements of the Intelligence Community;

(7) Shall ensure that appropriate departments and agencies have access to intelligence and receive the support needed to perform independent analysis;

(8) Shall protect, and ensure that programs are developed to protect, intelligence sources, methods, and activities from unauthorized disclosure;

(9) Shall, after consultation with the heads of affected departments and agencies, establish guidelines for Intelligence Community elements for:

(A) Classification and declassification of all intelligence and intelligence-related information classified under the authority of the Director or the authority of the head of a department or Intelligence Community element; . . .

(14) Shall have ultimate responsibility for production and dissemination of intelligence produced by the Intelligence Community and authority to levy analytic tasks on intelligence production organizations within the Intelligence Community, in consultation with the heads of the Intelligence Community elements concerned; . . .

(16) Shall ensure the timely exploitation and dissemination of data gathered by national intelligence collection means, and ensure that the resulting intelligence is disseminated immediately to appropriate government elements, including military commands;

(17) Shall determine requirements and priorities for, and manage and direct the tasking, collection, analysis, production, and dissemination of, national intelligence by elements of the Intelligence Community, including approving requirements for collection and analysis and resolving conflicts in collection requirements and in the tasking of national collection assets of Intelligence Community elements (except when otherwise directed by the President or when the Secretary of Defense exercises collection tasking authority under plans and arrangements approved by the Secretary of Defense and the Director); . . .

(20) Shall ensure, through appropriate policies and procedures, the deconfliction, coordination, and integration of all intelligence activities conducted by an Intelligence Community element or funded by the National Intelligence Program. In accordance with these policies and procedures:

(A) The Director of the Federal Bureau of Investigation shall coordinate the clandestine collection of foreign intelligence collected through human sources or through human-enabled means and counterintelligence activities inside the United States;

(B) The Director of the Central Intelligence Agency shall coordinate the clandestine collection of foreign intelligence collected through human sources or through human-enabled means and counterintelligence activities outside the United States;

(C) All policies and procedures for the coordination of counterintelligence activities and the clandestine collection of foreign intelligence inside the United States shall be subject to the approval of the Attorney General; and

(D) All policies and procedures developed under this section shall be coordinated with the heads of affected departments and Intelligence Community elements; ...

(c) The Director's exercise of authorities in the Act and this order shall not abrogate the statutory or other responsibilities of the heads of departments of the United States Government or the Director of the Central Intelligence Agency. ...

1.4. *The Intelligence Community.* Consistent with applicable Federal law and with the other provisions of this order, and under the leadership of the Director, as specified in such law and this order, the Intelligence Community shall:

(a) Collect and provide information needed by the President and, in the performance of executive functions, the Vice President, the NSC, the Homeland Security Council, the Chairman of the Joint Chiefs of Staff, senior military commanders, and other executive branch officials and, as appropriate, the Congress of the United States;

(b) In accordance with priorities set by the President, collect information concerning, and conduct activities to protect against, international terrorism, proliferation of weapons of mass destruction, intelligence activities directed against the United States, international criminal drug activities, and other hostile activities directed against the United States by foreign powers, organizations, persons, and their agents;

(c) Analyze, produce, and disseminate intelligence; ...

(f) Protect the security of intelligence related activities, information, installations, property, and employees by appropriate means, including such investigations of applicants, employees, contractors, and other persons with similar associations with the Intelligence Community elements as are necessary; ...

(i) Perform such other functions and duties related to intelligence activities as the President may direct. ...

1.5. *Duties and Responsibilities of the Heads of Executive Departments and Agencies.* The heads of all departments and agencies shall:

(a) Provide the Director access to all information and intelligence relevant to the national security or that otherwise is required for the performance of the Director's duties ... except such information excluded by law, by the President, or by the Attorney General acting under this order at the direction of the President. ...

1.6. *Heads of Elements of the Intelligence Community.* The heads of elements of the Intelligence Community shall:

(a) Provide the Director access to all information and intelligence relevant to the national security or that otherwise is required for the performance of the Director's duties, to include administrative and other appropriate management information, except such information excluded by law, by the President, or by the Attorney General acting under this order at the direction of the President;

(b) Report to the Attorney General possible violations of Federal criminal laws by employees and of specified Federal criminal laws by any other person as provided in procedures agreed upon by the Attorney General and the head of the department, agency, or establishment concerned, in a manner consistent with the protection of intelligence sources and methods, as specified in those procedures;

(c) Report to the Intelligence Oversight Board, consistent with Executive Order 13462 of February 29, 2008, and provide copies of all such reports to the Director, concerning any intelligence activities of their elements that they have reason to believe may be unlawful or contrary to executive order or presidential directive;

(d) Protect intelligence and intelligence sources, methods, and activities from unauthorized disclosure in accordance with guidance from the Director;

(e) Facilitate, as appropriate, the sharing of information or intelligence, as directed by law or the President, to State, local, tribal, and private sector entities;

(f) Disseminate information or intelligence to foreign governments and international organizations under intelligence or counterintelligence arrangements or agreements established in accordance with section 1.3(b)(4) of this order; . . .

(h) Ensure that the inspectors general, general counsels, and agency officials responsible for privacy or civil liberties protection for their respective organizations have access to any information or intelligence necessary to perform their official duties.

1.7. *Intelligence Community Elements.* Each element of the Intelligence Community shall have the duties and responsibilities specified below, in addition to those specified by law or elsewhere in this order. Intelligence Community elements within executive departments shall serve the information and intelligence needs of their respective heads of departments and also shall operate as part of an integrated Intelligence Community, as provided in law or this order.

(a) *The Central Intelligence Agency.* The Director of the Central Intelligence Agency shall:

(1) Collect (including through clandestine means), analyze, produce, and disseminate foreign intelligence and counterintelligence;

(2) Conduct counterintelligence activities without assuming or performing any internal security functions within the United States;

(3) Conduct administrative and technical support activities within and outside the United States as necessary for cover and proprietary arrangements;

(4) Conduct covert action activities approved by the President. No agency except the Central Intelligence Agency (or the Armed Forces of the United States in time of war declared by the Congress or during any period covered by a report from the President to the Congress consistent with the War Powers Resolution, Public Law 93-148) may conduct any covert action activity unless the President determines that another agency is more likely to achieve a particular objective;

(5) Conduct foreign intelligence liaison relationships with intelligence or security services of foreign governments or international organizations consistent with section 1.3(b)(4) of this order;

(6) Under the direction and guidance of the Director, and in accordance with section 1.3(b)(4) of this order, coordinate the implementation of intelligence and counterintelligence relationships between elements of the Intelligence

Community and the intelligence or security services of foreign governments or international organizations; and

(7) Perform such other functions and duties related to intelligence as the Director may direct. . . .

(c) *The National Security Agency.* The Director of the National Security Agency shall:

(1) Collect (including through clandestine means), process, analyze, produce, and disseminate signals intelligence information and data for foreign intelligence and counterintelligence purposes to support national and departmental missions;

(2) Establish and operate an effective unified organization for signals intelligence activities, except for the delegation of operational control over certain operations that are conducted through other elements of the Intelligence Community. No other department or agency may engage in signals intelligence activities except pursuant to a delegation by the Secretary of Defense, after coordination with the Director;

(3) Control signals intelligence collection and processing activities, including assignment of resources to an appropriate agent for such periods and tasks as required for the direct support of military commanders;

(4) Conduct administrative and technical support activities within and outside the United States as necessary for cover arrangements;

(5) Provide signals intelligence support for national and departmental requirements and for the conduct of military operations; . . .

(g) *Intelligence Elements of the Federal Bureau of Investigation.* Under the supervision of the Attorney General and pursuant to such regulations as the Attorney General may establish, the intelligence elements of the Federal Bureau of Investigation shall:

(1) Collect (including through clandestine means), analyze, produce, and disseminate foreign intelligence and counterintelligence to support national and departmental missions, in accordance with procedural guidelines approved by the Attorney General, after consultation with the Director;

(2) Conduct counterintelligence activities; and

(3) Conduct foreign intelligence and counterintelligence liaison relationships with intelligence, security, and law enforcement services of foreign governments or international organizations in accordance with sections 1.3(b)(4) and 1.7(a)(6) of this order. . . .

(j) *The Office of the Director of National Intelligence.* The Director shall collect (overtly or through publicly available sources), analyze, produce, and disseminate information, intelligence, and counterintelligence to support the missions of the Office of the Director of National Intelligence, including the National Counterterrorism Center, and to support other national missions. . . .

1.10. *The Department of Defense.* The Secretary of Defense shall:

(a) Collect (including through clandestine means), analyze, produce, and disseminate information and intelligence and be responsive to collection tasking and advisory tasking by the Director;

(b) Collect (including through clandestine means), analyze, produce, and disseminate defense and defense related intelligence and counterintelligence, as required for execution of the Secretary's responsibilities;

(c) Conduct programs and missions necessary to fulfill national, departmental, and tactical intelligence requirements;

(d) Conduct counterintelligence activities in support of Department of Defense components and coordinate counterintelligence activities in accordance with section 1.3(b)(20) and (21) of this order;

(e) Act, in coordination with the Director, as the executive agent of the United States Government for signals intelligence activities; . . .

PART 2. *CONDUCT OF INTELLIGENCE ACTIVITIES* . . .

2.2. *Purpose.* . . . Set forth below are certain general principles that, in addition to and consistent with applicable laws, are intended to achieve the proper balance between the acquisition of essential information and protection of individual interests. Nothing in this Order shall be construed to apply to or interfere with any authorized civil or criminal law enforcement responsibility of any department or agency.

2.3. *Collection of Information.* Elements of the Intelligence Community are authorized to collect, retain or disseminate information concerning United States persons only in accordance with procedures established by the head of the Intelligence Community element concerned . . . and approved by the Attorney General . . . after consultation with the Director. Those procedures shall permit collection, retention, and dissemination of the following types of information: . . .

(b) Information constituting foreign intelligence or counterintelligence, including such information concerning corporations or other commercial organizations. Collection within the United States of foreign intelligence not otherwise obtainable shall be undertaken by the Federal Bureau of Investigation (FBI) or, when significant foreign intelligence is sought, by other authorized elements of the Intelligence Community, provided that no foreign intelligence collection by such elements may be undertaken for the purpose of acquiring information concerning the domestic activities of United States persons; . . .

(e) Information needed to protect foreign intelligence or counterintelligence sources, methods, and activities from unauthorized disclosure. Collection within the United States shall be undertaken by the FBI except that other elements of the Intelligence Community may also collect such information concerning present or former employees, present or former intelligence element contractors or their present or former employees, or applicants for such employment or contracting; . . .

2.4. *Collection Techniques.* Elements of the Intelligence Community shall use the least intrusive collection techniques feasible within the United States or directed against United States persons abroad. Elements of the Intelligence Community are not authorized to use such techniques as electronic surveillance, unconsented physical searches, mail surveillance, physical surveillance, or monitoring devices unless they are in accordance with procedures established by the head of the Intelligence Community element concerned or the head of a department containing such element and approved by the Attorney General, after consultation with the Director. Such procedures shall protect constitutional and other legal rights and limit use of such information to lawful governmental purposes. These procedures shall not authorize:

(a) The Central Intelligence Agency (CIA) to engage in electronic surveillance within the United States except for the purpose of training, testing, or conducting countermeasures to hostile electronic surveillance;

(b) Unconsented physical searches in the United States by elements of the Intelligence Community other than the FBI, except for:

(1) Searches by counterintelligence elements of the military services directed against military personnel within the United States or abroad for intelligence purposes, when authorized by a military commander empowered to approve physical searches for law enforcement purposes, based upon a finding of probable cause to believe that such persons are acting as agents of foreign powers; and

(2) Searches by CIA of personal property of non-United States persons lawfully in its possession;

(c) Physical surveillance of a United States person in the United States by elements of the Intelligence Community other than the FBI, except for:

(1) Physical surveillance of present or former employees, present or former intelligence element contractors or their present or former employees, or applicants for any such employment or contracting; and

(2) Physical surveillance of a military person employed by a non-intelligence element of a military service; and

(d) Physical surveillance of a United States person abroad to collect foreign intelligence, except to obtain significant information that cannot reasonably be acquired by other means.

2.5. *Attorney General Approval.* The Attorney General hereby is delegated the power to approve the use for intelligence purposes, within the United States or against a United States person abroad, of any technique for which a warrant would be required if undertaken for law enforcement purposes, provided that such techniques shall not be undertaken unless the Attorney General has determined in each case that there is probable cause to believe that the technique is directed against a foreign power or an agent of a foreign power. The authority delegated pursuant to this paragraph, including the authority to approve the use of electronic surveillance as defined in the Foreign Intelligence Surveillance Act of 1978, as amended, shall be exercised in accordance with that Act.

2.6. *Assistance to Law Enforcement and Other Civil Authorities.* Elements of the Intelligence Community are authorized to: . . .

(b) Unless otherwise precluded by law or this Order, participate in law enforcement activities to investigate or prevent clandestine intelligence activities by foreign powers, or international terrorist or narcotics activities; . . .

2.7. *Contracting.* Elements of the Intelligence Community are authorized to enter into contracts or arrangements for the provision of goods or services with private companies or institutions in the United States and need not reveal the sponsorship of such contracts or arrangements for authorized intelligence purposes. Contracts or arrangements with academic institutions may be undertaken only with the consent of appropriate officials of the institution.

2.8. *Consistency With Other Laws.* Nothing in this Order shall be construed to authorize any activity in violation of the Constitution or statutes of the United States.

2.9. *Undisclosed Participation in Organizations Within the United States.* No one acting on behalf of elements of the Intelligence Community may join or otherwise participate in any organization in the United States on behalf of any element within the Intelligence Community without disclosing such person's intelligence affiliation to appropriate officials of the organization, except in accordance with procedures established by the head of the Intelligence Community element concerned or the head of a department containing such element and approved by the Attorney General, after consultation with the Director. Such participation shall be authorized only if it is essential to achieving lawful purposes as determined by the Intelligence Community element head or designee. No such participation may be undertaken for the purpose of influencing the activity of the organization or its members except in cases where:

(a) The participation is undertaken on behalf of the FBI in the course of a lawful investigation; or

(b) The organization concerned is composed primarily of individuals who are not United States persons and is reasonably believed to be acting on behalf of a foreign power....

2.11. *Prohibition on Assassination.* No person employed by or acting on behalf of the United States Government shall engage in, or conspire to engage in, assassination.

2.12. *Indirect Participation.* No element of the Intelligence Community shall participate in or request any person to undertake activities forbidden by this Order.

2.13. *Limitation on Covert Action.* No covert action may be conducted which is intended to influence United States political processes, public opinion, policies, or media.

PART 3. *GENERAL PROVISIONS*

3.1. *Congressional Oversight.* The duties and responsibilities of the Director and the heads of other departments, agencies, elements, and entities engaged in intelligence activities to cooperate with the Congress in the conduct of its responsibilities for oversight of intelligence activities shall be implemented in accordance with applicable law, including title V of the [National Security Act of 1947, as amended]. The requirements of applicable law, including title V of the [National Security Act of 1947, as amended], shall apply to all covert action activities as defined in this Order....

3.5. *Definitions.* For the purposes of this Order, the following terms shall have these meanings:

(a) *Counterintelligence* means information gathered and activities conducted to identify, deceive, exploit, disrupt, or protect against espionage, other intelligence activities, sabotage, or assassinations conducted for or on behalf of foreign powers, organizations, or persons, or their agents, or international terrorist organizations or activities.

(b) *Covert action* means an activity or activities of the United States Government to influence political, economic, or military conditions abroad, where it is intended that the role of the United States Government will not be apparent or acknowledged publicly, but does not include:

(1) Activities the primary purpose of which is to acquire intelligence, traditional counterintelligence activities, traditional activities to improve or maintain the operational security of United States Government programs, or administrative activities;

(2) Traditional diplomatic or military activities or routine support to such activities;

(3) Traditional law enforcement activities conducted by United States Government law enforcement agencies or routine support to such activities; or

(4) Activities to provide routine support to the overt activities (other than activities described in paragraph (1), (2), or (3)) of other United States Government agencies abroad.

(c) *Electronic surveillance* means acquisition of a nonpublic communication by electronic means without the consent of a person who is a party to an electronic communication or, in the case of a nonelectronic communication, without the consent of a person who is visibly present at the place of communication, but not including the use of radio direction-finding equipment solely to determine the location of a transmitter....

(e) *Foreign intelligence* means information relating to the capabilities, intentions, or activities of foreign governments or elements thereof, foreign organizations, foreign persons, or international terrorists.

(f) *Intelligence* includes foreign intelligence and counter-intelligence.

(g) *Intelligence activities* means all activities that elements of the Intelligence Community are authorized to conduct pursuant to this order.

(h) *Intelligence Community* and agencies within the Intelligence Community refers to:

(1) The Office of the Director of National Intelligence;

(2) The Central Intelligence Agency;

(3) The National Security Agency;

(4) The Defense Intelligence Agency;

(5) The National Geospatial-Intelligence Agency;

(6) The National Reconnaissance Office;

(7) The other offices within the Department of Defense for the collection of specialized national foreign intelligence through reconnaissance programs;

(8) The intelligence and counterintelligence elements of the Army, the Navy, the Air Force, and the Marine Corps;

(9) The intelligence elements of the Federal Bureau of Investigation;

(10) The Office of National Security Intelligence of the Drug Enforcement Administration;

(11) The Office of Intelligence and Counterintelligence of the Department of Energy;

(12) The Bureau of Intelligence and Research of the Department of State;

(13) The Office of Intelligence and Analysis of the Department of the Treasury;

(14) The Office of Intelligence and Analysis of the Department of Homeland Security;

(15) The intelligence and counterintelligence elements of the Coast Guard; and

(16) Such other elements of any department or agency as may be designated by the President, or designated jointly by the Director and the head of the department or agency concerned, as an element of the Intelligence Community.

(i) *National Intelligence and Intelligence Related to National Security* means all intelligence, regardless of the source from which derived and including information gathered within or outside the United States, that pertains, as determined consistent with any guidance issued by the President, or that is determined for the purpose of access to information by the Director in accordance with section 1.3(a)(1) of this order, to pertain to more than one United States Government agency; and that involves threats to the United States, its people, property, or interests; the development, proliferation, or use of weapons of mass destruction; or any other matter bearing on United States national or homeland security.

(j) *The National Intelligence Program* means all programs, projects, and activities of the Intelligence Community, as well as any other programs of the Intelligence Community designated jointly by the Director and the head of a United States department or agency or by the President. Such term does not include programs, projects, or activities of the military departments to acquire intelligence solely for the planning and conduct of tactical military operations by United States Armed Forces.

(k) *United States person* means a United States citizen, an alien known by the intelligence element concerned to be a permanent resident alien, an unincorporated association substantially composed of United States citizens or permanent resident aliens, or a corporation incorporated in the United States, except for a corporation directed and controlled by a foreign government or governments....

1. The CIA

National Security Act of 1947
Pub. L. No. 80-253, 61 Stat. 495 (as amended)

50 U.S.C. §403-4a. DIRECTOR OF CENTRAL INTELLIGENCE AGENCY...

(d) Responsibilities. The Director of the Central Intelligence Agency shall—

(1) collect intelligence through human sources and by other appropriate means, except that the Director of the Central Intelligence Agency shall have no police, subpoena, or law enforcement powers or internal security functions;

(2) correlate and evaluate intelligence related to the national security and provide appropriate dissemination of such intelligence;

(3) provide overall direction for and coordination of the collection of national intelligence outside the United States through human sources by elements of the intelligence community authorized to undertake such collection and, in coordination with other departments, agencies, or elements of the United States Government which are authorized to undertake such collection, ensure that the most effective use is made of resources and that appropriate account is taken of the risks to the United States and those involved in such collection; and

(4) perform such other functions and duties related to intelligence affecting the national security as the President or the Director of National Intelligence may direct....

Clearly, the CIA is assigned HUMINT collection tasks outside the United States. No less clearly, at first glance, the National Security Act draws the line at the border and forbids "internal" security functions. Yet the 1947 Act, as amended, calls on the

DNI to take any actions necessary to "protect intelligence sources and methods from unauthorized disclosure." 50 U.S.C. §403-1(i)(1). Such actions are not geographically limited or defined. Protecting sources and methods also means protecting its own facilities, including those in the United States. In addition, the CIA is to "perform such other functions and duties related to intelligence affecting the national security as the President or the National Security Council may direct." According to Mark Reibling, this language originally provided "a pair of operational baggy pants," while CIA Counsel Scott Breckinridge called the "other functions" language a "banana-peel clause." Mark Riebling, *Wedge: The Secret War Between the FBI and CIA* 79 (1994). In fact, Executive Order No. 12,333 §1.7(a)(2)-(3) directs the CIA also to perform "counterintelligence activities without assuming or performing internal security within the United States," as well as "administrative and technical support activities within . . . the United States as necessary for cover and proprietary activities." The following materials show that these openings to activities inside the United States have created some tension with the "internal security" prohibition.

Select Committee to Study Governmental Operations with Respect to Intelligence Activities (Church Committee), Foreign and Military Intelligence
S. Rep. No. 94-755, bk. I, at 136-139 (1976)

The National Security Act of 1947 defines the duties of the CIA in terms of "intelligence" or "intelligence relating to the national security." The legislative history of the Act clearly shows that Congress intended the activities authorized by this language to be related to foreign intelligence. This construction is aided by the statute's provision that "the Agency shall have no police, subpoena, law enforcement power, or internal-security functions," 50 U.S.C. [§403-4a(d)(1), *supra*]. . . .

The legislative history of the Act shows that in establishing the CIA Congress contemplated an agency which not only would be limited to foreign intelligence operations but one which would conduct very few of its operations within the United States. It was contemplated that the Agency would have its headquarters here, and in House Committee hearings in executive session the possibility of seeking foreign intelligence information from private American citizens who traveled abroad was discussed with approval. But in public and in private it was generally agreed among legislators and representatives of the Executive that the CIA would be "confined out of the continental limits of the United States and in foreign fields," that it should have no "police power or anything else within the confines of this country," and that it was "supposed to operate only abroad." . . .

The CIA . . . has interpreted the internal security prohibition narrowly to exclude investigations of domestic activities of American groups for the purpose of determining foreign associations. But history indicates that at the time of enactment of the National Security Act, threats to "internal security" were widely understood to include domestic groups with foreign connections. Investigations by the FBI of American groups with no such connections, in fact, have been a recent phenomenon. The original order from President Roosevelt to J. Edgar Hoover to begin internal security operations was to investigate foreign communist and fascist influence within the United States. There is no evidence that by 1947 these investigations were considered foreign intelligence. . . .

...As authority for some of its operations within the United States, the Agency has relied upon Section 102(d)(3) of the National Security Act, [50 U.S.C. §403-1(i)(1)], which charges the Director of Central Intelligence [now the Director of National Intelligence] with responsibility to protect intelligence sources and methods from unauthorized disclosure.

The CIA has construed the sources and methods language broadly to authorize investigation of domestic groups whose activities, including demonstrations, have potential, however remote, for creating threats to CIA installations, recruiters or contractors. In the course of carrying out these investigations the Agency has collected general information about the leadership, funding activities, and policies of targeted groups. . . .

The sources and methods language was discussed only briefly in the recorded legislative history of the National Security Act. . . . Despite congressional concern, expressed again and again during hearings and floor debates on the bill, that the CIA was to have no potential for infringing upon the rights of American citizens and that it was to be virtually excluded from acting within the United States, no one questioned whether the sources and methods language would raise problems in this area. The lack of interest in the provision suggests that it was not viewed as conveying new authority to investigate; rather it charged the Director of the Central Intelligence Agency with responsibility to use the authority which he already had to protect sensitive intelligence information. . . .

Halkin v. Helms

United States Court of Appeals, District of Columbia Circuit, 1982
690 F.2d 977

MacKinnon, J. Plaintiffs appeal several orders of the district court which resulted in the dismissal of their complaint for legal and equitable relief on claims arising out of certain activities of the Central Intelligence Agency (CIA) in the period from 1967 to 1974. The complaint alleged violations of plaintiffs' first, fourth, fifth and ninth amendment rights, and of section 102(d)(3) of the National Security Act of 1947, 50 U.S.C. [§403-4a(d)(1)]. For the reasons set forth below, the judgment of the district court is affirmed.

Appellants are 21 individuals and 5 organizations who in the late 1960's and early 1970's were involved in various activities seeking to protest and secure an end to the involvement of the United States in the Vietnam War. The individual appellees are seven named persons and an unspecified number of John Does who at the time plaintiffs' claims arose were officials of the CIA or were otherwise agents or employees of the United States government. The seven appellees referred to hereinafter as the "individual appellees"[1] were sued for damages in their individual capacities. The appellees also include the heads of the CIA, FBI, Department of Defense and Secret Service, who were sued in their official capacities and with respect to whom plaintiffs sought injunctive and declaratory relief only.

---

1. The individual appellees are Richard Helms (former Director of Central Intelligence), William E. Colby (same), James R. Schlesinger (same and also former Secretary of Defense), Cord Meyer, Jr. (Assistant Director for Plans of the CIA), James J. Angleton (Chief of CIA Counterintelligence Staff), Richard Ober (CIA Counterintelligence Staff), and Howard Osborn (Director of Security of the CIA).

Plaintiffs filed suit in October 1975, after disclosures by the press and by the President's Commission on CIA Activities Within the United States[6] (the Rockefeller Commission) revealed that government agencies, including the FBI and the CIA, had conducted intelligence operations that resulted in surveillance of United States citizens who opposed the war in Vietnam. These operations included intelligence gathering activities both within and without the United States. Two such intelligence gathering programs are the focus of the present litigation.

A.   OPERATION CHAOS

The first program, designated by the CIA as Operation CHAOS, was an intelligence-gathering activity conducted by the CIA originally at the request of President Johnson which sought to determine the extent to which foreign governments or political organizations[8] exerted influence on or provided support to domestic critics of the government's Vietnam policies.[9] CHAOS was begun in 1967 by appellee Helms, who at the time was Director of Central Intelligence.[10] . . .

Over the course of several years, Operation CHAOS produced six reports for the White House and some thirty-four reports for cabinet-level officials, dealing with the subject of foreign influence on the domestic antiwar movement. In the normal course of its operations, CHAOS also produced a steady stream of reports to the FBI and other agencies detailing the results of its various intelligence activities with respect to the antiwar movement.

Discovery conducted by plaintiffs in the district court revealed that among the several thousand computerized files it maintained on Americans involved in various aspects of the antiwar movement,[12] Operation CHAOS ultimately developed files on 15 of the individual appellants and the five appellant organizations. The gravamen of plaintiffs' claims with respect to Operation CHAOS concerned the several known methods whereby the CIA compiled information on plaintiffs' activities. . . .

. . . [B]eginning in late 1969, the CHAOS office developed its own network of informants for the purposes of infiltrating various foreign antiwar groups located in foreign countries that might have had ties to domestic antiwar activity. Although the principal focus of such infiltration was foreign groups, it is now known that informants destined for such assignments were directed to infiltrate antiwar circles within the United States for the purpose of gaining knowledge of their operations and credibility as antiwar activists. In the course of these preliminary associations,

6. The Commission was established by Executive Order of President Ford on January 4, 1975, Executive Order No. 11828 (1975) and filed its final Report in June 1975.
8. Early CHAOS documents indicate the program's concern with the influence of "Soviets, Chicoms [Chinese Communists], Cubans and other Communist countries. . . . Of particular interest is any evidence of foreign direction, control, training or funding."
9. According to early CHAOS documents, the domestic groups suspected of receiving such support included "radical students, anti-Vietnam war activists, draft resisters and deserters, black nationalists, anarchists, and assorted 'New Leftists.' "
10. Helms testified before the Rockefeller Commission that although the President never specifically directed the CIA to institute a program devoted to gathering this information, "the setting up of this unit [CHAOS] was what I conceived to be a proper action" to respond to "almost daily and weekly" requests of the President.
12. In addition to files containing information on the subject individual or group, the CIA's computer system indexed over 100,000 names of persons upon whom separate files were not maintained.

CHAOS agents apparently supplied information on the activities of domestic antiwar groups, and this information was placed in the general CHAOS data base.[16]

 . . . Operation CHAOS made use of the facilities of other ongoing CIA surveillance programs. These included: (1) the CIA letter-opening program, which was directed at letters passing between the United States and the Soviet Union, and involved the examination of correspondence to and from individuals or organizations placed on a "watchlist";[17] (2) the Domestic Contact Service, a CIA office which solicits foreign intelligence information overtly from willing sources within the United States; (3) the CIA's "Project 2," which was directed at the infiltration of foreign intelligence targets by agents posing as dissident sympathizers and which, like CHAOS, had placed agents within domestic radical organizations for the purposes of training and establishment of dissident credentials; (4) the CIA's Project MERRIMAC, operated by the Office of Security, which was designed to infiltrate domestic antiwar and radical organizations thought to pose a threat to the security of CIA property and personnel; and (5) Project RESISTANCE, also a creature of the Office of Security, which gathered information on domestic groups without any actual infiltration.

From its inception, CHAOS also regularly received information from the FBI on that agency's investigations of the domestic antiwar movement.

B. INTERNATIONAL ELECTRONIC COMMUNICATIONS

In addition to the surveillance activities carried out under the aegis of Operation CHAOS, plaintiffs complained of the CIA's practice of obtaining the contents of international communications (telephone, telegraph and radio transmissions) by submitting subjects' names on "watchlists" to the National Security Agency (NSA). NSA possesses the technology to scan the mass of signals transmitted through various communications systems and then to select out by computer those messages in which certain words or phrases occur. It is thereby possible for that agency to acquire all communications over a monitored system in which, for example, a person's name is mentioned. Between 1967 and 1973, the FBI, the Secret Service, and military intelligence agencies, as well as the CIA, submitted the names of domestic individuals and organizations on watchlists to NSA, and ultimately acquired through NSA the international communications of over a thousand American citizens. . . .

C. HISTORY OF THE LITIGATION

1. Discovery

Since this action was filed in October 1976, the parties have fought the bulk of their dispute on the battlefield of discovery. Shortly after filing their complaint,

---

16. The CIA admitted that CHAOS agents associated with at least one plaintiff within the United States and with an unspecified number of plaintiffs traveling in foreign countries; however, it refused to identify these plaintiffs.

17. In addition to the mail of persons who had been "watchlisted," the letter-opening program also examined randomly-selected letters moving between the United States and the Soviet Union.

plaintiffs sought the production of documents concerning (1) the conduct of Operation CHAOS in general, and (2) CHAOS surveillance of plaintiff individuals and organizations in particular. A large number of documents responsive to plaintiffs' request were produced, but with portions claimed to disclose sensitive information redacted. Approximately 200 responsive documents were withheld in their entirety.[27] Subsequently, as public reports further disclosed the extent of CIA domestic activities, plaintiffs in July 1977 sought additional discovery in the form of (3) requests for admissions that the CIA or foreign "liaison services" had conducted various types of surveillance against each plaintiff or against nonparty organizations to which plaintiffs belonged; (4) further interrogatories seeking more detailed justification of the redaction and withholding of documents previously requested; (5) a request for the production of [other] documents. . . .

The CIA declined to supply all of the information requested by plaintiffs. With respect to the identification of plaintiffs who had been the subjects of surveillance under the CHAOS program or by virtue of watchlists submitted by the CIA to NSA, the CIA claimed that more than the limited disclosure already given[28] would reveal the identities of covert sources and disclose the existence of liaison relationships with foreign intelligence services, and that therefore this information was privileged from discovery. The CIA declined . . . to answer plaintiffs' interrogatories seeking more detailed explanations of the redactions in the documents it had produced. . . . Finally, it refused to disclose whether any plaintiffs' names had been submitted on watchlists to NSA by the Special Operations Group.

In January 1978, plaintiffs pursuant to Fed. R. Civ. P. 37 filed a motion to compel the Director of the CIA to respond to plaintiffs' interrogatories and requests for production of documents. The CIA responded with two affidavits by then-Director Stansfield Turner formally claiming that the requested information was protected from discovery by the state secrets privilege. . . .

In a memorandum opinion filed August 30, 1978, the district court upheld the CIA's claim of the state secrets privilege and denied plaintiffs' motion to compel. . . .

Plaintiffs explicitly conceded in the district court that the successful invocation of the state secrets privilege by the Director of Central Intelligence made it impossible for them to go forward with their claims for *damages* based on statutory and constitutional violations occurring as a result of Operation CHAOS. Without access to the facts about the identities of particular plaintiffs who were subjected to CIA surveillance (or to NSA interception at the instance of the CIA), direct injury in fact to any of the plaintiffs would not have been susceptible of proof. . . .

27. The CIA furnished brief descriptions of documents that were entirely withheld (e.g., "Dispatch dated 1 August 1968, information on dissident activity abroad, mentions [plaintiff] in passing").

28. The CIA had admitted in the course of discovery that various identified and unidentified plaintiffs were on several occasions the targets of CHAOS surveillance or were subjected to surveillance in the course of CHAOS operations directed at other subjects. Specifically, it appears that under Operation CHAOS, the CIA (1) opened and copied the mail of three identified plaintiffs within the United States; (2) targeted the mail of at least two identified plaintiffs for opening; (3) had CHAOS agents attend private meetings of unidentified plaintiff organizations; (4) collected nonpublic information on nine other identified plaintiffs; (5) electronically surveilled two unidentified plaintiffs abroad in the course of operations directed at other persons; (6) had two agents who "were associated" with at least one unidentified plaintiff within the United States; and (7) had agents who "associated" with an undisclosed number of unidentified plaintiffs abroad, in the course of operations directed at other persons.

. . . The district court was on solid ground in refusing to compel production of documents on the basis of the Director's claim as asserted in the public affidavit without resort to any more detailed justification. . . .

NOTES AND QUESTIONS

1. *Interpreting the 1947 Act.* What does it mean to say that "the Agency shall have no police, subpoena, or law enforcement powers or internal security functions"? There is no other express geographic limitation in the Act. To what extent may the CIA act within the United States? Are CIA authorities greater when operating abroad? Absent definitions in the Act, how should the CIA interpret the key terms "police," "law enforcement," and "internal security"?

2. *Authority for Operation CHAOS?* Did the domestic activities of Operation CHAOS exceed the statutory authority of the CIA? If the mission was to ascertain foreign influence on domestic dissident activities, was CIA accumulation of information on Americans needed to assess fairly whether the activities had foreign connections? Was CHAOS a legitimate program to protect CIA "sources and methods"? If you believe the operation exceeded statutory limits, does the Constitution supply the needed authority?

If you were responsible for approving staff requests to engage in surveillance of Americans, what criteria would you apply in deciding?

3. *Executive Order No. 12,333 and the National Security Act of 1947.* Compare §§1.7(a) and 2.3(b) of Executive Order No. 12,333, *supra,* to the National Security Act of 1947. Do you see any significant differences in the "such other functions and duties" authorizations in the Act and the Executive Order? What are they? How may the CIA "conduct counterintelligence activities" without performing any "internal security functions" within the United States? What do you suppose constitutes "foreign intelligence information not otherwise obtainable," and how may the CIA or NSA collect "significant" foreign intelligence within the United States without violating the proscription against collecting information on the domestic activities of United States persons? Executive Order No. 12,333 also anticipates that the CIA will engage in the "collection of foreign intelligence or counterintelligence within the United States," *id.* §1.8(a), and "participate in law enforcement activities to investigate or prevent clandestine intelligence activities by foreign powers or international terrorist or narcotics activities," *id.* §2.6(b). Can you reconcile these authorities with the "no police . . . or internal security" proviso in the 1947 Act?

4. *Weighing Government Misconduct and National Security Concerns.* In *Halkin,* the court's ruling against disclosure of the disputed evidence apparently made it impossible for individual plaintiffs to demonstrate any personal injury from government misconduct, resulting in dismissal of their claims for damages. Moreover, while several plaintiffs identified as subjects of CHAOS surveillance could establish standing to sue, they could not demonstrate such a cognizable danger of recurrent violation

of their rights as to entitle them to injunctive or declaratory relief. *Halkin*, 690 F.2d at 1003-1009.

Has the court concluded, in effect, that foreign policy considerations may excuse violations of the plaintiffs' statutory or constitutional rights? If the plaintiffs would otherwise have been entitled to damages under the Federal Tort Claims Act, is this an instance of uncompensated injury by the government without due process, in violation of the Fifth Amendment to the Constitution? *See Logan v. Zimmerman Brush Co.*, 455 U.S. 422, 428-431 (1982). The *Halkin* court observed:

> As in the other cases in which the need to protect sensitive information affecting the national security clashes with fundamental constitutional rights of individuals, we believe that "[t]he responsibility must be where the power is." *New York Times Co. v. United States*, 403 U.S. 713, 728 (1971) (Stewart, J., concurring). In the present context, where the Constitution compels the subordination of appellants' interest in the pursuit of their claims to the executive's duty to preserve our national security, this means that remedies for constitutional violations which cannot be proven under existing legal standards, if there are to be such remedies, must be provided by Congress. That is where the government's power to remedy wrongs is ultimately reposed. Consequently, that is where the responsibility for compensating those injured in the course of pursuing the ends of state must lie. [690 F.2d at 1001.]

If responsibility lies where the power is, what authority did the Executive have to launch Operation CHAOS without congressional authority?

Is it clear, as the court suggests, that the Constitution "compels" subordination of individual constitutional claims in cases like this one, or that the court in enforcing the organic law must prefer one part of it over another? In *United States Department of Justice v. Julian*, 486 U.S. 1, 13 (1988), the Supreme Court indicated that the state secrets privilege arises "as a result of judicial decision."

5. *Redefining the Scope of the Mission?* When Congress enacted the 2004 Intelligence Reform Act, the terms "national intelligence" and "intelligence related to national security" were defined to include "all intelligence, regardless of the source from which derived and including information gathered within or outside the United States, that pertains . . . to more than one . . . agency; and that involves threats to the United States, its people, property, or interests; the development, proliferation, or use of weapons of mass destruction; or any other matter bearing on United States national or homeland security." Intelligence Reform and Terrorism Prevention Act of 2004, Pub. L. No. 108-458, §1012, 118 Stat. 3638, 3662. How does this expansive definition affect the geographical boundaries of intelligence activities by the CIA? Is the implication of the amended Act that the CIA may lawfully collect intelligence through technical means inside the United States?

6. *The Director of National Intelligence and Internal Security.* Although the CIA internal security proviso remains after the enactment of the 2004 Intelligence Reform Act, no such constraint was imposed on the DNI by the Act. What are the legal and practical implications of omitting the internal security prohibition for the DNI?

Does the expanded definition of "national intelligence" noted above undercut the internal security prohibition for the CIA?

7. *Is Further Reform Needed?* Do the continuing ambiguities in the law concerning the domestic role of the CIA and its relationship to the FBI suggest a need for further statutory reform? Would it be preferable to list activities that the CIA may lawfully perform inside the United States, rather than to maintain a blanket prohibition of uncertain scope? Reviewing the 1947 Act and its 2004 amendments, along with Executive Order No. 12,333, can you come up with such a list? How would you describe the justifications for CIA collection activities inside the United States? Which methods of collection should be authorized and which ones prohibited, if any? Can you add language that would ensure coordination of CIA activities with those of the FBI and provide a mechanism for ensuring respect for the rights of U.S. persons? Should the "no internal security" proviso be amended to say "except as otherwise permitted by law"? *See* Grant T. Harris, *The CIA Mandate and the War on Terror*, 23 Yale L. & Pol'y Rev. 529, 571-576 (2005) (suggesting such changes).

2. The FBI

The Attorney General is expressly vested with "primary investigative authority for all Federal crimes of terrorism." 18 U.S.C. §2332b(f) (2006). The FBI, in contrast, has scant statutory authority to carry out its mission. Lacking a legislative charter, the FBI operates on the basis of the Attorney General's authority found in 28 U.S.C. §533 (2006) to appoint officials:

(1) to detect and prosecute crimes against the United States;
(2) to assist in the protection of the person of the President; and ...
(4) to conduct such other investigations regarding official matters under the control of the Department of Justice and the Department of State as may be directed by the Attorney General.

The FBI also draws investigative authority from statutes authorizing specific methods or purposes for collection, such as the Foreign Intelligence Surveillance Act (FISA), analyzed in Chapter 7.

All FBI investigations are conducted according to guidelines promulgated by the Attorney General and Executive Order No. 12,333. On September 29, 2008, Attorney General Michael Mukasey announced the issuance of the *Attorney General's Guidelines for Domestic FBI Operations, available at* http://www.usdoj.gov/ag/readingroom/guidelines.pdf, which took effect on December 1, 2008. The consolidated guidelines combine nearly uniform standards for all FBI domestic investigations and replace five sets of previously discrete guidance on crimes investigation, national security investigations, and foreign intelligence investigations.

Unlike the CIA or any other intelligence collector, the FBI therefore operates under the direction of the nation's highest law enforcement officer and within a culture of law enforcement. Nevertheless, the FBI has also sometimes strayed from its lawful domestic role and has undertaken efforts to disrupt domestic groups.

Select Committee to Study Governmental Operations with Respect to Intelligence Activities (Church Committee), Intelligence Activities and the Rights of Americans

S. Rep. No. 94-755, bk. II, at 86-89 (1976)

The FBI's initiation of COINTELPRO operations against the Ku Klux Klan, "Black Nationalists" and the "New Left" brought to bear upon a wide range of domestic groups the techniques previously developed to combat Communists and persons who happened to associate with them.

The start of each program coincided with significant national events. The Klan program followed the widely-publicized disappearance in 1964 of three civil rights workers in Mississippi. The "Black Nationalist" program was authorized in the aftermath of the Newark and Detroit riots in 1967. The "New Left" program developed shortly after student disruption of the Columbia University campus in the spring of 1968. While the initiating memoranda approved by Director Hoover do not refer to these specific events, it is clear that they shaped the context for the Bureau's decisions.

These programs were not directed at obtaining evidence for use in possible criminal prosecutions arising out of those events. Rather, they were secret programs — "under no circumstances" to be "made known outside the Bureau" — which used unlawful or improper acts to "disrupt" or "neutralize" the activities of groups and individuals targeted on the basis of imprecise criteria.

(1) *Klan and "White Hate" COINTELPRO.* — The expansion of Klan investigations, in response to pressure from President Johnson and Attorney General Kennedy, was accompanied by an internal Bureau decision to shift their supervision from the General Investigative Division to the Domestic Intelligence Division. One internal FBI argument for the transfer was that the Intelligence Division was "in a position to launch a disruptive counterintelligence program" against the Klan with the "same effectiveness" it had against the Communist Party.

Accordingly, in September 1964 a directive was sent to seventeen field offices instituting a COINTELPRO against the Klan and what the FBI considered to be other "White Hate" organizations (e.g., American Nazi Party, National States Rights Party) "to expose, disrupt, and otherwise neutralize" the activities of the groups, "their leaders, and adherents."

During the 1964-1971 period, when the program was in operation, 287 proposals for COINTELPRO actions against Klan and "White Hate" groups were authorized by FBI headquarters. Covert techniques used in this COINTELPRO included creating new Klan chapters to be controlled by Bureau informants and sending an anonymous letter designed to break up a marriage.

(2) *"Black Nationalist" COINTELPRO.* — The stated strategy of the "Black Nationalist" COINTELPRO instituted in 1967 was "to expose, disrupt, misdirect, discredit, or otherwise neutralize" such groups and their "leadership, spokesmen, members, and supporters." The larger objectives were to "counter" their "propensity for violence" and to "frustrate" their efforts to "consolidate their forces" or to "recruit new or youthful adherents." Field offices were instructed to exploit conflicts within and between groups; to use news media contacts to ridicule and otherwise discredit groups; to prevent "rabble rousers" from spreading their "philosophy" publicly; and to gather information on the "unsavory backgrounds" of group leaders.

In March 1968, the program was expanded from twenty-three to forty-one field offices and the following long-range goals were set forth:

(1)   prevent the "coalition of militant black nationalist groups";
(2)   prevent the rise of a "messiah" who could "unify and electrify" the movement, naming specifically Dr. Martin Luther King, Jr., Stokely Carmichael, and Elijah Muhammed;
(3)   prevent violence by pinpointing "potential troublemakers" and "neutralizing" them before they "exercise their potential for violence";
(4)   prevent groups and leaders from gaining "respectability" by discrediting them to the "responsible" Negro community, the "responsible" white community, "liberals" with "vestiges of sympathy" for militant black nationalist and "Negro radicals"; and
(5)   "prevent these groups from recruiting young people."

After the Black Panther Party emerged as a group of national stature, FBI field offices were instructed to develop "imaginative and hard-hitting counterintelligence measures aimed at crippling the BPP." Particular attention was to be given to aggravating conflicts between the Black Panthers and rival groups in a number of cities where such conflict had already taken on the character of "gang warfare with attendant threats of murder and reprisals."

During 1967-1971, FBI headquarters approved 379 proposals for COINTELPRO actions against "black nationalists." These operations utilized dangerous and unsavory techniques which gave rise to the risk of death and often disregarded the personal rights and dignity of the victims.

(3) *"New Left" COINTELPRO.* — The most vaguely defined and haphazard of the COINTELPRO operations was that initiated against the "New Left" in May 1968. It was justified to the FBI Director by his subordinates on the basis of the following considerations:

The nation was "undergoing an era of disruption and violence" which was "caused to a large extent" by individuals "generally connected with the New Left."

Some of these "activists" were urging "revolution" and calling for "the defeat of the United States in Vietnam."

The problem was not just that they committed "unlawful acts," but also that they "falsely" alleged police brutality, and that they "scurrilously attacked the Director and the Bureau" in an attempt to "hamper" FBI investigations and to "drive us off the college campuses."

Consequently, the COINTELPRO was intended to "expose, disrupt, and otherwise neutralize" the activities of "this group" and "persons connected with it." The lack of any clear definition of "New Left" meant, as an FBI supervisor testified, that "legitimate" and nonviolent antiwar groups were targeted because they were "lending aid and comfort" to more disruptive groups.

Further directives issued soon after initiation of the program urged field offices to "vigorously and enthusiastically" explore "every avenue of possible embarrassment" of New Left adherents. Agents were instructed to gather information on the "immorality" and the "scurrilous and depraved" behavior, "habits, and living conditions" of the members of targeted groups. This message was reiterated several months later, when the offices were taken to task for their failure to remain alert for and seek specific data depicting the "depraved nature and moral looseness of the

New Left" and to "use this material in a vigorous and enthusiastic approach to neutralizing them."

In July 1968, the field offices were further prodded by FBI headquarters to:

(1) prepare leaflets using "the most obnoxious pictures" of New Left leaders at various universities;
(2) instigate "personal conflicts or animosities" between New Left leaders;
(3) create the impression that leaders are "informants for the Bureau or other law enforcement agencies" (the "snitch jacket" technique);
(4) send articles from student or "underground" newspapers which show "depravity" ("use of narcotics and free sex") of New Left leaders to university officials, donors, legislators, and parents;
(5) have members arrested on marijuana charges;
(6) send anonymous letters about a student's activities to parents, neighbors and the parents' employers;
(7) send anonymous letters about New Left faculty members (signed "A Concerned Alumni" or "A Concerned Taxpayer") to university officials, legislators, Board of Regents, and the press;
(8) use "cooperative press contacts";
(9) exploit the "hostility" between New Left and Old Left groups;
(10) disrupt New Left coffee houses near military bases which are attempting to "influence members of the Armed forces";
(11) use cartoons, photographs, and anonymous letters to "ridicule" the New Left;
(12) use "misinformation" to "confuse and disrupt" New Left activities, such as by notifying members that events have been cancelled.

During the period 1968-1971, 291 COINTELPRO actions against the "New Left" were approved by headquarters. Particular emphasis was placed upon preventing the targeted individuals from public speaking or teaching and providing "misinformation" to confuse demonstrators.

NOTES AND QUESTIONS

1. *Suing the FBI over COINTELPRO.* In 1976, several Washington area residents who had been politically active in anti-war and civil rights activities in the 1960s and early 1970s brought suit against the FBI and District of Columbia officials for alleged violations of constitutional rights related to the FBI COINTELPRO program. In *Hobson v. Wilson,* 737 F.2d 1, 10 (D.C. Cir. 1984), *cert. denied sub nom. Brennan v. Hobson,* 470 U.S. 1084 (1985), the plaintiffs prevailed against most of the defendants. The Court of Appeals stated, "Government action taken with the intent to disrupt or destroy lawful organizations, or to deter membership in those groups, is absolutely unconstitutional." 737 F.2d at 29. What likely explains the different outcomes in *Halkin* and *Hobson?*

2. *Investigatory Authorizations Under Executive Order No. 12,333.* What constitutes a "lawful" FBI investigation within the meaning of Executive Order No. 12,333? What are the likely elements of a probable cause determination under §2.5? Review §2.4. Does any agency other than the FBI have authority to conduct physical searches inside the United States? Is the answer the same for physical surveillance of U.S. persons

within the United States? Under what circumstances may the FBI engage in physical surveillance of a U.S. person abroad?

3. *Authority for FBI Guidelines.* Do you think Congress should provide more explicit statutory authority for the FBI to conduct national security investigations? *See* Tom Lininger, *Sects, Lies, and Videotape: The Surveillance and Infiltration of Religious Groups,* 89 Iowa L. Rev. 1201 (2004) (so arguing).

4. *Relationship to Other Guidelines and Policies.* The 2008 *Attorney General's Guidelines for Domestic FBI Operations* repealed and replaced several existing sets of guidelines, including separate sets for criminal investigation, national security investigation, and foreign intelligence collection. Other Department of Justice guidelines affecting FBI activities remain in effect, including the *Attorney General's Guidelines on Federal Bureau of Investigation Undercover Operations* (May 2002), *available at* http://www.usdoj.gov/olp/fbiundercover.pdf; the *Attorney General's Guidelines Regarding the Use of FBI Confidential Human Sources* (Dec. 13, 2006), *available at* http://www.fas.org/irp/agency/doj/fbi/chs-guidelines.pdf; and *Guidance Regarding the Use of Race by Federal Law Enforcement Agencies* (June 2003, updated July 2008), *available at* http://www.usdoj.gov/crt/split/documents/guidance_on_race.php. The 2008 *Guidelines for Domestic FBI Operations* do not apply to extraterritorial operations carried out by FBI agents or human sources in foreign countries. Attorney General Mukasey announced in September 2008 that he would be issuing new *Attorney General's Guidelines for Extraterritorial FBI Operations. See Memorandum from the Attorney General to Heads of Department Components* (Sept. 29, 2008), *available at* http://www.usdoj.gov/ag/readingroom/guidelines-memo.pdf. Notwithstanding the general repeal of the earlier guidelines, the Attorney General directed that existing guidelines remain in effect in their application to extraterritorial operations until the new guidelines are issued. *Id.*

5. *Predicated Investigations.* The Guidelines state that predicated investigations are generally based on "allegations, reports, facts or circumstances indicative of possible criminal or national security-threatening activity, or the potential for acquiring information responsive to foreign intelligence requirements . . . [where] supervisory approval must be obtained." *Guidelines for Domestic FBI Operations* §II. Does the Constitution require some predicate activity before the FBI may launch an investigation? Would you infer such a requirement from statutes, or from Executive Order No. 12,333? What is the value of supervisory approval in predicated investigations?

6. *Infiltration.* Is CIA or FBI infiltration of domestic organizations permitted by Executive Order No. 12,333? On the basis of what information will the "agency head or designee" determine that infiltration is "essential to achieving lawful purposes"? If infiltration is authorized outside the limits of the order, what redress would be available to aggrieved persons? *See* Seth Kreimer, *Watching the Watchers: Surveillance, Transparency, and Political Freedom in the War on Terror,* 7 U. Pa. J. Const. L. 133 (2004).

7. *Assessments of the Guidelines.* The FBI's interpretation of the 2008 *Guidelines* was made public when it released, in response to a Freedom of Information Act (FOIA) lawsuit, its *Domestic Investigations and Operations Guide* (Dec. 16, 2008), *available at* http://s3.amazonaws.com/nytdocs/docs/264/264.pdf. Prior to the opening of a

formal investigation, FBI "assessments" may be undertaken without any predicate suspicion or threat. According to the *Domestic Investigations and Operations Guide*, the basis for opening an assessment "cannot be arbitrary or groundless suspicion," but the standard is "difficult to define." What is their value? Does the FBI have statutory authority to conduct these assessments? A former FBI agent stated that the *Guide* "raises fundamental questions about whether a domestic intelligence agency can protect civil liberties if they feel they have a right to collect broad personal information about people they don't even suspect of wrongdoing." Charlie Savage, *Loosening of F.B.I. Rules Stirs Privacy Concerns*, N.Y. Times, Oct. 29, 2009. According to a document released pursuant to a Freedom of Information Act request, the FBI initiated 11,667 assessments of people and groups in the four months between December 2008 and March 2009. Charlie Savage, *F.B.I. Casts Wide Net Under Relaxed Rules for Terror Inquiries, Data Show*, N.Y. Times, Mar. 26, 2011.

Note that the FBI may recruit human sources or task existing ones in an assessment. The *Attorney General's Guidelines Regarding the Use of FBI Confidential Human Sources* (Dec. 13, 2006), *supra*, provide detailed guidance on the use of human sources. Do you see any potential legal problems with the use of human sources in conducting an assessment?

In addition, the FBI may engage in physical surveillance in an assessment. Physical surveillance had been available to the Bureau in general crimes investigations at the assessment level. Do you see any legal issues in extending physical surveillance to this broader set of guidelines? Might these rules encourage the FBI to engage in fishing expeditions that waste resources and damage the reputations of innocent people?

8. *The Use of Race or Religion.* Section II of the 2003 *Guidance Regarding the Use of Race by Federal Law Enforcement Agencies* states that "federal law enforcement officers who are protecting national security...may consider race, ethnicity and other relevant factors to the extent permitted by our laws and the Constitution." When engaged in traditional law enforcement activities, officers may not use race or ethnicity to any degree, except that officers may rely on race or ethnicity in a specific suspect description. Is there any reason not to apply the same direction to national security investigations? To foreign intelligence investigations? Do you suppose that the assessments engaged in by the FBI might focus on members of a racial group? A religious group? Following the outing of an FBI informant who had infiltrated a California mosque in November 2010, Muslim organizations complained that overreaching FBI investigative tactics have damaged the relationship between the Muslim groups and the Bureau. Jerry Markon, *Mosque Infiltration Feeds Muslims' Distrust of FBI*, Wash. Post, Dec. 5, 2010. Should investigations be limited to circumstances where possible criminal or national security-threatening activity has been received by the FBI?

9. *Creation of a U.S. MI5?* MI5 (Military Intelligence, Section 5) is charged with counterintelligence and counterterrorism activities within the United Kingdom. It is headed by a permanent civil service employee (the Director General) answerable to the Home Secretary, and it does not have general law enforcement responsibilities. In recent years, some have suggested that the United States should create a domestic intelligence service patterned after MI5. *See, e.g.*, William E. Odom, *Fixing Intelligence for a More Secure America* 180-182 (2d ed. 2003). Creating an American MI5 would avoid the conflict or competition between counterterrorism or counterintelligence and law

enforcement, it is asserted, and thus make the FBI more effective at its counter-tasks. Instead of relying on the FBI to perform domestic intelligence gathering, an MI5-type agency might be separate from both the FBI and CIA (although, like them, it would report to the DNI). The FBI would then revert to what it has historically done best — fighting crime by building cases against criminals. The domestic intelligence agency, in contrast, would collect intelligence in the United States to guard against ongoing and future espionage or terrorist plots. The potential targets of the new agency could be wholly homegrown, like the Ku Klux Klan or domestic terrorists, or those with foreign origins or connections, such as Al Qaeda.

Would creation of a such a new agency be a good idea? If our MI5 reported to the DNI instead of directly to the President, and was no longer supervised by the chief law enforcement officer of the United States, are you satisfied that the agency would avoid the politically driven operations that bedeviled the nation in the Nixon years?

3.   The NSA

The NSA is the largest agency within the intelligence community. It is devoted to communications security and to collecting and disseminating SIGINT. NSA's predecessor, the Armed Forces Security Agency (AFSA), was established within the Department of Defense in 1949, but because each military service branch continued to collect SIGINT for its own use, AFSA proved ineffectual in coordinating SIGINT activities. In October 1952, President Truman signed a secret directive to create the NSA in order to provide an effective structure for coordinating SIGINT activities for civilian and military consumers. Richard A. Best Jr., *The National Security Agency: Issues for Congress* 16 (Cong. Res. Serv. RL30740), Jan. 16, 2001; *see* Jeffrey T. Richelson, *The U.S. Intelligence Community* 30-37 (5th ed. 2008). Apart from annual appropriations for the NSA based on secret briefings about SIGINT activities before the appropriations committees, the first major legislation dealing with NSA was the National Security Agency Act of 1959, Pub. L. No. 86-36, 73 Stat. 63. It authorized the Secretary of Defense to "establish such positions, and to appoint . . . such officers and employees, in the National Security Agency, as may be necessary to carry out the functions of such agency." *Id.* §2. However, this measure dealt mostly with housekeeping matters inside the Agency and did not describe the functions of NSA.

Until it was revealed that U.S. intelligence agencies were spying on domestic groups opposed to the Vietnam War, there was little interest in the NSA among members of Congress or the public and little knowledge about the secretive agency. During the Church Committee hearings in 1976, NSA Director Lieutenant General Lew Allen Jr. provided the first open-session congressional testimony about NSA SIGINT activities and the NSA practice of establishing "watch lists," discussed in *Halkin, supra.* Although the Church Committee and its House counterpart, known as the Pike Committee, acknowledged the continuing importance of NSA's foreign intelligence collection activities, both committees also recommended specific authorizing legislation for NSA that would include strict limits on the monitoring of communications by U.S. citizens. *See* Church Committee, *supra* p. 127, bk. I, at 464; *Recommendations of the Final Report of the House Select Comm. on Intelligence,* H.R. Rep. No. 94-833, at 3 (1976). The congressional initiative toward a "legislative charter" for the intelligence agencies, including NSA, died in the 1979-1980 congressional session amidst partisan disputes, when the Soviet invasion of Afghanistan caught the

United States by surprise and provoked new efforts to invigorate intelligence capabilities.

Congress did, however, enact FISA in 1978, authorizing and regulating electronic surveillance in the United States to obtain foreign intelligence. Because the NSA conducts electronic surveillance, FISA became an important part of the NSA's regulatory framework. We address FISA in detail in Chapters 7 and 8.

In 1992, the National Security Act of 1947 was amended to state that

> the Secretary of Defense shall ensure . . . through the National Security Agency (except as otherwise directed by the President or the National Security Council), the continued operation of an effective unified organization for the conduct of signals intelligence activities and shall ensure that the product is disseminated in a timely manner to authorized recipients. [Intelligence Authorization Act for Fiscal Year 1993, Pub. L. No. 102-496, §706, 106 Stat. 3180, 3194-3195 (1992) (codified as amended at 50 U.S.C. §403-5(b)(1) (2006).]

Additional guidance for the NSA has been provided by executive order.

Executive Order No. 12,333, United States Intelligence Activities

(as amended by Executive Order Nos. 13,284 (2003),
13,355 (2004), and 13,470 (2008))
73 Fed. Reg. 45,325 (July 30, 2008)

1.12. Intelligence Components Utilized by the Secretary of Defense.... [T]he Secretary of Defense is authorized to utilize the following: . . .

(b) National Security Agency, whose responsibilities shall include:

(1) Establishment and operation of an effective unified organization for signals intelligence activities, except for the delegation of operational control over certain operations that are conducted through other elements of the Intelligence Community. No other department or agency may engage in signals intelligence activities except pursuant to a delegation by the Secretary of Defense;

(2) Control of signals intelligence collection and processing activities, including assignment of resources to an appropriate agent for such periods and tasks as required for the direct support of military commanders;

(3) Collection of signals intelligence information for national foreign intelligence purposes in accordance with guidance from the Director of Central Intelligence;

(4) Processing of signals intelligence data for national foreign intelligence purposes in accordance with guidance from the Director of Central Intelligence;

(5) Dissemination of signals intelligence information for national foreign intelligence purposes to authorized elements of the Government, including the military services, in accordance with guidance from the Director of Central Intelligence;

(6) Collection, processing and dissemination of signals intelligence information for counterintelligence purposes;

(7) Provision of signals intelligence support for the conduct of military operations in accordance with tasking, priorities, and standards of timeliness assigned by the Secretary of Defense. If provision of such support requires use of national

collection systems, these systems will be tasked within existing guidance from the Director of Central Intelligence;

(8) Executing the responsibilities of the Secretary of Defense as executive agent for the communications security of the United States Government; . . .

(10) Protection of the security of its installations, activities, property, information, and employees by appropriate means, including such investigations of applicants, employees, contractors, and other persons with similar associations with the NSA as are necessary. . . .

The power of NSA computers to collect massive amounts of data is staggering. NSA "employs more mathematicians than any other organization in the world and [its facilities contain] the densest concentration of computer power on the planet." Patrick Radden Keefe, *Chatter: Dispatches from the Secret World of Global Eavesdropping* 8 (2005). It uses sophisticated key-word searching and other techniques (often lumped together and referred to as "data mining") to perform some analysis on large amounts of material before it is delivered to other agencies. Its technical capacity actually far outstrips the human capacity to evaluate or use all the information it collects.

The Agency does not act upon the intelligence it collects. Instead, NSA passes that intelligence along to other civilian and military agencies and officials. *Id.* In its communications security role, NSA uses its SIGINT capabilities to detect espionage and other intelligence activities directed against the United States. For example, early in the Cold War NSA conducted a program code-named VENONA that used signal intercepts to detect Soviet espionage in the United States. Between 1943 and 1957, VENONA helped identify Alger Hiss, Julius Rosenberg, Klaus Fuchs, and others who served as Soviet agents. *See* Robert L. Benson, *The Venona Story* (National Security Agency/Central Security Service) (n.d.), *available at* http://www.nsa.gov/publications/publi00039.cfm. Many of the released intercepts may be viewed at http://www.nsa.gov/venona/. Additional background on the NSA may be found in three books by James Bamford, *The Shadow Factor: The Ultra-Secret NSA from 9/11 to the Eavesdropping on America* (2008); *Body of Secrets: Anatomy of the Ultra-Secret National Security Agency* (2001); and *Puzzle Palace* (1982).

NOTES AND QUESTIONS

1. *Authority to Create the NSA?* What authority did President Truman have to establish the NSA in 1952? The National Security Act of 1947, Pub. L. No. 80-253, 61 Stat. 495 (codified as amended in scattered sections of 10 & 50 U.S.C.), created a Secretary of Defense and states that "[u]nder the direction of the President and subject to the provisions of this Act he shall . . . [e]stablish general policies and programs for the National Military Establishment and for all the departments and agencies therein." Pub. L. No. 80-253, §202(a)(1), 61 Stat. 495, 500. If this provision is insufficient, does the President possess constitutional authority to create an agency to collect SIGINT for foreign intelligence purposes? To collect SIGINT in the United States?

2. *Watch Lists.* If the *Halkin* court had reached the merits, how should it have ruled on the plaintiffs' complaints concerning the NSA's use of watch lists? Watch lists were developed by identifying individual names, subjects, locations, and the like within a mass of communications to separate useful intelligence from background "noise." Watch lists were thus precursors to contemporary data-mining techniques, including those at issue in the post–September 11 NSA domestic eavesdropping program. See *infra* pp. 222-232.

During the Vietnam War period, congressional investigators learned of an NSA project known as Shamrock in which copies of international telegrams were provided on a daily basis to NSA by three telegraph companies. Church Committee, *supra* p. 127, bk. III, at 765-776. Pursuant to what legal authority would this project have been conducted? The congressional desire to bring practices such as these under legislative control helped assure the 1978 enactment of FISA, examined in Chapter 7.

3. *Contemporary Authorities.* To what extent, if at all, does the 1959 National Security Agency Act authorize the activities of the NSA? Does the 1992 amendment to the National Security Act of 1947 constitute an adequate legislative charter for the NSA's activities? If not, what changes or additions would you recommend? To what extent do the provisions of Executive Order No. 12,333 supply the necessary details? What questions do you have about what the NSA may and may not do after reading these two measures?

4. *ECHELON.* An NSA program called ECHELON allegedly used data-mining techniques aimed at telecommunications from Europe for economic espionage. *Keefe, supra,* at 194-208. Sophisticated listening stations in the United States and Great Britain reportedly tracked these communications. *Id.* at 52-54. European leaders claimed that ECHELON was employed to steal secrets from European countries and pass them on to U.S. competitors. European Parliament, *Report of the Existence of a Global System for the Interception of Private and Commercial Communications (ECHELON Interception System),* July 11, 2001, *available at* http://www.fas.org/irp/program/process/rapport_echelon_en.pdf.

Does the NSA have the authority to conduct a program like ECHELON? Some in the United States countered the European complaints by maintaining that ECHELON was used to observe bribes by European companies of government officials in furtherance of their commercial interests. Keefe, *supra,* at 194-198. Do you see any legal problems with these techniques or with their objectives?

D.   SHARING COLLECTED INTELLIGENCE

Some of the September 11 hijackers lived openly in the United States when their names or names of their close associates were on intelligence "watch lists." The watch-list information was not shared in a timely fashion among federal agencies, which might have been able to detect the hijackers' plot before it was implemented. Because intelligence about would-be terrorists might be obtained by the FBI, CIA, NSA, or agencies inside the Defense Department, or by a state or local law enforcement agency, the challenges of sharing intelligence are staggering. Moreover, the FBI, long embedded in its role as the federal government's chief law enforcement agency, has struggled to reshape its mission to incorporate a vigorous counterterrorism component. How should information classified by one agency be shared with another agency? How should a federal agency share with a state or local agency? How can information be shared in a secure way without jeopardizing the privacy interests of those identified in the intelligence?

Some coordination is required by Executive Order No. 12,333, and ODNI provides guidance to federal, state, and local agencies on sharing information through its Information Sharing Environment. *See Information Sharing Environment* (updated regularly), *at* http://www.ise.gov/. The FBI leads and coordinates foreign intelligence and counterintelligence activities in the United States, and the CIA, Department of Defense, and military intelligence entities must coordinate with the FBI. Executive Order No. 12,333 §§1.8(a), 1.11(d), 1.14, 1.12(d)(1). Outside the United States, all the intelligence agencies are required to coordinate with the CIA. *Id.* §§1.8(d), 1.11(d), 1.12(d)(1), 1.14(a). In practice, coordination has sometimes been difficult to achieve.

1.   Bridging the Law Enforcement/Intelligence Collection Divide

The National Security Act of 1947 declares that the CIA shall have no "internal security" functions. It was thus determined by Congress that the already functioning FBI would continue to serve as the nation's domestic security agency. At the same time, it was understood early on that the "internal security" prohibition in the 1947 Act would not forbid the CIA from coordinating or collecting *foreign* intelligence information in the United States. However, there was nothing in the Act to provide for CIA and FBI coordination, and no rules to say when the CIA could play a counterintelligence role in the United States. In theory, law enforcement and intelligence collection roles, activities, and methods had been legally and functionally separated to protect the integrity of their tasks and to protect the civil liberties of those targeted for investigation by the government. *See* Jonathan M. Fredman, *Intelligence Agencies, Law Enforcement, and the Prosecution Team,* 16 Yale L. & Pol'y Rev. 331, 336-337 (1998). Thus, the 1947 Act "cut the man down the middle . . . between domestic and foreign counterespionage." Mark Riebling, *Wedge: The Secret War Between the FBI and CIA* 78 (1994).

While the FBI has expanded its extraterritorial role to acquire information about transnational threats, the CIA and agencies inside the Departments of Homeland Security and Defense have also stepped up their efforts in support of counterterrorism. Intelligence gathering for counterterrorism must anticipate threats before they are carried out, while law enforcement typically reacts after the event. However, because terrorism and international crime pose national security threats that transcend both national borders *and* the borders between law enforcement and intelligence collection, coordination and cooperation are required among intelligence agencies and between the intelligence and law enforcement arms of the FBI.

As amended in 1996, the National Security Act permits agencies of the intelligence community, upon the request of a law enforcement agency, to "collect information outside the United States about individuals who are not United States persons." 50 U.S.C. §403-5a. Executive Order No. 12,333 establishes a legal presumption that agencies of the Intelligence Community may "participate in law enforcement activities

to investigate or prevent clandestine intelligence activities by foreign powers, or international terrorist or narcotics activities" unless "otherwise precluded by law or this
Order." *Id.* §2.6. The order also explicitly charges the DNI with developing guidelines
for sharing of intelligence information by the intelligence community, subject to
approval by the Attorney General. *Id.* §1.3(a)(2). The DNI also "shall ensure, through
appropriate policies and procedures, the deconfliction, coordination, and integration
of all intelligence activities conducted by an Intelligence Community element or
funded by the National Intelligence Program." *Id.* §1.3(b)(20).

A USA Patriot Act provision authorizes a greater degree of interagency cooperation and sharing of information than was permitted previously. The Act permits,
"[n]otwithstanding any other provision of law . . . foreign or counterintelligence . . .
information obtained as part of a criminal investigation to be disclosed to any Federal
law enforcement, intelligence, protective, immigration, national defense, or national
security official in order to assist the official receiving that information in the performance of his official duties." Pub. L. No. 107-56, §203(d)(1), 115 Stat. 272, 281
(2001), amending 50 U.S.C. §403-5(d). The same discretion is given for the sharing
of grand jury information. *Id.* §203(a)(1), 115 Stat. 278-279, amending 18 U.S.C.
§6(e)(3)(C).

In the Intelligence Reform and Terrorism Prevention Act of 2004 (IRTPA), Pub.
L. No. 108-458, 118 Stat. 3638, Congress created a National Counterterrorism Center
(NCTC). *Id.* §1021m, 118 Stat. 3672. The Senate-confirmed Director of the NCTC
reports to the DNI generally, but to the President on the planning and implementation of joint counterterrorism operations. *Id.* The IRTPA vests in the DNI the "principal authority to ensure maximum availability of and access to intelligence information
within the intelligence community consistent with national security." *Id.* §1011(a), 118
Stat. 3650. IRTPA also requires a "coordinated environment" in which intelligence
information can be "provided in its more shareable form." *Id.* §1016(b)(2), (d)(1),
118 Stat. 3665-3666.

2.   Coordinating the FBI

Owing at least in part to the FBI's long-standing tradition of performing the
federal law enforcement role, intelligence collection and analysis efforts were long
regarded inside the Bureau as of secondary importance. Even as additional resources
and staff were devoted to intelligence collection and analysis inside the FBI during the
1990s, the intelligence function was still not central to the FBI mission. In addition to
the perception among many that engaging heavily in intelligence work would only
compromise the effectiveness of FBI law enforcement, the Bureau's reluctance to
embrace an intelligence mission wholeheartedly was also due in part to our nation's
cultural and historical antipathy to a domestic intelligence service. Images of the
sinister omnipresence of the German Gestapo and the Soviet KGB were firmly etched
into the public consciousness.

A few months after Congress created a revised intelligence community structure
in December 2004, President Bush issued an order creating a new National Security
Division (NSD) within the FBI that is subject to the overall direction of the DNI. *See*
Douglas Jehl, *Bush to Create New Unit in F.B.I. for Intelligence*, N.Y. Times, June 30, 2005.
The restructuring was designed to break down historic barriers between the FBI and
CIA, while elevating the relative importance of the intelligence mission inside the FBI.

Id. The new division, called the National Security Service, includes counterterrorism and counterintelligence divisions and an intelligence directorate. A new position of Assistant Attorney General for National Security, in charge of counterterrorism, counterintelligence, and the Office of Intelligence Policy Review, was approved by Congress in the USA Patriot Improvement and Reauthorization Act of 2005, Pub. L. No. 109-177, §506(a), 120 Stat. 192, 247 (2006).

NOTES AND QUESTIONS

1. *Intelligence Reform and the FBI.* The restructuring accomplished by Congress in the IRTPA and later in the Patriot Reauthorization Act was "intended to break down old walls between foreign and domestic intelligence activities." Douglas Jehl, *Bush to Create New Unit in F.B.I. for Intelligence,* N.Y. Times, June 30, 2005. Do you see any downside risk in tearing down the wall between foreign and domestic intelligence? In lowering the historic barrier between the FBI and the CIA? To what extent will the FBI now be subject to the authority of the DNI? Whose job is it to ensure that the National Security Service not undertake activities that violate U.S. laws?

2. *Utility of the Information-Sharing Requirements.* Are the USA Patriot Act and IRTPA information-sharing provisions clearly advisable? Do these provisions raise the possibility that the CIA will collect information in the United States about Americans? In light of the complexities of mounting an effective counterterrorism strategy, can you think of any good alternatives to these information-sharing mechanisms? Can you think of ways to create greater accountability for their use?

What legal measures might improve information sharing across these jurisdictional lines? Between agencies? *See* Peter P. Swire, *Privacy and Information Sharing in the War on Terrorism,* 51 Vill. L. Rev. 951 (2006) (suggesting a due diligence checklist for information-sharing projects).

3. *Checks and Balances vs. Efficiency.* Is competition between the CIA and the FBI inevitable? If the coordination and competition problems *can* be solved, *should* they be solved? Or is it part of our nation's character "to chafe at bureaucratic inefficiency... [but] to distrust the centralization of power needed to correct it"? Riebling, *supra,* at 460. Are the agencies' missions so different that their work cannot be coordinated? Is the reluctance to vest one agency with both foreign and domestic security responsibility a sign of healthy skepticism about the dangers of the accumulation of power in one entity? In the end, is the foreign/domestic dichotomy that continues to dominate the law of internal security workable? Is it constitutionally defensible? Is the better dividing line one between intelligence collection and law enforcement?

6

The Fourth Amendment and Counterterrorism

Since the birth of our nation, Americans have worried about espionage committed by hostile foreign agents. In recent times, we have also become the targets of violent terrorist acts at home and abroad. To gather information about these threats to national security, we have employed many of the same techniques that are used in ordinary criminal investigations, including wiretaps, undercover agents and informants, physical searches of persons and places, and, more recently, sophisticated computer technologies, including e-mail intercepts and data mining.

In almost every instance, these measures have succeeded in protecting the American people from harm. In the process, however, government officials have occasionally lost sight of their mission, or strayed from it, and have violated individual privacy rights, just as in any criminal investigation gone awry. Where the subject of a probe is a possible terrorist act, which may be politically motivated, First Amendment freedoms of assembly and expression may be implicated as well. Special care is thus required in sorting out protected activities from those that could lead to violence or serious disruption of society and in selecting appropriate investigative techniques for each.

This sorting-out process is often complicated by a lack of information about the exact nature of suspected threats. While no one argues that a mere hunch about anticipated violent acts or subversion will justify surveillance of potential targets, something less than a completed illegal act must suffice. Thus, the development of standards for approval of investigations into national security threats is a critical legal issue.

In this and the succeeding five chapters we focus on intelligence collection within the United States and abroad — electronic surveillance; physical searches; the collection of tangible and electronic transactional records, such as travel records, telephone dialing and billing information, bank records, and library records; data mining of the resulting data bases; and watch list and screening measures for mass transit and other public places.

In this chapter, we start in Part A with a short primer on the Fourth Amendment and the "special needs" exceptions. In Part B, we examine the Supreme Court's seminal analysis of the President's claim of inherent authority to conduct warrantless electronic surveillance in domestic security investigations. In Part C, we consider whether subsequent lower court case law recognized a "foreign intelligence exception" to the warrant requirement of the Fourth Amendment.

In Chapter 7, we turn to statutory authority for electronic foreign intelligence surveillance in the Foreign Intelligence Surveillance Act (FISA) and related legislation. Chapter 8 examines the most recent extension of FISA procedures to permit programmatic surveillance without regard to particularized targets. In Chapter 9, we take up statutory authority for investigatory collection of tangible and electronic transactional records held by third parties, using court orders, national security letters, and subpoenas. In Chapter 10, we consider a range of other surveillance and collection techniques used to profile and "watchlist" terrorist suspects and to screen access to transportation systems, critical infrastructure, and other possible targets for terrorism. Finally, in Chapter 11, we shift our focus from domestic intelligence collection to the U.S. law governing national security surveillance abroad.

A.   THE FOURTH AMENDMENT FRAMEWORK

An introduction to the Fourth Amendment necessarily starts in colonial America. The British used a "general warrant" to conduct searches without probable cause — essentially fishing expeditions.

> The British general warrant was a search tool employed without limitation on location, and without any necessity to precisely describe the object or person sought. British authorities were simply given license to "break into any shop or place suspected" wherever they chose. With that kind of unfettered discretion, the general warrant could be, and often was, used to intimidate. General warrants executed during the reign of Charles I sought to intimidate dissidents, authors, and printers of seditious material by ransacking homes and seizing personal papers. In 1765, the courts declared general warrants illegal, and Parliament followed a year later.
>   In the colonies, complaints that royal officials were violating the privacy of colonists through the use of writs of assistance, equivalent to general warrants, grew. Because English law did not, as yet, recognize a right of personal privacy, the crown's abuses in the colonies were not remediable at law. It was thus no surprise that the new American Constitution and the government it created would respect a series of individual freedoms. . . . [William C. Banks & M.E. Bowman, *Executive Authority for National Security Surveillance*, 50 Am. U. L. Rev. 1, 92-94 (2001).]

In reaction to the general warrant, the Framers adopted the Fourth Amendment to the U.S. Constitution. It provides:

> The right of the people to be secure in their persons, houses, papers, and effects, against unreasonable searches and seizures shall not be violated, and no Warrants shall issue, but upon probable cause, supported by Oath or affirmation, and particularly describing the place to be searched, and the persons or things to be seized.

The Amendment presents several threshold issues. First, federal agents can "search" a property just by looking at it from the street, as any member of the public can. Does the Fourth Amendment apply to such a search? In *Katz v. United States*, 389 U.S. 347 (1967), FBI agents placed an electronic listening device on the roof of a public telephone booth in Los Angeles. They did not seek a warrant. The agents recorded the voice of Charles Katz as he engaged in illegal gambling with contacts in other cities. Repudiating earlier Supreme Court precedents that limited Fourth

Amendment coverage to situations in which a physical penetration of a constitution-ally protected place occurred, the *Katz* Court ruled that "the Fourth Amendment protects people, not places." 389 U.S. at 351. But if the applicability of Fourth Amend-ment privacy focuses on people rather than places, what circumstances determine whether personal privacy concerns trigger the protection of the Constitution? Con-curring, Justice Harlan suggested that Fourth Amendment coverage turns on the subjective existence of "a reasonable expectation of privacy." 389 U.S. at 360. The Harlan formulation thus supplies an answer to the question about a "search" of property in the public view. The Fourth Amendment does not bar such a search because the property owners have no reasonable expectation of privacy from public scrutiny. The "reasonable expectation of privacy" also guides courts in deciding whether a "search" has occurred. *See United States v. Jacobsen,* 466 U.S. 109 (1984); *Skinner v. Railway Labor Executives' Ass'n,* 489 U.S. 602 (1989).

Second, how does the warrant requirement in the Fourth Amendment relate to the reasonableness requirement? Is a warrantless search unreasonable *per se?* In 1967, the Supreme Court held that warrantless searches "are *per se* unreasonable — subject only to a few specifically established and well-delineated exceptions." *Katz, supra,* 389 U.S. at 357. It is the neutral determination of probable cause to issue a warrant that makes the warranted search reasonable; without a warrant, a search is presumptively unreasonable, unless it fits an exception.

Warrants, however, are now "more the exception than the rule." Joshua Dress-ler & Alan C. Michaels, *Understanding Criminal Procedure, Volume I: Investigation* 311 (4th ed. 2006). Some exceptions, said to be grounded in necessity, have been declared even in criminal investigations:

- searches incident to arrest, *United States v. Robinson,* 414 U.S. 218 (1973)
- automobile searches, *Michigan v. Long,* 463 U.S. 1032 (1983)
- "hot pursuit" or exigent circumstance searches, *Michigan v. Tyler,* 436 U.S. 499 (1978)
- "stop and frisk" searches, *Terry v. Ohio,* 392 U.S. 1 (1968)

Other exceptions have been recognized for searches conducted for purposes other than criminal investigation, such as accident prevention, protection of public health, or administrative compliance:

- the use of pen register devices, *Smith v. Maryland,* 442 U.S. 735 (1979)
- the contents of banking records, *United States v. Miller,* 425 U.S. 435 (1976)
- searches to prevent railroad accidents that cause "great human loss," *Skinner v. Railway Labor Executives' Ass'n,* 489 U.S. 602, 628 (1989)
- searches to help prevent the spread of disease or contamination during a public health crisis. *Camara v. Municipal Court,* 387 U.S. 523, 539 (1967)

Finally, some warrantless searches are permitted at borders and on the high sea on theories of traditional border control and/or public safety:

- searches of persons and things entering and leaving the United States, *United States v. Montoya de Hernandez,* 473 U.S. 531 (1985)

- searches of boats on navigable waters, *United States v. Villamonte-Marquez*, 462 U.S. 579 (1983)

- searches of airplanes. *United States v. Nigro*, 727 F.2d 100 (6th Cir. 1984) (en banc)

The last two groups of exceptions are sometimes labeled "special needs exceptions," because "special needs, beyond the normal need for [criminal] law enforcement, make the warrant and probable-cause requirement impracticable." *Griffin v. Wisconsin*, 483 U.S. 868, 872 (1987) (quoting *New Jersey v. T.L.O.*, 469 U.S. 325, 351 (1985) (Blackmun, J., concurring in judgment)). Although "special needs" may be "no more than a label that indicates a lax standard will apply," William J. Stuntz, *Implicit Bargains, Government Power, and the Fourth Amendment*, 44 Stan. L. Rev. 553, 554 (1992), that standard is still the reasonableness balancing standard. Dressler & Michaels, *supra*, at 327.

In view of the devastation wrought by the airline hijackings on September 11, 2001, it is not hard to find a special need for warrantless preboarding airplane searches:

> When the risk is the jeopardy to hundreds of human lives and millions of dollars of property inherent in the pirating or blowing up of a large airplane, that danger alone meets the test of reasonableness, so long as the search is conducted in good faith for the purpose of preventing hijacking or like damage and with reasonable scope, and the passenger has been given notice of his liability to such a search so that he can avoid it by choosing not to travel by air. [*United States v. Edwards*, 498 F.2d 496, 500 (2d Cir. 1974).]

See also John Rogers, *Bombs, Borders, and Boarding: Combating International Terrorism at United States Airports and the Fourth Amendment*, 20 Suffolk Transnat'l L. Rev. 501 (1997); Chapter 8.

What about a search prompted by nothing more than an anonymous tip of a planned bombing? In one case the Supreme Court remarked that it did not need to

> speculate about the circumstances under which the danger alleged in an anonymous tip might be so great as to justify a search even without a showing of reliability. We do not say, for example, that a report of a person carrying a bomb need bear the indicia of reliability we demand for a report of a person carrying a firearm before the police can constitutionally conduct a frisk. [*Florida v. J.L.*, 529 U.S. 266, 273-274 (2000).]

How does the anonymous tip case compare to the exceptional cases just mentioned? What additional facts about the bomb threat or the government's proposal concerning who or what was searched would you want to know before authorizing the search?

Should concern for national security justify warrantless electronic surveillance of Americans suspected in some way of being connected to terrorist threats? Should it provide the basis for video surveillance of streets, parks, and other public places? If there is a national security exception to the warrant requirement, what is the scope of the exception, and what procedures should substitute for the warrant process? Consider the following assessment.

William C. Banks & M.E. Bowman, Executive
Authority for National Security Surveillance

50 Am. U. L. Rev. 1, 92-94 (2001)

Although the Fourth Amendment eliminated the abuses of general warrants, its commands remain unclear, especially in the face of technological progress. Moreover, the Fourth Amendment was designed to protect against overreaching in investigations of criminal enterprises. Investigations of politically motivated threats to our national security, such as terrorism or espionage, were simply not contemplated. . . .

Terrorism presents a unique set of challenges in the United States. First, current criminal laws and traditional law enforcement processes cannot provide absolute protection against terrorist acts. While arrest, prosecution, and incarceration serve well to help prevent most crimes from occurring, the risk of catastrophic harm from terrorist attacks forces us to consider other means of prevention. Moreover, traditional Fourth Amendment requirements may thwart many investigations of terrorism, which depend on stealth to prevent terrorist plans before they are carried out.

Second, while terrorism is at its core a national security problem, it represents an unusual confluence of phenomena for the investigative community — the primary purpose of the investigation may be simultaneously and in equal measure law enforcement and national security. With few exceptions, the rules for gathering intelligence about terrorism in the United States are no different from the rules for ordinary criminal investigations.

Third, most prognostications are for more threats of terrorism in the United States in coming years, largely due to the perception that our defenses against conventional attacks are so formidable. Greater threats thus place an additional premium on greater intelligence resources and successes.

The tradition of liberty in the United States casts a shadow over all national security surveillance, and is an overriding problem in addressing terrorism concerns. The core openness of our society permits all of us, including the potential terrorist, considerable freedom to move about, to associate with others, and to act in furtherance of political aims. As recent terrorist incidents in the United States have created a sense of urgency among citizens and government officials to find better preventive strategies, reflection has also reminded us that hasty actions to thwart terrorism may threaten the freedoms that permit an open society. Thus, in seeking ways to investigate potential terrorist activity, just as in fashioning better responses to terrorist incidents, the measures adopted must not undermine our basic freedoms.

B.   A NATIONAL SECURITY EXCEPTION?

Foreign Intelligence Surveillance Act of 1977

S. Rep. No. 95-604, at 9-12 (1977)
[hereinafter *Senate Report No. 604*]

. . . In 1928, the Supreme Court in *Olmstead v. United States* [277 U.S. 468] held that wiretapping was not within the coverage of the Fourth Amendment. Three years later, Attorney General William D. Mitchell authorized telephone wiretapping, upon the personal approval of bureau chiefs, of syndicated bootleggers and in "exceptional cases where the crimes are substantial and serious, and the necessity is great and [the bureau chief and the Assistant Attorney General] are satisfied that the persons whose wires are to be tapped are of the criminal type." These general guidelines governed the Department's practice through the thirties and telephone wiretapping was considered to be an important law enforcement tool.

Congress placed the first restrictions on wiretapping in the Federal Communications Act of 1934, which made it a crime for any person "to intercept and divulge or publish the contents of wire and radio communications." [48 Stat. 1103.] The Supreme Court construed this section to apply to Federal agents and held that evidence obtained from the interception of wire and radio communications and the fruits of the evidence, were inadmissible in court. [*Nardone v. United States*, 302 U.S. 379 (1937); 308 U.S. 338 (1939).] However, the Justice Department did not interpret the Federal Communications Act or the *Nardone* decision as prohibiting the interception of wire communications per se; rather only the interception and divulgence of their contents outside the Federal establishment was considered to be unlawful. Thus, the Justice Department found continued authority for its national security wiretaps.

In 1940, President Roosevelt issued a memorandum to the Attorney General stating his view that electronic surveillance would be proper under the Constitution where "grave matters involving defense of the nation" were involved. The President authorized and directed the Attorney General "to secure information by listening devices [directed at] the conversation or other communications of persons suspected of subversive activities against the Government of the United States, including suspected spies." The Attorney General was requested "to limit these investigations so conducted to a minimum and to limit them insofar as possible to aliens."

This practice was continued in successive administrations....

In the early fifties, however, Attorney General J. Howard McGrath took the position that he would not approve or authorize the installation of microphone surveillances by means of trespass. This policy was quickly reversed by Attorney General Herbert Brownell in 1954 in a sweeping memorandum to FBI Director Hoover instructing him that the Bureau was indeed authorized to conduct such trespassory surveillances regardless of the fact of surreptitious entry, and without the need to first acquire the Attorney General's authorization. Such surveillance was simply authorized whenever the Bureau concluded that the "national interest" so required....

In *Katz v. United States*, 389 U.S. 347 (1967), the Supreme Court finally discarded the *Olmstead* doctrine and held that the Fourth Amendment's warrant provision did apply to electronic surveillance. The Court explicitly declined, however, to extend its holding to cases "involving the national security." 389 U.S. at 358 n.23. The next year, Congress followed suit: responding to the *Katz* case, Congress enacted the Omnibus Crime Control and Safe Streets Act (18 U.S.C. §§2510-2520). Title III of that Act established a procedure for the judicial authorization of electronic surveillance for the investigation and prevention of specified types of serious crimes and the use of the product of such surveillance in court proceedings. It prohibited wiretapping and electronic surveillance by persons other than duly authorized law enforcement officers, personnel of the Federal Communications Commission, or communication common carriers monitoring communications in the normal course of their employment.

Title III, however, disclaimed any intention of legislating in the national security area....

Associate Justice Lewis F. Powell Jr.

Copyright © 1986, Ken Heinen.

United States v. United States District Court (*Keith*)[1]

United States Supreme Court, 1972
407 U.S. 297

Mr. JUSTICE POWELL delivered the opinion of the Court. The issue before us is an important one for the people of our country and their Government. It involves the delicate question of the President's power, acting through the Attorney General, to authorize electronic surveillance in internal security matters without prior judicial approval. . . . This case brings the issue here for the first time. Its resolution is a matter of national concern, requiring sensitivity both to the Government's right to protect itself from unlawful subversion and attack and to the citizen's right to be secure in his privacy against unreasonable Government intrusion.

This case arises from a criminal proceeding in the United States District Court for the Eastern District of Michigan, in which the United States charged three defendants with conspiracy to destroy Government property in violation of 18 U.S.C. §371. One of the defendants, Plamondon, was charged with the dynamite bombing of an office of the Central Intelligence Agency in Ann Arbor, Michigan.

During pretrial proceedings, the defendants moved to compel the United States to disclose certain electronic surveillance information and to conduct a hearing to determine whether this information "tainted" the evidence on which the indictment was based or which the Government intended to offer at trial. In response, the Government filed an affidavit of the Attorney General, acknowledging that its agents had overheard conversations in which Plamondon had participated. The affidavit also stated that the Attorney General approved the wiretaps "to gather intelligence information deemed necessary to protect the nation from attempts of domestic organizations to attack and subvert the existing structure of the Government." The logs of the surveillance were filed in a sealed exhibit for in camera inspection by the District Court.

On the basis of the Attorney General's affidavit and the sealed exhibit, the Government asserted that the surveillance was lawful, though conducted without prior judicial approval, as a reasonable exercise of the President's power (exercised through the Attorney General) to protect the national security. The District Court held that the surveillance violated the Fourth Amendment, and ordered the Government to make full disclosure to Plamondon of his overheard conversations.

[1. This case is commonly referred to by the name of the federal district court judge who first heard it, Damon J. Keith. — Eds.]

... [T]he Court of Appeals for the Sixth Circuit ... held that the surveillance was unlawful and that the District Court had properly required disclosure of the overheard conversations. ...

I

Title III of the Omnibus Crime Control and Safe Streets Act, 18 U.S.C. §§2510-2520, authorizes the use of electronic surveillance for classes of crimes carefully specified in 18 U.S.C. §2516. Such surveillance is subject to prior court order. Section 2518 sets forth the detailed and particularized application necessary to obtain such an order, as well as carefully circumscribed conditions for its use. The Act represents a comprehensive attempt by Congress to promote more effective control of crime while protecting the privacy of individual thought and expression. Much of Title III was drawn to meet the constitutional requirements for electronic surveillance enunciated by this Court in *Berger v. New York*, 388 U.S. 41 (1967), and *Katz v. United States*, 389 U.S. 347 (1967).

Together with the elaborate surveillance requirements in Title III, there is the following proviso, 18 U.S.C. §2511(3):

Nothing contained in this chapter or in section 605 of the Communications Act of 1934 (48 Stat. 1143; 47 U.S.C. 605) shall limit the constitutional power of the President to take such measures as he deems necessary to protect the Nation against actual or potential attack or other hostile acts of a foreign power, to obtain foreign intelligence information deemed essential to the security of the United States, or to protect national security information against foreign intelligence activities. *Nor shall anything contained in this chapter be deemed to limit the constitutional power of the President to take such measures as he deems necessary to protect the United States against the overthrow of the Government by force or other unlawful means, or against any other clear and present danger to the structure or existence of the Government.* The contents of any wire or oral communication intercepted by authority of the President in the exercise of the foregoing powers may be received in evidence in any trial hearing, or other proceeding only where such interception was reasonable, and shall not be otherwise used or disclosed except as is necessary to implement that power. (Emphasis supplied.)

The Government relies on §2511(3). It argues that "in excepting national security surveillances from the Act's warrant requirement Congress recognized the President's authority to conduct such surveillances without prior judicial approval." The section thus is viewed as a recognition or affirmance of a constitutional authority in the President to conduct warrantless domestic security surveillance such as that involved in this case.

We think the language of §2511(3), as well as the legislative history of the statute, refutes this interpretation. The relevant language is that: "Nothing contained in this chapter ... shall limit the constitutional power of the President to take such measures as he deems necessary to protect ..." against the dangers specified. At most, this is an implicit recognition that the President does have certain powers in the specified areas. Few would doubt this, as the section refers—among other things—to protection "against actual or potential attack or other hostile acts of a foreign power." But so far as the use of the President's electronic surveillance power is concerned, the language is essentially neutral.

Section 2511(3) certainly confers no power, as the language is wholly inappropriate for such a purpose. It merely provides that the Act shall not be interpreted to limit or disturb such power as the President may have under the Constitution. In short, Congress simply left presidential powers where it found them....

... [I]t would have been incongruous for Congress to have legislated with respect to the important and complex area of national security in a single brief and nebulous paragraph. This would not comport with the sensitivity of the problem involved or with the extraordinary care Congress exercised in drafting other sections of the Act. We therefore think the conclusion inescapable that Congress only intended to make clear that the Act simply did not legislate with respect to national security surveillances....

... [V]iewing §2511(3) as a congressional disclaimer and expression of neutrality, we hold that the statute is not the measure of the executive authority asserted in this case. Rather, we must look to the constitutional powers of the President.

II

It is important at the outset to emphasize the limited nature of the question before the Court. This case raises no constitutional challenge to electronic surveillance as specifically authorized by Title III of the Omnibus Crime Control and Safe Streets Act of 1968. Nor is there any question or doubt as to the necessity of obtaining a warrant in the surveillance of crimes unrelated to the national security interest. Further, the instant case requires no judgment on the scope of the President's surveillance power with respect to the activities of foreign powers, within or without this country. The Attorney General's affidavit in this case states that the surveillances were "deemed necessary to protect the nation from attempts of *domestic organizations* to attack and subvert the existing structure of Government" (emphasis supplied). There is no evidence of any involvement, directly or indirectly, of a foreign power.[8]

Our present inquiry, though important, is therefore a narrow one. It addresses a question left open by *Katz*: "Whether safeguards other than prior authorization by a magistrate would satisfy the Fourth Amendment in a situation involving the national security...." The determination of this question requires the essential Fourth Amendment inquiry into the "reasonableness" of the search and seizure in question, and the way in which that "reasonableness" derives content and meaning through reference to the warrant clause.

... [T]he President of the United States has the fundamental duty, under Art. II, §1, of the Constitution, to "preserve, protect and defend the Constitution of the United States." Implicit in that duty is the power to protect our Government against those who would subvert or overthrow it by unlawful means. In the discharge of this

---

8. Section 2511(3) refers to "the constitutional power of the President" in two types of situations: (i) where necessary to protect against attack, other hostile acts or intelligence activities of a "foreign power"; or (ii) where necessary to protect against the overthrow of the Government or other clear and present danger to the structure or existence of the Government. Although both of the specified situations are sometimes referred to as "national security" threats, the term "national security" is used only in the first sentence of §2511(3) with respect to the activities of foreign powers. This case involves only the second sentence of §2511(3), with the threat emanating—according to the Attorney General's affidavit—from "domestic organizations." Although we attempt no precise definition, we use the term "domestic organization" in this opinion to mean a group or organization (whether formally or informally constituted) composed of citizens of the United States and which has no significant connection with a foreign power, its agents or agencies. No doubt there are cases where it will be difficult to distinguish between "domestic" and "foreign" unlawful activities directed against the Government of the United States where there is collaboration in varying degrees between domestic groups or organizations and agents or agencies of foreign powers. But this is not such a case.

duty, the President — through the Attorney General — may find it necessary to employ electronic surveillance to obtain intelligence information on the plans of those who plot unlawful acts against the Government. The use of such surveillance in internal security cases has been sanctioned more or less continuously by various Presidents and Attorneys General since July 1946. . . .

Though the Government and respondents debate their seriousness and magnitude, threats and acts of sabotage against the Government exist in sufficient number to justify investigative powers with respect to them. The covertness and complexity of potential unlawful conduct against the Government and the necessary dependency of many conspirators upon the telephone make electronic surveillance an effective investigatory instrument in certain circumstances. The marked acceleration in technological developments and sophistication in their use have resulted in new techniques for the planning, commission, and concealment of criminal activities. It would be contrary to the public interest for Government to deny to itself the prudent and lawful employment of those very techniques which are employed against the Government and its law-abiding citizens. . . .

But a recognition of these elementary truths does not make the employment by Government of electronic surveillance a welcome development — even when employed with restraint and under judicial supervision. There is, understandably, a deep-seated uneasiness and apprehension that this capability will be used to intrude upon cherished privacy of law-abiding citizens. We look to the Bill of Rights to safeguard this privacy. Though physical entry of the home is the chief evil against which the wording of the Fourth Amendment is directed, its broader spirit now shields private speech from unreasonable surveillance. Our decision in *Katz* refused to lock the Fourth Amendment into instances of actual physical trespass. Rather, the Amendment governs "not only the seizure of tangible items, but extends as well to the recording of oral statements . . . without any 'technical trespass under . . . local property law.'" . . . *Katz, supra*, at 353. . . .

National security cases, moreover, often reflect a convergence of First and Fourth Amendment values not present in cases of "ordinary" crime. Though the investigative duty of the executive may be stronger in such cases, so also is there greater jeopardy to constitutionally protected speech. "Historically the struggle for freedom of speech and press in England was bound up with the issue of the scope of the search and seizure power," *Marcus v. Search Warrant*, 367 U.S. 717, 724 (1961). History abundantly documents the tendency of Government — however benevolent and benign its motives — to view with suspicion those who most fervently dispute its policies. Fourth Amendment protections become the more necessary when the targets of official surveillance may be those suspected of unorthodoxy in their political beliefs. The danger to political dissent is acute where the Government attempts to act under so vague a concept as the power to protect "domestic security." Given the difficulty of defining the domestic security interest, the danger of abuse in acting to protect that interest becomes apparent. . . .

III

As the Fourth Amendment is not absolute in its terms, our task is to examine and balance the basic values at stake in this case: the duty of Government to protect the domestic security, and the potential danger posed by unreasonable surveillance to individual privacy and free expression. If the legitimate need of Government to safeguard domestic security requires the use of electronic surveillance, the question is whether the needs of citizens for privacy and free expression may not be better protected by requiring a warrant before such surveillance is undertaken. We must also ask whether a warrant requirement would unduly frustrate the efforts of Government to protect itself from acts of subversion and overthrow directed against it.

Though the Fourth Amendment speaks broadly of "unreasonable searches and seizures," the definition of "reasonableness" turns, at least in part, on the more specific commands of the warrant clause. . . .

. . . [W]here practical, a governmental search and seizure should represent both the efforts of the officer to gather evidence of wrongful acts and the judgment of the magistrate that the collected evidence is sufficient to justify invasion of a citizen's private premises or conversation. Inherent in the concept of a warrant is its issuance by a "neutral and detached magistrate." The further requirement of "probable cause" instructs the magistrate that baseless searches shall not proceed.

These Fourth Amendment freedoms cannot properly be guaranteed if domestic security surveillances may be conducted solely within the discretion of the Executive Branch. . . . The historical judgment, which the Fourth Amendment accepts, is that unreviewed executive discretion may yield too readily to pressures to obtain incriminating evidence and overlook potential invasions of privacy and protected speech.

It may well be that, in the instant case, the Government's surveillance of Plamondon's conversations was a reasonable one which readily would have gained prior judicial approval. But this Court "has never sustained a search upon the sole ground that officers reasonably expected to find evidence of a particular crime and voluntarily confined their activities to the least intrusive means consistent with that end." *Katz, supra,* at 356-357. The Fourth Amendment contemplates a prior judicial judgment, not the risk that executive discretion may be reasonably exercised. This judicial role accords with our basic constitutional doctrine that individual freedoms will best be preserved through a separation of powers and division of functions among the different branches and levels of Government. The independent check upon executive discretion is not satisfied, as the Government argues, by "extremely limited" post-surveillance judicial review. Indeed, post-surveillance review would never reach the surveillances which failed to result in prosecutions. . . .

It is true that there have been some exceptions to the warrant requirement. But those exceptions are few in number and carefully delineated; in general, they serve the legitimate needs of law enforcement officers to protect their own wellbeing and preserve evidence from destruction. Even while carving out those exceptions, the Court has reaffirmed the principle that the "police must, whenever practicable, obtain advance judicial approval of searches and seizures through the warrant procedure," *Terry v. Ohio,* [392 U.S. 1, 20 (1968)].

The Government argues that the special circumstances applicable to domestic security surveillances necessitate a further exception to the warrant requirement. It is urged that the requirement of prior judicial review would obstruct the President in the discharge of his constitutional duty to protect domestic security. We are told further that these surveillances are directed primarily to the collecting and maintaining of intelligence with respect to subversive forces, and are not an attempt to gather evidence for specific criminal prosecutions. It is said that this type of surveillance should not be subject to traditional warrant requirements which were established to govern investigation of criminal activity, not ongoing intelligence gathering.

The Government further insists that courts "as a practical matter would have neither the knowledge nor the techniques necessary to determine whether there was probable cause to believe that surveillance was necessary to protect national security." These security problems, the Government contends, involve "a large number of complex and subtle factors" beyond the competence of courts to evaluate.

As a final reason for exemption from a warrant requirement, the Government believes that disclosure to a magistrate of all or even a significant portion of the information involved in domestic security surveillances "would create serious potential dangers to the national security and to the lives of informants and agents. . . . Secrecy is the essential ingredient in intelligence gathering; requiring prior judicial authorization would create a greater 'danger of leaks . . . because in addition to the judge, you have the clerk, the stenographer and some other officer like a law assistant or bailiff who may be apprised of the nature' of the surveillance." . . .

. . . There is, no doubt, pragmatic force to the Government's position.

But we do not think a case has been made for the requested departure from Fourth Amendment standards. . . . Security surveillances are especially sensitive because of the inherent vagueness of the domestic security concept, the necessarily broad and continuing nature of intelligence gathering, and the temptation to utilize such surveillances to oversee political dissent. We recognize, as we have before, the constitutional basis of the President's domestic security role, but we think it must be exercised in a manner compatible with the Fourth Amendment. In this case we hold that this requires an appropriate prior warrant procedure.

We cannot accept the Government's argument that internal security matters are too subtle and complex for judicial evaluation. Courts regularly deal with the most difficult issues of our society. There is no reason to believe that federal judges will be insensitive to or uncomprehending of the issues involved in domestic security cases. . . . If the threat is too subtle or complex for our senior law enforcement officers to convey its significance to a court, one may question whether there is probable cause for surveillance.

Nor do we believe prior judicial approval will fracture the secrecy essential to official intelligence gathering. The investigation of criminal activity has long involved imparting sensitive information to judicial officers who have respected the confidentialities involved. Judges may be counted upon to be especially conscious of security requirements in national security cases. Title III of the Omnibus Crime Control and Safe Streets Act already has imposed this responsibility on the judiciary in connection with such crimes as espionage, sabotage, and treason, §2516(1)(a) and (c), each of which may involve domestic as well as foreign security threats. Moreover, a warrant application involves no public or adversary proceedings: it is an *ex parte* request before a magistrate or judge. Whatever security dangers clerical and secretarial personnel may pose can be minimized by proper administrative measures, possibly to the point of allowing the Government itself to provide the necessary clerical assistance.

Thus, we conclude that the Government's concerns do not justify departure in this case from the customary Fourth Amendment requirement of judicial approval prior to initiation of a search or surveillance. Although some added burden will be imposed upon the Attorney General, this inconvenience is justified in a free society to protect constitutional values. Nor do we think the Government's domestic surveillance powers will be impaired to any significant degree. A prior warrant establishes presumptive validity of the surveillance and will minimize the burden of justification in post-surveillance judicial review. By no means of least importance will be the reassurance of the public generally that indiscriminate wiretapping and bugging of law-abiding citizens cannot occur.

IV

. . . [W]e do not hold that the same type of standards and procedures prescribed by Title III are necessarily applicable to this case. We recognize that domestic security surveillance may involve different policy and practical considerations from the surveillance of "ordinary crime." The gathering of security intelligence is often long range and involves the interrelation of various sources and types of information. The exact targets of such surveillance may be more difficult to identify than in surveillance operations against many types of crime specified in Title III. Often, too, the emphasis of domestic intelligence gathering is on the prevention of unlawful activity or the enhancement of the Government's preparedness for some possible future crisis or emergency. Thus, the focus of domestic surveillance may be less precise than that directed against more conventional types of crime.

Given these potential distinctions between Title III criminal surveillances and those involving the domestic security, Congress may wish to consider protective standards for the latter which differ from those already prescribed for specified crimes in Title III. Different standards may be compatible with the Fourth Amendment if they are reasonable both in relation to the legitimate need of Government for intelligence information and the protected rights of our citizens. For the warrant application may vary according to the governmental interest to be enforced and the nature of citizen rights deserving protection. . . .

. . . We . . . hold . . . that prior judicial approval is required for the type of domestic security surveillance involved in this case and that such approval may be made in accordance with such reasonable standards as the Congress may prescribe.

V

As the surveillance of Plamondon's conversations was unlawful, because conducted without prior judicial approval, the courts below correctly held that *Alderman v. United States*, 394 U.S. 165 (1969), is controlling and that it requires disclosure to the accused of his own impermissibly intercepted conversations. As stated in *Alderman*, "the trial court can and should, where appropriate, place a defendant and his counsel under enforceable orders against unwarranted disclosure of the materials which they may be entitled to inspect." 394 U.S. at 185.

The judgment of the Court of Appeals is hereby affirmed.

The CHIEF JUSTICE concurs in the result.

[The concurring opinions of DOUGLAS and WHITE, JJ., are omitted.]

NOTES AND QUESTIONS

1. *The Nature of the Privacy Interest.* Has your phone ever been tapped, or have you suspected that it was? Ever had your mail opened? Your e-mail or the history of your Internet use read by others without your permission? How did you feel (or how do you

think you would feel) upon discovering such an intrusion? Would you feel better knowing that a judge had issued a warrant to authorize it?

While acknowledging that "physical entry of the home is the chief evil" addressed by the Fourth Amendment, the Court found in *Keith*, as it had in *Katz*, that the "broader spirit" of the Amendment protects telephone conversations as well. But what is it about electronic surveillance that the Court found objectionable? Is it that a "search" of private conversations is being conducted, or is it the "convergence of First and Fourth Amendment values"? Does the privacy protected by the Court cover just governmental acquisition of personal or intimate information? By analogy, should the protection extend to information we reveal to others? *See* Chapter 9.

Arguably, a physical search may be less intrusive than a wiretap, especially if the electronic surveillance continues for weeks or months after the initial intrusion. *See Olmstead v. United States*, 277 U.S. 438, 473 (1928) (Brandeis, J., dissenting); *Berger v. New York*, 388 U.S. 41, 60 (1967).

Why is this freedom from unreasonable searches important to individuals? What purpose does it serve in society? *See generally* Alan Westin, *Privacy and Freedom* (1967).

2. *Inherent Surveillance Authority?* Does Article II, Section 1, implicitly authorize the President to conduct electronic surveillance? *See In re Neagle*, 135 U.S. 1 (1890). Does Article II distinguish between domestic and foreign national security threats?

If the President possesses some independent constitutional authority to engage in domestic electronic surveillance, why, according to the *Keith* Court, is an exception to the warrant requirement not appropriate?

3. *The Baseline for Comparison: Ordinary Criminal (Title III) Electronic Surveillance.* Title III requires that an application for authorization to conduct electronic surveillance contain detailed information about the alleged criminal offense, the facilities and communication sought to be intercepted, the identity of the target (if known), the period of time sought for surveillance, and an explanation of whether other investigative methods have failed or why they are unlikely to succeed or are too dangerous. 18 U.S.C. §2518(1)(b)-(d) (2006). A court may issue an order for electronic surveillance only if it finds probable cause that communications related to the commission of a crime will be obtained through the surveillance. *Id.* §2518(3)(b). Can you see why intelligence agencies would seek to avoid the strictures of Title III in conducting electronic surveillance for intelligence purposes?

Title III also requires a warrant before the government may obtain access to stored communications, such as e-mail, during the first 180 days of storage. 18 U.S.C. §2703(a) (2006 & Supp. III 2009). After 180 days, the government may obtain access to stored communications pursuant to a search warrant or, after notice to the subscriber, pursuant to an administrative or grand jury subpoena or a court order. *Id.* §2703. See Chapter 9. Likewise, cell phones, display pagers, and voice pagers are protected by Title III. 18 U.S.C. §2510(1), (12) (2006).

4. *Deciding Whether a Warrant Should Issue.* Is probable cause the sole criterion for authorizing a warrant? Might it be appropriate for a magistrate to consider the extent to which the information sought is of an intimate nature? Or what uses the government intends for the information? *See* Russell D. Covey, *Pervasive Surveillance and the Future of the Fourth Amendment*, 80 Miss. L.J. 1289 (2011) (so arguing).

5. *Balancing Away the Warrant Requirement.* Does the Warrant Clause of the Fourth Amendment adequately protect privacy interests? What is the function of a "neutral and detached magistrate" in a warrant proceeding? Why did the government object to the warrant procedure for electronic surveillance in *Keith*?

Orin Kerr argues that the Warrant Clause plays only a modest role in national security investigations because courts are poorly equipped to decide whether a warrant requirement would be reasonable in the national security setting. Orin S. Kerr, *The Modest Role of the Warrant Clause in National Security Investigations*, 88 Tex. L. Rev. 1669 (2010). Professor Kerr explains that, unlike the usual Fourth Amendment case, in which police conduct a search and the court then decides whether the already executed, judicially warranted search met Fourth Amendment requirements, judges in national security investigations must decide in advance about hypothetical facts concerning hypothetical investigations, based on an unclear standard:

> Under . . . *Keith* . . . whether a warrant is required is based on whether requiring a warrant is workable, but that depends on what standard is required for obtaining a warrant. . . . [W]hat standard is required for obtaining a warrant depends on what kind of standard would make a warrant standard workable. [*Id.* at 1675-1676.]

Does Professor Kerr accurately describe the way the Warrant Clause was applied in *Keith*? Would you expect the Warrant Clause to diminish in importance in national security investigations? If so, what would take its place?

How did the *Keith* Court balance the President's Article II powers against the Fourth Amendment warrant requirement for domestic subjects? Did the Court fairly reconcile "the Government's right to protect itself from unlawful subversion and attack" with "the citizen's right to be secure in his privacy against unreasonable Government intrusion"? Should the Court have attached more importance to the fact that a magistrate's role could be performed more efficiently by after-the-fact judicial review where surveillance abuses are alleged?

6. *Warrantless Surveillance "To Save American Lives."* In December 2005, the *New York Times* revealed the existence of a four-year, large-scale warrantless electronic surveillance program that intercepted communications of some U.S. citizens. James Risen & Eric Lichtblau, *Bush Lets U.S. Spy on Callers Without Courts*, N.Y. Times, Dec. 16, 2005. At a White House press conference, President Bush offered this explanation for the warrantless surveillance:

> . . . We know that a two-minute phone conversation between somebody linked to al Qaeda here and an operative overseas could lead directly to the loss of thousands of lives. To save American lives, we must be able to act fast and to detect these conversations so that we can prevent new attacks.
>
> So, consistent with U.S. law and the Constitution, I authorized the interception of international communications of people with known links to al Qaeda and related terrorist organizations. . . .
>
> . . . I've reauthorized this program more than 30 times since the September 11th attacks, and I intend to do so for so long as our nation . . . faces the continuing threat of an enemy that wants to kill American citizens. [Press Conference of the President (Dec. 19, 2005).]

Assuming, arguendo, that Congress has enacted no applicable statute, would you agree, based on *Keith*, that the program described by the President is constitutional? Other aspects of this program are considered in Chapter 8.

7. *Domestic vs. Foreign Threats.* Justice Powell's interpretation of §2511(3) may have been crucial to the outcome of the case. His willingness to draw a sharp distinction between a "domestic organization" and "foreign" activities in the United States became the predicate for establishing the Fourth Amendment warrant requirement for "domestic" national security investigations. Why is the power to protect "domestic security" viewed with greater skepticism by the Court than the power to protect against foreign perils? Are the two concepts really different? Are foreign threats to national security necessarily greater than domestic ones? Does §2511(3) clearly reflect such a sharp distinction in the origin of national security threats?

Justice Powell also concluded that §2511(3) "is essentially neutral" regarding presidential power. Do you agree? Consider the provision's last sentence.

C.   A FOREIGN INTELLIGENCE EXCEPTION?

In *Keith*, Justice Powell suggested that national security wiretaps may not have to meet all the Fourth Amendment requirements applicable in criminal investigations, but he did not specify what alternative processes might be appropriate in such cases. Nor did the Court refer to the constitutional requirements for other forms of surveillance, such as searches of the home and person. The Court also emphasized that *Keith* did not involve any foreign power, but was strictly a case involving "domestic security."

Meanwhile, the agencies within the intelligence community had, since their inception after World War II, been developing their own guidelines for national security surveillance. After *Keith*, several lower courts considered the applicability of the Fourth Amendment to surveillance to obtain foreign intelligence.

...The Fifth Circuit in *United States v. Brown*, 484 F.2d 418 (5th Cir. 1973), *cert. denied*, 415 U.S. 960 (1974), upheld the legality of a surveillance in which the defendant, an American citizen, was incidentally overheard as a result of a warrantless wiretap authorized by the Attorney General for foreign intelligence purposes. The court found that on the basis of "the President's constitutional duty to act for the United States in the field of foreign affairs, and his inherent power to protect national security in the conduct of foreign affairs . . . the President may constitutionally authorize warrantless wiretaps for the purpose of gathering foreign intelligence." [484 F.2d at 426.]

In *United States v. Butenko*, 494 F.2d 593 (3d Cir. 1974) (en banc), *cert. denied sub nom. Ivanov v. United States*, 419 U.S. 881 (1974), the Third Circuit similarly held that electronic surveillance conducted without a warrant would be lawful so long as the primary purpose was to obtain foreign intelligence information. The court found that such surveillance would be reasonable under the Fourth Amendment without a warrant even though it might involve the overhearing of conversations.

However, in *Zweibon v. Mitchell*, 516 F.2d 594 (D.C. Cir. 1975), *cert. denied*, 425 U.S. 944 (1976), the Circuit Court of Appeals for the District of Columbia, in the course of an opinion requiring that a warrant must be obtained before a wiretap is installed on a domestic organization that is neither the agent of, nor acting in collaboration with, a foreign power, questioned whether any national security exception to the warrant requirement would be constitutionally permissible.

Although the holding of *Zweibon* was limited to the case of a domestic organization without ties to a foreign power, the plurality opinion of the court—in legal analysis closely patterned on *Keith*—concluded "that an analysis of the policies implicated by foreign security surveillance indicates that, absent exigent circumstances, all warrantless electronic surveillance is unreasonable and therefore unconstitutional." [*Senate Report No. 604, supra* p. 170, at 14, 15.]

Note that the Supreme Court declined to hear the appeals in each of these cases.

Zweibon was a suit for damages by members of the Jewish Defense League (JDL) for unlawful electronic surveillance. Although the JDL is a U.S. organization, JDL protest actions directed against Soviet facilities inside the United States risked a significant foreign relations problem with the Soviet Union. Despite the fact that "Soviet officials vigorously and continuously protested these activities, for which they held the United States Government responsible," 516 F.2d at 608, 609, the D.C. Circuit refused to rule that this foreign affairs tension was cause to waive the Fourth Amendment warrant requirement. *Id.* at 614. A similar result was reached in *Berlin Democratic Club v. Rumsfeld*, 410 F. Supp. 144 (D.D.C. 1976), where a warrant was required to wiretap Americans living in West Germany despite Department of Defense arguments about dangers to United States forces and to American foreign policy. *Id.* at 157.

While these lower court decisions about a possible foreign intelligence exception to the warrant requirement concerned wiretaps to collect foreign intelligence, the FBI also conducted warrantless physical searches. The Church Committee found that

> [b]efore 1966, the FBI conducted over two hundred "black bag jobs." These warrantless surreptitious entries were carried out for intelligence purposes *other than* microphone installation, such as physical search and photographing or seizing documents.
>
> ... [T]here is no indication that the FBI informed any Attorney General about its use of "black bag jobs."
>
> Surreptitious entries were performed by teams of FBI agents with special training in subjects such as "lock studies." Their missions were authorized in writing by FBI Director Hoover or his deputy, Clyde Tolson. A "Do Not File" procedure was utilized, under which most records of surreptitious entries were destroyed soon after an entry was accomplished.
>
> The use of surreptitious entries against domestic targets dropped drastically after J. Edgar Hoover banned "black bag jobs" in 1966. . . . [S. Select Comm. to Study Governmental Operations with Respect to Intelligence Activities (Church Committee), *Intelligence Activities and the Rights of Americans*, S. Rep. No. 94-755, bk. III, at 355 (1976).]

One such black bag job was challenged in the following case, in which the government raised the defense of a foreign intelligence exception to the warrant requirement.

United States v. Ehrlichman

United States District Court, District of Columbia, 1974
376 F. Supp. 29, *aff'd*, 546 F.2d 910 (D.C. Cir. 1976),
cert. denied, 429 U.S. 1120 (1977)

GESELL, J. Five defendants stand indicted for conspiring to injure a Los Angeles psychiatrist [Dr. Lewis Fielding] in the enjoyment of his Fourth Amendment rights by entering his offices without a warrant for the purpose of obtaining the doctor's medical records relating to one of his patients, a Daniel Ellsberg, then under Federal indictment for revealing top secret documents. They now claim that broad pretrial discovery into the alleged national security aspects of this case is essential to the presentation of their defense, in that it will establish (1) that the break-in was legal under the Fourth Amendment because the President authorized it for reasons of national security, and (2) that even in the absence of such authorization the national security information available to the defendants at that time led them to the good-faith, reasonable belief that the break-in was legal and justified in the national interest. The Court has carefully considered these assertions, which have been fully briefed and argued over a two-day period, and finds them to be unpersuasive as a matter of law. . . .

The Fourth Amendment protects the privacy of citizens against unreasonable and unrestrained intrusion by Government officials and their agents. It is not theoretical. It lies at the heart of our free society. As the Supreme Court recently remarked, "no right is held more sacred." *Terry v. Ohio*, 392 U.S. 1, 9 (1968). Indeed, the American Revolution was sparked in part by the complaints of the colonists against the issuance of writs of assistance, pursuant to which the King's revenue officers conducted unrestricted, indiscriminate searches of persons and homes to uncover contraband. James Otis' famous argument in Lechmere's Case, challenging the writ as a "monster of oppression" and a "remnant of Star Chamber tyranny," sowed one of the seeds of the coming rebellion. The Fourth Amendment was framed against this background; and every state in the Union, by its own constitution, has since reinforced the protections and the security which that Amendment was designed to achieve.

Thus the security of one's privacy against arbitrary intrusion by governmental authorities has proven essential to our concept of ordered liberty. When officials have attempted to justify law enforcement methods that ignore the strictures of this Amendment on grounds of necessity, such excuses have proven fruitless, for the Constitution brands such conduct as lawless, irrespective of the end to be served. Throughout the years the Supreme Court of the United States, regardless of changes in its composition or contemporary issues, has steadfastly applied the Amendment to protect a citizen against the warrantless invasion of his home or office, except under carefully delineated emergency circumstances. No right so fundamental should now, after the long struggle against governmental trespass, be diluted to accommodate conduct of the very type the Amendment was designed to outlaw.

The break-in charged in this indictment involved an unauthorized entry and search by agents of the Executive branch of the Federal Government. It is undisputed that no warrant was obtained and no Magistrate gave his approval. Moreover, none of the traditional exceptions to the warrant requirement are claimed and none existed; however desirable the break-in may have appeared to its instigators, there is no indication that it had to be carried out quickly, before a warrant could have been obtained. On the contrary, it had been meticulously planned over a period of more than a month. The search of Dr. Fielding's office was therefore clearly illegal under the unambiguous mandate of the Fourth Amendment.

Defendants contend that even though the Fourth Amendment would ordinarily prohibit break-ins of this nature, the President has the authority, by reason of his special responsibilities over foreign relations and national defense, to suspend its requirements, and that he did so in this case. Neither assertion is accurate. Many of the landmark Fourth Amendment cases in this country and in England concerned citizens accused of disloyal or treasonous conduct, for history teaches that such suspicions foster attitudes within a government that generate conduct inimical to individual rights. See *United States v. United States District Court*, 407 U.S. 297, 314 (1972). The judicial response to such Executive overreaching has been consistent and emphatic: the Government must comply with the strict constitutional and statutory limitations on trespassory searches and arrests even when known foreign agents are involved. To hold otherwise, except under the most exigent circumstances, would be to abandon the Fourth Amendment to the whim of the Executive in total disregard of the Amendment's history and purpose.

Defendants contend that, over the last few years, the courts have begun to carve out an exception to this traditional rule for purely intelligence-gathering searches deemed necessary for the conduct of foreign affairs. However, the cases cited are carefully limited to the issue of wiretapping, a relatively nonintrusive search, *United States v. Butenko*, 494 F.2d 593 (3d Cir. 1974); *United States v. Brown*, 484 F.2d 418 (5th Cir. 1973); *Zweibon v. Mitchell*, 363 F. Supp. 936 (D.D.C. 1973), and the Supreme Court has reserved judgment in this unsettled area. *United States v. United States District Court*, 407 U.S. 297, 322 n.20 (1972). The Court cannot find that this recent, controversial judicial response to the special problem of national security wiretaps indicates an intention to obviate the entire Fourth Amendment whenever the President determines that an American citizen, personally innocent of wrongdoing, has in his possession information that may touch upon foreign policy concerns.[4] Such a doctrine, even in the context of purely information-gathering searches, would give the Executive a blank check to disregard the very heart and core of the Fourth Amendment and the vital privacy interests that it protects....

The facts presented pretrial lead the Court to conclude as a matter of law that the President not only lacked the authority to authorize the Fielding break-in but also that he did not in fact give any specific directive permitting national security break-ins, let alone this particular intrusion. The President has repeatedly and publicly denied prior knowledge or authorization of the Fielding break-in, and the available transcripts of the confidential tape recordings support that claim.... [The evidence reflected] intense Presidential concern with the need to plug the national security leaks and a belief that Dr. Ellsberg might be involved, but no specific reference either to Dr. Fielding or to trespassory searches....

Defendants adopt the fall-back position that even if the President did not specifically authorize the Fielding break-in, he properly delegated to one or more of the defendants or unindicted co-conspirators the authority to approve national security break-ins. Of course, since the President had no such authority in the first place, he could not have delegated it to others. Beyond this, however, the Court rejects the contention that the President could delegate his alleged power to suspend constitutional rights to non-law enforcement officers in the vague, informal, inexact terms noted above. Even in the wiretap cases the courts have stressed the fact that the

---

4. The doctrine of the President's inherent authority as "the sole organ of the nation in its external relations," 10 Annals of Cong. 613 (1800) (remarks of John Marshall), has been developed by a series of Supreme Court decisions dealing with the President's power to enter into international agreements and to prohibit commercial contracts which impede American foreign policy. *United States v. Curtiss-Wright Export Corp.*, 299 U.S. 304 (1936). None of these cases purport to deal with the constitutional rights of American citizens or with Presidential action in defiance of congressional legislation. When such issues have arisen, Executive assertions of inherent authority have been soundly rejected. See *Kent v. Dulles*, 357 U.S. 116 (1958); *Youngstown Sheet & Tube Co. v. Sawyer*, 343 U.S. 579 (1952).

President had specifically delegated the authority over "national security" wiretaps to his chief legal officer, the Attorney General, who approved each such tap. *See, e.g., Katz v. United States*, 389 U.S. 347, 364 (1967) (White, J., concurring). Whatever accommodation is required between the guarantees of the Fourth Amendment and the conduct of foreign affairs, it cannot justify a casual, ill-defined assignment to White House aides and part-time employees granting them an uncontrolled discretion to select, enter and search the homes and offices of innocent American citizens without a warrant. *Cf. Ex parte Milligan*, 71 U.S. (4 Wall.) 2 (1866); *Ex parte Merryman*, 17 Fed. Cas. p. 144, 151 (No. 9,487) (C.C. Md. 1861)....

Defendants' motions for discovery are granted to the extent set forth above and are denied in all other respects. The motion for dismissal because of the danger of exposing national security information is denied.

NOTES AND QUESTIONS

1. *Comparing Searches and Electronic Surveillance.* Is physical entry of the home more threatening to civil liberties than a wiretap? Microphone surveillance at one time required entry to install the device, which would, like a wiretap, transmit all conversations, including those not subject to the investigation. If a physical search is controlled, it will take less time and may focus only on material relevant to the investigation. Yet for many of us, invasion of our physical space is more threatening than the prospect of electronic surveillance. Why is that so?

2. *Accountability for the Exception.* While the D.C. Circuit Court affirmed the conviction in *United States v. Ehrlichman*, 546 F.2d 910 (D.C. Cir. 1976), *cert. denied*, 429 U.S. 1120 (1977), the panel was more circumspect than Judge Gesell. The court merely held that no "national security" exception to the warrant requirement could be invoked without specific authorization by the President or Attorney General. *Id.* at 925. Judge Wilkey elaborated:

> The danger of leaving delicate decisions of propriety and probable cause to those actually assigned to ferret out "national security" information is patent, and is indeed illustrated by the intrusion undertaken in this case, without any more specific Presidential direction than that ascribed to Henry II vexed with Becket.[68] As a constitutional matter, if Presidential approval is to replace judicial approval for foreign intelligence gathering, the personal authorization of the President — or his alter ego for these matters, the Attorney General — is necessary to fix accountability and centralize responsibility for insuring the least intrusive surveillance necessary and preventing zealous officials from misusing the President's prerogative. [*Id.* at 926.]

3. *Executive (or Congressional) Approval as a Warrant Substitute?* Would the substitution of the President's or Attorney General's approval for a search compensate for the loss of the warrant procedure? The Attorney General at the time of the Fielding break-in was John N. Mitchell, who was subsequently sent to prison for perjury and conspiracy in connection with efforts to cover up the burglary of the Democratic National

---

68. Attributed as "Who will free me from this turbulent priest?" [Thomas Becket, the Archbishop of Canterbury, was murdered in 1170 by followers of Henry II, who are said to have interpreted Henry's remarks as a royal command. — Eds.]

Committee headquarters at the Watergate in Washington. The President was Richard M. Nixon, who was named an unindicted co-conspirator in the same affair. *See United States v. Haldeman*, 559 F.2d 31, 51 (D.C. Cir. 1976). Would presidential or attorney general approval of a search be a lawful substitute for probable cause if Congress approved such a regime by statute? See Chapter 7.

   4. *A Domestic Intelligence Exception?* At the time of the break-in, Ellsberg had been indicted for disclosing the *Pentagon Papers* (a classified account of American involvement in the Vietnam War) to reporters. Ehrlichman and his co-defendants argued that "the search was legal because [it was] undertaken pursuant to a delegated Presidential power to authorize such a search in the field of foreign affairs." *Ehrlichman*, 546 F.2d at 913. However, there was no accusation that Ellsberg or his psychiatrist had any relationship to a foreign power. What does Judge Wilkey's dictum, *supra* Note 2, suggest about the parameters of any such "national security" exception to the warrant requirement?
   Consider again the warrantless surveillance program described by President Bush, *supra.* Does the *Ehrlichman* decision change your view about the constitutionality of the more recent surveillance program, again assuming no controlling legislative authority?

   5. *Applying the Exception to Other Searches.* If there is some "national security" exception to the warrant requirement, is there a principled basis for limiting the exception to electronic surveillance? *See United States v. Ehrlichman*, 546 F.2d at 938 (Leventhal, J., concurring); David S. Eggert, Note, *Executive Order 12,333: An Assessment of the Validity of Warrantless National Security Searches*, 1983 Duke L.J. 611, 627-628. *See also* Banks & Bowman, *supra* p. 170, at 67 ("In light of the potentially greater intrusiveness of electronic surveillance, it may be reasonable to expect greater executive discretion to conduct warrantless searches than warrantless wiretaps."). In addition to the degree of intrusion, what factors should be taken into account in deciding whether the warrant requirement applies? *See id.* at 67-68.
   Should place matter? Although the Supreme Court in *Katz* famously proclaimed that the Fourth Amendment protects people, not places, even in *Katz* the defendant's use of a telephone booth became a "temporarily private place whose momentary occupants' expectations of freedom from intrusion are recognized as reasonable." 389 U.S. at 361 (Harlan, J., concurring). The distinction between people and places may thus be blurry, perpetuated by Justice Harlan's reasonable expectation of privacy test. Can you think of a better test that takes into account the nature of the intrusion, the type of privacy at risk, and the government's interests in acquiring and perhaps using the information?
   Unlike a physical search, most computer searches involve the remote collection of digital electronic data. Is a computer search therefore a "search" under the Fourth Amendment? Under what circumstances are computer data "seized," and when would such a search or seizure be "reasonable"? Computer searches "challenge several of the basic assumptions underlying Fourth Amendment doctrine. Computers are like containers in a physical sense, homes in a virtual sense, and vast warehouses in an informational sense." Orin S. Kerr, *Searches and Seizures in a Digital World*, 119 Harv. L. Rev. 531, 533 (2005). Which perspective do you find most helpful in thinking about application of the Fourth Amendment to Internet and computer searches?

United States v. Truong Dinh Hung

United States Court of Appeals, Fourth Circuit, 1980
629 F.2d 908, *cert. denied*, 454 U.S. 1144 (1982)

WINTER, J. Truong Dinh Hung, more familiarly known as David Truong, and Ronald Humphrey were convicted of espionage, conspiracy to commit espionage and several espionage-related offenses for transmitting classified United States government information to representatives of the government of the Socialist Republic of Vietnam. In these appeals, they seek reversal of their convictions because of warrantless surveillance and searches. . . .

We hold that the warrantless searches and surveillance did not violate the Fourth Amendment. . . .

David Truong, a Vietnamese citizen and son of a prominent Vietnamese political figure, came to the United States in 1965. At least since his arrival in the United States, Truong has pursued an active scholarly and political interest in Vietnam and the relationship between Vietnam and the United States. In 1976, Truong met Dung Krall, a Vietnamese-American, the wife of an American Naval Officer, who had extensive contacts among the Vietnamese community in Paris. Truong persuaded Krall to carry packages for him to Vietnamese in Paris. The recipients were representatives of the Socialist Republic of Vietnam at the time of the 1977 Paris negotiations between that country and the United States. The packages contained copies of diplomatic cables and other classified papers of the United States government dealing with Southeast Asia. Truong procured the copies from Ronald Humphrey, an employee of the United States Information Agency, who obtained the documents surreptitiously, copied them, removed their classification markings and furnished the copies to Truong. In a statement given after his arrest, Humphrey said that his motive was to improve relations between the North Vietnamese government and the United States so that he could be reunited with a woman whom he loved who was a prisoner of the North Vietnamese government.

Unknown to Truong, Krall was a confidential informant employed by the CIA and the FBI. Krall kept these agencies fully informed of Truong's activities and presented the packages Truong had given her to the FBI for inspection, copying and approval before she carried the documents to Paris. The FBI permitted this operation to continue, while monitoring it closely, from approximately September, 1976, until January 31, 1978.

When the intelligence agencies first learned that Truong was transmitting classified documents to Paris, they were understandably extremely anxious to locate Truong's source for his data. Toward that end, the government conducted a massive surveillance of Truong. Truong's phone was tapped and his apartment was bugged from May, 1977 to January, 1978. The telephone interception continued for 268 days and every conversation, with possibly one exception, was monitored and virtually all were taped. The eavesdropping device was operative for approximately 255 days and it ran continuously. No court authorization was ever sought or obtained for the installation and maintenance of the telephone tap or the bug. The government thus ascertained that Humphrey was providing Truong with the copies of secret documents. This leak of sensitive information of course ceased when Truong and Humphrey were arrested on January 31, 1978. . . .

The defendants raise a substantial challenge to their convictions by urging that the surveillance conducted by the FBI violated the Fourth Amendment and that all the evidence uncovered through that surveillance must consequently be suppressed. As has been stated, the government did not seek a warrant for the eavesdropping on Truong's phone conversations or the bugging of his apartment. Instead, it relied upon a "foreign intelligence" exception to the Fourth Amendment's warrant requirement. In the area of foreign intelligence, the government contends, the President may authorize surveillance without seeking a judicial warrant because of his constitutional prerogatives in the area of foreign affairs. On this basis, the FBI sought and received approval for the surveillance from the President's delegate, the Attorney General. This approval alone, according to the government, is constitutionally sufficient to authorize foreign intelligence surveillance such as the surveillance of Truong....

...Although the Supreme Court has never decided the issue which is presented to us, it formulated the analytical approach which we employ here in an analogous case, *United States v. United States District Court* (*Keith*), 407 U.S. 297 (1972)....

For several reasons, the needs of the executive are so compelling in the area of foreign intelligence, unlike the area of domestic security, that a uniform warrant requirement would, following *Keith,* "unduly frustrate" the President in carrying out his foreign affairs responsibilities. First of all, attempts to counter foreign threats to the national security require the utmost stealth, speed, and secrecy. A warrant requirement would add a procedural hurdle that would reduce the flexibility of executive foreign intelligence initiatives, in some cases delay executive response to foreign intelligence threats, and increase the chance of leaks regarding sensitive executive operations.

More importantly, the executive possesses unparalleled expertise to make the decision whether to conduct foreign intelligence surveillance, whereas the judiciary is largely inexperienced in making the delicate and complex decisions that lie behind foreign intelligence surveillance. The executive branch, containing the State Department, the intelligence agencies, and the military, is constantly aware of the nation's security needs and the magnitude of external threats posed by a panoply of foreign nations and organizations. On the other hand, while the courts possess expertise in making the probable cause determination involved in surveillance of suspected criminals, the courts are unschooled in diplomacy and military affairs, a mastery of which would be essential to passing upon an executive branch request that a foreign intelligence wiretap be authorized. Few, if any, district courts would be truly competent to judge the importance of particular information to the security of the United States or the "probable cause" to demonstrate that the government in fact needs to recover that information from one particular source.

Perhaps most crucially, the executive branch not only has superior expertise in the area of foreign intelligence, it is also constitutionally designated as the preeminent authority in foreign affairs. The President and his deputies are charged by the constitution with the conduct of the foreign policy of the United States in times of war and peace. See *United States v. Curtiss-Wright Corp.,* 299 U.S. 304 (1936). Just as the separation of powers in *Keith* forced the executive to recognize a judicial role when the President conducts domestic security surveillance, so the separation of powers requires us to acknowledge the principal responsibility of the President for foreign affairs and concomitantly for foreign intelligence surveillance.

In sum, because of the need of the executive branch for flexibility, its practical experience, and its constitutional competence, the courts should not require the executive to secure a warrant each time it conducts foreign intelligence surveillance.[4]

However, because individual privacy interests are severely compromised any time the government conducts surveillance without prior judicial approval, this foreign intelligence exception to the Fourth Amendment warrant requirement must be carefully limited to those situations in which the interests of the executive are paramount. First, the government should be relieved of seeking a warrant only when the object of the search or the surveillance is a foreign power, its agent or collaborators. In such cases, the government has the greatest need for speed, stealth, and secrecy, and the surveillance in such cases is most likely to call into play difficult and subtle judgments about foreign and military affairs. When there is no foreign connection, the executive's needs become less compelling; and the surveillance more closely resembles the surveillance of suspected criminals, which must be authorized by warrant. Thus, if the government wishes to wiretap the phone of a government employee who is stealing sensitive documents for his personal reading or to leak to a newspaper, for instance, the absence of a foreign connection and the importance of individual privacy concerns contained within the Fourth Amendment lead to a requirement that the executive secure advance judicial approval for surveillance. . . .

Second . . . the executive should be excused from securing a warrant only when the surveillance is conducted "primarily" for foreign intelligence reasons. We think that the district court adopted the proper test, because once surveillance becomes primarily a criminal investigation, the courts are entirely competent to make the usual probable cause determination, and because, importantly, individual privacy interests come to the fore and government foreign policy concerns recede when the government is primarily attempting to form the basis for a criminal prosecution. We thus reject the government's assertion that, if surveillance is to any degree directed at gathering foreign intelligence, the executive may ignore the warrant requirement of the Fourth Amendment.

The defendants urge that the "primarily" test does not go far enough to protect privacy interests. They argue that the government should be able to avoid the warrant requirement only when the surveillance is conducted "solely" for foreign policy reasons. The proposed "solely" test is unacceptable, however, because almost all foreign intelligence investigations are in part criminal investigations. Although espionage prosecutions are rare, there is always the possibility that the targets of the investigation will be prosecuted for criminal violations. Thus, if the defendants' "solely" test were adopted, the executive would be required to obtain a warrant almost every time it undertakes foreign intelligence surveillance, and, as indicated above, such a

---

4. Since the surveillance was conducted in this case, Congress has enacted the Foreign Intelligence Surveillance Act of 1978, 50 U.S.C. §1801 et seq. . . . While the Act suggests that it is possible for the executive branch to conduct at least some types of foreign intelligence surveillance while being subject to a warrant requirement, the complexity of the statute also suggests that the imposition of a warrant requirement, beyond the constitutional minimum described in this opinion, should be left to the intricate balancing performed in the course of the legislative process by Congress and the President. The elaborate structure of the statute demonstrates that the political branches need great flexibility to reach the compromises and formulate the standards which will govern foreign intelligence surveillance. Thus, the Act teaches that it would be unwise for the judiciary, inexpert in foreign intelligence, to attempt to enunciate an equally elaborate structure for core foreign intelligence surveillance under the guise of a constitutional decision. Such an attempt would be particularly ill-advised because it would not be easily subject to adjustment as the political branches gain experience in working with a warrant requirement in the foreign intelligence area.

requirement would fail to give adequate consideration to the needs and responsibilities of the executive in the foreign intelligence area.

In this case, the district court concluded that on July 20, 1977, the investigation of
Truong had become primarily a criminal investigation. Although the Criminal Division of the Justice Department had been aware of the investigation from its inception,
until summer the Criminal Division had not taken a central role in the investigation.
On July 19 and July 20, however, several memoranda circulated between the Justice
Department and the various intelligence and national security agencies indicating
that the government had begun to assemble a criminal prosecution. . . .

Therefore, because there was more than enough evidence to indicate that
Truong had collaborated with the Vietnamese government and because the district
court did not err in choosing July 20 as the date when the investigation became
primarily a criminal investigation, we do not disturb the decision of the district
court to exclude all evidence obtained through the surveillance after July 20 but to
permit the government to introduce evidence secured through the surveillance
before July 20.

Because the Fourth Amendment warrant requirement is a critical constitutional
protection of individual privacy, this discussion should conclude by underscoring the
limited nature of this foreign intelligence exception to the warrant requirement
which we recognize in the instant case. The exception applies only to foreign powers,
their agents, and their collaborators. Moreover, even these actors receive the protection of the warrant requirement if the government is primarily attempting to put
together a criminal prosecution. . . .

NOTES AND QUESTIONS

1. *The "Primary Purpose" Doctrine.* The court in *Truong* concluded that the standard for deciding the constitutionality of warrantless foreign intelligence surveillance
that eventually became a criminal investigation was whether the "primary purpose" of
the search was in fact to obtain foreign intelligence information. At what point does
an investigation change from "primarily" foreign intelligence collection to "primarily" law enforcement? Does the "primary purpose" rule adequately accommodate the
competing interests? Although FISA had been enacted by the time of the *Truong*
decision, the surveillance of Truong was conducted before FISA and therefore not
governed by its terms. However, the "primary purpose" standard became influential
in construing the FISA authorization for intelligence surveillance. See Chapter 7.

2. *Deciding Reasonableness.* The court also found that intercepting Truong's
phone calls and listening to conversations with visitors to Truong's apartment were
"reasonable" efforts to locate the source of the purloined documents. 629 F.2d at 916-
917. In light of the court's conclusion that no warrant was required for at least part of
the surveillance, does it necessarily follow that the surveillance was reasonable?
According to what criteria should reasonableness be determined?

3. *Package Searches.* Although the discussion of surveillance in *Truong* is not specifically directed to either electronic or non-electronic surveillance as such, the court
did independently consider the constitutionality of the searches of packages Truong
sent to Paris with Krall. The search of a letter and package conducted with executive

authorization but without a warrant before the July 20 date at which the surveillance became, in the court's view, criminal in nature, was treated as governed by a foreign intelligence exception to the warrant requirement. *Id.* at 916-917. Another package searched without either the authorization of the Attorney General or a warrant was not covered by a foreign intelligence exception to the warrant requirement but was nonetheless constitutional, according to the court, because Truong had no reasonable expectation of privacy in the package. *Id.*

4. *Reconciling the Cases?* Is there any way to square the reasoning of the court in *Truong* with the holding of the Supreme Court in *Keith?* With the holding by Judge Gesell in *Ehrlichman?* Does the *Truong* court's reasoning apply equally to inspection of sealed parcels and to installation of surveillance cameras in a target's workplace or home?

5. *Less Intrusive Surveillance.* First and Fourth Amendment interests have not always received such extensive judicial protection where arguably less intrusive information collection techniques are employed. For example, in an area that is open to visual surveillance, the monitoring of beeper signals from a radio transmitter placed in contraband material and picked up by a police radio receiver does not trigger Fourth Amendment protections, because the target has no legitimate expectation of privacy. *United States v. Knotts*, 460 U.S. 276, 284-285 (1983). The same result applies when the police use the beeper signal to monitor movements, so long as visual surveillance could have performed the monitoring. *Id.* at 285.

What are the implications of this extension of *Katz* — that someone who "knowingly exposes" her movements to others in a public place has no reasonable expectation of privacy — when others, including police or intelligence officials, take note of or record those movements? *Katz v. United States*, 389 U.S. 347, 351 (1967). Does this reduced expectation insulate from constitutional challenge the use of evolving technologies such as video cameras, video tracking devices, radio transmitting devices, visual magnification, and biometrics and face recognition for surveillance in public places? *See* Marc Jonathan Blitz, *Video Surveillance and the Constitution of Public Space: Fitting the Fourth Amendment to a World That Tracks Image and Identity*, 82 Tex. L. Rev. 1349, 1375-1398 (2004). Can you say which places are public and which are private? Is it conceivable that the growing use of evolving technologies to provide physical, or visual surveillance of individuals may become so pervasive and intense that it will constitute a Fourth Amendment search? *See* Afsheen John Radsan, *The Case for Stewart over Harlan on 24/7 Physical Surveillance*, 88 Tex. L. Rev. 1475, 1480 (2010) (so arguing).

In *Laird v. Tatum*, 408 U.S. 1, 10 (1972), the Supreme Court dismissed on standing grounds a complaint against an Army program that investigated civil disturbances by collecting personal information about individuals and organizations. *See also Socialist Workers Party v. Attorney Gen.*, 510 F.2d 253 (2d Cir. 1974) (approving undercover FBI surveillance of convention of Young Socialists of America). *But see Philadelphia Yearly Meeting of the Religious Soc'y of Friends v. Tate*, 519 F.2d 1335 (3d Cir. 1975) (approving photography and compilation of records on political demonstrators but not the sharing of information with private employers or broadcasters). Constitutional protections generally have not been extended to investigations based on the use of informants and the examination of financial records held by third parties. *See* John Elliff, *The Attorney General's Guidelines for FBI Investigations*,

69 Cornell L. Rev. 785, 788-789 (1984). Should the courts be more solicitous of individual rights in these cases?

6. *Effect of New Technologies on Fourth Amendment Law.* Does changing technology affect what privacy deserves constitutional protection? In *Kyllo v. United States*, 533 U.S. 27 (2001), decided a few months before 9/11, the police used thermal imaging technology to measure the heat radiating from the exterior walls of a private home to verify suspicions that high-intensity lamps were being used to grow marijuana indoors. Because the sense-enhancing technology permitted intrusion into the home that would not otherwise have been possible without physical intrusion, and because the thermal imaging technique is not in general public use, the Court found that the homeowner had a reasonable expectation of privacy that was violated. *Id.* at 34-35. What are the implications of the holding of *Kyllo* today, when weapons of mass destruction (WMD) terrorism threats may be monitored by nanotech sensors and scanning devices not yet in general use that may help prevent deployment of a WMD in a major city? *See* Covey, *supra* p. 179.

In 2010, the Supreme Court explained that the *Katz* Court "relied on its own knowledge and experience" in finding a reasonable expectation of privacy in a telephone booth, *City of Ontario v. Quon*, 130 S. Ct. 2619 (2010), but cautioned that "[i]t is not so clear that courts at present are on so sure a ground." *Id.* at 2629. The Court noted that

> [r]apid changes in the dynamics of communication and information transmission are evident not just in the technology itself but in what society accepts as proper behavior. . . .
> . . . Cell phone and text message communications are so pervasive that some persons may consider them to be essential means or necessary instruments for self-expression, even self-identification. [*Id.* at 2629-2630.]

In the 1980s, the Supreme Court decided two cases involving the use of a government-installed locating device — a beeper — to monitor a suspect's location. In *United States v. Knotts*, 460 U.S. 276 (1983), no warrant was required when the surveillance revealed the location of the beeper in a public place, while in *United States v. Karo*, 468 U.S. 705 (1984), a warrant was required when the beeper was traced to the inside of a home. As we write, the equivalent issue is the use of global positioning system (GPS) devices for surveillance. GPS "is a satellite-based technology that reveals information about the location, speed, and direction of a targeted subject." Renee McDonald Hutchins, *Tied Up in Knotts? GPS Technology and the Fourth Amendment*, 55 UCLA L. Rev. 409, 414 (2007). Law enforcement authorities may use GPS technology for real-time tracking of targets in a range of settings. Are GPS devices sufficiently different from beepers that their use should require a traditional warrant? *See* Alison M. Smith, *Law Enforcement Use of Global Positioning (GPS) Devices to Monitor Motor Vehicles: Fourth Amendment Considerations* (Cong. Res. Serv. R41663), Feb. 28, 2011.

In many cities today, public cameras are ubiquitous, and video surveillance in stores, banks, mass transit facilities, and other places where crowds gather is now commonplace. Do individuals have important privacy interests in these public places that are threatened by the new surveillance systems? What predictions can you make about constitutional challenges to these new surveillance technologies? *See* Radsan, *supra*, 88 Tex. L. Rev. at 1490-1493; Covey, *supra*.

Congressional Authority for Foreign Intelligence Surveillance

7

Communications and surveillance technologies have undergone explosive growth since the digital and dot-com revolutions of the 1980s and 1990s. Both ordinary and Internet communications can be intercepted, and cell phone calls can be traced to the phone's location. Hidden recorders may preserve conversations, while parabolic microphones capture voices at long distances. Video surveillance cameras permit government officials to monitor public areas by closed-circuit television. Global positioning system (GPS) devices and electronic toll systems permit remote, 24/7 tracing of an individual's movements. Computer-driven scanners can search through millions of e-mail messages in a heartbeat. Emerging nanotechnology and bio-engineering will expand further the horizons of the government's capabilities for surveillance.

By providing the means to watch and listen to people and to trace their movements, electronic surveillance can help to detect and prevent terrorism and other security threats. It also may help to find those responsible for security-related crimes after the fact.

Yet unlike physical searches for particular information or things, electronic surveillance records everything a target says or does. Especially when undertaken over a long period on a continual basis, electronic surveillance casts a wide and open-ended net, capturing data that may be at best irrelevant and at worst deeply personal.

The Constitution contains two provisions that can guard against government abuses of such advanced technology. The Fourth Amendment was included in the Bill of Rights to counter any tendency toward the kind of intimidation practiced by the English Crown against its citizens. The First Amendment was added as a bulwark against government intrusions that could dampen political expression.

This chapter turns from the evolution of Fourth Amendment and national security surveillance law in the courts, discussed in Chapter 6, to statutory authorization for foreign intelligence surveillance in the Foreign Intelligence Surveillance Act (FISA), 50 U.S.C. §§1801-1881g (2006 & Supp. III 2009), as amended by Pub. L. No. 111-259, §801, 124 Stat. 2654, 2746 (2010). In Part A, we introduce the core FISA requirements and procedures for electronic surveillance and physical searches. (We separately examine FISA authorizations for pen registers, trap and trace devices, and the collection of business records in Chapter 9.) In Part B, we consider the tension — and, for a time, the "wall" — between surveillance to collect evidence for criminal law enforcement and surveillance to collect foreign intelligence. Finally, in Part C, we briefly assess trends in FISA electronic and physical surveillance.

A.   THE FOREIGN INTELLIGENCE SURVEILLANCE ACT (FISA): CORE REQUIREMENTS AND PROCEDURES

Two events prompted congressional enactment of FISA in 1978. First, the Supreme Court decision in *Keith* ended by asserting that "Congress may wish to consider protective standards for [domestic security surveillance] . . . which differ from those already prescribed for specified crimes in Title III." *United States v. United States District Court (Keith)*, 407 U.S. 297, 322 (1972), *supra* p. 172. Second, in addition to the Watergate scandal in 1973, the early 1970s saw startling revelations of illegal spying and other activities by U.S. intelligence agencies, including the FBI and CIA, and by the IRS and the military. These agencies sought to target and disrupt politically active domestic groups (principally civil rights and anti-war organizations), see *supra* pp. 147-171, and they engaged in widespread warrantless surveillance. The Senate Select Committee to Study Government Operations with Respect to Intelligence Activities, known as the Church Committee, for its chairman Senator Frank Church, summarized the effects of these domestic intelligence abuses in a 1976 report:

> . . . FBI headquarters alone has developed over 500,000 domestic intelligence files, and these have been augmented by additional files at FBI Field Offices. The FBI opened 65,000 of these domestic intelligence files in 1972 alone. In fact, substantially more individuals and groups are subject to intelligence scrutiny than the number of files would appear to indicate, since typically, each domestic intelligence file contains information on more than one individual or group, and this information is readily retrievable through the FBI General Name Index.
>
> The number of Americans and domestic groups caught in the domestic intelligence net is further illustrated by the following statistics:
>
> - Nearly a quarter of a million first class letters were opened and photographed in the United States by the CIA between 1953-1973, producing a CIA computerized index of nearly one and one-half million names.
> - At least 130,000 first class letters were opened and photographed by the FBI between 1940-1966 in eight U.S. cities.
> - Some 300,000 individuals were indexed in a CIA computer system and separate files were created on approximately 7,200 Americans and over 100 domestic groups during the course of CIA's Operation CHAOS (1967-1973).
> - Millions of private telegrams sent from, to, or through the United States were obtained by the National Security Agency from 1947 to 1975 under a secret arrangement with three United States telegraph companies.
> - An estimated 100,000 Americans were the subjects of United States Army intelligence files created between the mid-1960's and 1971.
> - Intelligence files on more than 11,000 individuals and groups were created by the Internal Revenue Service between 1969 and 1973 and tax investigations were started on the basis of political rather than tax criteria.
> - At least 26,000 individuals were at one point catalogued on an FBI list of persons to be rounded up in the event of a "national emergency."

[S. Select Comm. to Study Government Operations with Respect to Intelligence Activities (Church Committee), *Intelligence Activities and the Rights of Americans,* S. Rep. No. 94-755, bk. II, at 6-7 (1976).]

Most of these surveillance and collection abuses were rationalized as foreign intelligence gathering. When Congress finally responded to the Supreme Court's invitation in *Keith,* therefore, it enacted standards for *foreign intelligence surveillance* inside the United States, not domestic security surveillance. In *United States v. Duggan,* 743 F.2d 59 (2d Cir. 1984), the court opined that

> Congress passed FISA to settle what it believed to be the unresolved question of the applicability of the Fourth Amendment warrant requirement to electronic surveillance for foreign intelligence purposes, and to "remove any doubt as to the lawfulness of such surveillance." H.R. Rep. 1283, pt. I, 95th Cong., 2d Sess. 25 (1978) ("House Report"). FISA reflects both Congress's "legislative judgment" that the court orders and other procedural safeguards laid out in the Act "are necessary to insure that electronic surveillance by the U.S. Government within this country conforms to the fundamental principles of the fourth amendment," S. Rep. No. 701, 95th Cong., 2d Sess. 13, *reprinted in* 1978 U.S. Code Cong. & Ad. News 3973, 3982 ("Senate Report 95-701"), and its attempt to fashion a "secure framework by which the Executive Branch may conduct legitimate electronic surveillance for foreign intelligence purposes within the context of this Nation's commitment to privacy and individual rights." S. Rep. No. 604, 95th Cong., 1st Sess. 15, *reprinted in* 1978 U.S. Code Cong. & Ad. News 3904, 3916 ("Senate Report 95-604"). [743 F.2d at 73.]

Domestic security surveillance, on the other hand, was by default left subject to the existing Title III criminal law enforcement framework.

Consider how FISA applied to the defendants in the following case.

United States v. Rosen

United States District Court, Eastern District of Virginia, 2006
447 F. Supp. 2d 538

ELLIS, District Judge. Defendants, Steven J. Rosen and Keith Weissman, are charged . . . with one count of conspiring to communicate national defense information to persons not entitled to receive it, in violation of 18 U.S.C. §793(d), (e) and (g). More specifically, Count One . . . alleges that between April 1999 and continuing until August 2004, Rosen and Weissman along with alleged co-conspirator Lawrence Franklin, then an employee of the Department of Defense ("DOD"), were engaged in a conspiracy to communicate information relating to the national defense to those not entitled to receive it. According to the superseding indictment, Franklin and certain other unnamed government officials with authorized possession of classified national defense information communicated that information to Rosen and Weissman, who were employed at the time as lobbyists for the American-Israel Public Affairs Committee (AIPAC). It is further alleged that Rosen and Weissman then communicated the information received from their government sources to members of the media, other foreign policy analysts, and certain foreign officials, none of whom were authorized to receive this information. . . .

In the course of its investigation of the alleged conspiracy, the government sought and obtained orders issued by the Foreign Intelligence Surveillance Court ("FISC") pursuant to the Foreign Intelligence Surveillance Act ("FISA"), 50 U.S.C. §1801 *et seq.*, authorizing certain physical searches and electronic surveillance. As the investigation pertained to national security, these applications and orders were classified. Because the government intends to offer evidence obtained or derived from physical searches and electronic surveillance authorized by these orders, defendants seek by motion (1) to obtain disclosure of the classified applications submitted to the FISC, the FISC's orders, and related materials, and/or (2) to suppress the evidence obtained or derived from any searches or surveillance conducted pursuant to the issued FISA orders. . . .

I.

FISA, enacted in 1978, was Congress's response to three related concerns: (1) the judicial confusion over the existence, nature and scope of a foreign intelligence exception to the Fourth Amendment's warrant requirement that arose in the wake of the Supreme Court's 1972 decision in *United States v. United States District Court*, 407 U.S. 297 (1972); (2) the Congressional concern over perceived Executive Branch abuses of such an exception;[2] and (3) the felt need to provide the Executive Branch with an appropriate means to investigate and counter foreign intelligence threats.[3] FISA accommodates these concerns by establishing a detailed process the Executive Branch must follow to obtain orders allowing it to collect foreign intelligence information "without violating the rights of citizens of the United States." *United States v. Hammoud*, 381 F.3d 316, 332 (4th Cir. 2004) (en banc), *vacated on other grounds*, 543 U.S. 1097 (2005), *reinstated in pertinent part*, 405 F.3d 1034 (2005). Although originally limited to electronic surveillance, FISA's coverage has now been expanded to include physical searches, as well. . . .[4]

FISA's detailed procedure for obtaining orders authorizing electronic surveillance or physical searches of a foreign power or an agent of a foreign power begins with the government's filing of an *ex parte*, under seal application with the FISC.[5] Such an application must be approved by the Attorney General and must include certain specified information. *See* 50 U.S.C. §§1804(a) and 1823(a). A FISC judge considering the application may also require the submission of additional information necessary to make the requisite findings under §§1805(a) and 1824(a).

---

2. *See* S. Rep. No. 95-604(I), at 7, 1978 U.S.C.C.A.N. 3904, 3908 [hereinafter S. Judiciary Comm. Rep.] ("This legislation is in large measure a response to the revelations that warrantless electronic surveillance in the name of national security has been seriously abused.").

3. *See generally* William C. Banks and M.E. Bowman, *Executive Authority for National Security Surveillance*, 50 Am. U. L. Rev. 1, 75-76 (2000) (describing the impetus for FISA).

4. *See* Intelligence Authorization Act for Fiscal Year 1995, Pub. L. No. 103-359, 108 Stat. 3443 (1994) (codified as amended at 50 U.S.C. §1821 *et seq.*). And, in 1998, Congress further amended FISA to create slightly different procedures for authorizing the use of pen registers and trap and trace devices for foreign intelligence information, *see* Intelligence Authorization Act for Fiscal Year 1999, Pub. L. No. 105-272, 112 Stat. 2405 (1998) (codified as amended at 50 U.S.C. §1841 *et seq.*), and to allow the executive branch access to business records for foreign intelligence and international terrorism investigations. *See* 18 U.S.C. §§1861-63. The parties' dispute involves only electronic surveillance and physical searches conducted pursuant to FISA.

5. The FISC consists of eleven district court judges selected by the Chief Justice from at least seven judicial circuits and serving staggered seven year terms. *See* 50 U.S.C. §1803(a). At least three of the FISC's judges must reside within twenty miles of Washington, D.C. *Id.* In the unlikely event that a FISA application is denied by a judge of the FISC, the government may seek review of such denial in the Foreign Intelligence Surveillance Court of Review (FISCR), and if necessary, in the Supreme Court of the United States. *See* 50 U.S.C. §1803(b).

After review of the application, a single judge of the FISC must enter an *ex parte* Order granting the government's application for electronic surveillance or a physical search of a foreign power or an agent of a foreign power provided the judge makes certain specific findings, including most importantly, that on the basis of the facts submitted by the applicant there is probable cause to believe that—

(1) the target of the electronic surveillance or physical search is a foreign power or an agent of a foreign power, except that no United States person may be considered a foreign power or an agent of a foreign power solely upon the basis of activities protected by the First Amendment to the Constitution of the United States; and

(2) for electronic surveillance, each of the facilities or places at which the electronic surveillance is directed is being used, or is about to be used, by a foreign power or an agent of a foreign power; or

(3) for physical searches, the premises or property to be searched is owned, used, possessed by, or is in transit to or from an agent of a foreign power or a foreign power.

See 50 U.S.C. §§1805(a) and 1823(a).[6] If the FISC judge's findings reflect that the government has satisfied the statute's requirements, the judge must issue an order approving the surveillance or search. Such an order must describe the target, the information sought, and the means of acquiring such information. *See* 50 U.S.C. §§1805(c)(1) and 1824(c)(1). The order must also set forth the period of time during which the electronic surveillance or physical searches are approved, which is generally ninety days or until the objective of the electronic surveillance or physical search has been achieved. *See* 50 U.S.C. §§1805(e)(1) and 1824(d)(1). Applications for a renewal of the order must generally be made upon the same basis as the original application and require the same findings by the FISC. *See* 50 U.S.C. §§1805(e)(2) and 1824(d)(2).

Although FISA is chiefly directed to obtaining "foreign intelligence information,"[7] the Act specifically contemplates cooperation between federal authorities conducting electronic surveillance and physical searches pursuant to FISA and federal law enforcement officers investigating clandestine intelligence activities. In this respect,

---

6. In addition to these probable cause findings, the FISC judge must also find that: (1) the President has authorized the Attorney General to approve applications for electronic surveillance or physical searches for foreign intelligence information; (2) that the application has been made by a Federal officer and approved by the Attorney General; (3) that the proposed minimization procedures meet the respective definitions of minimization procedures for electronic surveillance and physical searches; and (4) that the application contains all statements and certifications required by 50 U.S.C. §1804 for electronic surveillance and 50 U.S.C. §1823 for physical searches and, if the target is a United States person, the certification or certifications are not clearly erroneous on the basis of the statement made under sections 1804(a)(7)(E) and 1823(a)(7)(E) of title 18 and any other information furnished under sections 1804(d) and 1823(c) of this title. *See* 50 U.S.C. §§1805(a) and 1823(a).

7. FISA defines "foreign intelligence information" as—

(1) information that relates to, and if concerning a United States person is necessary to, the ability of the United States to protect against—

(A) actual or potential attack or other grave hostile acts of a foreign power or an agent of a foreign power;

(B) sabotage or international terrorism by a foreign power or an agent of a foreign power; or

(C) clandestine intelligence activities by an intelligence service or network of a foreign power or by an agent of a foreign power; or

(2) information with respect to a foreign power or foreign territory that relates to, and if concerning a United States person is necessary to—

(A) the national defense or the security of the United States; or

(B) the conduct of the foreign affairs of the United States.

50 U.S.C. §1801(e).

FISA explicitly allows the use of evidence derived from FISA surveillance and searches in criminal prosecutions. *See* 50 U.S.C. §§1806(k) and 1825(k).

If the Attorney General approves the use of evidence collected pursuant to FISA in a criminal prosecution, and the government intends to use or disclose FISA evidence at the trial of an "aggrieved person,"[8] the government must first notify the aggrieved person and the district court that the government intends to disclose or use the FISA evidence. *See* 50 U.S.C. §§1806(c) and 1825(d). On receiving such notification, an aggrieved person may seek to suppress any evidence derived from FISA surveillance or searches on the grounds that: (1) the evidence was unlawfully acquired; or (2) the electronic surveillance or physical search was not conducted in conformity with the Order of authorization or approval. *See* 50 U.S.C. §§1806(e) and 1825(f). And, if an aggrieved person moves to suppress FISA evidence or to obtain FISA material, then upon the filing of an affidavit by the Attorney General stating under oath that disclosure of such material would harm national security, the district court must review the FISA warrant applications and related materials *in camera* and *ex parte* to determine whether the surveillance or search "of the aggrieved person was lawfully authorized and conducted." 50 U.S.C. §§1806(f) and 1825(g).

This review is properly *de novo*, especially given that the review is *ex parte* and thus unaided by the adversarial process. Thus, the government's contention here that a reviewing district court must accord the FISC's probable cause determination "substantial deference" cannot be sustained in light of the Fourth Circuit's clear contrary statement on the issue. But the government is correct that the certifications contained in the applications should be "presumed valid." *See* 50 U.S.C. §1805(a)(5) (applying "clearly erroneous" standard to factual averments contained in certification when the target is a United States person)....

II.

At the threshold, defendants seek disclosure of the FISA applications, orders, and related materials at issue in this case so they may effectively participate in the review process. On this point FISA is clear: It allows a reviewing court to disclose such materials "only where such disclosure is necessary to make an accurate determination of the legality of the surveillance." 50 U.S.C. §1806(f). Defendants claim this condition is met, by arguing (1) that the FISC's determination that they were agents of a foreign power was surely wrong; and (2) that evidence of the government's evident failure to comply with FISA's minimization procedures requires disclosure. Neither argument is persuasive....

Review of the FISA applications, orders and other materials in this case presented none of the concerns that might warrant disclosure to defendants. The FISA dockets contained no facial inconsistencies, nor did they disclose any reason to doubt any of the representations made by the government in its applications.

---

8. FISA defines an "aggrieved person" with respect to electronic surveillance as "a person who is the target of an electronic surveillance or any other person whose communications or activities were subject to electronic surveillance." 50 U.S.C. §1801(k). With respect to physical searches, FISA similarly defines an "aggrieved person" as a "person whose premises, property, information, or material is the target of physical search or any other person whose premises, property, information, or material was subject to physical search." 50 U.S.C. §1821(2).

Likewise, the targets of the surveillance are precisely defined. Finally, although defendants claim that the discovery obtained from the government contains a significant amount of non-foreign intelligence information, this contention relies upon an inordinately narrow view of what constitutes foreign intelligence information, and therefore is unavailing. For these reasons, and given the government's legitimate national security interest in maintaining the secrecy of the information contained in the FISA applications, disclosure of the FISA materials to defendants is not warranted in this case.

III. . . .

Defendants' attack on the lawfulness of the FISA surveillance in this case focuses chiefly on two issues: (1) whether the FISC had probable cause to believe that the targets of the sanctioned surveillance were "agents of a foreign power," as required by FISA, and (2) whether there was proper compliance with the minimization procedures subsequent to the surveillance. Review of the FISA material confirms that both of these issues must be resolved in favor of the lawfulness of the surveillance.

Defendants' necessarily speculative contention that the FISC must have erred when it found probable cause to believe that the targets are agents of a foreign power is without merit. An agent of a foreign power is defined by the statute, in pertinent part, as any person who —

(A) knowingly engages in clandestine intelligence gathering activities for or on behalf of a foreign power, which activities involve or may involve a violation of the criminal statutes of the United States;

(B) pursuant to the direction of an intelligence service or network of a foreign power, knowingly engages in any other clandestine intelligence activities for or on behalf of such power, which activities involve or are about to involve a violation of the criminal statutes of the United States; . . . or

(E) knowingly aids or abets any person in the conduct of activities described in [the subparagraphs above] or knowingly conspires with any person to engage in activities described in [the subparagraphs above].

50 U.S.C. §1801(b)(2). Although the phrase "clandestine intelligence gathering activities" is not defined in FISA, the legislative history demonstrates that the drafters viewed these "activities" in light of the criminal espionage laws, including 18 U.S.C. §§793 and 794, and considered that such "activities" would include, for example, "collection or transmission of information or material that is not generally available to the public." See S. Rep. No. 95-701, at 21-22 (1978), 1978 U.S.C.C.A.N. 3973, 3990-91 [hereinafter S. Intelligence Rep.]. . . .

Importantly, FISA is clear that in determining whether there is probable cause to believe that a potential target of FISA surveillance or a FISA search is an agent of a foreign power, the FISC judge may not consider a United States person an agent of a foreign power "*solely* upon the basis of activities protected by the First Amendment." 50 U.S.C. §1805(a) (emphasis added). From this plain language, it follows that the probable cause determination may rely in part on activities protected by the First Amendment, provided the determination also relies on activities not protected by the First Amendment. This issue received extensive treatment in the legislative history, which, consistent with the statute's plain language, makes clear that First Amendment activities cannot form the *sole* basis for concluding a U.S. person is an agent of a foreign power. The following excerpt from the legislative history illustrates this point:

> The Bill is not intended to authorize electronic surveillance when a United States person's activities, even though secret and conducted for a foreign power, consist entirely of lawful acts such as lobbying or the use of confidential contacts to influence public officials, directly or indirectly, through the dissemination of information. Individuals exercising their right to lobby public officials or to engage in political dissent from official policy may well be in contact with representatives of foreign governments and groups when the issues concern foreign affairs or international economic matters.
>
> They must continue to be free to communicate about such issues and to obtain information or exchange views with representatives of foreign governments or with foreign groups, free from any fear that such contact might be the basis for probable cause to believe they are acting at the direction of a foreign power thus triggering the government's power to conduct electronic surveillance.

See S. Intelligence Rep. at 29.

The legislative history makes equally clear, however, that this protection extends only to the "*lawful* exercise of First Amendment rights of speech, petition, assembly and association." *Id.* (emphasis added). Similarly, the House Report (Intelligence Committee) emphasized that FISA "would not authorize surveillance of ethnic Americans who *lawfully* gather political information and perhaps even *lawfully* share it with the foreign government of their national origin." *See In re Sealed Case*, 310 F.3d 717, 739 (FISCR 2002) (emphasis added) (quoting H. Rep. No. 95-1283, at 40). For example, electronic surveillance might be appropriate if there is probable cause to believe that —

> foreign intelligence services [are] hid[ing] behind the cover of some person or organization in order to influence American political events and deceive Americans into believing that the opinions or influence are of domestic origin and initiative and such deception is willfully maintained in violation of the Foreign Agents Registration Act.

S. Intelligence Rep. at 29. Thus, if the FISC judge has probable cause to believe that the potential target is engaged in *unlawful* activities in addition to those protected by the First Amendment, the FISC may authorize surveillance of a U.S. person.

In this respect, it is important to emphasize the significant difference between FISA's probable cause requirement and the government's ultimate burden to prove the existence of criminal activity beyond a reasonable doubt. Indeed, the Fourth Circuit has described probable cause in this context as "a fluid concept — turning on the assessment of probabilities in particular factual contexts — not readily, or even usefully, reduced to a neat set of rules." *United States v. Hammoud*, 381 F.3d [316 (4th Cir. 2004),] at 332 (upholding probable cause finding that Hammoud was an agent of Hizballah). Furthermore, "[i]n evaluating whether probable cause exists, it is the task of the issuing judge 'to make a practical, common-sense decision, whether, given all the circumstances set forth in the affidavit, there is a fair probability' that the search will be fruitful." *Id.* (quoting *Illinois v. Gates*, 462 U.S. 213, 238 (1983)); *see also Mason v. Godinez*, 47 F.3d 852, 855 (7th Cir. 1995) ("Probable cause means more than bare suspicion but less than absolute certainty that a search will be fruitful."). And, in making the probable cause determination, FISA permits a judge to "consider past activities of the target, as well as facts and circumstances relating to current or future activities of the target." 50 U.S.C. §1805(b). Furthermore, with respect to those U.S. persons suspected of involvement in clandestine intelligence activities, the probable cause determination "does not necessarily require a showing of an imminent violation of criminal law" because "Congress clearly intended a lesser showing of probable cause for these activities than that applicable to ordinary cases." *In re Sealed Case*, 310 F.3d at 738. Illustrative of this intent is FISA's description of clandestine intelligence activities as those that "involve or *may* involve a violation of the criminal statutes of the United States." 50 U.S.C. §1801(b)(2)(A); *see In re Sealed Case*, 310 F.3d at 738. As FISA's drafters made clear: "The term 'may involve' not only requires less information regarding the crime involved, but also permits electronic surveillance at some point prior to the time when a crime sought to be prevented, as for example, the transfer of classified documents, actually occurs." *In re Sealed Case*, 310 F.3d at 738 (quoting H. Rep. No. 95-1283, at 40). Thus, while the statute is intended to avoid permitting electronic surveillance solely on the basis of First Amendment activities, it plainly allows a FISC judge to issue an order allowing the surveillance or physical search if there is probable cause to believe that the target, even if engaged in First Amendment activities, may also be involved in unlawful clandestine intelligence activities, or in knowingly aiding and abetting such activities. In these circumstances, the fact that a target is also involved in protected First Amendment activities is no bar to electronic surveillance pursuant to FISA.

A thorough review of the FISA dockets in issue confirms that the FISC had ample probable cause to believe that the targets were agents of a foreign power quite apart from their First Amendment lobbying activities. While the defendants' lobbying activities are generally protected by the First Amendment, willful violations of §793 are not, and as is demonstrated by the allegations contained in the superseding indictment, the FISC had probable cause to believe that such violations had occurred in this case.

Defendants' second argument in support of their motion is that the government failed to follow the applicable minimization procedures. In this regard, it is true that once the electronic surveillance or the physical search has been approved, the government must apply the specific minimization procedures contained in the application to the FISC. These minimization procedures are "designed to protect, as far as reasonable, against the acquisition, retention, and dissemination of nonpublic information which is not foreign intelligence information." *In re Sealed Case*, 310 F.3d 717, 731 (FISCR 2002). While the specific minimization procedures for each application are classified, they must meet the definition of minimization procedures under §1801(h) for electronic surveillance and §1821(4) for physical searches. FISA minimization procedures include, in pertinent part —

> (1) specific procedures adopted by the Attorney General that are reasonably designed in light of the purpose and technique of the particular surveillance or search, to minimize the acquisition and retention, and prohibit the dissemination, of nonpublicly available information concerning unconsenting United States persons consistent with the need of the United States to obtain, produce, and disseminate foreign intelligence information;
>
> (2) procedures that require that nonpublicly available information, which is not foreign intelligence information, shall not be disseminated in a manner that identifies any United States person, without such person's consent, unless such person's identity is necessary to understand foreign intelligence information or assess its importance;

(3) notwithstanding paragraphs (1) and (2), procedures that allow for the retention and dissemination of information that is evidence of a crime which has been, is
being, or is about to be committed and that is to be retained or disseminated for law
enforcement purposes.

See 50 U.S.C. §§1801(h) and 1821(4). Congress intended these minimization procedures to act as a safeguard for U.S. persons at the acquisition, retention and dissemination phases of electronic surveillance and searches. *See* S. Intelligence Rep. at 39.
Thus, for example, minimization at the acquisition stage is designed to insure that the
communications of non-target U.S. persons who happen to be using a FISA target's
telephone, or who happen to converse with the target about non-foreign intelligence
information, are not improperly disseminated. *See id.* Similarly, minimization at the
retention stage is intended to ensure that "information acquired, which is not necessary for obtaining, producing, or disseminating foreign intelligence information, be
destroyed where feasible." *See In re Sealed Case,* 310 F.3d at 731 (quoting H. Rep.
No. 95-1283, at 56). Finally, the dissemination of foreign intelligence information
"needed for an approved purpose...should be restricted to those officials with a
need for such information." *Id.* As the Foreign Intelligence Surveillance Court of
Review has recently made clear, these procedures do not prohibit the sharing of
foreign intelligence information between FBI intelligence officials and criminal prosecutors when there is evidence of a crime. *Id.*

FISA's minimization procedures are meant to parallel the minimization procedures of Title III, which courts have sensibly construed as not requiring the
total elimination of innocent conversation. *See* S. Intelligence Rep. at 39 (citing *United
States v. Bynum,* 485 F.2d 490, 500 (2d Cir. 1973), *cert. denied,* 423 U.S. 952 (1975)).[15]
On the contrary, "[i]n assessing the minimization effort, the Court's role is to determine whether 'on the whole the agents have shown a high regard for the right of
privacy and have done all they reasonably could to avoid unnecessary intrusion.'"
Id. at 39-40 (quoting *United States v. Tortorello,* 480 F.2d 764 (2d Cir.), *cert. denied,* 414
U.S. 866 (1973)). Thus, "[a]bsent a charge that the minimization procedures have
been disregarded completely, the test of compliance is 'whether a good faith effort to
minimize was attempted.'" *Id.* (quoting *United States v. Armocida,* 515 F.2d 29, 44 (3d
Cir. 1975)).

Obviously, the extent of the government's minimization will depend largely on
its construction of the term "foreign intelligence information." And in this respect,
"foreign intelligence information" includes, among other things, "information that
relates to, and if concerning a United States person is necessary to, the ability of the
United States to protect against...clandestine intelligence activities by an intelligence service or network of a foreign power or by an agent of a foreign power." 50
U.S.C. §1801(e). Acknowledging the inherent difficulty in determining whether
something is related to clandestine activity, courts have construed "foreign intelligence information" broadly and sensibly allowed the government some latitude in its

---

15. Title III's minimization procedures provide, in pertinent part, that:

Every order and extension thereof shall contain a provision that the authorization to intercept shall
be executed as soon as practicable, shall be conducted in such a way as to minimize the interception
of communications not otherwise subject to interception under this chapter, and must terminate
upon attainment of the authorized objective, or in any event in thirty days.

See 18 U.S.C. §2518(5).

determination of what is foreign intelligence information. As the Fourth Circuit pointed out, "[i]t is not always immediately clear" whether a particular conversation must be minimized because "[a] conversation that seems innocuous on one day may later turn out to be of great significance, particularly if the individuals involved are talking in code." *Hammoud,* 381 F.3d at 334. For this reason, "when the government eavesdrops on clandestine groups . . . investigators often find it necessary to intercept all calls in order to record possible code language or oblique references to the illegal scheme." *United States v. Truong,* 629 F.2d 908, 917 (4th Cir. 1980). This latitude was intended by FISA's drafters who understood that it may be necessary to "acquire, retain and disseminate information concerning . . . the known contacts" of a U.S. person engaged in clandestine intelligence activities even though some of those contacts will invariably be innocent of any wrong-doing. H. Rep. No. 95-1283, at 58.

Given the breadth of the term "foreign intelligence information" in the context of investigating clandestine intelligence activities and the rule of reason that applies to the government's obligation to minimize non-pertinent information, defendants' motion to suppress for failure to properly minimize must be denied. The *ex parte, in camera* review of the FISA dockets discloses that any failures to minimize properly the electronic surveillance of the defendants were (i) inadvertent, (ii) disclosed to the FISC on discovery, and (iii) promptly rectified. . . .

NOTES AND QUESTIONS

a. Title III Warrants for Ordinary Criminal Investigations

The general standard for searches in criminal investigations is set out in Federal Rule of Criminal Procedure 41. Among other things, Rule 41 permits warrants for a search and seizure of property that constitutes evidence of or is related to the commission of a crime. Rule 41 also requires that the target receive a copy of the warrant and an inventory of seized property, and that the investigator show "reasonable cause" for serving the warrant at night rather than in daylight.

As you read the following Notes and Questions, consider how FISA orders for electronic surveillance or physical searches are different, and why. After reading *Rosen,* would you say that FISA supplies a constitutionally adequate substitute for the traditional law enforcement warrant? What advantages does FISA provide for intelligence officials? What drawbacks are there to the FISA process, from the investigators' point of view? If FISA had not been enacted, how and pursuant to what authority would investigators have learned about the alleged criminal activities of the co-conspirators charged in *Rosen*? To what extent does the legality of FISA surveillance turn on whether the objective of the investigation is a criminal prosecution?

b. The Scope of FISA Electronic Surveillance and Physical Searches

1. *Foreign Intelligence Information.* Review the definition of "foreign intelligence information" quoted in *Rosen, supra* p. 197. "International terrorism," which forms part of that definition, is itself defined in FISA to include activities that—

(1) involve violent acts or acts dangerous to human life that . . . would be a criminal violation if committed within the jurisdiction of the United States or any State;

(2) appear to be intended
  (A) to intimidate or coerce a civilian population;
  (B) to influence the policy of a government by intimidation or coercion; or
  (C) to affect the conduct of a government by assassination or kidnapping; and
(3) occur totally outside the United States, or transcend national boundaries in terms of the means by which they are accomplished, the persons they appear intended to coerce or intimidate, or the locale in which their perpetrators operate or seek asylum. [50 U.S.C. §1801(c).]

Can you think of some kinds of information that investigators of possible terrorism would be interested in having that could not be collected pursuant to FISA?

2. *Electronic Surveillance.* The form of the electronic surveillance used in *Rosen* was not specified. However, FISA defines four categories of electronic surveillance, some of which go beyond conventional telephone wiretaps and hidden microphones:

(f) "Electronic surveillance" means—
(1) the acquisition by an electronic, mechanical, or other surveillance device of the contents of any wire or radio communication sent by or intended to be received by a particular, known United States person who is in the United States, if the contents are acquired by intentionally targeting that United States person, under circumstances in which a person has a reasonable expectation of privacy and a warrant would be required for law enforcement purposes;
(2) the acquisition by an electronic, mechanical, or other surveillance device of the contents of any wire communication to or from a person in the United States, without the consent of any party thereto, if such acquisition occurs in the United States...;
(3) the intentional acquisition by an electronic, mechanical, or other surveillance device of the contents of any radio communication, under circumstances in which a person has a reasonable expectation of privacy and a warrant would be required for law enforcement purposes, and if both the sender and all intended recipients are located within the United States; or
(4) the installation or use of an electronic, mechanical, or other surveillance device in the United States for monitoring to acquire information, other than from a wire or radio communication, under circumstances in which a person has a reasonable expectation of privacy and a warrant would be required for law enforcement purposes. [50 U.S.C. §1801(f)(1)-(4).]

Does this definition cover surveillance by hidden microphones installed in a person's home or office? What about a listening device in a person's car? Is video surveillance covered? *See United States v. Koyomejian,* 946 F.2d 1450, 1451 (9th Cir. 1991), *aff'd in part, rev'd in part,* 970 F.2d 536 (9th Cir. 1992) (en banc), *cert. denied,* 506 U.S. 1005 (1992) (technique is covered).

3. *The Geographical Scope of FISA Electronic Surveillance.* Are there geographical limits to the communications subject to FISA electronic surveillance? Does FISA cover the surveillance of communications from Afghanistan to the United States? From the United States to Afghanistan? From one city to another within Afghanistan? If not the last, why do you think Congress did not require FISA authorization for such communications? Upon what authority would such surveillance be conducted?

4. *Physical Searches.* A "physical search" under FISA involves a "physical intrusion within the United States into premises or property . . . under circumstances in which a person has a reasonable expectation of privacy and a warrant would be required for law enforcement purposes." 50 U.S.C. §1821(5). What do you suppose counts as a "physical intrusion"? See *supra* p. 192, discussing *Kyllo v. United States*, 533 U.S. 27 (2001). The substantive provisions for physical searches track those for electronic surveillance. The procedures are somewhat different. A physical search may be approved "for the period necessary to achieve its purpose, or for ninety days, whichever is less." 50 U.S.C. §1824(d)(1). But a search may continue for up to one year if it is directed against a foreign power," or up to 120 days if the target is an agent of a foreign power. *Id.* §1824(d)(1)(A) and (B). Unlike the usual procedure for a search pursuant to a warrant, FISA does not require that agents knock before entry, supply notice of the search, particularize the object of the search, or inventory what is found for the target. The difference is based on practical considerations:

> Physical searches to gather foreign intelligence information depend upon stealth. If the targets of such searches discover that the United States Government had obtained significant information about their activities, those activities would likely be altered, rendering the information useless. [William F. Brown & Americo R. Cinquegrana, *Warrantless Physical Searches for Foreign Intelligence Purposes: Executive Order 12,333 and the Fourth Amendment*, 35 Cath. L. Rev. 97, 131 (1985).]

Does this explanation provide constitutional justification for either the FISA procedure or a wholly untethered warrantless search? *See* Daniel J. Malooly, *Physical Searches Under FISA: A Constitutional Analysis*, 35 Am. Crim. L. Rev. 411, 420-423 (1998).

5. *Who May Be Targeted?* In an espionage prosecution, it may be easy to see how the target of FISA surveillance falls within the definition of "agent of a foreign power." How do you suppose these determinations are made in national security or counterterrorism investigations? In addition to the portions of definitions reproduced in *Rosen*, FISA sets out two kinds of potential targets:

§1801. Definitions.

As used in this subchapter:
(a) "Foreign power" means—
(1) a foreign government or any component thereof, whether or not recognized by the United States;
(2) a faction of a foreign nation or nations, not substantially composed of United States persons;
(3) an entity that is openly acknowledged by a foreign government or governments to be directed and controlled by such foreign government or governments;
(4) a group engaged in international terrorism or activities in preparation therefor;
(5) a foreign-based political organization, not substantially composed of United States persons; or
(6) an entity that is directed and controlled by a foreign government or governments.
(b) "Agent of a foreign power" means—
(1) any person other than a United States person, who—
(A) acts in the United States as an officer or employee of a foreign power, or as a member of a foreign power as defined in subsection (a)(4) of this section;

(B) acts for or on behalf of a foreign power which engages in clandestine intelligence activities in the United States contrary to the interests of the United States, when the circumstances of such person's presence in the United States indicate that such person may engage in such activities in the United States, or when such person knowingly aids or abets any person in the conduct of such activities or knowingly conspires with any person to engage in such activities;

(C) engages in international terrorism or activities in preparation therefore [*sic*]; . . .

(2) any person who — . . .

(C) knowingly engages in sabotage or international terrorism, or activities that are in preparation therefor, for or on behalf of a foreign power;

(D) knowingly enters the United States under a false or fraudulent identity for or on behalf of a foreign power or, while in the United States, knowingly assumes a false or fraudulent identity for or on behalf of a foreign power. . . .

Can you now describe the categories of targets that may be subjected to electronic surveillance or a physical search pursuant to FISA? Taking into account that to be an "agent of a foreign power" requires that the target work for or act on behalf of a "foreign power" (except for the "lone wolf" category described below) can you think of examples of a "foreign power" or "agent of foreign power"? Under what circumstances could a "United States person" be treated as an agent of a foreign power? How did these definitions apply to the subjects of surveillance in *Rosen*?

The so-called "lone wolf" provision, 50 U.S.C. §1801(b)(1)(C), was added by §6001 of the Intelligence Reform and Terrorism Prevention Act of 2004, Pub. L. No. 108-458, 118 Stat. 3638, 3742. If the lone wolf need not be linked in any way to a foreign power, has the "foreign agent" requirement effectively been eliminated for foreign intelligence surveillance? Can you identify any downside risks to the expanded definition? *See* Patricia L. Bellia, *The "Lone Wolf" Amendment and the Future of Foreign Intelligence Surveillance Law*, 50 Vill. L. Rev. 425, 428-429, 455-456 (2005); Elizabeth B. Bazan, *Intelligence Reform and Terrorism Prevention Act of 2004: "Lone Wolf" Amendment to the Foreign Intelligence Surveillance Act* (Cong. Res. Serv. RS22011), Dec. 29, 2004. Although the lone wolf provision has been subject to periodic sunsets since enactment, its authority was recently extended to June 1, 2015. Pub. L. No. 112-14, §2(b), 125 Stat. 216 (2011).

On the basis of what information would investigators make a "foreign agency" determination before seeking FISA surveillance? Can the FBI make such a determination without the surveillance permitted by FISA? See Chapter 8.

c.   The FISA Application Process for Electronic Surveillance or a Physical Search

1. *The Special Court.* Congress relied on its Article III power to "ordain and establish" the lower federal courts when it created the Foreign Intelligence Surveillance Court (FISC). For background on the FISC and its procedures, *see* Elizabeth B. Bazan, *The U.S. Foreign Intelligence Surveillance Court and the U.S. Foreign Intelligence Surveillance Court of Review: An Overview* (Cong. Res. Serv. RL 33833), Jan. 24, 2007; *United States Foreign Intelligence Surveillance Court, Rules of Procedure*, Nov. 1, 2010, *available at* http://www.uscourts.gov/uscourts/RulesAndPolicies/rules/FISC_Rules_of_ Procedure.pdf.

2. *An Overview of the Process for Obtaining a FISA Order for Electronic Surveillance or a Physical Search.* As shown by the flow chart below, after an investigation indicates a need for foreign intelligence, an application is prepared (by lawyers in the Department of Justice, typically supported by one or more affidavits from investigating agencies) and submitted to the FISC. The FISC considers the application in camera and ex parte; the targets of the proposed surveillance are not informed. If the FISC approves the order, it is executed by the NSA or the FBI in most cases. If the government subsequently seeks to introduce information obtained from the FISA surveillance as evidence in a criminal prosecution, the government must inform the defendant of that intent, as it did in *Rosen*. The defendant may then seek to suppress the materials on the grounds that the evidence was unlawfully acquired or that the surveillance or search was not conducted in conformity with the FISC order. In *Rosen*, the defendant sought disclosure of the FISA application and supporting materials in connection with its motion to suppress. If the Attorney General avers that such disclosure would harm national security, the criminal court will review the materials in camera and ex parte to decide de novo whether the FISC order and its execution by the government were lawful. The *Rosen* court was thus taking a "second look" at the FISA order, but its nominally de novo review standard considers only, for U.S. persons, whether the certifications contained in the original FISA application were "clearly erroneous" (which *Rosen* construes to make such certifications "presum[ptively] valid") or, for all other targets, whether the certifications were complete.

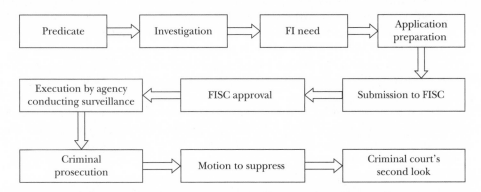

3. *What Must an Application Contain?* What are the essential components of an application for FISA surveillance? How do they differ from the elements of an application for a traditional warrant for law enforcement purposes?

In addition to the requirements summarized in *Rosen*, the Attorney General must find that the information sought "cannot reasonably be obtained by normal investigative techniques." 50 U.S.C. §1804(a)(7)(C). The application also must describe any past surveillance involving the target, the surveillance devices to be employed, the means of installation (including whether physical entry will be required), and the period of time for conducting the surveillance. *Id.* §1804(a)(8), (9), (10).

Due to the growing complexity of FISA applications, in 2001 the FBI developed FISA verification procedures (the so-called Woods Procedures, named for their author, FBI lawyer Michael J. Woods) to better ensure the accuracy of the facts in each FISA application, particularly concerning what FISA calls "probable cause," and the existence and nature of any parallel criminal processes or prior or ongoing asset relationship involving the target. The procedures include FBI computer database searches and requirements to check the status of the proposed target with the Asset and Informant Unit and Criminal Division. The Woods Procedures were declassified in 2002 and are available at http://www.fas.org/irp/agency/doj/fisa/woods/pdf. Are these likely to improve the accuracy of the FISA process? How will Congress or the public know of their success or failure?

4. *The FISA Order for Electronic Surveillance or a Physical Search.*

a. *Foreign Power or Agent Target.* FISA "probable cause" is fundamentally different from Title III probable cause. Under FISA, the FISC must find probable cause to believe what? Is the FISA probable cause standard quoted in *Rosen* more or less onerous than the general criminal probable cause standard?

Both FISA and federal criminal laws require something like the probability of a certain fact. But unlike Title III warrants, FISA orders are based "upon the probability of a possibility; the probability to believe that the foreign target of the order *may* engage in spying, or the probability to believe that the American target of the order *may* engage in criminal spying activities." Charles Doyle, *Memorandum to Senate Select Committee on Intelligence: Probable Cause, Reasonable Suspicion, and Reasonableness Standards in the Context of the Fourth Amendment and the Foreign Intelligence Surveillance Act* (Cong. Res. Serv.), Jan. 30, 2006, *available at* http://www.fas.org/sgp/crs/intel/m013006.pdf. Under what circumstances and according to what standard may the FISC question the determinations made in the application for surveillance? *See* William C. Banks & M.E. Bowman, *Executive Authority for National Security Surveillance*, 50 Am. U. L. Rev. 1, 83 (2001); Brown & Cinquegrana, *supra* p. 205, at 129-131.

What justifies the lesser probable cause requirement in FISA? The purpose of law enforcement is to prosecute those guilty of committing a crime, while intelligence investigations have a broader scope and seek to protect the nation from foreign enemies. Foreign intelligence investigations are often more open-ended. What are the legal implications if law enforcement and intelligence surveillance objectives blur or even merge, when intelligence information produces evidence that is used in a criminal prosecution? What answer does *Rosen* suggest?

b. *Foreign Power or Agent Locus.* The FISC must also find that there is probable cause to believe that the locus of the surveillance is being used or about to be used by, or, for physical searches, owned, used, or possessed by or in transit to or from, a foreign power or agent of a foreign power. This seemingly simple requirement was complicated by the increasing use of cell phones instead of the geographically fixed landlines that existed when FISA was adopted in 1978.

To cope with this change in technology, Federal Rule of Criminal Procedure 41(a) was amended in 2001 to permit a single law enforcement warrant to be used "in any district in which activities related to the terrorism may have occurred" in conducting "an investigation of domestic terrorism or international terrorism." USA Patriot Act §219, 115 Stat. 291. FISA was also amended in 2001 to permit the FISC to order these so-called "roving wiretaps." A roving wiretap permits investigators to listen in on any phone a target might use. If the judge "finds that the actions of the target of the application may have the effect of thwarting" the ability of the investigators to identify a specific communications carrier, Internet service provider, or other person needed to assist in the effective and secret execution of the surveillance, the order may authorize such assistance from multiple parties. USA Patriot Act §206, 115 Stat. 282 (amending 50 U.S.C. §1805(c)(2)(B)).

To complete the authorization for roving wiretaps, the FISA requirement that the FISC "specify... the nature and location of each of the facilities or places at which the electronic surveillance will be directed" was also amended by adding "if known" at the end. Intelligence Authorization Act for Fiscal Year 2002, Pub. L. No. 107-108, §314(a)(2)(A), 115 Stat. 1394, 1402 (amending 50 U.S.C. §1805(c)(1)(B)).

These provisions do not require that investigators first determine that the target is using the phone to be tapped. Does this authority permit investigators to tap a homeowner's phone if the target enters the home? Could they monitor the Internet use at the public library if the target enters the library?

In the 2006 USA Patriot Improvement and Reauthorization Act, Congress added a provision for orders when the "nature and location of... the facilities or places at which the surveillance will be directed is unknown." Within ten days after surveillance begins, investigators must provide the FISC with a description of the facility or place brought under surveillance, the reasons to believe that it is being used by the target, and any necessary minimization procedures. Pub. L. No. 109-177, §108, 120 Stat. 192, 203 (2006) (amending 50 U.S.C. §1805(c)(1)(B)). The roving wiretap authorities, originally sunsetted, were recently extended to June 1, 2015. Pub. L. No. 112-14, §2(a), 125 Stat. 216 (2011).

c. *Minimization.* The FISC must also find that proposed minimization procedures meet statutory requirements. What is minimization, and why is it required? Do you agree with the *Rosen* court that the potential minimization breach in the *Rosen* investigation did not justify suppressing the FISA-derived evidence? Does the "rule of reason" standard adopted by the court adequately safeguard personal information?

The minimization procedures are classified, "although the internal review mechanisms include standard goals for all applications, as well as for situation-specific assessments for individual applications." Banks & Bowman, *supra* p. 170, at 89. Minimization plays an especially important role in protecting privacy when FISA processes are utilized to collect large quantities of personal information through data-mining techniques. The role of minimization in programmatic surveillance is considered in Chapter 8.

5. *Provisions for Emergency Surveillance.* FISA authorizes electronic surveillance without a court order in certain emergency circumstances. Such surveillance is permitted for up to a year when directed solely at communications between or among foreign powers or focused on their property, when there is "no substantial likelihood" that a communication involving a U.S. person will be acquired. 50 U.S.C. §1802.

More importantly, FISA states that when the Attorney General reasonably determines that "an emergency situation exists" regarding the employment of electronic surveillance to obtain foreign intelligence information "before an order authorizing such surveillance can with due diligence be obtained" and that there is a "factual basis for issuance of an order," the Attorney General may authorize the surveillance if a FISC judge is simultaneously informed and if an application is made to that judge "as soon as practicable, but not more than 72 hours" after the Attorney General authorization. 50 U.S.C. §1805(f). If the FISC does not issue a judicial order, the surveillance must stop "when the information sought is obtained, when the application for the order is denied, or after the expiration of 72 hours from the time of authorization by the Attorney General, whichever is earliest." *Id.* If no order is obtained, the information collected may not be used without consent "except with the approval of the Attorney General if the information indicates a threat of death or serious bodily harm to any person." *Id.*

Provision for physical searches in emergency circumstances is made on a basis parallel to that for electronic surveillance; the authority lasts for up to 72 hours, by which time an application for approval must be made to the FISC. 50 U.S.C. §§1822(a), 1824(e), (f). *See also* 50 U.S.C. §§1843(a), (b) (parallel emergency authorities for pen register and trap and trace devices).

Between FISA's enactment in 1978 and September 11, 2001, Attorneys General issued 47 emergency authorizations under FISA. In the 18 months after September 11, 2001, the Attorney General authorized more than 170 emergency wiretaps and/or physical searches under FISA. Dan Eggen & Robert O'Harrow Jr., *U.S. Steps Up Secret Surveillance*, Wash. Post, Mar. 23, 2003. Under 50 U.S.C. §1808(a)(2), the Attorney General must report annually to the intelligence committees the total number of emergency employments of electronic surveillance. The reports are not publicly available.

Are you troubled by the absence of a prior judicial check on these executive decisions? How can responsible officials be certain that these decisions satisfy statutory and constitutional norms? Given the availability of these FISA emergency provisions, can you envision any emergency that would justify foreign intelligence surveillance in the United States without complying with FISA? This question is addressed *infra* p. 228.

6. *Judicial Review of FISA Surveillance.* If no criminal prosecution is initiated following FISA surveillance, how would an individual subjected to unlawful surveillance under FISA be able to challenge the illegal conduct in court? The FISC does not publish its decisions, and its orders are sealed. Proceedings are ex parte and are thus normally not known to the targets of surveillance. 50 U.S.C. §§1802(a)(3), 1806(f)-(g).

As the *Rosen* defendants learned, even if targets of surveillance do find out, they may not be able to examine materials related to the surveillance as part of the criminal court's "second look" if the Attorney General files a claim of privilege under FISA §1806(f). Can you see why FISA permits the government to withhold the applications and accompanying affidavits and certifications from discovery in an adversarial proceeding? If the reviewing judge exercises his statutory discretion not to disclose portions of the documents, how will the targets of surveillance be able to appeal the judge's decision? On what basis could a court of appeals overturn the nondisclosure decision? *See ACLU v. Barr*, 952 F.2d 457 (D.C. Cir. 1991) (reviewing court may overturn a nondisclosure decision if the certifications of compliance with FISA requirements are clearly erroneous); *see also United States v. Rahman*, 189 F.3d 88 (2d Cir. 1999), *cert. denied*, 528 U.S. 982 (2000).

d.   Constitutional Concerns

1. *Article III Case or Controversy?* The FISC receives applications and issues orders solely on an ex parte basis without any adversarial proceedings. Do such matters meet the Article III "case or controversy" requirements? *United States v. Megahey*, 553 F. Supp. 1180 (E.D.N.Y. 1982), held that FISA proceedings before the FISC "involve

concrete questions respecting the application of the Act and are in a form such that a judge is capable of acting on them." 553 F. Supp. at 1197. *See also United States v. Johnson,* 952 F.2d 565 (2d Cir. 1991), *cert. denied,* 506 U.S. 816 (1992); *United States v. Cavanaugh,* 807 F.2d 787 (9th Cir. 1987); *In re Kevork,* 788 F.2d 566 (9th Cir. 1986); *United States v. Falvey,* 540 F. Supp. 1306, 1313 (E.D.N.Y. 1982).

2. *Political Question Doctrine.* The courts that have heard challenges to FISA surveillance orders have ruled that their review itself is not barred by the political question doctrine. *See, e.g., United States v. Duggan,* 743 F.2d 59, 74-75 (2d Cir. 1984) (limited judicial role in determining whether the target of a warrant is properly subject to the prescribed procedure does not threaten political question values and does not inject courts into the making of foreign policy).

3. *Fourth Amendment.* In *United States v. Duggan,* 743 F.2d 59 (2d Cir. 1984), alleged members of the Provisional Irish Republican Army (PIRA) faced a number of charges relating to export, transportation, and delivery of explosives and firearms. Some of the evidence against them was derived from electronic surveillance pursuant to FISA. Defendants contended that FISA is unconstitutional on grounds that it violates the probable cause requirement of the Fourth Amendment. The court rejected their argument:

> We regard the procedures fashioned in FISA as a constitutionally adequate balancing of the individual's Fourth Amendment rights against the nation's need to obtain foreign intelligence information. The governmental concerns . . . make reasonable the adoption of prerequisites to surveillance that are less stringent than those precedent to the issuance of a warrant for a criminal investigation. . . .
> We conclude that these requirements provide an appropriate balance between the individual's interest in privacy and the government's need to obtain foreign intelligence information, and that FISA does not violate the probable cause requirement of the Fourth Amendment. . . . [*Id.* at 73-74.]

Although the Supreme Court has not considered the constitutionality of FISA, the lower courts have uniformly followed *Duggan* in upholding the FISA procedures. *See, e.g., Johnson, supra,* 952 F.2d at 575 (FISA satisfies Fourth Amendment requirements); *United States v. Pelton,* 835 F.2d 1067, 1075 (4th Cir. 1987) (same); *United States v. Ott,* 827 F.2d 473, 475-477 (9th Cir. 1987) (ex parte review procedures do not violate Fourth or Fifth Amendments); *Cavanaugh, supra,* 807 F.2d at 790 (FISA satisfies the Fourth Amendment).

One of us has written that "FISA was the product of a set of compromises unique to their time. . . . While . . . suspicion of criminal activity was an essential part of . . . FISA, . . . Congress did not intend for FISA to authorize surveillance for the purpose of enforcing the criminal laws." William C. Banks, *The Death of FISA,* 91 U. Minn. L. Rev. 1209, 1228 (2007). How does this "FISA as compromise" view compare with your understanding of the constitutionality of FISA?

4. *Confrontation.* Did the *Rosen* court's refusal to disclose the FISA materials to the defendants violate their due process confrontation rights? Although the Supreme Court has never decided a FISA appeal, the Court did deny review in a challenge to the government's refusal to disclose materials that supported an application for

FISA surveillance. In *United States v. Squillicote*, 221 F.3d 542 (4th Cir. 2000), *cert. denied*, 532 U.S. 971 (2001), a married couple were convicted of conspiring to commit espionage on behalf of East Germany, the Soviet Union, Russia, and South Africa. The FBI obtained 20 separate FISA orders for surveillance that lasted 550 days. Based almost exclusively on the FISA-derived evidence, the parties were sentenced to 22 and 17 years in prison, respectively. Although FISA and the Due Process Clause entitled the accused to question the basis for the government's surveillance, counsel for the accused spies were never permitted to see the underlying documentation that supported the applications for surveillance because the government invoked §1806(f) and filed a claim of privilege. Does §1806(f) comply with the Due Process Clause? Why do you think that the Supreme Court has declined to review a conviction on this basis?

5. *First Amendment.* What protections does FISA provide against surveillance that would burden expressive freedoms? What is meant by the prohibition against finding a U.S. person to be an agent of a foreign power "solely upon the basis of activities protected by the first amendment"? 50 U.S.C. §1805(a)(3)(A). The 1978 Senate Judiciary Committee report on FISA stated that activities protected by the First Amendment may not "form *any part* of the basis" for identifying a FISA target. *See Foreign Intelligence Surveillance Act of 1978: Hearing Before the Subcomm. on Criminal Laws and Procedures of the S. Comm. on the Judiciary*, 95th Cong. 13, 23 (1977) (emphasis added). Did the *Rosen* court take this legislative history into account in evaluating the rules for identifying a potential FISA target?

Did the court in *Rosen* fairly separate the defendants' activities that might be protected from those that are not so protected? What other information could be available to investigators that would permit the application to go forward without being "solely" based on protected First Amendment activities?

Review the definition of "agent of a foreign power" set out *supra* p. 199. Could the FISC grant a surveillance order based on an investigators' assessment that advocacy or fund raising on the part of a potential target constitutes "activities that are in preparation" for terrorism? Problems of profiling targets on the basis of their expressive activities are considered *infra* p. 307.

6. *Reprise: FISA and the Constitution.* After September 11, the Department of Justice maintained that "FISA . . . is not required by the Constitution." Letter from Daniel J. Bryant, Assistant Attorney General, to Senator Bob Graham, Chairman, S. Select Comm. on Intelligence (Aug. 6, 2002) (copy on file with authors). Do you agree?

B.   FISA, LAW ENFORCEMENT, AND "THE WALL"

Some defendants in criminal cases have moved to suppress FISA-acquired evidence on the ground that the FISA surveillance was unlawful, because the evidence was originally sought as part of a criminal investigation. They maintain that the government has thus misused FISA to do an end run around Title III and the ordinary warrant and probable cause requirements of the Fourth Amendment. The government usually replies that the investigators sought only foreign intelligence information. Is it possible, indeed likely, that both sides are correct? In *Duggan, supra*, 743 F.2d at 78, the court concluded that an "otherwise valid FISA surveillance is not tainted" simply because the government anticipates that its fruits *may* be used in a criminal prosecution. But how can a judge determine that the government has not used FISA simply to avoid having to comply with Rule 41? *See United States v. Rahman,* 861 F. Supp. 247 (S.D.N.Y. 1994), *aff'd,* 189 F.2d 88 (2d Cir. 1999) (refusing to find an end run).

Before 2002, courts followed *United States v. Truong Dinh Hung,* 629 F.2d 908 (4th Cir. 1980), *supra* p. 187, and allowed evidence gathered during FISA surveillance to support a criminal conviction only after finding that intelligence collection was the "primary" purpose of the surveillance, *United States v. Johnson,* 952 F.2d 565 (1st Cir. 1991), *cert. denied,* 506 U.S. 816 (1992), or at least *a* purpose (not necessarily primary), *United States v. Sarkissian,* 841 F.2d 959, 964 (9th Cir. 1988). The assumption seemed to be that if the original purpose of the surveillance was intelligence gathering, there was no reason not to use the collected information in a criminal prosecution.

In the days and weeks after the September 11, 2001, terrorist attacks, it was widely reported that an investigative failure may have permitted a twentieth hijacker to escape pre-attack detection because of a concern based on "primary purpose." Zacarias Moussaoui was arrested on immigration charges a few weeks before the attacks. Officials at a private flight-training school had grown suspicious when Moussaoui said that he wanted to learn to fly large jet aircraft, but that he had no interest in becoming a commercial pilot. At about the same time, a French intelligence agency warned the FBI in a classified cable that Moussaoui had "Islamic extremist beliefs." David Johnston & Philip Shenon, *F.B.I. Curbed Scrutiny of Man Now a Suspect in Attacks,* N.Y. Times, Oct. 6, 2001. When FBI field agents in Minneapolis sought headquarters approval for a FISA search, they were turned down, apparently because there was insufficient indication that Moussaoui was an agent of a foreign power. The field agents then also failed to persuade headquarters to open a criminal investigation that would have employed grand jury subpoenas and law enforcement warrants to examine Moussaoui's computer and telephone records. Apparently, this request was denied because senior FBI officials worried that an open criminal investigation might thwart a later FISA application by defeating the primary purpose requirement. They were concerned in part because FISC Chief Judge Royce Lamberth had recently questioned the candor of Justice Department officials who sought FISA orders for targets who were already the subjects of criminal investigations. A criminal case was eventually opened and a FISA order was obtained, but only after the September 11 attacks. *Id.*

The belief that a full investigation of Moussaoui before September 11 might have led to exposure of the hijackers' plot helped spur enactment of the USA Patriot Act and, three years later, the lone-wolf provision in the Intelligence Reform and Terrorism Prevention Act of 2004. See *supra* p. 206. The criminal prosecution of Moussaoui is considered *infra* p. 657.

Concerns about the primary purpose requirement produced an amendment to FISA in the USA Patriot Act. The meaning and constitutionality of the amendment are addressed in the following case.

In re: Sealed Case Nos. 02-001, 02-002

Foreign Intelligence Surveillance Court of Review, 2002
310 F.3d 717

GUY, Senior Circuit Judge, presiding; SILBERMAN and LEAVY, Senior Circuit Judges.

PER CURIAM: This is the first appeal from the Foreign Intelligence Surveillance Court to the Court of Review since the passage of the Foreign Intelligence

Surveillance Act (FISA), 50 U.S.C. §§1801-1862 (West 1991 and Supp. 2002), in 1978. The appeal is brought by the United States from a FISA court surveillance order which imposed certain restrictions on the government. . . .

I.

. . . [T]he court ordered that

law enforcement officials shall not make recommendations to intelligence officials concerning the initiation, operation, continuation or expansion of FISA searches or surveillances. Additionally, the FBI and the Criminal Division [of the Department of Justice] shall ensure that law enforcement officials do not direct or control the use of the FISA procedures to enhance criminal prosecution, and that advice intended to preserve the option of a criminal prosecution does not inadvertently result in the Criminal Division's directing or controlling the investigation using FISA searches and surveillances toward law enforcement objectives.

To ensure the Justice Department followed these strictures the court also fashioned what the government refers to as a "chaperone requirement"; that a unit of the Justice Department, the Office of Intelligence Policy and Review (OIPR) (composed of 31 lawyers and 25 support staff), "be invited" to all meetings between the FBI and the Criminal Division involving consultations for the purpose of coordinating efforts "to investigate or protect against foreign attack or other grave hostile acts, sabotage, international terrorism, or clandestine intelligence activities by foreign powers or their agents." If representatives of OIPR are unable to attend such meetings, "OIPR shall be appri[s]ed of the substance of the meetings forthwith in writing so that the Court may be notified at the earliest opportunity."

These restrictions are not original to the order appealed. They were actually set forth in an opinion written by the former Presiding Judge of the FISA court on May 17 of this year. [*See In re All Matters Submitted to the Foreign Intelligence Surveillance Court*, 218 F. Supp. 2d 611 (2002).] . . .

. . . [T]he May 17 opinion of the FISA court . . . appears to proceed from the assumption that FISA constructed a barrier between counterintelligence/intelligence officials and law enforcement officers in the Executive Branch — indeed, it uses the word "wall" popularized by certain commentators (and journalists) to describe that supposed barrier.

The "wall" emerges from the court's implicit interpretation of FISA. The court apparently believes it can approve applications for electronic surveillance only if the government's objective is *not* primarily directed toward criminal prosecution of the foreign agents for their foreign intelligence activity. But the court neither refers to any FISA language supporting that view, nor does it reference the Patriot Act amendments, which the government contends specifically altered FISA to make clear that an application could be obtained even if criminal prosecution is the primary counter mechanism. . . .

II.

The government makes two main arguments. The first . . . is that the supposed pre-Patriot Act limitation in FISA that restricts the government's intention to use foreign intelligence information in criminal prosecutions is an illusion; it finds no support in either the language of FISA or its legislative history. The government does recognize that several courts of appeals, while upholding the use of FISA surveillances, have opined that FISA may be used only if the government's primary purpose in pursuing foreign intelligence information is not criminal prosecution, but the government argues that those decisions, which did not carefully analyze the statute, were incorrect in their statements, if not incorrect in their holdings.

Alternatively, the government contends that even if the primary purpose test was a legitimate construction of FISA prior to the passage of the Patriot Act, that Act's amendments to FISA eliminate that concept. . . .

The 1978 FISA

We turn first to the statute as enacted in 1978. . . . [The court reviewed the definitions of "foreign intelligence information" and "agent of a foreign power" and noted that each is concerned with national security crimes.]

In light of these definitions, it is quite puzzling that the Justice Department, at some point during the 1980s, began to read the statute as limiting the Department's ability to obtain FISA orders if it intended to prosecute the targeted agents — even for foreign intelligence crimes. To be sure, section 1804, which sets forth the elements of an application for an order, required a national security official in the Executive Branch — typically the Director of the FBI — to certify that "the purpose" of the surveillance is to obtain foreign intelligence information (amended by the Patriot Act to read "a significant purpose"). But as the government now argues, the definition of foreign intelligence information includes evidence of crimes such as espionage, sabotage or terrorism. Indeed, it is virtually impossible to read the 1978 FISA to exclude from its purpose the prosecution of foreign intelligence crimes, most importantly because, as we have noted, the definition of an agent of a foreign power — if he or she is a U.S. person — is grounded on criminal conduct. . . .

The origin of what the government refers to as the false dichotomy between foreign intelligence information that is evidence of foreign intelligence crimes and that which is not appears to have been a Fourth Circuit case decided in 1980. *United States v. Truong Dinh Hung*, 629 F.2d 908 (4th Cir. 1980). That case, however, involved an electronic surveillance carried out prior to the passage of FISA and predicated on the President's executive power. In approving the district court's exclusion of evidence obtained through a warrantless surveillance subsequent to the point in time when the government's investigation became "primarily" driven by law enforcement objectives, the court held that the Executive Branch should be excused from securing a warrant only when "the object of the search or the surveillance is a foreign power, its agents or collaborators," and "the surveillance is conducted 'primarily' for foreign intelligence reasons." *Id.* at 915. . . .

. . . [S]ome time in the 1980s — the exact moment is shrouded in historical mist — the Department [of Justice] applied the *Truong* analysis to an interpretation of the FISA statute. What is clear is that in 1995 the Attorney General adopted "Procedures for Contacts Between the FBI and the Criminal Division Concerning Foreign Intelligence and Foreign Counterintelligence Investigations."

Apparently to avoid running afoul of the primary purpose test used by some courts, the 1995 Procedures limited contacts between the FBI and the Criminal Division in cases where FISA surveillance or searches were being conducted by the FBI for foreign intelligence (FI) or foreign counterintelligence (FCI) purposes.

The procedures state that "the FBI and Criminal Division should ensure that advice intended to preserve the option of a criminal prosecution does not inadvertently result in either the fact or the appearance of the Criminal Division's *directing or controlling* the FI or FCI investigation toward law enforcement objectives." 1995 Procedures at 2, ¶6 (emphasis added). Although these procedures provided for significant information sharing and coordination between criminal and FI or FCI investigations, based at least in part on the "directing or controlling" language, they eventually came to be narrowly interpreted within the Department of Justice, and most particularly by OIPR, as requiring OIPR to act as a "wall" to prevent the FBI intelligence officials from communicating with the Criminal Division regarding ongoing FI or FCI investigations. . . .

The Patriot Act and the FISA Court's Decision

The passage of the Patriot Act altered and to some degree muddied the landscape. In October 2001, Congress amended FISA to change "the purpose" language in 1804(a)(7)(B) to "a significant purpose." It also added a provision allowing "Federal officers who conduct electronic surveillance to acquire foreign intelligence information" to "consult with Federal law enforcement officers to coordinate efforts to investigate or protect against" attack or other grave hostile acts, sabotage or international terrorism, or clandestine intelligence activities, by foreign powers or their agents. 50 U.S.C. §1806(k)(1). And such coordination "shall not preclude" the government's certification that a significant purpose of the surveillance is to obtain foreign intelligence information, or the issuance of an order authorizing the surveillance. *Id.* §1806(k)(2). Although the Patriot Act amendments to FISA expressly sanctioned consultation and coordination between intelligence and law enforcement officials, in response to the first applications filed by OIPR under those amendments, in November 2001, the FISA court for the first time adopted the 1995 Procedures, as augmented by the January 2000 and August 2001 Procedures, as "minimization procedures" to apply in all cases before the court.

The Attorney General interpreted the Patriot Act quite differently. On March 6, 2002, the Attorney General approved new "Intelligence Sharing Procedures" to implement the Act's amendments to FISA. The 2002 Procedures supersede prior procedures and were designed to permit the complete exchange of information and advice between intelligence and law enforcement officials. They eliminated the "direction and control" test and allowed the exchange of advice between the FBI, OIPR, and the Criminal Division regarding "the initiation, operation, continuation, or expansion of FISA searches or surveillance." On March 7, 2002, the government filed a motion with the FISA court, noting that the Department of Justice had adopted the 2002 Procedures and proposing to follow those procedures in all matters before the court. The government also asked the FISA court to vacate its orders adopting the prior procedures as minimization procedures in all cases and imposing special "wall" procedures in certain cases.

Unpersuaded by the Attorney General's interpretation of the Patriot Act, the court ordered that the 2002 Procedures be adopted, *with modifications*, as minimization procedures to apply in all cases. The court emphasized that the definition of minimization procedures had not been amended by the Patriot Act, and reasoned that the 2002 Procedures "cannot be used by the government to amend the Act in ways Congress has not." . . .

Undeterred, the government submitted the application at issue in this appeal on July 19, 2002, and expressly proposed using the 2002 Procedures *without modification.* In an order issued the same day, the FISA judge hearing the application granted an order for surveillance of the target but modified the 2002 Procedures consistent with the court's May 17, 2002 *en banc* order. It is the July 19, 2002 order that the government appeals....

... [T]he Patriot Act amendments clearly disapprove the primary purpose test. And as a matter of straightforward logic, if a FISA application can be granted even if "foreign intelligence" is only a significant — not a primary — purpose, another purpose can be primary. One other legitimate purpose that could exist is to prosecute a target for a foreign intelligence crime....

... [I]t is our task to do our best to read the statute to honor congressional intent. The better reading, it seems to us, excludes from the purpose of gaining foreign intelligence information a sole objective of criminal prosecution. We therefore reject the government's argument to the contrary. Yet this may not make much practical difference. Because, as the government points out, when it commences an electronic surveillance of a foreign agent, typically it will not have decided whether to prosecute the agent (whatever may be the subjective intent of the investigators or lawyers who initiate an investigation). So long as the government entertains a realistic option of dealing with the agent other than through criminal prosecution, it satisfies the significant purpose test.

The important point is — and here we agree with the government — the Patriot Act amendment, by using the word "significant," eliminated any justification for the FISA court to balance the relative weight the government places on criminal prosecution as compared to other counterintelligence responses. If the certification of the application's purpose articulates a broader objective than criminal prosecution — such as stopping an ongoing conspiracy — and includes other potential non-prosecutorial responses, the government meets the statutory test. Of course, if the court concluded that the government's sole objective was merely to gain evidence of past criminal conduct — even foreign intelligence crimes — to punish the agent rather than halt ongoing espionage or terrorist activity, the application should be denied.

... It can be argued, however, that by providing that an application is to be granted if the government has only a "significant purpose" of gaining foreign intelligence information, the Patriot Act allows the government to have a primary objective of prosecuting an agent for a non-foreign intelligence crime. Yet we think that would be an anomalous reading of the amendment. For we see not the slightest indication that Congress meant to give that power to the Executive Branch. Accordingly, the manifestation of such a purpose, it seems to us, would continue to disqualify an application. That is not to deny that ordinary crimes might be inextricably intertwined with foreign intelligence crimes. For example, if a group of international terrorists were to engage in bank robberies in order to finance the manufacture of a bomb, evidence of the bank robbery should be treated just as evidence of the terrorist act itself. But the FISA process cannot be used as a device to investigate wholly unrelated ordinary crimes....

III. ...

The FISA court expressed concern that unless FISA were "construed" in the fashion that it did, the government could use a FISA order as an improper substitute for an ordinary criminal warrant under Title III. That concern seems to suggest that the FISA court thought Title III procedures are constitutionally mandated if the government has a prosecutorial objective regarding an agent of a foreign power. But in *United States v. United States District Court* (*Keith*), 407 U.S. 297, 322 (1972) — in which the Supreme Court explicitly declined to consider foreign intelligence surveillance — the Court indicated that, even with respect to domestic national security intelligence gathering for prosecutorial purposes where a warrant was mandated, Title III procedures were not constitutionally required: "[W]e do not hold that the same type of standards and procedures prescribed by Title III are necessarily applicable to this case. We recognize that domestic security surveillance may involve different policy and practical considerations from the surveillance of 'ordinary crime.'" Nevertheless, in asking whether FISA procedures can be regarded as reasonable under the Fourth Amendment, we think it is instructive to compare those procedures and requirements with their Title III counterparts. Obviously, the closer those FISA procedures are to Title III procedures, the lesser are our constitutional concerns....

... [W]hile Title III contains some protections that are not in FISA, in many significant respects the two statutes are equivalent, and in some, FISA contains additional protections. Still, to the extent the two statutes diverge in constitutionally relevant areas — in particular, in their probable cause and particularity showings — a FISA order may not be a "warrant" contemplated by the Fourth Amendment.... We do not decide the issue but note that to the extent a FISA order comes close to meeting Title III, that certainly bears on its reasonableness under the Fourth Amendment....

Ultimately, the question becomes whether FISA, as amended by the Patriot Act, is a reasonable response based on a balance of the legitimate need of the government for foreign intelligence information to protect against national security threats with the protected rights of citizens....

It will be recalled that the case that set forth the primary purpose test as constitutionally required was *Truong*. The Fourth Circuit thought that *Keith*'s balancing standard implied the adoption of the primary purpose test. We reiterate that *Truong* dealt with a pre-FISA surveillance based on the President's constitutional responsibility to conduct the foreign affairs of the United States. 629 F.2d at 914. Although *Truong* suggested the line it drew was a constitutional minimum that would apply to a FISA surveillance, *see id.* at 914 n.4, it had no occasion to consider the application of the statute carefully. The *Truong* court, as did all the other courts to have decided the issue, held that the President did have inherent authority to conduct warrantless searches to obtain foreign intelligence information.... We take for granted that the President does have that authority and, assuming that is so, FISA could not encroach on the President's constitutional power. The question before us is the reverse, does FISA amplify the President's power by providing a mechanism that at least approaches a classic warrant and which therefore supports the government's contention that FISA searches are constitutionally reasonable....

... [The *Truong*] analysis, in our view, rested on a false premise and the line the court sought to draw was inherently unstable, unrealistic, and confusing. The false premise was the assertion that once the government moves to criminal prosecution, its "foreign policy concerns" recede. As we have discussed in the first part of the opinion, that is simply not true as it relates to counterintelligence. In that field the government's primary purpose is to halt the espionage or terrorism efforts, and criminal prosecutions can be, and usually are, interrelated with other techniques used to frustrate a foreign power's efforts....

CONCLUSION

...Even without taking into account the President's inherent constitutional authority to conduct warrantless foreign intelligence surveillance, we think the procedures and government showings required under FISA, if they do not meet the minimum Fourth Amendment warrant standards, certainly come close. We, therefore, believe firmly, applying the balancing test drawn from *Keith*, that FISA as amended is constitutional because the surveillances it authorizes are reasonable....

NOTES AND QUESTIONS

1. *The Holding.* What is the holding of *In re Sealed Case*? Is the holding based on FISA, on the Constitution, or both? Can you reconcile the holding with *Keith*? Does *Truong* have any continuing relevance to the law of national security surveillance?

2. *Purpose vs. Use.* The *Sealed Case* decision emphasized the importance of preserving the foreign intelligence objectives of FISA. In view of those objectives, on what basis did the FISCR object to barring the Criminal Division from directing or controlling the use of FISA procedures? Was the FISC order found defective because of the Patriot Act amendments to FISA, or would it have been reversed even if FISA had not been amended?

Is the FBI now permitted to conduct a secret search or wiretap for the primary purpose of investigating possible criminal activity even though there is no probable cause to suspect the commission of a crime? Although terrorism itself is criminal, terrorists may also engage in common criminal activities — credit card fraud, for example. If the Patriot Act amendment makes it easier for the FBI to manage parallel criminal and intelligence investigations, is the gain in effectiveness worth the risk of misuse of the process?

3. *"Special Needs."* In an omitted portion of the opinion, the FISCR analogized its support of the lowered wall to the Supreme Court's approval of warrantless and sometimes suspicionless searches that are designed to serve the government's "special needs, beyond the normal need for law enforcement." *In re Sealed Case*, 310 F.3d at 743, quoting *Vernonia School Dist. 47J v. Acton*, 515 U.S. 646, 653 (1995) (quoting *Griffin v. Wisconsin*, 483 U.S. 868, 873 (1987) (internal quotation marks omitted)). As noted in Chapter 6, the Court has upheld searches that do not satisfy conventional Fourth Amendment standards for suspicionless drug-testing of student athletes, government employees, and railroad workers, along with administrative searches of residences and certain highly regulated businesses. Are you persuaded that the Supreme Court's "special needs" cases are based on considerations analogous to the Justice Department procedures at issue in the principal case? The special needs doctrine is discussed by the FISCR in a second decision *infra* p. 233.

4. *The Aftermath.* In 2003, the FBI issued a classified field directive to further dismantle the wall between law enforcement and intelligence investigations. The directive spelled out the Model Counterterrorism Investigations Strategy (MCIS) and requirements that criminal and intelligence investigators physically work as part of the same teams investigating terrorism. Dan Eggen, *FBI Applies New Rules to*

Surveillance, Wash. Post, Dec. 13, 2003. In 2006 a National Security Division (NSD) was created at the Department of Justice by the USA Patriot Reauthorization and Improvement Act, *supra* p. 209. Creation of the NSD consolidated the former Office of Intelligence Policy and Review (OIPR) (now the Office of Intelligence) and the Counterterrorism and Counterespionage sections of the Criminal Division to ensure full coordination between intelligence investigators and criminal prosecutors. *See* http://www.justice.gov/nsd/about-nsd.html. Do the revised structures satisfy the requirements outlined in the FISCR decision? Is the new strategy constitutional?

C. FISA TRENDS

The FISC has been active. More than 20,000 applications for surveillance or searches have been approved by the FISC since 1979. Brief annual FISA reports from the Attorney General, including the volume of applications approved for the year, are posted at http://www.fas.org/irp/agency/doj/fisa/#rept. During calendar year 2010, 1,579 applications were made to conduct electronic surveillance and physical searches (1,511 included requests to conduct electronic surveillance). Five applications were withdrawn by the government prior to a FISC ruling. The FISC did not deny any applications in whole or in part, and it made modifications to the proposed orders in 14 applications submitted by the government in 2010. *See* Letter from Ronald Weich, Assistant Attorney General, to Senator Harry Reid (Apr. 29, 2011), *available at* http://www.fas.org/irp/agency/doj/fisa/2010rept.pdf. Although the most recent data show a reduction in the aggregate number of FISA applications for electronic surveillance since peaking at more than 2,000 annually in 2005, the lower number reflects congressional approval of programmatic surveillance in 2007 and 2008 (see Chapter 8), not an actual reduction in surveillance or in the workload of the FISC or DOJ. Spencer S. Hsu, *As Approvals Drop, Work on Secret Wiretaps Grows, U.S. Government Sources Say*, Wash. Post, Dec. 24, 2010. By comparison, an average of about 600-700 requests for electronic surveillance are submitted to federal courts by law enforcement officials under 18 U.S.C. §2518 annually. What do the numbers suggest?

Notwithstanding the ever-increasing use of FISA and the FISC, foreign intelligence surveillance of suspected terrorists under the terms and conditions of FISA has not been a panacea. In part, this is because

> experience demonstrates three harsh realities: first, it is often difficult to isolate U.S. persons from one or more foreign surveillance targets in a place or through electronic monitoring; second, it is often impossible to determine the relationship of a potential terrorist to a foreign power early in an investigation; and third ... U.S. persons are as capable as any other of wreaking catastrophic havoc. [Banks & Bowman, *supra* p. 170, at 95.]

The lone wolf provision, *supra* p. 206, is supposed to address the second of these concerns.

Programmatic Electronic Surveillance for Foreign Intelligence

8

With the ongoing revolution in digital communications, the idea of a geographic border has become an increasingly less viable marker for legal authorities and their limits. So has the citizenship or status of a target of electronic surveillance. Using the Internet, packets of data that constitute messages travel in disparate ways through global networks, many of which come through or end up in the United States. Those packets and countless Skype calls and instant and text messages originate from the United States in growing numbers, although the senders or recipients may be in the United States or abroad. Moreover, it may or may not be possible to identify senders or recipients by the e-mail addresses or phone numbers they use to communicate.

Do we think of our international communications as being somehow less private than our domestic calls? When FISA was enacted in 1978, Congress apparently exempted surveillance conducted abroad because in that era most Americans' communications did not travel along international wires. Now our message packets may travel abroad, even if we are in the United States corresponding by e-mail with a friend who is in the same city.

Because FISA was written to apply to broadly defined categories of "electronic surveillance" inside the United States, these recent developments in technology have brought the interception of many previously unregulated communications — e-mail is the most prominent example — inside the FISA scheme. Thus, with FISA's traditional focus on domestic collection, even a foreign-to-foreign text message intercepted from a server inside the United States requires compliance with FISA procedures.

Evolving technologies have also turned the traditional sequence of FISA processes on its head. We discovered after 9/11 that investigators could enter transactional data about potential terrorists and come up with a list that included four of the hijackers — a sort of reverse of a typical FISA investigation. Now data mining — the application of algorithms or other database techniques to reveal hidden characteristics or relationships — may be used to develop a list of targets for traditional FISA surveillance. In order to collect foreign intelligence data to mine, officials claim that they need access to telecom switches inside the United States, or that they need records of Internet traffic residing on servers in the United States. In either instance, of course, the collected data would almost certainly include information about U.S. persons.

In this chapter we first examine programmatic surveillance — collection of data without court orders identifying individual targets — conducted by the George W. Bush administration. The so-called Terrorist Surveillance Program (TSP) was hidden from public view for more than four years, in part at least because it was so controversial. We then explore congressional responses to technological change and to the TSP. In 2008 Congress codified programmatic surveillance as a new subtitle of FISA and, in doing so, ushered in a new era of warrantless surveillance, the legal parameters of which are still being formed. The second published decision of the Foreign Intelligence Surveillance Court of Review (FISCR), reproduced below, provides an early test of the legal efficacy of programmatic surveillance.

A.   CASE STUDY: THE TERRORIST SURVEILLANCE PROGRAM

On December 16, 2005, the *New York Times* reported that, according to government officials, "President Bush secretly authorized the National Security Agency to eavesdrop on Americans and others inside the United States to search for evidence of terrorist activity without the court-approved warrants ordinarily required for domestic spying." James Risen & Eric Lichtblau, *Bush Lets U.S. Spy on Callers Without Courts*, N.Y. Times, Dec. 16, 2005. Pursuant to a still-secret executive order signed by the President in October 2001, the NSA had without warrants monitored the telephone and e-mail communications of thousands of persons inside the United States, where one end of the communication was outside the United States, in an effort to learn more about possible terrorist plots. *Id.* Later called the Terrorist Surveillance Program (TSP) by the Administration, the NSA surveillance created a major controversy, drawing out prominent critics and proponents alike, provoking hearings in Congress, prompting lawsuits by civil liberties organizations and by defendants who challenged their previous pleas or convictions, and generating countless op-ed pieces, blog debates, and commentary.

The Bush administration vigorously defended the TSP. President Bush first authorized the program for about 45 days and then renewed the authorization at the end of each succeeding 45-day period. *President's Radio Address* (Dec. 17, 2005), *at* http://georgewbush-whitehouse.archives.gov/news/releases//2005/12/20051217. html. According to the President, the program had to be approved "by our nation's top legal officials, including the Attorney General and the Counsel to the President." *Id.* Shortly after the story broke in the *New York Times*, the Justice Department's Office of Legislative Affairs immediately prepared a letter for congressional leaders summarizing its legal rationale for the NSA surveillance. Excerpts from that letter follow:

Letter from William E. Moschella, Assistant Attorney General, to The Honorable Pat Roberts, Chairman, Senate Select Committee on Intelligence et al.

Dec. 22, 2005
available at http://www.fas.org/irp/agency/doj/fisa/doj122205.pdf

As you know, in response to unauthorized disclosures in the media, the President has described certain activities of the National Security Agency ("NSA") that he has authorized since shortly after September 11, 2001. As described by the President, the

NSA intercepts certain international communications into and out of the United States of people linked to al Qaeda or an affiliated terrorist organization. The purpose of these intercepts is to establish an early warning system to detect and prevent another catastrophic terrorist attack on the United States. The President has made clear that he will use his constitutional and statutory authorities to protect the American people from further terrorist attacks, and the NSA activities the President described are part of that effort. Leaders of the Congress were briefed on these activities more than a dozen times.

The purpose of this letter is to provide an additional brief summary of the legal authority supporting the NSA activities described by the President.

As an initial matter, I emphasize a few points. The President stated that these activities are "crucial to our national security." The President further explained that "the unauthorized disclosure of this effort damages our national security and puts our citizens at risk. Revealing classified information is illegal, alerts our enemies, and endangers our country." These critical national security activities remain classified. All United States laws and policies governing the protection and nondisclosure of national security information, including the information relating to the activities described by the President, remain in full force and effect. The unauthorized disclosure of classified information violates federal criminal law. The Government may provide further classified briefings to the Congress on these activities in an appropriate manner. Any such briefings will be conducted in a manner that will not endanger national security.

Under Article II of the Constitution, including in his capacity as Commander in Chief, the President has the responsibility to protect the Nation from further attacks, and the Constitution gives him all necessary authority to fulfill that duty. *See, e.g., Prize Cases*, 67 U.S. (2 Black) 635, 668 (1863) (stressing that if the Nation is invaded, "the President is not only authorized but bound to resist by force . . . without waiting for any special legislative authority"); *Campbell v. Clinton*, 203 F.3d 19, 27 (D.C. Cir. 2000) (Silberman, J., concurring) ("[T]he *Prize Cases* . . . stand for the proposition that the President has independent authority to repel aggressive acts by third parties even without specific congressional authorization, and courts may not review the level of force selected."); *id.* at 40 (Tatel, J., concurring). The Congress recognized this constitutional authority in the preamble to the Authorization for the Use of Military Force ("AUMF") of September 18, 2001, 115 Stat. 224 (2001) ("[T]he President has authority under the Constitution to take action to deter and prevent acts of international terrorism against the United States."), and in the War Powers Resolution, *see* 50 U.S.C. §1541(c) ("The constitutional powers of the President as Commander in Chief to introduce United States Armed Forces into hostilities [] . . . [extend to] a national emergency created by attack upon the United States, its territories or possessions, or its armed forces.").

This constitutional authority includes the authority to order warrantless foreign intelligence surveillance within the United States, as all federal appellate courts, including at least four circuits, to have addressed the issue have concluded. *See, e.g., In re Sealed Case*, 310 F.3d 717, 742 (FISA Ct. of Rev. 2002) ("[A]ll the other courts to have decided the issue [have] held that the President did have inherent authority to conduct warrantless searches to obtain foreign intelligence information. . . . We take for granted that the President does have that authority. . . ."). The Supreme Court has said that warrants are generally required in the context of purely *domestic* threats, but it expressly distinguished *foreign* threats. *See United States v. United States*

District Court, 407 U.S. 297, 308 (1972). As Justice Byron White recognized almost 40 years ago, Presidents have long exercised the authority to conduct warrantless surveillance for national security purposes, and a warrant is unnecessary "if the President of the United States or his chief legal officer, the Attorney General, has considered the requirements of national security and authorized electronic surveillance as reasonable." *Katz v. United States*, 389 U.S. 347, 363-364 (1967) (White, J., concurring).

The President's constitutional authority to direct the NSA to conduct the activities he described is supplemented by statutory authority under the AUMF. The AUMF authorizes the President "to use all necessary and appropriate force against those nations, organizations, or persons he determines planned, authorized, committed, or aided the terrorists attacks of September 11, 2001, . . . in order to prevent any future acts of international terrorism against the United States." §2(a). The AUMF clearly contemplates action within the United States, *see also id.* pmbl. (the attacks of September 11 "render it both necessary and appropriate that the United States exercise its rights to self-defense and to protect United States citizens both at home and abroad"). The AUMF cannot be read as limited to authorizing the use of force against Afghanistan, as some have argued. Indeed, those who directly "committed" the attacks of September 11 resided in the United States for months before those attacks. The reality of the September 11 plot demonstrates that the authorization of force covers activities both on foreign soil and in America.

In *Hamdi v. Rumsfeld*, 542 U.S. 507 (2004), the Supreme Court addressed the scope of the AUMF. At least five Justices concluded that the AUMF authorized the President to detain a U.S. citizen in the United States because "detention to prevent a combatant's return to the battlefield is a fundamental incident of waging war" and is therefore included in the "necessary and appropriate force" authorized by the Congress. *Id.* at 518-519 (plurality opinion of O'Connor, J.); *see id.* 587 (Thomas, J., dissenting). These five Justices concluded that the AUMF "clearly and unmistakably authorize[s]" the "fundamental incident[s] of waging war." *Id.* at 518-19 (plurality opinion); *see id.* at 587 (Thomas, J., dissenting).

Communications intelligence targeted at the enemy is a fundamental incident of the use of military force. Indeed, throughout history, signals intelligence has formed a critical part of waging war. In the Civil War, each side tapped the telegraph lines of the other. In the World Wars, the United States intercepted telegrams into and out of the country. The AUMF cannot be read to exclude this long-recognized and essential authority to conduct communications intelligence targeted at the enemy. We cannot fight a war blind. Because communications intelligence activities constitute, to use the language of *Hamdi*, a fundamental incident of waging war, the AUMF *clearly and unmistakably authorizes* such activities directed against the communications of our enemy. Accordingly, the President's "authority is at its maximum." *Youngstown Sheet & Tube Co. v. Sawyer*, 343 U.S. 579, 635 (1952) (Jackson, J., concurring); *see Dames & Moore v. Regan*, 453 U.S. 654, 668 (1981); *cf. Youngstown*, 343 U.S. at 585 (noting the absence of a statute "from which [the asserted authority] c[ould] be fairly implied").

The President's authorization of targeted electronic surveillance by the NSA is also consistent with the Foreign Intelligence Surveillance Act ("FISA"). Section 2511(2)(f) of title 18 provides, as relevant here, that the procedures of FISA and two chapters of title 18 "shall be the exclusive means by which electronic surveillance . . . may be conducted." Section 109 of FISA, in turn, makes it unlawful to conduct electronic surveillance, "except as authorized by statute." 50 U.S.C. §1809(a)(1). Importantly, section 109's exception for electronic surveillance "authorized by statute" is broad, especially considered in the context of surrounding provisions. *See* 18 U.S.C. §2511(1) ("Except as otherwise specifically provided *in this chapter* any person who — (a) intentionally intercepts . . . any wire, oral or electronic communication [] . . . shall be punished . . . .") (emphasis added); *id.* §2511(2)(e) (providing a defense to liability to individuals "conduct[ing] electronic surveillance, . . . as authorized by *that Act [FISA]*") (emphasis added).

By expressly and broadly excepting from its prohibition electronic surveillance undertaken "as authorized by statute," section 109 of FISA permits an exception to the "procedures" of FISA referred to in U.S.C. §2511(2)(f) where authorized by another statute, even if the other authorizing statute does not specifically amend section 2511(2)(f). The AUMF satisfies section 109's requirement for statutory authorization of electronic surveillance, just as a majority of the Court in *Hamdi* concluded that it satisfies the requirement in 18 U.S.C. §4001(a) that no U.S. citizen be detained by the United States "except pursuant to an Act of Congress." *See Hamdi*, 542 U.S. at 519 (explaining that "it is of no moment that the AUMF does not use specific language of detention"); *see id.* at 587 (Thomas, J., dissenting).

Some might suggest that FISA could be read to require that a subsequent statutory authorization must come in the form of an amendment to FISA itself. But under established principles of statutory construction, the AUMF and FISA must be construed in harmony to avoid any potential conflict between FISA and the President's Article II authority as Commander in Chief. *See, e.g., Zadvydas v. Davis*, 533 U.S. 678, 689 (2001); *INS v. St. Cyr*, 533 U.S. 289, 300 (2001). Accordingly, any ambiguity as to whether the AUMF is a statute that satisfies the requirements of FISA and allows electronic surveillance in the conflict with al Qaeda without complying with FISA procedures must be resolved in favor of an interpretation that is consistent with the President's long-recognized authority.

The NSA activities described by the President are also consistent with the Fourth Amendment and the protection of civil liberties. The Fourth Amendment's "central requirement is one of reasonableness." *Illinois v. McArthur*, 531 U.S. 326, 330 (2001) (internal quotation marks omitted). For searches conducted in the course of ordinary criminal law enforcement, reasonableness generally requires securing a warrant. *See Bd. of Educ. v. Earls*, 536 U.S. 822, 828 (2002). Outside the ordinary criminal law enforcement context, however, the Supreme Court has, at times, dispensed with the warrant, instead adjudging the reasonableness of a search under the totality of circumstances. *See United States v. Knights*, 534 U.S. 112, 118 (2001). In particular, the Supreme Court has long recognized that "special needs, beyond the normal need for law enforcement," can justify departure from the usual warrant requirement. *Vernonia School Dist. 47J v. Acton*, 515 U.S. 646, 653 (1995); *see also City of Indianapolis v. Edmond*, 531 U.S. 32, 41-42 (2000) (striking down checkpoint where "primary purpose was to detect evidence of ordinary criminal wrongdoing").

Foreign intelligence collection, especially in the midst of an armed conflict in which the adversary has already launched catastrophic attacks within the United States, fits squarely within the "special needs" exception to the warrant requirement. Foreign intelligence collection undertaken to prevent further devastating attacks on our Nation serves the highest purpose through means other than traditional law enforcement. *See In re Sealed Case*, 310 F.3d at 745; *United States v. Duggan*, 743 F.2d 59, 72 (2d Cir. 1984) (recognizing that the Fourth Amendment implications of foreign intelligence surveillance are far different from ordinary wiretapping, because they are not principally used for criminal prosecution).

Intercepting communications into and out of the United States of persons linked to al Qaeda in order to detect and prevent a catastrophic attack is clearly *reasonable*. Reasonableness is generally determined by "balancing the nature of the intrusion on the individual's privacy against the promotion of legitimate governmental interests." *Earls*, 536 U.S. at 829. There is undeniably an important and legitimate privacy interest at stake with respect to the activities described by the President. That must be balanced, however, against the Government's compelling interest in the security of the Nation, *see, e.g., Haig v. Agee*, 453 U.S. 280, 307 (1981) ("It is obvious and unarguable that no governmental interest is more compelling than the security of the Nation.") (citation and quotation marks omitted). The fact that the NSA activities are reviewed and reauthorized approximately every 45 days to ensure that they continue to be necessary and appropriate further demonstrates the reasonableness of these activities.

As explained above, the President determined that it was necessary following September 11 to create an early warning detection system. FISA could not have provided the speed and agility required for the early warning detection system. In addition, any legislative change, other than the AUMF, that the President might have sought specifically to create such an early warning system would have been public and would have tipped off our enemies concerning our intelligence limitations and capabilities. Nevertheless, I want to stress that the United States makes full use of FISA to address the terrorist threat, and FISA has proven to be a very important tool, especially in longer-term investigations. In addition, the United States is constantly assessing all available legal options, taking full advantage of any developments in the law.

We hope this information is helpful.

Sincerely,
William E. Moschella
Assistant Attorney General

NOTES AND QUESTIONS

1. *Nature of the Terrorist Surveillance Program.* What did the NSA actually do, as best you can tell from the Department of Justice (DOJ) letter? Were there any internal procedural controls? If so, what were they? Did they adequately safeguard any privacy rights that might have been implicated?

2. *The Predicate Legal Standard for Surveillance.* As indicated in the Justice Department letter, the TSP conducted surveillance of persons "linked to al Qaeda or an affiliated terrorist organization." How do you suppose it was determined whether a person fit that description? What legal standard would govern such a determination? In written answers to questions raised by Senators at a July 26, 2006, Senate Judiciary Committee hearing, NSA Director Keith B. Alexander stated that

professional intelligence officers at [NSA], with the assistance of other elements of the Intelligence Community and subject to appropriate and vigorous oversight by the NSA Inspector General and General Counsel, among others, would rely on the best available intelligence information to determine whether there are reasonable grounds to believe that a party to an international communication is affiliated with al Qaeda. [Senator Edward M. Kennedy, *FISA for the 21st Century: Questions for Lt. General Keith B. Alexander* (July 26, 2006), *available at* http://www.fas.org/irp/congress/2006_hr/ alexander-qfr.pdf.]

Do you see any legal shortcomings in this description of the decision process and the legal standard for implementing TSP surveillance?

3. *Applicability of FISA.* Although FISA's scope is summarized in *United States v. Rosen* and the Notes and Questions following that case in Chapter 7, in considering the applicability of FISA to the TSP you will want to look in particular at the language of §1801(f), quoted *supra* p. 204. Consider also the complete text of 18 U.S.C. §2511(2)(e) and (f), governing ordinary criminal warrants:

(e) Notwithstanding any other provision of this title or section 705 or 706 of the Communications Act of 1934, it shall not be unlawful for an officer, employee, or agent of the United States in the normal course of his official duty to conduct electronic surveillance, as defined in section 101 of the Foreign Intelligence Surveillance Act of 1978, as authorized by that Act.

(f) Nothing contained in this chapter or chapter 121 or 206 of this title, or section 705 of the Communications Act of 1934, shall be deemed to affect the acquisition by the United States Government of foreign intelligence information from international or foreign communications, or foreign intelligence activities conducted in accordance with otherwise applicable Federal law involving a foreign electronic communications system, utilizing a means other than electronic surveillance as defined in section 101 [50 U.S.C. section 1801] of the Foreign Intelligence Surveillance Act of 1978, and procedures in this chapter or chapter 121 and the Foreign Intelligence Surveillance Act of 1978 shall be the exclusive means by which electronic surveillance, as defined in section 101 of such Act, and the interception of domestic wire, oral, and electronic communications may be conducted.

In addition, consider §1809(a)(1) of FISA (making unauthorized electronic surveillance a criminal offense):

A person is guilty of an offense if he intentionally—
(1) engages in electronic surveillance under color of law except as authorized by statute; or
(2) discloses or uses information obtained under color of law by electronic surveillance, knowing or having reason to know that the information was obtained through electronic surveillance not authorized by statute. [50 U.S.C. §1809(a)(1).]

Are you persuaded by the DOJ analysis that FISA is inapplicable to the TSP?

Does it affect your answer that on January 17, 2007, Attorney General Gonzales wrote to Senators Leahy and Specter of the Senate Judiciary Committee and advised them that on January 10, a FISC judge "issued orders authorizing the Government to target for collection international communications into or out of the United States where there is probable cause to believe that one of the communicants is a member or agent of al Qaeda or an associated terrorist organization"? Letter from Attorney General Alberto R. Gonzales to Sens. Leahy and Specter (Jan. 17, 2007), *available at* http://www.fas.org/irp/congress/2007_cr/fisa011707.html. According to the

Attorney General, these orders would "allow the necessary speed and agility" and, accordingly, all surveillance previously occurring under the TSP would thereafter be conducted with the approval of the FISC.

4. *Why Not FISA?* The government has an enviable track record in the FISC. See *supra* p. 220. Why did it not seek a FISA order for the TSP? In a January 2006 address, Attorney General Alberto R. Gonzales defended the decision not to rely on FISA:

> We have to remember that we're talking about a wartime foreign intelligence program. It is an "early warning system" with only one purpose: To detect and prevent the next attack on the United States from foreign agents hiding in our midst. It is imperative for national security that we can detect RELIABLY, IMMEDIATELY, and WITHOUT DELAY whenever communications associated with al Qaeda enter or leave the United States. That may be the only way to alert us to the presence of an al Qaeda agent in our country and to the existence of an unfolding plot.
>
> Consistent with the wartime intelligence nature of this program, the optimal way to achieve the necessary speed and agility is to leave the decisions about particular intercepts to the judgment of professional intelligence officers, based on the best available intelligence information. They can make that call quickly. If, however, those same intelligence officers had to navigate through the FISA process for each of these intercepts, that would necessarily introduce a significant factor of DELAY, and there would be critical holes in our early warning system.
>
> Some have pointed to the provision in FISA that allows for so-called "emergency authorizations" of surveillance for 72 hours without a court order. There's a serious misconception about these emergency authorizations. People should know that we do not approve emergency authorizations without knowing that we will receive court approval within 72 hours. FISA requires the Attorney General to determine IN ADVANCE that a FISA application for that particular intercept will be fully supported and will be approved by the court before an emergency authorization may be granted. That review process can take precious time. Thus, to initiate surveillance under a FISA emergency authorization, it is not enough to rely on the best judgment of our intelligence officers alone. Those intelligence officers would have to get the sign-off of lawyers at the NSA that all provisions of FISA have been satisfied, then lawyers in the Department of Justice would have to be similarly satisfied, and finally as Attorney General, I would have to be satisfied that the search meets the requirements of FISA. And we would have to be prepared to follow up with a full FISA application within the 72 hours. [Prepared Remarks for Attorney General Alberto R. Gonzales, Georgetown University Law Center, Jan. 24, 2006, *available at* http://www.usdoj.gov/ag/speeches/2006/ag_speech_0601241.html.]

In evaluating the Attorney General's statement, consider FISA's emergency surveillance provisions, quoted *supra* p. 209. Do you believe he was justified in bypassing the FISA procedures?

5. *The AUMF as Authority for the TSP?* Recall that the September 18, 2001, Authorization for the Use of Military Force (AUMF), *supra* p. 87, authorizes the President to

> use all necessary and appropriate force against those nations, organizations, or persons he determines planned, authorized, committed, or aided the terrorist attacks that occurred on September 11, 2001, or harbored such organizations, or persons, in order to prevent any future acts of international terrorism against the United States by such nations, organizations or persons. [Pub. L. No. 107-40, §2(a), 115 Stat. 224 (2001).]

Did it thereby authorize the TSP? (The Supreme Court's construction of the AUMF appears in the *Hamdi* case, *infra* p. 445.) Is it relevant to your answer that in the USA Patriot Act, enacted in October 2001, *after* enacting the AUMF, Congress amended FISA by, *inter alia*, extending the period of emergency surveillance from 24 hours to 72 hours, or that it left in place the following FISA provision?

> Notwithstanding any other law, the President, through the Attorney General, may authorize electronic surveillance without a court order under this subchapter to acquire foreign intelligence information for a period not to exceed fifteen calendar days following a declaration of war by the Congress. [50 U.S.C. §1811 (2006 & Supp. III 2009).]

In light of the comprehensive scheme detailed in FISA, should the more open-ended grant of authority in the AUMF be read to authorize the TSP?

In *Greene v. McElroy*, 360 U.S. 474 (1959), the Supreme Court declined to find authority for security clearance procedures employed by the Executive in the absence of explicit approval by either the President or Congress. *See also Kent v. Dulles*, 357 U.S. 116 (1958) (declining to find authority for the Secretary of State to restrict the right of travel absent explicit delegation from Congress). *But see Haig v. Agee*, 453 U.S. 280 (1981) (inferring authority to restrict the right of travel from congressional acquiescence in State Department policy). The *Greene* Court cited *Ex parte Endo*, 323 U.S. 283, 303 n.24 (1944), in which the Court declared that under the circumstances of that case a claim of Executive authority based on an appropriation would have to "plainly show a purpose to bestow the precise authority which is claimed." There the Court found no authorization for the continued imprisonment of loyal Japanese-Americans during World War II "where a lump appropriation was made for the overall program of the [War Relocation] Authority and no sums were earmarked for the single phase of the total program [there] involved." *Id.* Should a "clear statement" requirement apply to prevent reliance on the AUMF as authority for the TSP?

6. *Inherent Constitutional Authority?* In light of all the foregoing, did President Bush have inherent constitutional authority to order the TSP? Consider the President's exchange with a reporter at a December 19, 2005, press conference:

Q . . . [W]hy did you skip the basic safeguards of asking courts for permission for the intercepts?

THE PRESIDENT: First of all, I — right after September the 11th, I knew we were fighting a different kind of war. And so I asked people in my administration to analyze how best for me and our government to do the job people expect us to do, which is to detect and prevent a possible attack. That's what the American people want. We looked at the possible scenarios. And the people responsible for helping us protect and defend came forth with the current program, because it enables us to move faster and quicker. And that's important. We've got to be fast on our feet, quick to detect and prevent.

We use FISA still — you're referring to the FISA court in your question — of course, we use FISA. But FISA is for long-term monitoring. What is needed in order to protect the American people is the ability to move quickly to detect.

Now, having suggested this idea, I then, obviously, went to the question, is it legal to do so? I am — I swore to uphold the laws. Do I have the legal authority to do this? And the answer is, absolutely. As I mentioned in my remarks, the legal authority is derived from the Constitution, as well as the authorization of force by the United States Congress.

Are you persuaded by the President's statement? Consider the arguments made in the Justice Department letter. If you think there is a clash between the President's claim of authority and the statutes — placing the TSP in Justice Jackson's third category — how should we resolve it?

7. *The Fourth Amendment.* If the President has inherent constitutional authority for the TSP, notwithstanding any statute, does he also escape the strictures of the Fourth Amendment? If not, is the program constitutional? A few weeks after the September 11 attacks, Office of Legal Counsel (OLC) lawyers John Yoo and Robert Delahunty prepared a memorandum for White House Counsel Gonzales and DOD General Counsel William J. Haynes II, offering advice on the authority for the use of military force to prevent or deter terrorist activity inside the United States. *Memorandum for Alberto R. Gonzales & William J. Haynes, II, Authority for Use of Military Force to Combat Terrorist Activities Within the United States* (Oct. 23, 2001, *available at* http://www.fas.org/irp/agency/doj/olc/milforce.pdf. The authors argued that the President has expanded wartime powers that trump Fourth Amendment requirements:

> [H]owever well suited the warrant and probable cause requirements may be as applied to criminal investigations or to other law enforcement activities, they are unsuited to the demands of wartime and the military necessity to successfully prosecute a war against an enemy. In the circumstances of September 11, the Constitution provides the Government with expanded powers to prosecute the war effort. . . . In light of the well-settled understanding that constitutional constraints must give way in some respects to the exigencies of war, we think that the better view is that the Fourth Amendment does *not* apply to domestic military operations designed to deter and prevent further terrorist attacks. [*Id.* at 24-25 (emphasis in original).]

Are you persuaded?

8. *The End of TSP?* In his January 2007 letter to Senators Leahy and Specter, *supra* Note 3, Attorney General Gonzales concluded by stating that the President would not reauthorize the TSP when its current authorization expired. *Id.* Why would the President have chosen to discontinue the TSP? Did he do it because he was able to obtain the functional equivalent of the TSP through orders from the FISC? Review §§1804 and 1805 of FISA, described in *United States v. Rosen, supra* p. 195, and in the Notes and Questions that follow it. Can you imagine what the FISC orders say? At least one FISC judge may have agreed to treat the international telecom switches inside the United States as FISA "facilities." Assuming that communications involving Al Qaeda passed through telecom switches in the United States, obtaining such orders from the FISC gave the government access to nearly all international telecom traffic coming and going from the United States. *See* William C. Banks, *Programmatic Surveillance and FISA: Of Needles in Haystacks,* 88 Tex. L. Rev. 1633, 1643 (2010). How should a FISC judge have responded to the inevitable fact that the rest of America was using those switches at the same time? Whatever the content of the orders, do you think they ended the legal controversy over the TSP?

9. *The Lawsuits Challenging TSP.* Private plaintiffs filed lawsuits against agencies and/or officials of the government allegedly involved in the TSP. In *American Civil Liberties Union v. National Security Agency,* 438 F. Supp. 2d 754 (E.D. Mich. 2006), a district court actually declared the TSP unlawful for violating both FISA and the

Fourth Amendment. The Court of Appeals reversed, 493 F.3d 644 (6th Cir. 2007), ruling that the plaintiffs lacked standing because they could not prove that they had been subjected to the surveillance. In addition, the plaintiffs could not rely on discovery to develop their proof of injury because of the state secrets doctrine. *Id.* at 683, 687-688.

In *Al-Haramain Islamic Foundation v. Bush*, 451 F. Supp. 2d 1215 (D. Or. 2006), *rev'd*, 507 F.3d 1190 (9th Cir. 2007), the plaintiff Foundation had, through government error in the discovery process in different litigation involving the Foundation and the Treasury Department, obtained documents showing that the government had recorded telephone conversations between one of its Saudi Arabia-based officers and two of its U.S.-based lawyers. Although the federal District Court in Oregon allowed the plaintiffs to rely on the documents as evidence that they were subjected to the TSP, 451 F. Supp. at 1227, 1229, the Ninth Circuit Court of Appeals reversed, but remanded the case to determine whether FISA preempts the state secrets privilege. 507 F.3d at 1193. Eventually all the remaining TSP lawsuits were transferred to the Northern District of California, where in 2008 Judge Vaughn Walker ruled that, in some circumstances, FISA preempts the state secrets privilege. *In re Telecommunications Records Litig.*, 564 F. Supp. 2d 1109, 1119 (N.D. Cal. 2008). But he dismissed the Foundation's case without prejudice after ruling that the accidentally disclosed documents remained subject to the state secrets privilege and thus could not provide the necessary proof of injury to establish standing. 564 F. Supp. 2d at 1137. In January 2011, Judge Walker dismissed the lawsuit after concluding that the plaintiffs lack standing to assert their claims. *In re National Security Agency Telecommunications Records Litig.*, Case No. 3:07-cv-01115-vrw (N.D. Cal. 2011), *available at* http://www.court housenews.com/2011/02/01/Government wiretaps.pdf.

If the courts are not likely to determine the lawfulness of TSP, can you think of other mechanisms that could provide some accountability for the TSP under FISA and the Constitution? *See* Kathleen Clark, *The Architecture of Accountability: A Case Study of the Warrantless Surveillance Program*, 2010 BYU L. Rev. 357, 390-404 (suggesting transparency mechanisms).

   10. *Investigating the DOJ Lawyers?* In March 2004, Deputy Attorney General James B. Comey, acting for a hospitalized Attorney General John Ashcroft, refused to sign off on a reauthorization of the TSP. The expiring TSP was reauthorized the next day without DOJ approval. Comey considered resigning, and he learned that Ashcroft, FBI Director Mueller, and OLC head Jack Goldsmith would join him. Harold H. Bruff, *Bad Advice: Bush's Lawyers in the War on Terror* 152-154 (2009). In a later speech to the staff at NSA, Comey said that the lawyer is

> the custodian of our Constitution and the rule of law. It is the job of a good lawyer to say "yes." It is as much the job of a good lawyer to say "no." "No" is much, much harder. "No" must be spoken into a storm of crisis, with loud voices all around, with lives hanging in the balance. . . . It takes an understanding that, in the long run, intelligence under law is the only sustainable intelligence in this country. [James B. Comey, *Intelligence Under the Law*, 10 Green Bag 2d 439, 444 (2007).]

In 2006 more than 40 members of Congress requested that the Department of Justice Office of Professional Responsibility (OPR) investigate whether DOJ lawyers acted properly early on in approving the TSP. After OPR opened an investigation, the head of OPR requested that he and six OPR employees be given security clearances so that they could start their work. Apparently on the advice of Attorney General Alberto Gonzales, President Bush denied the clearances, blocking the investigation. Clark, *supra*, 2010 BYU L. Rev. at 402. What standards would have determined whether the DOJ lawyers acted properly?

11. *Amending FISA.* After one FISC judge reportedly approved some version of the TSP, a different FISC judge decided in May 2007 not to continue its approval. The Bush administration immediately urged Congress to pass statutory authorization for the program. In August 2007, Congress enacted the Protect America Act, Pub. L. No. 110-55, 121 Stat. 552, which permitted the DNI and the Attorney General to authorize collection of foreign intelligence concerning persons reasonably believed to be outside the United States, without obtaining an order from the FISC, even if one party to the communication was a U.S. citizen inside the United States. The Protect America Act expired by its own terms in February 2008, leading to the enactment on July 10, 2008, of the FISA Amendments Act.

B. THE FISA AMENDMENTS ACT AND THE FUTURE OF PROGRAMMATIC SURVEILLANCE

In July 2008, Congress enacted the FISA Amendments Act (FAA), Pub. L. No. 110-261, 122 Stat. 2436, 50 U.S.C. §§1881a et seq., which authorized until December 31, 2012, sweeping and suspicionless programmatic surveillance targeting individuals outside the United States. The core of the new subtitle of FISA contains this broad authorization:

> **§1881a. Procedures for Targeting Certain Persons Outside the United States Other than United States Persons.**
>
> (a) Authorization — Notwithstanding any other provision of law, upon the issuance of an order in accordance with subsection (i)(3) or a determination under subsection (c)(2), the Attorney General and the Director of National Intelligence may authorize jointly, for a period of up to 1 year from the effective date of the authorization, the targeting of persons reasonably believed to be located outside the United States to acquire foreign intelligence information.
>
> (b) Limitations — An acquisition authorized under subsection (a) —
>
> (1) may not intentionally target any person known at the time of acquisition to be located in the United States;
>
> (2) may not intentionally target a person reasonably believed to be located outside the United States if the purpose of such acquisition is to target a particular, known person reasonably believed to be in the United States;
>
> (3) may not intentionally target a United States person reasonably believed to be located outside the United States;
>
> (4) may not intentionally acquire any communication as to which the sender and all intended recipients are known at the time of the acquisition to be located in the United States; and
>
> (5) shall be conducted in a manner consistent with the fourth amendment to the Constitution of the United States. . . .

The prohibition on intentionally targeting a United States person abroad, like the other limitations in subsection (b), applies only to the *programmatic* surveillance authorized in subsection (a). The FAA expressly permits *individually targeted* electronic surveillance of United States persons abroad, subject to the traditional FISA requirements, including probable cause of foreign agency. 50 U.S.C. §1881b.

To enable programmatic surveillance, the FISC need not find probable cause of foreign agency or otherwise review individualized surveillance applications under the FAA. *Id.* §1881a(c)(4). Instead, the Attorney General and DNI merely certify to the FISC that acquisitions under the program will meet the targeting objectives and limitations set out above, and that they will satisfy traditional FISA minimization procedures. *Id.* §1881a(g). The certification also must state that the Attorney General had adopted guidelines to ensure that statutory procedures are complied with, that the targeting and minimization procedures and guidelines are consistent with the Fourth Amendment, and that a significant purpose of the programmatic collection is to obtain foreign intelligence information. *Id.*

Judicial review of the certifications, as well as targeting and minimization procedures, must be conducted prior to implementation of an authorization for surveillance, §1881a(i), unless the Attorney General and the DNI determine that "time does not permit" the prior review, in which case the authorization must be sought as soon as practicable, but not more than seven days after the determination is made. §1881a(g)(1)(B). In any event, the judicial review role of the FISC is quite limited:

§1881a(I). Judicial Review of Certifications and Procedures — ...

(3) Orders —
(A) Approval — If the Court finds that a certification submitted in accordance with subsection (g) contains all the required elements and that the targeting and minimization procedures adopted in accordance with subsections (d) and (e) are consistent with the requirements of those subsections and with the fourth amendment to the Constitution of the United States, the Court shall enter an order approving the certification and the use . . . of the procedures for the acquisition. . . .

After a FISC judge approves the program features, the Attorney General and DNI authorize the surveillance program — without the need to obtain judicial orders for individual targets — and issue directives requesting (or compelling) communications carriers to assist. *Id.* §1881a(h). Such a directive was the basis for the following heavily redacted decision of the FISCR, only the second one issued in its 30-year history.

In re Directives [Redacted Text]* Pursuant to Section 105B of the Foreign Intelligence Surveillance Act

Foreign Intelligence Surveillance Court of Review, 2008
551 F.3d 1004

[This decision was based on the temporary Protect America Act, but it concerned some of the core provisions retained in the FISA Amendments Act. It was rendered on August 22, 2008, but only published in redacted form on January 12, 2009.]

* The text and footnotes that have been redacted from this opinion contain classified information.

SELYA, Chief Judge. This petition for review stems from directives issued to the petitioner [redacted text] pursuant to a now-expired set of amendments to the Foreign Intelligence Surveillance Act of 1978 (FISA), [50 U.S.C.A. §§1801-1871 (West 2003 & Supp. 2008)]. Among other things, those amendments, known as the Protect America Act of 2007 (PAA), Pub. L. No. 110-55, 121 Stat. 552, authorized the United States to direct communications service providers to assist it in acquiring foreign intelligence when those acquisitions targeted third persons (such as the service provider's customers) reasonably believed to be located outside the United States. Having received [redacted text] such directives, the petitioner challenged their legality before the Foreign Intelligence Surveillance Court (FISC). When that court found the directives lawful and compelled obedience to them, the petitioner brought this petition for review. . . .

I. THE STATUTORY FRAMEWORK

On August 5, 2007, Congress enacted the PAA, codified in pertinent part at 50 U.S.C. §§1805a to 1805c, as a measured expansion of FISA's scope. Subject to certain conditions, the PAA allowed the government to conduct warrantless foreign intelligence surveillance on targets (including United States persons) "reasonably believed" to be located outside the United States. 50 U.S.C. §1805b(a). This proviso is of critical importance here.

Under the new statute, the Director of National Intelligence (DNI) and the Attorney General (AG) were permitted to authorize, for periods of up to one year, "the acquisition of foreign intelligence information concerning persons reasonably believed to be outside the United States" if they determined that the acquisition met five specified criteria. [They are set out in §1881a(b) above.] . . . Pursuant to this authorization, the DNI and the AG were allowed to issue directives to "person[s]" — a term that includes agents of communications service providers — delineating the assistance needed to acquire the information. *Id.* §1805b(e); *see id.* §1805b(a)(3).

The PAA was a stopgap measure. By its terms, it sunset[ted] on February 16, 2008. Following a lengthy interregnum, the lapsed provisions were repealed on July 10, 2008, through the instrumentality of the FISA Amendments Act of 2008, Pub. L. No. 110-261, §403, 122 Stat. 2436, 2473 (2008). But because the certifications and directives involved in the instant case were issued during the short shelf life of the PAA, they remained in effect. *See* FISA Amendments Act of 2008 §404(a)(1). We therefore assess the validity of the actions at issue here through the prism of the PAA. [redacted text]

II. BACKGROUND

Beginning in [redacted text] 2007, the government issued directives to the petitioner commanding it to assist in warrantless surveillance of certain customers [redacted text and footnote]. These directives were issued pursuant to certifications that purported to contain all the information required by the PAA.

The certifications require certain protections above and beyond those specified by the PAA. For example, they require the AG and the National Security Agency (NSA) to follow the procedures set out under Executive Order 12333 §2.5, 46 Fed. Reg. 59,941, 59,951 (Dec. 4, 1981), before any surveillance is undertaken. Moreover, affidavits supporting the certifications spell out additional safeguards to be employed in effecting the acquisitions. This last set of classified procedures has not been included in the information transmitted to the petitioner. In essence, as implemented, the certifications permit surveillances conducted to obtain foreign intelligence for national security purposes when those surveillances are directed against foreign powers or agents of foreign powers reasonably believed to be located outside the United States.

The . . . petitioner . . . refused to comply with the directives. On [redacted text], the government moved to compel compliance. Following amplitudinous briefing, the FISC handed down a meticulous opinion validating the directives and granting the motion to compel. . . .

III.   ANALYSIS . . .

B.   The Fourth Amendment Challenge. . . .

The petitioner's remonstrance has two main branches. First, it asserts that the government, in issuing the directives, had to abide by the requirements attendant to the Warrant Clause of the Fourth Amendment. Second, it argues that even if a foreign intelligence exception to the warrant requirements exists and excuses compliance with the Warrant Clause, the surveillances mandated by the directives are unreasonable and, therefore, violate the Fourth Amendment. The petitioner limits each of its claims to the harm that may be inflicted upon United States persons. . . .

2.   The Foreign Intelligence Exception.

The recurrent theme permeating the petitioner's arguments is the notion that there is no foreign intelligence exception to the Fourth Amendment's Warrant Clause. The FISC rejected this notion, positing that our decision in *In re Sealed Case* [310 F.3d 717, 721 (FISA Ct. Rev. 2002)] confirmed the existence of a foreign intelligence exception to the warrant requirement.

While the *Sealed Case* court avoided an express holding that a foreign intelligence exception exists by assuming arguendo that whether or not the warrant requirements were met, the statute could survive on reasonableness grounds, *see* 310 F.3d at 741-42, we believe that the FISC's reading of that decision is plausible.

The petitioner argues correctly that the Supreme Court has not explicitly recognized such an exception; indeed, the Court reserved that question in *United States v. United States District Court* (*Keith*), 407 U.S. 297, 308-09 (1972). But the Court has recognized a comparable exception, outside the foreign intelligence context, in so-called "special needs" cases. In those cases, the Court excused compliance with the Warrant Clause when the purpose behind the governmental action went beyond routine law enforcement and insisting upon a warrant would materially interfere with the accomplishment of that purpose. *See, e.g., Vernonia Sch. Dist. 47J v. Acton*, 515 U.S. 646, 653 (1995) (upholding drug testing of high-school athletes and explaining that the exception to the warrant requirement applied "when special needs, beyond the normal need for law enforcement, make the warrant and probable-cause requirement[s] impracticable" (quoting *Griffin v. Wisconsin*, 483 U.S. 868, 873 (1987))); *Skinner v. Ry. Labor Execs. Ass'n*, 489 U.S. 602, 620 (1989) (upholding regulations instituting drug and alcohol testing of railroad workers for safety reasons);

cf. Terry v. Ohio, 392 U.S. 1, 23-24 (1968) (upholding pat-frisk for weapons to protect officer safety during investigatory stop).

The question, then, is whether the reasoning of the special needs cases applies by analogy to justify a foreign intelligence exception to the warrant requirement for surveillance undertaken for national security purposes and directed at a foreign power or an agent of a foreign power reasonably believed to be located outside the United States. Applying principles derived from the special needs cases, we conclude that this type of foreign intelligence surveillance possesses characteristics that qualify it for such an exception.

For one thing, the purpose behind the surveillances ordered pursuant to the directives goes well beyond any garden-variety law enforcement objective. It involves the acquisition from overseas foreign agents of foreign intelligence to help protect national security. Moreover, this is the sort of situation in which the government's interest is particularly intense.

The petitioner has a fallback position. Even if there is a narrow foreign intelligence exception, it asseverates, a definition of that exception should require the foreign intelligence purpose to be the primary purpose of the surveillance. For that proposition, it cites the Fourth Circuit's decision in *United States v. Truong Dinh Hung,* 629 F.2d 908, 915 (4th Cir. 1980). That dog will not hunt.

This court previously has upheld as reasonable under the Fourth Amendment the Patriot Act's substitution of "a significant purpose" for the talismanic phrase "primary purpose." . . . In our view the more appropriate consideration is the programmatic purpose of the surveillances and whether — as in the special needs cases — that programmatic purpose involves some legitimate objective beyond ordinary crime control.

Under this analysis, the surveillances authorized by the directives easily pass muster. Their stated purpose centers on garnering foreign intelligence. There is no indication that the collections of information are primarily related to ordinary criminal-law enforcement purposes. Without something more than a purely speculative set of imaginings, we cannot infer that the purpose of the directives (and, thus, of the surveillances) is other than their stated purpose.

We add, moreover, that there is a high degree of probability that requiring a warrant would hinder the government's ability to collect time-sensitive information and, thus, would impede the vital national security interests that are at stake. *See, e.g., Truong Dinh Hung,* 629 F.2d at 915 (explaining that when the object of a surveillance is a foreign power or its collaborators, "the government has the greatest need for speed, stealth, and secrecy"). [redacted text] Compulsory compliance with the warrant requirement would introduce an element of delay, thus frustrating the government's ability to collect information in a timely manner. [redacted text]

For these reasons, we hold that a foreign intelligence exception to the Fourth Amendment's warrant requirement exists when surveillance is conducted to obtain foreign intelligence for national security purposes and is directed against foreign powers or agents of foreign powers reasonably believed to be located outside the United States.

3.   Reasonableness.

This holding does not grant the government carte blanche: even though the foreign intelligence exception applies in a given case, governmental action intruding on individual privacy interests must comport with the Fourth Amendment's reasonableness requirement. Thus, the question here reduces to whether the PAA, as applied through the directives, constitutes a sufficiently reasonable exercise of governmental power to satisfy the Fourth Amendment.

. . . To determine the reasonableness of a particular governmental action, an inquiring court must consider the totality of the circumstances. *Samson v. California*, 547 U.S. 843, 848 (2006); *Tennessee v. Garner*, 471 U.S. 1, 8-9 (1985). This mode of approach takes into account the nature of the government intrusion and how the intrusion is implemented. The more important the government's interest, the greater the intrusion that may be constitutionally tolerated.

The totality of the circumstances model requires the court to balance the interests at stake. If the protections that are in place for individual privacy interests are sufficient in light of the governmental interest at stake, the constitutional scales will tilt in favor of upholding the government's actions. If, however, those protections are insufficient to alleviate the risks of government error and abuse, the scales will tip toward a finding of unconstitutionality.

Here, the relevant governmental interest — the interest in national security — is of the highest order of magnitude. *See Haig v. Agee*, 453 U.S. 280, 307 (1981); *In re Sealed Case*, 310 F.3d at 746. Consequently, we must determine whether the protections afforded to the privacy rights of targeted persons are reasonable in light of this important interest.

At the outset, we dispose of two straw men — arguments based on a misreading of our prior decision in *Sealed Case*. First, the petitioner notes that we found relevant six factors contributing to the protection of individual privacy in the face of a governmental intrusion for national security purposes. *See In re Sealed Case*, 310 F.3d at 737-41 (contemplating prior judicial review, presence or absence of probable cause, particularity, necessity, duration, and minimization). On that exiguous basis, it reasons that our decision there requires a more rigorous standard for gauging reasonableness.

This is a mistaken judgment. In *Sealed Case*, we did not formulate a rigid six-factor test for reasonableness. That would be at odds with the totality of the circumstances test that must guide an analysis in the precincts patrolled by the Fourth Amendment. We merely indicated that the six enumerated factors were relevant under the circumstances of that case.

Second, the petitioner asserts that our *Sealed Case* decision stands for the proposition that, in order to gain constitutional approval, the PAA procedures must contain protections equivalent to the three principal warrant requirements: prior judicial review, probable cause, and particularity. That is incorrect. What we said there — and reiterate today — is that the more a set of procedures resembles those associated with the traditional warrant requirements, the more easily it can be determined that those procedures are within constitutional bounds. We therefore decline the petitioner's invitation to reincorporate into the foreign intelligence exception the same warrant requirements that we already have held inapplicable.

Having placed *Sealed Case* into perspective, we turn to the petitioner's contention that the totality of the circumstances demands a finding of unreasonableness here. That contention boils down to the idea that the protections afforded under the PAA are insufficiently analogous to the protections deemed adequate in *Sealed Case* because the PAA lacks (i) a particularity requirement, (ii) a prior judicial review requirement for determining probable cause that a target is a foreign power or an agent of a foreign power, and (iii) any plausible proxies for the omitted protections. For good measure, the petitioner suggests that the PAA's lack of either a necessity requirement or a reasonable durational limit diminishes the overall reasonableness of surveillances conducted pursuant thereto.

The government rejoins that the PAA, as applied here, constitutes reasonable governmental action. It emphasizes both the protections spelled out in the PAA itself and those mandated under the certifications and directives. This matrix of safeguards comprises at least five components: targeting procedures, minimization procedures, a procedure to ensure that a significant purpose of a surveillance is to obtain foreign intelligence information, procedures incorporated through Executive Order 12333 §2.5, and [redacted text] procedures [redacted text] outlined in an affidavit supporting the certifications.

The record supports the government. Notwithstanding the parade of horribles trotted out by the petitioner, it has presented no evidence of any actual harm, any egregious risk of error, or any broad potential for abuse in the circumstances of the instant case. Thus, assessing the intrusions at issue in light of the governmental interest at stake and the panoply of protections that are in place, we discern no principled basis for invalidating the PAA as applied here. In the pages that follow, we explain our reasoning.

The petitioner's arguments about particularity and prior judicial review are defeated by the way in which the statute has been applied. When combined with the PAA's other protections, the [redacted text] procedures and the procedures incorporated through the Executive Order are constitutionally sufficient compensation for any encroachments.

The [redacted text] procedures [redacted text] are delineated in an ex parte appendix filed by the government. They also are described, albeit with greater generality, in the government's brief. [redacted text] Although the PAA itself does not mandate a showing of particularity, see 50 U.S.C. §1805b(b), this pre-surveillance procedure strikes us as analogous to and in conformity with the particularity showing contemplated by *Sealed Case*. 310 F.3d at 740. [redacted text]

The procedures incorporated through section 2.5 of Executive Order 12333, made applicable to the surveillances through the certifications and directives, serve to allay the probable cause concern. That section states in relevant part:

> The Attorney General hereby is delegated the power to approve the use for intelligence purposes, within the United States or against a United States person abroad, of any technique for which a warrant would be required if undertaken for law enforcement purposes, provided that such techniques shall not be undertaken unless the Attorney General has determined in each case that there is *probable cause* to believe that the technique is directed against *a foreign power or an agent of a foreign power.*

46 Fed. Reg. at 59,951 (emphasis supplied). Thus, in order for the government to act upon the certifications, the AG first had to make a determination that probable cause existed to believe that the targeted person is a foreign power or an agent of a foreign power. Moreover, this determination was not made in a vacuum. The AG's decision was informed by the contents of an application made pursuant to Department of

Defense (DOD) regulations. *See* DOD, Procedures Governing the Activities of DOD Intelligence Components that Affect United States Persons, DOD 5240.1-R, Proc. 5, Pt. 2.C (Dec.1982). Those regulations required that the application include a statement of facts demonstrating both probable cause and necessity. *See id.* They also required a statement of the period—not to exceed 90 days—during which the surveillance was thought to be required.[7] *See id.*

[redacted text and footnote]

The petitioner's additional criticisms about the surveillances can be grouped into concerns about potential abuse of executive discretion and concerns about the risk of government error (including inadvertent or incidental collection of information from non-targeted United States persons). We address these groups of criticisms sequentially.

The petitioner suggests that, by placing discretion entirely in the hands of the Executive Branch without prior judicial involvement, the procedures cede to that Branch overly broad power that invites abuse. But this is little more than a lament about the risk that government officials will not operate in good faith. That sort of risk exists even when a warrant is required. In the absence of a showing of fraud or other misconduct by the affiant, the prosecutor, or the judge, a presumption of regularity traditionally attaches to the obtaining of a warrant.

Here—where an exception affords relief from the warrant requirement—common sense suggests that we import the same presumption. Once we have determined that protections sufficient to meet the Fourth Amendment's reasonableness requirement are in place, there is no justification for assuming, in the absence of evidence to that effect, that those prophylactic procedures have been implemented in bad faith.

Similarly, the fact that there is some potential for error is not a sufficient reason to invalidate the surveillances. [redacted text]

Equally as important, some risk of error exists under the original FISA procedures—procedures that received our imprimatur in *Sealed Case,* 310 F.3d at 746. A prior judicial review process does not ensure that the types of errors complained of here [redacted text] would have been prevented.

It is also significant that effective minimization procedures are in place. These procedures serve as an additional backstop against identification errors as well as a means of reducing the impact of incidental intrusions into the privacy of non-targeted United States persons. The minimization procedures implemented here are almost identical to those used under FISA to ensure the curtailment of both mistaken and incidental acquisitions. These minimization procedures were upheld by the FISC in this case, and the petitioner stated at oral argument that it is not quarreling about minimization but, rather, about particularity. Thus, we see no reason to question the adequacy of the minimization protocol.

The petitioner's concern with incidental collections is overblown. It is settled beyond peradventure that incidental collections occurring as a result of constitutionally permissible acquisitions do not render those acquisitions unlawful. *See, e.g., United*

---

7. At oral argument, the government augmented this description, stating that, under the DOD procedure, the NSA typically provides the AG with a two-to-three-page submission articulating the facts underlying the determination that the person in question is an agent of a foreign power; that the National Security Division of the Department of Justice writes its own memorandum to the AG; and that an oral briefing of the AG ensues.

States v. Kahn, 415 U.S. 143, 157-58 (1974). The government assures us that it does not maintain a database of incidentally collected information from non-targeted United States persons, and there is no evidence to the contrary. On these facts, incidentally collected communications of non-targeted United States persons do not violate the Fourth Amendment.

To the extent that the petitioner may be concerned about the adequacy of the targeting procedures, it is worth noting that those procedures include provisions designed to prevent errors. [redacted text] Furthermore, a PAA provision codified at 50 U.S.C. §1805b(d) requires the AG and the DNI to assess compliance with those procedures and to report to Congress semi-annually. . . .

5. Recapitulation.

After assessing the prophylactic procedures applicable here, including the provisions of the PAA, the affidavits supporting the certifications, section 2.5 of Executive Order 12333, and the declaration mentioned above, we conclude that they are very much in tune with the considerations discussed in *Sealed Case.* Collectively, these procedures require a showing of particularity, a meaningful probable cause determination, and a showing of necessity. They also require a durational limit not to exceed 90 days — an interval that we previously found reasonable.[11] *See In re Sealed Case,* 310 F.3d at 740. Finally, the risks of error and abuse are within acceptable limits and effective minimization procedures are in place.

Balancing these findings against the vital nature of the government's national security interest and the manner of the intrusion, we hold that the surveillances at issue satisfy the Fourth Amendment's reasonableness requirement.

IV.   CONCLUSION

Our government is tasked with protecting an interest of utmost significance to the nation — the safety and security of its people. But the Constitution is the cornerstone of our freedoms, and government cannot unilaterally sacrifice constitutional rights on the altar of national security. Thus, in carrying out its national security mission, the government must simultaneously fulfill its constitutional responsibility to provide reasonable protections for the privacy of United States persons. The judiciary's duty is to hold that delicate balance steady and true.

We believe that our decision to uphold the PAA as applied in this case comports with that solemn obligation. In that regard, we caution that our decision does not constitute an endorsement of broad-based, indiscriminate executive power. Rather, our decision recognizes that where the government has instituted several layers of serviceable safeguards to protect individuals against unwarranted harms and to minimize incidental intrusions, its efforts to protect national security should not be frustrated by the courts. This is such a case.

---

11. This time period was deemed acceptable because of the use of continuing minimization procedures. *In re Sealed Case,* 310 F.3d at 740. Those minimization procedures are nearly identical to the minimization procedures employed in this case. *See* text *supra.*

We need go no further. The decision granting the government's motion to compel is affirmed; the petition for review is denied and dismissed; and the motion for a stay is denied as moot.

So ordered.

ORDER

Whereas,

1. An opinion that addresses and resolves issues of statutory and constitutional significance has been filed under seal;

2. It would serve the public interest and the orderly administration of justice to publish this opinion;

3. Publication of an unredacted opinion would disclose materials that have been properly classified by the Executive Branch;

4. Redactions, after consultation with the Executive Branch, can be made to exclude such classified materials without distorting the content of the discussion of the statutory and constitutional issues;

5. Such redactions have been made by the Court;

It Is Hereby Ordered that:

1. The redacted opinion shall be published . . . .

2. Notwithstanding the publication of the redacted opinion, the parties and their counsel, and any agent of, or other person(s) working in concert with, any party or counsel, shall continue to handle and safeguard all classified information pertaining to this case in accordance with applicable security requirements and regulations and applicable orders issued by this Court or the FISC. . . .

NOTES AND QUESTIONS

a. The FISA Amendments Act

1. *Changing Technologies.* The original 1978 definition of "electronic surveillance" excluded from FISA coverage the collection of foreign-to-foreign and foreign-to-domestic communications by tapping analog lines outside the United States or by intercepting satellite signals. With digitization and related technological changes, new collection techniques brought interceptions that had been conducted outside FISA within the definition of "electronic surveillance" and thus within FISA. A substantial share of the world's Internet traffic now passes through U.S.-based servers on its way from origins to destinations, allowing government agencies to gain access to communications from virtually everywhere from telecom facilities inside the United States. Thus, changing technologies have forced statutory reform in multiple ways. Are you persuaded that these changes in technology justify the programmatic surveillance authorized by the FAA?

2. *How Does the FAA Operate in Practice?* The FAA preserves the long-term FISA principle of relying on the location of the potential target of surveillance and then her U.S. person/non-U.S. person status as bases for regulation. Just how reliable a marker

is location in the digital age? How would the government know that an e-mail message sent from gmail.com or any similar provider originates from outside the United States? Or that a cell phone call placed from a phone with a New York City area code is actually being made by a terrorist suspect who is planning a terrorist attack from inside his home in Yemen? Can you see how over- and under-collection occurs under the FAA, using the assumptions embedded in the Act?

As was apparently the case with the TSP, the FAA does not limit the government to surveillance of particular, known persons reasonably believed to be outside the United States, but instead authorizes what are sometimes characterized as "basket warrants" for surveillance and eventual data mining. 50 U.S.C. §1881a(a). Non-U.S. person targets do not have to be suspected of being an agent of a foreign power, nor, for that matter, must they be suspected of involvement in terrorism or any national security or other crime. *Id.* Does it matter under the FAA that potential targets may be communicating with innocent persons inside the United States?

Presumably, once a specific target for further surveillance is identified through the FAA processes, the government applies to the FISC for an order to conduct traditional FISA electronic surveillance. Are you satisfied that this sequential use of FISA assures that collection objectives are met while protecting the Fourth and First Amendment rights of innocent persons who may be overheard?

3. *Targeting Under the FAA.* The programmatic collection provisions of FAA treat geography as a proxy for U.S. person status, and thus for targeting. Unlike the practice with traditional FISA applications, the government is not required to obtain an FISC order identifying the facilities, telephone lines, e-mail addresses, places, or property where any surveillance will be directed. Given the breadth of the authorization for programmatic surveillance in the FAA, what do you suppose are the targeting criteria? Who decides? Might targets include a terrorist organization? A large set of telephone numbers or e-mail addresses? An entire area code or ISP? Although details of the implementation of the program authorized by the FAA remain classified, experts guess that the government uses a broad vacuum-cleaner-like first stage of collection, focusing on transactional data, in which wholesale collection occurs after some filtering criteria are developed. A more particularized identification of content follows by mining the collected data. *See* Richard A. Posner, *Privacy, Surveillance, and Law,* 75 U. Chi. L. Rev. 254, 253 (2008).

Because of the difficulty of ascertaining a target's location, and because the location and identity of targets' correspondents are impossible to predict, over-collection seems unavoidable. For example, despite the statutory prohibition on deliberately targeting U.S. persons, incidental acquisition of U.S. person communications will occur whenever such a person uses any foreign telecommunications services, including the Internet. *Id.* at 252. Can you describe some protocol that would prevent, or at least reduce, such over-collection? Should the probable cause standard applicable in traditional FISA surveillance be imported into the FAA? Some flexible approach, with higher standards for relatively minor threats and lower standards for more serious threats?

Can you see how under-collection is also likely under the FAA? Consider a Saudi Al Qaeda operative who is located in Pakistan using a cell phone with a Washington, D.C., area code. Although subject to warrantless surveillance under the FAA, government officials might assume, on the basis of his cell phone information, that he is a U.S. person. Can you think of a statutory solution to the under-collection problem?

4. *FAA Minimization.* The minimization requirements for collection under-taken pursuant to the FAA are identical to those for traditional FISA surveillance described *supra* p. 209. 50 U.S.C. §1881a(e). The FISC does not review the imple-mentation of minimization procedures or practices for the programmatic surveil-lance it approves, and the Act permits the government to retain and disseminate information relating to U.S. persons so long as the government determines that it is "foreign intelligence information." *Id.* §1801(h)(1). Do you see any potential for abuse of discretion in the retention and dissemination of information under the FAA that does not exist in traditional FISA collection? What could be done to reduce any such potential?

As an alternative to relying on minimization practices, some experts have pro-posed that collection limitations be relaxed in return for robust restrictions on the ability of government officials to access or use the information collected. Proposals include using automated filters to segregate communications involving U.S. persons from others, allowing the latter to be handled without much restriction; setting limits on the use of data that has been collected (e.g., for foreign intelligence purposes, not for unrelated criminal prosecution); requiring judicial approval before disseminating collected data; and using audit trails to hold officials accountable if they use data for impermissible purposes. *See* Markle Found., *Mobilizing Information to Prevent Terrorism* 65-71 (2006). Do you think that some version of the proposed authorized-use rules would be preferable to minimization?

5. *Extending FISA to U.S. Persons Abroad.* For the first time, FAA subjects surveil-lance intentionally targeting a U.S. person reasonably believed to be abroad to tradi-tional FISA foreign agency/probable cause procedures. 50 U.S.C. §§1881b,1881c. Congress has thus undertaken to regulate a critical national security activity of the President outside the United States. Do you suppose the President was constrained in any way in such surveillance before FAA? Might the extension of FAA abroad raise constitutional questions that would not exist in its domestic application? Could, or should, the individual targeting requirement be applied to non-U.S. persons abroad? Some answers to these questions may be found in Chapter 11.

6. *Privacy in the Digital Age.* Should our conceptions of privacy be updated for the digital/social networking era? Is privacy now more about keeping information secret from the government than in the past? Is it about retaining control over how our personal information is made available to others, including the government? Or is privacy needed as a shield from excessive government power?

7. *Congressional Oversight.* The FAA requires that

not less frequently than once every 6 months, the Attorney General shall fully inform, in a manner consistent with national security, the congressional intelligence committees and the Committees on the Judiciary of the Senate and the House of Representatives, consistent with the Rules of the House of Representatives, [and] the . . . Rules of the Senate . . . concerning the implementation of this title. . . . [50 U.S.C. §1881f.]

Similar assessments must be provided to the FISC, and the DOJ Inspector General and other IG offices of agencies authorized to collect information under the FAA may review compliance with FAA targeting and minimization procedures and guidelines.

The first semiannual assessments provided by the Attorney General and DNI found violations of the targeting and minimization procedures. The assessments state that the number of violations is small when compared to the volume of activity. *Semiannual Assessment of Compliance with Procedures and Guidelines Issued Pursuant to Section 702 of the Foreign Intelligence Surveillance Act, Submitted by the Attorney General and the Director of National Intelligence* (Dec. 2009), *available at* http://www.aclu.org/files/pdfs/natsec/faafoia20101129/FAAODNI0001.pdf.

8. *Fine-Tuning the FAA?* In view of the indeterminacy of target location and the lack of other targeting criteria in the FAA, should or *must* Congress revise the authorization for programmatic surveillance to satisfy Fourth Amendment requirements? According to one commentator, Congress should authorize automated monitoring under the FAA to identify potential threats, so long as there is

> a circumscribed but authorized procedure for follow-up monitoring or investigation of initial suspicion derived from automated monitoring. . . . [W]hat is needed, in my view, is the electronic surveillance equivalent of a *Terry* stop. [Kim Taipale, *The Ear of Dionysus: Rethinking Foreign Intelligence Surveillance*, 9 Yale J.L. & Tech. 128, 160 (2007).]

The initial automated monitoring presumably would consist of collecting telephone numbers and analyzing patterns of their use. Neither it nor the follow-up investigation would, according to Taipale's proposal, be subject to FISA procedures or would collect "content" for Fourth Amendment purposes. *Terry v. Ohio,* 392 U.S. 1 (1968), held that police may detain a suspect ("stop and frisk") for a brief period based on reasonable suspicion that a crime has been committed. Do you think the *Terry* case is analogous? Could officials collect, say, fragments of phone calls or e-mail messages, then check some database to learn whether the fragments lead to suspicion about a potential target? Presumably then officials would follow traditional FISA processes to conduct a full-blown collection. Can you see the value of granting officials discretion to make the follow-up monitoring Taipale advocates? What downside risks could you imagine?

9. *Exclusivity Redux.* The FAA includes this language regarding exclusivity:

> (a) Except as provided in subsection (b), the procedures of chapters 119, 121, and 206 of title 18, United States Code, and this Act shall be the exclusive means by which electronic surveillance and the interception of domestic wire, oral, or electronic communications may be conducted.
> (b) Only an express statutory authorization for electronic surveillance or the interception of domestic wire, oral, or electronic communications, other than as an amendment to this Act or chapters 119, 121, or 206 of title 18, United States Code, shall constitute an additional exclusive means for the purpose of subsection (a). [50 U.S.C. §1812]

Does this provision adequately express congressional determination to provide the exclusive rules for conducting electronic surveillance for foreign intelligence purposes? Could the President ever have a legal justification for circumventing the FAA?

10. *Testing the Constitutionality of the FAA in Court?* A mix of individuals and groups involved in human rights, media, law, and labor challenged the constitutionality of the core provision of the FAA that authorizes targeting non-U.S. persons outside the

United States for purposes of collecting foreign intelligence. The plaintiffs demonstrated that they incurred costs to adjust their means of communicating out of fear that the government would intercept their communications under the FAA. In *Amnesty International USA v. Clapper*, 638 F.3d 118 (2d Cir. 2011), a panel of the Second Circuit reversed a dismissal of the lawsuit and concluded that the plaintiffs have standing to sue because "the plaintiffs have established that they have a reasonable fear of injury and have incurred costs to avoid it." *Id.* at 122. On the merits, the plaintiffs claim that the FAA procedures violate the Fourth and First Amendments, Article III, and the principles of separation of powers. If the federal courts reach the merits in this lawsuit, how should the plaintiffs' claims be decided?

b. The *In re Directives* Decision

1. *Comparing Procedural Protections in FISA and the PAA.* The petitioning telecom relied on the FISCR's *In re Sealed Case* decision in arguing that the procedural protections provided by the PAA were insufficient, including requirements of particularity and prior judicial review for probable cause of foreign agency. Are you satisfied that the protections in the PAA (which are practically the same in the FAA) satisfy the Fourth Amendment?

2. *Special Needs Redux.* Recall that in its first decision the FISCR relied in part on the special needs doctrine to uphold DOJ guidelines in 2002 that tore down the wall between intelligence officials and criminal and prosecutors. See *supra* p. 212. There the "special need" was foreign intelligence collection. Is the special needs doctrine better suited to programmatic surveillance than to traditional FISA collection? Are you persuaded that the special needs doctrine justifies a foreign intelligence exception to the Warrant Clause?

3. *Reasonableness Redux.* According to the FISCR, Fourth Amendment reasonableness was satisfied in part by a variety of safeguards found within and outside the PAA. How did the FISCR make its decision about reasonableness? Why did the court not inquire into the government's compliance with minimization requirements as an aspect of reasonableness? In addition, the FISCR relied on Executive Order No. 12,333 and a secret affidavit spelling out safeguards in deciding that there were adequate protections for the telecom. Do you agree with the court that redactions "can be made to exclude such classified materials without distorting the content of the discussion of the statutory and constitutional issues"?

9

Third-Party Records and Data Mining

The conventional wisdom after 9/11 was that U.S. national security agencies failed to "connect the dots" before the attacks. But some experts have noted that while there "certainly was a lack of dot-connecting before September 11," the more critical failure was that "[t]here were too few useful dots." Robert Bryant et al., *America Needs More Spies*, The Economist, July 12, 2003, at 30. In this chapter, we explore both parts of this insight.

In Part A we revisit privacy themes addressed in earlier chapters to test their portability to third-party records—personal information voluntarily turned over to others. Next, in Part B, we consider how so-called national security letters (NSLs) and Foreign Intelligence Surveillance Act (FISA) §215 orders are used to collect dots in quantity—transactional data—from third-party record holders like banks, telephone companies, Internet service providers, and travel agencies. Finally, in Part C, we look at how dots are connected by computer "data mining" to perform link analysis or pattern recognition.

A. FINDING THE DOTS — THIRD-PARTY RECORDS

1. Expectations of Privacy Regarding Third-Party Records

Smith v. Maryland
United States Supreme Court, 1979
442 U.S. 735

Mr. Justice BLACKMUN delivered the opinion of the Court. This case presents the question whether the installation and use of a <u>pen register</u>[1] constitutes a "search"

---

1. "A pen register is a mechanical device that records the numbers dialed on a telephone by monitoring the electrical impulses caused when the dial on the telephone is released. It does not overhear oral communications and does not indicate whether calls are actually completed." *United States v. New York Tel. Co.*, 434 U.S. 159, 161 n.1 [(1977)]. A pen register is "usually installed at a central telephone facility [and] records on a paper tape all numbers dialed from [the] line" to which it is attached. *United States v. Giordano*, 416 U.S. 505, 549 n.1 (1974).

within the meaning of the Fourth Amendment, made applicable to the States through the Fourteenth Amendment.

On March 5, 1976, in Baltimore, Md., Patricia McDonough was robbed. She gave the police a description of the robber and of a 1975 Monte Carlo automobile she had observed near the scene of the crime. After the robbery, McDonough began receiving threatening and obscene phone calls from a man identifying himself as the robber. On one occasion, the caller asked that she step out on her front porch; she did so, and saw the 1975 Monte Carlo she had earlier described to police moving slowly past her home. On March 16, police spotted a man who met McDonough's description driving a 1975 Monte Carlo in her neighborhood. By tracing the license plate number, police learned that the car was registered in the name of petitioner, Michael Lee Smith.

The next day, the telephone company, at police request, installed a pen register at its central offices to record the numbers dialed from the telephone at petitioner's home. The police did not get a warrant or court order before having the pen register installed. The register revealed that on March 17 a call was placed from petitioner's home to McDonough's phone. On the basis of this and other evidence, the police obtained a warrant to search petitioner's residence. The search revealed that a page in petitioner's phone book was turned down to the name and number of Patricia McDonough; the phone book was seized. Petitioner was arrested, [convicted, and sentenced to six years' imprisonment.] . . .

. . . In determining whether a particular form of government-initiated electronic surveillance is a "search" within the meaning of the Fourth Amendment, our lodestar is *Katz v. United States*, 389 U.S. 347 (1967)[5] . . . .

In applying the *Katz* analysis to this case, it is important to begin by specifying precisely the nature of the state activity that is challenged. The activity here took the form of installing and using a pen register. Since the pen register was installed on telephone company property at the telephone company's central offices, petitioner obviously cannot claim that his "property" was invaded or that police intruded into a "constitutionally protected area." Petitioner's claim, rather, is that, notwithstanding the absence of a trespass, the State, as did the Government in *Katz*, infringed a "legitimate expectation of privacy" that petitioner held. Yet a pen register differs significantly from the listening device employed in *Katz*, for pen registers do not acquire the *contents* of communications. This Court recently noted:

> "Indeed, a law enforcement official could not even determine from the use of a pen register whether a communication existed. These devices do not hear sound. They disclose only the telephone numbers that have been dialed—a means of establishing communication. Neither the purport of any communication between the caller and the recipient of the call, their identities, nor whether the call was even completed is disclosed by pen registers." *United States v. New York Tel. Co.*, 434 U.S. 159, 167 (1977).

---

5. Situations can be imagined, of course, in which *Katz*'s two-pronged inquiry would provide an inadequate index of Fourth Amendment protection. For example, if the Government were suddenly to announce on nationwide television that all homes henceforth would be subject to warrantless entry, individuals thereafter might not in fact entertain any actual expectation of privacy regarding their homes, papers, and effects. Similarly, if a refugee from a totalitarian country, unaware of this Nation's traditions, erroneously assumed that police were continuously monitoring his telephone conversations, a subjective expectation of privacy regarding the contents of his calls might be lacking as well. In such circumstances, where an individual's subjective expectations had been "conditioned" by influences alien to well-recognized Fourth Amendment freedoms, those subjective expectations obviously could play no meaningful role in ascertaining what the scope of Fourth Amendment protection was. In determining whether a "legitimate expectation of privacy" existed in such cases, a normative inquiry would be proper.

Given a pen register's limited capabilities, therefore, petitioner's argument that its installation and use constituted a "search" necessarily rests upon a claim that he had a "legitimate expectation of privacy" regarding the numbers he dialed on his phone.

This claim must be rejected. First, we doubt that people in general entertain any actual expectation of privacy in the numbers they dial. All telephone users realize that they must "convey" phone numbers to the telephone company, since it is through telephone company switching equipment that their calls are completed. All subscribers realize, moreover, that the phone company has facilities for making permanent records of the numbers they dial, for they see a list of their long-distance (toll) calls on their monthly bills. In fact, pen registers and similar devices are routinely used by telephone companies "for the purposes of checking billing operations, detecting fraud and preventing violations of law." *United States v. New York Tel. Co.*, 434 U.S., at 174-175....

...Most phone books tell subscribers, on a page entitled "Consumer Information," that the company "can frequently help in identifying to the authorities the origin of unwelcome and troublesome calls." Telephone users, in sum, typically know that they must convey numerical information to the phone company; that the phone company has facilities for recording this information; and that the phone company does in fact record this information for a variety of legitimate business purposes. Although subjective expectations cannot be scientifically gauged, it is too much to believe that telephone subscribers, under these circumstances, harbor any general expectation that the numbers they dial will remain secret....

... [E]ven if petitioner did harbor some subjective expectation that the phone numbers he dialed would remain private, this expectation is not "one that society is prepared to recognize as 'reasonable.' " This Court consistently has held that a person has no legitimate expectation of privacy in information he voluntarily turns over to third parties. E.g., *United States v. Miller*, 425 U.S. [435] at 442-444 [1976]. In *Miller*, for example, the Court held that a bank depositor has no "legitimate 'expectation of privacy' " in financial information "voluntarily conveyed to...banks and exposed to their employees in the ordinary course of business." 425 U.S. at 442. The Court explained:

> "The depositor takes the risk, in revealing his affairs to another, that the information will be conveyed by that person to the Government.... This Court has held repeatedly that the Fourth Amendment does not prohibit the obtaining of information revealed to a third party and conveyed by him to Government authorities, even if the information is revealed on the assumption that it will be used only for a limited purpose and the confidence placed in the third party will not be betrayed." *Id.* at 443.

Because the depositor "assumed the risk" of disclosure, the Court held that it would be unreasonable for him to expect his financial records to remain private.

This analysis dictates that petitioner can claim no legitimate expectation of privacy here. When he used his phone, petitioner voluntarily conveyed numerical information to the telephone company and "exposed" that information to its equipment in the ordinary course of business. In so doing, petitioner assumed the risk that the company would reveal to police the numbers he dialed. The switching equipment that processed those numbers is merely the modern counterpart of the operator who, in an earlier day, personally completed calls for the subscriber. Petitioner concedes that if he had placed his calls through an operator, he could claim no legitimate expectation of privacy. We are not inclined to hold that a different constitutional result is required because the telephone company has decided to automate....

... We therefore conclude that petitioner in all probability entertained no actual expectation of privacy in the phone numbers he dialed, and that, even if he did, his expectation was not "legitimate." The installation and use of a pen register, consequently, was not a "search," and no warrant was required....

Mr. Justice POWELL took no part in the consideration or decision of this case.

Mr. Justice STEWART, with whom Mr. Justice BRENNAN joins, dissenting.... The numbers dialed from a private telephone—although certainly more prosaic than the conversation itself—are not without "content." Most private telephone subscribers may have their own numbers listed in a publicly distributed directory, but I doubt there are any who would be happy to have broadcast to the world a list of the local or long distance numbers they have called. This is not because such a list might in some sense be incriminating, but because it easily could reveal the identities of the persons and the places called, and thus reveal the most intimate details of a person's life....

Mr. Justice MARSHALL, with whom Mr. Justice BRENNAN joins, dissenting.... [E]ven assuming ... that individuals "typically know" that a phone company monitors calls for internal reasons, it does not follow that they expect this information to be made available to the public in general or the government in particular. Privacy is not a discrete commodity, possessed absolutely or not at all. Those who disclose certain facts to a bank or phone company for a limited business purpose need not assume that this information will be released to other persons for other purposes.

The crux of the Court's holding, however, is that whatever expectation of privacy petitioner may in fact have entertained regarding his calls, it is not one "society is prepared to recognize as 'reasonable.'" In so ruling, the Court determines that individuals who convey information to third parties have "assumed the risk" of disclosure to the government. This analysis is misconceived in two critical respects.

Implicit in the concept of assumption of risk is some notion of choice. At least in the third-party consensual surveillance cases, which first incorporated risk analysis into Fourth Amendment doctrine, the defendant presumably had exercised some discretion in deciding who should enjoy his confidential communications. By contrast here, unless a person is prepared to forgo use of what for many has become a personal or professional necessity, he cannot help but accept the risk of surveillance. It is idle to speak of "assuming" risks in contexts where, as a practical matter, individuals have no realistic alternative.

More fundamentally, to make risk analysis dispositive in assessing the reasonableness of privacy expectations would allow the government to define the scope of Fourth Amendment protections. For example, law enforcement officials, simply by announcing their intent to monitor the content of random samples of first-class mail or private phone conversations, could put the public on notice of the risks they would thereafter assume in such communications. Yet, although acknowledging this implication of its analysis, the Court is willing to concede only that, in some circumstances, a further "normative inquiry would be proper." No meaningful effort is made to explain what those circumstances might be, or why this case is not among them.

In my view, whether privacy expectations are legitimate within the meaning of *Katz* depends not on the risks an individual can be presumed to accept when imparting information to third parties, but on the risks he should be forced to assume in a free and open society....

The use of pen registers, I believe, constitutes such an extensive intrusion. To hold otherwise ignores the vital role telephonic communication plays in our personal and professional relationships, as well as the First and Fourth Amendment interests implicated by unfettered official surveillance. Privacy in placing calls is of value not only to those engaged in criminal activity. The prospect of unregulated governmental monitoring will undoubtedly prove disturbing even to those with nothing illicit to hide. Many individuals, including members of unpopular political organizations or journalists with confidential sources, may legitimately wish to avoid disclosure of their personal contacts. Permitting governmental access to telephone records on less than probable cause may thus impede certain forms of political affiliation and journalistic endeavor that are the hallmark of a truly free society. Particularly given the Government's previous reliance on warrantless telephonic surveillance to trace reporters' sources and monitor protected political activity, I am unwilling to insulate use of pen registers from independent judicial review....

NOTES AND QUESTIONS

1. *Pen Registers and Trap and Trace vs. Wiretaps.* What is it about a pen register or trap and trace device that makes it so different from a wiretap? Should the differences have such constitutional significance? Consider the analogy to a mailed letter. The letter contains protected content, while the envelope contains only the mailing and return addresses and postage information. Thus, the contents of the letter are afforded protection, but the envelope is not. *See* Orin S. Kerr, *Internet Surveillance Law After the USA Patriot Act: The Big Brother That Isn't*, 97 Nw. U. L. Rev. 607, 611-616 (2003). Does the same contents/envelope distinction fit the pen register/trap and trace scenarios? Consider the views of Justices Stewart and Marshall. What "content" is arguably revealed by a pen register? *See* Daniel J. Solove, *Reconstructing Electronic Surveillance Law*, 72 Geo. Wash. L. Rev. 1264, 1286-1287 (2004).

2. *Comparing Katz.* Is the privacy interest recognized by the Court in *Katz* different in any appreciable way from the interest asserted in *Smith*? If the telephone company had the technical means to listen in on the phone calls in both cases, why protect one caller but not the other? Are the phone numbers dialed private? Should they be? *See* Patricia Bellia, *Surveillance Law Through Cyberlaw's Lens*, 72 Geo. Wash. L. Rev. 1375, 1405 (2004). Why should providing that information to a private third party matter so much in deciding what information the government can acquire? When you provide phone numbers to the phone company, do you expect that it will turn them over to Big Brother? Have you knowingly and willingly "assumed the risk" of such disclosure?

Alternatively, is the outcome in *Smith* best understood as reflecting a judgment that it doesn't really matter much, because the phone numbers were not of much value to the individual? *See* Daniel J. Solove, *Digital Dossiers and the Dissipation of Fourth Amendment Privacy*, 75 S. Cal. L. Rev. 1083 (2002).

3. *Extending Smith to the Internet.* Is *Smith* authority for searching e-mail subject lines and URLs without a warrant?

4. *A Statutory Remedy?* After *Smith*, Congress enacted the Pen Register Act, 18 U.S.C. §§3121-3127 (2006). The Act imposes a warrant requirement before the government may obtain a pen register. *Id.* §3121(a). However, in contrast to a traditional Fourth Amendment warrant based on probable cause, the government may obtain an order for a pen register simply by showing that its use is "relevant to an ongoing investigation." *Id.* §3123(a). The USA Patriot Act extended the pen register and trap and trace authorities to include addressing information on e-mail and to ISP and URL addresses. Pub. L. No. 107-56, §216, 115 Stat. 272, 288-290 (2001) (amending 18 U.S.C. §3127(3), (4)). Are these statutory provisions constitutional?

5. *The Implications of Smith. Smith* laid the foundation for more than just pen registers. If people have no legitimate expectation of privacy in information they voluntarily convey to the phone company in the normal course of business, then they also arguably have no such expectation in the transactional information they convey to hundreds of other third parties in the ordinary course of business. Congress therefore authorized the Foreign Intelligence Surveillance Court (FISC) to issue orders for transactional records pursuant to FISA §215 and enacted several other statutes authorizing the FBI to obtain transactional data by issuing NSLs without prior court order. These are described in the table on the next page. In calendar year 2005, the government reported that it had obtained 155 §215 orders and issued 9,254 NSLs related to U.S. persons (excluding NSLs for subscriber information). Letter from William E. Moschella (Assistant Attorney General, Dep't of Justice) to J. Dennis Hastert (Speaker, House of Representatives) (Apr. 28, 2006). Aggregate FBI use of NSLs increased from 8,500 requests in 2000 to 47,000 in 2005, while the percentage of NSLs used to investigate U.S. persons increased from 39 percent in 2003 to 57 percent in 2006. Charles Doyle, *National Security Letters in Foreign Intelligence Investigations: Legal Background and Recent Amendments* 13, 15 (Cong. Res. Serv. RL33320), Sept. 8, 2009.

6. *Some of the Dots: Transactional Data.* "'Transactional' information broadly describes information that documents financial or communications transactions without necessarily revealing the substance of those transactions." Michael J. Woods, *Counterintelligence and Access to Transactional Records: A Practical History of USA PATRIOT Act Section 215*, 1 J. Nat'l Security L. & Pol'y 37, 41 (2005). Such information includes telephone billing records that list numbers dialed, an Internet service provider's records showing a customer's Internet use, records of banking transactions and money transfers, credit card records, and travel records. It has reportedly proven invaluable in counterterrorist investigations. Terrorists can try to encrypt or otherwise disguise the substance of their communications, but "[i]t is far more difficult for them to cover their transactional footsteps." *Id.* at 41-42. Counterterrorist analysts can use transactional information to perform "link analysis" to tie suspects together and thus help identify terror cells. *See* McCormick Tribune Found., *Counterterrorism Technology and Privacy* (Cantigny Conf. Rep.) 53 (Patrick J. McMahon

Profile of the Current NSL Statutes

NSL Statute	18 U.S.C. 2709	12 U.S.C. 3414	15 U.S.C. 1681u	15 U.S.C. 1681v	50 U.S.C. 436
Addressee	communications providers	financial institutions	consumer credit agencies	consumer credit agencies	financial institutions, consumer credit agencies, travel agencies
Certifying officials	senior FBI officials and SACs	senior FBI officials and SACs	senior FBI officials and SACs	supervisory official of an agency investigating, conducting intelligence activities relating to or analyzing int'l terrorism	senior officials no lower than Ass't Secretary or Ass't Director of agency w/employees w/access to classified material
Information covered	identified customer's name, address, length of service, and billing info	identified customer financial records	identified consumer's name, address, former address, place and former place of employment	all information relating to an identified consumer	all financial information relating to consenting, identified employee
Standard/ purpose	relevant to an investigation to protect against int'l terrorism or clandestine intelligence activities	sought for foreign counter-intelligence purposes to protect against int'l terrorism or clandestine intelligence activities	sought for an investigation to protect against int'l terrorism or clandestine intelligence activities	necessary for the agency's investigation, activities, or analysis relating to int'l terrorism	necessary to conduct a law enforcement investigation, counter-intelligence inquiry or security determination
Dissemination	only per Att'y Gen. guidelines	only per Att'y Gen. guidelines	w/i FBI, to secure approval for intell. investigation, to military investigators when inform. relates to military member	no statutory provision	only to agency of employee under investigation, DoJ for law enforcement or intell. purposes, or fed. agency when clearly relevant to mission
Immunity/fees	no provisions	no provisions	fees; immunity for good faith compliance with an NSL	immunity for good faith compliance with an NSL	reimbursement; immunity for good faith compliance with an NSL

Charles Doyle, National Security Letters: Proposals in the 112th Congress (Cong. Res. Serv. R41619) 9, Feb. 1, 2011.

rapporteur, 2005). An example is the retrospective link analysis of the 9/11 hijackers. Woods, *supra*, at 42. It can also be used for pattern recognition and data matching to identify suspects.

7. *The Expectation of Privacy in Transactional Records.* Do you, subjectively, have any expectation of privacy when you convey data to a bank or commercial vendor, dial a telephone number, or transmit an e-mail message? Of course, you do not expect to keep the information private from the bank, vendor, phone company, or Internet service provider. The entities with which you deal directly need the data to complete the transaction that you initiate. But do you also expect those entities to share the information with others? In fact, don't some vendors promise you just the opposite, and sometimes even provide a box to check or button to indicate whether you want such data to be shared?

Have the dramatic changes in patterns of commercial activity and communications in the decades since *Smith* and *Miller* made such an expectation reasonable? *See* Christopher Slobogin & Joseph E. Schumacher, *Reasonable Expectations of Privacy and Autonomy in Fourth Amendment Cases: An Empirical Look at "Understandings Recognized and Permitted by Society,"* 42 Duke L.J. 727 (1993) (reporting a survey suggesting that the public finds government perusal of bank records highly invasive). Was the reasonableness of such an expectation altered by the events of September 11, 2001? Consider the following case.

United States v. Warshak

United States Court of Appeals, Sixth Circuit, 2010
631 F.3d 266

BOGGS, Circuit Judge. Berkeley Premium Nutraceuticals, Inc., was an incredibly profitable company that served as the distributor of Enzyte, an herbal supplement purported to enhance male sexual performance. In this appeal, defendants Steven Warshak ("Warshak"), Harriet Warshak ("Harriet"), and TCI Media, Inc. ("TCI"), challenge their convictions stemming from a massive scheme to defraud Berkeley's customers. . . .

I. STATEMENT OF THE FACTS . . .

[During a criminal investigation of Steven Warshak for mail and wire fraud, money laundering, and related federal offenses, the government obtained an order from a United States Magistrate Judge directing an internet service provider, NuVox Communications, ("ISP") to turn over to government agents information pertaining to Warshak's e-mail account, including (1) customer account information, such as application information, "account identifiers," "[b]illing information to include bank account numbers," contact information, and "[any] other information pertaining to the customer, including set up, synchronization, etc."; (2) "[t]he contents of wire or electronic communications (not in electronic storage unless greater than 181 days old) that were placed or stored in directories or files owned or controlled" by the ISP; and (3) "[a]ll Log files and backup tapes." At a later date, Warshak was informed of the order and sought unsuccessfully to suppress evidence derived from his e-mails in his criminal trial.]

II. ANALYSIS

A. The Search & Seizure of Warshak's Emails

Warshak argues that the government's warrantless, *ex parte* seizure of approximately 27,000 of his private emails constituted a violation of the Fourth Amendment's prohibition on unreasonable searches and seizures.[12] The government counters that, even if government agents violated the Fourth Amendment in obtaining the emails, they relied in good faith on the Stored Communications Act ("SCA"), 18 U.S.C. §§2701 et seq., a statute that allows the government to obtain certain electronic communications without procuring a warrant. The government also argues that any hypothetical Fourth Amendment violation was harmless. We find that the government *did* violate Warshak's Fourth Amendment rights by compelling his Internet Service Provider ("ISP") to turn over the contents of his emails. However, we agree that agents relied on the SCA in good faith, and therefore hold that reversal is unwarranted.

1. The Stored Communications Act

The Stored Communications Act ("SCA"), 18 U.S.C. §§2701 et seq., "permits a 'governmental entity' to compel a service provider to disclose the contents of [electronic] communications in certain circumstances." *Warshak II*, 532 F.3d at 523. As this court explained in *Warshak II*:

> Three relevant definitions bear on the meaning of the compelled-disclosure provisions of the Act. "[E]lectronic communication service[s]" permit "users . . . to send or receive wire or electronic communications," [18 U.S.C.] §2510(15), a definition that covers basic e-mail services, *see* Patricia L. Bellia et al., *Cyberlaw: Problems of Policy and Jurisprudence in the Information Age* 584 (2d ed. 2004). "[E]lectronic storage" is "any temporary, intermediate storage of a wire or electronic communication . . . and . . . any storage of such communication by an electronic communication service for purposes of backup protection of such communication." 18 U.S.C. §2510(17). "[R]emote computing service[s]" provide "computer storage or processing services" to customers, *id.* §2711(2), and are designed for longer-term storage, *see* Orin S. Kerr, *A User's Guide to the Stored Communications Act, and a Legislator's Guide to Amending It*, 72 Geo. Wash. L. Rev. 1208, 1216 (2004).
>   The compelled-disclosure provisions give different levels of privacy protection based on whether the e-mail is held with an electronic communication service or a remote computing service and based on how long the e-mail has been in electronic storage. The government may obtain the contents of e-mails that are "in electronic storage" with an electronic communication service for 180 days or less "only pursuant to a warrant." 18 U.S.C. §2703(a). The government has three options for obtaining communications stored with a remote computing service and communications that have been in electronic storage with an electronic service provider for more than 180 days: (1) obtain a warrant; [(2) use a generic form of authorization issued by the investigating agency;] or (3) obtain a court order under §2703(d). *Id.* §2703(a), (b).

532 F.3d at 523-24 (some alterations in original).

---

12. This is not the first time Warshak has raised this argument. In *Warshak v. United States*, 490 F.3d 455 (6th Cir. 2007) ("*Warshak I*"), a panel of this court determined that Warshak did indeed have a privacy interest in the contents of his emails. That decision was vacated on ripeness grounds. *See Warshak v. United States*, 532 F.3d 521 (6th Cir. 2008) (en banc) ("*Warshak II*"). In the present case, Warshak's claim is ripe for review.

2. Factual Background

Email was a critical form of communication among Berkeley personnel. As a consequence, Warshak had a number of email accounts with various ISPs, including an account with NuVox Communications. In October 2004, the government formally requested that NuVox prospectively preserve the contents of any emails to or from Warshak's email account. The request was made pursuant to [statute] and it instructed NuVox to preserve all future messages. NuVox acceded to the government's request and began preserving copies of Warshak's incoming and outgoing emails — copies that would not have existed absent the prospective preservation request. Per the government's instructions, Warshak was not informed that his messages were being archived. In January 2005, the government obtained a subpoena [authorized by statute] and compelled NuVox to turn over the emails that it had begun preserving the previous year. In May 2005, the government served NuVox with an *ex parte* court order under §2703(d) that required NuVox to surrender any additional email messages in Warshak's account. In all, the government compelled NuVox to reveal the contents of approximately 27,000 emails. Warshak did not receive notice of either the subpoena or the order until May 2006.

3. The Fourth Amendment ...

Not all government actions are invasive enough to implicate the Fourth Amendment. "The Fourth Amendment's protections hinge on the occurrence of a "search," a legal term of art whose history is riddled with complexity." *Widgren v. Maple Grove Twp.*, 429 F.3d 575, 578 (6th Cir. 2005). A "search" occurs when the government infringes upon "an expectation of privacy that society is prepared to consider reasonable." *United States v. Jacobsen*, 466 U.S. 109, 113 (1984). This standard breaks down into two discrete inquiries: "first, has the [target of the investigation] manifested a subjective expectation of privacy in the object of the challenged search? Second, is society willing to recognize that expectation as reasonable?" *California v. Ciraolo*, 476 U.S. 207, 211 (1986) (citing *Smith v. Maryland*, 442 U.S. 735, 740 (1979)).

Turning first to the subjective component of the test, we find that Warshak plainly manifested an expectation that his emails would be shielded from outside scrutiny. As he notes in his brief, his "entire business and personal life was contained within the ... emails seized." Appellant's Br. at 39-40. Given the often sensitive and sometimes damning substance of his emails, we think it highly unlikely that Warshak expected them to be made public, for people seldom unfurl their dirty laundry in plain view. *See, e.g., United States v. Maxwell*, 45 M.J. 406, 417 (C.A.A.F. 1996) ("[T]he tenor and content of e-mail conversations between appellant and his correspondent, 'Launchboy,' reveal a[n] ... expectation that the conversations were private."). Therefore, we conclude that Warshak had a subjective expectation of privacy in the contents of his emails.

The next question is whether society is prepared to recognize that expectation as reasonable. *See Smith*, 442 U.S. at 740. This question is one of grave import and enduring consequence, given the prominent role that email has assumed in modern communication. *Cf. Katz*, 389 U.S. at 352 (suggesting that the Constitution must be read to account for "the vital role that the public telephone has come to play in private communication"). Since the advent of email, the telephone call and the letter have waned in importance, and an explosion of Internet-based communication has taken place. People are now able to send sensitive and intimate information, instantaneously, to friends, family, and colleagues half a world away. Lovers exchange sweet nothings, and businessmen swap ambitious plans, all with the click of a mouse button. Commerce has also taken hold in email. Online purchases are often documented in email accounts, and email is frequently used to remind patients and clients of imminent appointments. In short, "account" is an apt word for the conglomeration of stored messages that comprises an email account, as it provides an account of its owner's life. By obtaining access to someone's email, government agents gain the ability to peer deeply into his activities. Much hinges, therefore, on whether the government is permitted to request that a commercial ISP turn over the contents of a subscriber's emails without triggering the machinery of the Fourth Amendment.

In confronting this question, we take note of two bedrock principles. First, the very fact that information is being passed through a communications network is a paramount Fourth Amendment consideration. *See ibid.; United States v. U.S. Dist. Court,* 407 U.S. 297, 313 (1972) ("[T]he broad and unsuspected governmental incursions into conversational privacy which electronic surveillance entails necessitate the application of Fourth Amendment safeguards."). Second, the Fourth Amendment must keep pace with the inexorable march of technological progress, or its guarantees will wither and perish. *See Kyllo v. United States,* 533 U.S. 27 (2001) (noting that evolving technology must not be permitted to "erode the privacy guaranteed by the Fourth Amendment"); *see also* Orin S. Kerr, *Applying the Fourth Amendment to the Internet: A General Approach,* 62 Stan. L. Rev. 1005, 1007 (2010) (arguing that "the differences between the facts of physical space and the facts of the Internet require courts to identify new Fourth Amendment distinctions to maintain the function of Fourth Amendment rules in an online environment").

With those principles in mind, we begin our analysis by considering the manner in which the Fourth Amendment protects traditional forms of communication. In *Katz,* the Supreme Court was asked to determine how the Fourth Amendment applied in the context of the telephone. There, government agents had affixed an electronic listening device to the exterior of a public phone booth, and had used the device to intercept and record several phone conversations. *See* 389 U.S. at 348. The Supreme Court held that this constituted a search under the Fourth Amendment, *see id.* at 353, notwithstanding the fact that the telephone company had the capacity to monitor and record the calls, *see Smith,* 442 U.S. at 746-47 (Stewart, J., dissenting). In the eyes of the Court, the caller was "surely entitled to assume that the words he utter[ed] into the mouthpiece w[ould] not be broadcast to the world." *Katz,* 389 U.S. at 352. The Court's holding in *Katz* has since come to stand for the broad proposition that, in many contexts, the government infringes a reasonable expectation of privacy when it surreptitiously intercepts a telephone call through electronic means. *Smith,* 442 U.S. at 746 (Stewart, J., dissenting) ("[S]ince *Katz,* it has been abundantly clear that telephone conversations are fully protected by the Fourth and Fourteenth Amendments.").

Letters receive similar protection. *See Jacobsen,* 466 U.S. at 114 ("Letters and other sealed packages are in the general class of effects in which the public at large has a legitimate expectation of privacy[.]"); *Ex Parte Jackson,* 96 U.S. 727, 733 (1877). While a letter is in the mail, the police may not intercept it and examine its contents unless they first obtain a warrant based on probable cause. *Ibid.* This is true despite the fact that sealed letters are handed over to perhaps dozens of mail carriers, any one of whom could tear open the thin paper envelopes that separate the private words from the world outside. Put another way, trusting a letter to an intermediary does not necessarily defeat a reasonable expectation that the letter will remain private.

See Katz, 389 U.S. at 351 ("[W]hat [a person] seeks to preserve as private, even in an area accessible to the public, may be constitutionally protected.").

Given the fundamental similarities between email and traditional forms of communication, it would defy common sense to afford emails lesser Fourth Amendment protection. *See* Patricia L. Bellia & Susan Freiwald, *Fourth Amendment Protection for Stored E-Mail,* 2008 U. Chi. Legal F. 121, 135 (2008) (recognizing the need to "eliminate the strangely disparate treatment of mailed and telephonic communications on the one hand and electronic communications on the other"); *City of Ontario v. Quon,* 130 S. Ct. 2619, 2631 (2010) (implying that "a search of [an individual's] personal e-mail account" would be just as intrusive as "a wiretap on his home phone line"); *United States v. Forrester,* 512 F.3d 500, 511 (9th Cir. 2008) (holding that "[t]he privacy interests in [mail and e-mail] are identical"). Email is the technological scion of tangible mail, and it plays an indispensable part in the Information Age. Over the last decade, email has become "so pervasive that some persons may consider [it] to be [an] essential means or necessary instrument[ ] for self-expression, even self-identification." *Quon,* 130 S. Ct. at 2630. It follows that email requires strong protection under the Fourth Amendment; otherwise, the Fourth Amendment would prove an ineffective guardian of private communication, an essential purpose it has long been recognized to serve. *See U.S. Dist. Court,* 407 U.S. at 313; *United States v. Waller,* 581 F.2d 585, 587 (6th Cir. 1978) (noting the Fourth Amendment's role in protecting "private communications"). As some forms of communication begin to diminish, the Fourth Amendment must recognize and protect nascent ones that arise. *See Warshak I,* 490 F.3d at 473 ("It goes without saying that like the telephone earlier in our history, e-mail is an ever-increasing mode of private communication, and protecting shared communications through this medium is as important to Fourth Amendment principles today as protecting telephone conversations has been in the past.").

If we accept that an email is analogous to a letter or a phone call, it is manifest that agents of the government cannot compel a commercial ISP to turn over the contents of an email without triggering the Fourth Amendment. An ISP is the intermediary that makes email communication possible. Emails must pass through an ISP's servers to reach their intended recipient. Thus, the ISP is the functional equivalent of a post office or a telephone company. As we have discussed above, the police may not storm the post office and intercept a letter, and they are likewise forbidden from using the phone system to make a clandestine recording of a telephone call — unless they get a warrant, that is. *See Jacobsen,* 466 U.S. at 114; *Katz,* 389 U.S. at 353. It only stands to reason that, if government agents compel an ISP to surrender the contents of a subscriber's emails, those agents have thereby conducted a Fourth Amendment search, which necessitates compliance with the warrant requirement absent some exception.

In *Warshak I,* the government argued that this conclusion was improper, pointing to the fact that NuVox contractually reserved the right to access Warshak's emails for certain purposes. While we acknowledge that a subscriber agreement might, in some cases, be sweeping enough to defeat a reasonable expectation of privacy in the contents of an email account, *see Warshak I,* 490 F.3d at 473; *Warshak II,* 532 F.3d at 526-27, we doubt that will be the case in most situations, and it is certainly not the case here.

As an initial matter, it must be observed that the mere *ability* of a third-party intermediary to access the contents of a communication cannot be sufficient to extinguish a reasonable expectation of privacy. In *Katz,* the Supreme Court found it reasonable to expect privacy during a telephone call despite the ability of an operator to listen in. *See Smith,* 442 U.S. at 746-47 (Stewart, J., dissenting). Similarly, the ability of a rogue mail handler to rip open a letter does not make it unreasonable to assume that sealed mail will remain private on its journey across the country. Therefore, the threat or possibility of access is not decisive when it comes to the reasonableness of an expectation of privacy.

Nor is the *right* of access. As the Electronic Frontier Foundation points out in its *amicus* brief, at the time *Katz* was decided, telephone companies had a right to monitor calls in certain situations. Specifically, telephone companies could listen in when reasonably necessary to "protect themselves and their properties against the improper and illegal use of their facilities." *Bubis v. United States*, 384 F.2d 643, 648 (9th Cir. 1967). In this case, the NuVox subscriber agreement tracks that language, indicating that "NuVox *may* access and use individual Subscriber information in the operation of the Service and as necessary to protect the Service." Acceptable Use Policy, *available at* http://business.windstream.com/Legal/acceptableUse.htm (last visited Aug. 12, 2010). Thus, under *Katz*, the degree of access granted to NuVox does not diminish the reasonableness of Warshak's trust in the privacy of his emails.

Our conclusion finds additional support in the application of Fourth Amendment doctrine to rented space. Hotel guests, for example, have a reasonable expectation of privacy in their rooms. *See United States v. Allen*, 106 F.3d 695, 699 (6th Cir. 1997). This is so even though maids routinely enter hotel rooms to replace the towels and tidy the furniture. Similarly, tenants have a legitimate expectation of privacy in their apartments. *See United States v. Washington*, 573 F.3d 279, 284 (6th Cir. 2009). That expectation persists, regardless of the incursions of handymen to fix leaky faucets. Consequently, we are convinced that some degree of routine access is hardly dispositive with respect to the privacy question.

Again, however, we are unwilling to hold that a subscriber agreement will *never* be broad enough to snuff out a reasonable expectation of privacy. As the panel noted in *Warshak I*, if the ISP expresses an intention to "audit, inspect, and monitor" its subscriber's emails, that might be enough to render an expectation of privacy unreasonable. *See* 490 F.3d at 472-73 (quoting *United States v. Simons*, 206 F.3d 392, 398 (4th Cir. 2000)). But where, as here, there is no such statement, the ISP's "control over the [e-mails] and ability to access them under certain limited circumstances will not be enough to overcome an expectation of privacy." *Id.* at 473.

We recognize that our conclusion may be attacked in light of the Supreme Court's decision in *United States v. Miller*, 425 U.S. 435 (1976). In *Miller*, the Supreme Court held that a bank depositor does not have a reasonable expectation of privacy in the contents of bank records, checks, and deposit slips. *Id.* at 442. The Court's holding in *Miller* was based on the fact that bank documents, "including financial statements and deposit slips, contain only information voluntarily conveyed to the banks and exposed to their employees in the ordinary course of business." *Ibid.* The Court noted,

> The depositor takes the risk, in revealing his affairs to another, that the information will be conveyed by that person to the Government. . . . [T]he Fourth Amendment does not prohibit the obtaining of information revealed to a third party and conveyed by him to Government authorities, even if the information is revealed on the assumption that it will be used only for a limited purpose and the confidence placed in the third party will not be betrayed.

Id. at 443 (citations omitted).

But *Miller* is distinguishable. First, *Miller* involved simple business records, as opposed to the potentially unlimited variety of "confidential communications" at issue here. *See ibid.* Second, the bank depositor in *Miller* conveyed information to the bank so that the bank could put the information to use "in the ordinary course of business." *Ibid.* By contrast, Warshak received his emails through NuVox. NuVox was an *intermediary,* not the intended recipient of the emails. *See* Bellia & Freiwald, *Stored E-Mail,* 2008 U. Chi. Legal F. at 165 ("[W]e view the best analogy for this scenario as the cases in which a third party carries, transports, or stores property for another. In these cases, as in the stored e-mail case, the customer grants access to the ISP because it is essential to the customer's interests."). Thus, *Miller* is not controlling.

Accordingly, we hold that a subscriber enjoys a reasonable expectation of privacy in the contents of emails "that are stored with, or sent or received through, a commercial ISP." *Warshak I,* 490 F.3d at 473; *see Forrester,* 512 F.3d at 511 (suggesting that "[t]he contents [of e-mail messages] may deserve Fourth Amendment protection"). The government may not compel a commercial ISP to turn over the contents of a subscriber's emails without first obtaining a warrant based on probable cause. Therefore, because they did not obtain a warrant, the government agents violated the Fourth Amendment when they obtained the contents of Warshak's emails. Moreover, to the extent that the SCA purports to permit the government to obtain such emails warrantlessly, the SCA is unconstitutional....

[The court held that the government violated Warshak's Fourth Amendment rights by compelling the ISP to turn over e-mail without first obtaining a warrant based on probable cause. However, because the agents relied in good faith on provisions in the Stored Communications Act, the exclusionary rule did not apply.]

KEITH, Circuit Judge, concurring. Although I concur in the result the majority reaches, I write separately to provide clarification concerning whether Warshak's emails, obtained in violation of the Fourth Amendment, should have been excluded from trial under the exclusionary rule....

Here, we are presented with a unique situation. As the majority notes, because the government requested a secret subpoena to confiscate Warshak's personal emails without his knowledge pursuant to §2703(b) and (d) of the Stored Communications Act ("SCA"), there is no need to exclude the evidence. The officers took these actions in good faith reliance upon these statutes. They requested the emails from NuVox via a §2703(b) subpoena and a §2703(d) order. Though the government failed to give notice within ninety days after the initial request, it did so only after the emails had been obtained and after an initial showing that notice should be delayed. While we today declare these statutes unconstitutional insofar as they permit the government to obtain such emails without a warrant, it does not follow that the evidence should have been excluded from Warshak's trial. Such an exclusion would not have a substantial deterrent effect on future Fourth Amendment violations enacted by the legislature. *See Herring v. United States,* 555 U.S. 135 (2009) (focusing on "the efficacy of the rule in deterring Fourth Amendment violations in the future"). Therefore, the majority rightfully affirms the district court's refusal to suppress Warshak's emails. With this I agree.

However, there is a further wrongdoing that troubles me today. Specifically, the government's request that NuVox preserve Warshak's stored and future email communications without Warshak's knowledge and without a warrant pursuant to §2703(f). Under §2703(f), "[a] provider of wire or electronic communication services or a remote computing service, upon the request of a governmental entity, shall take all necessary steps to *preserve* records and other evidence *in its possession* pending the issuance of a court order or other process." 18 U.S.C. §2703(f) (emphasis added). This subsection was added to the SCA in 1996 in an effort to supplement law enforcement resources and security. The Antiterrorism Act of 1996, Pub. L. 104-132, 110 Stat. 1305. While added in a completely different context from the creation of the statute, it is worthwhile to review the purpose of the statute as a whole when considering the meaning of this subsection.

Section 2703, as part of the Electronic Communications Privacy Act ("ECPA"), was enacted in 1986 as part of Congress's effort to maintain "a fair balance between the privacy expectations of American citizens and the legitimate needs of law enforcement agencies." S. Rep. 99-541, at 4, 1986 U.S.C.C.A.N. 3555, 3559. Moreover, the advent of the ECPA was precipitated by concerns about advancements in technology and the desire to protect personal and business information which individuals can no longer "lock away" with ease. The plain language of §2703(f) permits only the preservation of emails in the service provider's possession at the time of the request, not the preservation of future emails. Moreover, the Department of Justice, along with some theorists, emphasize that these requests "have no prospective effect." *See, e.g.,* Deirdre K. Mulligan, *Reasonable Expectations in Electronic Communications: A Critical Perspective on the Electronic Communications Privacy Act,* 72 Geo. Wash. L. Rev. 1557, 1565 (2004); U.S. Dep't of Justice, Searching and Seizing Computers and Obtaining Electronic Evidence in Criminal Investigations, Chapter III, §G(1) (2009), *available at* http://www.cybercrime.gov/ssmanual/03ssma.html ("[Section] 2703(f) letters should not be used prospectively to order providers to preserve records not yet created. If agents want providers to record information about future electronic communications, they should comply with the [Wiretap Act and the Pen/Trap statute].""). I find this statutory interpretation persuasive.

Following NuVox's policy, the provider would have destroyed Warshak's old emails but for the government's request that they maintain all current and prospective emails for almost a year without Warshak's knowledge. In practice, the government used the statute as a means to monitor Warshak after the investigation started without his knowledge and without a warrant. Such a practice is no more than backdoor wiretapping. I doubt that such actions, if contested directly in court, would withstand the muster of the Fourth Amendment. Email, much like telephone, provides individuals with a means to communicate in private. *See Warshak v. United States,* 490 F.3d 455, 469-70 (6th Cir. 2007), *vacated,* 532 F.3d 521 (6th Cir. 2008) (en banc). The government cannot use email collection as a means to monitor citizens without a warrant anymore than they can tap a telephone line to monitor citizens without a warrant. The purpose of §2703, along with the Stored Communications Act as a whole, is to maintain the boundaries between a citizen's reasonable expectation of privacy and crime prevention in light of quickly advancing technology. S. Rep. 99-541, at 4, 1986 U.S.C.C.A.N. 3555, 3559. To interpret §2703(f) as having both a retroactive and prospective effect would be contrary to the purpose of the statute as a whole.

While it was not the issue in today's decision, a policy whereby the government requests emails prospectively without a warrant deeply concerns me. I am furthermore troubled by the majority's willingness to disregard the current reading of §2703(f) without concern for future analysis of this statute. Nevertheless, because the government's violation of the Fourth Amendment stems from the order and/or subpoena to obtain Warshak's email communications pursuant to §2703(b) and (d), the government acted in good faith upon the statute. The fact that their policy likely exceeded the parameters of §2703(f) is irrelevant to this analysis as they did not rely upon §2703 as a whole in requesting the secret subpoena and order to obtain these emails. Accordingly, the majority was correct in holding that the evidence falls within the good faith exception to the exclusionary rule. . . .

NOTES AND QUESTIONS

1. *E-mail Privacy.* Is the expansion of privacy protections to e-mail a reasonable and predictable extension of the line of cases from *Katz* to *Smith* and *Miller*? Are you persuaded by the court's analogies to telephones and letters? Is a search of a personal e-mail account as intrusive as a wiretap on a land line or cell phone? Is surveillance of the Internet significantly different from surveillance of the physical world? *See* Orin S. Kerr, *Applying the Fourth Amendment to the Internet: A General Approach*, 62 Stan. L. Rev. 1005, 1032 (2010) (no); Christopher Slobogin, *Privacy at Risk: The New Government Surveillance and the Fourth Amendment* (2007) (yes).

2. *Content vs. Non-Content.* In *United States v. Forrester*, 512 F. 3d 500 (9th Cir. 2008), the Ninth Circuit ruled, based on *Smith*, that the government did not trigger Fourth Amendment requirements when it asked an ISP to install a monitoring device that recorded the target's IP addresses, to/from addresses for e-mails, and the volume of messages sent from the account. How closely analogous are the pen register in *Smith* and Internet surveillance approved in *Forrester*? Do most Internet users expect privacy in both their content and non-content information? Does the assumption that a person does not retain a reasonable expectation of privacy in information disclosed to a third party apply equally to the Internet and the physical world? Should it matter legally whether the third party is merely an intermediary that does not need to access or analyze the electronic communications — a phone company, for example — as opposed to a bank that receives electronic deposits and withdrawals?

In a suit brought by a city police officer against city and police officials for violating the Fourth Amendment when police supervisors reviewed the contents of stored text messages sent and received on the officer's city-issued alphanumeric pager, the Supreme Court was willing to assume for the sake of argument that the police officer had a reasonable expectation of privacy in the messages. It held that the assumed search was nevertheless reasonable on the strength of the "special needs" exception. *City of Ontario v. Quon*, 130 S. Ct. 2619 (2010). The Court explained its reluctance to find an express privacy right:

> The Court must proceed with care when considering the whole concept of privacy expectations in communications made on electronic equipment owned by a government employer. The judiciary risks error by elaborating too fully on the Fourth Amendment implications of emerging technology before its role in society has become clear. In *Katz*, the Court relied on its own knowledge and experience to conclude that there is a reasonable expectation of privacy in a telephone booth. See [*Katz, supra,*] at 360-361 (Harlan, J., concurring). It is not so clear that courts at present are on so sure a ground. Prudence counsels caution before the facts in the instant case are used to establish far-reaching premises that define the existence, and extent, of privacy expectations enjoyed by employees when using employer-provided communication devices.

Rapid changes in the dynamics of communication and information transmission are evident not just in the technology itself but in what society accepts as proper behavior....

Id. at 2629.

3. *The Role of the ISP and Privacy Policies.* Do you understand why the subscriber agreement between Warshak and NuVox did not defeat Warshak's reasonable expectation of privacy? Can you draft the language of an agreement that *would* extinguish the privacy expectation? Does the analogy to rented hotel rooms hold up in the world of the Internet and ISPs? In *Quon, supra,* the police department policy in effect stated that the city "reserves the right to monitor and log all network activity including e-mail and Internet use, with or without notice. Users should have no expectation of privacy or confidentiality when using these resources." *Id.* at 2625. The policy statement did not apply, on its face, to text messaging, although the city made clear to employees that the city would treat text messages the same way it treated e-mails. *Id.* However, unlike an e-mail sent on a city computer and transmitted through the city's own servers, a text message sent from a city pager was transmitted using wireless radio frequencies to a receiving station owned by a private ISP, where it was in turn routed from the ISP's transmitting station nearest to the recipient's pager or cell phone. *Id.* The holding in *Quon* is thus limited to stored text messages held by a third-party provider. According to the Court in *Quon,* "employer policies concerning communications will...shape the reasonable expectations of their employees, especially to the extent that such policies are clearly communicated." *Id.* at 2630. Is this assertion harmonious with what the *Katz* Court said about expectations of privacy?

4. *Comparing Business Records.* Is the contrast to bank records in *Miller* as starkly different from confidential e-mail communications as portrayed by the court? Does the fact that NuVox was an intermediary place the ISP in a fundamentally different legal posture from the bank in *Miller?* *See* Orin S. Kerr, *The Case for the Third-Party Doctrine,* 107 Mich. L. Rev. 561 (2009). Do you think that *Miller* would be decided the same way today?

5. *Repairing the Stored Communications Act?* Do you agree with Judge Keith that the government's warrantless request that NuVox preserve future as well as currently stored e-mails amounts to backdoor wiretapping in violation of the Fourth Amendment? How should Congress repair these shortcomings of the SCA? Would the imposition of traditional warrant procedures satisfy the objections? Would such a procedure be workable? If not, what kind of substitute would satisfy the government and the Fourth Amendment? *See* Orin S. Kerr, *A User's Guide to the Stored Communications Act, and a Legislator's Guide to Amending It,* 72 Geo. Wash. L. Rev. 1208 (2004).

2.   Techniques and Authorities for Collection of Transactional Data

Building on the privacy theory of *Smith,* Congress enacted several statutes that authorized the FBI to use NSLs — issued without any prior judicial order — to obtain transactional records from third-party record holders. Here is a redacted example of such a letter, followed by a judicial decision in a case testing its legitimacy.

SEC~~R~~ET

ALL INFORMATION CONTAINED
HEREIN IS UNCLASSIFIED EXCEPT
WHERE SHOWN OTHERWISE

U.S. Department of Justice

Federal Bureau of Investigation

In Reply, Please Refer to
File No

[Drafting] Field Division
[Street Address]
[City, State, Zip]

[Month Date, Year]

[Mr /Mrs.] [COMPANY POINT OF CONTACT]
[TITLE]
[COMPANY]
[STREET ADDRESS]
[CITY, STATE No Zip Code]

Dear [Mr /Mrs] [LAST NAME]:

     Under the authority of Executive Order 12333, dated
December 4, 1981, and pursuant to Title 18, United States Code
(U S.C), Section 2709 (as amended, October 26, 2001), you are
hereby directed to provide the Federal Bureau of Investigation

b2-2
b7E-1

     In accordance with Title 18, U.S.C., Section 2709(b), I
certify that the information sought is relevant to an authorized
investigation to protect against international terrorism or
clandestine intelligence activities, and that such an
investigation of a United States person is not conducted solely
on the basis of activities protected by the first amendment of
the Constitution of the United States

     You are further advised that Title 18, U.S C , Section
2709(c), prohibits any officer, employee or agent of yours from
disclosing to any person that the FBI has sought or obtained
access to information or records under these provisions.

b2-2
b7E-1

CLASSIFIED DECISIONS FINALIZED BY
DEPARTMENT REVIEW COMMITTEE (DRC)
DATE: 07-03-2004

CA# 03-2522

CLASSIFIED BY 65179 dmb/bcs/amw   6/5/2004
REASON: 1.4 (c)
DECLASSIFY ON: X 6/5/2029

Patriot Act II-828

SEC~~R~~ET

DECLASSIFIED BY 65179 dmb/bcs/amw
ON 8/3/2004

SECRET

[Mr /Mrs] [COMPANY POINT OF CONTACT]

Your cooperation in this matter is greatly appreciated

Sincerely,

[ADIC/SAC Name]
Assistant Director/Special

Agent in Charge

CLASSIFIED DECISIONS FINALIZED BY
DEPARTMENT REVIEW COMMITTEE (DRC)
DATE: 07-01-2004

CA# 03-2522

ALL INFORMATION CONTAINED
HEREIN IS UNCLASSIFIED EXCEPT
WHERE SHOWN OTHERWISE

CLASSIFIED BY 65179 dnh/bce/smw   6/30/2004
REASON: 1.4 (c)
DECLASSIFY ON: X 6/30/2025

2

Patriot Act II-829

SECRET

DECLASSIFIED BY 65129 dmb/bce/fmw
ON 8/3/2004

Doe v. Ashcroft (*Doe I*)

United States District Court, Southern District of New York, 2004
334 F. Supp. 2d 471
vacated and remanded sub nom. Doe v. Gonzales,
449 F.3d 415 (2d Cir. 2006)

MARRERO, J. . . .

I. INTRODUCTION

Plaintiffs in this case challenge the constitutionality of 18 U.S.C. §2709 ("§2709").[1] That statute authorizes the Federal Bureau of Investigation ("FBI") to compel communications firms, such as internet service providers ("ISPs") or telephone companies, to produce certain customer records whenever the FBI certifies that those records are "relevant to an authorized investigation to protect against international terrorism or clandestine intelligence activities." [*Id.*] The FBI's demands under §2709 *are* issued in the form of national security letters ("NSLs"), which constitute a unique form of administrative subpoena cloaked in secrecy and pertaining to national security issues. The statute bars all NSL recipients from ever disclosing that the FBI has issued an NSL.

The lead plaintiff, called "John Doe" ("Doe") for purposes of this litigation, is described in the complaint as an internet access firm that received an NSL. . . .

II. BACKGROUND . . .

A. Doe's Receipt of an NSL

After receiving a call from an FBI agent informing him that he would be served with an NSL, Doe received a document, printed on FBI letterhead, which stated that, "pursuant to Title 18, United States Code (U.S.C.), Section 2709" Doe was "directed" to provide certain information to the Government. As required by the terms of §2709, in the NSL the FBI "certif[ied] that the information sought [was] relevant to an authorized investigation to protect against international terrorism or clandestine intelligence activities." Doe was "further advised" that §2709(c) prohibited him, or his officers, agents, or employees, "from disclosing to *any person* that the FBI has sought or obtained access to information or records under these provisions." Doe was "requested to provide records responsive to [the] request *personally*" to a designated individual, and to not transmit the records by mail or even mention the NSL in *any* telephone conversation. . . .

. . . Doe has not complied with the NSL request, and has instead engaged counsel to bring the present lawsuit.

B. §2709 in General

As stated above, §2709 authorizes the FBI to issue NSLs to compel communications firms to produce certain customer records whenever the FBI certifies that those

---

[1. This section was amended by the Patriot Improvement Act in 2006, *infra* p. 281, as explained in the following Notes and Questions. — Eds.]

records are relevant to an authorized international terrorism or counterintelligence investigation, and the statute also categorically bars NSL recipients from disclosing the inquiry. In relevant part, it states:

> (a) Duty to provide. — A wire or electronic communication service provider shall comply with a request for subscriber information and toll billing records information, or electronic communication transactional records in its custody or possession made by the Director of the Federal Bureau of Investigation under subsection (b) of this section.
>
> (b) Required certification. — The Director of the Federal Bureau of Investigation, or his designee in a position not lower than Deputy Assistant Director at Bureau head-quarters or a Special Agent in Charge in a Bureau field office designated by the Director, may — (1) request the name, address, length of service, and local and long distance toll billing records of a person or entity if the Director (or his designee) certifies in writing to the wire or electronic communication service provider to which the request is made that the name, address, length of service, and toll billing records sought are relevant to an authorized investigation to protect against international terrorism or clandestine intelligence activities, provided that such an investigation of a United States person is not conducted solely on the basis of activities protected by the first amendment to the Constitution of the United States. . . .
>
> (c) Prohibition of certain disclosure. — No wire or electronic communication service provider, or officer, employee, or agent thereof, shall disclose to any person that the Federal Bureau of Investigation has sought or obtained access to information or records under this section. . . .

Section 2709 is one of only a handful of statutes authorizing the Government to issue NSLs. The other NSL statutes authorize the Government to compel disclosure of certain financial and credit records which it certifies are relevant to international terrorism or counter-intelligence investigations, and to compel disclosure of certain records of current or former government employees who have (or have had) access to classified information.[17]

C. Legislative History

Section 2709 was enacted as part of Title II of the Electronic Communications Privacy Act of 1986 ("ECPA"),[19] which sought to "protect privacy interests" in "stored wire and electronic communications" while also "protecting the Government's legitimate law enforcement needs."[20] . . .

. . . As first enacted, §2709 required electronic communication service providers to produce subscriber information," "toll billing records information," or "electronic communication transactional records," upon the FBI's internal certification that (1) the information was "relevant to an authorized foreign counterintelligence investigation" and that (2) there were "specific and articulable facts giving reason to believe that the person or entity to whom the information sought pertains [was] a foreign power or an agent of a foreign power." . . .

---

17. See 12 U.S.C. §3414 (financial records); 15 U.S.C. §§1681u, 1681v (credit records); 50 U.S.C. §436 (government employee records).
19. Pub. L. No. 99-508, §201, 100 Stat. 1848, 1867 (1986).
20. S. Rep. No. 99-541, at 3 (1986), *reprinted in* 1986 U.S.C.C.A.N. 3555, 3557.

The . . . most recent major revision to §2709 occurred in October 2001,[2] as part of the USA PATRIOT Act of 2001 ("Patriot Act").[39] In short, the Patriot Act removed the previous requirement that §2709 inquiries have a nexus to a foreign power, replacing that prerequisite with a broad standard of relevance to investigations of terrorism or clandestine intelligence activities. In hearings before the House Judiciary Committee on September 24, 2001, the Administration submitted the following explanation for the proposed change:

> NSL authority requires both a showing of relevance and a showing of links to an "agent of a foreign power." In this respect, [it is] substantially more demanding than the analogous criminal authorities, which require only a certification of relevance. Because the NSLs require documentation of the facts supporting the "agent of a foreign power" predicate and because they require the signature of a high-ranking official at FBI headquarters, they often take months to be issued. This is in stark contrast to criminal subpoenas, which can be used to obtain the same information, and are issued rapidly at the local level. In many cases, counter-intelligence and counterterrorism investigations suffer substantial delays while waiting for NSLs to be prepared, returned from headquarters, and served. The section would streamline the process of obtaining NSL authority. . . .

The House Judiciary Committee agreed that "[s]uch delays are unacceptable" and stated in its October 11, 2001, report that the Patriot Act would "harmonize[]" §2709 "with existing criminal law where an Assistant United States Attorney may issue a grand jury subpoena for all such records in a criminal case."

D. NSLs and Other Information-Gathering Authority

It is instructive to place the Government's NSL authority in the context of other means by which the Government gathers information of the type covered by §2709 because Congress (in passing and amending the NSL statutes) and the parties here (in contesting §2709's constitutionality) have drawn analogies to those other authorities as grounds for or against its validity. The relationship of §2709 to other related statutes supplies a backdrop for assessing congressional intent and judging the validity of the law on its face and as applied. In addition, an analysis of these analogous information-gathering methods indicates that NSLs such as the ones authorized by §2709 provide fewer procedural protections to the recipient than any other information-gathering technique the Government employs to procure information similar to that which it obtains pursuant to §2709.

1. Administrative Subpoenas

The most important set of statutes relevant to this case are those authorizing federal agencies to issue administrative subpoenas for the purpose of executing the particular agency's function. Ordinary administrative subpoenas, which are far more common than NSLs, may be issued by most federal agencies, as authorized by the hundreds of applicable statutes in federal law. For example, the Internal Revenue

---

[2. The statute was amended again in 2006 by the Patriot Improvement Act, *infra* p. 281, as explained in the following Notes and Questions. — Eds.]

39. *See* Pub. L. No. 107-56, §505, 115 Stat. 272, 365 (2001). . . .

Service (IRS) may issue subpoenas to investigate possible violations of the tax code, and the Securities Exchange Commission (SEC) may issue subpoenas to investigate possible violations of the securities laws. . . .

There is a wide body of law which pertains to administrative subpoenas generally. According to the Government's central theory in this case, those standing rules would presumably also apply to NSLs, even if not so explicitly stated in the text of the statute. Where an agency seeks a court order to enforce a subpoena against a resisting subpoena recipient, courts will enforce the subpoena as long as: (1) the agency's investigation is being conducted pursuant to a legitimate purpose, (2) the inquiry is relevant to that purpose, (3) the information is not already within the agency's possession, and (4) the proper procedures have been followed. The Second Circuit has described these standards as "minimal." Even if an administrative subpoena meets these initial criteria to be enforceable, its recipient may nevertheless affirmatively challenge the subpoena on other grounds, such as an allegation that it was issued with an improper purpose or that the information sought is privileged.

Unlike the NSL statutes, most administrative subpoena laws either contain no provision requiring secrecy, or allow for only limited secrecy in special cases. For example, some administrative subpoena statutes permit the investigating agency to apply for a court order to temporarily bar disclosure of the inquiry, generally during specific renewable increments or for an appropriate period of time fixed by the court, where such disclosure could jeopardize the investigation. . . .

2.   Subpoena Authority in the Criminal Context

In its role as a party to a federal criminal proceeding (including a grand jury proceeding), the Government has broad authority to issue a subpoena to obtain witness testimony or "*any* books, papers, documents, data, or other objects the subpoena designates."[52] Although such subpoenas "are issued in the name of the district court over the signature of the clerk, they are issued pro forma and in blank to anyone requesting them," and the "court exercises no prior control whatsoever upon their use."[53]

The court becomes involved in the subpoena process only if the subpoenaed party moves to quash the request as "unreasonable or oppressive,"[54] or if the Government seeks to compel compliance with the subpoena. The reasonableness of a subpoena depends on the context. For example, to survive a motion to quash, a subpoena issued in connection with a criminal trial "must make a reasonably specific request for information that would be both relevant and admissible at trial."[55] By contrast, a grand jury subpoena is generally enforced as long as there is a "reasonable possibility that the category of materials the Government seeks will produce information relevant to the general subject of the grand jury's investigation."[56] Considering the grand jury's broad investigatory power and minimal court supervision, it is accurate to observe, as the Second Circuit did long ago, that "[b]asically the grand jury is a law enforcement agency."[57]

---

52. Fed. R. Crim. P. 17(a), (c)(1) (emphasis added).
53. *In re Grand Jury Proceedings*, 486 F.2d 85, 90 (3d Cir. 1973).
54. Fed. R. Crim. P. 17(c)(2).
55. *United States v. R. Enters., Inc.*, 498 U.S. 292, 299 (1991) (*citing United States v. Nixon*, 418 U.S. 683, 700 (1974)).
56. *Id.* at 301.
57. *United States v. Cleary*, 265 F.2d 459, 461 (2d Cir. 1959).

While materials presented in a criminal trial setting are generally public, the federal rules impose stringent secrecy requirements on certain grand jury participants, including the attorneys, court reporters, and grand jurors.[59] ...

In certain contexts, the Government may issue subpoenas related to criminal investigations even without initiating a formal criminal proceeding. For example, the United States Attorney General is authorized to issue administrative subpoenas, without convening a grand jury, to investigate federal narcotics crimes, racketeering crimes, health care related crimes, and crimes involving the exploitation of children. In each of these instances, the administrative process is governed by the general rules described above, providing safeguards of judicial review.

3. Background Rules Governing Disclosure of Stored Electronic Communications

Title II of the ECPA [also called the Stored Communications Act], in which §2709 was enacted, sets forth an intricate framework by which electronic communications providers, such as ISPs and phone companies, may be compelled to disclose stored electronic information to the Government. The framework described below operates independently of the rules governing NSLs issued pursuant to §2709, but may aid with interpretation of §2709.

The Government may obtain basic subscriber information[69] merely by issuing an authorized administrative subpoena, trial subpoena, or grand jury subpoena, and the Government need not notify the subscriber of the request.

If the Government gives prior notice to the subscriber, or otherwise complies with certain delayed notice procedures, the Government may also subpoena the *contents* of electronic communications which are either (1) retained on a system for storage purposes (*e.g.*, opened email which remains on an ISP's server), or (2) retained, for more than 180 days, in intermediate or temporary storage (*e.g.*, unopened email on an ISP's server). For the Government to obtain the contents of electronic communications kept for 180 days or less in intermediate or temporary storage (e.g., unopened email on an ISP's server), it must obtain a search warrant under Federal Rule of Criminal Procedure 41, or the state equivalent. In other words, the Government would have to appear before a neutral magistrate and make a showing of probable cause. The Government may also obtain a court order requiring an electronic communications service provider to turn over transactional and content information by setting forth "specific and articulable facts showing that there are reasonable grounds to believe that" the information sought is "relevant and material to an ongoing criminal investigation."[75]

The ECPA permits the Government to seek a court order prohibiting the communications provider from revealing the Government's inquiry "for such period as the court deems appropriate" if the court determines that such disclosure, among

---

59. *See* Fed. R. Crim. P. 6(e).

69. Basic subscriber information includes: (1) a subscriber's name and (2) address; (3) the subscriber's local and long distance telephone connection records, or records of session times and durations; (4) the subscriber's length of service and types of service he has utilized; (5) any telephone or instrument number or other subscriber number or identity, including any temporarily assigned network address; and (6) the subscriber's means and source of payment for the service. *See* 18 U.S.C. §2703(c)(2).

75. 18 U.S.C. §2703(d).

other things, would result in "destruction of or tampering with evidence" or "seriously jeopardizing an investigation or unduly delaying a trial."[76]

4. Mail

Government law enforcement agencies are authorized to request the Postal Inspector to initiate a so-called "mail cover" to obtain any information appearing on the outside of a particular piece of mail.[77] Among other grounds, the law enforcement agency can obtain a mail cover by "specify[ing] the reasonable grounds to demonstrate the mail cover is necessary" to "[p]rotect the national security" or to "[o]btain information regarding the commission or attempted commission of a crime." There is no requirement that the mail sender or recipient be notified of the mail cover.

The Government must obtain a warrant based upon probable cause to open and inspect sealed mail because the contents of mail are protected by the Fourth Amendment. As the Supreme Court established long ago: "Whilst in the mail, [a person's papers] can only be opened and examined under like warrant, issued upon similar oath or affirmation, particularly describing the thing to be seized, as is required when papers are subjected to search in one's own household."[80]

5. Pen Registers and Trap and Trace Devices

Pen registers and trap and trace devices record certain electronic communications data indicating the origins and destinations of various "dialing, routing, addressing, or signaling information," *e.g.*, the phone numbers dialed to and from a telephone.[81] In criminal investigations, the Government must apply for a court order, renewable in 60-day increments, to install or collect data from such devices, though the standard for issuing such an order is relatively low. The Government need only show that "the information likely to be obtained by such installation and use is relevant to an ongoing criminal investigation."[83]

The person owning the communications device is prohibited, unless otherwise directed by court order, from disclosing the fact that a pen register or trap and trace device is in effect.

6. Wiretaps and Electronic Eavesdropping

The Fourth Amendment protects against warrantless Government wiretapping. Federal legislation specifies the procedures by which law enforcement officials may obtain a court order to conduct wiretaps and other forms of electronic eavesdropping. The requirements are rigorous. Among other things, the Government must show that: (1) "there is probable cause for belief that an individual is committing, has committed, or is about to commit" one of a list of enumerated crimes; (2) "there is probable cause for belief that particular communications concerning that offense will be obtained through such interception"; and (3) "normal investigative procedures

---

76. *Id.* §2705(b).
77. *See* 39 C.F.R. §233.3.
80. *See Ex parte Jackson*, 96 U.S. 727, 733 (1877).
81. *See* 18 U.S.C. §3127(3)-(4).
83. *Id.* §3123(a).

have been tried and have failed or reasonably appear to be unlikely to succeed if tried or to be too dangerous."[87] Such orders are not available "for any period longer than is necessary to achieve the objective of the authorization," subject to a renewable maximum of 30 days.[88] The communications provider is prohibited from disclosing that a wiretap or electronic surveillance is in place, "except as may otherwise be required by legal process and then only after prior notification" to the appropriate law enforcement authorities.[89]

7. Foreign Intelligence Surveillance Act . . .

[The court summarized the procedures for obtaining an order from the Foreign Intelligence Surveillance Court for electronic surveillance under FISA.]

The FISA also authorizes the Government to apply to the FISA court "for an order requiring the production of any tangible things (including books, records, papers, documents, and other items) for an investigation to obtain foreign intelligence information not concerning a United States person or to protect against international terrorism or clandestine intelligence activities. . . ."[99] Such an application need only specify that the inquiry is part of an authorized investigation and in accordance with the appropriate guidelines. Recipients of such an order are prohibited from disclosing to anyone (except those whose assistance is necessary to comply with the subpoena) that the inquiry was made.

Finally, FISA authorizes the Government to apply to the FISA court for an order, renewable in 90-day increments, to install a pen register or trap and trace device as part of "any investigation to obtain foreign intelligence information not concerning a United States person or to protect against international terrorism or clandestine intelligence activities." The Government need only certify to the court that it will likely obtain information relevant to a proper inquiry. Just as in the criminal context, the person owning the communications device is prohibited, unless otherwise directed by court order, from disclosing the fact that a pen register or trap and trace device is in effect. . . .

IV. DISCUSSION . . .

B. As Applied Here, Section 2709 Lacks Procedural Protections Necessary to Vindicate Constitutional Rights

1. Section 2709 and The Fourth Amendment[118] . . .

. . . The Fourth Amendment's protection against unreasonable searches applies to administrative subpoenas, even though issuing a subpoena does not involve a literal

---

87. *Id.* §2518(3).

88. *Id.* §2518(5).

89. *Id.* §2511(2)(a)(ii).

99. 50 U.S.C. §1861(a). [This authority was added by §215 of the USA Patriot Act, Pub. L. No. 107-108, §215, 115 Stat. 272, 287-288 (2001), and is therefore sometimes called a "Section 215 Order." It was amended by the Patriot Improvement Act, as explained in the Notes and Questions that follow this decision. — Eds.]

118. To be clear, the Fourth Amendment rights at issue here belong to the person or entity receiving the NSL, not to the person or entity to whom the subpoenaed records pertain. Individuals possess a limited Fourth Amendment interest in records which they voluntarily convey to a third party. *See* [Smith v.

physical intrusion or search. In so doing, the Supreme Court explained that the Fourth Amendment is not "confined literally to searches and seizures as such, but extends as well to the orderly taking under compulsion of process."[122]

However, because administrative subpoenas are "at best, constructive searches," there is no requirement that they be issued pursuant to a warrant or that they be supported by probable cause. Instead, an administrative subpoena needs only to be "reasonable," which the Supreme Court has interpreted to mean that (1) the administrative subpoena is "within the authority of the agency;" (2) that the demand is "not too indefinite;" and (3) that the information sought is "reasonably relevant" to a proper inquiry.[124]

While the Fourth Amendment reasonableness standard is permissive in the context of administrative subpoenas, the constitutionality of the administrative subpoena is predicated on the availability of a neutral tribunal to determine, after a subpoena is issued, whether the subpoena actually complies with the Fourth Amendment's demands. In contrast to an actual physical search, which must be justified by the warrant and probable cause requirements occurring *before* the search, an administrative subpoena "is regulated by, and its justification derives from, [judicial] process" available *after* the subpoena is issued.[125]

Accordingly, the Supreme Court has held that an administrative subpoena "may not be made and enforced" by the administrative agency; rather, the subpoenaed party must be able to "obtain judicial review of the reasonableness of the demand prior to suffering penalties for refusing to comply."[126] In sum, longstanding Supreme Court doctrine makes clear that an administrative subpoena statute is consistent with the Fourth Amendment when it is subject to "judicial supervision" and "surrounded by every safeguard of judicial restraint."[127]

Plaintiffs contend that §2709 violates this Fourth Amendment process-based guarantee because it gives the FBI alone the power to issue as well as enforce its own NSLs, instead of contemplating some form of judicial review. Although Plaintiffs appear to concede that the statute does not authorize the FBI to literally enforce the terms of an NSL by, for example, unilaterally seizing documents or imposing fines, Plaintiffs contend that §2709 has the *practical* effect of coercing compliance....

The crux of the problem is that the form NSL, like the one issued in this case, which is preceded by a personal call from an FBI agent, is framed in imposing language on FBI letterhead and which, citing the authorizing statute, orders a combination of disclosure in person and in complete secrecy, essentially coerces the

---

Maryland, 442 U.S. 735, 742-746 (1979); United States v. Miller, 425 U.S. 435, 440-443 (1976).] Nevertheless, as discussed below, many potential NSL recipients may have particular interests in resisting an NSL, *e.g.,* because they have contractually obligated themselves to protect the anonymity of their subscribers or because their own rights are uniquely implicated by what they regard as an intrusive and secretive NSL regime. For example, since the definition of "wire or electronic communication service provider," 18 U.S.C. §2709(a), is so vague, the statute could (and may currently) be used to seek subscriber lists or other information from an association that also provides electronic communication services (e.g., email addresses) to its members, or to seek records from libraries that many, including the *amici* appearing in this proceeding, fear will chill speech and use of these invaluable public institutions....

122. [*See United States v. Morton Salt Co.*, 338 U.S. 632, 651-652 (1950).]

124. *Id.* at 652.

125. *United States v. Bailey (In re Subpoena Duces Tecum)*, 228 F.3d 341, 348 (4th Cir. 2000).

126. *See v. City of Seattle*, 387 U.S. 541, 544-45 (1967); *see also Oklahoma Press Publishing Co. v. Walling*, 327 U.S. 186, 217 (1946).

127. *Oklahoma Press*, 327 U.S. at 217.

reasonable recipient into immediate compliance. Objectively viewed, it is improbable that an FBI summons invoking the authority of a certified "investigation to protect against international terrorism or clandestine intelligence activities," and phrased in tones sounding virtually as biblical commandment, would not be perceived with some apprehension by an ordinary person and therefore elicit passive obedience from a reasonable NSL recipient. The full weight of this ominous writ is especially felt when the NSL's plain language, in a measure that enhances its aura as an expression of public will, prohibits disclosing the issuance of the NSL to "any person." Reading such strictures, it is also highly unlikely that an NSL recipient reasonably would know that he may have a right to contest the NSL, and that a process to do so may exist through a judicial proceeding.

Because neither the statute, nor an NSL, nor the FBI agents dealing with the recipient say as much, all but the most mettlesome and undaunted NSL recipients would consider themselves effectively barred from consulting an attorney or anyone else who might advise them otherwise, as well as bound to absolute silence about the very existence of the NSL....

The evidence in this case bears out the hypothesis that NSLs work coercively in this way. The ACLU obtained, via the Freedom of Information Act ("FOIA"), and presented to the Court in this proceeding, a document listing all the NSLs the Government issued from October 2001 through January 2003. Although the entire substance of the document is redacted, it is apparent that hundreds of NSL requests were made during that period. Because §2709 has been available to the FBI since 1986 (and its financial records counterpart in RFPA since 1978), the Court concludes that there must have been hundreds more NSLs issued in that long time span. The evidence suggests that, until now, none of those NSLs was ever challenged in any court....

... The Court thus concludes that in practice NSLs are essentially unreviewable because, as explained, given the language and tone of the statute as carried into the NSL by the FBI, the recipient would consider himself, in virtually every case, obliged to comply, with no other option but to immediately obey and stay quiet....

Accordingly, the Court concludes that §2709, as applied here, must be invalidated because in all but the exceptional case it has the effect of authorizing coercive searches effectively immune from any judicial process, in violation of the Fourth Amendment....

2. NSLs May Violate ISP Subscribers' Rights

Plaintiffs have focused on the possibility that §2709 could be used to infringe subscribers' First Amendment rights of anonymous speech and association. Though it is not necessary to precisely define the scope of ISP subscribers' First Amendment rights, the Court concludes that §2709 may, in a given case, violate a subscriber's First Amendment privacy rights, as well as other legal rights, if judicial review is not readily available to an ISP that receives an NSL....

The Supreme Court has recognized the First Amendment right to anonymous speech at least since *Talley v. California*,[161] which invalidated a California law requiring that handbills distributed to the public contain certain identifying information about the source of the handbills. The Court stated that the "identification requirement would tend to restrict freedom to distribute information and thereby freedom of

161. 362 U.S. 60 (1960).

expression."[162] The Supreme Court has also invalidated identification requirements pertaining to persons distributing campaign literature, persons circulating petitions for state ballot initiatives, and persons engaging in door-to-door religious advocacy.

In a related doctrine, the Supreme Court has held that "compelled disclosure of affiliation with groups engaged in advocacy" amounts to a "restraint on freedom of association" where disclosure could expose the members to "public hostility."[166] Laws mandating such disclosures will be upheld only where the Government interest is compelling.

The Court concludes that such First Amendment rights may be infringed by application of §2709 in a given case. For example, the FBI theoretically could issue to a political campaign's computer systems operator a §2709 NSL compelling production of the names of all persons who have email addresses through the campaign's computer systems. The FBI theoretically could also issue an NSL under §2709 to discern the identity of someone whose anonymous online web log, or "blog," is critical of the Government. Such inquiries might be beyond the permissible scope of the FBI's power under §2709 because the targeted information might not be relevant to an authorized investigation to protect against international terrorism or clandestine intelligence activities, or because the inquiry might be conducted solely on the basis of activities protected by the First Amendment. These prospects only highlight the potential danger of the FBI's self-certification process and the absence of judicial oversight.

Other rights may also be violated by the disclosure contemplated by the statute; the statute's reference to "transactional records" creates ambiguity regarding the scope of the information required to be produced by the NSL recipient. If the recipient—who in the NSL is called upon to exercise judgment in determining the extent to which complying materials constitute transactional records rather than content—interprets the NSL broadly as requiring production of all e-mail header information, including subject lines, for example, some disclosures conceivably may reveal information protected by the subscriber's attorney-client privilege, *e.g.*, a communication with an attorney where the subject line conveys privileged or possibly incriminating information. Indeed, the practical absence of judicial review may lead ISPs to disclose information that is protected from disclosure by the NSL statute itself, such as in a case where the NSL was initiated solely in retaliation for the subscriber's exercise of his First Amendment rights, as prohibited by §2709(b)(1)-(b)(2). Only a court would be able to definitively construe the statutory and First Amendment rights at issue in the "First Amendment retaliation" provision of the statute, and to strike a proper balance among those interests.

The Government asserts that disclosure of the information sought under §2709 could not violate a subscriber's rights (and thus demands no judicial process) because the information which a §2709 NSL seeks has been voluntarily conveyed to the ISP who receives the NSL. According to the Government, an internet speaker relinquishes any interest in any anonymity, and any protected claim to that information, as soon as he releases his identity and other information to his ISP. In support of its position, the Government cites the Supreme Court's holding [in *Smith* and *Miller*] that, at least in the Fourth Amendment context involving the Government installing a pen register or obtaining bank records, when a person voluntarily conveys

162. *Id.* at 64.
166. *NAACP v. State of Alabama ex rel. Patterson,* 357 U.S. 449, 462 (1958).

information to third parties, he assumes the risk that the information will be turned over to the Government. . . .

The evidence on the record now before this Court demonstrates that the information available through a §2709 NSL served upon an ISP could easily be used to disclose vast amounts of anonymous speech and associational activity. For instance, §2709 imposes a duty to provide "electronic communication transactional records," a phrase which, though undefined in the statute, certainly encompasses a log of email addresses with whom a subscriber has corresponded and the web pages that a subscriber visits. Those transactional records can reveal, among other things, the anonymous message boards to which a person logs on or posts, the electronic newsletters to which he subscribes, and the advocacy websites he visits. Moreover, §2709 imposes a duty on ISPs to provide the names and addresses of subscribers, thus enabling the Government to specifically identify someone who has written anonymously on the internet.[175] As discussed above, given that an NSL recipient is directed by the FBI to turn over all information *"which you consider to be* an electronic communication transactional record," the §2709 NSL could also reasonably be interpreted by an ISP to require, at minimum, disclosure of all e-mail header information, including subject lines.

In stark contrast to this potential to compile elaborate dossiers on internet users, the information obtainable by a pen register is far more limited. As the Supreme Court in *Smith* was careful to note:

> [Pen registers] disclose only the telephone numbers that have been dialed — a means of establishing communication. Neither the purport of any communication between the caller and the recipient of the call, their identities, nor whether the call was even completed is disclosed by pen registers.[177]

The Court doubts that the result in *Smith* would have been the same if a pen register operated as a key to the most intimate details and passions of a person's private life.

The more apt Supreme Court case for evaluating the assumption of risk argument at issue here is *Katz v. United States,*[178] the seminal decision underlying both *Smith* and *Miller. Katz* held that the Fourth Amendment's privacy protections applied where the Government wiretapped a telephone call placed from a public phone booth. Especially noteworthy and pertinent to this case is the Supreme Court's remark that: "The Government's activities in electronically listening to and recording the petitioner's words violated the privacy upon which he justifiably relied while using the telephone booth and thus constituted a 'search and seizure' within the meaning of the Fourth Amendment."[180] The Supreme Court also stated that a person entering a phone booth who "shuts the door behind him" is "surely entitled to assume that the words he utters into the mouthpiece will not be broadcast to the world," and held

---

175. NSLs can potentially reveal far more than constitutionally-protected associational activity or anonymous speech. By revealing the websites one visits, the Government can learn, among many other potential examples, what books the subscriber enjoys reading or where a subscriber shops. As one commentator has observed, the records compiled by ISPs can "enable the government to assemble a profile of an individual's finances, health, psychology, beliefs, politics, interests, and lifestyle." Daniel J. Solove, *Digital Dossiers and the Dissipation of Fourth Amendment Privacy,* 75 S. Cal. L. Rev. 1083, 1084 (2002).

177. *Smith,* 442 U.S. at 741 (citation omitted).

178. 389 U.S. 347 (1967).

180. *Id.* at 353.

that, "[t]o read the Constitution more narrowly is to ignore the vital role that the public telephone has come to play in private communication."[181]

Applying that reasoning to anonymous internet speech and associational activity is relatively straightforward. A person who signs onto an anonymous forum under a pseudonym, for example, is essentially "shut[ting] the door behind him," and is surely entitled to a reasonable expectation that his speech, whatever form the expression assumes, will not be accessible to the Government to be broadcast to the world absent appropriate legal process. To hold otherwise would ignore the role of the internet as a remarkably powerful forum for private communication and association. Even the Government concedes here that the internet is an "important vehicle for the free exchange of ideas and facilitates associations."

To be sure, the Court is keenly mindful of the Government's reminder that the internet may also serve as a vehicle for crime. The Court equally recognizes that circumstances exist in which the First Amendment rights of association and anonymity must yield to a more compelling Government interest in obtaining records from internet firms. To this end, the Court re-emphasizes that it does not here purport to set forth the scope of these First Amendment rights in general, or define them in this or any other case. The Court holds only that such fundamental rights are certainly implicated in some cases in which the Government may employ §2709 broadly to gather information, thus requiring that the process incorporate the safeguards of some judicial review to ensure that if an infringement of those rights is asserted, they are adequately protected through fair process in an independent neutral tribunal. Because the necessary procedural protections are wholly absent here, the Court finds on this ground additional cause for invalidating §2709 as applied.

C. Constitutionality of the Non-Disclosure Provision

Finally, the Court turns to the issue of whether the Government may properly enforce §2709(c), the non-disclosure provision, against Doe or any other person who has previously received an NSL. Section 2709(c) states: "No wire or electronic communication service provider, or officer, employee, or agent thereof, shall disclose to any person that the Federal Bureau of Investigation has sought or obtained access to information or records under this section."

A threshold question concerning this issue is whether, as Plaintiffs contend, §2709(c) is subject to strict scrutiny as either a prior restraint on speech or a content-based speech restriction, or whether, as the Government responds, §2709(c) is subject to the more relaxed judicial review of intermediate scrutiny. The difference is crucial. A speech restriction which is either content-based or which imposes a prior restraint on speech is presumed invalid and may be upheld only if it is "narrowly tailored to promote a compelling Government interest." If "less restrictive alternatives would be at least as effective in achieving the legitimate purpose that the statute was enacted to serve," then the speech restriction is not narrowly tailored and may be invalidated. Under intermediate scrutiny, a speech restriction may be upheld as long as "it advances important governmental interests unrelated to the suppression of free speech and does not burden substantially more speech than necessary to further those interests."

---

181. *Id.* at 352.

The Court agrees with Plaintiffs that §2709(c) works as both a prior restraint on speech and as a content-based restriction, and hence, is subject to strict scrutiny. First, axiomatically the categorical non-disclosure mandate embodied in §2709(c) functions as prior restraint because of the straightforward observation that it prohibits speech before the speech occurs. As the Supreme Court articulated the threshold inquiry: "The relevant question is whether the challenged regulation authorizes suppression of speech in advance of its expression."[189] ...

Second, the Court considers §2709(c) to be a content-based speech restriction. ...

The Government ... argues that §2709(c) is content-neutral because it prohibits certain disclosures irrespective of any particular speaker's views on NSLs, terrorism, or anything else. ...

The Government's argument is unpersuasive. It fails to recognize that even a *viewpoint*-neutral restriction can be *content*-based, if the restriction pertains to an entire category of speech. ...

The Government's claim to perpetual secrecy surrounding the FBI's issuance of NSLs, by its theory as advanced here an authority neither restrained by the FBI's own internal discretion nor reviewable by any form of judicial process, presupposes a category of information, and thus a class of speech, that, for reasons not satisfactorily explained, must forever be kept from public view, cloaked by an official seal that will always overshadow the public's right to know. In general, as our sunshine laws and judicial doctrine attest, democracy abhors undue secrecy, in recognition that public knowledge secures freedom. Hence, an unlimited government warrant to conceal, effectively a form of secrecy *per se*, has no place in our open society. Such a claim is especially inimical to democratic values for reasons borne out by painful experience. Under the mantle of secrecy, the self-preservation that ordinarily impels our government to censorship and secrecy may potentially be turned on ourselves as a weapon of self-destruction. When withholding information from disclosure is no longer justified, when it ceases to foster the proper aims that initially may have supported confidentiality, a categorical and uncritical extension of non-disclosure may become the cover for spurious ends that government may then deem too inconvenient, inexpedient, merely embarrassing, or even illicit to ever expose to the light of day. At that point, secrecy's protective shield may serve not as much to secure a safe country as simply to save face. ...

... Section 2709(c) does not countenance the possibility that the FBI could permit modification of the NSL's no-disclosure order even in those or any other similar situations no longer implicating legitimate national security interests and presenting factual or legal issues that any court could reasonably adjudicate. Bluntly stated, the statute simply does not allow for that balancing of competing public interests to be made by an independent tribunal at any point. In this regard, it is conceivable that "less restrictive alternatives would be at least as effective in achieving the legitimate purpose that the statute was enacted to serve." For instance, Congress could require the FBI to make at least *some* determination concerning need before requiring secrecy, and ultimately it could provide a forum and define at least *some* circumstances in which an NSL recipient could ask the FBI or a court for a subsequent determination whether continuing secrecy was still warranted. ...

---

189. *Ward v. Rock Against Racism*, 491 U.S. 781, 795 n.5 (1989) (emphasis omitted).

In this Court's judgment, . . . authorities persuasively confirm that the Government should be accorded a due measure of deference when it asserts that secrecy is necessary for national security purposes in a *particular situation* involving *particular persons* at a *particular time.* Here, however, the Government cites no authority supporting the open-ended proposition that it may universally apply these general principles to impose perpetual secrecy upon an entire category of future cases whose details are unknown and whose particular twists and turns may not justify, for all time and all places, demanding unremitting concealment and imposing a disproportionate burden on free speech. . . .

VI. CONCLUSION

To summarize, the Court concludes that the compulsory, secret, and unreviewable production of information required by the FBI's application of 18 U.S.C. §2709 violates the Fourth Amendment, and that the non-disclosure provision of 18 U.S.C. §2709(c) violates the First Amendment. The Government is therefore enjoined from issuing NSLs under §2709 or from enforcing the non-disclosure provision in this or any other case, but enforcement of the Court's judgment will be stayed pending appeal, or if no appeal is filed, for 90 days. . . .

A different district court also found that the nondisclosure provisions of the NSL legislation violated the First Amendment. *Doe v. Gonzales,* 386 F. Supp. 2d 66 (D. Conn. 2005) (*Doe II*). The two cases were consolidated on appeal.

NOTES AND QUESTIONS

1. *Matching Legal Thresholds and Processes with Government Surveillance and Collection Techniques.* Professor Orin Kerr identifies the following legal thresholds (standards for obtaining the information) and attendant processes (administrative or judicial or both) for government surveillance, in ascending order of strictness:

   a. No standard or legal process. The government just gets the information it seeks.
   b. Internal administrative process. There is no bifurcation between the issuing and enforcing authority.
   c. Grand jury or administrative subpoena. The issuing and enforcing authority are bifurcated.
   d. Certification court order. The government needs a court order, but gets it simply by certifying relevancy. The court does not decide whether the certification is justified.
   e. Articulable facts court order. The government needs a court order and must offer specific and articulable facts to establish relevancy.
   f. Probable cause search warrant. The traditional criminal law standard and the predicate preferred by the Fourth Amendment.
   g. "Super" search warrant. Same, but government must first exhaust all other investigatory techniques or meet some other "plus" requirement beyond showing probable cause.
   h. Prohibition. The government is forbidden from getting the information.

Adapted from Orin Kerr, *Internet Surveillance Law After the USA Patriot Act: The Big Brother That Isn't,* 97 Nw. U. L. Rev. 607, 620-621 (2003). Match one of these

thresholds to each of the surveillance and collection techniques catalogued in
Doe v. Ashcroft.

Recall that FISA electronic surveillance has its own unique threshold. Where
would you place it in the hierarchy of thresholds? What about the threshold
for national security surveillance ordered by the President on the basis of his own
claimed unilateral authority? You may need to prepare a table of techniques and
standards to do this exercise. Is there any logic or pattern to the matches reflected
in your table?

Should one have to make a table to figure all this out? Looking just at electronic
surveillance techniques, Professor Daniel Solove remarks, "The intricacy of electronic
surveillance law is remarkable because it is supposed to apply not just to the FBI, but to
state and local police — and even to private citizens. Given its complexity, however, it is
unfair to expect these varying groups to comprehend what they can and cannot do."
Daniel J. Solove, *Reconstructing Electronic Surveillance Law,* 72 Geo. Wash. L. Rev. 1264,
1293 (2004). If you agree, and if you believe that inclusion of nonelectronic surveillance techniques only compounds the complexity, should the law be simplified? How?

2. *Pen Registers and Trap and Trace Devices.* Before 1998, pen register and trap and
trace devices were presumed to be included within the definition of "electronic
surveillance," so that orders could be obtained using FISA processes subject to the
requirements for gaining FISC approval to conduct electronic surveillance. Beginning in 1998, Congress amended FISA to enable the government to obtain pen
register and trap and trace orders under less demanding standards. The authorities
were amended again in the USA Patriot Act, Pub. L. No. 107-56, §214, 115 Stat. 272,
286 (2001).

First, the definitions of "pen register" and "trap and trace device" were changed
to include "dialing, routing, addressing, or signaling information transmitted by an
instrument or facility from which a wire or electronic communication is transmitted,
provided . . . that such information shall not include the contents of any communication." *Id.* §216(c), 115 Stat. 290 (amending 18 U.S.C. §3127(3), (4)). In Internet or
e-mail communications, does FISA's "contents" restriction really protect the substantive content of these communications? If the FBI can record search terms used at a
given Web site visited by the target, how will it sort "addressing" information from
contents? Is government access to e-mail and Web addresses any more threatening to
privacy interests than access to telephone numbers? How so?

Second, nothing approaching "probable cause" is required for an order for pen
registers or trap and trace devices. Instead, the 2001 amendments to FISA require
only a certification by the applicant

> that the information likely to be obtained is foreign intelligence information not con-
> cerning a United States person or is relevant to an ongoing investigation to protect against
> international terrorism or clandestine intelligence activities, provided that such investiga-
> tion of a United States person is not conducted solely upon the basis of activities protected
> by the first amendment. . . ." [USA Patriot Act §214(a)(2), 115 Stat. 286.]

The amendment was made at the same time that language was deleted that had
required an investigation to be in pursuit of "foreign intelligence information or
information concerning international terrorism," substituting a requirement that

the investigation serve instead "to obtain foreign intelligence information not concerning a United States person or to protect against international terrorism or clandestine intelligence activities." *Id.* §214(a)(1). Can you see what operational effect the changed targeting language will have? Who may be targeted by pen register or trap and trace devices now?

In 2006 the authorities were further amended to permit the government to obtain records of past calls and e-mail use. 50 U.S.C. §1842(d)(2)(c). A FISA pen register or trap and trace order may issue if "the information likely to be obtained is foreign intelligence information not concerning a United States person or is relevant to an ongoing investigation to protect against international terrorism or clandestine intelligence activities." 50 U.S.C. §1842(c)(2). When may FISA pen register/trap and trace authorities be used to investigate a U.S. person?

3. *Access to Business Records.* As enacted in 1978, FISA did not specifically authorize the government to obtain "documents" or other "tangible things." In 1998, FISA was amended to permit the government to apply to the FISC for an order to obtain "records" from "a common carrier, public accommodation facility, physical storage facility or vehicle rental facility." 50 U.S.C. §1862(a). The 2001 USA Patriot Act provided authorization under FISA for orders for the production of "any tangible things (including books, records, papers, documents, and other items)." USA Patriot Act §215, 115 Stat. 287 (codified at 50 U.S.C. §1861(a)(1) (2006)). Can you see why investigators sought the business records authorities? Further amendments followed in 2006 and 2008, partly due to sunset provisions. In 2011, the business records provision was extended to June 1, 2015. Pub. L. No. 112-14, §2(a), 125 Stat. 216.

4. *The Relevancy Standard.* Prior to the USA Patriot Act, FISA orders for selected business records required a showing of a counterintelligence purpose and of "specific and articulable facts giving reason to believe that the person to whom the records pertain is a foreign power or agent of a foreign power." Pub. L. No. 105-272, §602, 112 Stat. 2396, 2411. The USA Patriot Act broadened eligible information to "tangible things," and it substituted a showing that the production was for an authorized investigation to protect against international terrorism, and that such an investigation of a U.S. person was not based solely upon activities protected by the First Amendment. USA Patriot Act, Pub. L. No. 107-56, §215, 115 Stat. 287. This was effectively a relevancy standard. The same criteria were adopted for NSLs. *Id.* §214, 112 Stat. 286.

How did the substitution of the relevancy standard for the FISA probable cause standard affect the scope of government surveillance authority? Consider the following assessment.

Previously, the FBI could get the credit card records of anyone suspected of being a foreign agent. Under the PATRIOT Act, broadly read, the FBI can get the entire database of the credit card company. Under prior law, the FBI could get library borrowing records only with a subpoena in a criminal investigation, and generally had to ask for the records of a specific patron. Under the PATRIOT Act, broadly read, the FBI can go into a public library and ask for the records on everybody who ever used the library, or who used it on a certain day, or who checked out certain kinds of books. It can do the same at any bank, telephone company, hotel or motel, hospital, or university — merely upon the claim that the information is . . . sought for . . . an investigation to protect against international terrorism or clandestine intelligence activities. [*Terrorism Investigations and the Constitution: Hearing Before the Subcomm. on the Constitution of the H. Comm. on the Judiciary*, 108th Cong. (2003) (statement of James X. Dempsey, Executive Director, Center for Democracy & Technology), *available at* 2003 WL 21153545.]

The relevancy standard has been defended on the basis of the Supreme Court's reasoning in *Smith* and *Miller* that a person who voluntarily conveys information to a third party to consummate a transaction has no legitimate privacy interest in the information. Section 215, however, is not on its face limited to transactional information; it applies to "any tangible things (including books, records, papers, documents, and other items). . . ." 50 U.S.C. §1861(a)(1). Does the Court's reasoning, even if correct, support the full breadth of §215? Suppose you entrust your personal diary to your brother. Would a §215 order to your brother be supported by the Court's reasoning?

5. *Tightening the Relevancy Standard?* Although USA Patriot Act §215 requires a prior FISC order for FBI access to "tangible things," its relevancy standard is so low that the order is arguably boilerplate. The government itself has suggested that the FISC's role is simply to ascertain that the government has made the required certification of relevancy, not to determine that the certification is justified. *See* Letter from Jamie E. Brown, Acting Assistant Attorney General, Office of Legislative Affairs, U.S. Dep't of Justice, to F. James Sensenbrenner Jr., Chair, House Comm. on the Judiciary (May 13, 2003).

In the USA Patriot Improvement and Reauthorization Act of 2005, Pub. L. No. 109-177, 120 Stat. 192 (2006) (hereinafter Patriot Improvement Act), §106, Congress amended FISA §215 to clarify the relevancy standard. The government must now supply a "statement of facts" demonstrating that there are "reasonable grounds" to believe that the order is relevant to a counterterrorist investigation, although a requested order is deemed "presumptively relevant" to an authorized foreign intelligence or counterterrorist investigation if the government can show that the tangible things pertain to a foreign power or agent or suspected agent of a foreign power under FISA, or to "an individual in contact with, or known to, a suspected agent of a foreign power who is the subject of such authorized investigation." *Id.* The request must also provide a particularized description of the records sought. *Id.* Does this amendment make it easier or harder for the government to obtain a §215 order?

6. *Judicial Review of NSLs.* NSLs have been described as "the intelligence corollary to . . . administrative subpoena[s]." Lee S. Strickland, *New Information-Related Laws and the Impact on Civil Liberties*, Bull. Am. Soc'y for Info. Sci. & Tech., Feb./Mar. 2002, *available at* http://www.asis.org/Bulletin/Mar-02/strickland2. html. Neither administrative subpoenas nor NSLs require a prior court order. *See* Charles Doyle, *Administrative Subpoenas in Criminal Investigations: A Brief Legal Analysis* (Cong. Res. Serv. RL33321), Mar. 17, 2006; Charles Doyle, *Administrative Subpoenas and National Security Letters in Criminal and Foreign Intelligence Investigations: Background and Proposed Adjustments* (Cong. Res. Serv. RL 32880), Apr. 15, 2005. Why are the former lawful under the Fourth Amendment but not the latter, according to the court in *Doe v. Ashcroft?* How, if at all, can the infirmity of NSLs be cured without compromising national security?

In the Patriot Improvement Act, *supra*, §115, Congress for the first time authorized reciprocal means (described further in the next Note) for a recipient and the government to obtain judicial review after issuance of an NSL. A recipient of an NSL may petition a federal court to modify or set aside the letter "if compliance would be unreasonable, oppressive, or otherwise unlawful." (It also authorized the government to seek enforcement of an NSL from a federal court.) Does the opportunity for judicial review now afforded the NSL recipient satisfy the Fourth Amendment concern identified in the principal case?

7. *First Amendment Issues.* In *Doe v. Ashcroft*, the court found that NSLs for electronic communications records may impermissibly infringe First Amendment rights. Whose rights? (Hint: more than one category of person.) How are they infringed? How is this infringement different from that resulting from pen registers? How, if at all, could this infirmity be cured without compromising national security?

A former chief of the FBI's National Security Law Unit writes that the pre-9/11 "regulatory scheme governing counterintelligence, the higher legal standards for counterintelligence authorities, and even the 'wall' separating intelligence and criminal law enforcement have all functioned to counter-balance and contain a tendency toward excessive secrecy in this area." Woods, *supra* p. 251, at 67. Does the post-9/11 lowering of the legal standards and dismantling of the wall upset that balance, supporting the conclusion that the nondisclosure provisions of the NSL statutes fail strict scrutiny?

In partial response to *Doe I* and *II*, in §§115-116 of the Patriot Improvement Act Congress enacted a sort of reciprocal notice procedure as a means of initiating judicial review. The Act authorized a recipient of an NSL to disclose the letter for the purpose of obtaining legal advice regarding her response and to petition a court to challenge the NSL, as noted above. A recipient also may seek a judicial order setting aside the nondisclosure requirement by showing "that there is no reason to believe that disclosure may endanger the national security of the United States, interfere with a criminal, counterterrorism, or counterintelligence investigation, interfere with diplomatic relations, or endanger the life or physical safety of any person." The government's certification to the contrary is conclusive, however. If, on the other hand, the petition is filed more than a year after the NSL is delivered, then the government must permit disclosure within 90 days unless it recertifies that disclosure would so endanger or interfere. A recertification is also treated as conclusive.

The *Doe I* plaintiffs did not think that this amendment laid the First Amendment issues to rest, and the Court of Appeals remanded for further consideration in light of the Patriot Improvement Act. What First Amendment arguments would you make for the plaintiffs on remand? Does the "conclusive" treatment of government certifications render this First Amendment protection toothless?

8. *Library Records.* You have to tell the library what book you are borrowing. Do you intend that the library, in turn, will tell the government? Although as of April 2005, the government denied having yet used NSLs for library records, *see Attorney General Defends Patriot Act*, CNN.com, Apr. 5, 2005, *at* http://www.cnn.com/2005/POLITICS/04/05/patriot.act/, "John Doe II" turned out to be four Connecticut librarians who had received an NSL demanding library records. American Library Ass'n, *Library Connection Is "John Doe"—Board Speaks About NSL Order for Library Records*

(May 30, 2006), *available at* http://www.ala.org/Printer Template.cfm?Template=/ ContentManagement/HTMLDisplay.cfm&Content ID=128280.

No potential application of §215 has drawn more criticism than its possible use to obtain library records. Can you guess why? Do you think the Fourth Amendment and/ or the First Amendment is implicated? If library records enjoy a distinct First Amendment protection, should they be excluded from §215 authority?

In the USA Patriot Act Additional Reauthorizing Amendments Act of 2006, Congress excluded libraries from the definition of "wire or electronic communication service provider" for purposes of NSLs issued to obtain subscriber information and toll billing records information or electronic communication transactional records. Pub. L. No. 109-178, §§4(b) and 5, 120 Stat. 280, 281 (2006), *codified at* 18 U.S.C. §2709(f). *See*Yeh, *supra*, at 14-15 (describing dispute over construction of library exemption from "ISP" definition). It left libraries subject to §215 orders, however, although it also limited the number of FBI officials who could approve §215 applications for library records, as well as "book sales records, book customer lists, firearms sales records, tax return records, educational records, or medical records containing information that would identify a person." Patriot Improvement Act, *supra* p. 281, §106. Do all of these different kinds of information present the same constitutional issues?

9. *Inspector General's Reports and "Exigent Letters."* In the Patriot Improvement Act, Congress instructed the DOJ Inspector General (IG) to report on the FBI's use of NSLs. In a series of reports, the IG found a dramatic increase in the use of NSLs, as well as a significant number of violations of statutory authority, the *Attorney General Guidelines*, and internal FBI policies. Office of the Inspector Gen., U.S. Dep't of Justice, *A Review of the FBI's Use of National Security Letters* 121-124 (Mar. 2007), *available at* http://www.usdoj.gov/oig/special/s0703b.final.pdf. The IG also found that the FBI had sometimes obtained telephone billing records and subscriber information prior to serving NSLs or grand jury subpoenas by use of "exigent letters" and other informal methods outside the authorities for NSLs. *Id.* at 90. The exigent letters were premised on long-standing exceptions to Fourth Amendment requirements in the face of exigent circumstances, such as the destruction of evidence or danger to the officers. *See Richards v. Wisconsin,* 520 U.S. 385, 391 (1997). The Report indicated that the dominant use of NSLs was to develop evidence to support applications for FISA orders. *A Review of the FBI's Use of National Security Letters, supra,* at 65. A later report found that "the FBI's use of exigent letters became so casual, routine, and unsupervised that employees of all three communications providers sometimes generated exigent letters for FBI personnel to sign and return to them." *Report by the Office of the Inspector General of the Department of Justice on the Federal Bureau of Investigation's Use of Exigent Letters and Other Informal Requests for Telephone Records: Hearing Before the Subcomm. on the Constitution, Civil Rights, and Civil Liberties of the H. Comm. on the Judiciary,* 111th Cong. 14 (2010). Communication carriers assigned employees to FBI offices, where relaxed practices included offering sneak peeks—providing the FBI with a preview of the information available for a selected phone number before preparing documentation to justify a request. One FBI official observed that "it [was] like having the ATM in your living room." *Id.* at 15. The IG Reports indicated that corrective action was being taken.

10. *Continuing Litigation.* While consolidated appeals from the two district court cases were pending in the Second Circuit, Congress passed the Patriot Improvement Act,

and the government inadvertently revealed the names of the plaintiffs in *Doe II*. The Court of Appeals, in a per curiam opinion, dismissed *Doe II* as moot and vacated *Doe I* in part as moot, remanding the remainder for reconsideration in light of the Patriot Improvement Act. *Doe v. Gonzales*, 449 F.3d 415, 419 (2d Cir. 2006) (*Doe III*). On remand, the district court ruled that the amended statute still violated the First Amendment, because the nondisclosure requirement constituted a prior restraint and failed strict scrutiny under the First Amendment. *Doe v. Gonzales*, 500 F. Supp. 2d 379 (S.D.N.Y. 2007) (*Doe IV*). Although the government had a compelling national security interest, the Act vested executive officials with too much discretion without necessary procedural safeguards. The court also found that the judicial review standard and procedures violated separation of powers and failed the narrow tailoring required to meet First Amendment requirements. The Court of Appeals agreed for the most part, *John Doe, Inc. v. Mukasey*, 549 F.3d 861 (2d Cir. 2008) (*Doe V*), ruling that because judicial review must "place on the Government the burden to show a good reason to believe that disclosure may result in an enumerated harm, i.e., a harm related to an authorized investigation to protect against international terrorism or clandestine intelligence activities," *id.* at 881, such review may not be bound by a conclusive certification of harm as permitted in the statute. If the government uses the reciprocal notice procedure as a means of initiating judicial review, it may include notice of a recipient's opportunity to contest the nondisclosure requirement in an NSL. *Id.* at 883.

On further remand, under the procedure suggested by the Court of Appeals, the district court held that the government had met its burden. *Doe v. Holder*, 665 F. Supp. 2d 426 (S.D.N.Y. 2009) (*Doe VI*). Subsequently, the court granted partial disclosure of material the FBI had requested, including the name, address, telephone number, account number, e-mail address, and billing information of a subscriber, but found that the government had met its burden to show harm from disclosure of the remaining information. *Doe v. Holder*, 703 F. Supp. 2d 313 (S.D.N.Y. 2010) (*Doe VII*).

Would you say that Congress, the executive branch, and the courts have worked out a reasonable and constitutionally adequate scheme for using NSLs?

B. CONNECTING THE DOTS — DATA MINING

In May 2006, a news article asserted that the National Security Agency had, with the cooperation of three telecommunication companies, been secretly collecting telephone call data (external or "envelope" data, but not internal or "content" data) on "tens of millions of Americans" in order (in the words of an anonymous source) to "create a database of every call ever made" within the nation's borders. Leslie Cauley, *NSA Has Massive Database of Americans' Phone Calls*, USA Today, May 11, 2006. Similar revelations of an alleged NSA program code-named "Stellar Wind" were reported in December 2008. Michael Isikoff, *The Fed Who Blew the Whistle*, Newsweek, Dec. 22, 2008. The information collected may include calling and called phone numbers, dates, times, and perhaps lengths of completed calls. The data may be used in programs that identify patterns of calling that could indicate particular activity of interest to investigators. For example, a computer using these programs to search phone calls by members of the Yemeni immigrant community in Buffalo might identify several phone numbers of interest. The calling records of these numbers would then be searched, yielding perhaps 100 other numbers with which each phone number of interest had repeated contact.

If we began with 100 interesting phone numbers from the community under inspection, we now have 10,000 active phone taps. Everything is computer-driven so far, and a single workday at Fort Meade is not yet over. . . .

Social nets of people whom the computers think make "interesting phone calls" to each other are defined and stored, presumably forever, as persons of interest. Computers compare these government lists to others. . . .

Establishing the social networks within communities and among individuals requires tapping phones without probable cause. Computers must be free to crawl through their databases and open every phone line along the way. Of necessity, many phone taps are brief and will be discarded. After all, only four "degrees of separation" will get you to all 100 million households in the United States when each phone has 100 contacts, all of them available in phone bill records.

Finding groups is a good way to find conspiracies. Unfortunately and despite attempts to be selective, a system with geometrical expansion will yield many false positives. At some point, therefore, human analysts inspect the computer harvest we have been discussing. It is possible that a court might be asked for a paper-based search warrant. . . . [J.I. Nelson, *How the NSA Warrantless Wiretap System Works: An Educated Guess* (rev. June 9, 2006), *available at* http://wiretapfacts. notlong.com/.]

This outline of a massive domestic intelligence program, including warrantless wire-taps, is, of course, simply an educated guess, as its author acknowledges. The government has not yet admitted the existence of the program, much less its details.

The use of pen registers and trap and trace devices contemplated in *Smith v. Maryland* represents a relatively limited, "retail" form of surveillance. The NSA call data program, by contrast, apparently involves a "wholesale" collection effort to create a megadatabase of domestic calls by everyone in the United States. Such a database can be analyzed or "mined" to create new, more useful sets of information.

Data mining involves the use of sophisticated data analysis tools to discover previously unknown, valid patterns and relationships in large data sets. . . .

Data mining applications can use a variety of parameters to examine the data. They include association (patterns where one event is connected to another event, such as purchasing a pen and purchasing paper), sequence or path analysis (patterns where one event leads to another event, such as the birth of a child and purchasing diapers), classification (identification of new patterns, such as coincidences between duct tape purchases and plastic sheeting purchases), clustering (finding and visually documenting groups of previously unknown facts, such as geographic location and brand preferences), and forecasting (discovering patterns from which one can make reasonable predictions regarding future activities, such as the prediction that people who join an athletic club may take exercise classes). [Jeffrey W. Seifert, *Data Mining and Homeland Security: An Overview* (Cong. Res. Serv. RL 31798), Aug. 27, 2008.]

According to the Department of Homeland Security,

Data mining uses mathematical algorithms to construct statistical models that estimate the value of an unobserved variable—for example, the probability that an individual will engage in illegal activity. Data mining is best understood as an iterative process consisting of two separate stages: machine learning, where algorithms are applied against known data; and probabilistic inference, where the models built from algorithms are applied against unknown data to make predictions. [DHS Privacy Office, *Data Mining: Technology and Policy: 2008 Report to Congress* 31-32 (Dec. 2008).]

In a counterterrorism effort, "data mining can be a potential means to identify terrorist activities, such as money transfers and communications, and to identify and track individual terrorists themselves, such as through travel and immigration records." Seifert, *supra*, summary. *See generally* K.A. Taipale, *Data Mining and Domestic Security: Connecting the Dots to Make Sense of Data*, 5 Colum. Sci. & Tech. L. Rev. 2 (2003) (describing and assessing the technology). The NSA call data program is only the latest example of data mining for counterterrorism purposes. The following data-mining programs have also come to light:

- *The Total (Later Terrorist) Information Awareness Program (TIA)*. This was a research project of the Defense Advanced Research Projects Agency (DARPA) in 2002 to develop technology programs to "counter asymmetric threats by achieving *total information awareness* useful for preemption, national security warning, and national security decision making." Department of Def., *Report to Congress Regarding the Terrorism Information Awareness Program, Detailed Information* 1 (May 20, 2003) (emphasis added). Serious public relations mistakes (placing TIA under the direction of a principal in the Iran-Contra scandal and adopting a logo with an all-seeing eye atop a pyramid over the globe with the motto "*scientia est potentia*" (knowledge is power)), *see* http://www.richardgingras.com/tia/, contributed to Congress's decision to cut off funding for TIA in its original form. *See generally* Seifert, *supra*, at 5-7; Gina Marie Stevens, *Privacy: Total Information Awareness Programs and Related Information Access* (Cong. Res. Serv. RL31730), Mar. 21, 2003.

- *Computer-Assisted Passenger Prescreening System (CAPPS II)*. CAPPS II was an airline passenger prescreening program that used computer-generated profiles to select passengers for additional security screening — technically data-matching. It would have relied on commercial data to calculate "scores" for passengers. In fact, the Transportation Security Administration obtained such data from at least four airlines and two travel companies. But litigation made airlines wary of voluntarily sharing such data, the European Union objected, and Congress became concerned about false positives and a lack of procedures for correcting errors. In 2005, Congress prohibited the use of appropriated funds for CAPPS II or its successor, Secure Flight, until the Government Accountability Office certified that the system met certain privacy requirements. Seifert, *supra*, at 7-11. TSA put the Secure Flight requirements into effect in 2009, and airlines fully implemented the program in November 2010. *See* TSA, *Secure Flight — Frequently Asked Questions* (n.d.), *at* http://www.tsa.gov/what_we_do/layers/secureflight/faqs.shtm.

- *Investigative Data Warehouse (IDW)*. The IDW serves as a centralized data access point for FBI agents nationwide. Apart from its utility in investigations, critics have accused the FBI of using IDW with data exploitation tools to predict future crimes from past behavior. Electronic Frontier Found., *Report on the Investigative Data Warehouse* (Apr. 2009), *at* http://www.eff.org/issues/foia/investigative-data-warehouse.report.

Several other new tools for data search, analysis, and fusion are described in a report to Congress from the ODNI, Office of the Director of National Intelligence, *2010 Data Mining Report*, 2010, *available at* http://www.fas.org/irp/dni/datamining11.pdf.

NOTES AND QUESTIONS

1. *Just Finding Clues?* Police investigators have always conducted "link analysis" when they interview witnesses who saw a crime committed or who know the victim, then looked for connections in the information obtained in the interviews. "Data mining is no more than the computational automation of traditional investigative skills — that is, the intelligent analysis of myriad 'clues' in order to develop a theory of the case." Taipale, *supra*, at 21. Does it follow that "using computers to analyze data is similar to a police officer examining the same information and does not violate personal privacy"? *Counterterrorism Technology and Privacy, supra* p. 251, at 27. Do the two processes have different implications for personal privacy or expectations of privacy? Should we distinguish, for example, between subject-specific searches and generalized undirected data mining to derive or to match patterns? If so, how is computerized pattern matching different, from a privacy perspective, from a police officer's observation of a masked individual running on a public street? *See* Taipale, *supra*, at 64.

2. *The Question Smith and Miller Did Not Ask.* Attorney General Alberto R. Gonzales defended the NSA call data program, without admitting its existence, by arguing that "[t]here is no reasonable expectation of privacy in those kinds of records," citing *Smith.* Walter Pincus, *Gonzales Defends Phone-Data Collection,* Wash. Post, May 24, 2006. But the Supreme Court focused in *Smith* and *Miller* on the surveillance and collection techniques (pen registers recording dialed numbers and subpoenas for bank records), not on what became of the information they yielded. The Court's focus was understandable from the perspective of traditionally reactive "retail" criminal law enforcement, which builds one case at a time.

But in the fight against terrorism, reactive law enforcement has given way to proactive and preventive law enforcement. *See* Peter Raven-Hansen, *Security's Conquest of Law Enforcement,* in *In Democracy's Shadow* ch. 12 (Marcus G. Raskin & A. Carl LeVan eds., 2005); Daniel J. Steinbock, *Data Matching, Data Mining, and Due Process,* 40 Ga. L. Rev. 1, 16-17 (2005). Data are collected and stored in databases, perhaps indefinitely, for the continuing "wholesale" preventive effort. Even if they are not immediately archived with other data, they can be "virtually aggregated" at any moment to create a dynamic megadatabase. *See* Taipale, *supra*, at 42.

Does the prospect of such indefinite retention and aggregation have any bearing on the expectation of privacy? Do you have a greater expectation of privacy in your aggregated data than in their parts? For example, are you willing to risk that airlines will disclose your travel plans to the government, yet not want those data linked to your other consumer and credit information? Should courts gauge the legitimacy of privacy expectations in each collected item of personal information by the possibility that it will be aggregated for data mining to establish personal behavior patterns and profiles?

> [W]hen combined together, bits and pieces of data begin to form a portrait of a person. The whole becomes greater than the parts. This occurs because combining information creates synergies. When analyzed, aggregated information can reveal new facts about a person that she did not expect would be known about her when the original, isolated data was collected. [Daniel J. Solove, *A Taxonomy of Privacy,* 154 U. Pa. L. Rev. 477, 507 (2006).]

Does your answer depend on the length of time that information may be maintained by a government agency? On the purpose for which the information was originally collected? *See* Laurence H. Tribe, Op-Ed., *Bush Stomps on Fourth Amendment*, Boston Globe, May 16, 2006, at A15 ("Even if one trusts the president's promise not to connect all the dots to the degree the technology permits, the act of collecting all those dots in a form that *permits* their complete connection at his whim is a 'search,'" and "[d]oing it to all Americans...is an 'unreasonable search' if those Fourth Amendment words have any meaning at all.").

In *United States Department of Justice v. Reporters Committee for Freedom of the Press*, 489 U.S. 749 (1989), Justice Stevens, writing for the Court, acknowledged that even public personal data enjoy a certain "practical obscurity" that may be altered by its aggregation into an easily searched database. Posing the issue as "whether the compilation of otherwise hard-to-obtain information alters the privacy interest implicated by disclosure of that information," he asserted that "there is a vast difference between the public records" accessible by diligent effort in sundry locations throughout the country and "a computerized summary located in a single clearinghouse of information." *Id.* at 764. But today many public records exist in easily searchable computer databases. Are any computerized records still "practically obscure," in the same sense that hard-copy records at the courthouse or land office once were? Does the ever-increasing use of data mining—in both the public and private sectors—suggest a diminishing expectation of privacy in data? *See Kyllo v. United States*, 533 U.S. 27, 34 (2001) (finding that the use of heat-sensing technology was an unreasonable search, "*at least where (as here) the technology in question is not in general public use*") (emphasis added)). *See also City of Ontario v. Quon*, 130 S. Ct. 2619, 2623 (2010) ("[r]apid changes in the dynamics of communication and information transmission" are causing privacy expectations to evolve).

3. *False Positives.* Credit card data have several attributes that contribute to the success of data mining: a large number of valid transactions, a large number of fraudulent transactions, repetitive fraudulent use that generates common data patterns, and a relatively low cost to "false positives"—valid purchases that are incorrectly flagged as fraudulent—since they usually simply trigger a confirming phone call to the credit card holder. *See* Peter P. Swire, *Privacy and Information Sharing in the War on Terrorism*, 51 Vill. L. Rev. 951 (2006). In contrast, the number of terrorist attacks is extremely low, terrorist attacks are far less likely to be repetitive, rather than one of a kind, and the cost of false positives is far higher, both to the falsely identified innocent person and to the government, which must use substantial resources to investigate that person. *Id. But see* Paul Rosenzweig, *Proposals for Implementing the Terrorist Information Awareness System* (Heritage Found. Legal Memorandum) 4 (Aug. 7, 2003) (suggesting that costs of false positives are "relatively modest"). These differences do not rule out data mining for counterterrorism purposes, but they might suggest the need for special rules for dealing with false positives. *See* Rosenzweig, *supra* (suggesting that "robust" mechanisms to correct false positives from counterterrorist data mining would make the high false positive rate acceptable in light of the consequences of failing to data mine); Steinbock, *supra* p. 287 (suggesting due process protections for persons against whom government action will be taken because of data matching, such as persons denied boarding because of a match on a terrorist watch list). Can you think of special rules to address these differences?

4. *Statutory Protection?* In *Whalen v. Roe*, 429 U.S. 589 (1977), the Court upheld a state law requiring disclosure of certain prescription information to the state, which could enter it into an electronic database. The Court stated, however,

> We are not unaware of the threat to privacy implicit in the accumulation of vast amounts of personal information in computerized data banks or other massive government files.... The right to collect and use such data for public purposes is typically accompanied by a concomitant statutory or regulatory duty to avoid unwarranted disclosures. Recognizing that in some circumstances that duty arguably has its roots in the Constitution, nevertheless New York's statutory scheme, and its implementing administrative procedures, evidence a proper concern with, and protection of, the individual's interest in privacy. [*Id.* at 605.]

Congress has required inter-agency agreements for computer-matching among federal agencies, *see* Computer Matching and Privacy Protection Act of 1988, Pub. L. No. 100-153, §1, 102 Stat. 2507 (1988), but it has also enacted Privacy Act exemptions for computer-matching and inter-agency data sharing for national security and law enforcement purposes. *See* 5 U.S.C. §§552a(a)(8)(B)(vi), 552a(b)(7), 552a(j) (2006). Numerous other statutes regulate particular databases, usually with broad exemptions for law enforcement. *See* Taipale, *supra*, at 53 n.223.

In 2006, Congress deferred regulating data mining and instead required the Attorney General to provide a report on any initiatives to "develop pattern-based data-mining technology." Patriot Improvement Act, §126(b)(1), 120 Stat. 228. It defined "data mining" as

> a query or search or other analysis of one or more electronic databases, where (A) at least one of the databases was obtained from or remains under the control of a non-Federal entity, or the information was acquired initially by another department or agency of the Federal Government for purposes other than intelligence or law enforcement; (B) the search does not use personal identifiers of a specific individual or does not utilize inputs that appear on their face to identify or be associated with a specified individual to acquire information; and (C) a department or agency of the Federal Government is conducting the query or search or other analysis to find a pattern indicating terrorist or other criminal activity. [*Id.*]

How much counterterrorist data mining falls outside this definition? The definition expressly excludes "telephone directories, information publicly available via the Internet or available by any other means to any member of the public, any databases maintained, operated, or controlled by a State, local, or tribal government (such as a State motor vehicle database), or databases of judicial and administrative opinions." Even for what remains within the definition, however, Congress merely required the executive branch to give it a report.

What protections, if any, should Congress enact with respect to data mining by the government for counterterrorism purposes? *See* Department of Defense, Technology and Privacy Advisory Comm., *Safeguarding Privacy in the Fight Against Terrorism* (Mar. 2004) (recommending, *inter alia*, that Congress authorize the FISC to oversee government data mining but excluding data mining not involving U.S. persons or based on particularized suspicion); Rosenzweig, *supra*.

5. *The Inevitability of Data Mining in Counterterrorism?* In 2008, a committee of the National Research Council found that "automated identification of terrorists through data mining is neither feasible as an objective nor desireable as a goal of technology development efforts." Committee on Technical & Privacy Dimensions of Info. for Terrorism Prevention & Other Nat'l Goals et al., National Research Council of the Nat'l Academies, *Protecting Individual Privacy in the Struggle Against Terrorists: A Framework for Program Assessment* 3-4 (2008), *available at* http://epic.org/misc/nrc_rept_100708.pdf. The committee noted the serious privacy intrusions that are an incident of data mining, but it also noted that much of the data collected in countering terrorism leads to false positives, that data mining is vulnerable to countermeasures, and, at most, data-mining techniques should be used as a "preliminary screening method for identifying individuals who merit additional follow-up investigation." *Id.* at 4. *See generally* The Constitution Project, *Principles for Government Data Mining: Preserving Civil Liberties in the Information Age* (Nov. 20, 2010), *available at* http://www.constitutionproject.org/pdf/DataMiningPublication.pdf. For surveillance conducted pursuant to FISA, presumably the preliminary screening would be subject to minimization requirements, supervised by the FISC. In light of the opaqueness of minimization procedures for FISA surveillance, can you imagine how supervision and oversight of a preliminary screening program to counter terrorism based on data-mining techniques could be structured and implemented? *See* William C. Banks, *Programmatic Surveillance and FISA: Of Needles and Haystacks,* 88 Tex. L. Rev. 1633, 1658-1666 (2010).

Screening for Security —————10

On September 11, 2001, Mohamed Atta and Abdul Aziz al Omari boarded a 6 A.M. flight from Portland, Maine, to Boston's Logan International Airport.[1] A program called Computer Assisted Passenger Prescreening System (CAPPS) selected Atta for special security measures, which consisted at the time of holding his checked bags until he was on board the airplane. At Logan, Atta and al Omari, and eight colleagues who joined them, went through security checkpoints to board two different planes, both bound for Los Angeles. They were screened by metal detectors calibrated to detect items with the metal content of at least a .22-caliber handgun. Some of these men are now thought to have carried box cutters or pocket utility knives (defined as having blades less than four inches long and permitted on flights at the time).

In the meantime, four out of five more colleagues were flagged by CAPPS at Dulles International Airport en route to board another flight bound for Los Angeles. Two of them — brothers — were selected for extra scrutiny by the airline customer representative at the check-in counter because one of the brothers lacked a photo identification and could not speak English, and they seemed suspicious. Both brothers had dark hair and swarthy complexions, and one had a dark mustache. Again the consequence was that their bags were held until they were on board the airplane. Several of the men at Dulles set off the metal detectors at the security checkpoint and were hand-wanded before being passed. One had his carry-on bag swiped by an explosive trace detector. All were videotaped at the checkpoint. Four additional colleagues boarded yet another Los Angeles–bound plane in Newark at about the same time.

Of the 19 men who eventually boarded the fateful flights in this fashion on September 11, 7 used Virginia driver's licenses as their identification at check-in. None of them lived in Virginia. They had obtained the licenses there because they

---

1. These and other details in this introduction are drawn from *Final Report of the National Commission on Terrorist Attacks Upon the United States* (*9/11 Report*) (2004) (*9/11 Commission Report*) and *Protecting Our National Security from Terrorist Attacks: A Review of Criminal Terrorism Investigations and Prosecutions: Hearing Before the S. Comm. on the Judiciary*, 108th Cong. (2003) (statement of Paul McNulty, U.S. Attorney, E.D. Va.).

learned that one could get a genuine driver's license in Virginia in one day for approximately $100 cash, with no questions asked.

The *9/11 Commission Report* tells the rest of the story.

> The 19 men were aboard four transcontinental flights. They were planning to hijack these planes and turn them into large guided missiles, loaded with up to 11,400 gallons of jet fuel. By 8:00 A.M. on the morning of Tuesday, September 11, 2001, they had defeated all the security layers that America's civil aviation system then had in place to prevent a hijacking. [*9/11 Commission Report* at 4.]

This chapter explores some of the legal issues raised by this defeat of what was and still is essentially a system designed to screen terrorists from entry to transportation systems and other high-risk targets. In Part A we explore issues of checkpoint searches. In Part B we consider the narrower concerns of identification and watch-list screening. Finally, in Part C we examine the difficult question of profiling.

A.   CHECKPOINT SEARCHES

The government has been screening persons seeking entry into the country since the first Congress passed a customs statute exempting border searches from probable cause requirements. *See* 5 Wayne R. LaFave, *Search and Seizure* §10.5(a) (4th ed. 2004), *citing* Act of July 31, 1789, ch. 5, 1 Stat. 29, 43 (1789). Border searches without a warrant or probable cause have consistently been held reasonable as tools of national self-protection that are justified by "considerations specifically related to the need to police the border." *City of Indianapolis v. Edmond*, 531 U.S. 32, 38 (2000) (dictum).

Such searches are often conducted at airports where international flights land. At first, fear of airplane hijacking — "skyjacking" — in the 1960s, and then fear of bombs led to screening of air travelers. Such screening was upheld partly as a border search, and partly as an administrative or "regulatory" search:

> [S]creening searches of airline passengers are conducted as part of a general regulatory scheme in furtherance of an administrative purpose, namely, to prevent the carrying of weapons or explosives aboard aircraft, and thereby to prevent hijackings. The essential purpose of the scheme is not to detect weapons or explosives or to apprehend those who carry them, but to deter persons carrying such material from seeking to board at all. [*United States v. Davis*, 482 F.2d 893, 908 (9th Cir. 1973).]

The intrusiveness of the screening program had to match the "special need," leading to the conclusion that there was no justification for the compelled search of a person who elected not to board a plane. *Id. See generally* LaFave, *supra*, §10.6(c).

We have all grown accustomed to — if sometimes still annoyed by — security lines and checks at airports and to booting up our laptops as we go through the checkpoint. But have you had TSA agents or other security personnel look through the files on your computer? Does this process "prevent the carrying of weapons or explosives aboard aircraft," the ostensible special need for regulatory searches at airports. If it does not, is it lawful?

United States v. Arnold

United States Court of Appeals, Ninth Circuit, 2008
533 F.3d 1003, *cert. denied*, 129 S. Ct. 1312 (2009)

O'SCANNLAIN, Circuit Judge: We must decide whether customs officers at Los Angeles International Airport may examine the electronic contents of a passenger's laptop computer without reasonable suspicion.

I...

[Michael Arnold arrived at Los Angeles International Airport from the Philippines and proceeded to customs, where he was selected by a U.S. Customs and Border Patrol (CBP) officer for secondary questioning. His laptop was booted up and an inspection of the files revealed several nude photographs. Special agents with the United States Department of Homeland Security, Immigration and Customs Enforcement (ICE) were then called in to question Arnold and to examine his computer. They found numerous images depicting what they believed to be child pornography. Arnold was released but later arrested on various child pornography charges.

The district court granted Arnold's motion to suppress, finding that: (1) reasonable suspicion was indeed necessary to search the laptop; and (2) the government had failed to meet the burden of showing that the CBP officers had reasonable suspicion to search. This appeal by the government followed.]

II

Arnold argues that the district court was correct in concluding that reasonable suspicion was required to search his laptop at the border because it is distinguishable from other containers of documents based on its ability to store greater amounts of information and its unique role in modern life.

Arnold argues that "laptop computers are fundamentally different from traditional closed containers," and analogizes them to "homes" and the "human mind." Arnold's analogy of a laptop to a home is based on his conclusion that a laptop's capacity allows for the storage of personal documents in an amount equivalent to that stored in one's home. He argues that a laptop is like the "human mind" because of its ability to record ideas, e-mail, internet chats and web-surfing habits....

III

A

The Fourth Amendment states that "[t]he right of the people to be secure in their persons, houses, papers, and effects, against unreasonable searches and seizures, shall not be violated...." U.S. Const. amend. IV. Searches of international passengers at American airports are considered border searches because they occur at the "functional equivalent of a border." *Almeida-Sanchez v. United States*, 413 U.S. 266, 273 (1973) ("For...example, a search of the passengers and cargo of an airplane arriving at a St. Louis airport after a non-stop flight from Mexico

City would clearly be the functional equivalent of a border search."). "It is axiomatic that the United States, as sovereign, has the inherent authority to protect, and a paramount interest in protecting, its territorial integrity." *United States v. Flores-Montano*, 541 U.S. 149, 153 (2004). Generally, "searches made at the border . . . are reasonable simply by virtue of the fact that they occur at the border. . . ." *United States v. Ramsey*, 431 U.S. 606, 616 (1977).

The Supreme Court has stated that:

> The authority of the United States to search the baggage of arriving international travelers is based on its inherent sovereign authority to protect its territorial integrity. By reason of that authority, it is entitled to require that whoever seeks entry must establish the right to enter and to bring into the country whatever he may carry.

Torres v. Puerto Rico, 442 U.S. 465, 472-73 (1979). In other words, the "Government's interest in preventing the entry of unwanted persons and effects is at its zenith at the international border." *Flores-Montano*, 541 U.S. at 152. Therefore, "[t]he luggage carried by a traveler entering the country may be searched at random by a customs officer . . . no matter how great the traveler's desire to conceal the contents may be." *United States v. Ross*, 456 U.S. 798, 823 (1982). . . .

B

Courts have long held that searches of closed containers and their contents can be conducted at the border without particularized suspicion under the Fourth Amendment. Searches of the following specific items have been upheld without particularized suspicion: (1) the contents of a traveler's briefcase and luggage, *United States v. Tsai*, 282 F.3d 690, 696 (9th Cir. 2002); (2) a traveler's "purse, wallet, or pockets," *Henderson v. United States*, 390 F.2d 805, 808 (9th Cir. 1967); (3) papers found in containers such as pockets, see *United States v. Grayson*, 597 F.2d 1225, 1228-29 (9th Cir. 1979) (allowing search without particularized suspicion of papers found in a shirt pocket); and (4) pictures, films and other graphic materials. *See United States v. Thirty-Seven Photographs*, 402 U.S. 363, 376 (1971); *see also United States v. 12,200-Ft. Reels of Super 8MM. Film*, 413 U.S. 123, 124-25 (1973) ("Import restrictions and searches of persons or packages at the national borders rest on different considerations and different rules of constitutional law from domestic regulations.").

Nevertheless, the Supreme Court has drawn some limits on the border search power. Specifically, the Supreme Court has held that reasonable suspicion is required to search a traveler's "alimentary canal," *United States v. Montoya de Hernandez*, 473 U.S. 531, 541 (1985), because "[t]he interests in human dignity and privacy which the Fourth Amendment protects forbid any such intrusion [beyond the body's surface] on the mere chance that desired evidence might be obtained." *Id.* at 540 n.3 (quoting *Schmerber v. California*, 384 U.S. 757, 769 (1966)). However, it has expressly declined to decide "what level of suspicion, *if any*, is required for non-routine border searches such as strip, body cavity, or involuntary x-ray searches." *Id.* at 541 n.4 (emphasis added). Furthermore, the Supreme Court has rejected creating a balancing test based on a "routine" and "non-routine" search framework, and has treated the terms as purely descriptive. *See United States v. Cortez-Rocha*, 394 F.3d 1115, 1122 (9th Cir. 2005).

Other than when "intrusive searches of *the person*" are at issue, *Flores-Montano*, 541 U.S. at 152 (emphasis added), the Supreme Court has held open the possibility, "that some searches of *property* are so destructive as to require" particularized suspicion. *Id.* at 155-56 (emphasis added) (holding that complete disassembly and reassembly of a car gas tank did not require particularized suspicion). Indeed, the Supreme Court has left open the question of "'whether, and under what circumstances, a border search might be deemed "unreasonable" because of the particularly offensive manner in which it is carried out.'" *Id.* at 155 n.2 (quoting *Ramsey*, 431 U.S. at 618 n.13).

C

In any event, the district court's holding that particularized suspicion is required to search a laptop, based on cases involving the search of the person, was erroneous. . . .

The Supreme Court has stated that "[c]omplex balancing tests to determine what is a 'routine' search of a vehicle, as opposed to a more 'intrusive' search of a person, have no place in border searches of vehicles." *Flores-Montano*, 541 U.S. at 152. Arnold argues that the district court was correct to apply an intrusiveness analysis to a laptop search despite the Supreme Court's holding in *Flores-Montano*, by distinguishing between one's privacy interest in a vehicle compared to a laptop. However, this attempt to distinguish *Flores-Montano* is off the mark. The Supreme Court's analysis determining what protection to give a vehicle was not based on the unique characteristics of vehicles with respect to other property, but was based on the fact that a vehicle, as a piece of property, simply does not implicate the same "dignity and privacy" concerns as "highly intrusive searches of the person." *Flores-Montano*, 541 U.S. at 152.

Furthermore, we have expressly repudiated this type of "least restrictive means test" in the border search context. *See Cortez-Rocha*, 394 F.3d at 1123 (refusing to fashion a "least restrictive means test for border control vehicular searches, and . . . refus[ing] to tie the hands of border control inspectors in such a fashion"). Moreover, in both *United States v. Chaudhry*, 424 F.3d 1051, 1054 (9th Cir. 2005) (finding the distinction between "routine" and "non-routine" inapplicable to searches of property) and *Cortez-Rocha*, 394 F.3d at 1122-23, we have recognized that *Flores-Montano* rejected our prior approach of using an intrusiveness analysis to determine the reasonableness of property searches at the international border.

Therefore, we are satisfied that reasonable suspicion is not needed for customs officials to search a laptop or other personal electronic storage devices at the border.

IV

While the Supreme Court left open the possibility of requiring reasonable suspicion for certain border searches of property in *Flores-Montano*, 541 U.S. at 155-56, the district court did not base its holding on the two narrow grounds left open by the Supreme Court in that case.

Arnold has never claimed that the government's search of his laptop damaged it in any way; therefore, we need not consider whether "exceptional damage to property" applies. Arnold does raise the "particularly offensive manner" exception to the government's broad border search powers. But, there is nothing in the record to indicate that the manner in which the CBP officers conducted the search was "particularly offensive" in comparison with other lawful border searches. According to Arnold, the CBP officers simply "had me boot [the laptop] up, and looked at what I had inside. . . ."

Whatever "particularly offensive manner" might mean, this search certainly does not meet that test. Arnold has failed to distinguish how the search of his laptop and its electronic contents is logically any different from the suspicionless border searches of travelers' luggage that the Supreme Court and we have allowed. *See Ross*, 456 U.S. at 823; *see also Vance*, 62 F.3d at 1156 ("In a border search, a person is subject to search of luggage, contents of pockets and purse without any suspicion at all.").

With respect to these searches, the Supreme Court has refused to draw distinctions between containers of information and contraband with respect to their quality or nature for purposes of determining the appropriate level of Fourth Amendment protection. Arnold's analogy to a search of a home based on a laptop's storage capacity is without merit. The Supreme Court has expressly rejected applying the Fourth Amendment protections afforded to homes to property which is "*capable of functioning as a home*" simply due to its size, or, distinguishing between "'worthy' and 'unworthy' containers." *California v. Carney*, 471 U.S. 386, 393-94 (1985).

In *Carney*, the Supreme Court rejected the argument that evidence obtained from a warrantless search of a mobile home should be suppressed because it was "*capable of functioning as a home.*" *Id.* at 387-88, 393-94. The Supreme Court refused to treat a mobile home differently from other vehicles just because it could be used as a home. *Id.* at 394-95. The two main reasons that the Court gave in support of its holding, were: (1) that a mobile home is "readily movable," and (2) that "the expectation [of privacy] with respect to one's automobile is significantly less than that relating to one's home or office." *Id.* at 391 (quotation marks omitted).

Here, beyond the simple fact that one cannot live in a laptop, *Carney* militates against the proposition that a laptop is a home. First, as Arnold himself admits, a laptop goes with the person, and, therefore is "readily mobile." *Carney*, 471 U.S. at 391. Second, one's "expectation of privacy [at the border] . . . is significantly less than that relating to one's home or office." *Id.*

Moreover, case law does not support a finding that a search which occurs in an otherwise ordinary manner, is "particularly offensive" simply due to the storage capacity of the object being searched. *See California v. Acevedo*, 500 U.S. 565, 576 (1991) (refusing to find that "looking inside a closed container" when already properly searching a car was unreasonable when the Court had previously found "destroying the interior of an automobile" to be reasonable in *Carroll v. United States*, 267 U.S. 132 (1925)).

Because there is no basis in the record to support the contention that the manner in which the search occurred was "particularly offensive" in light of other searches allowed by the Supreme Court and our precedents, the district court's judgment cannot be sustained. . . .

VI

For the foregoing reasons, the district court's decision to grant Arnold's motion to suppress must be

Reversed.

NOTES AND QUESTIONS

1. *Regulatory or Special Needs Search?* Requiring the air traveler to boot up her laptop may serve the special need of keeping explosives off planes because it presumably helps show that the laptop is a laptop, and not a box for carrying explosives,

like the dummy printers that Al Qaeda in the Arabian Peninsula reportedly tried to ship to the United States as air freight. But searching through your files and images, or address books and calendars on other electronic devices such as cell phones, cannot be similarly justified. Such searches may be justified, if at all, only as border searches. There the rationale is simply the sovereign's authority to control its borders. Note that this justification is not anchored in the legislative power to enact immigration laws; it extends even to traveling U.S. citizens who cross our borders.

2. *Consent.* Some of the airport screening cases argue that with notice of the screening programs, a passenger who elects travel by air impliedly consents to the screening. LaFave, *supra* p. 292, §10.6(g). If she consents, she waives her privacy interest. Is this logic compelling for air travelers? *See United States v. Davis*, 482 F.2d 893, 905 (9th Cir. 1973) (asserting that it would violate the principle that government cannot "avoid the restrictions of the Fourth Amendment by notifying the public that all telephone lines would be tapped or that all homes would be searched"); LaFave, *supra*, §10.6(g) (theory of implied consent "diverts attention from the more fundamental question of whether the nature of the regulation undertaken by the government is in fact reasonable under the Fourth Amendment").

3. *The Walk-Away Option.* Closely related to the consent theory is one that travelers have notice of the inspection and therefore can always refuse inspection and take alternative transportation. A few courts condition their finding that a screening program is reasonable upon the program's inclusion of this option. *See Davis, supra*, 482 F.2d at 910. Does this logic take into account the impact of the walk-away option on the government's security interest? A few courts have reasoned that "such an option would constitute a one-way street for the benefit of a party planning airplane mischief, since there is no guarantee that if he were allowed to leave he might not return and be more successful," and that "the very fact that a safe exit is available if apprehension is threatened would, by diminishing risk, encourage attempts." *United States v. Skipwith*, 482 F.2d 1272, 1282 (5th Cir. 1973) (Aldrich, J., dissenting, but this discussion adopted by majority). Does the apparently heightened risk of terrorism to transportation systems after 9/11 now justify finding that a screening system without this option can still be reasonable? Then-Circuit Judge Alito, writing for the Third Circuit Court of Appeals, thought so in *United States v. Hartwell*, 436 F.3d 174, 179 (3d Cir. 2006) (upholding a nonconsensual hand-wanding of Hartwell after he set off the metal detector at an airport).

4. *Laptop Searches.* A 2008 letter from Congressman Bernie Thompson to the CBP described such searches:

> These practices include opening individual laptops; reading documents saved on the devices; accessing email accounts and reading through emails that have been sent and received; examining photographs; looking through personal calendars; and going through telephone numbers saved in cellular phones. Further, individuals have raised claims that these searches can sometimes last for hours and cause significant delay, while the subject of the search — often a U.S. citizen — is delayed entering the country and must sit by as the information contained in their personal devices [is] copied, confiscated or compromised. [Letter from Bennie G. Thompson, Chairman, U.S. House of Representatives, Committee on Homeland Security, to W. Ralph Basham, Commissioner, U.S. Customs and Border Protection (July 1, 2008).]

Arnold poses several limits on border searches? What are they? Why do they not apply to laptop searches for files and images? Should it make a difference if the laptop is removed from the border and searched elsewhere? If it is kept for months? *See* Constitution Project, *Suspicionless Border Searches of Electronic Devices: Legal and Privacy Concerns with the Department of Homeland Security's Policy* 5 (2011) (describing six-month retention of laptop seized at border and DHS policy permitting off-site retention for a "reasonable period"). One study concluded that even if laptop border searches are lawful, DHS policies permitting detention of electronic devices at a location and a time remote from the original border crossing "may impermissibly invade expectations of privacy and contravene well-settled Fourth Amendment principles." *Id.* at 6. *But see United States v. Cotterman*, 637 F.3d 1068 (9th Cir. 2011) ("travelers [do not] somehow have a constitutionally protected expectation that their property will not be removed from the border for search and, therefore, the Government must either staff every POE [point of entry] with the equipment and personnel needed to fully search all incoming property or otherwise be forced to blindly shut its eyes and hope for the best absent some particularized suspicion").

5. *Whole Body Imaging.* In 2010, TSA introduced whole body imaging (WBI) systems at airport checkpoints, and they are now the primary screening method at the busiest airports. Bart Elias, *Changes in Airport Passenger Screening Technologies and Procedures: Frequently Asked Questions* 1 (Cong. Res. Serv. R41502), Jan. 26, 2011. WBI systems notoriously capture a crude image of a passenger's body, causing some critics to call a WBI scan a "virtual strip search." *Id.* But TSA gives passengers the option of submitting to a pat-down search instead.

Does *Arnold* provide authority for the legality of WBI searches? Or are they "nonroutine" and intrusive searches that require particularized suspicion? What arguments would you make based on the case law set out in *Arnold* to decide the legality of WBI searches? Does the pat-down option affect your answer?

6. *Subway and Train Searches.* After terrorist bombings of trains killed more than 200 in Madrid in 2004, and subway bombings killed 52 in London in 2005, the New York subway system instituted a random container inspection program, whereby subway passengers were randomly selected for inspection of knapsacks, parcels, and purses (confined to "what is minimally necessary to ensure that the . . . item does not contain an explosive device."). Selected passengers were afforded the option of leaving rather than submitting to inspection.

Arnold supplies no precedent for upholding the legality of this inspection program. Can you see why? On the other hand, the regulatory or special need rationale does apply. In a challenge to the program, a court described the rationale as follows:

> First, as a threshold matter, the search must "serve as [its] immediate purpose an objective distinct from the ordinary evidence gathering associated with crime investigation." *Nicholas v. Goord,* 430 F.3d 652, 663 (2d Cir. 2005). Second, once the government satisfies that threshold requirement, the court determines whether the search is reasonable by balancing several competing considerations. These balancing factors include (1) the weight and immediacy of the government interest, *Earls,* 536 U.S. at 834; (2) "the nature of the privacy interest allegedly compromised by" the search, *id.* at 830; (3) "the character of the intrusion imposed" by the search, *id.* at 832; and (4) the efficacy of the search in advancing the government interest. [*MacWade v. Kelly,* 460 F.3d 260, 268-269 (2d Cir. 2006).]

The court then found that the New York subway container inspection program served the immediate and substantial "special need of preventing a terrorist attack on the subway." While it acknowledged the subway rider's full expectation of privacy in his containers, it also found the search "minimally intrusive" and "reasonably effective" (a question given the walk-away option), and therefore, that the program was, on balance, constitutional. *Id.* at 270, 273-275. Will any inspection program intended to prevent a terrorist attack *ever* be, on balance, unconstitutional? What kind of subway security check would fail the special needs test?

7. *Building Entry Screening.* The balancing test articulated in the airport screening cases and adapted for the container-inspection program in *MacWade* is fact-sensitive. Do the factors carry the same weight when the government screens entry into a building? How is that different? In *Barrett v. Kunzig*, 331 F. Supp. 266, 274 (M.D. Tenn. 1971), the court found that "[w]hen the interest in protection of the government property and personnel from destruction is balanced against any invasion to the entrant's personal dignity, privacy, and constitutional rights, the government's substantial interest in conducting the cursory [article] inspection [at building entry] outweighs the personal inconvenience suffered by the individual." But there the court also emphasized the relatively unobtrusive nature of the article inspection and its neutral application to all entrants. Suppose the screening includes frisks? Body searches? Suppose, using a watch list, the security personnel select particular entrants for a second search? Does it matter whether the search is conducted at the Pentagon or the Smithsonian Museum of Natural History? Professor LaFave's answer is that "what is required is a judicial assessment of the magnitude of the danger and a judicial determination of what screening procedures will suffice to meet it." LaFave, *supra*, §10.7(a). How would you perform this requirement for these building searches?

B. IDENTIFICATION AND WATCH-LISTING

Two of the 9/11 hijackers had been identified by the CIA as possible terrorist suspects and added to a State Department watch list of such suspects called "TIPOFF" on August 24, 2001. *9/11 Commission Report, supra* p. 291 n.1, at 270. TIPOFF was intended primarily to keep terrorists from getting visas to the United States. It was not shared with the FAA, which maintained a separate "no-fly list" of persons banned for air travel because of the threat they were thought to pose to civil aviation, as well as a "selectee list" of persons selected for further screening, such as hand-wanding and questioning. None of the hijackers were on either FAA list. *The 9/11 Investigations* 27 (Steve Strasser ed., 2004).

In 2003, President George W. Bush issued Homeland Security Presidential Directive 6 (HSPD-6) (Sept. 16, 2003), establishing a Terrorist Screening Center to consolidate the government's watch listing and screening. *See generally* William J. Krouse & Bart Elias, *Terrorist Watchlist Checks and Air Passenger Prescreening* 2 (Cong. Res. Serv. RL33645), Dec. 30, 2009. Subsequently, based partly on TIPOFF data, the National Counterterrorism Center (NCTC), under the Office of the Director of National Intelligence, created the Terrorist Identities Datamart Environment (TIDE) as the master repository for international terrorism data. TIDE "includes . . . all information the U.S. government possesses related to identities of individuals known or appropriately suspected to be or have been involved in activities constituting, in preparation for, in aid of, or related to [international] terrorism." National Counterterrorism Center, *Terrorist Identities Datamart Environment (TIDE)* (n.d.), *available at* http://www.nctc.gov/docs/Tide_Fact_Sheet.pdf. By 2008, it had more than 540,000 names (though only 450,000 identities, because of aliases and name variants), fewer than 5 percent of which were for U.S. persons. *Id.*

In theory, the watch-list process begins when a member of the intelligence community shares newly acquired information about suspected terrorists or their supporters with NCTC's TIDE. See the chart below. The standards applied are not public, although some anecdotal evidence suggests that they are at least partly subjective, that they may rest on indirect and possibly innocent connections to suspected terrorists as well as informant information of doubtful reliability, and that they err on the side of inclusion. Daniel J. Steinbock, *Designating the Dangerous: from Blacklists to Watch Lists*, 30 Seattle U. L. Rev. 65 (2006). NCTC nominates some of these persons, and the FBI-administered inter-agency Terrorist Screening Center (TSC) decides whether to accept the nomination for inclusion in the Consolidated Terrorist Screening Database (TSDB). Krouse & Elias, *supra*, at 203. The FBI also provides data about domestic terrorist suspects to the TSDB. As of 2009, it was reported that the TSDB contained more than one million records for more than 400,000 individuals.

The TSC then distributes TSDB-generated watch lists to end users — including all frontline screening agencies — such as the Transportation Security Administration (administering the no-fly and selectee lists), U.S. Customs and Border Protection, and the State Department's Bureau of Consular Affairs, as well as the FBI, and state and local governments through the National Crime Information Center. A 2007 study identified nine different end users, although the number and names of users has changed since then. *See* Peter M. Shane, *The Bureaucratic Due Process of Government Watch Lists*, 75 Geo. Wash. L. Rev. 804 (2007).

Terrorist Watch Listing and Screening Under HSPD-6

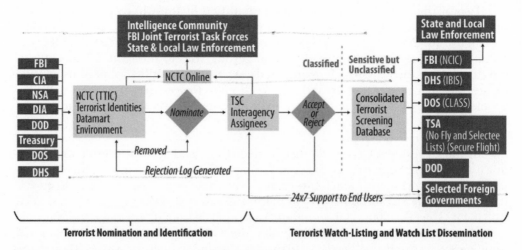

From William J. Krouse & Bart Elias, *Terrorist Watchlist Checks and Air Passenger Prescreening* 2 (Cong. Res. Serv. RL33645), Dec. 30, 2009.

The 9/11 Commission expressly recommended expanding traveler intelligence and traveler screening, with priority given to screening airline passengers for explosives. *9/11 Commission Report, supra,* at 385, 393. After a number of false starts, TSA has adopted the Secure Flight program for screening air travelers based in part on the collection of pre-flight information from passengers. No-fly and selectee watch lists were consolidated into the TSDB sometime in 2004, although they form only a small subset of the TSDB. In 2007, the head of TSA testified to efforts by TSA and TSC to reduce the number of persons on the no-fly list by as much as 50 percent, partly in response to the DHS Privacy Office's criticism of the quality of the list. Krouse & Elias, *supra,* at 12-13. It was reported then that the no-fly list includes about 4,000 individuals, while the selectee list includes some 14,000 names.

Before boarding a plane, a passenger must first supply some identification. What authority does the government have to require identification in the screening process? The following case provides some answers, and subsequent notes and questions address the related question of whether we should require a national identifier.

Gilmore v. Gonzales

United States Court of Appeals, Ninth Circuit, 2006
435 F.3d 1125, *cert. denied,* 549 U.S. 1110 (2007)

PAEZ, Circuit Judge. John Gilmore ("Gilmore") sued Southwest Airlines and the United States Attorney General, Alberto R. Gonzales, among other defendants, alleging that the enactment and enforcement of the Government's civilian airline passenger identification policy is unconstitutional. The identification policy requires airline passengers to present identification to airline personnel before boarding or be subjected to a search that is more exacting than the routine search that passengers who present identification encounter. Gilmore alleges that when he refused to present identification or be subjected to a more thorough search, he was not allowed to board his flights to Washington, D.C. Gilmore asserts that because the Government refuses to disclose the content of the identification policy, it is vague and uncertain and therefore violated his right to due process. He also alleges that when he was not allowed to board the airplanes, Defendants violated his right to travel, right to be free from unreasonable searches and seizures, right to freely associate, and right to petition the government for redress of grievances. . . .

[The government contended that the Security Directive authorizing the Transportation Security Administration to require passenger identification as a condition of boarding was "sensitive security information" that could not be shown to Gilmore or disclosed to the public. The court accepted this claim, but reviewed the Directive in camera.]

III. RIGHT TO TRAVEL

Gilmore alleges that the identification policy violates his constitutional right to travel because he cannot travel by commercial airlines without presenting identification, which is an impermissible federal condition. We reject Gilmore's right to travel argument because the Constitution does not guarantee the right to travel by any particular form of transportation. . . .

...Gilmore does not possess a fundamental right to travel by airplane even though it is the most convenient mode of travel for him. Moreover, the identification policy's "burden" is not unreasonable. The identification policy requires that airline passengers either present identification or be subjected to a more extensive search. The more extensive search is similar to searches that we have determined were reasonable and "consistent with a full recognition of appellant's constitutional right to travel." *United States v. Davis*, 482 F.2d 893, 912-13 (9th Cir. 1973).

...Additionally, Gilmore was free to decline both options and use a different mode of transportation. In sum, by requiring Gilmore to comply with the identification policy, Defendants did not violate his right to travel.

IV. FOURTH AMENDMENT

Gilmore next alleges that both options under the identification policy—presenting identification or undergoing a more intrusive search—are subject to Fourth Amendment limitations and violated his right to be free from unreasonable searches and seizures.

Request for Identification

Gilmore argues that the request for identification implicates the Fourth Amendment because "the government imposes a severe penalty on citizens who do not comply." Gilmore highlights the fact that he was once arrested at an airport for refusing to show identification and argues that the request for identification "[i]mposes the severe penalty of arrest." Gilmore further argues that the request for identification violates the Fourth Amendment because it constitutes "a warrantless general search for identification" that is unrelated to the goals of detecting weapons or explosives.

The request for identification, however, does not implicate the Fourth Amendment. "[A] request for identification by the police does not, by itself, constitute a Fourth Amendment seizure." *INS v. Delgado*, 466 U.S. 210, 216 (1984). Rather, "[a]n individual is seized within the meaning of the fourth amendment only if, in view of all of the circumstances surrounding the incident, a reasonable person would have believed that he was not free to leave." *United States v. $25,000 U.S. Currency*, 853 F.2d 1501, 1504 (9th Cir. 1988) (internal quotation marks omitted). In *Delgado*, the Supreme Court held that INS agents' questioning of factory workers about their citizenship status did not constitute a Fourth Amendment seizure. In *$25,000 U.S. Currency*, we held that a DEA agent's request for identification from a person waiting to board a flight was not a Fourth Amendment seizure.

Similarly, an airline personnel's request for Gilmore's identification was not a seizure within the meaning of the Fourth Amendment. Gilmore's experiences at the Oakland and San Francisco airports provide the best rebuttal to his argument that the requests for identification imposed a risk of arrest and were therefore seizures. Gilmore twice tried to board a plane without presenting identification, and twice left the airport when he was unsuccessful. He was not threatened with arrest or some other form of punishment; rather he simply was told that unless he complied with the policy, he would not be permitted to board the plane. There was no penalty for noncompliance.

Request to Search

[The Court rejected the Fourth Amendment challenge to the selectee search option, relying on the balancing analysis of *United States v. Davis*, 482 F.2d 893 (9th Cir. 1973), noted *supra* p. 292.]

CONCLUSION

In sum, we conclude that Defendants did not violate Gilmore's constitutional rights by adopting and implementing the airline identification policy. Therefore, his claims fail on the merits and we deny his petition for review....

NOTES AND QUESTIONS

a.   Identification Requirements

1. *Identification for Screening Purposes and the Fourth Amendment.* "Effective checking of names against watch lists ... requires that every person carry an accurate and secure form of identification." Steinbock, *Designating the Dangerous, supra,* at 113. Watch-listing is thus linked closely to the asserted need for more secure identification and to more frequent identification stops or checkpoints. *Id.*

Identification is mandatory for boarding flights. As *Gilmore* suggests, the Fourth Amendment poses no barrier to suspicionless government requests for identification at check-in or the security checkpoint, provided that a reasonable requested person would feel free to terminate the encounter. David J. Steinbock, *National Identity Cards: Fourth and Fifth Amendment Issues,* 56 Fla. L. Rev. 697, 711-714 (2004). Furthermore, the *MacWade* analysis suggests that "regulatory" (administrative) demands for identification at airport, transit system, and many building checkpoints would pass Fourth Amendment muster as well. *Id.* at 725-743. How would you apply that analysis to mandatory identification at the entrance to a federal building? What about a random demand for "your papers, please" made by police in a public street?

Of course, good identification serves not just a governmental interest, but also an individual interest in avoiding wrong matching. *See* Paul Rosenzweig & Jeff Jonas, *Correcting False Positives: Redress and the Watch List Conundrum,* 17 Legal Mem. (Heritage Found.) 10-11 (June 17, 2005), *available at* http://www.heritage.org/Research/ HomelandDefense/lm17.cfm. For this reason in part but, more important, as a personal convenience, most persons voluntarily provide identification. That is, we voluntarily show our government-issued identification — usually a driver's license — to cash checks, to register for classes, and to obtain other privileges. Such voluntary disclosure presents no Fourth Amendment concern. Why not?

2. *A National Identity Card or Other Identifier?* Some have argued that after 9/11, we need a national identity card system. *See* Alan Dershowitz, *Why Fear National ID Cards?,* N.Y. Times, Oct. 13, 2001. *See generally* Steinbock, *Designating the Dangerous, supra* (citing proponents). An effective system "necessitates mandatory participation, both in the sense of having an identity within the system and in presenting identification when required." Steinbock, *National Identity Cards, supra,* 56 Fla. L. Rev. at 708.

A mandatory national identifier requirement would pose at least three kinds of legal issues. First, there may be a Fourth Amendment question if identification is demanded randomly in some places, such as public streets, as suggested above. "[O]ne of the primary reasons that governments created passports and identity cards was to restrict movement, alter patterns of migration, and control the movements of poor people and others viewed as undesirable." Daniel J. Solove, *A Taxonomy of Privacy*, 154 U. Pa. L. Rev. 477, 514 n.183 (2006).

Second, the "main point of identity checking is to make a connection between the identified individual and collection of data." Steinbock, *National Identity Cards*, *supra*, 56 Fla. L. Rev. at 700. A national identifier "would likely be but one component of a large and complex nationwide identity system, the core of which could be a database of personal information on the U.S. population." Computer Sci. & Telecomms. Bd., National Research Council, *IDs — Not That Easy: Questions About Nationwide Identity Systems* 7 (Stephen T. Kent & Lynette I. Millet eds., 2002). The legality of a national identifier system thus turns in part on the legality of the associated database or watch list.

Third, identity checking may also generate data that can be used to track movements and purchases (e.g., subject was identified at 11:06 A.M. on June 20, 2006, at Constitution Ave. entrance to Department of Justice). The use of such data in a computer database raises some of the same privacy concerns created by government access to and use of third-party records. By providing identification on demand, does a person waive her privacy interest in the data? *See* Steinbock, *National Identity Cards*, *supra*, 56 Fla. L. Rev. at 748-752 (no, because identification is different from providing telephone numbers or banking information). Even if a single identification encounter does not offend privacy, does its aggregation into a database do so?

3. *The REAL ID Act — A Step in the Direction of a National ID Card?* In 2005, Congress enacted the REAL ID Act. Emergency Supplemental Appropriations Act for Defense, the Global War on Terror, and Tsunami Relief, Pub. L. No. 109-13, div. B, 119 Stat. 231, 302, *codified at* 49 U.S.C. §30301 note (2006). *See* Office of the Press Secretary, *Statement by Deputy Press Secretary Matt Chandler on DHS' Efforts to Enhance Driver's License Security* (Dec. 18, 2009), *available at* http://www.dhs.gov/ynews/releases/pr_1261170524591.shtm (extending deadline for material compliance). The REAL ID Act forbids any federal agency, three years after the Act's enactment, from accepting for any official purpose a state-issued driver's license or identification card unless it meets certain requirements. The identification must include name, address, date of birth, gender, a digital photo, signature, anti-tampering security features, and "[a] common machine-readable technology, with defined minimum data elements." 119 Stat. at 312. In addition, the state must insist on and verify certain identifying information and evidence of lawful status to issue such an identification. Finally, each state must "provide electronic access to all other States to information contained in the motor vehicle database of the States," which must include, at a minimum, "all data fields printed on drivers' licenses and identification cards issued by the State." *Id.* at 316. How is the REAL ID different from a national identity card? Which poses the larger privacy concern, the REAL ID or the database the Act requires? In *Whalen v. Roe*, 429 U.S. 589 (1977), the Supreme Court found reasonable a mandatory prescription-reporting system tied to a centralized database, but only because the system limited access to the database and criminalized

unauthorized disclosures. What protections, if any, are necessary to make the motor vehicle database contemplated by the REAL ID Act reasonable?

b.   Watch Lists and Other Identification-Related Databases

1. *Blacklists and Watch Lists.* Watch lists are automated databases used to identify individuals or entities for consequences (such as denial of entry or boarding) based solely on their inclusion ("listing") in the database. *See* Government Accounting Office, *Terrorist Watch Lists Should Be Consolidated to Promote Better Integration and Sharing* 3 (GAO-03-322), Apr. 15, 2003, *available at* http://www.gao.gov/new.items/ d03322.pdf; Steinbock, *Designating the Dangerous, supra.* Their use did not start with the counterterrorist efforts of the 1990s and later. The infamous "blacklists" of the McCarthy Era — listing "known" Communists and their "fellow travelers" — are a disturbing antecedent. Professor Steinbock summarizes the blacklists and the loyalty screening programs with which they were associated, as follows:

> Little or no effort was made to identify particular workers whose presence would actually pose some realistic threat to national security. Because Communist Party membership or "sympathetic association" with "subversive organizations," even long in the past, were [*sic*] deemed to be adequate proxies for dangerousness, large numbers of people were labeled disloyal or security threats who factually were not. In practice these programs often amounted, instead, to widespread punishment for the exercise of rights of belief, speech, and association. More broadly, they were also about public shaming and enforcing ideological conformity. [*Id.*]

Some procedural protections were eventually required by the courts or by Congress to protect victims of blacklisting and loyalty screening programs. Remarkably, "even [these] are wholly absent from twenty-first century listing. The result [today], in all likelihood, is a glut of both false positives and false negatives." *Id.*

2. *Mission Creep?* Watch lists are already used to control visa eligibility, entry, and departure, to screen airline passengers, to screen employees for sensitive jobs, and to trigger surveillance. *See id.* "Mission creep" — using lists for more and more purposes, including ordinary criminal and regulatory purposes, such as denial of firearms purchases — is a continuing risk. The Japanese-American internment experience suggests a more frightening mission — preventive detention in a perceived emergency. Indeed, the Japanese Americans who were detained in World War II were selected from a "custodial detention list" prepared by the FBI. *Id.* The FBI also prepared lists for use under the Emergency Detention Act of 1950, Pub. L. No. 81-831, 64 Stat. 1019. By 1966, the FBI's "Security Index" had grown to 26,000 names. Steinbock, *Designating the Dangerous, supra.* Does the reasonableness of a watch list turn in part on some statutory control of the purposes for which it may be used? *See Whalen v. Roe,* 429 U.S. 589 (1977); Solove, *supra* p. 304, at 520-522.

3. *False Positives and Protected Interests.* When an innocent person is erroneously included on a watch list or has the same name as someone on the list, the listing generates a "false positive." With approximately 8 percent of all air travelers being stopped each day and an estimated 70 million secondary screening searches being

conducted annually, even a small rate of false positives will snare many innocent travelers. *See* Rosenzweig & Jonas, *supra* p. 303, at 2 n.3.

Does a person have a right to due process in the no-fly decision, or, more plausibly, in the making or correction of the no-fly list? To establish a claim to due process, a person must first show that the challenged government action deprives her of life or a constitutionally protected liberty or property interest. *See American Mfrs. Mut. Ins. Co. v. Sullivan*, 526 U.S. 40, 59 (1999). The Supreme Court has held that something more than a mere reputational injury or "stigma" from the government action is required to make out a liberty interest. It requires "stigma-plus," the plus being some tangible burden such as loss of employment or of the opportunity to purchase alcohol. *See Wisconsin v. Constantineau*, 400 U.S. 433 (1971); *Paul v. Davis*, 424 U.S. 693 (1976). Does a person who is singled out for further screening or barred from boarding by his identification on a no-fly list meet the requirement? The court in *Green v. Transportation Security Administration*, 351 F. Supp. 2d 1119 (W.D. Wash. 2005), held no.

> As Plaintiffs point out, there can be little doubt that association with a government terrorist watch-list "might seriously damage [Plaintiffs'] standing and associations in [their] community," *Vanelli* [*v. Reynolds Sch. Dist. No. 7*, 667 F.2d 773, 777 n.5 (9th Cir. 1982) (citation omitted)], and Defendants have not argued otherwise.
>
> However, Plaintiffs fail to satisfy the "plus" prong of the stigma-plus doctrine....
>
> Plaintiffs, in the present matter, argue that their status has been altered because they are no longer able to travel like other airline passengers because of their alleged association with the No-Fly List. While Plaintiffs have a right to travel throughout the United States "uninhibited by statutes, rules, and regulations which unreasonably burden or restrict movement," *Saenz v. Roe*, 526 U.S. 489, 499 (1999), it is also true that "burdens on a single mode of transportation do not implicate the right to interstate travel." *Miller v. Reed*, 176 F.3d 1202, 1205 [(9th Cir. 1999)]. Thus, Plaintiffs do not have a right to travel without any impediments whatsoever. Indeed, Plaintiffs do not allege that they have suffered impediments different than the general traveling public.
>
> Plaintiffs also argue that their status has been altered because they have been publicly associated with the No-Fly List in full view of co-workers and the general traveling public. However, "injury to reputation alone is insufficient to establish a deprivation of a liberty interest protected by the Constitution." *Ulrich* [*v. City & County of San Francisco*, 308 F.3d 968, 982 (9th Cir. 2002)]. Plaintiffs have not alleged any tangible harm to their personal or professional lives that is attributable to their association with the No-Fly List, and which would rise to the level of a Constitutional deprivation of a liberty right. Furthermore, Plaintiffs have not alleged any injury to a property interest as a result of the disclosure of allegedly stigmatizing statements. Plaintiffs have not plead[ed] any tangible harm that satisfies the "plus" prong. Therefore, Plaintiffs have failed to state a stigma-plus Fifth Amendment claim. [*Green*, 351 F. Supp. 2d at 1129-1130.]

Do you agree? If you are denied boarding on a transcontinental flight because of your misidentification on a no-fly list, have you suffered any tangible burden? Suppose you have to get to the other coast as quickly as possible to see a dying relative? Is the court confusing the right to travel with the burden constituting a "plus factor"? *See* Shane, *supra* p. 300 ("court's analysis seems flatly wrong"); Justin Florence, Note, *Making the No Fly List: A Due Process Model for Terrorist Watchlists*, 115 Yale L.J. 2148, 2161 (2006) (asserting that the right to travel by plane is a liberty interest).

4. *Process Due in Watch-List Making or Correction.* If, notwithstanding the *Green* decision, you think a watch-listed traveler has a constitutionally protected liberty

interest, what process is due her? *See Mathews v. Eldridge*, 424 U.S. 319 (1976) (which is discussed so often in national security cases, see *infra* pp. 449-452, that we do not repeat it here.)

Critics of watch lists have suggested several procedural fixes for false positives and misidentification. A "front-end" fix is to institute more careful vetting procedures for placing a name on the list and tighter, more transparent standards. *See* Shane, *supra*, at 19-26. Professor Steinbock, however, raises the question whether the cost of such additional procedure and/or higher evidentiary standards for watch-listing may be too high for effective prevention of terrorist entry. Given the magnitude of the risk, shouldn't doubts be resolved in favor of inclusion? *See* Steinbock, *Designating the Dangerous, supra* p. 300.

Another fix is "back-end": providing some procedure for the victim of misidentification or other false positive to clear his name from the list. *See* Rosenzweig & Jonas, *supra* (suggesting administrative procedures for deciding passenger complaints, with a right of appeal to federal court, as well as "wrong matching" procedures for full attribution of list entries and for a wrongly matched person to supply additional information to correct an error); Shane, *supra*, at 31; Florence, *supra*, at 2166-2178 (suggesting that passengers be given "advance notice" of watch-listing on inquiry and a right to an administrative hearing about the alleged listing error through a government-appointed and security-cleared "compensatory counsel"). Professor Steinbock suggests a different and simpler kind of back-end protection: restricting the consequences of being listed just to selection for further investigation, thus "putting the *watch* back in watch lists." Steinbock, *Designating the Dangerous, supra.*

The Intelligence Reform and Terrorism Prevention Act of 2004, Pub. L. No. 108-458, §4012(a)(1), 118 Stat. 3638, 3714-3715 (codified at 49 U.S.C. §44903(j)(2)(C)(iii)(I) (2006)), required TSA and DHS to create appeals procedures for listed persons to challenge their listings. DHS therefore established a Traveler Redress Inquiry Program (TRIP) for taking complaints. Congress also conditioned implementation of "Secure Flight" — the program for collecting preflight information on passengers for watch-list screening — on development of procedures for protecting privacy and providing redress for victims of false positives. Department of Homeland Security Appropriations Act of 2006, Pub. L. No. 109-90, §518, 119 Stat. 2064, 2085. *See generally* Office of Inspector Gen., Dep't of Justice, *Review of the Terrorist Screening Center's Efforts to Support the Secure Flight Program* (Aug. 2005), *available at* http://www.usdoj.gov/oig/reports/FBI/a0534/index.htm.

C. PROFILING

Farag v. United States

United States District Court, Eastern District of New York, 2008
587 F. Supp. 2d 436

BLOCK, Senior District Judge: . . . On August 22, 2004, weeks away from the third anniversary of 9/11, plaintiffs Tarik Farag ("Farag") and Amro Elmasry ("Elmasry"), both Arabs, flew from San Diego to New York's John F. Kennedy Airport ("JFK") on American Airlines Flight 236. Farag and Elmasry, longtime friends, were flying to JFK after vacationing in California. Both were born in Egypt, but Farag, 36, had moved to the United States in 1971 at age five and later became an American citizen. He was a retired New York City police officer, and was then employed by the United States Bureau of Prisons as a corrections officer. Elmasry, 37, was an Egyptian citizen; he was employed in Egypt by General Electric as an area sales manager for its Africa-East Mediterranean region and had a valid U.S. visa.] They claim that when they deplaned they were met by at least ten armed police officers in SWAT gear with shotguns and police dogs, ordered to raise their hands, frisked, handcuffed and taken to a police station, where they were placed in jail cells; they were not released until about four hours later, after having been interrogated at length during their imprisonment regarding suspected terrorist surveillance activity aboard the plane. The investigation yielded absolutely no evidence of wrongdoing.

Alleging that they were unlawfully seized and imprisoned, Farag and Elmasry have each brought an action under *Bivens v. Six Unknown Named Agents of Federal Bureau of Narcotics*, 403 U.S. 388 (1971), against defendants FBI Special Agent William Ryan Plunkett ("Plunkett") and New York City Police Department Detective Thomas P. Smith ("Smith"), two counterterrorism agents responsible for plaintiffs' seizures, detentions and interrogations.... Plunkett and Smith seek summary judgment as to plaintiffs' *Bivens* claims on the ground of qualified immunity....

THE GOVERNMENT'S JUSTIFICATION FOR ITS CONDUCT

The Government lists the following actions of Farag and Elmasry on the aircraft, which, they argue, supported the agents' "concern that [plaintiffs] may [have been] conducting [terrorist] surveillance or probing operations," Gov't Br. at 5,[20] and justified the agents' seizures, detentions, and interrogations of plaintiffs:

— At the beginning of the flight, despite sitting on opposite sides of the aisle, plaintiffs spoke to each other over the heads of other passengers in a mixture of Arabic and English;

— Elmasry made an allegedly "unusual" initial seat change "from a window seat ... to a middle seat ... between two other male passengers";

— After Elmasry changed seats, he and Farag talked to each other "loudly" over the heads of other passengers in a mixture of Arabic and English;

— Elmasry looked at his watch when the plane took off, when the plane landed, and at other points during the flight;

— After the meal service, Elmasry "got out of his seat ..., went into the aisle, leaned over to Farag, and spoke a 'very short sentence' to Farag in a mixture of Arabic and English";

— Immediately thereafter, plaintiffs moved together to the back of the plane, and did not take their carry-on luggage with them;

— Plaintiffs got up to return to the front of the cabin at the very end of the flight, after the "fasten seatbelt" indicator was lit;

20. In particular, the Government argues that "there was probable cause to believe that Plaintiffs were violating the Destruction of Aircraft Act, 18 U.S.C. §32, and the federal conspiracy statute, 18 U.S.C. §371, both of which have been upheld by the Second Circuit as providing legitimate grounds for prosecuting potential terrorist plots against United States-flag aircraft." Gov't Br. at 25 (citing *United States v. Yousef*, 327 F.3d 56, 86-88 (2d Cir. 2003)).

—Upon returning to the front of the plane, Farag did not sit in his original seat (17E), but rather, in Elmasry's original seat (18A), which was located directly behind Smith;

—After the plane landed, Elmasry took out his cellular phone and deleted five or six numbers;

—While the plane was taxiing to the gate, Elmasry told Smith that "he is from Egypt, that he works for GE, and that '[his] work is always traveling.'"

See Gov't Br. at 14-16.

The Government lists the following events that took place in the terminal at JFK, after plaintiffs were first detained, as further support for the agents' actions:

—Farag told Smith that "after 9/11, when the CIA had c[o]me into the Federal Bureau of Prisons, my supervisors had asked me to translate documents, to translate tapes, [and] in fact I did translate tapes";

—Farag told Smith that "I had guns pointed at me as a police officer";

—While Farag was telling these things to Smith, Farag was "jittery" and "shaking" and "[his] speech was not calm." He appeared "nervous" and seemed "jumpy and agitated," and he raised his voice.

See Gov't Br. at 25-26....

II. ANALYSIS

A. Were Plaintiffs Arrested?

[The court held that the plaintiffs were arrested.] . . .

B. Was There Probable Cause for the Arrests?

Probable cause to arrest exists "where the arresting officer has 'knowledge or reasonably trustworthy information of facts and circumstances that are sufficient to warrant a person of reasonable caution in the belief that the person to be arrested has committed or is committing a crime.'" [*United States v. Delossantos*, 536 F.3d 155, 158 (2d Cir. 2008) (quoting *Walczyk v. Rio*, 496 F.3d 139, 156 (2d Cir. 2007))]. Only "those facts available to the officer at the time of the arrest and immediately before it" may be considered. *Lowth v. Town of Cheektowaga*, 82 F.3d 563, 569 (2d Cir. 1996) (citation omitted). Moreover, "[p]robable cause is to be assessed on an objective basis[,]" *Zellner v. Summerlin*, 494 F.3d 344, 369 (2d Cir. 2007); thus, "[a]n arresting officer's state of mind (*except for the facts that he knows*) is irrelevant. . . . " *Id.* The standard is a "fluid and contextual" one, requiring "examin[ation of] the totality of the circumstances of a given arrest." *Delossantos*, 536 F.3d at 159 (citations omitted). . . .

1. Was There Probable Cause Based on Non-Ethnic Factors Alone?

The Government contends that even if the Court does not consider that plaintiffs were Arabs and that they were at times conversing in Arabic, the other factors relied upon by the Government constitute probable cause. The Court disagrees. The Government tacks together a number of benign circumstances in the apparent belief that their numerosity will carry the day. The Court acknowledges that the Second Circuit has cautioned district courts not to "engage[ ] in erroneous 'divide-and-conquer analysis'" by "declining to give weight to [individual] observation[s] 'that [were] by [themselves] readily susceptible to . . . innocent explanation[s.]'" *Id.* at 161 (quoting *United States v. Arvizu*, 534 U.S. 266, 274 (2002)); *accord* [*United States v. Sokolow*, 490 U.S. 1, 9 (1989)] ("Any one of these factors is . . . quite consistent with innocent travel. But we think taken together they amount to reasonable suspicion."). Yet, even viewing all of these circumstances as a whole, it cannot rationally be held that if, hypothetically, the plaintiffs were two Caucasian traveling companions speaking French, or another non-Arabic language which the agents did not understand, "a person of reasonable caution" would have believed that they were engaged in terrorist surveillance. *Delossantos*, 536 F.3d at 158.

Principally, the Government relies on the agents' observations of plaintiffs' seat-changing and Elmasry's "timing" events with his watch. But the agents acknowledged in their incident report that they knew the plaintiffs were friends; quite logically, friends would want to sit as close to each other as possible, and they would also logically return to the vicinity of their original seats when the plane was landing to retrieve their carry-on luggage. As for Elmasry looking at his watch upon takeoff, landing, and at various other times during the flight, the proportion of airline passengers who do this is probably higher than the proportion who do not. *See United States v. Jones*, 149 F.3d 364, 369 (5th Cir. 1998) ("A factual condition which is consistent with [criminal activity] will not predicate reasonable suspicion, if that factual condition occurs even more frequently among the law abiding public. . . .").

The Government also argues that Elmasry's deletion of five or six telephone numbers from his cellular phone while he waited for the plane to reach the gate "could have been interpreted as destroying evidence[,]" Gov't Br. at 16. This conclusion, however, is utter speculation; the Government's Rule 56.1 Statement does not assert that Elmasry made any telephone calls during or after the flight, and the record gives no indication that Elmasry suspected he was about to be caught sufficient to imbue his acts with a suggestion of guilt.

Most troubling, the heavy reliance which the Government places on the plaintiffs' speaking "loudly" to each other over the heads of other passengers and otherwise drawing attention to themselves is counterintuitive: it simply makes no sense that if Elmasry were a terrorist on a surveillance mission, he would speak "loudly" across the aisle to his companion before takeoff, seek out and converse with the flight attendant, relocate to a seat "between two large men," or volunteer to one of those "large men" that he was from Egypt. What terrorist engaged in surveillance activity would behave so conspicuously? One would expect that such activity would be characterized by secrecy.

Nor could plaintiffs' conduct in the terminal be reasonably viewed as an escalation of events that would then have given rise to probable cause. The Court fails to grasp the significance of Farag telling Smith that because he spoke Arabic he had been asked by the Bureau of Prisons to translate tapes, and that guns had been pointed at him as a police officer—both logical consequences of his past and present employments.

Reliance on Farag's nervousness and raised voice is also problematic. *See, e.g., United States v. Ten Thousand Seven Hundred Dollars and No Cents in U.S. Currency*, 258 F.3d 215, 226-27 (3d Cir. 2001) ("[C]laimants' apparent nervousness is of minimal probative value, given that many, if not most, individuals can become nervous or agitated when detained by police officers." (citation omitted)). Moreover, Farag's "nervous" response to an unlawful show of force could not retroactively justify plaintiffs' arrests.

In sum, viewed in the light most favorable to plaintiffs, the non-ethnic factors cited by the Government do not constitute probable cause.

2. Would Consideration of Plaintiffs' Ethnicity Warrant a Finding of Probable Cause?

Allowing consideration of the plaintiffs' ethnicity and their use of Arabic would still not warrant a finding, in the context of the defendants' summary-judgment motion, that there was probable cause to arrest them. In other words, if the plaintiffs' view of events holds up at trial, their conduct was so benign that the ethnicity factor — even if it could be considered — would not change the outcome.

Nonetheless, the Court will address the ethnicity issue since the Government, given the importance it ascribes to the issue, would otherwise undoubtedly raise it at trial; moreover, the issue would probably surface if Smith and Plunkett were to take an interlocutory appeal from the Court's denial of that aspect of their motion seeking qualified immunity.

3. Can Plaintiffs' Arab Ethnicity Serve as a Probable Cause Factor?

The Government argues that plaintiffs' Arab ethnicity and use of the Arabic language are relevant factors in the probable-cause, as well as the reasonable-suspicion, calculus because "all of the persons who participated in the 9/11 terrorist attacks were Middle Eastern males[,]" Tr. of Oral Argument, July 18, 2008, at 18, and "the United States continues to face a very real threat of domestic terrorism from Islamic terrorists." Gov't Br. at 17.

The Government's position has some superficial appeal. After all, probable cause, and undoubtedly reasonable suspicion as well, is, once again, "a practical, nontechnical conception that deals with the factual and practical considerations of everyday life," *Delossantos*, 536 F.3d at 159 (internal quotation marks and citation omitted), and what American would not acknowledge that everyday life has changed in myriad ways, both great and small, since 9/11? Indeed, earlier this fall, the Second Circuit upheld a government program "that singled out male immigrants from two dozen predominantly Arab and Muslim countries for accelerated deportation after the Sept. 11, 2001, terrorist attacks[,]" Mark Hamblett, *Circuit Upholds Post-9/11 Effort That Singled Out Muslim Men*, N.Y.L.J., Sept. 25, 2008 at 1, finding it a "plainly rational attempt to enhance national security." *Rajah v. Mukasey*, 544 F.3d 427, [439 (2d Cir. 2008)].

Rajah, however, did not deal with ethnicity in the context of probable cause or reasonable suspicion. Indeed, the Government recognizes that "[t]here is no single precedent that resolves this case," Tr. of Oral Argument, July 18, 2008, at 17, which presumably accounts for its view of the case as one of first impression. Nevertheless, the interplay between race[33] and the Fourth Amendment is not a recent

33. For present purposes, the Court treats the "technically" distinct concepts of race and ethnicity as legal equivalents. *Iqbal v. Hasty*, 490 F.3d 143, 148 n.2 (2d Cir. 2007), *cert. granted sub nom. Ashcroft v. Iqbal*, — U.S. ——, 128 S. Ct. 2931 (2008). Moreover, the Court considers the fact that the plaintiffs spoke their native tongue, Arabic — as opposed to some other language equally unfamiliar to the agents — as inextricably related to, and legally indistinguishable from, plaintiffs' ethnicity per se.

phenomenon; courts and commentators have long struggled with the issue of whether and to what extent race can be a relevant consideration in the decision to detain an individual. *See, e.g.,* Samuel R. Gross & Katherine Y. Barnes, *Road Work: Racial Profiling and Drug Interdiction on the Highway,* 101 Mich. L. Rev. 651 (2002); Anthony C. Thompson, *Stopping the Usual Suspects: Race and the Fourth Amendment,* 74 N.Y.U. L. Rev. 956 (1999); Tracey Maclin, *Race and the Fourth Amendment,* 51 Vanderbilt L. Rev. 333 (1998); Sheri Lynn Johnson, *Race and the Decision to Detain a Suspect,* 93 Yale L.J. 214, 237 (1983). That legal backdrop obviously bears on the Court's analysis here.

At the outset, it should be understood that the Fourth Amendment — unlike the Equal Protection Clause — imposes no *a priori* restriction on race-based governmental action. As the Supreme Court noted in *Whren v. United States,* 517 U.S. 806 (1996):

> [T]he Constitution prohibits selective enforcement of the law based on considerations such as race. But the constitutional basis for objecting to intentionally discriminatory application of laws is the Equal Protection Clause, not the Fourth Amendment. Subjective intentions play no role in ordinary, probable-cause Fourth Amendment analysis.

Id. at 813; *see also United States v. Scopo,* 19 F.3d 777, 786 (2d Cir. 1994) (Newman, J., concurring) ("Though the Fourth Amendment permits a pretext arrest, if otherwise supported by probable cause, the Equal Protection Clause still imposes restraint on impermissibly class-based discriminations.").

In *Whren,* the existence of probable cause based on non-racial factors was conceded. *See* 517 U.S. at 810 ("Petitioners accept that Officer Soto had probable cause to believe that various provisions of the District of Columbia traffic code had been violated."). Thus, the Court opined only that an officer's subjective, potentially race-based motivations were irrelevant to the Fourth Amendment *once probable cause is established;* it was not called upon to address whether race might be relevant to the probable-cause analysis itself.

Although the Fourth Amendment does not single out race as a matter of special concern, it does impose a general requirement that *any* factor considered in a decision to detain must contribute to "a particularized and objective basis for suspecting the particular person stopped of criminal activity." *United States v. Cortez,* 449 U.S. 411, 417-18 (1981). Thus, as one commentator has observed, "race cannot affect probable cause or reasonable suspicion calculations unless it is statistically related to suspected criminal activity." Johnson, 93 Yale L.J. at 237. Whether such a relationship exists in a given case is necessarily a fact-specific inquiry; nevertheless, the case law reveals some recurring themes.

Perhaps the least controversial use of race in the context of the Fourth Amendment is its use as an *identifying* factor. If the victim of, or witness to, a crime describes the perpetrator as a young white male wearing a white shirt and black pants, there can be little doubt that law enforcement officials may consider that description in deciding whom to detain, even though the description is based, in part, on race.

Courts have also confronted the so-called "racial incongruity" argument — i.e., that race is indicative of criminality when members of a particular race seem "out of place" in a particular location. Some courts — including the Second Circuit — have sidestepped the issue by finding probable cause or reasonable suspicion based on other, non-racial factors. For example, in *United States v. Magda,* 409 F. Supp. 734 (S.D.N.Y. 1976), the district court found reasonable suspicion lacking where "[t]he reason for the stop was primarily because of an observed exchange...between a young black man and a young white man in an area of the city defined as 'narcotics prone.'" *Id.* at 740. The Second Circuit reversed, concluding that the circumstances and location of the transaction were sufficient to create reasonable suspicion; the circuit court made no mention of the race of the participants. *See United States v. Magda*, 547 F.2d 756, 758-59 (2d Cir. 1976); *see also United States v. Richard*, 535 F.2d 246, 248-249 (3d Cir. 1976) (noting that "the presence of two black males cruising in a car in a predominately white neighborhood is, by itself, insufficient cause for a belief that those persons have participated in a recent crime in the neighborhood," but reversing suppression order based on other factors); *State v. Wilson*, 775 So. 2d 1051, 1052 (La. 2000) ("[T]he officer made clear...that while racial incongruity 'did factor in,' he considered other circumstances more important in his decision to make an investigatory stop.").

Those courts that have squarely addressed the incongruity argument have uniformly rejected it. *See People v. Bower*, 24 Cal. 3d 638 (1979) ("[T]he presence of an individual of one race in an area inhabited primarily by members of another race is not a sufficient basis to suggest that crime is afoot."); *State v. Barber*, 118 Wash. 2d 335 (1992) ("It is the law that racial incongruity, i.e., a person of any race being allegedly 'out of place' in a particular geographic area, should never constitute a finding of reasonable suspicion of criminal activity"); *Phillips v. State*, 781 So. 2d 477, 479 (Fla. Dist. Ct. App. 2001) ("Clearly, the fact that a black person is merely walking in a predominantly white neighborhood does not indicate that he has committed, is committing, or is about to commit a crime.")....

But this case involves neither identification nor racial incongruity. Rather, <u>defendants' argument that plaintiffs' Arab ethnicity is a relevant consideration is premised on the notion that Arabs have a greater *propensity* than non-Arabs toward criminal activity—namely, terrorism.</u>

In support of this argument, defendants rely principally on language from the Supreme Court's opinion in *United States v. Brignoni-Ponce*, 422 U.S. 873 (1975). There, a roving border patrol agent had made a traffic stop based on nothing more than "the apparent Mexican ancestry" of the car's occupants. *Id.* at 885. The Supreme Court held that "this factor alone would [not] justify...a reasonable [suspicion]" of an immigration violation. *Id.* at 886. But it stated—in dictum—that "[t]he likelihood that any given person of Mexican ancestry is an alien is high enough to make Mexican appearance *a relevant factor*" in the Fourth Amendment calculus, if it were not *the only* basis for suspicion. *Id.* at 886-87 (emphasis added).[34]

Brignoni-Ponce's dictum was predicated on 1970 census figures establishing that in the border states between 8.5% and 20.4% of the ethnic-Mexican population self-registered as aliens. *Id.* at 886-87 & n.12. To the Court's knowledge, no court has ever marshaled statistics to conclude that racial or ethnic appearance is correlated with, and thus probative of, any type of criminal conduct *other than* immigration violations.

34. A year after *Brignoni-Ponce*, the Supreme Court held that officials at a border-control checkpoint could constitutionally single out motorists for inspection "even if it be assumed that such referrals are made largely on the basis of apparent Mexican ancestry." *United States v. Martinez-Fuerte*, 428 U.S. 543, 563 (1976). The Court recognized that such a criterion "would not sustain a roving-patrol stop," *id.*, but concluded that border-control checkpoints were exempt from the usual Fourth Amendment requirement of individualized suspicion. *See id.* at 562 ("[W]e hold that the stops and questioning at issue may be made in the absence of any individualized suspicion at reasonably located checkpoints."). Since there is obviously no contention that a traditional arrest or *Terry* stop is similarly exempt from that requirement, *Martinez-Fuerte* cannot support plaintiffs' detention.

See, e.g., United States v. Avery, 137 F.3d 343, 354 (6th Cir. 1997) ("[A]lthough the Court in *Brignoni-Ponce* stated 'the likelihood that any given person of Mexican ancestry is an alien is high enough to make Mexican appearance a relevant factor,' we refuse to adopt, by analogy, the concept that 'the likelihood that any given person of African ancestry is involved in drug trafficking is high enough to make African ancestry a relevant fact' in investigating drug trafficking....." (citation omitted)).

Moreover, the statistical rationale behind the *Brignoni-Ponce* dictum does not translate to the present case: Even granting that all of the participants in the 9/11 attacks were Arabs, and even assuming *arguendo* that a large proportion of would-be anti-American terrorists are Arabs, the likelihood that *any given airline passenger* of Arab ethnicity is a terrorist is so negligible that Arab ethnicity has no probative value in a particularized reasonable-suspicion or probable-cause determination. *Accord United States v. Ramos,* [591 F. Supp. 2d 93, 104 (D. Mass. 2008)] (considering, in dicta, the applicability of *Brignoni-Ponce* to Arabs suspected of terrorist activity post-9/11, and noting that "[a]mong other things, the type of statistics relied upon in *Brignoni-Ponce*... have not been presented here.")[, *aff'd,* 629 F.3d 60 (1st Cir. 2010)].

Indeed, the Ninth Circuit, whose judgment the Supreme Court upheld in *Brignoni-Ponce,* revisited *Brignoni-Ponce*'s dictum 25 years later and held, albeit also in dicta, that the statistical inference on which it was based was no longer valid, even in its original illegal-immigration context:

> *Brignoni-Ponce* was handed down in 1975, some twenty-five years ago. Current demographic data demonstrate that the statistical premises on which its dictum relies are no longer applicable. The Hispanic population of this nation, and of the Southwest and Far West in particular, has grown enormously.... Accordingly, Hispanic appearance is of little or no use in determining which particular individuals among the vast Hispanic populace should be stopped by law enforcement officials on the lookout for illegal aliens. Reasonable suspicion requires *particularized* suspicion, and in an area in which a large number of people share a specific characteristic, that characteristic casts too wide a net to play any part in a particularized reasonable suspicion determination.

[*United States v. Montero-Camargo,* 208 F.3d 1122 (9th Cir. 2000),] at 1133-34 (emphasis in original). Notably, the Supreme Court has never revisited its dictum in *Brignoni-Ponce,* nor has it ever addressed whether, *absent* compelling statistical evidence, race or ethnicity may be used as a factor in the Fourth Amendment calculus to indicate criminal propensity. Accordingly, the Court finds that *Brignoni-Ponce* offers no support for the Government's position....

There is no doubt that the specter of 9/11 looms large over this case. Although this is the first post-9/11 case to address whether race may be used to establish criminal propensity under the Fourth Amendment, the Court cannot subscribe to the notion that in the wake of 9/11 this may now be permissible. As the Second Circuit recently admonished, "the strength of our system of constitutional rights derives from the steadfast protection of those rights in both normal and unusual times." *Iqbal v. Hasty,* 490 F.3d 143, 159 (2d Cir. 2007)[, *rev'd on other grounds and remanded sub nom. Ashcroft v. Iqbal,* 129 S. Ct. 1937, 1954 (2009), *cert. granted and remanded,* 129 S. Ct. 2430 (2009), *cert. granted and remanded sub nom. Sawyer v. Iqbal,* 129 S. Ct. 2431 (2009)].

History teaches much the same lesson: The Supreme Court's approval of the internment of large numbers of Japanese-Americans during World War II, *see Korematsu v. United States,* 323 U.S. 214 (1945), is now widely regarded as a black mark on our constitutional jurisprudence. The daughter of two such internees—Kiyo Matsumoto—recently became the third Asian-American woman to be elevated to the federal bench. At her induction ceremony, Judge Matsumoto recalled the closing words of Justice Murphy's dissent in *Korematsu*; they are equally apt here:

> All residents of this nation are kin in some way by blood or culture to a foreign land. Yet they are primarily and necessarily a part of the new and distinct civilization of the United States. They must accordingly be treated at all times as the heirs of the American experiment and as entitled to all the rights and freedoms guaranteed by the Constitution.

323 U.S. at 206.

The Court "fully recognize[s] the gravity of the situation that confront[s] investigative officials of the United States as a consequence of the 9/11 attack[,]" *Iqbal*, 490 F.3d at 159 (2d Cir. 2007), and that the mindset of airline travelers has understandably been altered by 9/11. This justifiable apprehension must be assuaged by ensuring that security is strictly enforced, and by the passage of time without, hopefully, other episodic affronts to our country; but fear cannot be a factor to allow for the evisceration of the bedrock principle of our Constitution that no one can be arrested without probable cause that a crime has been committed. . . .

CONCLUSION

For the reasons described above, the Court grants summary judgment in the Government's favor with respect to plaintiffs' conspiracy claims, plaintiffs' common-law claims against Smith, and plaintiffs' §1981 claims. The Court denies summary judgment with respect to plaintiffs' *Bivens* claims against Smith and Plunkett, plaintiffs' FTCA claims against the United States, and Smith and Plunkett's qualified-immunity defense.

So ordered.

NOTES AND QUESTIONS

a. Legal Analysis of Profiling

1. *The Easy Case: Individualized Description.* The Department of Justice has issued guidance for federal law enforcement agencies on the use of race or ethnicity in conducting investigations. Civil Rights Div., U.S. Dep't of Justice, *Guidance Regarding the Use of Race by Federal Law Enforcement Agencies* (June 2003) ("*DOJ Guidance*"). It asserts:

> In conducting activities in connection with a specific investigation, Federal law enforcement officers may consider race and ethnicity only to the extent that there is trustworthy information, relevant to the locality or time frame, that links persons of a particular race or ethnicity to an identified criminal incident, scheme, or organization. This standard applies even where the use of race or ethnicity might otherwise be lawful . . . .

This guidance reflects the generally accepted principle that law enforcement agents may use race or an ethnic characteristic when it is part of the description of a particular suspect. *See* Sharon L. Davies, *Profiling Terror*, 1 Ohio St. J. Crim. L. 45, 54 & n.38

(2003) (citing decisions). "To act on the basis of a particular suspect's description as belonging to a given race is certainly to take race into account," Professor Ellmann explains, "but it is not to take *generalizations* about race into account." Stephen J. Ellmann, *Racial Profiling and Terrorism*, 46 N.Y.U. L. Rev. 675, 676 n.4 (2003). But the *DOJ Guidance*'s approval of profiling in some counterterrorism investigations may suggest how easily "the identification of a group of offenders by race tends to transform the physical description into a negative predictor and then into a mark of social status." Albert W. Alshuler, *Racial Profiling and the Constitution*, 2002 U. Chi. Legal F. 163, 265-266. Is being on the lookout for "Middle Eastern men" in their early 20s merely taking into account the fact that the original Al Qaeda membership seemed overwhelmingly to have included such men, or does it assume that they are more likely to commit future terrorist acts than Swedish grandmothers? Does the "lookout" profile stigmatize all young Middle Eastern men?

2. *Fourth Amendment Analysis: Mere "Relevance"?* The Fourth Amendment "special needs" (administrative search) analysis of racial profiling in security screening asks whether the race or ethnic factor in the profile is "clearly . . . relevant to the law enforcement need to be served." *United States v. Martinez-Fuerte*, 428 U.S. 543, 564 n.17 (1976). That it may constitute purposeful discrimination does not make the search or seizure unreasonable under the Fourth Amendment. *Whren v. United States*, 517 U.S. 806, 813 (1996). Thus, the Supreme Court has upheld secondary screening of persons at a border checkpoint made largely on the basis of apparent Mexican ancestry. *United States v. Martinez-Fuerte*, 428 U.S. 543, 563 (1976), relying in part on its earlier decision in *United States v. Brignoni-Ponce*, 422 U.S. 873 (1975), discussed in *Farag*.

The *DOJ Guidance* excerpted above permits the consideration of ethnicity in some law enforcement encounters. Did it permit such consideration in the encounter described in *Farag*? Was what the court called the "Arab ethnicity" of Farag and Elmasry relevant to a law enforcement need?

3. *Equal Protection Analysis: Stricter Scrutiny and Necessity?* Even if the arrest of Farag and Elmasry had survived a Fourth Amendment challenge, it would have raised questions under the Equal Protection Clause. At least as early as 1944, the Supreme Court declared that "all legal restrictions which curtail the rights of a single racial group are immediately suspect" and therefore subject to the "most rigid scrutiny." *Korematsu v. United States*, 323 U.S. 214, 216 (1944). The scrutiny actually applied by the Court, however, did not overturn the government's program to intern 120,000 Japanese-Americans following the attack on Pearl Harbor. Although the Court acknowledged that "[n]othing short of apprehension by the proper military authorities of the gravest imminent danger to the public safety can constitutionally justify" such race-based discrimination, the Court deferred to the judgment of military authorities and found that exclusion of Japanese-Americans from certain areas "has a definite and close relationship to the prevention of crime and sabotage." 323 U.S. at 218.

Since *Korematsu*, the Court has refined equal protection analysis. When government action is challenged on equal protection grounds, "the issue is whether the government can identify a sufficiently important objective for its discrimination. What is a sufficient justification depends entirely on the type of discrimination." Erwin Chemerinsky, *Constitutional Law* 669-670 (3d ed. 2006). When the government discriminates on the basis of race, national origin, or, for some actions, alienage, its justification will be subject to "strict scrutiny" and upheld only "if it is proven necessary to achieve a compelling government purpose." *Id.* at 529 (footnote omitted). Other classifications may require only "rational basis" review, under which the law need only be rationally related to a legitimate government purpose, or "intermediate scrutiny." *Id.*

Can you formulate an argument for the legality of ethnic profiling of Farag and Elmasry under modern equal protection analysis?

4. *Ethnic Profiling at the Airport.* The *DOJ Guidance* also provides this example of appropriate increased scrutiny of certain ethnic groups to protect the nation's borders:

> Example: U.S. intelligence sources report that terrorists from a particular ethnic group are planning to use commercial jetliners as weapons by hijacking them at an airport in California during the next week. Before allowing men of that ethnic group to board commercial airplanes in California airports during the next week, Transportation Security Administration personnel, and other federal and state authorities, may subject them to heightened scrutiny. . . . [*DOJ Guidance, supra,* at 703.]

Would this guideline have justified the selection of Mohamed Atta or his colleagues for further screening at Logan Airport on September 11? What about the selection of persons like them for scrutiny *after* 9/11?

Could you justify their selection if it had been based only on the gate agent's suspicion of their "Middle Eastern" appearance? See *supra* p. 291. Consider the *DOJ Guidance*'s conclusion that "reliance solely upon generalized stereotypes is forbidden," for which it offers the following example:

> Example: At the security entrance to a Federal courthouse, a man who appears to be of a particular ethnicity properly submits his briefcase for x-ray screening and passes through the metal detector. The inspection of the briefcase reveals nothing amiss, the man does not activate the metal detector, and there is nothing suspicious about his activities or appearance. In the absence of any threat warning, the federal security screener may not order the man to undergo a further inspection solely because he appears to be of a particular ethnicity.

Reasonable suspicion is not required for border searches, as *Arnold* indicated. Indeed, a border officer need not give a reason for a search. What then is to prevent otherwise "forbidden" profiling by airport and border personnel? One study concludes that "the absence of any requisite level of suspicion to conduct border searches opens the door to racial or religious profiling." Constitution Project, *supra* p. 298, at 6. *See also* Yule Kim, *Border Searches of Laptops and Other Electronic Storage Devices* (Cong. Res. Serv. RL 34404), Nov. 16, 2009.

Might the screening be based on a *combination* of racial or ethnic characteristics *and* behavioral factors? Would it then satisfy the equal protection analysis and meet the standard set out in the *DOJ Guidance*? *See* Davies, *supra,* at 60-61 (noting that courts have required profiles to be based on more than racial or ethnic elements alone to withstand equal protection challenge).

b. Practical Problems and Assessment of Profiling

1. *Problems of Applying Racial and Ethnic Classifications in Screening.* The *DOJ Guidance* is (deliberately?) vague about classification for profiling in counterterrorism

cases: it refers just to "ethnic groups." But "defenses of racial and ethnic profiling depend upon the ability of law enforcement officers to do it — to distinguish racial and ethnic groups from one another." Alschuler, *supra*, at 224. Does the legality not therefore depend partly on how the "ethnic group" is described and how much discretion that leaves checkpoint screeners or law enforcement officers?

One journalist characterized the New York subway system's random container inspection as an "obvious absurdity" and an "appalling waste of effort." Charles Krauthammer, *Give Grandma a Pass: Politically Correct Screening Won't Catch Jihadists*, Wash. Post, July 29, 2005. Since "jihadist terrorism has been carried out . . . by young Muslim men," he reasoned, we should give "special scrutiny to young Islamic men." *Id. See also* Milton Hirsch & David O. Markus, *Fourth Amendment Forum*, 27 Champion 34 (Mar. 2003) ("since 9/11 attacks were perpetrated by "Arab Muslim men," there "exists a demonstrable, verifiable nexus between" such characteristics when used to select travelers for high-level screening "and conduct that American officials have a public duty to interdict").

Could you explain to subway security officers how to identify "Islamic men"? What about persons "of Middle Eastern appearance"? *See* John Derbyshire, *At First Glance: Racial Profiling, Burning Hotter*, Nat'l Rev. Online (Oct. 5, 2001), *at* http://www.nationalreview.com/derbyshire/derbyshire100501.shtml. What about "Arab-looking"? *See* Stuart Taylor Jr., *D.C. Dispatch: Politically Incorrect Profiling: A Matter of Life or Death*, Nat'l J., Nov. 6, 2001; Davies, *supra*, at 51 n.29 ("It is a common misconception that all Arabs are racially identifiable by their darker skin. In fact, Arabs may have white skin and blue eyes, olive or dark skin and brown eyes, and hair in a variety of textures.").

One danger of vague classifications is that they leave the screeners too much discretion, creating space for conscious or unconscious application of the screeners' own prejudices. The same may be true even of profiling that includes behavioral factors, such as unusual passenger nervousness or sweating or failure to make eye contact, in a profile together with racial or ethnic factors. After 9/11, for example, the American Civil Liberties Union reported that 67 percent of airline passengers subjected to personal searches upon entering the United States were people of color; black and Latino Americans were four to nine times as likely as white Americans to be x-rayed after being frisked or patted down; and black women were more likely than any other U.S. citizens to be strip-searched. *See* R. Spencer McDonald, Note, *Rational Profiling in America's Airports*, 17 BYU J. Pub. L. 113, 136 (2002) (citing American Civil Liberties Union press release (Mar. 26, 2002)).

In light of these considerations, were the "non-ethnic" factors that caused agents to "arrest" Farag and Elmasry objective or subjective — reasonable intuitions or masked discrimination? Consider this view:

> To insist that an experienced bomb-dog handler or baggage screener ignore any hunches while mindlessly sticking to random passenger screening is, at best, a waste of limited resources. Sky marshals, Transportation Security Administration screeners, and others on the front lines of counterterrorism should be afforded sufficient discretion to draw upon their common sense and experience regarding people who exhibit nonbehavioral risk factors. [John Winn, *The Legitimacy of Profiling*, Wash. Times, Dec. 30, 2009.]

Should the court in *Farag* have paid more deference to the "common sense and experience" of security professionals?

2. *Empirical Nexus?* In <u>*United States v. Lopez,*</u> 328 F. Supp. 1077 (E.D.N.Y. 1971), the court initially upheld the use of a passenger profile in the pre-1973 selective anti-skyjacking screening program and follow-up frisk. But when discovery revealed that the airline had unilaterally eliminated one element of the FAA-established profile and added "an ethnic element for which there was no experimental basis, thus raising serious equal protection problems," the court suppressed the evidence from the frisk. *Id.* at 1101. "The approved [FAA] system survives constitutional scrutiny only by its careful adherence to absolute objectivity and neutrality," the court explained. "When elements of discretion and prejudice are interjected it becomes constitutionally impermissible." *Id.*

<u>Does this mean that any ethnic, religious, or national origin element of a screening profile must have at least "an experimental basis" to find a nexus between the element and the probability of a terrorist act?</u> If so, does "Islamic men" or "Middle Eastern appearance" have such a nexus to terrorism, in light of the fact that all of the 9/11 hijackers were apparently Muslims from the Middle East? *Compare* Thomas W. Joo, *Presumed Disloyal: Executive Power, Judicial Deference, and the Construction of Race Before and After September 11,* 34 Colum. Hum. Rts. L. Rev. 1, 41-42 (2002) (the "categories of 'Arab' and 'Muslim' are simply too broad"; "even if a man of Arab descent is relatively more likely to be a terrorist than a non-Arab, the likelihood that any given Arab man is a terrorist remains negligible"), *with* Ellmann, *supra,* at 698 ("People sharing all of Al Qaeda's background characteristics still seem more likely to be our adversaries than most of the people who share none of them — even though the great majority of people sharing all of these characteristics have no connection to terrorism whatsoever.").

Professor Alshuler suggests that "when a police practice systematically subjects the members of a race to searches and seizures at a higher rate than their rate of offending, a court should hold the practice unconstitutional unless it is appropriately tailored to advance a significant state interest." Alshuler, *supra,* at 223. Would profiling of "Middle Eastern men" satisfy this test? *See id.* at 265 ("special screening of people of Arab ethnicity at airports...should be impermissible"). How would we measure their "rate of offending"?

Professor Harcourt suggests that the success and justification of profiling depend on more than "identifying a stable group trait that correlates with higher offending." It also depends on "how responsive different groups are to the targeted policing and whether they engage in forms of substitution" by recruiting from nonprofiled groups or substituting different types of attacks that are more immune to profiling. *See* Bernard E. Harcourt, *Muslim Profiles Post 9/11: Is Racial Profiling an Effective Counterterrorist Measure and Does It Violate the Right to Be Free from Discrimination?* (Univ. of Chi. Law Sch., John M. Olin Law & Econ. Working Paper No. 288 (2d Series), at 9-10, Mar. 2006), *available at* http://ssrn.com/abstract=893905.

> The central question [is] whether racial profiling of young Muslim men in the New York subways will likely detect a terrorist attack or instead lead to the recruitment of non-profiled persons and the substitution of other acts for subway attacks — in other words, whether profiling will detect or increase terrorist attacks. The answer to this question is pure speculation. In the end, then, there is no need or reason to engage in a rights trade-off by racial profiling as part of any subway screening. [*Id.* at 27-28.]

That is, without empirical evidence that racial profiling works, there is no need for it. Do you agree?

3. *Costs and Benefits of Profiling.* Proponents of counterterrorism profiling have argued that the cost to a victim of frequent false positives "is minuscule," while the cost to society of a false negative (letting a terrorist through) could be enormous. They conclude that racial profiling is justified by a cost-benefit analysis. *See* LaFave, *supra* p. 292 (summarizing arguments of some proponents); Ellman, *supra*, at 698-707. Does this analysis consider all the costs? What about the risk that Al Qaeda will respond to the profile by selecting terrorists who do not look "Islamic" or "Middle Eastern" (if you can figure out what this means), including Americans like Jose Padilla (see *infra* p. 444), thus increasing the rate of false negatives? What about the cost of creating hostility and anxiety in the U.S. community of persons from the Middle East, and discouraging its members from voluntary cooperation? *See generally* Ellman, *supra*, at 705-707; Davies, *supra* p. 315, at 73-74. How would you inventory and balance all the benefits and costs of racial profiling in security screening and counterterrorism investigations?

c. National Origin and Religious Profiling

1. *National Origin Profiling of Post-9/11 Detainees and Interviewees.* Following the September 11 attacks, law enforcement and immigration authorities detained more than 1,100 persons as part of their investigation. On November 27, 2001, the Bush administration provided a breakdown of some 600 persons still being held. According to the report, 548 detained on immigration charges hailed from 47 countries, including more than 200 from Pakistan, and smaller numbers from Egypt, Turkey, Yemen, and India. Dan Eggen, *About 600 Still Held in Connection with Attacks, Ashcroft Says*, Wash. Post, Nov. 28, 2001. An earlier newspaper investigation of 235 detainees found that the largest numbers were from Saudi Arabia, Egypt, and Pakistan, and that almost all of them were men in their 20s and 30s. Amy Goldstein, *A Deliberate Strategy of Disruption*, Wash. Post, Nov. 4, 2001. When these figures were reported, none of the detainees had been charged with any terrorist activity. Subsequently, the Administration conducted "voluntary" interviews targeting 5,000 mostly Middle Eastern aliens holding tourist, student, or business visas. *See* Allan Lengel, *Arab Men in Detroit to Be Asked to See U.S. Attorney*, Wash. Post, Nov. 27, 2001.

Did these actions constitute constitutionally suspect profiling? Did they violate the *DOJ Guidance? Compare* Davies, *supra*, at 80-81, *and* Ellmann, *supra*, at 726-727 (because mass interviews were based on stigmatizing racial generalization that promoted public stereotypes, created great resentment in the targeted community, and probably generated few, if any leads, they were "unjustifiable discrimination"), *with* Samuel R. Gross & Debra Livingston, *Racial Profiling Under Attack*, 102 Colum. L. Rev. 1413, 1436 (2002) (concluding that the interview campaign was profiling to the extent that the FBI assumed that Middle Eastern men were more likely than others to commit acts of terror but was not profiling to the extent that FBI agents were "pursuing case-specific information about the September 11 attacks, albeit in dragnet fashion"). Does it matter? Professors Gross and Livingston suggest that how the FBI selects its interviewees matters less than how they carry out the interviews. *Id.* at 1436-1437 ("Are the interviews conducted respectfully...?"). Do you agree?

The Second Circuit Court of Appeals rejected a claim by Muslim men who were detained for immigration violations after they had been identified as persons of "high interest" in the investigation following 9/11, that they had been impermissibly selected on the basis of their national origin.

[P]laintiffs point to no authority clearly establishing an equal protection right to be free of selective enforcement of the immigration laws based on national origin, race, or religion at the time of plaintiffs' detentions. *See Reno v. American-Arab Anti-Discrimination Comm.*, 525 U.S. 471, 490-91 (1999) ("What will be involved in deportation cases is not merely the disclosure of normal domestic law enforcement priorities and techniques, but often the disclosure of foreign-policy objectives and (as in this case) foreign-intelligence products and techniques. The Executive should not have to disclose its 'real' reasons for deeming nationals of a particular country a special threat — or indeed for simply wishing to antagonize a particular foreign country by focusing on that country's nationals — and even if it did disclose them a court would be ill equipped to determine their authenticity and utterly unable to assess their adequacy"); *see also Zadvydas* [*v. Davis*, 533 U.S. 678, 696 (2001)] ("terrorism" might warrant "special arguments" for "heightened deference to the judgments of the political branches with respect to matters of national security"); *Mathews v. Diaz*, 426 U.S. 67, 81-82 (1976) ("The reasons that preclude judicial review of political questions also dictate a narrow standard of review of decisions made by the Congress or the President in the area of immigration and naturalization."); *but see Iqbal v. Hasty*, 490 F.3d 143, 175 (2d Cir.2007) (determining that *Reno* "does not stand for the proposition that the Government may subject members of a particular race, ethnicity, or religion to more restrictive conditions of confinement than members of other races, ethnic backgrounds, or religions"), rev'd on other grounds and remanded, *Ashcroft v. Iqbal*, 129 S.Ct. 1937, 1954 (2009). [*Turkmen v. Ashcroft*, 589 F.3d 542, 550 (2d Cir. 2009).]

2. *Religious Profiling?* In *Tabbaa v. Chertoff*, 509 F.3d 89 (2d Cir. 2007), the CBP had received classified information giving them reason to believe that terrorists or persons with terrorist ties would be attending a Muslim religious conference in Canada, which drew 13,000 individuals from across North America. They therefore, without particularizied suspicion, stopped a group of Muslim U.S. citizens at the border on their return from the conference and frisked, fingerprinted, photographed, questioned, and detained them for four to six hours, without telling them why they had been pulled aside. When these citizens challenged these actions in court, the court of appeals ultimately ruled that, as "routine" border searches, the actions did not violate the Fourth Amendment. It also held that the actions did not violate the plaintiffs' First Amendment rights of association or religious freedom under a strict scrutiny test, because they served a compelling counterterrorism need, and, *at the border*, this need could not have been satisfied by any significantly less restrictive means. *Id.* at 102-105.

3. *Profiling and National Identity Cards.* One commentator has argued that "[a] national identity card could facilitate greater civil liberties for groups targeted by racial and ethnic stereotyping and profiling. Membership would alleviate harassment because presentation of the card would result in an immediate check of one's identity with the national computerized data system." John Dwight Ingram, *Racial and Ethnic Profiling*, 29 T. Marshall L. Rev. 55, 83 (2003). Do you agree?

Surveillance Abroad   11

The United States has long conducted law enforcement and intelligence investigations overseas. Such investigations are critical in detecting threats to national security. In this chapter we examine the question whether, when U.S. investigators go abroad, the Constitution travels with them to limit their activities and, if so, to what extent. In particular, we consider whether the protections of the Fourth Amendment apply outside the United States and, if they do, whether they apply to aliens the same way they do to U.S. citizens. And we ask how such protections might be influenced by practical considerations.

Reid v. Covert

United States Supreme Court, 1957
354 U.S. 1

[Mrs. Covert murdered her husband, a U.S. Air Force sergeant, at an airbase in England. Pursuant to a "status-of-forces" executive agreement with that country, she was tried and convicted by U.S. court-martial without a jury trial under the Uniform Code of Military Justice (UCMJ). On a petition for a writ of habeas corpus, she attacked her conviction on the grounds that it violated her Fifth and Sixth Amendment rights to be tried by a jury after indictment by a grand jury. The District Court granted the petition, and this appeal followed. Mrs. Covert's appeal was consolidated with a like appeal by Mrs. Smith, who was convicted in a similar fashion of murdering her husband, an Army officer, in Japan.]

Mr. Justice BLACK announced the opinion of the Court and delivered an opinion, in which the Chief Justice, Mr. Justice DOUGLAS, and Mr. Justice BRENNAN join. . . . At the beginning we reject the idea that when the United States acts against citizens abroad it can do so free of the Bill of Rights. The United States is entirely a creature of the Constitution. Its power and authority have no other source. It can only act in accordance with all the limitations imposed by the Constitution. When the Government reaches out to punish a citizen who is abroad, the shield which the Bill of Rights and other parts of the Constitution provide to protect his life and liberty should not be stripped away just because he happens to be in another land. . . .

322

The rights and liberties which citizens of our country enjoy are not protected by custom and tradition alone, they have been jealously preserved from the encroachments of Government by express provisions of our written Constitution.

Among those provisions, Art. III, §2 and the Fifth and Sixth Amendments are directly relevant to these cases. Article III, §2 lays down the rule that:

> "The Trial of all Crimes, except in Cases of Impeachment, shall be by Jury; and such Trial shall be held in the State where the said Crimes shall have been committed; but when not committed within any State, the Trial shall be at such Place or Places as the Congress may by Law have directed."

The Fifth Amendment declares:

> "No person shall be held to answer for a capital, or otherwise infamous crime, unless on a presentment or indictment of a Grand Jury, except in cases arising in the land or naval forces, or in the Militia, when in actual service in time of War or public danger; ...."

And the Sixth Amendment provides:

> "In all criminal prosecutions, the accused shall enjoy the right to a speedy and public trial, by an impartial jury of the State and district wherein the crime shall have been committed...."

The language of Art. III, §2 manifests that constitutional protections for the individual were designed to restrict the United States Government when it acts outside of this country, as well as here at home. After declaring that all criminal trials must be by jury, the section states that when a crime is "not committed within any State, the Trial shall be at such Place or Places as the Congress may by Law have directed." If this language is permitted to have its obvious meaning, §2 is applicable to criminal trials outside of the States as a group without regard to where the offense is committed or the trial held. From the very first Congress, federal statutes have implemented the provisions of §2 by providing for trial of murder and other crimes committed outside the jurisdiction of any State "in the district where the offender is apprehended, or into which he may first be brought." The Fifth and Sixth Amendments, like Art. III, §2, are also all inclusive with their sweeping references to "no person" and to "all criminal prosecutions."

This Court and other federal courts have held or asserted that various constitutional limitations apply to the Government when it acts outside the continental United States. While it has been suggested that only those constitutional rights which are "fundamental" protect Americans abroad, we can find no warrant, in logic or otherwise, for picking and choosing among the remarkable collection of "Thou shalt nots" which were explicitly fastened on all departments and agencies of the Federal Government by the Constitution and its Amendments. Moreover, in view of our heritage and the history of the adoption of the Constitution and the Bill of Rights, it seems peculiarly anomalous to say that trial before a civilian judge and by an independent jury picked from the common citizenry is not a fundamental right.... Trial by jury in a court of law and in accordance with traditional modes of procedure after an indictment by grand jury has served and remains one of our most vital barriers to governmental arbitrariness. These elemental procedural safeguards were embedded in our Constitution to secure their inviolateness and sanctity against the passing demands of expediency or convenience. . . .

The [holding in *In re Ross*, 140 U.S. 453 (1891),] that the Constitution has no applicability abroad has long since been directly repudiated by numerous cases. That approach is obviously erroneous if the United States Government, which has no power except that granted by the Constitution, can and does try citizens for crimes committed abroad. . . . At best, the *Ross* case should be left as a relic from a different era.

[Last term the Court] relied on the *"Insular Cases"* to support its conclusion that Article III and the Fifth and Sixth Amendments were not applicable to the trial of Mrs. Smith and Mrs. Covert.[22] We believe that reliance was misplaced. The *"Insular Cases,"* which arose at the turn of the [twentieth] century, involved territories which had only recently been conquered or acquired by the United States. These territories, governed and regulated by Congress under Art. IV, §3, had entirely different cultures and customs from those of this country. . . .

Moreover, it is our judgment that neither the cases nor their reasoning should be given any further expansion. The concept that the Bill of Rights and other constitutional protections against arbitrary government are inoperative when they become inconvenient or when expediency dictates otherwise is a very dangerous doctrine and if allowed to flourish would destroy the benefit of a written Constitution and undermine the basis of our government. If our foreign commitments become of such nature that the Government can no longer satisfactorily operate within the bounds laid down by the Constitution, that instrument can be amended by the method which it prescribes. But we have no authority, or inclination, to read exceptions into it which are not there. . . .

Mr. Justice HARLAN, concurring in the result. . . . As I have already stated, I do not think that it can be said that these safeguards of the Constitution are never operative without the United States, regardless of the particular circumstances. On the other hand, I cannot agree with the suggestion that every provision of the Constitution must always be deemed automatically applicable to American citizens in every part of the world. For *Ross* and the *Insular Cases* do stand for an important proposition, one which seems to me a wise and necessary gloss on our Constitution. The proposition is, of course, not that the Constitution "does not apply" overseas, but that there are provisions in the Constitution which do not *necessarily* apply in all circumstances in every foreign place. . . . In other words, what *Ross* and the *Insular Cases* hold is that the particular local setting, the practical necessities, and the possible alternatives are relevant to a question of judgment, namely, whether jury trial should be deemed a necessary condition of the exercise of Congress' power to provide for the trial of Americans overseas. . . .

And so I agree with my brother Frankfurter that, in view of *Ross* and the *Insular Cases*, we have before us a question analogous, ultimately, to issues of due process; one can say, in fact, that the question of which specific safeguards of the Constitution are appropriately to be applied in a particular context overseas can be reduced to the issue of what process is "due" a defendant in the particular circumstances of a particular case.

---

22. *Downes v. Bidwell*, 182 U.S. 244; *Territory of Hawaii v. Mankichi*, 190 U.S. 197; *Dorr v. United States*, 195 U.S. 138; *Balzac v. Porto Rico*, 258 U.S. 298.

On this basis, I cannot agree with the sweeping proposition that a full Article III trial, with indictment and trial by jury, is required in every case for the trial of a civilian dependent of a serviceman overseas. The Government, it seems to me, has made an impressive showing that at least for the run-of-the-mill offenses committed by dependents overseas, such a requirement would be as impractical and anomalous as it would have been to require jury trial for Balzac in Porto Rico. . . .

So far as capital cases are concerned, I think they stand on quite a different footing than other offenses. In such cases the law is especially sensitive to demands for that procedural fairness which inheres in a civilian trial where the judge and trier of fact are not responsive to the command of the convening authority. I do not concede that whatever process is "due" an offender faced with a fine or a prison sentence necessarily satisfies the requirements of the Constitution in a capital case. . . . The number of such cases would appear to be so negligible that the practical problems of affording the defendant a civilian trial would not present insuperable problems.

On this narrow ground I concur in the result in these cases.

[The opinions of FRANKFURTER, J., concurring, and of CLARK, J., dissenting, are omitted.]

United States v. Verdugo-Urquidez
United States Supreme Court, 1990
494 U.S. 259

Chief Justice REHNQUIST delivered the opinion of the Court. The question presented by this case is whether the Fourth Amendment applies to the search and seizure by United States agents of property that is owned by a nonresident alien and located in a foreign country. We hold that it does not.

[Respondent René Martin Verdugo-Urquidez was a citizen and resident of Mexico who was apprehended by Mexican police and delivered to U.S. border authorities in response to a U.S. warrant for his arrest on drug-smuggling charges. Following his arrest, and while he was incarcerated in the United States, DEA agents searched Verdugo-Urquidez's property in Mexico with the approval of Mexican authorities, but without a U.S. warrant, and seized certain documents that were subsequently offered as evidence against him. The defendant sought to have that evidence excluded.]

The Fourth Amendment provides:

"The right of the people to be secure in their persons, houses, papers, and effects, against unreasonable searches and seizures, shall not be violated, and no Warrants shall issue, but upon probable cause, supported by Oath or affirmation, and particularly describing the place to be searched, and the persons or things to be seized."

That text, by contrast with the Fifth and Sixth Amendments, extends its reach only to "the people." Contrary to the suggestion of *amici curiae* that the Framers used this phrase "simply to avoid [an] awkward rhetorical redundancy," "the people" seems to have been a term of art employed in select parts of the Constitution. The Preamble declares that the Constitution is ordained and established by "the People of the

United States." The Second Amendment protects "the right of the people to keep and bear Arms," and the Ninth and Tenth Amendments provide that certain rights and powers are retained by and reserved to "the people." See also U.S. Const., Amdt. 1 ("Congress shall make no law...abridging...*the right of the people* peaceably to assemble") (emphasis added); Art. I, §2, cl. 1 ("The House of Representatives shall be composed of Members chosen every second Year *by the People of the several States*") (emphasis added). While this textual exegesis is by no means conclusive, it suggests that "the people" protected by the Fourth Amendment, and by the First and Second Amendments, and to whom rights and powers are reserved in the Ninth and Tenth Amendments, refers to a class of persons who are part of a national community or who have otherwise developed sufficient connection with this country to be considered part of that community. The language of these Amendments contrasts with the words "person" and "accused" used in the Fifth and Sixth Amendments regulating procedure in criminal cases.

What we know of the history of the drafting of the Fourth Amendment also suggests that its purpose was to restrict searches and seizures which might be conducted by the United States in domestic matters.... The available historical data show, therefore, that the purpose of the Fourth Amendment was to protect the people of the United States against arbitrary action by their own Government; it was never suggested that the provision was intended to restrain the actions of the Federal Government against aliens outside of the United States territory.

There is likewise no indication that the Fourth Amendment was understood by contemporaries of the Framers to apply to activities of the United States directed against aliens in foreign territory or in international waters. Only seven years after the ratification of the Amendment, French interference with American commercial vessels engaged in neutral trade triggered what came to be known as the "undeclared war" with France. In an Act to "protect the Commerce of the United States" in 1798, Congress authorized President Adams to "instruct the commanders of the public armed vessels which are, or which shall be employed in the service of the United States, to subdue, seize and take any armed French vessel, which shall be found within the jurisdictional limits of the United States, or elsewhere, on the high seas." §1 of An Act Further to Protect the Commerce of the United States, ch. 68, 1 Stat. 578.... Some commanders were held liable by this Court for unlawful seizures because their actions were beyond the scope of the congressional grant of authority, *see, e.g., Little v. Barreme*, 2 Cranch 170, 177-178 (1804); *cf. Talbot v. Seeman*, 1 Cranch 1, 31 (1801) (seizure of neutral ship lawful where American captain had probable cause to believe vessel was French), but it was never suggested that the Fourth Amendment restrained the authority of congress or of United States agents to conduct operations such as this.

The global view taken by the Court of Appeals of the application of the Constitution is also contrary to this Court's decisions in the *Insular Cases*, which held that not every constitutional provision applies to governmental activity even where the United States has sovereign power. In *Dorr v. United States*, 195 U.S. 138 (1904), we declared the general rule that in an unincorporated territory—one not clearly destined for statehood—Congress was not required to adopt "a system of laws which shall include the right of trial by jury, and that *the Constitution does not, without legislation and of its own force, carry such right to territory so situated.*" 195 U.S. at 149 (emphasis added). Only "fundamental" constitutional rights are guaranteed to inhabitants of those territories.... [C]ertainly, it is not open to us in light of the *Insular Cases* to endorse the view that every constitutional provision applies wherever the United States Government exercises its power.

Indeed, we have rejected the claim that aliens are entitled to Fifth Amendment rights outside the sovereign territory of the United States. In *Johnson v. Eisentrager*, 339 U.S. 763 (1950), the Court held that enemy aliens arrested in China and imprisoned in Germany after World War II could not obtain writs of habeas corpus in our federal courts on the ground that their convictions for war crimes had violated the Fifth Amendment and other constitutional provisions. The *Eisentrager* opinion acknowledged that in some cases constitutional provisions extend beyond the citizenry; "[t]he alien . . . has been accorded a generous and ascending scale of rights as he increases his identity with our society." *Id.*, at 770. But our rejection of extraterritorial application of the Fifth Amendment was emphatic:

> "Such extraterritorial application of organic law would have been so significant an innovation in the practice of governments that, if intended or apprehended, it could scarcely have failed to excite contemporary comment. Not one word can be cited. No decision of this Court supports such a view. *Cf. Downes v. Bidwell*, 182 U.S. 244 [(1901)]. None of the learned commentators on our Constitution has even hinted at it. The practice of every modern government is opposed to it." *Id.*, at 784.

If such is true of the Fifth Amendment, which speaks in the relatively universal term of "person," it would seem even more true with respect to the Fourth Amendment, which applies only to "the people."

To support his all-encompassing view of the Fourth Amendment, respondent points to language from the plurality opinion in *Reid v. Covert*, 354 U.S. 1 (1957). . . . Four Justices "reject[ed] the idea that when the United States acts *against citizens* abroad it can do so free of the Bill of Rights." *Id.*, at 5 (emphasis added). The plurality went on to say:

> "The United States is entirely a creature of the Constitution. Its power and authority have no other source. It can only act in accordance with all the limitations imposed by the Constitution. When the Government reaches out to punish *a citizen* who is abroad, the shield which the Bill of Rights and other parts of the Constitution provide to protect his life and liberty should not be stripped away just because he happens to be in another land." *Id.*, at 5-6 (emphasis added; footnote omitted).

Respondent urges that we interpret this discussion to mean that federal officials are constrained by the Fourth Amendment wherever and against whomever they act. But the holding of *Reid* stands for no such sweeping proposition: it decided that United States citizens stationed abroad could invoke the protection of the Fifth and Sixth Amendments. The concurring opinions by Justices Frankfurter and Harlan in *Reid* resolved the case on much narrower grounds than the plurality and declined even to hold that United States citizens were entitled to the full range of constitutional protections in all overseas criminal prosecutions. *See id.*, at 75 (Harlan, J., concurring in result) ("I agree with my brother Frankfurter that . . . we have before us a question analogous, ultimately, to issues of due process; one can say, in fact, that the question of which specific safeguards of the Constitution are appropriately to be applied in a particular context overseas can be reduced to the issue of what process is 'due' a defendant in the particular circumstances of a particular case"). Since respondent is not a United States citizen, he can derive no comfort from the *Reid* holding.

Verdugo-Urquidez also relies on a series of cases in which we have held that aliens enjoy certain constitutional rights. *See, e.g., Plyler v. Doe,* 457 U.S. 202, 211-212 (1982) (illegal aliens protected by Equal Protection Clause); *Kwong Hai Chew v. Colding,* 344 U.S. 590, 596 (1953) (resident alien is a "person" within the meaning of the Fifth Amendment); *Bridges v. Wixon,* 326 U.S. 135, 148 (1945) (resident aliens have First Amendment rights); *Russian Volunteer Fleet v. United States,* 282 U.S. 481 (1931) (Just Compensation Clause of Fifth Amendment); *Wong Wing v. United States,* 163 U.S. 228, 238 (1896) (resident aliens entitled to Fifth and Sixth Amendment rights); *Yick Wo v. Hopkins,* 118 U.S. 356, 369 (1886) (Fourteenth Amendment protects resident aliens). These cases, however, establish only that aliens receive constitutional protections when they have come within the territory of the United States and developed substantial connections with this country. Respondent is an alien who has had no previous significant voluntary connection with the United States, so these cases avail him not....

Not only are history and case law against respondent, but as pointed out in *Johnson v. Eisentrager,* 339 U.S. 763 (1950), the result of accepting his claim would have significant and deleterious consequences for the United States in conducting activities beyond its boundaries. The rule adopted by the Court of Appeals would apply not only to law enforcement operations abroad, but also to other foreign policy operations which might result in "searches or seizures." The United States frequently employs armed forces outside this country—over 200 times in our history—for the protection of American citizens or national security. Congressional Research Service, *Instances of Use of United States Armed Forces Abroad, 1798-1989* (E. Collier ed. 1989). Application of the Fourth Amendment to those circumstances could significantly disrupt the ability of the political branches to respond to foreign situations involving our national interest. Were respondent to prevail, aliens with no attachment to this country might well bring actions for damages to remedy claimed violations of the Fourth Amendment in foreign countries or in international waters. *See Bivens v. Six Unknown Federal Narcotics Agents,* 403 U.S. 388 (1971).... The Members of the Executive and Legislative Branches are sworn to uphold the Constitution, and they presumably desire to follow its commands. But the Court of Appeals' global view of its applicability would plunge them into a sea of uncertainty as to what might be reasonable in the way of searches and seizures conducted abroad. Indeed, the Court of Appeals held that absent exigent circumstances, United States agents could not effect a "search or seizure" for law enforcement purposes in a foreign country without first obtaining a warrant—which would be a dead letter outside the United States—from a magistrate in this country. Even if no warrant were required, American agents would have to articulate specific facts giving them probable cause to undertake a search or seizure if they wished to comply with the Fourth Amendment as conceived by the Court of Appeals....

For better or for worse, we live in a world of nation-states in which our Government must be able to "function effectively in the company of sovereign nations." *Perez v. Brownell,* 356 U.S. 44, 57 (1958). Some who violate our laws may live outside our borders under a regime quite different from that which obtains in this country. Situations threatening to important American interests may arise halfway around the globe, situations which in the view of the political branches of our Government require an American response with armed force. If there are to be restrictions on searches and seizures which occur incident to such American action, they must be imposed by the political branches through diplomatic understanding, treaty, or legislation.

The judgment of the Court of Appeals is accordingly

Reversed.

Justice KENNEDY, concurring. . . . I take it to be correct, as the plurality opinion in *Reid v. Covert* sets forth, that the Government may act only as the Constitution authorizes, whether the actions in question are foreign or domestic. *See* 354 U.S., at 6. But this principle is only a first step in resolving this case. The question before us then becomes what constitutional standards apply when the Government acts, in reference to an alien, within its sphere of foreign operations. . . . [Various cases], as well as *United States v. Curtiss-Wright Export Corp.*, 299 U.S. 304, 318 (1936), stand for the proposition that we must interpret constitutional protections in light of the undoubted power of the United States to take actions to assert its legitimate power and authority abroad. Justice Harlan made this observation in his opinion concurring in the judgment in *Reid v. Covert*:

> "I cannot agree with the suggestion that every provision of the Constitution must always be deemed automatically applicable to American citizens in every part of the world. For *Ross* and the *Insular Cases* do stand for an important proposition, one which seems to me a wise and necessary gloss on our Constitution. The proposition is, of course, not that the Constitution 'does not apply' overseas, but that there are provisions in the Constitution which do not *necessarily* apply in all circumstances in every foreign place. In other words, it seems to me that the basic teaching of *Ross* and the *Insular Cases* is that there is no rigid and abstract rule that Congress, as a condition precedent to exercising power over Americans overseas, must exercise it subject to all the guarantees of the Constitution, no matter what the conditions and considerations are that would make adherence to a specific guarantee altogether impracticable and anomalous." 354 U.S., at 74.

The conditions and considerations of this case would make adherence to the Fourth Amendment's warrant requirement impracticable and anomalous. . . . The absence of local judges or magistrates available to issue warrants, the differing and perhaps unascertainable conceptions of reasonableness and privacy that prevail abroad, and the need to cooperate with foreign officials all indicate that the Fourth Amendment's warrant requirement should not apply in Mexico as it does in this country. For this reason, in addition to the other persuasive justifications stated by the Court, I agree that no violation of the Fourth Amendment has occurred in the case before us. The rights of a citizen, as to whom the United States has continuing obligations, are not presented by this case.

I do not mean to imply, and the Court has not decided, that persons in the position of the respondent have no constitutional protection. The United States is prosecuting a foreign national in a court established under Article III, and all of the trial proceedings are governed by the Constitution. All would agree, for instance, that the dictates of the Due Process Clause of the Fifth Amendment protect the defendant. Indeed, as Justice Harlan put it, "the question of which specific safeguards . . . are appropriately to be applied in a particular context . . . can be reduced to the issue of what process is 'due' a defendant in the particular circumstances of a particular case." *Reid, supra*, at 75. Nothing approaching a violation of due process has occurred in this case.

[The opinion of Justice STEVENS, concurring in the judgment on the grounds that, although the Fourth Amendment applied, the search was reasonable, is omitted.]

Justice BRENNAN, with whom Justice MARSHALL joins, dissenting.... The Court today creates an antilogy: the Constitution authorizes our Government to enforce our criminal laws abroad, but when Government agents exercise this authority, the Fourth Amendment does not travel with them. This cannot be. At the very least, the Fourth Amendment is an unavoidable correlative of the Government's power to enforce the criminal law....

When we tell the world that we expect all people, wherever they may be, to abide by our laws, we cannot in the same breath tell the world that our law enforcement officers need not do the same. Because we cannot expect others to respect our laws until we respect our Constitution, I respectfully dissent.

Justice BLACKMUN, dissenting. I cannot accept the Court of Appeals' conclusion, echoed in some portions of Justice Brennan's dissent, that the Fourth Amendment governs every action by an American official that can be characterized as a search or seizure. American agents acting abroad generally do not purport to exercise sovereign authority over the foreign nationals with whom they come in contact. The relationship between these agents and foreign nationals is therefore fundamentally different from the relationship between United States officials and individuals residing within this country.

I am inclined to agree with Justice Brennan, however, that when a foreign national is held accountable for purported violations of United States criminal laws, he has effectively been treated as one of "the governed" and therefore is entitled to Fourth Amendment protections. Although the Government's exercise of *power* abroad does not ordinarily implicate the Fourth Amendment, the enforcement of domestic criminal law seems to me to be the paradigmatic exercise of sovereignty over those who are compelled to obey. In any event, as Justice Stevens notes, respondent was lawfully (though involuntarily) within this country at the time the search occurred. Under these circumstances I believe that respondent is entitled to invoke protections of the Fourth Amendment. I agree with the Government, however, that an American magistrate's lack of power to authorize a search abroad renders the Warrant Clause inapplicable to the search of a noncitizen's residence outside this country.

The Fourth Amendment nevertheless requires that the search be "reasonable." And when the purpose of a search is the procurement of evidence for a criminal prosecution, we have consistently held that the search, to be reasonable, must be based upon probable cause. Neither the District Court nor the Court of Appeals addressed the issue of probable cause, and I do not believe that a reliable determination could be made on the basis of the record before us. I therefore would vacate the judgment of the Court of Appeals and remand the case for further proceedings.

NOTES AND QUESTIONS

1. *Does the Constitution Follow the Flag?* At the beginning of his opinion for a plurality in *Reid v. Covert*, Justice Black famously declared that "[t]he United States is entirely a creature of the Constitution. Its power and authority have no other

source." 354 U.S. at 5-6. Given the context of the case, he was clearly referring to the extraterritorial authority of the federal government. This statement stands in sharp contrast to Justice Sutherland's opinion for the majority in *United States v. Curtiss-Wright Corp.*, 299 U.S. 304, 315-316 (1936), in which he remarked, "The broad statement that the federal government can exercise no powers except those specifically enumerated in the Constitution, and such implied powers as are necessary and proper to carry into effect the enumerated powers, is categorically true only in respect of our internal affairs."

Whatever the source of the foreign affairs power, both decisions recognize that the power is limited. *Reid* stated that the government "can only act in accordance with all the limitations imposed by the Constitution," 345 U.S. at 6, while *Curtiss-Wright* indicated that even its powers in international relations must be exercised "in subordination to the applicable provisions of the Constitution." 299 U.S. at 320. Such statements might suggest that the Bill of Rights is more of a structural limit on government power than a recital of individual protections. *See* Akhil Reed Amar, *The Bill of Rights as a Constitution*, 100 Yale L.J. 1131 (1991). Can these statements be squared with the *Verdugo-Urquidez* majority's declaration that not "every constitutional provision applies wherever the United States Government exercises its power"? *See generally* Kal Raustiala, *Does the Constitution Follow the Flag? The Evolution of Territoriality in American Law* (2009).

2. *Citizens vs. Aliens.* How did the citizenship of the defendants affect the outcomes in *Reid* and *Verdugo-Urquidez*? Chief Justice Rehnquist pointed out in *Verdugo-Urquidez* that aliens inside this country generally enjoy the same constitutional protections that U.S. citizens do. Can that equal treatment of citizens and aliens inside the United States be reconciled with his "textual exegesis" of the various Amendments — distinguishing between "persons" and "the people" — to make them apply differently to citizens and aliens abroad?

The majority in *Verdugo-Urquidez* indicated that in drafting the Fourth Amendment "it was never suggested that the provision was intended to restrain the actions of the Federal Government against aliens outside of the United States territory." 454 U.S. at 266. The Court also found no evidence that the Framers intended for the Amendment to constrain wartime military operations against enemies. Does it follow logically that the Framers therefore intended that the Fourth Amendment *not* apply to aliens abroad? Should we assume that they considered the matter at all? Can you think of any reason why the Framers might have wanted to guarantee freedom from unreasonable searches abroad to citizens but not aliens? *See generally* J. Andrew Kent, *A Textual and Historical Case Against a Global Constitution*, 95 Geo. L.J. 463, 465 (2007) (arguing, based on extensive analysis of the record, that "noncitizens outside the United States are to be protected only by diplomacy, treaties, the law of nations . . . , and nonconstitutional policy choices of the political branches").

3. *Sufficient Connection.* The *Verdugo-Urquidez* Court declared that the Fourth Amendment is inapplicable to aliens abroad who lack a "sufficient connection" to the United States. Can this limitation be found in the text of the Constitution?

What is a sufficient connection? The Court said only that Verdugo-Urquidez's connection was not sufficient to extend the protection of the Fourth Amendment to him, even though he was issued a green card in 1970 that he insisted was still valid, and even though the government claimed that he was engaged in trade (drug-trafficking) within the United States. Subsequent lower court decisions are inconsistent. *See, e.g., United States v. Defreitas,* 701 F. Supp. 2d 297 (E.D.N.Y. 2010) (alleged conspiracy to commit terrorist attack in the United States not a sufficient "voluntary connection"); *Martinez-Aguero v. Gonzalez,* 459 F.3d 618 (5th Cir. 2006) (regular and lawful entry into the United States sufficient). *See generally* Douglas I. Koff, *Post-Verdugo-Urquidez: The Sufficient Connection Test — Substantially Ambiguous, Substantially Unworkable,* 25 Colum. Hum. Rts. L. Rev. 435, 455-465 (1994). The resulting ambiguity makes it difficult for U.S. officials engaged in overseas surveillance of aliens to know how to proceed. The differentiation among aliens also means that disparate standards may apply to co-defendants engaged in the same conduct, suspected of the same crimes, and subjected to the same search. What kind of connection did Justice Blackmun, dissenting, say makes the Fourth Amendment applicable to Verdugo-Urquidez?

Should courts draw a bright line? If so, what should it be? *Compare* Randall K. Miller, *The Limits of U.S. International Law Enforcement After Verdugo-Urquidez: Resurrecting Rochin,* 58 U. Pitt. L. Rev. 867, 885 n.88 (1997) (drawing the line at the border, thus denying Fourth Amendment protections to all aliens searched abroad, regardless of their connection to the United States), *with* Koff, *supra,* at 485 (extending Fourth Amendment protections to all persons except nonresident enemy aliens searched incident to a military confrontation).

4. *Justice Harlan's "Practical Necessities."* Justice Harlan, concurring in *Reid,* argued that some "provisions of the Constitution . . . do not *necessarily* apply in all circumstances in every foreign place." 354 U.S. at 74 (emphasis in original). Whether they apply, he wrote, depends on the "particular circumstances of a particular case." *Id.* at 75. Justice Black emphatically disagreed, warning that it would be "very dangerous" to allow "the Bill of Rights and other constitutional protections against arbitrary government [to become] inoperative when they become inconvenient or when expediency dictates otherwise." *Id.* at 14.

Is Harlan's theory of conditional applicability based in the Constitution? If not, what is its source? Is it "very dangerous"? How is that theory reflected in Justice Kennedy's concurring opinion in *Verdugo-Urquidez?* Does it provide an answer to the majority's worry that application of the Fourth Amendment abroad would plunge government officials into a "sea of uncertainty"?

5. *Conditional Applicability of Verdugo-Urquidez?* The *Verdugo-Urquidez* majority stated that in *Johnson v. Eisentrager,* its 1950 habeas corpus case, "our rejection of extraterritorial application of the Fifth Amendment was emphatic." 494 U.S. at 269. But that rejection was also conditional. The 1950 Court noted that "[i]f the Fifth Amendment confers its rights on all the world . . . the same must be true of the companion civil-rights Amendments, for none of them is limited by its express terms, territorially or as to persons." 339 U.S. at 784. Whether at home or abroad, the Court then pointed out, the "disabilities this country lays upon the alien who becomes also an enemy are imposed temporarily as an incident of war and not as an incident of alienage." 494 U.S. at 272. The petitioners for a writ of habeas corpus in *Eisentrager* admittedly were German soldiers in a declared war. The defendant in *Verdugo-Urquidez* was not, of course, a wartime enemy alien.

In a 2008 case involving aliens held at Guantánamo as "enemy combatants," the Supreme Court, relying heavily on Harlan's practical necessities theory, indicated that the *Eisentrager* Court's refusal to extend the Fifth Amendment to aliens abroad was conditional in another way. *Boumediene v. Bush*, 553 U.S. 723 (2008) (*infra* p. 401). Justice Kennedy wrote the opinion for the majority, declaring that

> if the Government's reading of *Eisentrager* were correct, the opinion would have marked not only a change in, but a complete repudiation of, the *Insular Cases*' (and later *Reid*'s) functional approach to questions of extraterritoriality. We cannot accept the Government's view. Nothing in *Eisentrager* says that *de jure* sovereignty is or has ever been the only relevant consideration in determining the geographic reach of the Constitution or of habeas corpus. Were that the case, there would be considerable tension between *Eisentrager*, on the one hand, and the *Insular Cases* and *Reid*, on the other. Our cases need not be read to conflict in this manner. A constricted reading of *Eisentrager* overlooks what we see as a common thread uniting the *Insular Cases, Eisentrager*, and *Reid*: the idea that questions of extraterritoriality turn on objective factors and practical concerns, not formalism. [*Id.* at 726-727.]

So saying, the Court ruled that the Guantánamo prisoners could apply for a writ of habeas corpus, although it expressly withheld any opinion about their substantive rights. Justice Scalia, dissenting, warned that the decision paved the way for "the extraterritorial reach of other constitutional protections as well." *Id.* at 850.

Is *Verdugo-Urquidez* still good law after *Boumediene?* Can you make the argument that application of the Fourth Amendment to aliens abroad now requires consideration of the practical necessities of each case, as urged by Justices Harlan and Kennedy? How would such a requirement affect the day-to-day work of law enforcement agents abroad?

In re Terrorist Bombings of U.S. Embassies in East Africa (Fourth Amendment Challenges)

United States Court of Appeals, Second Circuit, 2008
552 F.3d 157

[Two other opinions in the same case were filed the same day, dealing with, respectively, the admissibility, sufficiency, and alleged withholding of evidence, and sentencing, 552 F.3d 93; and Fifth and Sixth Amendment challenges, 552 F.3d 177.]

JOSÉ A. CABRANES, Circuit Judge. Defendant-appellant Wadih El-Hage, a citizen of the United States, challenges his conviction in the United States District Court for the Southern District of New York (Leonard B. Sand, Judge) on numerous charges arising from his involvement in the August 7, 1998 bombings of the American Embassies in Nairobi, Kenya and Dar es Salaam, Tanzania . . . .

El-Hage contends that the District Court erred by (1) recognizing a foreign intelligence exception to the Fourth Amendment's warrant requirement, (2) concluding that the search of El-Hage's home and surveillance of his telephone lines qualified for inclusion in that exception . . . . Because we hold that the Fourth Amendment's requirement of reasonableness — and not the Warrant Clause — governs extraterritorial searches of U.S. citizens and that the searches challenged on this appeal were reasonable, we find no error in the District Court's denial of El-Hage's [motion to suppress illegally obtained evidence] . . . . El-Hage's challenge to his conviction is therefore without merit.

I. BACKGROUND

A. Factual Overview

American intelligence became aware of al Qaeda's presence in Kenya by mid-1996 and identified five telephone numbers used by suspected al Qaeda associates. *United States v. Bin Laden*, 126 F. Supp. 2d 264, 269 (S.D.N.Y. 2000). From August 1996 through August 1997, American intelligence officials monitored these telephone lines, including two El-Hage used: a phone line in the building where El-Hage lived and his cell phone. *See id.* The Attorney General of the United States then authorized intelligence operatives to target El-Hage in particular. *Id.* This authorization, first issued on April 4, 1997, was renewed in July 1997. *Id.* Working with Kenyan authorities, U.S. officials searched El-Hage's home in Nairobi on August 21, 1997, pursuant to a document shown to El-Hage's wife that was "identified as a Kenyan warrant authorizing a search for 'stolen property.'" *Id.* At the completion of the search, one of the Kenyan officers gave El-Hage's wife an inventory listing the items seized during the search. *Id.* El-Hage was not present during the search of his home. *Id.* It is uncontested that the agents did not apply for or obtain a warrant from a U.S. court. . . .

II. DISCUSSION . . .

B. The District Court's Denial of El-Hage's Motion to Suppress Evidence . . .

2. Extraterritorial Application of the Fourth Amendment

In order to determine whether El-Hage's suppression motion was properly denied by the District Court, we must first determine whether and to what extent the Fourth Amendment's safeguards apply to overseas searches involving U.S. citizens. In *United States v. Toscanino*, a case involving a Fourth Amendment challenge to overseas wiretapping of a non-U.S. citizen, we observed that it was "well settled" that "the Bill of Rights has extraterritorial application to the conduct abroad of federal agents directed against United States citizens." 500 F.2d 267, 280-81 (2d Cir. 1974); *see also United States v. Verdugo-Urquidez*, 494 U.S. 259, 283 n.7 (1990) (Brennan, J., dissenting) (recognizing "the rule, accepted by every Court of Appeals to have considered the question, that the Fourth Amendment applies to searches conducted by the United States Government against United States citizens abroad"). Nevertheless, we have not yet determined the specific question of the applicability of the Fourth Amendment's Warrant Clause to overseas searches. Faced with that question now, we hold that the Fourth Amendment's warrant requirement does not govern searches conducted abroad by U.S. agents; such searches of U.S. citizens need only satisfy the Fourth Amendment's requirement of reasonableness. . . .

. . . While never addressing the question directly, the Supreme Court provided some guidance on the issue in *United States v. Verdugo-Urquidez* . . . . [That guidance] and the following reasons weigh against imposing a warrant requirement on overseas searches.

First, there is nothing in our history or our precedents suggesting that U.S. officials must first obtain a warrant before conducting an overseas search. El-Hage has pointed to no authority — and we are aware of none — directly supporting the proposition that warrants are necessary for searches conducted abroad by U.S. law enforcement officers or local agents acting in collaboration with them; nor has El-Hage identified any instances in our history where a foreign search was conducted pursuant to an American search warrant. This dearth of authority is not surprising in light of the history of the Fourth Amendment and its Warrant Clause as well as the history of international affairs.... [Here the court reviews the *Verdugo-Urquidez* Court's analysis of the history of the drafting of the Fourth Amendment.] Accordingly, we agree with the Ninth Circuit's observation that "foreign searches have neither been historically subject to the warrant procedure, nor could they be as a practical matter." *United States v. Barona*, 56 F.3d 1087, 1092 n.1 (9th Cir. 1995).[7]

Second, nothing in the history of the foreign relations of the United States would require that U.S. officials obtain warrants from foreign magistrates before conducting searches overseas or, indeed, [lead us] to suppose that all other states have search and investigation rules akin to our own. As the Supreme Court explained in *Verdugo-Urquidez*:

> For better or for worse, we live in a world of nation-states in which our Government must be able to function effectively in the company of sovereign nations. Some who violate our laws may live outside our borders under a regime quite different from that which obtains in this country. Situations threatening to important American interests may arise halfway around the globe, situations which in the view of the political branches of our Government require an American response with armed force. If there are to be restrictions on searches and seizures which occur incident to such American action, they must be imposed by the political branches through diplomatic understanding, treaty, or legislation.

494 U.S. at 275 (internal citation, quotation marks, and brackets omitted). The American procedure of issuing search warrants on a showing of probable cause simply does not extend throughout the globe and, pursuant to the Supreme Court's instructions, the Constitution does not condition our government's investigative powers on the practices of foreign legal regimes "quite different from that which obtains in this country." *Id.*

Third, if U.S. judicial officers were to issue search warrants intended to have extraterritorial effect, such warrants would have dubious legal significance, if any, in a foreign nation. *Cf. The Schooner Exchange v. M'Faddon*, 11 U.S. 116, 135 (1812) ("The jurisdiction of the nation within its own territory is necessarily exclusive and absolute. It is susceptible of no limitation not imposed by itself."). As a District Court in this Circuit recently observed, "it takes little to imagine the diplomatic and legal complications that would arise if American government officials traveled to another

7. A U.S. citizen who is a target of a search by our government executed in a foreign country is not without constitutional protection — namely, the Fourth Amendment's guarantee of reasonableness which protects a citizen from unwarranted government intrusions. Indeed, in many instances, as appears to have been the case here, searches targeting U.S. citizens on foreign soil will be supported by probable cause.

The interest served by the warrant requirement in having a "neutral and detached magistrate" evaluate the reasonableness of a search is, in part, based on separation of powers concerns — namely, the need to interpose a judicial officer between the zealous police officer ferreting out crime and the subject of the search. These interests are lessened in the circumstances presented here for two reasons. First, a domestic judicial officer's ability to determine the reasonableness of a search is diminished where the search occurs on foreign soil. Second, the acknowledged wide discretion afforded the executive branch in foreign affairs ought to be respected in these circumstances.

A warrant serves a further purpose in limiting the scope of the search to places described with particularity or "the persons or things to be seized" in the warrant. U.S. Const. amend. IV. In the instant case, we are satisfied that the scope of the searches at issue was not unreasonable. *See* Parts II.B.3, *post.*

sovereign country and attempted to carry out a search of any kind, professing the authority to do so based on an American-issued search warrant." *United States v. Vilar*, No. 05-CR-621, 2007 WL 1075041, at *52 (S.D.N.Y. Apr. 4, 2007). We agree with that observation. A warrant issued by a U.S. court would neither empower a U.S. agent to conduct a search nor would it necessarily compel the intended target to comply. It would be a nullity, or in the words of the Supreme Court, "a dead letter." *Verdugo-Urquidez*, 494 U.S. at 274.

Fourth and finally, it is by no means clear that U.S. judicial officers could be authorized to issue warrants for overseas searches, *cf. Weinberg v. United States*, 126 F.2d 1004, 1006 (2d Cir. 1942) (statute authorizing district court to issue search warrants construed to limit authority to the court's territorial jurisdiction), although we need not resolve that issue here.

For these reasons, we hold that the Fourth Amendment's Warrant Clause has no extraterritorial application and that foreign searches of U.S. citizens conducted by U.S. agents are subject only to the Fourth Amendment's requirement of reasonableness.

The District Court's recognition of an exception to the warrant requirement for foreign intelligence searches finds support in the pre-FISA law of other circuits. *See United States v. Truong Dinh Hung*, 629 F.2d 908, 913 (4th Cir. 1980); *United States v. Buck*, 548 F.2d 871, 875 (9th Cir. 1977); *United States v. Butenko*, 494 F.2d 593, 605 (3d Cir. 1974); *United States v. Brown*, 484 F.2d 418, 426 (5th Cir. 1973). We decline to adopt this view, however, because the exception requires an inquiry into whether the "primary purpose" of the search is foreign intelligence collection. *See Bin Laden*, 126 F. Supp. 2d at 277. This distinction between a "primary purpose" and other purposes is inapt. As the U.S. Foreign Intelligence Surveillance Court of Review has explained:

> [The primary purpose] analysis, in our view, rested on a false premise and the line the court sought to draw was inherently unstable, unrealistic, and confusing. The false premise was the assertion that once the government moves to criminal prosecution, its "foreign policy concerns" recede. . . . [T]hat is simply not true as it relates to counterintelligence. In that field the government's primary purpose is to halt the espionage or terrorism efforts, and criminal prosecutions can be, and usually are, interrelated with other techniques used to frustrate a foreign power's efforts.

In re Sealed Case No. 02-001, 310 F.3d 717, 743 (Foreign Int. Surv. Ct. Rev. 2002). In addition, the purpose of the search has no bearing on the factors making a warrant requirement inapplicable to foreign searches—namely, (1) the complete absence of any precedent in our history for doing so, (2) the inadvisability of conditioning our government's surveillance on the practices of foreign states, (3) a U.S. warrant's lack of authority overseas, and (4) the absence of a mechanism for obtaining a U.S. warrant. Accordingly, we cannot endorse the view that the normal course is to obtain a warrant for overseas searches involving U.S. citizens unless the search is "primarily" targeting foreign powers.

3. The Kenyan Searches Were Reasonable and Therefore Did Not Violate the Fourth Amendment.

. . . First, El-Hage insists that his Nairobi home deserves special consideration in light of the home's status as "the most fundamental bastion of privacy protected by the Fourth Amendment." Second, he contends that the electronic surveillance was far broader than necessary because it encompassed "[m]any calls, if not the predominant amount, [that] were related solely to legitimate commercial purposes, and/or purely family and social matters."

To determine whether a search is reasonable under the Fourth Amendment, we examine the "totality of the circumstances" to balance "on the one hand, the degree to which it intrudes upon an individual's privacy and, on the other, the degree to which it is needed for the promotion of legitimate governmental interests." *Samson v. California*, 547 U.S. 843, 848 (2006) (quoting *United States v. Knights*, 534 U.S. 112, 118-19 (2001)) (internal quotation marks omitted)....

a. The Search of El-Hage's Home in Nairobi Was Reasonable....

Applying that test to the facts of this case, we first examine the extent to which the search of El-Hage's Nairobi home intruded upon his privacy. The intrusion was minimized by the fact that the search was not covert; indeed, U.S. agents searched El-Hage's home with the assistance of Kenyan authorities, pursuant to what was identified as a "Kenyan warrant authorizing [a search]." *Bin Laden*, 126 F. Supp. 2d at 269. The search occurred during the daytime, *id.* at 285, and in the presence of El-Hage's wife, *id.* at 269. At the conclusion of the search, an inventory listing the items seized during the search was prepared and given to El-Hage's wife. *Id.* at 269. In addition, the District Court found that "[t]he scope of the search was limited to those items which were believed to have foreign intelligence value[,] and retention and dissemination of the evidence acquired during the search were minimized." *Id.* at 285.

As described above, U.S. intelligence officers became aware of al Qaeda's presence in Kenya in the spring of 1996. *Id.* at 268-69. At about that time, they identified five telephone lines used by suspected al Qaeda associates, one of which was located in the same building as El-Hage's Nairobi home; another was a cellular phone used by El-Hage. *Id.* After these telephone lines had been monitored for several months, the Attorney General of the United States authorized surveillance specifically targeting El-Hage. *Id.* That authorization was renewed four months later, and, one month after that, U.S. agents searched El-Hage's home in Nairobi. *Id.* This sequence of events is indicative of a disciplined approach to gathering indisputably vital intelligence on the activities of a foreign terrorist organization. U.S. agents did not breach the privacy of El-Hage's home on a whim or on the basis of an unsubstantiated tip; rather, they monitored telephonic communications involving him for nearly a year and conducted surveillance of his activities for five months before concluding that it was necessary to search his home. In light of these findings of fact, which El-Hage has not contested as clearly erroneous, we conclude that the search, while undoubtedly intrusive on El-Hage's privacy, was restrained in execution and narrow in focus.

Balanced against this restrained and limited intrusion on El-Hage's privacy, we have the government's manifest need to investigate possible threats to national security. As the District Court noted, al Qaeda "declared a war of terrorism against all members of the United States military worldwide" in 1996 and later against American civilians. *Id.* at 269. The government had evidence establishing that El-Hage was working with al Qaeda in Kenya. *Id.* On the basis of these findings of fact, we agree with the District Court that, at the time of the search of El-Hage's home, the government had a powerful need to gather additional intelligence on al Qaeda's activities in Kenya, which it had linked to El-Hage.

Balancing the search's limited intrusion on El-Hage's privacy against the manifest need of the government to monitor the activities of al Qaeda, which had been connected to El-Hage through a year of surveillance, we hold that the search of El-Hage's Nairobi residence was reasonable under the Fourth Amendment.

b. The Surveillance of El-Hage's Kenyan Telephone Lines Was Also Reasonable.

El-Hage appears to challenge the reasonableness of the electronic surveillance of the Kenyan telephone lines on the grounds that (1) they were overbroad, encompassing calls made for commercial, family or social purposes and (2) the government failed to follow procedures to "minimize" surveillance. Indeed, pursuant to defense counsel's analysis, "as many as 25 percent of the calls were either made by, or to" a Nairobi businessman not alleged to have been associated with al Qaeda. El-Hage also criticizes the government for retaining transcripts of irrelevant calls — such as conversations between El-Hage and his wife about their children — despite the government's assurance to the District Court that the surveillance had been properly "minimized." *See United States v. Ruggiero*, 928 F.2d 1289, 1302 (2d Cir. 1991) ("[A]ny [electronic] interception 'shall be conducted in such a way as to minimize the interception of communications not otherwise subject to interception.'" (quoting 18 U.S.C. §2518(5))).

It cannot be denied that El-Hage suffered, while abroad, a significant invasion of privacy by virtue of the government's year-long surveillance of his telephonic communications. The Supreme Court has recognized that, like a physical search, electronic monitoring intrudes on "the innermost secrets of one's home or office" and that "[f]ew threats to liberty exist which are greater than that posed by the use of eavesdropping devices." *Berger v. New York*, 388 U.S. 41, 63 (1967); *cf. Katz v. United States*, 389 U.S. 347, 352-54 (1967). For its part, the government does not contradict El-Hage's claims that the surveillance was broad and loosely "minimized." Instead, the government sets forth a variety of reasons justifying the breadth of the surveillance. These justifications, regardless of their merit, do not lessen the intrusion El-Hage suffered while abroad, and we accord this intrusion substantial weight in our balancing analysis.

Turning to the government's interest, we encounter again the self-evident need to investigate threats to national security presented by foreign terrorist organizations. When U.S. intelligence learned that five telephone lines were being used by suspected al Qaeda operatives, the need to monitor communications traveling on those lines was paramount, and we are loath to discount — much less disparage — the government's decision to do so.

Our balancing of these compelling, and competing, interests turns on whether the scope of the intrusion here was justified by the government's surveillance needs. We conclude that it was, for at least the following four reasons.

First, complex, wide-ranging, and decentralized organizations, such as al Qaeda, warrant sustained and intense monitoring in order to understand their features and identify their members. *See In re Sealed Case No. 02-001*, 310 F.3d 717, 740-41 (Foreign Int. Surv. Ct. Rev. 2002) ("Less minimization in the acquisition stage may well be justified to the extent... 'the investigation is focusing on what is thought to be a widespread conspiracy[,] [where] more extensive surveillance may be justified in an attempt to determine the precise scope of the enterprise.'" (quoting *Scott v. United States*, 436 U.S. 128, 140 (1978) (alteration in original))).

Second, foreign intelligence gathering of the sort considered here must delve into the superficially mundane because it is not always readily apparent what information is relevant. *Cf. United States v. Rahman*, 861 F. Supp. 2d 247, 252-53 (S.D.N.Y. 1994) (recognizing the "argument that when the purpose of surveillance is to gather intelligence about international terrorism, greater flexibility in acquiring and storing information is necessary, because innocent-sounding conversations may later prove to be highly significant, and because individual items of information, not apparently significant when taken in isolation, may become highly significant when considered together over time").

Third, members of covert terrorist organizations, as with other sophisticated criminal enterprises, often communicate in code, or at least through ambiguous language. *See, e.g., United States v. Salameh*, 152 F.3d 88, 108 (2d Cir. 1998) ("Because Ajaj was in jail and his telephone calls were monitored, Ajaj and Yousef spoke in code when discussing the bomb plot."). Hence, more extensive and careful monitoring of these communications may be necessary.

Fourth, because the monitored conversations were conducted in foreign languages, the task of determining relevance and identifying coded language was further complicated.

Because the surveillance of suspected al Qaeda operatives must be sustained and thorough in order to be effective, we cannot conclude that the scope of the government's electronic surveillance was overbroad. While the intrusion on El-Hage's privacy was great, the need for the government to so intrude was even greater. Accordingly, the electronic surveillance, like the search of El-Hage's Nairobi residence, was reasonable under the Fourth Amendment.

In sum, because the searches at issue on this appeal were reasonable, they comport with the applicable requirement of the Fourth Amendment and, therefore, El-Hage's motion to suppress the evidence resulting from those searches was properly denied by the District Court.

III. CONCLUSION . . .

For these reasons, and for those set forth in *In re Terrorist Bombings of U.S. Embassies in East Africa*, [552 F.3d 177] (2d Cir. 2008), the judgment of conviction entered by the District Court against El-Hage is **AFFIRMED** in all respects except that the sentence is **VACATED**, and the case is **REMANDED** to the District Court for the sole purpose of resentencing El-Hage as directed in *In re Terrorist Bombings of U.S. Embassies in East Africa*, [552 F.3d 93] (2d Cir. 2008).

NOTES AND QUESTIONS

1. *Foreign Intelligence Exception?* The District Court in El-Hage's case found a foreign intelligence exception to the Fourth Amendment's warrant requirement. Why did the Court of Appeals not base its decision on such an exception? Isn't foreign intelligence collection always a "significant purpose" of any overseas surveillance of suspected terrorists, as that term was used in *In re Sealed Case, supra* p. 213?

2. *Warrants for Searches Abroad?* The court in *In re Terrorist Bombings* recalled its own declaration in an earlier case that it was "well settled" that "the Bill of Rights has extraterritorial application to the conduct abroad of federal agents directed against United States citizens." *United States v. Toscanino,* 500 F.2d 267, 280-281 (2d Cir. 1974). Yet its application of the Fourth Amendment, omitting the warrant requirement, reflects Justice Harlan's pragmatism more than Justice Black's absolutism in *Reid v. Covert.* What practical considerations prompted the court to suspend this requirement?

Do you think a judicial warrant should be required for a foreign search? If so, how would you address the practical concerns described by the court? *See* Justin M. Sandberg, Comment, *The Need for Warrants Authorizing Foreign Intelligence Searches of American Citizens Abroad: A Call for Formalism,* 69 U. Chi. L. Rev. 403 (2002) (urging judicial creation of warrant requirement); Carrie Truehart, Comment, *United States v. Bin Laden and the Foreign Intelligence Exception to the Warrant Requirement for Searches of "United States Persons" Abroad,* 82 B.U. L. Rev. 555 (2002) (urging statutory implementation of asserted constitutional warrant requirement).

The USA Patriot Act, enacted shortly after the September 11, 2001, terrorist attacks, authorizes a federal magistrate "in any district in which activities related to terrorism may have occurred" to issue a warrant for a search of property or a person "within or outside the district." Pub. L. No. 107-56, §219, 115 Stat. 272, 291 (2001). Should this provision be interpreted to require judicial authorization for searches abroad?

3. *Reasonableness of Searches Abroad.* The *In re Terrorist Bombings* court held that even though the warrant requirement is inapplicable, searches of U.S. citizens conducted abroad still must be reasonable. How does the court test for reasonableness? Was its test for the physical search of El-Hage's home different from that for the tap on his telephone? Can you derive a general test from its analysis?

In *United States v. Barona,* 56 F.3d 1087 (9th Cir. 1995), a divided court came up with different tests for reasonableness of warrantless surveillance of U.S. citizens abroad in a drug-smuggling investigation. The majority looked to good faith compliance with the law of the foreign country where the surveillance was conducted, absent conduct that shocks the conscience. *Id.* at 1103. In fact, the United States has entered into a growing number of bilateral mutual legal assistance treaties (MLATs), which independently require U.S. officials operating abroad to comply with the law of the foreign state. *See, e.g.,* Treaty Between the United States and the Government of Mexico on Mutual Legal Assistance in Criminal Matters, Dec. 9, 1987, U.S.-Mex., art. 12, 1987 U.S.T. LEXIS 208 ("A request for search, seizure, and delivery of any object acquired thereby to the requesting State shall be executed if it includes the information justifying such action *under the laws of the requested Party.*") (emphasis supplied). Such treaties confer no private rights, but their very existence may support the *Barona* court's incorporation of a compliance-with-foreign-law requirement into the Fourth Amendment's reasonableness standard. (They also create formal methods for U.S. law enforcement authorities to obtain help with investigations abroad.)

Judge Reinhardt dissented vigorously. Under the majority's reasoning, he argued, Americans are not only relegated to the "vagaries of foreign law," they are given

> *even less* protection than foreign law since ... the Constitution does not even require foreign officials to comply with their own law; all that is required is that American officials have a good faith belief that they did so.... [W]hen Americans enter Iraq, Iran, Singapore,

Kuwait, China, or other similarly inclined foreign lands, they can be treated by the United States government exactly the way those foreign nations treat their own citizens — at least for Fourth Amendment purposes. [56 F.3d at 1101.]

Instead, Judge Reinhardt argued, the government still must have probable cause for a foreign search, even if a warrant is impractical. On a motion to suppress, a court would make a post hoc determination of probable cause based on the government's explanation of why it initiated the search. "Because judicial scrutiny of the search will always take place *after* it has been conducted, there is no conceivable way that imposing such a requirement would hinder law enforcement efforts abroad — except to the extent that those efforts violate our own Constitution." *Id.* at 1102.

In determining the reasonableness of requiring a judicial warrant in domestic terrorism investigations, the Supreme Court in *United States v. United States District Court (Keith)*, 407 U.S. 297 (1972), *supra* p. 172, expressed concern that "unreviewed executive discretion may yield too readily to pressures to obtain incriminating evidence and overlook potential invasions of privacy and protected speech." 407 U.S. at 317. How did the *In re Terrorist Bombings* court address this concern? The *Barona* court?

4. *The Silver Platter Doctrine.* Suppose the Kenyan police *alone* had conducted the warrantless surveillance of El-Hage without probable cause and in flagrant violation of their own laws. Should a U.S. court suppress the fruits of such a foreign police surveillance? With two exceptions noted below, the courts have uniformly held no. *See, e.g., United States v. Defreitas*, 701 F. Supp. 2d 297, 304-305 (E.D.N.Y. 2010). Because the Bill of Rights does not protect Americans from the acts of foreign sovereigns and because applying the exclusionary rule to such acts would not deter them, such evidence can be turned over to U.S. law enforcement officials on a "silver platter" and admitted in U.S. criminal prosecutions. *See generally* Eric Bentley, *Toward an International Fourth Amendment: Rethinking Searches and Seizures After Verdugo-Urquidez*, 27 Vand. J. Transnat'l L. 329, 374-375 (1994); Robert L. King, *The International Silver Platter and the "Shocks the Conscience" Test: U.S. Law Enforcement Overseas*, 67 Wash. U. L.Q. 489, 511 (1989).

5. *The Joint Venture Exception.* Courts have recognized an exception to the silver platter doctrine for searches that are "joint ventures" between U.S. and foreign officials. Unfortunately, the courts have not reached a consensus on what constitutes a joint venture. Most agree that merely providing a tip to foreign police will not trigger the protections of the Fourth Amendment, and many hold that U.S. agents may request, be present during, or even participate in a search as long as they did not initiate and control it. *See* Bentley, *supra*, at 400 nn.297-314; Koff, *supra* p. 332, at 492 n.19. The *Restatement* declares, unhelpfully, that the exclusionary rule applies only when "the participation of United States law enforcement officers in the investigation, arrest, search, or interrogation through which the evidence was obtained was so substantial as to render the action that of the United States." *Restatement (Third) of Foreign Relations Law of the United States* §433(3) (1987). The Second Circuit has cut its own path by asking whether foreign police are acting as agents of the United States or whether U.S. law enforcement agents are evading our law by using foreign police. *See United States v. Maturo*, 982 F.2d 57, 61 (2d Cir. 1992). Apparently, U.S.

participation in the Kenyan search was so substantial that the government did not contest responsibility.

6. *The Shocks-the-Conscience Exception.* A second exception to the silver platter doctrine exists for conduct that shocks the judicial conscience. It was articulated in *United States v. Toscanino*, 500 F.2d 267 (2d Cir. 1974), a forcible abduction case, and applied in *United States v. Fernandez-Caro*, 677 F. Supp. 893 (S.D. Tex. 1987), in which Mexican authorities "threatened to kill [the defendant], beat him about the face and body, poured water through his nostrils while he was stripped, bound, and gagged, and applied electrical shocks to his wet body, among other things." *Id.* at 894. Exclusion of a forced confession is "not based on our Fourth Amendment jurisprudence," said the majority in *Barona*, "but rather on the recognition that we may employ our supervisory powers when absolutely necessary to preserve the integrity of the criminal justice system." 56 F.3d at 1091. Such evidence may be excluded even when obtained by foreign officials not acting as agents of the United States. *Maturo, supra*, 982 F.2d at 60-61.

The joint venture and shocks-the-conscience exceptions to the silver platter doctrine are explored further in Chapter 19, where we consider the U.S. practice of rendering terrorist suspects to a third country for interrogation (and likely harsh treatment) by that country's police or intelligence officials.

7. *Statutory Authorization of Collection Abroad.* Six years after *Verdugo*, Congress authorized elements of the intelligence community (excluding the military service branches) to collect information outside the United States against non-U.S. persons at the request of law enforcement agencies, "notwithstanding that the law enforcement agency intends to use the information collected for purposes of a law enforcement investigation or counterintelligence investigation." 50 U.S.C. §403-5a(a) (2006).

In the FISA Amendments Act of 2008, Pub. L. No. 110-261, 122 Stat. 2436 (adding 50 U.S.C. §§1881-1885c (Supp. III 2009)), Congress authorized the Attorney General and the Director of National Intelligence, acting jointly, to approve the programmatic targeting of "persons reasonably believed to be located outside the United States to acquire foreign intelligence information." 50 U.S.C. §1881a. The measure responds to a dramatic increase in communications using the Internet and fiber-optic cable and to greater concern about the threat of international terrorism after 9/11. Once the Foreign Intelligence Surveillance Court approves a program for collection, based on assurances that a "significant purpose" of any acquisition is to obtain foreign intelligence information and that the usual FISA minimization procedures will be followed, intelligence agencies like the NSA may monitor and collect electronic data—e-mail and telephone calls, for example—on a wholesale basis, without an individualized judicial order normally required for the targeting of any particular person. The collected data are then apparently mined, using key-word and pattern-recognition algorithms, for whatever information might be of interest. The FISA Amendments Act also authorized for the first time collections inside the United States of electronic data about U.S. persons located abroad, 50 U.S.C. §1881b, and collections abroad against U.S. persons. *Id.* §1881c. In these latter two instances the FISC must approve the collection on an individualized basis, applying generally the same standards that it does for domestic targets. The 2008 legislation is analyzed in greater detail *supra* pp. 232-245. *See* William C. Banks, *Programmatic Surveillance and FISA: Of Needles and Haystacks*, 88 Tex. L. Rev. 1633 (2010).

Applying the lessons learned in this chapter, do you think these two measures satisfy the requirements of the Fourth Amendment? Specifically, will information collected following the statutory procedures described here be admissible as evidence in a criminal trial? Will a targeted individual be successful in a *Bivens* claim asserting that the collection violated her privacy rights?

IV

Detaining Terrorist Suspects

Preventive Detention by Civil Authorities

12

The FBI began investigating the September 11 terrorist attacks (dubbed the PENTTBOM investigation) even before the last plane crashed.[1] But it was not only trying to identify, apprehend, and convict the perpetrators in the time-honored fashion of criminal investigations. Assistant Attorney General Michael Chertoff explained:

> In past terrorist investigations, you usually had a defined event and you're investigating it after the fact. That's not what we had here.... From the start, there was every reason to believe that there is more to come.... So we thought that we were getting information to prevent more attacks, which was even more important than trying any case that came out of the attacks. [*Quoted in* Toobin, *infra* n.1.]

The FBI immediately checked passenger manifests, airport terminal and parking garage videotapes, car rental agreements, credit card receipts, telephone records, and numerous other data sources to help identify the hijackers. It then extended its investigation to persons who lived or worked with the hijackers or otherwise crossed paths with them. Most of those interviewed were foreign nationals.

The FBI itself detained some or had state and local authorities detain them on suspicion of committing a variety of minor crimes. In addition, the FBI detained a few persons as "material witnesses." The Bureau asked the INS to detain many others who were in technical violation of their immigration status (out-of-status immigrants). In January 2002, the government initiated the "Absconder Apprehension Initiative" to locate and deport 6,000 Arabs and Muslims with outstanding deportation orders (among more than 300,000 foreign nationals subject to similar orders). By May 2003,

---

1. Background for this brief history was drawn from The Constitution Project, *Report on Post-9/11 Detentions* (June 2, 2004); Amnesty Int'l, *United States of America: Amnesty International's Concerns Regarding Post September 11 Detentions in the USA* (AMR 51/044/2002), Mar. 14, 2002; Jeffrey Rosen, *Holding Pattern,* New Republic, Dec. 10, 2001; *Hearing on DOJ Oversight: Preserving Our Freedom While Defending Against Terrorism, Before the S. Comm. on the Judiciary,* 107th Cong. (2001) (statements of John Ashcroft, Attorney General, and Michael Chertoff, Assistant Attorney General); Dan Eggen, *Many Held on Tenuous Ties to Sept. 11,* Wash. Post, Nov. 29, 2001; Department of Justice, *Attorney General Ashcroft Provides Total Number of Federal Criminal Charges and INS Detainees* (Nov. 27, 2001); Jeffrey Toobin, *Crackdown,* New Yorker, Nov. 5, 2001, at 56; Amy Goldstein, *A Deliberate Strategy of Disruption; Massive, Secretive Detention Effort Aimed Mainly at Preventing More Terror,* Wash. Post, Nov. 4, 2001.

another 2,747 noncitizens had been detained as part of a special registration program directed at Arabs and Muslims.

"We're clearly not standing on ceremony, and if there is a basis to hold them we're going to hold them," Chertoff said in reference to the detentions. *Id.* Attorney General John Ashcroft was even more blunt: "We have waged a deliberate campaign of arrest and detention to remove suspected terrorists who violate the law from our streets." *Hearing on DOJ Oversight, supra* n.1.

Within weeks of the 9/11 attacks, the media reported that more than 1,100 persons had been or were being detained by law enforcement authorities. Although the government declined to release a breakdown of this number, a newspaper investigation of 235 detainees whom it could identify indicated that the largest number were from Egypt, Saudi Arabia, and Pakistan. By the end of November, federal criminal charges had been brought against 104 individuals (most relating to possession of false identification or other fraud), of whom 55 were then in custody, while the INS had detained 548 persons for immigration violations.

This chapter explores the legality of detentions by civil authorities of suspected terrorists and persons with possible knowledge about terrorists in the wake of 9/11. We start in Part A by exploring the constitutional framework for arrest and detention, and the absence in U.S. law of a general statutory authority for preventive detention — detention to prevent a future harm or minimize the risk of harm. In Part B, we consider essentially pretextual criminal arrests and detention for "spitting on the sidewalk" — minor crimes — of persons suspected of some connection to or having information about terrorism. In Part C, we turn to the detention and removal of "high interest" (also called "special interest") immigrants, those suspected of being involved in terrorism or having information about terrorism. In Part D, we explore statutory authority for "investigatory detention" of "material witnesses" and how it was used or abused in the PENTTBOM investigation. Succeeding chapters deal with detention by the military before and after 9/11 of persons viewed as threatening national security.

A.   CONSTITUTIONAL BASIS FOR PREVENTIVE DETENTION

One scholar has described circumstances in which the government might want to detain a suspected terrorist but is not ready "to file charges in open court as required for a criminal prosecution."

> The government may have learned of the individual from a confidential or foreign-government source that it cannot publicly disclose, or from an ongoing investigation. It may lack sufficient evidence to convict beyond a reasonable doubt, but have substantial grounds to believe that the individual was actively engaged in armed conflict for al Qaeda. The disclosures necessary for a public trial might seriously compromise the military struggle against the Taliban and al Qaeda. U.S. law has no formal statutory mechanism by which the government could detain such a person. [David Cole, *Out of the Shadows: Preventive Detention, Suspected Terrorists, and War,* 97 Cal. L. Rev. 693 (2009).]

Civil detention of persons who have not been convicted of a crime has been found reasonable for criminal arrestees who are flight risks or dangers to the community, aliens facing deportation, the mentally ill when they pose a danger, sexual offenders even after they have completed their sentences, people with communicable diseases (see Chapter 23), and various persons (drunks, addicts, and the homeless) for their own protection. *See* Adam Klein & Benjamin Wittes, *Preventive Detention in American Theory and Practice*, 2 Harv. Nat'l Sec. J. 85 (2011) (exploring each kind of existing detention authority). Some scholars have therefore argued that the presumption against preventive detention is a "civic myth," *id.* at 87, and others agree that "[p]reventive detention is in fact an established part of U.S. law." Cole, *supra*, at 695.

The relevant law is largely framed by the Fourth Amendment, which insists on "[t]he right of the people to be secure in their persons . . . against unreasonable . . . seizures," and which provides that no arrest warrants shall issue except upon probable cause. Since there is no probable cause (as that term is used in the Fourth Amendment) to believe that a preventive detainee has committed or is committing a crime, the detention must be reasonable in the circumstances. If the detainee is a U.S. citizen, the "Non-Detention Act," 18 U.S.C. §4001(a) (2006), provides, "No citizen shall be imprisoned or otherwise detained by the United States except pursuant to an Act of Congress." Civil detention of U.S. citizens thus appears to require explicit statutory authority.

In fact, none of the preventive detentions described here was said to be based on a naked exercise of executive power. *See* Stephanie Cooper Blum, *Preventive Detention in the War on Terror: A Comparison of How the United States, Britain, and Israel Detain and Incapacitate Terrorist Suspects*, Homeland Sec. Aff., Oct. 2008, at 1 (contrasting Israel's and Britain's preventive detention laws enacted by Parliament and "not just executive usurpations of power").

Moreover, there are strong reasons to be skeptical of preventive detention.

> First, preventive detention rests on a prediction about future behavior, and no one can predict the future. Decision makers all too often fall back on stereotypes and prejudices as proxies for dangerousness. . . . Second, the risk of unnecessarily detaining innocent people is high, because decision makers are likely to err on the side of detention. . . . Third, preventive detention is inconsistent with basic notions of human autonomy and free will. We generally presume that individuals have a choice to conform their conduct to the law. Thus, we do not criminalize thought or intentions, but only actions. . . . Thus, . . . [w]hile it is not always explicitly rationalized in such terms, constitutional doctrine governing preventive detention is best understood as reflecting a strong presumption that the criminal process is the preferred means for addressing socially dangerous behavior. [Cole, *supra*, at 696-697.]

NOTES AND QUESTIONS

1. *The Constitutional Standards for Detention.* Generally, the Fourth Amendment requires that police, before making an arrest, have probable cause to believe that a suspect has committed a crime. However, they are allowed to stop a person when there is an "articulable suspicion that the person has been, is, or is about to be engaged in criminal activity." *United States v. Place*, 462 U.S. 696, 702 (1983). *See Terry v. Ohio*, 392 U.S. 1, 9 (1968). Nevertheless, "reasonable suspicion of criminal activity," short of probable cause, only "warrants a temporary seizure for the purpose of questioning limited to the purpose of the stop." *Florida v. Royer*, 460 U.S. 491, 498 (1983).

The INS may stop and detain persons for questioning about their citizenship upon a *reasonable suspicion* that they are illegal aliens. *United States v. Brignoni-Ponce*, 422 U.S. 873, 882-883 (1975). Congress has authorized the arrest and detention of such aliens pending a decision about their removal. 8 U.S.C. §1226 (2006). But the Supreme Court has ruled that after a decision to remove, continued indefinite detention would present a serious due process issue, at least as to aliens already in the country, who enjoy Fifth Amendment protection. *Zadvydas v. Davis*, 533 U.S. 678 (2001).

Zadvydas, however, did not involve an alien suspected of terrorism. The Court emphasized that the detention there at issue "d[id] not apply narrowly to 'a small segment of particularly dangerous individuals,' say suspected terrorists." *Id.* at 691 (quoting *Kansas v. Hendricks*, 521 U.S. 346, 368 (1997) (involving preventive detention of convicted sexual predator until he is no longer dangerous)). "Neither do we consider terrorism or other special circumstances," it added, "where special arguments might be made for forms of preventive detention and for heightened deference to the judgments of the political branches with respect to matters of national security." *Zadvydas, supra*, 533 U.S. at 696.

Is the Court suggesting a "national security exception" to the Fifth Amendment guarantee of due process? In the same vein, could there be such an exception to the Fourth Amendment's protection against unreasonable seizure? (Recall that, before enactment of the Foreign Intelligence Surveillance Act (FISA) in 1978, some lower courts found a national security exception to the warrant requirement for some kinds of searches and electronic surveillance.) How would you define such an exception? What limitations, if any, would the Fourth or Fifth Amendment place on the preventive detention of suspected alien terrorists in the United States?

2. *Due Process Requirements for Statutory Detention.* In *Denmore v. Hyung Joon Kim*, 538 U.S. 510 (2003), Justice Souter summarized the due process requirements for preventive detention as follows:

> [D]ue process requires a "special justification" for physical detention that "outweighs the individual's constitutionally protected interest in avoiding physical restraint" as well as "adequate procedural protections." "There must be a 'sufficiently compelling' governmental interest to justify such an action, usually a punitive interest in imprisoning the convicted criminal or a regulatory interest in forestalling danger to the community." The class of persons subject to confinement must be commensurately narrow and the duration of confinement limited accordingly.... Finally, procedural due process requires, at a minimum, that a detainee have the benefit of an impartial decisionmaker able to consider particular circumstances on the issue of necessity. [*Id.* at 557 (Souter, J., concurring in part and dissenting in part).]

Compare Klein & Wittes, *supra*, at 89 (arguing for "a relatively simply test" for counterterrorism detention: "Does America really need to do it, and if so, how can it do it in a fashion that minimizes erroneous incarcerations?"); Ian S. Speir, *Detention as Seizure: Deriving a Constitutional Infrastructure for U.S. Detention Policy* (Oct. 16, 2009), *available at* http://ssrn.com/abstract=1444928 (arguing that Fourth Amendment "constitutional infrastructure" consists of reasonableness, proportionality, and judicial review).

Applying similar standards in *United States v. Salerno*, 481 U.S. 739 (1987), a divided Supreme Court upheld the provisions of §3142(e) of the Bail Reform Act of 1984, 18 U.S.C. §§3141-3150, 3156 (2006 & Supp. III 2009), which authorized preventive detention (denial of bail) of arrestees on the grounds of flight risk or future dangerousness. The majority found that the Act authorized a "regulatory," rather than punitive, detention that was reasonably related to compelling government interests. The Court noted that regulatory interests in community safety can outweigh an individual's liberty interest, "[f]or example, in times of war and insurrection." *Salerno*, 481 U.S. at 748. But the Court emphasized that the Bail Reform Act authorized detention of an arrestee only when: (a) he has been arrested and indicted on probable cause of having committed one or more specified extremely dangerous offenses, (b) a court conducts a full-blown adversary hearing on the denial of bail, at which the arrestee is entitled to be represented by his own counsel, (c) the government persuades the court by clear and convincing evidence that no conditions of release can assure the presence of the arrestee or the safety of the community, and (d) the arrestee is given a right of appeal from the court's decision.

Did the post–September 11 detentions described above satisfy the Court's due process standards? Even if they did, does the Bail Reform Act occupy the field of preventive detention (leaving aside immigration detentions)?

3. *Cold War Detentions and the Non-Detention Act.* In 1950, Congress passed, over President Truman's veto, the Emergency Detention Act. Pub. L. No. 81-831, 64 Stat. 1019. Following a lengthy litany of the dangers of a "world communist movement," it authorized the President to declare an "Internal Security Emergency" in the event of an invasion, declaration of war by Congress, or "Insurrection within the United States in aid of a foreign enemy." *Id.* §102(a). In such an emergency, the President, acting through the Attorney General, was empowered to "apprehend and by order detain . . . each person as to whom there is reasonable ground to believe that such person probably will engage in, or probably will conspire with others to engage in, acts of espionage or of sabotage." *Id.* §103(a). The Justice Department constructed a half-dozen detention "camps" around the country pursuant to the Act, and during the Vietnam era it was suggested that war protests might be regarded for purposes of the Act as an "Insurrection within the United States in aid of a foreign enemy." *See* Alan M. Dershowitz, *The Role of Law During Times of Crisis: Would Liberty Be Suspended?*, in *Civil Disorder and Violence* 140-141 (Harry M. Cloor ed., 1972).

The Act was repealed unused by Pub. L. No. 92-129, 85 Stat. 348 (1971). The legislative history of the repealer cites First and Fifth Amendment violations and declares that "the concentration camp implications of the legislation render it abhorrent." H.R. Rep. No. 92-116, at 4 (1971), *reprinted in* 1971 U.S.C.C.A.N. 1438. But does the threat of further terrorist attacks after September 11, 2001, justify reenactment of the measure or one like it, permitting preventive detention of citizens and noncitizens alike as a counterterrorist measure? *See* Thomas F. Powers, *When to Hold 'Em*, Legal Aff. (Sept./Oct. 2004) (yes).

At the same time that it repealed the Emergency Detention Act, Congress adopted the Non-Detention Act, 18 U.S.C. §4001(a) (2006), set forth above. Does this Act apply to the detention of suspected terrorists? *See* Louis Fisher, *Detention of U.S. Citizens* (Cong. Res. Serv. RS22130), Apr. 28, 2005 (concluding from legislative history of the Non-Detention Act that Congress "intended the statutory language to restrict all detentions by the executive branch, not merely those by the Attorney General"). *See also Howe v. Smith*, 452 U.S. 473, 479 n.3 (1981) (the Act proscribes "detention of

any kind by the United States, absent a congressional grant of authority to detain")
(emphasis in original). Application of the Non-Detention Act was considered in
Hamdi v. Rumsfeld, 542 U.S. 507 (2004) (*infra* p. 445).

B.   "SPITTING ON THE SIDEWALK" — PRETEXTUAL(?) CRIMINAL DETENTION

Explaining the PENTTBOM detentions, Attorney General Ashcroft likened
some of the arrests for minor crimes to Attorney General Robert Kennedy's policy
of "arrest[ing] mobsters [for] spitting on the sidewalk if it would help in the battle
against organized crime." Goldstein, *supra* p. 347 n.1. Identity fraud, credit card
fraud, forgery, and larceny were among the criminal charges brought against some
of the detainees. Prosecution of suspected terrorists for crimes directly related to acts
of terrorism is addressed in Chapters 21 and 22.

NOTES AND QUESTIONS

1. *Pretextual?* A terror suspect who is arrested for "spitting on the sidewalk" has
been arrested on a pretext: the government's real reason for the arrest is that it
suspects he will commit a terrorist act or knows information about a planned future
act. Is a pretextual arrest lawful? The Supreme Court said yes in *Whren v. United States,*
517 U.S. 806, 813 (1996), as long as there is objective probable cause for the actual
arrest: "[s]ubjective intent [to detain the arrestee for terrorism-related conduct or
information] . . . does not make otherwise lawful conduct [the arrest] unlawful or
unconstitutional."

2. *The Practical Problem.* One difficulty with the spitting-on-the-sidewalk policy is
that persons charged with such minor offenses are usually released on bail. Indeed,
even *conviction* on such a charge often yields no term of imprisonment. Rising to the
occasion, however, one federal magistrate denied bail for an immigrant from El
Salvador who had allegedly helped some of the September 11 hijackers obtain
false identity papers (apparently without knowing that they were terrorists), explaining that "[o]ne of the unspoken issues today is, after the events of September 11, is it
going to be business as usual? I suspect not. The defendant, either wittingly or unwit-
tingly, certainly contributed [to the attacks]." T.R. Reid & Allen Lengel, *Scotland Yard
Says Hijackers May Have Trained in Britain; Terror Suspects Arrested in Spain, Holland,*
Wash. Post, Sept. 27, 2001.

3. *PENTTBOM Convictions.* In mid-2005, the Bush administration asserted that
terrorism investigations had resulted in charges against more than 400 suspects, half
of whom were convicted. A *Washington Post* study of the Department of Justice's own
list of prosecutions, however, indicated that only 39 of these convictions were for
crimes related to terrorism or national security. Dan Eggen & Julie Tate, *U.S. Campaign Produces Few Convictions on Terrorism Charges,* Wash. Post, June 12, 2005. The
majority were for minor crimes such as fraud, making false statements, and passport
violations, for which the median sentence was just 11 months.

The Justice Department defended the numbers by arguing that many defendants were prosecuted for such crimes in exchange for nonpublic information that was valuable in other terrorism probes. *Id.* The former Associate Attorney General who headed the Office of Legal Policy had an additional explanation: "You're talking about a violation of law that may or may not rise to the level of what might usually be called a federal case. But the calculation does not happen in isolation; you are not just talking about the [minor] crime itself, but the suspicion of terrorism. . . . That skews the calculation in favor of prosecution." *Id.* (quoting Viet D. Dinh). In other words, the *Post* paraphrased, "the primary strategy is to use 'prosecutorial discretion' to detain suspicious individuals by charging them with minor crimes." *Id.* Replied a defense attorney, "That's fine if you take it as a given that you have the devil here," citing Al Capone (who was eventually prosecuted for income tax evasion) as an example, but "[t]he problem is . . . that you're going to make mistakes and you're going to hurt innocent people." *Id.*

C. DETENTION OF "HIGH INTEREST" OR "SPECIAL INTEREST" IMMIGRANTS

The largest number of persons detained in the PENTTBOM investigation were immigrants arrested for visa violations. The Department of Justice adopted a "hold until cleared" policy for such detainees. An affidavit of an FBI agent opposing an immigrant detainee's bond request helps explain the process. Following the affidavit, a report of the Inspector General (IG) of the Department of Justice describes the "hold until cleared" policy and the conditions of detention for many of those detained. Detainees eventually challenged the policy and conditions of confinement in the case that follows the IG Report.

Affidavit of Michael E. Rolince, U.S. Dep't of Justice, Exec. Office for Immigration Review, Immigration Court

reprinted in Human Rights Watch, *Presumption of Guilt: Human Rights Abuses of Post-September 11 Detainees* app. B (Aug. 2002)
available at http://www.hrw.org/reports/2002/us911/USA0802.pdf

In Bond Proceedings
RE: ALI ABUBAKR ALI AL-MAQTARI

Pursuant to 28 U.S.C. §1736, I, Michael E. Rolince, hereby declare as follows:

1. I have been employed by the Federal Bureau of Investigation (FBI) since September 1974 as a Special Agent, and since August 1998, I have been the Section Chief of the Counterterrorism Division's International Terrorism Operations Section (ITOS) at FBI Headquarters in Washington D.C. . . .

3. As the ITOS Section Chief, I am personally involved in and have significant supervisory responsibilities for the nationwide FBI investigation initiated in response to a series of deadly terrorist attacks which occurred on September 11,

2001. As such, I am privy both to the broad scope of and to particular details from the investigation. . . .

5. The FBI has identified nineteen suspected hijackers, some of whose legal immigration status had expired. Based on a review of intelligence and other source information, the FBI has reason to believe that the hijackers were associated with al Qaeda, aka "the Base," an international network of terrorist cells controlled by Osama bin Laden, which has been formally designated by the Department of State as a foreign terrorist organization since October 8, 1999. Prior to the September 11, 2001 attacks, Osama bin Laden was being sought by the FBI in connection with the August 7, 1998 bombings of the United States embassies in Dar es Salaam, Tanzania, and Nairobi, Kenya, which killed over 200 individuals.

6. At the direction of President George W. Bush and Attorney General John Ashcroft, the FBI has initiated a nationwide investigation to identify and apprehend individuals involved in the hijackings and to prevent future acts of terrorism within the United States. To date the FBI has received or generated more than 250,000 leads from its web site, special hot line, a toll-free WATTS line, and in the FBI field offices, and additional leads are coming in every day. The investigation has yielded over 300 searches, and more than 100 court orders and 3000 subpoenas. There is still a great deal of information to be collected before the FBI will be in a position to determine the full scope of the terrorist conspiracy and to determine the full extent of damage that the terrorists intended to cause.

7. The FBI has come to believe that associates of the hijackers with connections to foreign terrorist organizations may still be in the United States. The tips received and the leads developed in our field offices have enabled the FBI to identify individuals who may have information about these associates, or, in fact, be among the participants. As explained below, the number of people of interest to the FBI is constantly changing as leads are followed and more information is obtained.

8. Information available to the FBI indicates a potential for additional terrorist incidents. As a result, the FBI has requested that all law enforcement agencies nationwide be on heightened alert. When there is threat information about a specific target, the FBI shares that information with appropriate state and local authorities. Several city and state officials have been contacted over the last few weeks to alert them to potential threats.

9. On September 23, 2001, the FBI issued a nationwide alert based on information indicating the possibility of attacks using crop-dusting aircraft. The FBI assesses the uses of this type of aircraft to distribute chemical or biological weapons of mass destruction as potential threats to Americans. At this point, there is no clear indication of the intended time or place of any such attack. The FBI has confirmed that Mohammed Atta, one of the suspected hijackers, was acquiring knowledge of crop-dusting aircraft prior to the attacks on September 11th. . . .

10. The investigation has also uncovered several individuals, including individuals who may have links to the hijackers, who fraudulently have obtained, or attempted to obtain, licenses to transport hazardous material.

11. In the context of this terrorism investigation, the FBI identified individuals whose activities warranted further inquiry. When such individuals were identified as aliens who were believed to have violated their immigration status, the FBI notified the Immigration and Naturalization Service (INS). The INS detained such aliens under the authority of the Immigration and Nationality Act. At this point, the FBI must consider the possibility that these aliens are somehow linked to, or may possess knowledge useful to the investigation of, the terrorist attacks on the World Trade Center and the Pentagon. The respondent, Ali Abubakr Ali Al-Maqtari (AL-MAQTARI), is one such individual.

12. As a result of a search previously described to the court, the FBI continues to download the hard drive of a computer. (The computer was found in a car belonging to Al-Maqtari's wife.) When interviewed by the FBI, Al-Maqtari said he had not used the laptop but purchased it used for $250 from a customer at the convenience store where he works. Al-Maqtari said that the customer obtained the computer from a third party. At present, the download of the hard drive is still running. Once this process is completed, the FBI will need several days to review the information obtained.

13. The FBI continues to actively pursue this investigation.

14. The business of counterterrorism intelligence gathering in the United States is akin to the construction of a mosaic. At this stage of the investigation, the FBI is gathering and processing thousands of bits and pieces of information that may seem innocuous at first glance. We must analyze all that information, however, to see if it can be fit into a picture that will reveal how the unseen whole operates. The significance of one item of information may frequently depend upon knowledge of many other items of information. What may seem trivial to some may appear of great moment to those within the FBI or the intelligence community who have a broader context within which to consider a questioned item or isolated piece of information. At the present stage of this vast investigation, the FBI is gathering and culling information that may corroborate or diminish our current suspicions of the individuals that have been detained. The Bureau is approaching that task with unprecedented resources and a nationwide urgency. In the meantime, the FBI has been unable to rule out the possibility that respondent is somehow linked to, or possesses knowledge of, the terrorist attacks on the World Trade Center and the Pentagon. To protect the public, the FBI must exhaust all avenues of investigation while ensuring that critical information does not evaporate pending further investigation.

I declare under penalty of perjury that the foregoing is true and correct. Executed on October 11, 2001, in Washington, D.C.

Michael E. Rolince
Federal Bureau of Investigation

Office of the Inspector General, Department of Justice, Press Release, The September 11 Detainees: A Review of the Treatment of Aliens Held on Immigration Charges in Connection with the Investigation of the September 11 Attacks

June 2, 2003, *available at* http://www.usdoj.gov/oig/special/0306/press.pdf

After the September 11 terrorist attacks, the Department of Justice (Department) used federal immigration laws to detain aliens in the United States who were suspected of having ties to the attacks or connections to terrorism, or who were encountered during the course of the Federal Bureau of Investigation's (FBI) investigation into the attacks. In the 11 months after the attacks, 762 aliens were detained in connection with the FBI terrorism investigation for various immigration offenses, including overstaying their visas and entering the country illegally.

The Office of the Inspector General (OIG) examined the treatment of these detainees, including their processing, bond decisions related to them, the timing of their removal from the United States or their release from custody, their access to counsel, and their conditions of confinement. . . .

Among the specific findings in the OIG's report:

Arrest, Charging & Assignment to a Detention Facility

The FBI in New York City made little attempt to distinguish between aliens who were subjects of the FBI terrorism investigation (called "PENTTBOM") and those encountered coincidentally to a PENTTBOM lead. The OIG report concluded that, even in the chaotic aftermath of the September 11 attacks, the FBI should have expended more effort attempting to distinguish between aliens who it actually suspected of having a connection to terrorism from [*sic*] those aliens who, while possibly guilty of violating federal immigration law, had no connection to terrorism but simply were encountered in connection with a PENTTBOM lead.

The INS did not consistently serve the September 11 detainees with notice of the charges under which they were being held within the INS's stated goal of 72 hours. The review found that some detainees did not receive these charging documents (called a "Notice to Appear" or NTA) for more than a month after being arrested. This delay affected the detainees' ability to understand why they were being held, obtain legal counsel, and request a bond hearing. . . .

The Department instituted a policy that all aliens in whom the FBI had an interest in connection with the PENTTBOM investigation required clearance by the FBI of any connection to terrorism before they could be removed or released. Although not communicated in writing, this "hold until cleared" policy was clearly understood and applied throughout the Department. The policy was based on the belief — which turned out to be erroneous — that the FBI's clearance process would proceed quickly. FBI agents responsible for clearance investigations often were assigned other duties and were not able to focus on the detainee cases. The result was that detainees remained in custody — many in extremely restrictive conditions of confinement — for weeks and months with no clearance investigations being conducted. The OIG review found that, instead of taking a few days as anticipated, the FBI clearance process took an average of 80 days, primarily because it was understaffed and not given sufficient priority by the FBI.

Bond and Removal Issues

The Department instituted a "no bond" policy for all September 11 detainees as part of its effort to keep the detainees confined until the FBI could complete its clearance investigations. The OIG review found that the INS raised concerns about this blanket "no bond" policy, particularly when it became clear that the FBI's clearance process was much slower than anticipated and the INS had little information in many individual cases on which to base its continued opposition to bond in immigration hearings. INS officials also were concerned about continuing to hold detainees while the FBI conducted clearance investigations where detainees had received a final removal or voluntary departure order. The OIG review found that the INS and the Department did not timely address conflicting interpretations of federal immigration law about detaining aliens with final orders of removal who wanted and were able to leave the country, but who had not been cleared by the FBI.

In January 2002, when the FBI brought the issue of the extent of the INS's detention authority to the Department's attention, the Department abruptly changed its position as to whether the INS should continue to hold aliens after they had received a final departure or removal order until the FBI had completed the clearance process. After this time, the Department allowed the INS to remove aliens with final orders without FBI clearance. In addition, in many cases the INS failed to review the detainees' custody determination as required by federal regulations.

The FBI's initial assessment of the September 11 detainees' possible connections to terrorism and the slow pace of the clearance process had significant ramifications on the detainees' conditions of confinement. Our review found that 84 September 11 detainees were housed at the MDC [Metropolitan Detention Center] in Brooklyn under highly restrictive conditions. These conditions included "lock down" for at least 23 hours per day; escort procedures that included a "4-man hold" with hand-cuffs, leg irons, and heavy chains any time the detainees were moved outside their cells; and a limit of one legal telephone call per week and one social call per month.

Among the OIG review's findings regarding the treatment of detainees held at the MDC and Passaic are:

Conditions of Confinement

BOP officials imposed a communications blackout for September 11 detainees immediately after the terrorist attacks that lasted several weeks. After the blackout period ended, the MDC's designation of the September 11 detainees as "Witness Security" inmates frustrated efforts by detainees' attorneys, families, and even law enforcement officials, to determine where the detainees were being held. We found that MDC staff frequently — and mistakenly — told people who inquired about a specific September 11 detainee that the detainee was not held at the facility when, in fact, the opposite was true.

The MDC's restrictive and inconsistent policies on telephone access for detainees prevented some detainees from obtaining legal counsel in a timely manner. Most of the September 11 detainees did not have legal representation prior to their detention at the MDC. Consequently, the policy developed by the MDC that permitted detainees one legal call per week — while complying with broad BOP national standards — severely limited the detainees' ability to obtain and consult with legal counsel. In addition, we found that in many instances MDC staff did not ask detainees if they wanted their one legal call each week. We also found that the list of pro bono attorneys provided to the detainees contained inaccurate and outdated information.

With regard to allegations of abuse at the MDC, the evidence indicates a pattern of physical and verbal abuse by some correctional officers at the MDC against some September 11 detainees, particularly during the first months after the attacks and during intake and movement of prisoners. Although the allegations of abuse have been declined for criminal prosecution, the OIG is continuing to investigate these matters administratively.

The OIG review found that certain conditions of confinement at the MDC were unduly harsh, such as subjecting the September 11 detainees to having two lights illuminated in their cells 24 hours a day for several months longer than necessary, even after electricians rewired the cellblock to allow the lights to be turned off individually. We also found that MDC staff failed to inform MDC detainees in a timely manner about the process for filing formal complaints about their treatment.

By contrast, the OIG review found that the detainees confined at Passaic had much different, and significantly less harsh, experiences than the MDC detainees. According to INS data, Passaic housed 400 September 11 detainees from the date of the terrorist attacks through May 30, 2002, the largest number of September 11 detainees held at any single U.S. detention facility. Passaic detainees housed in the general population were treated like "regular" INS detainees who also were held at the facility. Although we received some allegations of physical and verbal abuse, we did not find the evidence indicated a pattern of abuse at Passaic. However, the INS did not conduct sufficient and regular visits to Passaic to ensure the September 11 detainees' conditions of confinement were appropriate.

"The Justice Department faced enormous challenges as a result of the September 11 terrorist attacks, and its employees worked with dedication to meet these challenges," [Inspector General] Fine said. "The findings of our review should in no way diminish their work. However, while the chaotic situation and the uncertainties surrounding the detainees' connections to terrorism explain some of the problems we found in our review, they do not explain them all," Fine said. . . .

Iqbal v. Hasty

United States Court of Appeals, Second Circuit, 2007
490 F.3d 143
rev'd and remanded on other grounds, 129 S. Ct. 1937 (2009)

JON O. NEWMAN, Circuit Judge. . . .

[Javaid Iqbal is a Muslim Pakistani who was arrested by agents of the FBI and the Immigration and Naturalization Service on November 2, 2001, and charged with conspiracy to defraud and identity fraud. Following his arrest, he was detained in the MDC's (Metropolitan Detention Center in Brooklyn) general prison population until January 8, 2002, when he was removed from the general prison population and assigned to a special section of the MDC known as the Administrative Maximum Special Housing Unit ("ADMAX SHU"), where he remained until he was reassigned to the general prison population at the end of July 2002. He alleged that he was arrested and detained as a person "of high interest" solely because of his race, religion, and national origin, and not because of any involvement in terrorism. The complaint also alleged that Attorney General John Ashcroft and FBI Director Robert Mueller approved a policy of holding detainees "of high interest" in highly restrictive conditions until they were "cleared" by the FBI. Iqbal further alleged that he was kept in solitary confinement, mistreated in detention, handcuffed, shackled, beaten, and denied adequate food, and that the MDC staff called him, among other things, a "terrorist" and a "Muslim killer."

Iqbal pled guilty to non-terrorism charges, was sentenced, and eventually was removed to Pakistan. He brought this suit against his jailers, the Director of the FBI, and the Attorney General for damages based on violations of his constitutional and statutory rights as a result of the conditions of his confinement. Defendants moved to dismiss on grounds of qualified immunity. The lower court denied the motion, and this interlocutory appeal followed.] . . .

I. GENERAL PRINCIPLES OF QUALIFIED IMMUNITY . . .

. . . A defendant will be entitled to qualified immunity if either (1) his actions did not violate clearly established law or (2) it was objectively reasonable for him to believe that his actions did not violate clearly established law. . . .

. . . Several Defendants contend that even if the Plaintiff's complaint would survive a motion to dismiss in the face of a qualified immunity defense under normal circumstances, the post-9/11 context requires a different outcome. This argument is advanced on three fronts. First, some Defendants contend that the Government was entitled to take certain actions that might not have been lawful before 9/11 because the Government's interests assumed special weight in the post-9/11 context. Second, some Defendants contend that, even if the law was clearly established as to the existence of a right claimed to have been violated, it was not clearly established in the extraordinary circumstances of the 9/11 attack and its aftermath. Third, some Defendants contend that the post-9/11 context renders their actions objectively reasonable, an argument we do not reach in view of our disposition of their second contention.

We fully recognize the gravity of the situation that confronted investigative officials of the United States as a consequence of the 9/11 attack. We also recognize that some forms of governmental action are permitted in emergency situations that would exceed constitutional limits in normal times. *See Home Building & Loan Association v. Blaisdell,* 290 U.S. 398, 425-26 (1934) ("While emergency does not create power, emergency may furnish the occasion for the exercise of power."). But most of the rights that the Plaintiff contends were violated do not vary with surrounding circumstances, such as the right not to be subjected to needlessly harsh conditions of confinement, the right to be free from the use of excessive force, and the right not to be subjected to ethnic or religious discrimination. The strength of our system of constitutional rights derives from the steadfast protection of those rights in both normal and unusual times.

With some rights, for example, the right to be free from unreasonable searches, the existence of exigent circumstances might justify governmental action that would not otherwise be permitted. But, as we discuss below, the exigent circumstances of the post-9/11 context do not diminish the Plaintiff's right not to be needlessly harassed and mistreated in the confines of a prison cell by repeated strip and body-cavity searches. This and other rights, such as the right to be free from use of excessive force and not to be subjected to ethnic or religious discrimination, were all clearly established prior to 9/11, and they remained clearly established even in the aftermath of that horrific event. To whatever extent exigent circumstances might affect the lawfulness of the Defendants' actions or might have justified an objectively reasonable belief that their actions did not violate clearly established law, we consider the argument in connection with a particular claim.

With these general principles in mind, we turn to the Plaintiff's specific claims. . . .

III. CONDITIONS OF CONFINEMENT . . .

Because the Plaintiff was a pretrial detainee during his detention in the ADMAX SHU, his challenge to the conditions of his confinement arises from the substantive component of the Due Process Clause of the Fifth Amendment and not from the cruel and unusual punishment standards of the Eighth Amendment. *See Benjamin v. Fraser*, 343 F.3d 35, 49 (2d Cir. 2003). Pretrial detainees have not been convicted of a crime and thus "may not be punished in any manner — neither cruelly and unusually nor otherwise." *Id.* at 49-50. Courts considering challenges to confinement brought by pretrial detainees must first consider whether the circumstances of the particular confinement render the confinement punitive; since some restraint is necessary to confine a pretrial detainee, not all uncomfortable conditions or restrictions are necessarily punitive. *Id.* at 50. In *Bell v. Wolfish*, [441 U.S. 520 (1979)], the seminal case on the substantive due process claims of pretrial detainees, the Supreme Court recognized the following factors as relevant to the determination of whether a condition of confinement is punitive:

> "Whether the sanction involves an affirmative disability or restraint, whether it has historically been regarded as a punishment, whether it comes into play only on a finding of *scienter*, whether its operation will promote the traditional aims of punishment — retribution and deterrence, whether the behavior to which it applies is already a crime, whether an alternative purpose to which it may rationally be connected is assignable for it, and whether it appears excessive in relation to the alternative purpose assigned. . . ."

441 U.S. at 537-38 (quoting [*Kennedy v. Mendoza-Martinez*, 372 U.S. 144, 168-169 (1963)]). A court may infer that a condition of confinement is intended as punishment if it is not reasonably related to a legitimate government objective.

The complaint alleges, among other things, that MDC staff placed the Plaintiff in solitary confinement, deliberately subjected him to extreme hot and cold temperatures, shackled him every time he left his cell, and repeatedly subjected him to strip and body-cavity searches, and that these conditions were intended to be, and were in fact, punitive. Applying *Wolfish*, Judge Gleeson found these allegations sufficient to state a substantive due process claim, observing that whether the conditions were reasonably related to legitimate government objectives could not be determined on a motion to dismiss. . . .

The Plaintiff has alleged the purposeful infliction of restraints that were punitive in nature. Accordingly, the District Court need not have considered whether a Defendant was "deliberately indifferent" in inflicting the restraints or whether the restraints constituted cruel and unusual punishment. The right of pretrial detainees to be free from punitive restraints was clearly established at the time of the events in question, and no reasonable officer could have thought that he could punish a pretrial detainee by subjecting him to the practices and conditions alleged by the Plaintiff. . . .

VIII. RACIAL AND RELIGIOUS DISCRIMINATION

The Defendants argue that they are entitled to qualified immunity on the Plaintiff's First Amendment claim of religious discrimination and Fifth Amendment claim of racial or ethnic discrimination on three grounds: (1) the Plaintiff has failed to state a violation of clearly established rights, (2) the Plaintiff's allegations of discriminatory intent are too conclusory, and (3) the Plaintiff has not alleged the personal involvement of Ashcroft and Mueller.

The arguments of Ashcroft and Mueller challenging the sufficiency of the Plaintiff's race, ethnic, and religious discrimination claims misunderstand his complaint. They contend that his "complaint amounts to an objection that most of those persons determined to be of high interest to the 9/11 investigation were Muslim or from certain Arab countries," which they justify by pointing out that the 9/11 hijackers were Muslims from Arab countries. However, what the Plaintiff is alleging is that he was deemed to be "of high interest," and accordingly was kept in the ADMAX SHU under harsh conditions, solely because of his race, ethnicity, and religion. The Plaintiff also alleges that "Defendants specifically targeted [him] for mistreatment because of [his] race, religion, and national origin." These allegations are sufficient to state a claim of animus-based discrimination that any "reasonably competent officer" would understand to have been illegal under prior case law. *See Malley* [*v. Briggs*, 475 U.S. 335 (1986)], at 341. Accordingly, the Plaintiff's racial, ethnic, and religious discrimination claims cannot be dismissed on qualified immunity grounds at this stage of the litigation.

Hasty [former Warden of the MDC] also argues that the Plaintiff has failed to state a claim of discrimination. Citing *Reno v. American-Arab Anti-Discrimination Committee*, 525 U.S. 471 (1999) ("*AAADC*"), he argues that the Equal Protection Clause does not apply in the context of proceedings to remove illegal aliens and that the Government can permissibly deem nationals of a particular country to be a special threat. In *AAADC*, the Supreme Court concluded that a provision of the Illegal Immigration Reform and Immigrant Responsibility Act of 1996, 8 U.S.C. §1252(g), deprived the federal courts of jurisdiction to consider an illegal alien's selective enforcement challenge to deportation. *See* 525 U.S. at 487. The Court rejected the argument that it nevertheless had jurisdiction to consider an alien's constitutional arguments, holding that "an alien unlawfully in this country has no constitutional right to assert selective enforcement as a defense against his deportation," *see id.* at 488, even when the Government deports the alien "for the additional reason that it believes him to be a member of an organization that supports terrorist activity," *id.* at 492. *AAADC* affords the Defendants no relief. The Plaintiff is not challenging his deportation or even his arrest on criminal charges. Moreover, *AAADC* does not stand for the proposition that the Government may subject members of a particular race, ethnicity, or religion to more restrictive conditions of confinement than members of other races, ethnic backgrounds, or religions. . . .

The Plaintiff's allegations suffice to state claims of racial, ethnic, and religious discrimination. He alleges in particular that the FBI Defendants classified him "of high interest" solely because of his race, ethnic background, and religion and not because of any evidence of involvement in terrorism. He offers additional factual support for this allegation, stating that "within the New York area, all Arab Muslim men arrested on criminal or immigration charges while the FBI was following an investigative lead into the September 11th attacks — however unrelated the arrestee was to the investigation — were immediately classified as "of interest" to the post-September 11th investigation." We need not consider at this stage of the litigation whether these allegations are alone sufficient to state a clearly established constitutional violation under the circumstances presented because they are sufficient to state a violation when combined with the Plaintiff's allegation that, under the policy created and implemented by the Defendants, he was singled out for unnecessarily punitive conditions of confinement based on his racial, ethnic, and religious characteristics. . . .

CONCLUSION . . .

In sum, the serious allegations of gross mistreatment set forth in the complaint suffice, except as noted in this opinion, to defeat the Defendants' attempt to terminate the lawsuit at a preliminary stage, but, consistent with the important policies that justify the defense of qualified immunity, the defense may be reasserted in advance of trial after the carefully controlled and limited discovery that the District Court expects to supervise.

Affirmed in part, reversed in part, and remanded.

[Concurring opinion of JOSÉ A. CABRANES, J., omitted.]

Ashcroft v. Iqbal

United States Supreme Court, 2009
556 U.S. 662

Justice KENNEDY delivered the opinion of the Court. . . . Respondent's account of his prison ordeal could, if proved, demonstrate unconstitutional misconduct by some governmental actors. But the allegations and pleadings with respect to these actors are not before us here. This case instead turns on a narrower question: Did respondent, as the plaintiff in the District Court, plead factual matter that, if taken as true, states a claim that petitioners deprived him of his clearly established constitutional rights. We hold respondent's pleadings are insufficient. . . .

IV. . . .

[The Court applied the federal "plausibility pleading" standard first announced in *Bell Atlantic Corp. v. Twombly*, 550 U.S. 544 (2007) (asking whether the "well-pleaded" — non-conclusory — allegations of the complaint "plausibly" state a claim) to the claims that Attorney General Ashcroft and FBI Director Mueller adopted a policy of discriminatory detention and treatment in detention.]

The September 11 attacks were perpetrated by 19 Arab Muslim hijackers who counted themselves members in good standing of al Qaeda, an Islamic fundamentalist group. Al Qaeda was headed by another Arab Muslim — Osama bin Laden — and composed in large part of his Arab Muslim disciples. It should come as no surprise that a legitimate policy directing law enforcement to arrest and detain individuals because of their suspected link to the attacks would produce a disparate, incidental impact on Arab Muslims, even though the purpose of the policy was to target neither Arabs nor Muslims. On the facts respondent alleges the arrests Mueller oversaw were likely lawful and justified by his nondiscriminatory intent to detain aliens who were illegally present in the United States and who had potential connections to those who committed terrorist acts. As between that "obvious alternative explanation" for the arrests, and the purposeful, invidious discrimination respondent asks us to infer, discrimination is not a plausible conclusion.

But even if the complaint's well-pleaded facts give rise to a plausible inference that respondent's arrest was the result of unconstitutional discrimination, that inference alone would not entitle respondent to relief. It is important to recall that respondent's complaint challenges neither the constitutionality of his arrest nor his initial detention in the MDC. Respondent's constitutional claims against petitioners rest solely on their ostensible "policy of holding post-September-11th detainees" in the ADMAX SHU once they were categorized as "of high interest." To prevail on that theory, the complaint must contain facts plausibly showing that petitioners purposefully adopted a policy of classifying post-September-11 detainees as "of high interest" because of their race, religion, or national origin.

This the complaint fails to do. Though respondent alleges that various other defendants, who are not before us, may have labeled him a person of "of high interest" for impermissible reasons, his only factual allegation against petitioners accuses them of adopting a policy approving "restrictive conditions of confinement" for post-September-11 detainees until they were "'cleared' by the FBI." Accepting the truth of that allegation, the complaint does not show, or even intimate, that petitioners purposefully housed detainees in the ADMAX SHU due to their race, religion, or national origin. All it plausibly suggests is that the Nation's top law enforcement officers, in the aftermath of a devastating terrorist attack, sought to keep suspected terrorists in the most secure conditions available until the suspects could be cleared of terrorist activity. Respondent does not argue, nor can he, that such a motive would violate petitioners' constitutional obligations. He would need to allege more by way of factual content to "nudg[e]" his claim of purposeful discrimination "across the line from conceivable to plausible." *Twombly*, 550 U.S. at 570. . . .

It is important to note, however, that we express no opinion concerning the sufficiency of respondent's complaint against the defendants who are not before us. Respondent's account of his prison ordeal alleges serious official misconduct that we need not address here. Our decision is limited to the determination that respondent's complaint does not entitle him to relief from [Ashcroft and Mueller.] . . .

V

We hold that respondent's complaint fails to plead sufficient facts to state a claim for purposeful and unlawful discrimination against petitioners. The Court of Appeals should decide in the first instance whether to remand to the District Court so that respondent can seek leave to amend his deficient complaint.

The judgment of the Court of Appeals is reversed, and the case is remanded for further proceedings consistent with this opinion.

It is so ordered.

[The dissenting opinion of Justice SOUTER, with whom Justice STEVENS, Justice GINSBURG, and Justice BREYER join, and separate dissenting opinion of Justice BREYER are omitted.]

NOTES AND QUESTIONS

1. *Immigration Detentions.* Aliens who have been found either inadmissible or removable for terrorist activity are subject to mandatory detention under the immigration laws until their removal can be effected. 8 U.S.C. §§1182(a)(3)(B), 1227(a)(4)(B) (2006 & Supp. 2009). *See generally* 8 Charles Gordon et al., *Immigration Law and Procedure* §108.02[2][b] (2005). Most of the September 11 detainees, however, were not charged with terrorist activity. For example, as the Rolince affidavit, *supra* p. 353, ¶11, suggests, Al-Maqtari was arrested for a minor immigration violation: overstaying his visa. *See* Goldstein, *supra* p. 347 n.1.

Prolonged detention for minor "overstays" is highly unusual, according to immigration lawyers. *See* Pat Leisner, *Detention After Attacks Challenged*, AP Online, Dec. 1, 2001. INS regulations before the September 11 attacks provided that persons suspected of immigration violations could be held for 24 hours before being charged. After the attacks, the Department of Justice lengthened the period to 48 hours, then authorized the Attorney General to stay for ten days the release of immigrants granted bond in order to allow the government to appeal. *Review of Custody Determinations*, 66 Fed. Reg. 54,909 (Oct. 31, 2001). Asked to explain what standard he used for staying releases ordered by immigration judges, Attorney General Ashcroft testified that "if the attorney general develops an understanding that it's against the national interest and would in some way potentially violate or jeopardize the national security, then those orders are overruled." *Hearing on DOJ Oversight, supra* p. 347. *See also Continued Detention of Aliens Subject to Final Orders of Removal*, 66 Fed. Reg. 56,967 (Nov. 14, 2001) (providing for indefinite detention of suspected terrorist aliens after expiration of removal period); Jess Bravin, *U.S. Issues Rules to Indefinitely Detain Illegal Aliens Who Are Potentially Terrorists*, Wall St. J., Nov. 15, 2001. Authorities explained that immigration charges are a good way to detain persons suspected of terrorist connections when the government lacks sufficient evidence to prove the connections. *Id.*

After March 2003, the government filed immigration charges against more than 500 people who were under scrutiny in terrorism investigations. Mary Beth Sheridan, *Immigration Law as an Anti-Terrorism Tool*, Wash. Post, June 13, 2005. The *Washington Post* reported in 2005 that 768 suspects were "secretly processed on immigration charges" in the 9/11 investigations, and most were deported after being cleared of terrorism connections. *Id.*

2. *The Burden of Proof.* In the final analysis, the FBI affidavit sought to justify the detention of Al-Maqtari on the basis that the Bureau was "unable to rule out the possibility that respondent is somehow linked to, or possesses knowledge of,

the terrorist attacks on the World Trade Center and the Pentagon." Rolince Aff. ¶14. Is this rationale consistent with the Fourth Amendment? With a presumption of innocence? Or was the FBI suggesting a new standard or presumption for detentions intended to prevent terrorist attacks?

3. *Pretextual Immigration Detention.* In *Turkmen v. Ashcroft*, No. 02 CV 2307(JG), 2006 WL 1662663 (E.D.N.Y. June 14, 2006), *aff'd in part and vacated in part*, 589 F.3d 542 (2d Cir. 2009), a group of post-9/11 immigration detainees, all but one of whom were Muslims of Middle Eastern origin, challenged their detention in part on the Fourth Amendment ground that they were really detained for criminal investigation without probable cause. The court rejected the challenge:

> [P]laintiffs' entire detention was authorized by the post-removal period [immigration] detention statute. [8 U.S.C. §1231(a)(2).] That the government may have been motivated by a desire to keep terrorism suspects in jail pending further investigation does not alter the legality of the detention. It is well-established that the government's "[s]ubjective intent . . . does not make otherwise lawful conduct illegal or unconstitutional." *Whren v. United States*, 517 U.S. 806, 813 (1996) (internal quotation marks omitted). Accordingly, even accepting as true plaintiffs' allegations regarding defendants' motives, the detention of plaintiffs was authorized pursuant to the post-removal detention statute and thus did not violate the Fourth Amendment. [*Turkmen, supra*, 2006 WL 1662663, at *41.]

Can the statute invoked here have overcome limits imposed by the Fourth Amendment on government action?

4. *Profiling? Discriminatory Immigration Detention?* The overwhelming majority of the immigrants detained in the PENTTBOM investigation were Arab men. Moreover, they were detained for visa violations for which other nationalities were often released or bonded. "The approach is basically to target the Muslim and Arab community with a kind of zero-tolerance immigration policy. No other community is treated to zero-tolerance enforcement," said Professor David Cole. Sheridan, *supra.*

In *Turkmen*, the plaintiffs challenged the legality of selective enforcement of the immigration laws. On appeal, a two-judge panel (the third panel member, Judge Sotomayor, was elevated to the Supreme Court before the panel decision) found that there was no clearly established right to non-selective enforcement.

> [P]laintiffs point to no authority clearly establishing an equal protection right to be free of selective enforcement of the immigration laws based on national origin, race, or religion at the time of plaintiffs' detentions. *See Reno v. American-Arab Anti-Discrimination Comm.*, 525 U.S. 471, 490-91, (1999) ("What will be involved in deportation cases is not merely the disclosure of normal domestic law enforcement priorities and techniques, but often the disclosure of foreign-policy objectives and (as in this case) foreign-intelligence products and techniques. The Executive should not have to disclose its 'real' reasons for deeming nationals of a particular country a special threat — or indeed for simply wishing to antagonize a particular foreign country by focusing on that country's nationals — and even if it did disclose them a court would be ill equipped to determine their authenticity and utterly unable to assess their adequacy."); *see also Zadvydas*, 533 U.S. at 696 ("terrorism" might warrant "special arguments" for "heightened deference to the judgments of the political branches with respect to matters of national

security"); *Matthews v. Diaz*, 426 U.S. 67, 81-82 (1976) ("The reasons that preclude judicial review of political questions also dictate a narrow standard of review of decisions made by the Congress or the President in the area of immigration and naturalization."). [*Turkmen v. Ashcroft*, 589 F.3d 542, 550 (2d Cir. 2009).]

Is this two-judge panel's decision consistent with the panel decision in *Iqbal?* After the Supreme Court reversed and remanded *Iqbal*, what discrimination theory should the lower court apply to plaintiffs' remaining claims?

5. *The USA Patriot Act Preventive Detention Provision.* Immediately after the 9/11 attacks, Attorney General Ashcroft asked Congress for authority to hold suspected alien terrorists indefinitely. Bravin, *supra.* Would such legislation be constitutional? Congress rebuffed this request, providing instead in the USA Patriot Act that the INS could hold immigrants for up to seven days before charging them and then hold them while immigration proceedings were pending if the Attorney General certified, at least every six months, that their release would threaten national security. Pub. L. No. 107-56, §412, 115 Stat. 272, 350-351 (2001). How, if at all, might you argue that this legislation affected the legality of subsequent immigration detentions in the PENTTBOM investigation?

6. *The Ethics of Immigration Bond Hearings.* As the OIG report suggests, immigration laws, like the Bail Reform Act, authorize immigration judges to deny bond for a detained immigrant if the government provides evidence of flight risk or dangerousness. The FBI, however, provided no information to sustain such determinations in many cases. Nevertheless, INS lawyers were apparently ordered to argue the "no bond" position in court without any evidence, using "boilerplate" language like that in the Rolince affidavit. *See* Office of the Inspector Gen., U.S. Dep't of Justice, *The September 11 Detainees: A Review of the Treatment of Aliens Held on Immigration Charges in Connection with the Investigation of the September 11 Attacks* 78-80 (Apr. 2003), *available at* http://www.justice.gov/oig/special/0306/full.pdf. Was this ethical? *See id.* at 79, 81. In some cases, the alien succeeded in obtaining a bond order and in posting bond, but the INS, without appealing the order, continued to hold him anyway. Was this lawful? *See id.* at 87 (reporting that one INS official admitted not knowing what to tell the immigrant's lawyer, "because I cannot bring myself to say that the INS no longer feels compelled to obey the law"). How far may a government lawyer go in defending preventive detention if she is instructed that it is essential to a terrorism investigation?

7. *The Length of Immigration Detentions.* In *Denmore v. Hyung Joon Kim*, 538 U.S. 510 (2003), the Supreme Court revisited the issue of immigration detention, this time considering a statutory provision for mandatory detention of criminal aliens pending their removal hearings. Admitting that individualized bond hearings might be feasible, the majority nevertheless concluded that "when the Government deals with deportable aliens, the Due Process Clause does not require it to employ the least burdensome means to accomplish its goal." *Id.* at 528. It therefore upheld the mandatory detention law but emphasized that such detentions pending removal were for less than 90 days in the majority of cases. Joining in the opinion, Justice Kennedy noted that if the removal proceedings were unreasonably delayed, "it could become necessary then to inquire whether the detention is not to facilitate

deportation, or to protect against risk of flight or dangerousness, but to incarcerate for other reasons." *Id.* at 532-533 (Kennedy, J., concurring). How would the post–September 11 immigration detentions described in the OIG report fare by these standards?

8. *Rights of Detainees.* Ordinarily, immigrant detainees have a due process right to counsel at their own expense. *See generally* Gordon, *supra*, §108.04[2][b]. The Department of Justice said it afforded the September 11 detainees that right, although some detainees reportedly found it difficult to exercise it. *See, e.g., Hearing on DOJ Oversight, supra* p. 347 n.1 (questions by Senator Feingold to Attorney General Ashcroft); Amnesty Int'l, *supra* p. 347 n.1, at 4-6 (reporting that many detainees were effectively denied access to a lawyer for substantial periods). Shortly after publication of the OIG report, a divided panel of the D.C. Circuit Court of Appeals found that various public interest groups had no right under the Freedom of Information Act or the First Amendment to assorted information about the post–September 11 detentions, which they sought in part to ascertain the legality of the detentions and conditions of confinement. *Center for Nat'l Sec. Studies v. United States Dep't of Justice,* 331 F.3d 918 (D.C. Cir. 2003), *cert. denied,* 540 U.S. 1104 (2004). Based presumably on the government's representations, a majority of the panel assumed that the immigrant detainees "have had access to counsel, and the INS has provided detainees with lists of attorneys willing to represent them. . . . They have also been free to disclose their names to the public." *Id.* at 921. In light of the OIG report, were these assumptions warranted? *See* The Constitution Project, *Recommendations for Reforming our Immigration Detention System and Promoting Access to Counsel in Immigration Proceedings* 2 (2009) (recommending improved access for immigrants in detention because "the laws governing removal are complex and may prove overwhelming for individuals with little or no knowledge of English, especially when held far from their families and other support networks.").

9. *International Legal Rights of Alien Detainees.* Detainees also have rights under international law. The Vienna Convention on Consular Relations, Apr. 24, 1963, 21 U.S.T. 77, 596 U.N.T.S. 261, which the United States has ratified, gives a foreign arrestee the right to have his government notified of his arrest. *Id.* art. 361(b). *See Sanchez-Llamas v. Oregon,* 548 U.S. 331 (2006) (assuming, without deciding, that the Convention grants individuals enforceable rights, violations will not be enforced by applying an exclusionary rule, and enforceability is conditioned on compliance with state procedural rules). What purpose do you think this right serves? State law enforcement authorities have notoriously disregarded this right, *see* Sean D. Murphy, *United States Practice in International Law 1999-2000,* at 39 & n.1 (2002), despite the primacy of the Convention under the Supremacy Clause. Apart from the Supremacy Clause, can you think of any policy reason why the United States should honor the Convention's notification requirement?

The International Covenant on Civil and Political Rights art. 9, Dec. 16, 1966, 999 U.N.T.S. 171, ratified by the United States in 1992, states that "[n]o one shall be subjected to arbitrary arrest or detention," and that "[a]nyone who is deprived of his liberty by arrest or detention shall be entitled to take proceedings before a court, in order that that court may decide without delay on the lawfulness of his detention." Were these provisions violated by the PENTTBOM detentions?

D.   MATERIAL WITNESS DETENTIONS

The material witness statute, 18 U.S.C. §3144 (2006), provides as follows:

> If it appears from an affidavit filed by a party that the testimony of a person is material in a criminal proceeding, and if it is shown that it may become impracticable to secure the presence of the person by subpoena, a judicial officer may order the arrest of the person and treat the person in accordance with the provisions of section 3142 of this title [governing release on bond and requiring a judicial hearing]. No material witness may be detained because of inability to comply with any condition of release if the testimony of such witness can adequately be secured by deposition, and if further detention is not necessary to prevent a failure of justice. Release of a material witness may be delayed for a reasonable period of time until the deposition of the witness can be taken pursuant to the Federal Rules of Criminal Procedure.

The statute apparently was first used in a terrorism investigation to detain Terry Nichols, who was eventually convicted in connection with the Oklahoma City bombing. *See United States v. McVeigh,* 940 F. Supp. 1541, 1562 (D. Colo. 1996) (finding that Nichols's renunciation of U.S. citizenship and his association with Timothy McVeigh sufficiently showed probable cause to believe that it "may become impracticable" to rely on a subpoena to secure his testimony). After 9/11, it was used for the first time on a broader scale to detain persons suspected of having a connection with or information about terrorism. Although the government has not disclosed exactly how many persons it held as material witnesses in the PENTTBOM and subsequent counterterrorist investigations, Human Rights Watch reported that its research identified 70 such individuals as of June 2005. Human Rights Watch, *Witness to Abuse: Human Rights Abuses Under the Material Witness Law Since September 11,* 17 Hum. Rts. Watch 1 (June 2005). The plaintiff in the following case may be typical.

Attorney General

Ashcroft v. al-Kidd

United States Supreme Court, 2011
131 S. Ct. 2074

[Abdullah al-Kidd was born in Kansas and converted to Islam while attending the University of Idaho. In the spring of 2003, al-Kidd was arrested at the airport on "a material witness warrant" as he prepared to fly to Saudi Arabia to study Arabic and Islamic law on a scholarship. The warrant had been issued on the strength of an FBI affidavit asserting that al-Kidd was believed to have information crucial to the criminal prosecution of Sami Omar Al-Hussayen for visa fraud and false statements. Al-Kidd was handcuffed, interrogated, and then detained for 16 days, during which he was strip-searched on multiple occasions, handcuffed and shackled, confined in a high-security unit, and allowed to leave his continuously lit cell for only one to two hours each day.

He was released under supervision after he surrendered his passport. These conditions were only lifted 15 months later, after Al-Hussayen's trial was completed. (Al-Hussayen, a suspected webmaster of an allegedly jihadist Web site, was not convicted of any charges against him but was deported to Saudi Arabia for visa violations.) Al-Kidd was never called as a witness, and no evidence of any criminal activity by him was ever discovered. He was fired from his job, separated from his wife, deprived of his scholarship for study in Saudi Arabia, and unable afterward to find steady employment.

Al-Kidd then sued Attorney General Ashcroft and others for injuries resulting from the alleged misuse of material witness detention and for the conditions of his confinement. After the district court denied the defendants' motion to dismiss, they appealed. A divided panel of the United States Court of Appeals for the Ninth Circuit affirmed, holding that the Fourth Amendment prohibits pretextual arrests absent probable cause of criminal wrongdoing, and that Ashcroft could not claim qualified or absolute immunity. A divided court then denied rehearing en banc, with eight judges voting to rehear the case. Defendants then petitioned for certiorari, and the Supreme Court granted their petition.]

Justice SCALIA delivered the opinion of the Court. . . .

II

Qualified immunity shields federal and state officials from money damages unless a plaintiff pleads facts showing (1) that the official violated a statutory or constitutional right, and (2) that the right was "clearly established" at the time of the challenged conduct. *Harlow v. Fitzgerald*, 457 U.S. 800, 818 (1982). . . . In this case, the Court of Appeals' analysis at both steps of the qualified-immunity inquiry needs correction.

A

The Fourth Amendment protects "[t]he right of the people to be secure in their persons, houses, papers, and effects, against unreasonable searches and seizures." An arrest, of course, qualifies as a "seizure" of a "person" under this provision, *Dunaway v. New York*, 442 U.S. 200, 207-208 (1979), and so must be reasonable under the circumstances. Al-Kidd does not assert that Government officials would have acted unreasonably if they had used a material-witness warrant to arrest him for the purpose of securing his testimony for trial. He contests, however (and the Court of Appeals here rejected), the reasonableness of using the warrant to detain him as a suspected criminal.

Fourth Amendment reasonableness "is predominantly an objective inquiry." [*Indianapolis v. Edmond*, 531 U.S. 32, 47 (2000).] We ask whether "the circumstances, viewed objectively, justify [the challenged] action." *Scott v. United States*, 436 U.S. 128, 138 (1978). If so, that action was reasonable "*whatever* the subjective intent" motivating the relevant officials. *Whren v. United States*, 517 U.S. 806, 814 (1996). This approach recognizes that the Fourth Amendment regulates conduct rather than thoughts, *Bond v. United States*, 529 U.S. 334, 338, n.2 (2000); and it promotes even-handed, uniform enforcement of the law, *Devenpeck v. Alford*, 543 U.S. 146, 153-154 (2004).

Two "limited exception[s]" to this rule are our special-needs and administrative-search cases, where "actual motivations" do matter. *United States v. Knights*, 534 U.S. 112, 122 (2001) (internal quotation marks omitted). A judicial warrant and probable cause are not needed where the search or seizure is justified by "special needs, beyond the normal need for law enforcement," such as the need to deter drug use in public schools, *Vernonia School Dist. 47J v. Acton*, 515 U.S. 646, 653 (1995) (internal quotation marks omitted), or the need to assure that railroad employees engaged in train operations are not under the influence of drugs or alcohol, *Skinner v. Railway Labor Executives' Assn.*, 489 U.S. 602 (1989); and where the search or seizure is in execution of an administrative warrant authorizing, for example, an inspection of fire-damaged premises to determine the cause, *Michigan v. Clifford*, 464 U.S. 287, 294 (1984) (plurality opinion), or an inspection of residential premises to assure compliance with a housing code, *Camara v. Municipal Court of City and County of San Francisco*, 387 U.S. 523, 535-538 (1967). But those exceptions do not apply where the officer's purpose is not to attend to the special needs or to the investigation for which the administrative inspection is justified. The Government seeks to justify the present arrest on the basis of a properly issued judicial warrant — so that the special-needs and administrative-inspection cases cannot be the basis for a purpose inquiry here.

Apart from those cases, we have almost uniformly rejected invitations to probe subjective intent. See *Brigham City v. Stuart*, 547 U.S. 398, 404 (2006). There is one category of exception, upon which the Court of Appeals principally relied. In *Edmond*, 531 U.S. 32, we held that the Fourth Amendment could not condone suspicionless vehicle checkpoints set up for the purpose of detecting illegal narcotics. Although we had previously approved vehicle checkpoints set up for the purpose of keeping off the road unlicensed drivers, *Delaware v. Prouse*, 440 U.S. 648, 663 (1979), or alcohol-impaired drivers, *Michigan Dept. of State Police v. Sitz*, 496 U.S. 444 (1990); and for the purpose of interdicting those who illegally cross the border, *United States v. Martinez-Fuerte*, 428 U.S. 543 (1976); we found the drug-detection purpose in *Edmond* invalidating because it was "ultimately indistinguishable from the general interest in crime control," 531 U.S., at 44. In the Court of Appeals' view, *Edmond* established that "'programmatic purpose' is relevant to Fourth Amendment analysis of programs of seizures without probable cause." 580 F.3d, at 968.

That was mistaken. It was not the absence of probable cause that triggered the invalidating-purpose inquiry in *Edmond*. To the contrary, *Edmond* explicitly said that it would approve checkpoint stops for "general crime control purposes" that were based upon merely "some quantum of individualized suspicion." 531 U.S., at 47. Purpose was relevant in *Edmond* because "programmatic purposes may be relevant to the validity of Fourth Amendment intrusions undertaken *pursuant to a general scheme without individualized suspicion*," *id.*, at 45-46 (emphasis added).

Needless to say, warrantless, "suspicionless intrusions pursuant to a general scheme," *id.*, at 47, are far removed from the facts of this case. A warrant issued by a neutral Magistrate Judge authorized al-Kidd's arrest. The affidavit accompanying the warrant application (as al-Kidd concedes) gave individualized reasons to believe that he was a material witness and that he would soon disappear. The existence of a judicial warrant based on individualized suspicion takes this case outside the domain of not only our special-needs and administrative-search cases, but of *Edmond* as well.

A warrant based on individualized suspicion in fact grants more protection against the malevolent and the incompetent than existed in most of our cases eschewing inquiries into intent. In *Whren* and *Devenpeck*, we declined to probe the motives behind seizures supported by probable cause but lacking a warrant approved by a detached magistrate. *Terry v. Ohio*, 392 U.S. 1, 21-22 (1968), and *Knights*, 534 U.S., at 121-122, applied an objective standard to warrantless searches justified by a lesser showing of reasonable suspicion. We review even some suspicionless searches for objective reasonableness. See *Bond*, 529 U.S., at 335-336, 338, n.2. If concerns about improper motives and pretext do not justify subjective inquiries in those less protective contexts, we see no reason to adopt that inquiry here.

Al-Kidd would read our cases more narrowly. He asserts that *Whren* establishes that we ignore subjective intent only when there exists "probable cause to believe that a violation of law has occurred," 517 U.S., at 811 — which was not the case here. That is a distortion of *Whren*. Our unanimous opinion held that we would not look behind an objectively reasonable traffic stop to determine whether racial profiling or a desire to investigate other potential crimes was the real motive. In the course of our analysis, we dismissed Whren's reliance on our inventory-search and administrative-inspection cases by explaining that those cases do not "endors[e] the principle that ulterior motives can invalidate police conduct that is justifiable on the basis of probable cause to believe that a violation of law has occurred," *id.*, at 811. But to say that ulterior motives do *not* invalidate a search that is legitimate because of probable cause to believe a crime has occurred is not to say that it *does* invalidate all searches that are legitimate for other reasons.

"[O]nly an undiscerning reader," *ibid.*, would think otherwise. We referred to probable cause to believe that a violation of law had occurred because that was the legitimating factor in the case at hand. But the analysis of our opinion swept broadly to reject inquiries into motive generally. See *id.*, at 812-815. We remarked that our special-needs and administrative-inspection cases are unusual in their concern for pretext, and do nothing more than "explain that the exemption from the need for probable cause (and warrant), which is accorded to searches made for the purpose of inventory or administrative regulation, is not accorded to searches that are *not* made for those purposes," *id.*, at 811-812. And our opinion emphasized that we had at that time (prior to *Edmond*) rejected every request to examine subjective intent outside the narrow context of special needs and administrative inspections. Thus, al-Kidd's approach adds an "only" to a sentence plucked from the *Whren* opinion, and then elevates that sentence (as so revised) over the remainder of the opinion, and over the consistent holdings of our other cases.

Because al-Kidd concedes that individualized suspicion supported the issuance of the material-witness arrest warrant; and does not assert that his arrest would have been unconstitutional absent the alleged pretextual use of the warrant; we find no Fourth Amendment violation.[3] Efficient and evenhanded application of the law demands that we look to whether the arrest is objectively justified, rather than to the motive of the arresting officer.

B

A Government official's conduct violates clearly established law when, at the time of the challenged conduct, "[t]he contours of [a] right [are] sufficiently clear" that every "reasonable official would have understood that what he is doing violates that

---

3. The concerns of Justices Ginsburg and Sotomayor about the validity of the warrant in this case are beside the point. The validity of the warrant is not our "opening assumption," it is the premise of al-Kidd's argument. Al-Kidd does not claim that Ashcroft is liable because the FBI agents failed to obtain a valid warrant. He takes the validity of the warrant as a given, and argues that his arrest nevertheless violated the Constitution because it was motivated by an illegitimate purpose. His separate Fourth Amendment and statutory claims against the FBI agents who sought the material-witness warrant, which are the focus of both concurrences, are not before us.

right." *Anderson v. Creighton*, 483 U.S. 635, 640 (1987). We do not require a case directly on point, but existing precedent must have placed the statutory or constitutional question beyond debate. See *ibid.*; *Malley v. Briggs*, 475 U.S. 335, 341 (1986). The constitutional question in this case falls far short of that threshold.

At the time of al-Kidd's arrest, not a single judicial opinion had held that pretext could render an objectively reasonable arrest pursuant to a material-witness warrant unconstitutional. . . .

The Court of Appeals also found clearly established law lurking in the broad "history and purposes of the Fourth Amendment." 580 F.3d, at 971. We have repeatedly told courts—and the Ninth Circuit in particular, see *Brosseau v. Haugen*, 543 U.S. 194, 198-199 (2004) (*per curiam*) — not to define clearly established law at a high level of generality. The general proposition, for example, that an unreasonable search or seizure violates the Fourth Amendment is of little help in determining whether the violative nature of particular conduct is clearly established.

The same is true of the Court of Appeals' broad historical assertions. The Fourth Amendment was a response to the English Crown's use of general warrants, which often allowed royal officials to search and seize whatever and whomever they pleased while investigating crimes or affronts to the Crown. According to the Court of Appeals, Ashcroft should have seen that a pretextual warrant similarly "gut[s] the substantive protections of the Fourth Amendmen[t]" and allows the State "to arrest upon the executive's mere suspicion." 580 F.3d, at 972.

Ashcroft must be forgiven for missing the parallel, which escapes us as well. The principal evil of the general warrant was addressed by the Fourth Amendment's particularity requirement which Ashcroft's alleged policy made no effort to evade. The warrant authorizing al-Kidd's arrest named al-Kidd and only al-Kidd. It might be argued, perhaps, that when, in response to the English abuses, the Fourth Amendment said that warrants could only issue "on probable cause" it meant only probable cause to suspect a violation of law, and not probable cause to believe that the individual named in the warrant was a material witness. But that would make *all* arrests pursuant to material-witness warrants unconstitutional, whether pretextual or not— and that is not the position taken by al-Kidd in this case. . . .

Qualified immunity gives government officials breathing room to make reasonable but mistaken judgments about open legal questions. When properly applied, it protects "all but the plainly incompetent or those who knowingly violate the law." *Malley*, 475 U.S., at 341. Ashcroft deserves neither label, not least because eight Court of Appeals judges agreed with his judgment in a case of first impression. He deserves qualified immunity even assuming—contrafactually—that his alleged detention policy violated the Fourth Amendment.

* * *

We hold that an objectively reasonable arrest and detention of a material witness pursuant to a validly obtained warrant cannot be challenged as unconstitutional on the basis of allegations that the arresting authority had an improper motive. Because Ashcroft did not violate clearly established law, we need not address the more difficult question whether he enjoys absolute immunity. The judgment of the Court of Appeals is reversed, and the case is remanded for further proceedings consistent with this opinion.

It is so ordered.

Justice KAGAN took no part in the consideration or decision of this case.

Justice KENNEDY, with whom Justice GINSBURG, Justice BREYER, and Justice SOTO-MAYOR join as to Part I, concurring. I join the opinion of the Court in full. In holding that the Attorney General could be liable for damages based on an unprecedented constitutional rule, the Court of Appeals for the Ninth Circuit disregarded the purposes of the doctrine of qualified immunity. This concurring opinion makes two additional observations.

I

The Court's holding is limited to the arguments presented by the parties and leaves unresolved whether the Government's use of the Material Witness Statute in this case was lawful. See *ante*, at ____ (noting that al-Kidd "does not assert that his arrest would have been unconstitutional absent the alleged pretextual use of the warrant"). Under the statute, a Magistrate Judge may issue a warrant to arrest someone as a material witness upon a showing by affidavit that "the testimony of a person is material in a criminal proceeding" and "that it may become impracticable to secure the presence of the person by subpoena." 18 U.S.C. §3144. The scope of the statute's lawful authorization is uncertain. For example, a law-abiding citizen might observe a crime during the days or weeks before a scheduled flight abroad. It is unclear whether those facts alone might allow police to obtain a material witness warrant on the ground that it "may become impracticable" to secure the person's presence by subpoena. *Ibid.* The question becomes more difficult if one further assumes the traveler would be willing to testify if asked; and more difficult still if one supposes that authorities delay obtaining or executing the warrant until the traveler has arrived at the airport. These possibilities resemble the facts in this case.

In considering these issues, it is important to bear in mind that the Material Witness Statute might not provide for the issuance of warrants within the meaning of the Fourth Amendment's Warrant Clause. The typical arrest warrant is based on probable cause that the arrestee has committed a crime; but that is not the standard for the issuance of warrants under the Material Witness Statute. See *ante*, at 11 (reserving the possibility that probable cause for purposes of the Fourth Amendment's Warrant Clause means "only probable cause to suspect a violation of law"). If material witness warrants do not qualify as "Warrants" under the Fourth Amendment, then material witness arrests might still be governed by the Fourth Amendment's separate reasonableness requirement for seizures of the person. Given the difficulty of these issues, the Court is correct to address only the legal theory put before it, without further exploring when material witness arrests might be consistent with statutory and constitutional requirements. . . .

Justice GINSBURG, with whom Justice BREYER and Justice SOTOMAYOR join, concurring in the judgment. Is a former U.S. Attorney General subject to a suit for damages on a claim that he instructed subordinates to use the Material Witness Statute as a pretext to detain terrorist suspects preventively? Given *Whren v. United States*, 517 U.S. 806 (1996), I agree with the Court that no "clearly established law" renders Ashcroft answerable in damages for the abuse of authority al-Kidd charged. But I join Justice Sotomayor in objecting to the Court's disposition of al-Kidd's Fourth Amendment claim on the merits; as she observes, *post*, at 1 (opinion concurring in judgment), that claim involves novel and trying questions that will "have no effect on the outcome of th[is] case." *Pearson v. Callahan*, 555 U.S. 223, 236-237 (2009).

In addressing al-Kidd's Fourth Amendment claim against Ashcroft, the Court assumes at the outset the existence of a *validly obtained* material witness warrant. That characterization is puzzling. See *post*, at 2 (opinion of Sotomayor, J.).[1] Is a warrant "validly obtained" when the affidavit on which it is based fails to inform the issuing Magistrate Judge that "the Government has no intention of using [al-Kidd as a witness] at [another's] trial," *post*, at 1, and does not disclose that al-Kidd had cooperated with FBI agents each of the several times they had asked to interview him . . . ?

Casting further doubt on the assumption that the warrant was validly obtained, the Magistrate Judge was not told that al-Kidd's parents, wife, and children were all citizens and residents of the United States. In addition, the affidavit misrepresented that al-Kidd was about to take a one-way flight to Saudi Arabia, with a first-class ticket costing approximately $5,000; in fact, al-Kidd had a round-trip, coach-class ticket that cost $1,700. Given these omissions and misrepresentations, there is strong cause to question the Court's opening assumption — a valid material-witness warrant — and equally strong reason to conclude that a merits determination was neither necessary nor proper.

I also agree with Justice Kennedy that al-Kidd's treatment presents serious questions, unaddressed by the Court, concerning "the [legality of] the Government's use of the Material Witness Statute in this case." In addition to the questions Justice Kennedy poses, and even if the initial material witness classification had been proper, what even arguably legitimate basis could there be for the harsh custodial conditions to which al-Kidd was subjected: Ostensibly held only to secure his testimony, al-Kidd was confined in three different detention centers during his 16 days' incarceration, kept in high-security cells lit 24 hours a day, strip-searched and subjected to body-cavity inspections on more than one occasion, and handcuffed and shackled about his wrists, legs, and waist. Cf. *Bell v. Wolfish*, 441 U.S. 520, 539, n.20 (1979) ("[L]oading a detainee with chains and shackles and throwing him in a dungeon may ensure his presence at trial and preserve the security of the institution. But it would be difficult to conceive of a situation where conditions so harsh, employed to achieve objectives that could be accomplished in so many alternative and less harsh methods, would not support a conclusion that the purpose for which they were imposed was to punish.").

However circumscribed al-Kidd's *Bivens* claim against Ashcroft may have been, see *Bivens v. Six Unknown Fed. Narcotics Agents*, 403 U.S. 388 (1971), his remaining claims against the FBI agents who apprehended him invite consideration of the issues Justice Kennedy identified. His challenges to the brutal conditions of his confinement have been settled. But his ordeal is a grim reminder of the need to install safeguards against disrespect for human dignity, constraints that will control officialdom even in perilous times.

Justice SOTOMAYOR, with whom Justice GINSBURG and Justice BREYER join, concurring in the judgment. I concur in the Court's judgment reversing the Court of Appeals because I agree with the majority's conclusion that Ashcroft did not violate clearly

---

1. Nowhere in al-Kidd's complaint is there any concession that the warrant gained by the FBI agents was validly obtained.

established law. I cannot join the majority's opinion, however, because it unnecessarily "resolve[s] [a] difficult and novel questio[n] of constitutional . . . interpretation that will 'have no effect on the outcome of the case.'" *Ante*, at 3 (quoting *Pearson v. Callahan*, 555 U.S. 223, 237 (2009)).

Whether the Fourth Amendment permits the pretextual use of a material witness warrant for preventive detention of an individual whom the Government has no intention of using at trial is, in my view, a closer question than the majority's opinion suggests. Although the majority is correct that a government official's subjective intent is generally "irrelevant in determining whether that officer's actions violate the Fourth Amendment," *Bond v. United States*, 529 U.S. 334, 338, n.2 (2000), none of our prior cases recognizing that principle involved prolonged detention of an individual without probable cause to believe he had committed any criminal offense. We have never considered whether an official's subjective intent matters for purposes of the Fourth Amendment in that novel context, and we need not and should not resolve that question in this case. All Members of the Court agree that, whatever the merits of the underlying Fourth Amendment question, Ashcroft did not violate clearly established law. . . .

NOTES AND QUESTIONS

1. *Material Witness Detentions in PENTTBOM.* Review the material witness statute, *supra* p. 368. What aspect of the procedure for detaining material witnesses might deter the government from making wider use of this legal basis for detention? Under what circumstances might material witness detention appeal to the government?

2. *Obtaining Testimony?* Human Rights Watch found that fewer than half of the 9/11 material witnesses were ever brought before a grand jury or court to testify; many were apparently held as suspects rather than as witnesses. *Witness to Abuse, supra* p. 368, at 2. The government has not been shy about explaining this use of the statute. For example, after acknowledging that the United States has no general preventive detention law, one architect of the post-9/11 detention policy said that "the material witness statute *gives the government effectively the same power.* . . . To the extent that it is a suspect involved in terror, you hold them on a material witness warrant, and you get the information until you find out what's going on." *Id.* at 19 (quoting Mary Jo White, former U.S. Attorney for the Southern District of New York) (emphasis added). In another case in which the material witness's lawyer argued that the government was holding his client as a criminal suspect, not as a witness, the government responded, "Based on evidence collected to date, the government cannot exclude the possibility that [the detainee] was criminally, rather than innocently, involved in how his fingerprint got to Spain." *Quoted in* Ricardo J. Bascuas, *The Unconstitutionality of "Hold Until Clear": Reexamining Material Witness Detentions in the Wake of the September 11th Dragnet*, 58 Vand. L. Rev. 677, 679 (2005) (citation omitted).

Here is what the Court of Appeals said about the government's motives in detaining al-Kidd:

— Al-Kidd's arrest was sought a month *after* Al-Hussayen was indicted, and more than a year *before* trial began, temporally distant from the time any testimony would have been needed.

— The FBI had previously investigated and interviewed al-Kidd, but had never suggested, let alone demanded, that he appear as a witness.

— The FBI conducted lengthy interrogations with al-Kidd while in custody, including about matters apparently unrelated to Al-Hussayen's alleged visa violations.

— Al-Kidd *never actually testified* for the prosecution in Al-Hussayen's or any other case, despite his assurances that he would be willing to do so.

— Ashcroft's immediate subordinate, FBI Director Mueller, testified before Congress that al-Kidd's *arrest* (rather than, say, the obtaining of the evidence he was supposedly going to provide against Al-Hussayen) constituted a "major success[ ]" in "identifying and dismantling terrorist networks." [*Al-Kidd v. Ashcroft*, 580 F.3d 949, 963-964 (9th Cir. 2009).]

Is there any doubt that al-Kidd was not detained primarily (or at all) to obtain his testimony for the Al-Hussayen case?

3. *Testimony: A Key to the Material Witness's Jail Cell?* The material witness statute makes a deposition an alternative to detention for obtaining grand jury testimony, effectively giving the detainee a key to his jail cell. Human Rights Watch reports, however, that the government has consistently opposed depositions or stalled taking them, citing national security reasons. *Witness to Abuse, supra,* at 79. Moreover, the government reportedly failed to advise many detainees of the reasons for their arrests, of their right to an attorney and to have an attorney present at their interrogations, and of their right to remain silent. *Id.* at 4.

4. *Probable Cause.* The Ninth Circuit had distinguished *Whren* on the grounds that it presupposes "ordinary" probable cause to believe that the arrestee has committed a crime, and that material witness arrests are based neither on ordinary probable cause nor even reasonable suspicion to believe that the arrestee has committed or is committing a crime. What was the Supreme Court's answer? It asserted that al-Kidd conceded that "individualized suspicion" justified his search, but individualized suspicion of what?

Has the Court definitively decided the legality of material witness detentions? If not, what is left open? Under what circumstances would a material witness arrest be unlawful, either under the statute or under the Constitution? Consider this assessment:

[I]t is quite possible that section 3144 going forward will turn out to be problematic under the Fourth Amendment quite apart from the question of pretext, at least when applied in some settings that appear particularly harsh. Second, the lingering prospect of *Bivens* liability for FBI agents who misstate or misrepresent facts in the underlying 3144 warrant application to some degree will check the prextual use of 3144. . . . Where the case can actually be made that the person's testimony is needed and at risk, however, this decision should pave the way for reliance on 3144 even if the underlying motivation is primarily to incapacitate a potentially dangerous person . . . . [Robert Chesney, *Supreme Court Rejects Fourth Amendment Challenge to Material Witness Detention in Al-Kidd v. Ashcroft* (May 31, 2011), *at* http://www.lawfareblog.com/2011/05/supreme-court-rejects-fourth-amendment-challenge-to-material-witness-detention-in-al-kidd-v-ashcroft/.]

5. *An Alternative Holding?* Should the majority have considered whether using the material witness statute for preventive detention fits under some national security exception to the Fourth Amendment's protection against unreasonable seizures? *See United States v. United States District Court (Keith)*, 407 U.S. 297 (1972), *supra* p. 172. How would you define such an exception?

6. *Clearly Established?* The Court unanimously held (with Justice Kagan recused) that Ashcroft did not violate clearly established law. Was the rest of the majority opinion necessary to the result?

The Great Writ: Habeas Corpus Before 9/11

13

The common law writ of habeas corpus is a guard against arbitrary, indefinite executive imprisonment that predates the Constitution by centuries. Blackstone sang its praises in 1759:

> Of great importance to the public is the preservation of this personal liberty: for if once it were left in the power of any, the highest, magistrate to imprison arbitrarily whomever he or his officers thought proper ... there would soon be an end of all other rights and immunities. ... To bereave a man of life, or by violence to confiscate his estate, without accusation or trial, would be so gross and notorious an act of despotism, as must at once convey the alarm of tyranny throughout the whole kingdom. But confinement of the person, by secretly hurrying him to gaol, where his sufferings are unknown or forgotten; is a less public, a less striking, and therefore a more dangerous engine of arbitrary government. ...
>
> To make imprisonment lawful, it must either be, by process from the courts of judicature, or by warrant from some legal officer, having authority to commit to prison; which warrant must be in writing, under the hand and seal of the magistrate, and express the causes of the commitment, in order to be examined into (if necessary) upon a *habeas corpus*. If there be no cause expressed, the gaoler is not bound to detain the prisoner. For the law judges in this respect, ... that it is unreasonable to send a prisoner, and not to signify withal the crimes alleged against him. [1 William Blackstone, *Commentaries* *132-133.]

Alexander Hamilton quoted from this same passage in The *Federalist No. 84*, at 444 (George Carey & James McClellan eds., 2001). And, as Justice Scalia has said, "The two ideas central to Blackstone's understanding—due process as the right secured, and habeas corpus as the instrument by which due process could be insisted upon by a citizen illegally imprisoned—found expression in the Constitution's Due Process and Suspension Clauses. *See* Amdt. 5; Art. I, §9, cl. 2." *Hamdi v. Rumsfeld*, 542 U.S. 507, 554-556 (2004) (Scalia, J., dissenting). The Suspension Clause did not create the privilege of the writ; that privilege already existed as part of our common law heritage from England. Instead, the Clause forbids suspension of "[t]he Privilege of the Writ of Habeas Corpus ... unless when in Cases of Rebellion or Invasion the public Safety may require it." Art. I, §9, cl. 2.

378

Congress has recognized the privilege by statute, as noted below. "The habeas statute clearly has expanded habeas corpus 'beyond the limits that obtained during the 17th and 18th centuries,'" the Supreme Court has observed, "[b]ut '[a]t its historical core, the writ of habeas corpus has served as a means of reviewing the legality of Executive detention, and it is in that context that its protections have been strongest.'" *Rasul v. Bush*, 524 U.S. 466, 474 (2004) (internal citations omitted).

We begin this chapter in Part A with a look at the current statutory basis for habeas corpus jurisdiction in federal courts. In Part B we consider when and how the writ may be suspended or restricted, and by whom. Finally, in Part C we inquire whether the writ was available to nonresident aliens before 9/11.

A. STATUTORY BASIS FOR HABEAS CORPUS

The current habeas corpus statute describes the qualifications of persons entitled to seek the writ, as well as basic procedures for a court to follow in considering a petition for a writ. What kind of hearing does the statute prescribe?

Habeas Corpus
28 U.S.C. §§2241-2255 (2006 & Supp. III 2009)

§2241. Power to Grant Writ

(a) Writs of habeas corpus may be granted by the Supreme Court, any justice thereof, the district courts and any circuit judge within their respective jurisdictions. . . .

(c) The writ of habeas corpus shall not extend to a prisoner unless—

(1) He is in custody under or by color of the authority of the United States or is committed for trial before some court thereof; or

(2) He is in custody for an act done or omitted in pursuance of an Act of Congress, or an order, process, judgment or decree of a court or judge of the United States; or

(3) He is in custody in violation of the Constitution or laws or treaties of the United States; or

(4) He, being a citizen of a foreign state and domiciled therein is in custody for an act done or omitted under any alleged right, title, authority, privilege, protection, or exemption claimed under the commission, order or sanction of any foreign state, or under color thereof, the validity and effect of which depend upon the law of nations; or

(5) It is necessary to bring him into court to testify or for trial. . . .

§2243. Issuance of Writ; Return; Hearing; Decision

A court, justice or judge entertaining an application for a writ of habeas corpus shall forthwith award the writ or issue an order directing the respondent to show cause why the writ should not be granted, unless it appears from the application that the applicant or person detained is not entitled thereto.

The writ, or order to show cause shall be directed to the person having custody of the person detained. It shall be returned within three days unless for good cause additional time, not exceeding twenty days, is allowed.

The person to whom the writ or order is directed shall make a return certifying the true cause of the detention.

When the writ or order is returned a day shall be set for hearing, not more than five days after the return unless for good cause additional time is allowed.

Unless the application for the writ and the return present only issues of law the person to whom the writ is directed shall be required to produce at the hearing the body of the person detained.

The applicant or the person detained may, under oath, deny any of the facts set forth in the return or allege any other material facts....

The court shall summarily hear and determine the facts, and dispose of the matter as law and justice require.

B.   SUSPENDING THE WRIT

Although the Suspension Clause appears in that part of the Constitution devoted to an enumeration of legislative powers, there is no other textual clue about who possesses the power to suspend the writ. The question arose in an early Civil War era case, *Ex parte Merryman*, 17 F. Cas. 144 (C.C.D. Md. 1861) (No. 9487), when Chief Justice Taney ordered the release of a Southern sympathizer imprisoned at Fort McHenry. Merryman had been seized after President Lincoln signed an order authorizing suspension of the writ of habeas corpus. Said the Chief Justice, "I had supposed it to be one of those points in constitutional law upon which there was no difference of Opinion ... that the privilege of the writ could not be suspended, except by act of congress." *Id.* at 148. However, Taney's decree was ignored by the President, and Merryman remained in prison for a time. A month later, in a message to a special session of Congress, Lincoln remarked that Taney's interpretation of the constitutional requirement would allow

President Lincoln in Spring 1861.

Photographer unknown. Courtesy of the Abraham Lincoln Presidential Library and Museum.

all the laws, but one, to go unexecuted, and the government itself go to pieces, lest that one be violated.... [T]he Constitution itself, is silent as to which, or who, is to exercise the power; and as the provision was plainly made for a dangerous emergency, it cannot be believed the framers of the instrument intended, that in every case, the danger should run its course, until Congress could be called together; the very assembling of which might be prevented, as was intended in this case, by the rebellion. [4 *The Collected Works of Abraham Lincoln* 430-431 (Roy P. Basler ed., 1953).]

Five years later, the full Supreme Court made it clear that under some circumstances the writ can properly be suspended.

Ex parte Milligan

United States Supreme Court, 1866
71 U.S. (4 Wall.) 2

[During the Civil War, Congress passed a statute in 1863 authorizing President Abraham Lincoln to suspend the writ of habeas corpus subject to certain limitations. The statute was summarized in the headnotes to this case as follows:

> The first section authorizes the suspension, during the Rebellion, of the writ of habeas corpus, throughout the United States, by the President.
>
> Two following sections limited the authority in certain respects.
>
> The second section required that lists of all persons, being citizens of States in which the administration of the laws had continued unimpaired in the Federal courts, who were then held, or might thereafter be held, as prisoners of the United States, under the authority of the President, otherwise than as prisoners of war, should be furnished by the Secretary of State and Secretary of War to the judges of the Circuit and District Courts. These lists were to contain the names of all persons, residing within their respective jurisdictions, charged with violation of national law. And it was required, in cases where the grand jury in attendance upon any of these courts should terminate its session without proceeding by indictment or otherwise against any prisoner named in the list, that the judge of the court should forthwith make an order that such prisoner, desiring a discharge, should be brought before him or the court to be discharged, on entering into recognizance, if required, to keep the peace and for good behavior, or to appear, as the court might direct, to be further dealt with according to law. Every officer of the United States having custody of such prisoners was required to obey and execute the judge's order, under penalty, for refusal or delay, of fine and imprisonment.
>
> The third section enacts, in case lists of persons other than prisoners of war then held in confinement, or thereafter arrested, should not be furnished within twenty days after the passage of the act, or, in cases of subsequent arrest, within twenty days after the time of arrest, that any citizen, after the termination of a session of the grand jury without indictment or presentment, might, by petition alleging the facts and verified by oath, obtain the judge's order of discharge in favor of any person so imprisoned, on the terms and conditions prescribed in the second section. [*Ex parte Milligan*, 71 U.S. 2, 4-5 (1866).]

Lambdin P. Milligan, a resident of Indiana, was arrested at his home in October 1864 by order of General Alvin P. Hovey, commander of the military district of Indiana, and held in close confinement "otherwise than as [a] prisoner[] of war." He was then brought before a military tribunal in Indianapolis, tried on charges ranging from conspiracy against the government to inciting insurrection, found guilty, and sentenced to be hanged.

In the meantime, on January 2, 1865, the United States Circuit Court for Indiana had met at Indianapolis and empanelled a grand jury to inquire whether any laws of the United States had been broken by anyone and to make presentments. The grand jury did not find any bill of indictment or make any presentment against Milligan, and on January 27 the court adjourned after discharging the grand jury from further service.

Milligan then petitioned the Circuit Court for his release, citing the foregoing statute and arguing that the military tribunal had no jurisdiction to try him. Although only the first part of the resulting opinion treats the suspension of the writ of habeas corpus, we provide an excerpt here of the full majority and concurring opinions in order to convey accurately the Court's view of the importance of the issues it presented. We take up later parts of the majority opinion *infra* pp. 436 and 678.]

Mr. Justice DAVIS delivered the opinion of the court. . . . The importance of the main question presented by this record cannot be overstated; for it involves the very framework of the government and the fundamental principles of American liberty.

During the late wicked Rebellion, the temper of the times did not allow that calmness in deliberation and discussion so necessary to a correct conclusion of a purely judicial question. *Then*, considerations of safety were mingled with the exercise of power; and feelings and interests prevailed which are happily terminated. *Now* that the public safety is assured, this question, as well as all others, can be discussed and decided without passion or the admixture of any element not required to form a legal judgment. . . .

Milligan claimed his discharge from custody by virtue of the act of Congress "relating to *habeas corpus* and regulating judicial proceedings in certain cases," approved March 3d, 1863. Did that act confer jurisdiction on the Circuit Court of Indiana to hear this case?

In interpreting a law, the motives which must have operated with the legislature in passing it are proper to be considered. This law was passed in a time of great national peril, when our heritage of free government was in danger. An armed rebellion against the national authority, of greater proportions than history affords an example of, was raging; and the public safety required that the privilege of the writ of *habeas corpus* should be suspended. The President had practically suspended it, and detained suspected persons in custody without trial; but his authority to do this was questioned. It was claimed that Congress alone could exercise this power; and that the legislature, and not the President, should judge of the political considerations on which the right to suspend it rested. The privilege of this great writ had never before been withheld from the citizen; and as the exigence of the times demanded immediate action, it was of the highest importance that the lawfulness of the suspension should be fully established. It was under these circumstances, which were such as to arrest the attention of the country, that this law was passed. The President was authorized by it to suspend the privilege of the writ of *habeas corpus*, whenever, in his judgment, the public safety required; and he did, by proclamation, bearing date the 15th of September, 1863, reciting, among other things, the authority of this statute, suspend it. The suspension of the writ does not authorize the arrest of any one, but simply denies to one arrested the privilege of this writ in order to obtain his liberty.

It is proper, therefore, to inquire under what circumstances the courts could rightfully refuse to grant this writ, and when the citizen was at liberty to invoke its aid.

The second and third sections of the law are explicit on these points. The language used is plain and direct, and the meaning of the Congress cannot be mistaken. The public safety demanded, if the President thought proper to arrest a suspected person, that he should not be required to give the cause of his detention on return to a writ of *habeas corpus*. But it was not contemplated that such person should be detained in custody beyond a certain fixed period, unless certain judicial proceedings, known to the common law, were commenced against him. . . .

Milligan, in his application to be released from imprisonment, averred the existence of every fact necessary under the terms of this law to give the Circuit Court of Indiana jurisdiction. If he was detained in custody by the order of the President, otherwise than as a prisoner of war; if he was a citizen of Indiana and had never been in the military or naval service, and the grand jury of the district had met, after he had been arrested, for a period of twenty days, and adjourned without taking any proceedings against him, *then* the court had the right to entertain his petition and determine the lawfulness of his imprisonment. . . .

The controlling question in the case is this: Upon the *facts* stated in Milligan's petition, and the exhibits filed, had the military commission mentioned in it *jurisdiction*, legally, to try and sentence him? . . .

No graver question was ever considered by this court, nor one which more nearly concerns the rights of the whole people; for it is the birthright of every American citizen when charged with crime, to be tried and punished according to law. The power of punishment is, alone through the means which the laws have provided for that purpose, and if they are ineffectual, there is an immunity from punishment, no matter how great an offender the individual may be, or how much his crimes may have shocked the sense of justice of the country, or endangered its safety. By the protection of the law human rights are secured; withdraw that protection, and they are at the mercy of wicked rulers, or the clamor of an excited people. If there was law to justify this military trial, it is not our province to interfere; if there was not, it is our duty to declare the nullity of the whole proceedings. The decision of this question does not depend on argument or judicial precedents, numerous and highly illustrative as they are. These precedents inform us of the extent of the struggle to preserve liberty and to relieve those in civil life from military trials. The founders of our government were familiar with the history of that struggle; and secured in a written constitution every right which the people had wrested from power during a contest of ages. By that Constitution and the laws authorized by it this question must be determined. The provisions of that instrument on the administration of criminal justice are too plain and direct, to leave room for misconstruction or doubt of their true meaning. Those applicable to this case are found in that clause of the original Constitution which says, "That the trial of all crimes, except in case of impeachment, shall be by jury;" and in the fourth, fifth, and sixth articles of the amendments. The fourth proclaims the right to be secure in person and effects against unreasonable search and seizure; and directs that a judicial warrant shall not issue "without proof of probable cause supported by oath or affirmation." The fifth declares "that no person shall be held to answer for a capital or otherwise infamous crime unless on presentment by a grand jury, except in cases arising in the land or naval forces, or in the militia, when in actual service in time of war or public danger, nor be deprived of life, liberty, or property, without due process of law." And the sixth guarantees the right of trial by jury, in such manner and with such regulations that with upright judges, impartial juries, and an able bar, the innocent will be saved and the guilty punished. . . .

Time has proven the discernment of our ancestors; for even these provisions, expressed in such plain English words, that it would seem the ingenuity of man could not evade them, are *now*, after the lapse of more than seventy years, sought to be avoided. Those great and good men foresaw that troublous times would arise, when rulers and people would become restive under restraint, and seek by sharp and decisive measures to accomplish ends deemed just and proper; and that the principles of constitutional liberty would be in peril, unless established by irrepealable law. The history of the world had taught them that what was done in the past might be attempted in the future. The Constitution of the United States is a law for rulers and people, equally in war and in peace, and covers with the shield of its protection all classes of men, at all times, and under all circumstances. No doctrine, involving more pernicious consequences, was ever invented by the wit of man than that any of its provisions can be suspended during any of the great exigencies of government. Such a doctrine leads directly to anarchy and despotism, but the theory of necessity on which it is based is false; for the government, within the Constitution, has all the powers granted to it, which are necessary to preserve its existence; as has been happily proved by the result of the great effort to throw off its just authority.

Have any of the rights guaranteed by the Constitution been violated in the case of Milligan? and if so, what are they?

Every trial involves the exercise of judicial power; and from what source did the military commission that tried him derive their authority? Certainly no part of the judicial power of the country was conferred on them; because the Constitution expressly vests it "in one supreme court and such inferior courts as the Congress may from time to time ordain and establish," and it is not pretended that the commission was a court ordained and established by Congress. They cannot justify on the mandate of the President; because he is controlled by law, and has his appropriate sphere of duty, which is to execute, not to make, the laws; and there is "no unwritten criminal code to which resort can be had as a source of jurisdiction."

But it is said that the jurisdiction is complete under the "laws and usages of war."

It can serve no useful purpose to inquire what those laws and usages are, whence they originated, where found, and on whom they operate; they can never be applied to citizens in states which have upheld the authority of the government, and where the courts are open and their process unobstructed. This court has judicial knowledge that in Indiana the Federal authority was always unopposed, and its courts always open to hear criminal accusations and redress grievances; and no usage of war could sanction a military trial there for any offence whatever of a citizen in civil life, in nowise connected with the military service. Congress could grant no such power; and to the honor of our national legislature be it said, it has never been provoked by the state of the country even to attempt its exercise. One of the plainest constitutional provisions was, therefore, infringed when Milligan was tried by a court not ordained and established by Congress, and not composed of judges appointed during good behavior.

Why was he not delivered to the Circuit Court of Indiana to be proceeded against according to law? No reason of necessity could be urged against it; because Congress had declared penalties against the offences charged, provided for their punishment, and directed that court to hear and determine them. And soon after this military tribunal was ended, the Circuit Court met, peacefully transacted its business, and adjourned. It needed no bayonets to protect it, and required no military aid to execute its judgments. It was held in a state, eminently distinguished for patriotism, by judges commissioned during the Rebellion, who were provided with juries, upright, intelligent, and selected by a marshal appointed by the President. The government had no right to conclude that Milligan, if guilty, would not receive in that court merited punishment; for its records disclose that it was constantly engaged in the trial of similar offences, and was never interrupted in its administration of criminal justice. If it was dangerous, in the distracted condition of affairs, to leave Milligan unrestrained of his liberty because he "conspired against the government, afforded aid and comfort to rebels, and incited the people to insurrection," the *law* said arrest him, confine him closely, render him powerless to do further mischief; and then present his case to the grand jury of the district, with proofs of his guilt, and, if indicted, try him according to the course of the common law. If this had been done, the Constitution would have been vindicated, the law of 1863 enforced, and the securities for personal liberty preserved and defended. . . .

When peace prevails, and the authority of the government is undisputed, there is no difficulty of preserving the safeguards of liberty; for the ordinary modes of trial are never neglected, and no one wishes it otherwise; but if society is disturbed by civil commotion — if the passions of men are aroused and the restraints of law weakened, if not disregarded — these safeguards need, and should receive, the watchful care of those intrusted with the guardianship of the Constitution and laws. In no other way can we transmit to posterity unimpaired the blessings of liberty, consecrated by the sacrifices of the Revolution.

It is claimed that martial law covers with its broad mantle the proceedings of this military commission. The proposition is this: that in a time of war the commander of an armed force (if in his opinion the exigencies of the country demand it, and of which he is to judge), has the power, within the lines of the military district, to suspend all civil rights and their remedies, and subject citizens as well as soldiers to the *rule* of his will; and in the exercise of his lawful authority cannot be restrained, except by his superior officer or the President of the United States.

If this position is sound to the extent claimed, then when war exists, foreign or domestic, and the country is subdivided into military departments for mere convenience, the commander of one of them can, if he chooses, within his limits, on the plea of necessity, with the approval of the Executive, substitute military force for and to the exclusion of the laws, and punish all persons, as he thinks right and proper, without fixed or certain rules.

The statement of this proposition shows its importance; for, if true, republican government is a failure, and there is an end of liberty regulated by law. Martial law, established on such a basis, destroys every guarantee of the Constitution, and effectually renders the "military independent of and superior to the civil power" — the attempt to do which by the King of Great Britain was deemed by our fathers such an offence, that they assigned it to the world as one of the causes which impelled them to declare their independence. Civil liberty and this kind of martial law cannot endure together; the antagonism is irreconcilable; and, in the conflict, one or the other must perish.

This nation, as experience has proved, cannot always remain at peace, and has no right to expect that it will always have wise and humane rulers, sincerely attached to the principles of the Constitution. Wicked men, ambitious of power, with hatred of liberty and contempt of law, may fill the place once occupied by Washington and Lincoln; and if this right is conceded, and the calamities of war again befall us, the dangers to human liberty are frightful to contemplate. If our fathers had failed to provide for just such a contingency, they would have been false to the trust reposed in them. They knew — the history of the world told them — the nation they were founding, be its existence short or long, would be involved in war; how often or how long continued, human foresight could not tell; and that unlimited power, wherever lodged at such a time, was especially hazardous to freemen. For this, and other equally weighty reasons, they secured the inheritance they had fought to maintain, by incorporating in a written constitution the safeguards which *time* had proved were essential to its preservation. Not one of these safeguards can the President, or Congress, or the Judiciary disturb, except the one concerning the writ of *habeas corpus.*

It is essential to the safety of every government that, in a great crisis, like the one we have just passed through, there should be a power somewhere of suspending the writ of *habeas corpus.* In every war, there are men of previously good character, wicked enough to counsel their fellow-citizens to resist the measures deemed necessary by a good government to sustain its just authority and overthrow its enemies; and their influence may lead to dangerous combinations. In the emergency of the times, an immediate public investigation according to law may not be possible; and yet, the peril to the country may be too imminent to suffer such persons to go at large. Unquestionably, there is then an exigency which demands that the government, if it should see fit in the exercise of a proper discretion to make arrests, should not be required to produce the persons arrested in answer to a writ of *habeas corpus.* The Constitution goes no further. It does not say after a writ of *habeas corpus* is denied a citizen, that he shall be tried otherwise than by the course of the common law. . . .

It will be borne in mind that this is not a question of the power to proclaim martial law, when war exists in a community and the courts and civil authorities are overthrown. Nor is it a question what rule a military commander, at the head of his army, can impose on states in rebellion to cripple their resources and quell the insurrection. The jurisdiction claimed is much more extensive. The necessities of the service, during the late Rebellion, required that the loyal states should be placed within the limits of certain military districts and commanders appointed in them; and, it is urged, that this, in a military sense, constituted them the theatre of military operations; and, as in this case, Indiana had been and was again threatened with invasion by the enemy, the occasion was furnished to establish martial law. The conclusion does not follow from the premises. If armies were collected in Indiana, they were to be employed in another locality, where the laws were obstructed and the national authority disputed. On *her* soil there was no hostile foot; if once invaded, that invasion was at an end, and with it all pretext for martial law. Martial law cannot arise from a *threatened* invasion. The necessity must be actual and present; the invasion real, such as effectually closes the courts and deposes the civil administration.

It is difficult to see how the *safety* for the country required martial law in Indiana. If any of her citizens were plotting treason, the power of arrest could secure them, until the government was prepared for their trial, when the courts were open and ready to try them. It was as easy to protect witnesses before a civil as a military tribunal; and as there could be no wish to convict, except on sufficient legal evidence, surely an ordained and established court was better able to judge of this than a military tribunal composed of gentlemen not trained to the profession of the law.

It follows, from what has been said on this subject, that there are occasions when martial rule can be properly applied. If, in foreign invasion or civil war, the courts are actually closed, and it is impossible to administer criminal justice according to law, *then,* on the theatre of active military operations, where war really prevails, there is a necessity to furnish a substitute for the civil authority, thus overthrown, to preserve the safety of the army and society; and as no power is left but the military, it is allowed to govern by martial rule until the laws can have their free course. As necessity creates the rule, so it limits its duration; for, if this government is continued *after* the courts are reinstated, it is a gross usurpation of power. Martial rule can never exist where the courts are open, and in the proper and unobstructed exercise of their jurisdiction. It is also confined to the locality of actual war. Because, during the late Rebellion it could have been enforced in Virginia, where the national authority was overturned and the courts driven out, it does not follow that it should obtain in Indiana, where that authority was never disputed, and justice was always administered. And so in the case of a foreign invasion, martial rule may become a necessity in one state, when, in another, it would be "mere lawless violence." . . .

If the military trial of Milligan was contrary to law, then he was entitled, on the facts stated in his petition, to be discharged from custody by the terms of the act of Congress of March 3d, 1863. . . .

The CHIEF JUSTICE delivered the following opinion [in which WAYNE, SWAYNE, and MILLER, JJ., concurred].... [The Chief Justice agreed that the military commission was without lawful jurisdiction to try Milligan.] But the opinion which has just been read goes further; and as we understand it, asserts not only that the military commission held in Indiana was not authorized by Congress, but that it was not in the power of Congress to authorize it....

We think that Congress had power, though not exercised, to authorize the Military Commission which was held in Indiana....

Congress cannot direct the conduct of campaigns, nor can the President, or any commander under him, without the sanction of Congress, institute tribunals for the trial and punishment of offences, either of soldiers or civilians, unless in cases of a controlling necessity, which justifies what it compels, or at least insures acts of indemnity from the justice of the legislature.

We by no means assert that Congress can establish and apply the laws of war where no war has been declared or exists.

Where peace exists the laws of peace must prevail. What we do maintain is, that when the nation is involved in war, and some portions of the country are invaded, and all are exposed to invasion, it is within the power of Congress to determine in what states or district such great and imminent public danger exists as justifies the authorization of military tribunals for the trial of crimes and offences against the discipline or security of the army or against the public safety....

NOTES AND QUESTIONS

1. *Presidential Authority to Suspend the Writ?* Although the privilege of the writ has been suspended on a number of other occasions, the question raised by *Merryman* has not yet reached the full Supreme Court. *But see Ex parte Bollman*, 8 U.S. (4 Cranch) 75, 101 (1807) ("If at any time the public safety should require the suspension of the powers vested by this act in the courts of the United States, it is for the legislature to say so. That question depends on political considerations, on which the legislature is to decide."). Do you see any danger in allowing the President, acting alone, to suspend the writ, as Lincoln did? *See* Michael Stokes Paulsen, *The Merryman Power and the Dilemma of Autonomous Executive Branch Interpretation,* 15 Cardozo L. Rev. 81, 88-99 (1993); (Chief Justice) William H. Rehnquist, *All the Laws But One: Civil Liberties in Wartime* 11-45 (1998) (criticizing Chief Justice Taney); Harold C. Relyea, *National Emergency Powers: A Brief Overview of Presidential Suspensions of the Habeas Corpus Privilege and Invocations of Martial Law* (Cong. Res. Serv.), Sept. 20, 1976; John T. Sharer, *Power, Idealism, and Compromise: The Coordinate Branches and the Writ of Habeas Corpus,* 26 Emory L.J. 149 (1977); and Martin S. Sheffer, *Presidential Power to Suspend Habeas Corpus: The Taney-Bates Dialogue and Ex parte Merryman,* 11 Okla. City U. L. Rev. 1 (1986).

What about a danger in not allowing the President, acting alone, to suspend? How, if at all, could the Suspension Clause be interpreted to balance the dangers?

2. *The Effect of Suspension.* What was the effect of President Lincoln's suspension of the privilege of the writ of habeas corpus? You should be clear that suspension provides no legal authority for either arrest or detention; it only prevents a court from requiring the Executive to justify its act. *See* Jared A. Goldstein, *Habeas Without Rights,*

2007 Wis. L. Rev. 1165, 1169 ("As Chief Justice John Marshall framed the habeas inquiry: 'The question is, what authority has the jailor to detain him?'") (footnotes omitted). Without the judicial safeguard of habeas review, the Executive has the *power* to detain, but its *legal authority to do so* must derive from something other than the fact of suspension. Much of the *Milligan* decision after the discussion of the suspension statute is devoted to exploring the question of authority for trial by military commission, to which we return in depth in Chapter 22.

3. *Congress's Authority to Restrict Suspension by the President?* How had Congress limited the suspension authority it vested in President Lincoln? How did the arrest and military trial of Milligan violate the statutory limits Congress had established?

Is there any limit on Congress's ability to regulate the President's authority to suspend the writ? Did the *Milligan* decision shed any light on this question?

4. *Construing to Avoid the Constitutional Question.* By the usual rules of statutory construction, courts should construe legislation or executive orders, when "fairly possible," to avoid significant constitutional questions. *See Immigration & Naturalization Service v. St. Cyr*, 533 U.S. 289, 299-300 (2001). It may be especially desirable to avoid having to decide whether the executive alone may cut off access to the courts, because, "[a]t its historical core, the writ of habeas corpus has served as a means of reviewing the legality of executive detention, and it is in that context that its protections have been the strongest." *Id.* at 301. Thus, in *St. Cyr*, the Court construed a statute to allow habeas access to the courts, even though the statute was entitled "Elimination of Custody Review by Habeas Corpus." The Court insisted that any effort to restrict the privilege of seeking the writ must be clearly stated! *Id.* at 308-309 (finding that the title was not controlling, where the actual statutory text never mentioned habeas review).

5. *Congressional Limits on Routes to Review.* Could Congress, exercising its authority under Article III, Section 2, of the Constitution, limit judicial scrutiny of a suspension of the writ either by Congress or by the President? After the *Milligan* decision, Congress expressly provided for appeals to the Supreme Court from lower federal court decisions in habeas corpus proceedings. Act of Feb. 5, 1867, 14 Stat. 385. When a Southern newspaper editor was arrested and held for trial by a military commission on charges of libel and inciting insurrection, he applied for a writ of habeas corpus first to a federal circuit court and then to the Supreme Court. During the pendency of his appeal, Congress repealed the appellate jurisdiction of the Supreme Court under the 1867 Act. 15 Stat. 44 (1868). This apparent end run around *Milligan* was upheld in *Ex parte McCardle*, 74 U.S. (7 Wall.) 506 (1868), although the Court noted an alternate route to Supreme Court review. The Court then granted a petition for a *writ of certiorari* in another case involving the trial of a civilian in a military court. *Ex parte Yerger*, 75 U.S. (8 Wall.) 85 (1868). It based its decision on the appellate jurisdiction conferred on the Supreme Court by the Judicial Act of 1789 and by the Constitution to hear petitions for writs of habeas corpus. *Id.* at 96-106. Uncertainty about the constitutional necessity for an avenue of appeal to the Supreme Court is explored in William W. Van Alstyne, *A Critical Guide to Ex Parte McCardle*, 15 Ariz. L. Rev. 229 (1973); and Leonard G. Ratner, *Congressional Power Over the Appellate Jurisdiction of the Supreme Court*, 109 U. Pa. L. Rev. 157 (1960).

6. *Habeas Corpus After September 11.* In the massive PENTTBOM investigation that followed the terrorist attacks on September 11, 2001, the Justice Department extended by regulation from 24 to 48 hours the time that an alien suspected of an immigration violation could be held without criminal charges, and it provided for indefinite detention of suspected terrorist aliens. Do you think any of the several hundred persons detained for questioning for an extended period was entitled to a writ of habeas corpus?

C. AVAILABILITY OF THE WRIT TO NONRESIDENT ALIENS BEFORE 9/11

Johnson v. Eisentrager

United States Supreme Court, 1950
339 U.S. 763

Mr. Justice JACKSON delivered the opinion of the Court. The ultimate question in this case is one of jurisdiction of civil courts of the United States *vis-à-vis* military authorities in dealing with enemy aliens overseas. . . .

[U.S. armed forces captured 21 German nationals in service of German armed forces in China. A U.S. military commission sitting in China tried and convicted them of violating laws of war, namely, engaging in, permitting, or ordering continued military activity against the United States after the surrender of Germany and before the surrender of Japan. After conviction, their sentences were reviewed and approved by military reviewing authority. They were then repatriated to the U.S.-run Landsberg Prison in Germany to serve their sentences.

They filed a petition for a writ of habeas corpus in the District of Columbia, naming the Secretary of Defense, among others, and asserting that their trial, conviction, and imprisonment violated Articles I and III of the Constitution, the Fifth Amendment, and provisions of the Geneva Convention governing the treatment of prisoners of war.]

We are cited to no instance where a court, in this or any other country where the writ is known, has issued it on behalf of an alien enemy who, at no relevant time and in no stage of his captivity, has been within its territorial jurisdiction. Nothing in the text of the Constitution extends such a right, nor does anything in our statutes. . . .

I.

Modern American law has come a long way since the time when outbreak of war made every enemy national an outlaw, subject to both public and private slaughter, cruelty and plunder. But even by the most magnanimous view, our law does not abolish inherent distinctions recognized throughout the civilized world between citizens and aliens, nor between aliens of friendly and of enemy allegiance, nor between resident enemy aliens who have submitted themselves to our laws and nonresident enemy aliens who at all times have remained with, and adhered to, enemy governments.

With the citizen we are now little concerned, except to set his case apart as untouched by this decision and to take measure of the difference between his status and that of all categories of aliens. . . .

The alien, to whom the United States has been traditionally hospitable, has been accorded a generous and ascending scale of rights as he increases his identity with our society. Mere lawful presence in the country creates an implied assurance of safe conduct and gives him certain rights....

But, in extending constitutional protections beyond the citizenry, the Court has been at pains to point out that it was the alien's presence within its territorial jurisdiction that gave the Judiciary power to act. In the pioneer case of *Yick Wo v. Hopkins,* the Court said of the Fourteenth Amendment, "These provisions are universal in their application, to all persons within the territorial jurisdiction, without regard to any differences of race, of color, or of nationality; * * *." 118 U.S. 356, 369....

Since most cases involving aliens afford this ground of jurisdiction, and the civil and property rights of immigrants or transients of foreign nationality so nearly approach equivalence to those of citizens, courts in peace time have little occasion to inquire whether litigants before them are alien or citizen.

It is war that exposes the relative vulnerability of the alien's status. The security and protection enjoyed while the nation of his allegiance remains in amity with the United States are greatly impaired when his nation takes up arms against us. While his lot is far more humane and endurable than the experience of our citizens in some enemy lands, it is still not a happy one. But disabilities this country lays upon the alien who becomes also an enemy are imposed temporarily as an incident of war and not as an incident of alienage....

... [T]he nonresident enemy alien, especially one who has remained in the service of the enemy, does not have even this qualified access to our courts, for he neither has comparable claims upon our institutions nor could his use of them fail to be helpful to the enemy. Our law on this subject first emerged about 1813 when the Supreme Court of the State of New York had occasion, in a series of cases, to examine the foremost authorities of the Continent and of England. It concluded the rule of the common law and the law of nations to be that alien enemies resident in the country of the enemy could not maintain an action in its courts during the period of hostilities. This Court has recognized that rule, and it continues to be the law throughout this country and in England.

II.

The foregoing demonstrates how much further we must go if we are to invest these enemy aliens, resident, captured and imprisoned abroad, with standing to demand access to our courts.

We are here confronted with a decision whose basic premise is that these prisoners are entitled, as a constitutional right, to sue in some court of the United States for a writ of *habeas corpus.* To support that assumption we must hold that a prisoner of our military authorities is constitutionally entitled to the writ, even though he (a) is an enemy alien; (b) has never been or resided in the United States; (c) was captured outside of our territory and there held in military custody as a prisoner of war; (d) was tried and convicted by a Military Commission sitting outside the United States; (e) for offenses against laws of war committed outside the United States; (f) and is at all times imprisoned outside the United States.

We have pointed out that the privilege of litigation has been extended to aliens, whether friendly or enemy, only because permitting their presence in the country implied protection. No such basis can be invoked here, for these prisoners at no relevant time were within any territory over which the United States is sovereign, and the scenes of their offense, their capture, their trial and their punishment were all beyond the territorial jurisdiction of any court of the United States.

Another reason for a limited opening of our courts to resident aliens is that among them are many of friendly personal disposition to whom the status of enemy is only one imputed by law. But these prisoners were actual enemies, active in the hostile service of an enemy power....

A basic consideration in *habeas corpus* practice is that the prisoner will be produced before the court. This is the crux of the statutory scheme established by the Congress; indeed, it is inherent in the very term *"habeas corpus."* ... To grant the writ to these prisoners might mean that our army must transport them across the seas for hearing. This would require allocation of shipping space, guarding personnel, billeting and rations. It might also require transportation for whatever witnesses the prisoners desired to call as well as transportation for those necessary to defend legality of the sentence. The writ, since it is held to be a matter of right, would be equally available to enemies during active hostilities as in the present twilight between war and peace. Such trials would hamper the war effort and bring aid and comfort to the enemy. They would diminish the prestige of our commanders, not only with enemies but with wavering neutrals. It would be difficult to devise more effective fettering of a field commander than to allow the very enemies he is ordered to reduce to submission to call him to account in his own civil courts and divert his efforts and attention from the military offensive abroad to the legal defensive at home. Nor is it unlikely that the result of such enemy litigiousness would be a conflict between judicial and military opinion highly comforting to enemies of the United States....

III.

The Court of Appeals dispensed with all requirement of territorial jurisdiction based on place of residence, captivity, trial, offense, or confinement. It could not predicate relief upon any intraterritorial contact of these prisoners with our laws or institutions. Instead, it gave our Constitution an extraterritorial application to embrace our enemies in arms. Right to the writ, it reasoned, is a subsidiary procedural right that follows from possession of substantive constitutional rights. These prisoners, it considered, are invested with a right of personal liberty by our Constitution and therefore must have the right to the remedial writ. The court stated the steps in its own reasoning as follows: *"First.* The Fifth Amendment, by its terms, applies to 'any person.' *Second.* Action of Government officials in violation of the Constitution is void. This is the ultimate essence of the present controversy. *Third.* A basic and inherent function of the judicial branch of a government built upon a constitution is to set aside void action by government officials, and so to restrict executive action to the confines of the constitution. In our jurisprudence, no Government action which is void under the Constitution is exempt from judicial power. *Fourth.* The writ of habeas corpus is the established, time-honored process in our law for testing the authority of one who deprives another of his liberty, — 'the best and only sufficient defense of personal freedom.' * * *" 174 F.2d 961, 963-964....

When we analyze the claim prisoners are asserting and the court below sustained, it amounts to a right not to be tried at all for an offense against our armed forces. If the Fifth Amendment protects them from military trial, the Sixth Amendment as clearly prohibits their trial by civil courts. The latter requires in all criminal prosecutions that "the accused" be tried "by an impartial jury of the State and district wherein the crime shall have been committed, which district shall have been previously ascertained by law." And if the Fifth be held to embrace these prisoners because it uses the inclusive term "no person," the Sixth must, for it applies to all "accused." No suggestion is advanced by the court below or by prisoners of any constitutional method by which any violations of the laws of war endangering the United States forces could be reached or punished, if it were not by a Military Commission in the theatre where the offense was committed. . . .

If this Amendment invests enemy aliens in unlawful hostile action against us with immunity from military trial, it puts them in a more protected position than our own soldiers. American citizens conscripted into the military service are thereby stripped of their Fifth Amendment rights and as members of the military establishment are subject to its discipline, including military trials for offenses against aliens or Americans. . . .

The decision below would extend coverage of our Constitution to nonresident alien enemies denied to resident alien enemies. The latter are entitled only to judicial hearing to determine what the petition of these prisoners admits: that they are really alien enemies. When that appears, those resident here may be deprived of liberty by Executive action without hearing. While this is preventive rather than punitive detention, no reason is apparent why an alien enemy charged with having committed a crime should have greater immunities from Executive action than one who it is only feared might at some future time commit a hostile act.

If the Fifth Amendment confers its rights on all the world except Americans engaged in defending it, the same must be true of the companion civil-rights Amendments, for none of them is limited by its express terms, territorially or as to persons. Such a construction would mean that during military occupation irreconcilable enemy elements, guerrilla fighters, and "were-wolves" [German nationals trained to conduct terrorist activities in postwar Germany] could require the American Judiciary to assure them freedoms of speech, press, and assembly as in the First Amendment, right to bear arms as in the Second, security against "unreasonable" searches and seizures as in the Fourth, as well as rights to jury trial as in the Fifth and Sixth Amendments.

Such extraterritorial application of organic law would have been so significant an innovation in the practice of governments that, if intended or apprehended, it could scarcely have failed to excite contemporary comment. Not one word can be cited. No decision of this Court supports such a view. None of the learned commentators on our Constitution has ever hinted at it. The practice of every modern government is opposed to it.

We hold that the Constitution does not confer a right of personal security or an immunity from military trial and punishment upon an alien enemy engaged in the hostile service of a government at war with the United States. . . .

IV. . . .

These prisoners do not assert, and could not, that anything in the Geneva Convention makes them immune from prosecution or punishment for war crimes.[14]

---

14. We are not holding that these prisoners have no right which the military authorities are bound to respect. The United States, by the Geneva Convention of July 27, 1929, 47 Stat. 2021, concluded with forty-six other countries, including the German Reich, an agreement upon the treatment to be accorded

Article 75 thereof expressly provides that a prisoner of war may be detained until the end of such proceedings and, if necessary, until the expiration of the punishment. . . .

V. . . .

Since in the present application we find no basis for invoking federal judicial power in any district, we need not debate as to where, if the case were otherwise, the petition should be filed.

For reasons stated, the judgment of the Court of Appeals is reversed and the judgment of the District Court dismissing the petition is affirmed.

Reversed.

Mr. Justice BLACK, with whom Mr. Justice DOUGLAS and Mr. Justice BURTON concur, dissenting. . . . In Parts I, II, and III of its opinion, the Court apparently holds that no American court can even consider the jurisdiction of the military tribunal to convict and sentence these prisoners for the alleged crime. . . . [T]his holding . . . is based on the facts that (1) they were enemy aliens who were belligerents when captured, and (2) they were captured, tried, and imprisoned outside our realm, never having been in the United States.

The contention that enemy alien belligerents have no standing whatever to contest conviction for war crimes by habeas corpus proceedings has twice been emphatically rejected by a unanimous Court [citing *Ex parte Quirin,* 317 U.S. 1 (1942), and *In re Yamashita,* 327 U.S. 1 (1946)]. . . . That we went on to deny the requested writ [in both cases] in no way detracts from the clear holding that habeas corpus jurisdiction is available even to belligerent aliens convicted by a military tribunal for an offense committed in actual acts of warfare.

. . . Does a prisoner's right to test legality of a sentence then depend on where the Government chooses to imprison him? Certainly the *Quirin* and *Yamashita* opinions lend no support to that conclusion, for in upholding jurisdiction they place no reliance whatever on territorial location. The Court is fashioning wholly indefensible doctrine if it permits the executive branch, by deciding where its prisoners will be tried and imprisoned, to deprive all federal courts of their power to protect against a federal executive's illegal incarcerations.

If the opinion thus means, and it apparently does, that these petitioners are deprived of the privilege of habeas corpus solely because they were convicted and imprisoned overseas, the Court is adopting a broad and dangerous principle. . . .

. . . It has always been recognized that actual warfare can be conducted successfully only if those in command are left the most ample independence in the theatre of operations. Our Constitution is not so impractical or inflexible that it unduly restricts such necessary independence. It would be fantastic to suggest that alien enemies could hail our military leaders into judicial tribunals to account for their day to day activities on the battlefront. Active fighting forces must be free to fight while hostilities are in progress. But that undisputable axiom has no bearing on this case or the general problem from which it arises. . . .

---

captives. These prisoners claim to be and are entitled to its protection. It is, however, the obvious scheme of the Agreement that responsibility for observance and enforcement of these rights is upon political and military authorities. . . .

The question here involves a far narrower issue. Springing from recognition that our government is composed of three separate and independent branches, it is whether the judiciary has power in habeas corpus proceedings to test the legality of criminal sentences imposed by the executive through military tribunals in a country which we have occupied for years. . . .

Though the scope of habeas corpus review of military tribunal sentences is narrow, I think it should not be denied to these petitioners and others like them. We control that part of Germany we occupy. These prisoners were convicted by our own military tribunals under our own Articles of War, years after hostilities had ceased. However illegal their sentences might be, they can expect no relief from German courts or any other branch of the German Government we permit to function. Only our own courts can inquire into the legality of their imprisonment. Perhaps, as some nations believe, there is merit in leaving the administration of criminal laws to executive and military agencies completely free from judicial scrutiny. Our Constitution has emphatically expressed a contrary policy. . . .

. . . Our nation proclaims a belief in the dignity of human beings as such, no matter what their nationality or where they happen to live. Habeas corpus, as an instrument to protect against illegal imprisonment, is written into the Constitution. Its use by courts cannot in my judgment be constitutionally abridged by Executive or by Congress. I would hold that our courts can exercise it whenever any United States official illegally imprisons any person in any land we govern. Courts should not for any reason abdicate this, the loftiest power with which the Constitution has endowed them.

NOTES AND QUESTIONS

1. *Comparing Milligan and Eisentrager.* How were *Milligan* and *Eisentrager* different factually in ways that might have affected the availability of the writ to the petitioners? Which of those ways, if any, were reflected in the text of the Constitution? In the respective extant habeas statutes? In concerns about separation of powers? In U.S. history? In practical considerations relating to the competence of courts? How did each Court weigh these factors?

2. *Substantive Constitutional Rights?* The Court of Appeals in *Eisentrager* was said to have reasoned that "[r]ight to the writ . . . is a subsidiary procedural right that follows from possession of substantive constitutional rights." 339 U.S. at 781. Was the Court justified in regarding the "procedural" right to the writ of habeas corpus as "subsidiary"?

Forty years on, in *United States v. Verdugo-Urquidez,* 494 U.S. 259 (1990), the Court declared categorically that in *Eisentrager* it had emphatically "rejected the claim that aliens are entitled to Fifth Amendment rights outside the sovereign territory of the United States." *Id.* at 269. Is this an accurate characterization of the Court's 1950 decision? If not, did the Court have some other basis for rejecting the *Eisentrager* petitioners' application for the writ?

Did the *Eisentrager* Court necessarily have to determine the existence of substantive rights before deciding on the availability of the writ to vindicate such rights? In other words, does the Suspension Clause confer some substantive as well as procedural rights?

3. *Other Factors Influencing the Outcome?* In Part II of its opinion, the Court listed six factors that differentiated the petitioners from other prisoners. How important do you think each factor was in determining the availability of the writ? Were they all necessary to deny access to habeas? How did these factors interact?

4. *Alienage.* How important a role did the citizenship of the petitioners play in *Eisentrager?* What is the constitutional basis for the "inherent distinctions . . . between citizens and aliens" mentioned by the Court? Between friendly and enemy aliens? The Court referred to "a generous and ascending scale of rights" accorded to aliens by the courts. Can you describe the scale and name the rights? *See United States v. Verdugo-Urquidez, supra,* 494 U.S. at 270-273. Where did the *Eisentrager* petitioners fall on that scale?

5. *Impracticality of Giving Prisoners of War Habeas Access.* Suppose the Court had found that Eisentrager and other enemy soldiers with the same status *did have* the right to petition for a writ of habeas corpus. What practical difficulties might such a decision have raised for courts? What would have been the implications for national defense efforts in 1950? How about today?

6. *An Incident of War?* The *Eisentrager* Court explained that "[i]t is war that exposes the relative vulnerability of the alien's status." Was the United States still at war in 1950, when the case came to the Court? If the President's authority to imprison the petitioners depended on the existence of a war, in the same way that President Lincoln's authority to capture depended on the existence of a war in the *Prize Cases, supra* p. 69, was the United States engaged in a war as defined in that 1863 case? *See generally* Stephen I. Vladeck, *Ludecke's Lengthening Shadow: The Disturbing Prospect of War Without End,* 2 J. Nat'l Security L. & Pol'y 53 (2006).

7. *Soldiers' Rights and Human Rights in 1950.* The Court expressed concern that extending Fifth Amendment due process protections to Eisentrager and his fellow prisoners would "put them in a more protected position than our own soldiers." 339 U.S. at 783. This was a backhanded reference to the still primitive state of military justice at the time. The Uniform Code of Military Justice only became effective in 1951, a year after *Eisentrager,* and it took many years for it to evolve into the robust and procedurally fair system that it is today. International humanitarian law and international human rights also developed significantly after *Eisentrager.* See Chapter 2. Do these developments undercut the majority's treatment of the *Eisentrager* petitioner's right to personal freedom? If so, do they justify reinterpreting the holding, or does *Eisentrager* remain controlling precedent until it is expressly discarded by the Supreme Court?

8. *Availability of the Writ After 9/11.* It is often stated that "everything changed" after the terrorist attacks of 9/11. Did the events of that fateful day, with the resulting heightened awareness of our vulnerability to highly unpredictable attacks from elusive enemies, require us to rethink the meaning of the Suspension Clause? If they did, how is the meaning now different, and how can any such difference be put into practice?

The Great Writ: Habeas Corpus After 9/11 ——————14

As the last chapter suggests, by 1950 it seemed reasonably clear that a U.S. citizen detained by her government was entitled to petition a federal court for a writ of habeas corpus (e.g., *Ex parte Milligan*), while an alien detained abroad for acts committed abroad could not (e.g., *Johnson v. Eisentrager*).

What then of aliens detained inside the United States? During the Second World War, the government had to decide what to do with eight German saboteurs who were caught in the United States. President Roosevelt opted to try them by military commission (a court composed of military officers) in Washington, D.C., because a commission could impose death sentences, unlike the civilian courts at the time. *See* David J. Danelski, *The Saboteurs' Case*, 1 J. S. Ct. Hist. 61 (1996). But the President also told his Attorney General, "I won't hand them over to any United States marshal armed with a writ of habeas corpus. Understand?" *Id.* The presidential proclamation establishing the military commission dealt with this eventuality by providing that defendants "shall not be privileged to seek any remedy or maintain any proceeding directly or indirectly, or to have any such remedy or proceeding brought on their behalf, in the courts of the United States," except under such regulations as the Attorney General might issue. Proclamation No. 2561, 7 Fed. Reg. 5101 (July 2, 1942). This transparent attempt to suspend the writ ultimately fared poorly in court, however. The Supreme Court concluded that nothing in the proclamation "foreclose[d] consideration by the courts of petitioners' contentions that the Constitution and the laws of the United States constitutionally enacted forbid their trial by military commission." *Ex parte Quirin*, 317 U.S. 1, 25 (1942). Thus, even aliens had a right to petition for habeas when they were detained inside the United States.

A later World War II case involved an enemy soldier who petitioned for a writ of habeas corpus after being tried by a military commission in the then-unincorporated U.S. territory of the Phillipines. The Court declared that Congress "has not withdrawn, and the Executive branch of the government could not, unless there was suspension of the writ, withdraw from the courts the duty and power to make such inquiry into the authority of the commission as may be made by habeas corpus." *Application of Yamashita*, 327 U.S. 1, 9 (1946). Indeed, Justice Murphy characterized the claim that courts could not make such inquiries as an "obnoxious doctrine," which he said the Court "rejected fully and unquestionably." *Id.* at 30. Thus, it seemed that aliens in unincorporated U.S. territories had the right to petition for habeas.

396

After the 9/11 attacks, President George W. Bush issued a military order in November 2001 providing for the military detention and trial by military commission of noncitizens he designated as members of Al Qaeda or persons involved in acts of international terrorism. The language of the order closely resembled that used in the order issued by President Roosevelt in 1942. The order included the following provision:

Military Order of November 13, 2001, Detention, Treatment, and Trial of Certain Non-Citizens in the War Against Terrorism

66 Fed. Reg. 57,833 (Nov. 13, 2001)

SEC. 7. RELATIONSHIP TO OTHER LAW AND FORUMS ...

(b) With respect to any individual subject to this order —
(1) military tribunals shall have exclusive jurisdiction with respect to offenses by the individual; and
(2) the individual shall not be privileged to seek any remedy or maintain any proceeding, directly or indirectly, or to have any such remedy or proceeding sought on the individual's behalf, in
(i) any court of the United States, or any State thereof,
(ii) any court of any foreign nation, or
(iii) any international tribunal. ...

Within a short time, persons captured by (or rendered to) U.S. forces in Afghanistan began to be imprisoned at the Guantánamo Bay Naval Station in Cuba, raising the question whether *they* were entitled to petition for habeas.

This chapter is devoted to an examination of the privilege of the writ of habeas corpus since the terrorist attacks of 9/11. In Part A, we note two Supreme Court decisions involving the availability of the writ to Guantánamo detainees. In Part B, we consider whether the writ is available to noncitizens imprisoned by the United States abroad. These materials present difficult but profoundly important questions of constitutional interpretation and statutory construction. They also test, once again, the role of courts in providing for national security.

One final introductory note concerns language. Some of the jargon used here is freighted with technical meaning, so it must be employed with care. Other terms may be chosen for their political or emotional content. An example of the latter is the word "detainee," which has come into vogue since 9/11 as a kinder, gentler euphemism for "prisoner." We use the two words here interchangeably.

A.   EXTENDING THE STATUTORY WRIT TO GUANTÁNAMO BAY DETAINEES

Soon after U.S. military operations against Al Qaeda and the Taliban commenced in Afghanistan in fall 2001, U.S. troops captured a number of individuals on the battlefield. Following a period of detention (and sometimes interrogation) in Afghanistan, many of these individuals were transferred to Guantánamo Bay, as noted

Detainees at Camp X-Ray, Guantánamo Bay Naval Base, Cuba.

DOD photo by Petty Officer 1st Class Shane T. McCoy, U.S. Navy.

above. Eventually, some Al Qaeda suspects captured or rendered to U.S. custody in other countries were also transferred to Guantánamo.

In 2002, two Australian citizens and twelve Kuwaiti citizens who were detained at Guantánamo filed habeas petitions in the U.S. District Court for the District of Columbia (on the theory that their custodian or jailor was located there), invoking the Habeas Corpus Act, 28 U.S.C. §§2241-2255 (2006 & Supp. III 2009). The lower courts rejected their petitions, citing *Johnson v. Eisentrager*, 339 U.S. 763 (1950), for the proposition that "aliens detained outside the sovereign territory of the United States [may not] invok[e] a petition for a writ of habeas corpus." *Rasul v. Bush*, 215 F. Supp. 2d 55, 68 (D.D.C. 2002), *aff'd sub nom. Al Odah v. Bush*, 321 F.3d 1134 (D.C. Cir. 2003).

The Supreme Court reversed. It found the Guantánamo petitioners different from the *Eisentrager* detainees in important respects:

> They are not nationals of countries at war with the United States, and they deny that they have engaged in or plotted acts of aggression against the United States; they have never been afforded access to any tribunal, much less charged with and convicted of wrongdoing; and for more than two years they have been imprisoned in territory over which the United States exercises exclusive jurisdiction and control. [*Rasul v. Bush*, 542 U.S. 466, 467 (2004).]

It also held that *Eisentrager* dealt only with "the question of the prisoners' *constitutional* entitlement to habeas corpus," and made no more than "a passing reference" to the absence of "*statutory* authorization." *Id.* (emphasis in original). It then found that intervening case law had extended statutory habeas jurisdiction to encompass the petitioners' claims against a custodian in the District of Columbia. *Id.*

> In the end, the answer to the question presented is clear. Petitioners contend that they are being held in federal custody in violation of the laws of the United States.[15] No party questions the District Court's jurisdiction over petitioners' custodians. Cf. *Braden* [*v. 30th Judicial Circuit Court of Ky.*, 410 U.S. 484 (1973)], at 495. Section 2241, by its terms,

---

15. Petitioners' allegations — that, although they have engaged neither in combat nor in acts of terrorism against the United States, they have been held in Executive detention for more than two years in territory subject to the long-term, exclusive jurisdiction and control of the United States, without access to counsel and without being charged with any wrongdoing — unquestionably describe "custody in violation of the Constitution or laws or treaties of the United States." 28 U.S.C. §2241(c)(3).

requires nothing more. We therefore hold that §2241 confers on the District Court jurisdiction to hear petitioners' habeas corpus challenges to the legality of their detention at the Guantanamo Bay Naval Base. [*Rasul*, 542 U.S. at 483.]

NOTES AND QUESTIONS

1. *The Military Order's "Suspension" of the Writ.* Assuming that some of the petitioners in *Rasul* were detained pursuant to the Military Order of November 13, 2001, why did §7 of the order not cut off their access to the courts? First, consider whether, in light of §7's pedigree, it was intended to suspend the writ. Next, consider whether, in light of the "clear statement" rule declared in *Immigration & Naturalization Service v. St. Cyr*, 533 U.S. 289 (2001), *supra* p. 388, any such intent was stated with the required clarity.

2. *Eisentrager's "Dire Warning."* Sharply dissenting in *Rasul*, Justice Scalia quoted the "dire warning" in *Johnson v. Eisentrager*, 339 U.S. 763 (1950), to suggest that the Court's ruling would open the floodgates to habeas petitions by enemy aliens after we captured large numbers in battle. Indeed, alien detainees at Guantánamo quickly pressed habeas petitions in U.S. courts. *See In re Guantanamo Detainee Cases*, 355 F. Supp. 2d 443 (D.D.C. 2005) (reporting that 13 cases involving more than 60 detainees had been filed by July 2004). Can you think of an answer to this concern? *Ex parte Milligan* and the statute it applied in 1866 suggest one answer. What is it? See the Detainee Treatment Act of 2005, *infra* Note 6.

In an apparent effort to close, or at least control, the floodgates, the Pentagon announced shortly after the Supreme Court's decision in *Rasul* that it was creating a Combatant Status Review Tribunal (CSRT), to be staffed by military officers, before whom detainees could contest their combatant status. Memorandum for the Secretary of the Navy from Deputy Secretary of Defense Paul Wolfowitz, *Order Establishing Combatant Status Review Tribunal* (July 7, 2004), *available at* http://www.defense.gov/news/jul2004/d20040707review.pdf. Detainees would have the assistance of a "personal representative" assigned by the government, but not a lawyer, and they would have to overcome a "rebuttable presumption in favor of the government's evidence." *Id.* ¶¶c. and g.(12). Do you think this program could stem the tide of habeas petitions to federal courts? If you represented one of the Guantánamo prisoners, could you think of a way to challenge the CSRT program? *See* Mark Denbeaux & Joshua W. Denbeaux, *No-Hearing Hearings — CSRT: The Modern Habeas Corpus?* (Seton Hall Pub. Law Research Paper No. 951245, 2006), *available at* http://ssrn.com/abstract=951245.

3. *The Inner Realm of Military Affairs: What's Left of Eisentrager?* Justice Kennedy joined in the *Rasul* judgment by preserving part of *Eisentrager*. He found that *Eisentrager* approved of "a realm of political authority over military affairs where the judicial power may not enter," but also that the Guantánamo Bay detentions, far removed from hostilities and attended by no status-determining procedures, even by the military, fell outside that realm. If the *Rasul* majority had embraced those qualifications, what would be left of *Eisentrager*?

4. *The Detainees' Constitutional Rights. Rasul* was strictly a jurisdictional decision, finding that the Guantánamo detainees had the right to petition for habeas. It did not reach the next question, which is whether they could assert any constitutional rights

that were violated by their detention. But consider footnote 15, above, from the majority opinion. What answer to that question does the footnote suggest? Is the answer holding or dictum?

5. *Contextual Influences.* Speculation about the Court's motives is always treacherous. Yet between the oral arguments in *Rasul*, in which the government assured the Court that the detainees were being treated in compliance with basic international human rights principles, and the Court's decision, the press broke the scandal about abuse of prisoners in Iraq and possible use of torture by the United States in the interrogation of detainees. Might the reports of mistreatment and of possible violations of international laws against torture have influenced the Court's decision on opening access to Article III courts?

6. *"Statutory Entitlement" and the Detainee Treatment Act of 2005. Rasul* ruled that the Guantánamo detainees had a "statutory entitlement" to petition for habeas. Congress responded quickly to *Rasul* by amending the relevant habeas statute in an effort to narrow that entitlement:

Detainee Treatment Act of 2005 (DTA)

Pub. L. No. 109-148, §1001-1006, 119 Stat. 2680, 2739-2744 (2005)

§1005. PROCEDURES FOR STATUS REVIEW OF DETAINEES OUTSIDE THE UNITED STATES...

(e) Judicial Review of Detention of Enemy Combatants.—
(1) In General.—Section 2241 of title 28, United States Code, is amended by adding at the end the following:

"(e) Except as provided in section 1005 of the Detainee Treatment Act of 2005, no court, justice, or judge shall have jurisdiction to hear or consider—
(1) an application for a writ of habeas corpus filed by or on behalf of an alien detained by the Department of Defense at Guantanamo Bay, Cuba; or
(2) any other action against the United States or its agents relating to any aspect of the detention by the Department of Defense of an alien at Guantanamo Bay, Cuba, who—
(A) is currently in military custody; or
(B) has been determined by the United States Court of Appeals for the District of Columbia Circuit in accordance with the procedures set forth in section 1005(e) of the Detainee Treatment Act of 2005 to have been properly detained as an enemy combatant.".

Section 1005(e)(2) and (e)(3) of the Act provided limited judicial review in the D.C. Circuit of the procedural validity of final decisions of CSRTs and of Military Commissions, but not review of the merits of such decisions.

Within months, however, a divided Supreme Court decided in *Hamdan v. Rumsfeld*, 548 U.S. 557 (2006), that federal courts *still* had statutory jurisdiction to hear a Guantánamo detainee's petition for the writ in a challenge to his prospective trial by military commission. Concerning military commissions, see generally Chapter 22.

The *Hamdan* majority reasoned that Congress had not clearly expressed an intent to withdraw habeas jurisdiction from pending cases like Hamdan's. *Id.* at 575-584.

B.   EXTENDING THE CONSTITUTIONAL WRIT TO GUANTÁNAMO BAY DETAINEES (AND OTHERS?)

After extended negotiations with the Bush administration in which, according to most observers, the Administration prevailed, Congress responded to *Hamdan v. Rumsfeld* by enacting the Military Commissions Act of 2006 (MCA 2006), Pub. L. No. 109-366, 120 Stat. 2600. Section 7 of MCA 2006 was intended to further amend the habeas statute by cutting off all access to the courts for "an alien detained by the United States who has been determined by the United States to have been properly detained as an enemy combatant or is awaiting such determination," except for the limited review provided by DTA §1005(2) and (3), as noted above. Detainees promptly challenged the new act, as described in the following case.

Boumediene v. Bush
United States Supreme Court, 2008
553 U.S. 723

Justice KENNEDY delivered the opinion of the Court. Petitioners are aliens designated as enemy combatants and detained at the United States Naval Station at Guantanamo Bay, Cuba. There are others detained there, also aliens, who are not parties to this suit.

Petitioners present a question not resolved by our earlier cases relating to the detention of aliens at Guantanamo: whether they have the constitutional privilege of habeas corpus, a privilege not to be withdrawn except in conformance with the Suspension Clause, Art. I, §9, cl. 2. We hold these petitioners do have the habeas corpus privilege. Congress has enacted a statute, the Detainee Treatment Act of 2005 (DTA), 119 Stat. 2739, that provides certain procedures for review of the detainees' status. We hold that those procedures are not an adequate and effective substitute for habeas corpus. Therefore, §7 of the Military Commissions Act of 2006 (MCA), 28 U.S.C.A. §2241(e) (Supp. 2007), operates as an unconstitutional suspension of the writ. We do not address whether the President has authority to detain these petitioners nor do we hold that the writ must issue. These and other questions regarding the legality of the detention are to be resolved in the first instance by the District Court.

I . . .

Interpreting the AUMF [Authorization for Use of Military Force, Pub. L. No. 107-40 (2001), *supra* p. 86], the Department of Defense ordered the detention of these petitioners, and they were transferred to Guantanamo. Some of these individuals were apprehended on the battlefield in Afghanistan, others in places as far away from there as Bosnia and Gambia. All are foreign nationals, but none is a citizen of a nation now at war with the United States. Each denies he is a member of the al Qaeda terrorist network that carried out the September 11 attacks or of the Taliban regime that provided sanctuary for al Qaeda. Each petitioner appeared before a separate CSRT [Combatant Status Review Tribunal]; was determined to be an enemy combatant; and has sought a writ of habeas corpus in the United States District Court for the District of Columbia.

[These initial petitions culminated in the Supreme Court's decision in *Rasul v. Bush*, 524 U.S. 466 (2004), extending *statutory* habeas corpus jurisdiction to Guantanamo. The Court there did not reach the question of *constitutional* habeas corpus jurisdiction, which is presented in the instant cases.] . . .

II

As a threshold matter, we must decide whether MCA §7 denies the federal courts jurisdiction to hear habeas corpus actions pending at the time of its enactment. We hold the statute does deny that jurisdiction, so that, if the statute is valid, petitioners' cases must be dismissed.

As amended by the terms of the MCA, §2241(e) now provides:

(1) No court, justice, or judge shall have jurisdiction to hear or consider an application for a writ of habeas corpus filed by or on behalf of an alien detained by the United States who has been determined by the United States to have been properly detained as an enemy combatant or is awaiting such determination.

(2) Except as provided in [§1005(e)(2) and (e)(3) of the DTA] no court, justice, or judge shall have jurisdiction to hear or consider any other action against the United States or its agents relating to any aspect of the detention, transfer, treatment, trial, or conditions of confinement of an alien who is or was detained by the United States and has been determined by the United States to have been properly detained as an enemy combatant or is awaiting such determination. . . .

III . . .

We begin with a brief account of the history and origins of the writ. Our account proceeds from two propositions. First, protection for the privilege of habeas corpus was one of the few safeguards of liberty specified in a Constitution that, at the outset, had no Bill of Rights. In the system conceived by the Framers the writ had a centrality that must inform proper interpretation of the Suspension Clause. Second, to the extent there were settled precedents or legal commentaries in 1789 regarding the extraterritorial scope of the writ or its application to enemy aliens, those authorities can be instructive for the present cases.

A

The Framers viewed freedom from unlawful restraint as a fundamental precept of liberty, and they understood the writ of habeas corpus as a vital instrument to secure that freedom. Experience taught, however, that the common-law writ all too often had been insufficient to guard against the abuse of monarchial power. That history counseled the necessity for specific language in the Constitution to secure the writ and ensure its place in our legal system. . . .

This history was known to the Framers. It no doubt confirmed their view that pendular swings to and away from individual liberty were endemic to undivided, uncontrolled power. The Framers' inherent distrust of governmental power was the driving force behind the constitutional plan that allocated powers among three independent branches. This design serves not only to make Government accountable but also to secure individual liberty. Because the Constitution's separation-of-powers structure, like the substantive guarantees of the Fifth and Fourteenth Amendments, *see Yick Wo v. Hopkins*, 118 U.S. 356, 374 (1886), protects persons as well as citizens, foreign nationals who have the privilege of litigating in our courts can seek to enforce separation-of-powers principles, see, *e.g., INS v. Chadha*, 462 U.S. 919, 958-959 (1983).

That the Framers considered the writ a vital instrument for the protection of individual liberty is evident from the care taken to specify the limited grounds for its suspension: "The Privilege of the Writ of Habeas Corpus shall not be suspended, unless when in Cases of Rebellion or Invasion the public Safety may require it." Art. I, §9, cl. 2; *see* Amar, *Of Sovereignty and Federalism*, 96 Yale L.J. 1425, 1509 n.329 (1987) ("[T]he non-suspension clause is the original Constitution's most explicit reference to remedies"). . . .

In our own system the Suspension Clause is designed to protect against these cyclical abuses. The Clause protects the rights of the detained by a means consistent with the essential design of the Constitution. It ensures that, except during periods of formal suspension, the Judiciary will have a time-tested device, the writ, to maintain the "delicate balance of governance" that is itself the surest safeguard of liberty. *See Hamdi* [*v. Rumsfeld*, 542 U.S. 507 (2004)], at 536 (plurality opinion). The Clause protects the rights of the detained by affirming the duty and authority of the Judiciary to call the jailer to account. The separation-of-powers doctrine, and the history that influenced its design, therefore must inform the reach and purpose of the Suspension Clause.

B . . .

To support their arguments, the parties in these cases have examined historical sources to construct a view of the common-law writ as it existed in 1789 — as have *amici* whose expertise in legal history the Court has relied upon in the past. The Government argues the common-law writ ran only to those territories over which the Crown was sovereign. Petitioners argue that jurisdiction followed the King's officers. Diligent search by all parties reveals no certain conclusions. . . .

. . . We decline, therefore, to infer too much, one way or the other, from the lack of historical evidence on point.

IV

Drawing from its position that at common law the writ ran only to territories over which the Crown was sovereign, the Government says the Suspension Clause affords petitioners no rights because the United States does not claim sovereignty over the place of detention.

Guantanamo Bay is not formally part of the United States. *See* DTA §1005(g), 119 Stat. 2743. And under the terms of the lease between the United States and Cuba, Cuba retains "ultimate sovereignty" over the territory while the United States exercises "complete jurisdiction and control." *See* Lease of Lands for Coaling and Naval Stations, Feb. 23, 1903, U.S.-Cuba, Art. III, T.S. No. 418 (hereinafter 1903 Lease Agreement); *Rasul*, 542 U.S., at 471. Under the terms of the 1934 Treaty, however, Cuba effectively has no rights as a sovereign until the parties agree to modification of the 1903 Lease Agreement or the United States abandons the base. *See* Treaty Defining Relations with Cuba, May 29, 1934, U.S.-Cuba, Art. III, 48 Stat. 1683, T.S. No. 866.

The United States contends, nevertheless, that Guantanamo is not within its sovereign control. This was the Government's position well before the events of September 11, 2001. And in other contexts the Court has held that questions of sovereignty are for the political branches to decide. Even if this were a treaty interpretation case that did not involve a political question, the President's construction of the lease agreement would be entitled to great respect.

We therefore do not question the Government's position that Cuba, not the United States, maintains sovereignty, in the legal and technical sense of the term, over Guantanamo Bay. But this does not end the analysis. Our cases do not hold it is improper for us to inquire into the objective degree of control the Nation asserts over foreign territory....

A

The Court has discussed the issue of the Constitution's extraterritorial application on many occasions. These decisions undermine the Government's argument that, at least as applied to noncitizens, the Constitution necessarily stops where *de jure* sovereignty ends.

[The Court reviewed cases, including the *Insular Cases* and *Reid v. Covert*, 345 U.S. 1 (1957), as standing for the proposition that "whether a constitutional provision has extraterritorial effect depends upon the 'particular circumstances, the practical necessities, and the possible alternatives which Congress had before it' and, in particular, whether judicial enforcement of the provision would be 'impracticable and anomalous.'" (quoting Justice Harlan in *Reid*).] ...

Practical considerations weighed heavily as well in *Johnson v. Eisentrager*, 339 U.S. 763 (1950), where the Court addressed whether habeas corpus jurisdiction extended to enemy aliens who had been convicted of violating the laws of war. The prisoners were detained at Landsberg Prison in Germany during the Allied Powers' postwar occupation. The Court stressed the difficulties of ordering the Government to produce the prisoners in a habeas corpus proceeding. It "would require allocation of shipping space, guarding personnel, billeting and rations" and would damage the prestige of military commanders at a sensitive time. *Id.*, at 779. In considering these factors the Court sought to balance the constraints of military occupation with constitutional necessities. *Id.*, at 769-779; *see Rasul*, 542 U.S., at 475-476 (discussing the factors relevant to *Eisentrager*'s constitutional holding); 542 U.S., at 486 (Kennedy, J., concurring in judgment) (same).

True, the Court in *Eisentrager* denied access to the writ, and it noted the prisoners "at no relevant time were within any territory over which the United States is sovereign, and [that] the scenes of their offense, their capture, their trial and their punishment were all beyond the territorial jurisdiction of any court of the United States." 339 U.S., at 778. The Government seizes upon this language as proof positive that the *Eisentrager* Court adopted a formalistic, sovereignty-based test for determining the reach of the Suspension Clause. We reject this reading for three reasons.

First, we do not accept the idea that the above-quoted passage from *Eisentrager* is the only authoritative language in the opinion and that all the rest is dicta.

The Court's further determinations, based on practical considerations, were integral to Part II of its opinion and came before the decision announced its holding. *See* 339 U.S., at 781.

. . . Even if we assume the *Eisentrager* Court considered the United States' lack of formal legal sovereignty over Landsberg Prison as the decisive factor in that case, its holding is not inconsistent with a functional approach to questions of extraterritoriality. The formal legal status of a given territory affects, at least to some extent, the political branches' control over that territory. *De jure* sovereignty is a factor that bears upon which constitutional guarantees apply there.

Third, if the Government's reading of *Eisentrager* were correct, the opinion would have marked not only a change in, but a complete repudiation of, the *Insular Cases'* (and later *Reid's*) functional approach to questions of extraterritoriality. We cannot accept the Government's view. Nothing in *Eisentrager* says that *de jure* sovereignty is or has ever been the only relevant consideration in determining the geographic reach of the Constitution or of habeas corpus. Were that the case, there would be considerable tension between *Eisentrager,* on the one hand, and the *Insular Cases* and *Reid,* on the other. Our cases need not be read to conflict in this manner. A constricted reading of *Eisentrager* overlooks what we see as a common thread uniting the *Insular Cases, Eisentrager,* and *Reid:* the idea that questions of extraterritoriality turn on objective factors and practical concerns, not formalism.

B

The Government's formal sovereignty-based test raises troubling separation-of-powers concerns as well. The political history of Guantanamo illustrates the deficiencies of this approach. The United States has maintained complete and uninterrupted control of the bay for over 100 years. . . . The necessary implication of the argument is that by surrendering formal sovereignty over any unincorporated territory to a third party, while at the same time entering into a lease that grants total control over the territory back to the United States, it would be possible for the political branches to govern without legal constraint.

Our basic charter cannot be contracted away like this. The Constitution grants Congress and the President the power to acquire, dispose of, and govern territory, not the power to decide when and where its terms apply. Even when the United States acts outside its borders, its powers are not "absolute and unlimited" but are subject "to such restrictions as are expressed in the Constitution." *Murphy v. Ramsey,* 114 U.S. 15, 44 (1885). Abstaining from questions involving formal sovereignty and territorial governance is one thing. To hold the political branches have the power to switch the Constitution on or off at will is quite another. The former position reflects this Court's recognition that certain matters requiring political judgments are best left to the political branches. The latter would permit a striking anomaly in our tripartite system of government, leading to a regime in which Congress and the President, not this Court, say "what the law is." *Marbury v. Madison,* 1 Cranch 137, 177 (1803).

These concerns have particular bearing upon the Suspension Clause question in the cases now before us, for the writ of habeas corpus is itself an indispensable mechanism for monitoring the separation of powers. The test for determining the scope of this provision must not be subject to manipulation by those whose power it is designed to restrain.

C

As we recognized in *Rasul,* 542 U.S., at 476; *id.,* at 487 (Kennedy, J., concurring in judgment), the outlines of a framework for determining the reach of the Suspension Clause are suggested by the factors the Court relied upon in *Eisentrager.* In addition to the practical concerns discussed above, the *Eisentrager* Court found relevant that each petitioner:

> "(a) is an enemy alien; (b) has never been or resided in the United States; (c) was captured outside of our territory and there held in military custody as a prisoner of war; (d) was tried and convicted by a Military Commission sitting outside the United States; (e) for offenses against laws of war committed outside the United States; (f) and is at all times imprisoned outside the United States." 339 U.S., at 777.

Based on this language from *Eisentrager,* and the reasoning in our other extraterritoriality opinions, we conclude that at least three factors are relevant in determining the reach of the Suspension Clause: (1) the citizenship and status of the detainee and the adequacy of the process through which that status determination was made; (2) the nature of the sites where apprehension and then detention took place; and (3) the practical obstacles inherent in resolving the prisoner's entitlement to the writ.

Applying this framework, we note at the onset that the status of these detainees is a matter of dispute. The petitioners, like those in *Eisentrager,* are not American citizens. But the petitioners in *Eisentrager* did not contest, it seems, the Court's assertion that they were "enemy alien[s]." In the instant cases, by contrast, the detainees deny they are enemy combatants. They have been afforded some process in CSRT proceedings to determine their status; but, unlike in *Eisentrager,* there has been no trial by military commission for violations of the laws of war. The difference is not trivial. The records from the *Eisentrager* trials suggest that, well before the petitioners brought their case to this Court, there had been a rigorous adversarial process to test the legality of their detention. The *Eisentrager* petitioners were charged by a bill of particulars that made detailed factual allegations against them. To rebut the accusations, they were entitled to representation by counsel, allowed to introduce evidence on their own behalf, and permitted to cross-examine the prosecution's witnesses.

In comparison, the procedural protections afforded to the detainees in the CSRT hearings are far more limited, and, we conclude, fall well short of the procedures and adversarial mechanisms that would eliminate the need for habeas corpus review. Although the detainee is assigned a "Personal Representative" to assist him during CSRT proceedings, the Secretary of the Navy's memorandum makes clear that person is not the detainee's lawyer or even his "advocate." The Government's evidence is accorded a presumption of validity. The detainee is allowed to present "reasonably available" evidence, but his ability to rebut the Government's evidence against him is limited by the circumstances of his confinement and his lack of counsel at this stage. And although the detainee can seek review of his status determination in the Court of Appeals, that review process cannot cure all defects in the earlier proceedings. *See* Part V, *infra.*

As to the second factor relevant to this analysis, the detainees here are similarly situated to the *Eisentrager* petitioners in that the sites of their apprehension and detention are technically outside the sovereign territory of the United States. As noted earlier, this is a factor that weighs against finding they have rights under the Suspension Clause. But there are critical differences between Landsberg Prison, circa

1950, and the United States Naval Station at Guantanamo Bay in 2008. Unlike its present control over the naval station, the United States' control over the prison in Germany was neither absolute nor indefinite. Like all parts of occupied Germany, the prison was under the jurisdiction of the combined Allied Forces. The United States was therefore answerable to its Allies for all activities occurring there. The Court's holding in *Eisentrager* was thus consistent with the *Insular Cases,* where it had held there was no need to extend full constitutional protections to territories the United States did not intend to govern indefinitely. Guantanamo Bay, on the other hand, is no transient possession. In every practical sense Guantanamo is not abroad; it is within the constant jurisdiction of the United States.

As to the third factor, we recognize, as the Court did in *Eisentrager,* that there are costs to holding the Suspension Clause applicable in a case of military detention abroad. Habeas corpus proceedings may require expenditure of funds by the Government and may divert the attention of military personnel from other pressing tasks. While we are sensitive to these concerns, we do not find them dispositive. Compliance with any judicial process requires some incremental expenditure of resources. Yet civilian courts and the Armed Forces have functioned along side each other at various points in our history. *See, e.g., Duncan v. Kahanamoku,* 327 U.S. 304 (1946); *Ex parte Milligan,* 4 Wall. 2 (1866). The Government presents no credible arguments that the military mission at Guantanamo would be compromised if habeas corpus courts had jurisdiction to hear the detainees' claims. And in light of the plenary control the United States asserts over the base, none are apparent to us.

The situation in *Eisentrager* was far different, given the historical context and nature of the military's mission in post-War Germany. When hostilities in the European Theater came to an end, the United States became responsible for an occupation zone encompassing over 57,000 square miles with a population of 18 million. In addition to supervising massive reconstruction and aid efforts the American forces stationed in Germany faced potential security threats from a defeated enemy. In retrospect the post-War occupation may seem uneventful. But at the time *Eisentrager* was decided, the Court was right to be concerned about judicial interference with the military's efforts to contain "enemy elements, guerilla fighters, and 'werewolves.'" 339 U.S., at 784.

Similar threats are not apparent here; nor does the Government argue that they are. The United States Naval Station at Guantanamo Bay consists of 45 square miles of land and water. The base has been used, at various points, to house migrants and refugees temporarily. At present, however, other than the detainees themselves, the only long-term residents are American military personnel, their families, and a small number of workers. The detainees have been deemed enemies of the United States. At present, dangerous as they may be if released, they are contained in a secure prison facility located on an isolated and heavily fortified military base.

There is no indication, furthermore, that adjudicating a habeas corpus petition would cause friction with the host government. No Cuban court has jurisdiction over American military personnel at Guantanamo or the enemy combatants detained there. While obligated to abide by the terms of the lease, the United States is, for all practical purposes, answerable to no other sovereign for its acts on the base. Were that not the case, or if the detention facility were located in an active theater of war, arguments that issuing the writ would be "impracticable or anomalous" would have more weight. *See Reid,* 354 U.S., at 74 (Harlan, J., concurring in result). Under the facts presented here, however, there are few practical barriers to the running of the writ.

To the extent barriers arise, habeas corpus procedures likely can be modified to address them.

It is true that before today the Court has never held that noncitizens detained by our Government in territory over which another country maintains *de jure* sovereignty have any rights under our Constitution. But the cases before us lack any precise historical parallel. They involve individuals detained by executive order for the duration of a conflict that, if measured from September 11, 2001, to the present, is already among the longest wars in American history. The detainees, moreover, are held in a territory that, while technically not part of the United States, is under the complete and total control of our Government. Under these circumstances the lack of a precedent on point is no barrier to our holding.

We hold that Art. I, §9, cl. 2, of the Constitution has full effect at Guantanamo Bay. If the privilege of habeas corpus is to be denied to the detainees now before us, Congress must act in accordance with the requirements of the Suspension Clause. *Cf. Hamdi*, 542 U.S., at 564 (Scalia, J., dissenting) ("[I]ndefinite imprisonment on reasonable suspicion is not an available option of treatment for those accused of aiding the enemy, absent a suspension of the writ"). This Court may not impose a *de facto* suspension by abstaining from these controversies. The MCA does not purport to be a formal suspension of the writ; and the Government, in its submissions to us, has not argued that it is. Petitioners, therefore, are entitled to the privilege of habeas corpus to challenge the legality of their detention.

V

In light of this holding the question becomes whether the statute stripping jurisdiction to issue the writ avoids the Suspension Clause mandate because Congress has provided adequate substitute procedures for habeas corpus. The Government submits there has been compliance with the Suspension Clause because the DTA review process in the Court of Appeals, *see* DTA §1005(e), provides an adequate substitute. Congress has granted that court jurisdiction to consider

> "(i) whether the status determination of the [CSRT] . . . was consistent with the standards and procedures specified by the Secretary of Defense . . . and (ii) to the extent the Constitution and laws of the United States are applicable, whether the use of such standards and procedures to make the determination is consistent with the Constitution and laws of the United States." §1005(e)(2)(C), 119 Stat. 2742. . . .

A

Our case law does not contain extensive discussion of standards defining suspension of the writ or of circumstances under which suspension has occurred. This simply confirms the care Congress has taken throughout our Nation's history to preserve the writ and its function. Indeed, most of the major legislative enactments pertaining to habeas corpus have acted not to contract the writ's protection but to expand it or to hasten resolution of prisoners' claims. . . .

. . . [Unlike those statutes], here we confront statutes, the DTA and the MCA, that were intended to circumscribe habeas review. Congress' purpose is evident not only from the unequivocal nature of MCA §7's jurisdiction-stripping language, 28 U.S.C.A. §2241(e)(1) (Supp. 2007) ("No court, justice, or judge shall have jurisdiction to hear or consider an application for a writ of habeas corpus...”), but also from a comparison of the DTA to the statutes at issue in [cases construing habeas-strengthening statutes].... When Congress has intended to replace traditional habeas corpus with habeas-like substitutes,... it has granted to the courts broad remedial powers to secure the historic office of the writ....

In contrast, the DTA’s jurisdictional grant is quite limited. The Court of Appeals has jurisdiction not to inquire into the legality of the detention generally but only to assess whether the CSRT complied with the “standards and procedures specified by the Secretary of Defense” and whether those standards and procedures are lawful. DTA §1005(e)(2)(C), 119 Stat. 2742. If Congress had envisioned DTA review as coextensive with traditional habeas corpus, it would not have drafted the statute in this manner.... [M]oreover, there has been no effort to preserve habeas corpus review as an avenue of last resort. No saving clause exists in either the MCA or the DTA. And MCA §7 eliminates habeas review for these petitioners....

To the extent any doubt remains about Congress’ intent, the legislative history confirms what the plain text strongly suggests....

It is against this background that we must interpret the DTA and assess its adequacy as a substitute for habeas corpus....

B

We do not endeavor to offer a comprehensive summary of the requisites for an adequate substitute for habeas corpus. We do consider it uncontroversial, however, that the privilege of habeas corpus entitles the prisoner to a meaningful opportunity to demonstrate that he is being held pursuant to “the erroneous application or interpretation” of relevant law. *St. Cyr,* 533 U.S. at 302. And the habeas court must have the power to order the conditional release of an individual unlawfully detained—though release need not be the exclusive remedy and is not the appropriate one in every case in which the writ is granted. These are the easily identified attributes of any constitutionally adequate habeas corpus proceeding. But, depending on the circumstances, more may be required.

Indeed, common-law habeas corpus was, above all, an adaptable remedy. Its precise application and scope changed depending upon the circumstances. It appears the common-law habeas court’s role was most extensive in cases of pretrial and noncriminal detention, where there had been little or no previous judicial review of the cause for detention....

The idea that the necessary scope of habeas review in part depends upon the rigor of any earlier proceedings accords with our test for procedural adequacy in the due process context. *See Mathews v. Eldridge,* 424 U.S. 319, 335 (1976) (noting that the Due Process Clause requires an assessment of, *inter alia,* “the risk of an erroneous deprivation of [a liberty interest;] and the probable value, if any, of additional or substitute procedural safeguards”)....

Accordingly, where relief is sought from a sentence that resulted from the judgment of a court of record, ... considerable deference is owed to the court that ordered confinement. Likewise in those cases the prisoner should exhaust adequate alternative remedies before filing for the writ in federal court. Both aspects of federal habeas corpus review are justified because it can be assumed that, in the usual course, a court of record provides defendants with a fair, adversary proceeding.... The present cases fall outside these categories, however; for here the detention is by executive order.

Where a person is detained by executive order, rather than, say, after being tried and convicted in a court, the need for collateral review is most pressing. A criminal conviction in the usual course occurs after a judicial hearing before a tribunal disinterested in the outcome and committed to procedures designed to ensure its own independence. These dynamics are not inherent in executive detention orders or executive review procedures. In this context the need for habeas corpus is more urgent. The intended duration of the detention and the reasons for it bear upon the precise scope of the inquiry. Habeas corpus proceedings need not resemble a criminal trial, even when the detention is by executive order. But the writ must be effective. The habeas court must have sufficient authority to conduct a meaningful review of both the cause for detention and the Executive's power to detain.

To determine the necessary scope of habeas corpus review, therefore, we must assess the CSRT process, the mechanism through which petitioners' designation as enemy combatants became final. Whether one characterizes the CSRT process as direct review of the Executive's battlefield determination that the detainee is an enemy combatant—as the parties have and as we do—or as the first step in the collateral review of a battlefield determination makes no difference in a proper analysis of whether the procedures Congress put in place are an adequate substitute for habeas corpus. What matters is the sum total of procedural protections afforded to the detainee at all stages, direct and collateral.

Petitioners identify what they see as myriad deficiencies in the CSRTs. The most relevant for our purposes are the constraints upon the detainee's ability to rebut the factual basis for the Government's assertion that he is an enemy combatant. As already noted, at the CSRT stage the detainee has limited means to find or present evidence to challenge the Government's case against him. He does not have the assistance of counsel and may not be aware of the most critical allegations that the Government relied upon to order his detention. *See* App. to Pet. for Cert. in No. 06-1196, at 156, ¶F(8) (noting that the detainee can access only the "unclassified portion of the Government Information"). The detainee can confront witnesses that testify during the CSRT proceedings. *Id.*, at 144, ¶g(8). But given that there are in effect no limits on the admission of hearsay evidence—the only requirement is that the tribunal deem the evidence "relevant and helpful," *ibid.*, ¶g(9)—the detainee's opportunity to question witnesses is likely to be more theoretical than real....

Even if we were to assume that the CSRTs satisfy due process standards, it would not end our inquiry. Habeas corpus is a collateral process that exists, in Justice Holmes' words, to "cu[t] through all forms and g[o] to the very tissue of the structure. It comes in from the outside, not in subordination to the proceedings, and although every form may have been preserved opens the inquiry whether they have been more than an empty shell." *Frank v. Mangum*, 237 U.S. 309, 346 (1915) (dissenting opinion). Even when the procedures authorizing detention are structurally sound, the Suspension Clause remains applicable and the writ relevant. *See* 2 Chambers, Course of Lectures on English Law 1767-1773, at 6 ("Liberty may be violated either by arbitrary *imprisonment* without law or the appearance of law, or by a lawful magistrate for an unlawful reason")....

Although we make no judgment as to whether the CSRTs, as currently constituted, satisfy due process standards, we agree with petitioners that, even when all the parties involved in this process act with diligence and in good faith, there is considerable risk of error in the tribunal's findings of fact. This is a risk inherent in any process that, in the words of the former Chief Judge of the Court of Appeals, is "closed and accusatorial." *See* [*Bismullah v. Gates*, 514 F.3d 1291, 1296 (D.C. Cir. 2008)] (Ginsburg, C.J., concurring in denial of rehearing en banc). And given that the consequence of error may be detention of persons for the duration of hostilities that may last a generation or more, this is a risk too significant to ignore.

For the writ of habeas corpus, or its substitute, to function as an effective and proper remedy in this context, the court that conducts the habeas proceeding must have the means to correct errors that occurred during the CSRT proceedings. This includes some authority to assess the sufficiency of the Government's evidence against the detainee. It also must have the authority to admit and consider relevant exculpatory evidence that was not introduced during the earlier proceeding. . . .

The extent of the showing required of the Government in these cases is a matter to be determined. We need not explore it further at this stage. We do hold that when the judicial power to issue habeas corpus properly is invoked the judicial officer must have adequate authority to make a determination in light of the relevant law and facts and to formulate and issue appropriate orders for relief, including, if necessary, an order directing the prisoner's release.

C

We now consider whether the DTA allows the Court of Appeals to conduct a proceeding meeting these standards. "[W]e are obligated to construe the statute to avoid [constitutional] problems" if it is "'fairly possible'" to do so. *St. Cyr*, 533 U.S., at 299-300 (quoting *Crowell v. Benson*, 285 U.S. 22, 62 (1932)). . . .

The DTA does not explicitly empower the Court of Appeals to order the applicant in a DTA review proceeding released should the court find that the standards and procedures used at his CSRT hearing were insufficient to justify detention. This is troubling. Yet, for present purposes, we can assume congressional silence permits a constitutionally required remedy. . . .

The absence of a release remedy and specific language allowing AUMF challenges are not the only constitutional infirmities from which the statute potentially suffers, however. The more difficult question is whether the DTA permits the Court of Appeals to make requisite findings of fact. The DTA enables petitioners to request "review" of their CSRT determination in the Court of Appeals, DTA §1005(e)(2)(B)(i), 119 Stat. 2742; but the "Scope of Review" provision confines the Court of Appeals' role to reviewing whether the CSRT followed the "standards and procedures" issued by the Department of Defense and assessing whether those "standards and procedures" are lawful. §1005(e)(C), *ibid.* Among these standards is "the requirement that the conclusion of the Tribunal be supported by a preponderance of the evidence . . . allowing a rebuttable presumption in favor of the Government's evidence." §1005(e)(C)(i), *ibid.*

Assuming the DTA can be construed to allow the Court of Appeals to review or correct the CSRT's factual determinations, as opposed to merely certifying that the tribunal applied the correct standard of proof, we see no way to construe the statute to allow what is also constitutionally required in this context: an opportunity for the detainee to present relevant exculpatory evidence that was not made part of the record in the earlier proceedings.

On its face the statute allows the Court of Appeals to consider no evidence outside the CSRT record. . . .

By foreclosing consideration of evidence not presented or reasonably available to the detainee at the CSRT proceedings, the DTA disadvantages the detainee by limiting the scope of collateral review to a record that may not be accurate or complete. In other contexts, *e.g.,* in post-trial habeas cases where the prisoner already has had a full and fair opportunity to develop the factual predicate of his claims, similar limitations on the scope of habeas review may be appropriate. In this context, however, where the underlying detention proceedings lack the necessary adversarial character, the detainee cannot be held responsible for all deficiencies in the record. . . .

Although we do not hold that an adequate substitute must duplicate §2241 in all respects, it suffices that the Government has not established that the detainees' access to the statutory review provisions at issue is an adequate substitute for the writ of habeas corpus. MCA §7 thus effects an unconstitutional suspension of the writ. In view of our holding we need not discuss the reach of the writ with respect to claims of unlawful conditions of treatment or confinement.

VI

A

In light of our conclusion that there is no jurisdictional bar to the District Court's entertaining petitioners' claims the question remains whether there are prudential barriers to habeas corpus review under these circumstances. . . .

In cases involving foreign citizens detained abroad by the Executive, it likely would be both an impractical and unprecedented extension of judicial power to assume that habeas corpus would be available at the moment the prisoner is taken into custody. If and when habeas corpus jurisdiction applies, as it does in these cases, then proper deference can be accorded to reasonable procedures for screening and initial detention under lawful and proper conditions of confinement and treatment for a reasonable period of time. Domestic exigencies, furthermore, might also impose such onerous burdens on the Government that here, too, the Judicial Branch would be required to devise sensible rules for staying habeas corpus proceedings until the Government can comply with its requirements in a responsible way. *Cf. Ex parte Milligan,* 4 Wall., at 127 ("If, in foreign invasion or civil war, the courts are actually closed, and it is impossible to administer criminal justice according to law, *then,* on the theatre of active military operations, where war really prevails, there is a necessity to furnish a substitute for the civil authority, thus overthrown, to preserve the safety of the army and society; and as no power is left but the military, it is allowed to govern by martial rule until the laws can have their free course"). Here, as is true with detainees apprehended abroad, a relevant consideration in determining the courts' role is whether there are suitable alternative processes in place to protect against the arbitrary exercise of governmental power.

The cases before us, however, do not involve detainees who have been held for a short period of time while awaiting their CSRT determinations. Were that the case, or were it probable that the Court of Appeals could complete a prompt review of their applications, the case for requiring temporary abstention or exhaustion of alternative remedies would be much stronger. These qualifications no longer pertain here. In some of these cases six years have elapsed without the judicial oversight that habeas corpus or an adequate substitute demands. And there has been no showing that the Executive faces such onerous burdens that it cannot respond to habeas corpus actions. To require these detainees to complete DTA review before proceeding with their habeas corpus actions would be to require additional months, if not years, of delay. The first DTA review applications were filed over a year ago, but no decisions on the merits have been issued. While some delay in fashioning new procedures is unavoidable, the costs of delay can no longer be borne by those who are held in custody. The detainees in these cases are entitled to a prompt habeas corpus hearing.

Our decision today holds only that the petitioners before us are entitled to seek the writ; that the DTA review procedures are an inadequate substitute for habeas corpus; and that the petitioners in these cases need not exhaust the review procedures in the Court of Appeals before proceeding with their habeas actions in the District Court. The only law we identify as unconstitutional is MCA §7, 28 U.S.C.A. §2241(e) (Supp. 2007). Accordingly, both the DTA and the CSRT process remain intact. Our holding with regard to exhaustion should not be read to imply that a habeas court should intervene the moment an enemy combatant steps foot in a territory where the writ runs. The Executive is entitled to a reasonable period of time to determine a detainee's status before a court entertains that detainee's habeas corpus petition. The CSRT process is the mechanism Congress and the President set up to deal with these issues. Except in cases of undue delay, federal courts should refrain from entertaining an enemy combatant's habeas corpus petition at least until after the Department, acting via the CSRT, has had a chance to review his status.

B

Although we hold that the DTA is not an adequate and effective substitute for habeas corpus, it does not follow that a habeas corpus court may disregard the dangers the detention in these cases was intended to prevent. . . . [T]he Suspension Clause does not resist innovation in the field of habeas corpus. Certain accommodations can be made to reduce the burden habeas corpus proceedings will place on the military without impermissibly diluting the protections of the writ.

In the DTA Congress sought to consolidate review of petitioners' claims in the Court of Appeals. Channeling future cases to one district court would no doubt reduce administrative burdens on the Government. This is a legitimate objective that might be advanced even without an amendment to §2241. . . .

Another of Congress' reasons for vesting exclusive jurisdiction in the Court of Appeals, perhaps, was to avoid the widespread dissemination of classified information. The Government has raised similar concerns here and elsewhere. We make no attempt to anticipate all of the evidentiary and access-to-counsel issues that will arise during the course of the detainees' habeas corpus proceedings. We recognize, however, that the Government has a legitimate interest in protecting sources and methods of intelligence gathering; and we expect that the District Court will use its discretion to accommodate this interest to the greatest extent possible. *Cf. United States v. Reynolds*, 345 U.S. 1, 10 (1953) (recognizing an evidentiary privilege in a civil damages case where "there is a reasonable danger that compulsion of the evidence will expose military matters which, in the interest of national security, should not be divulged").

These and the other remaining questions are within the expertise and competence of the District Court to address in the first instance.

* * *

In considering both the procedural and substantive standards used to impose detention to prevent acts of terrorism, proper deference must be accorded to the political branches. *See United States v. Curtiss-Wright Export Corp.,* 299 U.S. 304, 320 (1936). Unlike the President and some designated Members of Congress, neither the Members of this Court nor most federal judges begin the day with briefings that may describe new and serious threats to our Nation and its people. The law must accord the Executive substantial authority to apprehend and detain those who pose a real danger to our security.

Officials charged with daily operational responsibility for our security may consider a judicial discourse on the history of the Habeas Corpus Act of 1679 and like matters to be far removed from the Nation's present, urgent concerns. Established legal doctrine, however, must be consulted for its teaching. Remote in time it may be; irrelevant to the present it is not. Security depends upon a sophisticated intelligence apparatus and the ability of our Armed Forces to act and to interdict. There are further considerations, however. Security subsists, too, in fidelity to freedom's first principles. Chief among these are freedom from arbitrary and unlawful restraint and the personal liberty that is secured by adherence to the separation of powers. It is from these principles that the judicial authority to consider petitions for habeas corpus relief derives.

Our opinion does not undermine the Executive's powers as Commander in Chief. On the contrary, the exercise of those powers is vindicated, not eroded, when confirmed by the Judicial Branch. Within the Constitution's separation-of-powers structure, few exercises of judicial power are as legitimate or as necessary as the responsibility to hear challenges to the authority of the Executive to imprison a person. Some of these petitioners have been in custody for six years with no definitive judicial determination as to the legality of their detention. Their access to the writ is a necessity to determine the lawfulness of their status, even if, in the end, they do not obtain the relief they seek.

Because our Nation's past military conflicts have been of limited duration, it has been possible to leave the outer boundaries of war powers undefined. If, as some fear, terrorism continues to pose dangerous threats to us for years to come, the Court might not have this luxury. This result is not inevitable, however. The political branches, consistent with their independent obligations to interpret and uphold the Constitution, can engage in a genuine debate about how best to preserve constitutional values while protecting the Nation from terrorism. *Cf. Hamdan* [*v. Rumsfeld,* 548 U.S. 557 (2006)], at 636 (Breyer, J., concurring) ("[J]udicial insistence upon that consultation does not weaken our Nation's ability to deal with danger. To the contrary, that insistence strengthens the Nation's ability to determine — through democratic means — how best to do so").

It bears repeating that our opinion does not address the content of the law that governs petitioners' detention. That is a matter yet to be determined. We hold that petitioners may invoke the fundamental procedural protections of habeas corpus. The laws and Constitution are designed to survive, and remain in force, in extraordinary times. Liberty and security can be reconciled; and in our system they are reconciled within the framework of the law. The Framers decided that habeas corpus, a right of first importance, must be a part of that framework, a part of that law.

The determination by the Court of Appeals that the Suspension Clause and its protections are inapplicable to petitioners was in error. The judgment of the Court of Appeals is reversed. The cases are remanded to the Court of Appeals with instructions that it remand the cases to the District Court for proceedings consistent with this opinion.

It is so ordered.

[Concurring opinion of Justice SOUTER, with whom Justice GINSBURG and Justice BREYER join, is omitted.]

Chief Justice ROBERTS, with whom Justice SCALIA, Justice THOMAS, and Justice ALITO join, dissenting. Today the Court strikes down as inadequate the most generous set of procedural protections ever afforded aliens detained by this country as enemy combatants. The political branches crafted these procedures amidst an ongoing military conflict, after much careful investigation and thorough debate. The Court rejects them today out of hand, without bothering to say what due process rights the detainees possess, without explaining how the statute fails to vindicate those rights, and before a single petitioner has even attempted to avail himself of the law's operation. And to what effect? The majority merely replaces a review system designed by the people's representatives with a set of shapeless procedures to be defined by federal courts at some future date. One cannot help but think, after surveying the modest practical results of the majority's ambitious opinion, that this decision is not really about the detainees at all, but about control of federal policy regarding enemy combatants. . . .

. . . The important point for me, however, is that the Court should have resolved these cases on other grounds. Habeas is most fundamentally a procedural right, a mechanism for contesting the legality of executive detention. The critical threshold question in these cases, prior to any inquiry about the writ's scope, is whether the system the political branches designed protects whatever rights the detainees may possess. If so, there is no need for any additional process, whether called "habeas" or something else. . . .

II . . .

. . . After much hemming and hawing, the majority appears to concede that the DTA provides an Article III court competent to order release. The only issue in dispute is the process the Guantanamo prisoners are entitled to use to test the legality of their detention. . . .

A . . .

Hamdi merits scant attention from the Court — a remarkable omission, as *Hamdi* bears directly on the issues before us. The majority attempts to dismiss *Hamdi's* relevance by arguing that because the availability of §2241 federal habeas was never in doubt in that case, "the Court had no occasion to define the necessary scope of habeas review . . . in the context of enemy combatant detentions." Hardly. *Hamdi* was all about the scope of habeas review in the context of enemy combatant detentions. The petitioner, an American citizen held within the United States as an enemy combatant, invoked the writ to challenge his detention. After "a careful examination both of the writ . . . and of the Due Process Clause," this Court enunciated the "basic process" the Constitution entitled Hamdi to expect from a habeas court under §2241.

That process consisted of the right to "receive notice of the factual basis for his classification, and a fair opportunity to rebut the Government's factual assertions before a neutral decisionmaker." In light of the Government's national security responsibilities, the plurality found the process could be "tailored to alleviate [the] uncommon potential to burden the Executive at a time of ongoing military conflict." For example, the Government could rely on hearsay and could claim a presumption in favor of its own evidence.

Hamdi further suggested that this "basic process" on collateral review could be provided by a military tribunal. It pointed to prisoner-of-war tribunals as a model that would satisfy the Constitution's requirements. Only "[i]n the *absence* of such process" before a military tribunal, the Court held, would Article III courts need to conduct full-dress habeas proceedings to "ensure that the minimum requirements of due process are achieved." *Ibid.* (emphasis added). And even then, the petitioner would be entitled to no more process than he would have received from a properly constituted military review panel, given his limited due process rights and the Government's weighty interests.

Contrary to the majority, *Hamdi* is of pressing relevance because it establishes the procedures American *citizens* detained as enemy combatants can expect from a habeas court proceeding under §2241. The DTA system of military tribunal hearings followed by Article III review looks a lot like the procedure *Hamdi* blessed. If nothing else, it is plain from the design of the DTA that Congress, the President, and this Nation's military leaders have made a good-faith effort to follow our precedent.

The Court, however, will not take "yes" for an answer. . . .

III . . .

The majority rests its decision on abstract and hypothetical concerns. Step back and consider what, in the real world, Congress and the Executive have actually granted aliens captured by our Armed Forces overseas and found to be enemy combatants:

- The right to hear the bases of the charges against them, including a summary of any classified evidence.

- The ability to challenge the bases of their detention before military tribunals modeled after Geneva Convention procedures. Some 38 detainees have been released as a result of this process.

- The right, before the CSRT, to testify, introduce evidence, call witnesses, question those the Government calls, and secure release, if and when appropriate.

- The right to the aid of a personal representative in arranging and presenting their cases before a CSRT.

- Before the D.C. Circuit, the right to employ counsel, challenge the factual record, contest the lower tribunal's legal determinations, ensure compliance with the Constitution and laws, and secure release, if any errors below establish their entitlement to such relief.

In sum, the DTA satisfies the majority's own criteria for assessing adequacy. This statutory scheme provides the combatants held at Guantanamo greater procedural protections than have ever been afforded alleged enemy detainees — whether citizens or aliens — in our national history. . . .

I respectfully dissent.

Justice SCALIA, with whom THE CHIEF JUSTICE, Justice THOMAS, and Justice ALITO join, dissenting. . . . Contrary to my usual practice, . . . I think it appropriate to begin with a description of the disastrous consequences of what the Court has done today.

I

America is at war with radical Islamists. . . .

The game of bait-and-switch that today's opinion plays upon the Nation's Commander in Chief will make the war harder on us. It will almost certainly cause more Americans to be killed. That consequence would be tolerable if necessary to preserve a time-honored legal principle vital to our constitutional Republic. But it is this Court's blatant *abandonment* of such a principle that produces the decision today. The President relied on our settled precedent in *Johnson v. Eisentrager*, 339 U.S. 763 (1950), when he established the prison at Guantanamo Bay for enemy aliens. Citing that case, the President's Office of Legal Counsel advised him "that the great weight of legal authority indicates that a federal district court could not properly exercise habeas jurisdiction over an alien detained at [Guantanamo Bay]." Memorandum from Patrick F. Philbin and John C. Yoo, Deputy Assistant Attorneys General, Office of Legal Counsel, to William J. Haynes II, General Counsel, Dept. of Defense (Dec. 28, 2001). Had the law been otherwise, the military surely would not have transported prisoners there, but would have kept them in Afghanistan, transferred them to another of our foreign military bases, or turned them over to allies for detention. Those other facilities might well have been worse for the detainees themselves.

In the long term, then, the Court's decision today accomplishes little, except perhaps to reduce the well-being of enemy combatants that the Court ostensibly seeks to protect. In the short term, however, the decision is devastating. At least 30 of those prisoners hitherto released from Guantanamo Bay have returned to the battlefield. Some have been captured or killed. But others have succeeded in carrying on their atrocities against innocent civilians. . . .

These, mind you, were detainees whom *the military* had concluded were not enemy combatants. Their return to the kill illustrates the incredible difficulty of assessing who is and who is not an enemy combatant in a foreign theater of operations where the environment does not lend itself to rigorous evidence collection. Astoundingly, the Court today raises the bar, requiring military officials to appear before civilian courts and defend their decisions under procedural and evidentiary rules that go beyond what Congress has specified. As the Chief Justice's dissent makes clear, we have no idea what those procedural and evidentiary rules are, but they will be determined by civil courts and (in the Court's contemplation at least) will be more detainee-friendly than those now applied, since otherwise there would no reason to hold the congressionally prescribed procedures unconstitutional. If they impose a higher standard of proof (from foreign battlefields) than the current procedures require, the number of the enemy returned to combat will obviously increase.

But even when the military has evidence that it can bring forward, it is often foolhardy to release that evidence to the attorneys representing our enemies. And one escalation of procedures that the Court *is* clear about is affording the detainees increased access to witnesses (perhaps troops serving in Afghanistan?) and to classified information. During the 1995 prosecution of Omar Abdel Rahman, federal prosecutors gave the names of 200 unindicted co-conspirators to the "Blind Sheik's" defense lawyers; that information was in the hands of Osama Bin Laden within two weeks. In another case, trial testimony revealed to the enemy that the United States had been monitoring their cellular network, whereupon they promptly stopped using it, enabling more of them to evade capture and continue their atrocities. . . .

. . . The Court today decrees that no good reason to accept the judgment of the other two branches is "apparent." "The Government," it declares, "presents no credible arguments that the military mission at Guantanamo would be compromised if habeas corpus courts had jurisdiction to hear the detainees' claims." What competence does the Court have to second-guess the judgment of Congress and the President on such a point? None whatever. But the Court blunders in nonetheless. Henceforth, as today's opinion makes unnervingly clear, how to handle enemy prisoners in this war will ultimately lie with the branch that knows least about the national security concerns that the subject entails.

II

A . . .

. . . The Court admits that it cannot determine whether the writ historically extended to aliens held abroad, and it concedes (necessarily) that Guantanamo Bay lies outside the sovereign territory of the United States. Together, these two concessions establish that it is (in the Court's view) perfectly ambiguous whether the common-law writ would have provided a remedy for these petitioners. If that is so, the Court has no basis to strike down the Military Commissions Act, and must leave undisturbed the considered judgment of the coequal branches.

How, then, does the Court weave a clear constitutional prohibition out of pure interpretive equipoise? The Court resorts to "fundamental separation-of-powers principles" to interpret the Suspension Clause. According to the Court, because "the writ of habeas corpus is itself an indispensable mechanism for monitoring the separation of powers," the test of its extraterritorial reach "must not be subject to manipulation by those whose power it is designed to restrain."

That approach distorts the nature of the separation of powers and its role in the constitutional structure. The "fundamental separation-of-powers principles" that the Constitution embodies are to be derived not from some judicially imagined matrix, but from the sum total of the individual separation-of-powers provisions that the Constitution sets forth. Only by considering them one-by-one does the full shape of the *Constitution's* separation-of-powers principles emerge. It is nonsensical to interpret those provisions themselves in light of some general "separation-of-powers principles" dreamed up by the Court. Rather, they must be interpreted to mean what they were understood to mean when the people ratified them. And if the understood scope of the writ of habeas corpus was "designed to restrain" (as the Court says) the actions of the Executive, the understood *limits* upon that scope were (as the Court seems not to grasp) just as much "designed to restrain" the incursions of the Third Branch. "Manipulation" of the territorial reach of the writ by the Judiciary poses just as much a threat to the proper separation of powers as "manipulation" by the

Executive. As I will show below, manipulation is what is afoot here. The understood limits upon the writ deny our jurisdiction over the habeas petitions brought by these enemy aliens, and entrust the President with the crucial wartime determinations about their status and continued confinement.

B

The Court purports to derive from our precedents a "functional" test for the extraterritorial reach of the writ, which shows that the Military Commissions Act unconstitutionally restricts the scope of habeas. That is remarkable because the most pertinent of those precedents, *Johnson v. Eisentrager*, 339 U.S. 763, conclusively establishes the opposite. . . .

. . . *Eisentrager* nowhere mentions a "functional" test, and the notion that it is based upon such a principle is patently false . . . .

The category of prisoner comparable to these detainees are not the *Eisentrager* criminal defendants, but the more than 400,000 prisoners of war detained in the United States alone during World War II. Not a single one was accorded the right to have his detention validated by a habeas corpus action in federal court — and that despite the fact that they were present on U.S. soil. The Court's analysis produces a crazy result: Whereas those convicted and sentenced to death for war crimes are without judicial remedy, all enemy combatants detained during a war, at least insofar as they are confined in an area away from the battlefield over which the United States exercises "absolute and indefinite" control, may seek a writ of habeas corpus in federal court. And, as an even more bizarre implication from the Court's reasoning, those prisoners whom the military plans to try by full-dress Commission at a future date may file habeas petitions and secure release before their trials take place. . . .

III

Putting aside the conclusive precedent of *Eisentrager,* it is clear that the original understanding of the Suspension Clause was that habeas corpus was not available to aliens abroad, as Judge Randolph's thorough opinion for the court below detailed. . . .

. . . [A]ll available historical evidence points to the conclusion that the writ would not have been available at common law for aliens captured and held outside the sovereign territory of the Crown. Despite three opening briefs, three reply briefs, and support from a legion of *amici,* petitioners have failed to identify a single case in the history of Anglo-American law that supports their claim to jurisdiction. The Court finds it significant that there is no recorded case *denying* jurisdiction to such prisoners either. But a case standing for the remarkable proposition that the writ could issue to a foreign land would surely have been reported, whereas a case denying such a writ for lack of jurisdiction would likely not. At a minimum, the absence of a reported case either way leaves unrefuted the voluminous commentary stating that habeas was confined to the dominions of the Crown.

What history teaches is confirmed by the nature of the limitations that the Constitution places upon suspension of the common-law writ. It can be suspended only "in Cases of Rebellion or Invasion." Art. I, §9, cl. 2. The latter case (invasion) is plainly limited to the territory of the United States; and while it is conceivable that a rebellion could be mounted by American citizens abroad, surely the overwhelming majority of its occurrences would be domestic. If the extraterritorial scope of habeas turned on flexible, "functional" considerations, as the Court holds, why would the Constitution limit its suspension almost entirely to instances of domestic crisis? Surely there is an even greater justification for suspension in foreign lands where the United States might hold prisoners of war during an ongoing conflict. And correspondingly, there is less threat to liberty when the Government suspends the writ's (supposed) application in foreign lands, where even on the most extreme view prisoners are entitled to fewer constitutional rights. It makes no sense, therefore, for the Constitution generally to forbid suspension of the writ abroad if indeed the writ has application there. . . .

The Nation will live to regret what the Court has done today. I dissent.

NOTES AND QUESTIONS

1. *A Right to Habeas?* Although the Court treated *Boumediene* as a Suspension Clause case, there is nothing for Congress to suspend unless the detainees have a right to petition for habeas in the first place. The government, citing *Eisentrager*, argued that there is no right to habeas for noncitizen prisoners held abroad in a place, like the Landsberg prison, where the United States lacks "formal legal sovereignty." The Guantánamo prisoners thus had no habeas right, the government insisted, because Cuba retains "ultimate sovereignty" under its lease agreement with the United States.

How did the Court respond? How is the Guantánamo Bay Naval Station different from the Landsberg prison in Germany? Why did the Court say that the "Government's formal legal sovereignty test raises troubling separation-of-powers concerns"?

Ultimately, the Court chose function over form, suggesting a multifactor functional test for habeas. What is the functional framework it adopts, and how does it apply to the detainees? How is its application to them different from its application to the *Eisentrager* petitioners? For a vigorous argument that the majority's history was flatly wrong, *see* Raymond Randolph, *Originalism and History: the Case of Boumediene v. Bush*, 34 Harv. J.L. & Pub. Pol'y 89 (2010).

2. *Suspension?* Once the Court found that the detainees had a right to constitutional habeas, it immediately faced other questions. "If the privilege of habeas corpus is to be denied to the detainees," the Court observed, "Congress must act in accordance with the requirements of the Suspension Clause." 553 U.S. at 771. What does the Suspension Clause require? Did Congress seek to suspend the right when it enacted MCA 2006? If so, did it satisfy the requirements? What must Congress now do if it wants to suspend habeas for the Guantánamo detainees?

3. *Adequate Substitute?* The Court found that, without formally suspending the privilege of the writ, Congress could nevertheless restrict prisoners' access to the courts so long as it provided an "adequate substitute" for habeas corpus — one that preserves the "function" of habeas review. *Id.* at 773. In what respects did the processes established by MCA 2006 and the DTA fall short of preserving the writ's function?

Can you identify the baseline procedures for constitutional habeas? To put if differently, if you were a district court judge in the District of Columbia, could you determine from *Boumediene* what procedures you should use in entertaining habeas petitions from detainees in Guantánamo?

4. *Paying Deference to the Political Branches.* Isn't Justice Scalia clearly correct in asserting that the *Boumediene* majority's treatment of *Eisentrager* worked a "bait and switch" on the Bush administration? Note that *Eisentrager* was decided in 1950, just a year after the Geneva Conventions were signed and the same year that basic reforms were adopted in the U.S. system of military justice. Should the Administration have taken the "bait" without regard for the evolved and evolving regime of human rights, both at home and abroad?

If *Boumediene* worked a "switch," does it leave any room for practical necessity? For example, does it require habeas to be made available at the moment a prisoner is detained abroad? Do the same rules apply at home? What other accommodations does the Court make, or say that the district courts can make, to practical exigencies and administrative burdens?

5. *Does the Constitutional Writ Extend Beyond Guantánamo Bay?* While *Boumediene* dealt only with detainees held at Guantánamo, its functional test for extraterritorial application of habeas may apply elsewhere. In *Al Maqaleh v. Gates,* 605 F.3d 84 (D.C. Cir. 2010), the petitioners were three prisoners at Bagram Air Force Base in Afghanistan. The Court of Appeals rejected their argument that U.S. "control of Bagram under the lease of the military base is sufficient to trigger the extraterritorial application of the Suspension Clause.... Such an interpretation would seem to create the potential for the extraterritorial extension of the Suspension Clause to noncitizens held in any United States military facility in the world, and perhaps to an undeterminable number of other United States-leased facilities as well." *Id.* at 95.

Instead, it applied the multifaceted *Boumediene* functional test to decide the case. Regarding citizenship, the court found these petitioners (two Yemenis and a Tunisian) no different from those in *Boumediene.* The relatively scant process they received from an "Unlawful Enemy Combatant Review Board" (UECRB) weighed in their favor. But the location of their detention weighed the other way: "While it is certainly realistic to assert that the United States has *de facto* sovereignty over Guantánamo, the same simply is not true with respect to Bagram." *Id.* at 97. The tie-breaker was the third factor, "the practical obstacles inherent in resolving the prisoner's entitlement to the writ." Bagram was, the court noted, located in an active theater of war. "The United States asserts, and petitioners cannot credibly dispute, that all of the attributes of a facility exposed to the vagaries of war are present in Bagram." Accordingly, the court held, "We cannot, consistent with *Eisentrager* as elucidated by *Boumediene,* hold that the right to the writ of habeas corpus and the constitutional protections of the Suspension Clause extend to Bagram detention facility in Afghanistan." *Id.* at 97-98.

Did *Al Maqaleh* allow the Administration to create a new "black hole" for detainees? *See* Kal Raustiala, *Al Maqaleh v. Gates, 605 F.3d 84. U.S. Court of Appeals for the D.C. Circuit, May 21, 2010,* 104 Am. J. Int'l L. 647, 653 (2010) (wondering "whether the Obama administration's victory in *Al Maqaleh* will inevitably lead to charges that Bagram is simply a new Guantánamo — only even harsher and more remote."). Based on the analysis in *Al Maqaleh,* how would you decide the extraterritorial application of constitutional habeas to noncitizen detainees at a CIA detention facility in Poland? On a U.S. naval vessel in the Indian Ocean?

Did *Al Maqaleh* put too much weight on functionalism and too little on habeas as a limit on executive power? *See* Marc D. Falkoff & Robert Knowles, *Bagram, Boumediene, and Limited Government,* 59 DePaul L. Rev. 851, 898 (2010) (arguing that *Boumediene*'s central principle "lies beyond pragmatism: indefinite detention without any court review is fundamentally inconsistent with any exercise of government power under the U.S. Constitution."); Stephen I. Vladeck, *The Suspension Clause as a Structural Right*, 62 U. Miami L. Rev. 275, 278 (2008) (viewing the Suspension Clause as "'a structural right' . . . creating no rights whatsoever, but merely empowering Congress to do away with the writ of habeas corpus only when exigency demands.").

6. *Constitutional Rights to Be Vindicated by Habeas?* The writ of habeas corpus is merely a means to an end: the end of making the government justify the detention of its prisoner. But recall that the Court of Appeals in *Eisentrager* had reasoned from rights to a habeas remedy: that the prisoners had constitutional rights that they could only vindicate if they had access to habeas. What answer did the Supreme Court give in that case? *See also United States v. Verdugo-Urquidez*, 494 U.S. 259 (1990) (holding that the Fourth Amendment does not protect an alien without substantial connections to the United States). Did *Rasul* change that answer? What about *Boumediene?*

Rasul was released from Guantánamo Bay in 2004. In the following case, he sued for damages, asserting in part that the defendants had violated his Fifth Amendment right to due process and his Eighth Amendment protection against cruel and unusual treatment in detention.

Rasul v. Myers

United States Court of Appeals for the D.C. Circuit, 2010
563 F.3d 527

Before: HENDERSON and BROWN, Circuit Judges, and RANDOLPH, Senior Circuit Judge.

PER CURIAM: . . . The main question in *Boumediene* was whether a provision in the Military Commissions Act, Pub. L. No. 109-366, 120 Stat. 2600 (2006) (codified in part at 28 U.S.C. §2241 & note), depriving federal courts of habeas corpus jurisdiction over petitions filed by Guantánamo detainees, violated the clause of the Constitution governing suspension of the writ, Art. 1, §9, cl. 2. 128 S. Ct. at 2237. . . . The Court acknowledged that it had never before determined that the Constitution protected aliens detained abroad, *id.* at 2262, and explicitly confined its constitutional holding "only" to the extraterritorial reach of the Suspension Clause, *id.* at 2275. The Court stressed that its decision "does not address the *content of the law* that governs petitioners' detention." *Id.* at 2277 (emphasis added). With those words, the Court in *Boumediene* disclaimed any intention to disturb existing law governing the extraterritorial reach of any constitutional provisions, other than the Suspension Clause. *See, e.g., Johnson v. Eisentrager*, 339 U.S. 763 (1950) (holding that aliens detained on a U.S. military base outside sovereign U.S. territory have no due process rights); *United States v. Verdugo-Urquidez*, 494 U.S. 259 (1990) (holding that the Fourth Amendment does not protect nonresident aliens against unreasonable searches or seizures conducted outside sovereign U.S. territory).

Plaintiffs nevertheless maintain that *Boumediene* has eroded the precedential force of *Eisentrager* and its progeny. Whether that is so is not for us to determine; the Court has reminded the lower federal courts that it alone retains the authority to overrule its precedents. . . .

There is another reason why we should not decide whether *Boumediene* portends application of the Due Process Clause and the Cruel and Unusual Punishment Clause to Guantánamo detainees—and it is on this ground we will rest our decision on remand. The doctrine of qualified immunity shields government officials from civil liability to the extent their alleged misconduct "does not violate clearly established statutory or constitutional rights of which a reasonable person would have known." *Harlow v. Fitzgerald*, 457 U.S. 800, 818 (1982)....

... No reasonable government official would have been on notice that plaintiffs had any Fifth Amendment or Eighth Amendment rights. At the time of their detention,[2] neither the Supreme Court nor this court had ever held that aliens captured on foreign soil and detained beyond sovereign U.S. territory had any constitutional rights—under the Fifth Amendment, the Eighth Amendment, or otherwise. The Court in *Boumediene* recognized just that: "It is true that before today the Court has never held that noncitizens detained by our Government in territory over which another country maintains *de jure* sovereignty have any rights under our Constitution." 128 S. Ct. at 2262.

Eisentrager and *Verdugo-Urquidez* were thought to be the controlling Supreme Court cases on the Constitution's application to aliens abroad. *Eisentrager* rejected a habeas petition brought by German nationals imprisoned at a United States military base in Germany. 339 U.S. at 778. The Court held that these alien prisoners, who "at no relevant time were within any territory over which the United States is sovereign," were not entitled to invoke the protection of the writ or the Fifth Amendment. *Id.* The Court referred nine times to the decisive fact that the alien prisoners were, at all relevant times, outside sovereign U.S. territory. *See id.* at 777-78.

"[E]mphatic" is how the Court later described its rejection of the claim that aliens outside the sovereign territory of the United States are entitled to due process rights. *Verdugo-Urquidez*, 494 U.S. at 269 (citing *Eisentrager*, 339 U.S. at 770). Following *Eisentrager*, the Court in *Verdugo-Urquidez* concluded that the Fourth Amendment did not protect nonresident aliens against unreasonable searches or seizures conducted outside the sovereign territory of the United States. *Id.* at 274-75. The majority noted that although American citizens abroad can invoke some constitutional protections, *id.* at 270 (citing *Reid v. Covert*, 354 U.S. 1 (1957) (plurality opinion)), aliens abroad are in an altogether different situation. *Id.* at 271. The long line of cases dealing with constitutional rights of both lawful resident aliens and illegal aliens establishes "only that aliens receive constitutional protections when they have come within the territory of the United States and developed substantial connections with this country." *Id.* (citing *Plyler v. Doe*, 457 U.S. 202, 212 (1982) (The provisions of the Fourteenth Amendment "are universal in their application, *to all persons within the territorial jurisdiction....*") (emphasis added in *Verdugo-Urquidez*); *Kwong Hai Chew v. Colding*, 344 U.S. 590, 596 n.5 (1953) ("The Bill of Rights is a futile authority for the alien seeking admission for the first time to these shores. But *once an alien lawfully enters and resides in this country* he becomes invested with the rights guaranteed by the Constitution to all people within our borders.") (emphasis added in *Verdugo-Urquidez*)). Those cases could not help an alien who, like *Verdugo-Urquidez* and plaintiffs in this case, had at no relevant time been in the country and had "no previous significant voluntary connection with the United States," *id.*....

---

2. All four plaintiffs were released more than four years before the Supreme Court decided *Boumediene*, and months before the Court held even that statutory habeas corpus jurisdiction extended to Guantanamo. See *Rasul v. Bush*, 542 U.S. 466, 483-84 (2004). We do not require government employees to anticipate future developments in constitutional law.

In short, there was no authority for — and ample authority against — plaintiffs' asserted rights at the time of the alleged misconduct. The defendants are therefore entitled to qualified immunity against plaintiffs' *Bivens* claims. For the foregoing reasons, we affirm the district court's dismissal of [the claims based on petitioners' asserted constitutional rights.]

So ordered.

[Concurring opinion of Circuit Judge BROWN omitted.]

NOTES AND QUESTIONS

1. *Distinguishing Eisentrager and Verdugo-Urquidez?* The Court of Appeals treats the Supreme Court's decisions in *Eisentrager* and *Verdugo-Urquidez* as dispositive on the question of Rasul's constitutional rights, other than the right to habeas. But did the *Myers* court accurately characterize the holdings in those cases? If so, is there any way to distinguish between the *Eisentrager* prisoners and Rasul that could justify the recognition of Fifth Amendment rights for the latter? Is there any difference between Verdugo-Urquidez (a Mexican national who had no connections with the United States when his property was searched by U.S. agents in Mexico) and Rasul that could justify the recognition of Fourth Amendment rights in Rasul?

2. *Habeas for What?* *Myers* was *not* a habeas case, but its conclusions about Rasul's constitutional rights presumably apply to all current noncitizen detainees who lack any connection to the United States. Does it make sense to find a right to constitutional habeas and then conclude that the petitioner has no constitutional rights? Even if a detainee/petitioner has no *constitutional rights*, are there other rights he could assert? Or is it wrong to frame the questions as one of rights at all, given the limited historical scope of habeas to test the jailor's authority to detain? *See* Jared A. Goldstein, *Habeas Without Rights*, 2007 Wis. L. Rev. 1165, 1169 ("Habeas did not protect rights . . . for a simple reason: habeas predates rights.").

Military Detention
Before 9/11

15

In Chapter 12 we explored justifications for preventive detention by civilian authorities of suspected terrorists or persons with information about terrorism. In Chapters 13 and 14 we learned that suspension of the writ of habeas corpus does not by itself provide authority for detention; it merely cuts off the right of a detainee to make the government justify its detention in a court of law.

In this chapter we turn to legal theories for detention by military authorities of persons deemed threats to national security before 9/11. In Part A, we consider authority for the detention of noncombatants during a declared war or invasion. In Part B, we analyze traditional law-of-war authority for detention of enemy combatants in armed conflict. In the following chapter, we explore how the same authority has been used to detain U.S. citizens and resident aliens as combatants after 9/11.

A. MILITARY DETENTION OF NONCOMBATANTS BEFORE 9/11

Alien Enemy Act
50 U.S.C. §21 (2006)

Whenever there is a declared war between the United States and any foreign nation or government, or any invasion or predatory incursion is perpetrated, attempted, or threatened against the territory of the United States by any foreign nation or government, and the President makes public proclamation of the event, all natives, citizens, denizens, or subjects of the hostile nation or government, being of the age of fourteen years and upward, who shall be within the United States and not actually naturalized, shall be liable to be apprehended, restrained, secured, and removed as alien enemies. The President is authorized in any such event, by his proclamation thereof, or other public act, to direct the conduct to be observed, on the part of the United States, toward the aliens who become so liable; the manner and degree of the restraint to which they shall be subject and in what cases, and upon what security their residence shall be permitted, and to provide for the removal of those who, not being permitted to reside within the United States, refuse or neglect to depart therefrom; and to establish any other regulations which are found necessary in the premises and for the public safety.

Korematsu v. United States
United States Supreme Court, 1944
323 U.S. 214

Mr. Justice BLACK delivered the opinion of the Court. The petitioner, an American citizen of Japanese descent, was convicted in a federal district court for remaining in San Leandro, California, a "Military Area," contrary to Civilian Exclusion Order No. 34 of the Commanding General of the Western Command, U.S. Army, which directed that after May 9, 1942, all persons of Japanese ancestry should be excluded from that area. No question was raised as to petitioner's loyalty to the United States. The Circuit Court of Appeals affirmed, and the importance of the constitutional question involved caused us to grant certiorari.

It should be noted, to begin with, that all legal restrictions which curtail the civil rights of a single racial group are immediately suspect. That is not to say that all such restrictions are unconstitutional. It is to say that courts must subject them to the most rigid scrutiny. Pressing public necessity may sometimes justify the existence of such restrictions; racial antagonism never can.

In the instant case prosecution of the petitioner was begun by information charging violation of an Act of Congress, of March 21, 1942, 56 Stat. 173, which provides that

> ...whoever shall enter, remain in, leave, or commit any act in any military area or military zone prescribed, under the authority of an Executive order of the President, by the Secretary of War, or by any military commander designated by the Secretary of War, contrary to the restrictions applicable to any such area or zone or contrary to the order of the Secretary of War or any such military commander, shall, if it appears that he knew or should have known of the existence and extent of the restrictions or order and that his act was in violation thereof, be guilty of a misdemeanor and upon conviction shall be liable to a fine of not to exceed $5,000 or to imprisonment for not more than one year, or both, for each offense.

Exclusion Order No. 34, which the petitioner knowingly and admittedly violated, was one of a number of military orders and proclamations, all of which were substantially based upon Executive Order No. 9066, 7 Fed. Reg. 1407. That order, issued after we were at war with Japan, declared that "the successful prosecution of the war requires every possible protection against espionage and against sabotage to national-defense material, national-defense premises, and national-defense utilities. . . . " [The order also authorized the designation of "military areas . . . from which any and all persons may be excluded."]

One of the series of orders and proclamations, a curfew order, which like the exclusion order here was promulgated pursuant to Executive Order 9066, subjected all persons of Japanese ancestry in prescribed West Coast military areas to remain in their residences from 8 P.M. to 6 A.M. As is the case with the exclusion order here, that prior curfew order was designed as a "protection against espionage and against sabotage." In *Hirabayashi v. United States*, 320 U.S. 81, we sustained a conviction obtained for violation of the curfew order. The Hirabayashi conviction and this one thus rest on the same 1942 Congressional Act and the same basic executive and military orders, all of which orders were aimed at the twin dangers of espionage and sabotage.

The 1942 Act was attacked in the *Hirabayashi* case as an unconstitutional delegation of power; it was contended that the curfew order and other orders on which it rested were beyond the war powers of the Congress, the military authorities and of the President, as Commander in Chief of the Army; and finally that to apply the curfew order against none but citizens of Japanese ancestry amounted to a constitutionally prohibited discrimination solely on account of race. To these questions, we gave the consideration which their importance justified. We upheld the curfew order as an exercise of the power of the government to take steps necessary to prevent espionage and sabotage in an area threatened by Japanese attack.

In the light of the principles we announced in the *Hirabayashi* case, we are unable to conclude that it was beyond the war power of Congress and the Executive to exclude those of Japanese ancestry from the West Coast war area at the time they did. True, exclusion from the area in which one's home is located is a far greater deprivation than constant confinement to the home from 8 P.M. to 6 A.M. Nothing short of apprehension by the proper military authorities of the gravest imminent danger to the public safety can constitutionally justify either. But exclusion from a threatened area, no less than curfew, has a definite and close relationship to the prevention of espionage and sabotage. . . .

Here, as in the *Hirabayashi* case, *supra*, at p. 99, ". . . we cannot reject as unfounded the judgment of the military authorities and of Congress that there were disloyal members of that population, whose number and strength could not be precisely and quickly ascertained. We cannot say that the war-making branches of the Government did not have ground for believing that in a critical hour such persons could not readily be isolated and separately dealt with, and constituted a menace to the national defense and safety, which demanded that prompt and adequate measures be taken to guard against it." . . .

We uphold the exclusion order as of the time it was made and when the petitioner violated it. In doing so, we are not unmindful of the hardships imposed by it upon a large group of American citizens. But hardships are part of war, and war is an aggregation of hardships. All citizens alike, both in and out of uniform, feel the impact of war in greater or lesser measure. Citizenship has its responsibilities as well as its privileges, and in time of war the burden is always heavier. Compulsory exclusion of large groups of citizens from their homes, except under circumstances of direst emergency and peril, is inconsistent with our basic governmental institutions. But when under conditions of modern warfare our shores are threatened by hostile forces, the power to protect must be commensurate with the threatened danger. . . .

It is said that we are dealing here with the case of imprisonment of a citizen in a concentration camp solely because of his ancestry, without evidence or inquiry concerning his loyalty and good disposition towards the United States. Our task would be simple, our duty clear, were this a case involving the imprisonment of a loyal citizen in a concentration camp because of racial prejudice. Regardless of the true nature of the assembly and relocation centers — and we deem it unjustifiable to call them concentration camps with all the ugly connotations that term implies — we are dealing specifically with nothing but exclusion order. To cast this case into outlines of racial prejudice, without reference to the real military dangers which were presented, merely confuses the issue. Korematsu was not excluded from the Military Area because of hostility to him or his race. He *was* excluded because we are at war with the Japanese Empire, because the properly constituted military authorities feared an invasion of our West Coast and felt constrained to take proper security measures, because they decided that the military urgency of the situation demanded that all citizens of Japanese ancestry be segregated from the West Coast temporarily, and finally, because Congress, reposing its confidence in this time of war in our military leaders — as inevitably it must — determined that they should have the power to do just this. There was evidence of disloyalty on the part of some, the military authorities considered that the need for action was great, and time was short. We cannot — by availing ourselves of the calm perspective of hindsight — now say that at that time these actions were unjustified.

Affirmed.

Japanese-American heads of families line up for relocation, San Francisco, 1942.

Photo courtesy The National Archives.

Mr. Justice FRANKFURTER, concurring.... The provisions of the Constitution which confer on the Congress and the President powers to enable this country to wage war are as much part of the Constitution as provisions looking to a nation at peace. And we have had recent occasion to quote approvingly the statement of former Chief Justice Hughes that the war power of the Government is "the power to wage war successfully." *Hirabayashi v. United States,* supra at 93; and see *Home Bldg. & L. Assn. v. Blaisdell,* 290 U.S. 398, 426. Therefore, the validity of action under the war power must be judged wholly in the context of war. That action is not to be stigmatized as lawless because like action in times of peace would be lawless. To talk about a military order that expresses an allowable judgment of war needs by those entrusted with the duty of conducting war as "an unconstitutional order" is to suffuse a part of the Constitution with an atmosphere of unconstitutionality. The respective spheres of action of military authorities and of judges are of course very different. But within their sphere, military authorities are no more outside the bounds of obedience to the Constitution than are judges within theirs. "The war power of the United States, like its other powers . . . is subject to applicable constitutional limitations," *Hamilton v. Kentucky Distilleries Co.*, 251 U.S. 146, 156. To recognize that military orders are "reasonably expedient military precautions" in time of war and yet to deny them constitutional legitimacy makes of the Constitution an instrument for dialectic subtleties not reasonably to be attributed to the hard-headed Framers, of whom a majority had had actual participation in war. . . .

Mr. Justice MURPHY, dissenting. This exclusion of "all persons of Japanese ancestry, both alien and non-alien," from the Pacific Coast area on a plea of military necessity in the absence of martial law ought not to be approved. Such exclusion goes over "the very brink of constitutional power" and falls into the ugly abyss of racism.

In dealing with matters relating to the prosecution and progress of a war, we must accord great respect and consideration to the judgments of the military authorities who are on the scene and who have full knowledge of the military facts. The scope of their discretion must, as a matter of necessity and common sense, be wide. And their judgments ought not to be overruled lightly by those whose training and duties ill-equip them to deal intelligently with matters so vital to the physical security of the nation.

At the same time, however, it is essential that there be definite limits to military discretion, especially where martial law has not been declared. Individuals must not be left impoverished of their constitutional rights on a plea of military necessity that has neither substance nor support. Thus, like other claims conflicting with the asserted constitutional rights of the individual, the military claim must subject itself to the judicial process of having its reasonableness determined and its conflicts with other interests reconciled. "What are the allowable limits of military discretion, and whether or not they have been overstepped in a particular case, are judicial questions." *Sterling v. Constantin*, 287 U.S. 378, 401.

The judicial test of whether the Government, on a plea of military necessity, can validly deprive an individual of any of his constitutional rights is whether the deprivation is reasonably related to a public danger that is so "immediate, imminent, and impending" as not to admit of delay and not to permit the intervention of ordinary constitutional processes to alleviate the danger. *United States v. Russell*, 13 Wall. 623, 627-628; *Mitchell v. Harmony*, 13 How. 115, 134-135; *Raymond v. Thomas*, 91 U.S. 712, 716. Civilian Exclusion Order No. 34, banishing from a prescribed area of the Pacific Coast "all persons of Japanese ancestry, both alien and non-alien," clearly does not meet that test. Being an obvious racial discrimination, the order deprives all those within its scope of the equal protection of the laws as guaranteed by the Fifth Amendment. It further deprives these individuals of their constitutional rights to live and work where they will, to establish a home where they choose and to move about freely. In excommunicating them without benefit of hearings, this order also deprives them of all their constitutional rights to procedural due process. Yet no reasonable relation to an "immediate, imminent, and impending" public danger is evident to support this racial restriction which is one of the most sweeping and complete deprivations of constitutional rights in the history of this nation in the absence of martial law. . . .

Mr. Justice JACKSON, dissenting. . . . [T]he "law" which this prisoner is convicted of disregarding is not found in an act of Congress, but in a military order. Neither the Act of Congress nor the Executive Order of the President, nor both together, would afford a basis for this conviction. It rests on the orders of General DeWitt. And it is said that if the military commander had reasonable military grounds for promulgating the orders, they are constitutional and become law, and the Court is required to enforce them. There are several reasons why I cannot subscribe to this doctrine.

It would be impracticable and dangerous idealism to expect or insist that each specific military command in an area of probable operations will conform to conventional tests of constitutionality. When an area is so beset that it must be put under military control at all, the paramount consideration is that its measures be successful, rather than legal. The armed services must protect a society, not merely its Constitution. The very essence of the military job is to marshall physical force, to remove every obstacle to its effectiveness, to give it every strategic advantage. Defense measures will not, and often should not, be held within the limits that bind civil authority in peace. No court can require such a commander in such circumstances to act as a reasonable man; he may be unreasonably cautious and exacting. Perhaps he should be. But a commander in temporarily focusing the life of a community on defense is carrying out a military program; he is not making law in the sense that the courts know the term. He issues orders, and they may have a certain authority as military commands, although they may be very bad as constitutional law.

But if we cannot confine military expedients by the Constitution, neither would I distort the Constitution to approve all that the military may deem expedient. That is what the Court appears to be doing, whether consciously or not. I cannot say, from any evidence before me, that the orders of General DeWitt were not reasonably expedient military precautions, nor could I say that they were. But even if they were permissible military procedures, I deny that it follows that they are constitutional. If, as the Court holds, it does follow, then we may as well say that any military order will be constitutional and have done with it.

The limitation under which courts always will labor in examining the necessity for a military order [is] illustrated by this case. How does the Court know that these orders have a reasonable basis in necessity? No evidence whatever on that subject has been taken by this or any other court....

In the very nature of things, military decisions are not susceptible of intelligent judicial appraisal. They do not pretend to rest on evidence, but are made on information that often would not be admissible and on assumptions that could not be proved. Information in support of an order could not be disclosed to courts without danger that it would reach the enemy. Neither can courts act on communications made in confidence. Hence courts can never have any real alternative to accepting the mere declaration of the authority that issued the order that it was reasonably necessary from a military viewpoint.

Much is said of the danger to liberty from the Army program for deporting and detaining these citizens of Japanese extraction. But a judicial construction of the due process clause that will sustain this order is a far more subtle blow to liberty than the promulgation of the order itself. A military order, however unconstitutional, is not apt to last longer than the military emergency. Even during that period a succeeding commander may revoke it all. But once a judicial opinion rationalizes such an order to show that it conforms to the Constitution, or rather rationalizes the Constitution to show that the Constitution sanctions such an order, the Court for all time has validated the principle of racial discrimination in criminal procedure and of transplanting American citizens. The principle then lies about like a loaded weapon ready for the hand of any authority that can bring forward a plausible claim of an urgent need.

Every repetition imbeds that principle more deeply in our law and thinking and expands it to new purposes. . . .

I should hold that a civil court cannot be made to enforce an order which violates constitutional limitations even if it is a reasonable exercise of military authority. The courts can exercise only the judicial power, can apply only law, and must abide by the Constitution, or they cease to be civil courts and become instruments of military policy.

Of course the existence of a military power resting on force, so vagrant, so centralized, so necessarily heedless of the individual, is an inherent threat to liberty. But I would not lead people to rely on this Court for a review that seems to me wholly delusive. The military reasonableness of these orders can only be determined by military superiors. If the people ever let command of the war power fall into irresponsible and unscrupulous hands, the courts wield no power equal to its restraint. The chief restraint upon those who command the physical forces of the country, in the future as in the past, must be their responsibility to the political judgments of their contemporaries and to the moral judgments of history.

My duties as a justice as I see them do not require me to make a military judgment as to whether General DeWitt's evacuation and detention program was a reasonable military necessity. I do not suggest that the courts should have attempted to interfere with the Army in carrying out its task. But I do not think they may be asked to execute a military expedient that has no place in law under the Constitution. I would reverse the judgment and discharge the prisoner.

[The opinion of Justice ROBERTS, dissenting, is omitted.]

NOTES AND QUESTIONS

1. *Alien Enemies?* Why did the government not invoke the Alien Enemy Act to confine Korematsu and his fellow internees? Could the government have invoked it to justify the PENTTBOM (referring to the 9/11 investigation) detentions of immigrants described *supra* p. 347? If so, has Congress occupied the field of alien detention during war or invasion with the Alien Enemy Act?

2. *Constitutionality of Emergency Actions in Wartime.* Attorney General Francis Biddle wrote about the decision to create the internments,

> I do not think [President Roosevelt] was much concerned with the gravity or implications of this step. . . . Nor do I think the constitutional difficulty plagued him. The Constitution has not greatly bothered any wartime President. That was a question of law, which ultimately the Supreme Court must decide. And meanwhile—probably a long meanwhile—we must get on with the war. [Francis Biddle, *In Brief Authority* 219 (1962).]

Whatever the President's regard for fidelity to the Constitution, what is the significance of the Court's and Justice Frankfurter's constitutionalization of actions that in times of peace would be lawless? Consider Justice Jackson's warning on this point in his dissenting opinion. Professor Lobel indicates that throughout the twentieth century, but especially since World War II, the expanding U.S. role in global affairs and a nearly constant state of national crisis have promoted the development of a "relativistic" theory that finds emergency powers within the framework of the Constitution: the Commander in Chief and Executive Clauses, the President's inherent power in foreign affairs, and the presumed power of Congress to make laws anticipating every emergency. Jules Lobel, *Emergency Powers and the Decline of Liberalism*, 98 Yale L.J. 1385, 1399-1409 (1989).

If the Court is to review the constitutionality of emergency actions, what standards are to be applied? Are they found in the Constitution itself, or elsewhere?

These questions and others are considered in the classic contemporaneous criticisms of the principal case: Nanete Dembitz, *Racial Discrimination and the Military Judgment: The Supreme Court's Korematsu and Endo Decisions*, 45 Colum. L. Rev. 175 (1945); and Eugene Rostow, *The Japanese American Cases—A Disaster*, 54 Yale L.J. 489 (1945). *See also* Lobel, *supra*, at 1399-1412.

3. *Possible Significance of Citizenship and Loyalty.* In *Ex parte Endo*, 323 U.S. 283 (1944), decided the same day as *Korematsu*, the Court found that a Japanese-American citizen whose loyalty to the United States was conceded by the government could not be detained in a relocation center. The Court noted that

> [t]he Constitution when it committed to the Executive and to Congress the exercise of the war power necessarily gave them wider scope for the exercise of judgment and discretion so that war might be waged effectively and successfully [citing *Hirabayashi*]. At the same time, however, the Constitution is as specific in its enumeration of many of the civil rights of the individual as it is in the enumeration of the powers of his government. . . .
> . . . In interpreting a wartime measure we must assume that Congress' purpose was to allow for the greatest possible accommodation between civil liberties and the exigencies of war. [*Id.* at 298-300.]

So saying, the Court refused to find in either the 1942 congressional act or Executive Order No. 9066 any implied authority to detain an admittedly loyal citizen where none was expressly given. Should we infer from the Court's holding that internment based on race or ethnic background might be permissible if it were approved either by an act of Congress or by a clear presidential directive? Or does *Endo* stand for the proposition that an admittedly loyal American may not be locked up, even in time of war? If the latter, how could loyalty be established if it is not admitted, and who has the burden of proving its presence or absence?

A small number of German-Americans were interned during the war after individual loyalty hearings. Why were Japanese-Americans not given the same hearings before internment? After the war, one interned German-American sought compensation from the government. His claim was rejected. The court noted that after "three years of testimony from hundreds of witnesses, Congress concluded that Japanese Americans were detained en masse because of racial prejudice and demagoguery, while German Americans were detained in small numbers, and only after individual hearings about their loyalty." *Jacobs v. Barr*, 959 F.2d 313, 314 (D.C. Cir. 1992).

4. *Standard of Review.* One commentator argues that careful judicial scrutiny is appropriate, if not essential, in cases like *Hirabayashi* and *Korematsu*, "'where there is the most at stake in terms of personal freedom and the political branches are most likely to over-react'—when the government deems it necessary to restrict the most cherished liberties of American citizens to guard the nation's security." Eric R. Yamamoto, *Korematsu Revisited—Correcting the Injustice of Extraordinary Government Excess and Lax Judicial Review*, 26 Santa Clara L. Rev. 1, 48 (1986) (citation omitted). Heightened judicial

scrutiny is especially important in such cases, he suggests, because "it addresses the inherent weakness in the system of majority rule." *Id.* at 48-49.

How is this proposed standard of review different from the one set forth in the second paragraph of the *Korematsu* opinion? What standard of review was actually applied by the *Korematsu* Court? *See Adarand Constructors, Inc. v. Pena,* 515 U.S. 200, 214 (1995) (calling the *Korematsu* Court's application of its "most rigid scrutiny" standard "inexplicab[le]"). How do you think *Korematsu* would be decided today under modern equal protection law? For a description of that law, see *supra* p. 316.

5. *Belated Disclosure of Government Misconduct.* The *Korematsu* Court's extremely deferential review of the government's claim of military necessity enabled a stunning act of official fraud that was not revealed until nearly 40 years later. In 1982, Professor Peter Irons of the University of California at San Diego initiated a Freedom of Information Act request to obtain access to Justice Department records from its prosecution of the *Korematsu* case in 1944. His discoveries encouraged Fred Korematsu to file a petition for a writ of *coram nobis* in the court where he was tried 40 years earlier to vacate his conviction on grounds of government misconduct. Setting aside Korematsu's conviction, the court found that

> the government knowingly withheld information from the courts when they were considering the critical question of military necessity in this case. A series of correspondence regarding what information should be included in the government's brief before the Supreme Court culminated in two different versions of a footnote that was to be used to specify the factual data upon which the government relied for its military necessity justification. The first version read as follows:
>
>> The Final Report of General DeWitt (which is dated June 5, 1943, but which was not made public until January 1944) is relied on in this brief for statistics and other details concerning the actual evacuation and the events that took place subsequent thereto. *The recital of the circumstances justifying the evacuation as a matter of military necessity, however, is in several respects,* particularly with reference to the use of illegal radio transmitters and to shore-to-ship signalling by persons of Japanese ancestry, *in conflict with information in the possession of the Department of Justice. In view of the contrariety of the reports on this matter we do not ask the Court to take judicial notice of the recital of those facts contained in the Report.* Petitioner's Exhibit AA, Memorandum of John L. Burling to Assistant Attorney General Herbert Wechsler, September 11, 1944 [emphasis added]....
>
> The footnote that appeared in the final version of the brief merely read as follows:
>
>> The Final Report of General DeWitt (which is dated June 5, 1943, but which was not made public until January 1944), hereinafter cited as Final Report, is relied on in this brief for statistics and other details concerning the actual evacuation and the events that took place subsequent thereto. *We have specifically recited in this brief the facts relating to the justification for the evacuation, of which we ask the Court to take judicial notice, and we rely upon the Final Report only to the extent that it relates to such facts.*
>
> Brief for the United States, *Korematsu v. United States,* October Term, 1944, No. 22, at 11. The final version made no mention of the contradictory reports. The record is replete with protestations of various Justice Department officials that the government had the obligation to advise the courts of the contrary facts and opinions. In fact, several Department of Justice officials pointed out to their superiors and others the "wilful historical inaccuracies and intentional falsehoods" contained in the DeWitt Report....

... Omitted from the reports presented to the courts was information possessed by the Federal Communications Commission, the Department of the Navy, and the Justice Department which directly contradicted General DeWitt's statements. Thus, the court had before it a selective record. [*Korematsu v. United States*, 584 F. Supp. 1406, 1417-1419 (N.D. Cal. 1984).]

The circumstances leading up to the 1984 decision are described in Peter Irons, *Justice at War: The Story of the Japanese American Internment Cases* (1983).

In the first *Korematsu* case, the Supreme Court relied heavily on its earlier decision in *Hirabayashi v. United States*, 320 U.S. 81 (1943). Gordon Hirabayashi's conviction for violating a curfew based on Executive Order No. 9066 was also vacated in a later *coram nobis* proceeding. *Hirabayashi v. United States*, 828 F.2d 591 (9th Cir. 1987). Documents and commentary on the later proceedings may be found in *Justice Delayed: The Record of the Japanese American Internment Cases* (Peter Irons ed., 1989).

Aside from the government briefs to the Supreme Court in *Hirabayashi* and *Korematsu*, the Acting Solicitor General in 2011 suggested that those cases might have been decided differently if the Solicitor General at the time, Charles Fahy, had been candid in his oral arguments before the Court about the lack of any evidence of military necessity. Neal Katyal, *Confession of Error: The Solicitor General's Mistakes During the Japanese-American Internment Cases*, The Justice Blog (May 20, 2011), *at* http://blogs.usdoj.gov/blog/archives/1346. The oral arguments are described in Irons, *Justice at War, supra*, at 235-236, 316-317.

6. *The Role of Government Lawyers in Korematsu.* Why do you think the government lawyers behaved the way they did, both initially in approving the executive order, and later in deliberately misleading the Supreme Court? Some possible reasons are set forth in Peter Irons, *Politics and Principle: An Assessment of the Roosevelt Record on Civil Rights and Liberties*, 59 Wash. L. Rev. 693, 716-720 (1984).

7. *Military Necessity or Racism?* In 1980, Congress established the Commission on Wartime Relocation and Internment of Civilians to review the facts and circumstances surrounding Executive Order No. 9066 and its impact on American citizens and permanent resident aliens. Pub. L. No. 96-317, 94 Stat. 964. In its report, entitled *Personal Justice Denied* (1982), the Commission found that some 120,000 people were held without judicial review, "despite the fact that not a single documented act of espionage, sabotage, or fifth column activity was committed by an American citizen of Japanese ancestry or by a resident Japanese alien on the West Coast. . . . [T]here was no justification in military necessity for the exclusion, . . . there was no basis for the detention." *Id.* at 3, 10.

How, then, could this monstrous injustice have occurred? Part of the answer surely lies in the fear and anger that gripped the country in the wake of the attack on Pearl Harbor. But another part can be found in the longstanding hostility of California farmers, businesses, and labor unions toward Japanese immigrants. Within weeks, voices of racism, tribalism, and economic opportunism began calling for the evacuation of all ethnic Japanese, aliens and citizens alike, from the West Coast. For example, columnist Walter Lippmann wrote, "The Pacific Coast is in imminent danger of a combined attack from within and from without. . . . [S]ome part of it may at any moment be a battlefield. Nobody's constitutional rights include the right to reside and do business on a battlefield." *Quoted in* Jacobus tenBroek, Edward N. Barnhart & Floyd W. Matson, *Prejudice, War and the Constitution* 85 n.45 (1970). Another journalist added, "and to hell with habeas corpus." Westbrook Pegler, *quoted in* Biddle, *supra* p. 431, at 218. The clamor was joined by groups like the Native Sons and Daughters of the Golden West, the American Legion, the California Farm Bureau Federation, and the Grower-Shipper Vegetable Association, who reportedly were able to exert significant influence on General DeWitt and, importantly, President Roosevelt. *See generally* Irons, *Justice at War, supra.*

The military also bears some of the responsibility. But why was the Army involved in the internments, when troops were urgently needed elsewhere to fight the war? It was certainly not because civilian authorities were incapable of rounding up even this large group and imprisoning its members. The West Coast was not a battlefield, the courts remained open, and local governments continued to function. Furthermore, the internees were remarkably cooperative, albeit deeply resentful: there was little resistance to the internments and few reported efforts to escape from the camps. In other words, the Army's unique ability to exert massive force simply was not needed. Moreover, any threats to national security from individual saboteurs and spies were addressed by the FBI in the early weeks of the war, and prosecuted in the criminal justice system.

The Justice and War Departments were intimately involved in the internment decision, as was President Roosevelt. Congress and the courts also played important enabling roles. But do you think the internments could have been carried out without the military's involvement? If not, did the military usurp the authority of civilian government to accomplish what would otherwise have been impossible? Or did the civilian government utilize the military to do what it otherwise could not have? Can you describe a legal regime to reduce the risk of military control of the government, or to make it more difficult for civilian authorities to misuse military power? The domestic role of the military is addressed in depth in Chapter 24.

8. *Apology and Payment.* In 1948, Congress passed the American-Japanese Evacuation Claims Act, 50 U.S.C. app. §§1981-1987 (2006), authorizing payment of up to $100,000 to each internee for loss of real or personal property occasioned by the evacuation. On February 19, 1976, President Gerald Ford rescinded Executive Order No. 9066, 34 years to the day after its issuance. Proclamation No. 4417, 41 Fed. Reg. 7741 (Feb. 20, 1976).

Forty years later, after protracted debate, Congress voted to give $20,000 and an apology to each of 60,000 surviving internees. The measure was signed into law by President Reagan in 1988. 50 U.S.C. app. §§1989 to 1989c-8 (2006). Acceptance of the $20,000 payment "shall be in full satisfaction of all claims" against the government for damages. *Id.* §1989b-4(a)(6). *See* Chris K. Iijima, *Reparations and the "Model Minority" Ideology of Acquiescence: The Necessity to Refuse the Return to Original Humiliation,* 40 B.C. L. Rev. 385 (1998) (warning that reparations must not be used to excuse the racism that caused the internments); Sarah L. Brew, *Making Amends for History: Legislative Reparations for Japanese Americans and Other Minority Groups,* 8 Law & Inequality 179 (1989).

9. *Could It Happen Again?* On the fiftieth anniversary of the internments, Fred Korematsu remarked, "The constitutional violations that were committed have been

cleared. This will never happen again." Katherine Bishop, *Japanese-Americans Treat Pain of Internment in World War II*, N.Y. Times, Feb. 19, 1992. Do you think he was right?

It is suggested that General Dewitt was the evil genius whose singleminded racism was responsible for this sorry turn of events. *See, e.g., Hirabayashi*, 828 F.2d at 599-600. But should General Dewitt be asked to shoulder all or even a major part of the blame? Judge Marilyn Patel concluded her 1984 decision overturning Fred Korematsu's conviction with this warning about the Supreme Court's 1944 decision:

> *Korematsu* remains on the pages of our legal and political history. As a legal precedent it is now recognized as having very limited application. As historical precedent it stands as a constant caution that in times of war or declared military necessity our institutions must be vigilant in protecting constitutional guarantees. It stands as a caution that in times of distress the shield of military necessity and national security must not be used to protect governmental actions from close scrutiny and accountability. It stands as a caution that in times of international hostility and antagonisms our institutions, legislative, executive and judicial, must be prepared to exercise their authority to protect all citizens from the petty fears and prejudices that are so easily aroused. [584 F. Supp. at 1420.]

Taking her admonition to heart, can you describe some legal mechanism that would make us less likely to repeat our mistake? If you think some broader strategy will be required, can you say what it is? *See generally* Aya Gruber, *Raising the Red Flag: The Continued Relevance of the Japanese Internment in the Post-Hamdi World*, 54 U. Kan. L. Rev. 307 (2006).

For a fascinating account of *Korematsu*'s use as precedent since 1944, as well as the use and misuse of narrative in deciding the case, *see* Dean Masaru Hashimoto, *The Legacy of Korematsu v. United States: A Dangerous Narrative Retold*, 4 UCLA Asian Pac. Am. L.J. 72 (1996).

B.   MILITARY DETENTION OF COMBATANTS BEFORE 9/11

Both of the following opinions treat the law-of-war authority for the military *trial* of alleged enemy combatants during an armed insurrection or declared war, a topic which we take up in detail in Chapter 22. But the trial of these individuals presupposes their *detention*, and the opinions therefore also, by necessary implication, address authority for wartime detention.

Ex parte Milligan

United States Supreme Court, 1866
71 U.S. (4 Wall.) 2

[The opinion is set forth *supra* p. 381.]

Ex parte Quirin

United States Supreme Court, 1942
317 U.S. 1

[After war was declared between the United States and Germany, seven German nationals, and Herbert Hans Haupt, a dual U.S.-German national, were trained at a German sabotage school near Berlin. German submarines then carried the saboteurs with a supply of explosives to the United States. They landed on U.S. beaches wearing German Marine Infantry uniforms, which they immediately buried. Before they could engage in any act of sabotage, however, they were betrayed to the FBI by one of their number.

After their arrest, President Roosevelt issued an order declaring that nationals of enemy states or those who acted under their direction, who were charged with sabotage, espionage, or "violations of the law of war," were subject to the jurisdiction of military tribunals. Proclamation No. 2561, 7 Fed. Reg. 5101 (July 7, 1942). A military commission then conducted a secret 18-day trial of the saboteurs. Toward the end of the trial, the Supreme Court decided in an extraordinary expedited summer session to hear argument on the saboteurs' appeal from refusal of the lower courts to entertain their petitions for writs of habeas corpus. Less than 24 hours after argument, it ruled *per curiam* that the military commission was lawfully constituted and authorized to try the saboteurs, promising a full opinion later. Six of the saboteurs were executed eight days after the Supreme Court's *per curiam* ruling (Roosevelt commuted the sentences of the others to imprisonment). The Court issued its full opinion three months later.]

Mr. Chief Justice STONE delivered the opinion of the Court.... We are not here concerned with any question of the guilt or innocence of petitioners. Constitutional safeguards for the protection of all who are charged with offenses are not to be disregarded in order to inflict merited punishment on some who are guilty. *Ex parte Milligan*, [71 U.S. (4 Wall.) 2 (1866)]. But the detention and trial of petitioners — ordered by the President in the declared exercise of his powers as Commander in Chief of the Army in time of war and of grave public danger — are not to be set aside by the courts without the clear conviction that they are in conflict with the Constitution or laws of Congress constitutionally enacted.

Congress and the President, like the courts, possess no power not derived from the Constitution. But one of the objects of the Constitution, as declared by its preamble, is to "provide for the common defence." ...

[The Court then catalogued first Congress's, then the President's, national security authorities under the Constitution.]

The Constitution thus invests the President as Commander in Chief with the power to wage war which Congress has declared, and to carry into effect all laws passed by Congress for the conduct of war and for the government and regulation of the Armed Forces, and all laws defining and punishing offences against the law of nations, including those which pertain to the conduct of war.

By the Articles of War, 10 U.S.C. §§1471-1593, Congress has provided rules for the government of the Army.... But the Articles also recognize the "military commission" appointed by military command as an appropriate tribunal for the trial and punishment of offenses against the law of war not ordinarily tried by court martial.

See Arts. 12, 15. Articles 38 and 46 authorize the President, with certain limitations, to prescribe the procedure for military commissions. Articles 81 and 82 authorize trial, either by court martial or military commission, of those charged with relieving, harboring or corresponding with the enemy and those charged with spying. And Article 15 declares that "the provisions of these articles conferring jurisdiction upon courts-martial shall not be construed as depriving military commissions . . . or other military tribunals of concurrent jurisdiction in respect of offenders or offenses that by statute or by the law of war may be triable by such military commissions . . . or other military tribunals." . . .

From the very beginning of its history this Court has recognized and applied the law of war as including that part of the law of nations which prescribes, for the conduct of war, the status, rights and duties of enemy nations as well as of enemy individuals. By the Articles of War, and especially Article 15, Congress has explicitly provided, so far as it may constitutionally do so, that military tribunals shall have jurisdiction to try offenders or offenses against the law of war in appropriate cases. . . .

An important incident to the conduct of war is the adoption of measures by the military command not only to repel and defeat the enemy, but to seize and subject to disciplinary measures those enemies who in their attempt to thwart or impede our military effort have violated the law of war. It is unnecessary for present purposes to determine to what extent the President as Commander in Chief has constitutional power to create military commissions without the support of Congressional legislation. For here Congress has authorized trial of offenses against the law of war before such commissions. . . . We may assume that there are acts regarded in other countries, or by some writers on international law, as offenses against the law of war which would not be triable by military tribunal here, either because they are not recognized by our courts as violations of the law of war or because they are of that class of offenses constitutionally triable only by a jury. It was upon such grounds that the Court denied the right to proceed by military tribunal in *Ex parte Milligan, supra.* But as we shall show, these petitioners were charged with an offense against the law of war which the Constitution does not require to be tried by jury. . . .

. . . [B]y the reference in the 15th Article of War to "offenders or offenses that . . . by the law of war may be triable by such military commissions," Congress has incorporated by reference, as within the jurisdiction of military commissions, all offenses which are defined as such by the law of war, and which may constitutionally be included within that jurisdiction. Congress had the choice of crystallizing in permanent form and in minute detail every offense against the law of war, or of adopting the system of common law applied by military tribunals so far as it should be recognized and deemed applicable by the courts. It chose the latter course.

By universal agreement and practice the law of war draws a distinction between the armed forces and the peaceful populations of belligerent nations and also between those who are lawful and unlawful combatants. Lawful combatants are subject to capture and detention as prisoners of war by opposing military forces. Unlawful combatants are likewise subject to capture and detention, but in addition they are subject to trial and punishment by military tribunals for acts which render their belligerency unlawful. The spy who secretly and without uniform passes the military lines of a belligerent in time of war, seeking to gather military information and communicate it to the enemy, or an enemy combatant who without uniform comes secretly through the lines for the purpose of waging war by destruction of life or property, are familiar examples of belligerents who are generally deemed not to be entitled to the status of prisoners of war, but to be offenders against the law of war subject to trial and punishment by military tribunals....

Specification 1 states that petitioners "being enemies of the United States and acting for...the German Reich, a belligerent enemy nation, secretly and covertly passed, in civilian dress, contrary to the law of war, through the military and naval lines and defenses of the United States...and went behind such lines, contrary to the law of war, in civilian dress...for the purpose of committing...hostile acts, and, in particular, to destroy certain war industries, war utilities and war materials within the United States."

This specification...plainly alleges violation of the law of war....

Citizenship in the United States of an enemy belligerent does not relieve him from the consequences of a belligerency which is unlawful because in violation of the law of war. Citizens who associate themselves with the military arm of the enemy government, and with its aid, guidance and direction enter this country bent on hostile acts are enemy belligerents within the meaning of the Hague Convention and the law of war. It is as an enemy belligerent that petitioner Haupt is charged with entering the United States, and unlawful belligerency is the gravamen of the offense of which he is accused....

But petitioners insist that even if the offenses with which they are charged are offenses against the law of war, their trial is subject to the requirement of the Fifth Amendment that no person shall be held to answer for a capital or otherwise infamous crime unless on a presentment or indictment of a grand jury, and that such trials by Article III, §2, and the Sixth Amendment must be by jury in a civil court....

Presentment by a grand jury and trial by a jury of the vicinage where the crime was committed were at the time of the adoption of the Constitution familiar parts of the machinery for criminal trials in the civil courts. But they were procedures unknown to military tribunals, which are not courts in the sense of the Judiciary Article, and which in the natural course of events are usually called upon to function under conditions precluding resort to such procedures....

... [W]e must conclude that §2 of Article III and the Fifth and Sixth Amendments cannot be taken to have extended the right to demand a jury to trials by military commission, or to have required that offenses against the law of war not triable by jury at common law be tried only in the civil courts....

Petitioners, and especially petitioner Haupt, stress the pronouncement of this Court in the *Milligan* case that the law of war "can never be applied to citizens in states which have upheld the authority of the government, and where the courts are open and their process unobstructed." Elsewhere in its opinion, the Court was at pains to point out that Milligan, a citizen twenty years resident in Indiana, who had never been a resident of any of the states in rebellion, was not an enemy belligerent either entitled to the status of a prisoner of war or subject to the penalties imposed upon unlawful belligerents. We construe the Court's statement as to the inapplicability of the law of war to Milligan's case as having particular reference to the facts before it. From them the Court concluded that Milligan, not being a part of or associated with the armed forces of the enemy, was a non-belligerent, not subject to the law of war save as — in circumstances found not there to be present and not involved here — martial law might be constitutionally established.

The Court's opinion is inapplicable to the case presented by the present record. We have no occasion now to define with meticulous care the ultimate boundaries of the jurisdiction of military tribunals to try persons according to the law of war. It is enough that petitioners here, upon the conceded facts, were plainly within those boundaries, and were held in good faith for trial by military commission, charged with being enemies who, with the purpose of destroying war materials and utilities, entered or after entry remained in our territory without uniform — an offense against the law of war. We hold only that those particular acts constitute an offense against the law of war which the Constitution authorizes to be tried by military commission. . . .

It follows that the orders of the District Court should be affirmed, and that leave to file petitions for habeas corpus in this Court should be denied.

Justice MURPHY took no part in the consideration or decision of these cases.

NOTES AND QUESTIONS

1. *The Overarching Constitution and Historical Understandings. Milligan* seems to stand for the proposition that the Constitution controls in war as in peace, at least where U.S. citizens are concerned. But some argued that it was, in fact, a departure from the historical understanding, one that prevailed through much of the Civil War.

> [Charles] Sumner and others articulated a "dual" theory of the conflict and of the U.S. government's powers: when responding to war-like attacks by its own citizens, the United States had the discretion to choose how to respond: either as a "sovereign" or a "belligerent." The "rebels in arms" were "criminals" because they were committing treason and also "enemies because their combination has assumed the front and proportions of war." The U.S. government, it was argued, may choose "to proceed against them in either character, according to controlling considerations of policy." Then here is the rub: "If we treat them as criminals, then we are under the restraints of the Constitution; if we treat them as enemies, then we have all the latitude sanctioned by the rights of war;" indeed, "the rights against enemies, founded on war . . . are absolutely without constitutional limitation." The choice of means was discretionary; the applicable legal regime flowed from the choice of means made by the U.S. government.

Andrew Kent, *The Constitution and the Laws of War During the Civil War*, 85 Notre Dame L. Rev. 1839, 1851 (2010) (quoting Senator Sumner). Even if the "dual theory" was widely held during the Civil War, did it survive *Milligan*? When, if ever, may U.S. citizens be detained and tried by the military, according to *Milligan*? Does the government have a choice about how to treat them?

2. *Military Necessity.* In *Reid v. Covert*, 354 U.S. 1, 21 (1957), the Court emphasized that

> the jurisdiction of military tribunals is a very limited and extraordinary jurisdiction derived from the cryptic language of Art. I, §8, and, at most, was intended to be only a narrow exception to the normal and preferred method of trial in courts of law. Every extension of military jurisdiction is an encroachment on the jurisdiction of the civil courts, and, more important, acts as a deprivation of the right to jury trial and of other treasured constitutional protections.

At the same time, the *Reid* Court found that the "exigencies which have required military rule on the battlefront are not present . . . where no conflict exists. Military trial of civilians 'in the field' is an extraordinary jurisdiction and it should not be expanded at the expense of the Bill of Rights." *Id.* at 35.

What "exigencies" require military *detention*? Are they geographically limited? Did they apply to the military detention of Milligan? Did the existence of an exigency depend on whether there were reasonable alternatives to his military detention? Were there?

3. *Statutory Authority?* *Quirin* suggests that there was statutory authority for the commission that tried the German saboteurs. Indeed, Articles 81 and 82 of the Articles of War, which it cites, seemed to authorize the trial of spies, at least, by military commission. But the decision places chief reliance on Article 15, which it quotes *supra* p. 438. Does Article 15, which is now 10 U.S.C. §821 (2006), authorize military commissions or is it merely a savings clause? If the latter, what authority does it save? In another World War II case involving military commissions, *In re Yamashita*, 327 U.S. 1 (1946), the Supreme Court explained that "[b]y thus recognizing military commissions in order to preserve their traditional jurisdiction over enemy combatants unimpaired by the Articles, Congress gave sanction, as we held in *Ex parte Quirin*, to any use of the military commission contemplated by the *common law of war*." *Id.* at 20 (emphasis added).

Presumably the law of war also authorizes the military detention of enemy combatants. If so, is §821 or any statute necessary to authorize military detention as long as we are at war? *See Hamdan v. Rumsfeld*, 548 U.S. 557, 592 (2006) (refraining from deciding analogous question). Could Congress by statute regulate or prohibit such detentions? On what specific constitutional authority would Congress rely for such a statute?

4. *Declared State of War?* If military detention is authorized by the common law of war, must war be declared for the Commander in Chief to detain? War had, of course, been declared before *Quirin* and *Yamashita* were decided. One advantage of requiring a declared war to authorize military detention or trial is that the authority then has a temporal limit; it lasts "so long as a state of war exists from its declaration until peace is proclaimed." *Yamashita*, 327 U.S. at 11-12. "A declaration of war draws clear lines. It defines (or at least has traditionally done so) who the enemy is: another state, and all the nationals of that state. It marks a clear beginning, and (again traditionally) an end, with some act or instrument marking its conclusion." A.B.A. Task Force on Terrorism and the Law, *Report and Recommendations on Military Commissions* 5 (Jan. 4, 2002) (*ABA Task Force Report*).

But we have seen that Congress can authorize "imperfect" war without a formal declaration. Writing of one such war (the Quasi-War with France) in *Talbot v. Seeman*, 5 U.S. 1 (1801), Chief Justice Marshall observed that "congress may authorize general hostilities, in which case the general laws of war apply to our situation; or partial hostilities, in which case the laws of war, so far as they actually apply to our situation, must be noticed." Military detention and trials by military commissions were also common in the field and in occupied Confederate states during the undeclared Civil War.

Yet even those states of war each had a defined and discernible end. Does a war on terrorists have a discernible end? If a state of war triggers common law of war authority, did the Authorization for Use of Military Force (AUMF), Pub. L. No. 107-40, 115 Stat. 224 (2001), *supra* p. 86, approving the use of force against the perpetrators of the September 11 attacks, authorize a state of war permitting the President to direct military detention and to use military commissions? *See Hamdan v. Rumsfeld, supra*, 548 U.S. at 593-594 (yes, as to military commissions, but it does not expand the President's existing authority to convene such commissions). War against whom? Is the power to detain coextensive with the state of war authorized by the AUMF? How long is that? Might it continue longer? *See Hamdi v. Rumsfeld*, 542 U.S. 547 (2004).

5. *Violations of the Law of War.* Were the September 11 attacks acts of war, and did they violate the law of war? Traditionally, states carry out acts of war, and a state's deliberate attack on noncombatant civilians would clearly violate the laws of war. *See, e.g.*, Convention Relative to the Protection of Civilian Persons in Time of War (1949 Geneva Convention IV), Aug. 12, 1949, 6 U.S.T. 3516, 75 U.N.T.S. 287. Some have argued that "war crimes" must by definition either be committed during an international armed conflict between *states* or in an internal armed conflict, and that the war conducted by terrorists is neither. *See, e.g.*, Joan Fitzpatrick, *Jurisdiction of Military Commissions and the Ambiguous War on Terrorism*, 96 Am. J. Int'l L. 345 (2002).

But the law of war applies also to some nonstate actors, such as insurgents. *ABA Task Force Report, supra*, at 7. It also presumably applies to terrorists with state sponsors. But does one also violate the law of war by conspiring with or aiding and abetting al Qaeda? *See* Association of the Bar of the City of New York, Comm. on Military Aff. & Justice, *Inter Arma Silent Leges: In Times of Armed Conflict, Should the Laws Be Silent?* 16 (Dec. 2001) (*N.Y. City Bar Report*) (no). In *Hamdan v. Rumsfeld, supra*, a plurality of the Supreme Court found that conspiracy was not a crime traditionally triable under the law of war. 548 U.S. at 600. Congress responded by purportedly codifying "offenses that have traditionally been triable by military commissions," but then including not only "conspiracy," but also "providing material support for terrorism." Military Commissions Act of 2006, Pub. L. No. 109-366, §3(a), 120 Stat. 2600, 2630.

6. *Reconciling Milligan and Quirin.* Although Attorney General Biddle at first asked the Court in *Quirin* to overrule *Milligan*, he later backed off from this demand in his oral argument and asserted that the Court could uphold the use of the military commission to try the saboteurs "without touching a hair of the *Milligan* case." George Lardner Jr., *Nazi Saboteurs Captured!*, Wash. Post, Jan. 13, 2002, Magazine, at 23. How *did* the Court distinguish *Milligan*? Did it distinguish the defendants by their citizenship? *See Mudd v. Caldera*, 134 F. Supp. 2d 138 (D.D.C. 2001) (citizens and noncitizens alike may be subject to the jurisdiction of a military commission for violating the laws of war). By their acts? (Recall that Milligan was charged with "Violation of the laws of war."). If *Milligan* survived *Quirin*, as the later opinion suggests, how much of it is left?

The *Quirin* Court suggested that *Milligan* should be limited to its facts. On the other hand, Justice Black wrote to the other Justices in *Quirin* that "[i]n this case I want to go no further than to declare that these particular defendants are subject to the jurisdiction of a military tribunal because of the circumstances." *See* Evan P. Schultz, *Now and Later*, Legal Times, Dec. 24, 2001, at 54. Accordingly, the opinion for the Court stated, "We hold only that these particular facts constitute an offense against the law of nations which the Constitution authorizes to be tried by military commission." *Quirin*, 317 U.S. at 20. Do "these particular facts" include the fact of declared war with its attendant limits (including identification of enemy combatants)?

If *Quirin* is limited to *its* facts, and applicable to military detention (not just trial), could the military constitutionally detain a suspected terrorist apprehended in the United States while civilian courts are open? In view of the Court's characterization of the military commission as a "narrow exception to the normal and preferred method of trial in courts of law," should we read *Quirin* for all that its language may be worth, or as narrowly as possible? *Cf. ABA Task Force Report, supra,* at 16 (recommending that "any use of military commissions should be limited to narrow circumstances in which compelling security interests justify their use," and that they not be used against persons lawfully present in the United States or unconnected with the September 11 attacks absent additional specific authority from Congress); *N.Y. City Bar Report, supra,* at 8 (arguing that *Quirin* should be limited to declared war).

Military Detention After 9/11 ━━16

In late 2001, President George W. Bush issued a military order authorizing the detention of "[a]ny individual subject to this order...at an appropriate location designated by the Secretary of Defense outside or within the United States." Military Order of Nov. 13, 2001, *Detention, Treatment, and Trial of Certain Non-Citizens in the War Against Terrorism*, 66 Fed. Reg. 57,833, §3(a) (Nov. 13, 2001) (reproduced in full *infra* p. 685). It provided that

[t]he term "individual subject to this order" shall mean any individual who is not a United States citizen with respect to whom I determine from time to time in writing that:
(1) there is reason to believe that such individual, at the relevant times,
(i) is or was a member of the organization known as al Qaida;
(ii) has engaged in, aided or abetted, or conspired to commit, acts of international terrorism, or acts in preparation therefor, that have caused, threaten to cause, or have as their aim to cause, injury to or adverse effects on the United States, its citizens, national security, foreign policy, or economy; or
(iii) has knowingly harbored one or more individuals described in subparagraphs (i) or (ii) of subsection 2(a)(1) of this order; and
(2) it is in the interest of the United States that such individual be subject to this order. [*Id.* §2(a).]

Pursuant to the order, hundreds of noncitizens captured in Afghanistan or Pakistan were detained at the Guantánamo Bay Naval Station and in other locations abroad. A report by a multi-agency task force asserted that 779 individuals had been detained at Guantánamo, of whom 242 remained in detention as of January 2010. *Final Report: Guantánamo Review Task Force* (Jan. 22, 2010) ("Guantánamo Review"), *available at* http://www.justice.gov/ag/guantanamo-review-final-report.pdf. A year later the number had declined to 172. *See* Cheryl Pellerin, *Military Commission Panel Sentences Guantanamo Detainee*, Am. Forces Press Serv., Feb. 18, 2011.

One of them, however, Yasir Esam Hamdi, turned out to have been born in the United States. When this was discovered, he was transferred to the United States, but still detained in military custody as an "enemy combatant." Another U.S. citizen, Jose Padilla, was arrested as a material witness as he stepped off the plane at O'Hare International Airport in Chicago, and then also transferred into military custody in the United States. Subsequently, a lawfully resident noncitizen, Ali Saleh Kahlah al-Marri, was arrested at his home in Peoria, Illinois, as a material witness and later indicted for credit card fraud and making false statements to the FBI. The government then moved *ex parte* to dismiss the indictment based on an order signed by President Bush the same day, determining al-Marri to be an "enemy combatant" and ordering his detention as such in military custody in the United States.

This chapter explores the authority for what the Obama administration has called "law-of-war detention," a term we also use in this chapter to refer to laws of war that are recognized by our law or incorporated into our law by the 2001 Authorization for the Use of Military Force. We start in Part A with the Supreme Court's decision in *Hamdi v. Rumsfeld*, 542 U.S. 507 (2004). In Part B, we consider whether authority to detain Hamdi and other battlefield captives extends to the detention of persons like Padilla and al-Marri, who were captured in the United States and not on the battlefield abroad. In Part C, we examine the still-evolving case law about detention authority that is being generated by noncitizen habeas petitions in the D.C. federal courts, prompted by the Supreme Court's decision in *Boumediene v. Bush*, 553 U.S. 723 (2008). Finally, in Part D we review the Obama administration's efforts to close the Guantánamo Bay Detention Center, and Congress's responses.

A. MILITARY DETENTION OF BATTLEFIELD CAPTIVES

Hamdi v. Rumsfeld

United States Supreme Court, 2004
542 U.S. 507

Justice O'CONNOR announced the judgment of the Court and delivered an opinion, in which THE CHIEF JUSTICE, Justice KENNEDY, and Justice BREYER join....

[During the U.S. military operations in Afghanistan that followed the 9/11 terrorist attacks, petitioner Hamdi was captured by Afghan Northern Alliance forces. He was subsequently transferred to U.S. military custody in Afghanistan and sent to Guantánamo. When it was discovered that he had been born in Louisiana, making him a U.S. citizen, he was transferred to the United States as an enemy combatant and detained at a Navy brig in Charleston, South Carolina. Hamdi's father filed a habeas petition on behalf of his son under 28 U.S.C. §2241, alleging that the government held him in violation of the Fifth and Fourteenth Amendments. In the ensuing proceeding, the government filed an affidavit by Department of Defense official Michael Mobbs, setting forth the foregoing facts based on hearsay.]

II

The threshold question before us is whether the Executive has the authority to detain citizens who qualify as "enemy combatants." There is some debate as to the proper scope of this term, and the Government has never provided any court with the full criteria that it uses in classifying individuals as such. It has made clear, however, that, for purposes of this case, the "enemy combatant" that it is seeking to detain is an individual who, it alleges, was "part of or supporting forces hostile to the United States or coalition partners" in Afghanistan and who "engaged in an armed conflict against the United States" there. We therefore answer only the narrow question before us: whether the detention of citizens falling within that definition is authorized.

The Government maintains that no explicit congressional authorization is required, because the Executive possesses plenary authority to detain pursuant to Article II of the Constitution. We do not reach the question whether Article II provides such authority, however, because we agree with the Government's alternative position, that Congress has in fact authorized Hamdi's detention, through the AUMF.

Associate Justice Sandra Day O'Connor.

Photo by Dane Penland. Collection of the Supreme Court of the United States.

Our analysis on that point, set forth below, substantially overlaps with our analysis of Hamdi's principal argument for the illegality of his detention. He posits that his detention is forbidden by 18 U.S.C. §4001(a). Section 4001(a) states that "[n]o citizen shall be imprisoned or otherwise detained by the United States except pursuant to an Act of Congress." Congress passed §4001(a) in 1971 as part of a bill to repeal the Emergency Detention Act of 1950, 50 U.S.C. §811 *et seq.*, which provided procedures for executive detention, during times of emergency, of individuals deemed likely to engage in espionage or sabotage. Congress was particularly concerned about the possibility that the Act could be used to reprise the Japanese internment camps of World War II. The Government again presses two alternative positions. First, it argues that §4001(a), in light of its legislative history and its location in Title 18, applies only to "the control of civilian prisons and related detentions," not to military detentions. Second, it maintains that §4001(a) is satisfied, because Hamdi is being detained "pursuant to an Act of Congress" — the AUMF. Again, because we conclude that the Government's second assertion is correct, we do not address the first. In other words, for the reasons that follow, we conclude that the AUMF is explicit congressional authorization for the detention of individuals in the narrow category we describe (assuming, without deciding, that such authorization is required), and that the AUMF satisfied §4001(a)'s requirement that a detention be "pursuant to an Act of Congress" (assuming, without deciding, that §4001(a) applies to military detentions).

The AUMF authorizes the President to use "all necessary and appropriate force" against "nations, organizations, or persons" associated with the September 11, 2001, terrorist attacks. 115 Stat. 224. There can be no doubt that individuals who fought against the United States in Afghanistan as part of the Taliban, an organization known to have supported the al Qaeda terrorist network responsible for those attacks, are individuals Congress sought to target in passing the AUMF. We conclude that detention of individuals falling into the limited category we are considering, for the duration of the particular conflict in which they were captured, is so fundamental and accepted an incident to war as to be an exercise of the "necessary and appropriate force" Congress has authorized the President to use.

The capture and detention of lawful combatants and the capture, detention, and trial of unlawful combatants, by "universal agreement and practice," are "important incident[s] of war." *Ex parte Quirin,* 317 U.S. [1 (1942)], at 28. The purpose of detention is to prevent captured individuals from returning to the field of battle and taking up arms once again.

There is no bar to this Nation's holding one of its own citizens as an enemy combatant. In *Quirin,* one of the detainees, Haupt, alleged that he was a naturalized United States citizen. 317 U.S., at 20. We held that "[c]itizens who associate themselves with the military arm of the enemy government, and with its aid, guidance and direction enter this country bent on hostile acts, are enemy belligerents within the meaning of . . . the law of war." *Id.,* at 37-38. While Haupt was tried for violations of the law of war, nothing in *Quirin* suggests that his citizenship would have precluded his mere detention for the duration of the relevant hostilities. See *id.,* at 30-31. Nor can we see any reason for drawing such a line here. A citizen, no less than an alien, can be "part of or supporting forces hostile to the United States or coalition partners" and "engaged in an armed conflict against the United States"; such a citizen, if released, would pose the same threat of returning to the front during the ongoing conflict.

In light of these principles, it is of no moment that the AUMF does not use specific language of detention. Because detention to prevent a combatant's return to the battlefield is a fundamental incident of waging war, in permitting the use of "necessary and appropriate force," Congress has clearly and unmistakably authorized detention in the narrow circumstances considered here. . . .

Hamdi contends that the AUMF does not authorize indefinite or perpetual detention. Certainly, we agree that indefinite detention for the purpose of interrogation is not authorized. Further, we understand Congress' grant of authority for the use of "necessary and appropriate force" to include the authority to detain for the duration of the relevant conflict, and our understanding is based on longstanding law-of-war principles. If the practical circumstances of a given conflict are entirely unlike those of the conflicts that informed the development of the law of war, that understanding may unravel. But that is not the situation we face as of this date. Active combat operations against Taliban fighters apparently are ongoing in Afghanistan. The United States may detain, for the duration of these hostilities, individuals legitimately determined to be Taliban combatants who "engaged in an armed conflict against the United States." If the record establishes that United States troops are still involved in active combat in Afghanistan, those detentions are part of the exercise of "necessary and appropriate force," and therefore are authorized by the AUMF.

Ex parte Milligan, [71 U.S. (4 Wall.) 2 (1866)], does not undermine our holding about the Government's authority to seize enemy combatants, as we define that term today. In that case, the Court made repeated reference to the fact that its inquiry into whether the military tribunal had jurisdiction to try and punish Milligan turned in large part on the fact that Milligan was not a prisoner of war, but a resident of Indiana arrested while at home there. *Id.,* at 118, 131. That fact was central to its conclusion. Had Milligan been captured while he was assisting Confederate soldiers by carrying a rifle against Union troops on a Confederate battlefield, the holding of the Court might well have been different. The Court's repeated explanations that Milligan was not a prisoner of war suggest that had these different circumstances been present he could have been detained under military authority for the duration of the conflict, whether or not he was a citizen. . . .

III

Even in cases in which the detention of enemy combatants is legally authorized, there remains the question of what process is constitutionally due to a citizen who disputes his enemy-combatant status. . . .

A

Though they reach radically different conclusions on the process that ought to attend the present proceeding, the parties begin on common ground. All agree that, absent suspension, the writ of habeas corpus remains available to every individual detained within the United States. U.S. Const., Art. I, §9, cl. 2 ("The Privilege of the Writ of Habeas Corpus shall not be suspended, unless when in Cases of Rebellion or Invasion the public Safety may require it"). Only in the rarest of circumstances has Congress seen fit to suspend the writ. . . . All agree suspension of the writ has not occurred here. Thus, it is undisputed that Hamdi was properly before an Article III court to challenge his detention under 28 U.S.C. §2241. Further, all agree that §2241 and its companion provisions provide at least a skeletal outline of the procedures to be afforded a petitioner in federal habeas review. Most notably, §2243 provides that "the person detained may, under oath, deny any of the facts set forth in the return or allege any other material facts," and §2246 allows the taking of evidence in habeas proceedings by deposition, affidavit, or interrogatories.

The simple outline of §2241 makes clear both that Congress envisioned that habeas petitioners would have some opportunity to present and rebut facts and that courts in cases like this retain some ability to vary the ways in which they do so as mandated by due process. The Government recognizes the basic procedural protections required by the habeas statute, but asks us to hold that, given both the flexibility of the habeas mechanism and the circumstances presented in this case, the presentation of the Mobbs Declaration to the habeas court completed the required factual development. It suggests two separate reasons for its position that no further process is due.

B

First, the Government urges the adoption of the Fourth Circuit's holding below—that because it is "undisputed" that Hamdi's seizure took place in a combat zone, the habeas determination can be made purely as a matter of law, with no further hearing or factfinding necessary. This argument is easily rejected. As the dissenters from the denial of rehearing en banc noted, the circumstances surrounding Hamdi's seizure cannot in any way be characterized as "undisputed," as "those circumstances are neither conceded in fact, nor susceptible to concession in law, because Hamdi has not been permitted to speak for himself or even through counsel as to those circumstances." 337 F.3d 335, 357 (Luttig, J., dissenting from denial of rehearing en banc). Further, the "facts" that constitute the alleged concession are insufficient to support Hamdi's detention. Under the definition of enemy combatant that we accept today as falling within the scope of Congress' authorization, Hamdi would need to be "part of or supporting forces hostile to the United States or coalition partners" and "engaged in an armed conflict against the United States" to justify his detention in the United States for the duration of the relevant conflict. The habeas petition states only that "[w]hen seized by the United States Government, Mr. Hamdi resided in Afghanistan." An assertion that one *resided* in a country in which combat operations are taking place is not a concession that one was "*captured* in a zone of active combat operations in a foreign theater of war," 316 F.3d, at 459 (emphasis added), and certainly is not a concession that one was "part of or supporting forces hostile to the United States or coalition partners" and "engaged in an armed conflict against the United States." Accordingly, we reject any argument that Hamdi has made concessions that eliminate any right to further process.

C

The Government's second argument requires closer consideration. This is the argument that further factual exploration is unwarranted and inappropriate in light of the extraordinary constitutional interests at stake. Under the Government's most extreme rendition of this argument, "[r]espect for separation of powers and the limited institutional capabilities of courts in matters of military decision-making in connection with an ongoing conflict" ought to eliminate entirely any individual process, restricting the courts to investigating only whether legal authorization exists for the broader detention scheme. At most, the Government argues, courts should review its determination that a citizen is an enemy combatant under a very deferential "some evidence" standard. [Brief for Respondents] 34 ("Under the some evidence standard, the focus is exclusively on the factual basis supplied by the Executive to support its own determination" (citing *Superintendent, Mass. Correctional Institution at Walpole v. Hill*, 472 U.S. 445, 455-457 (1985) (explaining that the some evidence standard "does not require" a "weighing of the evidence," but rather calls for assessing "whether there is any evidence in the record that could support the conclusion"))). Under this review, a court would assume the accuracy of the Government's articulated basis for Hamdi's detention, as set forth in the Mobbs Declaration, and assess only whether that articulated basis was a legitimate one. In response, Hamdi emphasizes that this Court consistently has recognized that an individual challenging his detention may not be held at the will of the Executive without recourse to some proceeding before a neutral tribunal to determine whether the Executive's asserted justifications for that detention have basis in fact and warrant in law. *See, e.g., Zadvydas v. Davis*, 533 U.S. 678, 690 (2001)....

... The ordinary mechanism that we use for balancing such serious competing interests, and for determining the procedures that are necessary to ensure that a citizen is not "deprived of life, liberty, or property, without due process of law," U.S. Const., Amdt. 5, is the test that we articulated in *Mathews v. Eldridge*, 424 U.S. 319 (1976). *Mathews* dictates that the process due in any given instance is determined by weighing "the private interest that will be affected by the official action" against the Government's asserted interest, "including the function involved" and the burdens the Government would face in providing greater process. 424 U.S., at 335. The *Mathews* calculus then contemplates a judicious balancing of these concerns, through an analysis of "the risk of an erroneous deprivation" of the private interest if the process were reduced and the "probable value, if any, of additional or substitute safeguards." *Ibid.* We take each of these steps in turn.

1

It is beyond question that substantial interests lie on both sides of the scale in this case. Hamdi's "private interest . . . affected by the official action," *ibid.*, is the most elemental of liberty interests — the interest in being free from physical detention by one's own government. "In our society liberty is the norm," and detention without trial "is the carefully limited exception." [*United States v. Salerno*, 481 U.S. 739 (1987),] at 755. . . .

Nor is the weight on this side of the *Mathews* scale offset by the circumstances of war or the accusation of treasonous behavior, for "[i]t is clear that commitment for *any* purpose constitutes a significant deprivation of liberty that requires due process protection," *Jones v. United States*, 463 U.S. 354, 361 (1983) (emphasis added; internal quotation marks omitted), and at this stage in the *Mathews* calculus, we consider the interest of the *erroneously* detained individual. Indeed, as *amicus* briefs from media and relief organizations emphasize, the risk of erroneous deprivation of a citizen's liberty in the absence of sufficient process here is very real. See Brief for AmeriCares et al. as *Amici Curiae* 13-22 (noting ways in which "[t]he nature of humanitarian relief work and journalism present a significant risk of mistaken military detentions"). Moreover, as critical as the Government's interest may be in detaining those who actually pose an immediate threat to the national security of the United States during ongoing international conflict, history and common sense teach us that an unchecked system of detention carries the potential to become a means for oppression and abuse of others who do not present that sort of threat. . . .

2

On the other side of the scale are the weighty and sensitive governmental interests in ensuring that those who have in fact fought with the enemy during a war do not return to battle against the United States. As discussed above, the law of war and the realities of combat may render such detentions both necessary and appropriate, and our due process analysis need not blink at those realities. Without doubt, our Constitution recognizes that core strategic matters of warmaking belong in the hands of those who are best positioned and most politically accountable for making them. *Department of Navy v. Egan*, 484 U.S. 518, 530 (1988) (noting the reluctance of the courts "to intrude upon the authority of the Executive in military and national security affairs"); *Youngstown Sheet & Tube Co. v. Sawyer*, 343 U.S. 579, 587 (1952) (acknowledging "broad powers in military commanders engaged in day-to-day fighting in a theater of war").

The Government also argues at some length that its interests in reducing the process available to alleged enemy combatants are heightened by the practical difficulties that would accompany a system of trial-like process. In its view, military officers who are engaged in the serious work of waging battle would be unnecessarily and dangerously distracted by litigation half a world away, and discovery into military operations would both intrude on the sensitive secrets of national defense and result in a futile search for evidence buried under the rubble of war. To the extent that these burdens are triggered by heightened procedures, they are properly taken into account in our due process analysis.

3

Striking the proper constitutional balance here is of great importance to the Nation during this period of ongoing combat. But it is equally vital that our calculus not give short shrift to the values that this country holds dear or to the privilege that is American citizenship. It is during our most challenging and uncertain moments that our Nation's commitment to due process is most severely tested; and it is in those times that we must preserve our commitment at home to the principles for which we fight abroad.

With due recognition of these competing concerns, we believe that neither the process proposed by the Government nor the process apparently envisioned by the District Court below strikes the proper constitutional balance when a United States citizen is detained in the United States as an enemy combatant. That is, "the risk of erroneous deprivation" of a detainee's liberty interest is unacceptably high under the Government's proposed rule, while some of the "additional or substitute procedural safeguards" suggested by the District Court are unwarranted in light of their limited "probable value" and the burdens they may impose on the military in such cases. *Mathews*, 424 U.S., at 335.

We therefore hold that a citizen-detainee seeking to challenge his classification as an enemy combatant must receive notice of the factual basis for his classification, and a fair opportunity to rebut the Government's factual assertions before a neutral decisionmaker. "For more than a century the central meaning of procedural due process has been clear: 'Parties whose rights are to be affected are entitled to be heard; and in order that they may enjoy that right they must first be notified.' It is equally fundamental that the right to notice and an opportunity to be heard 'must be granted at a meaningful time and in a meaningful manner.'" *Fuentes v. Shevin*, 407 U.S. 67, 80 (1972). These essential constitutional promises may not be eroded.

At the same time, the exigencies of the circumstances may demand that, aside from these core elements, enemy combatant proceedings may be tailored to alleviate their uncommon potential to burden the Executive at a time of ongoing military conflict. Hearsay, for example, may need to be accepted as the most reliable available evidence from the Government in such a proceeding. Likewise, the Constitution would not be offended by a presumption in favor of the Government's evidence, so long as that presumption remained a rebuttable one and fair opportunity for rebuttal were provided. Thus, once the Government puts forth credible evidence that the habeas petitioner meets the enemy-combatant criteria, the onus could shift to the petitioner to rebut that evidence with more persuasive evidence that he falls outside the criteria. A burden-shifting scheme of this sort would meet the goal of ensuring that the errant tourist, embedded journalist, or local aid worker has a chance to prove military error while giving due regard to the Executive once it has put forth meaningful support for its conclusion that the detainee is in fact an enemy combatant. In the words of *Mathews*, process of this sort would sufficiently address the "risk of erroneous deprivation" of a detainee's liberty interest while eliminating certain procedures that have questionable additional value in light of the burden on the Government. 424 U.S., at 335.

We think it unlikely that this basic process will have the dire impact on the central functions of warmaking that the Government forecasts. The parties agree that initial captures on the battlefield need not receive the process we have discussed here; that process is due only when the determination is made to *continue* to hold those who have been seized. The Government has made clear in its briefing that documentation regarding battlefield detainees already is kept in the ordinary course of military affairs. Any factfinding imposition created by requiring a knowledgeable affiant to summarize these records to an independent tribunal is a minimal one. Likewise, arguments that military officers ought not have to wage war under the threat of litigation lose much of their steam when factual disputes at enemy-combatant hearings are limited to the alleged combatant's acts. This focus meddles little, if at all, in the strategy or conduct of war, inquiring only into the appropriateness of continuing to detain an individual claimed to have taken up arms against the United States. While we accord the greatest respect and consideration to the judgments of military authorities in matters relating to the actual prosecution of a war, and recognize that the scope of that discretion necessarily is wide, it does not infringe on the core role of the military for the courts to exercise their own time-honored and constitutionally mandated roles of reviewing and resolving claims like those presented here. Cf. *Korematsu v. United States*, 323 U.S. 214, 233-234 (1944) (Murphy, J., dissenting) ("[L]ike other claims conflicting with the asserted constitutional rights of the individual, the military claim must subject itself to the judicial process of having its reasonableness determined and its conflicts with other interests reconciled"); *Sterling v. Constantin*, 287 U.S. 378, 401 (1932) ("What are the allowable limits of military discretion, and whether or not they have been overstepped in a particular case, are judicial questions").

In sum, while the full protections that accompany challenges to detentions in other settings may prove unworkable and inappropriate in the enemy-combatant setting, the threats to military operations posed by a basic system of independent review are not so weighty as to trump a citizen's core rights to challenge meaningfully the Government's case and to be heard by an impartial adjudicator.

D

In so holding, we necessarily reject the Government's assertion that separation of powers principles mandate a heavily circumscribed role for the courts in such circumstances. Indeed, the position that the courts must forgo any examination of the individual case and focus exclusively on the legality of the broader detention scheme cannot be mandated by any reasonable view of separation of powers, as this approach serves only to *condense* power into a single branch of government. We have long since made clear that a state of war is not a blank check for the President when it comes to the rights of the Nation's citizens. *Youngstown Sheet & Tube*, 343 U.S., at 587. Whatever power the United States Constitution envisions for the Executive in its exchanges with other nations or with enemy organizations in times of conflict, it most assuredly envisions a role for all three branches when individual liberties are at stake. *Mistretta v. United States*, 488 U.S. 361, 380 (1989) (it was "the central judgment of the Framers of the Constitution that, within our political scheme, the separation of governmental powers into three coordinate Branches is essential to the preservation of liberty"); *Home Building & Loan Assn. v. Blaisdell*, 290 U.S. 398, 426 (1934) (The war power "is a power to wage war successfully, and thus it permits the harnessing of the entire energies of the people in a supreme cooperative effort to preserve the nation. But even the war power does not remove constitutional limitations safeguarding essential liberties"). Likewise, we have made clear that, unless Congress acts to suspend it, the Great Writ of habeas corpus allows the Judicial Branch to play a necessary role in maintaining this delicate balance of governance, serving as an important judicial check on the Executive's discretion in the realm of detentions. See *INS v. St. Cyr*, 533 U.S. 289, 301 (2001) ("At its historical core, the writ of habeas corpus has served as a means of reviewing the legality of Executive detention, and it is in that context that its protections have been strongest"). Thus, while we do not question that our due process assessment must pay keen attention to the particular burdens faced by the Executive in the context of military action, it would turn our system of checks and balances on its head to suggest that a citizen could not make his way to court with a challenge to the factual basis for his detention by his government, simply because the Executive opposes making available such a challenge. Absent suspension of the writ by Congress, a citizen detained as an enemy combatant is entitled to this process.

Because we conclude that due process demands some system for a citizen detainee to refute his classification, the proposed "some evidence" standard is inadequate. Any process in which the Executive's factual assertions go wholly unchallenged or are simply presumed correct without any opportunity for the alleged combatant to demonstrate otherwise falls constitutionally short. As the Government itself has recognized, we have utilized the "some evidence" standard in the past as a standard of review, not as a standard of proof. That is, it primarily has been employed by courts in examining an administrative record developed after an adversarial proceeding — one with process at least of the sort that we today hold is constitutionally mandated in the citizen enemy-combatant setting. This standard therefore is ill suited to the situation in which a habeas petitioner has received no prior proceedings before any tribunal and had no prior opportunity to rebut the Executive's factual assertions before a neutral decisionmaker.

Today we are faced only with such a case. Aside from unspecified "screening" processes, and military interrogations in which the Government suggests Hamdi could have contested his classification, Hamdi has received no process. An interrogation by one's captor, however effective an intelligence-gathering tool, hardly constitutes a constitutionally adequate factfinding before a neutral decisionmaker. Compare Brief for Respondents 42-43 (discussing the "secure interrogation environment," and noting that military interrogations require a controlled "interrogation dynamic" and "a relationship of trust and dependency" and are "a critical source" of "timely and effective intelligence") with *Concrete Pipe [and Products of California, Inc. v. Construction Laborers Pension Trust]*, 508 U.S. 602, 617-618 (1993) ("one is entitled as a matter of due process of law to an adjudicator who is not in a situation which would offer a possible temptation to the average man as a judge . . . which might lead him not to hold the balance nice, clear and true" (internal quotation marks omitted)). That even purportedly fair adjudicators "are disqualified by their interest in the controversy to be decided is, of course, the general rule." *Tumey v. Ohio*, 273 U.S. 510, 522 (1927). Plainly, the "process" Hamdi has received is not that to which he is entitled under the Due Process Clause.

There remains the possibility that the standards we have articulated could be met by an appropriately authorized and properly constituted military tribunal. Indeed, it is notable that military regulations already provide for such process in related instances, dictating that tribunals be made available to determine the status of enemy detainees who assert prisoner-of-war status under the Geneva Convention. See Enemy Prisoners of War, Retained Personnel, Civilian Internees and Other Detainees, Army Regulation 190-8, §1-6 (1997). In the absence of such process, however, a court that receives a petition for a writ of habeas corpus from an alleged enemy combatant must itself ensure that the minimum requirements of due process are achieved. . . . As we have discussed, a habeas court in a case such as this may accept affidavit evidence like that contained in the Mobbs Declaration, so long as it also permits the alleged combatant to present his own factual case to rebut the Government's return. We anticipate that a District Court would proceed with the caution that we have indicated is necessary in this setting, engaging in a factfinding process that is both prudent and incremental. We have no reason to doubt that courts faced with these sensitive matters will pay proper heed both to the matters of national security that might arise in an individual case and to the constitutional limitations safeguarding essential liberties that remain vibrant even in times of security concerns.

IV

Hamdi asks us to hold that the Fourth Circuit also erred by denying him immediate access to counsel upon his detention and by disposing of the case without permitting him to meet with an attorney. Since our grant of certiorari in this case, Hamdi has been appointed counsel, with whom he has met for consultation purposes on several occasions, and with whom he is now being granted unmonitored meetings. He unquestionably has the right to access to counsel in connection with the proceedings on remand. No further consideration of this issue is necessary at this stage of the case....

The judgment of the United States Court of Appeals for the Fourth Circuit is vacated, and the case is remanded for further proceedings.

It is so ordered.

Justice SOUTER, with whom Justice GINSBURG joins, concurring in part, dissenting in part, and concurring in the judgment.... The plurality rejects [the government's "some evidence"] limit on the exercise of habeas jurisdiction and so far I agree with its opinion. The plurality does, however, accept the Government's position that if Hamdi's designation as an enemy combatant is correct, his detention (at least as to some period) is authorized by an Act of Congress as required by §4001(a), that is, by the Authorization for Use of Military Force, 115 Stat. 224 (hereinafter Force Resolution). Here, I disagree and respectfully dissent....

II

The threshold issue is how broadly or narrowly to read the Non-Detention Act, the tone of which is severe: "No citizen shall be imprisoned or otherwise detained by the United States except pursuant to an Act of Congress."...For a number of reasons, the prohibition within §4001(a) has to be read broadly to accord the statute a long reach and to impose a burden of justification on the Government.

First, the circumstances in which the Act was adopted point the way to this interpretation. The provision superseded a cold-war statute, the Emergency Detention Act of 1950, which had authorized the Attorney General, in time of emergency, to detain anyone reasonably thought likely to engage in espionage or sabotage. That statute was repealed in 1971 out of fear that it could authorize a repetition of the World War II internment of citizens of Japanese ancestry; Congress meant to preclude another episode like the one described in *Korematsu v. United States,* 323 U.S. 214 (1944)...

...To appreciate what is most significant, one must only recall that the internments of the 1940's were accomplished by Executive action. Although an Act of

Congress ratified and confirmed an Executive order authorizing the military to exclude individuals from defined areas and to accommodate those it might remove, see *Ex parte Endo*, 323 U.S. 283, 285-288 (1944), the statute said nothing whatever about the detention of those who might be removed; internment camps were creatures of the Executive, and confinement in them rested on assertion of Executive authority. When, therefore, Congress repealed the 1950 Act and adopted §4001(a) for the purpose of avoiding another *Korematsu*, it intended to preclude reliance on vague congressional authority (for example, providing "accommodations" for those subject to removal) as authority for detention or imprisonment at the discretion of the Executive (maintaining detention camps of American citizens, for example). In requiring that any Executive detention be "pursuant to an Act of Congress," then, Congress necessarily meant to require a congressional enactment that clearly authorized detention or imprisonment.

Second, when Congress passed §4001(a) it was acting in light of an interpretive regime that subjected enactments limiting liberty in wartime to the requirement of a clear statement and it presumably intended §4001(a) to be read accordingly. This need for clarity was unmistakably expressed in *Ex parte Endo, supra*, decided the same day as *Korematsu*.... The petitioner was held entitled to habeas relief in an opinion that set out this principle for scrutinizing wartime statutes in derogation of customary liberty:

> "In interpreting a wartime measure we must assume that [its] purpose was to allow for the greatest possible accommodation between . . . liberties and the exigencies of war. We must assume, when asked to find implied powers in a grant of legislative or executive authority, that the law makers intended to place no greater restraint on the citizen than was clearly and unmistakably indicated by the language they used." *Id.*, at 300.

Congress's understanding of the need for clear authority before citizens are kept detained is itself therefore clear, and §4001(a) must be read to have teeth in its demand for congressional authorization.

Finally, even if history had spared us the cautionary example of the internments in World War II, even if there had been no *Korematsu*, and *Endo* had set out no principle of statutory interpretation, there would be a compelling reason to read §4001(a) to demand manifest authority to detain before detention is authorized. The defining character of American constitutional government is its constant tension between security and liberty, serving both by partial helpings of each. In a government of separated powers, deciding finally on what is a reasonable degree of guaranteed liberty whether in peace or war (or some condition in between) is not well entrusted to the Executive Branch of Government, whose particular responsibility is to maintain security. For reasons of inescapable human nature, the branch of the Government asked to counter a serious threat is not the branch on which to rest the Nation's entire reliance in striking the balance between the will to win and the cost in liberty on the way to victory; the responsibility for security will naturally amplify the claim that security legitimately raises. A reasonable balance is more likely to be reached on the judgment of a different branch, just as Madison said in remarking that "the constant aim is to divide and arrange the several offices in such a manner as that each may be a check on the other — that the private interest of every individual may be a sentinel over the public rights." The Federalist No. 51, p. 349 (J. Cooke ed. 1961). Hence the need for an assessment by Congress before citizens are subject to lockup, and likewise the need for a clearly expressed congressional resolution of the competing claims.

III

Under this principle of reading §4001(a) robustly to require a clear statement of authorization to detain, none of the Government's arguments suffices to justify Hamdi's detention.

A

First, there is the argument that §4001(a) does not even apply to wartime military detentions, a position resting on the placement of §4001(a) in Title 18 of the United States Code, the gathering of federal criminal law.... [The] legislative history indicates that Congress was aware that §4001(a) would limit the Executive's power to detain citizens in wartime to protect national security, and it is fair to say that the prohibition was thus intended to extend not only to the exercise of power to vindicate the interests underlying domestic criminal law, but to statutorily unauthorized detention by the Executive for reasons of security in wartime, just as Hamdi claims.[2]

B

Next, there is the Government's claim, accepted by the Court, that the terms of the Force Resolution are adequate to authorize detention of an enemy combatant under the circumstances described,[3] a claim the Government fails to support sufficiently to satisfy §4001(a) as read to require a clear statement of authority to detain. Since the Force Resolution was adopted one week after the attacks of September 11, 2001, it naturally speaks with some generality, but its focus is clear, and that is on the use of military power. It is fairly read to authorize the use of armies and weapons, whether against other armies or individual terrorists. But, like the statute discussed in *Endo*, it never so much as uses the word detention, and there is no reason to think Congress might have perceived any need to augment Executive power to deal with dangerous citizens within the United States, given the well-stocked statutory arsenal of defined criminal offenses covering the gamut of actions that a citizen sympathetic to terrorists might commit. See, *e.g.*, 18 U.S.C. §2339A (material support for various

---

2. Nor is it possible to distinguish between civilian and military authority to detain based on the congressional object of avoiding another *Korematsu v. United States*, 323 U.S. 214 (1944). Although a civilian agency authorized by Executive order ran the detention camps, the relocation and detention of American citizens was ordered by the military under authority of the President as Commander in Chief. See *Ex parte Endo*, 323 U.S. 283, 285-288 (1944). The World War II internment was thus ordered under the same Presidential power invoked here and the intent to bar a repetition goes to the action taken and authority claimed here.

3. ... [T]he Government argues that a required Act of Congress is to be found in a statutory authorization to spend money appropriated for the care of prisoners of war and of other, similar prisoners, 10 U.S.C. §956(5). It is enough to say that this statute is an authorization to spend money if there are prisoners, not an authorization to imprison anyone to provide the occasion for spending money.

terrorist acts); §2339B (material support to a foreign terrorist organization); §2332a (use of a weapon of mass destruction, including conspiracy and attempt); §2332b(a)(1) (acts of terrorism "transcending national boundaries," including threats, conspiracy, and attempt); 18 U.S.C.A. §2339C (financing of certain terrorist acts); see also 18 U.S.C. §3142(e) (pretrial detention).

C

Even so, there is one argument for treating the Force Resolution as sufficiently clear to authorize detention of a citizen consistently with §4001(a). Assuming the argument to be sound, however, the Government is in no position to claim its advantage.

Because the Force Resolution authorizes the use of military force in acts of war by the United States, the argument goes, it is reasonably clear that the military and its Commander in Chief are authorized to deal with enemy belligerents according to the treaties and customs known collectively as the laws of war. Accordingly, the United States may detain captured enemies, and *Ex parte Quirin*, 317 U.S. 1 (1942), may perhaps be claimed for the proposition that the American citizenship of such a captive does not as such limit the Government's power to deal with him under the usages of war. Thus, the Government here repeatedly argues that Hamdi's detention amounts to nothing more than customary detention of a captive taken on the field of battle: if the usages of war are fairly authorized by the Force Resolution, Hamdi's detention is authorized for purposes of §4001(a)....

By holding him incommunicado, however, the Government obviously has not been treating him as a prisoner of war, and in fact the Government claims that no Taliban detainee is entitled to prisoner of war status. This treatment appears to be a violation of the Geneva Convention provision that even in cases of doubt, captives are entitled to be treated as prisoners of war "until such time as their status has been determined by a competent tribunal." Art. 5, 6 U.S.T., at 3324....

Whether, or to what degree, the Government is in fact violating the Geneva Convention and is thus acting outside the customary usages of war are not matters I can resolve at this point. What I can say, though, is that the Government has not made out its claim that in detaining Hamdi in the manner described, it is acting in accord with the laws of war authorized to be applied against citizens by the Force Resolution. I conclude accordingly that the Government has failed to support the position that the Force Resolution authorizes the described detention of Hamdi for purposes of §4001(a).

It is worth adding a further reason for requiring the Government to bear the burden of clearly justifying its claim to be exercising recognized war powers before declaring §4001(a) satisfied. Thirty-eight days after adopting the Force Resolution, Congress passed the statute entitled Uniting and Strengthening America by Providing Appropriate Tools Required to Intercept and Obstruct Terrorism Act of 2001 (USA PATRIOT ACT), 115 Stat. 272; that Act authorized the detention of alien terrorists for no more than seven days in the absence of criminal charges or deportation proceedings, 8 U.S.C. §1226a(a)(5) (2000 ed., Supp. I). It is very difficult to believe that the same Congress that carefully circumscribed Executive power over alien terrorists on home soil would not have meant to require the Government to justify clearly its detention of an American citizen held on home soil incommunicado.

D

Since the Government has given no reason either to deflect the application of §4001(a) or to hold it to be satisfied, I need to go no further; the Government hints of a constitutional challenge to the statute, but it presents none here. I will, however, stray across the line between statutory and constitutional territory just far enough to note the weakness of the Government's mixed claim of inherent, extrastatutory authority under a combination of Article II of the Constitution and the usages of war. It is in fact in this connection that the Government developed its argument that the exercise of war powers justifies the detention, and what I have just said about its inadequacy applies here as well. Beyond that, it is instructive to recall Justice Jackson's observation that the President is not Commander in Chief of the country, only of the military. *Youngstown Sheet & Tube Co. v. Sawyer*, 343 U.S. 579, 643-644 (1952) (concurring opinion); see also *id.*, at 637-638 (Presidential authority is "at its lowest ebb" where the President acts contrary to congressional will).

There may be room for one qualification to Justice Jackson's statement, however: in a moment of genuine emergency, when the Government must act with no time for deliberation, the Executive may be able to detain a citizen if there is reason to fear he is an imminent threat to the safety of the Nation and its people (though I doubt there is any want of statutory authority). This case, however, does not present that question, because an emergency power of necessity must at least be limited by the emergency; Hamdi has been locked up for over two years. Cf. *Ex parte Milligan*, 4 Wall. 2, 127 (1866) (martial law justified only by "actual and present" necessity as in a genuine invasion that closes civilian courts)....

IV...

It should go without saying that in joining with the plurality to produce a judgment, I do not adopt the plurality's resolution of constitutional issues that I would not reach. It is not that I could disagree with the plurality's determinations (given the plurality's view of the Force Resolution) that someone in Hamdi's position is entitled at a minimum to notice of the Government's claimed factual basis for holding him, and to a fair chance to rebut it before a neutral decision maker; nor, of course, could I disagree with the plurality's affirmation of Hamdi's right to counsel. On the other hand, I do not mean to imply agreement that the Government could claim an evidentiary presumption casting the burden of rebuttal on Hamdi, or that an opportunity to litigate before a military tribunal might obviate or truncate enquiry by a court on habeas.

Subject to these qualifications, I join with the plurality in a judgment of the Court vacating the Fourth Circuit's judgment and remanding the case.

Justice SCALIA, with whom Justice STEVENS joins, dissenting. . . . Where the Government accuses a citizen of waging war against it, our constitutional tradition has been to prosecute him in federal court for treason or some other crime. Where the exigencies of war prevent that, the Constitution's Suspension Clause, Art. I, §9, cl. 2, allows Congress to relax the usual protections temporarily. Absent suspension, however, the Executive's assertion of military exigency has not been thought sufficient to permit detention without charge. No one contends that the congressional Authorization for Use of Military Force, on which the Government relies to justify its actions here, is an implementation of the Suspension Clause. Accordingly, I would reverse the decision below.

I

The very core of liberty secured by our Anglo-Saxon system of separated powers has been freedom from indefinite imprisonment at the will of the Executive. Blackstone stated this principle clearly:

> "Of great importance to the public is the preservation of this personal liberty: for if once it were left in the power of any, the highest, magistrate to imprison arbitrarily whomever he or his officers thought proper . . . there would soon be an end of all other rights and immunities. . . . To bereave a man of life, or by violence to confiscate his estate, without accusation or trial, would be so gross and notorious an act of despotism, as must at once convey the alarm of tyranny throughout the whole kingdom. But confinement of the person, by secretly hurrying him to gaol, where his sufferings are unknown or forgotten; is a less public, a less striking, and therefore a more dangerous engine of arbitrary government. . . .
> "To make imprisonment lawful, it must either be, by process from the courts of judicature, or by warrant from some legal officer, having authority to commit to prison; which warrant must be in writing, under the hand and seal of the magistrate, and express the causes of the commitment, in order to be examined into (if necessary) upon a *habeas corpus*. If there be no cause expressed, the gaoler is not bound to detain the prisoner. For the law judges in this respect, . . . that it is unreasonable to send a prisoner, and not to signify withal the crimes alleged against him." 1 W. Blackstone, Commentaries on the Laws of England 132-133 (1765) (hereinafter Blackstone).

These words were well known to the Founders. Hamilton quoted from this very passage in The Federalist No. 84, p. 444 (G. Carey & J. McClellan eds., 2001). The two ideas central to Blackstone's understanding — due process as the right secured, and habeas corpus as the instrument by which due process could be insisted upon by a citizen illegally imprisoned — found expression in the Constitution's Due Process and Suspension Clauses. See Amdt. 5; Art. I, §9, cl. 2.

The gist of the Due Process Clause, as understood at the founding and since, was to force the Government to follow those common-law procedures traditionally deemed necessary before depriving a person of life, liberty, or property. When a citizen was deprived of liberty because of alleged criminal conduct, those procedures typically required committal by a magistrate followed by indictment and trial. . . .

II

The allegations here, of course, are no ordinary accusations of criminal activity. Yaser Esam Hamdi has been imprisoned because the Government believes he participated in the waging of war against the United States. The relevant question, then, is whether there is a different, special procedure for imprisonment of a citizen accused of wrongdoing *by aiding the enemy in wartime*.

A

Justice O'Connor, writing for a plurality of this Court, asserts that captured enemy combatants (other than those suspected of war crimes) have traditionally been detained until the cessation of hostilities and then released. That is probably an accurate description of wartime practice with respect to enemy *aliens*. The tradition with respect to American citizens, however, has been quite different. Citizens aiding the enemy have been treated as traitors subject to the criminal process. . . .

The modern treason statute is 18 U.S.C. §2381; it basically tracks the language of the constitutional provision. Other provisions of Title 18 criminalize various acts of warmaking and adherence to the enemy. The only citizen other than Hamdi known to be imprisoned in connection with military hostilities in Afghanistan against the United States *was* subjected to criminal process and convicted upon a guilty plea. See *United States v. Lindh*, 212 F. Supp. 2d 541 (E.D. Va. 2002) (denying motions for dismissal).

B

There are times when military exigency renders resort to the traditional criminal process impracticable. English law accommodated such exigencies by allowing legislative suspension of the writ of habeas corpus for brief periods. Blackstone explained:

> "And yet sometimes, when the state is in real danger, even this [*i.e.*, executive detention] may be a necessary measure. But the happiness of our constitution is, that it is not left to the executive power to determine when the danger of the state is so great, as to render this measure expedient. For the parliament only, or legislative power, whenever it seems proper, can authorize the crown, by suspending the *habeas corpus* act for a short and limited time, to imprison suspected persons without giving any reason for so doing. . . . In like manner this experiment ought only to be tried in case of extreme emergency; and in these the nation parts with it[s] liberty for a while, in order to preserve it for ever." 1 Blackstone 132. . . .

Our Federal Constitution contains a provision explicitly permitting suspension, but limiting the situations in which it may be invoked: "The privilege of the Writ of Habeas Corpus shall not be suspended, unless when in Cases of Rebellion or Invasion the public Safety may require it." Art. I, §9, cl. 2. Although this provision does not state that suspension must be effected by, or authorized by, a legislative act, it has been so understood, consistent with English practice and the Clause's placement in Article I.

The Suspension Clause was by design a safety valve, the Constitution's only "express provision for exercise of extraordinary authority because of a crisis," *Youngstown Sheet & Tube Co. v. Sawyer*, 343 U.S. 579, 650 (1952) (Jackson, J., concurring). . . .

III . . .

Writings from the founding generation also suggest that, without exception, the only constitutional alternatives are to charge the crime or suspend the writ. In 1788, Thomas Jefferson wrote to James Madison questioning the need for a Suspension Clause in cases of rebellion in the proposed Constitution. His letter illustrates the constraints under which the Founders understood themselves to operate:

> "Why suspend the Hab. corp. in insurrections and rebellions? The parties who may be arrested may be charged instantly with a well defined crime. Of course the judge will remand them. If the publick safety requires that the government should have a man

imprisoned on less probable testimony in those than in other emergencies; let him be taken and tried, retaken and retried, while the necessity continues, only giving him redress against the government for damages." 13 Papers of Thomas Jefferson 442 (July 31, 1788) (J. Boyd ed. 1956)....

Further evidence comes from this Court's decision in *Ex parte Milligan*, [71 U.S. (4 Wall.) 2] (1866). There, the Court issued the writ to an American citizen who had been tried by military commission for offenses that included conspiring to overthrow the Government, seize munitions, and liberate prisoners of war. The Court rejected in no uncertain terms the Government's assertion that military jurisdiction was proper "under the 'laws and usages of war,'" *id.*, at 121:

"It can serve no useful purpose to inquire what those laws and usages are, whence they originated, where found, and on whom they operate; they can never be applied to citizens in states which have upheld the authority of the government, and where the courts are open and their process unobstructed." *Ibid.*[1]

Milligan is not exactly this case, of course, since the petitioner was threatened with death, not merely imprisonment. But the reasoning and conclusion of *Milligan* logically cover the present case. The Government justifies imprisonment of Hamdi on principles of the law of war and admits that, absent the war, it would have no such authority. But if the law of war cannot be applied to citizens where courts are open, then Hamdi's imprisonment without criminal trial is no less unlawful than Milligan's trial by military tribunal.

Milligan responded to the argument, repeated by the Government in this case, that it is dangerous to leave suspected traitors at large in time of war:

"If it was dangerous, in the distracted condition of affairs, to leave Milligan unrestrained of his liberty, because he 'conspired against the government, afforded aid and comfort to rebels, and incited the people to insurrection,' the *law* said arrest him, confine him closely, render him powerless to do further mischief; and then present his case to the grand jury of the district, with proofs of his guilt, and, if indicted, try him according to the course of the common law. If this had been done, the Constitution would have been vindicated, the law of 1863 enforced, and the securities for personal liberty preserved and defended." *Id.*, at 122.

Thus, criminal process was viewed as the primary means — and the only means absent congressional action suspending the writ — not only to punish traitors, but to incapacitate them.

The proposition that the Executive lacks indefinite wartime detention authority over citizens is consistent with the Founders' general mistrust of military power permanently at the Executive's disposal. In the Founders' view, the "blessings of liberty" were threatened by "those military establishments which must gradually poison its very fountain." The Federalist No. 45, p. 238 (J. Madison). No fewer than 10 issues of the Federalist were devoted in whole or part to allaying fears of oppression from the proposed Constitution's authorization of standing armies in peacetime. Many

1. As I shall discuss presently, the Court purported to limit this language in *Ex parte Quirin*, 317 U.S. 1, 45 (1942). Whatever *Quirin*'s effect on *Milligan*'s precedential value, however, it cannot undermine its value as an indicator of original meaning. Cf. *Reid v. Covert*, 354 U.S. 1, 30 (1957) (plurality opinion) (*Milligan* remains "one of the great landmarks in this Court's history").

safeguards in the Constitution reflect these concerns. Congress's authority "[t]o raise and support Armies" was hedged with the proviso that "no Appropriation of Money to that Use shall be for a longer Term than two Years." U.S. Const., Art. 1, §8, cl. 12. Except for the actual command of military forces, all authorization for their maintenance and all explicit authorization for their use is placed in the control of Congress under Article I, rather than the President under Article II. . . . A view of the Constitution that gives the Executive authority to use military force rather than the force of law against citizens on American soil flies in the face of the mistrust that engendered these provisions.

IV

The Government argues that our more recent jurisprudence ratifies its indefinite imprisonment of a citizen within the territorial jurisdiction of federal courts. It places primary reliance upon *Ex parte Quirin*, 317 U.S. 1 (1942), a World War II case upholding the trial by military commission of eight German saboteurs, one of whom, Hans Haupt, was a U.S. citizen. The case was not this Court's finest hour. The Court upheld the commission and denied relief in a brief *per curiam* issued the day after oral argument concluded; a week later the Government carried out the commission's death sentence upon six saboteurs, including Haupt. The Court eventually explained its reasoning in a written opinion issued several months later.

Only three paragraphs of the Court's lengthy opinion dealt with the particular circumstances of Haupt's case. The Government argued that Haupt, like the other petitioners, could be tried by military commission under the laws of war. In agreeing with that contention, *Quirin* purported to interpret the language of *Milligan* quoted above (the law of war "can never be applied to citizens in states which have upheld the authority of the government, and where the courts are open and their process unobstructed") in the following manner:

> "Elsewhere in its opinion . . . the Court was at pains to point out that Milligan, a citizen twenty years resident in Indiana, who had never been a resident of any of the states in rebellion, was not an enemy belligerent either entitled to the status of a prisoner of war or subject to the penalties imposed upon unlawful belligerents. We construe the Court's statement as to the inapplicability of the law of war to Milligan's case as having particular reference to the facts before it. From them the Court concluded that Milligan, not being a part of or associated with the armed forces of the enemy, was a nonbelligerent, not subject to the law of war. . . ." 317 U.S., at 45.

In my view this seeks to revise *Milligan* rather than describe it. *Milligan* had involved (among other issues) two separate questions: (1) whether the military trial of Milligan was justified by the laws of war, and if not (2) whether the President's suspension of the writ, pursuant to congressional authorization, prevented the issuance of habeas corpus. The Court's categorical language about the law of war's inapplicability to citizens where the courts are open (with no exception mentioned for citizens who were prisoners of war) was contained in its discussion of the first point. See 4 Wall., at 121. The factors pertaining to whether Milligan could reasonably be considered a belligerent and prisoner of war, while mentioned earlier in the opinion, were made relevant and brought to bear in the Court's later discussion of whether Milligan came within the statutory provision that effectively made an exception to Congress's authorized suspension of the writ for (as the Court described it) "all parties, not prisoners of war, resident in their respective jurisdictions, . . . who were citizens of states in which the administration of the laws in the Federal tribunals was unimpaired," *id.* at 116. *Milligan* thus understood was in accord with the traditional law of habeas corpus I have described: Though treason often occurred in wartime, there was, absent provision for special treatment in a congressional suspension of the writ, no exception to the right to trial by jury for citizens who could be called "belligerents" or "prisoners of war."

But even if *Quirin* gave a correct description of *Milligan,* or made an irrevocable revision of it, *Quirin* would still not justify denial of the writ here. In *Quirin* it was uncontested that the petitioners were members of enemy forces. They were "*admitted* enemy invaders," 317 U.S., at 47 (emphasis added), and it was "undisputed" that they had landed in the United States in service of German forces, *id.,* at 20. The specific holding of the Court was only that, "upon the *conceded* facts," the petitioners were "plainly within [the] boundaries" of military jurisdiction, *id.,* at 46 (emphasis added). But where those jurisdictional facts are *not* conceded — where the petitioner insists that he is *not* a belligerent — *Quirin* left the pre-existing law in place: Absent suspension of the writ, a citizen held where the courts are open is entitled either to criminal trial or to a judicial decree requiring his release.

V

It follows from what I have said that Hamdi is entitled to a habeas decree requiring his release unless (1) criminal proceedings are promptly brought, or (2) Congress has suspended the writ of habeas corpus. A suspension of the writ could, of course, lay down conditions for continued detention, similar to those that today's opinion prescribes under the Due Process Clause. But there is a world of difference between the people's representatives' determining the need for that suspension (and prescribing the conditions for it), and this Court's doing so.

The plurality finds justification for Hamdi's imprisonment in the Authorization for Use of Military Force, 115 Stat. 224. . . . This is not remotely a congressional suspension of the writ, and no one claims that it is. Contrary to the plurality's view, I do not think this statute even authorizes detention of a citizen with the clarity necessary to satisfy the interpretive canon that statutes should be construed so as to avoid grave constitutional concerns; with the clarity necessary to comport with cases such as *Ex parte Endo,* 323 U.S. 283, 300 (1944), and *Duncan v. Kahanamoku,* 327 U.S. 304, 314-316, 324 (1946); or with the clarity necessary to overcome the statutory prescription that "[n]o citizen shall be imprisoned or otherwise detained by the United States except pursuant to an Act of Congress." 18 U.S.C. §4001(a).[5] But even if it did, I would not permit it to overcome Hamdi's entitlement to habeas corpus relief. The Suspension Clause of the Constitution, which carefully circumscribes the

---

5. The plurality rejects any need for "specific language of detention" on the ground that detention of alleged combatants is a "fundamental incident of waging war." Its authorities do not support that holding in the context of the present case. Some are irrelevant because they do not address the detention of *American citizens.* The plurality's assertion that detentions of citizen and alien combatants are equally authorized has no basis in law or common sense. Citizens and noncitizens, even if equally dangerous, are not similarly situated. *See, e.g., Milligan, supra; Johnson v. Eisentrager,* 339 U.S. 763 (1950); Rev. Stat. 4067, 50 U.S.C. §21 (Alien Enemy Act). That captivity may be consistent with the principles of international law does not prove that it also complies with the restrictions that the Constitution places on the American Government's treatment of its own citizens. . . .

conditions under which the writ can be withheld, would be a sham if it could be evaded by congressional prescription of requirements *other than the common-law requirement of committal for criminal prosecution* that render the writ, though available, unavailing. If the Suspension Clause does not guarantee the citizen that he will either be tried or released, unless the conditions for suspending the writ exist and the grave action of suspending the writ has been taken; if it merely guarantees the citizen that he will not be detained unless Congress by ordinary legislation says he can be detained; it guarantees him very little indeed.

It should not be thought, however, that the plurality's evisceration of the Suspension Clause augments, principally, the power of Congress. As usual, the major effect of its constitutional improvisation is to increase the power of the Court. Having found a congressional authorization for detention of citizens where none clearly exists; and having discarded the categorical procedural protection of the Suspension Clause; the plurality then proceeds, under the guise of the Due Process Clause, to prescribe what procedural protections *it* thinks appropriate....

...This judicial remediation of executive default is unheard of. The role of habeas corpus is to determine the legality of executive detention, not to supply the omitted process necessary to make it legal....

There is a certain harmony of approach in the plurality's making up for Congress's failure to invoke the Suspension Clause and its making up for the Executive's failure to apply what it says are needed procedures—an approach that reflects what might be called a Mr. Fix-it Mentality. The plurality seems to view it as its mission to Make Everything Come Out Right, rather than merely to decree the consequences, as far as individual rights are concerned, of the other two branches' actions and omissions. Has the Legislature failed to suspend the writ in the current dire emergency? Well, we will remedy that failure by prescribing the reasonable conditions that a suspension should have included. And has the Executive failed to live up to those reasonable conditions? Well, we will ourselves make that failure good, so that this dangerous fellow (if he is dangerous) need not be set free. The problem with this approach is not only that it steps out of the courts' modest and limited role in a democratic society; but that by repeatedly doing what it thinks the political branches ought to do it encourages their lassitude and saps the vitality of government by the people.

VI

Several limitations give my views in this matter a relatively narrow compass. They apply only to citizens, accused of being enemy combatants, who are detained within the territorial jurisdiction of a federal court. This is not likely to be a numerous group; currently we know of only two, Hamdi and Jose Padilla. Where the citizen is captured outside and held outside the United States, the constitutional requirements may be different. Cf. *Johnson v. Eisentrager*, 339 U.S. 763, 769-771 (1950); *Reid v. Covert*, 354 U.S. 1, 74-75 (1957) (Harlan, J., concurring in result); *Rasul v. Bush*, [542 U.S. 466 (2004)] (Scalia, J., dissenting). Moreover, even within the United States, the accused citizen-enemy combatant may lawfully be detained once prosecution is in progress or in contemplation...

...If the situation demands it, the Executive can ask Congress to authorize suspension of the writ—which can be made subject to whatever conditions Congress deems appropriate, including even the procedural novelties invented by the plurality today. To be sure, suspension is limited by the Constitution to cases of rebellion or invasion. But whether the attacks of September 11, 2001, constitute an "invasion," and whether those attacks still justify suspension several years later, are questions for Congress rather than this Court. . . .

Justice THOMAS, dissenting. The Executive Branch, acting pursuant to the powers vested in the President by the Constitution and with explicit congressional approval, has determined that Yaser Hamdi is an enemy combatant and should be detained. This detention falls squarely within the Federal Government's war powers, and we lack the expertise and capacity to second-guess that decision. As such, petitioners' habeas challenge should fail, and there is no reason to remand the case. . . . I do not think that the Federal Government's war powers can be balanced away by this Court. Arguably, Congress could provide for additional procedural protections, but until it does, we have no right to insist upon them. But even if I were to agree with the general approach the plurality takes, I could not accept the particulars. The plurality utterly fails to account for the Government's compelling interests and for our own institutional inability to weigh competing concerns correctly. I respectfully dissent. . . .

NOTES AND QUESTIONS

1. *The AUMF.* The AUMF (see *supra* p. 86) authorizes the President to use "all necessary and appropriate force," but is completely silent about detention authority. Why does the Supreme Court find that it authorizes detention at all? Even if it does, the use of military force to detain would presumably itself have to be "necessary and appropriate." By what standards or principles does the Court measure necessity and appropriateness?

In 2011, the House Armed Services Committee approved a measure entitled *Affirmation of Armed Conflict with Al-Qaeda, the Taliban, and Associated Forces,* providing:

Congress affirms that—
(1) the United States is engaged in an armed conflict with al-Qaeda, the Taliban, and associated forces and that those entities continue to pose a threat to the United States and its citizens, both domestically and abroad;
(2) the President has the authority to use all necessary and appropriate force during the current armed conflict with al-Qaeda, the Taliban, and associated forces pursuant to the Authorization for Use of Military Force (Public Law 107-40; 50 U.S.C. 1541 note);
(3) the current armed conflict includes nations, organization, and persons who—
(A) are part of, or are substantially supporting, al-Qaeda, the Taliban, or associated forces that are engaged in hostilities against the United States or its coalition partners; or
(B) have engaged in hostilities or have directly supported hostilities in aid of a nation, organization, or person described in subparagraph (A); and
(4) the President's authority pursuant to the Authorization for Use of Military Force. (Public Law 107-40; 50 U.S.C. 1541 note) includes the authority to detain belligerents, including persons described in paragraph (3), until the termination of hostilities.
[National Defense Authorization Act for 2012, H.R. 1540, 112th Cong. §1034 (2011).]

Would this bill clarify or confuse the President's authority to detain under the "affirmed" AUMF?

2. *Necessity for Military Detention in Hamdi.* Authority to detain under the law of war is based on military necessity, a premise echoed in the AUMF authorization for use of "*necessary* and appropriate force." *See* §2(a), *supra* p. 87 (emphasis supplied).

According to Justice O'Connor, "The purpose of detention is to prevent captured individuals from returning to the field of battle and taking up arms once again." They are detained, in other words, both to enable U.S. forces to carry out their mission and to provide force protection. In addition, such individuals are detained to obtain operational intelligence by interrogation. Moreover, the conditions of detention may be important, because the isolation of detainees and their consequent dependence on their captors may induce them to talk. Bringing such persons immediately before a judge, or even holding some kind of hearing, may be impracticable in the midst of hostilities, while the bullets are flying. Moving detainees back from the front lines may not be a cure, because it is often still impractical to withdraw troops from the front to give testimony or to preserve evidence during the fighting. *Cf. Odah v. United States*, 321 F.3d 1134, 1150 (D.C. Cir. 2003) (Randolph, J., concurring) (asserting with respect to military detainees at Camp X-Ray in Guantánamo Naval Base, Cuba, that "[t]he historical meaning of 'in the field' was not restricted to the field of battle. It applied as well to 'organized camps stationed in remote places where civil courts did not exist.'"), *rev'd and remanded by Rasul v. Bush*, 542 U.S. 466 (2004).

Do you agree with the *Hamdi* Court's assessment of military necessity? Would it make a difference whether Hamdi — a U.S. citizen allegedly fighting alongside the enemy — was one of a kind or one of a thousand?

3. *"Longstanding Law-of-War Principles."* The *Hamdi* plurality appeals to "longstanding law-of-war principles." What, exactly, are those principles, and where can they be found? See Chapter 2. How are they relevant here?

The assertion of law-of-war principles presents several thorny questions. First, if their application presupposes a war or armed conflict, must U.S. involvement in that conflict be expressly authorized by Congress? If so, what is its scope, both geographical and temporal? If law-of-war principles apply, do all of the President's war powers apply, as well, or just some of them? *See Hamdan v. Rumsfeld*, 548 U.S. 557, 594 (2006) (declaring that "there is nothing in the text or legislative history of the AUMF even hinting that Congress intended to expand or alter" the President's existing authority to convene a military commission). Note that a use-of-force authorization apparently would not trigger the Alien Enemy Act, *supra* p. 425. Does the AUMF override the Alien Enemy Act? If not, does this mean that the President has law-of-war authority under the AUMF to detain U.S. citizen combatants but not aliens in the United States?

Second, how should we define "enemy combatants" — persons subject to military detention under the law of war? How does the *Hamdi* Court define them? Recall the differences in the status of Milligan and of Quirin. Is Hamdi more like Milligan or like Quirin? In this regard, note that the saboteurs in *Quirin*, unlike Hamdi, did not contest their status as enemy soldiers. What definition of "enemy combatant" would you construct from *Milligan*, *Quirin*, and *Hamdi*?

Or are we looking in the wrong place? If war is authorized by declaration or by a use-of-force statute, should we not look to the congressional authorization for a definition of the enemy, rather than the law of war? Suppose Congress had not authorized the use of force against terrorist organizations like Al Qaeda, but the President had gone ahead anyway on the theory of repelling attack. Would military detention of combatants in that war be authorized? How would they be defined? What about persons detained as terrorists generally in an undeclared "war on terrorism"?

Third, even if the AUMF suffices to authorize military detention in the field, does it apply in the United States? Unlike Afghanistan, where Hamdi was captured, in the United States civilian courts are open and the criminal process is available. Should this make a difference?

Fourth, the principles of the law of war may be "longstanding," but will they be long-lasting? Under what changed circumstances could the majority's understanding of these principles "unravel," as the plurality opinion warns?

4. *The Greater Includes the Lesser?* In *Hamdi*, the court assumed that Supreme Court precedents concerning trial by military commission, especially *Quirin*, were apposite to the legality of military detention. *Quirin* did say that both lawful and unlawful combatants "are subject to capture and *detention*," and that unlawful combatants are additionally subject to military trial and punishment. See *supra* p. 438 (emphasis supplied). A lower court in a separate detention case understood this to reflect the Supreme Court's belief that "detention alone . . . [is] certainly the lesser of the consequences an unlawful combatant could face." *Padilla ex rel. Newman v. Bush*, 233 F. Supp. 2d 564, 595 (S.D.N.Y. 2002), *rev'd sub nom. Rumsfeld v. Padilla*, 352 F.3d 685 (2d Cir. 2003), *rev'd and remanded*, 542 U.S. 426 (2004).

But is that always true? The unlawful combatant who is tried at least will see a resolution of his status. *See Rasul v. Bush*, 542 U.S. 466, 488 (2004) (Kennedy, J., concurring in the judgment) (distinguishing *Eisentrager*, which involved aliens detained after conviction a by military commission, from *Rasul*, involving aliens "being held indefinitely, and without benefit of any legal proceeding to determine their status"). Applying the reasoning in *Hamdi*, might a combatant not be detained by the military indefinitely without trial or even charges, or until the political branches determine that the war is over? If detention is not the "lesser" consequence for such a combatant, is case law establishing the legality of a military *trial* really apposite to the legality of *detention*?

5. *"Plenary" Military Authority.* In *Hamdi*, the government also argued that the Executive has plenary authority under Article II to detain enemy combatants, presumably a "war power" of the Commander in Chief. Though the plurality did not reach this claim, it agreed that the capture and military detention of combatants are "important incident[s] of war," quoting *Quirin*, and Justice Thomas dissented on the ground that Hamdi's "detention falls squarely within the Federal Government's war powers" vested in the executive branch. Does this mean that the President did not need the delegated authority of the AUMF? How would you describe the limits on the President's non-statutory power to detain?

6. *Justice Scalia's Dissent.* Justice Scalia, joined by Justice Stevens, relied on the Suspension Clause to find the detention of Hamdi unlawful. What theory of detention did he draw from the Clause? By that theory, what are the government's options

in detaining someone like Hamdi? Does the theory apply to detention of those held at Guantánamo Bay?

7. *The Process Point: Determining the Combatant Status of U.S. Citizens.* The plurality in *Hamdi* employed a due process balancing to describe procedures required for determining the detainee's status. To test your understanding of the Court's conclusion, consider the alternatives.

First, why was combatant status not an issue in *Quirin*? The answer is that the German saboteurs admitted their status. If there is no factual dispute, then even a due process balancing presumably does not require any procedure to decide that status. Why did the Court reject the government's argument that Hamdi's status was undisputed?

If the detainee's combatant status *is* disputed and he is entitled to petition for a writ of habeas corpus, then the habeas corpus statute, 28 U.S.C. §2243, *supra* p. 379, itself suggests some evidentiary proceeding. Can you see why from examining the statute?

But what evidence and what kind of proceeding? The government suggested that "some evidence" would suffice. The government therefore argued that a court's role in a habeas corpus proceeding was only to decide whether the evidence stated in the Mobbs Declaration was sufficient standing alone. Is that argument consistent with the habeas corpus statute? Or with due process?

The Court rejected the "some evidence" standard partly on the grounds that "it primarily has been employed by courts in examining an administrative record developed after an adversarial proceeding. . . ." *Hamdi*, 542 U.S. at 537. But the government asserted that it *had* developed an administrative record after an elaborate internal process for determining combatant status of U.S. citizens, incorporating information developed by the Department of Defense, the Central Intelligence Agency, and the Department of Justice; written assessments by the same agencies; a formal legal opinion by the Office of Legal Counsel; recommendations by the Attorney General and the Secretary of Defense; and a final recommendation to and briefing for the President by the White House Counsel.[1] If such procedures were actually used to designate Hamdi as an enemy combatant and to generate the factual predicates for his military detention, why was the "some evidence" standard not sufficient?

Finally, consider the procedures that the plurality in *Hamdi* found were required by a due process balancing. Are these procedures sufficient to reduce the risk of inaccuracy in light of the interests at stake? What more would Justices Souter and Ginsburg require if they found that Congress had authorized military detention? What would you find necessary if you performed the balancing? In light of the foregoing, are Justices Scalia and Stevens right—is this a job for Congress? If so, what procedures would you recommend that Congress require?

8. *Hamdi After Remand.* After the Supreme Court remanded, Hamdi and the government negotiated an agreement for his release to his family in Saudi Arabia. The government asserted that he no longer had any intelligence value and posed no

---

1. Alberto R. Gonzales, Counsel to the President, Remarks at the American Bar Ass'n Standing Comm. on Law and Nat'l Security, Feb. 24, 2004, transcript *available at* http://www.fas.org/irp/news/2004/02/gonzales.pdf (asserting also, however, that neither these procedures nor any other specific procedures were required by law, but were adopted only by administrative grace).

threat. Under the agreement, Hamdi gave up his U.S. citizenship, renounced terrorism, waived any civil claim he had for his detention, and accepted certain travel restrictions, including a ten-year ban on returning to the United States. *See* Motion to Stay Proceedings, *Hamdi v. Rumsfeld,* No. 2:02CV439 (E.D. Va. Sept. 24, 2004), *available at* http://notablecases.vaed.uscourts.gov/2:02-cv-00439/docs/70223/0.pdf.

B. MILITARY DETENTION OF PERSONS CAPTURED IN THE UNITED STATES

1. José Padilla

Al Qaeda operatives recruited Jose Padilla, a United States citizen, to train for jihad in Afghanistan in February 2000, while Padilla was on a religious pilgrimage to Saudi Arabia. Subsequently, Padilla met with al Qaeda operatives in Afghanistan, received explosives training in an al Qaeda-affiliated camp, and served as an armed guard at what he understood to be a Taliban outpost. When United States military operations began in Afghanistan, Padilla and other al Qaeda operatives moved from safehouse to safehouse to evade bombing or capture. Padilla was, on the facts with which we are presented, "armed and present in a combat zone during armed conflict between al Qaeda/Taliban forces and the armed forces of the United States." Padilla eventually escaped to Pakistan, armed with an assault rifle. Once in Pakistan, Padilla met with Khalid Sheikh Mohammad, a senior al Qaeda operations planner, who directed Padilla to travel to the United States for the purpose of blowing up apartment buildings, in continued prosecution of al Qaeda's war of terror against the United States. After receiving further training, as well as cash, travel documents, and communication devices, Padilla flew to the United States in order to carry out his accepted assignment. [*Padilla v. Hanft,* 423 F.3d 386, 389-390 (4th Cir. 2005) (describing facts that were stipulated for purposes of summary judgment motion).]

Padilla was arrested as a material witness when he stepped off the plane at O'Hare International Airport in Chicago. He was then moved to a civilian correctional facility in New York City, where a grand jury had been convened. While he was there, however, President George W. Bush declared Padilla "an enemy combatant" and ordered the Secretary of Defense to detain him "consistent with U.S. law and the laws of war...." Order by President George W. Bush to the Secretary of Defense (June 9, 2002), *reproduced in Padilla v. Rumsfeld,* 352 F.3d 695, 724-725 app. A (2d Cir. 2003). He was then transferred to military custody in South Carolina.

Initially, Padilla challenged his detention by filing a habeas petition in the Southern District of New York. After the district court held that the government was authorized to detain him if it could adduce "some evidence" that he was an enemy combatant, *Padilla ex rel. Newman v. Bush,* 233 F. Supp. 2d 564 (S.D.N.Y. 2002), the Second Circuit Court of Appeals reversed on the merits. *Padilla v. Rumsfeld,* 352 F.3d 695 (2d Cir. 2003). The Supreme Court, however, then reversed the Second Circuit on jurisdictional grounds, finding that Padilla had petitioned for habeas in the wrong court. *Rumsfeld v. Padilla,* 542 U.S. 426 (2004).

Padilla then refiled his habeas petition in a federal district court in South Carolina, where he was being held in military custody. That court granted the petition. *Padilla v. Hanft,* 389 F. Supp. 2d 678, 691-692 (D.S.C. 2005) (quoting amici curiae in *Rumsfeld v. Padilla, supra*). The Fourth Circuit Court of Appeals reversed.

423 F.3d 386 (4th Cir. 2005), *cert. denied*, 547 U.S. 1062 (2006). Before the Supreme Court could decide Padilla's petition for certiorari, however, the government announced that it was transferring Padilla back to law enforcement custody for criminal prosecution. He was then ultimately convicted of criminal conspiracy to commit murder and providing material support to terrorists, and sentenced to 17 years in prison.

Padilla's saga thus generated dueling appellate opinions concerning the authority for his law-of-war detention, but without any Supreme Court resolution of the conflict. The key differences are shown in the following table.

Padilla v. Rumsfeld, 352 F.3d 695 (2d Cir. 2003)	*Padilla v. Hanft*, 423 F.3d 386 (4th Cir. 2005)
While it may be possible to infer a power of detention from the Joint Resolution in the battlefield context where detentions are necessary to carry out the war, there is no reason to suspect from the language of the Joint Resolution that Congress believed it would be authorizing the detention of an American citizen already held in a federal correctional institution and not "arrayed against our troops" in the field of battle. 352 F.3d at 723.	[*Hamdi*'s] reasoning simply does not admit of a distinction between an enemy combatant captured abroad and detained in the United States, such as Hamdi, and an enemy combatant who escaped capture abroad but was ultimately captured domestically and detained in the United States, such as Padilla. 423 F.3d at 393.
[T]he *Quirin* Court's decision to uphold military jurisdiction rested on express congressional authorization of the use of military tribunals to try combatants who violated the laws of war.... Accordingly, *Quirin* does not speak to whether, or to what degree, the President may impose military authority upon United States citizens domestically without clear congressional authorization. 352 F.3d at 715-716.	[I]n no place in *Quirin* did the Court even purport to establish a clear statement rule.... In fact, to the extent that Quirin can be understood to have addressed the need for a clear statement of authority from Congress at all, the rule would appear the opposite: [T]he detention and trial of petitioners — ordered by the President in the declared exercise of his powers as Commander in Chief of the Army in time of war and of grave public danger — are not to be set aside by the courts without the clear conviction that they are in conflict with the Constitution or laws of Congress constitutionally enacted. 423 F.3d at 396 (quoting *Quirin*, 317 U.S. at 25.)
The plain language of the Joint Resolution contains nothing authorizing the detention of American citizens captured on United States soil, much less the express authorization required by section 4001(a) and the "clear," "unmistakable" language required by *Endo*. 352 F.3d at 723 (referring to *Ex parte Endo*, 323 U.S. 283 (1944)).	[E]ven were a clear statement by Congress required, the AUMF constitutes such a clear statement according to the Supreme Court. In *Hamdi*, stating that "it [was] of no moment that the AUMF does not use specific language of detention," the plurality held that the AUMF "clearly and unmistakably authorized" Hamdi's detention. 423 F.3d at 396 (citing *Hamdi v. Rumsfeld*, 542 U.S. 507, 593 (2004)).

[T]he petitioners in *Quirin* admitted that they were soldiers in the armed forces of a nation against whom the United States had formally declared war. The *Quirin* Court deemed it unnecessary to consider the dispositive issue here — the boundaries of the Executive's military jurisdiction — because the *Quirin* petitioners "upon the conceded facts, were plainly within those boundaries." Padilla makes no such concession.... Moreover, ... when *Quirin* was decided in 1942, section 4001(a) had not yet been enacted.... 352 F.3d at 716 (citing *Quirin*, 317 U.S. at 46).	As the Court in *Quirin* explained, the *Milligan* Court's reasoning had "particular reference to the facts before it," namely, that Milligan was not "a part of or associated with the armed forces of the enemy." ... Thus confined, *Milligan* is inapposite here because Padilla, unlike Milligan, associated with, and has taken up arms against the forces of the United States on behalf of, an enemy of the United States. 423 F.3d at 396-397 (citing *Quirin*, 317 U.S. at 45.)

The Fourth Circuit, unlike the Second Circuit, had the benefit of the Supreme Court's decision in *Hamdi*. Ultimately, the Fourth Circuit's decision rested on the court's inability to see any distinction between Padilla and Hamdi.

As the AUMF authorized Hamdi's detention by the President, so also does it authorize Padilla's detention. Under the facts as presented here, Padilla unquestionably qualifies as an "enemy combatant" as that term was defined for purposes of the controlling opinion in *Hamdi*. Indeed, under the definition of "enemy combatant" employed in *Hamdi*, we can discern no difference in principle between Hamdi and Padilla. Like Hamdi, Padilla associated with forces hostile to the United States in Afghanistan. And, like Hamdi, Padilla took up arms against United States forces in that country in the same way and to the same extent as did Hamdi. Because, like Hamdi, Padilla is an enemy combatant, and because his detention is no less necessary than was Hamdi's in order to prevent his return to the battlefield, the President is authorized by the AUMF to detain Padilla as a fundamental incident to the conduct of war. [423 F.3d at 391-392.]

---

2. Ali Saleh Kahlah al-Marri

Al-Marri was a lawful resident alien arrested in Peoria, Illinois, as a material witness, then was indicted for credit card fraud and lying to the FBI. When he moved to suppress certain evidence in civil court, the government moved *ex parte* to dismiss the indictment based on an order signed by the President, declaring al-Marri an enemy combatant and ordering him transferred to military custody. Al-Marri petitioned for a writ of habeas corpus, to which the government filed a declaration ("the Rapp Declaration") asserting that

al-Marri: (1) is "closely associated with al Qaeda, an international terrorist organization with which the United States is at war"; (2) trained at an al Qaeda terrorist training camp in Afghanistan sometime between 1996 and 1998; (3) in the summer of 2001, was introduced to Osama Bin Laden by Khalid Shaykh Muhammed; (4) at that time, volunteered for a "martyr mission" on behalf of al Qaeda; (5) was ordered to enter the United States sometime before September 11, 2001, to serve as a "sleeper agent" to facilitate terrorist activities and explore disrupting this country's financial system through computer hacking; (6) in the summer of 2001, met with terrorist financier Mustafa Ahmed al-Hawsawi, who gave al-Marri money, including funds to buy a laptop; (7) gathered technical information about poisonous chemicals on his laptop; (8) undertook efforts to obtain false identification, credit cards, and banking information, including stolen credit card numbers; (9) communicated with known terrorists, including Khalid Shaykh Muhammed and al-Hawsawi, by phone and e-mail; and (10) saved information about jihad, the September 11th attacks, and Bin Laden on his laptop computer. [*Al-Marri v. Pucciarelli*, 534 F.3d 213, 220 (4th Cir. 2008) (en banc), *vacated and remanded sub nom. Al-Marri v. Spagone*, 129 S. Ct. 1545 (2009).]

The district court denied relief, and al-Marri appealed. A divided panel of the Fourth Circuit reversed, and al-Marri petitioned for rehearing *en banc*. The sharply divided *en banc* court produced multiple concurring and dissenting opinions. Judge Motz first opined that the Executive lacked authority for the military detention of al-Marri, but only three other judges joined her on this question. Thus, a bare majority of the court upheld the military detention authority. Judge Traxler then abandoned that majority to form a different majority for the proposition that the process afforded al-Marri to challenge his designation did not meet due process standards. These five votes sufficed to send the case back to the district court.

Al-Marri v. Pucciarelli

United States Court of Appeals, Fourth Circuit (en banc), 2008
534 F.3d 213
vacated and remanded sub nom. Al-Marri v. Spagone,
129 S. Ct. 1545 (2009)

PER CURIAM: . . . Having considered the briefs and arguments of the parties, the *en banc* court now holds: (1) by a 5 to 4 vote (Chief Judge Williams and Judges Wilkinson, Niemeyer, Traxler, and Duncan voting in the affirmative; Judges Michael, Motz, King, and Gregory voting in the negative), that, if the Government's allegations about al-Marri are true, Congress has empowered the President to detain him as an enemy combatant; and (2) by a 5 to 4 vote (Judges Michael, Motz, Traxler, King, and Gregory voting in the affirmative; Chief Judge Williams and Judges Wilkinson, Niemeyer, and Duncan voting in the negative), that, assuming Congress has empowered the President to detain al-Marri as an enemy combatant provided the Government's allegations against him are true, al-Marri has not been afforded sufficient process to challenge his designation as an enemy combatant.

Accordingly, the judgment of the district court is reversed and remanded for further proceedings consistent with the opinions that follow.

Reversed and remanded.

DIANA GRIBBON MOTZ, Circuit Judge, concurring in the judgment: . . .

I. . . .

The Rapp Declaration does *not* assert that al-Marri: (1) is a citizen, or affiliate of the armed forces, of any nation at war with the United States; (2) was seized on, near, or having escaped from a battlefield on which the armed forces of the United States or its allies were engaged in combat; (3) was ever in Afghanistan during the armed conflict between the United States and the Taliban there; or (4) directly participated in any hostilities against United States or allied armed forces. . . .

II. . . .

A. . . .

[Judge Motz found that as a lawfully admitted alien with a substantial connection to the United States, al-Marri was entitled to due process before he could be deprived of his liberty. But she also acknowledged that in *Hamdi v. Rumsfeld*, 542 U.S. 507 (2004), the Supreme Court found that Congress had constitutionally authorized the President to order the military detention, without the criminal process ordinarily required by the Due Process Clause, of persons who qualify as "enemy combatants."]

B.

The Government's primary argument is that the AUMF, as construed by precedent and considered against "the legal background against which [it] was enacted," i.e., constitutional and law-of-war principles, empowers the President to order the military to seize and detain al-Marri as an enemy combatant. . . .

1.

Tellingly, the Deputy Solicitor General conceded at oral argument before the *en banc* court that the AUMF only authorizes detention of enemy combatants. Thus, the Government does *not* argue that the broad language of the AUMF authorizes the President to subject to indefinite military detention anyone he believes to have aided any "nation[ ], organization [ ], or person[ ]" related to the September 11th attacks. *See* §2(a), 115 Stat. 224. Such an interpretation would lead to absurd results that Congress could not have intended.

Under that reading of the AUMF, the President would be able to subject to indefinite military detention anyone, including an American citizen, whom the President believed was associated with any organization that the President believed in some way "planned, authorized, committed, or aided" the September 11th attacks, so long as the President believed this to be "necessary and appropriate" to prevent future acts of terrorism.

Under such an interpretation of the AUMF, if some money from a nonprofit charity that feeds Afghan orphans made its way to al Qaeda, the President could subject to indefinite military detention any donor to that charity. Similarly, this interpretation of the AUMF would allow the President to detain indefinitely any employee or shareholder of an American corporation that built equipment used by the

September 11th terrorists; or allow the President to order the military seizure and detention of an American-citizen physician who treated a member of al Qaeda. . . .

2.

. . . [T]he Government wisely limits its argument. It relies only on the scope of the AUMF as construed by precedent and considered in light of "the legal background against which [it] was enacted." Specifically, the Government contends that "[t]he Supreme Court's and this Court's prior construction of the AUMF govern[s] this case and compel[s] the conclusion that the President is authorized to detain al-Marri as an enemy combatant."

i.

The precedent interpreting the AUMF on which the Government relies for this argument consists of two cases: the Supreme Court's opinion in *Hamdi*, 542 U.S. 507, and our opinion in *Padilla v. Hanft*, 423 F.3d 386 (4th Cir. 2005). The "legal background" for the AUMF, which the Government cites, consists of two cases from earlier conflicts, *Ex Parte Quirin*, 317 U.S. 1 (1942) (World War II), and *Ex Parte Milligan*, 71 U.S. (4 Wall.) 2 (1866) (U.S. Civil War), as well as constitutional and law-of-war principles.

With respect to the latter, we note that American courts have often been reluctant to follow international law in resolving domestic disputes. In the present context, however, they, like the Government here, have relied on the law of war-treaty obligations including the Hague and Geneva Conventions and customary principles developed alongside them. The law of war provides clear rules for determining an individual's status during an international armed conflict, distinguishing between "combatants" (members of a nation's military, militia, or other armed forces, and those who fight alongside them) and "civilians" (all other persons).[11] *See, e.g.*, Geneva Convention Relative to the Treatment of Prisoners of War (Third Geneva Convention) arts. 2, 4, 5, Aug. 12, 1949, 6 U.S.T. 3316, 75 U.N.T.S. 135; Geneva Convention Relative to the Protection of Civilian Persons in Time of War (Fourth Geneva Convention) art. 4, Aug. 12, 1949, 6 U.S.T. 3516, 75 U.N.T.S. 287. American courts have repeatedly looked to these careful distinctions made in the law of war in identifying which individuals fit within the "legal category" of "enemy combatant" under our Constitution. *See, e.g.*, *Hamdi*, 542 U.S. at 518; *Quirin*, 317 U.S. at 30-31 & n.7; *Milligan*, 71 U.S. at 121-22; *Padilla*, 423 F.3d at 391. . . .

Quirin, *Hamdi*, and *Padilla* all emphasize that *Milligan*'s teaching — that our Constitution does not permit the Government to subject *civilians* within the United States

---

11. Thus, "civilian" is a term of art in the law of war, not signifying an innocent person, but rather someone in a certain legal category who is *not* subject to *military* seizure or detention. So, too, a "combatant" is by no means always a wrongdoer, but rather a member of a different "legal category" who is subject to *military* seizure and detention. *Hamdi*, 542 U.S. at 522 n.1. For example, our brave soldiers fighting in Germany during World War II were "combatants" under the law of war, and viewed from Germany's perspective they were "enemy combatants." While civilians are subject to trial and punishment in civilian courts for all crimes committed during wartime in the country in which they are captured and held, combatant status protects an individual from trial and punishment by the capturing nation, unless the combatant has violated the law of war. *See id.* at 518; *Quirin*, 317 U.S. at 28-31. Nations in international conflicts can summarily remove the adversary's "combatants," i.e., the "enemy combatants," from the battlefield and detain them for the duration of such conflicts, but no such provision is made for "civilians." *Hamdi*, 542 U.S. at 518; *Quirin*, 317 U.S. at 28-31.

to military jurisdiction — remains good law. The *Quirin* Court explained that while the petitioners before it were affiliated with the armed forces of an enemy nation and so were enemy belligerents, Milligan was a "non-belligerent" and so "not subject to the law of war." 317 U.S. at 45. The *Hamdi* plurality similarly took care to note that *Milligan* "turned in large part on the fact that Milligan was not a prisoner of war" (i.e., combatant) and suggested that "[h]ad Milligan been captured while he was assisting Confederate soldiers by carrying a rifle against Union troops on a Confederate battle-field, the holding of the Court might well have been different." 542 U.S. at 522. And in *Padilla*, we reaffirmed that "*Milligan* does not extend to enemy combatants" and so "is inapposite here because Padilla, unlike Milligan, associated with, and has taken up arms against the forces of the United States on behalf of, an enemy of the United States." 423 F.3d at 396-97. Thus, although *Hamdi*, *Quirin*, and *Padilla* distinguish *Milligan*, they recognize that its core holding remains the law of the land. That is, civilians within this country (even "dangerous enemies" like Milligan who perpetrate "enormous crime[s]" on behalf of "secret" enemy organizations bent on "overthrow-ing the Government" of this country) may not be subjected to military control and deprived of constitutional rights.

In sum, the holdings of *Hamdi* and *Padilla* share two characteristics: (1) they look to law-of-war principles to determine who fits within the "legal category" of enemy combatant; and (2) following the law of war, they rest enemy combatant status on affiliation with the military arm of an enemy nation.

ii.

In view of the holdings in *Hamdi* and *Padilla*, we find it remarkable that the Government contends that they "compel the conclusion" that the President may detain al-Marri as an enemy combatant. For unlike Hamdi and Padilla, al-Marri is not alleged to have been part of a Taliban unit, not alleged to have stood alongside the Taliban or the armed forces of any other enemy nation, not alleged to have been on the battlefield during the war in Afghanistan, not alleged to have even been in Afghanistan during the armed conflict there, and not alleged to have engaged in combat with United States forces anywhere in the world. *See* Rapp Declaration (alleg-ing none of these facts, but instead that "[a]l-Marri engaged in conduct in prepara-tion for acts of international terrorism intended to cause injury or adverse effects on the United States"). Indeed, unlike Hamdi and Padilla, al-Marri had been imprisoned in the United States by civil authorities on criminal charges for more than a year before being seized by the military and indefinitely confined in a Navy brig as an enemy combatant.

In place of the "classic wartime detention" that the Government argued justified Hamdi's detention as an enemy combatant, or the "classic battlefield" detention it maintained justified Padilla's, here the Government argues that al-Marri's seizure and indefinite detention by the military in this country are justified "because he engaged in, and continues to pose a very real threat of carrying out, . . . acts of international terrorism." And instead of seeking judicial deference to decisions of "military officers who are engaged in the serious work of waging battle," *Hamdi*, 542 U.S. at 531-32, the Government asks us to defer to the "multi-agency evaluation process" of government bureaucrats in Washington made eighteen months after al-Marri was taken into cus-tody. Neither the holding in *Hamdi* nor that in *Padilla* supports the Government's contentions here. . . .

...Instead, the *Hamdi* plurality emphasized the narrowness of its holding, and the "limited category" of individuals controlled by that holding. In *Padilla*, we similarly saw no need to embrace a broader construction of the AUMF than that adopted by the Supreme Court in *Hamdi*. Indeed, the Government itself *principally* argued that Padilla was an enemy combatant because he, like Hamdi, "engaged in armed conflict" alongside the Taliban "against our forces in Afghanistan."...

...*Hamdi* and *Padilla* evidence no sympathy for the view that the AUMF permits indefinite military detention beyond the "limited category" of people covered by the "narrow circumstances" of those cases....

3....

i.

...[T]he Supreme Court's most recent terrorism cases—*Hamdan* [*v. Rumsfeld*, 548 U.S. 557 (2006)] and *Boumediene*—provide no support for the dissenters' position. In *Hamdan*, the Court held that because the conflict between the United States and al Qaeda in Afghanistan is not "between nations," it is a "'conflict not of an international character'"—and so is governed by Common Article 3 of the Geneva Conventions.

Common Article 3 and other Geneva Convention provisions applying to non-international conflicts (in contrast to those applying to international conflicts) simply do *not* recognize the "legal category" of enemy combatant. *See* Third Geneva Convention, art. 3, 6 U.S.T. at 3318. As the International Committee of the Red Cross—the official codifier of the Geneva Conventions—explains, "an 'enemy combatant' is a person who, either lawfully or unlawfully, engages in hostilities for the opposing side in an *international* armed conflict;" in contrast, "[i]n non-international armed conflict combatant status *does not exist.*" Int'l Comm. of the Red Cross, Official Statement: The Relevance of IHL in the Context of Terrorism, at 1, 3 (Feb. 21, 2005), http://www.icrc.org/Web/Eng/siteeng0.nsf/htmlall/terrorismihl-210705 (emphasis added).

Perhaps for this reason, our dissenting colleagues and the Government ignore *Hamdan*'s holding that the conflict with al Qaeda in Afghanistan is a non-international conflict and ignore the fact that, in such conflicts, the legal category of enemy combatant does not exist....

...Furthermore, in *Boumediene*, the Court demonstrated no more sympathy for the Government's position than it had in any of the other recent terrorism cases. Rather, the Court expressly held that persons designated by the Executive "as enemy combatants" and held by United States forces at Guantánamo Bay must be afforded "the fundamental procedural protections of habeas corpus" guaranteed by our Constitution, even though they were foreign nationals who had been seized in foreign lands. The Court explained that "[t]he laws and Constitution are designed to survive, and remain in force, in extraordinary times."

...Because the legal status of enemy combatant does not exist in non-international conflicts, the law of war leaves the detention of persons in such conflicts to the applicable law of the detaining country. In al-Marri's case, the applicable law is our Constitution. Under our Constitution, even if the Supreme Court should hold that the Government may detain indefinitely Boumediene, Hamdan, and others like them, who were captured *outside* the United States and lack substantial and voluntary connections to this country, that holding would provide no support for approving al-Marri's military detention. For not only was al-Marri seized and detained *within* the United States, he also has substantial connections to the United States and so plainly is protected by the Due Process Clause.

ii. . . .

We recognize the understandable instincts of those who wish to treat domestic terrorists as "combatants" in a "global war on terror." Allegations of criminal activity in association with a terrorist organization, however, do not permit the Government to transform a civilian into an enemy combatant subject to indefinite military detention, just as allegations of murder in association with others while in military service do not permit the Government to transform a civilian into a soldier subject to trial by court martial. *See United States ex rel. Toth v. Quarles*, 350 U.S. 11, 23 (1955) (holding that ex-servicemen, "like other civilians, are entitled to have the benefit of safeguards afforded those tried in the regular courts authorized by Article III of the Constitution").

To be sure, enemy combatants may commit crimes just as civilians may. When an enemy combatant violates the law of war, that conduct will render the person an "unlawful" enemy combatant, subject not only to detention but also to military trial and punishment. *Quirin*, 317 U.S. at 31. But merely engaging in unlawful behavior does not make one an enemy combatant. *Quirin* illustrates these distinctions well. The *Quirin* petitioners were first enemy combatants — associating themselves with the military arm of the German government with which the United States was at war. They became *unlawful* enemy combatants when they violated the law of war by "without uniform com[ing] secretly through the lines for the purpose of waging war." *Id.* By doing so, in addition to being subject to military detention for the duration of the conflict as enemy combatants, they also became "subject to trial and punishment by military tribunals for acts which render their belligerency illegal." *Id.* Had the *Quirin* petitioners never "secretly and without uniform" passed our "military lines," *id.*, they still would have been enemy combatants, subject to military detention, but would not have been *unlawful* enemy combatants subject to military trial and punishment.

Neither *Quirin* nor any other precedent even suggests, as our dissenting colleagues seem to believe, that individuals with constitutional rights, unaffiliated with the military arm of any enemy government, can be subjected to military jurisdiction and deprived of those rights solely on the basis of their conduct on behalf of a terrorist organization. In fact, *Milligan* rejected the Government's attempt to do just this. There, the Court acknowledged that Milligan's conduct — "joining and aiding" a "secret political organization, armed to oppose the laws, and seek[ing] by stealthy means to introduce the enemies of the country into peaceful communities, there to . . . overthrow the power of the United States" — made him and his co-conspirators "dangerous enemies to their country." 71 U.S. at 6, 130. But the Government did not allege that Milligan took orders from any enemy government or took up arms against this country on the battlefield. And so the Court held that the Government could not subject Milligan to trial by military tribunal or treat him as an enemy combatant subject to military detention as a prisoner of war. Milligan was an "enem[y] of the country" and associated with an organization seeking to "overthrow[ ] the Government" of this country, but he was still a civilian and had to be treated as one. *Id.* . . .

iii. . . .

. . . [B]ecause the AUMF contains only a broad grant of war powers and lacks any specific language authorizing detention, the *Hamdi* plurality explained that its opinion "only finds legislative authority to detain under the AUMF once it is sufficiently clear that the individual *is*, in fact, an enemy combatant." 542 U.S. at 523 (emphasis added). Although the military detention of enemy combatants like Hamdi is certainly "a fundamental incident of waging war," *id.* at 519, the military detention of civilians like al-Marri just as certainly is not.

Even assuming the Constitution permitted Congress to grant the President such an awesome and unprecedented power, if Congress intended to grant this authority, it could and would have said so explicitly. The AUMF lacks the particularly clear statement from Congress that would, at a minimum, be necessary to authorize the indefinite military detention of *civilians* as enemy combatants. *See, e.g., Greene v. McElroy*, 360 U.S. 474, 508 (1959) (rejecting Government argument that executive orders and statutes permitted deprivation of liberty rights absent "explicit authorization"); *Duncan v. Kahanamoku*, 327 U.S. 304, 324 (1946) (rejecting Government argument that statute authorized trial of civilians by military tribunals because Congress could not have intended "to exceed the boundaries between military and civilian power, in which our people have always believed"); *Ex Parte Endo*, 323 U.S. 283, 300 (1944) (rejecting Government argument that a "wartime" executive order and statute permitted detention of citizen of Japanese heritage when neither "use[d] the language of detention"); *Brown v. United States*, 12 U.S. (8 Cranch) 110, 128-29 (1814) (rejecting Government argument that declaration of war authorized confiscation of enemy property because it did not clearly "declare[]" the legislature's "will"). We are exceedingly reluctant to infer a grant of authority that is so far afield from anything recognized by precedent or law-of-war principles, especially given the serious constitutional concerns it would raise. . . .

C.

Thus, we turn to the Government's final contention. The Government summarily argues that even if the AUMF does not authorize al-Marri's seizure and indefinite detention as an enemy combatant, the President has "inherent constitutional authority" to order the military to seize and detain al-Marri. According to the Government, the President's "war-making powers" afford him "inherent" authority to subject persons legally residing in this country and protected by our Constitution to military arrest and detention, without the benefit of any criminal process, if the President believes these individuals have "engaged in conduct in preparation for acts of international terrorism." *See* Rapp Declaration. Given that the Government has now acknowledged that aliens lawfully residing in the United States have the same due process rights as United States citizens, this is a breathtaking claim — and one that no member of the court embraces. . . .

1.

In contrast to the AUMF, which is silent on the detention of asserted alien terrorists captured and held within the United States, in the Patriot Act, enacted shortly after the AUMF, Congress carefully stated how it wished the Government to handle aliens believed to be terrorists who were seized and held within the United States. The Patriot Act provides the Executive with broad powers to deal with "terrorist aliens," but it *explicitly prohibits* their indefinite detention.

Section 412 of the Patriot Act, entitled "Mandatory Detention of Suspected Terrorists," permits the short-term "[d]etention of [t]errorist [a]liens." Patriot Act §412(a). The statute authorizes the Attorney General to detain any alien whom he "has reasonable grounds to believe": (1) "seeks to enter the United States" to "violate any law of the United States relating to espionage or sabotage" or to use "force, violence, or other unlawful means" in opposition to the government of the United States; (2) "has engaged in a terrorist activity"; or (3) is "likely to engage after entry in any terrorist activity," has "incited terrorist activity," is a "representative" or "member" of a "terrorist organization," is a "representative" of a "group that endorses or espouses terrorist activity," or "has received military-type training" from a terrorist organization. *Id.*; 8 U.S.C.A. §1182(a)(3)(A)-(B) (West 2007); *see also* 8 U.S.C.A. §1227(a)(4)(A)(i), (a)(4)(A)(iii), (a)(4)(B) (West 2007). In addition, the Patriot Act authorizes the Attorney General to detain any other alien who "is engaged in any other activity that endangers the national security of the United States." Patriot Act §412(a). In particular, the Patriot Act permits the Attorney General to "take into custody" any "terrorist aliens" based only on the Attorney General's "belie[fs]" as to the aliens' threat, with *no* process or evidentiary hearing, and judicial review available only through petition for habeas corpus. *Id.*

Recognizing the breadth of this grant of power, however, Congress also imposed strict limits in the Patriot Act on the duration of the detention of such "terrorist aliens" within the United States. Thus, the Patriot Act expressly prohibits unlimited "indefinite detention"; instead it requires the Attorney General either to begin "removal proceedings" or to "charge the alien with a criminal offense" "not later than 7 days after the commencement of such detention." *Id.* If a terrorist alien's removal "is unlikely for the reasonably foreseeable future," he "may be detained for additional periods of up to six months" if his release "will threaten the national security of the United States." *Id.* But no provision of the Patriot Act allows for unlimited indefinite detention. Moreover, the Attorney General must provide the legislature with reports on the use of this detention authority every six months, which must include the number of aliens detained, the grounds for their detention, and the length of the detention. *Id.* §412(c).

Therefore, the Patriot Act establishes a specific method for the Government to detain aliens affiliated with terrorist organizations who the Government believes have come to the United States to endanger our national security, conduct espionage and sabotage, use force and violence to overthrow the government, engage in terrorist activity, or are likely to engage in any terrorist activity. Congress could not have better described the Government's allegations against al-Marri — *and* Congress decreed that individuals so described are *not* to be detained indefinitely, but only for a limited time, and only by civilian authorities, prior to deportation or criminal prosecution.

In sum, Congress has carefully prescribed the process by which it wishes to permit detention of "terrorist aliens" within the United States, and it has expressly prohibited the indefinite detention the President seeks here. The Government's argument that the President may indefinitely detain al-Marri is thus contrary to Congress's expressed will. "When the President takes measures incompatible with the expressed or implied will of Congress, his power is at its lowest ebb, for then he can rely only upon his own constitutional powers minus any constitutional powers of Congress over the matter." *Youngstown [Sheet & Tube Co. v. Sawyer*, 343 U.S. 579 (1952),] at 637 (Jackson, J., concurring). As the Supreme Court has recently explained, "[w]hether or not the President has independent power . . . he may not disregard limitations that Congress has, in proper exercise of its own war powers, placed on his powers." *Hamdan*, 126 S. Ct. at 2774 n.23 (citing *Youngstown*, 343 U.S. at 637 (Jackson, J., concurring)). In such cases, "Presidential claim[s]" to power "must be scrutinized with caution, for what is at stake is the equilibrium established by our constitutional system." *Youngstown*, 343 U.S. at 638 (Jackson, J., concurring). . . .

3.

In light of al-Marri's due process rights under our Constitution and Congress's express prohibition in the Patriot Act on the indefinite detention of those civilians arrested as "terrorist aliens" within this country, we can only conclude that, in the case at hand, the President claims power that far exceeds that granted him by the Constitution.

We do not question the President's wartime authority over enemy combatants, but absent suspension of the writ of habeas corpus, the Constitution simply does not provide the President the power to exercise military authority over civilians within the United States. *See Toth*, 350 U.S. at 14 ("[A]ssertion of military authority over civilians cannot rest on the President's power as commander-in-chief."). The President cannot eliminate constitutional protections with the stroke of a pen by proclaiming a civilian, even a criminal civilian, an enemy combatant subject to indefinite military detention. Put simply, the Constitution does not empower the President to order the military to seize civilians residing within the United States and detain them indefinitely without criminal process, and this is so even if he calls them "enemy combatants."

A "well-established purpose of the Founders" was "to keep the military strictly within its proper sphere, subordinate to civil authority." *Reid [v. Covert*, 354 U.S. 1, 30 (1957)]. In the Declaration of Independence, our forefathers lodged the complaint that the King of Great Britain had "affected to render the Military independent of and superior to the Civil power" and objected that the King had "depriv[ed] us in many cases, of the benefits of Trial by Jury." *The Declaration of Independence* paras. 14, 20 (U.S. 1776). Thus, a resolute conviction that civilian authority should govern the military animated the framing of the Constitution. As Alexander Hamilton, no foe of executive power, observed, the President's Commander-in-Chief powers "amount to nothing more than the supreme command and direction of the military and naval forces." The Federalist No. 69, at 386 (Alexander Hamilton) (Clinton Rossiter ed., 1961). "That military powers of the Commander in Chief were not to supersede representative government of *internal affairs* seems obvious from the Constitution and from elementary American history." *Youngstown*, 343 U.S. at 644 (Jackson, J., concurring) (emphasis added). For this reason, in *Youngstown*, the Supreme Court rejected the President's claim to "inherent power" to use the military even to seize property within the United States, despite the Government's argument that the refusal would "endanger the well-being and safety of the Nation." *Id.* at 584 (majority opinion). . . .

To sanction such presidential authority to order the military to seize and indefinitely detain civilians, even if the President calls them "enemy combatants," would have disastrous consequences for the Constitution — and the country. For a court to uphold a claim to such extraordinary power would do more than render lifeless the Suspension Clause, the Due Process Clause, and the rights to criminal process in the

Fourth, Fifth, Sixth, and Eighth Amendments; it would effectively undermine all of the freedoms guaranteed by the Constitution. It is that power—were a court to recognize it—that could lead all our laws "to go unexecuted, and the government itself to go to pieces." We refuse to recognize a claim to power that would so alter the constitutional foundations of our Republic.

III. . . .

. . . We believe that it is unnecessary to litigate whether al-Marri is an enemy combatant, but joining in remand for the evidentiary proceedings outlined by Judge Traxler will at least place the burden on the Government to make an initial showing that normal due process protections are unduly burdensome and that the Rapp declaration is "the most reliable available evidence," supporting the Government's allegations before it may order al-Marri's military detention. Therefore, we concur in the per curiam opinion reversing and remanding for evidentiary proceedings to determine whether al-Marri actually is an enemy combatant subject to military detention.

Judges Michael, King, and Gregory have authorized me to indicate that they join in this opinion.

TRAXLER, Circuit Judge, concurring in the judgment: . . . I agree with my colleagues who hold that the [AUMF] . . . grants the President the power to detain enemy combatants in the war against al Qaeda, including belligerents who enter our country for the purpose of committing hostile and war-like acts such as those carried out by the al Qaeda operatives on 9/11. And, I agree that the allegations made by the government against al-Marri, if true, would place him within this category and permit the President to militarily detain him.

However, I depart from my dissenting colleagues on the issue of whether al-Marri has been afforded a fair opportunity to challenge the factual basis for his designation as an enemy combatant. Because the process afforded al-Marri by the district court to challenge the factual basis for his designation as an enemy combatant did not meet the minimal requirements of due process guaranteed by the Fifth Amendment, I would reverse the district court's dismissal of al-Marri's habeas petition and remand for further evidentiary proceedings on the issue of whether al-Marri is, in fact, an enemy combatant subject to military detention. . . .

II. THE AUTHORITY TO DETAIN. . . .

B. . . .

1. . . .

In my opinion . . . there is no doubt that individuals who are dispatched here by al Qaeda, the organization known to have carried out the 9/11 attacks upon our country, as sleeper agents and terrorist operatives charged with the task of committing additional attacks upon our homeland "are [also] individuals Congress sought to target in passing the AUMF." *Hamdi*, 542 U.S. at 518. Citing the right of the United States "to protect United States citizens *both at home and abroad*," the AUMF authorized the President's use of "all necessary and appropriate force against" the nations *and organizations* that "planned, authorized, committed, or aided" the 9/11 attacks, "or harbored such organizations or persons, in order to prevent any future acts of international terrorism against the United States." 115 Stat. 224. Clearly, Congress was not merely authorizing military retaliation against a reigning foreign government known to have *supported* the enemy force that attacked us in our homeland, but was also authorizing military action against al Qaeda operatives who, like the 9/11 hijackers, were sent by the al Qaeda organization to the United States to conduct additional terror operations here.

As persuasively pointed out by the government, it was the 9/11 attacks which triggered the passage of the AUMF. The al Qaeda operatives who successfully carried out those attacks entered this country under false pretenses for the purpose of carrying out al Qaeda orders and, while finalizing the preparations for these attacks, maintained a facade of peaceful residence until the very moment they boarded the commercial airliners that they used as weapons. The hijackers never engaged in combat operations against our forces on a foreign battlefield. Yet al-Marri would have us rule that when Congress authorized the President to deal militarily with those responsible for the 9/11 attacks upon our country, it did not intend to authorize the President to deal militarily with al Qaeda operatives identically situated to the 9/11 hijackers. There is nothing in the language of the AUMF that suggests that Congress intended to limit the military response or the presidential authorization to acts occurring in foreign territories, and it strains reason to believe that Congress, in enacting the AUMF in the wake of those attacks, did *not* intend for it to encompass al Qaeda operatives standing in the exact position as the attackers who brought about its enactment. Furthermore, Congress has not revised or revoked the AUMF since its enactment or since the Supreme Court decided *Hamdi.*

I am also unpersuaded by the claim that because al Qaeda itself is an international terrorist organization instead of a "nation state" or "enemy government," the AUMF cannot apply, consistent with the laws of war and our constitutional guarantees, to such persons. The premise of that claim seems to be that because al Qaeda is not technically in control of an enemy nation or its government, it cannot be considered as anything other than a criminal organization whose members are entitled to all the protections and procedures granted by our constitution. I disagree.

In my view, al Qaeda is much more and much worse than a criminal organization. And while it may be an unconventional enemy force in a historical context, it is an enemy force nonetheless. The fact that it allied itself with an enemy government of a foreign nation only underscores this point, rendering attempts to distinguish its soldiers or operatives as something meaningfully different from military soldiers in service to the Taliban government (or al Qaeda operatives such as Hamdi and Padilla, who fought beside them) equally strained. The President attacked the Taliban in Afghanistan as *retaliation* for al Qaeda's strike upon our nation *because* al Qaeda was centralized there and allied with the Taliban, and it also strains credulity to assert that while we are legitimately at war with the Taliban government, we cannot be at war with al Qaeda. . . .

2.

If the allegations of the Rapp Declaration are true, I am also of the view that al-Marri would fall within the category of persons who may be lawfully detained pursuant to the authority granted by the AUMF. . . .

III. DUE PROCESS

While I agree with my colleagues who would hold that the President has the legal authority under the AUMF to detain al-Marri as an enemy combatant for the duration of the hostilities, we part company on the issue of whether the process afforded al-Marri to challenge his detention was sufficient to meet the minimum requirements of due process of law. In my opinion, due process demands more procedural safeguards than those provided to al-Marri in the habeas proceedings below. . . .

C. . . .

. . . [I]n my opinion, the district court erred in the initial step of accepting the hearsay affidavit of Rapp "as the most reliable available evidence from the [g]overnment," *id.* at 534, without any inquiry into whether the provision of nonhearsay evidence would unduly burden the government, and erred in failing to then weigh the competing interests of the litigants in light of the factual allegations and burdens placed before it for consideration.

1. . . .

Although I do not rule out the possibility that hearsay evidence might ultimately prove to be the most reliable available evidence from the government in this case, *Hamdi* does not support such a categorical relaxation of the protections due persons who are detained within our borders. . . . The *Hamdi* plurality's acceptance of hearsay evidence from the government in such settings . . . clearly arose from the context of a battlefield detainee, the "exigencies of [such] circumstances," and the "uncommon potential to burden the Executive at a time of ongoing military conflict." *Id.* at 533. The relaxed evidentiary standard was accepted in the balance as appropriate in light of the facts of that case — a person initially detained abroad by our allies on a battlefield in Afghanistan. . . . [W]hile the plurality refused to categorically prohibit hearsay declarations, neither did it categorically approve the use of such hearsay declarations in all enemy-combatant proceedings. Hearsay declarations *may* be accepted upon a weighing of the burdens in time of warfare of "providing greater process" against the detainee's liberty interests. *Id.* at 529. But to decide whether a hearsay declaration is acceptable, the court must first take into account "the risk of erroneous deprivation" of the detainee's liberty interest, "the probable value, if any, of any additional or substitute procedural safeguards," and the availability of additional or substitute evidence which might serve the interests of both litigants. . . .

2.

In this case al-Marri's "private interest affected by the official action" is the same as that of Hamdi, *i.e.*, the liberty interest in being free from unlawful seizure and detention. *Hamdi*, 542 U.S. at 529. The risk of an erroneous deprivation of al-Marri's liberty interest, however, is not identical to the risk that was present in *Hamdi*. Al-Marri was not captured on the battlefields of Afghanistan or Iraq, nor even apprehended in a neighboring country where al Qaeda trains its soldiers. He was arrested by civilian federal authorities while residing in Illinois. I am acutely aware of the dangers of detention and imprisonment without compliance with criminal process safeguards, dangers that are even greater when the military detains persons inside the borders of the United States. In my view, the risk of erroneously detaining a civilian or citizen in this country as an enemy combatant is much greater inside the United States than in the very different context addressed by the Supreme Court in *Hamdi, i.e.,* a conventional battlefield within the borders of a foreign country in which we are fighting our enemies.

On the other hand, we must consider the government's interest "in detaining those who actually pose an immediate threat to the national security of the United States during ongoing international conflict," *Hamdi,* 542 U.S. at 530, and in "ensuring that those who have in fact fought with the enemy during a war do not return to battle against the United States," *id.* at 531, as well as "the burdens the [g]overnment would face in providing greater process," *id.* at 529.

Here, the government asserts that the Rapp Declaration, which summarizes the intelligence gathered on al-Marri's activities as an al Qaeda operative, is sufficient to meet its initial burden of proving that al-Marri was properly designated an enemy combatant. However, unlike in *Hamdi,* the government has presented *only* the Rapp Declaration. It has made no attempt to show that this hearsay evidence "need[s] to be accepted as the most reliable available evidence from the [g]overnment," *id.* at 533-34, or that additional protections to ensure that the innocent are not detained by our military would be "unworkable and inappropriate in th[is] enemy-combatant setting," *id.* at 535. Nor has there been any consideration of the "probable value, if any, of additional or substitute procedural safeguards" or the availability of more reliable evidence that might be presented by substitute methods which account for the government's weighty interests. *Id.* at 529.

. . . [A]l-Marri argued below that he believed the discovery [he] sought would be primarily from civilian agencies that could produce it without interfering with the war powers and war operations of this government. At a minimum, I believe the government should be required to demonstrate to the district court why this is not the case and why, in balancing the liberty interest of the detainee and the heightened risk of erroneous deprivation, the Rapp Declaration should be accepted as the most reliable available evidence the government can produce without undue burden or serious jeopardy to either its war efforts or its efforts to ensure the national security of this nation. . . .

GREGORY, Circuit Judge, concurring in the judgment [omitted].

WILLIAMS, Chief Judge, concurring in part and dissenting in part: . . .

I.

A. . . .

A distillation of [the *Milligan, Quirin,* and *Hamdi*] precedents, I believe, yields a definition of an enemy combatant subject to detention pursuant to Congressional authorizations as an individual who meets two criteria: (1) he attempts or engages in belligerent acts against the United States, either domestically or in a foreign combat zone; (2) on behalf of an enemy force.

Given the specific allegations against al-Marri, I have little difficulty concluding that he satisfies the first criterion. First, the allegations set forth in the Rapp

Declaration, if true, clearly show that al-Marri was on United States soil to commit acts of belligerency against the United States. *See Quirin*, 317 U.S. at 31 (stating that unlawful combatants include those who commit "hostile acts involving destruction of life or property" on United States soil).

According to the Rapp Declaration, al-Marri also meets what I view as the second requirement of an enemy combatant: that the belligerent acts be carried out on behalf of an enemy force. Unlike the plurality, I cannot accept al-Marri's contention that because he allegedly has ties only to al Qaeda, a terrorist organization that does not control any nation, he does not meet this portion of the definition of enemy combatant.

The plurality opinion may very well be correct that, under the traditional "law of war," persons not affiliated with the military of a *nation-state* may not be considered enemy combatants. And I recognize the respect domestic courts have long afforded the "law of nations." *See Murray v. Schooner Charming Betsy*, 6 U.S. (2 Cranch) 64, 118 (1804) ("[A]n act of Congress ought never to be construed to violate the law of nations if any other possible construction remains."). Here, however, Congress has, through the AUMF, addressed precisely this question by clearly authorizing the President to use force against "organizations," as well as against nation-states. *See Padilla v. Hanft*, 423 F.3d 386, 395-96 (4th Cir. 2005) (noting "the AUMF constitutes...a clear statement" in favor of detention). As a specific and targeted congressional directive, the AUMF controls the question of who may be detained, for purposes of domestic law — at least with respect to those individuals that fall within its scope....

I wish to emphasize that by permitting the President to militarily detain al-Marri pursuant to the AUMF I am not being expansive; in al-Marri we are dealing with someone *squarely* within the purposes of the AUMF, which was passed to target organizations, like al Qaeda, responsible for the September 11 attacks and to prevent future terrorist attacks. This case does not present what to me are more difficult issues regarding enemy combatants and the scope of AUMF, such as the status of an individual who joined al Qaeda after September 11, 2001, or an individual who is part of a designated foreign terrorist organization, that played no role in the September 11 attacks. Instead, al-Marri is clearly an "individual[ ] Congress sought to target in passing the AUMF." *Hamdi*, 542 U.S. at 518. In addition, while "indefinite detention" of enemy combatants is not permitted, *see generally Hamdi*, 542 U.S. at 519-20, we remain engaged against the forces of al Qaeda in the border regions of Afghanistan to this day....

B. . . .

. . . I view section 412 of the Patriot Act to refer to the President's power, under Article II §3, to "take Care that the Laws be faithfully executed." U.S. Const., art. II, §3. The statute refers to the Attorney General, the President's agent in implementing the Take Care Clause, and it is found nestled within the immigration code. Fairly read, the Patriot Act does not therefore purport to limit the President's separate Commander-in-Chief power. But the authorization granted in the AUMF, with its explicit reference to military force, relates to the Commander-in-Chief power. Whatever limitations are present in the Patriot Act, therefore, do not restrict the separate and distinct grant of power effected by the AUMF....

II.

I do not agree, however, with Judge Traxler's separate concurrence, which concludes that a remand is necessary to permit al-Marri to further challenge his detention. . . .

B. . . .

. . . I see nothing in *Hamdi* that forbids a sworn statement — like the Rapp Declaration — from providing sufficient "notice" of the allegations against al-Marri. Moreover . . . the magistrate judge required the Government to provide al-Marri the declaration in response to his request. . . .

Finally, and most importantly, *Hamdi* stressed the need for a "prudent" and "incremental" process. . . . By failing to participate, Al-Marri simply short-circuited the entire "incremental" process. . . .

Judge Duncan has authorized me to indicate that she joins in this opinion.

WILKINSON, Circuit Judge, concurring in part and dissenting in part: . . .

III. THE DETENTION OF AL-MARRI IS CONSISTENT WITH THE LIMITS ESTABLISHED BY OUR CONSTITUTION ON THE MILITARY DETENTION OF THOSE LAWFULLY ON AMERICAN SOIL. . . .

D. . . .

. . . [A]n "enemy" is any individual who is (1) a member of (2) an organization or nation against whom Congress has declared war or authorized the use of military force. Taken together, these two criteria closely track traditional law of war concepts that distinguish enemies from non-enemies. At the same time, they recognize that modern military threats include those posed by non-state actors.

I first address the criterion of membership. While the traditional requirement of residency or other affiliation with an enemy nation still applies, the advent of enemy organizations requires a functional equivalent to residency for this new stateless actor. This is achieved by the requirement of membership in the enemy organization. Because membership may be considered more amorphous than residency or citizenship, it is important that there be identifiable facts that indicate such affiliation with the enemy organization. Such indicia of membership may include: self-identification with the organization through verbal or written statements; participation in the group's hierarchy or command structure; or knowingly taking overt steps to aid or participate in the organization's activities. Thus, for example, someone who sends money to "a nonprofit charity that feeds Afghan orphans" that unknowingly makes "its way to al Qaeda" would not be a member of the al Qaeda organization, and it is beyond hyperbole for the plurality to suggest otherwise. Furthermore, the membership requirement is important because it aids in distinguishing those who are the enemy from those who merely sympathize with the enemy.

The second criterion — congressional authorization — recognizes that Congress may authorize the use of military force against non-state actors, such as terrorist organizations, as it has already with the AUMF. By contemplating such authorization, this second criterion appropriately excludes from the category of "enemy" those persons or groups against whom Congress has not authorized the use of military force. Thus, the notion that any individual affiliated with an organization engaged in purported terrorist activities — such as the "environmental group" mentioned by the plurality — could be considered an enemy combatant is completely unfounded. For certain, there are many individuals and organizations engaged in unlawful conduct, and even terrorism. But most of these individuals and organizations have nothing to do with al Qaeda, its affiliates, or the September 11 attacks. Under this criterion, such persons would not be eligible for military detention under the AUMF. This is both consistent with our traditional conception of who should and should not be eligible for detention and appropriate in light of the constitutional imperative that military detention be the exception and not the rule. Indeed, not to require congressional authorization for such detentions in this country splits the ground beneath the war powers right in two.

If the first two criteria address who in modern warfare is the enemy, the third criterion addresses who is the combatant. Historically, this distinction has separated those with military aims from those who do not present a threat to opposing forces. Though yesterday's soldier has been replaced, at least in part, by those who eschew the conventions of lawful warfare, the purpose underlying this distinction remains unchanged. In light of today's realities, a "combatant" is a person who knowingly plans or engages in conduct that harms or aims to harm persons or property for the purpose of furthering the military goals of an enemy nation or organization. Like the first two criteria, this requirement closely tracks the relevant traditional law of war rules.

Under this criterion, those who use military-like force against American soldiers or civilians obviously qualify as combatants. Similarly, members of an enemy sleeper terrorist cell that have taken steps, even if preliminary in nature, toward an act of destruction are also considered combatants. Conversely, persons traditionally considered civilians, such as members of the enemy organization who do not possess hostile or military designs, are non-combatants and may not be detained by the military. This includes persons who would clearly be non-combatants, such as a "physician who treated a member of al Qaeda," because they intend no harm to persons or property. Such persons would not be subject to military detention.

Two further examples may help illustrate the scope of this framework. First is a person who joins a terrorist organization after Congress has authorized the use of military force against the respective group. In the present conflict, this would include new recruits to al Qaeda or its affiliates after 9/11. Under the above criteria, such persons are clearly part of the "enemy," even if they were not members of the targeted organization at the time Congress initially acted. This is because it was the organization and its affiliates, and not just the then-members of such groups, against whom Congress authorized the use of force. *See* AUMF, 115 Stat. 224 (authorizing the use of "all necessary and appropriate force against those . . . organizations [that] . . . committed" the 9/11 attacks, "in order to prevent any future acts of international terrorism"). Thus, in the current conflict, any "individual can become part of a covered 'organization' by joining it after the September 11 attacks." As a result, such a person, if also a combatant, would be eligible for military detention.

Second is a person who commits, or plans to commit, a terrorist act but is not otherwise affiliated with an organization or country covered by a congressional proclamation. Timothy McVeigh is one example that comes to mind. Because such a person is not a member of an enemy organization, he may not be detained as an enemy combatant under the above criteria. Indeed, Congress has never declared war against a single individual or even a discrete conspiracy (unless the Barbary pirates qualify), and it is difficult to envision a scenario in which it would. This is unsurprising, in part because prosecutions of individual terrorists do not ordinarily present the same sort of logistical, informational, and evidentiary problems as large scale terrorist networks or nations. . . .

. . . [U]nder these criteria, there are at least three significant limitations on the executive's ability to militarily detain persons lawfully residing in the United States.

First, there is the significant political check of congressional authorization. Specifically, absent some limited inherent authority needed during times of emergency, the executive may only detain those persons against whom Congress has authorized the use of force. If history is any indicator, Congress does not take such a decision lightly. Indeed, it was the dire events of September 11th that gave rise to the use of military force in the present instance, and it is likely that only emergencies of similar magnitude will trigger a similar response.

Second, even if Congress were to authorize the use of military force against a particular group, it would not be authorizing the executive to make a sweep on the basis of mere membership. This is because membership, without more, is not enough to qualify as an enemy combatant under my proposed criteria. Rather, the person in question must have taken steps to further the military goals of the organization. Thus, McCarthy-like accusations of mere group membership would not suffice as a basis for detention.

Third, persons subject to military detention are afforded the opportunity to challenge the accuracy of their detention before a neutral decisionmaker in accordance with the framework articulated in *Hamdi*. This ensures that the government possesses sufficient evidence to justify a measure as serious as military detention. . . .

[The opinion of NIEMEYER, Circuit Judge, concurring in the judgment in part and dissenting in part, is omitted].

[The opinion of DUNCAN, Circuit Judge, concurring in part and dissenting in part, is omitted].

NOTES AND QUESTIONS

1. *The Non-Detention Act — Section 4001(a)*. The plurality in *Hamdi* assumed, but did not decide, that §4001(a) applies to military detentions, then found that it was satisfied by the AUMF. If §4001(a) does apply and the AUMF is invoked as a statutory exception within its contemplation, should we apply the clear statement requirement to the AUMF, as Justices Souter and Ginsburg insisted in *Hamdi*, and the Second Circuit did in *Padilla?* Even without insisting on a clear statement, does a natural reading of the AUMF embrace uses of force (and, by implication, military detention) *within* the United States, or just in Afghanistan or wherever else the armed forces are deployed in combat abroad? *See* Stephen I. Vladeck, Comment, *A Small Problem of Precedent: 18 U.S.C. §4001(a) and the Detention of U.S. Citizen "Enemy Combatants,"* 112 Yale L.J. 961, 967 (2003) (arguing that the AUMF fails to satisfy §4001(a)).

2. *Necessity for Military Detention in Padilla and Al-Marri.* If the arguments of necessity applied to Hamdi, did they also apply to Padilla and al-Marri? What if the government believes someone like Padilla to be an imminent threat to set off a dirty bomb, but lacks probable cause to arrest him? What response does Justice Souter suggest for such an emergency? Here is the District Court's answer, after Padilla refiled his habeas petition on remand from the Supreme Court:

> Simply stated, this is a law enforcement matter, not a military matter.... At the time that [Padilla] was arrested pursuant to the material arrest warrant, any alleged terrorist plans that he harbored were thwarted. From then on, he was available to be questioned — and was indeed questioned — just like any citizen accused of criminal conduct....
>
> There can be no debate that this country's laws amply provide for the investigation, detention and prosecution of citizen and non-citizen terrorists alike....
>
> ... The difference between invocation of the criminal process and the power claimed by the President here, however, is one of accountability. The criminal justice system requires that defendants and witnesses be afforded access to counsel, imposes judicial supervision over government action, and places congressionally imposed limits on incarceration.

[*Padilla v. Hanft*, 389 F. Supp. 2d 678, 691-692 (D.S.C. 2005), *rev'd*, 423 F.3d 387 (4th Cir. 2005), *cert. denied*, 547 U.S. 1062 (2006) (quoting *amici curiae* in *Rumsfeld v. Padilla*, 542 U.S. 426 (2004)).]

Although the Fourth Circuit panel disagreed, Padilla *was* eventually transferred back to law enforcement custody and convicted of a crime.

After the *en banc* decision, al-Marri promptly petitioned the Supreme Court for *certiorari*. The government then transferred him, as it had Padilla in similar circumstances, back to law enforcement custody, and the Supreme Court therefore vacated the *en banc* opinion and remanded with instructions to dismiss the appeal as moot. Al-Marri was indicted on two counts of providing material support to a foreign terrorist organization (see *infra* p. 604) and pleaded guilty to a single count. He was sentenced to eight years in prison and has a projected release date of 2015.

How would you reframe the authority for military detention to confine it strictly to situations of bona fide military necessity? Does the length of the detention affect the necessity, and, if so, how would you reflect this consideration in your specification of detention authority? Should military necessity be judged in light of the availability and practicality of the ordinary criminal process to detain?

Do the outcomes in *Hamdi*, *Padilla*, and *Al-Marri* cast any doubt on the propriety of judicial deference to executive claims of military necessity for military detention? (Consider also the aftermath of *Korematsu v. United States*, 323 U.S. 214 (1944), discussed in Chapter 15.) If so, how should courts view such claims?

3. *Defining Enemy Combatant.* All of the judges in *Al-Marri* seem agreed that the President's detention authority extends to enemy combatants, but they disagreed about who is an enemy combatant. We have now reviewed the circumstances of Milligan, Quirin, Hamdi, Padilla, and al-Marri. Can you say who among them are enemy combatants and who are not? Does your analysis suggest any comprehensive definition? Judge Williams remarked that al-Marri was "someone *squarely* within the purposes of the AUMF . . . ." *Al-Marri*, 534 F.3d at 286. Suppose al-Marri had never left

the United States, but affiliated with Al Qaeda through the Internet because he agreed with its aims. Would he still fall squarely within the AUMF?

One factor that seems *not* to figure in the definition is U.S. citizenship. One of the German saboteurs in *Quirin* a citizen, and as a lawfully resident alien al-Marri arguably enjoyed the constitutional rights of a citizen. If he could lawfully be detained, then arguably so could a U.S. citizen in similar circumstances.

4. *"Affirming" the AUMF?* Proposed legislation in 2011 "affirming" the AUMF is set forth *supra* p. 86. Would this measure cover someone like Padilla? Al-Marri? A Saudi who paid for al-Marri's tuition, believing that al-Marri was a "jihadist"? If you find the provision ambiguous, what language would you substitute to clarify the President's detention authority?

5. *The USA Patriot Act.* The Patriot Act provided limited detention authority for persons Judge Motz called "terrorist aliens." In fact, its provision seems tailor-made for someone like al-Marri. Why did the Patriot Act not occupy the field, in the same way that the Labor Management Relations Act occupied the field in *Steel Seizure* or that the statute authorizing interception of ships going to French ports occupied the field in *Little v. Barreme?* Did the judges who upheld detention authority in *al-Marri* find that Congress cannot occupy the field of law-of-war detention, or that it had not? What constitutional authority, if any, does Congress have to occupy this particular field? *See generally* Ingrid Wuerth, *The Captures Clause*, 76 U. Chi. L. Rev. 1683 (2009).

C. MILITARY DETENTION: EVOLVING LAW OF THE HABEAS CASES

While *Hamdi* involved a U.S. citizen, it set out a broader principle of law-of-war detention. Once the Supreme Court opened the door to habeas petitions from the Guantánamo detainees in *Boumediene v. Bush*, 553 U.S. 723 (2008), that principle was developed in the resulting habeas cases heard in the federal courts of the District of Columbia. As different district courts grappled with both substantive and procedural issues of detention, their opinions inevitably diverged. *See, e.g.,* Nathaniel H. Nesbitt, *Meeting Boumediene's Challenge: The Emergence of an Effective Habeas Jurisprudence and Obsolescence of New Detention Legislation*, 95 Minn. L. Rev. 244 (2010); Robert M. Chesney, *Who May Be Held? Military Detention Through the Habeas Lens*, 52 B.C. L. Rev. 769 (2011); Benjamin Wittes, Robert M. Chesney & Larkin Reynolds, *The Emerging Law of Detention 2.0: The Guantánamo Habeas Cases as Lawmaking* (updated May 12, 2011), *at* http://www.brookings.edu/papers/2011/05_guantanamo_wittes.aspx (analyzing emerging differences).

Substantively, the district courts have reached varying conclusions about whether law-of-war detention authority extends to supporters of Al Qaeda or the Taliban, "substantial" supporters, the Al Qaeda "command structure," or mere members, and whether the scope of such authority is informed or limited by the laws of war in light of the Administration's reliance strictly on the AUMF. Procedurally, the courts have also disagreed about whether (and how far) the government's evidentiary bar moves with the length of detention, an issue related to the substantive question whether detention status is permanent or might change over time. The courts have diverged less sharply on the quality of admissible hearsay and other evidentiary issues that *Hamdi* left to them.

The following decision by the D.C. Circuit Court of Appeals resolved some of these conflicts among the district court opinions, but left others.

Al-Bihani v. Obama

United States Court of Appeals, District of Columbia Circuit, 2010
590 F.3d 866, *rehearing denied en banc,* 619 F.3d 1 (D.C. Cir. 2010),
cert. denied, 131 S. Ct. 1814 (2011)

BROWN, Circuit Judge: . . .

[Ghaleb Nassar Al-Bihani is a Yemeni citizen who traveled to Afghanistan to defend the Taliban's Islamic state against the Northern Alliance. The government alleged that he stayed at Al Qaeda-affiliated guesthouses and may also have received instruction at Al Qaeda terrorist training camps. Al-Bihani did not dispute that he eventually accompanied and served as a cook for a paramilitary group allied with the Taliban, known as the 55th Arab Brigade, which included Al Qaeda members within its command structure and which fought on the front lines against the Northern Alliance. He carried a brigade-issued weapon, but never fired it in combat. Al-Bihani and the rest of the brigade eventually surrendered, under orders, to Northern Alliance forces, which kept him in custody until his handover to U.S. Coalition forces in early 2002. The U.S. military sent Al-Bihani to Guantánamo for detention and interrogation. Al-Bihani unsuccessfully petitioned for a writ of habeas corpus, then brought this appeal.]

II

Al-Bihani's many arguments present this court with two overarching questions regarding the detainees at the Guantánamo Bay naval base. The first concerns whom the President can lawfully detain pursuant to statutes passed by Congress. The second asks what procedure is due to detainees challenging their detention in habeas corpus proceedings. The Supreme Court has provided scant guidance on these questions, consciously leaving the contours of the substantive and procedural law of detention open for lower courts to shape in a common law fashion. In this decision, we aim to narrow the legal uncertainty that clouds military detention.

A

Al-Bihani challenges the statutory legitimacy of his detention by advancing a number of arguments based upon the international laws of war. He first argues that relying on "support," or even "substantial support" of Al Qaeda or the Taliban as an independent basis for detention violates international law. As a result, such a standard should not be read into the ambiguous provisions of the Authorization for

Use of Military Force (AUMF), Pub. L. No. 107-40, §2(a), 115 Stat. 224, 224 (2001), the Act empowering the President to respond to the attacks of September 11, 2001. Al-Bihani interprets international law to mean anyone not belonging to an official state military is a civilian, and civilians, he says, must commit a direct hostile act, such as firing a weapon in combat, before they can be lawfully detained. Because Al-Bihani did not commit such an act, he reasons his detention is unlawful. Next, he argues the members of the 55th Arab Brigade were not subject to attack or detention by U.S. Coalition forces under the laws of co-belligerency because the 55th, although allied with the Taliban against the Northern Alliance, did not have the required opportunity to declare its neutrality in the fight against the United States. His third argument is that the conflict in which he was detained, an international war between the United States and Taliban-controlled Afghanistan, officially ended when the Taliban lost control of the Afghan government. Thus, absent a determination of future danger-ousness, he must be released. *See* Geneva Convention Relative to the Treatment of Prisoners of War (Third Geneva Convention) art. 118, Aug. 12, 1949, 6 U.S.T. 3316, 75 U.N.T.S. 135. Lastly, Al-Bihani posits a type of "clean hands" theory by which any authority the government has to detain him is undermined by its failure to accord him the prisoner-of-war status to which he believes he is entitled by international law.

Before considering these arguments in detail, we note that all of them rely heavily on the premise that the war powers granted by the AUMF and other statutes are limited by the international laws of war. This premise is mistaken. There is no indica-tion in the AUMF, the Detainee Treatment Act of 2005 [DTA], Pub. L. No. 109-148, div. A, tit. X, 119 Stat. 2739, 2741-43, or the MCA of 2006 or 2009 [Military Commis-sions Act of 2006, Pub. L. No. 109-366, 120 Stat. 2600; Military Commissions Act of 2009, Pub. L. No. 111-84, 123 Stat. 2190], that Congress intended the international laws of war to act as extra-textual limiting principles for the President's war powers under the AUMF. The international laws of war as a whole have not been imple-mented domestically by Congress and are therefore not a source of authority for U.S. courts. *See* Restatement (Third) of Foreign Relations Law of the United States §111(3)-(4) (1987). Even assuming Congress had at some earlier point implemented the laws of war as domestic law through appropriate legislation, Congress had the power to authorize the President in the AUMF and other later statutes to exceed those bounds. *See id.* §115(1)(a). Further weakening their relevance to this case, the inter-national laws of war are not a fixed code. Their dictates and application to actual events are by nature contestable and fluid. *See id.* §102 cmts. b & c (stating there is "no precise formula" to identify a practice as custom and that "[i]t is often difficult to determine when [a custom's] transformation into law has taken place"). Therefore, while the international laws of war are helpful to courts when identifying the general set of war powers to which the AUMF speaks, *see Hamdi*, 542 U.S. at 520, their lack of controlling legal force and firm definition render their use both inapposite and inadvisable when courts seek to determine the limits of the President's war powers.

Therefore, putting aside that we find Al-Bihani's reading of international law to be unpersuasive, we have no occasion here to quibble over the intricate application of vague treaty provisions and amorphous customary principles. The sources we look to for resolution of Al-Bihani's case are the sources courts always look to: the text of relevant statutes and controlling domestic case law.

Under those sources, Al-Bihani is lawfully detained.... The statutes authorizing the use of force and detention not only grant the government the power to craft a workable legal standard to identify individuals it can detain, but also cabin the application of these definitions. The AUMF authorizes the President to "use all necessary and appropriate force against those nations, organizations, or persons he determines planned, authorized, committed, or aided the terrorist attacks that occurred on September 11, 2001, or harbored such organizations or persons." AUMF §2(a). The Supreme Court in *Hamdi* ruled that "necessary and appropriate force" includes the power to detain combatants subject to such force. 542 U.S. at 519. Congress, in the 2006 MCA, provided guidance on the class of persons subject to detention under the AUMF by defining "unlawful enemy combatants" who can be tried by military commission. 2006 MCA sec. 3, §948a(1). The 2006 MCA authorized the trial of an individual who "engaged in hostilities or who has purposefully and materially supported hostilities against the United States or its co-belligerents who is not a lawful enemy combatant (including a person who is part of the Taliban, al Qaeda, or associated forces)." *Id.* §948a(1)(A)(i). In 2009, Congress enacted a new version of the MCA with a new definition that authorized the trial of "unprivileged enemy belligerents," a class of persons that includes those who "purposefully and materially supported hostilities against the United States or its coalition partners." Military Commissions Act of 2009 sec. 1802, §§948a(7), 948b(a), 948c, 123 Stat. 2575-76. The provisions of the 2006 and 2009 MCAs are illuminating in this case because the government's detention authority logically covers a category of persons no narrower than is covered by its military commission authority. Detention authority in fact sweeps wider, also extending at least to traditional P.O.W.s, *see id.* §948a(6), and arguably to other categories of persons. But for this case, it is enough to recognize that any person subject to a military commission trial is also subject to detention, and that category of persons includes those who are part of forces associated with Al Qaeda or the Taliban or those who purposefully and materially support such forces in hostilities against U.S. Coalition partners.

In light of these provisions of the 2006 and 2009 MCAs, the facts that were both found by the district court and offered by Al-Bihani ... place Al-Bihani within the "part of" and "support" prongs of the relevant statutory definition. ... His acknowledged actions — accompanying the brigade on the battlefield, carrying a brigade-issued weapon, cooking for the unit, and retreating and surrendering under brigade orders — strongly suggest, in the absence of an official membership card, that he was part of the 55th. Even assuming, as he argues, that he was a civilian "contractor" rendering services, those services render Al-Bihani detainable under the "purposefully and materially supported" language of both versions of the MCA. That language constitutes a standard whose outer bounds are not readily identifiable. But wherever the outer bounds may lie, they clearly include traditional food operations essential to a fighting force and the carrying of arms. Viewed in full, the facts show Al-Bihani was part of and supported a group — prior to and after September 11 — that was affiliated with Al Qaeda and Taliban forces and engaged in hostilities against a U.S. Coalition partner. Al-Bihani, therefore, falls squarely within the scope of the President's statutory detention powers.[2]

2. In reaching this conclusion, we need not rely on the evidence suggesting that Al-Bihani attended Al Qaeda training camps in Afghanistan and visited Al Qaeda guesthouses. We do note, however, that evidence supporting the military's reasonable belief of either of those two facts with respect to a non-citizen seized abroad during the ongoing war on terror would seem to overwhelmingly, if not definitively, justify the government's detention of such a non-citizen. *Cf. Nat'l Comm'n on Terrorist Attacks upon the United States, the 9/11 Commission Report* 66-67.

The government can also draw statutory authority to detain Al-Bihani directly from the language of the AUMF. The AUMF authorizes force against those who "harbored . . . organizations or persons" the President determines "planned, authorized, committed, or aided the terrorist attacks of September 11, 2001." AUMF §2(a). It is not in dispute that Al Qaeda is the organization responsible for September 11 or that it was harbored by the Taliban in Afghanistan. It is also not in dispute that the 55th Arab Brigade defended the Taliban against the Northern Alliance's efforts to oust the regime from power. Drawing from these facts, it cannot be disputed that the actual and foreseeable result of the 55th's defense of the Taliban was the maintenance of Al Qaeda's safe haven in Afghanistan. This result places the 55th within the AUMF's wide ambit as an organization that harbored Al Qaeda, making it subject to U.S. military force and its members and supporters — including Al-Bihani — eligible for detention. . . .

With the government's detention authority established as an initial matter, we turn to the argument that Al-Bihani must now be released according to longstanding law of war principles because the conflict with the Taliban has allegedly ended. *See Hamdi*, 542 U.S. at 521. Al-Bihani offers the court a choice of numerous event dates — the day Afghans established a post-Taliban interim authority, the day the United States recognized that authority, the day Hamid Karzai was elected President — to mark the official end of the conflict. No matter which is chosen, each would dictate the release of Al-Bihani if we follow his reasoning. His argument fails on factual and practical grounds. First, it is not clear if Al-Bihani was captured in the conflict with the Taliban or with Al Qaeda; he does not argue that the conflict with Al Qaeda is over. Second, there are currently 34,800 U.S. troops and a total of 71,030 Coalition troops in Afghanistan, with tens of thousands more to be added soon. The principle Al-Bihani espouses — were it accurate — would make each successful campaign of a long war but a Pyrrhic prelude to defeat. The initial success of the United States and its Coalition partners in ousting the Taliban from the seat of government and establishing a young democracy would trigger an obligation to release Taliban fighters captured in earlier clashes. Thus, the victors would be commanded to constantly refresh the ranks of the fledgling democracy's most likely saboteurs. . . .

Even so, we do not rest our resolution of this issue on international law or mere common sense. The determination of when hostilities have ceased is a political decision, and we defer to the Executive's opinion on the matter, at least in the absence of an authoritative congressional declaration purporting to terminate the war. *See Ludecke v. Watkins*, 335 U.S. 160, 168-70 & n.13 (1948) ("[T]ermination [of a state of war] is a political act."). . . . In the absence of a determination by the political branches that hostilities in Afghanistan have ceased, Al-Bihani's continued detention is justified.

Al-Bihani also argues he should be released because the government's failure to accord him P.O.W. status violated international law and undermined its otherwise lawful authority to detain him. Even assuming Al-Bihani is entitled to P.O.W. status, we find no controlling authority for this "clean hands" theory in statute or in caselaw. The AUMF, DTA, and MCA of 2006 and 2009 do not hinge the government's detention authority on proper identification of P.O.W.s or compliance with international law in general. In fact, the MCA of 2006, in a provision not altered by the MCA of 2009, explicitly precludes detainees from claiming the Geneva conventions — which include criteria to determine who is entitled to P.O.W. status—as a source of rights. *See* 2006 MCA sec. 5(a)....

B...

Drawing upon *Boumediene*'s holding, Al-Bihani challenges numerous aspects of the habeas procedure devised by the district court....

Al-Bihani's argument clearly demonstrates error, but that error is his own. Habeas review for Guantánamo detainees need not match the procedures developed by Congress and the courts specifically for habeas challenges to criminal convictions. *Boumediene*'s holding explicitly stated that habeas procedures for detainees "need not resemble a criminal trial," 128 S. Ct. at 2269. It instead invited "innovation" of habeas procedure by lower courts, granting leeway for "[c]ertain accommodations [to] be made to reduce the burden habeas corpus proceedings will place on the military." *Id.* at 2276....

...Al-Bihani is a non-citizen who was seized in a foreign country. Requiring highly protective procedures at the tail end of the detention process for detainees like Al-Bihani would have systemic effects on the military's entire approach to war. From the moment a shot is fired, to battlefield capture, up to a detainee's day in court, military operations would be compromised as the government strove to satisfy evidentiary standards in anticipation of habeas litigation....

With Al-Bihani's limited procedural entitlement established as a general matter, we turn to the specific procedural claims warranting serious consideration. The question of what standard of proof is due in a habeas proceeding like Al-Bihani's has not been answered by the Supreme Court. *See Boumediene*, 128 S. Ct. at 2271 ("The extent of the showing required of the Government in these cases is a matter to be determined."). Attempting to fill this void, Al-Bihani argues the prospect of indefinite detention in this unconventional war augurs for a reasonable doubt standard or, in the alternative, at least a clear and convincing standard....

...[But] [i]n addition to the *Hamdi* plurality's approving treatment of military tribunal procedure, it also described as constitutionally adequate—even for the detention of U.S. citizens—a "burden-shifting scheme" in which the government need only present "credible evidence that the habeas petitioner meets the enemy-combatant criteria" before "the onus could shift to the petitioner to rebut that evidence with more persuasive evidence that he falls outside the criteria." *Hamdi*, 542 U.S. at 533-34. That description mirrors a preponderance standard....

...[T]raditional habeas review did not entail review of factual findings, particularly in the military context. *See In re Yamashita*, 327 U.S. 1, 8 (1946) ("If the military tribunals have lawful authority to hear, decide and condemn, their action is not subject to judicial review merely because they have made a wrong decision on disputed facts."). Where factual review has been authorized, the burden in some domestic circumstances has been placed *on the petitioner* to prove his case under a clear and convincing standard. *See* 28 U.S.C. §2254(e)(1) (regulating federal review of state court factual findings). If it is constitutionally permissible to place that higher burden on a citizen petitioner in a routine case, it follows a priori that placing a lower burden on the government defending a wartime detention—where national security interests are at their zenith and the rights of the alien petitioner at their nadir—is also permissible.

We find Al-Bihani's hearsay challenges to be similarly unavailing. Al-Bihani claims that government reports of his interrogation answers — which made up the majority, if not all, of the evidence on which the district court relied — and other informational documents were hearsay improperly admitted absent an examination of reliability and necessity. He contends, in fact, that government reports of his interrogation answers were "*double* hearsay" because his answers were first translated by an interpreter and then written down by an interrogator. We first note that Al-Bihani's interrogation answers themselves were not hearsay; they were instead party-opponent admissions that would have been admitted in any U.S. court. *See* Fed. R. Evid. 801(d)(2)(A). That they were translated does not affect their status. *See United States v. Da Silva,* 725 F.2d 828, 831-32 (2d Cir. 1983). However, that the otherwise admissible answers were relayed through an interrogator's account does introduce a level of technical hearsay because the interrogator is a third party unavailable for cross examination. Other information, such as a diagram of Al Qaeda's leadership structure, was also hearsay.

But that such evidence was hearsay does not automatically invalidate its admission — it only begins our inquiry. . . .

. . . [T]he question a habeas court must ask when presented with hearsay is not whether it is admissible — it is always admissible — but what probative weight to ascribe to whatever indicia of reliability it exhibits. . . .

In Al-Bihani's case, the district court clearly reserved that authority in its process and assessed the hearsay evidence's reliability as required by the Supreme Court. First, the district court retained the authority to assess the weight of the evidence. Second, the district court had ample contextual information about evidence in the government's factual return to determine what weight to give various pieces of evidence. Third, the district court afforded Al-Bihani the opportunity . . . to rebut the evidence and to attack its credibility. Further, Al-Bihani did not contest the truth of the majority of his admissions upon which the district court relied, enhancing the reliability of those reports. We therefore find that the district court did not improperly admit hearsay evidence. . . .

III

Al-Bihani's detention is authorized by statute and there was no constitutional defect in the district court's habeas procedure that would have affected the outcome of the proceeding. For these reasons, the order of the district court denying Al-Bihani's petition for a writ of habeas corpus is

Affirmed.

Brown, Circuit Judge, concurring: The Supreme Court in *Boumediene* and *Hamdi* charged this court and others with the unprecedented task of developing rules to review the propriety of military actions during a time of war, relying on common law tools. We are fortunate this case does not require us to demarcate the law's full substantive and procedural dimensions. But as other more difficult cases arise, it is important to ask whether a court-driven process is best suited to protecting both the rights of petitioners and the safety of our nation. The common law process depends on incrementalism and eventual correction, and it is most effective where there are a significant number of cases brought before a large set of courts, which in turn enjoy the luxury of time to work the doctrine supple. None of those factors exist in the Guantánamo context. The number of Guantánamo detainees is limited and the circumstances of their confinement are unique. The petitions they file, as the *Boumediene* Court counseled, are funneled through one federal district court and one appellate court. And, in the midst of an ongoing war, time to entertain a process of literal trial and error is not a luxury we have.

While the common law process presents these difficulties, it is important to note that the Supreme Court has not foreclosed Congress from establishing new habeas standards in line with its *Boumediene* opinion. . . . [T]he circumstances that frustrate the judicial process are the same ones that make this situation particularly ripe for Congress to intervene pursuant to its policy expertise, democratic legitimacy, and oath to uphold and defend the Constitution. These cases present hard questions and hard choices, ones best faced directly. Judicial review, however, is just that: *re*-view, an indirect and necessarily backward looking process. And looking backward may not be enough in this new war. The saying that generals always fight the last war is familiar, but familiarity does not dull the maxim's sober warning. In identifying the shape of the law in response to the challenge of the current war, it is incumbent on the President, Congress, and the courts to realize that the saying's principle applies to us as well. Both the rule of law and the nation's safety will benefit from an honest assessment of the new challenges we face, one that will produce an appropriately calibrated response. . . .

WILLIAMS, Senior Circuit Judge, concurring in part and concurring in the judgment: . . . The petitioner's detention is legally permissible by virtue of facts that he himself has conceded. . . .

Within the portion of the opinion addressing the petitioner's substantive argument that his activities in Afghanistan do not put him in the class of people whom the President may detain pursuant to the AUMF, the majority unnecessarily addresses a number of other points. Most notable is the paragraph that begins, "Before considering these arguments in detail," and that reaches the conclusion that "the premise that the war powers granted by the AUMF and other statutes are limited by the international laws of war . . . is mistaken." The paragraph appears hard to square with the approach that the Supreme Court took in *Hamdi*. See 542 U.S. at 521 (O'Connor, J.) (plurality opinion) ("[W]e understand Congress' grant of authority for the use of "necessary and appropriate force" to include the authority to detain for the duration of the relevant conflict, and our understanding is based on longstanding law-of-war principles."); *id.* at 548-49 (Souter, J., opinion concurring in part and dissenting in part) (advocating a more substantial role for the laws of war in interpretations of the President's authority under the AUMF). In any event, there is no need for the court's pronouncements, divorced from application to any particular argument. Curiously, the majority's dictum goes well beyond what even the *government* has argued in this case.

Because the petitioner's detention is lawful by virtue of facts that he has conceded—a conclusion that the majority seems not to dispute—the majority's analysis of the constitutionality of the *procedures* the district court used is unnecessary. . . .

NOTES AND QUESTIONS

1. *The Common Law Process of Lawmaking.* While some observers may despair of the divergent cases emerging from the D.C. District courts, the process is familiar. Common law is made incrementally when trial courts need to decide issues in the cases that come before them, and courts of appeals periodically—and with some lag—then resolve some of the differences in opinions that serve as binding precedent for later trial court decisions. *See generally Habeas Works: Federal Courts' Proven Capacity to Handle Guantánamo Cases: A Report from Retired Federal Judges* (Human Rights First and the Constitution Project, June 2010). (In addition to *Al-Bihani,* see *Bensayah v. Obama,* 610 F.3d 718 (D.C. Cir. 2010); *Barhoumi v. Obama,* 609 F.3d 416 (D.C. Cir. 2010); *Awad v. Obama,* 608 F.3d 1 (D.C. Cir. 2010).) The common law process, however, comes at the cost of at least temporarily fragmented law and disparate outcomes, and, some have argued, at the cost of creating a shaky foundation for a preventive detention regime. *See, e.g.,* Sophia Brill, *The National Security Court We Already Have,* 28 Yale L. & Pol'y Rev. 525 (2010).

2. *Law-of-War Limits?* Two judges in the *Al-Bihani* panel went out of their way to reject Al-Bihani's argument that any detention authority conferred by the AUMF was subject to or incorporated the limits set by the law of war. In other words, they considered detention authority to be exclusively a question of domestic law. The third member of the panel disassociated himself from what he described as *dicta* that went well beyond any argument that even the government had made. In denying *en banc* review, the full court agreed, asserting that determining "the role of international law-of-war principles in interpreting the AUMF . . . is not necessary to the disposition of the merits." *Al-Bihani v. Obama,* 619 F.3d 1, 1 (D.C. Cir. 2010).

So what is the role of international law-of-war principles? One view is that Congress was oblivious to law of war when it enacted the AUMF, and that the scope of the AUMF is be found entirely in its plain words (and perhaps, legislative intent). While "necessary and appropriate" is hardly helpful in describing the kinds of force the AUMF authorizes, its identification of the targets of force at least permits some group identification. It is left then to courts to determine individual identification—what degree of association with a targeted group is necessary to justify "AUMF detention."

But they do not do this in a vacuum. If the plain words and legislative history are not dispositive, courts interpret statutes against shared background understandings, often those reflected by like cases. There is a broad background understanding of law enforcement detention in U.S. law, driven by or under the shadow of the Fourth Amendment, but the understanding concerning wartime detention is reflected chiefly in *Milligan* and *Quirin.* Ironically, each discusses the law of war. In *Quirin,* the Court said that "[f]rom the very beginning of its history this Court has recognized and applied the law of war as including that part of the law of nations which prescribes, for the conduct of war, the status, rights and duties of enemy nations as well as of enemy individuals." *Ex parte Quirin,* 317 U.S. 1, 27 (1942). Our armed services have also long followed the law of war, dating back at least to the Lieber code. Is that law not therefore part of the background understanding for interpreting the AUMF?

Alternatively, is it unreasonable to assume that when Congress legislates about the use of force abroad, it does so against a background of international law that should be taken into account in interpreting its legislation? We have seen that courts construe statutes to avoid conflicts with international law where possible; should we assume that Congress, too, has legislated to avoid conflict, unless it clearly overrides international law? Is there anything in the AUMF that clearly overrides law-of-war principles?

Finally, is it possible to construe "appropriate" in the AUMF to *incorporate* relevant law-of-war principles? Congress clearly has the constitutional power to incorporate under the Define and Punish Clause, and in fact has done so; it acted under that clause when it passed the Articles of War, which were cited in *Quirin* as authority for trial by military commission. 317 U.S. at 28.

3. *What Law of War?* Judge Brown eschews law-of-war principles partly because they are "not a fixed code" and lack "firm definition." Assuming that they are relevant to interpreting the AUMF, what do they provide with respect to Al-Bihani? There clearly was an armed conflict in Afghanistan when he was captured. While this conflict has been characterized as one not of an international character, making most of the Geneva Conventions inapplicable to it, Common Article 3, *supra* p. 30, would still apply, as would Article 75 of AP I, *supra* p. 40. Neither specifies who may be detained, although both address conditions of detention, and Article 75 requires prompt release as soon as the circumstances justifying detention have ceased to exist.

4. *Status.* The AUMF targets organizations and persons who "planned, authorized, committed, or aided" the 9/11 attacks, or harbored such organizations or persons. In habeas litigation, the Administration proposed the following standard for detention under the AUMF:

> The President has the authority to detain persons that the President determines planned, authorized, committed, or aided the terrorist attacks that occurred on September 11, 2001, and persons who harbored those responsible for those attacks. The President also has the authority to detain persons who were part of, or substantially supported, Taliban or al Qaida forces or associated forces that are engaged in hostilities against the United States or its coalition partners, including any person who has committed a belligerent act, or has directly supported hostilities, in aid of such enemy armed forces. [*Hamlily v. Obama*, 616 F. Supp. 2d 63, 67 (D.D.C. 2009) (quoting government brief).]

The government has since explained that this standard is based on the AUMF and "draws on international laws of war to inform our interpretation of the statutory detention authority conferred by Congress in the AUMF." Remarks of Assistant Attorney General Tony West at the ABA Standing Comm. on Law and Nat'l Security Breakfast, Feb. 18, 2011, *available at* http://www.americanbar.org/content/dam/aba/multimedia/migrated/natsecurity/audio/national_security'matters.authcheckdam.mp3.

Al-Bihani was a brigade cook; the government made no claim that he was involved in the 9/11 attacks. Does he meet the Administration standard? If that standard is different from the AUMF standard, does he meet the latter? The court deemed cooking for a Taliban combat unit sufficient. But is that because he was present in the field with the brigade, because it had Al Qaeda members in its command structure, or because he carried a weapon (though he says he never fired it)? Suppose he was not in the field, but purchased food for the brigade in a Pakistani marketplace? Suppose he only donated money for that purpose? *See* Charlie Savage, *Obama Team Is Divided on Anti-Terror Tactics*, N.Y. Times, Mar. 28, 2010 (reporting that

Department of Justice's Office of Legal Counsel "found no precedents justifying detention of mere supporters of Al Qaeda who were picked up far away from enemy forces, [but] it was not prepared to state any definitive conclusion"). Suppose he quit as cook and left the brigade because he was unhappy with the pay? Suppose he was trained in an Al Qaeda camp, but as a cook, not a terrorist? *See* p. 493 n.2. Suppose he received weapons training in a camp in Pakistan, but the camp was neither Al Qaeda nor Taliban, but instead something like the local boy scouts? Can you see why the habeas courts might diverge in deciding who can be detained?

A recent district court habeas decision concluded (quoting from habeas opinions):

> "[T]here are no settled criteria," for determining who is "part of" the Taliban, al-Qaida, or an associated force. "That determination must be made on a case-by-case basis by using a functional rather than formal approach and by focusing on the actions of the individual in relation to the organization." The Court must consider the totality of the evidence to assess the individual's relationship with the organization. But being "part of["] the Taliban, al-Qaida, or an associated force requires "some level of knowledge or intent." *See also Bensayah*, 610 F.3d at 725 ("purely independent conduct of a freelancer is not enough" to demonstrate an individual was "part of" an organization.). [*Khan v. Obama*, 741 F. Supp. 2d 1, 5 (D.D.C. 2010) (omitting internal citations to habeas decisions).]

5. *"Spillover" Effects?* The diverging habeas opinions may affect not just the petitioners. One scholar notes that the opinions overhang other detention operations regardless of whether such operations are subject to judicial review, because military authorities are unlikely to ignore judicial opinions about detention authority. They may also affect targeting decisions, because such decisions also pose difficult problems of group and individual identification. Chesney, *supra* p. 490, 52 B.C. L. Rev. at 773-774. The habeas courts "have become, for better or worse, the central U.S. government institution engaged in the critical — and ultimately unavoidable — task of tailoring the laws governing military activity to suit the increasingly important scenario in which states classify clandestine non-state actors as strategic threats requiring a military response." *Id. See generally id.* at 776-781 (identifying possible "detention predicates" and "constraint criteria"). In short, they have reluctantly, and by congressional default, taken the lead in crafting new principles for asymmetric warfare. *See also* Geoffrey S. Corn, *The Role of the Courts in the War on Terror: The Intersection of Hyperbole, Military Necessity, and Judicial Review*, 43 New Eng. L. Rev. 17, 36 (2008) (asserting, approvingly, that "the government might finally be forced by [*Boumediene*] and continuing judicial oversight to clearly articulate and defend the rationale for the expansive application of the term "enemy combatant" that is at the heart of the concept of a "Global War on Terror").

6. *Lawmaking Competency.* It is possible to craft guidance by analogy from 1949 Geneva Convention III, or from customary law-of-war provisions for identifying lawful targets, *see* Chesney, *supra*, 52 B.C. L. Rev. at 793-797, but the project of law-interpreting then morphs quickly into a process of lawmaking. Do you agree with Judge Brown that this is a project for which Congress is better suited than the courts? *But see Habeas Works, supra* p. 498, at 13-16 (asserting that habeas courts have successfully engaged in traditional interpretation and application of detention standard

established by Congress); Nesbitt, *supra*, 95 Minn. L. Rev. at 247-248 (arguing that "while new detention legislation would have made sense during the first eighteen months of habeas litigation, the maturation of the jurisprudence has rendered this option unnecessary at best and counterproductive at worst. Habeas works. Congress should stand back and allow the courts to proceed.").

If this is a project for Congress, what detention standard should it adopt? *See, e.g.*, Chesney, *supra*, 52 B.C. L. Rev. at 857-858; Benjamin Wittes & Colleen A. Peppard, *Designing Detention: A Model Law for Terrorist Incapacitation* 3-4 (Brookings Inst. 2009), *available at* http://www.brookings.edu/papers/2009/0626_detention_wittes.aspx; Madeline Morris et al., *After Guantánamo: War, Crime, and Detention*, Harv. L. & Pol'y Rev. Online (July 14, 2009), http:// www.hlpronline.com/Morris_HLPR_071409.pdf (appending draft of proposed legislation).

D. CLOSING GUANTÁNAMO AND CHOOSING CRIMINAL PROCESS[2]

On May 21, 2009, President Barack Obama ordered "the closing of the prison camp at Guantánamo Bay." Remarks by President Barack Obama, *Protecting Our Security and Our Values*, National Archives, Washington, D.C., May 21, 2009. Asserting that "Guantánamo set back the moral authority that is America's strongest currency in the world," the President explained that the Administration would review the cases of the remaining detainees to decide who should be prosecuted in U.S. civil courts, who should be tried by improved military commissions, who should be transferred to another country, who could neither be prosecuted nor released because they pose a continuing clear danger to the American people, and "those we have been ordered [to] release[] by the courts." *Id.*

Congress, however, erected an obstacle to closing Guantánamo by blocking funding for the transfer of any non-citizen detainee from Guantánamo to the United States, unless the Administration prepared a detailed plan for each proposed transferee. Each plan had to include, "at a minimum — (1) an assessment of the risk that the individual . . . poses to the national security of the United States, its territories, or possessions; (2) a proposal for the disposition of each such individual; (3) the measures to be taken to mitigate any risks [posed by the transfer]; (4) the location or locations at which the individual will be held under the proposal for disposition . . . ; (5) the costs associated with executing the plan, including technical and financial assistance required to be provided to State and local law enforcement agencies, if necessary, to carry out the plan; (6) a summary of the consultation required [with state and local authorities of the transferee location in the United States] . . . ; and (7) a certification by the Attorney General that under the plan the individual poses little or no security risk to the United States, its territories, or Possessions. National Defense Authorization Act for Fiscal Year 2010, Pub. L. No. 111-84, §1041, 123 Stat. 2190, 2454-2455 (2009). The appropriations limitation, as a practical matter, made transfers from Guantánamo to the United States impossible.

---

2. *See generally* Michael John Garcia et al., *Closing the Guantánamo Detention Center: Legal Issues* (Cong. Res. Serv. RL40139), Feb. 11, 2011.

The initial review process ordered by the President was completed in January 2010. It approved 36 detainees for criminal prosecution in federal court (including alleged 9/11 mastermind, Khalid Sheikh Mohammed), 126 detainees for transfer to foreign custody (including 30 approved for "conditional" detention based on the security conditions in Yemen, the country to which they could eventually be transferred), and 48 for continued detention under the AUMF. *Guantánamo Review Task Force, supra* p. 444, at ii. Detainees were designated for continued detention based on their playing a "significant organizational role" within Al Qaeda, the Taliban, or associated forces, advanced training or combat experience, expressed recidivist intent, or "a history of associations with extremist activity." *Id.* at 24.

Congress, however, acted again to block the proposed criminal prosecutions. It included the following limitation in the defense authorization for fiscal year 2011:

> None of the funds authorized to be appropriated by this Act for fiscal year 2011 may be used to transfer, release, or assist in the transfer or release to or within the United States, its territories, or possessions of Khalid Sheikh Mohammed or any other detainee who (1) is not a United States citizen or a member of the Armed Forces of the United States; and (2) is or was held on or after January 20, 2009, at United States Naval Station, Guantánamo Bay, Cuba, by the Department of Defense.

Ike Skelton National Defense Authorization Act for Fiscal Year 2011, Pub. L. No. 111-383, §1032, 124 Stat. 4137, 4351 (2011). Not content with this restriction, Congress also prohibited any use of the authorized appropriation to modify or construct new detention facilities in the United States for Guantánamo detainees. *Id.* §1034(a), 124 Stat. 4353.

The President reluctantly signed the Authorization Act, stating:

> Section 1032 represents a dangerous and unprecedented challenge to critical executive branch authority to determine when and where to prosecute Guantánamo detainees, based on the facts and the circumstances of each case and our national security interests. The prosecution of terrorists in Federal court is a powerful tool in our efforts to protect the Nation and must be among the options available to us. Any attempt to deprive the executive branch of that tool undermines our Nation's counterterrorism efforts and has the potential to harm our national security.
>
> With respect to section 1033, the restrictions on the transfer of detainees to the custody or effective control of foreign countries interfere with the authority of the executive branch to make important and consequential foreign policy and national security determinations regarding whether and under what circumstances such transfers should occur in the context of an ongoing armed conflict. We must have the ability to act swiftly and to have broad flexibility in conducting our negotiations with foreign countries. [Statement by the President on H.R. 6523 (Jan. 7, 2011).]

If the Act's limitation is constitutional, it effectively prevents the President from shutting down Guantánamo as long as the Administration believes that any detainee now held there cannot be tried by a military commission for whatever reason but is too dangerous to release. It does not apply, however, to persons not detained at Guantánamo. Nor does it bar or condition the criminal prosecution of persons arrested in the United States for terrorist or related crimes.

Shortly after the report on the review process, Attorney General Eric Holder announced a decision to prosecute the man who tried to bomb a Northwest Airlines flight (popularly known as the "the underwear bomber"), following what he characterized as a long-standing "practice . . . to arrest and detain under federal criminal law all terrorist suspects who are apprehended inside the United States." Letter from Attorney General Eric Holder to Senator Mitch McConnell Regarding Umar Farouk Abdulmutallab (Feb. 3, 2010), *available at* http://www.justice.gov/cjs/docs/ag-letter-2-3-10.pdf. He noted that the initial transfers of both Jose Padilla and Ali Saleh Kahlah al-Marri into "law of war custody raised serious statutory and constitutional questions in the courts concerning the lawfulness of the government's actions and spawned lengthy litigation" that was only ended by their return to "law enforcement custody" and eventual criminal prosecution and imprisonment. *Id.* at 3.

In March 2011, the White House issued a new policy on the Guantánamo detainees, back-pedaling from the President's 2009 pledge to close the facility.

White House, Office of the Press Secretary, Fact Sheet: New Actions on Guantánamo and Detainee Policy

Mar. 7, 2011

In a speech nearly two years ago at the National Archives, the President advanced a four-part approach to closing the detention facility at Guantánamo Bay, keeping our country safe, and upholding the law: (1) to bring detainees to justice in prosecutions in either federal civilian courts or in reformed military commissions, (2) to comply with court-ordered releases of detainees, (3) to transfer detainees from Guantánamo whenever it is possible to do so safely and humanely, and (4) when neither prosecution nor other legal options are available, to hold these individuals in lawful military detention. He affirmed that "whenever feasible, we will try those who have violated American criminal laws in federal courts."

The Administration remains committed to closing the detention facility at Guantánamo Bay, and to maintain a lawful, sustainable and principled regime for the handling of detainees there, consistent with the full range of U.S. national security interests. In keeping with the strategy we laid out, we are proceeding today with the following actions:

Resumption of Military Commissions

The Secretary of Defense will issue an order rescinding his prior suspension on the swearing and referring of new charges in the military commissions. New charges in military commissions have been suspended since the President announced his review of detainee policy, shortly after taking office.

The Administration, working on a bipartisan basis with members of Congress, has successfully enacted key reforms, such as a ban on the use of statements taken as a result of cruel, inhuman or degrading treatment, and a better system for handling classified information. With these and other reforms, military commissions, along with prosecutions of suspected terrorists in civilian courts, are an available and important tool in combating international terrorists that fall within their jurisdiction while upholding the rule of law.

Executive Order on Periodic Review

In the Archives speech, the President recognized there are certain Guantánamo detainees who have not been charged, convicted, or designated for transfer, but must continue to be detained because they "in effect, remain at war with the United States." For this category of detainees, the President stated: "We must have a thorough process of periodic review, so that any prolonged detention is carefully evaluated and justified."

Today, the President issued an Executive Order establishing such a process for these detainees. . . .

. . . If a final determination is made that a detainee no longer constitutes a significant threat to our security, the Executive Order provides that the Secretaries of State and Defense are to identify a suitable transfer location outside the United States, consistent with the national security and foreign policy interests of the United States and applicable law. As the President has stated before, no Guantánamo detainee will be released into the United States. . . .

Continued Commitment to Article III Trials

Pursuant to the President's order to close Guantánamo, this Administration instituted the most thorough review process ever applied to the detainees held there. Among other things, for the first time, we consolidated all information available to the federal government about these individuals. That information was carefully examined by some of our government's most experienced prosecutors, a process that resulted in the referral of 36 individuals for potential prosecution. Since the time of those referrals, the Departments of Justice and Defense, with the advice of career military and civilian prosecutors, have been working to bring these defendants to justice, securing convictions in a number of cases and evaluating others to determine which system — military or civilian — is most appropriate based on the nature of the evidence and traditional principles of prosecution.

In recent months, some in Congress have sought to undermine this process. In December, Congress enacted restrictions on the prosecution of Guantánamo detainees in Federal courts. The Administration opposes these restrictions as a dangerous and unprecedented challenge to Executive authority to select the most effective means available to bring terrorists to justice and safeguard our security. The Executive Branch possesses the information and expertise necessary to make the best judgment about where a particular prosecution should proceed, and Congress's intrusion upon this function is inconsistent with the long-standing and appropriate allocation of authority between the Executive and Legislative branches. . . .

Military commissions should proceed in cases where it has been determined appropriate to do so. Because there are situations, however, in which our federal courts are a more appropriate forum for trying particular individuals, we will seek repeal of the restrictions imposed by Congress, so that we can move forward in the forum that is, in our judgment, most in line with our national security interests and the interests of justice.

We will continue to vigorously defend the authority of the Executive to make these well-informed prosecution decisions, both with respect to those detainees in our custody at Guantánamo and those we may apprehend in the future. A one-size-fits-all policy for the prosecution of suspected terrorists, whether for past or future cases, undermines our Nation's counterterrorism efforts and harms our national security.

Support for a Strong International Legal Framework

Because of the vital importance of the rule of law to the effectiveness and legitimacy of our national security policy, the Administration is announcing our support for two important components of the international legal framework that covers armed conflicts: Additional Protocol II and Article 75 of Additional Protocol I to the 1949 Geneva Conventions.

Additional Protocol II, which contains detailed humane treatment standards and fair trial guarantees that apply in the context of non-international armed conflicts, was originally submitted to the Senate for approval by President Reagan in 1987. The Administration urges the

Senate to act as soon as practicable on this Protocol, to which 165 States are a party. An extensive interagency review concluded that United States military practice is already consistent with the Protocol's provisions. . . .

Article 75 of Additional Protocol I, which sets forth fundamental guarantees for persons in the hands of opposing forces in an international armed conflict, is similarly important to the international legal framework. Although the Administration continues to have significant concerns with Additional Protocol I, Article 75 is a provision of the treaty that is consistent with our current policies and practice and is one that the United States has historically supported. Our adherence to these principles is also an important safeguard against the mistreatment of captured U.S. military personnel. The U.S. Government will therefore choose out of a sense of legal obligation to treat the principles set forth in Article 75 as applicable to any individual it detains in an international armed conflict, and expects all other nations to adhere to these principles as well.

NOTES AND QUESTIONS

1. *Constitutionality of Limitations.* The President "shall take Care that the Laws be faithfully executed," U.S. Const. art. II, §3. The Ike Skelton Act effectively prohibits execution of the criminal laws against Guantánamo detainees by criminal prosecution in a federal court, as there is no such court in Guantánamo. Is it unconstitutional? The Act also conditions any transfer of a detainee to foreign custody on a burdensome certification, not here reproduced. Is such a condition constitutional?

2. *The Choices Left.* If the Ike Skelton Act's limitations are constitutional, what choices are left for dealing with the remaining Guantánamo detainees? One is to prosecute them by military commission. See Chapter 22. Another is to continue their detention in Guantánamo, effectively leaving their future to the habeas process and the newly adopted process for periodic review. A third is to transfer them to foreign custody, if the arduous certification process imposed by the bill is satisfied. A recent bill would zero out appropriations for even such transfers. *See* Benjamin Wittes, *House GOP to Supreme Court: Bring Gitmo Detainees Here*, Lawfare, Feb. 23, 2011, *available at* http://www.lawfareblog.com/2011/02/a-house-gop-gift-to-habeas.

What choices are left for dealing with future captives? The Act's limitations only apply to Guantánamo detainees, so future captives presumably could be detained and/or criminally prosecuted in the United States. But given the Administration's professed desire still to close the Guantánamo Detention Center, and the political controversy that has attended efforts to try foreign terrorists in the United States, there may be a strong incentive to "outsource" their detention to allies in Afghanistan or Iraq. Alternatively, the detention quandary could be avoided altogether if military operations invariably kill rather than capture. *See* Chesney, *supra* p. 490, 52 B.C. L. Rev. at 804 (asserting, on this view, that the dramatic uptick in targeted killing during the Obama administration "is no surprise").

3. *Presumption for (or Against) Criminal Prosecution?* The White House Fact Statement asserts that although "[m]ilitary commissions should proceed in cases where it has been determined appropriate to do so, . . . there are situations . . . in which our federal courts are a more appropriate forum for trying particular individuals." The federal courts are open and have gained ever-increasing experience trying terrorism cases since 9/11, and the government has enjoyed a virtually unblemished record of victories in terrorism cases. Why should there not be a presumption in favor of criminal prosecution of terror suspects and criminal imprisonment of terror convicts?

V
Interrogating Terrorist Suspects

Interrogating Terrorist Suspects

17

The next three chapters are about the use of torture to extract intelligence information from detainees who will not willingly talk. Reliance on torture to extract confessions is at least as old as Ancient Greece. Before and during the Inquisition, trial by ordeal employed torture to supplement circumstantial evidence in a criminal case. If the accused confessed during torture, he could be convicted. John H. Langbein, *The Legal History of Torture*, in *Torture: A Collection* 93-95 (Sanford Levinson ed., 2004).

In intelligence investigations, especially those that take place during war or in the aftermath of a terrorist attack, investigators do not know in advance what the detainee knows that may be of value. Possible answers range from nothing to something significant. How should legal rules guide this uncertain quest for information? If the human tendency is to extract information by any means necessary, is abusive interrogation an inevitable result of any regime short of an absolute ban on abuse? *See* Joseph Margulies, *Guantanamo and the Abuse of Presidential Power* 29 (2006) (so arguing).

When grotesque photographs of detainees being abused by U.S. personnel at the Abu Ghraib detention facility in Iraq became prime time news in 2004, our nation's leaders engaged in an often vituperative debate about whether gathering intelligence through torture is effective — whether the gain is worth the pain. For example, two former U.S. military commanders wrote in 2007:

> ... These assertions that "torture works" may reassure a fearful public, but it is a false security . . . and any "flexibility" about torture at the top drops down the chain of command like a stone. . . . If we forfeit our values by signaling that they are negotiable in situations of grave or imminent danger, we drive those undecideds into the arms of the enemy. [Charles C. Krulak & Joseph P. Hoar, *It's Our Cage, Too*, Wash. Post, May 17, 2007.]

This chapter has two objectives. In Part A, we ask you first to review the report of a court-martial at the beginning of the twentieth century and the government's own account of "enhanced interrogation" techniques in the war on terror, then consider where you would draw the line between permissible interrogation and torture. In Part B, a judicial decision and Notes and Questions explore the legal landscape that governs interrogation for intelligence purposes.

In Chapter 18, we ask you to apply this legal framework to a case study of coercive interrogation during the war on terror. In Chapter 19, we consider whether sending suspects to foreign states for coercive interrogation (and detention without trial) avoids or changes that framework.

A. WHEN IS INTERROGATION TORTURE?

Part of the Spanish-American War was fought in the Philippines, where the U.S. defeat of the Spanish in Manila in 1898 was instrumental in affirming the independence of the Philippines from Spain. U.S. annexation of the Philippines after the war with Spain ended provoked a three-year insurgency by Philippine revolutionary forces. *See* Brian M. Linn, *The Philippine War: 1899-1902* (2000). During the insurrection, several U.S. military officers were court-martialed for war crimes. The report by the Judge Advocate General on the trial of one Army officer follows.

Court-Martial of Major Edwin F. Glenn[1]
Samar, Philippine Islands, April 1902
S. Doc. No. 213, 57th Cong. 20-28

War Department
Office of the Judge-Advocate-General
Washington July 18, 1902

THE SECRETARY OF WAR.

SIR: I beg leave to submit the following report upon the record of trial in the case of Maj. Edwin F. Glenn, Fifth U.S. Infantry.

The court-martial was appointed by the President in an Executive order dated April 30, 1902, and met at Catbalogan, in the island of Samar, on the 23d of May....

Major Glenn was tried on the following charge and specification.

CHARGE

Conduct to the prejudice of good order and military discipline, in violation of the sixty-second article of war.

SPECIFICATION

In that Maj. Edwin F. Glenn, Fifth U.S. Infantry... being on duty commanding the United States troops while at the pueblo of Igbarras, province of Iloilo, island of Panay, Philippine Islands, and having in his charge one Tobeniano Ealdama, presidente of the town on Igbarras aforesaid, did unlawfully order, direct, and, by his presence and authority, cause an officer and soldiers, subject to his the said Glenn's

[1. The report may be viewed in its entirety *at* http://web.lexis-nexis.com.lawezproxy.syr.edu/congcomp/document?_m=9c232820280cc08cf2cfdb65e96d8a09&_docnum=1&wchp=dGLbVlb-zSkSA&_md5=cd1516627794a8a5c487192fa20b3f30.—Eds.]

command, to execute upon him, the said Tobeniano Ealdama, a method of punishment commonly known in the Philippine Islands as the "water cure;" that is, did cause water to be introduced into the mouth and stomach of the said Ealdama against his will.

This at Igbarras, Panay, on or about the 27th day of November, 1900.

The accused pleads "Not guilty" to the charge and specification, but submitted the following statement, in the nature of an admission of fact, in connection with his arraignment: . . .

> I would like to state to the court, in explanation of this plea, the facts and circumstances that brought it about. . . . [A] short time since the commanding general of the Division of the Philippines called me into his office and said that he had just received a cablegram from the United States informing him that two enlisted men, now citizens, but formerly of the Twenty-sixth U.S. Volunteer Infantry, had testified before the United States Senate committee that I, while in command at Igbaras, Panay, of a detachment of United States troops had caused the water cure, so called, to be given to the presidente of that town. And the general added that his orders were to prefer charges against me and bring me to trial. . . .
>
> Subsequently this question came up between myself and the judge-advocate, and it was insisted that I should admit the word "water cure," and I have admitted it. My only reason for objection was that the word "water cure" is not a fixed term in its meaning. . . .

Tobeniano Ealdama, the native who was subjected to the water cure by Major Glenn's order, was called as a witness for the prosecution and testified (in Spanish) that . . . Major Glenn arrived at Igbarras in command of a detachment of United States troops, established his headquarters at the convent, and sent for witness (Ealdama). The witness was asked where General Delgado was, and replied that he was not in the town of Igbarras. He was then asked:

Q: What did they do to you then?
A: They told me if I did not tell I would be punished. They told me to take my shirt off, and they tied my arms. The captain and doctor and lieutenant sat at the table and there were some soldiers in the hallway. They laid me on my back and had some water with a faucet, and held my arms tight and proceeded to open my mouth. After they gave me some water for a little while the doctor told them to stop, and then asked me the whereabouts of General Delgado. I told them that I did not know where the general was, and they proceeded again with the water. They gave me water, some through the nose and some through the mouth. I had shortness of breath and pain in the stomach.
Q: Did it have any other effect on you?
A: My throat also hurt me on account of so much water put through it.
Q: How much water did you take in?
A: Four bottles, about four bottles, as best I know.
Q: What effect did that have upon you?
A: I had some pain in my throat.
Q: Did you retain this water on your stomach?
A: I kept it in my stomach.
Q: Did any come off of it?
A: Yes, sir; I did vomit some.
Q: What did they do with you then?
A: They asked me quite a number of questions and I did not know the answer to them, and the Major said, "All right, let him up."
Q: What did they do to you then?
A: I went to the table and sat down and waited, and they administered water to the school-teacher while I was waiting.

Q: Where did you go then?

A: I went downstairs.

Q: What did they do to you there?

A: They asked me if I was in communication with the insurrectos. I said that I was not.

Q: What did they do to you then?

A: They said, "You are a liar. Take off your clothes."

Q: Well, go on.

A: Then I was sleeping. (The interpreter said that he thought the witness meant that he was in a recumbent position.) They brought a kind of syringe.

Q: What did they do with it?

A: Open my mouth and put water in my mouth.

Q: What kind?

A: Salty.

Q: How much did they put in?

A: About one bottle.

Q: What effect did that have?

A: It was very bitter.

Q: Did it have any other effect?

A: My stomach and throat pained me, and also the nose where they passed the salt water through . . .

. . . [S]ubsequent to the occurrences above testified to, the witness (Tobeniano Ealdama) was tried by a military commission at Isiolo between June 7 and 14, 1901, under the charge of "being a war traitor," the specification alleging holding intercourse with the enemy by means of letters, contributing money, and food to the insurrectionary forces, and directing others, members of said forces, to collect contributions. He was also charged with "violating the laws of war" by joining and becoming a captain in the insurrectionary forces and recruiting and swearing into the Insurgent service the members of the local police force of Igbarras. He was found guilty of the offenses charged and sentenced to confinement at hard labor for ten years. He was released from confinement to enable him to testify as a witness in this case.

The accused admitted the facts in connection with the administration of the water cure, but undertook to show, in defense, that his act was not unlawful; that is, it was justified by military necessity and was warranted as a legitimate exercise of force by the laws of war.

In support of this defense it was attempted to show that Ealdama was a war traitor; that he acted as an officer of the insurgent forces; that he organized the native police of Igbarras as a part of such insurgent forces, and he collected contributions of money and supplies for the insurrectionary cause and transmitted them to their destination. The order announcing the result of Ealdama's trial by military commissions, which has already been mentioned, was introduced in support of this contention. . . .

. . . [The] resort to torture is attempted to be justified, not as an exceptional occurrence, but as the habitual method of obtaining information from individual insurgents. The accused took considerable pains to establish the fact that torture was the usual practice of the Spaniards; that it was practiced by the insurgents; and that when a native was punished by the Americans for refusing to assist them in their operations against the insurgents he was not subsequently punished by the insurrectionary leaders for giving such assistance. If this be admitted, the accused was attempting to justify his conduct, not as an act dictated by military necessity, but as a method of conducting operations.

When looked at from this point of view the defense falls completely, inasmuch as it is attempted to establish the principle that a belligerent who is at war with a savage or semicivilized enemy may conduct his operations in violation of the rules of civilized war. This no modern State will admit for an instant; nor was it the rule in the Philippine Islands. It is proper to observe that the several general officers who have exercised chief command in the Philippine Islands have, all of them, expressly forbidden practices like that of which the accused is here charged. Their principal subordinates have given similar instructions forbidding a resort to cruelty in the most positive terms. . . .

The rules respecting the treatment of guerrillas contemplate the existence of large armies which are annoyed in their operations by the presence of small guerrilla bands — that is, by the acts of small bodies of the enemy who are not a part of his combatant forces and who conduct their operations in violation of the rules of war. This was not the case in the Philippine Islands generally, where there were no large armies operating against each other as organized bodies. The troops were operating in detachments against isolated bands or bodies of insurgents, all of which were acting as guerrillas and were conducting their operations in flagrant disregard of the rules of civilized war. The situation thus presented was difficult and to the last degree exasperating, but it did not relieve the officers and men of the occupying forces of their obligation to adhere to the rules of war in the efforts put forth by them with a view to suppress the insurrection and restore public order. . . .

The accused was found guilty upon both charge and specification, and the following sentence was imposed:

> To be suspended from command for the period of one month, and to forfeit the sum of $50 for the same period. The court is thus lenient on account of the circumstances as shown in evidence.

Although the accused was tried for but a single administration of the water-cure — not for habitually resorting to it in the conduct of operations against the insurrectionary forces — the sentence imposed, in my opinion, was inadequate to the offense established by the testimony of the witnesses and the admission of the accused. The sympathy of the court seems to have been with the accused throughout the trial; the feeling of the [jury] members in that respect is also indicated by qualifying words which are added to the sentence, and by the unanimous recommendation to clemency which is appended to the record.

I . . . recommended that the sentence be confirmed and carried into effect.

Very respectfully,

George B. Davis
Judge-Advocate General

On April 16, 2009, the following memorandum, signed by Principal Deputy Assistant Attorney General Stephen G. Bradbury, was released pursuant to a Freedom of Information Act (FOIA) request. Apparently, the General Counsel of the CIA had sought the advice of the Office of Legal Counsel, Department of Justice, concerning the legality of a series of "enhanced interrogation techniques" that were employed by the CIA between 2002 and 2005 in Afghanistan (and perhaps elsewhere). Assistant

AG Bradbury first described the techniques, as he understood them, in the part of the memorandum reproduced here. He quoted an internal CIA document as his source, *Background Paper on CIA's Combined Use of Interrogation Techniques* (Dec. 30, 2004), also released following a FOIA request, and *available at* http://www.aclu.org/torturefoia/released/082409/olcremand/2004olc97.pdf.

Application of 18 U.S.C. §§2340-2340A to the Combined Use of Certain Techniques in the Interrogation of High Value al Qaeda Detainees

Office of Legal Counsel, U.S. Department of Justice (May 10, 2005)
http://www.fas.org/irp/agency/doj/olc/combined.pdf

Memorandum for: John A. Rizzo, Senior Deputy General Counsel,
                          Central Intelligence Agency

From: Stephen G. Bradbury, Principal Deputy Assistant Attorney General

Phases of the Interrogation Process

The first phase of the interrogation process, "Initial Conditions," does not involve interrogation techniques. . . . The "Initial Conditions" nonetheless set the stage for use of the interrogation techniques, which come later.

. . . [B]efore being flown to the site of interrogation, a detainee is given a medical examination. He then is "securely shackled and is deprived of sight and sound through the use of blindfolds, earmuffs, and hoods" during the flight. An onboard medical officer monitors his condition. Security personnel also monitor the detainee for signs of distress. Upon arrival at the site, the detainee "finds himself in complete control of Americans" and is subjected to "precise, quiet, and almost clinical" procedures designed to underscore "the enormity and suddenness of the change in environment, the uncertainty about what will happen next, and the potential dread [a detainee] may have of US custody." His head and face are shaved; his physical condition is documented through photographs taken while he is nude; and he is given medical and psychological interviews to assess his condition and to make sure there are no contraindications to the use of any particular interrogation techniques.

The detainee then enters the next phase, the "Transition to Interrogation." The interrogators conduct an initial interview, "in a relatively benign environment," to ascertain whether the detainee is willing to cooperate. The detainee is "normally clothed but seated and shackled for security purposes." The interrogators take "an open, non-threatening approach," but the detainee "would have to provide information on actionable threats and location information on High-Value targets at large — not lower-level information — for interrogators to continue with [this] neutral approach." If the detainee does not meet this "very high" standard, the interrogators submit a detailed interrogation plan to CIA headquarters for approval. If the medical and psychological assessments find no contraindications to the proposed plan, and if senior CIA officers at headquarters approve some or all of the plan through a cable transmitted to the site of the interrogation, the interrogation moves to the next phase.

Three interrogation techniques are typically used to bring the detainee to "a baseline, dependent state," "demonstrat[ing] to the [detainee] that he has no control over basic human needs" and helping to make him "perceive and value his personal welfare, comfort, and immediate needs more than the information he is protecting." The three techniques used to establish this "baseline" are nudity, sleep deprivation (with shackling and, at least at times, with use of a diaper), and dietary manipulation. These techniques . . . "require little to no physical interaction between the detainees and interrogator."

Other techniques, which "require physical interaction between the interrogator and detainee," are characterized as "corrective" and "are used principally to correct, startle, or achieve another enabling objective with the detainee." These techniques "are not used simultaneously but are often used interchangeably during an individual interrogation session." The insult slap is used "periodically throughout the interrogation process when the interrogator needs to immediately correct the detainee or provide a consequence to a detainee's response or non-response." The insult slap "can be used in combination with water dousing or kneeling stress positions"— techniques that are not characterized as "corrective." Another corrective technique, the abdominal slap, "is similar to the insult slap in application and desired result" and "provides the variation necessary to keep a high level of unpredictability in the interrogation process." The abdominal slap may be simultaneously combined with water dousing, stress positions, and wall standing. A third corrective technique, the facial hold, "is used sparingly throughout interrogation." It is not painful, but "demonstrates the interrogator's control over the [detainee]." It too may be simultaneously combined with water dousing, stress positions, and wall standing. Finally, the attention grasp "may be used several times in the same interrogation" and may be simultaneously combined with water dousing or kneeling stress positions.

Some techniques are characterized as "coercive." These techniques "place the detainee in more physical and psychological stress." Coercive techniques "are typically not used in combination, although some combined use is possible." Walling "[where a detainee is slammed against a false wall, and the loud sound of the impact creates the impression of a powerful impact] is one of the most effective interrogation techniques because it wears down the [detainee] physically, heightens uncertainty in the detainee about what the interrogator may do to him, and creates a sense of dread when the [detainee] knows he is about to be walled again." A detainee "may be walled one time (one impact with the wall) to make a point or twenty to thirty times consecutively when the interrogator requires a more significant response to a question," and "will be walled multiple times" during a session designed to be intense. Walling cannot practically be used at the same time as other interrogation techniques.

Water temperature and other considerations of safety established by OMS [Office of Medical Services] limit the use of another coercive technique, water dousing. The technique "may be used frequently within those guidelines." As suggested above, interrogators may combine water dousing with other techniques, such as stress positions, wall standing, the insult slap, or the abdominal slap.

The use of stress positions is "usually self-limiting in that temporary muscle fatigue usually leads to the [detainee's] being unable to maintain the stress position after a period of time." Depending on the particular position, stress positions may be combined with water dousing, the insult slap, the facial hold, and the attention grasp. Another coercive technique, wall standing, is "usually self-limiting" in the same way as stress positions. It may be combined with water dousing and the abdominal slap. OMS guidelines limit the technique of cramped confinement to no more than eight hours at a time and 18 hours a day, and confinement in the "small box" is limited to two hours. Cramped confinement cannot be used in simultaneous combination with corrective or other coercive techniques.

We understand that the CIA's use of all these interrogation techniques is subject to ongoing monitoring by interrogation team members who will direct that techniques be discontinued if there is a deviation from prescribed procedures and by medical and psychological personnel from OMS who will direct that any or all techniques be discontinued if in their professional judgment the detainee may otherwise suffer severe physical or mental pain or suffering.

A Prototypical Interrogation

In a "prototypical interrogation," the detainee begins his first interrogation session stripped of his clothes, shackled, and hooded, with the walling collar over his head and around his neck. The interrogators remove the hood and explain that the detainee can improve his situation by cooperating and may say that the interrogators "will do what it takes to get important information." As soon as the detainee does anything inconsistent with the interrogators' instructions, the interrogators use an insult slap or abdominal slap. They employ walling if it becomes clear that the detainee is not cooperating in the interrogation. This sequence "may continue for several more iterations as the interrogators continue to measure the [detainee's] resistance posture and apply a negative consequence to [his] resistance efforts." The interrogators and security officers then put the detainee into position for standing sleep deprivation, begin dietary manipulation through a liquid diet, and keep the detainee nude (except for a diaper). The first interrogation session, which could have lasted from 30 minutes to several hours, would then be at an end.

If the interrogation team determines there is a need to continue, and if the medical and psychological personnel advise that there are no contraindications, a second session may begin. The interval between sessions could be as short as an hour or as long as 24 hours. At the start of the second session, the detainee is released from the position for standing sleep deprivation, is hooded, and is positioned against the walling wall, with the walling collar over his head and around his neck. Even before removing the hood, the interrogators use the attention grasp to startle the detainee. The interrogators take off the hood and begin questioning. If the detainee does not give appropriate answers to the first questions, the interrogators use an insult slap or abdominal slap. They employ walling if they determine that the detainee "is intent on maintaining his resistance posture." This sequence "may continue for multiple iterations as the interrogators continue to measure the [detainee's] resistance posture." The interrogators then increase the pressure on the detainee by using a hose to douse the detainee with water for several minutes. They stop and start the dousing as they continue the interrogation. They then end the session by placing the detainee into the same circumstances as at the end of the first session: the detainee is in the standing position for sleep deprivation, is nude (except for a diaper), and is subjected to dietary manipulation. Once again, the session could have lasted from 30 minutes to several hours.

Again, if the interrogation team determines there is a need to continue, and if the medical and psychological personnel find no contraindications, a third session may follow. The session begins with the detainee positioned as at the beginning of the second. If the detainee continues to resist, the interrogators continue to use walling and water dousing. The corrective techniques — the insult slap, the abdominal slap, the facial hold, the attention grasp — "may be used several times during this session based on the responses and actions of the [detainee]." The interrogators integrate stress positions and wall standing into the session. Furthermore, "[i]ntense questioning and walling would be repeated multiple times." Interrogators "use one technique to support another." For example, they threaten the use of walling unless the detainee holds a stress position, thus inducing the detainee to remain in the position longer than he otherwise would. At the end of the session, the interrogators and security personnel place the detainee into the same circumstances as at the end of the first two sessions, with the detainee subject to sleep deprivation, nudity, and dietary manipulation.

In later sessions, the interrogators use those techniques that are proving most effective and drop the others. Sleep deprivation "may continue to the 70 to 120 hour range, or possibly beyond for the hardest resisters, but in no case exceed the 180-hour time limit." If the medical or psychological personnel find contraindications, sleep deprivation will end earlier. While continuing the use of sleep deprivation, nudity, and dietary manipulation, the interrogators may add cramped confinement. As the detainee begins to cooperate, the interrogators "begin gradually to decrease the use of interrogation techniques." They may permit the detainee to sit, supply clothes, and provide more appetizing food.

The entire process in this "prototypical interrogation" may last 30 days. If additional time is required and a new approval is obtained from headquarters, interrogation may go longer than 30 days. Nevertheless, "[o]n average, the actual use of interrogation techniques covers a period of three to seven days, but can vary upwards to fifteen days based on the resilience of the [detainee]." . . .

NOTES AND QUESTIONS

1. *Definitions: Do You Know It When You See It?* The ban on torture is widely said to be *jus cogens* — a universal norm. *See, e.g., Filartiga v. Peña-Irala*, 630 F.2d 876, 884 (2d Cir. 1980) (finding that "official torture is now prohibited by the law of nations"); *Tel-Oren v. Libyan Arab Republic*, 726 F.2d 774, 781, 791 n.20 (D.C. Cir. 1984) (Edwards, J., concurring), *cert. denied*, 470 U.S. 1003 (1985) (asserting that "commentators have begun to identify a handful of heinous actions — each of which violates definable, universal and obligatory norms," including, at a minimum, bans on governmental "torture").

We consider the attempted legal definitions of torture in the next part of this chapter, but if the ban on torture is *jus cogens*, do we need a legal definition? Should we simply know torture when we see it? Which, if any, of the techniques described above do you consider torture? Why? Does it matter to you that we have court-martialed our own soldiers for using such techniques? Would you give the same answer in any set of circumstances? Can a technique not be torture if applied alone, but constitute torture when combined with other techniques? That is, can a whole interrogation procedure amount to torture even if its parts, standing alone, do not?

Even if you are unclear whether a technique — or battery of techniques — is torture, you might well conclude that it is inhumane and offensive to human dignity.

For example, after objections to Israeli mistreatment of detainees during the Palestinian Intifada, the Israeli Supreme Court ruled that certain interrogation methods approved for use by Israel's security services — hooding, shaking, forced crouch on toes, painful handcuffing, seating detainees on low and inclined stools, sleep deprivation, and prolonged extremely loud music — violated the detainees' constitutional protections to a right of dignity, based on Israeli domestic law. *Public Committee Against Torture in Israel v. State of Israel*, HC, 5100/94 (1999). How would you characterize the techniques described in the court-martial report and the OLC memo set out above?

Would a universal definition of torture or inhumane treatment be a good idea? Would it matter? *See* Oren Gross, *Are Torture Warrants Warranted? Pragmatic Absolutism and Official Disobedience*, 88 Minn. L. Rev. 1481, 1487 (2004) ("preventive interrogational torture is far too complex to be addressed by definitional juggling"); Jeremy Waldron, *Torture and Positive Law: Jurisprudence for the White House*, 105 Colum. L. Rev. 1681, 1699 (2005) (a precise definition of torture is advisable, because "if the terms [are] . . . indeterminate, the person to whom the prohibition is addressed may not know exactly what is required of him"). *Compare* John T. Parry, *"Just For Fun": Understanding Torture and Understanding Abu Ghraib*, 1 J. Nat'l Security L. & Pol'y 253, 262-270 (2005) (asserting that the United States and other nations play a "definitional game" where governments parse language and deny responsibility for conduct that goes too far).

2. *Waterboarding*. The interrogation technique described in the *Glenn* court-martial — the "water cure," or more recently waterboarding — pre-dates the Inquisition and owes its longevity and apparent appeal to the fact that it causes extreme physical and mental suffering, but leaves no marks on the body. Eric Weiner, *Waterboarding: A Tortured History* (National Pub. Radio, Nov. 3, 2007), *available at http://www.npr.org/templates/story/story.php?storyId=15886834*. For another description of waterboarding, from another memo prepared for the CIA, *see Memorandum for John Rizzo, Acting General Counsel of the Central Intelligence Agency, from U.S. Department of Justice, Office of Legal Counsel Re: Interrogation of Al Qaeda Operative* 3-4 (Aug. 1, 2002). *See* Joby Warrick, *CIA Tactics Endorsed in Secret Memos*, Wash. Post, Oct. 15, 2008.

Does waterboarding constitute torture? Federal courts in the United States have punished law enforcement personnel for waterboarding, including local sheriffs and Philippine government agents. *See United States v. Lee*, 744 F.2d 1124 (5th Cir. 1984); *In re Estate of Ferdinand E. Marcos, Human Rights Litig.*, 910 F. Supp. 1460, 1463 (D. Haw. 1995). Can you draft language for a law that would forbid use of waterboarding? Would a ban on "torture" accomplish the objective?

3. *The CIA and Torture*. The 2005 Memorandum, written for the CIA, concludes that none of the "enhanced interrogation techniques" described there, alone or in combination, necessarily constitutes torture. Do you agree? What legal standards should be used to measure the CIA practices? Can you think of any reason why CIA rules for coercive interrogation should differ from those followed by the military? By civilian law enforcement personnel?

4. *Who Decides What Interrogation Conduct Is Unlawful?* The official policy of the United States is to condemn and prohibit torture. *See generally* U.S. Dep't of State, *Initial Report of the United States of America to the UN Committee Against Torture*

(Oct. 15, 1999), *available at* http://www.state.gov/www/global/human_rights/torture_intro.html ("Torture is prohibited by law throughout the United States. It is categorically denounced as a matter of policy and as a tool of state authority."); *Second Periodic Report of the United States of America to the Committee Against Torture* (May 6, 2005), *available at* http://www.state.gov/g/drl/rls/45738.htm ("United States is unequivocally opposed to the use and practice of torture. . . . No circumstance whatsoever . . . may be invoked as a justification for or defense to committing torture."). Who decides how to translate the policy into enforceable rules?

5. *The Ticking Bomb: Utilitarianism vs. Morality?* Is it *ever* justifiable to torture a detainee? One perspective emphasizes a range of practical problems that seriously limit the value of information obtained through torture, most importantly the fact that the person being interrogated can be expected to say whatever he thinks the interrogator wants to hear — in order to make the pain stop. Thus, the information is inherently unreliable. *See* Jeannine Bell, *"Behind This Mortal Bone": The (In)effectiveness of Torture*, 83 Ind. L.J. 339 (2008); *see also* J. M. Arrigo, *A Utilitarian Argument Against Torture Interrogation of Terrorists*, 10 Sci. & Eng'g Ethics 543 (2004). But the Bush administration consistently maintained that its harsh interrogation techniques produced intelligence that helped prevent terrorist attacks. For example, officials claimed that Khalid Sheikh Mohammed, the mastermind of the 9/11 attacks, provided detailed intelligence about the Al Qaeda network after being subjected to waterboarding, and that Abu Zubaydah, a top Al Qaeda strategist, implicated Jose Padilla in a dirty-bomb plot after coercive interrogation. Stephen Grey, *Ghost Plane: The True Story of the CIA Torture Program* 242-243 (2006). If this true, does it legitimate torture in some circumstances?

The mere possibility that coercive interrogation could save many lives creates an undoubted and morally complex tension between the need to obtain information and the condoning of torture. Assume, for example, that authorities have in custody someone whom they feel certain has placed an especially destructive explosive device somewhere in a large shopping mall. The explosive may go off at any time, and there may not be enough time to evacuate the mall. If the bomb detonates, thousands will die. The detainee is believed to be the only person with knowledge of the bomb, and he will not talk. Should the interrogators torture the detainee in hopes of learning the location of the bomb before it is too late? *Compare* Alan M. Dershowitz, *Why Terrorism Works* 142-149 (2002) (torture techniques may be morally and legally justified in some circumstances), *with* Association of the Bar of the City of New York, Comm. on Int'l Human Rights, Comm. on Military Affairs & Justice, *Human Rights Standards Applicable to the United States' Interrogation of Detainees* 8-9 (Apr. 30, 2004), *available at* http://www.abcny.org/pdf/HUMANRIGHTS.pdf ("Condoning torture under any circumstances erodes one of the most basic principles of international law and human rights and contradicts our values as a democratic state"), *and* David Luban, *Liberalism, Torture, and the Ticking Bomb*, 91 Va. L. Rev. 1425 (2005) (ticking-bomb scenarios may be used to rationalize institutionalized practices and procedures of torture). *See also* Kim Lane Scheppele, *Hypothetical Torture in the "War on Terrorism,"* 1 J. Nat'l Security L. & Pol'y 285 (2005) (taking a "hard line" against torture on sociological grounds). The Convention Against Torture, to which the United States is a party, says torture can never be justified. *See infra* p. 528. Professor Jeremy Waldron would not allow the authorization of torture even in the ticking-bomb scenario. Waldron argues that a line on what techniques are permitted has to be drawn "somewhere, and I say we should draw it where the law requires it, and where the human rights tradition has insisted that it should be drawn." Waldron, *supra*, at 1715.

How should we respond to the assertion that sometimes torture *works*—that it produces intelligence that exposes terrorist plots? Prominent examples include French claims that coercion exposed terrorist operations in Algeria, Adam Shatz, *The Torture of Algiers*, N.Y. Rev. of Books, Nov. 21, 2002, and U.S. claims that torturing suspects in the Philippines uncovered a plot to crash 11 commercial airliners into the Pacific in 1995. *See* Dershowitz, *supra*, at 137.

6. *Torture Warrants?* Professor Dershowitz would recognize a qualified prohibition on torture. He suggests a form of judicial "torture warrant" before permitting torture of suspected terrorists in interrogations. Dershowitz, *supra* at 148-149, 158-163. What might be the criteria for issuing such warrants? Should a judge, for example, try to balance the credibility or gravity of a threat against the suffering or injury to be inflicted on the recalcitrant detainee? Can you articulate a process that would be helpful to the court in doing that?

Another approach advocates an "emergency exception" to a ban on torture based on a written finding by the President of "an urgent and extraordinary need" reported "within a reasonable period" to appropriate congressional committees. The report would state the reason to believe that the information is known by the person to be interrogated, that it "concerns a specific plan that threatens U.S. lives," and that there are "no reasonable alternatives to save the lives in question." Philip B. Heymann & Juliette N. Kayyem, *Long-Term Legal Strategy Project for Preserving Security and Democratic Freedoms in the War on Terrorism* 25-26 (2004). Is this "findings" approach preferable to a torture warrant in the ticking-bomb case?

Alternatively, should we expect government officials confronted with the ticking-bomb case to engage in a form of official disobedience, hoping for ratification of the disobedient conduct after the fact? *See* Gross, *supra*, at 107. *Could* ratification by Congress or the President after the fact make lawful torture that was undertaken in disobedience of the law?

Which of these approaches is best? If you think torture might be permissible in some circumstances, can you think of other methods for keeping its "qualified" use in check?

B.   THE LEGAL STANDARDS AND THEIR APPLICATION

On March 30, 2006, Charles Emmanuel, also known as Chuckie Taylor, Charles Taylor Jr., and Roy Belfast, son of the infamous president of Liberia, Charles Taylor, was arrested when he attempted to enter the United States with a passport obtained through false statements on his passport application. After he pleaded guilty to the passport fraud charge and was sentenced to 11 months in prison in December 2007, a 2008 Justice Department indictment charged Emmanuel with participating in torture in Liberia between 1999 and 2003. The opinion below, issued in response to a pretrial motion to dismiss an indictment, is the first judicial interpretation of a federal statute that criminalizes acts of torture committed outside the United States if the offender is a U.S. national or, regardless of nationality, is present in the United States.

United States v. Charles Emmanuel

United States District Court, Southern District of Florida, 2007
2007 WL 2002452

CECILIA M. ALTONAGA, United States District Judge. This cause is before the Court on Defendant, Charles Emmanuel's Motion to Dismiss the Indictment Based on the Unconstitutionality of 18 U.S.C. §2340A. . . .

I. BACKGROUND

A. International and National Prohibitions of Torture

International prohibition against torture is a *jus cogens* norm of international law. *See Nuru v. Gonzales*, 404 F.3d 1207, 1222-23 (9th Cir. 2005) ("torture is illegal under the law of virtually every country in the world and under the international law of human rights") (internal footnotes omitted). The Universal Declaration of Human Rights, adopted by the United Nations in 1948, states that "no one shall be subjected to torture or to cruel, inhuman or degrading treatment or punishment." Universal Decl. of Human Rights, Dec. 10, 1948, U.N. Doc. A/810, art. 5. The International Covenant on Civil and Political Rights, Dec. 16, 1966, art. 7, 999 U.N.T.S. 171, 6 I.L.M. 368, states that "[n]o one shall be subjected to torture or to cruel, inhuman or degrading treatment or punishment."

On December 10, 1984, the United Nations General Assembly unanimously adopted the Convention Against Torture and Other Cruel, Inhuman or Degrading Treatment or Punishment ("Convention Against Torture" or "Convention"). G.A. Res. 39/46, U.N. GAOR, 39th Sess., Supp. No. 51 at 197, U.N. Doc. A/RES/39/46, S. Treaty Doc. No. 100-20, 1465 U.N.T.S. 85 (Dec. 10, 1984). It was adopted "with the stated purpose to 'make more effective the struggle against torture and other cruel, inhuman or degrading treatment or punishment throughout the world.'" *Auguste v. Ridge*, 395 F.3d 123, 130 (3d Cir. 2005) (quoting the Preamble to the Convention, S. Treaty Doc. No. 100-20, 1465 U.N.T.S. 85)). The Convention entered into force on June 26, 1987. *See id.* It has been described as the "most important U.N. treaty for controlling, regulating, and prohibiting torture and related practices." Winston Nagan & Lucie Atkins, *The International Law of Torture: From Universal Proscription to Effective Application and Enforcement*, 14 Harv. Hum. Rts. J. 87, 97 (2001).

On April 18, 1988, President Ronald Reagan signed the Convention, with the caveat that the United States reserved the right to communicate such reservations, interpretive understandings, or declarations as were deemed necessary. *See Auguste*, 395 F.3d at 130 (citations omitted). President Reagan submitted the Convention Against Torture to the Senate for advice and consent to ratification on May 20, 1988, with seventeen proposed conditions (four reservations, nine understandings, and four declarations). *Id.* at 131 (citing S. Exec. Rep. 101-30, at 2, 7 (1990)).

In January 1990, President George H.W. Bush submitted a revised and reduced list of proposed conditions. *See Auguste*, 395 F.3d at 131. One of the proposed conditions was that in order to constitute torture, the "act must be specifically intended to inflict severe physical or mental pain or suffering." *Id.* (quoting S. Exec. Rep. 101-30 at 9, 36). On January 30, 1990, the Senate Foreign Relations Committee held a hearing and thereafter, on August 30, 1990, issued a report recommending that the Senate give its advice and consent to ratification of the Convention Against Torture, subject to reservations, understandings and declarations.[2] S. Exec. Rep. 101-30 (1990). The full Senate gave its advice and consent to ratification, again, subject to several reservations, understandings and declarations. *See* S17, Cong. Rec. 486, S17491-92 (daily ed. 1990).

On October 21, 1994 and pursuant to Article 26 of the Convention, when President William Clinton deposited the instrument for ratification with the United Nations, *see Xuncax v. Gramajo,* 886 F. Supp. 162, 176 n.12 (D. Mass. 1995), the United States became a party to the Convention. Notably, the President included the Senate understandings in the instrument of ratification." *Auguste,* 395 F.3d at 132 (citing 1830 U.N.T.S. 320, 321, 322 (1994)); Declarations and Reservations made upon Ratification, accession, or Succession (visited Nov. 24, 2004) (http://untreaty.un.org/ENGLISH/bible/englishinternetbible/partI/chapterIV/treaty14.asp)).

In consenting to ratification of the Convention Against Torture, the Senate acknowledged that existing U.S. federal and state criminal statutes prohibited acts of torture occurring within the United States. *See Summary and Analysis of the Convention Against Torture and Other Cruel, Inhuman or Degrading Treatment,* S. Treaty Doc. 100-20, 9-10 (1988). The Senate recognized that in order for the United States to comply with its obligations under the treaty, it would need to enact a criminal statute prohibiting acts of torture by the defendants specified in Article 5 of the Convention, committed outside the United States. *Id.*

There are 144 parties to the Convention Against Torture, representing approximately 75% of the member states of the United Nations, including the United States and Liberia. The Convention defines "torture" as

> any act by which severe pain or suffering, whether physical or mental, is intentionally inflicted on a person for such purposes as obtaining from him or a third person information or a confession, punishing him for an act he or a third person has committed or is suspected of having committed, or intimidating or coercing him or a third person, or for any reason based on discrimination of any kind, when such pain or suffering is inflicted by or at the instigation of or with the consent or acquiescence of a public official or other person acting in an official capacity.

Convention, Article 1(1).

Article 2(1) of the Convention requires each State Party to "take effective legislative, administrative, judicial or other measures to prevent acts of torture in any territory under its jurisdiction." Article 4 requires each State Party to "ensure that all acts of torture are offences under its criminal law. The same shall apply to any attempt to commit torture and to any act by any person which constitutes complicity or participation in torture." Article 5(1) requires each State Party to "take such measures as may be necessary to establish its jurisdiction over the offences . . . (b) When the alleged offender is a national of that State," and "2. . . . where the alleged offender is present in any territory under its jurisdiction and it does not extradite him. . . ."

---

2. The Senate gave advice and consent subject to the reservation that the term "cruel, inhuman or degrading treatment or punishment" is to have a meaning as prohibited by the Fifth, Eighth, and/or Fourteenth Amendments to the U.S. Constitution, and subject to additional understandings, including that the provisions of the Convention are not self-executing. For a complete listing of the reservations, understandings and declarations of the United States Senate, see http://www.unhchr.ch/html/menu2/6/cat/treaties/convention-reserv.htm.

The Convention . . . was not intended to be self-executing. *See Reyes-Sanchez v. United States Attorney Gen.*, 369 F.3d 1239, 1240 n.1 (11th Cir. 2004); *Calderon v. Reno*, 39 F. Supp. 2d 943, 956 (N.D. Ill. 1998); *White v. Paulsen*, 997 F. Supp. 1380, 1383 (E.D. Wash. 1998). . . . The United States therefore enacted 18 U.S.C. §§2340-2340A of the United States Criminal Code pursuant to Articles 4 and 5 of the Convention. The Torture Convention Implementation Act ("Torture Act"), 18 U.S.C. §§2340 and 2340A, contains a definitional section, section 2340, and a section listing proscriptive elements and jurisdictional requirements, section 2340A.

The Torture Act states that "[w]hoever outside the United States commits or attempts to commit torture shall be fined . . . or imprisoned not more than 20 years, or both, and if death results . . . shall be punished by death or imprisoned for any term of years or for life." Federal courts have jurisdiction if "the alleged offender is a national of the United States; or the alleged offender is present in the United States, irrespective of the nationality of the victim or alleged offender." 18 U.S.C. §2340A(b). A person who conspires to commit an offense under the Act is subject to the same penalties prescribed for the offense under section 2340A(c).

Under the Torture Act, torture is defined in a slightly different manner from its definition in the Convention. Torture is defined in the Torture Act as "an act committed by a person acting under the color of law specifically intended to inflict severe physical or mental pain or suffering (other than pain or suffering incidental to lawful sanctions) upon another person within his custody or physical control." 18 U.S.C. §2340(1). "Severe mental pain or suffering" is

the prolonged mental harm caused by or resulting from—
    (A) the intentional infliction or threatened infliction of severe physical pain or suffering;
    (B) the administration or application, or threatened administration or application, of mind-altering substances or other procedures calculated to disrupt profoundly the senses or the personality;
    (C) the threat of imminent death; or
    (D) the threat that another person will imminently be subjected to death, severe physical pain or suffering, or the administration or application of mind-altering substances or other procedures calculated to disrupt profoundly the senses or personality.

18 U.S.C. §2340(2).

. . . Pursuant to Article 27 of the Convention, the Torture Act entered into force for the United States on November 20, 1994, thirty days after it was deposited for ratification with the United Nations. *See Xuncax*, 886 F. Supp. at 176 n.12. The conspiracy offense was added in the 2001 amendments. . . .

B. This Prosecution

On December 6, 2006, the Grand Jury returned an Indictment against Defendant, Charles Emmanuel, charging Defendant with conspiracy to commit, and the commission of acts of torture upon an unidentified person ("victim") in the country of Liberia. The Indictment alleges that Defendant was born in Boston, Massachusetts, was present in the United States as a result of his arrival at Miami International

Airport, and at relevant times, was present in the country of Liberia, located in West Africa. Because his father, Charles McArthur Taylor, was president of Liberia, Defendant allegedly had authority to command members of the Liberian Antiterrorist Unit and participated in activities of the Liberian security forces, including the Antiterrorist Unit, a Special Security Service, and the Liberian National Police. During 2002, Liberia had non-violent groups and armed rebel groups opposed to the presidency of Defendant's father.

Count One of the Indictment charges Defendant with knowingly conspiring with others to commit torture by conspiring with others to commit acts, under the color of law, with the specific intent to inflict severe physical pain and suffering upon a person within their custody and control. The object of the conspiracy was to obtain information from the alleged victim about actual, perceived, or potential opponents of the Taylor presidency by, *inter alia*, committing torture, in violation of Title 18, United States Code, §§2340A and 2340(1). The interrogation and torture are alleged to have taken place in various locations in Liberia, on or about July 24, 2002. Among other things, Defendant allegedly made the victim hold scalding water in his hands and repeatedly shocked the victim's genitalia and other body parts, and a co-conspirator poured scalding water on other locations of the victim's body, applied a hot iron to the victim's flesh, and rubbed salt into the victim's open wounds. All acts are alleged to violate 18 U.S.C. §2340A(c).

Count Two alleges that Defendant and others, while intending to inflict severe physical pain and suffering, committed and attempted to commit torture, while acting under color of law, by committing [the acts described above], in violation of 18 U.S.C. §§2340A and 2340(1), and 18 U.S.C. §2....

Defendant's Motion to Dismiss challenges the Indictment on several constitutional grounds. The "core problem with this case," according to Defendant, is that "the government seeks to oversee, through the open-ended terms of federal criminal law—the internal and wholly domestic actions of a foreign government." The essence of the challenge to the prosecution is the constitutional infirmity of 18 U.S.C. §2340A, a law that has been in place for over a decade, and under which Defendant is the first person to be prosecuted....

II. ANALYSIS

A. Congress' Power to Enact the Torture Act

To paraphrase Defendant, he argues that the Torture Act does not implement the Convention Against Torture, but rather, creates a different crime from the act of torture defined in the Convention. According to Defendant, the Torture Act has an expansive statutory prohibition of torture, where pain and suffering need not be inflicted for purposes of intimidation, coercion, or for obtaining a confession. That definition is at odds with the limited treaty terms, which define torture as an act by which severe pain or suffering is intentionally inflicted for such purposes as obtaining information or a confession when inflicted by a public official in an official capacity. Because the definition of torture in the Torture Act, in essence, a definition amounting to aggravated battery, does not track the treaty language, the definition varies sharply from the international understanding of torture as set forth in the Convention, and the statute thus cannot be said to effectuate, or be necessary to or proper for, compliance with the treaty.

Defendant's argument fails to persuade that Congress lacked authorization, under the Necessary and Proper Clause or the Offences Clause of Article I of the Constitution, to enact the Torture Act.

1. Necessary and Proper Clause and the Treaty Power

... Congress certainly had the authority to pass the Torture Act under the Necessary and Proper Clause of Article I, as an adjunct to the Executive's authority under Article II to enter into treaties, with the advice and consent of the Senate....

In determining the intended meaning of the parties, a court should look to a treaty's negotiating and drafting history, as well as the subsequent practice of the parties in their application of the treaty. *See Elcock v. United States*, 80 F. Supp. 2d 70, 78-79 (E.D.N.Y. 2000) (citations omitted). Also, because a treaty implicates questions of foreign policy, the construction given by the Executive Branch, although not binding on the court, is entitled to great weight. *See Factor v. Laubenheimer*, 290 U.S. 276, 295 (1933). Furthermore, "if a treaty fairly admits of two constructions, one restricting the rights that may be claimed under it, and the other enlarging it, the more liberal construction is to be preferred." *Id.* at 293-94. Lastly, a court is under a duty to interpret a statute in a manner consonant with treaty obligations, because "an act of Congress ought never to be construed to violate the law of nations, if any other possible construction remains...." *United States v. PLO*, 695 F. Supp. 1456, 1465 (S.D.N.Y. 1988) (quoting *Murray v. The Charming Betsy*, 6 U.S. (2 Cranch) 64, 118 (1804)).

When the Convention was ratified by the United States, it was explicitly ratified subject to certain understandings and restrictions. Those understandings and limitations were subsequently incorporated into the legislative scheme that effectuated it, including the statutory definition of torture. Defendant cites to no case that compels a finding that where legislation that implements a treaty varies from the language or scope of the treaty, it is constitutionally infirm, or is less necessary and proper to carry out the powers exercised by the Executive under Article II than legislation that mirrors verbatim the language used in the treaty....

Here, the definition of torture in the Torture Act admittedly does not "track the language of the Convention in all material respects." The statutory definition of torture does, however, parallel the definition found in the Convention, in that both texts define torture to include the intentional infliction of severe pain or suffering by a public official or person acting under color of law. The element missing from the statutory definition, that is, that the torture be inflicted for the purposes of obtaining a confession, for punishment, or for intimidation or coercion, does not take the Torture Act outside the authorization given Congress in the Necessary and Proper Clause. Indeed, the more expansive statutory definition, which captures more acts of torture than does the definition contained in the Convention, is consistent with the international community's near universal condemnation of torture and cruel, inhuman or degrading treatment, and is consistent with repeated calls for the international community to be more "effective [in] the struggle against torture." *Convention Preamble; see also Aldana v. Del Monte Fresh Produce, N.A., Inc.*, 416 F.3d 1242, 1247 (11th Cir. 2005) ("State-sponsored torture, unlike torture by private actors, likely violates international law....") (citation omitted)....

... [T]he Torture Act plainly bears a rational relationship to the stated objectives of the Convention, and thus passes constitutional muster under the Necessary and Proper Clause.

2. Offenses Clause

Alternatively, assuming Defendant was correct, and Congress' more expansive definition of torture took the Torture Act outside the realm of the Necessary and Proper Clause, one additional source of constitutional authority for the Torture Act may be found in Article I, §8, cl.10 of the Constitution, that is the "offences against the Law of Nations" Clause. That clause gives Congress the power "[t]o define and punish Piracies and Felonies on the high Seas, and Offences against the Law of Nations." *Id.* Because of the way the clause is written, and contrary to Defendant's proposed interpretation of it, Congress has the power to define and punish offenses against the law of nations, independent of any piracies or felonies that occur on the high seas. . . .

The prohibition against official torture has attained the status of a *jus cogens* norm, not merely the status of customary international law. *See* [*Siderman de Blake v. Republic of Argentina*, 965 F.2d 699, 714, 717 (9th Cir. 1992)] (collecting authorities). In reaching the not surprising conclusion that prohibition of official torture was a *jus cogens* norm, the Ninth Circuit explained:

> [W]e conclude that the right to be free from official torture is fundamental and universal, a right deserving of the highest status under international law, a norm of *jus cogens*. The crack of the whip, the clamp of the thumb screw, the crush of the iron maiden, and, in these more efficient modern times, the shock of the electric cattle prod are forms of torture that the international order will not tolerate. To subject a person to such horrors is to commit one of the most egregious violations of the personal security and dignity of a human being. That states engage in official torture cannot be doubted, but all states believe it is wrong, all that engage in torture deny it, and no state claims a sovereign right to torture its own citizens.

Id. at 717 (citations omitted).

It is beyond peradventure that torture and acts that constitute cruel, inhuman or degrading punishment, acts prohibited by *jus cogens*, are similarly abhorred by the law of nations. *See, e.g., Sosa v. Alvarez-Machain*, 542 U.S. 692, 732 (2004) ("'[F]or purposes of civil liability, the torturer has become — like the pirate and slave trader before him — *hostis humani generis*, an enemy of all mankind.'") (quoting *Filartiga v. Pena-Irala*, 630 F.2d 876, 890 (2d Cir. 1980)). Certainly the numerous international treaties and agreements, and several domestic statutes that contain varying proscriptions against torture, addressing both civil and criminal reparation, demonstrate the law of nations' repudiation of torture.

Over a century ago, the Supreme Court stated that "if the thing made punishable is one which the United States are required by their international obligations to use due diligence to prevent, it is an offense against the law of nations." *United States v. Arjona*, 120 U.S. 479, 488 (1887). In the present international community, it cannot be said that the Torture Act, legislation that criminalizes acts of torture by U.S. nationals or persons present in the United States, committed outside the United States, does not address an act made punishable by the Government's international obligations under the Convention, and which the Government is required to use due diligence to prevent. Thus, the Torture Act also finds constitutional protection as a law enacted by Congress to punish offences against the law of nations. . . .

D. Whether Sections 2340-2340A are Unconstitutionally Vague

Defendant argues that the Torture Act, 18 U.S.C. §§2340-2340A, does not give fair warning of what is outlawed, is void for vagueness, and therefore violates the Due Process Clause of the Fifth Amendment. Specifically, Defendant maintains that the definitions of "torture" and "severe mental pain or suffering," and the various terms used in those definitions, such as "acting under the color of law," and "incidental to lawful sanction," included in the Torture Act, 18 U.S.C. §2340, do "not provide the kind of notice that will allow ordinary people to understand what conduct is prohibited." Defendant also argues that because the statute is vague, a prosecutor may use it as a tool of foreign affairs, and it may consequently authorize or encourage arbitrary and discriminatory enforcement. Defendant challenges the Torture Act as vague on its face and as applied, and as additional support for his position regarding vagueness, Defendant submits with his Reply memorandum two Justice Department memoranda which offer varying interpretations of torture as defined in the Torture Act.[8]

. . . "Vagueness may invalidate a criminal statute if it either (1) fails 'to provide the kind of notice that will enable ordinary people to understand what conduct it prohibits' or (2) authorizes or encourages 'arbitrary and discriminatory enforcement.'" *United States v. Eckhardt,* 466 F.3d 938, 944 (11th Cir. 2006) (quoting *City of Chicago v. Morales,* 527 U.S. 41, 56 (1999) (citation omitted)); *see also* [*United States v. Hasner,* 340 F.3d 1261 (11th Cir. 2003),] at 1269 ("A statute is unconstitutionally vague if it fails to 'define the criminal offense with sufficient definiteness that ordinary people can understand what conduct is prohibited and in a manner that does not encourage arbitrary and discriminatory enforcement.'") (quoting *Kolender v. Lawson,* 461 U.S. 352, 357 (1983)). "[T]he presence of culpable intent as a necessary element of the offense does much to destroy any force in the argument" that a statute is unconstitutionally vague. *Boyce Motor Lines v. United States,* 342 U.S. 337, 342 (1952).

The Torture Statute contains specific intent as one of its elements, as it defines "torture" to be "an act committed by a person acting under the color of law specifically intended to inflict severe physical or mental pain or suffering. . . ." The Indictment informs Defendant that he and his coconspirators, acting under color of law and with the specific intent to inflict severe physical pain and suffering, burned the alleged victim's flesh with a hot iron, forced the alleged victim at gunpoint to hold scalding water in his hands, burned parts of the victim's body with scalding water, repeatedly shocked the genitalia and other parts of the body with an electrical device, and rubbed salt into the alleged victim's wounds. Such allegations, coupled with the statutory language contained in the Torture Statute, certainly advise the ordinary person of prohibited conduct with sufficient definiteness. The Torture Statute,

---

8. An August 1, 2002 memorandum from Assistant Attorney General Jay S. Bybee to Alberto R. Gonzales, then Counsel to the President, states, for example, that "certain acts may be cruel, inhuman, or degrading, but still not produce pain and suffering of the requisite intensity to fall within Section 2340A's proscription against torture." The memorandum goes on to examine possible defenses that would negate a claim that interrogation methods violate the statute. A December 30, 2004 Justice Department memorandum "supercedes" the August 2002 memorandum "in its entirety," because the discussion contained within the latter was "unnecessary."

enacted to fulfill the United States' treaty obligations with most of the countries of the world, certainly put the Defendant, a person born in the United States, on notice of conduct prohibited not only in this country, but in much of the civilized world. . . .

[The Court also held that, because the defendant is a U.S. citizen by birth, extraterritorial application of the Torture Statute does not violate Fifth Amendment Due Process Clause rights. Nor were his Sixth Amendment speedy trial or venue rights violated because, although his alleged crimes occurred years earlier in Liberia, the indictment was only months old and he had not shown that he would be unable to mount a constitutionally adequate defense in Miami.]

NOTES AND QUESTIONS

a.   The Convention Against Torture

1. *Interpreting the Convention Against Torture (CAT).* The torture ban in the CAT is explicit. Is the meaning of the prohibition clear? Note that the ban is unconditional: "No exceptional circumstances whatsoever, whether a state of war or a threat of war, internal political instability or any other public emergency, may be invoked as a justification of torture." CAT art. 2(2). Surely the CAT drafters were aware of the so-called "ticking bomb" scenario, in which torture is justified on grounds of saving lives in a crisis. Why do you suppose the CAT did not preserve an exception for the ticking bomb?

2. *Comparing the Definitions of Torture.* As noted in the *Charles Emmanuel* case, when the U.S. Senate gave its consent to the CAT in 1990, it attached a variety of reservations, declarations, and understandings. Included was an understanding about the meaning of the term "torture":

> . . . in order to constitute torture, an act must be specifically intended to inflict severe physical or mental pain or suffering and that mental pain or suffering refers to prolonged mental harm caused by or resulting from (1) the intentional infliction or threatened infliction of severe physical pain or suffering; (2) the administration or application, or threatened administration or application, of mind altering substances or other procedures calculated to disrupt profoundly the senses or the personality; (3) the threat of imminent death; or (4) the threat that another person will imminently be subjected to death, severe physical pain or suffering, or the administration or application of mind altering substances or other procedures calculated to disrupt profoundly the senses or personality.

Later, in its Initial Report to the U.N. Committee against Torture in 1999 (CAT/C/28/Add.5), the United States declared: "In 1994, Congress enacted a new federal law to implement the requirements of the Convention against Torture relating to acts of torture committed outside United States territory. . . . The statute adopts the Convention's definition of torture, consistent with the terms of United States ratification." *Id.* ¶47.

Compare the definitions of torture in the CAT, without the U.S. understanding, with the definition in the Torture Act, which is based on that understanding:

Convention Against Torture – Article 1(1)

For the purposes of this Convention, the term "torture" means any act by which severe pain or suffering, whether physical or mental, is intentionally inflicted on a person for such purposes as obtaining from him or a third person information or a confession, punishing him for an act he or a third person has committed or is suspected of having committed, or intimidating or coercing him or a third person, or for any reason based on discrimination of any kind, when such pain or suffering is inflicted by or at the instigation of or with the consent or acquiescence of a public official acting in an official capacity. It does not include pain or suffering arising only from, inherent in or incidental to lawful sanctions.

Torture Act. 18 U.S.C. §2340

As used in this chapter—
(1) "torture" means an act committed by a person acting under the color of law specifically intended to inflict severe physical or mental pain or suffering (other than pain or suffering incidental to lawful sanctions) upon another person within his custody or physical control;
(2) "severe mental pain or suffering" means the prolonged mental harm caused by or resulting from—
(A) the intentional infliction or threatened infliction of severe physical pain or suffering;
(B) the administration or application, or threatened administration or application, of mind-altering substances or other procedures calculated to disrupt profoundly the senses or the personality;
(C) the threat of imminent death; or
(D) the threat that another person will imminently be subjected to death, severe physical pain or suffering, or the administration or application of mind-altering substances or other procedures calculated to disrupt profoundly the senses or personality. . . .

How do the two authorities differ in their definitions of torture? How does the meaning of mental suffering differ?

Why would the Senate, in approving the CAT, and later Congress, in passing the Torture Act, have added a specific intent requirement to the definition? If causing pain is a purposeful means to the end of obtaining desired intelligence, is there a meaningful distinction between specific intent and knowledge of the consequences? Does an intention to gather intelligence (a legitimate purpose) somehow trump what would otherwise constitute specific intent to torture? If the interrogator specifically intends to cause suffering, does it matter legally why the interrogator causes the pain?

Can you say what interrogation techniques are permitted under the U.S. understanding about the definition of torture? Sleep deprivation? Starvation? Sensory deprivation or bombardment? Which of these, if any, would otherwise be forbidden by the CAT?

Would the Torture Act be improved by defining "the infliction of severe pain and suffering" as "the application of any physical stressors to detainees that are not applied to the detaining nation's own trainees in a nonpunitive setting"? *See* Michael W. Lewis, *A Dark Descent into Reality: Making the Case for an Objective Definition of Torture,* 67 Wash. & Lee L. Rev. 77, 119 (2010) (so arguing).

3. *The CAT and "Cruel, Inhuman, or Degrading Treatment."* Article 16 of the CAT requires that states "undertake to prevent . . . other acts of cruel, inhuman or degrading treatment or punishment which do not amount to torture." How does this requirement differ from the Convention's ban on torture?

One of the reservations attached to the CAT by the U.S. Senate provides that "the United States considers itself bound by the obligation under Article 16 to prevent 'cruel, inhuman or degrading treatment or punishment,' only insofar as [that term] means the cruel, unusual and inhumane treatment or punishment prohibited by the Fifth, Eighth, and/or Fourteenth Amendments to the Constitution of the United States." Resolution of Advice and Consent to the Ratification of the Convention Against Torture and Other Forms of Cruel, Inhuman or Degrading Treatment or Punishment ¶I(2), 136 Cong. Rec. S17,491 (Oct. 27, 1990). Why might the Senate have insisted on (and the President have supported) this reservation?

Why do you suppose that Congress failed to include criminal sanctions for cruel, inhuman, or degrading (CID) treatment in the Torture Act? How did this failure affect the U.S. obligation under the Torture Convention not to engage in such treatment?

4. *Deportation and the CAT.* Article 3 of the CAT explicitly prohibits any individual from being deported to a country where there are "substantial grounds for believing" that the individual would be in danger of being tortured. In *Khouzam v. Ashcroft,* 361 F.3d 161 (2d Cir. 2004), the Court overturned a Board of Immigration Appeals (BIA) decision that the abuse that Coptic Christian Khouzam would likely face from Egyptian police if deported to stand trial for an alleged murder does not amount to torture, because the police would not be acting with the consent or approval of government officials. The court acknowledged that the CAT excludes from the torture definition "suffering arising only from, inherent in or incidental to lawful sanctions," but the CAT also lists pain or suffering inflicted for the purpose of "obtaining a confession" as an example of torture. *Id.* The BIA apparently reasoned that cruel acts directed against Khouzam would not constitute torture because the abuse would be part of a lawful sanction. The court stated that it "would totally eviscerate the CAT to hold that once someone is accused of a crime it is a legal impossibility for any abuse inflicted on that person to constitute torture." *Id.* at 169. The court concluded that "torture requires only that government officials know of or remain willfully blind to an act and thereafter breach their legal responsibility to prevent it." *Id.* at 171.

5. *Aliens Held Abroad.* For the purposes of compliance with the CAT, would it matter where the mistreatment of a prisoner by U.S. officials took place? Suppose the CIA beats an alien abroad to force him to reveal the details of an anticipated terrorist

attack. Would such CIA conduct violate the CAT? If the measures of compliance with the CAT prohibition against "cruel, inhuman, or degrading treatment" are the Fifth, Eighth, and Fourteenth Amendments, as stated in the U.S. reservation upon ratification, do aliens held by the United States overseas have any protection from such treatment by U.S. officials under the CAT? *See United States v. Verdugo-Urquidez*, 494 U.S. 259 (1990) (holding Fourth Amendment inapplicable to the search abroad of an alien who lacks substantial connections to the United States); *Johnson v. Eisentrager*, 339 U.S. 763 (1950) (suggesting that the Fifth Amendment has no extraterroritorial application to aliens).

b. Incorporating the Geneva Conventions

1. *The War Crimes Act and Grave Breaches of the Geneva Conventions.* The four Geneva Conventions for the Protection of Victims of War, Aug. 12, 1949, *available at* http://www.icrc.org/Web/Eng/siteeng0.nsf/html/genevaconventions, regulate the treatment of noncombatants during armed conflict, including prisoners of war (POWs), the injured and sick, and civilians. See Chapter 2. The War Crimes Act (WCA), 18 U.S.C. §2441 (2006), provides criminal sanctions for, *inter alia*, "grave breaches" of the Geneva Conventions:

War Crimes Act
18 U.S.C. §2441 (2006)

(a) Offense. — Whoever, whether inside or outside the United States, commits a war crime, in any of the circumstances described in subsection (b), shall be fined under this title or imprisoned for life or any term of years, or both, and if death results to the victim, shall also be subject to the penalty of death.

(b) Circumstances. — The circumstances referred to in subsection (a) are that the person committing such war crime or the victim of such war crime is a member of the Armed Forces of the United States or a national of the United States....

(c) Definition. — As used in this section the term "war crime" means any conduct —

(1) defined as a grave breach in any of the international conventions signed at Geneva 12 August 1949, or any protocol to such convention to which the United States is a party... [or]

(3) which constitutes a grave breach of common Article 3....

Article 130 of Geneva Convention III on POWs defines a grave breach as

willful killing, torture or inhuman treatment, including biological experiments, willfully causing great suffering or serious injury to body or health, compelling a prisoner of war to serve in the forces of the hostile Power, or willfully depriving a prisoner of war of the rights of fair and regular trial prescribed in this Convention.

Before it was amended in 2006, War Crimes Act §2441(c)(3) defined as a war crime conduct that "constitutes a violation of common Article 3" of the Geneva Conventions. Common Article 3 reads in relevant part as follows:

Common Article 3, Geneva Conventions for the Protection of Victims of War

In the case of armed conflict not of an international character occurring in the territory of one of the High Contracting Parties, each Party to the conflict shall be bound to apply, as a minimum, the following provisions:

(1) Persons taking no active part in the hostilities, including members of armed forces who have laid down their arms and those placed *hors de combat* by sickness, wounds, detention, or any other cause, shall in all circumstances, be treated humanely, without any adverse distinction founded on race, color, religion or faith, sex, birth or wealth, or any other similar criteria.

To this end, the following acts are and shall remain prohibited at any time and in any place whatsoever with respect to the above-mentioned persons:

(a) violence to life and person, in particular murder of all kinds, mutilation, cruel treatment and torture; . . .

(c) outrages upon personal dignity, in particular humiliating and degrading treatment

(d) the passing of sentences and the carrying out of executions without previous judgment pronounced by a regularly constituted court, affording all the judicial guarantees which are recognized as indispensable by civilized peoples. . . . .

Applying the language of the Geneva Conventions, as incorporated through the pre- and post-2006 WCA, what threshold determinations must be made, and by whom?

a. *What Conduct Is Covered?* If not just "torture," however defined, but also "cruel treatment, . . . [and] outrages upon personal dignity, in particular humiliating and degrading treatment" are grave breaches under the Geneva Conventions, does it make sense to engage in hairsplitting definitional debates about permissible interrogation? For POWs, Article 17 of Geneva Convention III provides that "no physical or mental torture, nor any other form of coercion, may be inflicted on prisoners of war to secure from them information of any kind whatever." For protected civilians, Article 31 of Geneva Convention IV provides that "[n]o physical or moral coercion shall be exercised against [them], in particular to obtain information from them or from third parties." What interrogation techniques would be proscribed by these rules? *See* Jennifer K. Elsea, *Lawfulness of Interrogation Techniques Under the Geneva Conventions* 23-35 (Cong. Res. Serv. RL32567), Sept. 8, 2004.

b. *Are the Conventions Judicially Enforceable?* In *Hamdan v. Rumsfeld*, 548 U.S. 557 (2006), the Supreme Court held that Common Article 3 is applicable to the conflict with Al Qaeda in Afghanistan. Even though its protections fall "short of full protection under the Conventions," *id.* at 630, the Court ruled that Hamdan had to be tried by a "'regularly constituted court affording all the judicial guarantees which are recognized as indispensable by civilized peoples.'" *Id.* at 630, quoting from Common

Article 3(1)(d). Does it follow that the other provisions of Common Article 3 also apply to the conflict in Afghanistan?

In the next chapter, a case study of coercive interrogation in the war on terror provides an opportunity to apply the Geneva Conventions and WCA to actions of interrogators and their superiors in a range of settings.

2. *The International Covenant on Civil and Political Rights (ICCPR)*. The ICCPR, like the CAT, forbids torture and cruel, inhuman, and degrading conduct, and was approved as a treaty by the Senate. The ICCPR is non-self-executing, and lower federal courts have found that the ICCPR creates no privately enforceable rights in U.S. courts. *See Buell v. Mitchell*, 274 F.3d 337 (6th Cir. 2001). However, some courts cite the ICCPR as evidence that customary international law prohibits arbitrary arrest, prolonged detention, and torture. *See* Elsea, *supra*, at 12-13 (United States "has not officially proclaimed an emergency or named measures that would derogate from the ICCPR.").

3. *The Role of Customary International Law and Jus Cogens*. The substantive content of customary international law on the subject of torture is embodied in the CAT and ICCPR, among other instruments. The torture prohibition is also part of *jus cogens* and is so recognized by U.S. courts. *See Restatement (Third) of Foreign Relations Law of the United States* §702 (1986). It remains unclear, however, whether the prohibition against cruel, inhuman, or degrading treatment is also part of *jus cogens*.

c. **Domestic Law on Torture**

1. *A Domestic Baseline: How We Treat Our Own?* The U.S. reservation to Article 16 of the CAT limits "cruel, inhuman or degrading conduct" to that which violates that Fifth, Eighth, and/or Fourteenth Amendments. What is the content of those constitutional protections? For contrasting views, *see* Seth F. Kreimer, *Too Close to the Rack and the Screw: Constitutional Constraints on Torture in the War on Terror*, 6 U. Pa. J. Const. L. 278 (2003); and John T. Parry, *What Is Torture, Are We Doing It, and What If We Are?*, 64 U. Pitt. L. Rev. 237 (2003). It was not until 1936 that the Supreme Court barred the use in a state criminal trial of a confession obtained by brutally beating the suspects. In *Brown v. Mississippi*, 297 U.S. 278 (1936), the confessions were thrown out on the grounds that interrogation is part of the state machinery for obtaining convictions and is thus subject to the requirements of the Due Process Clause. In *Rogers v. Richmond*, 365 U.S. 534 (1961), the Court extended the Due Process Clause ban to abusive police conduct even where the reliability of a confession was not at issue.

In *Chavez v. Martinez*, 538 U.S. 760 (2003), a badly fractured Supreme Court ruled on claims of liability asserted by a plaintiff who had been subjected to persistent police questioning while he was in the hospital incapacitated by extreme pain. Five Justices voted to remand the question of whether the plaintiff could pursue a claim for violation of his substantive due process rights, but the Court could not agree about the scope and applicability of those rights or the related right against self-incrimination.

Three Justices joined in part of an opinion by Justice Thomas asserting that the interrogation was not egregious or conscience-shocking enough to violate the plaintiff's substantive due process rights. They reasoned that "freedom from unwanted police questioning is [not] a right so fundamental that it cannot be abridged absent a 'compelling state interest.'" *Id.* at 776. For them, it was enough that the questioning was justified by *some* government interest — here, the need to preserve critical evidence concerning a shooting by a police officer — and that it was not "conduct intended to injure in some way unjustifiable by any government interest." *Id.* at 775. Justice Stevens concluded that "the interrogation of respondent was the functional equivalent of an attempt to obtain an involuntary confession from a prisoner by torturous methods," which is "a classic example of a violation of a constitutional right 'implicit in the concept of ordered liberty.'" *Id.* at 788 (Stevens, J., concurring in part, dissenting in part).

Justice Kennedy (joined on this point by Justices Stevens and Ginsburg) agreed that the use of investigatory torture violates a person's fundamental right to liberty but noted that interrogating suspects who are in pain or anguish is not necessarily torture when the police have "legitimate reasons, borne of exigency... [such as] [l]ocating the victim of a kidnapping, ascertaining the whereabouts of a dangerous assailant or accomplice, or determining whether there is a rogue police officer." *Id.* at 796 (Kennedy, J., concurring in part, dissenting in part). On the other hand, he added, the police may not prolong or increase the suspect's suffering or threaten to do so to elicit a statement. The test for a constitutional violation, in Justice Kennedy's view, was whether the police "exploited" the suspect's pain to secure his statement. He found that they had done so in *Chavez.*

Under any of the tests in *Chavez* would torture in the United States of a suspected terrorist to obtain information about a possibly imminent terrorist attack violate substantive due process? How about practices such as hooding and sleep deprivation? Do military or civilian investigators in the war on terrorism have broader authority than the police do to use coercive interrogation techniques because of their different goals in an interrogation? *See* Marcy Strauss, *Torture,* 48 N.Y.L. Sch. L. Rev. 201, 251 (2003) (maintaining that it is unclear whether torture used to gain information violates the Fifth Amendment privilege against self-incrimination if the information is not used in a criminal prosecution; if so used, the right is violated).

Does the Eighth Amendment ban on "cruel and unusual punishment" supply an interpretive standard in the coercive interrogation context? If no judicially imposed punishment is contemplated by the interrogators, does the Eighth Amendment even apply? *See Ingraham v. Wright,* 430 U.S. 651, 671 n.40 (1977) ("[T]he State does not acquire the power to punish with which the Eighth Amendment is concerned until after it has secured a formal adjudication of guilt in accordance with due process of law.").

2. *A Congressional Prohibition.* In 2005, over the strenuous objection of the Bush administration, Congress enacted the Detainee Treatment Act, which provides in part:

Detainee Treatment Act

Pub. L. No. 109-148, §§1001-1006, 119 Stat. 2680, 2739-2744 (2005)

§1003. PROHIBITION ON CRUEL, INHUMAN, OR DEGRADING TREATMENT OR PUNISHMENT OF PERSONS UNDER CUSTODY OR CONTROL OF THE UNITED STATES GOVERNMENT.

(a) In General. — No individual in the custody or under the physical control of the United States Government, regardless of nationality or physical location, shall be subject to cruel, inhuman, or degrading treatment or punishment.

(b) Construction. — Nothing in this section shall be construed to impose any geographical limitation on the applicability of the prohibition against cruel, inhuman, or degrading treatment or punishment under this section.

(c) Limitation on Supersedure. — The provisions of this section shall not be superseded, except by a provision of law enacted after the date of the enactment of this Act which specifically repeals, modifies, or supersedes the provisions of this section.

(d) Cruel, Inhuman, or Degrading Treatment or Punishment Defined. — In this section, the term "cruel, inhuman, or degrading treatment or punishment" means the cruel, unusual, and inhumane treatment or punishment prohibited by the Fifth, Eighth, and Fourteenth Amendments to the Constitution of the United States, as defined in the United States Reservations, Declarations and Understandings to the United Nations Convention Against Torture and Other Forms of Cruel, Inhuman or Degrading Treatment or Punishment done at New York, December 10, 1984.

The same language appears in Pub. L. No. 109-163, §§1401-1406, 119 Stat. 3136, 3474-3480 (2006).

How important is the "regardless of nationality or physical location" language in determining the scope of the government's investigative authority and the rights of the detainee? The definition of "cruel, inhuman, or degrading treatment" mirrors that stated in the U.S. reservation to Article 16 of the CAT and covers only acts prohibited by the Fifth, Eighth, and Fourteenth Amendments. Does the Detainee Treatment Act thus require that persons (including aliens) in U.S. custody or control abroad not be subjected to treatment that would be unconstitutional if it occurred in the United States? If the meaning of the constitutional protections changes over time, the treatment forbidden by the Act presumably will change as well. How would you advise those responsible for supervising interrogations to keep abreast of their responsibilities?

3. *The Army Field Manual.* The Detainee Treatment Act also forbids exposure of persons in the custody or under the effective control of the Department of Defense (DOD) to any interrogation techniques not listed in the U.S. Army's field manual, *Intelligence Interrogation* (FM 34-52, Sept. 28, 1992). Pub. L. No. 109-148, §1002(a), 119 Stat. 2739; Pub. L. No. 109-163, §1402(a), 119 Stat. 3475. In September 2006, the Army replaced its 1992 manual with *Human Intelligence Collection Operations* (FM 2-22.3). The new field manual states that the only interrogation techniques permitted

are those it authorizes. The manual prohibits "any inhumane treatment — including abusive practices, torture, or cruel, inhuman, or degrading treatment or punishment" — and it asserts that "these unlawful and unauthorized forms of treatment are unproductive because they may yield unreliable results, damage subsequent collection efforts, and result in extremely negative consequences at national and international levels." *Id.* app. M-5. It also calls on non-DOD agencies that interrogate military detainees to follow its rules. FM 2-22.3 is considered again in a case study presented in the next chapter.

What is the legal significance of limiting DOD interrogators to techniques in an Army field manual? Why do you suppose that non-DOD interrogators are not subject to the same or some similar restrictions?

4. *The Military Commissions Act (MCA).* The Military Commissions Act of 2006 (MCA), Pub. L. No. 109-366, §6(b)(1)(A), 120 Stat. 2600, narrowed the offenses covered by the War Crimes Act by substituting a "grave breach" for a "violation" of Common Article 3. It also defined "grave breaches" to include "cruel or inhuman treatment," meaning "an act intended to inflict severe or serious physical or mental pain or suffering." *Id.* §6(b)(1)(B). Only "extreme" physical pain is covered. *Id.* The MCA did not criminalize degrading treatment. Nor did it specifically prohibit techniques such as waterboarding. It did, however, declare that the War Crimes Act, as amended, satisfies the U.S. obligation to punish grave breaches of Common Article 3, while authorizing the President to interpret the meaning and application of the Geneva Conventions. *Id.* §6(a)(2), (3). This added flexibility was supposed to allow the President to approve the CIA's use of "enhanced" interrogation techniques.

5. *The CIA.* On July 20, 2007, President Bush signed Executive Order 13,340, *Interpretation of the Geneva Conventions Common Article 3 as Applied to a Program of Detention and Interrogation Operated by the Central Intelligence Agency,* 72 Fed. Reg. 40,707. The executive order did not authorize the use of any particular interrogation techniques. Instead, it barred the CIA from certain practices, including those forbidden by the Torture Act, the DTA, and the MCA. However, the order did not proscribe techniques expressly prohibited from being used by the military under the 2006 Army Field Manual — such as waterboarding, hooding, sleep deprivation, or forced standing for long periods. President Obama revoked the Bush order in 2009:

Executive Order No. 13,491, Ensuring Lawful Interrogations
74 Fed. Reg. 4893 (Jan. 22, 2009)

By the authority vested in me by the Constitution and the laws of the United States of America, in order to improve the effectiveness of human intelligence-gathering, to promote the safe, lawful, and humane treatment of individuals in United States custody and of United States personnel who are detained in armed conflicts, to ensure compliance with the treaty obligations of the United States, including the Geneva Conventions, and to take care that the laws of the United States are faithfully executed, I hereby order as follows:

Section 1. Revocation.

Executive Order 13440 of July 20, 2007, is revoked. All executive directives, orders, and regulations inconsistent with this order, including but not limited to those issued to or by the Central Intelligence Agency (CIA) from September 11, 2001, to January 20, 2009, concerning detention or the interrogation of detained individuals, are revoked to the extent of their inconsistency with this order. . . .

Sec. 3. Standards and Practices for Interrogation of Individuals in the Custody or Control of the United States in Armed Conflicts.

(a) Common Article 3 Standards as a Minimum Baseline. Consistent with the requirements of the Federal torture statute, 18 U.S.C. 2340-2340A, section 1003 of the Detainee Treatment Act of 2005, 42 U.S.C. 2000dd, the Convention Against Torture, Common Article 3, and other laws regulating the treatment and interrogation of individuals detained in any armed conflict, such persons shall in all circumstances be treated humanely and shall not be subjected to violence to life and person (including murder of all kinds, mutilation, cruel treatment, and torture), nor to outrages upon personal dignity (including humiliating and degrading treatment), whenever such individuals are in the custody or under the effective control of an officer, employee, or other agent of the United States Government or detained within a facility owned, operated, or controlled by a department or agency of the United States.

(b) Interrogation Techniques and Interrogation-Related Treatment. Effective immediately, an individual in the custody or under the effective control of an officer, employee, or other agent of the United States Government, or detained within a facility owned, operated, or controlled by a department or agency of the United States, in any armed conflict, shall not be subjected to any interrogation technique or approach, or any treatment related to interrogation, that is not authorized by and listed in Army Field Manual 2-22.3 (Manual). Interrogation techniques, approaches, and treatments described in the Manual shall be implemented strictly in accord with the principles, processes, conditions, and limitations the Manual prescribes. Where processes required by the Manual, such as a requirement of approval by specified Department of Defense officials, are inapposite to a department or an agency other than the Department of Defense, such a department or agency shall use processes that are substantially equivalent to the processes the Manual prescribes for the Department of Defense. . . .

(c) Interpretations of Common Article 3 and the Army Field Manual. From this day forward, unless the Attorney General with appropriate consultation provides further guidance, officers, employees, and other agents of the United States Government may, in conducting interrogations, act in reliance upon Army Field Manual 2-22.3, but may not, in conducting interrogations, rely upon any interpretation of the law governing interrogation . . . issued by the Department of Justice between September 11, 2001, and January 20, 2009.

Sec. 4. Prohibition of Certain Detention Facilities, and Red Cross Access to Detained Individuals.

(a) CIA Detention. The CIA shall close as expeditiously as possible any detention facilities that it currently operates and shall not operate any such detention facility in the future.

(b) International Committee of the Red Cross Access to Detained Individuals. All departments and agencies of the Federal Government shall provide the International Committee of the Red Cross with notification of, and timely access to, any individual detained in any armed conflict in the custody or under the effective control of an officer, employee, or other agent of the United States Government or detained within a facility owned, operated, or controlled by a department or agency of the United States Government, consistent with Department of Defense regulations and policies. . . .

Sec. 6. Construction with Other Laws.

Nothing in this order shall be construed to affect the obligations of officers, employees, and other agents of the United States Government to comply with all pertinent laws and treaties of the United States governing detention and interrogation, including but not limited to: the Fifth and Eighth Amendments to the United States Constitution; the Federal torture statute, 18 U.S.C. 2340-2340A; the War Crimes Act, 18 U.S.C. 2441; the Federal assault statute, 18 U.S.C. 113; the Federal maiming statute, 18 U.S.C. 114; the Federal "stalking" statute, 18 U.S.C. 2261A; articles 93, 124, 128, and 134 of the Uniform Code of Military Justice, 10 U.S.C. 893, 924, 928, and 934; section 1003 of the Detainee Treatment Act of 2005, 42 U.S.C. 2000dd; section 6(c) of the Military Commissions Act of 2006, Public Law 109-366; the Geneva Conventions; and the Convention Against Torture. Nothing in this order shall be construed to diminish any rights that any individual may have under these or other laws and treaties. This order is not intended to, and does not, create any right or benefit, substantive or procedural, enforceable at law or in equity against the United States, its departments, agencies, or other entities, its officers or employees, or any other person.

In what respects does the Obama executive order change the law concerning interrogations for intelligence purposes? Is there any question of his constitutional authority to change the law, to the extent that he has? Are torture and cruel, inhuman, and degrading treatment now unlawful if carried out by any person working on behalf of the United States? How durable are the rules contained in the executive order? Should Congress codify them?

6. *Criminal Sanctions.* Why do you suppose Congress has not enacted a statute specifically outlawing torture within the United States?

The Uniform Code of Military Justice (UCMJ) provides for courts-martial to prosecute torture or inhumane acts committed within or outside the United States by members of the military and certain accompanying civilians. 10 U.S.C. §805 (UCMJ applies worldwide); *id.* §802 (to any service member); *id.* §802(a)(10) (to certain accompanying civilians); *id.* §818 (for an offense against the laws of war); *id.* §855 (torture or cruel or unusual punishment); *id.* §934 ("disorders and neglects to the prejudice of good order and discipline in the armed forces"). The admissibility in courts-martial of evidence concerning abusive interrogations is reviewed in Chapter 18.

7. *Criminal and Civil Defenses to Torture Actions.* One part of the Detainee Treatment Act, *supra* p. 535, provides a legal defense for U.S. personnel in any criminal or

civil action brought against them based on their involvement in an authorized inter-rogation of suspected foreign terrorists. The defense exists when the U.S. interroga-tor "did not know that the [interrogation] practices were unlawful and a person of ordinary sense and understanding would not know the practices were unlawful." Pub. L. No. 109-148, §1004(a), 119 Stat. 2740; Pub. L. No. 109-163, §1404, 119 Stat. 3475-3476. A good faith reliance on the advice of counsel may be "an important factor" in measuring the accused's culpability. *Id.* Could a claim of reliance on the memoran-dum from Stephen G. Bradbury, set out *supra* p. 514, thus immunize an interrogator from any liability?

8. *Civil Sanctions.* The Foreign Claims Act (FCA), 10 U.S.C. §2734(a) (2006), permits recovery of up to $100,000 from the United States for a claim brought by a resident of a foreign country where the injury occurred outside the United States "and is caused by, or is otherwise incident to [the] noncombat activities of" the U.S. military. *Id.* "Noncombat activity" is defined to include any "activity, other than combat, war or armed conflict, that is particularly military in character and has little parallel in the civilian community." 32 C.F.R. §842.41(c) (2010). Under the Act, claims commissions, consisting of commissioned officers, are established for each service branch and are in place wherever the military has a significant presence. However, experience with the FCA in Iraq and Afghanistan suggests that complex procedures and stringent policies have prevented most injured Afghans and Iraqis from obtaining compensation for their injuries. Scott Borrowman, *Sosa v. Alvarez-Machain and Abu Ghraib — Civil Remedies for Victims of Extraterritorial Torts by U.S. Military Personnel and Civilian Contractors*, 2005 BYU L. Rev. 371, 376; Lisa Magarrell & Lorna Peterson, *After Torture: U.S. Accountability and the Right to Redress* 14-15 (International Ctr. for Transitional Justice, Aug. 2010).

The Alien Tort Claims Act (ATCA), 28 U.S.C. §1350 (2006), confers jurisdiction on federal district courts over tort suits by aliens where a violation of the law of nations or a treaty of the United States is alleged. In *Sosa v. Alvarez-Machain*, 542 U.S. 692 (2004), the Supreme Court rejected the ATCA as a basis for jurisdiction in the federal courts over a tort claim related to the abduction of one Mexican national by another who acted with the approval of the Drug Enforcement Administration (DEA). The Court reasoned that the ATCA was intended to create jurisdiction to hear suits based on current international norms, but only those whose "content and acceptance among civilized nations" is no less definite than the small number of "historical paradigms" familiar when the statute was passed in 1789. *Id.* at 718. In the course of its opinion, however, the Court cited with evident approval the decision in *Filartiga v. Peña-Irala*, 630 F.2d 876 (2d Cir. 1980), which applied the ATCA in a torture case.

The Torture Victim Protection Act (TVPA), Pub. L. No. 102-256, 106 Stat. 73 (1992), codified at 28 U.S.C. §1350 note (2006), provides a civil remedy in the federal courts for individuals, including U.S. persons, who have been victims of torture or extrajudicial killing. The TVPA thus may offer relief for U.S. persons that would be unavailable under the ATCA. However, the TVPA only provides a cause of action for torture or extrajudicial killing "under color of law, of any foreign nation." *Id.* §2a. Do you think that the TVPA would support an action for improper removal by U.S. officials of an individual who might be subjected to torture abroad? Would it apply where U.S. officials allegedly direct foreign officials to carry out acts of torture against a non-U.S. citizen? *See Arar v. Ashcroft, infra* p. 567.

Case Study: Coercive Interrogation by U.S. Forces After 9/11

18

As early as December 2002, U.S. military and civilian interrogators are reported to have abused individuals captured and detained in the war on terrorism by beating them and subjecting them to prolonged sleep and sensory deprivation, as well as to sexual humiliation. The abuse began in Afghanistan, then spread to Guantánamo Bay, Cuba, and other offshore U.S. interrogation centers, and later to Iraq. Several investigations of these abuses revealed that serious injuries and deaths occurred among the detainees.

Our objective in Part A of this chapter is to tell the interrogation story from September 11 through the Abu Ghraib scandal in 2004, with pertinent updates to the present. Next, in Part B, we apply laws reviewed in the previous chapter to the interrogation of persons in U.S. custody after 9/11. We also try to determine whether the President enjoys constitutional or other powers that would excuse him from compliance with the rules.

A. THE EVOLVING HISTORY OF INTERROGATION OF SUSPECTED TERRORISTS[1]

In October 1996, Secretary of Defense William Perry spoke at a meeting of Western Hemisphere defense ministers in Argentina. Responding to criticisms of so-called "torture manuals" used to train Latin American intelligence officers at the U.S. Army School of the Americas in the 1980s and to a 1996 Intelligence Oversight Board report describing intelligence activities in Latin America, Perry said he was shocked when he found out about the manuals. He also declared that the Defense

---

1. Several collections of documents relating to U.S. interrogation of its detainees may be found online. Among the most extensive are New York Times, *A Guide to the Memos on Torture* (n.d.), *at* http://www. nytimes.com/ref/international/24MEMO-GUIDE.html; National Sec. Archive, *Torturing Democracy* (2008), *available at* http://www.gwu.edu/~nsarchiv/torturingdemocracy/timelines/index2.html; and American Civil Liberties Union, National Security Project, *Torture Report* (updated regularly), *at* http:// www.thetorturereport.org/node/1. The Department of Defense Web site also provides links to DOD reports, independent panel and inspector general reports, briefing transcripts, and news releases and articles, *at* http://www.defense.gov/news/detainee_investigations.html. Many of the key documents are collected in Mark Danner, *Torture and Truth: America, Abu Ghraib, and the War on Terror* (2004); and *The Torture Papers: The Road to Abu Ghraib* (Karen J. Greenberg & Joshua L. Dratel eds., 2005).

Department would never again advocate torture or other inhumane treatment in its training programs.[2]

Secretary Perry's assertion could not have taken into account September 11 and the war on terrorism that followed. Vice President Dick Cheney appeared on *Meet the Press* on the Sunday immediately after the attacks. Asked how the Administration planned to respond to the continuing threat of terrorism, the Vice President said that the United States would "have to work on the dark side . . . [and] use any means at our disposal."[3] According to Cofer Black, former director of the Central Intelligence Agency's (CIA's) counterterrorism unit, "after 9/11, the gloves came off."[4]

Beginning with the capture in Afghanistan of senior Al Qaeda operatives, the Bush administration had to determine how best to extract intelligence information from individuals detained by U.S. forces. "Setting" the methods and parameters of interrogation thus became an integral part of counterterrorism planning. Should Al Qaeda figures be questioned by the FBI, using traditional methods? By military interrogators, following service branch rules? By the CIA, perhaps using harsher techniques in secret locations?

Answering these questions became intensely political and legally contentious inside the Bush administration. Interrogations were conducted by both military and CIA personnel. At times the two sets of interrogators operated separately, at other times they were co-located, and military personnel often had responsibility for capturing and holding the suspects who were later subject to CIA interrogation. As a result, the two intelligence-gathering efforts tended to overlap if not merge. Meanwhile, the Administration's early legal guidance on interrogation was prepared for the CIA, but DOD then relied on some of the analysis in those memoranda to develop guidance for its own military interrogators. When abusive interrogations by U.S. officials began to be revealed, Congress adopted reforms that covered the military, but apparently not the CIA. Thus, as you review this narrative and questions that follow, recall that CIA and DOD interrogators were sometimes subject to different legal regimes, but that their practices were part of an overlapping and evolving legal picture that remained murky for years.

The Bush administration decided early on to detain indefinitely a number of persons seized in Afghanistan and elsewhere and to create a new detention facility at the U.S. Navy base at Guantánamo Bay to hold at least some of them. The first detainees taken there in January 2002 were designated "unlawful combatants" by President Bush.

Meanwhile, the President directed the CIA to detain and interrogate certain "high value" terrorism suspects. Because of statutory authorities said to enable the CIA to operate in secret (see *supra* Chapter 5), the Administration apparently believed it could hold detainees in secret prisons where no one would know who was being held or what the CIA was doing to them while detained. On September 17, 2001, President Bush authorized the CIA to rely on paramilitary forces to capture, detain, and interrogate suspected terrorists.[5] Yet the directive did not provide guidance on detention or interrogation, and because the CIA had little interrogation

2. Linda D. Kozaryn, *Perry Bans U.S. Training in Inhumane Techniques*, American Forces Information Serv., Oct. 9, 1996, *available at* http://osd.dtic.mil/news/Oct1996/n10091996_9610095.html.
3. Jane Mayer, *The Dark Side: The Inside Story of How the War on Terror Turned into a War on American Ideals* 9-10 (2008).
4. John Barry, Michael Hirsh & Michael Isikoff, *The Roots of Torture*, Newsweek, May 24, 2004, at 26.
5. David Johnston, *At a Secret Interrogation, Dispute Flared over Tactics*, N.Y. Times, Sept. 10, 2006.

experience,[6] the Agency sought guidance from decades-old manuals describing a "survive, evade, resist, escape" (SERE) program used in training U.S. service personnel to withstand the effects of torture.[7]

As U.S. forces began to detain fighters in Afghanistan in late 2001, those not held by the military and sent to Guantánamo, the so called "high-value" detainees, were held by the CIA. In early 2002, senior Al Qaeda operative Abu Zubaydah was captured in a firefight and flown to a secret CIA facility in Thailand. After the Federal Bureau of Investigation (FBI) interrogated Zubaydah in a non-coercive manner and learned that Khalid Sheikh Mohammed (KSM) was the apparent mastermind of the September 11 attacks, Zubaydah began to resist interrogation. The CIA then took over interrogation and subjected Zubaydah to waterboarding, reportedly ending his resistance. Eventually Zubaydah was moved to another CIA site in Poland and then to Guantánamo.[8] KSM was captured in March 2003 in Pakistan, then transported to Afghanistan and subsequently to the CIA site in Poland, where he was waterboarded and otherwise subjected to harsh interrogation techniques.[9] The CIA Inspector General later found that the CIA waterboarded Zubaydah 83 times in August 2002, and employed the same technique with KSM 183 times in March 2003.[10]

The President announced in a February 7, 2002, order, *Humane Treatment of Al Qaeda and Taliban Detainees,*[11] that the United States would voluntarily extend the protections of the Third Geneva Convention to captured Taliban fighters, although such fighters were not regarded as unlawful combatants entitled to prisoner-of-war (POW) status. Captured members of Al Qaeda would be treated "humanely," even though the Geneva Conventions were said not to apply to Al Qaeda members at all. This followed advice in a January 9, 2002, memorandum from the Justice Department Office of Legal Counsel (OLC) to the Defense Department, *Application of Treaties and Laws to Al Qaeda and Taliban Detainees,*[12] written by John Yoo and Robert Delahunty, concluding that the President had constitutional authority to suspend application of the Geneva Conventions in Afghanistan, or to decide that the Conventions did not apply to captured Al Qaeda and Taliban detainees. The "humane treatment" order applied only to the armed forces, however, not the CIA, which presumably was free to continue utilizing interrogation techniques described above and in the previous chapter.

In the summer of 2002, the Justice Department was asked to advise what interrogation techniques would violate U.S. or international law. In August, the OLC opined that

> for an act to constitute torture as defined in [the Torture Act], it must inflict pain that is difficult to endure. Physical pain amounting to torture must be equivalent in intensity to the pain accompanying serious physical injury, such as organ failure, impairment of

---

6. Mayer, *supra*, at 144-145.

7. Scott Shane, David Johnston & James Risen, *Secret U.S. Endorsement of Severe Interrogations,* N.Y. Times, Oct. 4, 2007.

8. Johnston, *supra* n.4; Scott Shane, *Inside a 9/11 Mastermind's Interrogation,* N.Y. Times, June 22, 2008.

9. Mayer, *supra* n.3, at 270-274.

10. *See* Office of Inspector Gen., Central Intelligence Agency, *Special Review: Counterterrorism Detention and Interrogation Activities (September 2001-October 2003)* 12-23, 44-45 (May 7, 2004), *at* http://luxmedia. com.edgesuite.net/aclu/IG_Report.pdf.

11. *Reprinted in The Torture Papers, supra* n.1, at 134.

12. *Reprinted id.* at 38.

bodily function, or even death. For purely mental pain or suffering to amount to torture . . . it must result in significant psychological harm of significant duration, e.g., lasting for months or even years. We conclude that the mental harm also must result from one of the predicate acts listed in the statute, namely: threats of imminent death; threats of the infliction of the kind of pain that would amount to physical torture; infliction of such physical pain as a means of psychological torture; use of drugs or other procedures designed to deeply disrupt the senses, or fundamentally alter an individual's personality; or threatening to do any of these things to a third party.[13]

The memorandum suggested that a one-time kick to a prisoner's stomach with military boots while forcing him into a kneeling position would not amount to "torture" that would be subject to prosecution. The OLC memorandum even concluded that torture might be justified in some circumstances, and that the statutory prohibition on torture would not apply to actions taken by the President as Commander in Chief. *Id.* at 33-39.

By the summer of 2002, there were about 600 detainees at Guantánamo. Military interrogators there knew from the President's order that the Geneva Convention POW protections did not apply, and that detainees should be treated "humanely," but they had no clear guidance on the limits of their interrogations other than the statutes reviewed in the last chapter. Reacting to what was characterized as "tenacious resistance by some detainees to existing interrogation methods,"[14] in October 2002 the commander at Guantánamo Bay sought permission to use new interrogation techniques that were more coercive than those authorized in the Army Field Manual, including the "use of stress positions (like standing), for a maximum of four hours"; isolation for up to 30 days; "deprivation of light and auditory stimuli"; hooding; removal of clothing; "forced grooming (shaving of facial hair, etc.)"; and using "fear of dogs . . . to induce stress."[15] A separate legal opinion by Army Lieutenant Colonel Diane Beaver evaluated a range of even more aggressive techniques — from exposure to cold weather or water to threats of death or severe pain to inducing the "misperception of asphyxiation" and "mild noninjurious physical contact."[16] Lieutenant Colonel Beaver found that these techniques were consistent with existing legal standards if they could "plausibly have been thought necessary . . . to achieve a legitimate governmental objective" and the force was applied "in a good faith effort and not maliciously or sadistically for the very purpose of causing harm."[17]

By December 2002, the media began reporting that so-called "stress and duress" tactics or "high pressure methods" were being used in secret detention centers overseas by Defense Department and CIA interrogators in pursuit of "actionable intelligence." Those methods included forcing detainees to stand or kneel for hours in

13. Office of Legal Counsel, U.S. Dep't of Justice, *Memorandum for Alberto R. Gonzales, Counsel to the President, Re: Standards of Conduct for Interrogation Under 18 U.S.C. §§2340-2340A,* at 1 (Aug. 1, 2002) (commonly referred to as the Bybee Memo, for Assistant Attorney General Jay S. Bybee, who signed it), *available at* http://www.gwu.edu/~nsarchiv/NSAEBB/NSAEBB127/02.08.01.pdf. The "organ failure" passage relies on public health statutes of questionable applicability to the interrogation setting.

14. *Final Report of the Independent Panel to Review DoD Detention Operations* 35 (Aug. 24, 2004) (hereinafter *Schlesinger Report*), *at* http://www.defense.gov/news/Aug2004/d20040824finalreport.pdf.

15. Memorandum for Chairman of the Joint Chiefs of Staff from James T. Hill, General, U.S. Army, *Counter-Resistance Techniques* (Oct. 25, 2002), *available at* http://www.gwu.edu/~nsarchiv/NSAEBB/NSAEBB127/02.10.25.pdf.

16. Diane E. Beaver, Joint Task Force 170, Department of Def., *Legal Brief on Proposed Counter-Resistance Strategies* (Oct. 11, 2002), *available at* http://www.gwu.edu/~nsarchiv/NSAEBB/NSAEBB127/02.10.11.pdf.

17. *Id.*

black hoods or spray-painted goggles, bombarding the detainees with lights 24 hours a day, withholding painkillers from wounded detainees, confining them in tiny rooms or binding them in painful positions, subjecting them to loud noises, and depriving them of sleep.[18] A special interrogation plan was authorized for high-value detainee Mohammed al-Qahtani, known then as the "twentieth hijacker" because he sought entry to the United States shortly before 9/11 after communicating with the hijackers. Apparently feeling unconstrained by Geneva Convention limits, interrogators went even further with Qahtani. They isolated him and interrogated him for up to 20 hours per day, threatened him with dogs, and subjected him to sexual humiliation.[19] A June 2004 statement from the Department of Defense confirmed that similarly harsh interrogation techniques were approved by Secretary Donald Rumsfeld on December 2, 2002, for general use in Guantánamo but were rescinded on January 15, 2003.[20] An August 2004 Army report found that interrogators in Afghanistan employed similar techniques beginning in December 2002.[21]

By early 2003, the apparent failure to obtain useful information from certain detainees at Guantánamo led Defense Secretary Rumsfeld to charge an "Interrogation Working Group" of senior Defense Department lawyers to develop guidance on parameters for interrogation. In April 2003, the Working Group, echoing the earlier Bybee Memo, advised that the President as Commander in Chief could authorize torture despite legal prohibitions. Secretary Rumsfeld's response to the Working Group's report is set forth below. The designation "(U)" means unclassified.

Counter-Resistance Techniques in the War on Terrorism

April 16, 2003
http://www.defense.gov/news/Jun2004/d20040622doc9.pdf

Memorandum for: Commander, US Southern Command

From: Donald Rumsfeld, Secretary of Defense

(U) I have considered the report of the Working Group that I directed be established on January 15, 2003.

(U) I approve the use of specified counter-resistance techniques, subject to the following:

(U) a. The techniques I authorize are those lettered A-X, set out at Tab A.

(U) b. These techniques must be used with all the safeguards described at Tab B.

(U) c. Use of these techniques is limited to interrogations of unlawful combatants held at Guantanamo Bay, Cuba.

---

18. *See* Dana Priest & Barton Gellman, *U.S. Decries Abuse But Defends Interrogations*, Wash. Post, Dec. 26, 2002.
19. *Army Regulation 15-6 Final Report: Investigation of FBI Allegations of Detainee Abuse at Guantanamo Bay, Cuba Detention Facility*, amended June 9, 2005, *reprinted in Administration of Torture: A Documentary Record from Washington to Abu Ghraib and Beyond* A-98, A-110-A-118 (Jameel Jaffer & Amrit Singh eds., 2007).
20. Department of Def. News Release, *DoD Provides Details on Interrogation Process* (June 22, 2004), *available at* http://www.defense.gov/releases/release.aspx?releaseid=7487.
21. Maj. Gen. George R. Fay, *AR 15-6 Investigation of the Abu Ghraib Prison and 205th Military Intelligence Brigade* 29 (Aug. 25, 2004) (hereinafter *Fay Report*), *at* http://www.dod.gov/news/Aug2004/d20040825fay.pdf.

(U) d. Prior to the use of these techniques, the Chairman of the Working Group on Detainee Interrogations in the Global War on Terrorism must brief you and your staff.

(U) I reiterate that US Armed Forces shall continue to treat detainees humanely and, to the extent appropriate and consistent with military necessity, in a manner consistent with the principles of the Geneva Conventions. In addition, if you intend to use techniques B, I, O, or X, you must specifically determine that military necessity requires its use and notify me in advance.

(U) If, in your view, you require additional interrogation techniques for a particular detainee, you should provide me, via the Chairman of the Joint Chiefs of Staff, a written request describing the proposed technique, recommended safeguards, and the rationale for applying it with an identified detainee.

(U) Nothing in this memorandum in any way restricts your existing authority to maintain good order and discipline among detainees.

TAB A. INTERROGATION TECHNIQUES

(U) The use of techniques A-X is subject to the general safeguards as provided below as well as specific implementation guidelines to be provided by the appropriate authority. Specific implementation guidance with respect to techniques A-Q is provided in Army Field Manual 34-52. Further implementation guidance with respect to techniques R-X will need to be developed by the appropriate authority.

(U) Of the techniques set forth below, the policy aspects of certain techniques should be considered to the extent those policy aspects reflect the views of other major U.S. partner nations. Where applicable, the description of the technique is annotated to include a summary of the policy issues that should be considered before application of the technique.

A. (U) Direct: Asking straightforward questions.

B. (U) Incentive/Removal of Incentive: Providing a reward or removing a privilege, above and beyond those that are required by the Geneva Convention, from detainees. (Caution: Other nations that believe that detainees are entitled to POW protections may consider that provision and retention of religious items (e.g., the Koran) are protected under international law (see, Geneva III, Article 34). Although the provisions of the Geneva Convention are not applicable to the interrogation of unlawful combatants, consideration should be given to these views prior to the application of the technique.)

C. (U) Emotional Love: Playing on the love a detainee has for an individual or group.

D. (U) Emotional Hate: Playing on the hatred a detainee has for an individual or group.

E. (U) Fear Up Harsh: Significantly increasing the fear level in a detainee.

F. (U) Fear Up Mild: Moderately increasing the fear level in a detainee.

G. (U) Reduced Fear: Reducing the fear level in a detainee.

H. (U) Pride and Ego Up: Boosting the ego of a detainee.

I. (U) Pride and Ego Down: Attacking or insulting the ego of a detainee, not beyond the limits that would apply to a POW. (Caution: Article 17 of the Geneva III provides, "Prisoners of war who refuse to answer may not be threatened, insulted, or exposed to any unpleasant or disadvantageous treatment of any kind." Other nations that believe that detainees are entitled to POW protections may consider this technique inconsistent with the provisions of Geneva. Although the provisions of Geneva are not applicable to the interrogation of unlawful combatants, consideration should be given to these views prior to application of the technique.)

J. (U) Futility: Invoking the feeling of futility of a detainee.

K. (U) We Know All: Convincing the detainee that the interrogator knows the answer to questions he asks the detainee.

L. (U) Establish Your Identity: Convincing the detainee that the interrogator has mistaken the detainee for someone else.

M. (U) Repetition Approach: Continuously repeating the same question to the detainee within interrogation periods of normal duration.

N. (U) File and Dossier: Convincing the detainee that the interrogator has a damning and inaccurate file, which must be fixed.

O. (U) Mutt and Jeff: A team consisting of a friendly and harsh interrogator. The harsh interrogator might employ the Pride and Ego Down technique. (Caution: Other nations that believe that POW protections apply to detainees may view this technique as inconsistent with the Geneva III, Article 13 which provides that POWs must be protected against acts of intimidation. Although the provisions of Geneva are not applicable to the interrogation of unlawful combatants, consideration should be given to these views prior to application of the technique.)

P. (U) Rapid Fire: Questioning in rapid succession without allowing detainee to answer.

Q. (U) Silence: Staring at the detainee to encourage discomfort.

R. (U) Change of Scenery Up: Removing the detainee from the standard interrogation setting (generally to a location more pleasant, but no worse).

S. (U) Change of Scenery Down: Removing the detainee from the standard interrogation setting and placing him in a setting that may be less comfortable; would not constitute a substantial change in environmental quality.

T. (U) Dietary Manipulation: Changing the diet of a detainee; no intended deprivation of food or water; no adverse medical or cultural effect and without intent to deprive subject of food or water, e.g., hot rations to MREs.

U. (U) Environmental Manipulation: Altering the environment to create moderate discomfort (e.g., adjusting temperature or introducing an unpleasant smell). Conditions would not be such that they would injure the detainee. Detainee would be accompanied by interrogator at all times. (Caution: Based on court cases in other countries, some nations may view application of this technique in certain circumstances to be inhumane. Consideration of these views should be given prior to use of this technique.)

V. (U) Sleep Adjustment: Adjusting the sleeping times of the detainee (e.g., reversing sleep cycles from night to day.) This technique is NOT sleep deprivation.

W. (U) False Flag: Convincing the detainee that individuals from a country other than the United States are interrogating him.

X. (U) Isolation: Isolating the detainee from other detainees while still complying with basic standards of treatment. (Caution: The use of isolation as an interrogation technique requires detailed implementation instructions, including specific guidelines regarding the length of isolation, medical and psychological review, and approval for extensions of the length of isolation by the appropriate level in the chain of command. This technique is not known to have been generally used for interrogation purposes for longer than 30 days. Those nations that believe detainees are subject to POW protections may view use of this technique as inconsistent with the requirements of Geneva III, Article 13 which provides that POWs must be protected against acts of intimidation; Article 14 which provides that POWs are entitled to respect for their person; Article 34 which prohibits coercion and Article 126 which ensures access and basic standards of treatment. Although the provisions of Geneva are not applicable to the interrogation of unlawful combatants, consideration should be given to these views prior to application of the technique.)

TAB B. GENERAL SAFEGUARDS

(U) Application of these interrogation techniques is subject to the following general safeguards: (i) limited to use only at strategic interrogation facilities; (ii) there is a good basis to believe that the detainee possesses critical intelligence; (iii) the detainee is medically and operationally evaluated as suitable (considering all techniques to be used in combination); (iv) interrogators are specifically trained for the technique(s); (v) a specific interrogation plan (including reasonable safeguards, limits on duration, intervals between applications, termination criteria and the presence or availability of qualified medical personnel) has been developed; (vi) there is appropriate supervision; and (vii) there is appropriate specified senior approval for use with any specific detainee (after considering the foregoing and receiving legal advice). . . .

After the United States and its allies invaded Iraq in March 2003, there reportedly was widespread confusion about permissible techniques for interrogating prisoners there. The Geneva Conventions clearly applied in Iraq to captured Iraqis, but the detention facilities also included members of Al Qaeda and other foreign fighters whose status was unclear, based on Administration determinations concerning those held at Guantanamo. A March 14, 2003, OLC opinion written by John Yoo, *Military Interrogation of Alien Unlawful Combatants Held Outside the United States,*[22] contains extensive analysis of supposed broad authorities of the President to make rules for interrogation that fail to comply with either the CAT or the Geneva Conventions. The opinion also suggested defenses that the President would have available if any executive official were charged with abusive interrogation. The opinion failed, however, to take into account application of the Uniform Code of Military Justice (UCMJ) or the Army Field Manual.

The U.S. military command authority initially ordered that standard Field Manual 34-52 rules be followed. In August 2003, however, Defense Secretary Rumsfeld sent the military overseer of interrogation at Guantánamo, Major General Geoffrey Miller, to Iraq to "rapidly exploit internees for actionable intelligence."[23] General Miller brought with him the list of techniques approved by Secretary Rumsfeld for Guantánamo, some of which exceeded the limits of the Army

---

22. *Available at* http://www.justice.gov/olc/docs/memo-combatantsoutsideunitedstates.pdf.
23. General Antonio M. Taguba, *Article 15-6 Investigation of the 800th Military Police Brigade* 7 (Jan. 31, 2004) (hereinafter *Taguba Report*), *available at* http://news.findlaw.com/hdocs/docs/iraq/tagubarpt.html.

Field Manual, although he noted that the Geneva Conventions were supposed to apply in Iraq. In September, the military commander in Iraq approved a policy on interrogation that included portions of the Guantánamo policy and elements of policies then used by special forces.[24] Central Command disapproved the September policy, however, and in October approved rules that mirrored an outdated version of Field Manual 34-52, which permitted interrogators to control "lighting and heating, as well as food, clothing, and shelter given to detainees."[25] The policy on interrogation in Iraq changed again later in October, the third amendment in less than 30 days.[26]

In January 2004, following public reports of detainee abuse, Lieutenant General Ricardo S. Sanchez, Commander of Combined Joint Task Force Seven in Iraq, requested an investigation of the operations of the 800th Military Police Brigade, the unit in charge of Abu Ghraib prison near Baghdad. Major General Antonio M. Taguba, who was appointed to conduct the investigation, found "numerous incidents of sadistic, blatant, wanton criminal abuses" at the prison, "intentionally perpetrated by several members of the military police guard force." The abuses included "punching, slapping, and kicking detainees," a litany of sexual and vulgar insults and attacks, and threats with loaded weapons.[27] In February 2004, the International Committee of the Red Cross (ICRC) issued a report detailing a number of serious human rights abuses by coalition forces in Iraq between March and November 2003.[28] A March 2004 classified report by the CIA Inspector General concluded that some of the interrogation techniques approved for CIA use by the Department of Justice in 2002 might violate the prohibition on "cruel, inhuman, or degrading" treatment in the Convention Against Torture.[29] Finally, in May 2004, public attention focused on Abu Ghraib after graphic photos of prisoner abuse were exposed by the media.[30]

In June 2004, the OLC memos were leaked. In August 2004, the American Bar Association condemned "any use of torture or other cruel, inhuman, or degrading treatment or punishment upon persons within the custody or under the physical control of the United States government [and] any endorsement or authorization of such measures by government lawyers."[31]

Two months after the public disclosure of abuses at Abu Ghraib, the August 2002 Bybee Memo, *supra* n.13, was withdrawn by OLC head Jack Goldsmith because he thought it was "sloppily reasoned, overbroad, and incautious in asserting

24. Subsequent investigators described a migration to Iraq of Guantánamo techniques—such as the use of dogs and forced nudity—to intimidate and dehumanize detainees. *See Schlesinger Report, supra* n.13, at 36; *Fay Report, supra* n.21, at 10.

25. *Schlesinger Report, supra* n.14, at 37-38; *see* Department of the Army, *Intelligence Interrogation* (FM 34-52) ch. 3 (Sept. 28, 1992).

26. *Fay Report, supra* n.21, at 28.

27. *Taguba Report, supra* n.23.

28. *Report of the International Committee of the Red Cross (ICRC) on the Treatment by the Coalition Forces of Prisoners of War and Other Protected Persons by the Geneva Conventions in Iraq During Arrest, Internment and Interrogation* (Feb. 2004), *available at* http://www.informationclearinghouse.info/pdf/icrc_iraq.pdf.

29. Douglas Jehl, *Report Warned on CIA's Tactics in Interrogation*, N.Y. Times, Nov. 9, 2005.

30. The Abu Ghraib photos are collected at http://www.salon.com/news/abu_ghraib/2006/03/14/introduction. In November 2009, Secretary of Defense Robert Gates blocked the release of 2,000 additional photos depicting detainee abuse in Iraq and Afghanistan. Gates acted on the basis of authority granted in a Department of Homeland Security Appropriations Act. *Gates Blocks Detainee Abuse Photos* (CBS News, Nov. 14, 2009), *at* http://www.cbc.ca/news/world/story/2009/11/14/prisoner-abuse-photos014.html.

31. ABA House of Delegates, *Resolution 10-B* (Aug. 9, 2004).

extraordinary constitutional authorities on behalf of the President."[32] A new opinion superseding the Bybee Memo was delivered on December 30, 2004.[33] The new memorandum questioned "the appropriateness and relevance of the non-statutory discussion ... and various aspects of the statutory analysis" in the earlier memo—namely, the assertion that torture required organ failure, impaired bodily function, or death.[34] However, the new memorandum did not disagree with any substantive conclusions offered by the 2002 memorandum. Moreover, it continued to maintain that it was unlikely that a person who "acted in good faith, and only after reasonable investigation establishing that his conduct would not inflict severe physical or mental pain or suffering," would possess the specific intent required to violate the torture statute.[35]

A March 2006 news story described the existence of a temporary, top-secret detention site at Camp Nana, near Baghdad, that since early 2004 included a "Black Room" where placards posted by soldiers stated, "No blood, no foul."[36] Detainee abuse attributed to the Special Operations unit at Camp Nana reflected "confusion over and, in some cases, disregard for" interrogation rules and standards for treatment of detainees.[37]

Since 2006, *WikiLeaks*, an international nonprofit whistle-blowing Web site, has published nearly 400,000 secret U.S. Army field reports. The reports indicate that U.S. authorities failed to investigate hundreds of reports of abuse, rape, and even murder by Iraqi police and U.S. soldiers. These reports, often supported by medical evidence, describe prisoners shackled, blindfolded, hung by wrists or ankles, and subjected to whipping, punching, kicking, or electric shocks. Six reports end with a detainee's apparent death.[38]

A February 2006 United Nations report on the Guantánamo Bay detentions, compiled by U.N. envoys who interviewed former detainees, their families, and their lawyers, along with U.S. officials, concluded that U.S. treatment of detainees there violated the detainees' rights to physical and mental health and, in some cases, constituted torture. United Nations Comm'n on Human Rights, *Situation of Detainees at Guantanamo Bay* (Feb. 15, 2006), *available at* http://www.usawatch.org/docs/E.CN.4.2006.120_.pdf. The United States replied to the U.N. report with a factual and legal defense, *Reply of the Government of the United States of America to the Report of the Five UNCHR Special Rapporteurs on Detainees in Guantanamo Bay, Cuba* (Mar. 10, 2006), *available at* http://www.asil.org/pdfs/ilib0603212.pdf.

In 2008, the Senate Armed Services Committee completed another investigation of detainee treatment:

---

32. Jack Goldsmith, *The Terror Presidency* 10 (2007).

33. Memorandum for James B. Comey, Deputy Attorney General, from Daniel Levin, Acting Assistant Attorney General, *Legal Standards Applicable Under 18 U.S.C. 2340-2340A* (Dec. 30, 2004), *at* http://www.justice.gov/olc/18usc23402340a2.htm.

34. *Id.* at 1-2.

35. *Id.* at 17.

36. Eric Schmitt & Carolyn Marshall, *In Secret Unit's "Black Room," A Grim Portrait of U.S. Abuse*, N.Y. Times, Mar. 19, 2006.

37. *Id.*

38. Nick Davies, Jonathan Steel & David Leigh, *Iraq War Logs: Secret Files Show How US Ignored Torture*, Guardian, Oct. 22, 2010.

Senate Armed Services Committee, Inquiry into the Treatment of Detainees in U.S. Custody

Nov. 20, 2008

http://armed-services.senate.gov/Publications/Detainee Report Final_April 22 2009.pdf

EXECUTIVE SUMMARY . . .

(U) The collection of timely and accurate intelligence is critical to the safety of U.S. personnel deployed abroad and to the security of the American people here at home. The methods by which we elicit intelligence information from detainees in our custody affect not only the reliability of that information, but our broader efforts to win hearts and minds and attract allies to our side.

(U) Al Qaeda and Taliban terrorists are taught to expect Americans to abuse them. They are recruited based on false propaganda that says the United States is out to destroy Islam. Treating detainees harshly only reinforces that distorted view, increases resistance to cooperation, and creates new enemies. In fact, the April 2006 National Intelligence Estimate "Trends in Global Terrorism: Implications for the United States" cited "pervasive anti U.S. sentiment among most Muslims" as an underlying factor fueling the spread of the global jihadist movement. Former Navy General Counsel Alberto Mora testified to the Senate Armed Services Committee in June 2008 that "there are serving U.S. flag-rank officers who maintain that the first and second identifiable causes of U.S. combat deaths in Iraq — as judged by their effectiveness in recruiting insurgent fighters into combat — are, respectively the symbols of Abu Ghraib and Guantanamo."

(U) The abuse of detainees in U.S. custody cannot simply be attributed to the actions of "a few bad apples" acting on their own. The fact is that senior officials in the United States government solicited information on how to use aggressive techniques, redefined the law to create the appearance of their legality, and authorized their use against detainees. Those efforts damaged our ability to collect accurate intelligence that could save lives, strengthened the hand of our enemies, and compromised our moral authority. This report is a product of the Committee's inquiry into how those unfortunate results came about. . . .

SENATE ARMED SERVICES COMMITTEE CONCLUSIONS

Conclusion 1: On February 7, 2002, President George W. Bush made a written determination that Common Article 3 of the Geneva Conventions, which would have afforded minimum standards for humane treatment, did not apply to al Qaeda or Taliban detainees. Following the President's determination, techniques such as waterboarding, nudity, and stress positions, used in SERE [Survival Evasion Resistance and Escape] training to simulate tactics used by enemies that refuse to follow the Geneva Conventions, were authorized for use in interrogations of detainees in U.S. custody.

Conclusion 2: Members of the President's Cabinet and other senior officials participated in meetings inside the White House in 2002 and 2003 where specific interrogation techniques were discussed. National Security Council Principals reviewed the CIA's interrogation program during that period.

Conclusions on SERE Training Techniques and Interrogations

Conclusion 3: The use of techniques similar to those used in SERE resistance training—such as stripping students of their clothing, placing them in stress positions, putting hoods over their heads, and treating them like animals—was at odds with the commitment to humane treatment of detainees in U.S. custody. Using those techniques for interrogating detainees was also inconsistent with the goal of collecting accurate intelligence information, as the purpose of SERE resistance training is to increase the ability of U.S. personnel to resist abusive interrogations and the techniques used were based, in part, on Chinese Communist techniques used during the Korean War to elicit false confessions.

Conclusion 4: The use of techniques in interrogations derived from SERE resistance training created a serious risk of physical and psychological harm to detainees. The SERE schools employ strict controls to reduce the risk of physical and psychological harm to students during training. Those controls include medical and psychological screening for students, interventions by trained psychologists during training, and code words to ensure that students can stop the application of a technique at any time should the need arise. Those same controls are not present in real world interrogations.

Conclusions on Senior Official Consideration of SERE Techniques for Interrogations

Conclusion 5: In July 2002, the Office of the Secretary of Defense General Counsel solicited information from the Joint Personnel Recovery Agency (JPRA) [an agency expert in training U.S. personnel to withstand interrogation techniques considered unlawful under the Geneva Conventions] on SERE techniques for use during interrogations. That solicitation, prompted by requests from Department of Defense General Counsel William J. Haynes II, reflected the view that abusive tactics similar to those used by our enemies should be considered for use against detainees in U.S. custody.

Conclusion 6: The Central Intelligence Agency's (CIA) interrogation program included at least one SERE training technique, waterboarding. Senior Administration lawyers, including Alberto Gonzales, Counsel to the President, and David Addington, Counsel to the Vice President, were consulted on the development of legal analysis of CIA interrogation techniques. Legal opinions subsequently issued by the Department of Justice's Office of Legal Counsel (OLC) interpreted legal obligations under U.S. anti-torture laws and determined the legality of CIA interrogation techniques. Those OLC opinions distorted the meaning and intent of anti-torture laws, rationalized the abuse of detainees in U.S. custody and influenced Department of Defense determinations as to what interrogation techniques were legal for use during interrogations conducted by U.S. military personnel.

Conclusions on JPRA Offensive Activities

Conclusion 7: Joint Personnel Recovery Agency (JPRA) efforts in support of "offensive" interrogation operations went beyond the agency's knowledge and expertise. JPRA's support to U.S. government interrogation efforts contributed to detainee abuse. JPRA's offensive support also influenced the development of policies that authorized abusive interrogation techniques for use against detainees in U.S. custody.

Conclusion 8: Detainee abuse occurred during JPRA's support to Special Mission Unit (SMU) Task Force (TF) interrogation operations in Iraq in September 2003. JPRA Commander Colonel Randy Moulton's authorization of SERE instructors, who had no experience in detainee interrogations, to actively participate in Task Force interrogations using SERE resistance training techniques was a serious failure in judgment. The Special Mission Unit Task Force Commander's failure to order that SERE resistance training techniques not be used in detainee interrogations was a serious failure in leadership that led to the abuse of detainees in Task Force custody. Iraq is a Geneva Convention theater and techniques used in SERE school are inconsistent with the obligations of U.S. personnel under the Geneva Conventions....

Conclusions on GTMO's Request for Aggressive Techniques

Conclusion 10: Interrogation techniques in Guantanamo Bay's (GTMO) October 11, 2002 request for authority submitted by Major General Michael Dunlavey, were influenced by JPRA training for GTMO interrogation personnel and included techniques similar to those used in SERE training to teach U.S. personnel to resist abusive enemy interrogations. GTMO Staff Judge Advocate Lieutenant Colonel Diane Beaver's legal review justifying the October 11, 2002 GTMO request was profoundly in error and legally insufficient. Leaders at GTMO, including Major General Dunlavey's successor, Major General Geoffrey Miller, ignored warnings from DoD's Criminal Investigative Task Force and the Federal Bureau of Investigation that the techniques were potentially unlawful and that their use would strengthen detainee resistance....

Conclusion 13: Secretary of Defense Donald Rumsfeld's authorization of aggressive interrogation techniques for use at Guantanamo Bay was a direct cause of detainee abuse there. Secretary Rumsfeld's December 2, 2002 approval of Mr. Haynes's recommendation that most of the techniques contained in GTMO's October 11, 2002 request be authorized, influenced and contributed to the use of abusive techniques, including military working dogs, forced nudity, and stress positions, in Afghanistan and Iraq.

Conclusion 14: Department of Defense General Counsel William J. Haynes II's direction to the Department of Defense's Detainee Working Group in early 2003 to consider a legal memo from John Yoo of the Department of Justice's OLC as authoritative, blocked the Working Group from conducting a fair and complete legal analysis and resulted in a report that, in the words of then Department of the Navy General Counsel Alberto Mora contained "profound mistakes in its legal analysis." Reliance on the OLC memo resulted in a final Working Group report that recommended approval of several aggressive techniques, including removal of clothing, sleep deprivation, and slapping, similar to those used in SERE training to teach U.S. personnel to resist abusive interrogations.

Conclusions on Interrogations in Iraq and Afghanistan

Conclusion 15: Special Mission Unit (SMU) Task Force (TF) interrogation policies were influenced by the Secretary of Defense's December 2, 2002 approval of aggressive interrogation techniques for use at GTMO. SMU TF interrogation policies in Iraq included the use of aggressive interrogation techniques such as military working dogs and stress positions. SMU TF policies were a direct cause of detainee abuse and influenced interrogation policies at Abu Ghraib and elsewhere in Iraq.

Conclusion 16: During his assessment visit to Iraq in August and September 2003, GTMO Commander Major General Geoffrey Miller encouraged a view that interrogators should be more aggressive during detainee interrogations.

Conclusion 17: Interrogation policies approved by Lieutenant General Ricardo Sanchez, which included the use of military working dogs and stress positions, were a direct cause of detainee abuse in Iraq. Lieutenant General Sanchez's decision to issue his September 14, 2003 policy with the knowledge that there were ongoing discussions as to the legality of some techniques in it was a serious error in judgment. The September policy was superseded on October 12, 2003 as a result of legal concerns raised by U.S. Central Command. That superseding policy, however, contained ambiguities and contributed to confusion about whether aggressive techniques, such as military working dogs, were authorized for use during interrogations.

Conclusion 18: U.S. Central Command (CENTCOM) failed to conduct proper oversight of Special Mission Unit Task Force interrogation policies. Though aggressive interrogation techniques were removed from Combined Joint Task Force 7 interrogation policies after CENTCOM raised legal concerns about their inclusion in the September 14, 2003 policy issued by Lieutenant General Sanchez, SMU TF interrogation policies authorized some of those same techniques, including stress positions and military working dogs.

Conclusion 19: The abuse of detainees at Abu Ghraib in late 2003 was not simply the result of a few soldiers acting on their own. Interrogation techniques such as stripping detainees of their clothes, placing them in stress positions, and using military working dogs to intimidate them appeared in Iraq only after they had been approved for use in Afghanistan and at GTMO. Secretary of Defense Donald Rumsfeld's December 2, 2002 authorization of aggressive interrogation techniques and subsequent interrogation policies and plans approved by senior military and civilian officials conveyed the message that physical pressures and degradation were appropriate treatment for detainees in U.S. military custody. What followed was an erosion in standards dictating that detainees be treated humanely.

B. APPLYING THE INTERROGATION LAWS

On April 16, 2009, President Obama authorized the release of four previously undisclosed OLC memos describing interrogation techniques used by the CIA between 2002 and 2005. One, quoted *supra* p. 542 and signed by Jay S. Bybee in 2002, purported to give the CIA legal approval for waterboarding and other harsh treatment, including forced nudity, slamming detainees into walls, and prolonged sleep deprivation. Three others, signed by Stephen G. Bradbury in May 2005, also concluded that the harsh techniques were lawful, even when multiple methods were used in combination. The memos are *available at* http://www.fas.org/irp/agency/doj/olc/index.html.

NOTES AND QUESTIONS

a. Legality Under International Law

1. *The Convention Against Torture.* Do any of the techniques in Defense Secretary Rumsfeld's April 16, 2003, memo on Guantánamo exceed the limits set out in

the Torture Convention or the U.S. understandings? See *supra* p. 529. Which techniques? Would the same methods be lawful in Iraq? At some undisclosed offshore location?

Do any of the techniques in Rumsfeld's memo exceed the limits of the Torture Act, 18 U.S.C. §§2340-2340B, *supra* p. 529. Recall that in August 2002 the Justice Department's OLC offered a very narrow definition of "torture," see *supra* p. 542, and argued that in any case the President could authorize torture. It also indicated that interrogation activities "may be cruel, inhuman, or degrading, but still not produce pain and suffering of the requisite intensity" to violate §2340. Bybee Memo, *supra* p. 543 n.13, at 1. The memorandum also asserted that a specific intent to torture is required to violate the torture statute. *Id.* at 4. How would you rate this definition of the key terms against those set out in the Torture Convention, the Torture Act, and the U.S. understanding? *See* Seth F. Kreimer, *"Torture Lite," "Full Bodied" Torture, and the Insulation of Legal Conscience*, 1 J. Nat'l Security L. & Pol'y 187 (2005); Duncan Campbell, *U.S. Interrogators Turn to "Torture Lite,"* Guardian, Jan. 25, 2003. Could the Bybee Memo effectively exempt the CIA from complying with the CAT and the Torture Act?

2. *Applying the Geneva Conventions.* Recall from our consideration of the Geneva Conventions in Chapter 2 that each one requires nations to criminalize "grave breaches," including acts of "torture or inhuman treatment." Each Convention also calls on nations to "take measures necessary for the suppression of all acts contrary to the provisions of the present Convention other than the grave breaches." One such provision important here is Common Article 3, which requires detainees of every description to be treated humanely, and which forbids "cruel treatment and torture," as well as "outrages on personal dignity, in particular, humiliating and degrading treatment." See *supra* p. 532. The War Crimes Act, *supra* p. 531, was supposed to satisfy U.S. obligations under the Geneva Conventions in this regard by criminalizing grave breaches and, before 2006 amendments by the Military Commissions Act, *supra* p. 536, all violations of Common Article 3.

The Bush administration took the position in early 2002 that Al Qaeda and Taliban prisoners were "unlawful combatants" not protected by the Geneva Convention Relative to the Treatment of Prisoners of War (Geneva III), the one most clearly relevant here. Because Geneva III was inapplicable, it argued, the War Crimes Act incorporating it by reference necessarily did not apply to U.S. officials interrogating such prisoners. The White House, President George W. Bush, *Memorandum for the Vice President et al.: Humane Treatment of al Qaeda and Taliban Detainees* (Feb. 7, 2002), *available at* http://www.aclu.org/files/assets/CIA.pdf. The Administration's arguments are reviewed in the following paragraphs.

a. *Terrorists as Protected Belligerents?* The Bush administration first argued that the Geneva Conventions did not apply to members of Al Qaeda, because Al Qaeda is not a High Contracting Party to the Conventions. On the other hand, members of the Taliban, as a group representing the de facto government of Afghanistan, a High Contracting Party, were said to be covered by the Conventions.

As a practical matter, of course, Al Qaeda depended heavily on Taliban support—bordering on sponsorship—in order to carry out its terrorist attacks against the United States. At the same time, the Taliban appear to have been heavily influenced by Al Qaeda. Under the circumstances, does it make sense to apply the Conventions differently to members of the two enemy groups?

b. *Character of the Conflict.* The Administration maintained that neither Al Qaeda nor Taliban members were entitled to the protection of Common Article 3, however, because the conflict was, at least initially, international, not one described as "not of an international character." Is this argument consistent with the contention that the Taliban were covered by the Conventions generally because the Taliban were the de facto government of Afghanistan? Can you say how the applicability of Common Article 3 to the Taliban might have changed after the election of the Karzai government in Afghanistan in June 2002, when the conflict became internal and foreign forces remained in the country at the invitation of the new government? Should it have changed?

c. *Location of the Fighting?* In *Hamdan v. Rumsfeld*, 548 U.S. 557 (2006), the Supreme Court found that Common Article 3 affords some protection to persons who are not associated with a signatory or nonsignatory "Power" but who are involved in a conflict "in the territory of" a signatory. The Court construed the phrase "not of an international character" literally to distinguish conflicts between nations. Do you think it is consistent with the purposes of the Geneva Conventions to make their application dependent upon where a prisoner is captured?

d. *Status as POWs?* The Administration also insisted that the Taliban were not entitled to protections afforded prisoners of war under Geneva III. Article 4 of the Convention defines POWs as combatants who have a "fixed distinctive sign recognizable at a distance," carry arms openly, and conduct operations in accordance with the laws and customs of war. It was supported in this argument in *United States v. Lindh*, 212 F. Supp. 2d 541 (E.D. Va. 2002). The requirements in question are designed to enable belligerents on one side to distinguish those on the other from noncombatants, who must not be attacked.

A POW must be "humanely treated," and he may not be required to divulge more than his name, rank, serial number, and age. Moreover,

> [n]o physical or mental torture, nor any other form of coercion, may be inflicted on prisoners of war to secure from them information of any kind whatever. Prisoners of war who refuse to answer may not be threatened, insulted, or exposed to unpleasant or disadvantageous treatment of any kind. [Geneva III, art. 17.]

POW status also brings other privileges, including the right to retain personal belongings, to quartering under conditions as favorable as those of the custodian, and to communicate with family members.

Once a prisoner of any sort is in custody, should his failure to fit the definition of a POW expose him to torture or inhumane treatment? Note that Common Article 3 applies to all prisoners, regardless of their status.

e. *Determination of Status.* Article 5 of Geneva Convention III entitles detainees to a determination of whether they are POWs or not by a "competent tribunal." The OLC asserted in its January 22, 2002, memorandum, however, that there can be no doubt about the POW status of any individual affiliated with the Taliban, because the organization was found not to meet the requirements of Article 4. Memorandum for Alberto R. Gonzales, Counsel to the President, and William J. Haynes II, General Counsel, Department of Defense, from Jay S. Bybee, Office of Legal Counsel,

Re: Application of Treaties and Laws to Al Qaeda and Taliban Detainees (Jan. 22, 2002), *available at* http://www.justice.gov/olc/docs/memo-laws-taliban-detainees.pdf. This position appeared to be at variance with U.S. practice in other settings. *See* Jennifer Elsea, *Treatment of "Battlefield Detainees" in the War on Terrorism* 36 (Cong. Res. Serv. RL31367), Jan. 23, 2007 (noting that the United States has in the past required an individualized assessment of detainee status before denying POW status). In the view of one observer, it is "discouraging . . . to see American lawyers arguing for the inapplicability of the Conventions on grounds that are strikingly similar . . . to those invoked by Germany" during World War II. Waldron, *supra*, at 1695.

Can you say what constitutes a "competent tribunal" for purposes of Article 5? Can the President be a "competent tribunal"? Did the U.S. refusal, at least initially, to employ such a tribunal to determine the status of each detainee constitute a violation of the Article 5? If so, would that violation provide an enemy with an argument for arbitrarily denying captured U.S. soldiers the protections of POW status?

f. *Prohibition of Torture as a Customary Norm?* Recall that the United States has recognized Article 75 of Geneva Protocol I as customary international law. See *supra* p. 40. It forbids "torture of all kinds, whether physical or mental," as well as "outrages upon personal dignity, in particular humiliating and degrading treatment, . . . any form of indecent assault, . . . and threats to commit any of the foregoing acts." Protocol I art. 75(2). Technically, Protocol I applies only to conflicts of an international character. But as customary law, does Article 75 set a baseline for *all* "persons who are in the power of a Party"?

g. *Treatment of Noncombatants?* In remarks about the detention facility at Guantánamo Bay in early 2002, Defense Secretary Rumsfeld declared that "[s]ometimes when you capture a big, large group there will be someone who just happened to be in there that didn't belong in there." *Secretary Rumsfeld Media Availability En Route to Camp X-Ray*, Jan. 27, 2002, *available at* http://www.defense.gov/transcripts/transcript.aspx?transcriptid=2338. What rights do such innocent bystanders have, once detained?

3. *The New Paradigm?* In 2002, White House Counsel Alberto R. Gonzales argued in a memorandum to President Bush that the "nature of the new war" and the "new paradigm render[] obsolete Geneva's strict limitations" on questioning and make other Geneva provisions "quaint." *Decision Re Application of the Geneva Convention on Prisoners of War to the Conflict with Al Qaeda and the Taliban* (Jan. 25, 2002), *available at* http://www.slate.com/features/whatistorture/LegalMemos.html. How would you rebut Gonzales's interpretation? Do Gonzales's arguments apply with equal force in Afghanistan and in Iraq? To detainees captured elsewhere? *See* Derek Jinks & David Sloss, *Is the President Bound by the Geneva Conventions?*, 90 Cornell L. Rev. 97 (2004) (concluding that the President is bound by the Geneva Conventions).

Review the provisions of the Detainee Treatment Act and Executive Order No. 13,491, *supra* pp. 535, 536. If these laws had been in place beginning in October 2001, in what respects, if at all, would the lawfulness of U.S. interrogation practices have been different? Do you think U.S. interrogations would have been conducted differently?

4. *Outsourcing and Hiding Torture?* Article 49 of the Fourth Geneva Convention prohibits "deportations of protected persons from occupied territory." Such a deportation or transfer or unlawful confinement of a protected person is a "grave breach"

of the convention. Geneva IV art. 147. On March 19, 2004, the OLC drafted a memo indicating that the CIA could transfer detainees out of Iraq for interrogation, despite the Geneva Convention, by construing the ban not to apply to illegal aliens who have no legal right to remain in Iraq. The memo concluded that the temporary relocation of persons not charged with a crime to face interrogation at another location outside Iraq is not akin to the wartime practices the Geneva Convention was designed to forbid. Draft Memorandum from Jack Goldsmith, Assistant Attorney General, to Alberto R. Gonzales, Counsel to the President, *Permissibility of Relocating Certain "Protected Persons" from Occupied Iraq* (Mar. 19, 2004), *available at* http://www.washingtonpost.com/wp-srv/nation/documents/doj_memo031904.pdf. The CIA then transported as many as a dozen detainees from Iraq to other countries between March and October of 2004. *See* Dana Priest, *Memo Lets CIA Take Detainees Out of Iraq,* Wash. Post, Oct. 24, 2004. (The practice of "extraordinary rendition" is addressed in Chapter 19.)

The CIA also reportedly held dozens, perhaps up to 100, persons in Iraq as "ghost detainees." In June or July 2003, for example, Hiwa Abdul Rahman Rashul, a suspected member of the Iraqi Al-Ansar terrorist group who was nicknamed "Triple X" by CIA and military officials, was captured by Kurdish fighters. He was turned over to the CIA, which rendered him to Afghanistan for interrogation, then brought him back to Iraq. Then-Director of Central Intelligence (DCI) George Tenet asked Defense Secretary Rumsfeld not to give Rashul a prisoner number and to hide him from the Red Cross. Rashul was then lost in the Iraqi prison system for seven months. When asked about the legal basis for hiding Rashul, Rumsfeld replied, "We know from our knowledge that [Tenet] has authority to do this." *Id.*; Eric Schmitt & Thom Shanker, *Rumsfeld Issued an Order to Hide Detainee in Iraq,* N.Y. Times, June 17, 2004. In late 2005, Human Rights Watch provided a list of 26 "ghost detainees" believed to be in U.S. custody. *U.S. Holding at Least Twenty-Six "Ghost Detainees"* (Dec. 1, 2005). One secret CIA prison was reportedly code-named Bright Light, where the most important Al Qaeda detainees were held in an undisclosed location. James Risen, *State of War: The Secret History of the CIA and the Bush Administration* 31 (2006).

What could be wrong with hiding a detainee in this fashion? How would you respond to the OLC's legal justification for rendering "ghost detainees"?

In a 2006 televised speech, President Bush stated that some individuals captured by the United States

> pose a significant threat, or may have intelligence that we and our allies need . . . and they withhold information that could save American lives. In these cases, it has been necessary to move these individuals to an environment where they can be held secretly, questioned by experts . . . . And so the CIA used an alternative set of procedures. [The White House, *President Discusses Creation of Military Commissions to Try Suspected Terrorists,* Sept. 6, 2006, *available at* http://georgewbush-whitehouse.archives.gov/news/releases/2006/09/20060906-3.html.]

On the basis of what authority would the President have ordered such an "alternative set of procedures"?

b. Responsibility for Abuse

1. *Assigning Responsibility.* Guidance for interrogations at Abu Ghraib prison came from three different sources at different times — from Army field manuals, from personnel who had worked earlier in Afghanistan, and from Guantánamo.

Craig Gordon, *High-Pressure Tactics: Critics Say Bush Policies — Post 9/11 — Gave Interrogators Leeway to Push Beyond Normal Limits*, Newsday, May 23, 2004. General Taguba found that operating procedures and copies of the Geneva Conventions were not distributed to the guards handling the prisoners. To complicate matters, senior military commanders called for interrogators to isolate and manipulate detainees who might have "significant intelligence value." R. Jeffrey Smith, *Memo Gave Intelligence Bigger Role: Increased Pressure Sought on Prisoners*, Wash. Post, May 21, 2004.

The overall detention and interrogation picture that has emerged from official statements and documents reveals "a trail of fitful ad hoc policymaking" where interrogation techniques were authorized, then rescinded or modified, at times leading to decisions made in the field or at the Pentagon on a case-by-case basis. Dana Priest & Bradley Graham, *U.S. Struggled Over How Far to Push Tactics*, Wash. Post, June 24, 2004. Unlike CIA requests for expanded interrogation authority that were reviewed by the Department of Justice and the National Security Council, Defense Department interrogation policy decisions were not subjected to outside review. *Id.*

2. *Investigating Interrogation Abuses.* An investigation led by former Secretary of Defense James Schlesinger found 300 allegations of abuse and 66 substantiated cases of confirmed or possible abuse in Iraq.[39] An Army investigation determined that the abuses "resulted from the failure of individuals to follow known standards of discipline and Army values and, in some cases, the failure of a few leaders to enforce those standards of discipline."[40] The Army decided not to charge any of those leaders with wrongdoing, however, finding some senior officers "responsible" but not "culpable."[41] By contrast, the Schlesinger investigation found that the abuses were "more than the failure of a few leaders to enforce proper discipline. There is both institutional and personal responsibility at higher levels."[42]

On March 22, 2006, an Army spokesman reported more than 600 accusations of detainee abuse in Iraq and Afghanistan since October 2001 and disciplinary actions against 251 soldiers.[43]

c.   Criminal Liability

1. *Prosecuting Abuses.* Seven Military Police and two military intelligence soldiers were convicted under the UCMJ of abusing detainees at Abu Ghraib, while 251 other soldiers and officers were punished in some way for detainee abuse in Iraq and Afghanistan.[44] Three of the five officers investigated by the Army for their role in the Abu Ghraib abuses were cleared; Colonel Thomas Pappas, commander of Abu Ghraib prison, was reprimanded and fined, while Brigadier General Janis Karpinski, another commander of Abu Ghraib, was demoted to the rank of colonel.[45] Although

---

39. *Schlesinger Report, supra* n.14, at 5.
40. U.S. Army News Release, *Army Releases Findings in Detainee-Abuse Investigations* (May 5, 2005), *at* http://news.findlaw.com/wash/s/20050506/20050506145910.html.
41. Josh White & Thomas E. Ricks, *Officers Won't Be Charged in Prison Scandal*, Wash. Post, Aug. 27, 2004.
42. *Schlesinger Report, supra* n.14, at 5.
43. Eric Schmitt, *Iraq Abuse Trial Is Again Limited to Lower Ranks*, N.Y. Times, Mar. 23, 2006.
44. *Id.*; Eric Schmitt, *Army Dog Handler Is Convicted in Detainee Abuse at Abu Ghraib*, N.Y. Times, Mar. 22, 2006.
45. U.S. Army News Release, *Army Releases Findings in Detainee-Abuse Investigations* (May 5, 2005), *at* http://news.findlaw.com/wash/s/20050506/20050506145910.html; Frontline, *The Torture Question: Frequently Asked Questions* (PBS, Oct. 18, 2005), *at* http://www.pbs.org/wgbh/pages/frontline/torture/etc/faqs.html#8.

Lieutenant Colonel Steven Jordan, director of the interrogation center at Abu Ghraib, was convicted for disobeying an order when he spoke with others about the Abu Ghraib investigation, his commanding general dismissed the charge and removed the conviction from Jordan's record.[46] Only one person connected to the post-9/11 interrogations has been criminally prosecuted in U.S. civilian courts for detainee abuse. David Passaro, a former CIA contractor, was convicted of assault for beating an Afghan detainee who later died.[47]

In June 2005 the Defense Department promoted or nominated for promotion the former deputy commander of U.S. forces in Iraq and the senior military lawyer for the U.S. command in Baghdad, both involved in overseeing or advising detention and interrogation operations during the Abu Ghraib scandal. The top intelligence officer in Iraq at that time was promoted earlier in the year. Eric Schmitt, *Army Moves to Advance 2 Linked to Abu Ghraib*, N.Y. Times, June 29, 2005. The *Schlesinger Report*, *supra* p. 543 n.14, had found those officers to be among those responsible for the abuses at Abu Ghraib, and the Fay Report, *supra* p. 544 n.21, faulted the commanders for issuing and revising the interrogation rules three times in 30 days, and faulted their legal staffs for giving bad advice—not warning that practices permitted at Guantánamo and in Afghanistan might not be lawful in Iraq. Nevertheless, the Army Inspector General cleared them of any wrongdoing. Inspector Gen., Department of the Army, *Detainee Operations Inspection* (July 21, 2004), *at* http://www.washingtonpost.com/wp-srv/world/iraq/abughraib/detaineereport.pdf.

Only low-level interrogators and handlers were disciplined for interrogation abuses in Afghanistan and at Guantánamo. A review by Air Force Lieutenant General Randall M. Schmidt of three years' practice and more than 24,000 interrogations at Guantánamo led to a recommendation of reprimand for Army Major General Geoffrey C. Miller, commander of the Guantánamo facility in 2002 and 2003, for failing to oversee the interrogation of a high-value detainee who was subjected to abusive treatment. *Army Regulation 15-6: Final Report, Investigation into FBI Allegations of Detainee Abuse at Guantanamo Bay, Cuba Detention Facility* (Apr. 1, 2005, amended June 9, 2005). Nevertheless, the Army's Inspector General decided that Miller had not violated the law or Defense Department policy. David S. Cloud, *Guantanamo Reprimand Was Sought, An Aide Says*, N.Y. Times, July 13, 2005. One suggested reason for the failure to hold senior officials accountable is the lack of an independent prosecutor inside the military, equivalent to a district attorney, who would have command authority to investigate up the chain of command. Eric Schmitt, *Iraq Abuse Trial Is Again Limited to Lower Ranks*, N.Y. Times, Mar. 23, 2006.

At a news conference called in response to the Abu Ghraib publicity in June 2004, White House Counsel Alberto Gonzales denied that "the president...authorized, ordered or directed" violations of "the standards of the torture conventions or the torture statute." *Transcript of Press Briefing by Alberto Gonzales* (June 22, 2004). What legal wiggle room does the Gonzales statement leave for the President? Does it mean that President Bush was not responsible for the reported abuses? What do the findings of the Senate Armed Services Committee suggest about the responsibility of the President and other high-ranking Administration officials for the abuses described in their report?

---

46. Josh White, *Army Officer Is Cleared in Abu Ghraib Scandal*, Wash. Post, Jan. 10, 2008.
47. Elizabeth Dunbar, *Ex-CIA Contractor Sentenced to Prison*, Wash. Post, Feb. 13, 2007.

Who do you think is responsible for the abuses at Guantánamo, Abu Ghraib, and Camp Nana?

2. *Possible Defenses to Torture Charges.*

a. *Necessity and Self-Defense.* The criminal law doctrine of self-defense permits the use of force to prevent harm to another person:

Model Penal Code §3.02. Justification Generally: Choice of Evils.

(1) Conduct that the actor believes to be necessary to avoid a harm or evil to himself or to another is justifiable, provided that:

(a) the harm or evil sought to be avoided by such conduct is greater than that sought to be prevented by the law defining the offense charged; and

(b) neither the Code nor other law defining the offense provides exceptions or defenses dealing with the specific situation involved; and

(c) a legislative purpose to exclude the justification claimed does not otherwise plainly appear. . . .

Does that doctrine apply in this setting to excuse otherwise unlawful torture or inhumane treatment by an interrogator of a prisoner? Must the information sought by interrogators be available by no other means than torture? Is an individual claim of self-defense portable to the entire executive branch in the war on terrorism? Would a necessity defense be available even where Congress clearly proscribed the conduct so defended, as it did in the Torture Act? *See* Wayne R. LaFave & Austin W. Scott, 1 *Substantive Criminal Law* §5.4, at 629 (1986). Might such a defense be available to someone charged with carrying out even a specious legal authorization of torture? *See Public Comm. Against Torture in Israel v. State of Israel,* H.C. 5100/94, 53(4) P.D. 817 (1999) (necessity defense available for conduct necessary to save a life from substantial danger of serious harm, absent alternative means for neutralizing the harm).

Does the presence of an arguable defense to an act of torture nullify the requirement that the torture be legally authorized? *See* William C. Banks & Peter Raven-Hansen, *Targeted Killing and Assassination: The U.S. Legal Framework,* 37 U. Rich. L. Rev. 667, 668 (2003) (basic rule of law requires positive legal authority for government actions).

b. *Reasonable Reliance on Official Advice?* The criminal law also provides a defense for ignorance or mistake in some limited circumstances:

Model Penal Code §2.04. Ignorance or Mistake.

(1) Ignorance or mistake as to a matter of fact or law is a defense if:

(a) the ignorance or mistake negatives the purpose, knowledge, belief, recklessness or negligence required to establish a material element of the offense . . . .

(3) A belief that conduct does not legally constitute an offense is a defense to a prosecution for that offense based upon such conduct when:

> (a) the statute or other enactment defining the offense is not known to the actor and has not been published or otherwise reasonably made available prior to the conduct alleged; or
>
> (b) he acts in reasonable reliance upon an official statement of the law, afterward determined to be invalid or erroneous, contained in ...
>
> > (iii) an administrative order or grant of permission; or
> >
> > (iv) an official interpretation of the public officer or body charged by law with responsibility for the interpretation, administration or enforcement of the law defining the offense.

Is the President's order "an administrative order" that could set up this defense? (Recall that White House Counsel Gonzales denied that the President "authorized, ordered or directed" violations of the standards of CAT or the Torture Act.) Is a legal opinion of the Office of Legal Counsel an "official interpretation"? Could any government interrogator "reasonably" rely upon either a presidential order or an OLC opinion to conduct the most coercive forms of interrogation? *See United States v. Barker,* 546 F.2d 940 (D.C. Cir. 1976) (split panel affirming availability of mistake defense to Watergate burglar, but on different rationales). How is this defense different from the "Nuremberg defense" — "I was only following orders" — "a notion from which our criminal justice system, one based on individual accountability and responsibility, has historically recoiled"? *United States v. North,* 910 F.2d 843, 881 (D.C. Cir. 1990).

c. *Article II as a Trump Card?* The January 2002 OLC memo, *supra* p. 542, at 36, 39, asserted that "Congress can no more interfere with the President's conduct of the interrogation of enemy combatants than it can dictate strategic or tactical decisions on the battlefield." In what particular settings is the Article II argument most persuasive? *See* Michael D. Ramsey, *Torturing Executive Power,* 93 Geo. L.J. 1213 (2005). Unlike the Bybee Memo, *supra* p. 543 n.13, the December 30, 2004, OLC memo, *supra* p. 548, made no mention of the constitutional authority of the President to disregard statutory or treaty obligations regarding torture. Of what significance is the revision?

Compare detention and on-the-spot interrogations of those seized on the battlefield during combat with long-term detentions in remote locations away from the battle. Al Qaeda reportedly continues to plan and carry out terrorist acts that threaten national security. Does that ongoing threat give the Commander in Chief a tactical choice to capture and interrogate Al Qaeda operatives using torture?

If you agree that there is a constitutional limit to the authority of Congress to regulate interrogation, can you construe the laws reviewed in this section to avoid the potential constitutional problem? Is the constitutional authority of the President relevant to the international legality of the abusive conduct? *See* W. Michael Reisman, Editorial Comment, *Holding the Center of the Law of Armed Conflict,* 100 Am. J. Int'l L. 852, 854 (2006) (no).

3. *Prosecuting Civilian Contractors?* In June 2004 a federal grand jury in North Carolina indicted a contractor employed by the CIA on assault charges for allegedly beating a detainee in Afghanistan over two days in 2003. The detainee died the next day. The former contractor was found guilty of assault and sentenced to eight years and four months in prison. Elizabeth Dunbar, *Ex-CIA Contractor Sentenced to Prison,*

Wash. Post, Feb. 13, 2007. How might the War Crimes Act, 18 U.S.C. §2441, *supra* p. 531, apply to the accused in this case?

Generally, the UCMJ has not been used to criminally prosecute civilians accompanying military units in peacetime. *See, e.g., Willenburg v. Neurauter,* 48 M.J. 152, 157 (C.A.A.F. 1998). The Military Extraterritorial Jurisdiction Act of 2000 (MEJA), however, provides for federal jurisdiction over crimes committed abroad by civilians who are "accompanying or employed by" the U.S. military. 18 U.S.C. §§3261-3267 (2006). MEJA creates no new substantive crimes but incorporates a range of existing offenses, such as murder, assault, sexual abuse, and deprivation of rights under color of law. Still, after the 2004 *Taguba Report, supra* p. 547 n.23, named the contracting firms Titan Corporation and CACI International, Inc. as having provided translators and interrogators accused of engaging in detainee abuse at the Abu Ghraib prison, it appeared that the jurisdictional provisions of the MEJA would not reach the contractors that employed the accused individuals, because they were not "accompanying or employed by the military." Moreover, CACI's contract was with the Department of the Interior rather than the Department of Defense (DOD). Scott Shane, *Some U.S. Prison Contractors May Avoid Charges,* Balt. Sun, May 24, 2004.

In response to this jurisdictional gap, the 2005 Defense Authorization Act broadened the range of potential defendants under MEJA to include civilian employees, contractors or subcontractors, and their employees, of DOD or "any other Federal agency, or any provisional authority, to the extent such employment relates to supporting the mission of the Department of Defense overseas." Pub. L. No. 108-375, §1088, 118 Stat. 1811, 2066-2067 (2004). Do these amendments to MEJA plug all the holes? Would they reach State Department or FBI contractors? CIA contractors? *See* Frederick A. Stein, *Have We Closed the Barn Door Yet? A Look at the Current Loopholes in the Military Extraterritorial Jurisdiction Act,* 27 Hous. J. Int'l L. 579 (2005).

Some observers suggest that doubts about the criminal liability of civilian contractors who engage in interrogational torture also point to broader questions about the wisdom of privatizing a range of national security activities normally undertaken by the government. How might these questions be addressed? *See* Jon D. Michaels, *Beyond Accountability: The Constitutional, Democratic, and Strategic Problems with Privatizing War,* 82 Wash. U. L.Q. 1001 (2004).

The National Defense Authorization Act for Fiscal Year 2010, Pub. L. No. 111-84, §1038, 123 Stat. 2190, 2451 (2009), prohibits contractor personnel from interrogating detainees under the control of the Department of Defense, unless the Secretary waives the ban for up to 60 days after he determines that the waiver is "vital to the national security interests of the United States." *Id.* §1038(d) The Secretary must provide written notice to Congress after issuance of a waiver. *Id.* The same provision expressly permits contractors to serve as linguists, interpreters, report writers, information technology technicians, and trainers and advisers to the interrogators, so long as the contractors are subject to the same laws and policies as the government interrogators and are overseen by Defense Department personnel. *Id.* §1038(b). The Defense Department has issued rules implementing the contractor restrictions. 48 C.F.R. §237.173, 75 Fed. Reg. 67,633 (Nov. 3, 2010). Do these provisions provide adequate controls on contract personnel?

4. *Lawyers and Their Role.* Many of the legal opinions in the Justice Department and Defense Department memoranda described and quoted above are highly controversial. Some commentators argued that the memoranda were designed primarily

to protect potentially culpable officials from prosecution for interrogation abuses. *See Lawyers' Statement on Bush Administration's Torture Memos* (Aug. 4, 2004), *at* http://www.sfcityattorney.org/Modules/ShowDocument.aspx?documentid=507 (letter signed by about 130 prominent lawyers); *Letter Sent to the United States Congress Regarding Recent Human Rights Issues in Iraq* (June 16, 2004), *at* http://www.lawprofessorblogs.com/taxprof/linkdocs/harvardimpeach.pdf (letter signed by more than 500 university professors). Others, including Defense Department investigators of detention and interrogation practices, found that the confusion and ambiguity fostered by these memoranda may have contributed to the abusive practices or to a "permissive climate in which abuses were more likely." Richard B. Bilder & Detlev F. Vagts, *Speaking Law to Power: Lawyers and Torture*, 98 Am. J. Int'l L. 689, 691 (2004) (citing, e.g., John Barry, Michael Hirsh & Michael Isikoff, *The Roots of Torture*, Newsweek, May 24, 2004, at 28). What are the legal and ethical responsibilities of government lawyers in the war on terror? *See* Bilder & Vagts, *supra*, at 691-695; *Symposium: Lawyers' Roles and the War on Terror*, 1 J. Nat'l Security L. & Poly. 357 (2005).

The *Schlesinger Report, supra* p. 543 n.14, found that in the development of Defense Department detention and interrogation policies in 2002 and 2003 "the legal resources of the Services' Judge Advocate General and General Counsels were not utilized to their full potential. Had the Secretary of Defense had a wider range of legal opinions and more robust debate regarding detainee policies and operations," the frequent policy changes between December 2002 and April 2003 might have been avoided. *Id.* at 8. Why would the Secretary not have sought more advice from JAG lawyers and General Counsels? What would have been gained by their perspectives?

At a Senate hearing in July 2005, the judge advocates general for the Army, Air Force, and Marines stated that they complained about the Justice Department's definition of "torture" and how it would be applied in the Working Group process early in 2003. Their objections apparently were overruled by the Defense Department General Counsel's office. Neil A. Lewis, *Military's Opposition to Harsh Interrogation Is Outlined*, N.Y. Times, July 28, 2005; Josh White, *Military Lawyers Fought Policy on Interrogations, JAGs Recount Objections to Definition of Torture*, Wash. Post, July 15, 2005. Why do you think the Secretary failed to heed the advice that was offered?

The Senate Armed Services Committee report, *supra* p. 550, also blamed senior Administration lawyers and the authors of the OLC opinions for enabling the abuses documented above. The Office of Professional Responsibility of the Department of Justice completed an investigation of OLC lawyers John Yoo and Keith Bybee in 2009, concluding that they engaged in "professional misconduct" by authorizing enhanced interrogation techniques. Office of Professional Responsibility, Department of Justice, *Report* 260 (2009), *available at* http://judiciary.house.gov/hearings/pdf/OPRFinalReport090729.pdf. A second report from the Associate Deputy Attorney General, David Margolis, said only that the two lawyers exercised "poor judgment," but that he would not recommend referring them for discipline because they did not, in his view, knowingly provide false advice. Memorandum to the Attorney General from David Margolis, Associate Deputy Attorney General (Jan. 5, 2010), *available at* http://judiciary.house.gov/hearings/pdf/DAGMargolisMemo100105.pdf. *See also* David D. Cole, *The Sacrificial Yoo: Accounting for Torture in the OPR Report*, 4 J. Nat'l Security L. & Pol'y 455 (2010).

The latter conclusion thus excused what might otherwise have been an obligation by the Department of Justice to refer Yoo and Bybee to state bar associations for disciplinary proceedings. President Obama also stated that he would not advocate prosecuting the OLC lawyers. *See* Press Release, The White House Office of the Press Sec'y, Statement of President Barack Obama on Release of the OLC Memos (Apr. 16, 2009), *available at* http://www.whitehouse.gov/the-press-office/statement-president-barack-obama-release-olc-memos ("[N]othing will be gained by spending our time and energy laying blame for the past."). Do you believe that these lawyers and/or their highest ranking superiors broke the law? Which laws? Do you agree that nothing would be gained by a prosecution? *See* Jordan J. Paust, *Criminal Responsibility of Bush Administration Officials with Respect to Unlawful Interrogation Tactics and the Facilitating Conduct of Lawyers*, in *The United States and Torture: Interrogation, Incarceration, and Abuse* 281 (Marjorie Kohn ed., 2011).

A Senate Judiciary Subcommittee hearing in 2009 focused on the role of the OLC in authorizing coercive interrogation methods. *See What Went Wrong: Torture and the Office of Legal Counsel in the Bush Administration: Hearing Before the Subcomm. on Administrative Oversight and the Courts of the S. Comm. on the Judiciary*, 111th Cong. (May 13, 2009), *available at* http://www.fas.org/irp/congress/2009_hr/wrong.html.

d.   Civil Liability

1. *Civil Liability for U.S. Government Interrogators?* The memoranda quoted and described above expose an underlying tension in setting the interrogation policy — providing maximum flexibility to pressure detainees to talk while ensuring immunity from criminal sanctions for interrogators if they cross lawful boundaries. This tension is most readily apparent in the January 9, 2002, OLC memorandum from John Yoo and Robert Delahunty, *supra* p. 542, arguing that the Geneva Conventions do not apply to captured Al Qaeda and Taliban detainees. Potential criminal liability is addressed *supra* p. 558.

In February 2006, a federal district court dismissed most of a civil suit for damages brought by Guantánamo Bay detainees who alleged that they were tortured in violation of the Geneva Conventions, the law of nations, and the Constitution. *Rasul v. Rumsfeld*, 414 F. Supp. 2d 26 (D.D.C. 2006). The court held that sovereign immunity barred the law of nations and Geneva Conventions claims, and that qualified immunity of individual government officials required dismissal of the constitutional claims because the rights at stake were not "clearly established." For sovereign immunity to apply to the international law claims, however, the court had to find that the defendants were acting within their scope of employment. How could U.S. officials act within their scope of employment when they torture detainees? The Court of Appeals voted to dismiss all the claims, *Rasul v. Myers*, 512 F.3d 644 (D.C. Cir. 2008), but the Supreme Court reversed and remanded to reconsider the constitutional claims in light of its 2008 decision in *Boumediene v. Bush*, 553 U.S. 723 (2008) (reproduced *supra* p. 401). 129 S. Ct. 763 (2008). On remand, the Court of Appeals again dismissed all the detainees' claims after concluding that the alien detainees lacked clearly established constitutional rights under the Fifth or Eighth Amendments, inasmuch as the Supreme Court has yet to squarely overrule the part of *Johnson v. Eisentrager*, 339 U.S. 763 (1950), suggesting that aliens abroad do not have Fifth Amendment rights). *Rasul v. Myers*, 563 F.3d 527 (D.C. Cir.), *cert. denied*, 130 S. Ct. 1013 (2009).

2. *Civil Liability for Lawyers?* In 2009, a federal district court refused to dismiss most parts of a civil suit by convicted terrorist Jose Padilla against former OLC lawyer

John Yoo. *Padilla v. Yoo*, 633 F. Supp. 2d 1005 (N.D. Cal. 2009). Padilla alleged that he was abused during his confinement at a military brig in South Carolina during his three-year, eight-month detention based on the orders of high-ranking government officials and the legal and policy justifications for abusive interrogation provided by Yoo. The court noted that Yoo is unlikely to be held accountable for his actions in any other forum, and that a reasonable lawyer in Yoo's position should have known that he was authorizing a violation of Padilla's constitutional rights. *Id.* A decision by the Ninth Circuit Court of Appeals on appeal by Yoo was pending at this writing.

      3. *Civil Liability of Contractors?* Relying on the Alien Tort Statute (ATS), 28 U.S.C. §1350 (2006), in 2004 the Center for Constitutional Rights sued two prime security contractors operating for the United States in Iraq — CACI International, Inc. and Titan Corp. — on behalf of Iraqi prisoners, alleging that the contractors conspired with government officials to abuse the detainees and failed adequately to supervise their employees. *See* Renae Merle, *CACI and Titan Sued Over Iraq Operations*, Wash. Post, June 10, 2004. The suit sought damages and an injunction to prevent the contractors from obtaining new government contracts. The Court of Appeals granted summary judgment in favor of both defendants because the contractors were conducting operations under military authority, and, like the military, contractors whose work is fully integrated in the military mission are exempt from the ATS because of the sovereign immunity of the U.S. government. State law tort claims were found to be similarly preempted by the federal interest in protecting military activities. *See Saleh v. Titan Corp.*, 436 F. Supp. 2d 55 (D.D.C. 2006), *aff'd in part and rev'd in part*, 580 F.3d 1 (D.C. Cir. 2009), *cert. denied*, 2011 WL 2518834 (U.S. June 27, 2011). In another lawsuit, *Al Shimari v. CACI Premier Technology, Inc.*, 657 F. Supp. 2d 700, 720-725 (E.D. Va. 2009), the court refused to find federal preemption of a state law tort claim based on abusive interrogation by a contractor, because the court concluded that interrogation was not a combat activity.

      If the first decision is correct, is there any other basis for imposing civil liability on contractors for interrogational torture? If not, and if civil suits against the government and government officials are also barred, as suggested above, will the prospect of criminal prosecution provide an adequate deterrence to official torture? Is your answer influenced by the official responses to reports of torture and abusive interrogation set forth in this chapter and the last one?

      If the *Al Shimari* decision is correct, are you prepared to say what is and is not "combat activity" in the ongoing struggle against the threat to national security posed by international terrorists? Should civil liability turn on such a distinction?

Extraordinary Rendition **19**

Rendition is generally understood to be the surrender of a person from one state to another state that has requested him, typically pursuant to an agreement or extradition treaty, for the purpose of criminal prosecution. In the mid-1990s, however, the United States began capturing suspected terrorist operatives and transferring them to foreign countries as part of a CIA program designed to disrupt and dismantle Al Qaeda terrorist operations. Michael Scheuer, *A Fine Rendition*, N.Y. Times, Mar. 11, 2005. The practice is commonly called "extraordinary rendition," because it involves no treaty or formal agreement and is attended by no judicial process.

The first such renditions were set up by senior officials working in the CIA's Islamic-militant unit and involved informal arrangements with the government of Egypt. As it happened, a few of the top Al Qaeda operatives were Egyptians who had been convicted in absentia of offenses in Egypt. The United States captured some of these and rendered them to Egypt, even though abusive interrogations by Egyptian interrogators, including torture, had long been documented by the State Department. *See* Bureau of Democracy, Human Rights & Labor, U.S. Dep't of State, *Egypt: Country Reports on Human Rights Practices* (Feb. 23, 2001), *at* http://www.state. gov/g/drl/rls/hrrpt/2000/nea/784.htm. The arrangement between U.S. and Egyptian intelligence services was such that the Americans could give questions to Egyptian interrogators they wanted put to detainees in the morning and get answers that same day. Scheuer, *supra.*

After September 11, extraordinary renditions expanded. Receiving nations included Syria, Jordan, Morocco, and Uzbekistan, as well as Egypt. The renditions were not limited to individuals wanted by third countries, but included transfers to third countries solely for the purpose of interrogation — to extract intelligence, as quickly as possible. Stephen Grey, *Ghost Plane: The True Story of the CIA Torture Program* 148-152 (2006). The legal bases for extraordinary rendition and potential judicial remedies for its abuses are addressed in the following decision and in notes and questions that follow it.

Arar v. Ashcroft

United States Court of Appeals, Second Circuit (en banc), 2009
585 F.3d 559, *cert. denied*, 130 S. Ct. 3409 (2010)

DENNIS JACOBS, Chief Judge: Maher Arar appeals from a judgment of the United States District Court for the Eastern District of New York (Trager, J.) dismissing his complaint against the Attorney General of the United States, the Secretary of Homeland Security, the Director of the Federal Bureau of Investigation, and others, including senior immigration officials. Arar alleges that he was detained while changing planes at Kennedy Airport in New York (based on a warning from Canadian authorities that he was a member of Al Qaeda), mistreated for twelve days while in United States custody, and then removed to Syria via Jordan pursuant to an intergovernmental understanding that he would be detained and interrogated under torture by Syrian officials. The complaint alleges a violation of the Torture Victim Protection Act ("TVPA") and of his Fifth Amendment substantive due process rights arising from the conditions of his detention in the United States, the denial of his access to counsel and to the courts while in the United States, and his detention and torture in Syria.

The district court dismissed the complaint (with leave to re-plead only as to the conditions of detention in the United States and his access to counsel and the courts during that period) and Arar timely appealed (without undertaking to amend). *Arar v. Ashcroft*, 414 F. Supp. 2d 250 (E.D.N.Y. 2006). A three-judge panel of this Court unanimously held that: (1) the District Court had personal jurisdiction over Thompson, Ashcroft, and Mueller; (2) Arar failed to state a claim under the TVPA; and (3) Arar failed to establish subject matter jurisdiction over his request for a declaratory judgment. *Arar v. Ashcroft*, 532 F.3d 157 (2d Cir. 2008). A majority of the panel also dismissed Arar's *Bivens* claims, with one member of the panel dissenting. *Id.* The Court voted to rehear the appeal *in banc*. We now affirm.

We have no trouble affirming the district court's conclusions that Arar sufficiently alleged personal jurisdiction over the defendants who challenged it, and that Arar lacks standing to seek declaratory relief. We do not reach issues of qualified immunity or the state secrets privilege. As to the TVPA, we agree with the unanimous position of the panel that Arar insufficiently pleaded that the alleged conduct of United States officials was done under color of foreign law. We agree with the district court that Arar insufficiently pleaded his claim regarding detention in the United States, a ruling that has been reinforced by the subsequent authority of *Bell Atlantic Corp. v. Twombly*, 550 U.S. 544, 570 (2007). Our attention is therefore focused on whether Arar's claims for detention and torture in Syria can be asserted under *Bivens v. Six Unknown Named Agents of Federal Bureau of Narcotics*, 403 U.S. 388 (1971) ("*Bivens*").

To decide the *Bivens* issue, we must determine whether Arar's claims invoke *Bivens* in a new context; and, if so, whether an alternative remedial scheme was available to Arar, or whether (in the absence of affirmative action by Congress) " 'special factors counsel[ ] hesitation.' " *See Wilkie v. Robbins*, 551 U.S. 537, 550 (2007) (quoting *Bush v. Lucas*, 462 U.S. 367, 378 (1983)). This opinion holds that "extraordinary rendition" is a context new to *Bivens* claims, but avoids any categorical ruling on alternative remedies — because the dominant holding of this opinion is that, in the context of extraordinary rendition, hesitation is warranted by special factors. We therefore affirm. . . .

Our ruling does not preclude judicial review and oversight in this context. But if a civil remedy in damages is to be created for harms suffered in the context of extraordinary rendition, it must be created by Congress, which alone has the institutional competence to set parameters, delineate safe harbors, and specify relief. If Congress chooses to legislate on this subject, then judicial review of such legislation would be available.

Applying our understanding of Supreme Court precedent, we decline to create, on our own, a new cause of action against officers and employees of the federal government. Rather, we conclude that, when a case presents the intractable "special factors" apparent here, it is for the Executive in the first instance to decide how to implement extraordinary rendition, and for the elected members of Congress — and not for us as judges — to decide whether an individual may seek compensation from government officers and employees directly, or from the government, for a constitutional violation. Administrations past and present have reserved the right to employ rendition, *see* David Johnston, *U.S. Says Rendition to Continue, but with More Oversight,* N.Y. Times, Aug. 24, 2009, and not withstanding prolonged public debate, Congress has not prohibited the practice, imposed limits on its use, or created a cause of action for those who allege they have suffered constitutional injury as a consequence.

I

Arar's complaint sets forth the following factual allegations.

Arar is a dual citizen of Syria, where he was born and raised, and of Canada, to which his family immigrated when he was 17.

While on vacation in Tunisia in September 2002, Arar was called back to work in Montreal. His itinerary called for stops in Zurich and New York.

Arar landed at Kennedy Airport around noon on September 26. Between planes, Arar presented his Canadian passport to an immigration official who, after checking Arar's credentials, asked Arar to wait nearby. About two hours later, Arar was fingerprinted and his bags searched. Between 4 p.m. and 9 p.m., Arar was interviewed by an agent from the Federal Bureau of Investigation ("FBI"), who asked (*inter alia*) about his relationships with certain individuals who were suspected of terrorist ties. Arar admitted knowing at least one of them, but denied being a member of a terrorist group. Following the FBI interview, Arar was questioned by an official from the Immigration and Nationalization Service ("INS") for three more hours; he continued to deny terrorist affiliations.

Arar spent the night alone in a room at the airport. The next morning (September 27) he was questioned by FBI agents from approximately 9 a.m. until 2 p.m.; the agents asked him about Osama Bin Laden, Iraq, Palestine, and other things. That evening, Arar was given an opportunity to return voluntarily to Syria. He refused, citing a fear of torture, and asked instead to go to Canada or Switzerland. Later that evening, he was transferred to the Metropolitan Detention Center ("MDC") in Brooklyn, where he remained until October 8.

On October 1, the INS initiated removal proceedings, and served Arar with a document stating that he was inadmissible because he belonged to a terrorist organization. Later that day, he called his mother-in-law in Ottawa — his prior requests to place calls and speak to a lawyer having been denied or ignored.

His family retained a lawyer to represent him and contacted the Canadian Consulate in New York.

A Canadian consular official visited Arar on October 3. The next day, immigration officers asked Arar to designate in writing the country to which he would want to be removed. He designated Canada. On the evening of October 5, Arar met with his attorney. The following evening, a Sunday, Arar was again questioned by INS officials. The INS District Director in New York left a voicemail message on the office phone of Arar's attorney that the interview would take place, but the attorney did not receive the message in time to attend. Arar was told that she chose not to attend. In days following, the attorney was given false information about Arar's whereabouts.

On October 8, 2002, Arar learned that the INS had: (1) ordered his removal to Syria, (2) made a (required) finding that such removal would be consistent with Article 3 of the Convention Against Torture ("CAT"), and (3) barred him from re-entering the United States for five years. He was found inadmissible to the United States on the basis of 8 U.S.C. §1182(a)(3)(B)(i)(V), which provides that any alien who "is a member of a terrorist organization" is inadmissible to the United States. The finding was based on Arar's association with a suspected terrorist and other (classified) information. Thereafter, Defendant J. Scott Blackman, an INS Regional Director, made a determination that Arar was clearly and unequivocally a member of Al Qaeda and inadmissible to the United States. A "Final Notice of Inadmissibility," dated October 8, and signed by Defendant Deputy Attorney General Larry Thompson, stated that Arar's removal to Syria would be consistent with the CAT, notwithstanding Arar's articulated fear of torture.

Later that day, Arar was taken to New Jersey, whence he flew in a small jet to Washington, D.C., and then to Amman, Jordan. When he arrived in Amman on October 9, he was handed over to Jordanian authorities who treated him roughly and then delivered him to the custody of Syrian officials, who detained him at a Syrian Military Intelligence facility. Arar was in Syria for a year, the first ten months in an underground cell six feet by three, and seven feet high. He was interrogated for twelve days on his arrival in Syria, and in that period was beaten on his palms, hips, and lower back with a two-inch-thick electric cable and with bare hands. Arar alleges that United States officials conspired to send him to Syria for the purpose of interrogation under torture, and directed the interrogations from abroad by providing Syria with Arar's dossier, dictating questions for the Syrians to ask him, and receiving intelligence learned from the interviews.

On October 20, 2002, Canadian Embassy officials inquired of Syria as to Arar's whereabouts. The next day, Syria confirmed to Canada that Arar was in its custody; that same day, interrogation ceased. Arar remained in Syria, however, receiving visits from Canadian consular officials. On August 14, 2003, Arar defied his captors by telling the Canadians that he had been tortured and was confined to a small underground cell. Five days later, after signing a confession that he had trained as a terrorist in Afghanistan, Arar was moved to various locations. On October 5, 2003, Arar was released to the custody of a Canadian embassy official in Damascus, and was flown to Ottawa the next day.

II

On January 22, 2004, Arar filed a four-count complaint in the Eastern District of New York seeking damages from federal officials for harms suffered as a result of his detention and confinement in the United States and his detention and interrogation in Syria. Count One of Arar's complaint seeks relief under the Torture Victim Protection Act ("TVPA"), 28 U.S.C. §1350 note (a)(1) (the "TVPA claim"). Counts Two and Three seek relief under the Fifth Amendment for Arar's alleged torture in Syria (Count Two) and his detention there (Count Three). Count Four seeks relief under the Fifth Amendment for Arar's detention in the United States prior to his removal to Syria. Arar also seeks a declaratory judgment that defendants' conduct violated his "constitutional, civil, and human rights." . . .

III . . .

At the outset, we conclude (as the panel concluded unanimously) that Arar: (1) sufficiently alleged personal jurisdiction over the defendants, and (2) has no standing to seek declaratory relief; in addition, because we dismiss the action for the reasons set forth below, we need not (and do not) reach the issues of qualified immunity or the state secrets privilege. . . .

IV

The TVPA creates a cause of action for damages against any "individual who, under actual or apparent authority, or color of law, of any foreign nation . . . subjects an individual to torture." 28 U.S.C. §1350 note (a)(1). Count One of Arar's complaint alleges that the defendants conspired with Jordanian and Syrian officials to have Arar tortured in direct violation of the TVPA.

Any allegation arising under the TVPA requires a demonstration that the defendants acted under color of foreign law, or under its authority. *Kadic v. Karadzic,* 70 F.3d 232, 245 (2d Cir. 1995). "In construing the term[ ] . . . 'color of law,' courts are instructed to look . . . to jurisprudence under 42 U.S.C. §1983. . . ." *Id.* (citing H.R. Rep. No. 367, 102d Cong., 2d Sess., at 5 (1991) *reprinted in* 1992 U.S.C.C.A.N. 84, 87). Under section 1983, "[t]he traditional definition of acting under color of state law requires that the defendant . . . have exercised power 'possessed by virtue of state law and made possible only because the wrongdoer is clothed with the authority of state law.' " *West v. Atkins,* 487 U.S. 42, 49 (1988) (quoting *United States v. Classic,* 313 U.S. 299, 326 (1941)). The determination as to whether a non-state party acts under color of state law requires an intensely fact-specific judgment unaided by rigid criteria as to whether particular conduct may be fairly attributed to the state. . . .

Accordingly, to state a claim under the TVPA, Arar must adequately allege that the defendants possessed power under Syrian law, and that the offending actions (*i.e.,* Arar's removal to Syria and subsequent torture) derived from an exercise of that power, or that defendants could not have undertaken their culpable actions absent such power. The complaint contains no such allegation. Arar has argued that his allegation of conspiracy cures any deficiency under the TVPA. But the conspiracy allegation is that United States officials encouraged and facilitated the exercise of power by Syrians in Syria, not that the United States officials had or exercised power or authority under Syrian law. The defendants are alleged to have acted under color of federal, not Syrian, law, and to have acted in accordance with alleged federal policies and in pursuit of the aims of the federal government in the international context. At most, it is alleged that the defendants encouraged or solicited certain conduct by foreign officials. Such conduct is insufficient to establish that the defendants were in some way clothed with the authority of Syrian law or that their conduct may otherwise be fairly attributable to Syria. *See, e.g., Harbury v. Hayden*, 444 F. Supp. 2d 19, 42-43 (D.D.C. 2006), *aff'd on other grounds*, 522 F.3d 413 (D.C. Cir. 2008). We therefore agree with the unanimous holding of the panel and affirm the District Court's dismissal of the TVPA claim.

V

Count Four of the complaint alleges that the conditions of confinement in the United States (prior to Arar's removal to Syria), and the denial of access to courts during that detention, violated Arar's substantive due process rights under the Fifth Amendment. The District Court dismissed this claim — without prejudice — as insufficiently pleaded, and invited Arar to re-plead the claim in order to "articulate more precisely the judicial relief he was denied" and to "name those defendants that were personally involved in the alleged unconstitutional treatment." *Arar*, 414 F. Supp. 2d at 286, 287. Arar elected (in his counsel's words) to "stand on the allegations of his original complaint."

On a motion to dismiss, courts require "enough facts to state a claim to relief that is plausible on its face." *Twombly*, 550 U.S. at 570; *see also Ashcroft v. Iqbal*, — U.S. —, 129 S. Ct. 1937, 1949-50 (2009). "Factual allegations must be enough to raise a right to relief above the speculative level. . . ." *Twombly*, 550 U.S. at 555. Broad allegations of conspiracy are insufficient; the plaintiff "must provide some factual basis supporting a meeting of the minds, such that defendants entered into an agreement, express or tacit, to achieve the unlawful end." *Webb v. Goord*, 340 F.3d 105, 110 (2d Cir. 2003) (internal quotation marks omitted) (addressing conspiracy claims under 42 U.S.C. §1985). Furthermore, a plaintiff in a *Bivens* action is required to allege facts indicating that the defendants were personally involved in the claimed constitutional violation. *See Ellis v. Blum*, 643 F.2d 68, 85 (2d Cir. 1981).

Arar alleges that "Defendants' — undifferentiated — 'denied Mr. Arar effective access to consular assistance, the courts, his lawyers, and family members" in order to effectuate his removal to Syria. But he fails to specify any culpable action taken by any single defendant, and does not allege the "meeting of the minds" that a plausible conspiracy claim requires. He alleges (in passive voice) that his requests to make phone calls "were ignored," and that "he was told" that he was not entitled to a lawyer, but he fails to link these denials to any defendant, named or unnamed. Given this omission, and in view of Arar's rejection of an opportunity to re-plead, we agree with the District Court and the panel majority that this Count of the complaint must be dismissed.

We express no view as to the sufficiency of the pleading otherwise, that is, whether the conduct alleged (if plausibly attributable to defendants) would violate a constitutionally protected interest. To the extent that this claim may be deemed to be a *Bivens*-type action, it may raise some of the special factors considered later in this opinion.

VI

Arar's remaining claims seek relief on the basis of torture and detention in Syria, and are cast as violations of substantive due process. At the outset, Defendants argue that the jurisdictional bar of the INA deprived the District Court of subject-matter jurisdiction over these counts because Arar's removal was conducted pursuant to a decision that was "at the discretion" of the Attorney General. . . .

. . . [W]e need not decide the . . . question of whether the INA bar defeats jurisdiction of Arar's substantive due process claims, because we conclude below that the case must be dismissed at the threshold for other reasons.

VII

In *Bivens*, the Supreme Court "recognized for the first time an implied private action for damages against federal officers alleged to have violated a citizen's constitutional rights." *Corr. Servs. Corp. v. Malesko*, 534 U.S. 61, 66 (2001). The plaintiff in *Bivens* had been subjected to an unlawful, warrantless search which resulted in his arrest. The Supreme Court allowed him to state a cause of action for money damages directly under the Fourth Amendment, thereby giving rise to a judicially-created remedy stemming directly from the Constitution itself.

The purpose of the *Bivens* remedy "is to deter individual federal officers from committing constitutional violations." *Malesko*, 534 U.S. at 70. So a *Bivens* action is brought against individuals, and any damages are payable by the offending officers. *Carlson v. Green*, 446 U.S. 14, 21 (1980). Notwithstanding the potential breadth of claims that would serve that objective, the Supreme Court has warned that the *Bivens* remedy is an extraordinary thing that should rarely if ever be applied in "new contexts." *See Malesko*, 534 U.S. at 69 (internal quotation marks omitted). In the 38 years since *Bivens*, the Supreme Court has extended it twice only: in the context of an employment discrimination claim in violation of the Due Process Clause, *Davis v. Passman*, 442 U.S. 228 (1979); and in the context of an Eighth Amendment violation by prison officials, *Carlson*, 446 U.S. 14. Since *Carlson* in 1980, the Supreme Court has declined to extend the *Bivens* remedy in any new direction at all. Among the rejected contexts are: violations of federal employees' First Amendment rights by their employers, *Bush v. Lucas*, 462 U.S. 367 (1983); harms suffered incident to military service, *United States v. Stanley*, 483 U.S. 669 (1987); denials of Social Security benefits, *Schweiker* [*v. Chilicky*, 487 U.S. 412 (1988),] at 412; claims against federal agencies, *FDIC v. Meyer*, 510 U.S. 471 (1994); claims against private corporations operating under federal contracts, *Malesko*, 534 U.S. 61 (2001); and claims of retaliation by federal officials against private landowners, *Wilkie* [*v. Robbins*, 551 U.S. 537 (2007),] at 562.

This case requires us to examine whether allowing this *Bivens* action to proceed would extend *Bivens* to a new "context," and if so, whether such an extension is advisable.

"Context" is not defined in the case law. At a sufficiently high level of generality, any claim can be analogized to some other claim for which a *Bivens* action is afforded, just as at a sufficiently high level of particularity, every case has points of distinction. We construe the word "context" as it is commonly used in law: to reflect a potentially recurring scenario that has similar legal and factual components.

The context of this case is international rendition, specifically, "extraordinary rendition." Extraordinary rendition is treated as a distinct phenomenon in international law. Indeed, law review articles that affirmatively advocate the creation of a remedy in cases like Arar's recognize "extraordinary rendition" as the context. *See, e.g.*, Peter Johnston, Note, *Leaving the Invisible Universe: Why All Victims of Extraordinary Rendition Need a Cause of Action Against the United States*, 16 J.L. & Pol'y 357, 363 (2007).

More particularly, the context of extraordinary rendition in Arar's case is the complicity or cooperation of United States government officials in the delivery of a noncitizen to a foreign country for torture (or with the expectation that torture will take place). This is a "new context": no court has previously afforded a *Bivens* remedy for extraordinary rendition.

Once we have identified the context as "new," we must decide whether to recognize a *Bivens* remedy in that environment of fact and law. The Supreme Court tells us that this is a two-part inquiry. In order to determine whether to recognize a *Bivens* remedy in a new context, we must consider: whether there is an alternative remedial scheme available to the plaintiff; and whether " 'special factors counsel[ ] hesitation' " in creating a *Bivens* remedy. *Wilkie*, 551 U.S. at 550 (quoting *Bush*, 462 U.S. at 378).

VIII ...

... [W]e need not decide whether an alternative remedial scheme was available because, "even in the absence of an alternative [remedial scheme], a *Bivens* remedy is a subject of judgment ... [in which] courts must ... pay particular heed ... to any special factors counselling hesitation before authorizing a new kind of federal litigation." *Wilkie*, 551 U.S. at 550. Such special factors are clearly present in the new context of this case, and they sternly counsel hesitation.

IX

When the *Bivens* cause of action was created in 1971, the Supreme Court explained that such a remedy could be afforded because that "case involve[d] no special factors counselling hesitation in the absence of affirmative action by Congress." *Bivens*, 403 U.S. at 396. This prudential limitation was expressly weighed by the Court in *Davis*, 442 U.S. at 245-46, and *Carlson*, 446 U.S. at 18-19, and such hesitation has defeated numerous *Bivens* initiatives, *see, e.g., Stanley*, 483 U.S. at 683-84; [*Chappell v. Wallace*, 462 U.S. 296 (1983)] at 304; *Wilkie*, 551 U.S. at 554-55; [*Dotson v. Griesa*, 398 F.3d 156 (2d Cir. 2005)] at 166-67. Among the "special factors" that have "counsel[ed] hesitation" and thereby foreclosed a *Bivens* remedy are: military concerns, *Stanley*, 483 U.S. at 683-84; *Chappell*, 462 U.S. at 304; separation of powers, *United States v. City of Philadelphia*, 644 F.2d 187, 200 (3d Cir. 1980); the comprehensiveness of available statutory schemes, *Dotson*, 398 F.3d at 166; national security concerns, *Beattie v. Boeing Co.*, 43 F.3d 559, 563 (10th Cir. 1994); and foreign policy considerations, *United States v. Verdugo-Urquidez*, 494 U.S. 259, 274 (1990).

Two principles emerge from this review of case law:

— "Special factors" is an embracing category, not easily defined; but it is limited in terms to factors that provoke "hesitation." While special factors should be substantial enough to justify the absence of a damages remedy for a wrong, no account is taken of countervailing factors that might counsel alacrity or activism, and none has ever been cited by the Supreme Court as a reason for affording a *Bivens* remedy where it would not otherwise exist.

— The only relevant threshold — that a factor "counsels hesitation" — is remarkably low. It is at the opposite end of the continuum from the unflagging duty to exercise jurisdiction. Hesitation is a pause, not a full stop, or an abstention; and to counsel is not to require. "Hesitation" is "counseled" whenever thoughtful discretion would pause even to consider.

With these principles in mind, we adduce, one by one, special factors that bear upon the recognition of a *Bivens* remedy for rendition.

X

Although this action is cast in terms of a claim for money damages against the defendants in their individual capacities, it operates as a constitutional challenge to policies promulgated by the executive. Our federal system of checks and balances provides means to consider allegedly unconstitutional executive policy, but a private action for money damages against individual policymakers is not one of them. A *Bivens* action is sometimes analogized to an action pursuant to 42 U.S.C. §1983, but it does not reach so far as to create the federal counterpart to an action under *Monell v. Department of Social Services*, 436 U.S. 658 (1978). Here, we need not decide categorically whether a *Bivens* action can lie against policymakers because in the context of extraordinary rendition, such an action would have the natural tendency to affect diplomacy, foreign policy, and the security of the nation, and that fact counsels hesitation. Our holding need be no broader.

A. Security and Foreign Policy

The Executive has practiced rendition since at least 1995. *See* Extraordinary Rendition in U.S. Counterterrorism Policy: The Impact on Transatlantic Relations: Joint Hearing Before the Subcomm. on International Organizations, Human Rights, and Oversight and the Subcomm. on Europe of the H. Comm. on Foreign Affairs, 110th Cong. 15 (2007) (statement of Michael F. Scheuer, Former Chief, Bin Laden Unit, CIA). Arar gives "the mid-1990s" as the date for the inception of the policy under which he was sent to Syria for torture. A suit seeking a damages remedy against senior officials who implement such a policy is in critical respects a suit against the government as to which the government has not waived sovereign immunity. Such a suit unavoidably influences government policy, probes government secrets, invades government interests, enmeshes government lawyers, and thereby elicits government funds for settlement. (Canada has already paid Arar $10 million.)

It is a substantial understatement to say that one must hesitate before extending *Bivens* into such a context. A suit seeking a damages remedy against senior officials who implement an extraordinary rendition policy would enmesh the courts ineluctably in an assessment of the validity and rationale of that policy and its implementation in this particular case, matters that directly affect significant diplomatic and national security concerns. It is clear from the face of the complaint that Arar explicitly targets the "policy" of extraordinary rendition; he cites the policy twice in his complaint, and submits documents and media reports concerning the practice. His claim cannot proceed without inquiry into the perceived need for the policy, the threats to which it responds, the substance and sources of the intelligence used to formulate it, and the propriety of adopting specific responses to particular threats in light of apparent geopolitical circumstances and our relations with foreign countries.

The Supreme Court has expressly counseled that matters touching upon foreign policy and national security fall within "an area of executive action 'in which courts have long been *hesitant* to intrude' " absent congressional authorization. *Lincoln v. Vigil*, 508 U.S. 182, 192 (1993) (emphasis added) (*quoting Franklin v. Massachusetts*, 505 U.S. 788, 819 (1992) (Stevens, J., concurring in part and concurring in the judgment)). It "has recognized 'the generally accepted view that foreign policy was the province and responsibility of the Executive.' . . . Thus, unless Congress specifically has provided otherwise, courts traditionally have been *reluctant* to intrude upon the authority of the Executive in military and national security affairs." *Dep't of Navy v. Egan*, 484 U.S. 518, 529-30 (1988) (emphasis added) (*quoting Haig v. Agee*, 453 U.S. 280, 293-94 (1981)). This "hesita[tion]" and "reluctan[ce]" is counseled by:

— the constitutional separation of powers among the branches of government, *see United States v. Curtiss-Wright Exp. Co.*, 299 U.S. 304, 320-22 (1936). . . .

— the limited institutional competence of the judiciary, *see Boumediene v. Bush,* — U.S. ——, 128 S. Ct. 2229, 2276-77 (2008) ("Unlike the President and some designated Members of Congress, neither the Members of this Court nor most federal judges begin the day with briefings that may describe new and serious threats to our Nation and its people. The law must accord the Executive substantial authority to apprehend and detain those who pose a real danger to our security."). . . .

B. Classified Information

The extraordinary rendition context involves exchanges among the ministries and agencies of foreign countries on diplomatic, security, and intelligence issues. The sensitivities of such classified material are "too obvious to call for enlarged discussion." *Dep't of Navy*, 484 U.S. at 529 (internal quotation marks omitted). Even the probing of these matters entails the risk that other countries will become less willing to cooperate with the United States in sharing intelligence resources to counter terrorism. "At its core," as the panel opinion observed, "this suit arises from the Executive Branch's alleged determination that (a) Arar was affiliated with Al Qaeda, and therefore a threat to national security, and (b) his removal to Syria was appropriate in light of U.S. diplomatic and national security interests." *Arar*, 532 F.3d at 181. To determine the basis for Arar's alleged designation as an Al Qaeda member and his subsequent removal to Syria, the district court would have to consider what was done by the national security apparatus of at least three foreign countries, as well as that of the United States. Indeed, the Canadian government—which appears to have provided the intelligence that United States officials were acting upon when they detained Arar—paid Arar compensation for its role in the events surrounding this lawsuit, but has *also* asserted the need for Canada itself to maintain the confidentiality of certain classified materials related to Arar's claims.

C. Open Courts

Allegations of conspiracy among government agencies that must often work in secret inevitably implicate a lot of classified material that cannot be introduced into the public record. Allowing Arar's claims to proceed would very likely mean that some documents or information sought by Arar would be redacted, reviewed *in camera*, and otherwise concealed from the public. Concealment does not bespeak wrongdoing: in such matters, it is just as important to conceal what has *not* been done. Nevertheless, these measures would excite suspicion and speculation as to the true nature and depth of the supposed conspiracy, and as to the scope and depth of judicial oversight. Indeed, after an inquiry at oral argument as to whether classified materials relating to Arar's claims could be made available for review *in camera*, Arar objected to the supplementation of the record with material he could not see. *See* Letter from David Cole, Counsel for Maher Arar (Dec. 23, 2008). After pointing out that such materials are unnecessary to the adjudication of a motion on the pleadings (where the allegations of the complaint must be accepted as true), Arar protested that any materials submitted *ex parte* and *in camera* would not be subject to adversarial testing and that consideration of such documents would be "presumptively unconstitutional" since they would result in a decision "on the basis of secret information available to only one side of the dispute."

The court's reliance on information that cannot be introduced into the public record is likely to be a common feature of any *Bivens* actions arising in the context of alleged extraordinary rendition. This should provoke hesitation, given the strong preference in the Anglo-American legal tradition for open court proceedings, a value incorporated into modern First and Sixth Amendment law. . . .

XI

A government report states that this case involves assurances received from other governments in connection with the determination that Arar's removal to Syria would be consistent with Article 3 of the CAT. Office of Inspector General, Dep't of Homeland Sec., (Unclassified) *The Removal of a Canadian Citizen to Syria* 5, 22, 26-27 (2008). This case is not unique in that respect. Cases in the context of extraordinary rendition are very likely to present serious questions relating to private diplomatic assurances from foreign countries received by federal officials, and this feature of such claims opens the door to graymail.

A. Assurances

The regulations promulgated pursuant to the [Foreign Affairs Reform and Restructuring Act of 1998 ("FARRA"), 8 U.S.C. §1231 note] explicitly authorize the removal of an alien to a foreign country following receipt from that country of sufficiently reliable assurances that the alien will not be tortured. *See* 8 C.F.R. §208.18(c). Should we decide to extend *Bivens* into the extraordinary rendition context, resolution of these actions will require us to determine whether any such assurances were received from the country of rendition and whether the relevant defendants relied upon them in good faith in removing the alien at issue.

Any analysis of these questions would necessarily involve us in an inquiry into the work of foreign governments and several federal agencies, the nature of certain classified information, and the extent of secret diplomatic relationships. An investigation into the existence and content of such assurances would potentially embarrass our government through inadvertent or deliberate disclosure of information harmful to our own and other states. Given the general allocation of authority over foreign relations to the political branches and the decidedly limited experience and knowledge of the federal judiciary regarding such matters, such an investigation would also implicate grave concerns about the separation of powers and our institutional competence. These considerations strongly counsel hesitation in acknowledging a *Bivens* remedy in this context.

B. Graymail

... [T]here is further reason to hesitate where, as in this case, the challenged government policies are the subject of classified communications: a possibility that such suits will make the government "vulnerable to 'graymail,'" *i.e.*, individual lawsuits brought to induce the [government] to settle a case (or prevent its filing) out of fear that any effort to litigate the action would reveal classified information that may undermine ongoing covert operations," or otherwise compromise foreign policy efforts. *Tenet v. Doe*, 544 U.S. 1, 11 (2005). We cast no aspersions on Arar, or his lawyers; this dynamic inheres in any case where there is a risk that a defendant might "disclose classified information in the course of a trial." *United States v. Pappas*, 94 F.3d 795, 799 (2d Cir. 1996). This is an endemic risk in cases (however few) which involve a claim like Arar's.

The risk of graymail is itself a special factor which counsels hesitation in creating a *Bivens* remedy. There would be hesitation enough in an ordinary graymail case, *i.e.*, where the tactic is employed against the *government*, which can trade settlement cash (or the dismissal of criminal charges) for secrecy. *See Tenet*, 544 U.S. at 11; *Pappas*, 94 F.3d at 799. But the graymail risk in a *Bivens* rendition case is uniquely troublesome. The interest in protecting military, diplomatic, and intelligence secrets is located (as always) in the *government;* yet a *Bivens* claim, by definition, is never pleaded against the government. *See, e.g., Malesko*, 534 U.S. at 70. So in a *Bivens* case, there is a dissociation between the holder of the non-disclosure interest (the government, which cannot be sued directly under *Bivens*) and the person with the incentive to disclose (the defendant, who cannot waive, but will be liable for any damages assessed). In a rendition case, the *Bivens* plaintiff could in effect pressure the individual defendants until the *government* cries uncle. Thus any *Bivens* action involving extraordinary rendition would inevitably suck the government into the case to protect its considerable interests, and — if disclosure is ordered — to appeal, or to suffer the disclosure, or to pay....

In the end, a *Bivens* action based on rendition is — in all but name — a claim against the government. It is not for nothing that Canada (the government, not an individual officer of it) paid Arar $10 million dollars.

XII

In the small number of contexts in which courts have implied a *Bivens* remedy, it has often been easy to identify both the line between constitutional and unconstitutional conduct, and the alternative course which officers should have pursued. The guard who beat a prisoner should not have beaten him; the agent who searched without a warrant should have gotten one; and the immigration officer who subjected an alien to multiple strip searches without cause should have left the alien in his clothes. This distinction may or may not amount to a special factor counseling hesitation in the implication of a *Bivens* remedy. But it is surely remarkable that the context of extraordinary rendition is so different, involving as it does a complex and rapidly changing legal framework beset with critical legal judgments that have not yet been made, as well as policy choices that are by no means easily reached.

Consider: should the officers here have let Arar go on his way and board his flight to Montreal? Canada was evidently unwilling to receive him; it was, after all, Canadian authorities who identified Arar as a terrorist (or did something that led their government to apologize publicly to Arar and pay him $10 million).

Should a person identified as a terrorist by his own country be allowed to board his plane and go on to his destination? Surely, that would raise questions as to what duty is owed to the other passengers and the crew.

Or should a suspected terrorist en route to Canada have been released on the Canadian border — over which he could re-enter the United States virtually at will? Or should he have been sent back whence his plane came, or to some third country? Should those governments be told that Canada thinks he is a terrorist? If so, what country would take him?

Or should the suspected terrorist have been sent to Guantanamo Bay or — if no other country would take him — kept in the United States with the prospect of release into the general population? *See Zadvydas v. Davis,* 533 U.S. 678, 699-700 (2001).

None of this is to say that extraordinary rendition is or should be a favored policy choice. At the same time, the officials required to decide these vexed issues are "subject to the pull of competing obligations." *Lombardi v. Whitman,* 485 F.3d 73, 83 (2d Cir. 2007). Many viable actions they might consider "clash with other equally important governmental responsibilities." *Pena v. DePrisco,* 432 F.3d 98, 114 (2d Cir. 2005) (internal quotation marks omitted). Given the ample reasons for pause already discussed, we need not and do not rely on this consideration in concluding that it is inappropriate to extend *Bivens* to this context. Still, Congress is the appropriate branch of government to decide under what circumstances (if any) these kinds of policy decisions — which are directly related to the security of the population and the foreign affairs of the country — should be subjected to the influence of litigation brought by aliens.

XIII

All of these special factors notwithstanding, we cannot ignore that, as the panel dissent put it, "there is a long history of judicial review of Executive and Legislative decisions related to the conduct of foreign relations and national security." *Arar,* 532 F.3d at 213 (Sack, J., concurring in part and dissenting in part). Where does that leave us? We recognize our limited competence, authority, and jurisdiction to make rules or set parameters to govern the practice called rendition. By the same token, we can easily locate that competence, expertise, and responsibility elsewhere: in Congress. Congress may be content for the Executive Branch to exercise these powers without judicial check. But if Congress wishes to create a remedy for individuals like Arar, it can enact legislation that includes enumerated eligibility parameters, delineated safe harbors, defined review processes, and specific relief to be afforded. Once Congress has performed this task, *then* the courts in a proper case will be able to review the statute and provide judicial oversight to the "Executive and Legislative decisions [which have been made with regard] to the conduct of foreign relations and national security." *Id....*

SACK, Circuit Judge, joined by Judges CALABRESI, POOLER, and PARKER, concurring in part and dissenting in part.... We disagree ... with the majority's continued insistence that Arar cannot employ a *Bivens* remedy to seek compensation for his injuries at the hands of government agents. The majority reaches that conclusion by artificially dividing the complaint into a domestic claim that does not involve torture—viz., "[Arar's] claim regarding detention in the United States," —and a foreign claim that does—viz., "[Arar's] claims for detention and torture in Syria." The majority then dismisses the domestic claim as inadequately pleaded and the foreign claim as one that cannot "be asserted under *Bivens*" in light of the opinion's "dominant holding" that "in the context of involuntary rendition, hesitation is warranted by special factors." . . .

As we will explain, . . . the complaint's allegations cannot properly be divided into claims for mistreatment in the United States and "claims for detention and torture in Syria." Arar's complaint of mistreatment sweeps more broadly than that, encompassing a chain of events that began with his interception and detention at New York's John F. Kennedy Airport ("JFK") and continued with his being sent abroad in shackles by government agents with the knowledge that he would likely be tortured as a result. Viewed in this light, we conclude that Arar's allegations do not present a "new context" for a *Bivens* action.

And even were it a new context, we disagree with what appears to be the *en banc* majority's test for whether a new *Bivens* action should be made available: the existence *vel non* of "special factors counselling hesitation." First, we think heeding "special factors" relating to secrecy and security is a form of double counting inasmuch as those interests are fully protected by the state-secrets privilege. Second, in our view the applicable test is not whether "special factors" exist, but whether after "paying particular heed to" them, a *Bivens* remedy should be recognized with respect to at least some allegations in the complaint. Applying that test, we think a *Bivens* remedy is available. . . .

Our overriding concern, however, is with the majority's apparent determination to go to whatever length necessary to reach what it calls its "dominant holding": that a *Bivens* remedy is unavailable. Such a holding is unnecessary inasmuch as the government assures us that this case could likely be resolved quickly and expeditiously in the district court by application of the state-secrets privilege. . . .

II. THE DISMISSAL OF THE FOURTH CLAIM FOR RELIEF . . .

A. Specification of Defendants' Acts and Conspiracy Allegations . . .

Arar should not have been required to "name those defendants [who] were personally involved in the alleged unconstitutional treatment." *Arar*, 414 F. Supp. 2d at 287. In actions pursuant to 42 U.S.C. §1983, which are "analog[s]" of the less-common *Bivens* action, *Ashcroft v. Iqbal*, —— U.S. ——, ——, 129 S. Ct. 1937, 1948 (2009) (citation omitted), we allow plaintiffs to "maintain[ ] supervisory personnel as defendants . . . until [they have] been afforded an opportunity through at least brief discovery to identify the subordinate officials who have personal liability." *Davis v. Kelly*, 160 F.3d 917, 921 (2d Cir. 1998) (citing Second Circuit authority).

> Similarly, courts have rejected the dismissal of suits against unnamed defendants described by roles . . . until the plaintiff has had some opportunity for discovery to learn the identities of responsible officials. Once the supervisory officer has inquired within the institution and identified the actual decision-makers of the challenged action, those officials may then submit affidavits based on their personal knowledge of the circumstances.

Id. (citations omitted). . . .

To be sure, the Supreme Court has recently set a strict pleading standard for supervisory liability claims under *Bivens* against a former Attorney General of the United States and the Director of the FBI. *See Iqbal, supra.* We do not think, however, that the Court has thereby permitted governmental actors who are unnamed in a complaint automatically to escape personal civil rights liability. A plaintiff must, after all, have some way to identify a defendant who anonymously violates his civil rights. We doubt that *Iqbal* requires a plaintiff to obtain his abusers' business cards in order to state a civil rights claim. Put conversely, we do not think that *Iqbal* implies that federal government miscreants may avoid *Bivens* liability altogether through the simple expedient of wearing hoods while inflicting injury. Some manner of proceeding must be made available for the reasons we recognized in *Davis.*

Whether or not there is a mechanism available to identify the "Doe" defendants, moreover, Arar's complaint *does* sufficiently name some individual defendants who personally took part in the alleged violation of his civil rights. The role of defendant J. Scott Blackman, formerly Director of the Regional Office of INS, for example, is, as reflected in the district court's explication of the facts, *see Arar*, 414 F. Supp. 2d at 252-54, set forth in reasonable detail in the complaint. So are at least some of the acts of the defendant Edward J. McElroy, District Director of the INS. . . .

C. Sufficient Pleading under *Iqbal*

More generally, we think the district court's extended recitation of the allegations in the complaint makes clear that the facts of Arar's mistreatment while within the United States — including the alleged denial of his access to courts and counsel and his alleged mistreatment while in federal detention in the United States — were pleaded meticulously and in copious detail. The assertion of relevant places, times, and events — and names when known — is lengthy and specific. Even measured in light of Supreme Court case law post-dating the district court's dismissal of the fourth claim, which instituted a more stringent standard of review for pleadings, the complaint here passes muster. It does not "offer[ ] 'labels and conclusions' or 'formulaic recitation of the elements of a cause of action.'" *Iqbal*, 129 S. Ct. at 1949 (quoting *Bell Atl. Corp. v. Twombly*, 550 U.S. 544, 555 (2007)). Nor does it "tender[ ] 'naked assertion[s]' devoid of 'further factual enhancement.'" *Id.* (quoting *Twombly*, 550 U.S. at 557). Its allegations of a constitutional violation are "'plausible on [their] face.'" *Id.* (quoting *Twombly*, 550 U.S. at 555). And, as we have explained, Arar has pled "factual content that allows the court to draw the reasonable inference that the defendant[s] [are] liable for the misconduct alleged." *Id.* (quoting *Twombly*, 550 U.S. at 556). We would therefore vacate the district court's dismissal of the Fourth Claim for Relief. . . .

IV. THE "CONTEXT" IN WHICH A *BIVENS* REMEDY IS SOUGHT

The majority's artificial interpretation of the complaint permits it to characterize the "context" of Arar's *Bivens* action as entirely one of "international rendition, specifically, 'extraordinary rendition.'" This permits the majority to focus on the part of the complaint that presents a "new context" for *Bivens* purposes. But when the complaint is considered in light of all of Arar's allegations, his due process claim for relief from his apprehension, detention, interrogation, and denial of access to counsel and courts in the United States, as well as his expulsion to Syria for further interrogation likely under torture, is not at all "new." . . .

C. The New Context Test ...

If the alleged facts of Arar's complaint were limited to his claim of "extraordinary rendition" to, and torture in, Syria—that is, limited to his allegations that he was transported by the United States government to Syria via Jordan pursuant to a conspiracy or other arrangement among the countries or their agents and mistreated in Syria as a result—as the majority would have it, then we might well agree that we are dealing with a "new context." But ... the complaint is not so limited. Incarceration in the United States without cause, mistreatment while so incarcerated, denial of access to counsel and the courts while so incarcerated, and the facilitation of torture by others, considered as possible violations of a plaintiff's procedural and substantive due process rights, are hardly novel claims, nor do they present us with a "new context" in any legally significant sense.

We have recognized implied *Bivens* rights of action pursuant to the Due Process Clause, so Arar's claims for relief are not new actions under *Bivens* in that sense. ... In *Iqbal*, for example, we considered a *Bivens* action brought on, *inter alia*, a Fifth Amendment substantive due process theory. The plaintiff alleged physical mistreatment and humiliation, as a Muslim prisoner, by federal prison officials, while he was detained at the MDC. After concluding, on interlocutory appeal, that the defendants were not entitled to qualified immunity, we returned the matter to the district court for further proceedings. We did not so much as hint either that a *Bivens* remedy was unavailable or that its availability would constitute an unwarranted extension of the *Bivens* doctrine. *Iqbal*, 490 F.3d at 177-78. ...

Indeed, even the most "international" of Arar's domestic allegations—that the defendants, acting within the United States, sent Arar to Syria with the intent that he be tortured—present no new context for *Bivens* purposes. Principles of substantive due process apply to a narrow band of extreme misbehavior by government agents acting under color of law: mistreatment that is "so egregious, so outrageous, that it may fairly be said to shock the contemporary conscience." *Lombardi v. Whitman*, 485 F.3d 73, 79 (2d Cir. 2007) (internal quotation marks omitted). Sending Arar from the United States with the intent or understanding that he will be tortured in Syria easily exceeds the level of outrageousness needed to make out a substantive due process claim. ...

To be sure, Arar alleges not that the defendants themselves tortured him; he says that they "outsourced" it. But we do not think that the question whether the defendants violated Arar's substantive due process rights turns on whom they selected to do the torturing, or that such "outsourcing" somehow changes the essential character of the acts within the United States to which Arar seeks to hold the defendants accountable. ...

V. DEVISING A NEW *BIVENS* DAMAGES ACTION ...

B. The Special Factors Identified by the Majority ...

... After *Iqbal*, it would be difficult to argue that Arar's complaint can survive as against defendants who are alleged to have been supervisors with, at most, "knowledge" of Arar's mistreatment. *See Iqbal*, 129 S. Ct. at 1949; *see also id.* at 1955 (Souter, J., dissenting). And to the extent that the United States remains a defendant, perhaps it should be dismissed for want of possible liability under *Bivens* too. But that does not dispose of the case against the lower-level defendants, such as Blackman, McElroy, and the Doe defendants, who are alleged to have personally undertaken purposeful unconstitutional actions against Arar.

It also may be that to the extent actions against "policymakers" can be equated with lawsuits against policies, they may not survive *Iqbal* either. But while those championing Arar's case may in fact wish to challenge extraordinary rendition policy writ large, the relief Arar himself seeks is principally compensation for an unconstitutional implementation of that policy. That is what *Bivens* actions are for. . . .

. . . The other "special factors" cited by the majority focus our attention on the ability of the executive to conduct the business of diplomacy and government in secret as necessary and to protect public and private security. It is beyond dispute that the judiciary must protect that concern. *See, e.g., Doe v. CIA*, 576 F.3d 95 (2d Cir. 2009). But inasmuch as there are established procedures for doing just that, we think treating that need as giving rise to "special factors counseling hesitation" is an unfortunate form of double counting. The problem can be, should be, and customarily is, dealt with case by case by employing the established procedures of the state-secrets doctrine, rather than by barring all such plaintiffs at the courtroom door without further inquiry.

C. Factors Weighing in Favor of a *Bivens* Action

At least some factors weigh in favor of permitting a *Bivens* action in this case. We assume, as we are required to, that Arar suffered a grievous infringement of his constitutional rights by one or more of the defendants, from his interception and detention while changing planes at an international airport to the time two weeks later when he was sent off in the expectation — perhaps the intent and expectation — that he would be tortured, all in order to obtain information from him. Breach of a constitutional or legal duty would appear to counsel in favor of some sort of opportunity for the victim to obtain a remedy for it. . . .

VI. THE STATE-SECRETS PRIVILEGE

[The dissenters argue that the state-secrets privilege is well suited to provide for a ruling on the merits of Arar's claims.] . . .

BARRINGTON D. PARKER, Circuit Judge, joined by Judges CALABRESI, POOLER, and SACK, dissenting: . . . My point of departure from the majority is the text of the Convention Against Torture, which provides that "[n]o exceptional circumstances whatsoever, whether a state of war or a threat of war, internal political instability or any other public emergency, may be invoked as a justification of torture." United Nations Convention Against Torture and Other Cruel, Inhuman, or Degrading Treatment or Punishment Art. 2, cl. 2, December 10, 1984, S. Treaty Doc. No. 100-20, 1465 U.N.T.S. 85 ("Convention Against Torture"). Because the majority has neglected this basic commitment and a good deal more, I respectfully dissent.

Maher Arar credibly alleges that United States officials conspired to ship him from American soil, where the Constitution and our laws apply, to Syria, where they do not, so that Syrian agents could torture him at federal officials' direction and behest. He also credibly alleges that, to accomplish this unlawful objective, agents of our government actively obstructed his access to this very Court and the protections established by Congress. *See* 8 U.S.C. §1252(a)(2)(D) (providing for judicial review of constitutional claims or questions of law raised by an order of removal).

While I broadly concur with my colleagues who dissent, I write separately to underscore the miscarriage of justice that leaves Arar without a remedy in our courts. The majority would immunize official misconduct by invoking the separation of powers and the executive's responsibility for foreign affairs and national security. Its approach distorts the system of checks and balances essential to the rule of law, and it trivializes the judiciary's role in these arenas. To my mind, the most depressing aspect of the majority's opinion is its sincerity....

Notably, the majority opinion does not appear to dispute the notion that Arar has stated an injury under the Fifth Amendment of the Constitution. That is heartening, because, by any measure, the notion that federal officials conspired to send a man to Syria to be tortured "shocks the conscience." *Rochin v. California*, 342 U.S. 165, 172 (1952). What is profoundly disturbing, however, is the Court's pronouncement that it can offer Arar no opportunity to prove his case and no possibility of relief. This conclusion is at odds with the Court's responsibility to enforce the Constitution's protections and cannot, in my view, be reconciled with *Bivens*. The majority is at odds, too, with our own State Department, which has repeatedly taken the position before the world community that this exact remedy is available to torture victims like Arar. If the Constitution ever implied a damages remedy, this is such a case—where executive officials allegedly blocked access to the remedies chosen by Congress in order to deliver a man to known torturers.

The Court's hesitation today immunizes official conduct directly at odds with the express will of Congress and the most basic guarantees of liberty contained in the Constitution. By doing so, the majority risks a government that can interpret the law to suits its own ends, without scrutiny....

I...

When presented with an appropriate case or controversy, courts are entitled—indeed obliged—to act, even in instances where government officials seek to shield their conduct behind invocations of "national security" and "foreign policy." *See, e.g., Hamdan v. Rumsfeld*, 548 U.S. 557 (2006); *Reid v. Covert*, 354 U.S. 1, 23-30 (1957); *Youngstown* [*Sheet & Tube Co. v. Sawyer*, 343 U.S. 579 (1952)]. *Compare Ex parte Quirin*, 317 U.S. 1, 19 (1942) (observing the "duty which rests on the courts, in time of war as well as in time of peace, to preserve unimpaired the constitutional safeguards of civil liberty"), *with* Maj. Op. at 42 (suggesting that Arar's allegations do not trigger the Court's "unflagging duty to exercise [its] jurisdiction"). This authority derives directly from the Constitution and goes hand in hand with the responsibility of the courts to adjudicate all manner of cases put before them....

II...

... [C]ontrary to the majority's suggestion, the courts require no invitation from Congress before considering claims that touch upon foreign policy or national security. In fact, the Supreme Court has demonstrated its willingness to enter this arena against the express wishes of Congress. In *Boumediene v. Bush*, — U.S. ——, 128 S. Ct. 2229 (2008), the Supreme Court rebuffed legislative efforts to strip the courts of jurisdiction over detainees held at Guantanamo Bay. It held that the writ of habeas corpus extended to the naval base, and that neither Congress nor the executive branch could displace the courts without formally suspending the writ. Importantly, it did so despite the fact that this exercise of judicial power plainly affected the executive's detention of hundreds of enemy combatants and a centerpiece of the war on terror. The Court recognized that habeas proceedings "may divert the attention of military personnel from other pressing tasks" but refused to find these concerns "dispositive." *Id.* at 2261. . . .

POOLER, Circuit Judge, joined by Judges CALABRESI, SACK, and PARKER, dissenting. . . .

II. TVPA . . .

. . . In the Section 1983 context, the Supreme Court has held that private individuals may be liable for joint activities with state actors even where those private individuals had no official power under state law. *Dennis v. Sparks,* 449 U.S. 24, 27-28 (1980). In *Sparks,* the private individuals conspired with a state judge to enjoin the plaintiff's mining operation. The Court held:

> [T]o act "under color of" state law for §1983 purposes does not require that the defendant be an officer of the State. It is enough that he is a willful participant in joint action with the State or its agents. Private persons, jointly engaged with state officials in the challenged action, are acting "under color" of law for purposes of §1983 actions.

Id.; see also Khulumani v. Barclay Nat. Bank Ltd., 504 F.3d 254, 315 (2d Cir. 2007) (Korman, J., concurring in part). Arar alleges that U.S. officials, recognizing that Syrian law was more permissive of torture tha[n] U.S. law, contacted an agent in Syria to arrange to have Arar tortured under the authority of Syrian law. Specifically, Arar alleges that U.S. officials sent the Syrians a dossier containing questions, identical to those questions he was asked while detained in the U.S., including one about his relationship with a particular individual wanted for terrorism. He also alleges the Syrian officials supplied U.S. officials with information they extracted from him, citing a public statement by a Syrian official. Assuming the truth of these allegations, defendants' wrongdoing was only possible due to the latitude permitted under Syrian law and their joint action with Syrian authorities. The torture may fairly be attributed to Syria. . . .

Under Section 1983, non-state actors who willfully participate in joint action with state officials, acting under state law, themselves act under color of state law. By analogy, under the TVPA, non-Syrian actors who willfully participate in joint action with Syrian officials, acting under Syrian law, themselves act under color of Syrian law. In *Aldana v. Del Monte Fresh Produce,* 416 F.3d 1242, 1249, 1265 (11th Cir. 2005), the Eleventh Circuit sustained a TVPA claim where plaintiffs alleged that a U.S. corporation "hir[ed] and direct[ed] its employees and/or agents," including a Guatemalan mayor, "to torture the Plaintiffs and threaten them with death." 416 F.3d at 1265. The allegation that the corporation participated in joint action with the Guatemalan official was sufficient. I see no principled reason to apply different rules to the TVPA context than the Section 1983 context, to federal agent defendants than corporate defendants, or to actors in the United States than actors on foreign soil. Arar alleges that defendants, acting in concert with Syrian officials, interrogated him through torture under color of Syrian law, which they could not have accomplished under color of U.S. law alone. . . .

CALABRESI, Circuit Judge, joined by Judges POOLER, SACK, and PARKER, dissenting. . . . In its utter subservience to the executive branch, its distortion of *Bivens* doctrine, its unrealistic pleading standards, its misunderstanding of the TVPA and of §1983, as well as in its persistent choice of broad dicta where narrow analysis would have sufficed, the majority opinion goes seriously astray. It does so, moreover, with the result that a person — whom we must assume (a) was totally innocent and (b) was made to suffer excruciatingly (c) through the misguided deeds of individuals acting under color of federal law — is effectively left without a U.S. remedy. . . .

All this, as the other dissenters have powerfully demonstrated, is surely bad enough. I write to discuss one last failing, an unsoundness that, although it may not be the most significant to Arar himself, is of signal importance to us as federal judges: the majority's unwavering willfulness. It has engaged in what properly can be described as extraordinary judicial activism. It has violated long-standing canons of restraint that properly must guide courts when they face complex and searing questions that involve potentially fundamental constitutional rights. It has reached out to decide an issue that should not have been resolved at this stage of Arar's case. Moreover, in doing this, the court has justified its holding with side comments (as to other fields of law such as torts) that are both sweeping and wrong. That the majority — made up of colleagues I greatly respect — has done all this with the best of intentions, and in the belief that its holding is necessary in a time of crisis, I do not doubt. But this does not alter my conviction that in calmer times, wise people will ask themselves: how could such able and worthy judges have done that? . . .

NOTES AND QUESTIONS

a. The Rendition Program

1. *Scope of the Operations.* No one knows for sure how many extraordinary renditions have occurred. Some estimate that more than 100 persons have been thus rendered by the United States since the September 11 attacks. Dana Priest, *CIA's Assurances on Transferred Suspects Doubted*, Wash. Post, Mar. 17, 2005.

In June 2005, Italian police officials issued arrest warrants for 22 alleged U.S. intelligence operatives in connection with the rendering of an Islamic cleric, Osama Nasr (also known as Abu Omar) from Italy to Egypt without the approval of the Italian government. Although some reported that Italian authorities knew of and consented to the rendition, the Italian government denied those reports. Craig Whitlock, *Italy Denies Complicity in Alleged CIA Action*, Wash. Post, July 1, 2005. The Italian justice minister nevertheless declined to forward a prosecutor's extradition request to Washington for the 22 accused CIA officers. Peter Kiefer, *Italian Minister Declines to Seek Extradition of C.I.A. Operatives*, N.Y. Times, Apr. 13, 2006. Eventually, however, nine Italians and 26 Americans were indicted, and in November 2009, 22 suspected CIA agents and their aides and two Italian secret service officials were convicted (most in absentia) for an illegal abduction and rendition to Egypt. Rachel Donadio, *Italy Convicts 23 Americans for CIA Renditions*, N.Y. Times, Nov. 4, 2009.

2. *Why Do It?* Why would the United States sponsor or participate in extraordinary renditions? One unnamed official with experience in so rendering detainees explained: "We don't kick the [expletive] out of them. We send them to other countries so they can kick the [expletive] out of them." Dana Priest & Barton Gellman, *U.S. Decries Abuse but Defends Interrogations; "Stress and Duress" Tactics Used on Terrorism Suspects Held in Secret Overseas Facilities*, Wash. Post, Dec. 26, 2002.

3. *The Byproducts of Rendition.* Transfer of a prisoner to the custody of a third country for interrogation always involves the risk that the information derived, whether or not by abusive methods, will be unreliable. Indeed, unless U.S. agents are present during the interrogation, information divulged by the prisoner may be misinterpreted or even misrepresented by his interrogators. Consider the case of Ibn Al-Libi, an Al Qaeda operative, who was captured in Afghanistan in 2002, questioned by FBI agents at Bagram airbase, but then removed from their custody and flown by CIA agents to Egypt. Al-Libi was forced to confess to numerous offenses while in Egyptian custody, and his confessions became the source of false information linking Iraq and Al Qaeda. *See* Gray, *supra*, at 43.

4. *CIA Charter Flights.* An apparently private charter company, Aero Contractors, is actually a domestic centerpiece of the CIA's secret air service, which conducted flights to render suspects abroad. *See* Scott Shane, *CIA Expanding Terror Battle Under Guise of Charter Flights*, N.Y. Times, May 31, 2005. One 2005 analysis of 26 planes operated by CIA companies showed 307 flights in Europe since September 2001. Ian Fisher, *Reports of Secret U.S. Prisons in Europe Draw Ire and Otherwise Red Faces*, N.Y. Times, Dec. 1, 2005.

Binyam Mohamed, an Ethiopian national and British resident, was detained in Pakistan in 2002 and, for two years, was moved between "black sites" in Pakistan, Morocco, and Afghanistan, and then to Guantánamo, where he remained until he was released to Britain in 2009. Before his release, lawyers for Mohamed sued in Britain to obtain disclosure of any information in the possession of the U.K. government that would support Mohamed's claims that he had been tortured by the United States. Eventually, the U.K. courts ordered the release of limited summaries that confirm that Mohamed was subjected to cruel, inhuman, and degrading treatment by U.S. authorities. Richard Norton-Taylor, *Binyam Mohamed Torture Evidence Must Be Revealed*, Guardian, Feb. 10, 2010. Mohamed and other victims of CIA extraordinary rendition then brought suit under the Alien Tort Statute (ATS) against Jeppesen Dataplan, a company allegedly involved in providing flight services that enabled the CIA to carry out the renditions of Mohamed and his co-plaintiffs. *Mohamed v. Jeppesen Dataplan, Inc.*, 579 F.3d 943 (9th Cir. 2009) (en banc). During a corporate meeting, Jeppesen executive Bob Overby stated to his colleagues, "We do all of the extraordinary rendition flights — you know, the torture flights." Jane Mayer, *Outsourcing Torture: The Secret History of America's "Extraordinary Rendition" Program*, New Yorker, Feb. 14, 2005. If the state secrets privilege had not effectively ended the lawsuit against Jeppesen Dataplan, how should the court have ruled on Mohamed's claims on the merits?

5. *"Black Sites" and the Use of Contractors.* Although not publicly admitted, presumably the CIA used the services of private contractors to maintain the "black sites" and also to provide logistics and air travel for extraordinary renditions. What laws constrain the use of contractors in these settings, and what regulations would guide

their actions? Would a suspect tortured by a contractor in a "black site" have legal remedies in a U.S. court?

6. *Official Policy?* Officials denied that renditions have occurred for the purpose of torture. R. Jeffrey Smith, *Gonzales Defends Transfer of Detainees*, Wash. Post, Mar. 8, 2005 (quoting Attorney General Gonzales as stating that it is not U.S. policy to send persons "to countries where we believe or we know that they're going to be tortured"); Joel Brinkley, *U.S. Interrogations Are Saving European Lives, Rice Says*, N.Y. Times, Dec. 6, 2005 (quoting Secretary of State Condoleezza Rice as stating that "[t]he United States does not transport and has not transported detainees from one country to another for the purpose of interrogation using torture."). How much legal wiggle room do these statements preserve for the Administration? How, if at all, should these statements of U.S. policy affect Arar's likelihood of gaining relief in his lawsuit?

b.   Judicial Remedies for Extraordinary Rendition

1. *The Availability of Judicial Remedies.* The Second Circuit ruled that the TVPA does not support a claim where U.S. officials allegedly direct foreign officials to torture a non-U.S. citizen. Does the fact that U.S. officials were alleged to be acting under color of federal, not Syrian, law necessarily mean that those officials did not violate the TVPA? Of what value, then, is the TVPA to victims of torture directed by U.S. agents? Are you persuaded by the dissenters' analogy of the TVPA to Section 1983 suits involving joint action by non-state actors (in this case non-Syrian) and state actors?

2. *Bivens.* Why did the court decline to decide Arar's claim for damages arising out of alleged due process violations? Do you understand the legal basis for the exception to the *Bivens* doctrine, where "special factors counseling hesitation" that include foreign policy, military, and national security concerns bar the tort remedy for violation of Arar's constitutional rights? What sensitive issues of national security between the United States and Syria could justify declining to decide the tort claim?

Other courts have been similarly unwilling to extend *Bivens* liability. A claim by foreign nationals who alleged that they had been tortured by U.S. military personnel was dismissed after finding "special factors counseling hesitation" similar to those relied upon in *Arar* in *In re Iraq & Afghanistan Detainees*, 479 F. Supp. 2d 85 (D.D.C. 2007). The same result was reached in *Lebron v. Rumsfeld*, 764 F. Supp. 2d 787 (D.S.C. 2011) where the court found that "special factors" justified dismissal of a claim that Jose Padilla's constitutional rights were violated when he was allegedly mistreated while in military detention. *See supra* p. 469. Two district courts have allowed similar *Bivens* claims to survive motions to dismiss. *Padilla v. Yoo*, 633 F. Supp. 2d 1005 (N.D. Cal. 2009); *Vance v. Rumsfeld*, 694 F. Supp. 2d 957 (N.D. Ill. 2010). Decisions on appeal in the three most recent cases were pending at this writing.

3. *Assessing the Outcome in Arar.* Do the "what if" circumstances offered in part XII of the majority opinion persuade you that U.S. officials treated Arar reasonably and lawfully under the circumstances? Were there only two options available—let Arar go on to his destination or render him to Syria? If not, what should U.S. officials have done with Arar when he entered U.S. customs in New York City? For an argument that courts should reject the "categorical deference" to government officials

shown in *Arar* "if the government did not show that it had used a less intrusive alternative to extraordinary rendition in a similar case," *see* Peter Marguiles, *Judging Myopia in Hindsight: Bivens Actions, National Security Decisions, and the Rule of Law*, 96 Iowa L. Rev. 195, 243 (2010).

Do you agree with the majority that it is more appropriate for Congress than the courts to fashion a remedy for someone like Arar?

Why did the plausibility-pleading rule justify dismissing Arar's claims concerning the conduct of U.S. officials inside the United States? If senior government officials were involved in the diplomatic communications that led to Arar's removal, is it reasonable to surmise that those officials authorized the steps taken inside the United States to enable his rendition to Syria? *See* Marguiles, *supra*, 96 Iowa L. Rev. at 225 (yes).

4. *Extraterritorial Reach of the Constitution.* The apparent legal assumption of the lawyers who advised those creating the "black sites" and extraordinary rendition program was that if the abusive interrogations occurred outside the United States and the persons seized and interrogated were not U.S. citizens, the resulting abuses could not be challenged as violating the constitutional rights of the victim. Is the assumption correct? How, if at all, is your answer influenced by the decisions in *Reid v. Covert, supra* p. 322; *Verdugo-Urquidez v. United States, supra* p. 325; *Johnson v. Eisentrager,* noted *supra* p. 389; and *Boumediene v. Bush, supra* p. 401?

5. *Availability of Habeas Corpus.* In *Abu Ali v. Ashcroft,* 350 F. Supp. 2d 28 (D.D.C. 2004), U.S. citizen Omar Abu Ali challenged his ongoing detention in a prison in Saudi Arabia allegedly at the direction and with the ongoing supervision of the United States. When Abu Ali's parents sought habeas corpus for their son, the United States argued that the suit must be dismissed for lack of jurisdiction, "no matter how extensive a role the United States might have played and continues to play" in Abu Ali's detention, "for the sole reason that he is presently in a foreign prison." *Id.* at 40. The court held that the United States may not avoid habeas corpus jurisdiction by enlisting a foreign nation to detain an American citizen:

> This position is as striking as it is sweeping. The full contours of the position would permit the United States, at its discretion and without judicial review, to arrest a citizen of the United States and transfer her to the custody of allies overseas in order to avoid constitutional scrutiny; to arrest a citizen of the United States through the intermediary of a foreign ally and ask the ally to hold the citizen at a foreign location indefinitely at the direction of the United States; or even to deliver American citizens to foreign governments to obtain information through the use of torture. In short, the United States is in effect arguing for nothing less than the unreviewable power to separate an American citizen from the most fundamental of his constitutional rights merely by choosing where he will be detained or who will detain him. [*Id.*]

How, if at all, does the court's answer to the government affect those in a situation similar to Arar's?

c.   International Law Limits on Extraordinary Rendition

1. *The CAT and Implementing Legislation.* Review the discussion of the Convention Against Torture and its implementing legislation, *supra* p. 529. CAT Article 3

provides that "[n]o State Party shall expel, return ('refouler') or extradite a person to another State where there are substantial grounds for believing that he would be in danger of being subjected to torture." An understanding attached to the Convention by the Senate upon its advice and consent states that the requirement in Article 3 would apply when it is "more likely than not" that torture would follow such a rendition. S. Exec. Rep. No. 101-30, Resolution of Advice and Consent to Ratification (1990), ¶II(2). What information should lawyers take into account when asked to advise on a "more likely than not" determination? The CAT lacks a parallel provision regarding cruel, inhuman, or degrading treatment following rendition. What is the legal significance of this omission? *See* Michael John Garcia, *Renditions: Constraints Imposed by Laws on Torture* 7 (Cong. Res. Serv. RL32890), Sept. 8, 2009.

In 1998, Congress approved legislation purporting to implement Article 3 of the CAT. Pub. L. No. 105-277, §2242, 112 Stat. 2681, 2681-822 to -823. The measure states that it is

> the policy of the United States not to . . . effect the involuntary return of any person to a country in which there are substantial grounds for believing the person would be in danger of being subjected to torture, regardless of whether the person is physically present in the United States. *Id.* §2242(a).

The Act requires relevant federal agencies to adopt regulations to implement the policy. But it provides no penalties for violation. Article 4(1) of the CAT requires each state party to "ensure that all acts of torture are offenses under its criminal law. The same shall apply to an attempt to commit torture and to an act by any person which constitutes complicity or participation in torture." Does the 1998 legislation satisfy the U.S. obligation under Article 4(1)? How about current Department of Homeland Security regulations that prohibit the removal of all persons to states where they "more likely than not" would be tortured? 8 C.F.R. §§208.16-18, 1208.16-18 (2010). (CIA regulations concerning renditions, if any, are not publicly available.) *See* Garcia, *supra*, at 9.

The Torture Act, 18 U.S.C. §§2340, 2340A (2006), *supra* p. 529, expressly criminalizes acts of torture and attempts to commit torture outside the United States. *Id.* §2340A(a). It also provides punishment for conspiracy to do either of those things. *Id.* §2340A(c). It defines torture as an act "specifically intended to inflict severe physical or mental pain or suffering (other than pain or suffering incidental to lawful sanctions) upon another person within his custody or physical control." *Id.* §2340(1). What facts would have to be proven in order to hold a CIA official criminally liable under the statute who arranged for an extraordinary rendition that resulted in torture? Recall Attorney General Gonzales's comment, *supra* p. 556. Would a mere belief that a suspect might be tortured in the destination state be sufficient to make the CIA official criminally responsible for any torture that occurs there? Does this statute satisfy the U.S. obligation under CAT Article 4(1)?

A March 2002 memorandum to the General Counsel of the Defense Department, signed by Jay S. Bybee of the Office of Legal Counsel, asserted that "the United States is free from any constraints imposed by the Torture Convention in deciding whether to transfer detainees that it is holding abroad to third countries." *Memorandum for William J. Haynes from Jay Bybee, Re: The President's Power as Commander in Chief to Transfer Captured Terrorists to the Control and Custody of Foreign Nations* (Mar. 13, 2002), *available at* http://www.fas.org/irp/agency/doj/olc/index.html (maintaining that the treaty does not apply extraterritorially). Recall that the Bush administration also decided early in 2002 that the Geneva Conventions do not apply to captured Al Qaeda or Taliban detainees. Were these positions legally defensible in 2002? Are they defensible now?

2. *Assurances.* Regulations implementing the CAT provide that any transfers of a captive to another country must be accompanied by "sufficiently reliable" diplomatic assurances from the receiving country to the U.S. Secretary of State that it will not torture the suspect. 8 C.F.R. §208.18(c). CIA officials have stated that Agency guidelines require a receiving country to give assurances that a rendered prisoner will be treated humanely, and require that U.S. personnel monitor compliance with the assurances. Douglas Jehl & David Johnston, *Rule Change Lets CIA Freely Send Suspects Abroad to Jails,* N.Y. Times, Mar. 6, 2005. What capacity does the United States have to enforce promises that detainees are treated humanely? What was the *Arar* court's justification for not inquiring about any assurances regarding Arar's treatment? If courts do not review compliance with the policy expressed in the 1998 legislation excerpted in the previous Note, how can that policy be enforced?

3. *Geneva Convention Limits on Rendition.* An involuntary transfer of "protected persons" to another state is forbidden by Geneva Convention IV, Article 49. A violation constitutes a "grave breach" and is thus a war crime. *Id.* art. 147. Recall the Bush administration's arguments concerning the applicability of the Geneva Conventions in the post–September 11 campaign, *supra* p. 554. Which persons in what places are protected from rendition under the Geneva Conventions? Might these provisions have been helpful to Arar in his lawsuit?

Do the protections of Common Article 3, *supra* p. 532, apply to renditions of persons to countries where they may be tortured? *See* Garcia, *supra,* at 20 (probably not). Would the War Crimes Act, *supra* p. 531, prohibit renditions where torture is likely? *See id.* at 21 (yes, if U.S. personnel conspire with foreign officials and intend to so harm the victim).

4. *Customary International Law.* The *Restatement of the Foreign Relations Law of the United States* declares that "causing the disappearance of individuals" is absolutely prohibited under international law, that it violates the human rights of the victim, and that it constitutes a violation of a peremptory norm or *jus cogens. Id.* §702c cmts. a, c, n. *See* Jordan J. Paust, *Beyond the Law: The Bush Administration's Unlawful Responses in the "War" on Terror* 36-38 (2007).

5. *Effect of the Bush and Obama Executive Orders.* Executive Order No. 13,400, promulgated by President Bush on July 20, 2007, construed Common Article 3 of the Geneva Conventions as not applicable to members of Al Qaeda, the Taliban, or associated forces. The President also reasserted his authority as Commander in Chief to interpret the meaning of Common Article 3, while he stated that the CIA would follow guidelines not to engage in torture, or cruel and inhuman treatment, or to humiliate or degrade prisoners in a manner beyond the bounds of human decency. See *supra* p. 536. Could extraordinary renditions have been carried out lawfully on the basis of this executive order? President Obama repealed the Bush executive order when he issued Executive Order No. 13,491, 74 Fed. Reg. 4893 (Jan. 22, 2009), *supra* p. 536. Does the Obama order end U.S. participation in extraordinary rendition operations?

d.   Reforms

1. *Effect of the Detainee Treatment Act.* Review the language of the Detainee Treatment Act, *supra* p. 535. If this provision had been in effect when Arar was rendered to Syria, would the Act have been violated?

2. *Further Reforms?* The Obama executive order established the Special Task Force on Interrogation and Transfer Policies. On August 24, 2009, the Task Force issued recommendations to the President, including stronger procedures for obtaining and evaluating diplomatic assurances from a receiving country; a monitoring mechanism to ensure consistent access to transferred persons, with minimal notice to the detaining government; and annual, coordinated reports from the Inspectors General of the Departments of State, Defense, and Homeland Security on transfers that were made on the basis of assurances. Department of Justice, *Special Task Force on Interrogations and Transfer Policies Issues Its Recommendations to the President* (Aug. 24, 2009), *at* http://www.usdooj.gov/opa/pr/2009/August/09-ag-835.html. Do you think these reforms, if implemented, will put a stop to extraordinary renditions? If not, will they ensure that rendered prisoners will not be subjected to abusive interrogation? What other changes in law would you recommend in reforming the practice of extraordinary rendition? *See* Louis Fisher, *Extraordinary Rendition: The Price of Secrecy,* 57 Am. U. L. Rev. 1405 (2008).

VI

Prosecuting Threats to National Security

Criminalizing Terrorism and Material Support ──20

Generally, First Amendment protections for freedom of speech, assembly, and association pose no obstacle to prosecution of terrorists for committing terrorist acts. Murder and maiming enjoy no constitutional protection. But the prosecution of such primary offenders—if they survive the terrorist attack and are successfully hunted down—comes too late to prevent the harm. Nor is such prosecution likely to deter others who are religiously or politically motivated to commit terrorist attacks. Counterterrorist criminal law therefore necessarily searches up the chain of causation to secondary defendants who aid and abet, conspire, harbor, or otherwise assist the terrorists. And prosecution of either primary or secondary defendants is complicated when their conduct takes place abroad, given the normal presumption against extraterritorial application of U.S. law.

In Part A of this chapter, we consider a case that suggests that the hoary criminal laws of treason and sedition may be a poor fit for such prosecutions. In the 1990s, Congress therefore criminalized providing "material support" to terrorists or designated "foreign terrorist organizations." In Part B, we consider these laws and the issues they raise about criminalizing advocacy and association as well as personal guilt. Finally, in Part C, we consider the extraterritorial application of U.S. counterterrorism laws.

A. TREASON AND SEDITION

United States v. Rahman

United States Court of Appeals, Second Circuit, 1999
189 F.3d 88

PER CURIAM: These are appeals by ten defendants convicted of seditious conspiracy and other offenses arising out of a wide-ranging plot to conduct a campaign of urban terrorism. Among the activities of some or all of the defendants were rendering assistance to those who bombed the World Trade Center, planning to bomb bridges and tunnels in New York City, murdering Rabbi Meir Kahane, and planning to murder the President of Egypt. We affirm the convictions of all the defendants....

The Government adduced evidence at trial showing the following: Abdel Rahman, a blind Islamic scholar and cleric, was the leader of the seditious conspiracy, the purpose of which was *"jihad,"* in the sense of a struggle against the enemies of Islam. Indicative of this purpose, in a speech to his followers Abdel Rahman instructed that they were to "do *jihad* with the sword, with the cannon, with the grenades, with the missile . . . against God's enemies." Abdel Rahman's role in the conspiracy was generally limited to overall supervision and direction of the membership, as he made efforts to remain a level above the details of individual operations. However, as a cleric and the group's leader, Abdel Rahman was entitled to dispense *"fatwas,"* religious opinions on the holiness of an act, to members of the group sanctioning proposed courses of conduct and advising them whether the acts would be in furtherance of *jihad.*

According to his speeches and writings, Abdel Rahman perceives the United States as the primary oppressor of Muslims worldwide, active in assisting Israel to gain power in the Middle East, and largely under the control of the Jewish lobby. Abdel Rahman also considers the secular Egyptian government of Mubarak to be an oppressor because it has abided Jewish migration to Israel while seeking to decrease Muslim births. Holding these views, Abdel Rahman believes that *jihad* against Egypt and the United States is mandated by the Qur'an. Formation of a *jihad* army made up of small "divisions" and "battalions" to carry out this *jihad* was therefore necessary, according to Abdel Rahman, in order to beat back these oppressors of Islam including the United States. . . .

I. CONSTITUTIONAL CHALLENGES

A. Seditious Conspiracy Statute and the Treason Clause

Defendant Nosair (joined by other defendants) contends that his conviction for seditious conspiracy, in violation of 18 U.S.C. §2384, was illegal because it failed to satisfy the requirements of the Treason Clause of the U.S. Constitution, Art. III, §3.

Article III, Section 3 provides, in relevant part:

> Treason against the United States, shall consist only in levying War against them, or in adhering to their Enemies, giving them Aid and Comfort. No Person shall be convicted of Treason unless on the Testimony of two Witnesses to the same overt Act, or on Confession in open Court.

The seditious conspiracy statute provides:

> If two or more persons in any State or Territory, or in any place subject to the jurisdiction of the United States, conspire to overthrow, put down or to destroy by force the Government of the United States, or to levy war against them, or to oppose by force the authority thereof, or by force to prevent, hinder or delay the execution of any law of the United States, or by force to seize, take, or possess any property of the United States contrary to the authority thereof, they shall each be fined under this title or imprisoned not more than twenty years, or both.

18 U.S.C. §2384.

Nosair contends that because the seditious conspiracy statute punishes conspiracy to "levy war" against the United States without a conforming two-witness requirement, the statute is unconstitutional. He further claims that because his conviction for conspiracy to levy war against the United States was not based on the testimony of two witnesses to the same overt act, the conviction violates constitutional standards.

It is undisputed that Nosair's conviction was not supported by two witnesses to the same overt act. Accordingly the conviction must be overturned if the requirement of the Treason Clause applies to this prosecution for seditious conspiracy.

The plain answer is that the Treason Clause does not apply to the prosecution. The provisions of Article III, Section 3 apply to prosecutions for "treason." Nosair and his co-appellants were not charged with treason. Their offense of conviction, seditious conspiracy under Section 2384, differs from treason not only in name and associated stigma, but also in its essential elements and punishment....

Seditious conspiracy by levying war includes no requirement that the defendant owe allegiance to the United States, an element necessary to conviction of treason. *See* 18 U.S.C. §2381 (defining "allegiance to United States" as an element of treason)....

... The reference to treason in the constitutional clause necessarily incorporates the elements of allegiance and betrayal that are essential to the concept of treason.... Nosair was thus tried for a different, and lesser, offense than treason. We therefore see no reasonable basis to maintain that the requirements of the Treason Clause should apply to Nosair's prosecution.

B. Seditious Conspiracy Statute and the First Amendment

Abdel Rahman, joined by the other appellants, contends that the seditious conspiracy statute, 18 U.S.C. §2384, is an unconstitutional burden on free speech and the free exercise of religion in violation of the First Amendment. First, Abdel Rahman argues that the statute is facially invalid because it criminalizes protected expression and that it is overbroad and unconstitutionally vague. Second, Abdel Rahman contends that his conviction violated the First Amendment because it rested solely on his political views and religious practices.

1. Facial Challenge

a. *Restraint on Speech.* ... As Section 2384 proscribes "speech" only when it constitutes an agreement to use force against the United States, Abdel Rahman's generalized First Amendment challenge to the statute is without merit. Our court has previously considered and rejected a First Amendment challenge to Section 2384. *See United States v. Lebron*, 222 F.2d 531, 536 (2d Cir. 1955). Although *Lebron's* analysis of the First Amendment issues posed by Section 2384 was brief, the panel found the question was squarely controlled by the Supreme Court's then-recent decision in *Dennis v. United States*, 341 U.S. 494 (1951). In *Dennis*, the Court upheld the constitutionality of the Smith Act, which made it a crime to advocate, or to conspire to advocate, the overthrow of the United States government by force or violence. *See* 18 U.S.C. §2385; *Dennis*, 341 U.S. at 494. The *Dennis* Court concluded that, while the "element of speech" inherent in Smith Act convictions required that the Act be given close First Amendment scrutiny, the Act did not impermissibly burden the expression of protected speech, as it was properly "directed at advocacy [of overthrow of the government by force], not discussion." *See id.* at 502.

After *Dennis*, the Court broadened the scope of First Amendment restrictions on laws that criminalize subversive advocacy. It remains fundamental that while the state may not criminalize the expression of views — even including the view that violent overthrow of the government is desirable — it may nonetheless outlaw encouragement, inducement, or conspiracy to take violent action. Thus, in *Yates v. United States*, 354 U.S. 298, 318 (1957), overruled in part on other grounds, *Burks v. United States*, 437 U.S. 1, 7 (1978), the Court interpreted the Smith Act to prohibit only the advocacy of concrete violent action, but not "advocacy and teaching of forcible overthrow as an abstract principle, divorced from any effort to instigate action to that end." And in *Brandenburg v. Ohio*, 395 U.S. 444, 447 (1969) (per curiam), the Court held that a state may proscribe subversive advocacy only when such advocacy is directed towards, and is likely to result in, "imminent lawless action."

The prohibitions of the seditious conspiracy statute are much further removed from the realm of constitutionally protected speech than those at issue in *Dennis* and its progeny. To be convicted under Section 2384, one must conspire to *use* force, not just to *advocate* the use of force. We have no doubt that this passes the test of constitutionality. . . .

b. *Vagueness and Overbreadth.* Abdel Rahman also contends that Section 2384 is overbroad and void for vagueness.

(i) *Overbreadth.* A law is overbroad, and hence void, if it "does not aim specifically at evils within the allowable area of State control, but, on the contrary, sweeps within its ambit other activities that . . . constitute an exercise of freedom of speech or of the press." *Thornhill v. Alabama*, 310 U.S. 88, 97 (1940). . . .

We recognize that laws targeting "sedition" must be scrutinized with care to assure that the threat of prosecution will not deter expression of unpopular viewpoints by persons ideologically opposed to the government. But Section 2384 is drawn sufficiently narrowly that we perceive no unacceptable risk of such abuse.

Abdel Rahman argues that Section 2384 is overbroad because Congress could have achieved its public safety aims "without chilling First Amendment rights" by punishing only "substantive acts involving bombs, weapons, or other violent acts." One of the beneficial purposes of the conspiracy law is to permit arrest and prosecution before the substantive crime has been accomplished. The Government, possessed of evidence of conspiratorial planning, need not wait until buildings and tunnels have been bombed and people killed before arresting the conspirators. Accordingly, it is well established that the Government may criminalize certain preparatory steps towards criminal action, even when the crime consists of the use of conspiratorial or exhortatory words. Because Section 2384 prohibits only conspiratorial agreement, we are satisfied that the statute is not constitutionally overbroad.

(ii) *Vagueness.* Abdel Rahman also challenges the statute for vagueness. A criminal statute, particularly one regulating speech, must "define the criminal offense with sufficient definiteness that ordinary people can understand what conduct is prohibited and in a manner that does not encourage arbitrary and discriminatory enforcement." *Kolender v. Lawson*, 461 U.S. 352, 357 (1983). Abdel Rahman argues that Section 2384 does not provide "fair warning" about what acts are unlawful, leaving constitutionally protected speech vulnerable to criminal prosecution.

There is indeed authority suggesting that the word "seditious" does not sufficiently convey what conduct it forbids to serve as an essential element of a crime. *See Keyishian v. Board of Regents*, 385 U.S. 589, 598 (1967) (noting that "dangers fatal to First Amendment freedoms inhere in the word 'seditious,'" and invalidating law that provided, *inter alia*, that state employees who utter "seditious words" may be discharged). But the word "seditious" does not appear in the prohibitory text of the statute; it appears only in the caption. The terms of the statute are far more precise. The portions charged against Abdel Rahman and his co-defendants — conspiracy to levy war against the United States and to oppose by force the authority thereof — do not involve terms of such vague meaning. Furthermore, they unquestionably specify that agreement *to use force* is an essential element of the crime. Abdel Rahman therefore cannot prevail on the claim that the portions of Section 2384 charged against him criminalize mere expressions of opinion, or are unduly vague.

2. Application of Section 2384 to Abdel Rahman's Case

Abdel Rahman also argues that he was convicted not for entering into any conspiratorial agreement that Congress may properly forbid, but "solely for his religious words and deeds" which, he contends, are protected by the First Amendment. In support of this claim, Abdel Rahman cites the Government's use in evidence of his speeches and writings.

There are two answers to Abdel Rahman's contention. The first is that freedom of speech and of religion do not extend so far as to bar prosecution of one who uses a public speech or a religious ministry to commit crimes. Numerous crimes under the federal criminal code are, or can be, committed by speech alone. As examples: Section 2 makes it an offense to "counsel[ ]," "command[ ]," "induce[ ]" or "procure[ ]" the commission of an offense against the United States. 18 U.S.C. §2(a). Section 371 makes it a crime to "conspire . . . to commit any offense against the United States." 18 U.S.C. §371. Section 373, with which Abdel Rahman was charged, makes it a crime to "solicit[ ], command[ ], induce[ ], or otherwise endeavor[ ] to persuade" another person to commit a crime of violence. 18 U.S.C. §373(a). Various other statutes, like Section 2384, criminalize conspiracies of specified objectives, *see, e.g.,* 18 U.S.C. §1751(d) (conspiracy to kidnap); 18 U.S.C. §1951 (conspiracy to interfere with commerce through robbery, extortion, or violence); 21 U.S.C. §846 (conspiracy to violate drug laws). All of these offenses are characteristically committed through speech. Notwithstanding that political speech and religious exercise are among the activities most jealously guarded by the First Amendment, one is not immunized from prosecution for such speech-based offenses merely because one commits them through the medium of political speech or religious preaching. Of course, courts must be vigilant to insure that prosecutions are not improperly based on the mere expression of unpopular ideas. But if the evidence shows that the speeches crossed the line into criminal solicitation, procurement of criminal activity, or conspiracy to violate the laws, the prosecution is permissible.

The evidence justifying Abdel Rahman's conviction for conspiracy and solicitation showed beyond a reasonable doubt that he crossed this line. His speeches were not simply the expression of ideas; in some instances they constituted the crime of conspiracy to wage war on the United States under Section 2384 and solicitation of attack on the United States military installations, as well as of the murder of Egyptian President Hosni Mubarak under Section 373.

For example: Abdel Rahman told Salem he "should make up with God . . . by turning his rifle's barrel to President Mubarak's chest, and kill[ing] him." Tr. 4633.

On another occasion, speaking to Abdo Mohammed Haggag about murdering President Mubarak during his visit to the United States, Abdel Rahman told Haggag, "Depend on God. Carry out this operation. It does not require a fatwa. . . . You are ready in training, but do it. Go ahead." Tr. 10108.

The evidence further showed that Siddig Ali consulted with Abdel Rahman about the bombing of the United Nations Headquarters, and Abdel Rahman told him, "Yes, it's a must, it's a duty." Tr. 5527-5529.

On another occasion, when Abdel Rahman was asked by Salem about bombing the United Nations, he counseled against it on the ground that it would be "bad for Muslims," Tr. 6029, but added that Salem should "find a plan to destroy or to bomb or to . . . inflict damage to the American Army." Tr. 6029-6030.

Words of this nature — ones that instruct, solicit, or persuade others to commit crimes of violence — violate the law and may be properly prosecuted regardless of whether they are uttered in private, or in a public speech, or in administering the duties of a religious ministry. The fact that his speech or conduct was "religious" does not immunize him from prosecution under generally-applicable criminal statutes.

Abdel Rahman also protests the Government's use in evidence of his speeches, writings, and preachings that did not in themselves constitute the crimes of solicitation or conspiracy. He is correct that the Government placed in evidence many instances of Abdel Rahman's writings and speeches in which Abdel Rahman expressed his opinions within the protection of the First Amendment. However, while the First Amendment fully protects Abdel Rahman's right to express hostility against the United States, and he may not be prosecuted for so speaking, it does not prevent the use of such speeches or writings in evidence when relevant to prove a pertinent fact in a criminal prosecution. The Government was free to demonstrate Abdel Rahman's resentment and hostility toward the United States in order to show his motive for soliciting and procuring illegal attacks against the United States and against President Mubarak of Egypt.

Furthermore, Judge Mukasey properly protected against the danger that Abdel Rahman might be convicted because of his unpopular religious beliefs that were hostile to the United States. He explained to the jury the limited use it was entitled to make of the material received as evidence of motive. He instructed that a defendant could not be convicted on the basis of his beliefs or the expression of them — even if those beliefs favored violence. He properly instructed the jury that it could find a defendant guilty only if the evidence proved he committed a crime charged in the indictment.

We reject Abdel Rahman's claim that his conviction violated his rights under the First Amendment. . . .

NOTES AND QUESTIONS

1. *Treason.* "Treason" is the only crime expressly identified in the Constitution, which states that "Treason against the United States, shall consist only in levying War against them, or in adhering to their Enemies, giving them Aid and Comfort." U.S. Const. art. III, §3. Furthermore, the text supplies a special evidentiary rule for treason prosecutions: "No Person shall be convicted of Treason unless on the Testimony of two Witnesses to the same overt Act, or on Confession in open Court." *Id.* Why did the Framers single out treason for special mention and write an evidentiary rule for treason prosecutions directly into the Constitution, while leaving other crimes to legislative definition and evidentiary rules to the courts through the medium of the common law?

The restrictive nature of the constitutional rule of evidence suggests an answer: the Framers feared that the state would use treason prosecutions to suppress dissent.

> The treason clause is a product of the awareness of the Framers of the "numerous and dangerous excrescences" which had disfigured the English law of treason and was therefore intended to put it beyond the power of Congress to "extend the crime and punishment of treason." The debate in the Convention, remarks in the ratifying conventions, and contemporaneous public comment make clear that a restrictive concept of the crime was imposed and that ordinary partisan divisions within political society were not to be escalated by the stronger into capital charges of treason, as so often had happened in England. [S. Doc. No. 92-82, Congressional Research Service, *The Constitution of the United States of America: Analysis and Interpretation* (1973) (citations omitted), *updated version available at* http://www.law.cornell.edu/anncon/authorship.html.]

Indeed, the Framers provided additional protections for such partisan divisions by prohibiting Congress from enacting any law abridging freedom of speech, the press, assembly, petition, and (by judicial implication) association. U.S. Const. amend. I. *See* Ronald D. Rotunda & John E. Nowak, *Treatise on Constitutional Law* §20.41 (3d ed. Pocket Part 2005) (describing case law regarding freedom of association). Are the Framers' concerns about the crime of treason still valid? *See* Kristen Eichensehr, *Treason in an Age of Terrorism: An Explanation and Evaluation of Treason's Return in Democratic States,* 42 Vand. J. Transnat'l L. 1443 (2009).

Why did Abdel Rahman argue that he was effectively convicted of treason? Did the court's answer to his claim bypass the protections that the Framers built into the Treason Clause?

Should he have been prosecuted for treason? *See* Carlton F.W. Larson, *The Forgotten Constitutional Law of Treason and the Enemy Combatant,* 154 U. Pa. L. Rev. 863 (2006) (arguing that conspiracy to levy war is not seditious conspiracy, not treason, but urging revival of treason prosecutions for enemy combatants instead of military trial).

2. *Inciting Imminent Harm.* The *Rahman* court's synopsis of the constitutional law governing advocacy of lawless action makes it sound more consistent than it is. *See, e.g.,* Christina E. Wells, *Fear and Loathing in Constitutional Decision-Making,* 2005 Wis. L. Rev. 115. In a World War I case under the 1918 Sedition Act, the Supreme Court declared that the government could constitutionally criminalize the utterance of "words . . . used in such circumstances . . . as to create a clear and present danger that they will bring about the substantive evils that Congress has a right to prevent." *Schenck v. United States,* 249 U.S. 47, 52 (1919). The Court seemed to relax the clear-and-present-danger test in *Dennis v. United States,* 341 U.S. 494 (1951), by finding that the harm from an overthrow of the government would be so grave that the government need not show its imminence or probability in order to punish advocacy of the overthrow. Dennis and his co-defendants were convicted and sentenced to long prison terms for violating the Smith Act, which made it unlawful "to knowingly or willfully advocate, abet, advise, or teach the duty, necessity, desirability, or propriety of overthrowing or destroying any government in the United States by force or violence. . . ." Act of June 28, 1940, 54 Stat. 670, 671 (1940). What were their criminal

acts? Apparently, according to the evidence adduced by the government, assembling to discuss and plan future teaching of books by Stalin, Marx and Engels, and Lenin. Finally, without disavowing these chilling precedents, the Court reversed a conviction for "criminal syndicalism" in *Brandenberg v. Ohio*, 395 U.S. 444 (1969). There, the defendant had given a racist and anti-Semitic speech at a Ku Klux Klan rally. The Court held that a State could not criminalize "advocacy of the use of force or of law violation except where such advocacy is directed to inciting or producing imminent lawless action *and* is *likely* to incite or produce such action." *Id.* at 447 (emphasis added).

How does Section 2384 fare under these tests? Did the *Rahman* court apply them correctly? *See* John Alan Cohan, *Seditious Conspiracy, the Smith Act, and Prosecution for Religious Speech Advocating the Violent Overthrow of Government*, 17 St. John's J. Legal Comment. 199 (2003).

3. *Expression as Evidence.* Are not Rahman's religious expressions, quoted in the case, quintessentially protected speech? Why was it constitutional to base his criminal prosecution in part on them? *See generally* Cohan, *supra*.

B.   MATERIAL SUPPORT CRIMES

Congress has criminalized a range of terrorist activities — from using weapons of mass destruction to bombing public places or government facilities. *See* 18 U.S.C. §§2331-2339D (2006 & Supp. III 2009). But because terrorists often evade capture or die in the attack, and their supporters are easier to locate and prosecute, prosecutors have more often turned to laws criminalizing material support for terrorism. These make it a crime not only to provide support in preparation for or carrying out terrorist acts, but also to provide support to an organization that the Secretary of State has designated a "foreign terrorist organization" (FTO). 8 U.S.C. §1189(a)(1) (2006).

The Secretary may designate a foreign organization as an FTO if she finds that it engages in "terrorism," defined as "premeditated, politically motivated violence perpetrated against noncombatant targets by subnational groups or clandestine agents," 22 U.S.C. §2656f(d)(2) (2006), or "terrorist activity," defined as

any activity which is unlawful under the laws of the place where it is committed (or which, if it had been committed in the United States, would be unlawful under the laws of the United States or any State) and which involves any of the following:

(I) The highjacking or sabotage of any conveyance (including an aircraft, vessel, or vehicle).

(II) The seizing or detaining, and threatening to kill, injure, or continue to detain, another individual in order to compel a third person (including a governmental organization) to do or abstain from doing any act as an explicit or implicit condition for the release of the individual seized or detained.

(III) A violent attack upon an internationally protected person (as defined in section 1116(b)(4) of Title 18) or upon the liberty of such a person.

(IV) An assassination.

(V) The use of any—

(a) biological agent, chemical agent, or nuclear weapon or device, or

(b) explosive, firearm, or other weapon or dangerous device (other than for mere personal monetary gain),

with intent to endanger, directly or indirectly, the safety of one or more individuals or to cause substantial damage to property.

(VI) A threat, attempt, or conspiracy to do any of the foregoing.

[8 U.S.C. §1182(a)(3)(B)(iii) (2006).]

The courts have held that an organization with a U.S. presence is entitled to notice and an opportunity to be heard before it is designated as an FTO, but they have been deferential to the Secretary in making the determination and have rejected claims that she must reveal classified information that forms part of the basis for the designation. *See, e.g., People's Mojahedin Org. of Iran v. United States Dep't of State*, 613 F.3d 220 (D.C. Cir. 2010). The Secretary had designated 48 FTOs as of May 2011, including Hamas (Islamic Resistance Movement), Hizballah (Party of God), Kongra-Gel (KGK, formerly Kurdistan Workers' Party, PKK, KADEK), Liberation Tigers of Tamil Eelam (LTTE), Al Qaeda (AQ), Real IRA (RIRA), and the Revolutionary Armed Forces of Colombia (FARC). Office of the Coordinator for Counterterrorism, U.S. Dep't of State, *Foreign Terrorist Organizations* (May 19, 2011), *available at* http://www.state.gov/s/ct/rls/other/des/123085.htm. The process for designating FTOs is analyzed in Chapter 25.

The material support statutes are excerpted below, followed by a Supreme Court decision rejecting a constitutional challenge to 18 U.S.C. §2339B, which criminalizes material support for an FTO.

---

18 U.S.C. §2339A. Providing material support to terrorists

(a) Offense. — Whoever provides material support or resources or conceals or disguises the nature, location, source, or ownership of material support or resources, knowing or intending that they are to be used in preparation for, or in carrying out, a violation of [various specific terrorist crimes] or in preparation for, or in carrying out, the concealment of an escape from the commission of any such violation, or attempts or conspires to do such an act, shall be fined under this title, imprisoned not more than 15 years, or both, and, if the death of any person results, shall be imprisoned for any term of years or for life. A violation of this section may be prosecuted in any Federal judicial district in which the underlying offense was committed, or in any other Federal judicial district as provided by law.

(b) Definitions. — As used in this section —

(1) the term "material support or resources" means any property, tangible or intangible, or service, including currency or monetary instruments or financial securities, financial services, lodging, training, expert advice or assistance, safehouses, false documentation or identification, communications equipment, facilities, weapons, lethal substances, explosives, personnel (1 or more individuals who may be or include oneself), and transportation, except medicine or religious materials.

(2) the term "training" means instruction or teaching designed to impart a specific skill, as opposed to general knowledge; and

(3) the term "expert advice or assistance" means advice or assistance derived from scientific, technical or other specialized knowledge.

**18 U.S.C. §2339B. Providing material support or resources to designated
foreign terrorist organizations**

(a)(1) Unlawful conduct. — Whoever knowingly provides material support or resources to a foreign terrorist organization, or attempts or conspires to do so, shall be fined under this title or imprisoned not more than 15 years, or both, and, if the death of any person results, shall be imprisoned for any term of years or for life. To violate this paragraph, a person must have knowledge that the organization is a designated terrorist organization . . . , that the organization has engaged or engages in terrorist activity . . . , or that the organization has engaged or engages in terrorism. . . .

(g) Definitions. — As used in this section — . . .

(4) the term "material support or resources" has the same meaning given that term in section 2339A. . . .

(h) Provision of personnel. — No person may be prosecuted under this section in connection with the term "personnel" unless that person has knowingly provided, attempted to provide, or conspired to provide a foreign terrorist organization with 1 or more individuals (who may be or include himself) to work under that terrorist organization's direction or control or to organize, manage, supervise, or otherwise direct the operation of that organization. Individuals who act entirely independently of the foreign terrorist organization to advance its goals or objectives shall not be considered to be working under the foreign terrorist organization's direction and control.

(i) Rule of construction. — Nothing in this section shall be construed or applied so as to abridge the exercise of rights guaranteed under the First Amendment to the Constitution of the United States. . . .

18 U.S.C. §2339C. Prohibitions against the financing of terrorism

(a) Offenses. —

(1) In general. — Whoever, in a circumstance described in subsection (b) [prescribing jurisdictional attributes of crime], by any means, directly or indirectly, unlawfully and willfully provides or collects funds with the intention that such funds be used, or with the knowledge that such funds are to be used, in full or in part, in order to carry out — . . .

(B) any . . . act intended to cause death or serious bodily injury to a civilian, or to any other person not taking an active part in the hostilities in a situation of armed conflict, when the purpose of such act, by its nature or context, is to intimidate a population, or to compel a government or an international organization to do or to abstain from doing any act, shall be punished as prescribed in subsection (d)(1). . . .

Holder v. Humanitarian Law Project

United States Supreme Court, 2010
130 S. Ct. 2705

Chief Justice ROBERTS delivered the opinion of the Court. . . . [The plaintiffs are two U.S. citizens, the Humanitarian Law Project (HLP) (a human rights organization with consultative status to the United Nations), Ralph Fertig (the HLP's president), and others who want to provide support to the Kurdistan Workers' Party (PKK) (founded to establish an independent Kurdish state in southeastern Turkey), and the Liberation Tigers of Tamil Eelam (LTTE) (founded to create an independent Tamil state in Sri Lanka). The PKK and LTTE were each designated a foreign terrorist organization by the United States based on evidence that they committed numerous terrorist attacks, some of which harmed U.S. citizens. Plaintiffs claimed, however, that they want to support only the lawful humanitarian and political activities of the PKK and LTTE with monetary contributions, other tangible aid, legal training, and political advocacy.]

II

. . . Plaintiffs challenge §2339B's prohibition on four types of material support — "training," "expert advice or assistance," "service," and "personnel." They raise three constitutional claims. First, plaintiffs claim that §2339B violates the Due Process Clause of the Fifth Amendment because these four statutory terms are impermissibly vague. Second, plaintiffs claim that §2339B violates their freedom of speech under the First Amendment. Third, plaintiffs claim that §2339B violates their First Amendment freedom of association.

Plaintiffs do not challenge the above statutory terms in all their applications. Rather, plaintiffs claim that §2339B is invalid to the extent it prohibits them from engaging in certain specified activities. With respect to the HLP and Judge Fertig, those activities are: (1) "train[ing] members of [the] PKK on how to use humanitarian and international law to peacefully resolve disputes"; (2) "engag[ing] in political advocacy on behalf of Kurds who live in Turkey"; and (3) "teach[ing] PKK members how to petition various representative bodies such as the United Nations for relief." With respect to the other plaintiffs, those activities are: (1) "train[ing] members of [the] LTTE to present claims for tsunami-related aid to mediators and international bodies"; (2) "offer[ing] their legal expertise in negotiating peace agreements between the LTTE and the Sri Lankan government"; and (3) "engag[ing] in political advocacy on behalf of Tamils who live in Sri Lanka." . . .

III

Plaintiffs claim, as a threshold matter, that we should affirm the Court of Appeals without reaching any issues of constitutional law. They contend that we should interpret the material-support statute, when applied to speech, to require proof that a defendant intended to further a foreign terrorist organization's illegal activities. That interpretation, they say, would end the litigation because plaintiffs' proposed activities consist of speech, but plaintiffs do not intend to further unlawful conduct by the PKK or the LTTE.

We reject plaintiffs' interpretation of §2339B because it is inconsistent with the text of the statute. Section 2339B(a)(1) prohibits "knowingly" providing material support. It then specifically describes the type of knowledge that is required: "To violate this paragraph, a person must have knowledge that the organization is a designated terrorist organization . . . , that the organization has engaged or engages in terrorist activity . . . , or that the organization has engaged or engages in terrorism. . . ." *Ibid.* Congress plainly spoke to the necessary mental state for a violation of §2339B, and it chose knowledge about the organization's connection to terrorism, not specific intent to further the organization's terrorist activities.

Plaintiffs' interpretation is also untenable in light of the sections immediately surrounding §2339B, both of which do refer to intent to further terrorist activity. See §2339A(a) (establishing criminal penalties for one who "provides material support or resources . . . knowing or intending that they are to be used in preparation for, or in carrying out, a violation of" statutes prohibiting violent terrorist acts); §2339C(a)(1) (setting criminal penalties for one who "unlawfully and willfully provides or collects funds with the intention that such funds be used, or with the knowledge that such funds are to be used, in full or in part, in order to carry out" other unlawful acts). Congress enacted §2339A in 1994 and §2339C in 2002. See §120005(a), 108 Stat. 2022 (§2339A); §202(a), 116 Stat. 724 (§2339C). Yet Congress did not import the intent language of those provisions into §2339B, either when it enacted §2339B in 1996, or when it clarified §2339B's knowledge requirement in 2004.

Finally, plaintiffs give the game away when they argue that a specific intent requirement should apply only when the material-support statute applies to speech. There is no basis whatever in the text of §2339B to read the same provisions in that statute as requiring intent in some circumstances but not others. It is therefore clear that plaintiffs are asking us not to interpret §2339B, but to revise it. "Although this Court will often strain to construe legislation so as to save it against constitutional attack, it must not and will not carry this to the point of perverting the purpose of a statute." *Scales v. United States*, 367 U.S. 203, 211 (1961).

Scales is the case on which plaintiffs most heavily rely, but it is readily distinguishable. That case involved the Smith Act, which prohibited membership in a group advocating the violent overthrow of the government. The Court held that a person could not be convicted under the statute unless he had knowledge of the group's illegal advocacy and a specific intent to bring about violent overthrow. *Id.*, at 220-222, 229. This action is different: Section 2339B does not criminalize mere membership in a designated foreign terrorist organization. It instead prohibits providing "material support" to such a group. Nothing about *Scales* suggests the need for a specific intent requirement in such a case. The Court in *Scales,* moreover, relied on both statutory text and precedent that had interpreted closely related provisions of the Smith Act to require specific intent. Plaintiffs point to nothing similar here.

We cannot avoid the constitutional issues in this litigation through plaintiffs' proposed interpretation of §2339B.

IV

We turn to the question whether the material-support statute, as applied to plaintiffs, is impermissibly vague under the Due Process Clause of the Fifth Amendment. "A conviction fails to comport with due process if the statute under which it is obtained fails to provide a person of ordinary intelligence fair notice of what is prohibited, or is so standardless that it authorizes or encourages seriously discriminatory enforcement." *United States v. Williams*, 553 U.S. 285, 304 (2008). We consider whether a statute is vague as applied to the particular facts at issue, for "[a] plaintiff who engages in some conduct that is clearly proscribed cannot complain of the vagueness of the law as applied to the conduct of others." *Hoffman Estates v. Flipside, Hoffman Estates, Inc.*, 455 U.S. 489, 495 (1982). We have said that when a statute "interferes with the right of free speech or of association, a more stringent vagueness test should apply." *Id.*, at 499. "But 'perfect clarity and precise guidance have never been required even of regulations that restrict expressive activity.'" *Williams, supra*, at 304 (quoting *Ward v. Rock Against Racism*, 491 U.S. 781, 794 (1989))....

. . . [Cases establish the] rule that "[a] plaintiff who engages in some conduct that is clearly proscribed cannot complain of the vagueness of the law as applied to the conduct of others." *Hoffman Estates, supra*, at 495. That rule makes no exception for conduct in the form of speech. Thus, even to the extent a heightened vagueness standard applies, a plaintiff whose speech is clearly proscribed cannot raise a successful vagueness claim under the Due Process Clause of the Fifth Amendment for lack of notice. And he certainly cannot do so based on the speech of others. Such a plaintiff may have a valid overbreadth claim under the First Amendment, but our precedents make clear that a Fifth Amendment vagueness challenge does not turn on whether a law applies to a substantial amount of protected expression. Otherwise the doctrines would be substantially redundant.

Under a proper analysis, plaintiffs' claims of vagueness lack merit. Plaintiffs do not argue that the material-support statute grants too much enforcement discretion to the Government. We therefore address only whether the statute "provide[s] a person of ordinary intelligence fair notice of what is prohibited." *Williams*, 553 U.S., at 304.

As a general matter, the statutory terms at issue here are quite different from the sorts of terms that we have previously declared to be vague. We have in the past "struck down statutes that tied criminal culpability to whether the defendant's conduct was 'annoying' or 'indecent' — wholly subjective judgments without statutory definitions, narrowing context, or settled legal meanings." *Id.*, at 306; see also *Papachristou v. Jacksonville*, 405 U.S. 156, n.1 (1972) (holding vague an ordinance that punished "vagrants," defined to include "rogues and vagabonds," "persons who use juggling," and "common night walkers" (internal quotation marks omitted)). Applying the statutory terms in this action — "training," "expert advice or assistance," "service," and "personnel" — does not require similarly untethered, subjective judgments.

Congress also took care to add narrowing definitions to the material-support statute over time. These definitions increased the clarity of the statute's terms. See §2339A(b)(2) ("'training' means instruction or teaching designed to impart a specific skill, as opposed to general knowledge"); §2339A(b)(3) ("'expert advice or assistance' means advice or assistance derived from scientific, technical or other specialized knowledge"); §2339B(h) (clarifying the scope of "personnel"). And the knowledge requirement of the statute further reduces any potential for vagueness, as we have held with respect to other statutes containing a similar requirement.

Of course, the scope of the material-support statute may not be clear in every application. But the dispositive point here is that the statutory terms are clear in their application to plaintiffs' proposed conduct, which means that plaintiffs' vagueness challenge must fail. Even assuming that a heightened standard applies because the material-support statute potentially implicates speech, the statutory terms are not vague as applied to plaintiffs.

Most of the activities in which plaintiffs seek to engage readily fall within the scope of the terms "training" and "expert advice or assistance." Plaintiffs want to "train members of [the] PKK on how to use humanitarian and international law to peacefully resolve disputes," and "teach PKK members how to petition various representative bodies such as the United Nations for relief." 552 F.3d at 921 n.1. A person of ordinary intelligence would understand that instruction on resolving disputes through international law falls within the statute's definition of "training" because it imparts a "specific skill," not "general knowledge." §2339A(b)(2). Plaintiffs' activities also fall comfortably within the scope of "expert advice or assistance": A reasonable person would recognize that teaching the PKK how to petition for humanitarian relief before the United Nations involves advice derived from, as the statute puts it, "specialized knowledge." §2339A(b)(3). In fact, plaintiffs themselves have repeatedly used the terms "training" and "expert advice" throughout this litigation to describe their own proposed activities, demonstrating that these common terms readily and naturally cover plaintiffs' conduct.

Plaintiffs respond by pointing to hypothetical situations designed to test the limits of "training" and "expert advice or assistance." They argue that the statutory definitions of these terms use words of degree — like "specific," "general," and "specialized" — and that it is difficult to apply those definitions in particular cases. . . .

Whatever force these arguments might have in the abstract, they are beside the point here. Plaintiffs do not propose to teach a course on geography, and cannot seek refuge in imaginary cases that straddle the boundary between "specific skills" and "general knowledge." We emphasized this point in *Scales*, holding that even if there might be theoretical doubts regarding the distinction between "active" and "nominal" membership in an organization — also terms of degree — the defendant's vagueness challenge failed because his "case present[ed] no such problem." 367 U.S. at 223. . . .

Plaintiffs also contend that they want to engage in "political advocacy" on behalf of Kurds living in Turkey and Tamils living in Sri Lanka. They are concerned that such advocacy might be regarded as "material support" in the form of providing "personnel" or "service[s]," and assert that the statute is unconstitutionally vague because they cannot tell.

As for "personnel," Congress enacted a limiting definition in IRTPA that answers plaintiffs' vagueness concerns. Providing material support that constitutes "personnel" is defined as knowingly providing a person "to work under that terrorist organization's direction or control or to organize, manage, supervise, or otherwise direct the operation of that organization." §2339B(h). The statute makes clear that "personnel" does not cover *independent* advocacy: "Individuals who act entirely independently of the foreign terrorist organization to advance its goals or objectives shall not be considered to be working under the foreign terrorist organization's direction and control." *Ibid.*

"[S]ervice" similarly refers to concerted activity, not independent advocacy. See Webster's Third New International Dictionary 2075 (1993) (defining "service" to mean "the performance of work commanded or paid for by another: a servant's duty: attendance on a superior"; or "an act done for the benefit or at the command of another"). Context confirms that ordinary meaning here. The statute prohibits providing a service "*to* a foreign terrorist organization." §2339B(a)(1) (emphasis added). The use of the word "to" indicates a connection between the service and the foreign group. We think a person of ordinary intelligence would understand that independently advocating for a cause is different from providing a service to a group that is advocating for that cause. . . .

V

A

We next consider whether the material-support statute, as applied to plaintiffs, violates the freedom of speech guaranteed by the First Amendment. Both plaintiffs and the Government take extreme positions on this question. Plaintiffs claim that Congress has banned their "pure political speech." It has not. Under the material-support statute, plaintiffs may say anything they wish on any topic. They may speak and write freely about the PKK and LTTE, the governments of Turkey and Sri Lanka, human rights, and international law. They may advocate before the United Nations. As the Government states: "The statute does not prohibit independent advocacy or expression of any kind." Brief for Government 13. Section 2339B also "does not prevent [plaintiffs] from becoming members of the PKK and LTTE or impose any sanction on them for doing so." *Id.*, at 60. Congress has not, therefore, sought to suppress ideas or opinions in the form of "pure political speech." Rather, Congress has prohibited "material support," which most often does not take the form of speech at all. And when it does, the statute is carefully drawn to cover only a narrow category of speech to, under the direction of, or in coordination with foreign groups that the speaker knows to be terrorist organizations....

[But] [t]he Government is wrong that the only thing actually at issue in this litigation is conduct....[Section] 2339B regulates speech on the basis of its content. Plaintiffs want to speak to the PKK and the LTTE, and whether they may do so under §2339B depends on what they say. If plaintiffs' speech to those groups imparts a "specific skill" or communicates advice derived from "specialized knowledge" — for example, training on the use of international law or advice on petitioning the United Nations — then it is barred. On the other hand, plaintiffs' speech is not barred if it imparts only general or unspecialized knowledge....

B

The First Amendment issue before us is more refined than either plaintiffs or the Government would have it. It is not whether the Government may prohibit pure political speech, or may prohibit material support in the form of conduct. It is instead whether the Government may prohibit what plaintiffs want to do — provide material support to the PKK and LTTE in the form of speech.

Everyone agrees that the Government's interest in combating terrorism is an urgent objective of the highest order. Plaintiffs' complaint is that the ban on material support, applied to what they wish to do, is not "necessary to further that interest." The objective of combating terrorism does not justify prohibiting their speech, plaintiffs argue, because their support will advance only the legitimate activities of the designated terrorist organizations, not their terrorism.

Whether foreign terrorist organizations meaningfully segregate support of their legitimate activities from support of terrorism is an empirical question. When it enacted §2339B in 1996, Congress made specific findings regarding the serious threat posed by international terrorism. See AEDPA §§301(a)(1)-(7), 110 Stat. 1247, note following 18 U.S.C. §2339B (Findings and Purpose). One of those findings explicitly rejects plaintiffs' contention that their support would not further the terrorist activities of the PKK and LTTE: "[F]oreign organizations that engage in terrorist activity are so tainted by their criminal conduct that *any contribution to such an organization* facilitates that conduct." §301(a)(7) (emphasis added).

Plaintiffs argue that the reference to "any contribution" in this finding meant only monetary support. There is no reason to read the finding to be so limited, particularly because Congress expressly prohibited so much more than monetary support in §2339B. Congress's use of the term "contribution" is best read to reflect a determination that any form of material support furnished "to" a foreign terrorist organization should be barred, which is precisely what the material-support statute does. Indeed, when Congress enacted §2339B, Congress simultaneously removed an exception that had existed in §2339A(a) (1994 ed.) for the provision of material support in the form of "humanitarian assistance to persons not directly involved in" terrorist activity. AEDPA §323, 110 Stat. 1255. That repeal demonstrates that Congress considered and rejected the view that ostensibly peaceful aid would have no harmful effects.

We are convinced that Congress was justified in rejecting that view. The PKK and the LTTE are deadly groups. "The PKK's insurgency has claimed more than 22,000 lives." Declaration of Kenneth R. McKune, App. 128, ¶5. The LTTE has engaged in extensive suicide bombings and political assassinations, including killings of the Sri Lankan President, Security Minister, and Deputy Defense Minister. *Id.*, at 130-132; Brief for Government 6-7. "On January 31, 1996, the LTTE exploded a truck bomb filled with an estimated 1,000 pounds of explosives at the Central Bank in Colombo, killing 100 people and injuring more than 1,400. This bombing was the most deadly terrorist incident in the world in 1996." McKune Affidavit, App. 131, ¶6.h. It is not difficult to conclude as Congress did that the "tain[t]" of such violent activities is so great that working in coordination with or at the command of the PKK and LTTE serves to legitimize and further their terrorist means. AEDPA §301(a)(7), 110 Stat. 1247.

Material support meant to "promot[e] peaceable, lawful conduct," Brief for Plaintiffs 51, can further terrorism by foreign groups in multiple ways. "Material support" is a valuable resource by definition. Such support frees up other resources within the organization that may be put to violent ends. It also importantly helps lend legitimacy to foreign terrorist groups—legitimacy that makes it easier for those groups to persist, to recruit members, and to raise funds—all of which facilitate more terrorist attacks. "Terrorist organizations do not maintain *organizational* "firewalls' that would prevent or deter . . . sharing and commingling of support and benefits." McKune Affidavit, App. 135, ¶11. "[I]nvestigators have revealed how terrorist groups systematically conceal their activities behind charitable, social, and political fronts." M. Levitt, Hamas: Politics, Charity, and Terrorism in the Service of Jihad 2-3 (2006). "Indeed, some designated foreign terrorist organizations use social and political components to recruit personnel to carry out terrorist operations, and to provide support to criminal terrorists and their families in aid of such operations." McKune Affidavit, App. 135, ¶11; Levitt, *supra*, at 2 ("Muddying the waters between its political activism, good works, and terrorist attacks, Hamas is able to use its overt political and charitable organizations as a financial and logistical support network for its terrorist operations").

Money is fungible, and "[w]hen foreign terrorist organizations that have a dual structure raise funds, they highlight the civilian and humanitarian ends to which such moneys could be put." McKune Affidavit, App. 134, ¶9. But "there is reason to believe that foreign terrorist organizations do not maintain legitimate *financial* firewalls between those funds raised for civil, nonviolent activities, and those ultimately used to support violent, terrorist operations." *Id.*, at 135, ¶12. Thus, "[f]unds raised ostensibly for charitable purposes have in the past been redirected by some terrorist groups to fund the purchase of arms and explosives." *Id.*, at 134, ¶10. See also Brief for Anti-Defamation League as *Amicus Curiae* 19-29 (describing fundraising activities by the PKK, LTTE, and Hamas); *Regan v. Wald*, 468 U.S. 222, 243 (1984) (upholding President's decision to impose travel ban to Cuba "to curtail the flow of hard currency to Cuba—currency that could then be used in support of Cuban adventurism"). There is evidence that the PKK and the LTTE, in particular, have not "respected the line between humanitarian and violent activities." McKune Affidavit, App. 135, ¶13 (discussing PKK); see *id.*, at 134 (LTTE).

The dissent argues that there is "no natural stopping place" for the proposition that aiding a foreign terrorist organization's lawful activity promotes the terrorist organization as a whole. But Congress has settled on just such a natural stopping place: The statute reaches only material support coordinated with or under the direction of a designated foreign terrorist organization. . . .

C

In analyzing whether it is possible in practice to distinguish material support for a foreign terrorist group's violent activities and its nonviolent activities, we do not rely exclusively on our own inferences drawn from the record evidence. We have before us an affidavit stating the Executive Branch's conclusion on that question. The State Department informs us that "[t]he experience and analysis of the U.S. government agencies charged with combating terrorism strongly suppor[t]" Congress's finding that all contributions to foreign terrorist organizations further their terrorism. McKune Affidavit, App. 133, ¶8. See *Winter v. Natural Resources Defense Council, Inc.*, 129 S. Ct. 365, 376-377 (2008) (looking to similar affidavits to support according weight to national security claims). In the Executive's view: "Given the purposes, organizational structure, and clandestine nature of foreign terrorist organizations, it is highly likely that any material support to these organizations will ultimately inure to the benefit of their criminal, terrorist functions—regardless of whether such support was ostensibly intended to support non-violent, non-terrorist activities." McKune Affidavit, App. 133, ¶8.

That evaluation of the facts by the Executive, like Congress's assessment, is entitled to deference. This litigation implicates sensitive and weighty interests of national security and foreign affairs. The PKK and the LTTE have committed terrorist acts against American citizens abroad, and the material-support statute addresses acute foreign policy concerns involving relationships with our Nation's allies. See *id.*, at 128-133, 137. We have noted that "neither the Members of this Court nor most federal judges begin the day with briefings that may describe new and serious threats to our Nation and its people." *Boumediene v. Bush*, 553 U.S. 723, 797 (2008). It is vital in this context "not to substitute . . . our own evaluation of evidence for a reasonable evaluation by the Legislative Branch." *Rostker v. Goldberg*, 453 U.S. 57, 68 (1981).

Our precedents, old and new, make clear that concerns of national security and foreign relations do not warrant abdication of the judicial role. We do not defer to the

Government's reading of the First Amendment, even when such interests are at stake. We are one with the dissent that the Government's "authority and expertise in these matters do not automatically trump the Court's own obligation to secure the protection that the Constitution grants to individuals." But when it comes to collecting evidence and drawing factual inferences in this area, "the lack of competence on the part of the courts is marked," *Rostker, supra,* at 65, and respect for the Government's conclusions is appropriate.

One reason for that respect is that national security and foreign policy concerns arise in connection with efforts to confront evolving threats in an area where information can be difficult to obtain and the impact of certain conduct difficult to assess. The dissent slights these real constraints in demanding hard proof—with "detail," "specific facts," and "specific evidence"—that plaintiffs' proposed activities will support terrorist attacks. That would be a dangerous requirement. In this context, conclusions must often be based on informed judgment rather than concrete evidence, and that reality affects what we may reasonably insist on from the Government. The material-support statute is, on its face, a preventive measure—it criminalizes not terrorist attacks themselves, but aid that makes the attacks more likely to occur. The Government, when seeking to prevent imminent harms in the context of international affairs and national security, is not required to conclusively link all the pieces in the puzzle before we grant weight to its empirical conclusions. See *Zemel v. Rusk,* 381 U.S., at 17 ("[B]ecause of the changeable and explosive nature of contemporary international relations, . . . Congress . . . must of necessity paint with a brush broader than that it customarily wields in domestic areas"). . . .

We also find it significant that Congress has been conscious of its own responsibility to consider how its actions may implicate constitutional concerns. First, §2339B only applies to designated foreign terrorist organizations. There is, and always has been, a limited number of those organizations designated by the Executive Branch, see, *e.g.,* 74 Fed. Reg. 29742 (2009); 62 Fed. Reg. 52650 (1997), and any groups so designated may seek judicial review of the designation. Second, in response to the lower courts' holdings in this litigation, Congress added clarity to the statute by providing narrowing definitions of the terms "training," "personnel," and "expert advice or assistance," as well as an explanation of the knowledge required to violate §2339B. Third, in effectuating its stated intent not to abridge First Amendment rights, see §2339B(i), Congress has also displayed a careful balancing of interests in creating limited exceptions to the ban on material support. The definition of material support, for example, excludes medicine and religious materials. See §2339A(b)(1). In this area perhaps more than any other, the Legislature's superior capacity for weighing competing interests means that "we must be particularly careful not to substitute our judgment of what is desirable for that of Congress." *Rostker, supra,* at 68. Finally, and most importantly, Congress has avoided any restriction on independent advocacy, or indeed any activities not directed to, coordinated with, or controlled by foreign terrorist groups.

At bottom, plaintiffs simply disagree with the considered judgment of Congress and the Executive that providing material support to a designated foreign terrorist organization—even seemingly benign support—bolsters the terrorist activities of that organization. That judgment, however, is entitled to significant weight, and we have persuasive evidence before us to sustain it. Given the sensitive interests in national security and foreign affairs at stake, the political branches have adequately substantiated their determination that, to serve the Government's interest in preventing terrorism, it was necessary to prohibit providing material support in the form of training, expert advice, personnel, and services to foreign terrorist groups, even if the supporters meant to promote only the groups' nonviolent ends.

We turn to the particular speech plaintiffs propose to undertake. First, plaintiffs propose to "train members of [the] PKK on how to use humanitarian and international law to peacefully resolve disputes." 552 F.3d at 92 n.1. Congress can, consistent with the First Amendment, prohibit this direct training. It is wholly foreseeable that the PKK could use the "specific skill[s]" that plaintiffs propose to impart, §2339A(b)(2), as part of a broader strategy to promote terrorism. The PKK could, for example, pursue peaceful negotiation as a means of buying time to recover from short-term setbacks, lulling opponents into complacency, and ultimately preparing for renewed attacks. See generally A. Marcus, Blood and Belief: The PKK and the Kurdish Fight for Independence 286-295 (2007) (describing the PKK's suspension of armed struggle and subsequent return to violence). A foreign terrorist organization introduced to the structures of the international legal system might use the information to threaten, manipulate, and disrupt. This possibility is real, not remote.

Second, plaintiffs propose to "teach PKK members how to petition various representative bodies such as the United Nations for relief." 552 F.3d at 921 n.1. The Government acts within First Amendment strictures in banning this proposed speech because it teaches the organization how to acquire "relief," which plaintiffs never define with any specificity, and which could readily include monetary aid. Indeed, earlier in this litigation, plaintiffs sought to teach the LTTE "to present claims for tsunami-related aid to mediators and international bodies," 552 F.3d at 921 n.1, which naturally included monetary relief. Money is fungible, and Congress logically concluded that money a terrorist group such as the PKK obtains using the techniques plaintiffs propose to teach could be redirected to funding the group's violent activities.

Finally, plaintiffs propose to "engage in political advocacy on behalf of Kurds who live in Turkey," and "engage in political advocacy on behalf of Tamils who live in Sri Lanka." 552 F.3d at 921 n.1. As explained above, plaintiffs do not specify their expected level of coordination with the PKK or LTTE or suggest what exactly their "advocacy" would consist of. Plaintiffs' proposals are phrased at such a high level of generality that they cannot prevail in this preenforcement challenge. See [*Washington State Grange v. Washington State Republican Party*, 552 U.S. 442, 454 (2008)]; *Zemel*, 381 U.S., at 20....

All this is not to say that any future applications of the material-support statute to speech or advocacy will survive First Amendment scrutiny. It is also not to say that any other statute relating to speech and terrorism would satisfy the First Amendment. In particular, we in no way suggest that a regulation of independent speech would pass constitutional muster, even if the Government were to show that such speech benefits foreign terrorist organizations. We also do not suggest that Congress could extend the same prohibition on material support at issue here to domestic organizations. We simply hold that, in prohibiting the particular forms of support that plaintiffs seek to provide to foreign terrorist groups, §2339B does not violate the freedom of speech.

VI

Plaintiffs' final claim is that the material-support statute violates their freedom of association under the First Amendment. Plaintiffs argue that the statute criminalizes the mere fact of their associating with the PKK and the LTTE, thereby running afoul of [prior] decisions . . . and cases in which we have overturned sanctions for joining the Communist Party.

The Court of Appeals correctly rejected this claim because the statute does not penalize mere association with a foreign terrorist organization. As the Ninth Circuit put it: "The statute does not prohibit being a member of one of the designated groups or vigorously promoting and supporting the political goals of the group. . . . What [§2339B] prohibits is the act of giving material support. . . ." 205 F.3d at 1133. Plaintiffs want to do the latter. Our decisions scrutinizing penalties on simple association or assembly are therefore inapposite. *See, e.g., Robel, supra,* at 262 ("It is precisely because th[e] statute sweeps indiscriminately across all types of association with Communist-action groups, without regard to the quality and degree of membership, that it runs afoul of the First Amendment"). . . .

* * *

The Preamble to the Constitution proclaims that the people of the United States ordained and established that charter of government in part to "provide for the common defence." As Madison explained, "[s]ecurity against foreign danger is . . . an avowed and essential object of the American Union." The Federalist No. 41, p. 269 (J. Cooke ed. 1961). We hold that, in regulating the particular forms of support that plaintiffs seek to provide to foreign terrorist organizations, Congress has pursued that objective consistent with the limitations of the First and Fifth Amendments.

The judgment of the United States Court of Appeals for the Ninth Circuit is affirmed in part and reversed in part, and the cases are remanded for further proceedings consistent with this opinion.

It is so ordered.

Justice BREYER, with whom Justices GINSBURG and SOTOMAYOR join, dissenting. Like the Court, and substantially for the reasons it gives, I do not think this statute is unconstitutionally vague. But I cannot agree with the Court's conclusion that the Constitution permits the Government to prosecute the plaintiffs criminally for engaging in coordinated teaching and advocacy furthering the designated organizations' lawful political objectives. In my view, the Government has not met its burden of showing that an interpretation of the statute that would prohibit this speech- and association-related activity serves the Government's compelling interest in combating terrorism. And I would interpret the statute as normally placing activity of this kind outside its scope.

I. . . .

"Coordination" with a group that engages in unlawful activity also does not deprive the plaintiffs of the First Amendment's protection under any traditional "categorical" exception to its protection. The plaintiffs do not propose to solicit a crime. They will not engage in fraud or defamation or circulate obscenity. Cf. *United States v. Stevens*, 130 S. Ct. 1577, 1585 (2010) (describing "categories" of unprotected speech). And the First Amendment protects advocacy even of *unlawful* action so long as that advocacy is not "directed to inciting or producing *imminent lawless action* and . . . *likely to incite or produce* such action." *Brandenburg v. Ohio*, 395 U.S. 444, 447 (1969) (*per curiam*) (emphasis added). Here the plaintiffs seek to advocate peaceful, *lawful* action to secure *political* ends; and they seek to teach others how to do the same. No one contends that the plaintiffs' speech to these organizations can be prohibited as incitement under *Brandenburg*.

Moreover, the Court has previously held that a person who associates with a group that uses unlawful means to achieve its ends does not thereby necessarily forfeit the First Amendment's protection for freedom of association. See *Scales v. United States*, 367 U.S. 203, 229 (1961) ("[Q]uasi-political parties or other groups that may embrace both legal and illegal aims differ from a technical conspiracy, which is defined by its criminal purpose"); see also [*NAACP v. Claiborne Hardware Co.*, 458 U.S. 886, 908 (1982)] ("The right to associate does not lose all constitutional protection merely because some members of the group may have participated in conduct or advocated doctrine that itself is not protected"). Rather, the Court has pointed out in respect to associating with a group advocating overthrow of the Government through force and violence: "If the persons assembling have committed crimes elsewhere . . . , they may be prosecuted for their . . . violation of valid laws. But it is a different matter when the State, instead of prosecuting them for such offenses, seizes upon mere participation in a peaceable assembly and a lawful public discussion as the basis for a criminal charge." [*De Jonge v. Oregon*, 299 U.S. 353, 365 (1937)] (striking down conviction for attending and assisting at Communist Party meeting because "[n]otwithstanding [the party's] objectives, the defendant still enjoyed his personal right of free speech and to take part in peaceable assembly having a lawful purpose"). . . .

Not even the "serious and deadly problem" of international terrorism can require *automatic* forfeiture of First Amendment rights. §301(a)(1), 110 Stat. 1247, note following 18 U.S.C. §2339B. Cf. §2339B(i) (instructing courts not to "constru[e] or appl[y the statute] so as to abridge the exercise of rights guaranteed under the First Amendment"). After all, this Court has recognized that not "'[e]ven the war power . . . remove[s] constitutional limitations safeguarding essential liberties.'" *United States v. Robel*, 389 U.S. 258, 264 (1967) (quoting *Home Building & Loan Assn. v. Blaisdell*, 290 U.S. 398, 426 (1934)). See also *Abrams v. United States*, 250 U.S. 616, 628 (1919) (Holmes, J., dissenting) ("[A]s against dangers peculiar to war, as against others, the principle of the right to free speech is always the same"). Thus, there is no general First Amendment exception that applies here. If the statute is constitutional in this context, it would have to come with a strong justification attached. . . .

The Government does identify a compelling countervailing interest, namely, the interest in protecting the security of the United States and its nationals from the threats that foreign terrorist organizations pose by denying those organizations financial and other fungible resources. I do not dispute the importance of this interest. But I do dispute whether the interest can justify the statute's criminal prohibition. To put the matter more specifically, precisely how does application of the statute to the protected activities before us *help achieve* that important security-related end?

The Government makes two efforts to answer this question. *First*, the Government says that the plaintiffs' support for these organizations is "fungible" in the same sense as other forms of banned support. Being fungible, the plaintiffs' support could, for example, free up other resources, which the organization might put to terrorist ends.

The proposition that the two very different kinds of "support" are "fungible," however, is not *obviously* true. There is no *obvious* way in which undertaking advocacy for political change through peaceful means or teaching the PKK and LTTE, say, how to petition the United Nations for political change is fungible with other resources that might be put to more sinister ends in the way that donations of money, food, or computer training are fungible. It is far from obvious that these advocacy activities can themselves be redirected, or will free other resources that can be directed, towards terrorist ends. Thus, we must determine whether the Government has come forward with evidence to support its claim.

The Government has provided us with no empirical information that might convincingly support this claim. . . .

Second, the Government says that the plaintiffs' proposed activities will "bolste[r] a terrorist organization's efficacy and strength in a community" and "undermin[e] this nation's efforts to *delegitimize and weaken* those groups." Government Brief 56 (emphasis added). In the Court's view, too, the Constitution permits application of the statute to activities of the kind at issue in part because those activities could provide a group that engages in terrorism with "legitimacy." The Court suggests that, armed with this greater "legitimacy," these organizations will more readily be able to obtain material support of the kinds Congress plainly intended to ban — money, arms, lodging, and the like. . . .

But this "legitimacy" justification cannot by itself warrant suppression of political speech, advocacy, and association. Speech, association, and related activities on behalf of a group will often, perhaps always, help to legitimate that group. Thus, were the law to accept a "legitimating" effect, in and of itself and without qualification, as providing sufficient grounds for imposing such a ban, the First Amendment battle would be lost in untold instances where it should be won. Once one accepts this argument, there is no natural stopping place. The argument applies as strongly to "independent" as to "coordinated" advocacy. That fact is reflected in part in the Government's claim that the ban here, so supported, prohibits a lawyer hired by a designated group from filing on behalf of that group an *amicus* brief before the United Nations or even before this Court. . . .

Regardless, the "legitimacy" justification itself is inconsistent with critically important First Amendment case law. Consider the cases involving the protection the First Amendment offered those who joined the Communist Party intending only to further its peaceful activities. In those cases, this Court took account of congressional findings that the Communist Party not only advocated theoretically but also sought to put into practice the overthrow of our Government through force and violence. The Court had previously accepted Congress' determinations that the American Communist Party was a "Communist action organization" which (1) acted under the "control, direction, and discipline" of the world Communist movement, a movement that sought to employ "espionage, sabotage, terrorism, and any other means deemed necessary, to establish a Communist totalitarian dictatorship," and (2) "endeavor[ed]" to bring about "the overthrow of existing governments by . . . force if necessary." *Communist Party of United States v. Subversive Activities Control Bd.*, 367 U.S. 1, 5-6 (1961) (internal quotation marks omitted).

Nonetheless, the Court held that the First Amendment protected an American's right to belong to that party — despite whatever "legitimating" effect membership might have had — as long as the person did not share the party's unlawful purposes. . . . The Government's "legitimating" theory would seem to apply to these cases with equal justifying force; and, if recognized, it would have led this Court to conclusions other than those it reached. . . .

II

For the reasons I have set forth, I believe application of the statute as the Government interprets it would gravely and without adequate justification injure interests of the kind the First Amendment protects. Thus, there is "a serious doubt" as to the statute's constitutionality. [*Crowell v. Benson*, 285 U.S. 22, 62 (1932)]. And where that is so, we must "ascertain whether a construction of the statute is fairly possible by which the question may be avoided." *Ibid.*

I believe that a construction that would avoid the constitutional problem is "fairly possible." In particular, I would read the statute as criminalizing First-Amendment-protected pure speech and association only when the defendant knows or intends that those activities will assist the organization's unlawful terrorist actions. Under this reading, the Government would have to show, at a minimum, that such defendants provided support that they knew was significantly likely to help the organization pursue its unlawful terrorist aims.

A person acts with the requisite knowledge if he is aware of (or willfully blinds himself to) a significant likelihood that his or her conduct will materially support the organization's terrorist ends. On the other hand, for the reasons I have set out, knowledge or intent that this assistance (aimed at lawful activities) could or would help further terrorism simply by helping to legitimate the organization is not sufficient. . . .

Thus, textually speaking, a statutory requirement that the defendant *knew* the support was material can be read to require the Government to show that the defendant knew that the consequences of his acts had a significant likelihood of furthering the organization's terrorist, not just its lawful, aims.

I need not decide whether this is the only possible reading of the statute in cases where "material support" takes the form of "currency," "property," "monetary instruments," "financial securities," "financial services," "lodging," "safehouses," "false documentation or identification," "weapons," "lethal substances," or "explosives," and the like. §2339A(b)(1). Those kinds of aid are inherently more likely to help an organization's terrorist activities, either directly or because they are fungible in nature. Thus, to show that an individual has provided support of those kinds will normally prove sufficient for conviction (assuming the statute's other requirements are met). But where support consists of pure speech or association, I would indulge in no such presumption. Rather, the Government would have to prove that the defendant knew he was providing support significantly likely to help the organization pursue its unlawful terrorist aims (or, alternatively, that the defendant intended the support to be so used). . . .

III

Having interpreted the statute to impose the *mens rea* requirement just described, I would remand the cases so that the lower courts could consider more specifically the precise activities in which the plaintiffs still wish to engage and determine whether and to what extent a grant of declaratory and injunctive relief were [*sic*] warranted. . . .

NOTES AND QUESTIONS

1. *The Anti-Terrorist Prosecutor's Weapon of Choice?* As we noted above, the apparent expansion of the suicide terrorist threat in the 1990s, and the difficulty of identifying

and arresting would-be suicide terrorists in time, has caused the government to begin searching more vigorously up the chain of causation not only for those who plan, but also for those who support, acts of terrorism. Abdel Rahman's prosecution was a way station in this shift in prosecutorial focus to "precursor crimes," because he was prosecuted for "overall supervision and direction of the membership," as the *Rahman* court put it, not for involvement in "individual operations." Yet the "seditious conspiracy" crime that the government there charged was anachronistic, notwithstanding the eventual success of the prosecution. *But see* Carlton F.W. Larson, *The Forgotten Constitutional Law of Treason and the Enemy Combatant Problem*, 154 U. Pa. L. Rev. 863 (2006) (urging prosecution of enemy combatants for treason and noting the historical applicability of the offense not just to citizens, but to anyone within the United States). Prosecutors needed a tool better suited to interdicting material support and, thereby, suicide terrorism.

When Congress responded by enacting the material support provision of AEDPA in 1996 and expanding material support liability in subsequent legislation, prosecutors used their new weapon enthusiastically. The material support charge is increasingly the government's weapon of choice against suspected terrorists. Data through September 2010 indicate that material support offenses ranked first in charges and convictions in the war on terrorism. Center on Law & Sec., *Terrorist Trial Report Card: September 11, 2001-September 11, 2010*, at 12-13 (2010), *available at* http://www.lawandsecurity.org/Portals/0/documents/01_TTRC2010Final1.pdf. *See generally* Norman Abrams, *The Material Support Terrorism Offenses: Perspectives Derived from the (Early) Model Penal Code*, 1 J. Nat'l Security L. & Pol'y 5 (2005); Robert M. Chesney, *The Sleeper Scenario: Terrorism-Support Laws and the Demands of Prevention*, 42 Harv. J. Legis. 3 (2005); Wayne McCormack, *Inchoate Terrorism: Liberalism Clashes with Fundamentalism*, 37 Geo. J. Int'l L. 1 (2005).

2. *Knowledge or Specific Intent?* The plaintiffs argued that §2339B required proof that a defendant intended to further an FTO's terrorist activities. What does the statute say? How do its scienter (state of mind) requirements compare to its companion material support statutes §§2339A and 2339C?

If the statute does not require specific intent, why is it not unconstitutional? In the Smith Act, Congress criminalized knowing membership in any organization that advocates the overthrow of the government by force or violence. 18 U.S.C. §2385 (2006). The Act came before the Supreme Court in *Scales v. United States*, 367 U.S. 203 (1961), in which the Court upheld a conviction for membership only on proof of *knowing* membership or affiliation *and specific intent* to further the group's unlawful goals. The Court explained its insistence on these elements of proof by rejecting the concept of guilt by association:

> In our jurisprudence guilt is personal, and when the imposition of punishment on a status or on conduct can only be justified by reference to the relationship of that status or conduct to other concededly criminal activity (here advocacy of violent overthrow), that relationship must be sufficiently substantial to satisfy the concept of personal guilt in order to withstand attack under the Due Process Clause of the Fifth Amendment. [*Id.* at 224-225.]

Specific intent implements the requirement of personal guilt by "tying the imposition of guilt to an individually culpable act." David Cole, *Hanging with the Wrong*

Crowd: Of Gangs, Terrorists, and the Right of Association, 1999 Sup. Ct. Rev. 203, 217. In First Amendment terms, the specific intent requirement "identifies the only narrowly tailored way to punish individuals for group wrongdoing (essentially by requiring evidence of individual wrongdoing), just as the *Brandenburg* test [*supra* p. 602] sets forth the narrowly tailored way to respond to advocacy of illegal conduct." Cole, *supra*, 1999 Sup. Ct. Rev. at 218. How does the Court distinguish *Scales?* Does §2339B make it a crime to be a member of an FTO?

3. *The Logic of Criminalizing Mere Knowing Support.* Some FTOs, such as Hamas, are dual-purpose organizations; they engage in terrorism, but they also provide social services. *Cf.* Michael Whidden, Note, *Unequal Justice: Arabs in America and United States Antiterrorism in Legislation,* 69 Fordham L. Rev. 2825, 2873 (2001) (asserting that FTOs Hamas and Hezbollah operate orphanages, hospitals, schools, and medical clinics for indigent Palestinians in addition to conducting terrorist activities). Some supporters want only to support the non-terrorist purposes of the FTO. Did Congress in §2339B make it a crime to write a check to Hamas to support its social services? If so, why? Why does the majority in *Holder* not reject Congress's reasoning? Why does the dissent? Did the majority defer too much to congressional "fact" finding? *See* Robert M. Chesney, *National Security Fact Deference,* 95 Va. L. Rev. 1361, 1362 (2009) ("'[N]ational security fact deference' is freighted with constitutional significance. On one hand, it may undermine the capacity of courts to guard against unlawful executive branch actions (in terms of both unjustified assertions of power and violations of individual rights). On the other hand, it may prevent the judicial power from encroaching inappropriately upon executive responsibilities relating to national security, while simultaneously helping to preserve the judiciary's institutional legitimacy. National security fact deference claims, in short, implicate competing values of great magnitude").

4. *Vagueness.* A law is unconstitutionally vague if a reasonable person cannot tell what expression is prohibited and what is permitted. "Material support," as used in §2339B, is defined in §2339A(b). Is the statute vague as applied to the provision of explosives or safehouses to a terrorist or FTO? What about the donation of money to an FTO? If these applications don't seem unconstitutionally vague, what about providing personnel, training, or expert advice? Why did the majority reject the vagueness challenge to the latter terms?

Did the Court rule that there are no applications of these terms that would be unconstitutionally vague? Consider the case of a lawyer for a convicted terrorist who meets periodically with her client in prison and secretly conveys messages between him and his associates (including members of an FTO) outside prison. Is the term "personnel" unconstitutionally vague as applied to prosecute that lawyer for providing *herself* as "personnel" to a terrorist or FTO? *See United States v. Sattar,* 272 F. Supp. 2d 348 (S.D.N.Y. 2003) (*Sattar I*) (yes; government's assertion in oral argument that "you know it when you see it" is an "insufficient guide by which a person can predict the legality of that person's conduct," whatever merit it may have as a way to identify obscenity). Is it too vague for prosecuting the lawyer for supplying *her client* as "personnel" to the FTO, by making him "available" through communications that she conveys? *See United States v. Sattar,* 314 F. Supp. 2d 279, 300 (S.D.N.Y. 2004), *cert. denied,* 130 S. Ct. 1924 (2010) (*Sattar II*) (no; "the 'provision' of 'personnel'—in this case, by making the imprisoned

Sheik Abdel Rahman available as a co-conspirator in a conspiracy to kill and kidnap persons in a foreign country—is conduct that plainly is prohibited by the statute" with sufficient definiteness). How about a U.S. citizen who joins the Taliban to fight alongside Al Qaeda fighters against U.S. armed forces in Afghanistan? *See United States v. Lindh*, 212 F. Supp. 2d 541, 574 (E.D. Va. 2002) (no; "personnel" is not unconstitutionally vague as applied to "employees" or "employee-like operatives" who were under the "direction and control" of an FTO). *See* James P. Fantetti, Comment, *John Walker Lindh, Terrorist? Or Merely a Citizen Exercising His Constitutional Freedom: The Limits of the Freedom of Association in the Aftermath of September Eleventh*, 71 U. Cinn. L. Rev. 1373 (2003).

Suppose a cab driver drives a person he knows to be a member of an FTO to the airport. Can he constitutionally be prosecuted for providing "transportation" to an FTO?

5. *Protected Expression.* Donating money is not membership, but it is also unlike donating weapons, safe houses, or transportation. "The right to join together 'for the advancement of beliefs and ideas' is diluted," the Supreme Court explained, "if it does not include the right to pool money through contributions, for funds are often essential if 'advocacy' is to be truly or optimally 'effective.'" *Buckley v. Valeo*, 424 U.S. 1, 65-66 (1974) (quoting *NAACP v. Alabama ex rel. Patterson*, 357 U.S. 449, 460 (1958)). Why is donating money to an FTO not protected political expression?

One answer is that it *is* protected expression, but that the protection is not absolute. What degree of scrutiny should a court then give to its regulation? *See* Cole, *supra*, 1999 Sup. Ct. Rev. at 237-238 (urging strict scrutiny—requiring a close relationship to a compelling government interest—when government's purpose is to regulate association as such). *See generally* Nina J. Crimm, *High Alert: The Government's War on the Financing of Terrorism and Implications for Donors, Domestic Charitable Organizations, and Global Philanthropy*, 45 Wm. & Mary L. Rev. 1341 (2004); David Cole, *The New McCarthyism: Repeating History in the War on Terrorism*, 38 Harv. C.R.-C.L. L. Rev. 1, 11 (2003).

In *Holder*, however, the plaintiffs were not making financial contributions to the FTOs; nor were they engaged simply in "pure political speech." Instead, they wanted to provide material support to FTOs "in the form of speech" — by providing training lectures and advice. How did prohibiting such support in the form of speech have a close relationship to the concededly compelling interest of preventing or making more difficult terrorist acts by FTOs? Does *Holder* "open[] the door for prohibiting any speech related to a terrorist organization, no matter how peaceful it is, as long as it is expressed in coordination with or under the direction of a terrorist organization"? Daphne Barak-Enez & David Scharia, *Freedom of Speech, Support for Terrorism, and the Challenge of Global Constitutional Law*, 2 Harv. Nat'l Security J. 1, 19 (2011).

The dissent in *Humanitarian Law Project v. Holder* had serious doubts that the prohibition bore the necessary relationship to the counterterrorism interest. How did it avoid the resulting constitutional issue? Does its solution interpret §2339B or rewrite it? Should Congress amend §2339B to require specific intent for support in the form of speech? *See* The Constitution Project, *Reforming the Material Support Laws: Constitutional Concerns Presented by Prohibitions on Material Support to "Terrorist Organizations"* (Nov. 17, 2009) (so arguing).

C.   THE LONG ARM OF THE LAW: EXTRATERRITORIAL CRIMINAL JURISDICTION

Congress has enacted a variety of statutes aimed at international terrorism. *See, e.g.,* 18 U.S.C. §§31-32 (2006) (hijacking or sabotaging aircraft); *id.* §§175-178 (developing or possessing biological or toxin weapons); 18 U.S.C. §§2331-2332 (2006 & Supp. III 2009) (killing or injuring U.S. citizens abroad); *id.* §2332a (directing weapons of mass destruction against Americans abroad or against anyone within the United States); *id.* §2339A (providing material support to terrorists); and 49 U.S.C. §§46,501-46,507 (2006) (committing air piracy). Most of these are now expressly extraterritorial in application. But some older criminal statutes are not. The following case discusses the interpretative principles governing extraterritorial application of U.S. criminal laws.

United States v. Bin Laden

United States District Court, Southern District of New York, 2000
92 F. Supp. 2d 189

SAND, District Judge. The sixth superseding indictment in this case ("the Indictment") charges fifteen defendants with conspiracy to murder United States nationals, to use weapons of mass destruction against United States nationals, to destroy United States buildings and property, and to destroy United States defense utilities. The Indictment also charges defendants Mohamed Sadeek Odeh, Mohamed Rashed Daoud al-'Owhali, and Khalfan Khamis Mohamed, among others, with numerous crimes in connection with the August 1998 bombings of the United States Embassies in Nairobi, Kenya, and Dar es Salaam, Tanzania, including 223 counts of murder....

I. EXTRATERRITORIAL APPLICATION

Odeh argues that Counts 5-8, 11-237, and 240-244 must be dismissed because (a) they concern acts allegedly performed by Odeh and his co-defendants outside United States territory, yet (b) are based on statutes that were not intended by Congress to regulate conduct outside United States territory. More specifically, Odeh argues that "the statutes that form the basis for the indictment fail clearly and unequivocally to regulate the conduct of foreign nationals for conduct outside the territorial boundaries of the United States."...

A. General Principles of Extraterritorial Application

It is well-established that Congress has the power to regulate conduct performed outside United States territory. It is equally well-established, however, that courts are to presume that Congress has not exercised this power—i.e., that statutes apply only to acts performed within United States territory—unless Congress manifests an intent to reach acts performed outside United States territory. This "clear manifestation" requirement does not require that extraterritorial coverage should be found only if the statute itself explicitly provides for extraterritorial application. Rather, courts should consider "all available evidence about the meaning" of the statute, e.g., its text, structure, and legislative history.

Furthermore, the Supreme Court has established a limited exception to this standard approach for "criminal statutes which are, as a class, not logically dependent on their locality for the Government's jurisdiction, but are enacted because of the right of the Government to defend itself against obstruction, or fraud wherever perpetrated, especially if committed by its own citizens, officers, or agents." *United States v. Bowman*, 260 U.S. 94, 98 (1922). As regards statutes of this type, courts may infer the requisite intent "from the nature of the offense" described in the statute, and thus need not examine its legislative history.[3] *Id.* The Court further observed that "to limit the [] locus [of such a statute] to the strictly territorial jurisdiction [of the United States] would be greatly to curtail the scope and usefulness of the statute and leave open a large immunity for frauds as easily committed by citizens on the high seas and in foreign countries as at home. . . ."

Odeh argues that *Bowman* is "not controlling precedent" because it "involved the application of [a] penal statute[] to United States citizens," i.e., not to foreign nationals such as himself. This argument is unavailing. . . .

. . . Under international law, the primary basis of jurisdiction is the "subjective territorial principle," under which "a state has jurisdiction to prescribe law with respect to . . . conduct that, wholly or in substantial part, takes place within its territory." *Restatement (Third) of the Foreign Relations Law of the United States* §402(1)(a) (1987). International law recognizes five other principles of jurisdiction by which a state may reach conduct *outside* its territory: (1) the objective territorial principle; (2) the protective principle; (3) the nationality principle; (4) the passive personality principle; and (5) the universality principle. The objective territoriality principle provides that a state has jurisdiction to prescribe law with respect to "conduct outside its territory that has or is intended to have substantial effect within its territory." *Restatement* §402(1)(c). The protective principle provides that a state has jurisdiction to prescribe law with respect to "certain conduct outside its territory by *persons not its nationals* that is directed against *the security of the state* or against a limited class of other state interests." *Id.* §402(3) (emphasis added). The nationality principle provides that a state has jurisdiction to prescribe law with respect to "the activities, interests, status, or relations of its nationals outside as well as within its territory." *Id.* §402(2). The passive personality principle provides that "a state may apply law — particularly criminal law — to an act committed outside its territory by a person not its national where the victim of the act was its national." *Id.* §402, cmt. g. The universality principle provides that, "[a] state has jurisdiction to define and prescribe punishment for certain offenses recognized by the community of nations as of universal concern, such as piracy, slave trade, attacks on or hijacking of aircraft, genocide, war crimes, and perhaps *certain acts of terrorism*," regardless of the locus of their occurrence. *Id.* §404 (emphasis added). Because Congress has the power to override international law if it so chooses, *Restatement* §402, cmt. I., none of these five principles places ultimate limits on Congress's power to reach extraterritorial conduct. At the same time, however, "[i]n determining whether a statute applies extraterritorially, [courts]

---

3. This is not necessarily to say, however, that legislative history is entirely irrelevant under the *Bowman* exception to the standard approach. Given that the *Bowman* rule is ultimately concerned with congressional intent, if the legislative history clearly indicates that Congress intended the statute in question to apply only within the United States, it would be inconsistent with *Bowman* to ignore this evidence, and conclude — in reliance on *Bowman* — that Congress intended the statute to apply extraterritorially. . . .

presume that Congress does not intend to violate principles of international law... [and] in the absence of an explicit Congressional directive, courts do not give extraterritorial effect to any statute that violates principles of international law." *United States v. Vasquez-Velasco*, 15 F.3d 833, 839 (9th Cir. 1994) (citing *McCulloch v. Sociedad Nacional de Marineros de Honduras*, 372 U.S. 10, 21-22 (1963)). Hence, courts that find that a given statute applies extraterritorially typically pause to note that this finding is consistent with one or more of the five principles of extraterritorial jurisdiction under international law.

The *Bowman* rule would appear to be most directly related to the protective principle, which, as noted, explicitly authorizes a state's exercise of jurisdiction over "conduct outside its territory *by persons not its nationals.*" *Restatement* §402(3). Hence, an application of the *Bowman* rule that results in the extraterritorial application of a statute to the conduct of foreign nationals is consistent with international law....

B. 18 U.S.C. §§844, 924, 930, 1114, and 2155

In light of the preceding general principles, we find that Congress intended each of the following statutory provisions to reach conduct by foreign nationals on foreign soil....

1. 18 U.S.C. §844(f), (h), and (n)

The Indictment predicates Count 5 on 18 U.S.C. §§844(f).... Subsection 844(f)(1) provides:

> Whoever maliciously damages or destroys, or attempts to damage or destroy, by means of fire or an explosive, any building, vehicle, or other personal or real property in whole or in part owned or possessed by, or leased to, the United States, or any department or agency thereof, shall be imprisoned for not less than 5 years and not more than 20 years, fined under this title, or both. [18 U.S.C. §844(f)(1).]
>
> Given (i) that this provision is explicitly intended to protect United States property, (ii) that a significant amount of United States property is located outside the United States, and (iii) that, accordingly, foreign nationals are in at least as good a position as are United States nationals to damage such property, we find, under *Bowman*, that Congress intended Section 844(f)(1) to apply extraterritorially—irrespective of the nationality of the perpetrator....

III. CONSTITUTIONAL AUTHORITY

Odeh argues that the Counts based on 18 U.S.C. §§2332 and 2332a must be dismissed because these statutes are unconstitutional in that they exceed Congress's authority to legislate under the Constitution. As noted above, Subsection 2332(b) provides in relevant part that "[w]hoever outside the United States... engages in a conspiracy to kill[] a national of the United States shall [be punished as further provided]," 18 U.S.C. §2332(b); and Section 2332a(a) provides in relevant part that, "[a] person who... uses, threatens, or attempts or conspires to use, a weapon of mass destruction... (1) against a national of the United States while such national is outside of the United States;... or (3) against any property that is owned, leased or used by the United States . . . , whether the property is within or outside of the United States, shall [be punished as further provided]." 18 U.S.C. §2332a(a).

Odeh suggests that there is but one constitutional grant of authority to legislate that could support these two statutory provisions: Article I, Section 8, Clause 10. Clause 10 grants Congress the authority "[t]o define and punish Piracies and Felonies committed on the high Seas, and Offenses against the Law of Nations." U.S. Const. art. I, §8, cl. 10. Odeh argues that, as "[t]he acts described in these two statutes . . . are not widely regarded as offenses 'against the law of nations,'" these statutes exceed Congress's authority under Clause 10.

There are two problems with this argument. First, even assuming that the acts described in Sections 2332 and 2332a are not *widely* regarded as violations of international law, it does not necessarily follow that these provisions exceed Congress's authority under Clause 10. Clause 10 does not merely give Congress the authority to punish offenses against the law of nations; it also gives Congress the power to "define" such offenses. Hence, provided that the acts in question are recognized by at least some members of the international community as being offenses against the law of nations, Congress arguably has the power to criminalize these acts pursuant to its power *to define* offenses against the law of nations. *See United States v. Smith*, 18 U.S. (5 Wheat.) 153, 159 (1820) (Story, J.) ("Offenses . . . against the law of nations, cannot, with any accuracy, be said to be completely ascertained and defined in any public code recognized by the common consent of nations. . . . [T]herefore . . . , there is a peculiar fitness in giving the power to define as well as to punish.").

Second, and more important, it is not the case that Clause 10 provides the only basis for Sections 2332 and 2332a. The Supreme Court has recognized that, with regard to foreign affairs legislation, "investment of the federal Government with the powers of external sovereignty did not depend upon the affirmative grants of the Constitution." *United States v. Curtiss-Wright Export Corp.*, 299 U.S. 304, 318 (1936). Rather, Congress's authority to regulate foreign affairs "exist[s] as inherently inseparable from the conception of nationality." *Id.* (citations omitted). More specifically, this "concept of essential sovereignty of a free nation clearly requires the existence and recognition of an inherent power in the state to protect itself from destruction." *United States v. Rodriguez*, 182 F. Supp. 479, 491 (S.D. Cal. 1960), *aff'd in part sub nom. Rocha v. United States*, 288 F.2d 545 (9th Cir.), *cert. denied*, 366 U.S. 948 (1961).

In penalizing extraterritorial conspiracies to kill nationals of the United States, Section 2332(b) is clearly designed to protect a vital United States interest. And, indeed, Congress expressly identified this protective function as the chief purpose of Section 2332. Therefore, we conclude, under *Curtiss-Wright*, that Congress acted within its authority in enacting these provisions. . . .

V. APPLICATION OF 18 U.S.C. §930(c) TO FOREIGN VICTIMS

Odeh argues that interpreting Section 930(c)[1] to reach "the deaths of Kenyan and Tanzanian citizens [as opposed to United States citizens] would be contrary to established principles of international law." More specifically, Odeh advances the

---

[1. 18 U.S.C. §930(c) provides that "[a] person who kills or attempts to kill any person in the course of a violation of subsection (a) or (b) [involving knowing possession of firearms or other dangerous weapons in a federal facility], or in the course of an attack on a Federal facility involving the use of a firearm or other dangerous weapon, shall be punished [as further provided]." — Eds.]

following two arguments. First, given (i) that "[u]nder 18 U.S.C. §930(c), the only arguable basis for jurisdiction over the deaths of foreign citizens is the principle of universality," (ii) that "[u]niversal jurisdiction results where there is *universal* condemnation of an offense, and a general interest in cooperating to suppress them, as reflected in *widely accepted* international agreements," and (iii) that "the universality principle does not encompass terrorist actions resulting in the deaths of individuals who are not diplomatic personnel," it follows that applying Section 930(c) to the deaths of "ordinary" foreign nationals on foreign soil would constitute a violation of international law.

There are two problems with this argument. First, because "universal jurisdiction is increasingly accepted for certain acts of terrorism, such as . . . indiscriminate violent assaults on people at large," Restatement §404, cmt. a, a plausible case could be made that extraterritorial application of Section 930(c) in this case *is* supported by the universality principle.

Second, it is not the case that the universality principle is the "only arguable basis for jurisdiction over the deaths of foreign citizens." As indicated by our conclusion . . . that Section 930(c) is designed to *protect* vital United States interests, the protective principle is also an "arguable basis" for the extraterritorial application of Section 930(c). . . . In providing for the death penalty where death results in the course of an attack on a Federal facility, Section 930(c) is clearly designed to deter attacks on Federal facilities. Given the likelihood that foreign nationals will be in or near Federal facilities located in foreign nations, this deterrent effect would be significantly diminished if Section 930(c) were limited to the deaths of United States nationals. . . .

Odeh argues, second, that, even if the universality principle (or one of the four other principles) did authorize the application of Section 930(c) to the deaths of ordinary foreign nationals on foreign soil, such application would violate international law nevertheless, because (i) "[e]ven where one of the principles authorizes jurisdiction, a nation is nevertheless precluded from exercising jurisdiction where jurisdiction would be 'unreasonable,'" and (ii) application of Section 930(c) to the deaths of ordinary foreign nationals on foreign soil would be unreasonable. *Id.* (citations omitted).

According to the Restatement, the following factors are to be taken into account for the purpose of determining whether exercise of extraterritorial jurisdiction is reasonable:

> (a) the link of the activity to the territory of the regulating state, i.e., the extent to which the activity takes place within the territory, or has substantial, direct, and foreseeable effect upon or in the territory;
> (b) the connections, such as nationality, residence, or economic activity, between the regulating state and the person principally responsible for the activity to be regulated, or between that state and those whom the regulation is designed to protect;
> (c) the character of the activity to be regulated, the importance of regulation to the regulating state, the extent to which other states regulate such activities, and the degree to which the desirability of such regulation is generally accepted;
> (d) the existence of justified expectations that might be protected or hurt by the regulation;
> (e) the importance of the regulation to the international political, legal, or economic system;

(f) the extent to which the regulation is consistent with the traditions of the international system;

(g) the extent to which another state may have an interest in regulating the activity; and

(h) the likelihood of conflict with regulation by another state.

Restatement §403(2). Given that factor (a) alludes to the subjective territorial principle and the objective territorial principle, it is not especially relevant to a statute, such as Section 930(c), based primarily on the protective principle. Much the same can be said of factor (b), as it alludes to the nationality principle, the subjective territorial principle, and the objective territorial principle. Factor (c), in contrast, is highly relevant to Section 930(c). It is important both to the United States and other nations to prevent the destruction of their facilities — regardless of their location; and such regulation is accordingly widely accepted among the nations of the world. As for factor (d), Section 930(c) protects the expectation of foreign nationals that they will be free of harm while on the premises of United States facilities. We can think of no "justified" expectation, however, that would be hurt by the extraterritorial application of Section 930(c). As for factor (e), in light of the prominent role played by the United States in "the international political, legal, and economic systems," the protection of United States facilities — regardless of their location — is highly important to the stability of these systems. Turning to factor (f), as indicated by the preceding discussion of factor (c), most, if not all, nations are concerned about protecting their facilities, both at home and abroad. Hence, Section 930(c) is highly consistent "with the traditions of the international system." As for (g), it must be acknowledged that when the United States facility is on foreign soil, and when the victims of the attack are nationals of the host nation, the host nation "has a keen interest in regulating and punishing [the] offenders." This is not to say, however, that the host nation has a greater interest than does the United States. Furthermore, even if it were the case that the host nation had a greater interest than the United States, this single factor would be insufficient to support the conclusion that application of Section 930(c) to the bombings of the two Embassies is unreasonable. Coming, finally, to factor (h), Odeh does not argue that application of Section 930(c) to the bombings would conflict with Kenyan and/or Tanzanian law, nor are we otherwise aware of such conflict. On the contrary, the Government informs the Court that "[t]he Kenyan Government voluntarily rendered Odeh (and [co-defendant] al-'Owhali) to the United States, and neither the Kenyan nor the Tanzanian Government has asserted any objection to the United States' exercise of jurisdiction in this case." Factor (h) thus counts in favor of the reasonableness of applying Section 930(c) to the bombings. . . .

NOTES AND QUESTIONS

1. *Extraterritoriality and the Constitution.* No one questions a sovereign state's authority to prescribe laws for its own territory, and the Constitution quite clearly vests limited authority to do so in Congress. But can Congress constitutionally make laws that apply abroad? The Constitution is silent on this question, but Article III states that when a crime is "not committed within any State," trial for the crime shall be conducted where Congress directs. U.S. Const. art. III, §2, cl. 3. Thus, the Framers clearly contemplated criminal sanctions against acts committed

outside any state of the union. Moreover, they vested Congress with the authority to define and punish "Offenses against the Law of Nations." *Id.* art. I, §8, cl. 10. Because such offenses may be committed abroad, this provision gives Congress extraterritorial lawmaking authority. On what basis does Odeh argue that 18 U.S.C. §§2332 and 2332a exceed Congress's lawmaking authority? Is the court's response consistent with a federal government of limited lawmaking authority?

Assuming that Congress can enact laws with extraterritorial effect, does the Constitution place any limit on extraterritoriality? Civil procedure students may suspect that some "minimum contact" by the defendant or her acts with the United States might be required as a matter of due process. Beyond that, however, customary international law principles of prescriptive jurisdiction might also establish limits as a part of our federal common law. Indeed, one commentator asserts that "[i]t is arguable that the Constitution permits Congress to make acts committed abroad crimes under United States law only to the extent permitted by international law." Andreas Lowenfeld, *U.S. Law Enforcement Abroad: The Constitution and International Law*, 83 Am. J. Int'l L. 880, 881 (1989). How does the *Bin Laden* court regard this assertion?

If international law does not limit extraterritorial lawmaking by Congress, what role, if any, does it play, according to the court? What rule of statutory construction is implicated by applicable international laws?

2. *Presumption Against Extraterritoriality.* Why should the courts presume that a statute applies locally only, unless Congress clearly manifests an intent to reach acts performed abroad? Sometimes such an intent is manifested by the plain language of the statute. The statute that makes it a crime to develop, produce, stockpile, transfer, acquire, retain, or possess any biological agent, toxin, or delivery system for use as a weapon, for example, expressly provides that "[t]here is extraterritorial Federal jurisdiction over an offense under this section committed by or against a national of the United States." 18 U.S.C. §175 (2006). Similarly, 18 U.S.C. §2332(b) (2006), expressly makes it a crime to engage in a conspiracy "outside the United States" to kill U.S. nationals. *Bowman* created an exception to the presumption against extraterritoriality. Why?

3. *The Territoriality and Nationality Principles of Extraterritorial Jurisdiction.* The court in *Bin Laden* catalogued principles of jurisdiction under customary international law, but such principles are not equally accepted by all nations, and they may not be helpful for other reasons. *See generally* Christopher L. Blakesley, *Extraterritorial Jurisdiction*, in 2 *International Criminal Law* 33 (M. Cherif Bassiouni ed., 2d ed. 1999). The territorial principle, for example, applies both to actors within a sovereign's territory ("subjective territoriality") and to effects in such territory resulting from acts abroad ("objective territoriality"), and it is reflected in *Restatement* §402(1). But while it is the most common and widely accepted principle of jurisdiction, it often will be unavailable for terrorist or other criminal acts performed abroad, including inchoate acts intended ultimately to cause injury in the United States. The nationality principle — allowing a sovereign to exercise jurisdiction over its nationals for their acts performed abroad — is also accepted by the practice of nations. Roman Boed, *United States Legislative Approach to Extraterritorial Jurisdiction in Connection with Terrorism*, in 2 *International Criminal Law, supra,* at 147. But international terrorists may not be U.S. nationals, just as most of the *Bin Laden* defendants were not.

4. *The Protective Principle of Extraterritorial Jurisdiction.* The protective principle is more likely to apply to acts of international terrorism, but it is limited to offenses against the security of the state or acts that threaten the integrity of government functions. *Restatement* §402(3) & cmt. f. (1981). It thus is easily applied to the embassy bombings. Would it apply to terrorist acts committed against private U.S. nationals abroad? "The lack of definition of the range of conduct encompassed by the protective principle and the principle's malleability," Professor Boed worries, "could lead to the principle's justification of a wide-ranging exercise of extraterritorial jurisdiction." Boed, *supra*, at 148.

5. *The Passive Personality Principle of Extraterritorial Jurisdiction.* Even if the protective principle does not apply to terrorist acts against private U.S. nationals, such acts would clearly fall under the passive personality principle. But this principle has not traditionally found wide support in the practice of states, Boed, *supra*, at 149, and it was squarely rejected by the United States until recently. *See* Blakesley, *supra*, at 69-70 ("The passive-personality theory traditionally has been anathema to U.S. law and practice.").

In the Omnibus Diplomatic Security and Antiterrorism Act of 1986, however, Congress made it a crime to kill or conspire to kill or cause physical violence to a U.S. national while such national is outside the United States. Pub. L. No. 99-399, §1202, 100 Stat. 853, 896, now codified at 18 U.S.C. §2332 (2006). The *Bin Laden* defendants were charged with this crime, and it would apply as well to acts of homicide or physical violence against private U.S. nationals traveling abroad. Does that mean that the United States could prosecute an Italian pickpocket for pushing a U.S. tourist in Rome as he extracted the tourist's wallet? Even Congress had doubts about reaching so far, so it added a limitation forbidding any prosecution except upon written certification by the Attorney General or his Deputy that "such offense was intended to coerce, intimidate, or retaliate against a government or a civilian population." 18 U.S.C. §2332(d). Here Congress attempted to narrow the offenses to terrorist offenses without defining them and thus to avoid extending the statute to barroom brawls or ordinary street crimes. But what new problem does this provision arguably create? Who creates jurisdiction under this law, and when is it created? *See* Lowenfeld, *supra*, at 891 (opining that the statute is unconstitutional).

Congress came back to passive personality jurisdiction in the Antiterrorism and Effective Death Penalty Act of 1996. Pub. L. No. 104-132, 110 Stat. 1214 (1996). In a section of that Act entitled "Clarification and Extension of Criminal Jurisdiction Over Certain Terrorism Offenses Overseas," Congress systematically amended multiple sections of the criminal code to supply the "clear manifestation" of extraterritoriality that is needed to overcome the presumption against extraterritoriality. *Id.* §721. These sections address aircraft piracy, destruction of aircraft, violence at international airports, murder of foreign officials and other persons, protection of the same, threats and extortion against the same, kidnaping of internationally protected persons, and developing or possessing biological weapons. *See* Boed, *supra*, at 159-173.

6. *The Universality Principle of Extraterritorial Jurisdiction.* Universality is perhaps the most controversial of the principles of extraterritorial jurisdiction, because it could theoretically result in a state's prosecuting a non-national for acts performed abroad against other non-nationals. *See* Kenneth C. Randall, *Universal Jurisdiction Under International Law,* 66 Tex. L. Rev. 785 (1988). It rests on the assumption that there are

some crimes so widely regarded as heinous that their perpetrators are enemies of mankind, subject to prosecution the world over. The prosecuting nation acts for all nations to protect their collective interest.

To which crimes does this principle apply, according to the *Bin Laden* court? Do they include terrorism? In 1984, Judge Edwards of the D.C. Circuit Court of Appeals asserted that he was unable to conclude "that the law of nations . . . outlaws politically motivated terrorism, no matter how repugnant it might be to our legal system." *Tel-Oren v. Libyan Arab Republic*, 726 F.2d 774, 796 (D.C. Cir. 1984), *cert. denied*, 470 U.S. 1003 (1985). Why do you suppose that the law of nations might not subject terrorism to universal jurisdiction? On the other hand, the law of nations is not static. *Restatement* §404 (quoted in *Bin Laden, supra* p. 622) would include "*perhaps* certain acts of terrorism" (emphasis supplied). Professor Blakesley argues that the law of nations has *already* condemned individual offenses (such as air piracy and hostage-taking) for which "terrorism" is merely a composite term. Blakesley, *supra*, at 72. What was the *Bin Laden* court's conclusion in 2000?

7. *The Rule of Reasonableness.* The *Restatement* suggests that traditional principles of extraterritoriality are not to be mechanically applied; a court must always consider whether exercising jurisdiction in the particular circumstances would be reasonable. Indeed, the malleability and overlap of the traditional principles of extraterritorial jurisdiction under international law have caused some to suggest that reasonableness is today the overriding principle, under which the availability or nonavailability of the traditional principles is just a factor in the equation. Blakesley, *supra*, at 41. Is extraterritorial jurisdiction in *Bin Laden* reasonable? Why or why not?

8. *"Substantial Nexus."* We suggested that the civil procedure student might speculate whether the Due Process Clause imposes a "minimum contacts" requirement for extraterritorial jurisdiction. In fact, a few cases have spoken of the need for a substantial nexus between the defendant or his acts and the state exercising extraterritorial jurisdiction. *See, e.g., United States v. Davis*, 905 F.2d 245 (9th Cir. 1990), *cert. denied*, 498 U.S. 1047 (1991). Most courts, however (including the *Bin Laden* court in a portion of the opinion not reproduced here), have concluded that if extraterritorial jurisdiction is justified by the international principles of extraterritorial jurisdiction, due process is satisfied. *Davis*, 905 F.2d at 249. This seems persuasive when jurisdiction is supported by the territoriality, nationality, or protective principle, because each presumes "contact." Can you explain how? But does it work for jurisdiction supported only by the passive personality or universality principle?

Prosecuting Accused Terrorists and Their Supporters in Criminal Courts

21

It is not just the crimes that pose legal problems in prosecuting accused terrorists and their supporters, but also the evidence. In 1996, Congress for the first time authorized the intelligence community, "upon the request of a United States law enforcement agency, [to] collect information outside the United States about individuals who are not United States persons . . . notwithstanding that the law enforcement agency intends to use the information collected for purposes of a law enforcement investigation or counterintelligence investigation." 50 U.S.C. §403-5a(a) (2006). Moreover, after 9/11, Congress expressly authorized and encouraged more sharing of information among intelligence and law enforcement agencies. When intelligence agencies are tasked with information collection for law enforcement and those agencies share their information, the information collected may be used or sought in criminal prosecutions against alleged terrorists or their supporters. *See generally* Note, *Secret Evidence in the War on Terror,* 118 Harv. L. Rev. 1962 (2005).

However, such use or access may compromise the security of the information itself, as well as intelligence sources or methods used to collect it. Moreover, as we saw in Chapters 17 and 18, some evidence may have been obtained by coercive interrogation. Such evidence poses issues of due process and confrontation, and it may not be trustworthy. Judge Wilkinson explained some of these problems in his opinion in *Al-Marri v. Pucciarelli,* 534 F.3d 213 (4th Cir. 2008) (en banc), *vacated and remanded sub nom. Al-Marri v. Spagone,* 129 S. Ct. 1545 (2009).

The problems presented by the criminal prosecution of terrorists are even more pronounced at trial . . . .

First, while a showcase of American values, an open and public criminal trial may also serve as a platform for suspected terrorists. Terror suspects may use the bully pulpit of a criminal trial in an attempt to recruit others to their cause. Likewise, terror suspects may take advantage of the opportunity to interact with others during trial to pass critical intelligence to their allies. . . .

Second, and relatedly, the prosecution of some terrorists could present security concerns of a different sort: witnesses and jurors may be subjected to threats of violence or become the targets of attack. . . .

Third, and finally, the plurality also neglects to discuss another serious concern: traditional criminal proceedings, especially public trials, may not be responsive to the executive's legitimate need to protect sensitive information. . . .

However, the government's desire to protect such sensitive intelligence may conflict with a defendant's confrontation and compulsory process rights. By employing those rights, a terror suspect like al-Marri may, in a tactic commonly referred to as "graymail," request highly sensitive materials. Such a request leaves the government facing a Hobson's Choice. The government can withdraw all or part of its case to protect its information, or proceed and surrender its sensitive intelligence and possibly its source. And even if the government is able to suppress the defendant's request, defense counsel will be able to insinuate that the government is hiding information that is favorable to the defendant. . . .

. . . Congress may certainly take [such concerns] into account in deciding that the criminal justice system is not the sole permissible means of dealing with suspected terrorists. . . . [*Al-Marri*, 534 F.3d at 307-308 (Wilkinson, J., concurring in part and dissenting in part.)]

This chapter is about how Congress, the courts, and the Executive have taken such problems into account in criminal prosecutions against accused terrorists and their supporters. First, in criminal cases, a defendant may invoke her constitutional, statutory, and rule-based rights of discovery to gain access to classified information in government hands that she says she needs to defend herself. Alternatively, she may already possess classified information as a current or former government employee, and she may threaten to use that information at trial to rebut or explain the charged conduct. To deal with the discovery and use of classified information in criminal cases, Congress enacted the Classified Information Procedures Act (CIPA) in 1980. We consider CIPA in Part A.

Second, the government may want to use information obtained from classified intelligence sources and methods as evidence against a suspected terrorist or other criminal. It may have to decide whether to proceed and disclose such evidence in open court, or to offer the evidence by methods that keep it from either the public or the defendant, or both. Such efforts are discussed in Part B of this chapter.

Third, criminal defendants may demand access to classified exculpatory evidence. In Part C, we explore the issues raised by such a demand in the criminal prosecution of Zacarias Moussaoui, who was accused of involvement in the 9/11 terrorist attacks.

Fourth, some of the evidence the government seeks to offer at the trial of a terror suspect may have been coerced from the defendant or derived from a witness who was coerced, either by U.S. interrogators or by others. Part D addresses issues surrounding the use of such coerced evidence in a criminal prosecution.

Some commentators — including former federal judge and Attorney General Michael B. Mukasey — have argued that Article III courts are not up to the task of dealing with problems like these, and that the record of criminal prosecutions of terror suspects to date prove it. They have therefore proposed that Congress create a new National Security Court to try terror suspects. In Part E, we consider that proposal.

A.   THE CLASSIFIED INFORMATION PROCEDURES ACT

Classified Information Procedures Act

18 U.S.C. app. 3 §§1-16 (2006 & Supp. III 2009)

§4. DISCOVERY OF CLASSIFIED INFORMATION BY DEFENDANTS

The court, upon a sufficient showing, may authorize the United States to delete specified items of classified information from documents to be made available to the defendant through discovery under the Federal Rules of Criminal Procedure, to substitute a summary of the information for such classified documents, or to substitute a statement admitting relevant facts that the classified information would tend to prove. The court may permit the United States to make a request for such authorization in the form of a written statement to be inspected by the court alone....

§5. NOTICE OF DEFENDANT'S INTENTION TO DISCLOSE CLASSIFIED INFORMATION

(a) Notice by defendant. If a defendant reasonably expects to disclose or to cause the disclosure of classified information in any manner in connection with any trial or pretrial proceeding involving the criminal prosecution of such defendant, the defendant shall, within the time specified by the court or, where no time is specified, within thirty days prior to trial, notify the attorney for the United States and the court in writing. Such notice shall include a brief description of the classified information. Whenever a defendant learns of additional classified information he reasonably expects to disclose at any such proceeding, he shall notify the attorney for the United States and the court in writing as soon as possible thereafter and shall include a brief description of the classified information....

§6. PROCEDURE FOR CASES INVOLVING CLASSIFIED INFORMATION

(a) Motion for hearing. Within the time specified by the court for the filing of a motion under this section, the United States may request the court to conduct a hearing to make all determinations concerning the use, relevance, or admissibility of classified information that would otherwise be made during the trial or pretrial proceeding. Upon such a request, the court shall conduct such a hearing. Any hearing held pursuant to this subsection (or any portion of such hearing specified in the request of the Attorney General) shall be held in camera if the Attorney General certifies to the court in such petition that a public proceeding may result in the disclosure of classified information. As to each item of classified information, the court shall set forth in writing the basis for its determination. Where the United States' motion under this subsection is filed prior to the trial or pretrial proceeding, the court shall rule prior to the commencement of the relevant proceeding.

(b) Notice.

(1) Before any hearing is conducted pursuant to a request by the United States under subsection (a), the United States shall provide the defendant with notice of the classified information that is at issue. Such notice shall identify the specific classified information at issue whenever that information previously has been made

available to the defendant by the United States. When the United States has not previously made the information available to the defendant in connection with the case, the information may be described by generic category, in such form as the court may approve, rather than by identification of the specific information of concern to the United States.

(2) Whenever the United States requests a hearing under subsection (a), the court, upon request of the defendant, may order the United States to provide the defendant, prior to trial, such details as to the portion of the indictment or information at issue in the hearing as are needed to give the defendant fair notice to prepare for the hearing.

(c) Alternative procedure for disclosure of classified information

(1) Upon any determination by the court authorizing the disclosure of specific classified information under the procedures established by this section, the United States may move that, in lieu of the disclosure of such specific classified information, the court order—

(A) the substitution for such classified information of a statement admitting relevant facts that the specific classified information would tend to prove; or

(B) the substitution for such classified information of a summary of the specific classified information.

The court shall grant such a motion of the United States if it finds that the statement or summary will provide the defendant with substantially the same ability to make his defense as would disclosure of the specific classified information. The court shall hold a hearing on any motion under this section. Any such hearing shall be held in camera at the request of the Attorney General.

(2) The United States may, in connection with a motion under paragraph (1), submit to the court an affidavit of the Attorney General certifying that disclosure of classified information would cause identifiable damage to the national security of the United States and explaining the basis for the classification of such information. If so requested by the United States, the court shall examine such affidavit in camera and ex parte. . . .

(e) Prohibition on disclosure of classified information by defendant, relief for defendant when United States opposes disclosure

(1) Whenever the court denies a motion by the United States that it issue an order under subsection (c) and the United States files with the court an affidavit of the Attorney General objecting to disclosure of the classified information at issue, the court shall order that the defendant not disclose or cause the disclosure of such information.

(2) Whenever a defendant is prevented by an order under paragraph (1) from disclosing or causing the disclosure of classified information, the court shall dismiss the indictment or information; except that, when the court determines that the interests of justice would not be served by dismissal of the indictment or information, the court shall order such other action, in lieu of dismissing the indictment or information, as the court determines is appropriate. Such action may include, but need not be limited to—

(A) dismissing specified counts of the indictment or information;

(B) finding against the United States on any issue as to which the excluded classified information relates; or

(C) striking or precluding all or part of the testimony of a witness. . . .

United States v. Lee

United States District Court, District of New Mexico, 2000
90 F. Supp. 2d 1324

CONWAY, Chief Judge. This matter came on for consideration of the Motion of Dr. Wen Ho Lee for a Declaration that Sections 5 and 6 of the Classified Information Procedures Act (CIPA) are Unconstitutional as Applied.... [Wen Ho Lee was being prosecuted on charges of espionage and mishandling of classified information at the Los Alamos National Laboratory.]

I. CIPA FRAMEWORK

The Classified Information Procedures Act (CIPA), 18 U.S.C. app. III §§1-16 (1988), provides for pretrial procedures to resolve questions of admissibility of classified information in advance of its use in open court.[1] Under CIPA procedures, the defense must file a notice briefly describing any classified information that it "reasonably expects to disclose or to cause the disclosure of" at trial. 18 U.S.C. app. III §5(a). Thereafter, the prosecution may request an *in camera* hearing for a determination of the "use, relevance and admissibility" of the proposed defense evidence. *Id.* at §6(a). If the Court finds the evidence admissible, the government may move for, and the Court may authorize, the substitution of unclassified facts or a summary of the information in the form of an admission by the government.[2] *See id.* at §6(c)(1). Such a motion may be granted if the Court finds that the statement or summary will provide the defendant with "substantially the same ability to make his defense as would disclosure of the specific classified information." *Id.* If the Court does not authorize the substitution, the government can require that the defendant not disclose classified information. *See id.* at §6(e). However, under §6(e)(2), if the government prevents a defendant from disclosing classified information at trial, the court may: (A) dismiss the entire indictment or specific counts, (B) find against the prosecution on any issue to which the excluded information relates, or (C) strike or preclude the testimony of particular government witnesses. *See* 18 U.S.C. app. III §6(e)(2). Finally, CIPA requires that the government provide the defendant with any evidence it will use to rebut the defendant's revealed classified information evidence. *See id.* at §6(f).

II. CONSTITUTIONALITY OF CIPA

Defendant Lee contends that, as applied to him, the notice and hearing requirements of §5 and §6 of CIPA are unconstitutional.... Although I find Defendant's claims unjustified, I will nevertheless address them in turn.[3] ...

---

1. Classified information is defined as including "information and material" subject to classification or otherwise requiring protection from public disclosure. *See* 18 U.S.C. app. III §1. Thus, CIPA applies to classified testimony as well as to classified documents.
2. If the court finds that the evidence is not admissible at trial, CIPA is no longer implicated. When determining the use, relevance and admissibility of the proposed evidence, the court may not take into account that the evidence is classified; relevance of classified information in a given case is governed solely by the standards set forth in the Federal Rules of Evidence.
3. Other courts that have considered the constitutionality of CIPA are in accord.

A. Defendant's Privilege Against Self-incrimination

Defendant Lee's first contention is that the notice and hearing requirements of §5 and §6 violate his Fifth Amendment privilege against self-incrimination because they force him to reveal classified aspects of his own trial testimony. Defendant argues that by forcing him to reveal portions of his potential testimony, CIPA unconstitutionally infringes upon his right to remain silent until and unless he decides to testify. Similarly, Defendant argues that if he chooses not to comply with the notice requirements, under the penalty of not being able to offer such testimony at trial, CIPA unconstitutionally denies him the right to testify on his own behalf. In either case, Defendant contends that CIPA forces him to pay a price in the form of a costly pretrial decision in order to preserve his constitutional rights at trial.

CIPA does not require that a defendant specify whether or not he will testify or what he will testify about. Instead, CIPA requires "merely a general disclosure as to what classified information the defense expects to use at trial, regardless of the witness or the document through which that information is to be revealed." *United States v. Poindexter*, 725 F. Supp. 13, 33 (D.D.C. 1989). Defendant's argument that if he discloses the classified information his right to remain silent has been compromised (or in the alternative that if he refuses to disclose the classified information his right to testify has been compromised) is misplaced. Despite CIPA's requirements, Defendant still has the option of not testifying. Similarly, if the defense does not disclose classified information as required by CIPA, the defendant retains the option of testifying, albeit with the preclusion of any classified information.

In addition, the pretrial disclosure of certain aspects of a criminal defense is hardly a novel concept. Examples of such requirements include Fed. R. Crim. P. 12.1 (alibi defense); Fed. R. Crim. P. 12.2 (insanity defense); Fed. R. Crim. P. 12.3 (public authority defense); and Fed. R. Crim. P. 16 (medical and scientific tests, and tangible objects and certain documents). Such provisions have consistently been held constitutional. . . . CIPA merely provides a mechanism for determining the admissibility of classified information so that classified information is not inadvertently disclosed during open proceedings. Defendant still has the choice of presenting the evidence during trial or not, after it has been deemed admissible. "That the defendant faces . . . a dilemma demanding a choice between complete silence and presenting a defense has never been thought an invasion of the privilege against compelled self-incrimination." *Williams v. Florida*, 399 U.S. 78, 84 (1970).

Defendant also argues that the burdens placed upon him by CIPA unconstitutionally violate his Fifth Amendment rights in that they do not advance any interests related to the fairness and accuracy of the criminal trial. However, Defendant's argument is unconvincing. CIPA is designed to "assure the fairness and reliability of the criminal trial" while permitting the government to "ascertain the potential damage to national security of proceeding with a given prosecution before trial." *See United States v. Ivy*, 1993 WL 316215 at *4 (citations omitted). As the Supreme Court has noted, "it is obvious and unarguable that no governmental interest is more compelling than the security of the Nation." *Poindexter*, 725 F. Supp. at 34 (quoting *Haig v. Agee*, 453 U.S. 280, 307 (1981)). CIPA serves that interest "by providing a mechanism for protecting both the unnecessary disclosure of sensitive national security information and by helping to ensure that those with significant access to such information will not escape the sanctions of the law applicable to others by use of the greymail route."[5] *Id.* at 34. Accordingly, I find that CIPA does not violate Defendant's privilege against self-incrimination by infringing upon either his right to remain silent or his right to testify on his own behalf.

B. Defendant's Right to Confront and Cross-examine Witnesses

Defendant Lee next argues that §5 and §6 of CIPA violate his Sixth Amendment right to confront and cross-examine government witnesses by forcing him to notify the government pretrial (and explain the significance) of all the classified information he reasonably expects to elicit from prosecution witnesses on cross-examination and all such information that will be contained in defense counsel's questions to those witnesses.[6]

Defendant contends that under CIPA, the "prosecution can shape its case-in-chief to blunt the force of the defense cross examination" and that the advance notice under CIPA "will impede effective defense cross-examination." However, the Confrontation Clause does not guarantee the right to undiminished surprise with respect to cross-examination of prosecutorial witnesses. . . .

CIPA does not require that the defense reveal its plan of cross-examination to the government. CIPA also does not require that the defendant reveal what questions his counsel will ask, in which order, and to which witnesses. Likewise, the defendant need not attribute the information to any particular witness. CIPA merely requires that the defendant identify the classified information he reasonably intends to use. Because the only cited tactical disadvantage that may accrue, minimization of surprise, is slight, defendant has failed to demonstrate that the requirements under CIPA render his opportunity for cross-examination ineffective.

C. Defendant's Right to Due Process

Defendant's due process argument is based on the contention that CIPA's disclosure requirements violate the Due Process Clause by imposing a one-sided burden on the defense, without imposing a mandatory reciprocal duty on the prosecution. However, due process is only denied where the balance of discovery is tipped against the defendant and in favor of the government. . . .

Here, the CIPA burdens are not one-sided. First, the government has already agreed to allow Defendant and his counsel access to all classified files at issue in the indictment. Second, the government must produce all discoverable materials before the defense is required to file a §5(a) notice. Third, before a §6 hearing is conducted, the government must reveal details of its case so as to give the defense fair notice to prepare for the hearing. *See* 18 U.S.C. app. III §6(b)(2). Specifically, the government must provide the defense with any portions of any material it may use to establish the

---

5. Greymail refers to a tactic employed by a defendant who threatens to disclose classified information with the hopes that the prosecution will choose not to prosecute in order to keep the information protected.

6. Under the Sixth Amendment, a criminal defendant "shall enjoy the right . . . to be confronted with the witnesses against him." U.S. Const. amend. VI. Pursuant to the right to confront the witnesses against him, a criminal defendant has the "fundamental right" to cross examine witnesses for the prosecution.

"national defense" element of any charges against Lee. Fourth, under §6(f), the government is required to provide notice of any evidence it will use to rebut classified information that the court permits the defense to use at trial. Finally, in addition to the discovery obligations under §6 of CIPA, the government must also comply with the Federal Rules of Criminal Procedure and *Brady v. Maryland*, 373 U.S. 83 (1963).

Despite the fact that the government's reciprocal duties under CIPA are not triggered until it decides to request a §6 hearing, the overall balance of discovery is not tipped against Lee. . . .

III. CONCLUSION

In summary, Defendant Lee has failed to show that the carefully balanced framework for determining the use of classified information by the defense set forth in CIPA violates his Fifth Amendment privilege against self-incrimination, his Fifth Amendment right to remain silent or his Fifth and Sixth Amendment rights to testify on his own behalf. Defendant has also failed to demonstrate that CIPA violates his Fifth Amendment right to due process of law or his Sixth Amendment right to confront and cross-examine witnesses.

NOTES AND QUESTIONS

1. *The Decision to Prosecute.* When the government decides whether to mount a criminal prosecution or initiate an immigration proceeding against an alleged terrorist, it must assess the risk that going forward will expose state secrets or classified information. Consequently, the Attorney General has instructed federal prosecutors, in deciding whether to prosecute, to weigh (a) the likelihood of such exposure, (b) the resulting damage to national security, (c) the likelihood of success if the case is brought, and (d) the nature and importance of other federal interests that prosecution would promote. U.S. Dep't of Justice, *Attorney General's Guidelines for Prosecutions Involving Classified Information* 4-6 (1981). Sometimes this weighing will dictate not prosecuting. How, if at all, would the enactment of CIPA have affected this process? The decision to prosecute and the government's conduct of the trial of Wen Ho Lee are dealt with extensively in Dan Stober & Ian Hoffman, *A Convenient Spy: Wen Ho Lee and the Politics of Nuclear Espionage* (2001).

2. *Is It Classified?* How did the *Lee* court decide whether CIPA was applicable — that is, whether the information Wen Ho Lee was planning to use was "classified"? Must the court simply defer to the government's classification stamp? If so, "the government could make C.I.P.A. applicable whenever it suited its purpose simply by rubber-stamping documents that had no relevance to the national security." 26 Charles Alan Wright & Kenneth W. Graham Jr., *Federal Practice and Procedure* §5672, at 748 (1992).

3. *Graymail.* In *United States v. Reynolds*, 345 U.S. 1, 12 (1953), the Supreme Court said that "it is unconscionable to allow [the government] to undertake prosecution and then invoke its governmental privileges to deprive the accused of anything which might be material to his defense." Rejected Federal Rule of Evidence 509 therefore

provided that when the state secrets privilege is sustained and a party is thereby deprived of material evidence, the court should make whatever orders "the interests of justice require, including striking the testimony of a witness, declaring a mistrial, finding against the government upon an issue as to which the evidence is relevant, or dismissing the action." 26 Wright & Graham, *supra*, at 417. *See generally* Louis Fisher, *In the Name of National Security: Unchecked Presidential Power and the Reynolds Case* (2006) (reviewing the history of the rule).

Can you see how these principles from civil litigation help set the stage for graymail in criminal trials? How does it work? Is it an unfair tactic by unscrupulous defendants or lawyers? Former Assistant Attorney General Philip Heymann has noted that "[i]t would be a mistake...to view the 'greymail' problem as limited to instances of unscrupulous or questionable conduct by defendants since wholly proper defense attempts to obtain or disclose classified information may present the government with the same 'disclose or dismiss' dilemma." S. Rep. No. 96-823, at 3 (1980), *reprinted in* 1980 U.S.C.C.A.N. 4294, 4296-4297. Into which category would the disclose-or-dismiss dilemma in the Wen Ho Lee case fall? *See* Bob Drogin, *Nuke Secrets Deemed Vital to Scientist's Case*, L.A. Times, June 16, 2000 (reporting that a member of Lee's legal team characterized as "graymailing the government" his request for complete computer records and 400,000 pages of classified data for nearly every U.S. nuclear weapon). Has the enactment of CIPA eliminated the possibility of graymail?

4. *Defendant's Discovery in Criminal Cases.* In criminal cases, defendants have certain limited rights to discovery. The Supreme Court has held that the prosecution must disclose evidence that is favorable to the defendant and "is material either to guilt or to punishment." *Brady v. Maryland*, 373 U.S. 83, 87 (1963). Specific defense requests thus require the prosecution to turn over all exculpatory evidence, which may include classified information in national security prosecutions. *See United States v. Rezaq*, 156 F.R.D. 514, 516-517 (D.D.C. 1994). In addition, the Jencks Act, 18 U.S.C. §3500 (2006), requires the prosecution to produce statements in its possession by witnesses who have testified on direct examination at trial in order to facilitate cross-examination by the defense. Such statements could include ones made by secret intelligence assets. For example, in the case that prompted enactment of the Act, the statements were confidential reports by paid government informants who were members of the Communist Party. *Jencks v. United States*, 353 U.S. 657 (1957). Finally, Federal Rule of Criminal Procedure 16(a)(1)(A)-(B) permits criminal defendants to discover their own statements, as well as documents and tangible objects in the possession, custody, or control of the government that are material to the defendant's defense, are intended for use by government as evidence, or were obtained from or belong to the defendant. Here again, the documents or tangible objects might include classified information, or their disclosure might reveal intelligence sources and methods. *See generally* Jonathan M. Fredman, *Intelligence Agencies, Law Enforcement, and the Prosecution Team*, 16 Yale L. & Pol'y Rev. 331 (1998).

Of course, intelligence agencies may hold back classified information or sources and methods and provide only unclassified information to the prosecution. Could the prosecution then argue that it had only the latter in its possession, custody, or control, thus avoiding discovery of classified information by the defense? The cases are neither clear nor consistent, but in general they hold that "federal discovery obligations extend to those government agencies that are so closely 'aligned' with the prosecution of a specific matter that justice requires their records be subject to the respective discovery obligations." *Id.* at 347. The *United States Attorneys' Manual* states that "an investigative or prosecutive agency becomes aligned with the government prosecutor when it becomes actively involved in the investigation or the prosecution of a particular case." *United States Attorneys' Manual* tit. 9, *Criminal Resource Manual* §2052(B)(1) (1997).

Does the tasking of an intelligence agency by the FBI under the 1996 law (quoted *supra* p. 630) constitute sufficient "active involvement" to align it with the prosecution? *See* Fredman, *supra* at 364 (opining that "a court could well [so] conclude"). Suppose the intelligence community on its own initiative forwards to the FBI foreign surveillance information suggesting criminal wrongdoing. Has it thereby aligned itself with the prosecutors if a criminal prosecution results? *Id.* (probably not). Here the *United States Attorneys' Manual* suggests that its role must first "exceed[] the role of providing mere tips or leads based on information generated independently of the criminal case." *Criminal Resource Manual, supra,* §2052(B)(1).

5. *CIPA and Discovery.* CIPA permits the government to argue ex parte against the discovery of classified information, 18 U.S.C. app. 3 §4, but it does not purport to change discovery standards. Nevertheless, some courts and commentators have read CIPA to narrow a defendant's rights or balance them against governmental interests. *See* 26 Wright & Graham, *supra,* §5672, at 745-746. In *United States v. Yunis,* 867 F.2d 617 (D.C. Cir. 1989), for example, the court arguably crafted a new relevancy standard for discovery of classified information by holding that "mere . . . theoretical relevance" was not enough; the defendant was obliged to show that the information is "at least 'helpful to the defense of [the] accused.'" *Id.* at 623 (quoting *Roviaro v. United States,* 353 U.S. 53, 60-61 (1957) (involving informer's privilege)).

When a court in a §4 proceeding *does* find that classified information is discoverable, the government is afforded the option of substituting a summary or a statement admitting relevant facts that the classified information would tend to prove. The courts have also inferred authority from CIPA to order defense counsel to obtain security clearances as a condition of seeing classified information or participating in hearings at which it may be disclosed. *See United States v. Bin Laden,* 58 F. Supp. 2d 113 (S.D.N.Y. 1999) (rejecting the claim that this requirement unconstitutionally interferes with defendant's choice of counsel).

6. *CIPA Notice and the Admissibility Hearing.* A defendant who wishes to disclose classified information in the case must give specific prior notice to the government pursuant to §5, on penalty of having the court exclude any classified information omitted from the notice. 18 U.S.C. app. 3 §5. Why is it not unconstitutional to thus require a defendant to tip his hand, according to *Lee?*

Following a §5 notice, the government may request a hearing concerning the use, relevancy, or admissibility of the identified information. 18 U.S.C. app. 3 §6. This hearing is usually held in camera. CIPA's legislative history is quite clear that it was not intended to change existing rules of evidence applicable in this hearing. *See* 26 Wright & Graham, *supra,* §5672, at 756-757 (discussing history). Some courts have taken this history to heart and even stated that they must disregard the classified nature of the information in ruling on its relevancy and admissibility. Others — notably the Fourth Circuit — have found that CIPA established "a more strict rule of admissibility" for classified information. *United States v. Smith*, 780 F.2d 1102, 1105 (4th Cir. 1985). *See* Note, *United States v. Smith: Construing the Classified Information Procedures Act as Restricting the Admissibility of Evidence*, 44 Wash. & Lee L. Rev. 720 (1987). Moreover, other courts have obtained the same results as *Smith* by narrowly construing defenses, such as reliance on CIA authority (*see United States v. Lopez-Lima*, 738 F. Supp. 1404 (S.D. Fla. 1990)), in order to rule the classified information irrelevant. *See* 26 Wright & Graham, *supra*, §5672, at 757-758.

7. *CIPA Substitution.* Courts may find classified information to be relevant and material. CIPA §6 then affords the government the option of moving to substitute an unclassified statement of admissions or an unclassified summary for the classified information. The court must grant that motion "if it finds that the statement or summary will provide the defendant with substantially the same ability to make his defense as would disclosure." 18 U.S.C. app. 3 §6(c)(1).

8. *CIPA: Disclose or Dismiss.* If, on the other hand, the court denies the motion, then the Attorney General must decide whether to disclose the information. *Id.* §6(e)(1). If she decides against disclosure, the court may dismiss all or part of the indictment, find against the government on an issue to which the withheld information relates, or strike testimony. *Id.* §6(e)(2). In deciding among these alternatives, the court is not supposed to balance interests, but instead to take whatever action is necessary "to make the defendant whole again." S. Rep. No. 96-823, at 9 (1980). For example, in *United States v. Fernandez*, 913 F.2d 148 (4th Cir. 1990), a prosecution of the CIA station chief in Costa Rica growing out of the Iran-Contra Affair, the defendant sought to introduce classified documents purporting to show the truth of statements he had made concerning the CIA's role in the resupply of the Contras. Using CIPA procedures, the Independent Counsel proposed that an unclassified summary of evidence be used in substitution for the documents, but the court found that the summary would not provide Fernandez with substantially the same ability to make his defense as would disclosure of the classified information. When the Attorney General refused to declassify the information, the court dismissed the indictment over the strenuous objections of the Independent Counsel. The government also ended the Wen Ho Lee prosecution by accepting his plea to a single count of the multi-count indictment, partly, it is reported, because senior Energy Department officials feared that the judge would order disclosure of classified information to Lee for use in his defense. *See* Bob Drogin, *How FBI's Flawed Case Against Lee Unraveled*, L.A. Times, Sept. 13, 2000.

9. *Another Option: Lying?* In 1983, a former CIA officer named Edwin P. Wilson was tried and convicted for illegally exporting explosives to Libya. He claimed that he was still working for the Agency and acting on its authority. During Wilson's trial, the government introduced an affidavit from a high-ranking CIA official denying Wilson's continued employment. The affidavit was a deliberate falsehood. Before Wilson was sentenced, attorneys at the CIA and the Justice Department learned of the fabrication, yet they failed to inform either the trial court or the appellate court. When the truth came to light 20 years later, Wilson's conviction was vacated. *United States v. Wilson*, 289 F. Supp. 2d 801 (S.D. Tex. 2003). A clearly incensed judge wrote, "Honesty comes hard to the government." *Id.* at 809.

B. USING "SILENT" WITNESSES AND SECRET EVIDENCE

United States v. Abu Ali

United States Court of Appeals, Fourth Circuit, 2008
528 F.3d 210, *cert. denied*, 129 S. Ct. 1312 (2009)

WILKINSON, MOTZ, and TRAXLER, Circuit Judges: [Ahmed Omar Abu Ali was born in
the United States and sent to Saudi Arabia for college. While attending school there,
he became affiliated with an Al Qaeda cell. In the course of meetings with Al Qaeda
operatives in Saudi Arabia, Abu Ali suggested "assassinations or kidnappings of members of the U.S. Senate, the U.S. Army, and the Bush administration, a plan to rescue
the prisoners at Guantánamo Bay, and plans to blow up American warplanes on U.S.
bases and at U.S. ports, similar to the USS Cole operation." The cell began his training to reenter the United States as a "sleeper," for purposes of conducting later
terrorist acts.

However, the Saudi counterterrorist agency Mabahith arrested Abu Ali before his
training was completed and interrogated him. It also notified the FBI, which suggested questions for the interrogation. Eventually, the Saudi authorities surrendered
Abu Ali to the United States, where he was tried for providing material support to a
foreign terrorist organization, among several counts, partly on the basis of statements
he made during the Saudi interrogation.]

Ahmed Omar Abu Ali was convicted by a jury of nine criminal counts arising from
his affiliation with an al-Qaeda terrorist cell located in Medina, Saudi Arabia, and its
plans to carry out a number of terrorist acts in this country. He was sentenced by the
district court to 360 months imprisonment and 360 months of supervised release
following imprisonment. Abu Ali appeals his convictions and the government
cross-appeals his sentence. For the following reasons, we affirm the conviction, but
we vacate and remand for purposes of resentencing.

Unlike some others suspected of terrorist acts and designs upon the United
States, Abu Ali was formally charged and tried according to the customary processes of the criminal justice system. Persons of good will may disagree over the
precise extent to which the formal criminal justice process must be utilized when
those suspected of participation in terrorist cells and networks are involved.
There should be no disagreement, however, that the criminal justice system
does retain an important place in the ongoing effort to deter and punish terrorist
acts without the sacrifice of American constitutional norms and bedrock values.
As will be apparent herein, the criminal justice system is not without those attributes of adaptation that will permit it to function in the post-9/11 world. These
adaptations, however, need not and must not come at the expense of the requirement that an accused receive a fundamentally fair trial. In this case, we are
satisfied that Abu Ali received a fair trial, though not a perfect one, and that
the criminal justice system performed those functions which the Constitution
envisioned for it. . . .

VI.

Abu Ali . . . challenges the district court's handling of certain classified information under the provisions of the Classified Information Procedures Act ("CIPA"), 18

U.S.C. App. 3, §§1-16 (West 2000 & Supp. 2007).[13] Abu Ali's primary contention is that the district court violated his Sixth Amendment Confrontation Clause rights by admitting as evidence unredacted versions of two classified documents that Abu Ali had only been permitted to view in a redacted form, and by refusing to allow Abu Ali and his lead trial counsel to attend and participate in the hearings conducted under CIPA to discuss the classified evidence. . . .

A.

The Sixth Amendment guarantees that "[i]n all criminal prosecutions, the accused shall enjoy . . . the right to be confronted with the witnesses against him." U.S. Const. amend. VI. Its "main and essential purpose . . . is to secure for the opponent the opportunity of cross-examination." *Delaware v. Van Arsdall,* 475 U.S. 673, 678 (1986). However, the right "means more than being allowed to confront the witness physically." *Id.* "[T]he principal evil at which the Confrontation Clause was directed was the civil-law mode of criminal procedure, and particularly its use of *ex parte* examinations as evidence against the accused." *Crawford v. Washington,* 541 U.S. 36, 54 (2004). Thus, while this is not the ordinary case, we think the criminal defendant's right to confront witnesses necessarily encompasses his right to also see any documentary evidence that such witnesses offer at trial as evidence to support a conviction. *Cf. Abourezk v. Reagan,* 785 F.2d 1043, 1060 (D.C. Cir.1986) ("It is a hallmark of our adversary system that we safeguard party access to evidence tendered in support of a requested court judgment. The openness of judicial proceedings serves to preserve both the appearance and the reality of fairness in the adjudications of United States courts. It is therefore the firmly held main rule that a court may not dispose of the merits of a case on the basis of *ex parte, in camera* submissions.").

A defendant's right to see the evidence that is tendered against him *during* trial, however, does not necessarily equate to a right to have classified information disclosed to him *prior* to trial. Evidentiary privileges may serve as valid bases to block the disclosure of certain types of evidence, and the validity of such privileges may be tested by in camera and ex parte proceedings before the court "for the limited purpose of determining whether the asserted privilege is genuinely applicable." *Id.* As a general rule, "[i]f the court finds that the claimed privilege does not apply, then the other side must be given access to the information." *Id.* If the court finds that the privilege does apply, then it may preclude access to the information. But neither scenario results in the conviction of a defendant "based upon evidence he was never permitted to see and to rebut." *Id.*

In the area of national security and the government's privilege to protect classified information from public disclosure, we look to CIPA for appropriate procedures. . . .

C.

With these principles in mind, we turn first to Abu Ali's Confrontation Clause challenge to the government's introduction at trial of two unredacted, classified documents that memorialized communications between Sultan Jubran [an Al

---

13. These issues were separately raised via classified briefs and argued in closed proceedings before this panel.

Qaeda operative] and Abu Ali in the days following the May 2003 safe house raids conducted by the Saudi officials in Medina, as well as to his exclusion from the CIPA proceedings in which these communications were discussed.

1. . . .

[Only one of Abu Ali's lawyers obtained a security clearance. The government disclosed to the security-cleared lawyer unredacted copies of evidence it intended to declassify and introduce at trial, but explained that it would take some precautions to prevent public disclosure of the unredacted documents. It afforded Abu Ali's uncleared lawyers access only to redacted versions of the same documents.]
. . . The first declassified document was dated May 27, 2003, and read as follows:

> Peace, How are you and how is your family? I hope they are good. I heard the news about the children's sickness. I wish them a speedy recovery, God willing. Anyway, please keep in touch. Greetings to the group, Hani.

The government intended to demonstrate that "Hani" was a known alias of Abu Ali and that "news about the children's sickness" was a coded reference to the raids conducted by the Mabahith and the arrest of the Medina cell members. The second declassified document was dated June 6, 2003, and read as follows:

> To my brother, Peace to you with God's mercy and blessings. Thank God, I am fine. I was saved from the accident by a great miracle. I ask God that I would be thankful to Him. I have no idea about the others. However, according to what one doctor mentioned, Adil was not with them, thank God. The important thing is to get yourself ready for the medical checkup because you may have an appointment soon. Therefore, you must keep yourself ready by refraining from eating high fat meals and otherwise.

With regard to this communication, the government intended to demonstrate that the term "accident" was also a coded reference to the safe house raids. According to the government's theory, Sultan Jubran was advising Abu Ali that he did not know which cell members had escaped and which were captured, but that he and al-Faq'asi (a/k/a "Adil"), had escaped, and warning that Abu Ali might also be at risk.

A comparison of the classified and unclassified documents reveals that the declassified versions provided the dates, the opening salutations, the entire substance of the communications, and the closings, and had only been lightly redacted to omit certain identifying and forensic information.

On October 19, 2005, the government filed an in camera, ex parte motion pursuant to §4 of CIPA, seeking a protective order prohibiting testimony and lines of questioning that would lead to the disclosure of the classified information during the trial. *See* 18 U.S.C. App. 3 §4. The government advised that the classified portions of the communications could not be provided to Abu Ali and his uncleared counsel because they contained highly sensitive information which, if confirmed in a public setting, would divulge information detrimental to national security interests. The district court granted the government's motion by in camera, ex parte, sealed order. However, the district court ruled that the United States could use the "silent witness rule" to disclose the classified information to the jury at trial.[18] . . .

3.

Having carefully considered the circumstances and evidence below, we conclude that the district court's determination that the redacted classified information need not be disclosed to the defendant, his uncleared counsel, and the public was not an abuse of discretion. Nor do we think that the district court's exclusion of Abu Ali and his uncleared counsel from the CIPA proceedings ran afoul of the Confrontation Clause. The district court's admission of the classified versions of the documents as evidence for consideration by the jury without disclosing the same versions to Abu Ali, however, was clearly contrary to the rights guaranteed to Abu Ali by the Confrontation Clause.

We begin with the district court's exclusion of Abu Ali and his uncleared counsel from the CIPA proceedings. The district court was presented with a §4 motion by the government to protect the classified information and a §5 motion, made at a later date, by Abu Ali that he be allowed to disclose that information. Initially, the district court found the redacted, unclassified version of the communications to be adequate to meet the defendant's need for information. CIPA expressly provides for such redactions of classified information from documents sought or required to be produced to the defendant, and the determination may be based upon an ex parte showing that the disclosure would jeopardize national security interests. The district court appropriately balanced the interests and made a reasonable determination that disclosure of the redacted information was not necessary to a fair trial.

There was likewise no abuse of discretion in the district court's decision to preclude Abu Ali's uncleared counsel from cross-examining the government's witnesses about the redacted information, which would have effectively disclosed the classified information that the court had already ruled need not be disclosed. A defendant and his counsel, if lacking in the requisite security clearance, must be excluded from hearings that determine what classified information is material and whether substitutions crafted by the government suffice to provide the defendant adequate means of presenting a defense and obtaining a fair trial. Thus, the mere exclusion of Abu Ali and his uncleared counsel from the CIPA hearings did not run afoul of CIPA or Abu Ali's Confrontation Clause rights.

We also conclude that the district court struck an appropriate balance between the government's national security interests and the defendant's right to explore the manner in which the communications were obtained and handled. Abu Ali and his uncleared counsel were provided with the substance of the communications, the

18. The "silent witness" rule was described in *United States v. Zettl*, 835 F.2d 1059, 1063 (4th Cir. 1987), as follows.

[T]he witness would not disclose the information from the classified document in open court. Instead, the witness would have a copy of the classified document before him. The court, counsel and the jury would also have copies of the classified document. The witness would refer to specific places in the document in response to questioning. The jury would then refer to the particular part of the document as the witness answered. By this method, the classified information would not be made public at trial but the defense would be able to present that classified information to the jury.

Id.

dates, and the parties involved, and CIPA-cleared defense counsel was provided with the classified versions and afforded unfettered opportunity to cross-examine the government's witnesses concerning these matters. At the conclusion of the examinations, defense counsel pointed to no specific problem with the issues explored. The district court also expressly considered Abu Ali's rights under the Confrontation Clause and determined that public examination of these witnesses was not necessary to prevent infringement of them. Having fully considered the record and the classified information ourselves, we agree. Uncleared defense counsel were not entitled to disclose the classified information via their questioning of the witnesses about their roles in extracting, sharing, transferring, and handling the communications, and Abu Ali, who was ably represented by counsel at the hearing on this issue, was not deprived of his right to confrontation or to a fair trial merely because he and his uncleared counsel were not also allowed to attend.

The error in the case, which appears to have originated in the October 2005 CIPA proceeding, was that CIPA was taken one step too far. The district court did not abuse its discretion in protecting the classified information from disclosure to Abu Ali and his uncleared counsel, in approving a suitable substitute, or in determining that Abu Ali would receive a fair trial in the absence of such disclosure. But, for reasons that remain somewhat unclear to us, the district court granted the government's request that the complete, unredacted classified document could be presented to the jury via the "silent witness" procedure. The end result, therefore, was that the jury was privy to the information that was withheld from Abu Ali.

As noted above, CIPA contemplates and authorizes district courts to prevent the disclosure of classified information, as was done in this case, so long as it does not deprive the defendant of a fair trial. CIPA also authorizes restrictions upon the questioning of the witnesses to ensure that classified information remains classified. Indeed, even the "silent witness" procedure contemplates situations in which the jury is provided classified information that is withheld from the public, but not from the defendant. In addition, CIPA provides district courts wide discretion to evaluate and approve suitable substitutions to be presented to the jury. CIPA does not, however, authorize courts to provide classified documents to the jury when only such substitutions are provided to the defendant. Nor could it. There is a stark difference between ex parte submissions from prosecutors which protect the disclosure of irrelevant, nonexculpatory, or privileged information, and situations in which the government seeks to use *ex parte* information in court as evidence to obtain a conviction. And, the notion that such "safeguards against wide-ranging discovery . . . would be sufficient to justify a conviction on secret evidence is patently absurd." [*United States v. Claudio*, 44 F.3d 10, 14 (1st Cir. 1995)]; *see also United States v. Innamorati*, 996 F.2d 456, 488 (1st Cir. 1993) (finding no error in prosecutor's ex parte submission of information for consideration as to whether it must be disclosed to the defendant, but noting that "there [was] no question . . . of convictions based upon secret evidence furnished to the factfinder but withheld from the defendants").

The same can be said for the evidence here. If classified information is to be relied upon as evidence of guilt, the district court may consider steps to protect some or all of the information from unnecessary public disclosure in the interest of national security and in accordance with CIPA, which specifically contemplates such methods as redactions and substitutions so long as these alternatives do not deprive the defendant of a fair trial. However, the government must at a minimum provide the same version of the evidence to the defendant that is submitted to the jury. We do not balance a criminal defendant's right to see the evidence which will be used to convict him against the government's interest in protecting that evidence from public disclosure. If the government does not want the defendant to be privy to information that is classified, it may either declassify the document, seek approval of an effective substitute, or forego its use altogether. What the government cannot do is hide the evidence from the defendant, but give it to the jury. Such plainly violates the Confrontation Clause.

D.

Having determined that submission of the classified documents to the jury ran afoul of Abu Ali's Confrontation Clause rights, we turn now to consider whether that error was harmless. We conclude that it was. . . .

VIII. . . .

For the foregoing reasons, the judgment is affirmed in part, reversed in part, and remanded for further proceedings consistent with this decision.

Affirmed in part, reversed in part, and remanded.

[Dissenting opinion of DIANA GRIBBON MOTZ, Circuit Judge (regarding sentencing), omitted.]

United States v. Rosen

United States District Court, Eastern District of Virginia, 2007
487 F. Supp. 2d 703

ELLIS, District Judge. This Espionage Act (18 U.S.C. §793) prosecution involves a substantial amount of classified information the government contends is information relating to the national defense ("NDI")[1] and for this reason the government seeks to avoid public disclosure of this material in the course of the trial. To this end, the government, by motion pursuant to §6 of the Classified Information Procedures Act ("CIPA"),[2] has proposed utilizing a procedure at trial whereby substantial quantities of classified information would be disclosed to the Court, the jury, and counsel, but withheld from the public. This novel proposal, if allowed, would effectively close a substantial portion of the trial. Accordingly, defendants challenge this proposed procedure on the grounds that it is neither authorized by CIPA nor constitutionally permissible.

---

1. It is important to recognize that NDI and classified material may not be coextensive sets. . . . While classified status may be probative of information's NDI status, it is not conclusive.
2. 18 U.S.C. App. 3.

I.

Both defendants are charged with conspiracy to communicate NDI to persons not authorized to receive it, in violation of 18 U.S.C. §793(g), (e). Rosen is additionally charged with aiding and abetting alleged co-conspirator Lawrence Franklin's unauthorized communication of NDI to persons not authorized to receive it, in violation of 18 U.S.C. §§793(d) and 2. The superceding indictment generally alleges that over a course of several years, defendants cultivated various sources of information within the United States government, obtained NDI from those sources, and then disseminated that NDI to others not authorized to receive it, including co-workers, journalists, and foreign government officials. . . .

III.

[After defendants proposed to offer classified information in their defense at trial and objected to the government's proposed substitutions pursuant to CIPA], "[t]he government . . . proposed a procedure for handling this material at trial and it is this proposal that is at issue here. The government's proposal is novel; no published opinion has been found or cited in which the precise procedure proposed here was judicially approved or used. Simply put, the government proposes that while the jury, the Court, and counsel will, for the most part, have access to the unredacted classified material, the public will not. Instead, the public, in the course of the trial, will see and hear only the substitutions that have passed through the CIPA §6(c) process. In other words, and putting to one side the not insubstantial practical problems inherent in conducting a trial pursuant to the government's proposed procedure, its use would surely exclude the public from substantial and critical parts of the trial. This result is evident from a more detailed description of the proposed procedure.

The government's proposal is, in effect, a variant and a substantial expansion of the so-called "silent witness rule," a rule that has been used and judicially approved in certain, but not all circumstances. . . . As noted, the effect of using the procedure in this case would be the exclusion of the public from substantial portions of the trial.

The proposed procedure would work as follows: for each classified document discussed at trial, the Court, the witness, counsel, and the jurors would have the unredacted classified document in front of them, either in paper form or via computer screens viewable only by those persons. The public, however, would see only a redacted version. When counsel or a witness wishes to direct the jury to a classified portion of the document, counsel and the witness would refer to the page, paragraph and line numbers, with the Court, opposing counsel, and the jury following along, but members of the public could not follow along because they would be unaware of the specific information referenced by counsel or the witness. And, the witness answering the questions about the document would not be permitted to refer to specific language or information in the document, except by use of certain codes. For example, to rebut the government's contention that certain material is NDI, defendants will likely wish to call witnesses to compare various public source documents with the alleged NDI. To do so effectively may well require the witness to refer to specific language or contents of both the public source document and the alleged NDI. Anticipating this, the government proposes that the witness would not speak the names of certain specific countries, foreign persons, etc., but would instead use a code (e.g., "Country A," "Report X," "Foreign Person Y," "Foreign Person Z," etc.)

provided also to counsel, the Court, and the jury. Moreover, this code would change with respect to different alleged overt acts, presumably to prevent the public from inferring the meaning of the generic designations or otherwise breaking the code. For example, if a witness discussing a particular alleged disclosure is instructed to refer to Monaco as Country A, a different witness (or even the same witness) discussing another alleged disclosure might use Country B or C to refer to Monaco.

Likewise, when recordings discussing classified information are played, the government proposes that the Court, counsel, witness, and jury listen on special headphones to the entire recording. The public, however, would not hear the full recording; instead, the recorded conversations would be played aloud in the courtroom, but where classified information is discussed in the recording, the public version would revert to static. Also, the public would receive only a redacted transcript of the conversations.

In sum, the novel and distinctive feature of the government's proposed procedure is that the public is walled off from seeing and hearing everything the jury, the Court, the attorneys and the witnesses see and hear. What the public does not see or hear is the heart of the case, namely the classified material the government claims is the NDI that the defendants allegedly received and distributed without authorization. A further, related novel and distinctive feature of the government's proposal relates to the jury. Although jurors will see and hear classified material, they, of course, will not have received security clearances for this purpose. Nor has this ever been otherwise in cases involving classified material, for a variety of reasons including the substantial time and effort typically required for such clearances to be completed and the substantial question whether it is constitutionally permissible to exclude jurors because they could not pass a security clearance investigation. The government's remedy for this anomaly is simply to have the jurors instructed that they cannot disclose to anyone the classified material they will see and hear during the trial.

With this description in mind, the analysis now proceeds to address the following questions:

(i) Whether the government's proposed procedure is explicitly or implicitly authorized by CIPA.
(ii) Whether the government's proposed procedure violates the right to a public trial, guaranteed to defendants by the Sixth Amendment and to the public by the First Amendment.

IV.

A.

The government urges that the use of the silent witness rule, codes, and redacted recordings are "substitutions" authorized by CIPA. Defendants disagree, noting the government's proposed procedure is nowhere authorized by CIPA, either explicitly or implicitly. Defendants are correct, a conclusion that follows from CIPA's plain language, but also from the fact that the government's proposed procedure simply cannot fit within CIPA's confines even assuming the statute's plain language would not otherwise preclude it.

Analysis of this statutory argument properly focuses on CIPA §6(c) and §8(b) .... As noted, CIPA §6(c) allows the government to move that in lieu of disclosing classified information at trial, a "substitution" be used, which could take the form of a summary of the information or a presumably sanitized statement of facts the classified statement would tend to prove. Importantly, no substitutions can be used unless there is a judicial finding that the substitution provides defendants with "substantially the same ability to make his defense as would disclosure of the specific classified information." Consistent with this, CIPA §8(b) also permits introduction and use at trial of redacted versions of classified materials unless "the whole ought in fairness to be considered."

Significantly, neither §6(c) nor §8(b) explicitly authorize[s] or state[s] that "substitutions" may be made available to the public and the jury on different terms. CIPA is at best silent on this issue. Yet, this silence should not be construed as implicitly authorizing the government's proposal. To the contrary, it seems clear that CIPA envisions that "substitutions," if not unfair to defendants, will be used at a public trial in identical form for both the jury and the public. While it is true, as reflected in CIPA's legislative history, that "Congress expected trial judges to fashion creative solutions in the interests of justice for classified information problems,"[9] there is no evidence that Congress expected this creativity to extend to adopting procedures that effectively close the trial to the public. Indeed, given the strong presumption in the law that trials will be open and that evidence will be fully aired in public, CIPA's silence about whether "substitutions" and "excisions" can be made available to the public and jury on different terms should be interpreted as a prohibition on doing so. Closing a trial, even partially, is a highly unusual result disfavored by the law. A statute, even one regulating the use of classified information, should not be construed as authorizing a trial closure based on Congress' mere silence or use of ambiguous language. Rather, because a trial closure implicates important constitutional rights, CIPA should not be read to authorize closure absent a clear and explicit statement by Congress in the statutory language.

In short, CIPA only authorizes the use of substitutions to avoid disclosure of classified information *to the public and the jury*, provided defendant's right to present a defense is not impaired; this authority is not the authority to close a trial to the public.

B.

Even assuming, *arguendo*, that the CIPA provision allowing "substitutions" might be stretched to encompass the government's proposed procedure, there is no doubt that the procedure would not pass muster under CIPA's fairness requirements. Where, as here, a central issue in the case is whether the government's alleged NDI is indeed genuinely NDI, and the proposed procedure would amount to a wholesale use of the silent witness rule to cover all of the alleged NDI, it cannot be said that the procedure affords defendants "substantially the same ability to make [their] defense as would disclosure of the specific classified information." CIPA §6(c). A few examples vividly illustrate this point.

As noted, the government in this case has the burden of proving beyond a reasonable doubt that the alleged NDI is indeed NDI. To this end, the government will likely invite witnesses to compare the substance of certain of defendants' emails, telephone

---

9. *United States v. North*, 713 F. Supp. 1452 (D.D.C. 1989) (citing H. Rep. No. 96-1436, 1980 U.S.C.C.A.N. 4294).

conversations, or faxes with certain alleged NDI to show that defendants had obtained NDI and were disseminating it without authorization. Defendants, of course, may wish to show, and indeed to emphasize, the dissimilarities between the alleged NDI and the information they obtained. Plainly, they would be significantly hobbled in doing so by use of the government's proposed procedure, inasmuch as the specific information could not be used in open court. The silent comparison of paragraphs or sentences, even where supplemented by codes, would effectively preclude defense counsel from driving home important points to the jury.

Similarly, it is apparent that defendants intend at trial to rebut the government's claim that certain material is NDI by having witnesses compare the alleged NDI to contemporaneous public domain material. Once again, the proposed procedure would unfairly impact defendants' ability to establish this defense. In this context, the silent witness rule, applied across the board as the government proposes here, essentially robs defendants of the chance to make vivid and drive home to the jury their view that the alleged NDI is no such thing, as essentially similar material was abundant in the public domain. Importantly in this respect, it is hard to see how defendants could effectively show, via the silent witness rule, that the details of differences between public source material and the alleged NDI are neither minor nor trivial. . . .

. . . In short, the use of codes would render virtually impossible an effective line of cross-examination vital to the defense. . . .

Yet another fatal defect in the fairness of the proposed procedure is apparent from the way in which it would hamper defendants should they choose to testify. Clearly, the proposed procedure would unfairly hinder defendants in their effort to explain why they believed any information they sought to obtain, the information they received, and the information they disclosed to others was not NDI. In this regard, defendants must be able to explain precisely what they knew and when, and from whom or what they learned it, and why they did not believe the material was NDI they were not authorized to have, or otherwise lacked the requisite *mens rea.* Yet, the proposed procedure would unfairly hinder defendants from doing so. For example, statements like "I heard from Foreign Person C the fact about Country X, reflected at Exhibit A page 3 paragraph 4 line 2—well, except for the last clause—and so when I asked Franklin for confirmation of that fact, I thought I was asking for a matter of public record," may provide some exculpatory description of defendants' state of mind, assuming the jury could decode the statement quickly enough to follow the questioning. Yet, it would be difficult, if not impossible, for defendants to explain fully why they believed the information they sought or had was in the public domain without revealing details about the information, the identity and reliability of Person C, etc. Because the proposed procedure shackles defendants in this way, it cannot pass muster under CIPA.

Finally, it must be noted that the government's proposed frequently-changing system of coded references not only invites juror confusion, but virtually guarantees it. Given the sheer number of substitutions and the proliferation of coded phrases, varying from witness to witness and overt act to overt act, the likelihood of juror confusion would be a sufficient ground, by itself, for rejecting the wholesale proposed substitutions under CIPA §6(c). . . .

V.

Defendants' challenge to the government's proposed procedure rests on constitutional as well as statutory grounds. Specifically, defendants argue that even if

CIPA's language can be stretched to cover the government's proposed procedure, that procedure nonetheless fails as a violation of defendants' Sixth Amendment right to a public trial and the public's First Amendment right to a trial open to public scrutiny. Thus, even if the procedure passed muster under CIPA, constitutional analysis is nonetheless required. This follows, defendants argue, because the proposed procedure effectively excludes the public from essential portions of the trial.[20]

Nor is there any doubt that the portions of the trial that would be closed to the public are critical portions of the trial. It is clear that the government's proposal precludes the public from hearing and evaluating the evidence on a crucial and contested element of the case, namely, whether the information at issue is NDI and whether defendants knew it to be such. Moreover, the quality and quantity of material the government proposes to exclude from public view is significant. Testimony about the putative NDI at issue in seven of the alleged nine disclosures would be partially closed to the public, as would the recordings and documents corresponding to this NDI. Notably, the government's proposed procedure would treat even certain related public domain documents, including news reports, as if they were classified documents. In short, in the circumstances of this case, the government's proposal is clearly equivalent to sealing essential aspects of the trial.

The analysis of defendants' constitutional argument properly begins with the recognition that defendants and the public have a fundamental right to a trial open to the public. The right to a public trial contributes to just adjudication, stimulates public confidence in the judicial system, and ensures that the public is fairly apprised of the proceedings in cases of public concern. A public trial contributes to just adjudication in several ways: (i) requiring witness[es]' testimony to be public deters perjury; (ii) requiring a judge's rulings to be made in public deters partiality and bias; and (iii) requiring prosecutors to present their charges and evidence publicly deters prosecutorial vindictiveness and abuse of power. In these ways, the presence of the public encourages accurate factfinding and wise use of judicial and prosecutorial discretion, thereby contributing to public confidence that justice has prevailed at trial. In short, justice must not only be done, it must be seen to be done.

Given the important interests at stake, it is now well-settled that defendants in criminal cases and the public both have a right to a trial open to public scrutiny. *See Press-Enterprise Co. v. Superior Court of California,* 464 U.S. 501, 510 (1984) (public's First Amendment right); *Waller v. Georgia,* 467 U.S. 39, 44-45 (1984) (defendant's Sixth Amendment right). It is also well-settled that the standard governing whether the public trial right has been infringed is the same whether the right is asserted by the press under the First Amendment or by a defendant under the Sixth Amendment. *Waller,* 467 U.S. at 46-47. Under this constitutional standard, a trial is presumptively

---

20. It is noteworthy in this respect that the government sensibly appears to have abandoned its original position that the proposed use of the silent witness rule, coded testimony, and redacted recordings does not close the trial because the public would be present in the courtroom. This argument, if credited, leads to the absurd result that a trial unintelligible to the public is still "open" to the public simply because the public is physically present to see and hear what they cannot understand. The public's physical presence, by itself, does not guarantee that a trial is public; it is also necessary that the trial be reasonably comprehensible to the physically present public.

open, and may be closed only if certain criteria are met. These criteria are set forth in *Press-Enterprise* and its progeny, as follows:

> (1) an "overriding interest" must exist to close the trial,
> (2) the closure is no broader than necessary to protect that interest,
> (3) the court considers reasonable alternatives to closure, and
> (4) the court makes specific findings on the record concerning the existence of the overriding interest, the breadth of the closure, and the unavailability of alternatives to facilitate appellate review.

Press-Enterprise, 464 U.S. at 510. As the proponent of closing the proceedings, the government bears a "weighty" burden to establish that closure is permissible. *Press-Enterprise*, 464 U.S. at 509-10. Decisions to close trials must be made on a case by case basis, with attention to the facts and circumstances of each case; statutes *per se* requiring closure in certain circumstances are impermissible. *Globe Newspaper Co. v. Superior Court*, 457 U.S. 596, 611 n.27 (1982). Finally, before trials may be closed, the public must be given notice and an opportunity to be heard. *In re Knight Publishing Co.*, 743 F.2d 231, 234-35 (4th Cir. 1984). An erroneous denial of a public trial is a structural error not amenable to harmless error analysis. *Bell*, 236 F.3d at 165 (citing cases).

Each of the four *Press-Enterprise* elements is separately considered.

1. Overriding Interest

The government claims that its interest in protecting classified information is a compelling and overriding one, and has cited numerous cases in support of this claim. While it is true, as an abstract proposition, that the government's interest in protecting classified information can be a qualifying compelling and overriding interest, it is also true that the government must make a specific showing of harm to national security in specific cases to carry its burden in this regard. The government's *ipse dixit* that information is damaging to national security is not sufficient to close the courtroom doors nor to obtain the functional equivalent, namely trial by code. *Press-Enterprise* and *In re Washington Post* require more; they require a judicial inquiry into the legitimacy of the asserted national security interest, and specific findings, sealed if necessary, about the harm to national security that would ensue if the request to close the trial is not granted. *See Press-Enterprise*, 464 U.S. at 510; *In re Washington Post*, 807 F.2d 383, 391-92 (4th Cir. 1986) (rejecting the government's argument that courts should defer to Executive Branch assertions that trial closures are necessary for national security reasons, and stating that a proceeding cannot be closed merely because the case implicated CIPA at an earlier stage). Moreover, the government's *ipse dixit* is insufficient whether it appears by way of classified status, or the bald assertion of counsel that information is damaging to national security. Thus, granting that national security concerns can justify appropriately tailored trial closures, the government nonetheless bears the burden of demonstrating, as a factual matter, that harm to national security would result from failing to close the trial.

Here, the government has not met its burden; instead, it has done no more than to invoke "national security" broadly and in a conclusory fashion, as to all the classified information in the case. Of course, classification decisions are for the Executive Branch, and the information's classified status must inform an assessment of the government's asserted interests under *Press-Enterprise*. But ultimately, trial judges must make their own judgment about whether the government's asserted interest in partially closing the trial is compelling or overriding. As noted, a generalized assertion of "national security interests," whether by virtue of the information's classified status or upon representation of counsel, is not alone sufficient to overcome the presumption in favor of open trials. Here, the government has not proffered any evidence about danger to national security from airing the evidence publicly, let alone an item-by-item description of the harm to national security that will result from disclosure at trial of each specific piece of information as to which closure is sought, as required by *Press-Enterprise.*

Moreover, quite aside from the government's failure to provide any evidence of harm to national security from an open trial, the government's assertion of an overriding interest justifying a trial closure is undermined by the substance of the proposed procedure, to wit, that the jury and uncleared witnesses will be permitted to receive unredacted classified information. Given that the government appears willing to trust its confidential information to jurors, alternates, and uncleared witnesses, including (potentially) defendants, it is difficult to credit fully the government's claim that the classified information at issue is deserving of rigorous protection.

The government urges that this proposed disclosure to the jury does not reflect any inconsistency on its part, because the jurors could be instructed never to disclose the classified information they received at trial. Yet such an instruction appears patently unfair here, because it would suggest to the jury that the information at issue is NDI. Nor is this a minor consideration given that the status of the information as NDI is a central issue in the case, and indeed an element of the charged crime as to which the government bears the burden of proof beyond a reasonable doubt. An instruction that the jurors must treat the information they receive as a closely-held government secret is not easily reconciled with the instruction that the jury is the sole judge of the facts of the case and that it alone determines whether the information at issue is NDI, *i.e.,* whether it is closely held and potentially damaging to national security if revealed. While the two instructions are not flatly contradictory, they would be beyond the capacity of most jurors to reconcile . . . .

In short, the government's asserted overriding interest is not treated as such by the government itself, given that the putative NDI will be disclosed to uncleared jurors and witnesses. And while the government's cited cases support the notion that national security interests *can be* sufficiently compelling to justify a partial closure of the trial, they also require that the government satisfy *Press-Enterprise* by adequately supporting its motion with a description of the specific harm to national security that would ensue from disclosure. The government has not done so here. Accordingly, its motion fails under the first prong of *Press-Enterprise.*

2. Narrowly Tailored

For the same reasons, there is no basis to conclude that the government's proposal is narrowly tailored to protect any national security interests. Since the government has not identified with specificity which of the classified information to be kept from public view would harm national security if disclosed to the broader public, or how the national security would be affected, it is impossible to evaluate whether the proposed closure is as narrowly tailored as possible to protect that asserted interest.

3. Alternatives

Likewise, assuming that an overriding interest exists here because disclosure of some or all of the classified information at issue would damage national security, it is evident that reasonable alternatives to closure exist here. To wit, the government could propose conventional CIPA §6(c) substitutions that would be given to the jury and the public in the same form. Whether these substitutions would pass CIPA §6(c) fairness standards is another question not here presented.

4. Findings

Although the conclusions concerning the other *Press-Enterprise* factors obviate the need for factual findings, the absence of any affidavit describing the ensuing harms to national security should the trial not be closed is noteworthy. A highly detailed explanation of the ensuing harms to national security is especially necessary to make the thorough factual findings required for a closure when, as here, much of the classified information at issue is not self-evidently damaging to national security....

VI.

To summarize, the wholesale use of the silent witness rule, coded testimony, and redacted recordings effectively closes the trial. This procedure is not a "substitution" authorized by CIPA, and even if it were, it would not afford defendants substantially the same opportunity to present their defense as the specific classified information. Moreover, even if the procedure passed muster under CIPA, it nonetheless would have to satisfy the *Press-Enterprise* test because it effectively closes portions of the trial. The proposed procedure does not; the government's showing of an overriding interest in protecting sensitive national security information has been insufficient to this point, and the government's claim that the information at issue is damaging to the national security if publicly disclosed is belied by its own proposal to release the information to uncleared persons. This opinion does not foreclose the government from proposing specific §6(c) substitutions that pass CIPA muster. Nor does this opinion foreclose consideration of or narrowly limited use of the silent witness rule where the government provides a specific factual basis for a claim that public disclosure would damage the national security.

For these reasons, defendants' motion to strike must be granted, and the government's motion to close the trial, styled a CIPA §6(c) motion, must be denied. At the government's request and with no objection from defendants, entry of an appropriate Order will be delayed to afford the government time to consider how to proceed with respect to the CIPA process.

NOTES AND QUESTIONS

1. *Excluding the Defendant and His Lawyers from the CIPA Hearing.* A court may hold a CIPA hearing to decide the relevance and admissibility of classified information. But courts also sometimes exclude a party and its lawyer from in camera hearings to

decide claims of privilege. Such exclusions are pretrial and said to be justified to protect the confidentiality of the putatively privileged information until the court can rule on the claim of privilege. How is the CIPA hearing different?

The court of appeals in *Abu Ali* said it is not different. Moreover, according to the court, defendant's security-cleared lawyer actually attended the CIPA hearing and "ably represented" Abu Ali, and the trial court carefully balanced the national security interests in deciding that providing only the redacted version to him and his uncleared lawyers would permit a sufficient defense. Do you agree with the court's analysis?

2. *Prosecutor's Use of Secret Evidence?* Look closely at the CIPA provisions. Do they permit the prosecutor to use classified information to *make the government's case* against the defendant, either secretly or in substituted or summarized form? If you are not sure, how should we resolve any ambiguity? *See Greene v. McElroy*, 360 U.S. 474 (1959).

After approving the district court's conduct of the pretrial CIPA hearing, the court of appeals in *Abu Ali* still found a fatal flaw in the decision below. The district court not only excluded Abu Ali from the CIPA hearing, it also would have prevented him from seeing the redacted part of the two documents it proposed to use to prove his guilt *at trial.* "There is a stark difference between ex parte submissions from prosecutors which protect the disclosure of irrelevant, nonexculpatory, or privileged information, and situations in which the government seeks to use *ex parte* information in court as evidence to obtain a conviction." 528 F.3d at 255. Indeed, the appeals court agreed with the First Circuit that it is "patently absurd" to think that limitations in discovery could be used to justify a conviction based on evidence kept secret from the defendant. *Id.*

What is the constitutional basis for the court's insistence that Abu Ali be entitled to see the evidence against him? In *Greene*, 360 U.S. at 496-497, the Supreme Court said:

> Certain principles have remained relatively immutable in our jurisprudence. One of these is that where governmental action seriously injures an individual, and the reasonableness of the action depends on fact findings, the evidence used to prove the Government's case must be disclosed to the individual so that he has an opportunity to show that it is untrue. While this is important in the case of documentary evidence, it is even more important where the evidence consists of the testimony of individuals whose memory might be faulty or who, in fact, might be perjurers or persons motivated by malice, vindictiveness, intolerance, prejudice, or jealousy. We have formalized these protections in the requirements of confrontation and cross-examination. They have ancient roots. They find expression in the Sixth Amendment which provides that in all criminal cases the accused shall enjoy the right "to be confronted with the witnesses against him."

In a case involving an immigration proceeding, not a criminal prosecution, the Ninth Circuit Court of Appeals cited the Due Process Clause of the Fifth Amendment to find unlawful the government's use of undisclosed classified information against the immigrants. It applied the balancing test of *Mathews v. Eldridge*, 424 U.S. 319 (1976), in which the Supreme Court held that the process constitutionally due before the government takes a person's life, liberty, or property is determined by balancing (1) the private interest affected by the government action, (2) the risk of erroneous deprivation through the procedures the government has used as well as the value of additional or substitute procedures, and (3) the government's interest in the action and in avoiding additional procedures. *American-Arab Anti-Discrimination Comm. v. Reno,* 70 F.3d 1045 (9th Cir. 1995). It stressed "an exceptionally high risk of erroneous deprivation when undisclosed information is used to determine the merits...." *Id.* at 1069.

3. *The Risk of Inaccuracy in Using Secret Evidence.* In *Jay v. Boyd,* 351 U.S. 345 (1956), decided before *Greene,* the Supreme Court found statutory authority for the government to use "confidential information" in an immigration proceeding over the vigorous dissent of Chief Justice Warren, and Justices Black, Frankfurter, and Douglas. Justice Black asked:

> What is meant by "confidential information"? According to officers of the Immigration Service it may be "merely information we received off the street"; or "what might be termed as hearsay evidence, which could not be gotten into the record..."; or "information from persons who were in a position to give us the information that might be detrimental to the interests of the Service to disclose that person's name..." or "such things, perhaps, as income-tax returns, or maybe a witness who didn't want to be disclosed, or where it might endanger their life, or something of that kind...." No nation can remain true to the ideal of liberty under law and at the same time permit people to have their homes destroyed and their lives blasted by the slurs of unseen and unsworn informers. There is no possible way to contest the truthfulness of anonymous accusations. The supposed accuser can neither be identified nor interrogated. He may be the most worthless and irresponsible character in the community. What he said may be wholly malicious, untrue, unreliable, or inaccurately reported. In a court of law the triers of fact could not even listen to such gossip, much less decide the most trifling issue on it. [*Id.* at 365.]

Illustrating these points, a former Director of Central Intelligence, representing a group of detained Iraqis, found "serious errors" in previously secret evidence used against his clients, including mistranslations, ethnic and religious stereotyping, and rumors derived from inter-group rivalry. *See* Susan M. Akram, *Scheherezade Meets Kafka: Two Dozen Sordid Tales of Ideological Exclusion,* 14 Geo. Immigr. L.J. 51, 87-88 (1999).

The risk of inaccuracy from using secret evidence also may be illustrated by a case described as "the only criminal case since the Sept. 11 attacks in which secret evidence was presented against the defendant." *See* Dale Russakoff, *N.J. Judge Unseals Transcript in Controversial Terror Case,* Wash. Post, June 25, 2003. Reportedly, local (nonfederal) prosecutors convinced a state judge during a bail hearing that evidence against a defendant whom they alleged had ties to terrorists was so sensitive that the defendant could not be allowed to see it. Months later, an appellate judge ruled that prosecutors had not shown the defendant to be a security risk, and the trial judge then unsealed the bail hearing transcript. *Id.*; Robert Hanley & Jonathan Miller, *4 Transcripts Are Released in Case Tied to 9/11 Hijackers,* N.Y. Times, June 25, 2003; Jennifer V. Hughes, *Supposed Links to Terrorism Revealed,* The Record (Bergen Cty., N.J.), June 25, 2003. Most of the evidence consisted of testimony by a detective about what he had heard from FBI agents regarding the defendant. Federal authorities, however, contradicted or denied knowledge of some of this information after release of the transcripts, and the defendant's attorney dismissed it as "slanderous, hearsay, double- and triple-hearsay, evidence which he claimed he could have rebutted if only he and the defendant had been allowed to see it." Russakoff, *supra*. "To think that they kept me in jail on this," the defendant said, after being held for six months as a suspected terrorist. *Id.* The state dropped all but one of 25 counts of selling fraudulent documents to Hispanic immigrants (none tied to terrorism).

What risk of inaccuracy was presented in *Abu Ali*, when Abu Ali's cleared counsel had seen the unredacted classified information?

4. *The Silent Witness Rule.* Suppose that the district court in *Abu Ali* had permitted Abu Ali and his uncleared counsel to see the unredacted evidence. The court would still be concerned about the disclosure of such evidence to the public in open court. (Abu Ali's ability to relay it to his confederates could presumably be controlled as long as he was in custody). The silent witness rule seemed to supply a solution, by having witnesses refer to specific parts of a classified document which was also shown to the jury so it could follow the testimony, without reading from the document in open court. Why did the court of appeals approve that procedure, while the district court in *Rosen* did not? Does CIPA authorize such a procedure? Is there any constitutional limitation on its use?

C. ACCESS TO SECRET EXCULPATORY TESTIMONY

United States v. Moussaoui

United States Court of Appeals, Fourth Circuit, 2004
365 F.3d 292, *amended on reh'g*, 382 F.3d 453,
cert. denied, 544 U.S. 931 (2005)

[Zacarias Moussaoui was arrested before the 9/11 attacks, then later indicted for acts in connection with those attacks. The government sought the death penalty on several of these charges. Subsequently, Witness **** (asterisks are used by the court to indicate redacted material), a suspected member of al Qaeda, was captured by the United States. Moussaoui moved for access to Witness ****, asserting that the witness would be an important part of his defense. Ultimately, he sought access from two additional witnesses in U.S. custody. The government opposed these requests.

The District Court found that the requested witnesses were material witnesses who might support Moussaoui's claim that he was not involved in the 9/11 attacks and that he should not receive the death penalty if convicted. It ordered their deposition by remote video, but the government appealed. The Court of Appeals remanded for the District Court to determine whether any substitution existed that would place Moussaoui in substantially the same position as would a deposition. The District Court rejected the government's proposed substitutions and again ordered deposition of the witnesses. When the government refused to comply with this order, the District Court dismissed the death notice and prohibited the government "from making any argument, or offering any evidence, suggesting that the defendant had any involvement in, or knowledge of, the September 11 attacks." This appeal followed.]

WILLIAM W. WILKINS, Chief Judge: . . .

III. . . .

A. Process Power

The Sixth Amendment guarantees that "[i]n all criminal prosecutions, the accused shall enjoy the right . . . to have compulsory process for obtaining witnesses in his favor." U.S. Const. amend. VI. The compulsory process right is circumscribed, however, by the ability of the district court to obtain the presence of a witness through service of process. The Government maintains that because the enemy combatant witnesses are foreign nationals outside the boundaries of the United States, they are beyond the process power of the district court and, hence, unavailable to Moussaoui. . . .

The Government's argument overlooks the critical fact that the enemy combatant witnesses are in the custody of an official of the United States Government. Therefore, we are concerned not with the ability of the district court to issue a subpoena to the witnesses, but rather with its power to issue a writ of habeas corpus *ad testificandum* ("testimonial writ") to the witnesses' custodian . . . .

[The court found that Secretary Rumsfeld was the proper custodian and that he was within the process power of the district court.]

IV.

The Government next argues that even if the district court would otherwise have the power to order the production of the witnesses, the January 30 and August 29 orders are improper because they infringe on the Executive's warmaking authority, in violation of separation of powers principles. . . .

B. Governing Principles . . .

This is not a case involving arrogation of the powers or duties of another branch. The district court orders requiring production of the enemy combatant witnesses involved the resolution of questions properly — indeed, exclusively — reserved to the judiciary. Therefore, if there is a separation of powers problem at all, it arises only from the burden the actions of the district court place on the Executive's performance of its duties.

The Supreme Court has explained on several occasions that determining whether a judicial act places impermissible burdens on another branch of government requires balancing the competing interests. *See, e.g., Nixon v. Admin'r of Gen. Servs.*, 433 U.S. 425, 443 (1977). . . .

C. Balancing

1. The Burden on the Government

The Constitution charges the Congress and the Executive with the making and conduct of war. It is not an exaggeration to state that the effective performance of these duties is essential to our continued existence as a sovereign nation. Indeed, "no governmental interest is more compelling than the security of the Nation." *Haig v. Agee*, 453 U.S. 280, 307 (1981). . . .

The Government alleges — and we accept as true — that **** the enemy combatant witnesses is critical to the ongoing effort to combat terrorism by al Qaeda. The witnesses are al Qaeda operatives **** Their value as intelligence sources can hardly be overstated. And, we must defer to the Government's assertion that interruption **** will have devastating effects on the ability to gather information from them. ****, it is not unreasonable to suppose that interruption **** could result in the loss of information that might prevent future terrorist attacks.

The Government also asserts that production of the witnesses would burden the Executive's ability to conduct foreign relations. The Government claims that if the Executive's assurances of confidentiality can be abrogated by the judiciary, the vital ability to obtain the cooperation of other governments will be devastated.

The Government also reminds us of the bolstering effect production of the witnesses might have on our enemies.... For example, al Qaeda operatives are trained to disrupt the legal process in whatever manner possible; indications that such techniques may be successful will only cause a redoubling of their efforts.

In summary, the burdens that would arise from production of the enemy combatant witnesses are substantial.

2. Moussaoui's Interest

The importance of the Sixth Amendment right to compulsory process is not subject to question — it is integral to our adversarial criminal justice system:

> The need to develop all relevant facts in the adversary system is both fundamental and comprehensive. The ends of criminal justice would be defeated if judgments were to be founded on a partial or speculative presentation of the facts. The very integrity of the judicial system and public confidence in the system depend on full disclosure of all the facts, within the framework of the rules of evidence. To ensure that justice is done, it is imperative to the function of the courts that compulsory process be available for the production of evidence needed either by the prosecution or by the defense.

United States v. Nixon, 418 U.S. 683, 709 (1974).

The compulsory process right does not attach to any witness the defendant wishes to call, however. Rather, a defendant must demonstrate that the witness he desires to have produced would testify "in his favor." Thus, in order to assess Moussaoui's interest, we must determine whether the enemy combatant witnesses could provide testimony material to Moussaoui's defense.

In the CIPA context,[12] we have adopted the standard articulated by the Supreme Court in *Roviaro v. United States,* 353 U.S. 53 (1957), for determining whether the government's privilege in classified information must give way. Under that standard, a defendant becomes entitled to disclosure of classified information upon a showing that the information " 'is relevant and helpful to the defense . . . or is essential to a fair

---

12. We adhere to our prior ruling that CIPA does not apply because the January 30 and August 29 orders of the district court are not covered by either of the potentially relevant provisions of CIPA: §4 (concerning deletion of classified information from *documents* to be turned over to the defendant during discovery) or §6 (concerning the disclosure of classified information by the defense during pretrial or trial proceedings). *See Moussaoui I,* 333 F.3d [509, 514-515 (4th Cir. 2003).] Like the district court, however, we believe that CIPA provides a useful framework for considering the questions raised by Moussaoui's request for access to the enemy combatant witnesses.

determination of a cause.' " [*United States v. Smith*, 780 F.2d 1102 (4th Cir. 1985)], at 1107 (quoting *Roviaro*, 353 U.S. at 60-61).

Because Moussaoui has not had — and will not receive — direct access to any of the witnesses, he cannot be required to show materiality with the degree of specificity that applies in the ordinary case. Rather, it is sufficient if Moussaoui can make a "plausible showing" of materiality. However, in determining whether Moussaoui has made a plausible showing, we must bear in mind that Moussaoui *does* have access to the **** summaries. . . .

. . . [T]he Government argues that even if the witnesses' testimony would tend to exonerate Moussaoui of involvement in the September 11 attacks, such testimony would not be material because the conspiracies with which Moussaoui is charged are broader than September 11. Thus, the Government argues, Moussaoui can be convicted even if he lacked any prior knowledge of September 11. This argument ignores the principle that the scope of an alleged conspiracy is a jury question, and the possibility that Moussaoui may assert that the conspiracy culminating in the September 11 attacks was distinct from any conspiracy in which he was involved. Moreover, even if the jury accepts the Government's claims regarding the scope of the charged conspiracy, testimony regarding Moussaoui's non-involvement in September 11 is critical to the penalty phase. If Moussaoui had no involvement in or knowledge of September 11, it is entirely possible that he would not be found eligible for the death penalty.

We now consider the rulings of the district court regarding the ability of each witness to provide material testimony in Moussaoui's favor.

The district court did not err in concluding that Witness **** could offer material evidence on Moussaoui's behalf. **** Several statements by Witness **** tend to exculpate Moussaoui. For example, the **** summaries state that **** This statement tends to undermine the theory (which the Government may or may not intend to advance at trial) that Moussaoui was to pilot a fifth plane into the White House. Witness **** has also **** This statement is significant in light of other evidence **** indicating that Moussaoui had no contact with any of the hijackers. **** This is consistent with Moussaoui's claim that he was to be part of a post-September 11 operation. . . .

. . . Moussaoui has made a sufficient showing that evidence from Witness **** would be more helpful than hurtful, or at least that we cannot have confidence in the outcome of the trial without Witness **** evidence. . . .

3. Balancing

Having considered the burden alleged by the Government and the right claimed by Moussaoui, we now turn to the question of whether the district court should have refrained from acting in light of the national security interests asserted by the Government. The question is not unique; the Supreme Court has addressed similar matters on numerous occasions. In all cases of this type — cases falling into "what might loosely be called the area of constitutionally guaranteed access to evidence," *Arizona v. Youngblood*, 488 U.S. 51, 55 (1988) (internal quotation marks omitted) — the Supreme Court has held that the defendant's right to a trial that comports with the Fifth and Sixth Amendments prevails over the governmental privilege. Ultimately, as these cases make clear, the appropriate procedure is for the district court to order production of the evidence or witness and leave to the Government the choice of whether to comply with that order. If the government refuses to produce the information at issue — as it may properly do — the result is ordinarily dismissal. . . .

In addition to the pronouncements of the Supreme Court in this area, we are also mindful of Congress' judgment, expressed in CIPA, that the Executive's interest in protecting classified information does not overcome a defendant's right to present his case. Under CIPA, once the district court determines that an item of classified information is relevant and material, that item must be admitted unless the government provides an adequate substitution. If no adequate substitution can be found, the government must decide whether it will prohibit the disclosure of the classified information; if it does so, the district court must impose a sanction, which is presumptively dismissal of the indictment.

In view of these authorities, it is clear that when an evidentiary privilege — even one that involves national security — is asserted by the Government in the context of its prosecution of a criminal offense, the "balancing" we must conduct is primarily, if not solely, an examination of whether the district court correctly determined that the information the Government seeks to withhold is material to the defense. We have determined that the enemy combatant witnesses can offer material testimony that is essential to Moussaoui's defense, and we therefore affirm the January 30 and August 29 orders. Thus, the choice is the Government's whether to comply with those orders or suffer a sanction.

V.

As noted previously, the Government has stated that it will not produce the enemy combatant witnesses for depositions (or, we presume, for any other purpose related to this litigation). We are thus left in the following situation: the district court has the power to order production of the enemy combatant witnesses and has properly determined that they could offer material testimony on Moussaoui's behalf, but the Government has refused to produce the witnesses. Under such circumstances, dismissal of the indictment is the usual course. Like the district court, however, we believe that a more measured approach is required. Additionally, we emphasize that no punitive sanction is warranted here because the Government has rightfully exercised its prerogative to protect national security interests by refusing to produce the witnesses.

Although, as explained above, this is not a CIPA case, that act nevertheless provides useful guidance in determining the nature of the remedies that may be available. Under CIPA, dismissal of an indictment is authorized only if the government has failed to produce an adequate substitute for the classified information, and the interests of justice would not be served by imposition of a lesser sanction. CIPA thus enjoins district courts to seek a solution that neither disadvantages the defendant nor penalizes the government (and the public) for protecting classified information that may be vital to national security.

A similar approach is appropriate here. Under such an approach, the first question is whether there is any appropriate substitution for the witnesses' testimony. Because we conclude, for the reasons set forth below, that appropriate substitutions are available, we need not consider any other remedy....

C. Instructions

... [W]e conclude that the district court erred in ruling that any substitution for the witnesses' testimony is inherently inadequate to the extent it is derived from the **** reports. To the contrary, we hold that the **** summaries (which, as the district court determined, accurately recapitulate the **** reports) provide an adequate basis for the creation of written statements that may be submitted to the jury in lieu of the witnesses' deposition testimony.

The crafting of substitutions is a task best suited to the district court, given its greater familiarity with the facts of the case and its authority to manage the presentation of evidence. Nevertheless, we think it is appropriate to provide some guidance to the court and the parties.

First, the circumstances of this case — most notably, the fact that the substitutions may very well support Moussaoui's defense — dictate that the crafting of substitutions be an interactive process among the parties and the district court. Second, we think that accuracy and fairness are best achieved by crafting substitutions that use the exact language of the **** summaries to the greatest extent possible. We believe that the best means of achieving both of these objectives is for defense counsel to identify particular portions of the **** summaries that Moussaoui may want to admit into evidence at trial. The Government may then argue that additional portions must be included in the interest of completeness. . . . If the substitutions are to be admitted at all (we leave open the possibility that Moussaoui may decide not to use the substitutions in his defense), they may be admitted only by Moussaoui. Based on defense counsel's submissions and the Government's objections, the district court could then create an appropriate set of substitutions. . . .

As previously indicated, the jury must be provided with certain information regarding the substitutions. While we leave the particulars of the instructions to the district court, the jury must be informed, at a minimum, that the substitutions are what the witnesses would say if called to testify; that the substitutions are derived from statements obtained under conditions that provide circumstantial guarantees of reliability; that the substitutions contain statements obtained **** ; and that neither the parties nor the district court has ever had access to the witnesses. . . .

Affirmed in part, vacated in part, and remanded.

[The opinions of WILLIAMS, Circuit Judge, and GREGORY, Circuit Judge, each concurring in part and dissenting in part, are omitted.]

NOTES AND QUESTIONS

1. *Deciding a Clash Between Branches: Formalism or Balancing?* The court concluded that the appropriate separation of powers analysis required by Moussaoui's insistence on access to **** is balancing, as prescribed by *Nixon v. Administrator of General Services*, 433 U.S. 425, 443 (1977) (stating that "the proper inquiry focuses on the extent to which [the judicial act of ordering access, in this instance] prevents the Executive Branch from accomplishing its constitutionally assigned functions, . . . [and whether] that impact is justified by an overriding need to promote objectives within the constitutional authority of [the court]"). But in *Public Citizen v. United States Department of Justice*, 491 U.S. 440, 485 (1989), Justice Kennedy indicated that there is "a line of cases of equal weight and authority, . . . where the Constitution by explicit text commits the power at issue to the exclusive control of the President, . . . [and the Court has] refused to tolerate *any* intrusion by [the courts]." Why is *Moussaoui*

not controlled by the latter line of cases? Doesn't the Commander in Chief Clause of Article II commit command of the armed forces in war to the President, and isn't the interrogation of enemy combatants in war part of that command? Does *Hamdi, supra* p. 445, or *Padilla, supra* p. 470, suggest any answers to these questions?

What other cases would you rely on in making the formalist argument for the government, or, by a balancing analysis, in arguing the extent to which court-ordered access to **** would prevent the President from conducting the war? In this regard, consider *Keith, supra* p. 172, *Korematsu, supra* p. 426, and *Zadvydas, supra* p. 350, Note 1. If the *Moussaoui* jury had been the target of serious threats of harm, how would you balance his Sixth Amendment right to trial by jury against the government's interest in protecting jurors by empaneling them secretly in a secure location to hear the trial by video?

2. *CIPA by Analogy.* In deciding the alternatives, the court determined that CIPA did not apply but relied on it anyway for a "useful framework." *See also United States v. Paracha*, No. 03 CR. 1197(SHS), 2006 WL 12768 (S.D.N.Y. Jan. 3, 2006) (using CIPA by analogy to impose *Moussaoui*-type solution to terror defendant's demand for access to witnesses in U.S. custody in Afghanistan), *aff'd*, 313 Fed. App'x 347 (2d Cir. 2008). Why did CIPA not apply? By what authority did the court undertake the relevance and balancing inquiries and order access to the summaries? Did the court, in effect, create a "wartime exception" to the Sixth Amendment after all? Is this another example of what Justice Scalia condemned as the "Mr. Fix-It Mentality" of courts? If CIPA is to be amended to cover the *Moussaoui* problem, why not leave that job to Congress?

3. *Switching Forums?* The district court invited the government to "reconsider whether the civilian criminal courts are the appropriate fora" for trying someone like Moussaoui. *United States v. Moussaoui*, No. Cr-01-455-A, 2003 WL 21263699, at *6 (E.D. Va. Mar. 10, 2003). The alternative is trial by military commission, which we explore in Chapter 22. Indeed, even Moussaoui's standby counsel appears to have invited this alternative, gratuitously conceding that the government's authority to try enemy combatants by military commission is "settled," and implying that the government can simply dismiss the criminal prosecution and proceed instead by a military commission to resolve the tension between Moussaoui's Sixth Amendment rights and the war powers. Brief of the Appellee at 3-4, *United States v. Moussaoui*, No. 03-4162 (4th Cir. May 13, 2003).

After you read the materials on military commissions, you can decide for yourself whether this was a wise concession. Do you agree with the apparent assumption upon which that concession and the District Court's invitation rested—that the government can switch forums in midstream? Even assuming that the government could lawfully have tried Moussaoui by military commission *ab initio*, does it necessarily follow that the government may start in a civilian court and then dismiss in favor of a military commission when it is unhappy with the civilian court's rulings? Would it matter how far the criminal prosecution had progressed beyond the indictment? If such a switch survived constitutional challenges, would it nevertheless violate the spirit of the law?

The government did, in fact, make a switch—actually a triple switch—in *Al-Marri v. Hanft*, 378 F. Supp. 2d 673 (D.S.C. 2005). After al-Marri lawfully entered the United States with his family to obtain a master's degree, he was initially arrested as a material witness in the 9/11 investigation. In the first switch, he was then rearrested and indicted for making false statements and for credit card fraud. More than two years later, President Bush interrupted the course of normal criminal proceedings (trial had not yet begun) by designating al-Marri an enemy combatant, after which he was transferred to military detention in South Carolina in the government's second switch. The government then successfully moved to drop the criminal indictment with prejudice.

Al-Marri argued that his criminal detention was sufficient to thwart any terrorist acts and that there was no necessity for military detention. The district court rejected his argument in part on the reasoning from case law asserting that when a federal investigation of criminal charges pending in state court reveals a federal crime, the state charges can be dismissed and the matter can be transferred to federal jurisdiction. *Id.* at 681. Is the analogy sound?

Al-Marri also protested that while he might have been acquitted of the criminal charges, he had no opportunity to prove his innocence in military detention. The court rejected this claim as well, reasoning that the purpose of military detention is preventive.

> This Court recognizes the natural response to this reasoning that, when a defendant is acquitted of criminal charges, society should not assume that he ever did nor that he will, in the future, engage in the activities for which he was charged. In this case, however, Petitioner was not charged with crimes of terrorism, and thus, an acquittal of various fraud charges does not lead to the conclusion that he will not, in the future, engage in acts of terrorism as alleged by the government.

Id. at 681 n.8.

As we saw in Chapter 16, after the Court of Appeals later divided sharply on the legality of al-Marri's detention as an enemy combatant and the adequacy of the procedure afforded him in deciding his status, the government switched forums for the third time, indicting al-Marri again. This time al-Marri entered a guilty plea to one count of conspiracy to provide material support to a foreign terrorist organization.

4. *Guilty Plea and Sentence.* On April 22, 2005, Moussaoui surprised everyone by pleading guilty to the key charges against him, while at the same time denying having any intention to commit mass murder. *See Moussaoui Pleads Guilty to Terror Charges* (CNN.com, Apr. 23, 2005), *at* http://www.cnn.com/2005/LAW/04/22/moussaoui/index.html. He was subsequently sentenced to life in prison. *United States v. Moussaoui,* No. 1:01CR00455-001, Judgment in a Criminal Case at 2 (E.D. Va. May 14, 2006).

5. *A Military Brig — the Better Forum?* The following assessment was written before the conclusion of the Moussaoui trial.

> The United States should drop all criminal charges against Zacarias Moussaoui, not because he is innocent, but because he is a foreign citizen who is (or was) a terrorist bent on killing innocent Americans, destroying American property, and disrupting American society. For less than a nanosecond, Moussaoui should be a free man again. . . .
>
> Before the nanosecond of Moussaoui's freedom ends, he should be transferred to the custody of the United States Department of Defense. After that, based on

recommendations coordinated by the National Security Council (NSC) for the President, the Executive Branch should implement a well-conceived decision about Moussaoui's next address. The NSC, rather than a particular United States agency, such as the Justice Department or the Defense Department, is the appropriate forum to vet such policies because they transcend the boundaries between domestic and international spheres, going beyond law enforcement and military issues. . . . The President, in making this decision on Moussaoui's next address, should consider our relations with foreign countries and the safety of our homeland. But whatever happens to Moussaoui, he did not — and does not — belong in criminal custody. [John Radsan, *The Moussaoui Case: The Mess from Minnesota,* 31 Wm. Mitchell L. Rev. 1417, 1417-1419 (2005).]

Do you agree? Did the system work? Or was the system distorted to accommodate national security? Do you think accused terrorists like Moussaoui and al-Marri should be tried by military commissions (a subject to which we turn in the next chapter)?

D. COERCED EVIDENCE

United States v. Ghailani

United States District Court, Southern District of New York, 2010
751 F. Supp. 2d 502

Lewis A. Kaplan, District Judge. Ahmed Khalfan Ghailani, an alleged member of Al Qaeda, was indicted in this Court in 1998 and charged with conspiring with Usama Bin Laden and others to kill Americans abroad by, among other means, bombing the United States Embassies in Nairobi, Kenya, and Dar es Salaam, Tanzania, bombings in which 224 people reportedly were killed. Years later, he was captured abroad by a foreign state and subsequently turned over to the Central Intelligence Agency ("CIA"). He was held and interrogated by the CIA at one or more secret locations outside the United States for a substantial period. He then was shifted to a secure facility at the United States naval base at Guantanamo where he remained until June 2009, at which time he was produced in this Court for prosecution on the indictment. Ghailani now moves to dismiss the indictment on the ground that he was tortured by the CIA in violation of his rights under the Due Process Clause of the Constitution.

I . . .

In this case, Ghailani has not identified explicitly the component of his due process rights that allegedly was violated. But he argues that both the CIA's use of "enhanced interrogation techniques" — in his word, torture — to question him and the fact that use of those techniques was authorized by "the highest levels of our government" are "'so fundamentally unfair,' 'shocking to our traditional sense of justice,' and 'outrageous'" that due process requires the indictment to be dismissed. He thereby invokes substantive rather than procedural due process.

The government does not here respond to Ghailani's assertions as to what was done to him while in CIA custody. Nor does it join issue on the question whether those assertions, if true, violated Ghailani's right to due process of law. Rather, it argues that Ghailani's allegations of pretrial custodial abuse are immaterial to this motion because dismissal of the indictment would not be a proper remedy for the government's alleged misconduct. In other words, the government argues that there is no legally significant connection between the alleged torture and any deprivation of the defendant's liberty that might result from this criminal prosecution.

If the government is correct in contending that Ghailani would not be entitled to dismissal of this criminal prosecution on due process grounds even if he was tortured in violation of his constitutional rights, it would be unnecessary for this Court to address the details of Ghailani's alleged treatment while in CIA custody. Nor in that event would it be appropriate to express any opinion as to whether that treatment violated his right to due process of law. The Court therefore passes directly to consideration of the government's argument.

II

The Due Process Clause, so far as is relevant here, protects against deprivations of liberty absent due process of law. The deprivation of liberty that Ghailani claims may occur if this case goes forward is his imprisonment in the event of conviction. In seeking dismissal of the indictment, however, he does not deny that he is being afforded every protection guaranteed to all in the defense of criminal prosecutions. Rather, Ghailani in effect argues that the case should be dismissed to punish the government for its mistreatment of him before he was presented in this Court to face the pending indictment.

For a due process violation to result in consequences adverse to the government in a criminal case — for example, the suppression of evidence or the dismissal of an indictment — there must be a causal connection between the violation and the deprivation of the defendant's life or liberty threatened by the prosecution. That is to say, relief against the government in a criminal case is appropriate if, and only if, a conviction otherwise would be a product of the government misconduct that violated the Due Process Clause. For only in such circumstances may it be said that the deprivation of life or liberty that follows from a criminal conviction flows from the denial of due process. This conclusion thus rests directly on the text of the Due Process Clause itself.

This point finds support also in the Supreme Court's consistent holdings that illegality in arresting or obtaining custody of a defendant does not strip a court of jurisdiction to try that defendant. "An illegal arrest, without more, has never been viewed as a bar to subsequent prosecution, nor as a defense to a valid conviction."

This doctrine, better known as the *Ker-Frisbie* rule,[14] dates back well over a century and "rests on the sound basis that due process of law is satisfied when one present in court is convicted of a crime after being fairly apprized of the charges against him and after a fair trial in accordance with constitutional procedural safeguards."[15] The Court repeatedly has reaffirmed this doctrine even as the concept of substantive due process has expanded. Moreover, the Court explicitly has refused to adopt an exclusionary rule that would operate on the defendant's person:

"Our numerous precedents ordering the exclusion of such illegally obtained evidence assume implicitly that the remedy does not extend to barring the prosecution altogether. So drastic a step might advance marginally some of the ends served by exclusionary rules,

14. *See Ker v. Illinois*, 119 U.S. 436 (1886); *Frisbie v. Collins*, 342 U.S. 519 (1952).
15. *Frisbie*, 342 U.S. at 522.

but it would also increase to an intolerable degree interference with the public interest in having the guilty brought to book."[17]

"[A defendant] is not himself a suppressible "fruit," and the illegality of his detention cannot deprive the Government of the opportunity to prove his guilt through the introduction of evidence wholly untainted by the police misconduct."[18] Rather, the proper remedy is money damages or criminal prosecution of the offending officers.

This case follows *a fortiori* from the rationale of the *Ker-Frisbie* rule. Ghailani is charged here with complicity in the murder of 224 people. The government here has stated that it will not use anything that Ghailani said while in CIA custody, or the fruits of any such statement, in this prosecution. In consequence, any deprivation of liberty that Ghailani might suffer as a result of a conviction in this case would be entirely unconnected to the alleged due process violation. Even if Ghailani was mistreated while in CIA custody and even if that mistreatment violated the Due Process Clause, there would be no connection between such mistreatment and this prosecution. If, as *Ker-Frisbie* holds, the illegal arrest of a defendant is not sufficiently related to a prosecution to warrant its dismissal, it necessarily follows that mistreatment of a defendant is not sufficient to justify dismissal where, as here, the connection between the alleged misconduct and the prosecution is non-existent or, at least, even more remote. Certainly the government should not be deprived here "of the opportunity to prove his guilt through the introduction of evidence wholly untainted by [any government] misconduct."[21] Any remedy for any such violation must be found outside the confines of this criminal case.

United States v. Toscanino[22] is not to the contrary. The defendant in that case allegedly was brought before the trial court as a result of being abducted and tortured by government agents, conduct that he claimed violated his right to due process of law. Upon conviction, he appealed on the ground that the agents' actions violated his right to due process and that the district court's jurisdiction over him was a product of that violation. The Second Circuit reversed the conviction and remanded to enable the defendant to attempt to prove that the agents' conduct was sufficiently outrageous to have violated the Due Process Clause. But *Toscanino* does not support Ghailani here.

As an initial matter, *Toscanino* was concerned with "denying the government the fruits of its exploitation of any deliberate and unnecessary lawlessness on its part." To whatever extent it is authoritative, a subject discussed below, the case is limited to situations in which the alleged outrageous government conduct brought the defendant within the court's jurisdiction, and thus was a but-for cause of any resulting conviction, and compromised the fairness and integrity of the criminal proceedings. There is no similar connection between Ghailani's alleged mistreatment while in CIA custody and this prosecution. Hence, to whatever extent that *Toscanino* remains viable, it does not apply here.

Second, as suggested already, it is doubtful that *Toscanino* remains authoritative. Several circuits have expressed doubt as to its continued viability in light of subsequent Supreme Court decisions. Moreover, the Second Circuit itself subsequently has

17. *United States v. Blue*, 384 U.S. 251, 255 (1966).
18. *United States v. Crews*, 445 U.S. 463, 474 (1980).
21. *Crews*, 445 U.S. at 474.
22. 500 F.2d 267 (2d Cir. 1974).

relied heavily on the *Ker-Frisbie* rule in deciding a case very similar to the one currently before this Court.

In *Brown v. Doe*,[27] a defendant convicted of felony murder and robbery in state court sought federal habeas corpus relief on the ground, *inter alia,* that his substantive due process rights had been violated by repeated brutal beatings by police following his arrest. He alleged that this pretrial custodial abuse "was so outrageous and so offensive to due process of law that it bar[red] his prosecution and require[d] dismissal of the indictment."[29]

In affirming the district court's denial of relief, the Second Circuit held that the Due Process Clause was the appropriate source of constitutional protection against the alleged pretrial abuse, but it concluded that the requested remedy was inappropriate. In light of the *Ker-Frisbie* line of cases, the court reasoned that "if there is no authority for barring the prosecution of a defendant who was illegally taken into custody, we are in no position to strip New York State of its power to try a defendant...who was lawfully arrested and convicted on untainted evidence."[30] Moreover, "the wrong committed by the police has its own remedies. It is unnecessary to remedy that wrong by absolving [petitioner] of his own crime, and there is no interest of justice served by a result in which the community suffers two unpunished wrongs."[31] The court concluded that "[t]he remedy of dismissal is not required to vindicate [petitioner's] due process rights. Other and more appropriate remedies are available," potentially including civil remedies under 42 U.S.C. §1983 and criminal prosecution of the police who assaulted him.[32]

Brown confirms this Court's view that *Toscanino,* if it retains any force, does so only where the defendant's presence before the trial court is procured by methods that offend the Due Process Clause. Dismissal of the indictment in the absence of a constitutional violation affecting the fairness of the criminal adjudication itself is unwarranted.

CONCLUSION

If, as Ghailani claims, he was tortured in violation of the Due Process Clause, he may have remedies. For the reasons set forth above, however, those remedies do not include dismissal of the indictment. The defendant's motion to dismiss the indictment on the grounds of allegedly outrageous government conduct in violation of his Fifth Amendment due process right is denied.

So ordered.

---

27. 2 F.3d 1236 (2d Cir. 1993).
29. *Id.* at 1242.
30. *Id.* at 1243.
31. *Id.*
32. *Id.*

United States v. Ghailani

United States District Court, Southern District of New York, 2010
743 F. Supp. 2d 261

LEWIS A. KAPLAN, District Judge. The question presented by this motion is whether the government may use in this criminal trial the testimony of a witness whom the government obtained only through information it allegedly extracted by physical and psychological abuse of the defendant. The government has elected not to litigate the details of what was done to the defendant. Instead, it has asked the Court to assume for purposes of the motion that everything the defendant said was coerced in violation of the Fifth Amendment. Accordingly, this decision, at the government's behest, proceeds on that premise. . . .

Ghailani eventually was apprehended in 2004 and turned over to the CIA. The CIA put him in a secret prison outside the United States and subjected him to so-called enhanced interrogation methods and other allegedly abusive treatment. It interrogated him in the secret prison for [REDACTED] Over time, Ghailani gave the CIA the information that led the government directly to Hussein Abebe "[REDACTED]

The government now proposes to call Abebe as a witness against Ghailani. Ghailani moves to preclude the government from doing so. He argues that the government's identification of Abebe and his procurement as a witness flowed directly from statements that he made under duress and that the receipt of Abebe's testimony would violate the Constitution.

The Fifth Amendment states that "[n]o person shall be compelled in any criminal case to be a witness against himself." But it does more. "When an incriminating statement has been obtained through coercion, the Fifth Amendment prohibits use of the statement or its "fruits'"[2] — that is to say, evidence derived from any statement coerced from the defendant — unless the evidence "has been come at . . . instead by means sufficiently distinguishable to be purged of the primary taint."[3] The government nevertheless argues that Abebe's testimony should be received because it is "attenuated" from the coercion to which Ghailani was subjected. It maintains that Abebe is willing to testify against Ghailani of his own free will, that Ghailani's coerced statements to the CIA played no part in securing Abebe's cooperation, and that the CIA was not motivated in its interrogation of Ghailani by any desire to obtain evidence for use against him in a criminal case. The Court finds that the government has not sustained its burden.

The temptation to allow our revulsion at these bombings, the human instinct for vengeance, and fear of terrorist attacks to overcome principles upon which our nation rests — principles that, although not always observed, are ideals to which we aspire — is powerful. If our nation is to continue as a bastion of liberty, however, we must remain true to our principles and overcome that temptation.

Among those principles is that which has been traced to Deuteronomy, that grew gradually through the long history of English law and in the American colonies, and that then was embodied in the Self Incrimination Clause in the Fifth Amendment. While the connection between fruits of a coerced statement — that is to say, evidence derived from a statement coerced from a defendant — may be so remote, so attenuated, from the coerced statement that the use of that derivative evidence does not

---

2. *Pillsbury Co. v. Conboy,* 459 U.S. 248, 278 (1983).
3. *Wong Sun v. United States,* 371 U.S. 471, 488 (1963).

violate the Fifth Amendment, the burden of proving attenuation is on the government.

In this case, the link between the CIA's coercion of Ghailani and Abebe's testimony is direct and close. Based on an extensive record, the Court's assessment of the credibility of witnesses the government called at the suppression hearing, and the lack of credible evidence to support key aspects of the government's argument, the government has not carried its burden of proving that Abebe's testimony would be so attenuated from Ghailani's coerced statements to permit its use. The motion to preclude Abebe's testimony is granted. . . .

[Substantial parts of the court's account of the facts are redacted with this note in the published opinion: "Text and associated footnote references redacted by government authorities in accordance with the Classified Information Procedures Act."]

II. THE EARLIER RULING . . .

To recapitulate briefly, illegally obtained evidence — including statements made by a defendant under government coercion — and the fruits of such evidence generally are not admissible against the defendant in a criminal trial. Nevertheless, the fruits of illegally obtained evidence are admissible where, insofar as remains relevant here, the government proves that the connection between the illegal government action and the evidence offered at trial — here, Abebe's testimony — is "so attenuated as to dissipate the taint." The ultimate question now before this Court therefore is whether the government has established that the connection between Abebe's testimony and Ghailani's unlawfully coerced statements is so remote as to permit Abebe to testify. . . .

III. ATTENUATION . . .

C. The Balance . . .

The government's strongest argument remains that related to deterrence. It initially contended that the CIA was motivated entirely by intelligence objectives and that exclusion here consequently would serve no deterrent purpose. Put another way, the suggestion was that the CIA would have done exactly the same thing irrespective of any law enforcement interest in prosecuting Ghailani.

The Court accepts that [REDACTED] Whether that means that absolutely no deterrent purpose would be served by suppression of Abebe's testimony here, however, is another matter in light of [REDACTED] And regardless of whether that is the case, deterrence is but one of the pertinent considerations.

In the last analysis, this Court concludes that exclusion of Abebe's testimony would be required here even if the government had identified and found him in otherwise comparable circumstances as a result of an illegal search or seizure, this notwithstanding the relative lack of deterrence of exclusion in these circumstances. If this were a search and seizure case, the relationship between the unlawful conduct and the identification and location would be just as close. Abebe's reluctance to testify and the fear of the authorities that nevertheless moves him to testify would be just as palpable. The government's failure to prove that the illegally seized evidence played no role in securing his cooperation would be just as glaring as [it is] here. These considerations would overcome the facts that the illegal search or seizure would have been a completed historical event and that the deterrent effect of exclusion, if any, would be considerably less than a certainty. But, it bears emphasis, this is not a Fourth Amendment search and seizure case. Hence, two factors make the case for exclusion here much stronger than if it were.

First, as this is a Fifth Amendment case, the receipt in evidence of Abebe's testimony itself would constitute a violation of the self-executing exclusionary rule inherent in the Constitution, not a matter of compliance with a purely utilitarian judge-made rule that was created in the twentieth century only to deter illegal searches and seizures.

Second, the deterrence analysis, which for reasons previously explained is of less importance here than in a Fourth Amendment case, is somewhat different. The CIA, acting upon the highest authority, used coercive methods to gain intelligence. This Court has declined to this point to express an opinion on the constitutionality of such methods, considered in and of themselves. It declines to do so now because that issue is not before it. What is before it, however, is the question whether the Fifth Amendment—which provides that "[n]o person . . . shall be compelled in any criminal case to be a witness against himself"—is violated if a Court receives in a criminal trial evidence that is the fruit of statements coerced from the defendant, at least where the relationship between the coerced statements and the evidence is [as] close as it is here. . . .

IV. CONCLUSION

In all the circumstances, this Court holds that the receipt in evidence of Abebe's testimony would violate the Fifth Amendment.[182] If the government is going to coerce a detainee to provide information to our intelligence agencies, it may not use that evidence—or fruits of that evidence that are tied as closely related to the coerced statements as Abebe's testimony would be here—to prosecute the detainee for a criminal offense. On these facts, the public interest in "making available to the trier of fact all concededly relevant and trustworthy evidence" is outweighed by the public and private interests protected by exclusion. The motion to preclude Abebe as a witness in this case is granted.

As the Court noted in its summary order dated October 5, 2010, it has not reached this conclusion lightly. It is acutely aware of the perilous world in which we live. But we must adhere to the basic principles that govern our nation not only when it is convenient to do so, but when perceived expediency tempts some to pursue a different course. The government may continue its prosecution of Ghailani without using this evidence. It probably may detain him as an enemy combatant as long as the present hostilities continue. What it cannot do is to use Abebe's testimony in its otherwise perfectly appropriate prosecution to convict him of the crimes with which he is charged.

The defendant's motion to preclude Hussein Abebe from testifying at trial is granted. The foregoing as well as the Court's previous opinion on this motion are the Court's findings of fact and conclusions of law.

So ordered.

---

182. It is very far from clear that Abebe's testimony would be admissible if Ghailani were being tried by military commission, even without regard to the question whether the Fifth Amendment would invalidate any more forgiving provisions of the rules of evidence otherwise applicable in such a proceeding. [These rules] . . . preclude or restrict the use of "statements obtained by torture or cruel, inhuman, or degrading treatment," and evidence derived therefrom, and could require exclusion of Abebe's testimony. Even if they did not, the Constitution might do so, even in a military commission proceeding.

NOTES AND QUESTIONS

1. *The Ker-Frisbie Doctrine.* As the court notes, the Supreme Court has declared that how a criminal defendant is brought to the court does not affect the court's jurisdiction over him. The *Ker-Frisbie* doctrine opened the door to abductions of suspects abroad (by a process sometimes called "informal rendition" — the converse of "extraordinary rendition" discussed in Chapter 19).

But *Toscanino* seemed to limit the *Ker-Frisbie* doctrine by refusing to exercise jurisdiction over a defendant who had been abducted by force that "shocked the conscience." How does the court in *Ghailani* distinguish *Toscanino*?

2. *Using Ghailani's Coerced Testimony Directly.* Suppose Ghailani confessed during his alleged torture. Would his coerced confession be admissible against him? The courts have traditionally excluded involuntary confessions for two reasons. First,

> because the methods used to extract them offend an underlying principle in the enforcement of our criminal law: that ours is an accusatorial and not an inquisitorial system — a system in which the State must establish guilt by evidence independently and freely secured and may not by coercion prove its charge against an accused out of his own mouth. "A coerced confession is offensive to basic standards of justice, not because the victim has a legal grievance against the police, but because declarations procured by torture are not premises from which a civilized forum will infer guilt." *Lyons* [*v. Oklahoma*], 322 U.S. [596, 605 (1944)]. [*United States v. Karake*, 443 F. Supp. 2d 8, 50 (D.D.C. 2006).]

Second, involuntary confessions may be untrue. "[W]hile a confession obtained by means of torture may be excluded on due process grounds as '[in]consistent with the fundamental principles of liberty and justice which lie at the base of all our civil and political institutions,' *Brown v. Mississippi*, 297 U.S. 278, 286 (1936), another legitimate reason to suppress it is the 'likelihood that the confession is untrue.' *Linkletter v. Walker*, 381 U.S. 618, 638 (1965) (quoting *Blackburn v. Alabama*, 361 U.S. 199, 207 (1960))." *Karake*, 443 F. Supp. 2d at 50-51.

3. *Using Ghailani's Coerced Testimony Indirectly: Fruit of the Poisonous Tree.* The government did not try to use Ghailani's confession, however. Instead it wanted to offer Abebe's testimony, which was allegedly voluntary. Because Abebe had been identified as a witness by Ghailani, Ghailani argued that Abebe's testimony was derived from and therefore tainted by Ghailani's own coercive interrogation — the fruit of the poisonous tree. Why did the court exclude Abebe's testimony?

Some of the evidence against detainees at Guantánamo Bay is derived from their own statements to interrogators, and some is from fellow detainees. Can you see problems these latter evidentiary sources could create for criminal prosecutions like Ghailani's? What is the solution? *Should* the *Ghailani* court have taken into account "the perilous world in which we live" in applying the relevant legal principles? These principles were, after all, chiefly developed in domestic cases involving police abuse of suspects (often with racist overtones). Are criminal prosecutions of accused terrorists who have been interrogated by military and CIA interrogators different?

4. *Ghailani's Conviction: Victory or Defeat?* After a jury trial from which Abebe's testimony was excluded, the jury convicted Ghailani on one count of conspiring to commit murder and acquitted him on 280 others. Charlie Savage, *Terror Verdict Tests Obama's Strategy on Trials*, N.Y. Times, Nov. 18, 2010. The court sentenced Ghailani to life in prison.

Representative Peter King called the outcome a "total miscarriage of justice," Editorial, *The Ghailani Verdict*, N.Y. Times, Nov. 19, 2010, and a "tragic wake-up call to the Obama administration to immediately abandon its ill-advised plan to try Guantanamo terrorists" in civilian courts, and he urged the Administration to try them in military commissions instead. Charlie Savage, *Ghailani Verdict Reignites Debate Over the Proper Court for Terrorism Trials*, N.Y. Times, Nov. 19, 2010. Justice Department spokespersons, on the other hand, declared it a victory, noting that the judge excluded key evidence (in the excerpted opinion) because of Ghailani's treatment during the prior Administration. *Id.* Others pointed out that neither costly security, public grandstanding by Ghailani, nor disclosures or leaks of classified information had resulted from the prosecution, contrary to critics' predictions. *Id.*

Was the mixed verdict a victory for the criminal justice option for dealing with accused terrorists or a defeat? Regarding Representative King's advice to the Administration, consider footnote 182 in the second *Ghailani* opinion. Had the jury found Ghailani not guilty on all counts, what would the Administration have done in light of Abebe's excluded testimony?

E. DO WE NEED A NATIONAL SECURITY COURT?

The mixed verdict in *Ghailani* renewed an acrimonious debate about the ability of the criminal process to handle terrorist cases. In addition to the problems of secret and coerced evidence discussed above, terror prosecutions potentially pose the following problems:

- whether the right to speedy trial has been violated by lengthy detention as an enemy combatant;
- whether the accused terrorist was entitled to *Miranda* warnings ("you have a right to remain silent. . . .") when he was arrested and detained abroad;
- whether the security of the jury and the judge requires special measures, including shackling the defendant or concealing the identity of jurors;
- whether tensions between the accused terrorist and his court-appointed lawyers render the assistance of counsel ineffective or threaten the conduct of the trial;
- whether the criminal justice system can afford the often lengthy, appeal-interrupted, pretrial motion practice and trial of accused terrorists.

See, e.g., ABA Comm. on Law & Nat'l Security, *Trying Terrorists in Article III Courts* (July 2009) (*Trying Terrorists*); Richard B. Zabel & James J. Benjamin Jr., *In Pursuit of Justice* (Human Rights First, May 2008); Robert Timothy Reagan, *National Security Case Studies: Special Case-Management Challenges* (Federal Judicial Ctr., Feb. 22, 2010); Robert Timothy Reagan, *Terrorism-Related Cases: Special Case-Management Challenges: Problems and Solutions* (Federal Judicial Ctr., Mar. 26, 2008).

Former federal judge and Attorney General Michael B. Mukasey cites Jose Padilla's saga as evidence that "current institutions and statutes are not well suited to even the limited task of supplementing . . . a military effort to combat Islamic terrorism."

Michael B. Mukasey, Op-Ed., *Jose Padilla Makes Bad Law*, Wall St. J., Aug. 22, 2007. He noted that Padilla's criminal case took three months to try, and that criminal cases involving the 1993 World Trade Center bombing, 1996 attacks on Khobar Towers, 1998 attacks on U.S. embassies in Africa, and the 2000 bombing of the *USS Cole* "have strained the financial resources and security resources of the federal courts near to the limit." *Id.* He also asserted that such prosecutions risk disclosing methods and sources of intelligence, and, when the courts relax evidentiary rules or criminal procedures, also can distort the rules applicable to ordinary criminal cases. *Id.*

Judge Mukasey therefore urged Congress to consider a proposal for the creation of a new Article III "national security court" to deal with national security prosecutions, including terrorism cases. *Id.* One such proposal would model the new court on the Foreign Intelligence Surveillance Court (or even "subsume the FISA court and its obligations within a new National Security Court") and staff it with Article III judges. Andrew C. McCarthy & Alykhan Velshi, *Outsourcing American Law: We Need a National Security Court* 24 & n.61 (American Enter. Inst. Working Paper No. 156, 2009), *available at* http://www.aei.org/docLib/20090820-Chapter6.pdf. Such a court would have concurrent jurisdiction with military commissions to try "alleged offenders . . . if those offenders qualify as alien enemy combatants . . . ." *Id.* at 26. Its priority would be "not justice for the individual but security of the American people," and it would therefore need "clear procedural rules which underscore that the overriding mission — into which the judicial function is being imported for very limited purposes — remains executive and military." *Id.* at 30. The proponents of this proposal are not specific about those rules, but they would apparently include a "credible and convincing evidence" standard of proof, a systemic "preference . . . that defendants be convicted and harshly sentenced," and strict limits on "judicial excess," to be enforced by a right of interlocutory appeal by the government to challenge any order "by which the court deviates from the procedural rules." *Id.* at 31-32. Finally, the court would be instructed by Congress to apply a much-narrowed *Brady* exculpatory evidence doctrine. *Id.* at 35. In short, they sum up, "[National Security Court] trials would add the Article III judges to the existing military commission format." *Id.* at 32.

Other proposals for a National Security Court would lengthen the speedy trial limitation, ease the government's burden to show a need for closing a trial to the public, require a two-thirds vote to find proof of guilt beyond a reasonable doubt, relax the hearsay and authentication rules of evidence, and, possibly, permit coerced statements into evidence in some circumstances (although this is unclear). *See* Kevin E. Lunday & Harvey Rishikof, *Due Process Is a Strategic Choice: Legitimacy and the Establishment of an Article III National Security Court*, 39 Cal. W. Int'l L.J. 87 (2008).

NOTES AND QUESTIONS

1. *A National Security Court for Detention Decisions.* A National Security Court has been proposed both to review detention cases and to try terrorism cases. *See, e.g.,* McCarthy & Velshi, *supra*, at 23-27; Lunday & Rishikof, *supra*, 39 Cal. W. Int'l L.J. at 113-118. Such a court would relieve the habeas courts of their burden of reviewing wartime detention and could also be given jurisdiction to authorize or review preventive detention under a new statute. Several scholars assert that the courts in the District of Columbia Circuit already are National Security Courts by default, because of their handling of habeas petitions by Guantánamo detainees. *See, e.g.,* Sophia M.

Brill, *The National Security Court We Already Have*, 28 Yale L. & Pol'y Rev. 525 (2010); Jack Goldsmith, *Long-Term Terrorist Detention and Our National Security Court* 6-8 (Series on Counterterrorism and American Statutory Law, Working Paper No. 5, 2009), *available at* http://www.brookings.edu/papers/2009/0209_detention_goldsmith.aspx.

2. *Need?* Proponents of a National Security Court cite the aforementioned problems, the length of terrorism trials, and the mixed verdict of *Ghailani* as evidence of the need for a new trial court, but is the anecdotal evidence compelling? Opponents note, first, that convictions were obtained in all of the cited cases. Although some scholars have criticized Department of Justice statistics for being over-inclusive and pointed to the surprisingly short *average* sentences handed out in cases that Justice has classified as terrorism-related, more nuanced evaluation of the statistics suggests that the government has obtained lengthy sentences for cases actually based on terrorism and material support charges. *See* Robert M. Chesney, *Federal Prosecution of Terrorism-Related Offenses: Conviction and Sentencing Data in Light of the "Soft-Sentence" and "Data-Reliability" Critiques*, 11 Lewis & Clark L. Rev. 851 (2007). In addition, a detailed study by former prosecutors of more than 100 criminal cases involving international terrorism concluded that, "contrary to the views of some critics, the court system is generally well-equipped to handle most terrorism cases," Zabel & Benjamin, *supra*, at 5, a conclusion echoed in part by a workshop of judges, prosecutors, and defense attorneys in terrorism cases. *See Trying Terrorists, supra*, at 8 ("Many of the *ad hoc* procedures developed by the courts to manage terrorism trials have been effective," although there can be a steep learning curve). Recall, too, that the court of appeals in *Abu Ali* emphasized that "the criminal justice system is not without those attributes of adaptation that will permit it to function in the post-9/11 world." *Abu Ali*, 528 F.3d at 221.

How much stress on the criminal justice system would suffice to justify creation of a National Security Court? On whom should the burden of proof fall, the proponents of such a court or their opponents? The current criminal justice system assumes that protection of the innocent is worth the cost of letting some guilty defendants go free. Does the same assumption apply to accused terrorists?

3. *Changing the Rules or Changing the Court?* Proposals for a National Security Court assume that evidentiary rules and standards of proof can be relaxed. But if this is true, could those rules and standards not be relaxed for ordinary criminal courts without any need to create a controversial new court? *See* Stephen I. Vladeck, *The Case Against National Security Courts*, 45 Willamette L. Rev. 505 (2009). If the answer is no because of constitutional limitations, would the same limitations not apply to the new Article III court?

> Either Congress can amend the Federal Rules of Evidence [or CIPA] to allow for the introduction [or the exclusion] of particular forms of evidence in particular cases, or the Constitution prohibits Congress from so acting. The former would suggest that a move to a national security court would be akin to using a bazooka to kill an ant; the latter would suggest that national security courts *couldn't* have a lesser evidentiary burden. [*Id.* at 519-520 (emphasis in original).]

In fact, the workshop mentioned above also concluded that "[s]ome of the challenges associated with terrorism trials are posed by constitutionally mandated safeguards, and thus, the use of an alternative forum to regulate Article III courts (such as a national security court) may not alleviate some of the challenges." *Trying Terrorists, supra*, at 8.

4. *Blowback.* Even if some of the challenges facing terrorist prosecutions could constitutionally be alleviated by simple rule changes, are they changes we would want to the ordinary criminal justice system? Judge Mukasey expressed concern that "if conventional legal rules are adapted to deal with a terrorist threat, whether by relaxed standards for conviction, searches, the admissibility of evidence or otherwise, those adaptions will infect and change the standards in ordinary cases with ordinary defendants in ordinary courts of law." Mukasey, *supra.* If such rule changes are confined to terrorism cases, then they could effectively convert the criminal court into a "National Security Court" anyway for purposes of terrorism cases. Historically, one protection against unfair rules has always been the fact that rules apply the same way to everyone, sometimes expressed in the aphorism that we are measured by how we treat our enemies. On the other hand, some of the innovations that judges have employed in terrorism cases were borrowed from drug or gang cases. Is concern about the "relaxation" or adaptation of rules in terrorism cases overblown?

5. *Legitimacy.* As *Rosen* stressed, an important attribute of American criminal justice is its transparency. Secret "Star Chamber" courts are contrary to our tradition, and some feel (perhaps unfairly) that the legitimacy of the Foreign Intelligence Surveillance Court is undercut by its closed hearings. Moreover, the United States has traditionally been critical of "special" security courts and military courts used in non-democratic states to stifle opponents and dissidents, as well as to try security risks. "Legitimacy remains a vital strategic weapon against terrorism." Lunday & Rishikof, *supra*, 39 Cal. W. Int'l L.J. at 131. Does not the legitimacy of the state's courts therefore also matter? Would a National Security Court have the same legitimacy as ordinary Article III courts have acquired over time? Should we be concerned not only about its legitimacy to Americans, but also about its legitimacy to our foreign allies and enemies?

Trial by Military Commission

22

Before deploying "necessary and appropriate force" against Al Qaeda and the Taliban in Afghanistan in November 2001, the Bush administration had to decide what it would do with those whom U.S. forces and their allies captured in the fight.

Apart from simply detaining them, one possibility was trying them in U.S. criminal courts. But the problems of secret evidence, which we explored in the previous chapter, not to mention concerns about security and efficiency, given the sheer numbers of anticipated captives, made this option impractical.

A second option was trying them before some ad hoc international tribunal. The surrender of control that this would entail, coupled with the Administration's repudiation of the International Criminal Court, made this option unappealing.

A third option was trying them by court-martial, using the same rules applicable to U.S. service personnel. This option would have used fair and time-tested procedures at the same time that it conformed with the laws of war. But the very fairness of the procedures may have been a strike against them; they may have seemed *too* fair and, partly as a result, too cumbersome for terrorists charged with horrific war crimes against civilians. *See* Jane Mayer, *The Hidden Power*, New Yorker, May 3, 2006, at 44 (quoting Vice President Dick Cheney on military commissions: "We think it guarantees that we'll have the kind of treatment of these individuals that we believe they deserve."). Their conformity with the laws of war could have been another strike against them, as long as the Administration insisted that such laws did not apply to terrorists.

Whatever the precise reasons, the Administration chose a fourth option: to try selected captives by "military commission" under procedures devised for the occasion. Military commissions are tribunals of military officers who sit as judge and jury. Historically, they have been used in the field to try spies, saboteurs, and others who violate the laws of war, and in occupied territories to try common crimes as well. In Chapter 15, we considered two pre-9/11 cases in reviewing the legal authority for *detention* by the military. In Part A of this chapter, we revisit these cases in exploring the legal authority for *trial* by military commission. In Part B, we examine the Military Order of November 13, 2001, which adopted the military commission option and the procedures implementing it, and the Supreme Court's 2006 decision in *Hamdan v. Rumsfeld* about the legal authority for military commissions. In Part C, we consider

Congress's responses to *Hamdan* and the use of military commissions pursuant to military commission legislation enacted after *Hamdan.*

A. TRIAL BY MILITARY COMMISSION BEFORE 9/11

Ex parte Milligan

United States Supreme Court, 1866
71 U.S. (4 Wall.) 2

[The opinion is set forth *supra* p. 381.]

Ex parte Quirin

United States Supreme Court, 1942
317 U.S. 1

[The opinion is set forth *supra* p. 437.]

NOTES AND QUESTIONS

[The notes and questions are set forth *supra* pp. 440-443.]

B. TRIAL BY MILITARY COMMISSION AFTER 9/11: THE FIRST PHASE

Before the Bush administration turned to the fourth option — trying enemy combatants by military commission — it tasked the Office of Legal Counsel with advising the President on the legality of using military commissions for this purpose. It provided him with an opinion on November 6, 2001, which is excerpted below. A week later, President Bush issued a Military Order authorizing trial by military commissions of persons he designated, which is also reproduced below. The Order delegated to the Secretary of Defense the task of promulgating procedures for such trials. Defense Secretary Donald Rumsfeld and the Department of Defense subsequently issued a host of implementing orders and instructions, many of which were repeatedly revised. *See, e.g.,* Department of Def., *Military Commission Order No. 1* (Mar. 21, 2002); Department of Def., *Military Commissions Instructions Nos. 1-10* (various dates).

Pursuant to the Order issued by President Bush, military commissions were instituted in November 2004 against four persons, including Salim Ahmed Hamdan, a Yemeni national captured during fighting in Afghanistan. Before they got under way, Hamdan challenged the legality of using the military commission to try him as an enemy combatant in a case that resulted in a seminal Supreme Court decision excerpted below. The decision effectively brought to a close what we call the first phase of post-9/11 military commissions, leading to statutory reforms.

Legality of the Use of Military Commissions to Try Terrorists

U.S. Department of Justice, Office of Legal Counsel
Nov. 6, 2001
2001 WL 36175681 (O.L.C.)

The President possesses inherent authority under the Constitution, as Chief Executive and Commander in Chief of the Armed Forces of the United States, to establish military commissions to try and punish terrorists captured in connection with the attacks of September 11 or in connection with U.S. military operations in response to those attacks.

Memorandum Opinion for: Counsel to the President

From: Patrick F. Philbin, Deputy Ass't Attorney General

You have asked us to consider whether terrorists captured in connection with the attacks of September 11 or in connection with ongoing U.S. operations in response to those attacks could be subject to trial before a military court. The Uniform Code of Military Justice ("UCMJ"), 10 U.S.C. §§801-946, authorizes military commissions to try "offenders or offenses that by statute or by the law of war may be tried by military commissions." 10 U.S.C. §821 (2000). The Supreme Court has interpreted identical language (then included in Article 15 of the Articles of War in effect during World War II) to incorporate customary practice and to authorize trial by military commission of any person subject to the laws of war for any offense under the laws of war. *See Ex parte Quirin*, 317 U.S. 1, 30 (1942).

We conclude that under 10 U.S.C. §821 and his inherent powers as Commander in Chief, the President may establish military commissions to try and punish terrorists apprehended as part of the investigation into, or the military and intelligence operations in response to, the September 11 attacks....

BACKGROUND

A military commission is a form of military tribunal typically used in three scenarios: (i) to try individuals (usually members of enemy forces) for violations of the laws of war; (ii) as a general court administering justice in occupied territory; and (iii) as a general court in an area where martial law has been declared and the civil courts are closed. *See generally* William Winthrop, *Military Law and Precedents* 836-40 (2d ed. 1920). The commission is convened by order of a commanding officer and consists of a board of officers who sit as adjudicators without a jury. *See id.* at 835. The commission's decision is subject to review by the convening authority and is not subject to direct judicial review.

Military commissions have been used throughout U.S. history to prosecute violators of the laws of war. "Since our nation's earliest days, such commissions have been
constitutionally recognized agencies for meeting many urgent governmental responsibilities related to war. They have been called our common law war courts." *Madsen v.
Kinsella*, 343 U.S. 341, 346-47 (1952). Military commissions have tried offenders drawn
from the ranks of aliens and citizens alike charged with war crimes arising as early as
the Revolutionary War, the Mexican-American War, and the Civil War, and as recently
as World War II. *See Quirin*, 317 U.S. at 32 n.10, 42 n.14. President Lincoln's assassins
and their accomplices were imprisoned and even executed pursuant to convictions
rendered by military commissions. Their offenses were characterized not as criminal
matters but rather as acts of rebellion against the government itself. *See Military Commissions*, 11 Op. Att'y Gen. 297 (1865); *Ex parte Mudd*, 17 F. Cas. 954 (S.D. Fla. 1868)
(No. 9899). Such use of military commissions has been repeatedly endorsed by federal courts, including as recently as this year. *See Mudd v. Caldera*, 134 F. Supp. 2d 138
(D.D.C. 2001).

Military commissions are not courts within Article III of the Constitution, nor are
they subject to the jury trial requirements of the Fifth and Sixth Amendments of the
Constitution. *See Quirin*, 317 U.S. at 40. Unlike Article III courts, the powers of military
commissions are derived not from statute, but from the laws of war. *See Ex parte
Vallandigham*, 68 U.S. (1 Wall.) 243, 249-53 (1863). That is, their authority derives
from the Constitution's vesting of the power of Commander in Chief in the President.
"Neither their procedure nor their jurisdiction has been prescribed by statute.
[Instead,] [i]t has been adapted in each instance to the need that called it forth."
Madsen, 343 U.S. at 347-48. "In general" [Congress] has left it to the President, and
the military commanders representing him, to employ the commission, as occasion
may require, for the investigation and punishment of violations of the laws of war." *Id.*
at 346 n.9 (quoting Winthrop, *supra* at 831).

I. MILITARY COMMISSIONS MAY BE USED TO TRY
ALL OFFENSES AGAINST THE LAWS OF WAR. . . .

A. Congress Has Sanctioned the Broad Jurisdiction of Military Commissions To Try All Offenses Against the Laws of War.

The UCMJ addresses the jurisdiction of military commissions in article 21, which
is section 821 of title 10 of the United States Code. Section 821 is phrased somewhat
unusually, because it does not *create* military commissions and define their functions
and jurisdiction. Instead, it refers to military commissions primarily to acknowledge
their existence and to *preserve* their existing jurisdiction. As explained more fully
below, military commissions had been created under the authority of the President
as Commander in Chief and used to try offenses against the laws of war before there
was any explicit statutory sanction for their use. Section 821, which is entitled "Jurisdiction of courts-martial not exclusive," thus states that "[t]he provisions of this
chapter conferring jurisdiction upon · courts-martial do not *deprive* military
commissions . . . of concurrent jurisdiction with respect to offenders or offenses
that by statute or by the law of war may be tried by military commissions." 10
U.S.C. §821 (emphasis added). The jurisdictional provision for courts-martial that
is cross-referenced is 10 U.S.C. §818 (2000), which defines the jurisdiction of general
courts-martial to include "jurisdiction to try any person who by the law of war is

subject to trial by a military tribunal." By its terms, section 821 takes the existence of military commissions as a given and clarifies that the establishment of broad jurisdiction in courts-martial will not curtail the powers of military commissions.

By expressly preserving the jurisdiction of military commissions, section 821 necessarily provides a congressional authorization and sanction for their use. Indeed, the Supreme Court has concluded that identical language in the predecessor provision to section 821 — article 15 of the Articles of War — "*authorized* trial of offenses against the laws of war before such commissions." *Quirin*, 317 U.S. at 29 (emphasis added)....

Indeed, if section 821 were read as restricting the use of military commissions and prohibiting practices traditionally followed, it would infringe on the President's express constitutional powers as Commander in Chief. *Cf. Quirin*, 317 U.S. at 47 (declining to "inquire whether Congress may restrict the power of the Commander in Chief to deal with enemy belligerents" by restricting use of military commissions); *id.* (declining also to "consider the question whether the President is compelled by the Articles of War to afford unlawful enemy belligerents a trial before subjecting them to disciplinary measures"). A clear statement of congressional intent would be required before a statute could be read to effect such an infringement on core executive powers. *See, e.g., Public Citizen v. Department of Justice*, 491 U.S. 440, 466 (1989).

The congressional sanction for the use of military commissions is a permissible exercise of Congress's powers under the Constitution. Congress has authority not only to "declare War," but also to "raise and support Armies," and "make Rules for the Government and Regulation of the land and naval Forces." U.S. Const. art. I, §8, cl. 11, 12, 14. To the extent military commissions are used for enforcing discipline within the armed forces of the United States, Congress has authority to sanction their use. In addition, Congress has authority to "define and punish . . . Offences against the Law of Nations." *Id.* art. I, §8, cl. 10. Authorizing the use of military commissions to enforce the laws of war — which are considered a part of the "Law of Nations" — is certainly a permissible exercise of these authorities. Or, to be more precise, it is permissible at least so long as any congressional regulations do not interfere with the President's authority as Commander in Chief. *Cf. Quirin*, 317 U.S. at 47 (declining to address "whether Congress may restrict the power of the Commander in Chief to deal with enemy belligerents" through regulations on military commissions); *cf. also Hamilton v. Dillin*, 88 U.S. (21 Wall.) 73, 87 (1874) (stating that the "President alone" is "constitutionally invested with the entire charge of hostile operations")....

B. Even if Congress Had Not Authorized Creation of Military Commissions, the President Would Have Authority as Commander in Chief To Convene Them....

The Commander in Chief Clause, U.S. Const. art. II, §2, cl. 1, vests in the President the full powers necessary to prosecute successfully a military campaign. It has long been understood that the Constitution provides the federal government all powers necessary for the execution of the duties the Constitution describes. As the Supreme Court explained in *Johnson v. Eisentrager*, "[t]he first of the enumerated powers of the President is that he shall be Commander-in-Chief of the Army and Navy of the United States. And, of course, grant of war power includes all that is necessary and proper for carrying these powers into execution." 339 U.S. 763, 788 (1950) (citation omitted); *see also Lichter v. United States*, 334 U.S. 742, 780 (1948)

("The powers of Congress and the President are only those which are to be derived from the Constitution but . . . the primary implication of a war power is that it shall be an effective power to wage the war successfully."); *Home Building & Loan Ass'n v. Blaisdell*, 290 U.S. 398, 426 (1934) (stating that "the war power of the federal government" is "a power to wage war successfully"). One of the necessary incidents of authority over the conduct of military operations in war is the power to punish enemy belligerents for violations of the laws of war. The laws of war exist in part to ensure that the brutality inherent in war is confined within some limits. It is essential for the conduct of a war, therefore, that an army have the ability to enforce the laws of war by punishing transgressions by the enemy. . . .

C. The Use of Military Commissions to Inflict Punishments Without the Procedures Provided for Criminal Trials under Article III, Section 2 and the Fifth and Sixth Amendments Is Constitutionally Permissible. . . .

At the time of the Founding, it was well settled that offenses under the laws of war were a distinct category of offense, unlike criminal offenses against the civil law, and were subject to trial in military tribunals without the benefits of the procedures of the common law enshrined in the Constitution. . . . Thus, under the settled understanding that the rights to jury trial and grand jury indictment do not extend beyond the cases where they were available at common law, those rights simply do not extend to trials before military tribunals for offenses against the laws of war. Such trials never included indictment or jury trial at the time of the Founding. . . .

The primary support for constitutional arguments to *restrict* the use of military commissions would be based on the Supreme Court's decision in *Ex parte Milligan*, 71 U.S. (4 Wall.) 2 (1866). . . .

We believe that the broad pronouncements in *Milligan* do not accurately reflect the requirements of the Constitution and that the case has properly been severely limited by the later decision in *Quirin*. . . .

Thus, the line that the Court ultimately drew in *Quirin* to distinguish *Milligan* may be read to suggest that a citizen (not in the U.S. military) can be tried by military commission *when he acts as a belligerent. See* 317 U.S. at 37. That condition was most clearly met where citizens "associate themselves with the military arm of the enemy government." *Id.* The distinction suggests that *Milligan* can be explained on the basis that the actions charged in *Milligan* did not amount to acts of belligerency. Even under this approach to *Quirin*, we conclude that in the context of the current conflict, any actions by U.S. citizens that amount to hostile acts against the United States or its citizens (and certainly participation in biological attacks, the attacks of September 11, or similar attacks) would make a person a "belligerent" subject to trial by military commission under *Quirin*.

We caution, however, that applying this standard may raise some ambiguities. The *Milligan* decision holds out at least the possibility that some charges that may be articulated under the law of war (such as the charge of giving aid and comfort to the enemy used in *Milligan*) may not, in some circumstances, amount to acts of belligerency triable by military commission. Exactly which acts place a person in the category of an "enemy belligerent" under *Quirin* thus may be a subject of litigation. In addition, it might be argued that *Quirin* should be read as imposing a brighter-line test under which citizens are triable by military commission when they "associate themselves with the military arm of the enemy government." 317 U.S. at 37. That standard, it could be claimed, is difficult to apply here because there are no organized armed forces of another belligerent nation facing the United States. For the reasons outlined above, we conclude that such an approach does not reflect the proper constitutional analysis and is not the proper reading of *Quirin*. Nonetheless, it raises a potential source of litigation risk....

2. Enemy aliens seized in the United States

Even if *Milligan* might raise litigation risks for the use of military commissions to try citizens, it should not raise the same difficulties for trying *aliens* charged with violations of the law of war....

II. THE PRESIDENT MAY CONCLUDE THAT THE LAWS OF ARMED CONFLICT APPLY TO THE TERRORIST ATTACKS.

As explained above, 10 U.S.C. §821 sanctions the full uses of the military commission established by custom and Executive practice in the United States military. That practice, as noted above, has permitted military commissions to try all offenses against the laws of war. The critical question for determining whether military commissions can properly be used here, therefore, is whether the terrorist attacks have created a situation to which the laws of war apply. That is, are the terrorist acts subject to the laws of war at all, or are they solely criminal matters to be treated under the municipal criminal law of the United States or a particular State?

As outlined below, it would be difficult—or impossible—to articulate any precise multi-pronged legal "test" for determining whether a particular attack or set of circumstances constitutes "war" justifying application of the laws of war—or to use the modern terminology, whether it is an "armed conflict" justifying use of the "laws of armed conflict." As the Supreme Court recognized long ago, determining whether a "war" exists depends largely on pragmatic considerations. As the Court put it in evaluating whether President Lincoln could properly invoke the laws of war by imposing a blockade on the southern states at the beginning of the Civil War, a conflict "becomes [a war] by its accidents—the number, power, and organization of the persons who originate and carry it on." *The Prize Cases*, 67 U.S. (2 Black) 635, 666 (1862). Precisely because it is a question that rests on pragmatic judgments that critically affect the national defense and vital matters of foreign policy, it is a determination that is properly left to the political branches, and particularly to the President. We explain in Part A below that the courts should defer to a Presidential determination that the laws of armed conflict apply. In Part B, we outline more specific principles that can be derived from precedents to demonstrate that the present attacks have created a set of circumstances that properly merit invocation of the laws of war. The scale of these attacks, the number of deaths they have caused, and the massive military response they have demanded makes it virtually self-evident that the present situation can be treated as an armed conflict subject to the laws of armed conflict.

A. Determining Whether War Exists Is a Question for the Political Branches....

By making the President Commander in Chief of the armed forces, the Constitution must be understood to grant him the full authorities required for him to effectively defend the Nation in the event of an armed attack. Necessarily included among those powers must be the ability to determine whether persons responsible for an attack should be subject to punishment under the laws of war. We outlined above our conclusion that the President's powers as Commander in Chief must include the authority to convene military commissions to enforce the laws of war. For largely the same reasons, the Commander in Chief's power should include authority to determine when the armed forces are engaged in a conflict that merits application of the laws of war. Use of the laws of war, after all, can be a key component in a strategy for conducting and regulating a military campaign. The ability to apply the laws of war means the ability to punish transgressions by an enemy against those laws, and thereby to compel an enemy to abide by certain standards of conduct. There can be no basis for withdrawing from the Commander in Chief the authority to determine when the Nation has been subjected to such an attack as warrants the use of the laws of war to deal with the enemy.

B. The Terrorist Attacks Have Created a Situation that Can Properly Be Considered War.

Although the determination whether the current situation merits application of the laws of war is properly committed to the discretion of the President as Commander in Chief, there are some standards that the President could take into account. Under principles that can be gleaned both from American precedents and sources addressing the international laws of armed conflict, these factors indicate that the laws of armed conflict are properly applicable here. As the Supreme Court put it in evaluating whether President Lincoln could properly invoke the laws of war by imposing a blockade on the southern states at the beginning of the Civil War, a conflict "becomes [a war] by its accidents — the number, power, and organization of the persons who originate and carry it on." *The Prize Cases*, 67 U.S. at 666. Where an organized force is carrying on a campaign of violence that reaches a sufficient level of intensity, it may be deemed an "armed conflict" by the President, thereby justifying application of the laws of armed conflict, including trials for the violation of those laws....

The critical question for determining whether the laws of armed conflict apply here, therefore, is whether the terrorist attacks were a sufficiently organized and systematic set of violent actions that they crossed a sufficient level of intensity to be considered "armed conflict." There can be no doubt that, whatever the "level of intensity" required to create an armed conflict, the gravity and scale of the violence inflicted on the United States on September 11 crossed that threshold....

III. UNDER THE LAWS OF WAR, THE TERRORISTS ARE UNLAWFUL COMBATANTS SUBJECT TO TRIAL AND PUNISHMENT FOR VIOLATIONS OF THE LAWS OF WAR....

As noted above, the terrorists involved in the attacks did not meet even the minimal conditions required to be recognized as lawful combatants. It is open to some doubt whether persons acting without authorization of a state could *ever* undertake hostile acts without violating the laws of war. But we need not reach that theory to conclude that the terrorists did not meet even the most basic requirements for complying with the laws of war as lawful combatants. They were not bearing arms openly and wearing fixed insignia. Thus, all of their hostile acts can be treated as violations of the laws of war. It is settled that any violation of the laws of war may be prosecuted as a "war crime." The U.S. Army Field Manual, *The Law of Land Warfare*, provides that "[a]ny person, whether a member of the armed forces or a civilian, who commits an act which constitutes a crime under international law is responsible therefor and liable to punishment." FM 27-10 ch. 8, par. 498. "The term 'war crime' is the technical expression for a violation of the law of war by any person or persons, military or civilian. Every violation of the laws of war is a war crime." *Id.* ch. 8, par. 499. Specific offenses here could include violations of the rule prohibiting "[u]se of civilian clothing by troops to conceal their military character," *id.* ch. 8, par. 504(g), the rule prohibiting "[f]iring on localities which are undefended and without military significance," *id.* ch. 8, par. 504(d), and the rule prohibiting deliberate targeting of civilian populations.

In addition, individuals can be prosecuted under the laws of armed conflict using standard theories of aiding and abetting and conspiracy. The U.S. Army Field Manual provides that "[c]onspiracy, direct incitement, and attempts to commit, as well as complicity in the commission of, crimes against peace, crimes against humanity, and war crimes are punishable." *Id.* ch. 8, par. 500. Commanders can also be held responsible for war crimes committed either under their orders or by those under their command.

Military Order of November 13, 2001, Detention, Treatment, and Trial of Certain Non-Citizens in the War Against Terrorism
66 Fed. Reg. 57,833 (Nov. 13, 2001)

By the authority vested in me as President and as Commander in Chief of the Armed Forces of the United States by the Constitution and the laws of the United States of America, including the Authorization for Use of Military Force Joint Resolution (Public Law 107-40, 115 Stat. 224) and sections 821 and 836 of title 10, United States Code, it is hereby ordered as follows:

SECTION 1. *FINDINGS.*

(a) International terrorists, including members of al Qaeda, have carried out attacks on United States diplomatic and military personnel and activities abroad and on citizens and property within the United States on a scale that has created a state of armed conflict that requires the use of the United States Armed Forces.

(b) In light of grave acts of terrorism and threats of terrorism, including the terrorist attacks on Sept. 11, 2001, on the headquarters of the United States Department of Defense in the national capital region, on the World Trade Center in New York, and on civilian aircraft such as in Pennsylvania, I proclaimed a national emergency on Sept. 14, 2001 (Proclamation 7463, Declaration of National Emergency by Reason of Certain Terrorist Attacks).

(c) Individuals acting alone and in concert involved in international terrorism possess both the capability and the intention to undertake further terrorist attacks against the United States that, if not detected and prevented, will cause mass deaths, mass injuries, and massive destruction of property, and may place at risk the continuity of the operations of the United States government.

(d) The ability of the United States to protect the United States and its citizens, and to help its allies and other cooperating nations protect their nations and their citizens, from such further terrorist attacks depends in significant part upon using the United States Armed Forces to identify terrorists and those who support them, to disrupt their activities, and to eliminate their ability to conduct or support such attacks.

(e) To protect the United States and its citizens, and for the effective conduct of military operations and prevention of terrorist attacks, it is necessary for individuals subject to this order pursuant to section 2 hereof to be detained, and, when tried, to be tried for violations of the laws of war and other applicable laws by military tribunals.

(f) Given the danger to the safety of the United States and the nature of international terrorism, and to the extent provided by and under this order, I find consistent with section 836 of title 10, United States Code, that it is not practicable to apply in military commissions under this order the principles of law and the rules of evidence generally recognized in the trial of criminal cases in the United States district courts.

(g) Having fully considered the magnitude of the potential deaths, injuries, and property destruction that would result from potential acts of terrorism against the United States, and the probability that such acts will occur, I have determined that an extraordinary emergency exists for national defense purposes, that this emergency constitutes an urgent and compelling government interest, and that issuance of this order is necessary to meet the emergency.

SECTION 2.   *DEFINITION AND POLICY.*

(a) The term "individual subject to this order" shall mean any individual who is not a United States citizen with respect to whom I determine from time to time in writing that:

(1) there is reason to believe that such individual, at the relevant times,

(i) is or was a member of the organization known as al Qaeda;

(ii) has engaged in, aided or abetted, or conspired to commit, acts of international terrorism, or acts in preparation therefor, that have caused, threaten to cause, or have as their aim to cause, injury to or adverse effects on the United States, its citizens, national security, foreign policy, or economy; or

(iii) has knowingly harbored one or more individuals described in subparagraphs (i) or (ii) of subsection 2(a)(1) of this order; and

(2) it is in the interest of the United States that such individual be subject to this order.

(b) It is the policy of the United States that the secretary of defense shall take all necessary measures to ensure that any individual subject to this order is detained in accordance with section 3, and, if the individual is to be tried, that such individual is tried only in accordance with section 4.

(c) It is further the policy of the United States that any individual subject to this order who is not already under the control of the Secretary of Defense but who is under the control of any other officer or agent of the United States or any state shall, upon delivery of a copy of such written determination to such officer or agent, forthwith be placed under the control of the Secretary of Defense.

SECTION 3. *DETENTION AUTHORITY OF THE SECRETARY OF DEFENSE.*

Any individual subject to this order shall be —

(a) detained at an appropriate location designated by the Secretary of Defense outside or within the United States;

(b) treated humanely, without any adverse distinction based on race, color, religion, gender, birth, wealth, or any similar criteria;

(c) afforded adequate food, drinking water, shelter, clothing, and medical treatment;

(d) allowed the free exercise of religion consistent with the requirements of such detention; and

(e) detained in accordance with such other conditions as the Secretary of Defense may prescribe.

SECTION 4. *AUTHORITY OF THE SECRETARY OF DEFENSE REGARDING TRIALS OF INDIVIDUALS SUBJECT TO THIS ORDER.*

(a) Any individual subject to this order shall, when tried, be tried by military commission for any and all offenses triable by military commission that such individual is alleged to have committed, and may be punished in accordance with the penalties provided under applicable law, including life imprisonment or death.

(b) As a military function and in light of the findings in section 1, including subsection (f) thereof, the Secretary of Defense shall issue such orders and regulations, including orders for the appointment of one or more military commissions, as may be necessary to carry out subsection (a) of this section.

(c) Orders and regulations issued under subsection (b) of this section shall include, but not be limited to, rules for the conduct of the proceedings of military commissions, including pretrial, trial, and post-trial procedures, modes of proof, issuance of process, and qualifications of attorneys, which shall at a minimum provide for —

(1) military commissions to sit at any time and any place, consistent with such guidance regarding time and place as the Secretary of Defense may provide;

(2) a full and fair trial, with the military commission sitting as the triers of both fact and law;

(3) admission of such evidence as would, in the opinion of the presiding officer of the military commission (or instead, if any other member of the commission so requests at the time the presiding officer renders that opinion, the opinion of the commission rendered at that time by a majority of the commission), have probative value to a reasonable person;

(4) in a manner consistent with the protection of information classified or classifiable under Executive Order 12958 of April 17, 1995, as amended, or any successor Executive Order, protected by statute or rule from unauthorized disclosure, or otherwise protected by law, (A) the handling of, admission into evidence of, and access to materials and information, and (B) the conduct, closure of, and access to proceedings;

(5) conduct of the prosecution by one or more attorneys designated by the Secretary of Defense and conduct of the defense by attorneys for the individual subject to this order;

(6) conviction only upon the concurrence of two-thirds of the members of the commission present at the time of the vote, a majority being present;

(7) sentencing only upon the concurrence of two-thirds of the members of the commission present at the time of the vote, a majority being present; and

(8) submission of the record of the trial, including any conviction or sentence, for review and final decision by me or by the Secretary of Defense if so designated by me for that purpose.

SECTION 5. *OBLIGATION OF OTHER AGENCIES TO ASSIST THE SECRETARY OF DEFENSE.*

Departments, agencies, entities, and officers of the United States shall, to the maximum extent permitted by law, provide to the Secretary of Defense such assistance as he may request to implement this order.

SECTION 6. *ADDITIONAL AUTHORITIES OF THE SECRETARY OF DEFENSE.*

(a) As a military function and in light of the findings in section 1, the Secretary of Defense shall issue such orders and regulations as may be necessary to carry out any of the provisions of this order.

(b) The Secretary of Defense may perform any of his functions or duties, and may exercise any of the powers provided to him under this order (other than under section 4(c)(8) hereof) in accordance with section 113(d) of title 10, United States Code.

SECTION 7. *RELATIONSHIP TO OTHER LAW AND FORUMS.*

(a) Nothing in this order shall be construed to —

(1) authorize the disclosure of state secrets to any person not otherwise authorized to have access to them;

(2) limit the authority of the President as Commander in Chief of the Armed Forces or the power of the President to grant reprieves and pardons; or

(3) limit the lawful authority of the Secretary of Defense, any military commander, or any other officer or agent of the United States or of any State to detain or try any person who is not an individual subject to this order.

(b) With respect to any individual subject to this order —

(1) military tribunals shall have exclusive jurisdiction with respect to offenses by the individual; and

(2) the individual shall not be privileged to seek any remedy or maintain any proceeding, directly or indirectly, or to have any such remedy or proceeding sought on the individual's behalf, in

(i) any court of the United States, or any State thereof,

(ii) any court of any foreign nation, or

(iii) any international tribunal.

(c) This order is not intended to and does not create any right, benefit, or privilege, substantive or procedural, enforceable at law or equity by any party, against the United States, its departments, agencies, or other entities, its officers or employees, or any other person.

(d) For purposes of this order, the term "state" includes any State, district, territory, or possession of the United States.

(e) I reserve the authority to direct the Secretary of Defense, at any time hereafter, to transfer to a governmental authority control of any individual subject to this order. Nothing in this order shall be construed to limit the authority of any such governmental authority to prosecute any individual for whom control is transferred.

SECTION 8.   *PUBLICATION.*

This order shall be published in the *Federal Register.*

George W. Bush

Hamdan v. Rumsfeld
United States Supreme Court, 2006
548 U.S. 557

[Salim Ahmed Hamdan, a Yemeni national, was captured in November 2001 by militia forces in Afghanistan and turned over to the U.S. military. In June 2002, he was transported to the military prison at Guantánamo Bay, Cuba. On July 3, 2003, President Bush determined that Hamdan (and five other detainees at Guantánamo Bay) were subject to the Military Order of November 13, 2001, and therefore triable by military commission. Military counsel was appointed for him, and his counsel promptly filed demands for charges and for a speedy trial pursuant to the Uniform Code of Military Justice (UCMJ), 10 U.S.C. §§801-946 (2006 & Supp. IV 2010). The demands were denied by a military official on the ground that Hamdan was not entitled to any of the protections of the UCMJ. On July 13, 2004, Hamdan was charged with conspiring with members of Al Qaeda to commit the offenses of "attacking civilians; attacking civilian objects; murder by an unprivileged belligerent; and terrorism." Among the overt acts listed in the charges was the claim that Hamdan acted as Osama bin Laden's "bodyguard and personal driver."

Before his trial could begin, Hamdan challenged the legality of the commission by habeas and mandamus petitions. The district court granted his petition for a writ of habeas corpus, but the Court of Appeals, in an opinion by then Judge Roberts, reversed. The Supreme Court granted certiorari and issued the following opinion.]

Justice STEVENS announced the judgment of the Court and delivered the opinion of the Court with respect to Parts I through IV, Parts VI through VI-D-iii, Part VI-D-v, and Part VII, and an opinion with respect to Parts V and VI-D-iv, in which Justice SOUTER, Justice GINSBURG, and Justice BREYER join.... [Hamdan] concedes that a court-martial constituted in accordance with the Uniform Code of Military Justice (UCMJ) would have authority to try him. His objection is that the military commission the President has convened lacks such authority, for two principal reasons: First, neither congressional Act nor the common law of war supports trial by this commission for the crime of conspiracy—an offense that, Hamdan says, is not a violation of the law of

war. Second, Hamdan contends, the procedures that the President has adopted to
try him violate the most basic tenets of military and international law, including
the principle that a defendant must be permitted to see and hear the evidence
against him. . . .

  For the reasons that follow, we conclude that the military commission convened
to try Hamdan lacks power to proceed because its structure and procedures violate
both the UCMJ and the Geneva Conventions. Four of us also conclude, see Part V,
infra, that the offense with which Hamdan has been charged is not an "offens[e] that
by . . . the law of war may be tried by military commissions." 10 U.S.C. §821. . . .

II

  [The Court found that the Detainee Treatment Act, *supra* p. 400, did not preclude review.]

III

  [The Court refused to abstain pending completion of the military commission
proceedings against Hamdan, noting that the comity considerations favoring abstention in *Schlesinger v. Councilman,* 420 U.S. 738 (1975), did not apply to Hamdan's
case.] . . .

  . . . First, Hamdan is not a member of our Nation's Armed Forces, so concerns
about military discipline do not apply. Second, the tribunal convened to try Hamdan
is not part of the integrated system of military courts, complete with independent
review panels, that Congress has established. Unlike the officer in *Councilman,* Hamdan has no right to appeal any conviction to the civilian judges of the Court of Military
Appeals (now called the United States Court of Appeals for the Armed Forces, see
Pub. L. 103-337, 108 Stat. 2831). Instead, under Dept. of Defense Military Commission Order No. 1 (Commission Order No. 1), which was issued by the President on
March 21, 2002, and amended most recently on August 31, 2005, and which governs
the procedures for Hamdan's commission, any conviction would be reviewed by a
panel consisting of three military officers designated by the Secretary of Defense.
Commission Order No. 1 §6(H)(4). Commission Order No. 1 provides that appeal
of a review panel's decision may be had only to the Secretary of Defense himself,
§6(H)(5), and then, finally, to the President, §6(H)(6).

  We have no doubt that the various individuals assigned review power under
Commission Order No. 1 would strive to act impartially and ensure that Hamdan
receive all protections to which he is entitled. Nonetheless, these review bodies clearly
lack the structural insulation from military influence that characterizes the Court of
Appeals for the Armed Forces, and thus bear insufficient conceptual similarity to state
courts to warrant invocation of abstention principles. . . .

IV

  The military commission, a tribunal neither mentioned in the Constitution nor
created by statute, was born of military necessity. See W. Winthrop, Military Law and
Precedents 831 (rev. 2d ed. 1920) (hereinafter Winthrop). . . .

  . . . As further discussed below, each aspect of that seemingly broad [military
commission] jurisdiction was in fact supported by a separate military exigency.

Generally, though, the need for military commissions during this period — as during the Mexican War — was driven largely by the then very limited jurisdiction of courts-martial: "The *occasion* for the military commission arises principally from the fact that the jurisdiction of the court-martial proper, in our law, is restricted by statute almost exclusively to members of the military force and to certain specific offences defined in a written code." *Id.*, at 831 (emphasis in original).

Exigency alone, of course, will not justify the establishment and use of penal tribunals not contemplated by Article I, §8 and Article III, §1 of the Constitution unless some other part of that document authorizes a response to the felt need. See *Ex parte Milligan*, [71 U.S.] 4 Wall. 2, 121 (1866) ("Certainly no part of the judicial power of the country was conferred on [military commissions.]"). And that authority, if it exists, can derive only from the powers granted jointly to the President and Congress in time of war. See *In re Yamashita*, 327 U.S. 1, 11 (1946).

The Constitution makes the President the "Commander in Chief" of the Armed Forces, Art. II, §2, cl. 1, but vests in Congress the powers to "declare War . . . and make Rules concerning Captures on Land and Water," Art. I, §8, cl. 11, to "raise and support Armies," *id.*, cl. 12, to "define and punish . . . Offences against the Law of Nations," *id.*, cl. 10, and "To make Rules for the Government and Regulation of the land and naval Forces," *id.*, cl. 14. The interplay between these powers was described by Chief Justice Chase in the seminal case of *Ex parte Milligan*:

> "The power to make the necessary laws is in Congress; the power to execute in the President. Both powers imply many subordinate and auxiliary powers. Each includes all authorities essential to its due exercise. But neither can the President, in war more than in peace, intrude upon the proper authority of Congress, nor Congress upon the proper authority of the President. . . . Congress cannot direct the conduct of campaigns, nor can the President, or any commander under him, without the sanction of Congress, institute tribunals for the trial and punishment of offences, either of soldiers or civilians, unless in cases of a controlling necessity, which justifies what it compels, or at least insures acts of indemnity from the justice of the legislature." 4 Wall., at 139-140.

Whether Chief Justice Chase was correct in suggesting that the President may constitutionally convene military commissions "without the sanction of Congress" in cases of "controlling necessity" is a question this Court has not answered definitively, and need not answer today. For we held in [*Ex parte Quirin*, 317 U.S. 1 (1942)] that Congress had, through Article of War 15, sanctioned the use of military commissions in such circumstances. 317 U.S., at 28 ("By the Articles of War, and especially Article 15, Congress has explicitly provided, so far as it may constitutionally do so, that military tribunals shall have jurisdiction to try offenders or offenses against the law of war in appropriate cases"). Article 21 of the UCMJ, the language of which is substantially identical to the old Article 15 and was preserved by Congress after World War II, reads as follows:

> "Jurisdiction of courts-martial not exclusive."
> "The provisions of this code conferring jurisdiction upon courts-martial shall not be construed as depriving military commissions, provost courts, or other military tribunals of concurrent jurisdiction in respect of offenders or offenses that by statute or by the law of war may be tried by such military commissions, provost courts, or other military tribunals." 64 Stat. 115.

We have no occasion to revisit *Quirin*'s controversial characterization of Article of War 15 as congressional authorization for military commissions. Contrary to the Government's assertion, however, even *Quirin* did not view the authorization as a sweeping mandate for the President to "invoke military commissions when he deems them necessary." Rather, the *Quirin* Court recognized that Congress had simply preserved what power, under the Constitution and the common law of war, the President had had before 1916 to convene military commissions — with the express condition that the President and those under his command comply with the law of war. See 317 U.S., at 28-29.[23] That much is evidenced by the Court's inquiry, *following* its conclusion that Congress had authorized military commissions, into whether the law of war had indeed been complied with in that case.

The Government would have us dispense with the inquiry that the *Quirin* Court undertook and find in either the AUMF [Authorization for Use of Military Force, Pub. L. No. 107-40, 115 Stat. 224 (2001)] or the DTA [Detainee Treatment Act of 2005, Pub. L. 109-148, 119 Stat. 2739] specific, overriding authorization for the very commission that has been convened to try Hamdan. Neither of these congressional Acts, however, expands the President's authority to convene military commissions. First, while we assume that the AUMF activated the President's war powers, see *Hamdi v. Rumsfeld*, 542 U.S. 507 (2004) (plurality opinion), and that those powers include the authority to convene military commissions in appropriate circumstances, there is nothing in the text or legislative history of the AUMF even hinting that Congress intended to expand or alter the authorization set forth in Article 21 of the UCMJ.[24]

Likewise, the DTA cannot be read to authorize this commission. Although the DTA, unlike either Article 21 or the AUMF, was enacted after the President had convened Hamdan's commission, it contains no language authorizing that tribunal or any other at Guantanamo Bay. The DTA obviously "recognize[s]" the existence of the Guantanamo Bay commissions in the weakest sense because it references some of the military orders governing them and creates limited judicial review of their "final decision[s]," DTA §1005(e)(3), 119 Stat. 2743. But the statute also pointedly reserves judgment on whether "the Constitution and laws of the United States are applicable" in reviewing such decisions and whether, if they are, the "standards and procedures" used to try Hamdan and other detainees actually violate the "Constitution and laws."

Together, the UCMJ, the AUMF, and the DTA at most acknowledge a general Presidential authority to convene military commissions in circumstances where justified under the "Constitution and laws," including the law of war. Absent a more specific congressional authorization, the task of this Court is, as it was in *Quirin*, to decide whether Hamdan's military commission is so justified. It is to that inquiry we now turn.

---

23. Whether or not the President has independent power, absent congressional authorization, to convene military commissions, he may not disregard limitations that Congress has, in proper exercise of its own war powers, placed on his powers. See *Youngstown Sheet & Tube Co. v. Sawyer*, 343 U.S. 579, 637 (1952) (Jackson, J., concurring). The Government does not argue otherwise.

24. On this point, it is noteworthy that the Court in *Ex parte Quirin*, 317 U.S. 1 (1942), looked beyond Congress' declaration of war and accompanying authorization for use of force during World War II, and relied instead on Article of War 15 to find that Congress had authorized the use of military commissions in some circumstances. Justice Thomas' assertion that we commit "error" in reading Article 21 of the UCMJ to place limitations upon the President's use of military commissions ignores the reasoning in *Quirin*.

V

The common law governing military commissions may be gleaned from past practice and what sparse legal precedent exists. Commissions historically have been used in three situations. First, they have substituted for civilian courts at times and in places where martial law has been declared. Their use in these circumstances has raised constitutional questions, see *Duncan v. Kahanamoku,* 327 U.S. 304 (1946); *Milligan,* 4 Wall., at 121-122, but is well recognized. Second, commissions have been established to try civilians "as part of a temporary military government over occupied enemy territory or territory regained from an enemy where civilian government cannot and does not function." *Duncan,* 327 U.S., at 314; see *Milligan,* 4 Wall., at 141-142 (Chase, C.J., concurring in judgment) (distinguishing "martial law proper" from "military government" in occupied territory)....

The third type of commission, convened as an "incident to the conduct of war" when there is a need "to seize and subject to disciplinary measures those enemies who in their attempt to thwart or impede our military effort have violated the law of war," *Quirin,* 317 U.S., at 28-29, has been described as "utterly different" from the other two. Not only is its jurisdiction limited to offenses cognizable during time of war, but its role is primarily a factfinding one — to determine, typically on the battlefield itself, whether the defendant has violated the law of war. The last time the U.S. Armed Forces used the law-of-war military commission was during World War II. In *Quirin,* this Court sanctioned President Roosevelt's use of such a tribunal to try Nazi saboteurs captured on American soil during the War. 317 U.S. 1. And in *Yamashita,* we held that a military commission had jurisdiction to try a Japanese commander for failing to prevent troops under his command from committing atrocities in the Philippines. 327 U.S. 1.

Quirin is the model the Government invokes most frequently to defend the commission convened to try Hamdan. That is both appropriate and unsurprising. Since Guantanamo Bay is neither enemy-occupied territory nor under martial law, the law-of-war commission is the only model available. At the same time, no more robust model of executive power exists; *Quirin* represents the high-water mark of military power to try enemy combatants for war crimes.

The classic treatise penned by Colonel William Winthrop, whom we have called "the 'Blackstone of Military Law,'" *Reid v. Covert,* 354 U.S. 1, 19, n.38 (1957) (plurality opinion), describes at least four preconditions for exercise of jurisdiction by a tribunal of the type convened to try Hamdan. First, "[a] military commission, (except where otherwise authorized by statute), can legally assume jurisdiction only of offenses committed within the field of the command of the convening commander." Winthrop 836. The "field of command" in these circumstances means the "theatre of war." *Ibid.* Second, the offense charged "must have been committed within the period of the war." *Id.,* at 837. No jurisdiction exists to try offenses "committed either before or after the war." *Ibid.* Third, a military commission not established pursuant to martial law or an occupation may try only "[i]ndividuals of the enemy's army who have been guilty of illegitimate warfare or other offences in violation of the laws of war" and members of one's own army "who, in time of war, become chargeable with crimes or offences not cognizable, or triable, by the criminal courts or under the Articles of war." *Id.,* at 838. Finally, a law-of-war commission has jurisdiction to try only two kinds of offense: "Violations of the laws and usages of war cognizable by military tribunals only," and "[b]reaches of military orders or regulations for which offenders are not legally triable by court-martial under the Articles of war." *Id.*, at 839.

... The question is whether the preconditions designed to ensure that a military necessity exists to justify the use of this extraordinary tribunal have been satisfied here.

The charge against Hamdan ... alleges a conspiracy extending over a number of years, from 1996 to November 2001.[30] All but two months of that more than 5-year-long period preceded the attacks of September 11, 2001, and the enactment of the AUMF — the Act of Congress on which the Government relies for exercise of its war powers and thus for its authority to convene military commissions.[31] Neither the purported agreement with Osama bin Laden and others to commit war crimes, nor a single overt act, is alleged to have occurred in a theater of war or on any specified date after September 11, 2001. None of the overt acts that Hamdan is alleged to have committed violates the law of war.

These facts alone cast doubt on the legality of the charge and, hence, the commission; as Winthrop makes plain, the offense alleged must have been committed both in a theater of war and *during*, not before, the relevant conflict. But the deficiencies in the time and place allegations also underscore — indeed are symptomatic of — the most serious defect of this charge: The offense it alleges is not triable by law-of-war military commission.

There is no suggestion that Congress has, in exercise of its constitutional authority to "define and punish ... Offences against the Law of Nations," U.S. Const., Art. I, §8, cl. 10, positively identified "conspiracy" as a war crime. As we explained in *Quirin*, that is not necessarily fatal to the Government's claim of authority to try the alleged offense by military commission;Congress, through Article 21 of the UCMJ, has "incorporated by reference" the common law of war, which may render triable by military commission certain offenses not defined by statute. 317 U.S., at 30. When, however, neither the elements of the offense nor the range of permissible punishments is defined by statute or treaty, the precedent must be plain and unambiguous. To demand any less would be to risk concentrating in military hands a degree of adjudicative and punitive power in excess of that contemplated either by statute or by the Constitution. ...

At a minimum, the Government must make a substantial showing that the crime for which it seeks to try a defendant by military commission is acknowledged to be an offense against the law of war. That burden is far from satisfied here. The crime of "conspiracy" has rarely if ever been tried as such in this country by any law-of-war military commission not exercising some other form of jurisdiction, and does not

---

30. The elements of this conspiracy charge have been defined not by Congress but by the President. See Military Commission Instruction No. 2, 32 C.F.R. §11.6 (2005).

31. Justice Thomas would treat Osama bin Laden's 1996 declaration of jihad against Americans as the inception of the war. But even the Government does not go so far; although the United States had for some time prior to the attacks of September 11, 2001, been aggressively pursuing al Qaeda, neither in the charging document nor in submissions before this Court has the Government asserted that the President's *war powers* were activated prior to September 11, 2001. Justice Thomas' further argument that the AUMF is "backward looking" and therefore authorizes *trial by military commission* of crimes that occurred prior to the inception of war is insupportable. If nothing else, Article 21 of the UCMJ requires that the President comply with the law of war in his use of military commissions. As explained in the text, the law of war permits trial only of offenses "committed within the period of the war." Winthrop 837; see also *Quirin*, 317 U.S., at 28-29 (observing that law-of-war military commissions may be used to try "those enemies *who in their attempt to thwart or impede our military effort* have violated the law of war" (emphasis added)). ...

appear in either the Geneva Conventions or the Hague Conventions—the major treaties on the law of war....

... [T]he only "conspiracy" crimes that have been recognized by international war crimes tribunals (whose jurisdiction often extends beyond war crimes proper to crimes against humanity and crimes against the peace) are conspiracy to commit genocide and common plan to wage aggressive war, which is a crime against the peace and requires for its commission actual participation in a "concrete plan to wage war." 1 Trial of the Major War Criminals Before the International Military Tribunal: Nuremberg, 14 November 1945-1 October 1946, p. 225 (1947)....

In sum, the sources that the Government and Justice Thomas rely upon to show that conspiracy to violate the law of war is itself a violation of the law of war in fact demonstrate quite the opposite. Far from making the requisite substantial showing, the Government has failed even to offer a "merely colorable" case for inclusion of conspiracy among those offenses cognizable by law-of-war military commission. Cf. *Quirin*, 317 U.S., at 36. Because the charge does not support the commission's jurisdiction, the commission lacks authority to try Hamdan.

The charge's shortcomings are not merely formal, but are indicative of a broader inability on the Executive's part here to satisfy the most basic precondition — at least in the absence of specific congressional authorization — for establishment of military commissions: military necessity. Hamdan's tribunal was appointed not by a military commander in the field of battle, but by a retired major general stationed away from any active hostilities. Cf. *Rasul v. Bush*, 542 U.S., at 487 (Kennedy, J., concurring in judgment) (observing that "Guantanamo Bay is...far removed from any hostilities"). Hamdan is charged not with an overt act for which he was caught redhanded in a theater of war and which military efficiency demands be tried expeditiously, but with an *agreement* the inception of which long predated the attacks of September 11, 2001 and the AUMF. That may well be a crime,[41] but it is not an offense that "by the law of war may be tried by military commissio[n]." 10 U.S.C. §821. None of the overt acts alleged to have been committed in furtherance of the agreement is itself a war crime, or even necessarily occurred during time of, or in a theater of, war. Any urgent need for imposition or execution of judgment is utterly belied by the record; Hamdan was arrested in November 2001 and he was not charged until mid-2004. These simply are not the circumstances in which, by any stretch of the historical evidence or this Court's precedents, a military commission established by Executive Order under the authority of Article 21 of the UCMJ may lawfully try a person and subject him to punishment.

VI

Whether or not the Government has charged Hamdan with an offense against the law of war cognizable by military commission, the commission lacks power to proceed. The UCMJ conditions the President's use of military commissions on compliance not only with the American common law of war, but also with the rest of the UCMJ itself, insofar as applicable, and with the "rules and precepts of the law of

41. Justice Thomas' suggestion that our conclusion precludes the Government from bringing to justice those who conspire to commit acts of terrorism is therefore wide of the mark. That conspiracy is not a violation of the law of war triable by military commission does not mean the Government may not, for example, prosecute by court-martial or in federal court those caught "plotting terrorist atrocities like the bombing of the Khobar Towers."

nations," *Quirin,* 317 U.S., at 28 — including, *inter alia,* the four Geneva Conventions signed in 1949. The procedures that the Government has decreed will govern Hamdan's trial by commission violate these laws.

A

The commission's procedures are set forth in Commission Order No. 1, which was amended most recently on August 31, 2005 — after Hamdan's trial had already begun. Every commission established pursuant to Commission Order No. 1 must have a presiding officer and at least three other members, all of whom must be commissioned officers. §4(A)(1). The presiding officer's job is to rule on questions of law and other evidentiary and interlocutory issues; the other members make findings and, if applicable, sentencing decisions. §4(A)(5). The accused is entitled to appointed military counsel and may hire civilian counsel at his own expense so long as such counsel is a U.S. citizen with security clearance "at the level SECRET or higher." §§4(C)(2)-(3).

The accused also is entitled to a copy of the charge(s) against him, both in English and his own language (if different), to a presumption of innocence, and to certain other rights typically afforded criminal defendants in civilian courts and courts-martial. See §§5(A)-(P). These rights are subject, however, to one glaring condition: The accused and his civilian counsel may be excluded from, and precluded from ever learning what evidence was presented during, any part of the proceeding that either the Appointing Authority or the presiding officer decides to "close." Grounds for such closure "include the protection of information classified or classifiable . . . ; information protected by law or rule from unauthorized disclosure; the physical safety of participants in Commission proceedings, including prospective witnesses; intelligence and law enforcement sources, methods, or activities; and other national security interests." §6(B)(3). Appointed military defense counsel must be privy to these closed sessions, but may, at the presiding officer's discretion, be forbidden to reveal to his or her client what took place therein. *Ibid.*

Another striking feature of the rules governing Hamdan's commission is that they permit the admission of *any* evidence that, in the opinion of the presiding officer, "would have probative value to a reasonable person." §6(D)(1). Under this test, not only is testimonial hearsay and evidence obtained through coercion fully admissible, but neither live testimony nor witnesses' written statements need be sworn. See §§6(D)(2)(b), (3). Moreover, the accused and his civilian counsel may be denied access to evidence in the form of "protected information" (which includes classified information as well as "information protected by law or rule from unauthorized disclosure" and "information concerning other national security interests," §§6(B)(3), 6(D)(5)(a)(v)), so long as the presiding officer concludes that the evidence is "probative" under §6(D)(1) and that its admission without the accused's knowledge would not "result in the denial of a full and fair trial." §6(D)(5)(b).[43] Finally, a presiding officer's determination that evidence "would not have probative

---

43. As the District Court observed, this section apparently permits reception of testimony from a confidential informant in circumstances where "Hamdan will not be permitted to hear the testimony, see the witness's face, or learn his name. If the government has information developed by interrogation of witnesses in Afghanistan or elsewhere, it can offer such evidence in transcript form, or even as summaries of transcripts." 344 F. Supp. 2d 152, 168 (D.D.C. 2004).

value to a reasonable person" may be overridden by a majority of the other commission members. §6(D)(1).

Once all the evidence is in, the commission members (not including the presiding officer) must vote on the accused's guilt. A two-thirds vote will suffice for both a verdict of guilty and for imposition of any sentence not including death (the imposition of which requires a unanimous vote). §6(F). Any appeal is taken to a three-member review panel composed of military officers and designated by the Secretary of Defense, only one member of which need have experience as a judge. §6(H)(4). The review panel is directed to "disregard any variance from procedures specified in this Order or elsewhere that would not materially have affected the outcome of the trial before the Commission." *Ibid.* Once the panel makes its recommendation to the Secretary of Defense, the Secretary can either remand for further proceedings or forward the record to the President with his recommendation as to final disposition. §6(H)(5). The President then, unless he has delegated the task to the Secretary, makes the "final decision." §6(H)(6). He may change the commission's findings or sentence only in a manner favorable to the accused. *Ibid.* . . .

C

In part because the difference between military commissions and courts-martial originally was a difference of jurisdiction alone, and in part to protect against abuse and ensure evenhandedness under the pressures of war, the procedures governing trials by military commission historically have been the same as those governing courts-martial. . . .

The uniformity principle is not an inflexible one; it does not preclude all departures from the procedures dictated for use by courts-martial. But any departure must be tailored to the exigency that necessitates it. See Winthrop 835, n.81. That understanding is reflected in Article 36 of the UCMJ, which provides:

> "(a) The procedure, including modes of proof, in cases before courts-martial, courts of inquiry, military commissions, and other military tribunals may be prescribed by the President by regulations which shall, so far as he considers practicable, apply the principles of law and the rules of evidence generally recognized in the trial of criminal cases in the United States district courts, but which may not be contrary to or inconsistent with this chapter.
> "(b) All rules and regulations made under this article shall be uniform insofar as practicable and shall be reported to Congress." 70A Stat. 50.

Article 36 places two restrictions on the President's power to promulgate rules of procedure for courts-martial and military commissions alike. First, no procedural rule he adopts may be "contrary to or inconsistent with" the UCMJ — however practical it may seem. Second, the rules adopted must be "uniform insofar as practicable." That is, the rules applied to military commissions must be the same as those applied to courts-martial unless such uniformity proves impracticable. . . .

. . . Without reaching the question whether any provision of Commission Order No. 1 is strictly "contrary to or inconsistent with" other provisions of the UCMJ, we conclude that the "practicability" determination the President has made is insufficient to justify variances from the procedures governing courts-martial. Subsection (b) of Article 36 was added after World War II, and requires a different showing of impracticability from the one required by subsection (a). Subsection (a) requires that the rules the President promulgates for courts-martial, provost courts, and military commissions alike conform to those that govern procedures in *Article III courts,* "so far as *he considers* practicable." 10 U.S.C. §836(a) (emphasis added). Subsection (b), by contrast, demands that the rules applied in courts-martial, provost courts, and military commissions — whether or not they conform with the Federal Rules of Evidence — be "uniform *insofar as practicable.*" §836(b) (emphasis added). Under the latter provision, then, the rules set forth in the Manual for Courts-Martial must apply to military commissions unless impracticable.

The President here has determined, pursuant to subsection (a), that it is impracticable to apply the rules and principles of law that govern "the trial of criminal cases in the United States district courts," §836(a), to Hamdan's commission. We assume that complete deference is owed that determination. The President has not, however, made a similar official determination that it is impracticable to apply the rules for courts-martial. And even if subsection (b)'s requirements may be satisfied without such an official determination, the requirements of that subsection are not satisfied here.

Nothing in the record before us demonstrates that it would be impracticable to apply court-martial rules in this case. There is no suggestion, for example, of any logistical difficulty in securing properly sworn and authenticated evidence or in applying the usual principles of relevance and admissibility. Assuming *arguendo* that the reasons articulated in the President's Article 36(a) determination ought to be considered in evaluating the impracticability of applying court-martial rules, the only reason offered in support of that determination is the danger posed by international terrorism. Without for one moment underestimating that danger, it is not evident to us why it should require, in the case of Hamdan's trial, any variance from the rules that govern courts-martial.

The absence of any showing of impracticability is particularly disturbing when considered in light of the clear and admitted failure to apply one of the most fundamental protections afforded not just by the Manual for Courts-Martial but also by the UCMJ itself: the right to be present. See 10 U.S.C.A. §839(c) (Supp. 2006). Whether or not that departure technically is "contrary to or inconsistent with" the terms of the UCMJ, 10 U.S.C. §836(a), the jettisoning of so basic a right cannot lightly be excused as "practicable."

Under the circumstances, then, the rules applicable in courts-martial must apply. Since it is undisputed that Commission Order No. 1 deviates in many significant respects from those rules, it necessarily violates Article 36(b).

The Government's objection that requiring compliance with the court-martial rules imposes an undue burden both ignores the plain meaning of Article 36(b) and misunderstands the purpose and the history of military commissions. The military commission was not born of a desire to dispense a more summary form of justice than is afforded by courts-martial; it developed, rather, as a tribunal of necessity to be employed when courts-martial lacked jurisdiction over either the accused or the subject matter. See Winthrop 831. Exigency lent the commission its legitimacy, but did not further justify the wholesale jettisoning of procedural protections. That history explains why the military commission's procedures typically have been the ones used by courts-martial. That the jurisdiction of the two tribunals today may sometimes overlap does not detract from the force of this history. Article 21 did not transform the military commission from a tribunal of true exigency into a more convenient adjudicatory tool. Article 36, confirming as much, strikes a careful balance between uniform procedure and the need to accommodate exigencies that may sometimes arise in a theater of war. That Article not having been complied with here, the rules specified for Hamdan's trial are illegal.

D

The procedures adopted to try Hamdan also violate the Geneva Conventions. The Court of Appeals dismissed Hamdan's Geneva Convention challenge on three independent grounds: (1) the Geneva Conventions are not judicially enforceable; (2) Hamdan in any event is not entitled to their protections; and (3) even if he is entitled to their protections,... abstention is appropriate....

i . . .

. . . We may assume that "the obvious scheme" of the 1949 Conventions is identical in all relevant respects to that of the 1929 Convention,[57] and even that scheme would, absent some other provision of law, preclude Hamdan's invocation of the Convention's provisions as an independent source of law binding the Government's actions and furnishing petitioner with any enforceable right. For, regardless of the nature of the rights conferred on Hamdan, cf. *United States v. Rauscher*, 119 U.S. 407 (1886), they are, as the Government does not dispute, part of the law of war. And compliance with the law of war is the condition upon which the authority set forth in Article 21 is granted.

ii . . .

The conflict with al Qaeda is not, according to the Government, a conflict to which the full protections afforded detainees under the 1949 Geneva Conventions apply because Article 2 of those Conventions (which appears in all four Conventions) renders the full protections applicable only to "all cases of declared war or of any other armed conflict which may arise between two or more of the High Contracting Parties." 6 U.S.T., at 3318. Since Hamdan was captured and detained incident to the conflict with al Qaeda and not the conflict with the Taliban, and since al Qaeda, unlike Afghanistan, is not a "High Contracting Party" — *i.e.,* a signatory of the Conventions, the protections of those Conventions are not, it is argued, applicable to Hamdan.[60]

We need not decide the merits of this argument because there is at least one provision of the Geneva Conventions that applies here even if the relevant conflict is not one between signatories. Article 3, often referred to as Common Article 3 because, like Article 2, it appears in all four Geneva Conventions, provides that in a "conflict not of an international character occurring in the territory of one of the

57. But see, *e.g.,* 4 Int'l Comm. of Red Cross, Commentary: Geneva Convention Relative to the Protection of Civilian Persons in Time of War 21 (1958) (hereinafter GCIV Commentary) (the 1949 Geneva Conventions were written "first and foremost to protect individuals, and not to serve State interests"); GCIII Commentary 91 ("It was not... until the Conventions of 1949... that the existence of 'rights' conferred on prisoners of war was affirmed").

60. The President has stated that the conflict with the Taliban is a conflict to which the Geneva Conventions apply.

High Contracting Parties, each Party to the conflict shall be bound to apply, as a minimum," certain provisions protecting "[p]ersons taking no active part in the hostilities, including members of armed forces who have laid down their arms and those placed *hors de combat* by . . . detention." *Id.*, at 3318. One such provision prohibits "the passing of sentences and the carrying out of executions without previous judgment pronounced by a regularly constituted court affording all the judicial guarantees which are recognized as indispensable by civilized peoples." *Ibid.*

The Court of Appeals thought, and the Government asserts, that Common Article 3 does not apply to Hamdan because the conflict with al Qaeda, being "'international in scope,'" does not qualify as a "'conflict not of an international character.'" That reasoning is erroneous. The term "conflict not of an international character" is used here in contradistinction to a conflict between nations. So much is demonstrated by the "fundamental logic [of] the Convention's provisions on its application." [415 F.3d 33, 44 (D.C. Cir. 2005) (Williams, J., concurring).] Common Article 2 provides that "the present Convention shall apply to all cases of declared war or of any other armed conflict which may arise between two or more of the High Contracting Parties." 6 U.S.T., at 3318 (Art. 2, ¶1). High Contracting Parties (signatories) also must abide by all terms of the Conventions vis-à-vis one another even if one party to the conflict is a nonsignatory "Power," and must so abide vis-à-vis the nonsignatory if "the latter accepts and applies" those terms. *Ibid.* (Art. 2, ¶3). Common Article 3, by contrast, affords some minimal protection, falling short of full protection under the Conventions, to individuals associated with neither a signatory nor even a nonsignatory "Power" who are involved in a conflict "in the territory of" a signatory. The latter kind of conflict is distinguishable from the conflict described in Common Article 2 chiefly because it does not involve a clash between nations (whether signatories or not). In context, then, the phrase "not of an international character" bears its literal meaning. See, *e.g.*, J. Bentham, Introduction to the Principles of Morals and Legislation 6, 296 (J. Burns & H. Hart eds. 1970) (using the term "international law" as a "new though not inexpressive appellation" meaning "betwixt nation and nation"; defining "international" to include "mutual transactions between sovereigns as such"). . . .

iii

Common Article 3, then, is applicable here and, as indicated above, requires that Hamdan be tried by a "regularly constituted court affording all the judicial guarantees which are recognized as indispensable by civilized peoples." 6 U.S.T., at 3320 (Art. 3, ¶1(d)). While the term "regularly constituted court" is not specifically defined in either Common Article 3 or its accompanying commentary, other sources disclose its core meaning. The commentary accompanying a provision of the Fourth Geneva Convention, for example, defines "'regularly constituted'" tribunals to include "ordinary military courts" and "definitely exclud[e] all special tribunals." GCIV Commentary 340 (defining the term "properly constituted" in Article 66, which the commentary treats as identical to "regularly constituted"). . . .

The Government offers only a cursory defense of Hamdan's military commission in light of Common Article 3. As Justice Kennedy explains, that defense fails because "[t]he regular military courts in our system are the courts-martial established by congressional statutes." At a minimum, a military commission "can be 'regularly constituted' by the standards of our military justice system only if some practical need explains deviations from court-martial practice." As we have explained, see Part VI-C, *supra*, no such need has been demonstrated here.

iv

Inextricably intertwined with the question of regular constitution is the evaluation of the procedures governing the tribunal and whether they afford "all the judicial guarantees which are recognized as indispensable by civilized peoples." 6 U.S.T., at 3320 (Art. 3, ¶1(d)). Like the phrase "regularly constituted court," this phrase is not defined in the text of the Geneva Conventions. But it must be understood to incorporate at least the barest of those trial protections that have been recognized by customary international law. . . .

We agree with Justice Kennedy that the procedures adopted to try Hamdan deviate from those governing courts-martial in ways not justified by any "evident practical need," and for that reason, at least, fail to afford the requisite guarantees. We add only that, as noted in Part VI-A, *supra*, various provisions of Commission Order No. 1 dispense with the principles, articulated in Article 75 [of Protocol I to the Geneva Conventions of 1949, June 8, 1977, 1125 U.N.T.S. 3, 16 I.L.M. 1391] and indisputably part of the customary international law, that an accused must, absent disruptive conduct or consent, be present for his trial and must be privy to the evidence against him. See §§6(B)(3), (D). That the Government has a compelling interest in denying Hamdan access to certain sensitive information is not doubted. But, at least absent express statutory provision to the contrary, information used to convict a person of a crime must be disclosed to him. . . .

VII

We have assumed, as we must, that the allegations made in the Government's charge against Hamdan are true. We have assumed, moreover, the truth of the message implicit in that charge—viz., that Hamdan is a dangerous individual whose beliefs, if acted upon, would cause great harm and even death to innocent civilians, and who would act upon those beliefs if given the opportunity. It bears emphasizing that Hamdan does not challenge, and we do not today address, the Government's power to detain him for the duration of active hostilities in order to prevent such harm. But in undertaking to try Hamdan and subject him to criminal punishment, the Executive is bound to comply with the Rule of Law that prevails in this jurisdiction.

The judgment of the Court of Appeals is reversed, and the case is remanded for further proceedings.

It is so ordered.

The CHIEF JUSTICE took no part in the consideration or decision of this case.

Justice BREYER, with whom Justice KENNEDY, Justice SOUTER, and Justice GINSBURG join, concurring. The dissenters say that today's decision would "sorely hamper the President's ability to confront and defeat a new and deadly enemy." They suggest that it undermines our Nation's ability to "preven[t] future attacks" of the grievous sort that we have already suffered. That claim leads me to state briefly what I believe the majority sets forth both explicitly and implicitly at greater length. The Court's conclusion ultimately rests upon a single ground: Congress has not issued the Executive a "blank check." Cf. *Hamdi v. Rumsfeld*, 542 U.S. 507, 536 (2004) (plurality opinion). Indeed, Congress has denied the President the legislative authority to create military commissions of the kind at issue here. Nothing prevents the President from returning to Congress to seek the authority he believes necessary.

Where, as here, no emergency prevents consultation with Congress, judicial insistence upon that consultation does not weaken our Nation's ability to deal with danger. To the contrary, that insistence strengthens the Nation's ability to determine — through democratic means — how best to do so. The Constitution places its faith in those democratic means. Our Court today simply does the same.

Justice KENNEDY, with whom Justice SOUTER, Justice GINSBURG, and Justice BREYER join as to Parts I and II, concurring in part. Military Commission Order No. 1, which governs the military commission established to try petitioner Salim Hamdan for war crimes, exceeds limits that certain statutes, duly enacted by Congress, have placed on the President's authority to convene military courts. This is not a case, then, where the Executive can assert some unilateral authority to fill a void left by congressional inaction. It is a case where Congress, in the proper exercise of its powers as an independent branch of government, and as part of a long tradition of legislative involvement in matters of military justice, has considered the subject of military tribunals and set limits on the President's authority. Where a statute provides the conditions for the exercise of governmental power, its requirements are the result of a deliberative and reflective process engaging both of the political branches. Respect for laws derived from the customary operation of the Executive and Legislative Branches gives some assurance of stability in time of crisis. The Constitution is best preserved by reliance on standards tested over time and insulated from the pressures of the moment. . . .

I join the Court's opinion, save Parts V and VI-D-iv. To state my reasons for this reservation, and to show my agreement with the remainder of the Court's analysis by identifying particular deficiencies in the military commissions at issue, this separate opinion seems appropriate.

I

Trial by military commission raises separation-of-powers concerns of the highest order. Located within a single branch, these courts carry the risk that offenses will be defined, prosecuted, and adjudicated by executive officials without independent review. Concentration of power puts personal liberty in peril of arbitrary action by officials, an incursion the Constitution's three-part system is designed to avoid. It is imperative, then, that when military tribunals are established, full and proper authority exists for the Presidential directive. . . .

II . . .

These structural differences between the military commissions and courts-martial — the concentration of functions, including legal decisionmaking, in a single executive official; the less rigorous standards for composition of the tribunal; and the creation of special review procedures in place of institutions created and regulated by Congress — remove safeguards that are important to the fairness of the proceedings and the independence of the court. Congress has prescribed these guarantees for courts-martial; and no evident practical need explains the departures here. For these reasons the commission cannot be considered regularly constituted under United States law and thus does not satisfy Congress' requirement that military commissions conform to the law of war.

Apart from these structural issues, moreover, the basic procedures for the commissions deviate from procedures for courts-martial, in violation of §836(b). As the Court explains, the Military Commission Order abandons the detailed Military Rules of Evidence, which are modeled on the Federal Rules of Evidence in conformity with §836(a)'s requirement of presumptive compliance with district-court rules. . . .

In sum, as presently structured, Hamdan's military commission exceeds the bounds Congress has placed on the President's authority in §§836 and 821 of the UCMJ. Because Congress has prescribed these limits, Congress can change them, requiring a new analysis consistent with the Constitution and other governing laws. At this time, however, we must apply the standards Congress has provided. By those standards the military commission is deficient.

III

In light of the conclusion that the military commission here is unauthorized under the UCMJ, I see no need to consider several further issues addressed in the plurality opinion by Justice Stevens and the dissent by Justice Thomas. . . .

Justice SCALIA, with whom Justice THOMAS and Justice ALITO join, dissenting. . . . [Justice Scalia found that the DTA deprived the Court of jurisdiction to hear Hamdan's case at this time. He then considered, assuming that the Court had jurisdiction, whether it should abstain from exercising it.]

. . . The principal opinion on the merits makes clear that it does not believe that the trials by military commission involve any "military necessity" *at all*: "The charge's shortcomings . . . are indicative of a broader inability on the Executive's part here to satisfy the most basic precondition . . . for establishment of military commissions: military necessity." This is quite at odds with the views on this subject expressed by our political branches. Because of "military necessity," a joint session of Congress authorized the President to "use all necessary and appropriate force," including military commissions, "against those nations, organizations, or persons [such as petitioner] he determines planned, authorized, committed, or aided the terrorist attacks that occurred on September 11, 2001." Authorization for Use of Military Force, §2(a), 115 Stat. 224, note following 50 U.S.C. §1541 (2000 ed., Supp. III). In keeping with this authority, the President has determined that "[t]o protect the United States and its citizens, and for the effective conduct of military operations and prevention of terrorist attacks, it is necessary for individuals subject to this order . . . to be detained, and, when tried, to be tried for violations of the laws of war and other applicable laws by military tribunals." Military Order of Nov. 13, 2001, 3 C.F.R. §918(e) (2002). It is not clear where the Court derives the authority—or the audacity—to contradict this determination. If "military necessities" relating to "duty" and "discipline" required abstention in *Councilman, supra*, at 757, military necessities relating to the disabling, deterrence, and punishment of the mass-murdering terrorists of September 11 require abstention all the more here.

The Court further seeks to distinguish *Councilman* on the ground that "the tribunal convened to try Hamdan is not part of the integrated system of military courts, complete with independent review panels, that Congress has established." ...

Even if we were to accept the Court's extraordinary assumption that the President "lack[s] the structural insulation from military influence that characterizes the Court of Appeals for the Armed Forces,"[8] the Court's description of the review scheme here is anachronistic. As of December 30, 2005, the "fina[l]" review of decisions by military commissions is now conducted by the D.C. Circuit pursuant to §1005(e)(3) of the DTA, and by this Court under 28 U.S.C. §1254(1). This provision for review by Article III courts creates, if anything, a review scheme *more* insulated from Executive control than that in *Councilman.* ...

Moreover, a third consideration counsels strongly in favor of abstention in this case.... Here, apparently for the first time in history, a District Court enjoined ongoing military commission proceedings, which had been deemed "necessary" by the President "[t]o protect the United States and its citizens, and for the effective conduct of military operations and prevention of terrorist attacks." Military Order of Nov. 13, 3 C.F.R. §918(e). Such an order brings the Judicial Branch into direct conflict with the Executive in an area where the Executive's competence is maximal and ours is virtually nonexistent. We should exercise our equitable discretion to *avoid* such conflict. Instead, the Court rushes headlong to meet it....

I would abstain from exercising our equity jurisdiction, as the Government requests....

Justice THOMAS, with whom Justice SCALIA joins, and with whom Justice ALITO joins in all but parts I, II-C-1, and III-B-2, dissenting....

I. ...

... [T]he President's decision to try Hamdan before a military commission for his involvement with al Qaeda is entitled to a heavy measure of deference. In the present conflict, Congress has authorized the President "to use all necessary and appropriate force against those nations, organizations, or persons *he determines* planned, authorized, committed, or aided the terrorist attacks that occurred on September 11, 2001 ... in order to prevent any future acts of international terrorism against the United States by such nations, organizations or persons." Authorization for Use of Military Force (AUMF), 115 Stat. 224, note following 50 U.S.C. §1541 (2000 ed., Supp. III) (emphasis added). As a plurality of the Court observed in *Hamdi*, the "capture, detention, and *trial* of unlawful combatants, by 'universal agreement and practice,' are 'important incident[s] of war,'" *Hamdi*, 542 U.S., at 518 (quoting *Quirin, supra,* at 28, 30; emphasis added), and are therefore "an exercise of the 'necessary and appropriate force' Congress has authorized the President to use." *Hamdi*, 542 U.S., at 518; *id.,* at 587 (Thomas, J., dissenting). *Hamdi*'s observation that military commissions are included within the AUMF's authorization is supported by this Court's previous recognition that "[a]n important incident to the conduct of war is the

---

8. The very purpose of Article II's creation of a *civilian* Commander in Chief in the President of the United States was to generate "structural insulation from military influence." See The Federalist No. 28 (A. Hamilton); *id.,* No. 69 (same). We do not live under a military junta. It is a disservice to both those in the Armed Forces and the President to suggest that the President is subject to the undue control of the military.

adoption of measures by the military commander, not only to repel and defeat the enemy, but to seize and subject to disciplinary measures those enemies who, in their attempt to thwart or impede our military effort, have violated the law of war." *In re Yamashita*, 327 U.S. 1, 11 (1946)....

...Nothing in the language of Article 21...suggests that it outlines the entire reach of congressional authorization of military commissions in all conflicts — quite the contrary, the language of Article 21 presupposes the existence of military commissions under an independent basis of authorization. Indeed, consistent with *Hamdi*'s conclusion that the AUMF itself authorizes the trial of unlawful combatants, the original sanction for military commissions historically derived from congressional authorization of "the initiation of war" with its attendant authorization of "the employment of all necessary and proper agencies for its due prosecution." W. Winthrop, Military Law and Precedents 831 (2d ed. 1920) (hereinafter Winthrop). Accordingly, congressional authorization for military commissions pertaining to the instant conflict derives not only from Article 21 of the UCMJ, but also from the more recent, and broader, authorization contained in the AUMF.[2]...

II...

A

...[A] law-of-war military commission may only assume jurisdiction of "offences committed within the field of the command of the convening commander," and...such offenses "must have been committed within the period of the war." See *id.*, at 836, 837. Here, as evidenced by Hamdan's charging document, the Executive has determined that the theater of the present conflict includes "Afghanistan, Pakistan and other countries" where al Qaeda has established training camps, and that the duration of that conflict dates back (at least) to Usama bin Laden's August 1996 "*Declaration of Jihad Against the Americans.*" Under the Executive's description of the conflict, then, every aspect of the charge, which alleges overt acts in "Afghanistan, Pakistan, Yemen and other countries" taking place from 1996 to 2001, satisfies the temporal and geographic prerequisites for the exercise of law-of-war military commission jurisdiction. And these judgments pertaining to the scope of the theater and duration of the present conflict are committed solely to the President in the exercise of his commander-in-chief authority. See [*The Prize Cases*, 67 U.S. (2 Black) 635, 670 (1863)] (concluding that the President's commander-in-chief judgment about the nature of a particular conflict was "a question to be decided *by him*, and this Court must be governed by the decisions and acts of the political department of the Government to which this power was entrusted")....

...The starting point of the present conflict (or indeed any conflict) is not determined by congressional enactment, but rather by the initiation of hostilities. See *Prize Cases, supra*, at 668 (recognizing that war may be initiated by "invasion of a foreign nation," and that such initiation, and the President's response, usually *precedes* congressional action). Thus, Congress' enactment of the AUMF did not mark the

---

2. Although the President very well may have inherent authority to try unlawful combatants for violations of the law of war before military commissions, we need not decide that question because Congress has authorized the President to do so. Cf. *Hamdi v. Rumsfeld*, 542 U.S. 507, 587 (2004) (Thomas, J., dissenting) (same conclusion respecting detention of unlawful combatants)....

beginning of this Nation's conflict with al Qaeda, but instead authorized the President to use force in the midst of an ongoing conflict. Moreover, while the President's "war powers" may not have been activated until the AUMF was passed, the date of such activation has never been used to determine the scope of a military commission's jurisdiction.[3] . . .

C

[Justice Thomas also concluded that, under the law of war, Hamdan could properly be charged with membership in a war-criminal enterprise and with conspiracy to commit war crimes.]

3

Ultimately, the plurality's determination that Hamdan has not been charged with an offense triable before a military commission rests not upon any historical example or authority, but upon the plurality's raw judgment of the "inability on the Executive's part here to satisfy the most basic precondition . . . for establishment of military commissions: military necessity." This judgment starkly confirms that the plurality has appointed itself the ultimate arbiter of what is quintessentially a policy and military judgment, namely, the appropriate military measures to take against those who "aided the terrorist attacks that occurred on September 11, 2001." AUMF §2(a), 115 Stat. 224. The plurality's suggestion that Hamdan's commission is illegitimate because it is not dispensing swift justice on the battlefield is unsupportable. Even a cursory review of the authorities confirms that law-of-war military commissions have wide-ranging jurisdiction to try offenses against the law of war in exigent and nonexigent circumstances alike. Traditionally, retributive justice for heinous war crimes is as much a "military necessity" as the "demands" of "military efficiency" touted by the plurality, and swift military retribution is precisely what Congress authorized the President to impose on the September 11 attackers in the AUMF.

Today a plurality of this Court would hold that conspiracy to massacre innocent civilians does not violate the laws of war. This determination is unsustainable. The judgment of the political branches that Hamdan, and others like him, must be held accountable before military commissions for their involvement with and membership in an unlawful organization dedicated to inflicting massive civilian casualties is supported by virtually every relevant authority, including all of the authorities invoked by the plurality today. It is also supported by the nature of the present conflict. We are not engaged in a traditional battle with a nation-state, but with a worldwide, hydra-

---

3. Even if the formal declaration of war were generally the determinative act in ascertaining the temporal reach of the jurisdiction of a military commission, the AUMF itself is inconsistent with the plurality's suggestion that such a rule is appropriate in this case. The text of the AUMF is backward looking, authorizing the use of "all necessary and appropriate force against those nations, organizations, or persons he determines planned, authorized, committed, or aided the terrorist attacks that occurred on September 11, 2001." Thus, the President's decision to try Hamdan by military commission—a use of force authorized by the AUMF—for Hamdan's involvement with al Qaeda prior to September 11, 2001, fits comfortably within the framework of the AUMF. In fact, bringing the September 11 conspirators to justice is the *primary point* of the AUMF. By contrast, on the plurality's logic, the AUMF would not grant the President the authority to try Usama bin Laden himself for his involvement in the events of September 11, 2001.

headed enemy, who lurks in the shadows conspiring to reproduce the atrocities of September 11, 2001, and who has boasted of sending suicide bombers into civilian gatherings, has proudly distributed videotapes of beheadings of civilian workers, and has tortured and dismembered captured American soldiers. But according to the plurality, when our Armed Forces capture those who are plotting terrorist atrocities like the bombing of the Khobar Towers, the bombing of the U.S.S. *Cole*, and the attacks of September 11 — even if their plots are advanced to the very brink of fulfillment — our military cannot charge those criminals with any offense against the laws of war. Instead, our troops must catch the terrorists "redhanded" in the midst of *the attack itself*, in order to bring them to justice. Not only is this conclusion fundamentally inconsistent with the cardinal principle of the law of war, namely protecting non-combatants, but it would sorely hamper the President's ability to confront and defeat a new and deadly enemy....

III

[Justice Thomas concluded that the Court should defer to the President's determination that court-martial procedures are not "practicable" for military commissions and therefore reject any requirement for uniformity of procedures. He also concluded that Common Article 3 was not judicially enforceable; that, if it were, the Court should defer to the President's "reasonable" interpretation of Common Article 3 as inapplicable to the "international" conflict with Al Qaeda; and, finally, that any claim Hamdan might have under Common Article 3 was not ripe.]

For these reasons, I would affirm the judgment of the Court of Appeals.

Justice ALITO, with whom Justices SCALIA and THOMAS join in parts I-III, dissenting. For the reasons set out in Justice Scalia's dissent, which I join, I would hold that we lack jurisdiction. On the merits, I join Justice Thomas' dissent with the exception of Parts I, II-C-1, and III-B-2, which concern matters that I find unnecessary to reach....

I...

In order to determine whether a court has been properly appointed, set up, or established, it is necessary to refer to a body of law that governs such matters. I interpret Common Article 3 as looking to the domestic law of the appointing country because I am not aware of any international law standard regarding the way in which such a court must be appointed, set up, or established, and because different countries with different government structures handle this matter differently. Accordingly, "a regularly constituted court" is a court that has been appointed, set up, or established in accordance with the domestic law of the appointing country....

III...

A...

In sum, I believe that Common Article 3 is satisfied here because the military commissions (1) qualify as courts, (2) that were appointed and established in accordance with domestic law, and (3) any procedural improprieties that might occur in particular cases can be reviewed in those cases.

B

The commentary on Common Article 3 supports this interpretation. The commentary on Common Article 3, ¶1(d) . . . states: ". . . *We must be very clear about one point: it is only 'summary' justice which it is intended to prohibit. . . .*" GCIV Commentary 39 (emphasis added).

It seems clear that the commissions at issue here meet this standard. Whatever else may be said about the system that was created by Military Commission Order No. 1 and augmented by the Detainee Treatment Act, §1005(e)(1), 119 Stat. 2742, this system — which features formal trial procedures, multiple levels of administrative review, and the opportunity for review by a United States Court of Appeals and by this Court — does not dispense "summary justice."

For these reasons, I respectfully dissent.

NOTES AND QUESTIONS

1. *Holding?* What, precisely, did *Hamdan* hold? Note that Justice Kennedy's vote was necessary to form a majority. Which parts of the decision are those of the plurality alone? Note also that the Chief Justice — who wrote the opinion for the Court of Appeals in *Hamdan* — did not participate. Is *Hamdan*'s holding unprecedented? *See* Stephen I. Vladeck, *Congress, the Commander-in-Chief, and the Separation of Powers After Hamdan*, 16 Transnat'l L. & Contemp. Probs. 933, 935-936 (2007) (no, citing *Little v. Barreme*, 6 U.S. (2 Cranch) 170 (1804)).

2. *Military Necessity Redux.* We saw in Chapter 15 that the military commission exception to the "preferred" method of civilian trial is justified by necessity. What is the necessity that the majority identified in *Hamdan*? Is it limited by time or place? Is it limited to acts for which a person is "caught redhanded in a theater of war and which military efficiency demands be tried expeditiously," as the plurality suggests? If so, is necessity a wasting justification? If necessity for trying Hamdan by military commission is no longer present, is there any necessity for continuing to detain him? What does the Court say and why? See *supra* p. 701.

Reread section 1 of the Military Order, especially section 1(e), *supra* p. 686. Has not the President already found military commissions necessary? Why does the Court not defer to his finding, as it did to the finding of military necessity in *Korematsu, supra* p. 426? Reread the AUMF, *supra* p. 86. Hasn't Congress found necessity and authorized the President to use all "necessary and appropriate force," as he determines? Why does the Court not defer to Congress? Which branch is best equipped to decide necessity?

When there is a "controlling necessity," does the President *need* any statutory authority to use military commissions? That is, does he have inherent authority to establish them? What does the majority say? What does Justice Thomas say? If so, is there any limit on that authority?

3. *Statutory Authority.* The Court does not reach the question of inherent presidential authority for military commissions, because it found that Article 21 preserved or incorporated the common law of war authority for military commissions.

Recall that the Court found that the AUMF authorized the military detention of Yaser Hamdi. *See Hamdi v. Rumsfeld*, 542 U.S. 507 (2004). Why does it not also authorize trial of Hamdan by military commission, especially since the AUMF was enacted after Article 21? Alternatively, why does the DTA not authorize such a trial?

4. *Law-of-War Limits on Military Commissions.* Article 21 is a two-headed coin: if it incorporates the common law of war and thus authorizes military commissions, it also incorporates any jurisdictional and procedural limits set by that law. What are those limits? By what constitutional authority may Congress directly, or by implication, impose any limits on the President's use of military commissions?

One law-of-war limit is temporal — military commission jurisdiction is only for charges committed within the period of war. When did that period commence? If it commenced by attack, was it the attack on 9/11 or the earliest attack by Al Qaeda against U.S. persons or property? Is Justice Thomas correct in arguing that *The Prize Cases* commits this decision to the President's conclusive discretion? If Congress took a different view by enacting the AUMF and referring to the 9/11 attacks, which branch prevails? *See generally* Barbara Salazar Torreon, *Periods of War* (Cong. Res. Serv. RS21405), Sept. 14, 2010.

5. *The UCMJ and the Uniformity Principle.* Article 36 of the UCMJ authorizes the President to prescribe procedures for military commissions. *See generally* Jennifer Elsea, *The Department of Defense Rules for Military Commissions: Analysis of Procedural Rules and Comparison with Proposed Legislation and the Uniform Code of Military Justice* (Cong. Res. Serv. RL31600), Jan. 18, 2005. What two restrictions does it place on the President's procedural power? Why were these restrictions not met by sections 1(f) and 1(g) of the Military Order of November 13, 2001? See *supra* p. 686. If the President had simply added "or the procedures of courts-martial recognized by the UCMJ" at the end of section 2(f), would that have satisfied the restriction? If not, what else would he have to find?

6. *The Geneva Conventions.* International treaties also impose procedural law-of-war limitations on military commissions. The majority in *Hamdan* held that Common Article 3 of the Geneva Conventions of 1949 applied to the conflict with Al Qaeda. It required trial by a tribunal that is "regularly constituted . . . ." Why did the majority think that a military commission established by the President's military order and operating under procedures promulgated with his authority was not such a court? How are courts "regularly constituted" in the United States? Could a military commission ever be "regularly constituted"? What was Justice Alito's answer to these questions? Did the Court sufficiently defer to the President in interpreting international law? *See* Julian Ku & John C. Yoo, *Hamdan v. Rumsfeld: The Functional Case for Foreign Affairs Deference to the Executive Branch*, 23 Const. Comment. 179 (2006) (no).

Common Article 3 also forbids "cruel treatment and torture," as well as "outrages upon personal dignity, in particular humiliating and degrading treatment." *Supra* p. 30. Does Common Article 3 now clearly govern investigatory torture of persons captured in the conflict against Al Qaeda, or can you distinguish *Hamdan*?

7. *Military Commission Procedures and Due Process.* In *In re Yamashita*, 327 U.S. 1 (1946), a military commission gave General Yamashita less than three weeks to

prepare for a massive trial that ultimately heard more than 200 witnesses; the commission permitted the government to add 59 new specifications to the 64 pending specifications just two days before trial, then denied his defense any extra time to meet them; it denied Yamashita access to the Army's investigative reports, which might have contained exculpatory materials; it admitted the rankest hearsay; and it even cut back cross-examination "as a means of saving time." *See* Stephen B. Ives Jr., *Vengeance Did Not Deliver Justice*, Wash. Post, Dec. 30, 2001. Most observers concluded that Yamashita did not receive a fair trial, but the Supreme Court refused to review the commission's rulings on the evidence or its conduct of the proceedings and therefore found it "unnecessary to consider what, in other situations, the Fifth Amendment might require." *Yamashita*, 327 U.S. at 23.

Justice Murphy dissented vehemently:

> The immutable rights of the individual, including those secured by the due process clause of the Fifth Amendment, belong not alone to the members of those nations that excel on the battlefield or that subscribe to the democratic ideology. They belong to every person in the world, victor or vanquished, whatever may be his race, color or beliefs. They rise above any status of belligerency or outlawry. They survive any popular passion or frenzy of the moment. No court or legislature or executive, not even the mightiest army in the world, can destroy them. . . .
>
> The failure of the military commission to obey the dictates of the due process requirements of the Fifth Amendment is apparent in this case. . . . No military necessity or other emergency demanded the suspension of the safeguards of due process. Yet petitioner was rushed to trial under an improper charge, given insufficient time to prepare an adequate defense, deprived of the benefits of some of the most elementary rules of evidence, and summarily sentenced to be hanged. [*Id.* at 26-28.]

Justice Rutledge agreed with Justice Murphy in dissent.

Does the Fifth Amendment apply to trial by military commission? Does it depend on where the defendant is captured or whether the military commission sits here or abroad? *See Rasul v. Bush*, 542 U.S. 466, 483 n.15 (2004); *Zadvydas v. Davis*, 533 U.S. 678, 693 (2001) ("[T]he Due Process Clause applies to all 'persons' within the United States, including aliens, whether their presence here is lawful, temporary, or permanent."); *cf. United States v. Verdugo-Urquidez*, 494 U.S. 259 (1990).

The district court found it unnecessary to reach the question whether Hamdan had any constitutional rights, although it noted that the Supreme Court's decision in *Rasul* "may contain some hint that non-citizens held at Guantánamo Bay have some Constitutional protection." 344 F. Supp. 2d 152, 173 n.19 (D.D.C. 2004), *rev'd*, 415 F.3d 33 (D.C. Cir. 2005), *rev'd and remanded*, 548 U.S. 557 (2006). The question of Hamdan's right to due process, if any, was therefore not before the Supreme Court.

C.   MILITARY COMMISSIONS AFTER *HAMDAN*[1]

Congress initially responded to *Hamdan* by enacting the Military Commissions Act of 2006, Pub. L. No. 109-366, 120 Stat. 2600. The Act delegated authority to the

---

1. *See generally* Jennifer K. Elsea, *The Military Commissions Act of 2009: Overview and Legal Issues* (Cong. Res. Serv. RL41163), Apr. 6, 2010; Jennifer K. Elsea, *Comparison of Rights in Military Commission Trials and Trials in Federal Criminal Court* (Cong. Res. Serv. R40932), Jan. 26, 2010, from which the facts in the

President to establish military commissions to try unlawful enemy combatants, and it defined offenses triable by such commissions. It also amended the UCMJ to establish procedures and rules of evidence for trial by military commissions. While the Act provided limited post-trial administrative review and more limited subsequent review by the federal courts, it also stripped all courts of habeas jurisdiction for petitions brought by enemy combatant detainees.

The government proceeded to try Hamdan, David Hicks (an Australian alleged to have fought alongside the Taliban in Afghanistan), and Ali Hamza Ahman Suliman al Bahlul (alleged to have served as Al Qaeda's propaganda chief) by military commission. Although Hicks pleaded guilty to providing material support to terrorism, and the other defendants were convicted, their prosecutions exposed many issues about military commission jurisdiction and procedures.

Upon taking office in 2009, President Obama halted military commissions in order to review their procedures and the detention program. In May 2009, the Administration announced that it was considering restarting the military commission system with upgraded procedures. Congress then incorporated some of these procedural changes and added others in the Military Commissions Act (MCA) of 2009, 10 U.S.C. §§948a-950t (Supp. III 2009).

In November 2009, Attorney General Holder announced plans to try five detainees by military commission, including Omar Khadr (the so-called "Child Terrorist"), a Canadian captured by U.S. forces at age 15 after a four-hour firefight in Afghanistan in July 2002, during which he is alleged to have thrown a hand grenade that fatally injured a U.S. soldier, and whose trial had actually begun in 2007. Holder also announced a plan to transfer five "high value detainees" to New York for trial in federal court. The latter plan was abandoned when it met with strong resistance from Congress, and the Administration said it would try these detainees in military commissions instead. *Statement of the Attorney General on the Prosecution of the 9/11 Conspirators*, Apr. 4, 2011, *available at* http://www.justice.gov/iso/opa/ag/speeches/2011/ag-speech-110404.html; Department of Def., *DOD Announces Charges Sworn Against Five Detainees Allegedly Responsible for 9/11 Attacks* (Mar. 31, 2011), *available at* http://www.defense.gov/releases/release.aspx?releaseid=14532.

The following materials identify selected issues of trial by military commission, with references to the completed trials of Hamdan and Khadr.

1. Personal Jurisdiction

A threshold jurisdictional question of military commission authority is jurisdiction over the person of the defendant. This question implicates the same thorny issues of status in armed conflicts that have sometimes divided the habeas courts. See Chapter 16. The Military Order of November 13, 2001, applied to persons whom the President designated in writing as falling within §2 of that order. The MCA of 2006 subsequently authorized the trial by military commission of an "alien unlawful enemy combatant," defined as a person who engaged in hostilities "or purposefully and materially supported hostilities against the United States or its

---

introduction are chiefly drawn. U.S. Military Commission rulings are collected in the *Military Commission Reporter*, *available at* http://www.wcl.american.edu/nimj/military_commission_law.cfm, and are also provided on a Department of Defense Web site, http://www.defense.gov/news/commissions.html.

co-belligerents who is not a lawful enemy combatant (including a person who is part of the Taliban, Al Qaeda, or associated forces)," or who was determined to be an unlawful enemy combatant by a Combatant Status Review Tribunal (CSRT) "or another competent tribunal established under the authority of the President or the Secretary of Defense." Pub. L. No. 109-366, §3, 120 Stat. 2601. The Act, however, expressly barred military commission jurisdiction over "lawful enemy combatants." *Id.*

NOTES AND QUESTIONS

1. *Personal Jurisdiction Under the Military Order.* If the Order was intended simply to exercise preexisting law-of-war authority, is the statement in §2 of what is, in effect, personal jurisdiction over prospective defendants within such authority? Reflecting concerns raised by the OLC memorandum, *supra* pp. 682-683, the Order did not apply to U.S. citizens. But aliens in the United States have been held to enjoy the same rights as citizens. Did the Order apply to them?

2. *Personal Jurisdiction Under MCA of 2006: Who Decides?* The MCA of 2006 gave military commissions jurisdiction over a person "determined to be an unlawful enemy combatant by a Combatant Status Review Tribunal [CSRT]." Pub. L. No. 109-366, §3, 120 Stat. 2601. CSRTs, however, were charged with deciding only whether a detainee was an enemy combatant, not whether he was lawful or unlawful. The military judge in the "Child Terrorist" case found:

> Without any determination of lawful or unlawful status, classification as an "enemy combatant" is sufficient to justify a detaining power's continuing detention of an individual captured in battle or taken into custody in the course of ongoing hostilities. However, under the well recognized body of customary international law relating to armed conflict, and specific provisions of GPW III, lawful combatants enjoy "combatant immunity" for their pre-capture acts of warfare, including the targeting, wounding, or killing of other human beings, provided those actions were performed in the context of ongoing hostilities against lawful military targets, and were not in violation of the law of war. *See Johnson v. Eisentrager,* 339 U.S. 763, 793 (1950) (Black, J. dissenting) ("Legitimate 'acts of warfare,' however murderous, do not justify criminal conviction.... It is no 'crime' to be a soldier....") (citing *Ex parte Quirin,* 317 U.S. 1, 30-31 (1942) ("Mere membership in the armed forces could not under any circumstances create criminal liability....")). Lawful enemy combatants enjoy all the privileges afforded soldiers under the law of war, including combatant immunity and the protections of the Geneva Conventions if wounded or sick, and while being held as prisoners of war (POWs). Additionally, lawful enemy combatants facing judicial proceedings for any of their actions in warfare that violate the law of war, or for post-capture offenses committed while they are POWs, are entitled to be tried by the same courts, and in accordance with the same procedures, that the detaining power would utilize to try members of its own armed forces (i.e., by court-martial for lawful enemy combatants held by the United States). See Arts. 84, 87 and 102, GPW III. [*United States v. Khadr,* CMCR 07-001, Opinion of the Court and Action on Appeal by the United States Filed Pursuant to 10 U.S.C. §950d (U.S. Mil. Comm'n Sept. 24, 2007).]

Defense lawyers for Hamdan and Khadr therefore challenged the military commissions' personal jurisdiction over these defendants, arguing they had not been found "*unlawful* enemy combatants" by CSRTs, and that the commission had no authority to make the jurisdictional finding itself. The military judge in Hamdan's case agreed, finding that the CSRT determination had been made by a different standard than the MCA of 2006, for the different purpose of "determining whether or not [Hamdan] was properly detained and not for the purpose of determining whether he was subject to trial by military commission." *United States v. Hamdan*, Decision and Order — Motion to Dismiss for Lack of Jurisdiction (U.S. Mil. Comm'n June 4, 2007). The judge also found that the President's determination applied to members of Al Qaeda as a group, "and did not represent an individualized determination" about the accused. On the same day, the military judge in Khadr's case reached the same conclusion, adding that nothing in the MCA of 2006 anticipated that the military commission itself would conduct a "mini-trial" to make the findings of fact necessary to assert jurisdiction. *United States v. Khadr*, Hearing Transcript at 17-22 (U.S. Mil. Comm'n June 4, 2007). Both judges dismissed the charges against the defendants.

The MCA of 2006 established and permitted an appeal to the U.S. Court of Military Commission Review. On the government's appeal of dismissal of the charges against Khadr, the Court of Military Commission Review reversed. It agreed that the CSRT designation did not establish jurisdiction. *United States v. Khadr*, 717 F. Supp. 2d 1215 (Ct. Mil. Comm'n Rev. 2007), *appeal dismissed for lack of jurisdiction*, 529 F.3d 1112 (D.C. Cir. 2008). But it held that the military commission could decide for itself whether a defendant was an unlawful enemy combatant and take evidence on that question. *Id.* at 1232. It therefore returned the case to the military commission. The military judge in *Hamdan* ruled that Hamdan qualified as an unlawful enemy combatant because he had taken a direct part in hostilities by driving "a vehicle to and towards the battlefield, containing missiles that could only be used against the United States and its co-belligerents," and he did not fit any of the Geneva Convention definitions of lawful combatants, as he was neither part of regular forces nor of a militia or volunteer forming part of such forces. *United States v. Hamdan*, On Reconsideration Ruling on Motion to Dismiss for Lack of Jurisdiction (U.S. Mil. Comm'n Dec. 19, 2007).

3. *Personal Jurisdiction and the MCA of 2009.* The MCA of 2009 now provides:

10 U.S.C. §948a. Definitions. . . .

(6) PRIVILEGED BELLIGERENT. — The term "privileged belligerent" means an individual belonging to one of the eight categories enumerated in Article 4 of the Geneva Convention Relative to the Treatment of Prisoners of War.

(7) UNPRIVILEGED ENEMY BELLIGERENT. — The term "unprivileged enemy belligerent" means an individual (other than a privileged belligerent) who —

(A) has engaged in hostilities against the United States or its coalition partners;

(B) has purposefully and materially supported hostilities against the United States or its coalition partners; or

(C) was a part of al Qaeda at the time of the alleged offense under this chapter.

10 U.S.C. §948c. Persons subject to military commissions

Any alien unprivileged enemy belligerent is subject to trial by military commission as set forth in this chapter.

10 U.S.C. §948d. Jurisdiction of military commissions

A military commission under this chapter shall have jurisdiction to try persons subject to this chapter for any offense made punishable by this chapter, sections 904 and 906 of this title (articles 104 and 106 of the Uniform Code of Military Justice), or the law of war, whether such offense was committed before, on, or after September 11, 2001, and may, under such limitations as the President may prescribe, adjudge any punishment not forbidden by this chapter, including the penalty of death when specifically authorized under this chapter. A military commission is a competent tribunal to make a finding sufficient for jurisdiction.

Does this solve the personal jurisdiction problem?

2.   Subject Matter Jurisdiction

Section 1(e) of the Military Order of November 13, 2001, found that it was "necessary for individuals subject to this order . . . when tried, to be tried for violations of the laws of war and other applicable laws by military tribunals." Section 4(a) referred to trial "for any and all offenses triable by military commission," begging the question of what those offenses were. The Order seemed to place law-of-war offenses within a military commission's jurisdiction, but left open the possibility of trial for violations of other, unidentified "applicable laws." If the Order extended subject matter jurisdiction beyond traditional law-of-war offenses, was it lawful?

The MCA of 2006 adopted a list of offenses that DOD had authorized for trial by military commission. The list was substantially retained in the MCA of 2009:

§950t. Crimes triable by military commission

The following offenses shall be triable by military commission under this chapter at any time without limitation:

(1) MURDER OF PROTECTED PERSONS. — Any person subject to this chapter who intentionally kills one or more protected persons shall be punished by death or such other punishment as a military commission under this chapter may direct.

(2) ATTACKING CIVILIANS. — Any person subject to this chapter who intentionally engages in an attack upon a civilian population as such, or individual civilians not taking active part in hostilities, shall be punished, if death results to one or more of the victims, by death or such other punishment as a military commission under this chapter may direct, and, if death does not result to any of the victims, by such punishment, other than death, as a military commission under this chapter may direct. . . .

(7) TAKING HOSTAGES. — Any person subject to this chapter who, having knowingly seized or detained one or more persons, threatens to kill, injure, or continue to detain such person or persons with the intent of compelling any nation, person other than the hostage, or group of persons to act or refrain from acting as an explicit or implicit condition for the safety or release of such person or persons, shall be punished, if death results to one or more of the victims, by death or such other punishment as a military commission under this chapter may direct, and, if death does not result to any of the victims, by such punishment, other than death, as a military commission under this chapter may direct. . . .

(9) USING PROTECTED PERSONS AS A SHIELD. — Any person subject to this chapter who positions, or otherwise takes advantage of, a protected person with the

intent to shield a military objective from attack or to shield, favor, or impede military operations, shall be punished, if death results to one or more of the victims, by death or such other punishment as a military commission under this chapter may direct, and, if death does not result to any of the victims, by such punishment, other than death, as a military commission under this chapter may direct.

(10) USING PROTECTED PROPERTY AS A SHIELD. — Any person subject to this chapter who positions, or otherwise takes advantage of the location of, protected property with the intent to shield a military objective from attack, or to shield, favor, or impede military operations, shall be punished as a military commission under this chapter may direct. . . .

(15) MURDER IN VIOLATION OF THE LAW OF WAR. — Any person subject to this chapter who intentionally kills one or more persons, including privileged belligerents, in violation of the law of war shall be punished by death or such other punishment as a military commission under this chapter may direct. . . .

(23) HIJACKING OR HAZARDING A VESSEL OR AIRCRAFT. — Any person subject to this chapter who intentionally seizes, exercises unauthorized control over, or endangers the safe navigation of a vessel or aircraft that is not a legitimate military objective shall be punished, if death results to one or more of the victims, by death or such other punishment as a military commission under this chapter may direct, and, if death does not result to any of the victims, by such punishment, other than death, as a military commission under this chapter may direct.

(24) TERRORISM. — Any person subject to this chapter who intentionally kills or inflicts great bodily harm on one or more protected persons, or intentionally engages in an act that evinces a wanton disregard for human life, in a manner calculated to influence or affect the conduct of government or civilian population by intimidation or coercion, or to retaliate against government conduct, shall be punished, if death results to one or more of the victims, by death or such other punishment as a military commission under this chapter may direct, and, if death does not result to any of the victims, by such punishment, other than death, as a military commission under this chapter may direct.

(25) PROVIDING MATERIAL SUPPORT FOR TERRORISM. —

(A) OFFENSE. — Any person subject to this chapter who provides material support or resources, knowing or intending that they are to be used in preparation for, or in carrying out, an act of terrorism (as set forth in paragraph (24) of this section), or who intentionally provides material support or resources to an international terrorist organization engaged in hostilities against the United States, knowing that such organization has engaged or engages in terrorism (as so set forth), shall be punished as a military commission under this chapter may direct.

(B) MATERIAL SUPPORT OR RESOURCES DEFINED. — In this paragraph, the term "material support or resources" has the meaning given that term in section 2339A(b) of title 18.

(26) WRONGFULLY AIDING THE ENEMY. — Any person subject to this chapter who, in breach of an allegiance or duty to the United States, knowingly and intentionally aids an enemy of the United States, or one of the co-belligerents of the enemy, shall be punished as a military commission under this chapter may direct. . . .

(29) CONSPIRACY. — Any person subject to this chapter who conspires to commit one or more substantive offenses triable by military commission under this subchapter, and who knowingly does any overt act to effect the object of the conspiracy, shall be punished, if death results to one or more of the victims, by death or such other punishment as a military commission under this chapter may direct, and, if death does not result to any of the victims, by such punishment, other than death, as a military commission under this chapter may direct. . . .

NOTES AND QUESTIONS

1. *Murder in Violation of the Law of War.* As the Court of Military Commission Review declared in *Khadr*, "lawful combatants enjoy 'combatant immunity' for their pre-capture acts of warfare, including the killing of other human beings, provided those actions were performed in the context of ongoing hostilities against lawful military targets, and were not in violation of the law of war." *Khadr, supra,* 717 F. Supp. 2d at 1221. While a civilian who kills a lawful combatant can be tried in civilian courts for murder, it is not clear that such a murder constitutes a violation of the law of war, or that the same principles govern in armed conflict not of an international character, where combatant immunity does not apply. *See* Elsea, *The Military Commissions Act of 2009, supra* p. 710 n.1, at 11 and authorities cited there. Murder of *protected persons* has been held a war crime, *id.,* but that crime is already covered under a distinct part of the MCA of 2009. *See* 10 U.S.C. §950t(1) (Supp. III 2009). *See generally* David Glazier, *A Court Without Jurisdiction: A Critical Assessment of the Military Charges Against Omar Khadr* 9-18 (Aug. 31, 2010), *available at* http://ssrn.com/abstract=1669946.

Khadr was charged with murder in violation of the law of war for allegedly throwing a grenade at U.S. soldiers during a firefight in which he was himself shot twice in the back and lost an eye. One scholar argues that this charge

> has the practical effect of converting this armed conflict into a human shooting season: the government asserts U.S. combatants had the right to shoot Khadr on sight (he was shot twice in the back based on his being a "hostile" rather than because he posed any particular threat at the time) yet criminally prosecuted him for fighting back. [Glazier, *supra*, at 15-16.]

Leaving aside the question whether a participant in an active firefight is a "particular threat" during the shooting, does this criticism require that Khadr be tried as a civilian in a criminal court, if he is to be tried for murder at all?

A military judge in *United States v. Jawad*, D-007, Ruling on Defense Motion to Dismiss — Lack of Subject Matter Jurisdiction (U.S. Mil. Comm'n Sept. 24, 2008), ruled that it was not enough for the government to show that the defendant was an unlawful enemy combatant who had committed a murder. "[T]hat the Accused might fail to qualify as a lawful combatant does not automatically lead to the conclusion that his conduct violated the law of war, and the propriety of the charges in this case must be based on the nature of the act, not simply on the status of the accused." *Id.* at 3. The government therefore also had to prove "that the method, manner or circumstances used violated the law of war." *Id.* at 2.

2. *Conspiracy?* A plurality in *Hamdan* found that conspiracy was not a recognized violation of the common law of war. But it also emphasized that "[t]here is no suggestion that Congress has, in exercise of its constitutional authority to 'define and punish . . . Offences against the Law of Nations,' U.S. Const., Art. I, §8, cl. 10, positively identified 'conspiracy' as a war crime." Now it has, in the MCA of 2009. Could Hamdan therefore be tried on remand pursuant to the MCA of 2009? Does its enactment cure the problem identified by the plurality?

3. *Material Support?* "Providing material support for terrorism" appears to be another new crime. This provision of the MCA of 2009 is borrowed from the domestic criminal laws that have been deployed so aggressively and successfully by U.S. prosecutors in federal courts. See Chapter 20. But does it run afoul of the common law of war for the same reasons as the conspiracy charges against Hamdan, or is it now lawful? The military judge in *Hamdan* concluded that it was, in fact, consistent with the common law of war, because military commissions tried defendants for cooperating with guerillas or "guerilla-marauders" in the Civil War. *See United States v. Hamdan,* D-012, Ruling on Motion to Dismiss (Ex Post Facto) (U.S. Mil. Comm'n July 14, 2008). Others have argued that the Civil War precedents were called into question by *Milligan* and that some of them appear to have involved distinguishable violations of martial law or occupation law rather than the law of war. Elsea, *The Military Commissions Act of 2009, supra,* at 13.

The Obama administration itself admitted doubt that material support crimes were offenses under the law of war.

[T]here are serious questions as to whether material support for terrorism or terrorist groups is a traditional violation of the law of war. The President has made clear that military commissions are to be used only to prosecute law of war offenses. . . . [O]ur experts believe that there is a significant risk that appellate courts will ultimately conclude that material support for terrorism is not a traditional law of war offense, thereby reversing hard-won convictions and leading to questions about the system's legitimacy. [*Legal Issues Regarding Military Commissions and the Trial of Detainees for Violations of the Law of War: Hearing Before the S. Comm. on Armed Servs.,* 111th Cong. 12 (2009) (submitted statement of David Kris, Assistant Attorney General).]

Congress included the material support crime in the MCA of 2009 in spite of the Administration's expressed reservation.

4. *Ex Post Facto Law?* The United States has recognized Article 75(4)(c) of 1977 Geneva Additional Protocol I as customary international law. It provides, in part, that "no one shall be accused or convicted of a criminal offence on account of any act or omission which did not constitute a criminal offence under the national or international law to which he was subject at the time when it was committed." Essentially the same rule applies to conflicts not of an international character. Glazier, *supra,* at 6. If Congress created new crimes in the MCA of 2009 (or 2006), would it violate Article 75 to charge defendants for acts that preceded enactment of the statute? Congress gave the following answer in the MCA of 2009:

The provisions of this subchapter codify offenses that have traditionally been triable by military commission. This chapter does not establish new crimes that did not exist before the date of the enactment of this subchapter, as amended [on October 28, 2009], but rather codifies those crimes for trial by military commission. Because the provisions of this subchapter codify offenses that have traditionally been triable under the law of war or otherwise triable by military commission, this subchapter does not preclude trial for offenses that occurred before the date of the enactment of this subchapter, as so amended. [10 U.S.C. §950p(d) (Supp. III 2009).]

Is it up to Congress, or may the courts independently decide such questions regarding their jurisdiction? Glazier, *supra* (arguing the latter).

5. *"Define and Punish" Authority?* The Constitution expressly vests Congress with the power to "define and punish offenses against the law of nations." U.S. Const. art. I, §8, cl. 10. Why does this power not provide a sufficient answer to the questions of subject matter jurisdiction raised by the foregoing notes? Can Congress not "define" as it sees fit? Or is this power "itself logically constrained in [']against the law of nations[']"? Glazier, *supra*, at 8. Did the Framers intend Congress simply to act as a scribe, or was it vested with a more creative task? *See id.* (arguing that "the purpose for including the clause . . . was to allow Congress to put Americans on notice as to the precise conduct that would constitute a crime where there might otherwise be ambiguity"). *See generally* Stephen I. Vladeck, *The Laws of War as a Constitutional Limit on Military Jurisdiction,* 4 J. Nat'l Security L. & Pol'y 295 (2010).

6. *Last in Time?* Does legislative authority rest *just* on the Define and Punish Clause? Why not on the clauses vesting power to make "rules concerning capture" or "rules for the government and regulation of the land and naval forces," or even just to make "all laws which shall be necessary and proper for carrying into execution" the power vested in the President as Commander in Chief for conducting armed conflict? U.S. Const. art. I, §8, cls. 11, 14, and 18, respectively. Does the international law of war restrict these legislative powers? In the event of a conflict between that body of law and the MCA of 2009, which prevails?

3.   Evidence Obtained by Coercion

The Military Order of November 13, 2001, permitted admission of such evidence as the presiding officer of the military commission found would "have probative value to a reasonable person." This rule would have permitted evidence obtained by torture or other coercion, if it had such probative value, as well as hearsay evidence that met the same standard. It thus seemingly tolerated evidence that would be inadmissible in a federal criminal court. The MCA of 2006 prohibited evidence obtained by torture, but allowed evidence obtained by coercion that does not amount to torture committed prior to the 2005 Detainee Treatment Act if the "totality of the circumstances" showed that it had probative value and the interests of justice would be served. Pub. L. No. 109-366, §3, 120 Stat. 2607 .

The MCA of 2009 is more restrictive:

10 U.S.C. §948r. Exclusion of statements obtained by torture or cruel, inhuman, or degrading treatment; prohibition of self-incrimination; admission of other statements of the accused

(a) EXCLUSION OF STATEMENTS OBTAIN[ED] BY TORTURE OR CRUEL, INHUMAN, OR DEGRADING TREATMENT. — No statement obtained by the use of torture or by cruel, inhuman, or degrading treatment (as defined by section 1003 of the Detainee Treatment Act of 2005 (42 U.S.C. 2000dd)), whether or not under color of law, shall be admissible in a military commission under this chapter, except against a person accused of torture or such treatment as evidence that the statement was made.

(b) SELF-INCRIMINATION PROHIBITED. — No person shall be required to testify against himself or herself at a proceeding of a military commission under this chapter.

(c) OTHER STATEMENTS OF THE ACCUSED. — A statement of the accused may be admitted in evidence in a military commission under this chapter only if the military judge finds —

(1) that the totality of the circumstances renders the statement reliable and possessing sufficient probative value; and

(2) that —

(A) the statement was made incident to lawful conduct during military operations at the point of capture or during closely related active combat engagement, and the interests of justice would best be served by admission of the statement into evidence; or

(B) the statement was voluntarily given.

(d) DETERMINATION OF VOLUNTARINESS. — In determining for purposes of subsection (c)(2)(B) whether a statement was voluntarily given, the military judge shall consider the totality of the circumstances, including, as appropriate, the following:

(1) The details of the taking of the statement, accounting for the circumstances of the conduct of military and intelligence operations during hostilities.

(2) The characteristics of the accused, such as military training, age, and education level.

(3) The lapse of time, change of place, or change in identity of the questioners between the statement sought to be admitted and any prior questioning of the accused....

In each of the following two cases, the defense cited this provision in support of a motion to suppress statements made by the defendant.

United States of America v. Mohammed Jawad

United States Military Commission, Sept. 24, 2008
D-008, Ruling on Defense Motion to Dismiss — Torture of Detainee

1. The defense asserts the Accused was subjected to an intentional sleep deprivation program and other abusive treatment while detained in U.S. custody which constitutes torture in violation of the law of war, U.S. law and DOD regulations and policy[1] and moves to dismiss the Charge and specifications with prejudice. The government opposes the motion, submitting that, even if the allegations are true, dismissal of charges is not the appropriate remedy, if one exists at all.

2. On or about December 17, 2002, in Kabul, Afghanistan, the Accused allegedly threw a hand grenade into a vehicle in which two American service members and their Afghan interpreter were riding. All suffered serious injuries. The Accused was immediately apprehended by Afghan police and transferred to U.S. custody the next day. He remained in continuous U.S. custody until his transfer to Guantanamo Bay, Cuba on or about February 6, 2003.

---

1. The President directed in Military Order 1, dated November 13, 2001, that detainees would be treated humanely. A February 7, 2002 White House memo reaffirmed this order and stated further they would be treated, "to the extent appropriate and consistent with military necessity, in a manner consistent with the principles of Geneva."

3. On December 25, 2003, the accused attempted suicide.

4. As early as November 2003, Joint Task Force-Guantanamo Bay personnel (JTF-GTMO) used a sleep deprivation measure to disorient selected detainees thought to have important intelligence data, disrupt their sleep cycles and biorhythms, make them more compliant and break down their resistance to interrogation. Pursuant to this technique, euphemistically referred to as the "frequent flyer" program, a detainee would be repeatedly moved from one detention cell to another in quick intervals, usually at night.

5. Shortly after assuming command of JTF-GTMO in March 2004, Major General (MG) Jay Hood ordered the "frequent flyer" program discontinued. Apparently unknown to MG Hood, the accused was subjected to the frequent flyer program and moved from cell to cell 112 times from 7 May 2004 to 20 May 2004, on average of about once every three hours. The accused was shackled and unshackled as he was moved from cell to cell. The Accused was not interrogated and the scheme was calculated to profoundly disrupt his mental senses.

6. While the "frequent flyer" program was intended to create a feeling of hopelessness and despair in the detainee and set the stage for successful interrogations, by March 2004 the accused was of no intelligence value to any government agency. The infliction of the "frequent flyer" technique upon the Accused thus had no legitimate interrogation purpose.

7. On or about June 2, 2008, the Accused was beaten, kicked, and pepper sprayed for not complying with a guard's instructions. He suffered, among other injuries, a broken nose.

8. The conditions experienced by the Accused while confined at Guantanamo Bay include excessive heat, constant lighting, loud noise, linguistic isolation (separating the accused from other Pashto speakers), and, on at least two separate occasions, 30 days physical isolation.

9. The Accused has not apparently suffered any permanent physical injuries as a result of his detention in U.S. custody. While the long term psychological impact of the Accused's detention is unclear, the Rule for Military Commission (RMC) 706 board concluded the Accused is "not currently suffering from a mental disease or defect," "does have sufficient present ability to consult with his lawyers with a reasonable degree of rational understanding" and "does have sufficient mental capacity to understand the nature of the proceedings against him and cooperate intelligently in his defense." Additionally, the Accused does not require immediate medical or psychological treatment.

10. The Military Commissions Act prohibits both the torture and cruel and inhuman treatment of detainees. Any degrading treatment carries a presumption it was imposed as a punitive not preventative measure.

11. The defense asserts that the government's conduct amounts to torture and violates the principles of due process of such a magnitude that dismissal of the charges is the only acceptable remedy.

12. This Commission finds that, under the circumstances, subjecting this Accused to the "frequent flyer" program from May 7-20, 2004 constitutes abusive conduct and cruel and inhuman treatment. Further, it came at least two months after the JTF-GTMO commander had ordered the program stopped. Its continuation was not simple negligence but flagrant misbehavior. Those responsible should face appropriate disciplinary action, if warranted under the circumstances.

13. That being said, the narrow issue before this Military Commission is whether dismissal of the charges against this Accused is appropriate for the conduct of an apparent few government agents. Answering this question does not require the Military Commission to decide as fact that this Accused was tortured. Assuming, but not deciding, that the government's actions against this Accused produced the pain and suffering of the requisite physical and/or mental intensity and of such duration to rise to the level of "torture," this Military Commission finds that the remedy sought by the defense is not warranted under the circumstances.

14. It is beyond peradventure that a Military Commission may dismiss charges because of abusive treatment of the Accused. However, when other remedies are available to adequately address the wrong, dismissal should be the last of an escalating list of options. Here, the Commission finds other remedies are available to adequately address the wrong inflicted upon the Accused, including, but not limited to, sentence credit towards any approved period of confinement, excluding statements and any evidence derived from the abusive treatment, and prohibiting persons who may have been involved in any improper actions against the Accused from testifying at trial. The Military Commission will rule upon the appropriate application of these, and other proposed remedies, as dictated by developments in this case.

15. Accordingly, the defense motion to dismiss based on torture of the Accused is DENIED.

So ordered this 24th day of September 2008.

Stephen R. Henley
Colonel, US Army
Military Judge

United States of America v. Omar Ahmed Khadr

United States Military Commission, Aug. 17, 2010
Suppression Motions, D-094, D-111, Ruling

1. The Defense moves to suppress certain statements made by the accused as set out in its briefs submitted in support of D094. The Defense alleges such statements are the product of torture, involuntary, unreliable, do not serve the interest of justice, and are fruit of the poisonous tree. Their admission, the defense further alleges, is prohibited under §948r of the Military Commissions Act of 2009 (MCA) and Military Commissions Rule of Evidence (M.C.R.E.) 304. The Defense also moves to suppress the videotape found at the compound where the firefight occurred as set out in its brief submitted in support of D-111. The Defense alleges the videotape was found only as a result of statements obtained improperly from the accused. The Government opposes both motions.

2. The Commission has considered the briefs, the witnesses' testimony, all the other evidence offered during the suppression hearing, and the oral arguments and finds as follows:

a. The accused engaged in a firefight with U.S. forces in Khost, Afghanistan, on 27 July 2002. The accused was severely wounded during the course of the firefight and was captured after the firefight ended. The U.S. forces treated the accused at the scene and transported him to Bagram Airfield, Afghanistan, where U.S. medical personnel operated on the accused and saved his life. The accused received world class medical care from the time he was captured and continues to receive the same world class medical care throughout his detention.

b. The accused was 15 years old at the time of his capture. The accused received limited formal education and received some home schooling prior to his capture; however, the accused speaks several languages, including English. The accused speaks English well enough that he did not need an interpreter to communicate effectively with U.S. forces, U.S. medical personnel, or any other U.S. personnel. At times the accused would volunteer to help translate for U.S. personnel and other detainees....

i. Interrogator #1 was the lead interrogator for the accused while the accused was at the Bagram detention center. He interrogated the accused 20-25 times. He always interrogated the accused in an interrogation room. He never interrogated the accused in the hospital. He used a "fear up" technique as a last resort with the accused. It is a technique used to attempt to raise the fear level of the detainee. He, at times, used a harsh tone of voice with the accused by yelling and cursing at the accused if he caught the accused in what he thought were lies. The accused told him he did not like the cursing and stopped talking to Interrogator #1 at one point because of the cursing. Interrogator #1 one time "got into the accused's face" by yelling at him and flipping a bench so it made a loud noise. The "fear up" technique included the use of stress positions on detainees who were healthy enough to endure that technique. Interrogator #1 never used the stress position technique on the accused. He never inflicted pain on or tried to injure the accused. He never used any dogs while interrogating the accused.

j. During one of the interrogations, Interrogator #1 told the accused a fictitious story about a detainee, an Afghan male, who lied to interrogators and was sent to a US prison for lying. There were "big, black guys" in the prison. The Afghan male was a kid away from home who they could not protect. The Afghan male got hurt when the "big, black guys" raped him in the showers. This fictitious story was unsuccessful in obtaining information from the accused. The "fear up" technique was also not successful in obtaining information from the accused.

k. Interrogator #1 used other types of techniques on the accused, such as a "love of freedom" and "pride/ego down." These were attempts to gather information through appealing to a person's desire to go home or implying that he was not really an important person and attempting to get him to talk about the people who really were important. He also used "fear of incarceration" as a technique. It was used in an attempt to gain cooperation in order to return to a normal life rather than being detained. These techniques did not amount to torture or abuse of the accused.

l. Guards would move detainees, to include the accused, with a hood over their heads. However, Interrogator #1 never interrogated the accused while he had a hood over his head. Interrogator #1 never threw cold water on the accused. He never bound the accused's hands to the ceiling and made him stand. He never made the accused carry heavy water bottles. He never used bright lights with the accused. He never tied a bag over the accused's head. He never pulled or yanked the accused off a stretcher.

m. The accused never told Interrogator #1 that there was a videotape (Appellate Exhibit (AE) 188 remarked as AE 230) in the house where the firefight took place. However, Interrogator #1 eventually obtained a copy of the videotape found in the house where the firefight took place. After he showed the videotape to the accused, the accused appeared somewhat shaken. The accused said that "the Americans know all." There was a dramatic change to the accused's cooperation after he saw the videotape. It was the use of the videotape which was successful in obtaining information from the accused rather than the other techniques used by Interrogator #1. . . .

4. . . .

c. There is no credible evidence the accused was ever tortured as that term in defined under M.C.R.E. 304(b)(3), even using liberal interpretation considering the accused's age. While Interrogator #1 told the accused a story about the rape of an Afghan youth in an America prison, there is no evidence that story caused the accused to make any incriminating statements then or in the future. In fact, the credible evidence is that the accused started to make incriminating statements only after he learned the Americans found the videotape at the compound where the firefight took place which shows the accused and others making improvised explosives and placing them along the roadside at night. No statement offered against the accused was derived from, the product of, or connected to any story Interrogator #1 told to the accused. . . .

e. The Commission concludes that, under the totality of the circumstances, the statements offered against the accused are reliable, possess sufficient probative value, were made voluntarily, are not the product of torture or mistreatment, and whose admission is in the interest of justice.

6. There is no evidence the accused made any statement to anyone about the existence of a videotape found at the scene of the firefight. There is no evidence to support the defense allegation that the commander made a decision to search the compound where the firefight occurred as a result of intelligence information obtained from the accused. The evidence is clear, and the Commission finds, the commander's decision to search the compound where the videotape was found was independent of and not derived from any interrogation of the accused. The videotape is not the "fruit of the poisonous tree" as there is no "poisonous tree."

7. The Commission finds the Government has met its burden to show the admissibility of the statements and videotape by a preponderance of the evidence. See MCRE 304(d)(1).

8. Accordingly, the motions to suppress the accused's statements and the videotape are denied.

So ordered this 17th day of August 2010.

Patrick J. Parish
COL, JA
Military Judge

NOTES AND QUESTIONS

1. *Evidence from "Torture Lite"?* The MCA of 2009 prohibits statements obtained by torture or cruel, inhuman, or degrading treatment, except as evidence of torture by the defendant. The military judge found that use of the "Frequent Flyer" program against Jawad constituted torture that would justify excluding evidence derived by the abusive treatment, although not the dismissal of the charges. Khadr was subject to the "Fear Up" technique instead, while he was recuperating from surgery, and still 15 years old. Why didn't this technique require exclusion of his statements? Should his age or condition make a difference? Khadr claimed that he was hooded, had his hands tied above a door for hours, threatened with dogs, and denied use of the washroom, forcing him to urinate on himself. Multiple government witnesses denied this, as reflected in omitted parts of the ruling, but his chief interrogator later pleaded guilty to abusing detainees to extract confessions after one detainee died in his custody. *See* Michelle Shepard, *Khadr's Military Interrogation Faces Scrutiny*, Toronto Star, Mar. 25, 2008.

Even if you disagree with the military judge in *Khadr*, the MCA ban is only on statements obtained by coercive treatment. The court found that it was after Khadr was shown a videotape seized from the compound where he was found, in which he is seen making and planting roadside bombs, that he started talking, and that his cooperation was fostered by FBI interrogators who treated him more gently. As to these statements, the "totality of the circumstances" arguably supported the finding of voluntariness, unless Khadr was still suffering from prior coercive treatment. *See* Peter Margulies, *The Military Commissions Act, Coerced Confessions, and the Role of the Courts* (Dec. 20, 2006), *available at* http://papers.ssrn.com/sol3/papers.cfm?abstract_id=954415; *cf.* Norman Abrams, *Terrorism Prosecutions in Federal Court: Exceptions to Constitutional Evidence Rules and the Development of a Cabined Exception for Coerced Confessions* (May 19, 2011), *available at* http://papers.ssrn.com/sol3/papers.cfm?abstract_id=1846963 (discussing modified rules for coerced confessions in federal terrorism trials).

2. *Evidence from Torture?* In a different military commission trial, it was revealed that statements were obtained after death threats to the detainee and his family. Do they constitute statements obtained by torture? See *supra* pp. 528-533 (defining torture). Not only were those statements suppressed, but also subsequent statements were suppressed because the circumstances did not sufficiently dissipate the coercive effect of the prior threats. *United States v. Jawad*, D-022, Ruling on Defense Motion to Suppress Out-of-Court Statements of the Accused to Afghan Authorities (U.S. Mil. Comm'n Oct. 28, 2008); *United States v. Jawad*, D-021, Ruling on Defense Motion to Suppress Out-of-Court Statements Made While in U.S. Custody (U.S. Mil. Comm'n Nov. 9, 2008).

Some statements by Khalid Sheikh Mohammed, the alleged mastermind of the 9/11 attacks, were obtained from repeated waterboarding. Scott Shane, *Waterboarding Used 266 Times on 2 Suspects*, N.Y. Times, Apr. 20, 2009. One reason members of Congress objected to the Administration's plan to try him in federal court was the likely inadmissibility of his statements in that forum. Would such statements be admissible in a trial by military commission? If not, can he now be successfully prosecuted before a military commission?

4. Other Evidentiary Rules

The Federal Rules of Evidence have elaborate rules against hearsay, but multiple exceptions as well. Fed. R. Evid. 801-807. There is no general rule against hearsay in formal, on-the-record administrative adjudication, in which "[a]ny oral or documentary evidence may be received, but the agency as a matter of policy shall provide for the exclusion of irrelevant, immaterial, or unduly repetitious evidence." Administrative Procedure Act, 5 U.S.C. §556 (2006).

The MCA of 2009 provides, in relevant part:

10 U.S.C. §949a(b)(3)

In making exceptions in the applicability in trials by military commission under this chapter from the procedures and rules otherwise applicable in general courts-martial, the Secretary of Defense may provide the following:

(A) Evidence seized outside the United States shall not be excluded from trial by military commission on the grounds that the evidence was not seized pursuant to a search warrant or authorization.

(B) A statement of the accused that is otherwise admissible shall not be excluded from trial by military commission on grounds of alleged coercion or compulsory self-incrimination so long as the evidence complies with the provisions of section 948r of this title.

(C) Evidence shall be admitted as authentic so long as —

(i) the military judge of the military commission determines that there is sufficient evidence that the evidence is what it is claimed to be; and

(ii) the military judge instructs the members that they may consider any issue as to authentication or identification of evidence in determining the weight, if any, to be given to the evidence.

(D) Hearsay evidence not otherwise admissible under the rules of evidence applicable in trial by general courts-martial may be admitted in a trial by military commission only if —

(i) the proponent of the evidence makes known to the adverse party, sufficiently in advance to provide the adverse party with a fair opportunity to meet the evidence, the proponent's intention to offer the evidence, and the particulars of the evidence (including information on the circumstances under which the evidence was obtained); and

(ii) the military judge, after taking into account all of the circumstances surrounding the taking of the statement, including the degree to which the statement is corroborated, the indicia of reliability within the statement itself, and whether the will of the declarant was overborne, determines that —

(I) the statement is offered as evidence of a material fact;

(II) the statement is probative on the point for which it is offered;

(III) direct testimony from the witness is not available as a practical matter, taking into consideration the physical location of the witness, the unique circumstances of military and intelligence operations during hostilities, and the adverse impacts on military or intelligence operations that would likely result from the production of the witness; and

(IV) the general purposes of the rules of evidence and the interests of justice will best be served by admission of the statement into evidence. . . .

NOTES AND QUESTIONS

1. *The Necessity for Relaxed Hearsay and Authentication Rules.* In *Hamdi,* the Supreme Court held that rules against hearsay "may need to be accepted as the most reliable available evidence from the Government" in a proceeding to decide enemy combatant status. *Hamdi v. Rumsfeld,* 542 U.S. 507, 533-534 (2004). Why should that be so? Does the same reasoning apply to evidence used to prosecute a detainee for war crimes? Khadr was seized during a firefight that destroyed much of the compound in which he had been found and left many dead and wounded. Do these circumstances affect your view of the evidentiary rules applicable to evidence in his trial by military commission? *See generally* Eun Young Choi, *Veritas, Not Vengeance: An Examination of the Evidentiary Rules for Military Commissions in the War on Terrorism,* 42 Harv. C.R.-C.L. L. Rev. 139 (2007) (written before enactment of the MCA of 2009).

2. *More "Totality of the Circumstances."* Does the MCA rule on hearsay sufficiently assure the reliability of evidence used in military commissions? If not, what rule would be better? Why should we adopt a stronger rule, when the Administrative Procedure Act provides a weaker one for formal administrative adjudications in the United States, such as actions to enforce a civil penalty against a respondent who is charged with violating an agency regulation?

3. *Classified Evidence.* The MCA of 2009 provides for the protection of classified information:

§949p-1. Protection of classified information: applicability of subchapter

(a) PROTECTION OF CLASSIFIED INFORMATION. — Classified information shall be protected and is privileged from disclosure if disclosure would be detrimental to the national security. Under no circumstances may a military judge order the release of classified information to any person not authorized to receive such information.

(b) ACCESS TO EVIDENCE. — Any information admitted into evidence pursuant to any rule, procedure, or order by the military judge shall be provided to the accused.

(c) DECLASSIFICATION. — Trial counsel shall work with the original classification authorities for evidence that may be used at trial to ensure that such evidence is declassified to the maximum extent possible, consistent with the requirements of national security. . . .

Provisions for defendant's access to classified information are partly modeled on the Classified Information Procedures Act (CIPA). In the *Hamdan* case, the defense requested access to "high value" detainees whom it hoped would testify that Hamdan was merely a driver, much as Zacarias Moussaoui requested access to a high-value detainee whom he hoped would testify that he was not operationally involved in the 9/11 attacks. See Chapter 21. The court granted the access subject to supervision by a government security officer, who would review each question and answer, and who would redact or summarize any answer by which he thought the detainee was attempting to communicate a secret message. *United States v. Hamdan,* P-004, On Reconsideration Ruling on Motion for Stay and for Access to High Value Detainees (U.S. Mil. Comm'n Mar. 14, 2008).

5. Assessment

Prior to the *Hamdan* decision, Justice Scalia, in an unguarded moment, reportedly said of proposals to try enemy combatants in civil courts:

> Give me a break. If he was captured by my army on the battlefield, that is where he belongs. I had a son on that battlefield and they were shooting at my son and I'm not about to give this man who was captured in a war a full jury trial. I mean it's crazy. [*Supreme Court: Detainees' Rights — Justice Scalia Speaks His Mind*, Newsweek, Apr. 3, 2006.]

Do you think it is crazy? In what ways is trial by military commission under the MCA of 2009 now different from a civil trial?

VII
Homeland Security

Homeland Security

23

Long before the 2001 attacks on the World Trade Center and the Pentagon, the U.S. government had begun to develop extensive plans for a response to asymmetric attacks on the homeland. In Chapters 5-19 we examined the elaborate federal apparatus for detecting and interdicting terrorist threats. Here we consider what to do if those prophylactic efforts fail.

Federal government plans for homeland security have evolved considerably, particularly since September 11. However, the planning documents, organization charts of the important players, and directives telling them what to do and when to do it have proven extremely ephemeral. Instead of tracing any particular plan for responding to a terrorist attack, we approach the problem functionally. To set the stage, in Part A we describe a credible worst-case scenario — an attack on the U.S. homeland using a weapon of mass destruction, and the responses of various government authorities. In Part B, we briefly review current federal government plans and authorities for responding to such an attack, particularly those involving interaction with first responders — local, state, and regional emergency personnel. In Part C, we consider the legal authorities for these first responders, focusing especially on the coordination of their roles. Part D examines federal authorities that may be invoked if a bioterrorist attack requires the compulsion of persons — isolation, quarantine, or vaccination — or commandeering of resources.

A. WORST-CASE SCENARIO: A PLAGUE ON YOUR CITY

Thomas V. Inglesby, Rita Grossman & Tara O'Toole, A Plague on Your City: Observations from TOPOFF

32 Clinical Infectious Diseases 436 (2001)
available at http://www.journals.uchicago.edu/CID/journal/issues/v32n3/001347/001347.html

May 17: An aerosol of pneumonic plague (*Yersinia pestis*) bacilli is released covertly from a fire extinguisher at a benefit concert in the Denver Performing Arts Center.

May 20: The Colorado Department of Public Health and Environment receives information that increasing numbers of persons began seeking medical attention at Denver area hospitals for cough and fever during the evening of May 19th. By early afternoon on May 20, 500 persons with these symptoms have received medical care, and 25 of those have died.

The Health Department notifies the CDC of the increased volume of sick. Plague is identified first by the state laboratory and subsequently confirmed in a patient specimen by the CDC lab at Ft. Collins. A public health emergency is declared by the State Health Officer, who immediately requests support from DHHS's Office of Emergency Preparedness. The Governor's Emergency Epidemic Response Committee assembles to respond to the unfolding crisis.

Thirty-one CDC staff are sent to Denver. Hospitals and clinics around the Denver area that just a day earlier were dealing with what appeared to be an unusual increase in influenza cases are now recalling staffs, implementing emergency plans, and seeking assistance in determining treatment protocols and protective measures. By late afternoon, hospital staff are beginning to call in sick, and antibiotics and ventilators are becoming more scarce. Some hospital staff have donned respiratory protective equipment.

The CDC and the FBI are notified by Denver police that a dead man has been found with terrorist literature and paraphernalia in his possession; his cause of death is unknown.

The Governor issues an executive order that restricts travel — including bus, rail and air travel — into or out of 14 Denver Metro counties, and commandeers all antibiotics that can be used to prevent or treat plague. At a press conference, the Governor informs the public that there is a plague outbreak in Denver as a result of a terrorist attack, and he announces his executive order. Citizens are instructed to seek treatment at a medical facility if feeling ill or if they have been in contact with a known or suspected case of plague. Those who are well are directed to stay in their homes and avoid public gatherings. The public is told that the disease is spread from person to person only "if you are within 6 feet of someone who is infected and coughing," and told that dust masks are effective at preventing the spread of disease.

Confirmed cases of plague are identified in Colorado locations other than Denver. Patient interviews suggest that most victims were at the Performing Arts Center days earlier. It is announced that the Governor is working with the President of the United States to resolve the crisis and that federal resources are being brought in to support the state agencies. By the end of the day, 783 cases of pneumonic plague have occurred, and 123 persons have died.

May 21: Broadcast media report that a "national crash effort" is underway to move large quantities of antibiotics to the region, as the CDC brings in its "national stockpile," but the quantity of available antibiotics is uncertain. The report explains that early administration of antibiotics is effective in treating plague but that antibiotics must be started within 24 hours of developing symptoms. A news story a few hours later reports that hospitals are running out of antibiotics.

A shipment from the National Pharmaceutical Stockpile (NPS) arrives in Denver, but there are great difficulties moving antibiotics from the airport to the persons who need it for treatment and prophylaxis. Out-of-state cases begin to be reported. The CDC officially notifies bordering states of the epidemic. Cases are reported in England and Japan. Both Japan and the World Health Organization request technical assistance from the CDC.

A number of hospitals in Denver are full to capacity and by the end of the day are unable to see or admit new patients. Thirteen hundred ventilators from the NPS are flown to Colorado. Bodies in hospital morgues are reported to have reached critical levels. The U.S. Surgeon General flies to Colorado to facilitate communications. Many states now are requesting supplies from the NPS. By the end of the day, 1,871 plague cases have been diagnosed throughout the U.S. and abroad. Of these, 389 persons have died.

May 22: Hospitals are under-staffed and have insufficient antibiotics, ventilators, and beds to meet demand. They cannot manage the influx of sick patients into the hospitals. Medical care is "beginning to shut down" in Denver.

Officials from the Health Department and the CDC have determined that a secondary spread of disease is occurring. The population in Denver is encouraged to wear face masks. The CDC advises that Colorado state borders be cordoned off in order to limit further spread of plague throughout the U.S. and other countries. Colorado officials express concern about their ability to get food and supplies into the state. The Governor's executive order is extended to prohibit travel into or out of the state of Colorado. By noon, there are 3,060 U.S. and international cases of pneumonic plague, 795 of whom have died.

The following day, May 23, 2000, this frightening exercise, called TOPOFF, was terminated. It had been organized by the Justice Department to test the ability of top officials at all levels of government to respond to a bioterrorist attack. Among the sobering results was the revelation that local health services—medical personnel, hospitals, and pharmaceutical supplies—were not nearly prepared to treat an outbreak of an infectious disease on such a large scale. Communications among local, state, and federal officials were unreliable. And responses were slowed by cumbersome decision-making processes or by a perception that no one was in charge. Other conclusions are described below.

The unfolding situation precipitated a series of increasingly stringent containment measures. By the end of the first day, [a travel advisory was issued] . . . that restricted travel in 16 Denver Metro counties. . . . Some people, in fact, were reported to be racing out of the state. As part of the travel advisory, persons were advised to stay home unless they were close contacts of diagnosed cases or were feeling sick; in the case of the latter they were directed to seek medical care. . . . [T]he police and National Guard admitted . . . that they would be unable to keep people at home. . . . [B]y the end of the exercise, "people had been asked to stay in their homes for 72 hours. . . . How were they supposed to get food or medicine?"

Throughout the unfolding epidemic, determining what information the public should be given and how quickly was an important and difficult issue. . . . It was clear that the public message itself would affect the capacity to control the epidemic, in that worried or panicked people might not seek the care they needed or, alternatively, might dangerously crowd health care facilities.

Balancing the rights of the uninfected with the rights of the infected was considered a critical issue. One observer commented that a citizen might be expected to respond to the series of advisories by saying, "You've told me I should just stay in my home, now you have an obligation to give me antibiotics." But there were not enough antibiotics to do this. . . .

Sometime into the exercise, (notional) civil unrest broke out. People had not been allowed to shop. Stores were closed. Food ran out because no trucks were being let into the state. Rioting began to occur. Gridlock occurred around the city, including around health care facilities. The use of snow-plows was proposed as a way of clearing the road of cars. Given the constraints of the exercise, it was not possible to gauge the true extent of social disorder that a bioterrorist attack might evoke, but most observers and participants agreed that serious civil disruption would be a genuine risk in such a crisis.

The wide spectrum of disease containment measures which were considered or implemented illustrated the uncertainty surrounding what measures would, in fact, be feasible and effective. One senior health participant said that sufficient legal powers seemed to exist to carry out the decisions that were being made, and noted that legal authorities were not the problem. The critical issue was having access to the necessary scientific, technical, practical and political expertise, and having sufficient reliable and timely information available (e.g., the number and location of sick persons, etc.) to make sound decisions about how to contain the epidemic....

...Perhaps the most striking observation overall is the recognition that the systems and resources now in place would be hard-pressed to successfully manage a bioweapons attack like that simulated in TOPOFF.... [*Id.*]

NOTES AND QUESTIONS

1. *Assessing the Emergency.* The escalating crisis in the TOPOFF exercise shows the importance of rapid recognition of the nature of an emergency. According to a Department of Homeland Security (DHS) study,

ER physicians, local hospital staff, infectious disease physicians, medical examiners, epidemiologists, and other public health officials should rapidly recognize the seriousness of the incident. Although laboratory methods to suspect preliminary diagnosis of the plague are available at many local public and private laboratories, there may be delayed recognition of the plague since most hospital ER and laboratory personnel in the United States and Canada have limited or no experience in identifying and/or treating plague.

...A rapid onset with large numbers of persons presenting at ERs with pneumonia should create high suspicion of a terrorist incident using the plague. Detection of the plague should also initiate laboratory identification of the plague strain and a determination of the potentiality of known antimicrobial drug resistance.... [Department of Homeland Sec./Homeland Sec. Council, *National Planning Scenarios* 4-5 (Version 21.3 Final Draft, Mar. 2006), *available at* http://info.publicintelligence.net/DHS%20-%20National%20Planning%20Scenarios%20March%202006.pdf.]

The Centers for Disease Control and Prevention (CDC) has developed a standard protocol for reporting possible outbreaks of diseases that might be weaponized by terrorists. *Interim Recommended Notification Procedures for Local and State Public Health Department Leaders in the Event of a Bioterrorist Incident* (Feb. 1, 2001), *at* http://emergency.cdc.gov/eMContact/Protocols.asp. If a local health official suspects that an outbreak of common symptoms might have been caused by a biological weapon, she should inform the state's health department, which will then notify the CDC. If a terrorist source is confirmed or thought by the state health department to be probable, the FBI and other predetermined response partners are to be notified. The CDC reporting protocol is not mandatory, however, and state and local governments have adopted it with some variations. Should it be mandatory?

2. *First Response.* As soon as a bioterrorist attack is detected, a concerted, immediate response will be required to limit the loss of life. What measures would the first responders to such an attack take? A DHS study includes this partial catalog:

> Persons with primary aerosol exposure to plague need to receive antibiotic therapy within 24 hours in order to prevent near certain fatality. The prevention of potential secondary person-to-person spread by fleeing victims will be a challenge. Epidemiological assessments, including contact investigation and notification, will be needed. Actions of incident-site personnel . . . include hazard identification and site control, establishment and operation of the ICS [federal Incident Command System], isolation and treatment of exposed victims, mitigation efforts, obtainment of PPE [personal protective equipment] and prophylaxis for responders, site remediation and monitoring, notification of airlines and other transportation providers, provision of public information, and effective coordination with national and international public health and governmental agencies.
>
> Evacuation and treatment of some victims will be required. Self-quarantine through shelter-in-place may be instituted.
>
> Tens of thousands of people will require treatment or prophylaxis with ventilators and antibiotics. Plague prompts antimicrobial prophylaxis of exposed persons, responders, and pertinent health care workers. Thousands will seek care at hospitals with many needing advanced critical care due to pneumonia caused by plague. Exposed persons will also need to be informed of signs and symptoms suggestive of plague as well as measures to prevent person-to-person spread. PPE (e.g., masks) for responders and health care providers should be available. Mobilization of the SNS [Strategic National Stockpile] for additional critical supplies and antibiotics will be necessary. Public information activities will be needed to promote awareness of potential signs and symptoms of plague. Proper control measures will include the need for rapid treatment; contact tracing; and, potentially, self-quarantine through shelter-in-place or other least restrictive means.
>
> Actions of incident-site personnel tested after the attack include protective action decisions, recognition of the hazard and scope, providing emergency response, communication, protection of special populations, treating victims with additional ventilators at hospitals, providing patient screening clinics, and providing treatment or drug distribution centers for prophylactic antibiotics. Mortuary requirements, animal-based surveillance to monitor potential spread of plague via natural methods, and veterinary services also will need to be considered. Since this is an international incident, the U.S. Department of State will provide appropriate assistance to U.S. citizens traveling or residing abroad, including the timely dissemination of information to allow citizens to make informed plans and decisions. [*National Planning Scenarios, supra* Note 1, at 4-6 to 4-7.]

Who should be expected to perform all these tasks — state and local personnel, federal officials, or both? What practical and legal problems can you foresee in implementing these measures?

3. *Controlling Public Information.* When word began to spread about the September 11, 2001, attacks on the World Trade Center and the Pentagon, Americans turned immediately to their televisions for news. They were rewarded with days of nonstop pictures, government press releases, and expert speculation about what had happened.

If an attack affects a wider area, as a chemical or radiological weapon might, or involves an infectious biological agent like plague, the public's involvement and cooperation in the response will be critically important. Members of the public cannot be expected to cooperate, of course, unless they receive some information about the nature of the emergency, as well as credible, authoritative instructions about how to respond. What form should that communication take? The CDC has prepared suggested media scripts, including this one:

- This is an urgent health message from the U.S. Department of Health and Human Services (HHS). Please pay careful attention to this message to protect your health and that of others.
- Public health officials believe that the bacteria that cause pneumonic plague may have been deliberately released into the air in the *xxx area.*
- Pneumonic plague is a life-threatening, serious infection of the lungs. It is caused by breathing in the plague bacteria.
- Plague can be spread from person to person. Avoid close and direct contact with people with plague symptoms.
- We have not confirmed the deliberate release of plague and do not know the extent or source of the outbreak....
- Local, state, and federal officials, including HHS, FBI, and Homeland Security, are working together. Updated announcements will be made as soon as officials know more.
- Ill persons should seek care immediately. Symptoms include fever, headache, muscle aches and chills, chest pain, and cough. Some people may cough up blood and have stomach pains. Most people develop symptoms within 1 to 4 days after exposure....
- ... By staying informed and following instructions from health officials, you can protect yourself, your family, and the community against this public health threat....

    For more information about the plague, visit the HHS Web site at http:www.hhs.gov, the Centers for Disease Control and Prevention's (CDC) plague page at http://www.bt.cdc.gov/agent/plague/, or call the CDC Hotline at 1-800-CDC-INFO for the latest information. [*Communicating in the First Hours, Bioterrorism Agents* (May 14, 2007), *at* http://emergency.cdc.gov/firsthours/.]

How would you react upon hearing this message on the radio or reading it on a smart phone? If your answer is, "I don't know," or "I would panic," how do you think the message could be crafted to evoke a more helpful response? What other steps could be taken that might secure the desired reaction from the public?

Can you think of reasons that the government might want to regulate media coverage? Do you think it should be able to impose limits on the dissemination of news? If so, can you say under what circumstances?

4. *Civil Unrest.* In the TOPOFF exercise, civil unrest (notionally, but predictably) broke out after a day or two. Can you suggest ways to avoid domestic violence in the wake of a terrorist attack? If such unrest is unavoidable, what government entity should be charged with responsibility for restoring order?

5. *Secondary Effects.* A WMD attack like the one described in TOPOFF is likely to have widespread ripple effects, including disruptions of the nation's financial infrastructure.

    As the financial world... begins to realize the likelihood of an epidemic, a sell-off occurs in the markets. There is a high absentee rate at banks, other financial institutions, and major corporations. Adding to these complications is the fact that bank and other financial customers may be staying home, afraid to venture into public places and trying instead to conduct business on the phone. As a result, the phone systems at financial institutions may become completely tied up, with far fewer transactions than normally occur. [*National Planning Scenarios, supra*, at 4-7.]

How could these kinds of impacts be limited?

6. *Exercising for Disaster.* While the TOPOFF exercise was under way in Denver in May 2000, simulated terrorist attacks involving chemical and radiological weapons were occurring in other cities. Subsequent large-scale exercises organized by DHS were based on notional attacks that also used radiological weapons and cyber warfare. *See generally* R. Eric Petersen et al., *Homeland Emergency Preparedness and the National Exercise Program: Background, Policy Implications, and Issues for Congress* (Cong. Res. Serv. RL34737), Nov. 10, 2008. Congress has ordered DHS to carry out national exercises at least every two years that are designed to be "as realistic as practicable, based on current risk assessments, including credible threats, vulnerabilities, and consequences, and designed to stress the national preparedness system." 6 U.S.C. §748 (2006 & Supp. III 2009). These exercises are part of a National Exercise Program, described in Petersen, *supra*, at 8-24. The Federal Emergency Management Agency (FEMA) has initiated a series of National Level Exercises focused on regional catastrophic response and recovery operations and collaboration between federal, regional, state, local, tribal, and private-sector participants. In 2011, for example, it practiced a response to a major earthquake in the central United States. *See FEMA National Level Exercise 2011: Fact Sheet* (Jan. 28, 2011), *at* http://www.fema.gov/media/fact_sheets/nle2011_fs.shtm.

DHS has also worked with other federal agencies to develop 15 all-hazards scenarios for use in homeland security preparedness activities. *See National Planning Scenarios, supra* p. 734. The *Scenarios* are marked "For Official Use Only," and DHS has not made them available to the public. Can you make an argument that such planning documents ought to be officially released?

B. THE FEDERAL RESPONSE ROLE

From 1950, when the Soviet Union tested its first atomic weapon, until the end of the Cold War, the American people lived in constant fear of a nuclear attack. For more than 40 years, the Civil Defense Act of 1950, ch. 1228, 64 Stat. 1245 (1951), as amended, directed the creation of a program to minimize the effects of such an attack on the civilian population and to deal with the resulting emergency conditions. Included in the program were planning for continuity of government, recruitment of emergency personnel, stockpiling of critical materials, and provision of warning systems and shelters. The Act purported to give the President broad powers in a civil defense emergency, for example, to take property "without regard to the limitation of any existing law," *id.* §303(a), 64 Stat. 1252, and to provide the government with immunity from suits for damages to property, personal injury, or death based on its actions during such an emergency. *Id.* §304, 64 Stat. 1253. The civil defense program, administered since 1979 by FEMA, was supposed to convince the American people and the Soviet leadership that the United States could not only survive a nuclear war, but also win one.

1.   Stafford Act Authorities

The Civil Defense Act also provided for federal responses to natural disasters, such as floods and hurricanes. It was augmented in 1974 by the Robert T. Stafford Disaster Relief and Emergency Assistance Act (Stafford Act), 42 U.S.C.A. §§5121-5207 (West 2009), *as amended by* Pub. L. No. 111-351, §§3, 4, 124 Stat. 3863, 3864 (2011). That statute provides broadly for federal assistance to states affected by various disasters. In 1994, the Civil Defense Act was repealed, then partially reenacted as an amendment to the Stafford Act. National Defense Authorization Act for Fiscal Year 1995, Pub. L. No. 103-337, §§3411, 3412, 108 Stat. 2663, 3100-3111 (1994). A House Armed Services Committee report declared at the time, ironically, that "the program has lost its defense emphasis. . . . Rather, the chief threats today come from tornadoes, earthquakes, floods, chemical spills, and the like." H.R. Rep. No. 103-499, at 5 (1994), *reprinted in* U.S.C.C.A.N. 2091, 2182-2183.

The Stafford Act may be invoked in the event of a presidentially declared major disaster or emergency, including "any natural catastrophe . . . or, regardless of cause, any fire, flood, or explosion," or on "any occasion for which, in the determination of the President, Federal assistance is needed to supplement State and local efforts and capabilities to save lives and to protect property and public health and safety, or to lessen or avert the threat of a catastrophe." 42 U.S.C. §§5122, 5170, 5191(a). While the President's declaration will usually be based on a state governor's request for help, the President may act without such a request when "the primary responsibility for response rests with the United States." *Id.* §5191(b). Moreover, the President may direct the DOD to perform any emergency work "essential for the preservation of life and property" for up to ten days. *Id.* §5170b(c). President Clinton declared an emergency under the Stafford Act on April 19, 1995, in response to the terrorist bombing that day of the Alfred P. Murrah Federal Building in Oklahoma City, and he ordered FEMA to direct and coordinate responses by other federal agencies and provide needed federal assistance. 60 Fed. Reg. 22,579 (May 8, 1995). *See also* 60 Fed. Reg. 21,819 (May 3, 1995) (declaring a "major disaster" and providing public and individual assistance). The Stafford Act was also invoked on September 11, 2001, when President Bush declared a "major disaster" in the State of New York in order to make available various forms of public and individual assistance, 66 Fed. Reg. 48,682-01, and was invoked on August 31, 2005, for Louisiana, Mississippi, and Alabama following the landfall of Hurricane Katrina. The White House, *The Federal Response to Hurricane Katrina: Lessons Learned* 33 (Feb. 2006).

2.   The Homeland Security Act and Related Directives

The Homeland Security Act of 2002, Pub. L. No. 107-296, 116 Stat. 2135 (2002) (codified as amended at 6 U.S.C. §§101-557 (2006) and scattered sections of other titles), directed the Secretary of the new Department of Homeland Security (DHS) to "build a comprehensive national incident management system with Federal, State, and local government personnel, agencies, and authorities, to respond to . . . [terrorist] attacks and disasters." 6 U.S.C. §312(5). The Act required the Secretary to "consolidate existing Federal Government emergency response plans into a single, coordinated national response plan." 6 U.S.C. §312(6). It merged all or portions of 22 federal agencies and 180,000 employees into the DHS. Included were the Coast Guard, Customs Service, Transportation Security Administration, FEMA, Secret

Service, parts of the Immigration and Naturalization Service, and a long list of less well-known federal entities. The Act designated DHS as the lead agency for coordinating disaster and emergency response and recovery assistance with state and local authorities. The startup of this huge new enterprise is traced in Harold C. Relyea, *Homeland Security: Department Organization and Management — Implementation Phase* (Cong. Res. Serv. RL31751), Jan. 3, 2005.

In February 2003, the White House published Homeland Security Presidential Directive/HSPD-5, entitled *Management of Domestic Incidents.* It is meant to "ensure that all levels of the government across the Nation have the capability to work efficiently and effectively together, using a national approach to domestic incident management," *id.* ¶(3), and it declares that the Secretary of Homeland Security is the "principal Federal official for domestic incident management." *Id.* ¶(4). The Secretary of Health and Human Services (HHS) shares responsibility with DHS for biological incidents, Sarah A. Lister, *An Overview of the U.S. Public Health System in the Context of Emergency Preparedness* 22 (Cong. Res. Serv. RL31719), Mar. 17, 2005, while the Attorney General is given lead responsibility for criminal investigations of terrorist threats or acts within the United States, and is directed to "coordinate the activities of other members of the law enforcement community to detect, prevent, preempt, and disrupt terrorist attacks against the United States." HSPD-5 ¶(8). In addition, the Defense Department may provide military support to civil authorities in a domestic incident, but always under the command of the Secretary of Defense. *Id.* ¶(9). While states have the primary role in responding to emergencies, DHS responsibilities are triggered when a federal agency acting under its own authority has requested DHS assistance, when state and local resources are overwhelmed and request federal assistance, when more than one federal agency has become involved in responding to the incident, or when the President directs the Secretary of Homeland Security to assume management of the incident. *Id.* ¶¶(4), (6).

HSPD-5 also orders the creation of a National Incident Management System (NIMS), to provide a flexible national framework within which governments at all levels and private entities can work together to manage domestic "incidents." The NIMS was rolled out a year later. Department of Homeland Sec., *National Incident Management System* (Mar. 1, 2004), *available at* http://www.fema.gov/pdf/emergency/NIMS/NIMS-core.pdf.

3.   The National Response Plan

HSPD-5 called for development of a National Response Plan (NRP) to replace existing national emergency response plans. The first NRP was published in January 2005. Like earlier plans, the NRP provided for a coordinated, all-hazards approach to "incident management," spelling out in broad terms the roles of all relevant elements of the national government and calling for communications and operational coordination by offices within DHS. It also set out a framework for federal interaction with state, local, and tribal governments and with the private sector in an emergency.

Weaknesses of the NRP were painfully exposed in the aftermath of Hurricane Katrina in 2005. White House investigators of the flawed federal response to the storm found that, while the NRP is sufficiently "flexible and scalable" to meet any threat or event, "the specific triggers" for the NRP and its components "are unclear." *The Federal Response to Hurricane Katrina, supra,* at 14. DHS Secretary Michael Chertoff declared Katrina to be an incident of national significance (INS) three days after the storm's landfall, on August 30, 2005, when two of the four triggering criteria listed in HSPD-5 ¶(4), noted above, had been met. *Id.* Yet there reportedly was confusion about whether the INS was triggered earlier by the President's emergency declaration under the Stafford Act. And according to the White House report, the NRP failed to articulate what actions should be taken by which agencies once an INS was declared. The lack of clear guidance was blamed for compromising the response. *Id.* at 15.

Congress reacted to these failures by amending the Stafford Act to allow accelerated federal assistance, without a state request, when necessary to save lives, prevent suffering, and mitigate severe damage. 42 U.S.C. §5170(a)(5). This enhanced authority to "push" federal response resources, rather than wait for the "pull" from the states, is limited to situations where the President declares a "major disaster." The same legislation created a National Preparedness System, providing a statutory foundation for intergovernmental and interagency homeland security and emergency management coordination. *See* Department of Homeland Sec., *National Preparedness Guidelines* (Sept. 2007), *at* http://www.dhs.gov/xlibrary/assets/National_ Preparedness_Guidelines.pdf.

4.   The National Response Framework

In January 2008 DHS released a reinvented NRP—the National Response Framework (NRF). FEMA is designated overall coordinator of the federal response, and the FEMA administrator is given the responsibility for initiating the federal response to a crisis.

Department of Homeland Security, National Response Framework

pages 7-11, Jan. 2008
http://www.fema.gov/pdf/emergency/nrf/nrf-core.pdf

. . . The *National Response Framework* is always in effect, and elements can be implemented at any level at any time. The *Framework* is capabilities based, which is to say that local governments, tribes, States, and the Federal Government all develop functional capabilities and identify resources that may be required based on hazard identification and risk assessment, threats, and other potential incidents. . . .

Scope

The *Framework* provides structures for implementing nationwide response policy and operational coordination for all types of domestic incidents. It can be partially or fully implemented in the context of a threat, in anticipation of a significant event, or in response to an incident. Selective implementation allows for a scaled response, delivery of the resources needed, and an appropriate level of coordination. . . .

It is not always obvious at the outset whether a seemingly minor event might be the initial phase of a larger, rapidly growing threat. The *Framework* incorporates standardized organizational structures that promote on-scene initiative, innovation, and sharing of essential resources drawn from all levels of government, NGOs, and the private sector. Response must be quickly scalable, flexible, and adaptable.

The *Framework* is also intended to accelerate the assessment and response to incidents that may require Federal assistance.... [The] coordination of Federal incident assessment and response efforts is intended to occur seamlessly, without the need for any formal trigger mechanism.

This *Framework*, therefore, eliminates the Incident of National Significance declaration....

Response Doctrine

... The overarching objective of response activities centers upon saving lives and protecting property and the environment....

Incidents begin and end locally, and most are wholly managed at the local level. Many incidents require unified response from local agencies, NGOs, and the private sector, and some require additional support from neighboring jurisdictions or the State. A small number require Federal support. National response protocols recognize this and are structured to provide additional, tiered levels of support when there is a need for more resources or capabilities to support and sustain the response and initial recovery. All levels should be prepared to respond, anticipating resources that may be required....

A basic premise of the *Framework* is that incidents are generally handled at the lowest jurisdictional level possible.

Scalable, Flexible, and Adaptable Operational Capabilities

As incidents change in size, scope, and complexity, the response must adapt to meet requirements. The number, type, and sources of resources must be able to expand rapidly to meet needs associated with a given incident. The *Framework*'s disciplined and coordinated process can provide for a rapid surge of resources from all levels of government, appropriately scaled to need....

Unity of Effort Through Unified Command

Effective unified command is indispensable to response activities and requires a clear understanding of the roles and responsibilities of each participating organization. Success requires unity of effort, which respects the chain of command of each participating organization while harnessing seamless coordination across jurisdictions in support of common objectives.

Use of the Incident Command System (ICS) is an important element across multijurisdictional or multiagency incident management activities....

The Department of Defense (DOD) is a full partner in the Federal response to domestic incidents, and its response is fully coordinated through the mechanisms of this *Framework*. Concepts of "command" and "unity of command" have distinct legal and cultural meanings for military forces and military operations. For Federal military forces, command runs from the President to the Secretary of Defense to the Commander of the combatant command to the DOD on-scene commander. Military forces will always remain under the operational and administrative control of the military chain of command, and these forces are subject to redirection or recall at any time. The ICS "unified command" concept is distinct from the military chain of command use of this term. And, as such, military forces do not operate under the command of the Incident Commander or under the unified command structure. . . .

Department of Homeland Security, National Response Framework, Catastrophic Incident Annex

pages 1-7, Nov. 2008
http://www.fema.gov/pdf/emergency/nrf/nrf_CatastrophicIncidentAnnex.pdf

Scope

A catastrophic incident, as defined by the *NRF*, is any natural or manmade incident, including terrorism, that results in extraordinary levels of mass casualties, damage, or disruption severely affecting the population, infrastructure, environment, economy, national morale, and/or government functions. A catastrophic incident could result in sustained nationwide impacts over a prolonged period of time; almost immediately exceeds resources normally available to State, tribal, local, and private-sector authorities in the impacted area; and significantly interrupts governmental operations and emergency services to such an extent that national security could be threatened. These factors drive the urgency for coordinated national planning to ensure accelerated Federal and/or national assistance.

Recognizing that Federal and/or national resources are required to augment overwhelmed State, tribal, and local response efforts, the *NRF-CIA* establishes protocols to preidentify and rapidly deploy key essential resources (e.g., medical teams, search and rescue teams, transportable shelters, medical and equipment caches, etc.) that are expected to be urgently needed/required to save lives and contain incidents.

Upon the occurrence of a catastrophic incident, or in advance if determined by the Secretary of Homeland Security, the Government will deploy Federal resources, organized into incident-specific "packages," in accordance with the *NRF-CIS* [an annual supplement to the *CIA*, published separately] and in coordination with the affected State and incident command structure.

Where State, tribal, or local governments are unable to establish or maintain an effective incident command structure due to catastrophic conditions, the Federal Government, at the direction of the Secretary of Homeland Security, may establish a unified command structure, led by the Unified Coordination Group (UCG), to save lives, protect property, maintain operation of critical infrastructure/key resources (CIKR), contain the event, and protect national security. The Federal Government shall transition to its role of coordinating and supporting the State, tribal, or local government when they are capable of reestablishing their incident command. . . .

Policies

A catastrophic incident will likely trigger a Presidential major disaster declaration and result in the Secretary of Homeland Security or a designee implementing the *NRF-CIA/CIS*.

All deploying Federal resources remain under the control of their respective Federal department or agency during mobilization and deployment. Some Federal departments and agencies have the authority, under their own statutes, to deploy directly to the incident scene.

Federal resources arriving at a National Logistics Staging Area (NLSA) remain there until requested by State/local incident command authorities, when they are integrated into the response effort. . . .

States are encouraged to conduct planning in collaboration with the Federal Government for catastrophic incidents as part of their steady-state preparedness activities.

The Federal Government, in collaboration with States, tribes, local governments, the private sector, and nongovernmental organizations (NGOs), develops proactive plans for activation and implementation of the *NRF-CIA*, to include situations where the need exceeds or challenges the resources and/or capabilities of State and local governments to respond and where the Federal Government may temporarily assume roles typically performed by State, tribal, and local governments.

The occurrence or threat of multiple or successive catastrophic incidents may significantly reduce the size, speed, and depth of the Federal response. If deemed necessary or prudent, the Federal Government may reduce the allocation of finite resources when multiple venues are competing for the same resources.

Situation

The initial response to a catastrophic incident starts on a local level with the local, tribal and/or State responders. However, there may be circumstances that exceed the capabilities of State, local, or tribal authorities in which they are unable to initially establish or maintain a command structure for incident response. In these[] instances, accelerated Federal response may be warranted, and the Department of Homeland Security (DHS)/Federal Emergency Management Agency (FEMA) will coordinate response activities until local, tribal, and/or State authorities are capable or have re-established their incident command structure.

Continuity of Operations (COOP)/Continuity of Government (COG)

Following a catastrophic event, segments of State, tribal, and local governments as well as NGOs and the private sector may be severely compromised. The Federal Government and its national partners must be prepared to fill potential gaps to ensure continuity of government and public- and private-sector operations. The incident may cause significant disruption of the impacted area's CIKR, such as energy, transportation, telecommunications, law enforcement, and public health and health care systems. . . .

Planning Assumptions

A catastrophic incident will result in large numbers of casualties and/or displaced persons, possibly in the tens to hundreds of thousands. During a catastrophic incident response, priority is given to human life-saving operations.

The nature and scope of a catastrophic incident will immediately overwhelm State, tribal, and local response capabilities and require immediate Federal support.

A detailed and credible common operating picture will not be achievable for 24 to 48 hours (or longer) after the incident. As a result, response activities may have to begin without the benefit of a detailed or complete situation and critical needs assessment.

The nature and scope of the catastrophic incident will include major natural or manmade hazards including chemical, biological, radiological, nuclear, or high-yield explosive attacks, and cyber attacks.

A catastrophic incident has unique dimensions/characteristics requiring that response plans/strategies be flexible enough to effectively address emerging needs and requirements.

A catastrophic incident will occur with little or no warning. Some incidents may be well underway before detection.

Multiple incidents will occur simultaneously or sequentially in contiguous and/ or noncontiguous areas. Some incidents, such as a biological WMD attack, may be dispersed over a large geographic area and lack a defined incident site.

A catastrophic incident will produce environmental impacts that severely challenge the ability and capacity of governments and communities to achieve a timely recovery.

Federal resources must be capable of mobilization and deployment before they are requested via normal *NRF* protocols.

Large-scale evacuations, organized or self-directed, may occur.

Existing health care systems in the impacted area are expected to be quickly overwhelmed, requiring evacuation of existing patients from these facilities to accommodate increased patient workload if the facility remains operational. Additionally, those persons with special needs, including residents of nursing homes and extended care facilities, will require special attention during evacuation.

Large numbers of people will be left temporarily or permanently homeless and may require prolonged temporary housing. Some displaced people will require specialized attention, health care assistance, and assistance with activities of daily living based on their special needs....

A catastrophic incident will have significant international dimensions, including impacts on the health and welfare of border community populations, cross-border trade, transit, law enforcement coordination, and others....

Federal Response ...

NRF-CIA actions that the Federal Government takes in response to a catastrophic incident include:...

> For no-notice/short-notice catastrophic events when there is little or no time to assess the requirements of the State, tribal, and local governments, Federal departments and agencies initiate actions to mobilize and deploy resources by scenario type as planned for in the *NRF-CIS*. To that end, the Department of Defense (DOD) is prepared to provide capabilities in the following support categories: aviation, communication, defense coordinating officer/defense coordinating element, medical treatment, patient evacuation, decontamination, and logistics.

All Federal departments and agencies and organizations assigned primary or supporting ESF responsibilities immediately begin implementation of those responsibilities, as appropriate or when directed by the President.

Incident-specific resources and capabilities (e.g., medical teams, search and rescue teams, equipment, transportable shelters, preventive and therapeutic pharmaceutical caches, etc.) are activated and prepared for deployment to an NLSA near the
incident site. . . .

Regional Federal facilities are activated and prepared to receive and treat casualties from the incident area. Federal facilities are directed to reprioritize services (in
some cases possibly reducing or postponing certain customary services) until life-
saving activities are concluded. . . .

NOTES AND QUESTIONS

1. *Adequacy of Emergency Response Authority.* As the excerpts above reveal, federal
plans for responses to terrorist attacks and other catastrophes are written in very
general terms. The NRF urges "[g]overnments at all levels . . . to develop detailed,
robust, all-hazards response plans." National Response Framework, *supra*, at 28, but
the Framework itself remains mostly vague and anodyne. The CIA is more detailed,
but only in comparison to the NRF.

If you were responsible for implementing the policies outlined in the NRF and
CIA, would you know how they required you to respond to a terrorist attack like the
release of pneumonic plague? If not, where would you look for guidance to determine
the scope of your duties?

2. *National Preparedness.* In 2011, President Obama signed Presidential Policy
Directive/PPD-8 (Mar. 30, 2011), *at* http://www.dhs.gov/xlibrary/assets/presidential-
policy-directive-8-national-preparedness.pdf. PPD-8 reviews and replaces an earlier
directive from President Bush, HSPD-8 (2003), and outlines a vision for strengthening the nation's security and resilience through preparation for threats. The new PPD
directs "the development of a national preparedness goal that identifies the core
capabilities necessary for preparedness and a national preparedness system to
guide activities that will enable the Nation to achieve the goal." *Id.* The national
preparedness goal "shall be informed by the risk of specific threats and
vulnerabilities—taking into account regional variations—and include concrete,
measurable, and prioritized objectives to mitigate the risk." *Id.* Based on this brief
description, and considering the provisions of the NRF excerpted above, can you
outline the "prioritized objectives" of a national preparedness goal and indicate
how to measure our progress in meeting those objectives?

3. *Assigning Agency Responsibilities.* Elimination of the "Incidents of National Significance" designation in the NRF means that the Framework and NIMS are always in
effect. Yet the NRF is unclear about most specific operations issues. For example,
HSPD-5 (*supra* p. 739) indicates that DHS should assume overall incident management responsibility when another federal agency requests DHS assistance, when state
and local resources are overwhelmed and request federal assistance, when more than
one federal agency becomes involved in responding to the incident, or when the
President directs the Secretary of Homeland Security to assume management of
the incident. These criteria are repeated in the NRF. But what does it mean in practical terms for state and local resources to be "overwhelmed," and which state or local
officials must make a request to trigger the federal role?

4. *Coordination with First Responders.* The concept of "unified command" is central to the NRF and NIMS. In contrast to a military-type chain of command, unified command takes into account that there may be multiple agencies and jurisdictions responding to an emergency. Designated leaders of those entities work together to establish a common set of objectives, and they agree upon a single operations plan (SOP) for responding to the event. In operational terms unified command under the NRF and NIMS is facilitated through a Joint Field Office (JFO). What will be required in practical terms to create a viable SOP and to implement it in a crisis?

FEMA also coordinates support through any of the 15 Emergency Support Functions (ESFs) described in the NRF. The ESFs are functionally organized, and are staffed by specialists from federal agencies and the private sector. They integrate capabilities in support of state and local response agencies. Each ESF is headed by a lead federal agency. What is needed to ensure that these functions are carried out as needed?

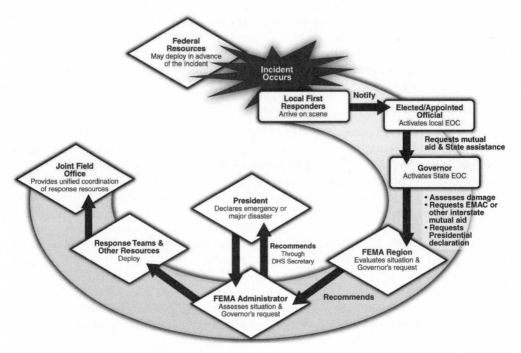

Overview of Stafford Act Support to States.

Department of Homeland Security, *Overview: ESF and Support Annexes Coordinating Federal Assistance in Support of the National Response Framework,* Jan. 2008, at 5.

5. *The Legal Status of the Federal Planning Documents.* Federal agency protocols designed for comprehensive application to government activities are often cast in the form of legislative rules (regulations) and are promulgated following the procedures of the Administrative Procedure Act (APA), 5 U.S.C. §§551-706 (2006).

The Homeland Security Act expressly grants rulemaking authority to DHS and states that the issuance of DHS regulations is generally governed by the APA. 6 U.S.C. §112(e). However, DHS took the position that because the National Response Framework and its associated planning documents were simply guidance documents, intended to create no binding or enforceable norms, it was not required to publish a Notice of Proposed Rulemaking or to invite public comments, as the APA normally requires for binding legislative regulations. Might a more transparent and participatory process produce better plans?

6. *A Military Role?* Each state's National Guard has elements trained and equipped to assist, under the direction of the state governor, in the response to a terrorist attack or a large natural disaster. See *infra* p. 785. At the federal level, the Stafford Act, the NRF, NRF/CIA, and other planning documents assign the Defense Department a supporting role in responding to a terrorist attack, including one involving a weapon of mass destruction. Should the military be given a larger role, or even lead agency responsibility? Consideration was given to such proposals in the wake of the flawed response to Hurricane Katrina. *See* David E. Sanger, *Bush Wants to Consider Broadening of Military's Powers During Natural Disasters*, N.Y. Times, Sept. 27, 2005. Do you think either state or federal governments could mount a fully effective response to such a calamity without the assistance of military forces? These questions are explored in Chapter 24.

7. *Regional Cooperation.* All 50 states, U.S. territories, and the District of Columbia have entered into a congressionally approved compact of mutual assistance, including help with evacuations. Emergency Management Assistance Compact, Pub. L. No. 104-321, 110 Stat. 3877 (1996). *See EMAC* (n.d.), *at* http://www.emacweb.org/?9. Regional mechanisms for response to disasters, or the lack thereof, were also the focus of reports assessing the 2005 response to Hurricane Katrina. *See The Federal Response to Hurricane Katrina, supra* p. 738; H. Select Bipartisan Comm. to Investigate the Preparation for and Response to Hurricane Katrina, *A Failure of Initiative* (2006), *available at* www.gpoaccess.gov/katrinareport/fullreport.pdf.

What advantages do regional response structures offer? What legal obstacles can you see to either the creation or implementation of these regional arrangements? Can one locality order its personnel or resources to help outside the locality? If such personnel are injured, who is liable? Who pays their salaries? Can the cost of lost or damaged equipment be recovered? How should such questions be answered?

8. *Viability of Plans?* Any response plans need to promise some predictability about the future. They should provide reasonable assurance that if all our defenses fail and we suffer another catastrophic terrorist attack, basic government structures will nevertheless survive, citizens will be protected from further harm, and normal life will eventually be substantially restored. Furthermore, both the existence of the plans and their viability must be made widely known. If the worst happens, members of the public must be convinced that it is in their best interests to cooperate in the implementation of the plan. The President should be convinced that even in a great crisis the rule of law can provide needed security — that she need not, for example, declare martial law. And potential terrorists should be deterred by the knowledge that if they attack, the American people will not lose faith in their government.

Do plans developed by DHS and other agencies provide these assurances? Any thoughtful answer must recognize the staggering complexity of the task, as well as the remarkable progress made since 9/11. Yet much remains to be done. One study at the end of the Bush administration offered this assessment:

> America is not ready for the next catastrophe. . . . There are still no detailed, government-wide plans to respond to a catastrophe. There is still considerable confusion over who will be in charge during a disaster. There are still almost no dedicated military forces on rapid alert to respond to a crisis here at home. There are still no guidelines to determine and assess the capabilities that states, cities, and towns should have to ensure they are prepared for the worst. [Christine E. Wormuth & Anne Witkowsky, *Managing the Next Domestic Catastrophe: Ready (Or Not)?* at vi (Center for Strategic & Int'l Studies, June 2008)]

See also David Heyman & James Jay Carafano, *Homeland Security 3.0: Building a National Enterprise to Keep America Safe, Free, and Prosperous* 1 (Heritage Found. & Center for Strategic & Int'l Studies, Sept. 18, 2008) (urging DHS to "foster better decision making in Congress and in the interagency process, support the development of a new generation of professionals, and facilitate information sharing throughout all elements of the enterprise[] . . . [and to] empower individuals and communities and extend international cooperation").

If you were named Homeland Security Secretary, what first steps would you take to prepare the nation for the next terrorist attack?

C. FIRST RESPONDERS: THE STATE AND LOCAL RESPONSE

1. State Law

Even if federal plans provide an overarching blueprint for emergency response, and the allure of federal funds entices states to adopt the NIMS mechanisms and complete the training and exercises that DHS and FEMA supply, the adage that "all incidents are local" has a close connection to reality, both practically and legally. State and local officials are always the first responders. The authority of these officials to act in anticipation of or in response to an emergency is part of a state's police powers. James G. Hodge, *The Role of New Federalism and Public Health Law*, 12 J.L. & Health 309 (1998). Those powers are at the core of state sovereignty and are derived from state constitutions and common law "police powers," and they are part of the reserved powers recognized by the Tenth Amendment to the U.S. Constitution. *See In re World Trade Ctr. Disaster Site Litig.*, 456 F. Supp. 2d 520, 550 (S.D.N.Y. 2006), *aff'd in part and dismissed in part*, 521 F.3d 169 (2d Cir. 2008) ("when an emergent disaster threatens society as a whole, the [common law] doctrine of *salus populi supreme lex* (the welfare of the people is the highest law) . . . encourage[s] immediate action to preserve society").

State constitutions and statutes typically give governors and public health officials broad discretion to act to protect public health and safety, and in an emergency to suspend laws and administrative rules, order evacuations and quarantines, commandeer resources, and control property. In the event of an attack with biological weapons, for example, these officials may prevent infected persons from spreading the disease to others. Healthy but exposed persons may be vaccinated or given medicine or have their movements restricted. *See* Edward A. Fallone, *Preserving the Public Health: A Proposal to Quarantine Recalcitrant AIDS Carriers*, 68 B.U. L. Rev. 441, 460-461 (1988). The federal government additionally has interstate and foreign quarantine authority, assessed *infra* pp. 755-759.

NOTES AND QUESTIONS

1. *Quarantine Authority.* The Supreme Court has long recognized the authority of the government to erect quarantines, both to confine persons and to exclude them, in order to prevent the spread of contagious or infectious diseases. In *Gibbons v. Ogden*, 22 U.S. 1, 25 (1824), the Supreme Court referred to a state's authority to quarantine, noting that even though quarantine laws affect commerce, their objective is to protect public health and they are thus within the authority of state and local governments. In recent times the Court approved the confinement of a sexually violent predator, declaring that

> we have never held that the Constitution prevents a State from civilly detaining those for whom no treatment is available, but who nevertheless pose a danger to others. A State could hardly be seen as furthering a "punitive" purpose by involuntarily confining persons afflicted with an untreatable, highly contagious disease. [*Kansas v. Hendricks*, 521 U.S. 346, 366 (1997).]

See also Jacobson v. Massachusetts, 197 U.S. 11 (1905) (upholding mandatory vaccinations following a smallpox outbreak); *Compagnie Francaise de Navigation a Vapeur v. Louisiana Bd. of Health*, 186 U.S. 380 (1902) (upholding a quarantine in New Orleans following a yellow fever outbreak). And while the Supreme Court has called the constitutional right to travel from one state to another "firmly imbedded in our jurisprudence," *Saenz v. Roe*, 526 U.S. 489, 498 (1999), other courts have held that the right may be curtailed in an emergency. *See, e.g., Smith v. Avino*, 91 F.3d 105 (11th Cir. 1996) (upholding a curfew in South Florida in wake of Hurricane Andrew). *See generally* Kathleen S. Swendiman & Jennifer K. Elsea, *Federal and State Quarantine and Isolation Authority* (Cong. Res. Serv. RL33201), Jan. 23, 2007.

According to one analysis, in the event of a bioterrorist attack, "[a]lmost certainly, a clash would occur between public health and legal officials at the local, state, and national levels about the measures necessary and the entity with jurisdiction to act." Smithson & Levy, *supra*, at 269. If state or local response efforts did come directly into conflict with federal measures, the former presumably would have to give way under the Supremacy Clause. Can you describe limits to the federal government's preemptive power to respond to a bioterrorist attack, aside from individual rights protections in the Bill of Rights that constrain all government actions? How about an attack using a chemical or radiological weapon? How could potential conflicts between federal and state or local response efforts be minimized?

2. *Erring on the Side of Caution?* How widely may government officials establish a cordon around an area suspected of containing infected persons or hazardous chemicals? How should doubts be resolved about the possible exposure of individuals to a contagion? In *Empire Kosher Poultry, Inc. v. Hallowell*, 816 F.2d 907 (3d Cir. 1987), a due process case involving a quarantine of poultry to combat avian influenza, the court

said that evidence of disease need not be shown before a quarantine is erected, since tests might not immediately reveal the existence of infection. Moreover, said the court, a broad buffer zone could be established to prevent the inadvertent movement of infected poultry out of the quarantine area.

3. *Enforcing a Quarantine.* One analysis of a 2000 federal TOPOFF exercise described above calls the quarantine of large groups of people "impractical," citing concern about the level of force needed for enforcement:

> Not only were local officials uncertain about their statutory authority to proceed with a quarantine, they believed that the public would probably not cooperate with compulsory orders to commandeer property, restrict movement of people, or forcibly remove them to designated locations. Traditionally, governments have counted upon the public to comply with public health orders on the basis that the good of the community overrides the rights of the individual. These days, however, citizens get angry at forced evacuations for such visible calamities as hurricanes, floods, and wildfires, not to mention a stay-at-home order for a microscopic killer that they may doubt is in their midst. Police also questioned whether their colleagues would recognize the authority of the public health officer to declare a quarantine or would even stick around to enforce the order. Finally, some wondered whether there were enough local and state police to quarantine a large metropolitan area in the first place. [Amy E. Smithson & Leslie-Anne Levy, *Ataxia: The Chemical and Biological Terrorism Threat and the U.S. Response* 269 (Henry L. Stimson Ctr. 2000).]

According to one police captain, "If police officers knew that a biological agent had been released, 99 percent of the cops would not be here. They would grab their families and leave." *Id.* at 270 n.225. Do these practical problems have legal solutions?

How would you describe the authority of law enforcement personnel who remained on duty? Could they, for example, shoot persons trying to escape the quarantine?

4. *Other Constraints on Individual Liberties.* In addition to quarantines, involuntary evacuations, and forced inoculations, government responses to a terrorist attack might include compulsory physical examinations to determine whether individuals are infected with a contagious disease, inspections of private property, and reviews of personal medical records. The Court has held that "regulatory" or "special needs" searches of individuals for noncriminal regulatory purposes (that is, not for the purpose of obtaining criminal evidence) do not offend the Fourth Amendment if the state's interest in the result is sufficiently compelling and the search is reasonable in the circumstances. *See, e.g., Vernonia Sch. Dist. 47J v. Acton,* 515 U.S. 646, 653 (1995) (upholding random drug tests of student athletes when "special needs, beyond the normal need for law enforcement, make the warrant and probable-cause requirement impracticable"); *National Treasury Employees Union v. Von Raab,* 489 U.S. 656 (1989) (approving drug tests of Customs Service employees); *cf. Ferguson v. City of Charleston,* 532 U.S. 67 (2001) (rejecting nonconsensual drug testing of obstetrics patients when results were to be given to police). In *Camara v. Municipal Court of San Francisco,* 387 U.S. 523, 539 (1967), the Court observed that warrantless inspections are "traditionally upheld in emergency situations." (Recall our consideration of these same exceptions to the Fourth Amendment's warrant requirement in connection with efforts to prevent terrorist attacks by surveillance, in Chapter 8, and screening for access to

public places and transportation systems, in Chapter 10.) In the wake of a bioterrorist attack, the government's interest in examining individuals and their property would be strong and immediate. Do you think it would outweigh individual privacy interests? *See* Barry Kellman, *Biological Terrorism: Legal Measures for Preventing Catastrophe*, 24 Harv. J.L. & Pub. Pol'y 417, 478-485 (2001).

Of course, state public health laws, including extreme measures such as quarantine, are also subject to constitutional due process constraints. Freedom from physical restraint is a classic "liberty" interest protected by the Fourteenth Amendment. *Kansas v. Hendricks, supra*, 521 U.S. at 356. How would you describe due process limits on state powers to respond to a terrorist attack? (Recall here our discussion in Chapter 16 of due process considerations in the imprisonment of terrorist suspects.)

2. The Model State Emergency Health Powers Act (MSEHPA)

State quarantine and vaccination laws, many of them decades old, do not reflect current disease or treatment science, and they are often targeted at particular diseases. *See* Lawrence O. Gostin, *The Law and the Public's Health: A Study of Infectious Disease Law in the United States*, 99 Colum. L. Rev. 59, 102-106 (1999).

Spurred by the 9/11 and anthrax attacks in 2001, states and cities began to reconsider a range of emergency response issues, including quarantine and isolation authorities. The Model State Emergency Health Powers Act (MSEHPA) (draft Dec. 21, 2001), *at* http://www.publichealthlaw.net/MSEHPA/MSEHPA.pdf, was drawn up in 2001 by public health experts at Georgetown and Johns Hopkins Universities. *See* Center for Law & the Public's Health, *Model State Public Health Laws* (n.d.), *at* http://www.publichealthlaw.net/ModelLaws/MSEHPA.php.

The MSEHPA borrows from various state laws and provides a template for sweeping state authorities that may be invoked in a public health emergency. It authorizes governors to declare a "public health emergency" after consulting with public health authorities or, in the absence of such consultation, "when the situation calls for prompt and timely action." MSEHPA §401. A "public health emergency" is defined as "an occurrence or imminent threat" of illness that is "believed to be caused" by bioterrorism or other disasters and poses "a high probability" of a large number of deaths, serious or long-term disabilities, or widespread exposure "that poses a significant risk of substantial harm to a large number of people in the affected population." *Id.* §104(m). During a public health emergency, a governor may suspend any statute concerning state government procedures or any agency rule or orders "to the extent that strict compliance with the same would prevent, hinder, or delay necessary action" in response to the public health emergency. *Id.* §403(a)(1). The public health emergency "shall" be terminated by a governor by executive order "upon finding that the occurrence of an illness or health condition that caused the emergency no longer poses a high probability of a large number of deaths in the affected population . . . or a significant risk of substantial future harm to a large number of people in the affected population." *Id.* §405(a). Otherwise, a public health emergency will terminate automatically after 30 days unless renewed by the governor or terminated earlier by majority vote of both chambers of a state legislature. *Id.* §405(b), (c).

In addition, during a public health emergency the MSEHPA authorizes state officials to close, evacuate, or decontaminate "any facility" or decontaminate or destroy "any material" where "there is a reasonable cause to believe that it may endanger the public health." *Id.* §501. Public health authorities are also given power to condemn or assume control over private property, control and manage health care facilities, and control routes and modes of transportation "if such action is reasonable and necessary to respond to the public health emergency." *Id.* §502.

The MSEHPA also includes these provisions concerning vaccination, treatment, isolation, and quarantine:

Model State Emergency Health Powers Act
draft Dec. 21, 2001
at http://www.publichealthlaw.net/MSEHPA/MSEHPA.pdf

ARTICLE VI.   SPECIAL POWERS DURING A STATE OF PUBLIC HEALTH EMERGENCY: PROTECTION OF PERSONS

Section 603. Vaccination and treatment.

During a state of public health emergency the public health authority may exercise the following emergency powers over persons as necessary to address the public health emergency—

(a) Vaccination. To vaccinate persons as protection against infectious disease and to prevent the spread of contagious or possibly contagious disease.

(1) Vaccination may be performed by any qualified person authorized to do so by the public health authority.

(2) A vaccine to be administered must not be such as is reasonably likely to lead to serious harm to the affected individual.

(3) To prevent the spread of contagious or possibly contagious disease the public health authority may isolate or quarantine, pursuant to Section 604, persons who are unable or unwilling for reasons of health, religion, or conscience to undergo vaccination pursuant to this Section.

(b) Treatment. To treat persons exposed to or infected with disease.

(1) Treatment may be administered by any qualified person authorized to do so by the public health authority.

(2) Treatment must not be such as is reasonably likely to lead to serious harm to the affected individual.

(3) To prevent the spread of contagious or possibly contagious disease the public health authority may isolate or quarantine, pursuant to Section 604, persons who are unable or unwilling for reasons of health, religion, or conscience to undergo treatment pursuant to this Section.

Section 604. Isolation and quarantine.

(a) Authorization. During the public health emergency, the public health authority may isolate...or quarantine...an individual or groups of individuals.... The public health authority may also establish and maintain places of isolation and quarantine, and set rules and make orders. Failure to obey these rules, orders, or provisions shall constitute a misdemeanor.

(b) Conditions and principles. The public health authority shall adhere to the following conditions and principles when isolating or quarantining individuals or groups of individuals:

(1) Isolation and quarantine must be by the least restrictive means necessary to prevent the spread of a contagious or possibly contagious disease to others and may include, but are not limited to, confinement to private homes or other private and public premises.

(2) Isolated individuals must be confined separately from quarantined individuals.

(3) The health status of isolated and quarantined individuals must be monitored regularly to determine if they require isolation or quarantine.

(4) If a quarantined individual subsequently becomes infected or is reasonably believed to have become infected with a contagious or possibly contagious disease he or she must promptly be removed to isolation.

(5) Isolated and quarantined individuals must be immediately released when they pose no substantial risk of transmitting a contagious or possibly contagious disease to others.

(6) The needs of persons isolated and quarantined shall be addressed in a systematic and competent fashion, including, but not limited to, providing adequate food, clothing, shelter, means of communication with those in isolation or quarantine and outside these settings, medication, and competent medical care.

(7) Premises used for isolation and quarantine shall be maintained in a safe and hygienic manner and be designed to minimize the likelihood of further transmission of infection or other harms to persons isolated and quarantined.

(8) To the extent possible, cultural and religious beliefs should be considered in addressing the needs of individuals, and establishing and maintaining isolation and quarantine premises. . . .

Section 605.   Procedures for isolation and quarantine.

During a public health emergency, the isolation and quarantine of an individual or groups of individuals shall be undertaken in accordance with the following procedures.

(a) Temporary isolation and quarantine without notice.

(1) Authorization. The public health authority may temporarily isolate or quarantine an individual or groups of individuals through a written directive if delay in imposing the isolation or quarantine would significantly jeopardize the public health authority's ability to prevent or limit the transmission of a contagious or possibly contagious disease to others. . . .

(4) Petition for continued isolation or quarantine. Within ten (10) days after issuing the written directive, the public health authority shall file a petition pursuant to Section 605(b) for a court order authorizing the continued isolation or quarantine of the isolated or quarantined individual or groups of individuals.

[Section 605(b) permits the public health authority to petition for isolation or quarantine with notice to affected individuals and a hearing within five days, with a ten-day extension possible in "extraordinary circumstances." The court will grant the state's petition if a preponderance of the evidence shows that isolation or quarantine is "reasonably necessary to prevent or limit the transmission of a contagious or possibly contagious disease to others."]

NOTES AND QUESTIONS

1. *Status of State Legislation.* According to the Center for Law and the Public's Health, as of July 2009, 38 states and the District of Columbia have enacted legislation that includes provisions from or closely related to the MSEHPA. A table documenting state legislative activity is available at http://www. publichealthlaw.net/Resources/ Modellaws.php. State representatives and various public health experts collaborated in 2003 to produce an alternative model that borrows some provisions from the MSEHPA, and provides a more comprehensive model for public health regulation. *See* State of Alaska, Health & Human Servs., *The Turning Point Model State Public Health Act* (June 21, 2004), *at* http://www.hss.state.ak.us/dph/improving/turningpoint/ MSPHA.htm.

2. *Constitutional?* Would the portions of the Model Act set out above survive a challenge to their constitutionality?

3. *Commandeering Resources.* Article V of the MSEHPA provides sweeping powers for a state public health authority to commandeer private resources during a public health emergency. In addition to the authority to close, evacuate, or decontaminate facilities or materials, and to gain access to and control of facilities, private property, and transportation modes, state officials would be given control over the procurement, rationing, and distribution of health care supplies. MSEHPA §§501-505. The Model Act anticipates that "just compensation" would be paid to any owner for property lawfully taken during the public health emergency. *Id.* §506. Under what circumstances would the provisions of Title V be implemented? If enacted, would these provisions be constitutional? Wise? How would you advise a state legislature interested in providing for these contingencies to ensure against the abuse of such powers?

4. *Compulsion of People.* Review the provisions of Article VI of the MSEHPA above. What is the difference between isolation and quarantine? What practical difference does it make whether a person is subject to an isolation or quarantine order? How useful are the conditions and principles set forth in §604(b) in deciding whether to impose isolation or quarantine? Are the public health needs and rights of affected individuals and other persons adequately served? Are the proposed procedures constitutional? Finally, who would actually enforce the quarantine, and how?

5. *Dealing with a Medical Surge.* Among the biggest challenges facing public health officials and other state and local decision makers in a crisis is the prospect of a medical surge — a demand for services and protection that far outstrips existing capacities. Under triage conditions criteria must be developed to strictly ration care. It may be important to waive licensing and certification requirements for care givers to permit the widespread use of volunteers, and to provide waivers of liability for those volunteers. Neither MSEHPA nor most existing state and local

laws provide expressly for such a medical surge. Federal law requires hospitals with emergency departments to provide medical screening and stabilization for every patient who arrives for care. 42 U.S.C. §1395dd (2006). How would you advise state decision makers to plan for a surge in patient demand that outstrips available resources?

6. *A Needed Set of Correctives?* Should state legislatures enact some version of the MSEHPA? What provisions would you say are most controversial, and why? Some scholars have claimed that the Model Act is unnecessary and is an overreaction to the need for incremental public health law reform. *See* LSU Program in Law, Sci. & Pub. Health, *White Paper #2: Review of the Model State Emergency Health Powers Act; Legislative Alternatives to the Model State Emergency Health Powers Act (MSEHPA)* (Apr. 2003), *available at* http://www.biotech.law.lsu.edu/blaw/bt/MSEHPA-review.htm; Erin M. Page, *Balancing Individual Rights and Public Health Safety During Quarantine: the U.S. and Canada,* 38 Case W. Res. J. Int'l L. 517 (2006-2007).

D. THE FEDERAL ROLE IN RESPONDING TO BIOTERRORIST ATTACKS

The federal responsibility for biological incidents is shared by several agencies, as noted earlier. Overall coordination is supposed to be provided by DHS. HHS, acting through the CDC, will play a leading role based on its specialized experience and expertise. Some of the statutory and regulatory authorities relevant to that role are set out below.

Public Health Service Act
42 U.S.C. §§201-300bbb (2006 & Supp. IV 2010)

§243. General Grant of Authority for Cooperation. . . .

(c) Development of plan to control epidemics and meet emergencies or problems resulting from disasters; . . .
(1) The Secretary [of Health and Human Services (the "Service")] is authorized to develop (and may take such action as may be necessary to implement) a plan under which personnel, equipment, medical supplies, and other resources of the Service and other agencies under the jurisdiction of the Secretary may be effectively used to control epidemics of any disease or condition and to meet other health emergencies or problems. . . .

§264. Regulations to Control Communicable Diseases

(a) Promulgation and Enforcement by Surgeon General. The Surgeon General, with the approval of the Secretary, is authorized to make and enforce such regulations as in his judgment are necessary to prevent the introduction, transmission, or spread of communicable diseases from foreign countries into the States or possessions, or from one State or possession into any other State or possession. For purposes of carrying out and enforcing such regulations, the Surgeon General may provide for such inspection, fumigation, disinfection . . . and other measures, as in his judgment may be necessary.

(b) Apprehension, detention, or conditional release of individuals. Regulations prescribed under this section shall not provide for the apprehension, detention, or conditional release of individuals except for the purpose of preventing the introduction, transmission, or spread of such communicable diseases as may be specified from time to time in Executive orders of the President upon the recommendation of the Secretary, in consultation with the Surgeon General. . . .

(d) (1) Apprehension and examination of persons reasonably believed to be infected. Regulations prescribed under this section may provide for the apprehension and examination of any individual reasonably believed to be infected with a communicable disease in a qualifying stage and (A) to be moving or about to move from a State to another State; or (B) to be a probable source of infection to individuals who, while infected with such disease in a qualifying stage, will be moving from a State to another State. Such regulations may provide that if upon examination any such individual is found to be infected, he may be detained for such time and in such manner as may be reasonably necessary. . . .

HHS has adopted the following regulations to implement this statutory authority:

Interstate Quarantine Regulations
42 C.F.R. pt. 70 (2010)

§70.2 Measures in the Event of Inadequate Local Control.

Whenever the Director of the Centers for Disease Control and Prevention determines that the measures taken by health authorities of any State or possession (including political subdivisions thereof) are insufficient to prevent the spread of any of the communicable diseases from such State or possession to any other State or possession, he/she may take such measures to prevent such spread of the diseases as he/she deems reasonably necessary, including inspection. . . .

§70.5 Certain Communicable Diseases; Special Requirements.

The following provisions are applicable with respect to any person who is in the communicable period of cholera, plague, smallpox, typhus or yellow fever, or who, having been exposed to any such disease, is in the incubation period thereof:

(a) Requirements relating to travelers.

(1) No such person shall travel from one State or possession to another, or on a conveyance engaged in interstate traffic, without a written permit of the Surgeon General or his/her authorized representative. . . .

§70.6 Apprehension and Detention of Persons with Specific Diseases.

Regulations prescribed in this part authorize the detention, isolation, quarantine, or conditional release of individuals, for the purpose of preventing the introduction, transmission, and spread of the communicable diseases listed in an Executive Order setting out a list of quarantinable communicable diseases, as provided under section 361(b) of the Public Health Service Act. Executive Order 13295, of April 4, 2003, contains the current revised list of quarantinable communicable diseases, and may be obtained at http://www.cdc.gov, or at http://www.archives. gov/federal_register/. If this Order is amended, HHS will enforce that amended order immediately and update this reference.

NOTES AND QUESTIONS

1. *Who's in Charge?* Can you tell from the authorities we have examined who will be responsible for coordinating and implementing all these federal, state, and local laws in a great crisis? In a portion of the federal statute not quoted above, the federal government may assist with or take over management of an intrastate incident if requested by a state or if the federal government determines that local efforts are not sufficient. 42 U.S.C. §264(e).

2. *Responding to Listed Pathogens.* The HHS regulations set out above have been amended several times since September 11, 2001, to expand the list of infectious agents for which the CDC may erect quarantines or detain persons. The executive order incorporated by reference in §70.6 lists cholera, diphtheria, infectious tuberculosis, plague, smallpox, yellow fever, and viral hemorrhagic fevers (including Lassa, Marburg, and Ebola). It also lists severe acute respiratory syndrome (SARS). Not listed are tularemia, botulism, and other contagions that could be weaponized and used by terrorists. Nor are there federal regulations authorizing the imposition of quarantine following an attack by chemical, radiological, or nuclear weapons, although federal authority may exist to prevent the transmission of disease that could occur as secondary effects of the contamination. An order aimed at halting the spread of bird flu adds "influenza caused by novel or reemergent influenza viruses that are causing, or have the potential to cause, a pandemic." Exec. Order No. 13,375 (Apr. 1, 2005). How should government authorities respond to the terrorist release of an infectious agent not listed or not immediately identifiable?

In May 2006, the Homeland Security Council issued its *Pandemic Influenza Implementation Plan, available at* http://www.pandemicflu.gov/professional/federal/ pandemic-influenza-implementation.pdf. At 233 pages, it sets out fairly elaborate guidance for U.S. planning in areas of primary federal responsibility, international efforts, controls of borders and transportation, protection of human and animal health, and public safety, emphasizing the roles of state and local governments wherever possible. Because a bird flu pandemic would present many of the legal and practical problems posed by a terrorist attack using plague or some other contagious disease, the *Implementation Plan* probably reflects the latest government thinking about large-scale, integrated planning for both kinds of catastrophe. Periodic updates of the *Implementation Plan* may be found at FLU.gov, *Federal Government* (n.d.), *at* http://www.flu.gov/professional/federal. *See generally* Sarah A. Lister, *Public Health and Medical Emergency Management: Issues in the 112th Congress* (Cong. Res. Serv. R41646), Feb. 18, 2011.

3. *Responding to Anthrax.* What measures need to be undertaken by federal officials to address the threat posed by terrorists sending anthrax spores through the mail, as happened in the aftermath of the September 11, 2001, attacks? Anthrax is extremely dangerous but not communicable. Can you explain how various federal agencies might cooperate in this effort? Do HHS and the CDC have the authority they need to be helpful? A Defense Department–sponsored report concluded that the anthrax letter attacks "revealed weaknesses in almost every aspect of U.S. biopreparedness and response." David Heyman, *Lessons from the Anthrax Attacks: Implications for U.S. Bioterrorism Preparedness* at viii (Apr. 2002), *available at* http://www.fas.org/irp/threat/cbw/dtra02.pdf. *See also* Keith Rhodes, *Diffuse Security Threats: Information on U.S. Domestic Anthrax Attacks* (GAO-03-0323T), Dec. 10, 2002, *available at* pp. 808-822 of another report found at http://www.fas.org/irp/congress/2002_rpt/911rept.pdf; General Accounting Office, *Bioterrorism: Public Health Responses to Anthrax Incidents of 2001* (GAO-04-152), Oct. 2003.

4. *Responding to Smallpox.* Reflecting growing fears that remaining supplies of smallpox virus might fall into the hands of terrorists, the CDC has published a plan for responding to an outbreak of a disease thought to have been eradicated in the 1970s. *See CDC Smallpox Response Plan and Guidelines (Version 3.0)* (June 23, 2004, with updates), *at* http://www.bt.cdc.gov/agent/smallpox/response-plan. The plan calls for employment of a "ring" strategy to isolate confirmed and suspected smallpox cases, vaccinate persons who may have come into contact with them, and keep all possible contacts under close surveillance. The size of a ring is to be determined by state and federal health officials.

5. *Federal Authority to Constrain Persons?* HHS's enabling legislation states that an "individual believed to be infected with a communicable disease in a communicable stage" may be "apprehended and examined." 42 U.S.C. §264(d). If found to be infected, the individual may then be "detained for such time and in such manner as may be reasonably necessary." *Id.* Do you think this language is meant to give the CDC authority to quarantine an entire city? Or to require vaccinations? What is the relationship between the HHS/CDC authorities and state law, whether or not a state has adopted something like the MSEHPA?

Do you think that principles of federalism and constitutional limits on the exercise of federal regulatory authority permit a federal quarantine within a single state? The Supreme Court has stated that Congress may "regulate those activities having a substantial relation to interstate commerce," *United States v. Lopez*, 514 U.S. 549, 555 (1995), but it has also ruled that Congress may not regulate non-economic activities within a state solely on the basis of the effect of those activities on interstate commerce. *United States v. Morrison*, 529 U.S. 598 (2000). A 2009 memorandum from the Attorney General to the Secretaries of HHS and DHS and other federal officials concluded that the authority to implement a federal quarantine intrastate is unclear. Memorandum for the President from the Attorney General, *Summary of Legal Authorities for Use in Response to an Outbreak of Pandemic Influenza* (Apr. 25, 2009), *available at* http://www.ncsl.org/IssuesResearch/Health/H1N1FluSwineFluPublicHealthAlert/tabid/17089/Default.aspx. Statutory and constitutional bases and limits for both state and federal public health regulations dealing with bioterrorism threats are briefed extensively in proposed CDC regulations. Department of Health & Human Servs., *Control of Communicable Diseases*, 70 Fed. Reg. 71,892-01, 71,893-71,896 (Nov. 30, 2005).

6. *Enforcing a Quarantine.* HHS and the CDC have no police force of their own to enforce a federal quarantine. Do you think such a quarantine could be enforced without the use of military forces? See *infra* pp. 783-788.

7. *Triage and Surge Control Redux.* The CDC maintains the Strategic National Stockpile (SNS) program. Within 12 hours of a terrorist attack, the Stockpile can deliver "push packages" containing needed pharmaceuticals and other medical supplies anywhere in the country. *See* CDC, *Strategic National Stockpile* (Apr. 14, 2005), *at* http://www.cdc.gov/phpr/stockpile.htm. Inventories are nevertheless limited, and they might not be adequate to treat every person affected by an outbreak of some diseases. Who do you think should receive such limited supplies first? Who should be empowered to choose among potential recipients? Would it be a good idea to decide such questions in advance of a terrorist attack or pandemic? If so, how?

Federal law also authorizes the waiver of various regulatory requirements in the event of a public health emergency. For example, the Food and Drug Administration (FDA) may permit the use of an unapproved drug or device in an emergency involving a biological, chemical, radiological, or nuclear agent. 21 U.S.C. §§360bbb-3(a) (2006).

The Military's
Domestic Role

24

Until recently the Defense Department had organized itself almost exclusively to fight a conventional war far from America's shores. In part this reflected the absence of the sort of domestic threats that have emerged in the last decade or so. It also demonstrated the public's antipathy toward any sort of military involvement in domestic life. During the Vietnam War, the Supreme Court noted "a traditional and strong resistance of Americans to any military intrusion into civilian affairs." *Laird v. Tatum*, 408 U.S. 1, 15 (1972). *See* W. Kent Davis, *Swords into Plowshares: The Dangerous Politicization of the Military in the Post-Cold War Era*, 33 Val. U. L. Rev. 61, 64-77 (1998). Thus, for most of our history the military's domestic role has consisted primarily of preparations for foreign wars and of occasional support for civilian authorities in curbing civil unrest and fighting the "war on drugs."

On September 11, 2001, however, the military's role, like so much else in this country, began to change. The following day the President described the terrorist attacks as "acts of war." The battlefield in this war obviously extends to the U.S. homeland. We saw in Chapters 16 and 22 that the military may be used to detain and try suspected terrorists. Should troops be deployed even more broadly on this new front? If so, should their Rules of Engagement (ROE) be different from those that guide military operations abroad? What legal authorities exist or would have to be created to accommodate these needed changes?

In Part A of this chapter we address the deep-seated American tradition of avoiding entanglement of the military in civilian life, as reflected in laws designed to limit that entanglement. Part B concerns the domestic intelligence role of the military. Finally, in Part C, we examine the military's role in responding to a terrorist attack on the homeland.

A. THE TRADITIONAL ROLE OF THE MILITARY IN AMERICAN SOCIETY

The domestic use of troops has been a fact of life and a matter of controversy at least since President Washington called out the militia to put down the Whiskey Rebellion in 1794. Many other Presidents have deployed federal military forces to help keep the peace, to aid local governments in natural disasters, and to enforce federal and state laws. State governors have called out their militias even more often, especially in the first three decades of the twentieth century. From the earliest days of the Republic, however, Americans have resisted any involvement by military forces in domestic matters.

1. The Posse Comitatus Act as a Background Principle

Could the President deploy troops to enforce a quarantine in the event of a bioterrorist attack like the one outlined in the plague scenario, *supra* p. 731? Could the troops detain looters? Could they shoot people trying to break out of the quarantine? The following decision may provide some guidance.

Bissonette v. Haig

United States Court of Appeals, Eighth Circuit, 1985
776 F.2d 1384, *aff'd*, 800 F.2d 812 (8th Cir. 1986) (en banc),
aff'd, 485 U.S. 264 (1988)

ARNOLD, J. This is an action for damages caused by defendants' alleged violations of the Constitution of the United States. . . .

This case arises out of the occupation of the village of Wounded Knee, South Dakota, on the Pine Ridge Reservation by an armed group of Indians on February 27, 1973. On the evening when the occupation began, members of the Federal Bureau of Investigation, the United States Marshals Service, and the Bureau of Indian Affairs Police sealed off the village by establishing roadblocks at all major entry and exit roads. The standoff between the Indians and the law enforcement authorities ended about ten weeks later with the surrender of the Indians occupying the village. . . .

In their amended complaint, plaintiffs allege . . . that they were unreasonably seized and confined in the village of Wounded Knee contrary to the Fourth Amendment and their rights to free movement and travel. Second, they claim that they were unreasonably searched by ground and aerial surveillance. In both cases, plaintiffs assert that the seizures and searches were unreasonable because "Defendants accomplished or caused to be accomplished those actions by means of the unconstitutional and felonious use of parts of the United States Army or Air Force. . . ." . . . This case comes to us on appeal from a dismissal for failure to state a claim, and we therefore accept for present purposes the factual allegations of the complaint.

These allegations must be viewed against the background of the Posse Comitatus Act of 1878, 18 U.S.C. §1385, which plaintiffs claim was violated here. The statute provides:

§1385. Use of Army and Air Force as Posse Comitatus[1]

Whoever, except in cases and under circumstances expressly authorized by the Constitution or Act of Congress, willfully uses any part of the Army or the Air Force as a posse

[1. The Latin term posse comitatus means, literally, "power or authority of the county," but it connotes a body of persons summoned by a sheriff to assist in preserving the peace or enforcing the law. The persons summoned to assist the sheriff might, of course, be either civilian or military. —Eds.]

comitatus or otherwise to execute the laws shall be fined not more than $10,000 or imprisoned not more than two years, or both.

A

The first two sets of claims raise the question whether a search or seizure, otherwise permissible, can be rendered unreasonable under the Fourth Amendment because military personnel or equipment were used to accomplish those actions. We believe that the Constitution, certain Acts of Congress, and the decisions of the Supreme Court embody certain limitations on the use of military personnel in enforcing the civil law, and that searches and seizures in circumstances which exceed those limits are unreasonable under the Fourth Amendment.

. . . Reasonableness is determined by balancing the interests for and against the seizure. Usually, the interests arrayed against a seizure are those of the individual in privacy, freedom of movement, or, in the case of a seizure by deadly force, life. Here, however, the opposing interests are more societal and governmental than strictly individual in character. They concern the special threats to constitutional government inherent in military enforcement of civilian law. That these governmental interests should weigh in the Fourth Amendment balance is neither novel nor surprising. In the typical Fourth Amendment case, the interests of the individual are balanced against those of the government. That some of those governmental interests are on the other side of the Fourth Amendment balance does not make them any less relevant or important.

Civilian rule is basic to our system of government. The use of military forces to seize civilians can expose civilian government to the threat of military rule and the suspension of constitutional liberties. On a lesser scale, military enforcement of the civil law leaves the protection of vital Fourth and Fifth Amendment rights in the hands of persons who are not trained to uphold these rights. It may also chill the exercise of fundamental rights, such as the rights to speak freely and to vote, and create the atmosphere of fear and hostility which exists in territories occupied by enemy forces.

The interest in limiting military involvement in civilian affairs has a long tradition beginning with the Declaration of Independence and continued in the Constitution, certain Acts of Congress, and decisions of the Supreme Court. The Declaration of Independence states among the grounds for severing ties with Great Britain that the King "has kept among us, in times of peace, Standing Armies without Consent of our Legislature . . . [and] has affected to render the Military independent of and superior to the Civil power." These concerns were later raised at the Constitutional Convention. Luther Martin of Maryland said, "when a government wishes to deprive its citizens of freedom, and reduce them to slavery, it generally makes use of a standing army."

The Constitution itself limits the role of the military in civilian affairs: it makes the President, the highest civilian official in the Executive Branch, Commander in Chief of the armed services (Art. II, §2); it limits the appropriations for armed forces to two years and grants to the Congress the power to make rules to govern the armed forces (Art. I, §8, cl. 14); and it forbids the involuntary quartering of soldiers in any house in time of peace (Third Amendment).

Congress has passed several statutes limiting the use of the military in enforcing the civil law [including the Posse Comitatus Act and the Insurrection Act, both addressed *infra*]. . . .

The Supreme Court has also recognized the constitutional limitations placed on military involvement in civilian affairs. A leading case is *Ex parte Milligan*, 71 U.S. 2, 124 (1866).... More recently, in *Laird v. Tatum*, 408 U.S. 1, 15-16 (1972), statements the Court made in dicta reaffirm these limitations....

The governmental interests favoring military assistance to civilian law enforcement are primarily twofold: first, to maintain order in times of domestic violence or rebellion; and second, to improve the efficiency of civilian law enforcement by giving it the benefit of military technologies, equipment, information, and training personnel. These interests can and have been accommodated by Acts of Congress to the overriding interest of preserving civilian government and law enforcement. At the time of the Wounded Knee occupation, Congress had prohibited the use of the military to execute the civilian laws, except when expressly authorized. 18 U.S.C. §1385. And it had placed specific limits on the President's power to use the national guard and military in emergency situations. 10 U.S.C. §§331-335. For example, under 10 U.S.C. §332, the President may call upon the military only after having determined that domestic unrest makes it "impracticable to enforce the laws of the United States by the ordinary course of judicial proceedings," and under 10 U.S.C. §334, he may do so only after having issued a proclamation ordering the insurgents to disperse. Those steps were not taken here.

We believe that the limits established by Congress on the use of the military for civilian law enforcement provide a reliable guidepost by which to evaluate the reasonableness for Fourth Amendment purposes of the seizures and searches in question here. Congress has acted to establish reasonable limits on the President's use of military forces in emergency situations, and in doing so has circumscribed whatever, if any, inherent power the President may have had absent such legislation. This is the teaching of *Youngstown Sheet & Tube Co. v. Sawyer*, 343 U.S. 579 (1952)....

B

... [T]he use of military force for domestic law-enforcement purposes is in a special category, and ... both the courts and Congress have been alert to keep it there. In short, if the use of military personnel is both unauthorized by any statute, and contrary to a specific criminal prohibition, and if citizens are seized or searched by military means in such a case, we have no hesitation in declaring that such searches and seizures are constitutionally "unreasonable." We do not mean to say that every search or seizure that violates a statute of any kind is necessarily a violation of the Fourth Amendment. But the statute prohibiting (if the allegations in the complaint can be proved) the conduct engaged in by defendants here is, as we have attempted to explain, not just any Act of Congress. It is the embodiment of a long tradition of suspicion and hostility towards the use of military force for domestic purposes.

Plaintiffs' Fourth Amendment case, therefore, must stand or fall on the proposition that military activity in connection with the occupation of Wounded Knee violated the Posse Comitatus Act.

In *United States v. Casper*, 541 F.2d 1275 (8th Cir. 1976) (per curiam), *cert. denied*, 430 U.S. 970 (1977), ... the District Court had found on a stipulated record that the following activities did not violate the Act: the use of Air Force personnel, planes, and cameras to fly surveillance; the advice of military officers in dealing with the disorder; and the furnishing of equipment and supplies. We affirmed "on the basis of the trial court's thorough and well-reasoned opinion." 541 F.2d at 1276.

... Therefore, unless plaintiffs now allege that the defendants took actions that went beyond those alleged in the *Casper* case, the actions alleged in the complaint now before us cannot violate the Act.

In *Casper*, quoting from Judge VanSickle's opinion for the District Court, 419 F. Supp. at 194, we approved the following standard for determining whether a violation of the Posse Comitatus Act had occurred:

> Were Army or Air Force personnel used by the civilian law enforcement officers at Wounded Knee in such a manner that the military personnel subjected the citizens to the exercise of military power which was regulatory, proscriptive, or compulsory in nature, either presently or prospectively?

541 F.2d at 1278....

When this concept is transplanted into the present legal context, we take it to mean that military involvement, even when not expressly authorized by the Constitution or a statute, does not violate the Posse Comitatus Act unless it actually regulates, forbids, or compels some conduct on the part of those claiming relief. A mere threat of some future injury would be insufficient....

... We of course have no way of knowing what plaintiffs would be able to prove if this case goes to trial, but the complaint, considered simply as a pleading, goes well beyond an allegation that defendants simply furnished supplies, aerial surveillance, and advice. It specifically charges that "the several Defendants maintained or caused to be maintained roadblocks and armed patrols constituting an armed perimeter around the village of Wounded Knee...." Defendants' actions, it is charged, "seized, confined, and made prisoners (of plaintiffs) against their will...." These allegations amount to a claim that defendants' activities, allegedly in violation of the Posse Comitatus Act, were "regulatory, proscriptive, or compulsory," in the sense that these activities directly restrained plaintiffs' freedom of movement. No more is required to survive a motion to dismiss....

As to the second set of claims, ... plaintiffs charge that they were searched and subjected to surveillance against their will by aerial photographic and visual search and surveillance. As we have already noted, *Casper* holds that this sort of activity does not violate the Posse Comitatus Act. It is therefore not "unreasonable" for Fourth Amendment purposes....

NOTES AND QUESTIONS

1. *Origins of the Posse Comitatus Act.* Early acts of Congress authorized the use of the militia to aid in law enforcement, although such use was never so extensive as it was after the Civil War. Reconstruction era abuses, culminating in the use of federal troops to police polling stations in Southern states (some say to influence the outcome of the presidential election of 1876), led to passage of the Posse Comitatus Act in 1878. The history is set forth in David E. Engdahl, *The New Civil Disturbances Regulations: The Threat of Military Intervention*, 49 Ind. L.J. 581, 597-603 (1974); and University of Colo. Law Revision Ctr., *A Comprehensive Study of the Use of Military Troops in Civil Disorders with Proposals for Legislative Reform*, 43 U. Colo. L. Rev. 399, 402-412 (1972). The Act is described generally in Jennifer Elsea, *The Posse Comitatus Act and Related Matters: A Sketch* (Cong. Res. Serv. RS20590), June 6, 2005; Matthew Carlton Hammond, Note, *The Posse Comitatus Act: A Principle in Need of Renewal*, 75 Wash. U.

L.Q. 953 (1997); and Sean J. Kealy, *Reexamining the Posse Comitatus Act: Toward a Right to Civil Law Enforcement,* 21 Yale L. & Pol'y Rev. 383 (2003).

2. *Elements of a Posse Comitatus Act Violation.* What exactly constitutes use of the armed forces "as a posse comitatus or otherwise to execute the laws"? To the "regulatory, proscriptive, or compulsory" standard set forth in *Bissonette,* we may add criteria from other cases growing out of the Wounded Knee incident: whether there was "direct, active" use of the military in civil law enforcement, *United States v. Red Feather,* 392 F. Supp. 916, 923 (D.S.D. 1975), or whether the use of the Army or the Air Force "pervaded the activities" of the civil law enforcement officers, *United States v. Jaramillo,* 380 F. Supp. 1375, 1379 (D. Neb. 1974), *appeal dismissed,* 510 F.2d 808 (8th Cir. 1975).

The Posse Comitatus Act may be inapplicable when the primary purpose of armed forces involvement is to enforce the Uniform Code of Military Justice or to achieve some distinctly military goal, and the benefits to civilian authorities are merely incidental — the so-called "military purpose" doctrine. *See Applewhite v. United States Air Force,* 995 F.2d 997, 1001 (10th Cir. 1993); *United States v. Thompson,* 33 M.J. 218 (C.M.A. 1991), *cert. denied,* 502 U.S. 1074 (1992).

Are you now prepared to say what particular military activities in aid of law enforcement are forbidden? Do you think the Posse Comitatus Act should be amended to make it easier to predict when the Act would apply? If so, how?

3. *Judicial Remedies for Violations.* There apparently never has been a criminal prosecution of anyone for violation of the Posse Comitatus Act. *See* Paul Jackson Rice, *New Laws and Insights Encircle the Posse Comitatus Act,* 104 Mil. L. Rev. 109, 111 (1984). Violations of the Posse Comitatus Act have, however, often been asserted as a defense to charges under other criminal statutes. For example, in *Red Feather* and *Jaramillo, supra,* American Indians at Wounded Knee were charged with interfering with a "law enforcement officer lawfully engaged in the lawful performance of his official duties." *See* 18 U.S.C. §231(a)(3) (2006). The defendants argued that the federal marshals and FBI agents were not performing their duties lawfully, within the meaning of the statute, because they enlisted military forces as a posse comitatus. *See also United States v. Mendoza-Cecelia,* 963 F.2d 1467, 1478 n.9 (11th Cir.), *cert. denied,* 506 U.S. 964 (1992).

Others apprehended by the military while attempting to smuggle drugs into the United States have argued that the evidence obtained in their arrests was inadmissible at trial. However, the federal courts have consistently refused to exclude such evidence in the absence of widespread and repeated Posse Comitatus Act violations. *See, e.g., Hayes v. Hawes,* 921 F.2d 100, 104 (7th Cir. 1990); *see also* Timothy J. Saviano, Note, *The Exclusionary Rule's Applicability to Violations of the Posse Comitatus Act,* Army Law., July 1995, at 61.

In *Bissonette v. Haig,* the appellants sought damages for infringement of their constitutional rights resulting from Posse Comitatus Act violations. Do such statutory violations give rise to a private cause of action separate and apart from any possible constitutional injury? *See Robinson v. Overseas Military Sales Corp.,* 21 F.3d 502 (2d Cir. 1994); *Lamont v. Haig,* 539 F. Supp. 552 (D.S.D. 1982) (no legislative intent to create a private right of action).

4. *Which Military Services Are Covered?* The Posse Comitatus Act expressly refers only to the Army and Air Force, and several cases have found that the Act does not restrict Navy law enforcement efforts. *See, e.g., Mendoza-Cecelia, supra,* 963 F.2d at 1477-1478; *but cf. United States v. Chon,* 210 F.3d 990 (9th Cir. 2000). Nevertheless, Navy

regulations have long prohibited the use of the Navy and Marine Corps as a posse comitatus, with certain exceptions, as a matter of Defense Department policy. *See* SECNAVINST 5820.7C (Jan. 26, 2006), *available at* http://www.hqmc.usmc.mil/PP&O/PS/psl/corrections/References/5820.7C.pdf.

Note that the Coast Guard presumably is not covered by the Posse Comitatus Act when, acting as a service of the Department of Homeland Security (DHS), it has a broad range of statutory law enforcement responsibilities. 14 U.S.C. §2. Otherwise, it is "a military service and a branch of the armed forces of the United States at all times"—specifically, a "service in the Navy." 14 U.S.C. §1. It assumes a military role "[u]pon the declaration of war or when the President directs." 14 U.S.C. §3.

In the event of a major terrorist attack or natural disaster, it is likely that unfederalized state National Guard troops will be dispatched to the scene before federal troops are considered or deployed. Several courts have held that until such forces are federalized they are not subject to the strictures of the Posse Comitatus Act. *See, e.g., United States v. Gilbert*, 165 F.3d 470 (6th Cir. 1999). Moreover, Congress has explicitly approved the states' use of the militia for "drug interdiction and counter-drug activities," so long as they remain under state control. 32 U.S.C. §112 (2006).

5. *Contemporary Vitality of the Posse Comitatus Act.* One might suspect that in our post-9/11 society, no one would likely object or even pay much attention to military involvement in civilian law enforcement, especially if it concerned a terrorist threat. But as the following case study suggests, strict compliance with the Posse Comitatus Act today could help avert the very problems that provoked passage of the Act in 1878.

CASE STUDY: RAID ON THE BRANCH DAVIDIANS[2]

After local law enforcement officials near Waco, Texas, reported to the Bureau of Alcohol, Tobacco, and Firearms (ATF) in May 1992 that the Branch Davidians, an obscure religious group, were stockpiling large quantities of firearms and black powder, officials worried that the sect's leader, known to his followers as David Koresh, was creating a military-type compound. An ATF investigation gathered enough evidence of illegal weapons activity to obtain search warrants for the compound. Although ATF had its own highly trained response team, agency officials determined that executing the warrants would require military support. Because ATF did not want to foot the bill for military support, however, agency staff essentially imagined a drug connection to the Branch Davidians, so that military expertise could be supplied without cost to the agency. Air surveillance of the compound revealed no drug activity, but ATF reported the possible presence of a methamphetamine laboratory on the grounds. Although ATF offered no proof of a drug connection, Department of Defense (DOD) drug enforcement officers furnished training facilities and equipment, including seven Bradley fighting vehicles. ATF also requested that Special Forces soldiers assist, including the conduct of "room clearing discriminate fire operations," the military equivalent of "close-quarter combat."

Command officers and their lawyers at Army Special Forces Command and the Judge Advocate General (JAG) office at Fort Bragg, North Carolina, soon grew

---

2. *See* Department of the Treasury, *Report of the Department of the Treasury on the Bureau of Alcohol, Tobacco, and Firearms Investigation of Vernon Wayne Howell also known as David Koresh* (1993), *available at* http://www.archive.org/details/reportofdepartme00unit; *Investigation into the Activities of Federal Law Enforcement Agencies Toward the Branch Davidians*, H.R. Rep. No. 104-749 (1996); Thomas R. Lujan, *Legal Aspects of Domestic Employment of the Army*, Parameters 82 (1997).

suspicious. After a review of plans for the operation — construction of a practice site, the ATF assault, provision of on-site medical services during the raid — the lawyers concluded that the military would be providing forbidden "active" participation in what amounted to law enforcement. Army personnel might find themselves treating injured civilians and searching arrested persons. If there was a drug lab at the site, soldiers could be involved in collecting evidence for prosecutions.

When military officers in Texas learned of the command officers' doubts, they argued that headquarters was an "unwarranted obstacle to mission success." Only after the command lawyers delivered a memorandum for the record to the Office of the Secretary of Defense did the local military officials conduct a more thorough review of the facts and the law. Soon thereafter, the military scaled back its offer of assistance to ATF to include safety, communications, and medical evaluation training. No soldiers would accompany ATF personnel to the compound.

When the raid was executed on February 28, 1993, the resulting firefight killed four agents and wounded more than 20; there were six deaths and four injuries among cult members. Then, after a 51-day siege, a fire swept through the compound, killing 74 Davidians. As tragic as they were, the raid, siege, and eventual fire might have been much worse in the public eye if Army Special Forces had been seen guiding ATF agents in an attack on a religious compound. In the end, the Posse Comitatus Act gave strength to the legal misgivings of headquarters JAG lawyers, and their resistance saved the Army from embarrassment and a backlash from an angry citizenry.

2. Exceptions to the Posse Comitatus Act

Recall that the Posse Comitatus Act prohibition applies "except in cases and under circumstances expressly authorized by the Constitution or Act of Congress." 18 U.S.C. §1850 (2006). The most important exception to the Act is a set of five statutes, referred to collectively as the Insurrection Act. It provides, in part:

Insurrection Act
10 U.S.C. §§331-335 (2006 & Supp. III 2009)

§332. Use of Militia and Armed Forces to Enforce Federal Authority

Whenever the President considers that unlawful obstructions, combinations, or assemblages, or rebellion against the authority of the United States, make it impracticable to enforce the laws of the United States in any State or Territory by the ordinary course of judicial proceedings, he may call into Federal service such of the militia of any State, and use such of the armed forces, as he considers necessary to enforce those laws or to suppress the rebellion.

§333. Major public emergencies; interference with State and Federal law

The President, by using the militia or the armed forces, or both, or by any other means, shall take such measures as he considers necessary to suppress, in a State, any insurrection, domestic violence, unlawful combination, or conspiracy, if it . . .
  (2) opposes or obstructs the execution of the laws of the United States or impedes the course of justice under those laws. . . .

§334. Proclamation to Disperse

Whenever the President considers it necessary to use the militia or the armed forces under this chapter, he shall, by proclamation, immediately order the insurgents or those obstructing the enforcement of the laws to disperse and retire peaceably to their abodes within a limited time.[3]

Military Cooperation with Law Enforcement Officials Act
10 U.S.C. §§371-382 (2006 & Supp. III 2009), as amended by Pub. L. No. 111-383, §1075(b)(10)(A), (B), 124 Stat. 4137, 4369 (2011)

§371. Use of information collected during military operations

(a) The Secretary of Defense may, in accordance with other applicable law, provide to Federal, State, or local civilian law enforcement officials any information collected during the normal course of military training or operations that may be relevant to a violation of any Federal or State law within the jurisdiction of such officials.

(b) The needs of civilian law enforcement officials for information shall, to the maximum extent practicable, be taken into account in the planning and execution of military training or operations.

(c) The Secretary of Defense shall ensure, to the extent consistent with national security, that intelligence information held by the Department of Defense and relevant to drug interdiction or other civilian law enforcement matters is provided promptly to appropriate civilian law enforcement officials. . . .

§375. Restriction on direct participation by military personnel

The Secretary of Defense shall prescribe such regulations as may be necessary to ensure that any activity (including the provision of any equipment or facility or the assignment or detail of any personnel) under this chapter does not include or permit direct participation by a member of the Army, Navy, Air Force, or Marine Corps in a search, seizure, arrest, or other similar activity unless participation in such activity by such member is otherwise authorized by law. . . .

§382. Emergency situations involving chemical or biological weapons of mass destruction

(a) In general. — The Secretary of Defense, upon the request of the Attorney General, may provide assistance in support of Department of Justice activities relating to the enforcement of section 175, 229, or 2332c of title 18 during an emergency situation involving a biological or chemical weapon of mass destruction. Department

---

[3. Section 331 provides for federal military assistance in putting down an insurrection against a state government. Section 335 makes the statutes applicable to Guam and the Virgin Islands. — Eds.]

of Defense resources, including personnel of the Department of Defense, may be used to provide such assistance if —

(1) the Secretary of Defense and the Attorney General jointly determine that an emergency situation exists; and

(2) the Secretary of Defense determines that the provision of such assistance will not adversely affect the military preparedness of the United States.

(b) Emergency situations covered. — In this section, the term "emergency situation involving a biological or chemical weapon of mass destruction" means a circumstance involving a biological or chemical weapon of mass destruction —

(1) that poses a serious threat to the interests of the United States; and

(2) in which —

(A) civilian expertise and capabilities are not readily available to provide the required assistance to counter the threat immediately posed by the weapon involved;

(B) special capabilities and expertise of the Department of Defense are necessary and critical to counter the threat posed by the weapon involved; and

(C) enforcement of section 175, 229, or 2332c of title 18 would be seriously impaired if the Department of Defense assistance were not provided.

(c) Forms of assistance. — The assistance referred to in subsection (a) includes the operation of equipment ... to monitor, contain, disable, or dispose of the weapon involved or elements of the weapon.

(d) Regulations. —

(1) The Secretary of Defense and the Attorney General shall jointly prescribe regulations concerning the types of assistance that may be provided under this section. Such regulations shall also describe the actions that Department of Defense personnel may take in circumstances incident to the provision of assistance under this section.

(2) (A) Except as provided in subparagraph (B), the regulations may not authorize the following actions:

(i) Arrest.

(ii) Any direct participation in conducting a search for or seizure of evidence related to a violation of section 175, 229, or 2332c of title 18.

(iii) Any direct participation in the collection of intelligence for law enforcement purposes.

(B) The regulations may authorize an action described in subparagraph (A) to be taken under the following conditions:

(i) The action is considered necessary for the immediate protection of human life, and civilian law enforcement officials are not capable of taking the action.

(ii) The action is otherwise authorized under subsection (c) or under otherwise applicable law. . . . [4]

[4. Other sections of the 1981 Act, as amended, deal variously with the use of military equipment and facilities, training and advising civilian law enforcement officials, maintenance and operation of equipment, reimbursement, the use of Coast Guard personnel for law enforcement, and impacts on military preparedness. References to sections 175 and 229 (which has replaced §2332c) of title 18 concern prohibitions on the possession or use of biological or chemical weapons, respectively. — Eds.]

Additional exceptions to the Posse Comitatus Act are considered in the following
Notes and Questions.

NOTES AND QUESTIONS

1. *The Insurrection Act.* The Insurrection Act had its origin in a 1792 law invoked
by President Washington in suppressing the Whiskey Rebellion. The history of its
component parts is traced in Stephen I. Vladeck, Note, *Emergency Power and the Militia
Acts,* 114 Yale L.J. 149, 159-167 (2004); William C. Banks, *Providing "Supplemental
Security"— The Insurrection Act and the Military Role in Responding to Domestic Crises,* 3
J. Nat'l Security L. & Pol'y 39, 56-72 (2009). In 1827 the Supreme Court indicated that
the President had broad discretion in determining when to use these statutes in
calling forth the militia, and that his determination was not subject to judicial review.
Martin v. Mott, 25 U.S. (12 Wheat.) 19, 29-32 (1827). *See also Luther v. Borden,* 48 U.S.
(7 How.) 1, 43-45 (1849); *The Prize Cases,* 67 U.S. (2 Black) 635, 668 (1863).

Since that time the Insurrection Act has been invoked for a variety of purposes,
including the breaking of the Pullman Strike in 1894. More recently, it has been used
to help integrate public schools and universities, to control racial unrest, to collect
intelligence about citizens, and to enforce a variety of state and federal laws. It was
invoked in 1992 to send federalized California National Guard troops, as well as
active-duty soldiers from Fort Ord and Marines from Camp Pendleton, to Los Angeles
to help control rioting in the wake of the Rodney King trial verdict. Exec. Order
No. 12,804, 57 Fed. Reg. 19,361 (May 1, 1992); Proclamation No. 6427, 57 Fed.
Reg. 19,359 (May 1, 1992).

2. *Insurrection Act as a Challenge to State Authority?* Section 333 of U.S.C. title 10 was
first enacted in 1956 in the form set out above. A half-century later a great natural
disaster prompted its amendment. The original language was then restored two years
later.

When Hurricane Katrina hit New Orleans in 2005, local police and other first
responders were overwhelmed. The Governor of Louisiana immediately asked the
White House for 40,000 soldiers to help in the recovery effort. The White House
delayed sending any active-duty military forces for five days, however, and then it
deployed only 7,200 troops. Apparently it was felt that the President would have had
to federalize Louisiana National Guard forces and invoke the Insurrection Act,
then maintain federal control of Guard troops to perform law enforcement duties
there — to stop looting and other lawlessness. While the Justice Department's Office
of Legal Counsel advised that federal military forces could be sent in, even over the
objections of local officials, the President reportedly wanted to avoid the perception
that he was seizing command from a female Southern governor of another party. *See*
Eric Lipton, Eric Schmitt & Thom Shanker, *Political Issues Snarled Plans for Troop Aid,* N.Y.
Times, Sept. 5, 2005. The eventual deployment of military forces, said to be the largest in
this country since the Civil War, is described in useful detail in *Failure of Initiative: Final
Report of the [House] Bipartisan Committee to Investigate the Preparation for and Response
to Hurricane Katrina* 201-238 (Feb. 15, 2006) [hereinafter *Failure of Initiative*].

Paradoxically, the President almost immediately suggested a need for expanded
authority for the use of federal troops in such an emergency. Asked whether DOD
should play a larger role, the President responded, "Clearly, in the case of a terrorist
attack that would be the case, but is there a natural disaster which — of a certain size

82nd Airborne troops patrol New Orleans after Hurricane Katrina.

U.S. Army photo by Daren Reehl.

that would then enable the Defense Department to become a lead agency in coordinating and leading the response effort? That's going to be a very important consideration for Congress to think about." *President's Remarks During Hurricane Rita Briefing
in Texas,* Sept. 25, 2005. A follow-on study, *The Federal Response to Hurricane Katrina:
Lessons Learned* (Feb. 2006), declared that "DOD capabilities must be better identified
and integrated into the Nation's response plans." *Id.* at 54. Moreover, it suggested, in
"extraordinary circumstances" it will be "appropriate for the Department of Defense
to lead the Federal response." *Id.* at 94. DOD and DHS were directed to revise the
National Response Plan to reflect this expanded role. *Id.*

At the Bush administration's urging, 10 U.S.C. §333 was amended in late 2006,
reportedly because of a desire to "clarify" the President's authority. As amended,
§333 provided in significant part:

> (a) Use of Armed Forces in Major Public Emergencies—
> (1) The President may employ the armed forces, including the National Guard in
> Federal service, to—
> (A) restore public order and enforce the laws of the United States when, as a
> result of a natural disaster, epidemic, or other serious public health emergency,
> terrorist attack or incident, or other condition in any State or possession of the
> United States, the President determines that—
> (i) domestic violence has occurred to such an extent that the constituted
> authorities of the State or possession are incapable of maintaining public order; and
> (ii) such violence results in a condition described in paragraph (2); or
> (B) suppress, in a State, any insurrection, domestic violence, unlawful combi-
> nation, or conspiracy if such insurrection, violation, combination, or conspiracy
> results in a condition described in paragraph (2).

(2) A condition described in this paragraph is a condition that—

(A) so hinders the execution of the laws of a State or possession, as applicable, and of the United States within that State or possession, that any part or class of its people is deprived of a right, privilege, immunity, or protection named in the Constitution and secured by law, and the constituted authorities of that State or possession are unable, fail, or refuse to protect that right, privilege, or immunity, or to give that protection; or

(B) opposes or obstructs the execution of the laws of the United States or impedes the course of justice under those laws. . . .

(b) Notice to Congress—The President shall notify Congress of the determination to exercise the authority in subsection (a)(1)(A) as soon as practicable after the determination and every 14 days thereafter during the duration of the exercise of that authority.

[Pub. L. No. 109-364, §1076, 120 Stat. 2083, 2404-2405 (2006).]

After the 2006 mid-term elections, the National Governors Association persuaded Congress that the amended law could in fact cause confusion and uncertainty about whether a governor or the President is primarily responsible in the event of an emergency, and Congress restored the earlier language. Banks, *supra*, 3 J. Nat'l Security L. & Pol'y at 76. Which version do you think makes it clearer when the President can employ troops domestically to help enforce the law? Might the "constructive ambiguity" of the original and now restored language encourage deliberation between state and federal officials? *See id.*

Did the 2006 amendment to §333 expand or restrict the President's authority? Can you think of any domestic emergency that could not be addressed by the President's using troops if one of the provisions of the Insurrection Act were invoked? Would the unwillingness of a state governor to ask for assistance ever be a bar to such use? Could troops so deployed make searches and arrests, direct traffic, enforce quarantines?

3. *The Military Cooperation with Law Enforcement Officials Act.* A dramatic surge in illicit drug traffic and related criminal activity during the 1970s and 1980s led President Reagan to declare a "war on drugs." *See* Christopher Simpson, *National Security Directives of the Reagan and Bush Administrations* 640-641 (1995). Congress responded in 1981 by enacting the Military Cooperation with Law Enforcement Officials Act, excerpted above, allowing the military to furnish equipment, facilities, and training to civilian law enforcement agencies, and to share relevant intelligence. 10 U.S.C. §§371-373. The Act also authorizes military personnel to operate equipment to intercept vessels or aircraft for law enforcement purposes. *Id.* §374. But it expressly forbids "direct participation by a member of the Army, Navy, Air Force, or Marine Corps in a search, seizure, arrest, or other similar activity unless . . . otherwise authorized by law." *Id.* §375. In separate legislation, the Defense Department was designated lead agency for the detection and monitoring of aerial and maritime shipments of illicit drugs into the United States. 10 U.S.C. §124 (2006). And in 1998 Congress expanded the permitted uses of military personnel to operate loaned equipment to include enforcement of terrorism laws. Pub. L. No. 105-277, §201, 112 Stat. 2681, 2681-567 (1998) (amending 10 U.S.C. §374).

Do you think this legislation added to powers already enjoyed by the President under the Insurrection Act? If not, why did Congress bother to pass it?

4. *Other Statutory Exceptions.* Another exception to the Posse Comitatus Act is found in H.R.J. Res. 1292, Pub. L. No. 90-331, 82 Stat. 170 (1968), which directs federal agencies (including the Department of Defense) to assist the Secret Service in the performance of its protective duties. This authority was used by President Johnson to deploy troops in Chicago during the Democratic National Convention in 1968 and by President Nixon to control antiwar demonstrations on several occasions. Congress has also approved emergency military assistance in enforcing a prohibition on the unauthorized possession or use of nuclear material. 18 U.S.C. §831(d), (e) (2006).

5. *Constitutional Exceptions.* The Posse Comitatus Act includes an exception for "circumstances expressly authorized by the Constitution." See *supra* p. 767. One possible express constitutional exception may be found in Article IV, section 4, which provides, "The United States shall guarantee to every State in this Union a Republican Form of Government, and shall protect each of them against invasion; and on Application of the Legislature, or of the Executive (when the Legislature cannot be convened) against domestic Violence." Can you describe the limits of the President's power to use troops for law enforcement under this provision? Do these clauses or the Article I Calling Forth Clause, alone or together, provide adequate authority to sustain the Insurrection Act, before or after the 2006 amendment? *See* Banks, *supra,* at 79-86 (no).

Defense Department regulations entitled "Employment of Military Resources in the Event of Civil Disturbances" refer to two "constitutional exceptions" to the Posse Comitatus Act "based upon the inherent legal right of the U.S. Government—a sovereign national entity under the Federal Constitution — to insure the preservation of public order and the carrying out of governmental operations within its territorial limits, by force if necessary." 32 C.F.R. §215.4(c)(1) (2010). One exception is described as emergency authority to take

> prompt and vigorous Federal action, including use of military forces, to prevent loss of life or wanton destruction of property and to restore governmental functioning and public order when sudden and unexpected civil disturbances, disasters, or calamities seriously endanger life and property and disrupt normal governmental functions to such an extent that duly constituted local authorities are unable to control the situations. [*Id.* §215.4(c)(1)(i).]

The other is for "protection of Federal property and functions." *Id.* §215.4(c)(1)(ii). *See also* DOD Dir. 5525.5, *DoD Cooperation with Civilian Law Enforcement Officials* (Dec. 20, 1989), at Encl. 4 §E4.1.2.3. President Johnson apparently believed that he was exercising such inherent powers when he ordered the military to suppress rioting in Washington, D.C., following the assassination of Dr. Martin Luther King Jr. in 1968. *See* Proclamation No. 3840, 33 Fed. Reg. 5495 (Apr. 9, 1968). This regulatory authority closely resembles one for "Immediate Responses," 32 C.F.R. §185.4(e) (2010), noted *infra* p. 785. The powers claimed in the regulations are not "expressly" set out in the constitutional text, of course.

Has Congress "occupied the field" by its enactment of the Posse Comitatus Act and its exceptions, precluding inconsistent exercise by the President of his inherent constitutional powers? Could Congress do so?

6. *Law Enforcement or War Fighting?* José Padilla was confined in a military brig for more than three years as an "enemy combatant" before finally being charged with criminal offenses related to terrorism. See *supra* p. 469. In responding to his petition for a writ of habeas corpus, one court remarked:

> Padilla argues also that his detention by the military violates the Posse Comitatus Act.... First, it is questionable whether that statute is enforceable in a habeas corpus proceeding to secure release from custody. *Cf. Robinson v. Overseas Military Sales Corp.*, 21 F.3d 502, 511 (2d Cir. 1994) (no private right of action to enforce Posse Comitatus Act). Moreover, the statute bars use of the military in civilian law enforcement. Padilla is not being detained by the military in order to execute a civilian law or for violating a civilian law, notwithstanding that his alleged conduct may in fact violate one or more such laws. He is being detained in order to interrogate him about the unlawful organization with which he is said to be affiliated and with which the military is in active combat, and to prevent him from becoming reaffiliated with that organization. Therefore, his detention by the military does not violate the Posse Comitatus Act. [*Padilla v. Bush*, 233 F. Supp. 2d 564, 588 n.9 (S.D.N.Y. 2002), *rev'd in part sub nom. Padilla v. Rumsfeld*, 352 F.3d 695 (2d Cir. 2003).]

Do you think the military can avoid application of the Posse Comitatus Act simply by characterizing a person it suspects of criminal activity as an "enemy combatant"? If you think the designation of enemy combatants might be subject to abuse, can you suggest some realistic process for distinguishing between law enforcement and war fighting, at least for this purpose? Or can you articulate some other principled basis for limiting the military's role in activities that involve both law enforcement and war fighting? What are the implications of the Military Commissions Act of 2009, *supra* p. 711, in answering these questions?

B.   THE MILITARY'S INTELLIGENCE ROLE IN HOMELAND SECURITY

Since the earliest days of the Republic, military intelligence units have supported domestic uses of military force. Chief Justice Marshall reportedly said of George Washington, "A general must be governed by his intelligence and must regulate his measures by his information. It is his duty to obtain correct information...." *Quoted in Tatum v. Laird*, 444 F.2d 947, 952-953 (D.C. Cir. 1971), *rev'd*, 408 U.S. 1 (1972). In principle, domestic intelligence collection for force protection or as part of DOD's homeland defense mission has never been controversial.

But military intelligence personnel have also been used at times to collect personal information about Americans who pose no real threat to national security. In this part of the chapter we look first at military intelligence activities at home during the Vietnam War, then turn to recent developments ostensibly related to the war on terrorism.

1.   Military Domestic Surveillance During the Vietnam War

Domestic military intelligence activity reached a peak in the late 1960s, when the Pentagon compiled data on more than 100,000 politically active Americans, in an effort to quell civil rights and anti–Vietnam War demonstrations and to discredit protestors. The Army deployed 1,500 plainclothes agents to watch demonstrators, infiltrate organizations, and circulate blacklists. Military officials claimed that they were preparing for the use of troops to put down insurrections. *See* Christopher H. Pyle, *Military Surveillance of Civilian Politics, 1961-1971* (1986). In 1976, the Church Committee, looking into a variety of intelligence community abuses, called the Army program "the worst intrusion that military intelligence has ever made into the civilian community." S. Select Comm. to Study Governmental Operations with Respect to Intelligence Activities, *Improper Surveillance of Private Citizens by the Military (Church Committee Report)*, S. Rep. No. 94-755, bk. III, at 792 (1976). Public disclosure of this activity precipitated the following case.

Laird v. Tatum

United States Supreme Court, 1972
408 U.S. 1

Mr. Chief Justice BURGER delivered the opinion of the Court. Respondents brought this class action in the District Court seeking declaratory and injunctive relief on their claim that their rights were being invaded by the Department of the Army's alleged "surveillance of lawful and peaceful civilian political activity." The petitioners in response describe the activity as "gathering by lawful means . . . (and) maintaining and using in their intelligence activities . . . information relating to potential or actual civil disturbances (or) street demonstrations." . . .

The President is authorized by 10 U.S.C. §331[2] to make use of the armed forces to quell insurrection and other domestic violence if and when the conditions described in that section obtain within one of the States. Pursuant to those provisions, President Johnson ordered federal troops to assist local authorities at the time of the civil disorders in Detroit, Michigan, in the summer of 1967 and during the disturbances that followed the assassination of Dr. Martin Luther King. Prior to the Detroit disorders, the Army had a general contingency plan for providing such assistance to local authorities, but the 1967 experience led Army authorities to believe that more attention should be given to such preparatory planning. The data-gathering system here involved is said to have been established in connection with the development of more detailed and specific contingency planning designed to permit the Army, when called upon to assist local authorities, to be able to respond effectively with a minimum of force. As the Court of Appeals observed,

> In performing this type function the Army is essentially a police force or the back-up of a local police force. To quell disturbances or to prevent further disturbances the Army needs the same tools and, most importantly, the same information to which local police forces have access. Since the Army is sent into territory almost invariably unfamiliar to most soldiers and their commanders, their need for information is likely to be greater than that of the hometown policeman.

---

2. "Whenever there is an insurrection in any State against its government, the President may, upon the request of its legislature or of its governor if the legislature cannot be convened, call into Federal service such of the militia of the other States, in the number requested by that State, and use such of the armed forces, as he considers necessary to suppress the insurrection." . . .

> No logical argument can be made for compelling the military to use blind force. When force is employed it should be intelligently directed, and this depends upon having reliable information — in time.... So we take it as undeniable that the military, *i.e.*, the Army, need a certain amount of information in order to perform their constitutional and statutory missions. 444 F.2d at 952-953 (footnotes omitted).

The system put into operation as a result of the Army's 1967 experience consisted essentially of the collection of information about public activities that were thought to have at least some potential for civil disorder, the reporting of that information to Army Intelligence headquarters at Fort Holabird, Maryland, the dissemination of these reports from headquarters to major Army posts around the country, and the storage of the reported information in a computer data bank located at Fort Holabird. The information itself was collected by a variety of means, but it is significant that the principal sources of information were the news media and publications in general circulation. Some of the information came from Army Intelligence agents who attended meetings that were open to the public and who wrote field reports describing the meetings, giving such data as the name of the sponsoring organization, the identity of speakers, the approximate number of persons in attendance, and an indication of whether any disorder occurred. And still other information was provided to the Army by civilian law enforcement agencies....

Our examination of the record satisfies us that the Court of Appeals properly identified the issue presented, namely, whether the jurisdiction of a federal court may be invoked by a complainant who alleges that the exercise of his First Amendment rights is being chilled by the mere existence, without more, of a governmental investigative and data-gathering activity that is alleged to be broader in scope than is reasonably necessary for the accomplishment of a valid governmental purpose. We conclude, however, that, having properly identified the issue, the Court of Appeals decided that issue incorrectly.

In recent years this Court has found in a number of cases that constitutional violations may arise from the deterrent, or "chilling," effect of governmental regulations that fall short of a direct prohibition against the exercise of First Amendment rights. In none of these cases, however, did the chilling effect arise merely from the individual's knowledge that a governmental agency was engaged in certain activities or from the individual's concomitant fear that, armed with the fruits of those activities, the agency might in the future take some other and additional action detrimental to that individual. Rather, in each of these cases, the challenged exercise of governmental power was regulatory, proscriptive, or compulsory in nature, and the complainant was either presently or prospectively subject to the regulations, proscriptions, or compulsions that he was challenging....

The decisions in these cases fully recognize that governmental action may be subject to constitutional challenge even though it has only an indirect effect on the exercise of First Amendment rights. At the same time, however, these decisions have in no way eroded the "established principle that to entitle a private individual to invoke the judicial power to determine the validity of executive or legislative action he must show that he has sustained, or is immediately in danger of sustaining, a direct injury as the result of that action...." *Ex parte Levitt*, 302 U.S. 633 (1937).

The respondents do not meet this test; their claim, simply stated, is that they disagree with the judgments made by the Executive Branch with respect to the type and amount of information the Army needs and that the very existence of the Army's data-gathering system produces a constitutionally impermissible chilling effect upon the exercise of their First Amendment rights. That alleged "chilling" effect may perhaps be seen as arising from respondents' very perception of the system as inappropriate to the Army's role under our form of government, or as arising from respondents' beliefs that it is inherently dangerous for the military to be concerned with activities in the civilian sector, or as arising from respondents' less generalized yet speculative apprehensiveness that the Army may at some future date misuse the information in some way that would cause direct harm to respondents. Allegations of a subjective "chill" are not an adequate substitute for a claim of specific present objective harm or a threat of specific future harm....

...[Plaintiffs] would have the federal courts as virtually continuing monitors of the wisdom and soundness of Executive action; such a role is appropriate for the Congress acting through its committees and the "power of the purse"; it is not the role of the judiciary, absent actual present or immediately threatened injury resulting from unlawful governmental action....

The concerns of the Executive and Legislative Branches in response to disclosure of the Army surveillance activities — and indeed the claims alleged in the complaint — reflect a traditional and strong resistance of Americans to any military intrusion into civilian affairs. That tradition has deep roots in our history and found early expression, for example, in the Third Amendment's explicit prohibition against quartering soldiers in private homes without consent and in the constitutional provisions for civilian control of the military. Those prohibitions are not directly presented by this case, but their philosophical underpinnings explain our traditional insistence on limitations on military operations in peacetime. Indeed, when presented with claims of judicially cognizable injury resulting from military intrusion into the civilian sector, federal courts are fully empowered to consider claims of those asserting such injury; there is nothing in our Nation's history or in this Court's decided cases, including our holding today, that can properly be seen as giving any indication that actual or threatened injury by reason of unlawful activities of the military would go unnoticed or unremedied.

Reversed.

Mr. Justice DOUGLAS, with whom Mr. Justice MARSHALL concurs, dissenting.

I

If Congress had passed a law authorizing the armed services to establish surveillance over the civilian population, a most serious constitutional problem would be presented. There is, however, no law authorizing surveillance over civilians, which in this case the Pentagon concededly had undertaken. The question is whether such authority may be implied. One can search the Constitution in vain for any such authority....

...[W]e have until today consistently adhered to the belief that "[i]t is an unbending rule of law, that the exercise of military power, where the rights of the citizen are concerned, shall never be pushed beyond what the exigency requires." *Raymond v. Thomas*, 91 U.S. 712, 716.

It was in that tradition that *Youngstown Sheet & Tube Co. v. Sawyer*, 343 U.S. 579, was decided, in which President Truman's seizure of the steel mills in the so-called Korean War was held unconstitutional. As stated by Justice Black:

> The order cannot properly be sustained as an exercise of the President's military power as Commander in Chief of the Armed Forces. The Government attempts to do so by citing a number of cases upholding broad powers in military commanders engaged in day-to-day fighting in a theater of war. Such cases need not concern us here. Even though "theater of war" be an expanding concept, we cannot with faithfulness to our constitutional system hold that the Commander in Chief of the Armed Forces has the ultimate power as such to take possession of private property in order to keep labor disputes from stopping production. This is a job for the Nation's lawmakers, not for its military authorities. *Id.* at 587. . . .

The act of turning the military loose on civilians even if sanctioned by an Act of Congress, which it has not been, would raise serious and profound constitutional questions. Standing as it does only on brute power and Pentagon policy, it must be repudiated as a usurpation dangerous to the civil liberties on which free men are dependent. For, as Senator Sam Ervin has said, "this claim of an inherent executive branch power of investigation and surveillance on the basis of people's beliefs and attitudes may be more of a threat to our internal security than any enemies beyond our borders." Privacy and Government Investigations, 1971 U. Ill. L.F. 137, 153.

II

The claim that respondents have no standing to challenge the Army's surveillance of them and the other members of the class they seek to represent is too transparent for serious argument. The surveillance of the Army over the civilian sector — a part of society hitherto immune from its control — is a serious charge. It is alleged that the Army maintains files on the membership, ideology, programs, and practices of virtually every activist political group in the country, including groups such as the Southern Christian Leadership Conference, Clergy and Laymen United Against the War in Vietnam, the American Civil Liberties Union, Women's Strike for Peace, and the National Association for the Advancement of Colored People. The Army uses undercover agents to infiltrate these civilian groups and to reach into confidential files of students and other groups. The Army moves as a secret group among civilian audiences, using cameras and electronic ears for surveillance. The data it collects are distributed to civilian officials in state, federal, and local governments and to each military intelligence unit and troop command under the Army's jurisdiction (both here and abroad); and these data are stored in one or more data banks.

Those are the allegations; and the charge is that the purpose and effect of the system of surveillance is to harass and intimidate the respondents and to deter them from exercising their rights of political expression, protest, and dissent "by invading their privacy, damaging their reputations, adversely affecting their employment and their opportunities for employment, and in other ways." Their fear is that "permanent reports of their activities will be maintained in the Army's data bank, and their 'profiles' will appear in the so-called 'Blacklist' and that all of this information will be released to numerous federal and state agencies upon request."

Judge Wilkey, speaking for the Court of Appeals, properly inferred that this Army surveillance "exercises a present inhibiting effect on their full expression and utilization of their First Amendment rights." 444 F.2d 947, 954. That is the test. The "deterrent effect" on First Amendment rights by government oversight marks an unconstitutional intrusion, *Lamont v. Postmaster General*, 381 U.S. 301, 307. Or, as stated by Mr. Justice Brennan, "inhibition as well as prohibition against the exercise of precious First Amendment rights is a power denied to government." *Id.* at 309....

The present controversy is not a remote, imaginary conflict. Respondents were targets of the Army's surveillance. First, the surveillance was not casual but massive and comprehensive. Second, the intelligence reports were regularly and widely circulated and were exchanged with reports of the FBI, state and municipal police departments, and the CIA. Third, the Army's surveillance was not collecting material in public records but staking out teams of agents, infiltrating undercover agents, creating command posts inside meetings, posing as press photographers and newsmen, posing as TV newsmen, posing as students, and shadowing public figures.

Finally, we know from the hearings conducted by Senator Ervin that the Army has misused or abused its reporting functions. Thus, Senator Ervin concluded that reports of the Army have been "taken from the Intelligence Command's highly inaccurate civil disturbance teletype and filed in Army dossiers on persons who have held, or were being considered for, security clearances, thus contaminating what are supposed to be investigative reports with unverified gossip and rumor. This practice directly jeopardized the employment and employment opportunities of persons seeking sensitive positions with the federal government or defense industry."[10]

Surveillance of civilians is none of the Army's constitutional business and Congress has not undertaken to entrust it with any such function....

[Dissenting opinion of Mr. Justice BRENNAN, with whom Mr. Justice STEWART and Mr. Justice MARSHALL join, omitted.]

NOTES AND QUESTIONS

1. *Military vs. Non-Military Intelligence.* Does the domestic collection of intelligence by the military differ in any constitutionally significant way from collection by, say, the FBI? Can you say how?

2. *Standing to Sue.* The *Laird* Court decided that the plaintiffs' claim was nonjusticiable, because they could not demonstrate standing to sue, which would have required a showing of "actual present or immediately threatened injury." What kind of injury did they claim to have suffered? Do you think Vietnam War protesters' fears of reprisal by government agencies were justified?

The *Laird* Court denied standing based on the plaintiffs' complaints about "the very existence of the Army's data-gathering system" and their "[a]llegation of a subjective 'chill' are not an adequate substitute for a claim of specific present objective harm or a threat of specific future harm." 408 U.S. at 13-14. In other words, the

10. Hearings on Federal Data Banks, Computers and The Bill of Rights, before the Subcommittee on Constitutional Rights of the Senate Committee on the Judiciary, 92d Cong., 1st Sess. (1971).

Laird plaintiffs did not allege any injuries. Instead they claimed that they *might* be injured if information collected by the military in the future were misused in some way. In *Amnesty International USA v. Clapper*, 638 F.3d 118 (2d Cir. 2011), plaintiffs who believed that they had been subject to surveillance authorized by Congress in the FISA Amendments Act of 2008 (*supra* p. 232) were found to have standing to challenge the constitutionality of the statute based on their assertions of concrete reasons to believe that they are likely to be overheard because their activities bring them into contact with the likely targets of the authorized surveillance. Based on the *Amnesty* and *Laird* decisions, can you predict whether future plaintiffs will be able to get a court to rule on the merits of a challenge to domestic surveillance activities by the military?

3. *Relevance of the Posse Comitatus Act?* According to the *Laird* majority, the Army was "essentially a police force" when it collected domestic intelligence, ostensibly in planning for a response to civil unrest. Did the Army's surveillance program therefore run afoul of the Posse Comitatus Act? Why do you suppose the Court did not refer to the Act? If it had, do you think its constitutional analysis would more nearly have resembled that of the *Bissonnette* court?

4. *Effect of the Insurrection Act?* The *Laird* Court cites 10 U.S.C. §331, one provision of the Insurrection Act (see *supra* p. 767), as authority for the deployment of military forces to help control rioting in several American cities in 1967 and 1968. It did not point to that same authority for the Army's surveillance program, which extended over a number of years. Could it have done so?

5. *Post-Vietnam Reforms.* In 1976, the Church Committee responded to the abuses outlined in *Laird* by proposing a "precisely drawn legislative charter" that would, *inter alia,* "limit military investigations to activities in the civilian community which are necessary and pertinent to the military mission, and which cannot feasibly be accomplished by civilian agencies." *Church Committee Report, supra,* bk. II, at 310-311. The Committee apparently believed that military intelligence units could make no unique contributions to the domestic security efforts of the FBI, local law enforcement, and other civilian agencies. Its proposal also may have reflected concern about conducting domestic intelligence collection under a military chain of command, whose priority is completion of its military mission, rather than under the Attorney General, whose priority is law enforcement.

Congress did not enact the charter suggested by the Church Committee, but it did pass the Privacy Act in 1974, 5 U.S.C. §552a (2006), as amended by Pub. L. No. 111-148, §6402(b)(2), 124 Stat. 119, 756 (2010), and Pub. L. No. 111-203, §1082, 124 Stat. 1376, 2080 (2010); and the Foreign Intelligence Surveillance Act (FISA), 50 U.S.C. §§1801-1881g (2006 & Supp. III 2009), as amended by Pub. L. No. 111-259, §801, 124 Stat. 2654, 2746 (2010). See *supra* pp. 192-245. Both measures limit the collection, retention, and sharing of information about how individuals exercise rights guaranteed by the First Amendment, as well as information not relevant to the mission of an agency. But serious doubts exist about the efficacy of these laws in safeguarding personal privacy. *See, e.g.,* William C. Banks, *Programmatic Surveillance and FISA: Of Needles and Haystacks,* 88 Tex. L. Rev. 1633 (2010); Orin S. Kerr, *Updating the Foreign Intelligence Surveillance Act,* 75 U. Chi. L. Rev. 225 (2008); Technology & Privacy Advisory Comm., *Safeguarding Privacy in the Fight Against Terrorism (TAPAC Report)* 25-26 (Mar. 2004).

The Defense Department's own rules now limit the domestic collection and use of personal information. For example, DOD Dir. 5200.27, *Acquisition of Information Concerning Persons and Organizations Not Affiliated with the Department of Defense* (Jan. 7, 1980), includes the following restrictions:

> 5.2. No information shall be acquired about a person or organization solely because of lawful advocacy of measures in opposition to Government policy....
>
> 5.5. There shall be no covert or otherwise deceptive surveillance or penetration of civilian organizations unless specifically authorized by the Secretary of Defense, or his designee....
>
> 5.7. No computerized data banks shall be maintained relating to individuals or organizations not affiliated with the Department of Defense, unless authorized by the Secretary of Defense, or his designee....
>
> 6.3. Access to information obtained under the provisions of this Directive shall be restricted to Governmental Agencies that require such information in the execution of their duties....

See also DOD Dir. 5240.1-R, *Procedures Governing the Activities of DoD Intelligence Components That Affect United States Persons* (Dec. 1982); Army Reg. 381-10, *U.S. Army Intelligence Activities* (Nov. 22, 2005), *available at* http://www.fas.org/irp/doddir/army/ar381-10.pdf.

Do these limitations on domestic intelligence collection address the concerns expressed by the Church Committee and by the dissenters in *Laird*? Are additional reforms needed?

2. Domestic Use of Military Intelligence Today

Several developments in the wake of 9/11 point to an expanding domestic role for the military intelligence agencies, which include the Defense Intelligence Agency and intelligence operations within each of the service branches. *See generally* Stephen Dycus, *The Role of Military Intelligence in Homeland Security*, 64 La. L. Rev. 779 (2004). DHS's Office of Intelligence & Analysis (I&A) receives, analyzes, and disseminates data about possible domestic terrorist threats from government and private sources, including the military's intelligence components. *See* Department of Homeland Sec., *Office of Intelligence and Analysis* (Mar. 2, 2011), *at* http://www.dhs.gov/xabout/structure/gc_1220886590914.shtm. The National Counterterrorism Center (NCTC), *supra* p. 164, performs many of the same functions. Military intelligence personnel work in both of these agencies, where they become both suppliers and recipients of personal information, some of which may have no clear relevance to the Pentagon's homeland defense mission. Congress has also approved the creation of an Under Secretary of Defense for Intelligence, 10 U.S.C. §137 (2006), who is supposed to provide "more coordinated, better focused intelligence support for pressing national concerns like homeland security." Department of Def., *Report to Congress on the Role of the Department of Defense in Supporting Homeland Security* 3 (Sept. 2003).

In 2002, DOD created the Northern Command (NORTHCOM), based in Colorado, to assist in homeland defense. *See generally* United States Northern Command, *Defending Our Homeland* (n.d.), *at* http://www.northcom.mil. Like DHS I&A and NCTC, NORTHCOM receives and "fuses" intelligence and law enforcement information from various sources, then redistributes it widely to federal, state, and local agencies. Unlike the two civilian agencies, however, NORTHCOM also collects domestic data directly from a Defense Intelligence Agency (DIA) Defense Counter-intelligence and Human Intelligence Center (DCHC), established in August 2008. *See* Department of Defense News Release, *DOD Activates Defense Counterintelligence and Human Intelligence Center* (Aug. 4, 2008), *at* http://www.defense.gov/releases/ release.aspx?releaseid=12106. While disclaiming any law enforcement activity or functions, DCHC develops "offensive counterintelligence operations" for DOD, potentially including efforts to penetrate, "deceive and disable foreign intelligence activities" directed against U.S. forces. Memorandum from the Deputy Secretary of Defense, *Establishment of the Defense Counterintelligence and Human Intelligence Center* (July 22, 2008), *available at* http://www.fas.org/irp/doddir/dod/dchc.pdf.

In June 2005, the Defense Department published *Strategy for Homeland Defense and Civil Support*, *available at* http://www.defense.gov/news/Jun2005/d20050630home land.pdf, declaring that DOD expected to "reorient its intelligence capabilities" to enable it to, *inter alia*, "[c]ollect homeland defense threat information from relevant private and public sector sources, consistent with US constitutional authorities and privacy law," and to "[d]evelop automated tools to improve data fusion, analysis, and management, to track systematically large amounts of data, and to detect, fuse, and analyze aberrant patterns of activity, consistent with US privacy protections." *Id.* at 21. The document pledges that DOD will work to "diminish existing cultural, technological, and bureaucratic obstacles to information sharing" among federal agencies, with state, local, and tribal governments, with private entities, and with "key foreign partners." *Id.* at 23.

Further evidence of DOD's expanding domestic intelligence role can be seen in the Pentagon's use of "noncompulsory" national security letters to collect banking and credit information about hundreds of Americans and others from U.S. financial institutions. *See* Eric Lichtblau & Mark Mazzetti, *Military Expands Intelligence Role in U.S.*, N.Y. Times, Jan. 14, 2007; DOD Instr. 5400.15, *Guidance on Obtaining Information from Financial Institutions* (Dec. 7, 2004), at Encl. 5. (The use of national security letters by the FBI is described *supra* pp. 262-284.)

NOTES AND QUESTIONS

1. *Legal Limits.* Do you think that current domestic intelligence activities out-lined here, including the role of military personnel in DHS's I&A Directorate and in the NCTC, fall within the limits imposed by the Posse Comitatus Act? Do they con-form to DOD's own rules?

If the Posse Comitatus Act is implicated, do any of its constitutional or statutory exceptions apply? Consider in this regard 10 U.S.C. §371, *supra* p. 768. It directs DOD to give "civilian law enforcement officials any information collected during the normal course of military training or operations that may be relevant to a violation of any Federal or State law," and it declares that the "needs of civilian law enforce-ment officials for information shall, to the maximum extent practicable, be taken into account in the planning and execution of military training or operations." *Id.* §371(a), (b). In light of this provision, are there any meaningful constraints on military intelligence collection?

2. *Implications for Civil Liberties.* As the military plays a larger domestic intelligence role, how would you weigh possible enhancements in security against possible losses in privacy and related liberties? What civil liberties safeguards apply to civilian intelligence activities that do not apply to the military? Are your answers affected by the availability of new data-mining technology described *supra* p. 284?

C. THE MILITARY'S ROLE IN RESPONDING TO DOMESTIC TERRORIST ATTACKS

Even before September 11, it was assumed that, for practical reasons, the military would be prominently involved in responding to a substantial terrorist attack at home. Several qualities recommend it for such a role. No other agency of government has as much equipment, training, and experience in the use of force as the Defense Department does (although some worry that such force may not be sufficiently refined for use at home). No other agency has such a durable communications system. And no other agency, especially if the National Guard is counted among its forces, is so widely dispersed around the country in places where its services may be urgently needed.

1. Leading or Supporting Role?

Thus far, government planners have prescribed a supporting role for the military. *Homeland Security Presidential Directive/HSPD-5* (Feb. 28, 2003) names the Secretary of Homeland Security as "principal Federal official for domestic incident management," and assigns "lead responsibility for criminal investigations of terrorist acts" to the Attorney General. Current plans generally call for use of the armed forces only when they could be uniquely helpful in responding to a serious emergency:

> The primary mission of the Department of Defense (DOD) and its components is national defense. Because of this critical role, resources are committed after approval by the Secretary of Defense or at the direction of the President. Many DOD components and agencies are authorized to respond to save lives, protect property and the environment, and mitigate human suffering under imminently serious conditions, as well as to provide support under their separate established authorities, as appropriate. The provision of defense support is evaluated by its legality, lethality, risk, cost, appropriateness, and impact on readiness. When Federal military and civilian personnel and resources are authorized to support civil authorities, command of those forces will remain with the Secretary of Defense. DOD elements in the incident area of operations and National Guard forces under the command of a Governor will coordinate closely with response organizations at all levels. [Federal Emergency Mgmt. Agency, *National Response Framework* 27 (Jan. 2008).]

The Defense Department's own regulations have long described its powers in the midst of a great domestic emergency as subordinate. For example, DOD Dir. 3025.1, *Military Support to Civil Authorities* §4.4.4.2 (Jan. 15, 1993), provides that "DOD resources are provided only when response or recovery requirements are beyond the capabilities of civil authorities (as determined by FEMA or another lead Federal agency for emergency response)." *See generally* Department of the Army, *Stability*

Operations and Support Operations (FM 3-07) (Feb. 20, 2003); DOD Dir. 3025.15, *Military Assistance to Civil Authorities* (Feb. 18, 1997).

In mid-2005, a DOD policy document appeared that may signal a significantly more expansive domestic role. Department of Def., *Strategy for Homeland Defense and Civil Support* (June 2005), *supra.* "Our adversaries consider US territory an integral part of a global theater of combat," it declares. "We must therefore have a strategy that applies to the domestic context the key principles that are driving the transformation of US power projection and joint expeditionary warfare." *Id.* at 1. The new policy envisions an "active, layered" defense that could deal with "simultaneous, mass casualty attacks." *Id.* at 7, 10. It also calls for significantly expanded domestic intelligence capabilities. *Id.* at 21-23. Finally, while recognizing that "[d]omestic security is primarily a civilian law enforcement function," the strategy declares that when "directed by the President, the Department will execute land-based military operations to detect, deter, and defeat foreign terrorist attacks within the United States." *Id.* at 26. Still, the Pentagon is careful to distinguish between "homeland defense (HD)," such as domestic air defense, for which DOD is the lead agency, and "homeland security." Jt. Pub. 3-26, *Homeland Security* at v-vi (Aug. 2, 2005), *available at* http://www.acq.osd.mil/ncbdp/nm/nmbook/references/DoD/2.40%20JP%203-26%20Homeland%20Security.pdf. "Except for HD missions," it says, "DOD will serve in a supporting role for domestic incident management." *Id.* at viii.

2.   Controlling Authorities

A "sense of Congress" provision in the Homeland Security Act of 2002 notes that existing laws, including the Insurrection Act and the Stafford Act, "grant the President broad powers that may be invoked in the event of domestic emergencies, including an attack against the Nation using weapons of mass destruction, and these laws specifically authorize the President to use the Armed Forces to help restore public order." 6 U.S.C. §466(a)(5) (2006).

The Stafford Act, 42 U.S.C.A. §§5121-5207 (West 2009), as amended by Pub. L. No. 111-351, §§3, 4, 124 Stat. 3863, 3864 (2011), gives the President authority to use any federal agency, including the Defense Department, to assist state governments in disaster relief operations, *id.* §5192, or specifically to use the armed forces to perform work "essential for the preservation of life and property." *Id.* §5170b(c). It has not been construed to permit the use of those forces to maintain law and order, however. *See* Jennifer K. Elsea & R. Chuck Mason, *The Use of Federal Troops for Disaster Assistance: Legal Issues* 7 (Cong. Res. Serv. RS22266), Nov. 28, 2008.

Several statutory exceptions to the Posse Comitatus Act, especially the Insurrection Act, 10 U.S.C. §§331-335, *supra* p. 767, give the President wide latitude to use troops for a variety of purposes, including law enforcement, in the aftermath of a terrorist attack or natural disaster. The military may turn over to law enforcement officials any information collected during "the normal course of . . . military operations," and in fact it must take law enforcement needs into account in planning and executing its operations. 10 U.S.C. §371. Treating any attack site as a crime scene, this measure could allow troops to assist in gathering evidence for a criminal prosecution, although a related provision bars any "direct participation" by military personnel in a "search, seizure, arrest, or other similar activity" unless otherwise authorized by law. 10 U.S.C. §375. And during an "emergency situation involving a biological or chemical weapon of mass destruction," military personnel may assist the Department of Justice in the collection of intelligence or in searches or seizures, if it is "necessary for the immediate protection of human life," and civilian law enforcement officials cannot do it. 10 U.S.C. §382. *See also* 18 U.S.C. §831(e) (emergency situation involving nuclear materials). *See generally* Charles Doyle & Jennifer Elsea, *Terrorism: Some Legal Restrictions on Military Assistance to Domestic Authorities Following a Terrorist Attack* (Cong. Res. Serv. RS21012), May 27, 2005.

Without reference to any specific enabling legislation, DOD regulations describing "immediate response authority" say that local military commanders may act in an emergency to "save lives, prevent human suffering, or mitigate great property damage." 32 C.F.R. §185.4(e) (2010). *See also id.* §215.4(c)(1), noted *supra* p. 773, and *id.* §501.2(a). This authority was cited when the military furnished medivac aircraft, ambulances, bomb detection dog teams, and various personnel to assist civilian officials following the Oklahoma City bombing in 1995. The regulations would also permit evacuation, restoration of essential public services, and traffic control. *See* Jim Winthrop, *The Oklahoma City Bombing: Immediate Response Authority and Other Military Assistance to Civil Authority (MACA)*, Army Law., July 1997, at 3. Do you think this authority should be spelled out in legislation?

3. Organizing for a Response

In 2002, NORTHCOM assumed responsibility for DOD's homeland defense efforts and for provision of military support to civil authorities. *See* William Knight & Steve Bowman, *Homeland Security: Evolving Roles and Missions for United States Northern Command* (Cong. Res. Serv. RS21322), Oct. 11, 2007. It manages military responses to all kinds of threats, from terrorism to hurricanes, working closely with DHS and directing the activities of the Joint Task Force-Civil Support. *See* United States Northern Command, *Joint Task Force Civil Support* (n.d.), *at* http://www.jtfcs.northcom.mil/JTFCS.aspx.

In October 2008, the first ever infantry combat brigade was assigned to NORTHCOM to help in responding to terrorist attacks, natural disasters, and civil unrest. Labeled the CBRNE Consequence Management Response Force, the unit is to receive special training in crowd and traffic control and the use of non-lethal weapons. *See* Gina Cavallaro, *Brigade Homeland Tours Start Oct. 1*, Army Times, Sept. 30, 2008, *available at* http://www.armytimes.com/news/2008/09/army_homeland_090708w/.

Regarding coordination between federal and state response efforts, the GAO reported in April 2008 that NORTHCOM was unfamiliar with state emergency response plans, and that a failure of NORTHCOM and the National Guard Bureau to define their respective response roles had resulted in confusion, duplication, and waste. Government Accountability Office, *Homeland Defense: Steps Have Been Taken to Improve U.S. Northern Command's Coordination with States and the National Guard Bureau, but Gaps Remain* (GAO-08-252), Apr. 2008.

The National Guard, with some 450,000 personnel, has a special role to play in the response to a terrorist attack. The nearly 5,000 Army and Air National Guard units scattered across the country have essentially the same relevant training and equipment as active-duty military elements, and they have extensive experience in firefighting, rescue, evacuation, and cleanup after storms and floods. The importance of the

Guard's role and the need for close coordination of the Guard's activities with those of active-duty military forces are spelled out in *Failure of Initiative, supra* p. 770, at 218-224, 228-231. Unless and until they are federalized by the President's order, however, Guard forces operate under the command of state governors. In this posture, as we have seen, *supra* p. 761, the Posse Comitatus Act does not apply. Thus, there may be an incentive to delay placing these forces under federal command in order to preserve the maximum flexibility in their use. *See generally* National Guard Bureau home page *at* http://www.ngb.army.mil/; William C. Banks, *The Normalization of Homeland Security After September 11: The Role of the Military in Counterterrorism Preparedness and Response,* 64 La. L. Rev. 735, 762-768 (2004).

The Pentagon has directed Guard forces to provide training and equipment for at least 70 specialized Weapons of Mass Destruction Civil Support Teams of 22 persons each who would be ready on a moment's notice for deployment to the scene of a chemical or biological weapons attack. *See* Department of the Army, *Weapons of Mass Destruction — Civil Support Team Operations, FM 3-11.22* (Mar. 31, 2009), *available at* http://www.fas.org/irp/doddir/army/fm3-11-22.pdf. *See also* GlobalSecurity.org, *Weapons of Mass Destruction Civil Support Teams* (Jan. 12, 2010), *at* http://www.globalsecurity.org/military/agency/army/wmd-cst.htm. Equipped with a mobile analytical laboratory and reliable communications gear, a team would assist state and local personnel in identifying dangerous agents, evacuating victims, and controlling access to affected areas. *See* GlobalSecurity.org, *Weapons of Mass Destruction Civil Support Teams* (n.d.), *at* http://www.globalsecurity.org/military/agency/army/wmd-cst.htm; 10 U.S.C. §12,310(c) (2006 & Supp. III 2009).

4.   New Rules After 9/11?

Six weeks after the terrorist attacks of 9/11, a 37-page Office of Legal Counsel (OLC) opinion described the domestic role of the military in these very expansive terms:

> [T]he President has ample constitutional and statutory authority to deploy the military against international or foreign terrorists operating within the United States. We further believe that the use of such military force generally is consistent with constitutional standards, and that it need not follow the exact procedures that govern law enforcement operations. [Memorandum for Alberto R. Gonzales, Counsel to the President, and William J. Haynes II, General Counsel, Department of Defense, from John C. Yoo, Deputy Assistant Attorney General, and Robert J. Delahunty, Special Counsel, Office of Legal Counsel, *Re: Authority for Use of Military Force to Combat Terrorist Activities Within the United States* (Oct. 23, 2001), *available at* http://www.usdoj.gov/opa/documents/memomilitaryforcecombatus10232001.pdf.]

The opinion was not released to the public when it was written, and the extent of its influence on military planning and policy is unknown.

Seven years later, the Yoo/Delahunty memorandum was repudiated in substantial part by another OLC opinion. Memorandum for the Files from Steven G. Bradbury, Principal Deputy Assistant Attorney General, *October 23, 2001 OLC Opinion Addressing the Domestic Use of Military Force to Combat Terrorist Activities* (Oct. 6, 2008), *available at* http://www.fas.org/irp/agency/doj/olc/caution.pdf. The new opinion urged "caution" in relying on the earlier one, describing several of its provisions as "either incorrect or highly questionable":

> The [2001] memorandum concludes...that the Fourth Amendment would not apply to domestic military operations, designed to deter and prevent further terrorist attacks. This conclusion does not reflect the current views of this Office. The Fourth Amendment is fully applicable to domestic military operations, though the application of the Fourth Amendment's essential "reasonableness" requirement to particular circumstances will be sensitive to the exigencies of military actions....
>
> ...[T]he memorandum also contains certain broad statements...suggesting that First Amendment speech and press rights and other guarantees of individual liberty under the Constitution would potentially be subordinated to overriding military necessities. These statements, too, were unnecessary to the opinion, are overbroad and general, and are not sufficiently grounded in the particular circumstances of a concrete scenario, and therefore cannot be viewed as authoritative.
>
> The memorandum concludes...that the domestic deployment of the Armed Forces by the President to prevent and deter terrorism would fundamentally serve a military purpose rather than a law enforcement purpose, and therefore the Posse Comitatus Act, 18 U.S.C. §1385 (2000), would not apply to such operations. Although the "military purpose" doctrine is a well-established limitation on the applicability of the Posse Comitatus Act, the broad conclusion...is far too general and divorced from specific facts and circumstances to be useful as an authoritative precedent of OLC.
>
> The memorandum treats the Authorization for Use of Military Force ("AUMF"), enacted by Congress in the immediate wake of 9/11, Pub. L. No. 107-40, 115 Stat. 224 (Sept. 18, 2001) [*supra* p. 86], as a statutory exception to the Posse Comitatus Act's restriction on the use of the military for domestic law enforcement. The better view, however, is that a reasonable and necessary use of military force taken under the authority of the AUMF would be a military action, potentially subject to the established "military purpose" doctrine, rather than a law enforcement action.
>
> The memorandum reasons...that in the aftermath of the 9/11 attacks, the Insurrection Act, 10 U.S.C. §333 (2000), would provide general authority for the President to deploy the military domestically to prevent and deter future terrorist attacks; whereas, consistent with the longstanding interpretation of the Executive Branch, any particular application of the Insurrection Act to authorize the use of the military for law enforcement purposes would require the presence of an actual obstruction of the execution of federal law or a breakdown in the ability of state authorities to protect federal rights. [*Id.* at 1-2.]

Neither the Yoo/Delahunty nor the Bradbury memorandum was made public until March 2, 2009, after the Obama administration took office.

NOTES AND QUESTIONS

1. *How the Military Can Help.* Review carefully the plague scenario set forth *supra* p. 731. What useful role could military forces have played in responding to the notional bioterrorist attack?

Do you agree that we should try to use other agencies whenever possible? If military forces are deployed in such an emergency, who should make the decisions about when and how to use them? What lessons can be learned from the federal response to Hurricane Katrina?

2.   *Need for New Rules?* One study suggests that "[t]here are currently adequate laws and structures in place to facilitate the use of the military in relief efforts in the event of a major catastrophe of whatever kind." ABA Standing Comm. on Law & Nat'l Sec. et al., *Hurricane Katrina Task Force Subcommittee Report* 23 (Feb. 2006). The 2001 Yoo/Delahunty OLC opinion described above apparently did not agree. Who was right?

Suppose the Yoo/Delahunty OLC opinion accurately stated the law after 9/11 — that domestic military counterterrorism operations would not be constrained by the First and Fourth Amendments, and that the AUMF could be read as a statutory exception to the Posse Comitatus Act. (Note that the 2008 Bradbury memo does not altogether dismiss this possibility.) What, if any, limits would then exist on the domestic employment of military forces?

3.   *Cooperation Between DOD and Other Agencies.* Based on the brief description of authorities and plans set out above, how would you rate the chances for a strong, efficient collaboration between the Departments of Defense and Justice in responding to a terrorist attack? What about DOD and FEMA? When the Principal Deputy Assistant Secretary of Defense (Homeland Defense) was asked in August 2005 whether he knew of a document issued by DHS that would help DOD determine the requirements for military assistance to civilian authorities, he replied, "To my knowledge, no such document exists." *See Failure of Initiative, supra* p. 770, at 203. What would you recommend to improve the chances of collaboration? *See generally* Jeffrey D. Brake, *Terrorism and the Military's Role in Domestic Crisis Management: Background and Issues for Congress* (Cong. Res. Serv. RL30938), Jan. 27, 2003.

4.   *The National Guard's Role.* Is the use of unfederalized National Guard forces in law enforcement consistent with the policies underlying the Posse Comitatus Act?

What advantages or disadvantages can you see to utilizing Guard forces under the control of state governors, rather than federalizing them, to respond to a terrorist attack? How, if at all, is your answer affected by the fact that Guard personnel in every state receive the same training and equipment prescribed by the Pentagon?

D.   MARTIAL LAW: WHEN PLANNING FAILS

If, in the event of an actual or threatened terrorist attack, or a large natural disaster, the execution of federal emergency plans fails to restore order, or if such plans are perceived as inadequate, martial law might be invoked as the option of last resort. Such a drastic step might seem advisable because of the military's extensive, coherent organization, its tradition of discipline, its robust communications systems, and its training in the use of force. Martial law could be declared by the President as Commander in Chief of U.S. armed forces, by a state governor as head of an unfederalized National Guard, or by a military officer in the field. Without specific guidance from higher authority, military leaders would then be governed only by rules fashioned by them to fit the situation. The content of the rules and the duration of their enforcement would, by definition, be impossible to predict. So, necessarily, would be the effect on Americans' civil liberties.

In the middle of the eighteenth century, Blackstone described martial law as

temporary excrescences bred out of the distemper of the state, and not any part of the permanent and perpetual laws of the kingdom. For martial law, which is built upon no settled principles, but is entirely arbitrary in its decisions, is . . . in truth and reality no law, but something indulged rather than allowed as a law. [2 William Blackstone, *Commentaries* *413.]

A century later, in a Civil War era case, the Supreme Court, in dictum, described the circumstances under which martial law might be invoked.

Ex parte Milligan
United States Supreme Court, 1866
71 U.S. (4 Wall.) 2

[The opinion is set forth *supra* p. 381.]

NOTES AND QUESTIONS

1. *The Necessity for Martial Law.* In an earlier case growing out of a rebellion in Rhode Island, the Court indicated that "a State may use its military power to put down an armed insurrection, too strong to be controlled by the civil authority. The power is essential to the existence of every government, essential to the preservation of order and free institutions, and is as necessary to the States of this Union as to any other government." *Luther v. Borden*, 48 U.S. (7 How.) 1, 44-45 (1849). In litigation arising in New Orleans, after that city had been captured by the Union Army in 1862 and placed under martial law, the Court declared that "[m]artial law is the law of military necessity in the actual presence of war." *United States v. Diekelman*, 92 U.S. (2 Otto) 520, 526 (1876). And in his concurring opinion in *Youngstown Sheet & Tube Co. v. Sawyer* (*Steel Seizure Case*), 343 U.S. 579, 650 n.19 (1952), Justice Jackson was careful to exclude from his discussion of emergency powers based on necessity, "as in a very limited category by itself, the establishment of martial law."

The governor of Hawaii declared martial law immediately after the Japanese attack on Pearl Harbor, as he was authorized to do by the Hawaii Organic Act §67, ch. 339, 31 Stat. 141, 153 (1900). Testing a military tribunal's power to try civilians for ordinary criminal offenses, the Court observed that "the term 'martial law' carries no precise meaning. The Constitution does not refer to 'martial law' at all and no Act of Congress had defined the term. It has been employed in various ways by different people and at different times." *Duncan v. Kahanamoku*, 327 U.S. 304, 315 (1946). Then, struggling to avoid describing the limits of executive or legislative power, the Court found that in using the term "martial law" Congress had not intended to authorize the supplanting of courts by military tribunals. The story is retold in fascinating detail in Harry N. Scheiber & Jane L. Scheiber, *Bayonets in Paradise: A Half-Century Retrospect on Martial Law in Hawai'i, 1941–1946*, 19 Haw. L. Rev. 477 (1997).

2. *Standby Martial Law?* In June 1955, the government conducted a massive civil defense exercise to simulate responses to a nuclear attack. To almost everyone's

surprise, President Eisenhower hypothetically declared nationwide martial law, suspended the writ of habeas corpus, and authorized military commanders to stop the functioning of local courts. His action was widely criticized as unnecessary and improper. *See, e.g.,* Robert S. Rankin & Winfried R. Dallmayr, *Freedom and Emergency Powers in the Cold War* 56-60 (1964). Nevertheless, throughout much of the Cold War the government had in place a comprehensive secret plan, called "Plan D," for responding to the threat of a nuclear attack. One element of that plan, Presidential Emergency Action Directive No. 21, apparently included a draft executive order declaring martial law.

In 1987, the *Miami Herald* reported that Lieutenant Colonel Oliver North and FEMA had drafted a new emergency plan calling for suspension of the Constitution, imposition of martial law, appointment of military commanders to run state and local governments, and detention of dissidents and Central American refugees. Miami Herald, July 5, 1987. *See* Jules Lobel, *Emergency Power and the Decline of Liberalism,* 98 Yale L.J. 1385, 1420 (1989) (noting that Lieutenant Colonel North denied drawing up such a plan).

Do you think the President should carry a draft order declaring martial law with her at all times? If so, do you think the terms of the order and criteria for its execution, or at least the fact of its existence, should be publicized?

3.   *Conditions for Martial Law.* One scholar argues that the Insurrection statutes, 10 U.S.C. §§331-335, delegate to the President the power to impose martial law. Vladeck, *supra* p. 770, at 152-153. If Congress has so conferred this power on the President, it has done no more to clarify the circumstances under which the power might be exercised. The Defense Department, on the other hand, has adopted regulations to cover such an eventuality:

> Martial law depends for its justification upon public necessity. Necessity gives rise to its creation; necessity justifies its exercise; and necessity limits its duration. The extent of the military force used and the actual measures taken, consequently, will depend upon the actual threat to order and public safety which exists at the time. In most instances the decision to impose martial law is made by the President.... However, the decision to impose martial law may be made by the local commander on the spot, if the circumstances demand immediate action, and time and available communications facilities do not permit obtaining prior approval from higher authority. [32 C.F.R. §501.4 (2010).]

How do these regulatory criteria for invocation of martial law compare with those articulated by the Supreme Court in *Ex parte Milligan?* Would it be possible, or wise, to try to develop more specific guidelines? Could you draft the guidelines? Is there any way to challenge the legitimacy of the DOD regulations before they can be used — or even afterward?

4.   *Planning to Avoid Martial Law.* As a practical matter, do you think any statutory or regulatory prescriptions could deter the President or military officials from declaring martial law in the wake of a terrorist attack involving a weapon of mass destruction, or in the aftermath of a great natural disaster? Can you think of any way to limit the resort to martial law in such a crisis?

VIII

Noncriminal Sanctions Against Terrorists and Their Supporters

Public Sanctions Against Terrorists and Their Supporters

25

Because the threat of terrorism is so grave and so complex, the United States has adopted a variety of countermeasures. In earlier chapters we examined the use of military force against terrorists and their state supporters. We then considered ways to detect such threats before they could be carried out, and to detain and interrogate individuals suspected of involvement in terrorist activities. We also reviewed criminal sanctions designed to punish and deter terrorism.

In this chapter we consider additional measures that do not involve the use of force. In Part A we take up efforts by sovereign states, acting in concert, to address the shared threat of terrorism. In Part B we turn to U.S. government economic sanctions intended to dissuade potential terrorists and deny them the resources they need to carry out their deadly mission.

A. INTERNATIONAL SANCTIONS

1. Developing a Consensus Among Nations to Fight Terrorism

a. The United States Reaches Out

If it was not apparent earlier, the events of September 11, 2001, made it abundantly clear that in the fight against terrorism the United States cannot go it alone. U.S. officials immediately began reaching out to other nations around the globe for assistance in gathering intelligence about terrorist suspects, apprehending persons believed to be connected with the attacks, freezing their financial assets, and mounting a military response against Osama bin Laden's supporters in Afghanistan. *See generally* Sean D. Murphy, *International Law, the United States, and the Non-Military "War" Against Terrorism*, 14 Eur. J. Int'l L. 347 (2003).

The United States also asked for help from international organizations. On the evening of the 11th, the NATO Council announced:

The NATO nations unanimously condemn these barbaric acts committed against a NATO member state. The mindless slaughter of so many innocent civilians is an unacceptable act of violence without precedent in the modern era. It underscores the urgency of intensifying the battle against terrorism, a battle that the NATO countries — indeed all civilised nations — must win. All Allies stand united in their determination to combat this scourge. [NATO Press Release PR/CP (2001) 122, Sept. 12, 2001.]

The next day, the U.N. Security Council passed a resolution calling on "all States to work together urgently to bring to justice the perpetrators, organizers, and sponsors of these terrorist attacks." S.C. Res. 1368, U.N. Doc. S/RES/1368 (Sept. 12, 2001). These declarations were followed by other commitments to cooperate in actions to combat terrorism, as outlined below.

The United States continues to rely on help from other nations, as well as from international organizations.

> The United States alone cannot eliminate every terrorist or terrorist organization that threatens our safety, security, or interests....The United States and its partners are engaged in the full range of cooperative [counterterrorism] activities — from intelligence sharing to joint training and operations and from countering radicalization to pursuing community resilience programs. [*National Strategy for Counterterrorism*, June 2011, at 6-7.]

Among many examples since 9/11, the United States and Russia entered into a bilateral agreement in 2006 to improve accounting for and physical protection of nuclear materials held by each nation, and to detect and interdict illicit trafficking in such materials. Eighty other nations have since joined their partnership. *See* U.S. Dep't of State, *The Global Initiative to Combat Nuclear Terrorism* (n.d.), http://www.state.gov/t/isn/c18406.htm. And the Group of Eight (G-8) (leading economic states) has agreed to develop travel document security standards, strengthen controls over shoulder-fired anti-aircraft missiles, and adopt other counterterrorism measures. *See G8 Statement on Counter-Terrorism*, July 8, 2005, http://www.g8.utoronto.ca/summit/2005gleneagles/index.html. Additional formal and informal collaborative measures are described below.

b.   International Commitment to Counterterrorism

Terrorist attacks at home are nothing new in many nations. Algeria, Colombia, France, Germany, Great Britain, India, Indonesia, Israel, Italy, the Philippines, Russia, Spain, and Sri Lanka are just a few of the states afflicted with this scourge in recent years. Individual nations around the globe have developed their own programs for combating terrorism. Some of these are described in annual reports by the U.S. State Department, *Country Reports on Terrorism, at* http://www.state.gov/s/ct/rls/crt/.

These individual nations have also agreed to cooperate in the fight against terrorism. This agreement can be seen in the following United Nations General Assembly resolution:

United Nations Global Counter-Terrorism Strategy
G.A. Res. 60/288, U.N. Doc. A/RES/60/288 (Sept. 20, 2006)

The General Assembly,
Guided by the purposes and principles of the Charter of the United Nations and *reaffirming* its role under the Charter, including on questions related to international peace and security, ...

Reaffirming that acts, methods and practices of terrorism in all its forms and manifestations are activities aimed at the destruction of human rights, fundamental freedoms and democracy, threatening territorial integrity, security of States and destabilizing legitimately constituted Governments, and that the international community should take the necessary steps to enhance cooperation to prevent and combat terrorism,

Reaffirming also that terrorism cannot and should not be associated with any religion, nationality, civilization or ethnic group, . . .

Affirming Member States' determination to continue to do all they can to resolve conflict, end foreign occupation, confront oppression, eradicate poverty, promote sustained economic growth, sustainable development, global prosperity, good governance, human rights for all and rule of law, improve intercultural understanding and ensure respect for all religions, religious values, beliefs or cultures, . . .

Adopts the present resolution . . . as the United Nations Global Counter-Terrorism Strategy. . . .

Plan of Action

We, the States Members of the United Nations, resolve:

1. To consistently, unequivocally and strongly condemn terrorism in all its forms and manifestations, committed by whomever, wherever and for whatever purposes, as it constitutes one of the most serious threats to international peace and security.

2. To take urgent action to prevent and combat terrorism in all its forms and manifestations and, in particular:

(a) To consider becoming parties without delay to the existing international conventions and protocols against terrorism, and implementing them, and to make every effort to reach an agreement on and conclude a comprehensive convention on international terrorism;

(b) To implement all General Assembly resolutions on measures to eliminate international terrorism, and relevant General Assembly resolutions on the protection of human rights and fundamental freedoms while countering terrorism. . . .

3. To recognize that international cooperation and any measures that we undertake to prevent and combat terrorism must comply with our obligations under international law, including the Charter of the United Nations and relevant international conventions and protocols, in particular human rights law, refugee law and international humanitarian law. . . .

The resolution includes commitments by member states to establish a single comprehensive database on biological incidents, modernize border and customs controls, improve the security of travel documents, deny financial and operational safe havens to terrorists, and protect human rights while countering terrorism, among other initiatives. Other U.N. General Assembly resolutions reflecting the same shared concern for the common threat of terrorism actually date back more than three decades. *See UN Action to Counter Terrorism* (n.d.), http://www.un.org/terrorism/.

It would be a mistake to assume that such resolutions have no practical value. It is true they tend to be cast in very broad, even aspirational, terms, and that they are understood to have no binding effect on member states. Yet while Resolution 60/288, set out above, was adopted without a roll-call vote, states often vote against such measures, suggesting that they are taken seriously. And although General Assembly resolutions may not represent a perfect consensus among nations, they both reflect and influence public opinion worldwide. They show a commitment to a common purpose and an agreement to cooperate in achieving that purpose. They may also provide domestic political "cover" for counterterrorist initiatives by individual states.

General Assembly resolutions often mark the beginning of a collaborative process that eventually leads to changes in international and domestic laws. Of particular importance here are resolutions approving proposed conventions aimed at combating terrorism. These "United Nations conventions" may then be opened for signature and ratification by all states, as noted below.

2.   Compulsory Actions by International Organizations

On October 15, 1999, the U.N. Security Council adopted a resolution "deploring the fact that the Taliban continues to provide safe haven to Usama bin Laden and to allow him . . . to use Afghanistan as a base from which to sponsor international terrorist operations." S.C. Res. 1267, U.N. Doc. S/RES/1267. Resolution 1267 set out limited measures designed to isolate the Taliban physically and financially. Its effect may have been blunted, however, by a new trading agreement between the Taliban and neighboring Iran. *See* Pamela Constable, *Iran Opening Eases Choke Hold of U.N. Sanctions on Afghans*, Wash. Post, Dec. 22, 1999. A little more than a year later, the Security Council adopted this more aggressive resolution:

United Nations Security Council, Resolution 1333
U.N. Doc. S/RES/1333 (Dec. 19, 2000)

The Security Council, . . .
Acting under Chapter VII of the Charter of the United Nations,
1. *Demands* that the Taliban . . . cease the provision of sanctuary and training for international terrorists and their organizations, take appropriate effective measures to ensure that the territory under its control is not used for terrorist installations and camps, or for the preparation or organization of terrorist acts against other States and their citizens, and cooperate with international efforts to bring indicted terrorists to justice;
2. *Demands also* that the Taliban . . . without further delay . . . turn over Usama bin Laden to appropriate authorities in a country where he has been indicted . . . or to appropriate authorities in a country where he will be arrested and effectively brought to justice;
3. *Demands further* that the Taliban should act swiftly to close all camps where terrorists are trained within the territory under its control . . .
5. *Decides* that all States shall:
(a) Prevent the direct or indirect supply, sale, and transfer to the territory of Afghanistan under Taliban control . . . of arms and related materiel of all types . . .
(b) Prevent the direct or indirect supply, sale, and transfer to the territory of Afghanistan under Taliban control . . . of technical advice, assistance, or training related to the military activities of the armed personnel under the control of the Taliban; . . .

8. *Decides* that all States shall take further measures:

(a) To close immediately and completely all Taliban offices in their territories . . .

(c) To freeze without delay funds and other assets of Usama bin Laden and individuals and entities associated with him as designated by the Committee [created by Resolution 1267, according to] . . . an updated list, based on information provided by States and regional organizations. . . .

9. *Demands* that the Taliban, as well as others, halt all illegal drugs activities and work to virtually eliminate the illicit cultivation of opium poppy, the proceeds of which finance Taliban terrorist activities; . . .

11. *Decides also* that all States are required to deny any aircraft permission to take off from, land in, or over-fly their territories if that aircraft has taken off from, or is destined to land at, a place in the territory of Afghanistan . . . unless the particular flight has been approved in advance . . . on the grounds of humanitarian need, including religious obligations such as the performance of the Hajj, or on the grounds that the flight promotes discussion of a peaceful resolution of the conflict in Afghanistan. . . .

If these resolutions created hardship for the Taliban, they nevertheless failed to dislodge bin Laden. Two weeks after the terrorist attacks on September 11, the Security Council adopted another resolution directing all States to criminalize the financing of terrorist activities, freeze terrorists' assets, suppress the recruitment of members by terrorist groups, eliminate the supply of weapons to terrorists, tighten border controls, and cooperate in exchanges of information and in the investigation and prosecution of terrorists. S.C. Res. 1373, U.N. Doc. S/RES/1373 (Sept. 28, 2001). This resolution echoed the language of the United Nations International Convention for the Suppression of the Financing of Terrorism, *opened for signature* Jan. 10, 2000, S. Treaty Doc. No. 106-49, 39 I.L.M. 270, excerpted below, which was approved earlier by the U.N. General Assembly, G.A. Res. 54/109, U.N. Doc. A/RES/54/109 (Dec. 9, 1999), but not yet in force. *See* Ilias Bantekas, *The International Law of Terrorist Financing*, 97 Am. J. Int'l L. 315, 325-327 (2003).

Resolutions 1267 and 1333 called for the creation of a list of individuals and entities associated with Osama bin Laden, Al Qaeda, and the Taliban, based on information provided by states and regional organizations. Listing required imposition of the sanctions noted above. In early 2011, the list contained some 485 entries. *See* Letter dated 13 April 2011 from the Chair of the Security Council Committee Established Pursuant to Resolution 1267 (1999) to the President of the Security Council, U.N. Doc. S/2011/245 (Apr. 13, 2011), http://www.un.org/ga/search/view_doc.asp?symbol=S/2011/245, at 9.

The Security Council has adopted a number of other resolutions addressing the threat of terrorism, including some concerned with weapons of mass destruction. *See, e.g.*, S.C. Res. 1540, U.N. Doc. S/RES/1540 (Apr. 28, 2004). They are available at *UN Action to Counter Terrorism: Security Council Resolutions* (updated regularly), http://www.un.org/terrorism/sc-res.shtml.

The Security Council resolutions described here differ from U.N. General Assembly resolutions in at least two important respects. First, their adoption requires the approval (or at least abstention) of all five permanent members of the Security Council. Second, such resolutions are binding on all member states, which agree in Article 25 of the United Nations Charter to "accept and carry out the decisions of the Security Council."

NOTES AND QUESTIONS

1. *Efficacy of Security Council Sanctions.* How effective are U.N. Security Council sanctions? Those aimed at Afghanistan and the Taliban regime did not lead to the capture of Osama bin Laden or to prevention of the terrorist attacks of 9/11, and they have not succeeded in shutting down all terrorist operations since then. Assessing the asset freeze, a U.N. committee reports that

> [l]isted groups affiliated with Al-Qaida and the Taliban continue to raise money through legal means, such as donations and legitimate business enterprises, and illegally, such as through kidnapping for ransom, extortion, drug trafficking and illegal taxation. Individual groups and cells raise money for their own operations and expenses, and there is no centralized disbursement of funds, except in some cases where the Taliban either collects or distributes money. The scale of financing varies from area to area and group to group, with the multimillion dollar business of the Taliban dwarfing groups like Al-Qaida in the Arabian Peninsula . . . . [Letter dated 13 April 2011, *supra,* at 18.]

See also Richard Barrett, *Time to Reexamine Regulation Designed to Counter the Financing of Terrorism,* 41 Case W. Res. J. Int'l L. 7 (2009) (describing the financing of the Taliban and Al Qaeda). The arms embargo and travel ban may have had a more significant effect. *See* Letter dated 13 April 2011, *supra,* at 21-23. "The key impact of the [1267 sanctions regime] is likely to be as a deterrent, particularly on potential financiers of Al-Qaida or the Taliban, for whom the consequences of sanctions can be acute." *Id.* at 9.

One indication that these measures have worked may be the Taliban's demand that its associates' names be removed from the 1267 list as part of the peace and reconciliation process in Afghanistan. *Id.* at 7.

> The impact of listing on a public figure is considerable. While subject to the sanctions measures, no senior government official can exercise effective authority, manage development aid, dispense patronage, or travel outside the country without specific Security Council agreement. Furthermore, the Taliban believe the List is a "kill or capture" list, which makes it harder for those who appear on it to take part in any political activity." [*Id.* at 10.]

Responding to these concerns and to a request from the government of Afghanistan, *see id.* at 10-12, in mid-2011 the Security Council split the Al Qaeda and Taliban sanctions regimes. S.C. Res. 1988, U.N. Doc. S/RES/1988 (June 17, 2011); S.C. Res. 1989, U.N. Doc. S/RES/1989 (June 17, 2011). *See* Security Council Committee Established Pursuant to Resolution 1988 (2011) (n.d.), http://www.un.org/sc/committees/1988/; Security Council Committee Pursuant to Resolutions 1267 (1999) and 1989 (2011) Concerning Al-Qaida and Associated Individuals and Entities (n.d.), http://www.un.org/sc/committees/1267/index.shtml. Resolution 1988 instructed a new committee administering a separate Taliban list to

> give due regard to requests for removal of individuals who meet the reconciliation conditions agreed to by the Government of Afghanistan and the international community, which include the renunciation of violence, no links to international terrorist organizations, including Al-Qaida, or any cell, affiliate, splinter group, or derivative thereof, and respect for the Afghan Constitution, including the rights of women and persons belonging to minorities. [S.C. Res. 1988, ¶18.]

Can you describe an organization and process for reviewing delisting requests that will help move Afghanistan toward a peaceful reconciliation? Can you think of other ways that the sanctions process might be employed to stop the spread of terrorism?

   2. *Accepting and Carrying Out the Resolutions.* Because they concern commitments under the United Nations Charter, which is a multilateral treaty, U.N. Security Council resolutions that are intended to be binding on member states have the same force in international law as other treaty obligations. They may in fact have greater force, since Article 103 of the U.N. Charter gives Security Council resolutions priority over other international obligations. *See* Michael Wood, *The UN Security Council and International Law* (Hersch Lauterpacht Memorial Lecture), Nov. 7, 2006, *available at* http://www.lcil.cam.ac.uk/Media/lectures/pdf/2006_hersch_lecture_3.pdf. Implementation of Resolution 1373, *supra*, is monitored and reported by the U.N. Counter-Terrorism Committee, *see* Security Council, *Counter-Terrorism Committee* (updated Aug. 8, 2011), *at* http://www.un.org/sc/ctc/, although the committee lacks enforcement authority.
   How would you expect Security Council resolutions to be enforced against states not in compliance? *See* Jimmy Gurulé, *Demise of the U.N. Economic Sanctions Regime to Deprive Terrorists of Funding*, 41 Case W. Res. J. Int'l L. 19, 55-63 (2009) (urging public admonishment of non-compliant states).

   3. *Do Those Listed Have Rights?* The Security Council addressed concerns about the fairness of some listings in S.C. Res. 1904, U.N. Doc. S/RES/1904 (Dec. 17, 2009), which created an ombudsperson to oversee the listing process. Member states' imposition of sanctions required by listing has been challenged, sometimes successfully, by individuals and organizations in a number of domestic courts, alleging insufficient evidence, lack of due process, and abridgement of various liberty interests. *See* Letter dated 13 April 2011, *supra*, at 13-14, 28-30; Part B, below. If your name were inadvertently placed on the 1267 list, how would you try to get it removed? *See* S.C. Res. 1904, ¶¶ 20-25 & Annex II (outlining procedure for review by an Ombudsperson of delisting requests). *See also* Craig Forcese & Kent Roach, *Limping into the Future: the U.N. 1267 Terrorism Listing Process at the Crossroads*, 42 Geo. Wash. Int'l L. Rev. 217, 219 (2010) (arguing that "even the new and improved 1267 listing process will not satisfy due process standards.").

3. Treaties Specifically Addressing Terrorism

   As of mid-2011, there are 14 major multilateral treaties, dating back to 1963, that specifically address international terrorism. *See* UN Action to Counter Terrorism, *International Instruments to Counter Terrorism* (n.d.), *at* http://www.un.org/terrorism/instruments.shtml (with links to relevant documents). Two that figure prominently in U.S. history are the Convention for the Suppression of Unlawful Seizure of Aircraft, Dec. 16, 1970, 22 U.S.T. 1641, and the International Convention Against the Taking of Hostages, Dec. 17, 1979, T.I.A.S. 11081. Both of these treaties and their implementing legislation are described in *United States v. Yunis*, 924 F.2d 1086 (D.C. Cir. 1991). The most recent such treaty at this writing is the Convention on the Suppression of Unlawful Acts Relating to International Civil Aviation (Beijing Convention), Sept. 10, 2010, *available at* http://www.icao.int/DCAS2010/restr/docs/

beijing_convention_multi.pdf. *See* Damien van der Toorn, *September 11 Inspired Aviation Counter-Terrorism Convention and Protocol Adopted*, ASIL Insights, Jan. 26, 2011, *at* http://www.asil.org/insights110126.cfm.

These treaties are generally concerned with particular terrorist acts, such as hostage taking, aircraft hijacking, bombings, and attacks on diplomats. Most of them require signatory states to pass laws criminalizing the terrorist acts addressed, then either to prosecute violators or to extradite them to other states having jurisdiction over them. *See* Donald Musch, *International Terrorism Agreements: Documents and Commentary* (2004); H. Comm. on Int'l Relations, 106th Cong., *International Terrorism: A Compilation of Major Laws, Treaties, Agreements, and Executive Documents* (Comm. Print 2000). There was at this writing no comprehensive convention to combat all forms of terrorism, although efforts to conclude one were continuing. *See, e.g.,* G.A. Res. 64/297, ¶8, U.N. Doc. A/RES/64/297 (Oct. 13, 2010).

International Convention for the Suppression of the Financing of Terrorism

opened for signature Jan. 10, 2000, S. Treaty Doc. No. 106-49, 39 I.L.M. 270

Article 2

1. Any person commits an offence within the meaning of this Convention if that person by any means, directly or indirectly, unlawfully and wilfully, provides or collects funds with the intention that they should be used or in the knowledge that they are to be used, in full or in part, in order to carry out:

(a) An act which constitutes an offence within the scope of and as defined in one of the treaties listed in the annex [addressing air hijacking, other threats to civil aviation, maritime navigation, internationally protected persons, hostage taking, protection of nuclear material, ocean platforms, and terrorist bombings]; or

(b) Any other act intended to cause death or serious bodily injury to a civilian, or to any other person not taking an active part in the hostilities in a situation of armed conflict, when the purpose of such act, by its nature or context, is to intimidate a population, or to compel a government or an international organization to do or to abstain from doing any act. . . .

4. Any person also commits an offence if that person attempts to commit an offence as set forth in paragraph 1 of this article.

5. Any person also commits an offence if that person:

(a) Participates as an accomplice in an offence as set forth in paragraph 1 or 4 of this article;

(b) Organizes or directs others to commit an offence as set forth in paragraph 1 or 4 of this article;

(c) Contributes to the commission of one or more offences as set forth in paragraphs 1 or 4 of this article by a group of persons acting with a common purpose. Such contribution shall be intentional and shall either:

(i) Be made with the aim of furthering the criminal activity or criminal purpose of the group, where such activity or purpose involves the commission of an offence as set forth in paragraph 1 of this article; or

(ii) Be made in the knowledge of the intention of the group to commit an offence as set forth in paragraph 1 of this article.

Article 3

This Convention shall not apply where the offence is committed within a single State, the alleged offender is a national of that State and is present in the territory of that State and no other State has a basis under article 7, paragraph 1, or article 7, paragraph 2, to exercise jurisdiction, except that the provisions of articles 12 to 18 [relating to cooperation and mutual assistance among states, extradition, and treatment of prisoners] shall, as appropriate, apply in those cases.

Article 4

Each State Party shall adopt such measures as may be necessary:
(a) To establish as criminal offences under its domestic law the offences set forth in article 2;
(b) To make those offences punishable by appropriate penalties which take into account the grave nature of the offences.

Article 5

1. Each State Party, in accordance with its domestic legal principles, shall take the necessary measures to enable a legal entity located in its territory or organized under its laws to be held liable when a person responsible for the management or control of that legal entity has, in that capacity, committed an offence set forth in article 2. Such liability may be criminal, civil or administrative....

Article 6

Each State Party shall adopt such measures as may be necessary, including, where appropriate, domestic legislation, to ensure that criminal acts within the scope of this Convention are under no circumstances justifiable by considerations of a political, philosophical, ideological, racial, ethnic, religious or other similar nature.

Article 7

1. Each State Party shall take such measures as may be necessary to establish its jurisdiction over the offences set forth in article 2 when:
(a) The offence is committed in the territory of that State;
(b) The offence is committed on board a vessel flying the flag of that State or an aircraft registered under the laws of that State at the time the offence is committed;
(c) The offence is committed by a national of that State.
2. A State Party may also establish its jurisdiction over any such offence when:
(a) The offence was directed towards or resulted in the carrying out of an offence referred to in article 2, paragraph 1, subparagraph (a) or (b), in the territory of or against a national of that State;
(b) The offence was directed towards or resulted in the carrying out of an offence referred to in article 2, paragraph 1, subparagraph (a) or (b), against a State or government facility of that State abroad, including diplomatic or consular premises of that State;

(c) The offence was directed towards or resulted in an offence referred to in article 2, paragraph 1, subparagraph (a) or (b), committed in an attempt to compel that State to do or abstain from doing any act; . . .

4. Each State Party shall likewise take such measures as may be necessary to establish its jurisdiction over the offences set forth in article 2 in cases where the alleged offender is present in its territory and it does not extradite that person to any of the States Parties that have established their jurisdiction in accordance with paragraphs 1 or 2. . . .

Article 8

1. Each State Party shall take appropriate measures, in accordance with its domestic legal principles, for the identification, detection and freezing or seizure of any funds used or allocated for the purpose of committing the offences set forth in article 2 as well as the proceeds derived from such offences, for purposes of possible forfeiture.

2. Each State Party shall take appropriate measures, in accordance with its domestic legal principles, for the forfeiture of funds used or allocated for the purpose of committing the offences set forth in article 2 and the proceeds derived from such offences. . . .

Article 9 . . .

2. Upon being satisfied that the circumstances so warrant, the State Party in whose territory the offender or alleged offender is present shall take the appropriate measures under its domestic law so as to ensure that person's presence for the purpose of prosecution or extradition. . . .

Article 10

1. The State Party in the territory of which the alleged offender is present shall, in cases to which article 7 applies, if it does not extradite that person, be obliged, without exception whatsoever and whether or not the offence was committed in its territory, to submit the case without undue delay to its competent authorities for the purpose of prosecution, through proceedings in accordance with the laws of that State. Those authorities shall take their decision in the same manner as in the case of any other offence of a grave nature under the law of that State. . . .

Article 11

1. The offences set forth in article 2 shall be deemed to be included as extraditable offences in any extradition treaty existing between any of the States Parties before the entry into force of this Convention. . . .

Article 12

1. States Parties shall afford one another the greatest measure of assistance in connection with criminal investigations or criminal or extradition proceedings in respect of the offences set forth in article 2, including assistance in obtaining evidence in their possession necessary for the proceedings.

2. States Parties may not refuse a request for mutual legal assistance on the ground of bank secrecy....

Article 14

None of the offences set forth in article 2 shall be regarded for the purposes of extradition or mutual legal assistance as a political offence or as an offence connected with a political offence or as an offence inspired by political motives....

Article 18

1. States Parties shall cooperate in the prevention of the offences set forth in article 2 by taking all practicable measures, *inter alia*, by adapting their domestic legislation, if necessary, to prevent and counter preparations in their respective territories for the commission of those offences within or outside their territories, including:...

(b) Measures requiring financial institutions and other professions involved in financial transactions to utilize the most efficient measures available for the identification of their usual or occasional customers, as well as customers in whose interest accounts are opened, and to pay special attention to unusual or suspicious transactions and report transactions suspected of stemming from a criminal activity. For this purpose, States Parties shall consider:

(i) Adopting regulations prohibiting the opening of accounts the holders or beneficiaries of which are unidentified or unidentifiable, and measures to ensure that such institutions verify the identity of the real owners of such transactions;...

(iii) Adopting regulations imposing on financial institutions the obligation to report promptly to the competent authorities all complex, unusual large transactions and unusual patterns of transactions, which have no apparent economic or obviously lawful purpose, without fear of assuming criminal or civil liability for breach of any restriction on disclosure of information if they report their suspicions in good faith;

(iv) Requiring financial institutions to maintain, for at least five years, all necessary records on transactions, both domestic or international.

2. States Parties shall further cooperate in the prevention of offences set forth in article 2 by considering:

(a) Measures for the supervision, including, for example, the licensing, of all money-transmission agencies;

(b) Feasible measures to detect or monitor the physical cross-border transportation of cash and bearer negotiable instruments....

The convention on terrorism financing echoes and implements some of the U.N. General Assembly and Security Council resolutions described above. It is in turn implemented by domestic statutes and other measures set out in Part B, below. This convention was approved by the U.N. General Assembly, G.A. Res. 54/109, U.N. Doc. A/RES/54/109 (Dec. 9, 1999), and signed by the United States on January 10, 2000, then submitted by President Clinton to the U.S. Senate on October 12, 2000, for its approval. The Senate gave its advice and consent to ratification on December 5, 2001, and it was ratified by President Bush on June 26, 2002. The House and Senate immediately got to work on the required domestic implementing legislation, some of which was enacted on June 25, 2002. Pub. L. No. 107-197, §§201-301, 116 Stat. 721, 724-728. That measure amended the material support statute, 18 U.S.C. §2339C, set forth in part *supra* p. 604.

The multilateral treaties entered into so far do not address every issue raised by the threat of international terrorism. *See* G.A. Res. 64/297, ¶8, U.N. Doc. A/RES/64/297 (Oct. 13, 2010) (urging states to conclude a comprehensive convention). Not all nations are parties to each of the treaties. (State signatories to each treaty are listed at Office of the Coordinator for Counterterrorism, U.S. Dep't of State, *International Conventions and Protocols on Terrorism*, Apr. 30, 2008, *at* http://www.state.gov/s/ct/rls/crt/2007/103717.htm.) Moreover, treaty provisions (for example, the requirement to enact criminal laws) may be difficult to enforce.

NOTES AND QUESTIONS

1. *Covered Activities?* What activities are proscribed by the Convention for the Suppression of the Financing of Terrorism? How does the definition of covered acts compare with the definitions of terrorism reviewed in Chapter 1? Does it cover advocacy (e.g., a speech at a fund-raiser for Hamas)?

2. *Enforcement.* Why might a state that has signed the Convention for the Suppression of the Financing of Terrorism subsequently decide not to abide by its terms, yet not withdraw from the convention? Does the convention do everything it could to minimize the influence of domestic politics in compliance?

How can the convention be enforced against a state that either does not enact implementing domestic law or, having done so, fails to apply that law to individuals or organizations within its jurisdiction that engage in forbidden activities? What about a state party that refuses to cooperate with other states as required by the convention?

Is the convention self-executing, that is, can it be invoked to provide relief in domestic courts? *See Restatement (Third) of Foreign Relations Law* §111 cmt. h (1987). Can you see why states might be reluctant to join such a convention if it were self-executing?

3. *Treaty as a Tactic.* Compare the terms of the convention set out above with U.N. Security Council Resolution 1333, *supra.* Which type of measure can be adopted more quickly, in response to unfolding events? Which is more narrowly targeted, and why? Which is more likely to achieve its goals, and why?

4.   Other Forms of International Cooperation

In addition to the U.N. Security Council resolutions and treaties described above, a number of non-binding agreements are aimed at combating terrorism. One important example is the Financial Action Task Force on Money Laundering (FATF), which augments the International Conventional for the Suppression of Terrorist Financing and the counterterrorism regimes created by Security Council resolutions 1267, 1333, and 1373. Created by the G-7 nations in 1989, FATF is an inter-governmental "'policy-making body' which works to generate the necessary political will to bring about national legislative and regulatory reforms . . . to combat money laundering and terrorist financing." FATF-GAFI, *About the FATF* (n.d.), http://www.fatf-gafi.org/pages/0,3417,%20en_32250379_32236836_1_1_1_1_1,00.html. FATF works closely with U.N. organizations, the International Monetary Fund (IMF), and the World Bank to set international standards, assess and monitor compliance with those standards, and encourage compliance through multilateral peer review.

Much of the practical day-to-day cooperation among nations in fighting terrorism is not, however, the product of any formal agreements or resolutions, and indeed may not be written down anywhere. Instead, it comes from states acting out of recognized self-interest in response to formal, but often private, diplomatic communications. It is also the product of informal relationships among military, intelligence, and law enforcement agencies and diplomatic corps based on shared interests, as well as the personal relationships of officials within those agencies. The weeks after September 11, for example, saw Defense Secretary Rumsfeld, Secretary of State Powell, and other U.S. officials traveling around the world in an effort to gain support for the American use of force in Afghanistan, and to arrange ad hoc alliances with Afghanistan's neighbors — Pakistan, Russia, the former Soviet republics of Uzbekistan and Tajikistan, and even Iran. These states were asked to assist by sharing intelligence, strengthening border controls, and in some instances permitting the basing of U.S. military forces on their territories.

While informal arrangements among officials of various nations may profoundly affect national security, they also may, like more formal actions, significantly affect civil liberties. Thus, it may make sense to document these cooperative measures, and, at least under some circumstances, to make the records available to the public. On the other hand, the prospect of public exposure might sometimes make such arrangements more difficult to reach.

B. DOMESTIC SANCTIONS

Domestic public sanctions are some of the most important tools of U.S. foreign policy, and they figure prominently in the war against terrorism. A number of them implement U.S. obligations found in treaties or U.N. Security Council resolutions, as noted above. Chief among these are measures designed to exert economic pressure. They may deny terrorists the material resources they need to carry out their attacks, and they hit the terrorists' supporters where it really hurts — in the pocketbook.

As the world's greatest economic power, the United States has considerable influence, even acting alone, over states that might provide financial support or safe haven for terrorists.

> With respect to nation-states, economic sanctions fall into six categories: restrictions on trading, technology transfer, foreign assistance, export credits and guarantees, foreign exchange and capital transactions, and economic access. Sanctions may include a total or partial trade embargo, embargo on financial transactions, suspension of foreign aid, restrictions on aircraft or ship traffic, or abrogation of a friendship, commerce, and navigation treaty. [Raphael Perl, *Terrorism, the Future, and U.S. Foreign Policy* 9 (Cong. Res. Serv. IB95112), Apr. 11, 2003.]

In addition, the United States has direct control over assets belonging to some terrorists, terrorist groups, or state supporters of terrorism. *See generally* Barry E. Carter,
International Economic Sanctions: Improving the Haphazard U.S. Legal Regime, 75 Cal. L.
Rev. 1159 (1987); Stanley J. Marcuss, *Grist for the Litigation Mill in U.S. Economic Sanctions Programs,* 30 Law & Pol'y Int'l Bus. 501 (1999).

1. Designation of Foreign Terrorist Organizations

People's Mojahedin Organization of Iran v. United States Department of State

United States Court of Appeals, District of Columbia Circuit, 2010
613 F.3d 220

Before: HENDERSON and TATEL, Circuit Judges, and WILLIAMS, Senior Circuit Judge.

PER CURIAM: This case is the fifth in a series of related actions challenging the
United States Secretary of State's designation of the Mojahedin-e Khalq Organization
(MEK) and its aliases as a Foreign Terrorist Organization (FTO). The MEK [is] also
called the People's Mojahedin Organization of Iran (PMOI)[1]. . . .
On July 15, 2008, . . . the PMOI petitioned State and its Secretary for revocation of
the PMOI's FTO designation. After assembling a record comprised of materials submitted by both the PMOI and the U.S. intelligence community, including classified
information, the Secretary rejected the PMOI's petition on January 12, 2009. The
PMOI now seeks review of the Secretary's decision. We conclude that the Secretary
failed to accord the PMOI the due process protections outlined in our previous
decisions and therefore remand.

I. . . .

A.

We begin by describing the Anti-Terrorism and Effective Death Penalty Act of
1996 (AEDPA), which was amended as part of the Intelligence Reform and Terrorist
Prevention Act of 2004, Pub. L. No. 108-458, §7119, 118 Stat. 3638, 3801 (2004).
Under AEDPA, the Secretary may designate an entity as an FTO if she determines
that (A) the entity is foreign, (B) it engages in "terrorist activity" or "terrorism" and
(C) the terrorist activity threatens the security of the United States or its nationals. 8
U.S.C. §1189(a)(1). "Terrorist activity" is defined in section 1182(a)(3)(B)(iii) and
includes hijacking, sabotage, kidnapping, assassination and the use of explosives,
firearms, or biological, chemical or nuclear weapons with intent to endanger people
or property, or a threat or conspiracy to do any of the foregoing. To "engage in
terrorist activity" involves, among other acts, soliciting funds or affording material
support for terrorist activities, *id.* §1182(a)(3)(B)(iv), while "terrorism" means "premeditated, politically motivated violence perpetrated against noncombatant targets
by subnational groups or clandestine agents," 22 U.S.C. §2656f(d)(2).

---

1. Because the petitioner in this case is the People's Mojahedin Organization of Iran, or the PMOI,
we refer to the MEK and all associated aliases as the PMOI.

The FTO designation has at least three consequences: the Secretary of the United States Treasury Department may freeze the FTO's assets, 8 U.S.C. §1189(a)(2)(C); FTO members are barred from entering the United States, *id.* §1182(a)(3)(B)(i)(IV), (V); and those who knowingly provide "material support or resources" to an FTO are subject to criminal prosecution, 18 U.S.C. §2339B(a)(1). A designated organization can attempt to avoid these consequences by seeking review in this court no later than thirty days after publication in the Federal Register of the Secretary's designation, amended designation or determination in response to a petition for revocation. *See* 8 U.S.C. §1189(c)(1). Our review is based "solely upon the administrative record, except that the Government may submit, for ex parte and in camera review, classified information" that the Secretary used to reach her decision. *Id.* §1189(c)(2). The review "sounds like the familiar procedure normally employed by the Congress to afford due process in administrative proceedings" and is "reminiscent of other administrative review." [*National Council of Resistance of Iran v. Department of State*, 251 F.3d 192 (D.C. Cir. 2001) (*NCRI I*)], at 196-97. Employing APA [Administrative Procedure Act]-like language, [*People's Mojahedin Org. of Iran v. U.S. Dep't of State*, 182 F.3d 17 (D.C. Cir. 1999) (*PMOI I*)], at 22, the statute requires that we "hold unlawful and set aside a designation, amended designation, or determination in response to a petition for revocation" that we find:

(A) arbitrary, capricious, an abuse of discretion, or otherwise not in accordance with law;
(B) contrary to constitutional right, power, privilege, or immunity;
(C) in excess of statutory jurisdiction, authority, or limitation, or short of statutory right;
(D) lacking substantial support in the administrative record taken as a whole or in classified information submitted to the court under paragraph (2), or
(E) not in accord with the procedures required by law.

8 U.S.C. §1189(c)(3). This standard of review applies only to the first and second requirements, namely, (1) that the organization is foreign and (2) that it engages in terrorism or terrorist activity or retains the capability and intent to do so. We have held that the third requirement that the organization's activities threaten U.S. nationals or national security presents an unreviewable political question. *PMOI I*, 182 F.3d at 23....

[The PMOI was originally designated an FTO in 1997, then redesignated as such in 1999, 2001, and 2003.]

C.

This action began in July 2008, when the PMOI filed a petition for revocation of its 2003 Redesignation....

After reviewing an administrative record consisting of both classified and unclassified information, the Secretary denied the PMOI's petition and published its denial in the Federal Register on January 12, 2009. *See* 74 Fed. Reg. at 1273-74. She also provided the PMOI with a heavily redacted 20-page administrative summary of State's review of the record, which summary referred to 33 exhibits, many of which were also heavily or entirely redacted. The Secretary's determination was based on the administrative record, "supporting exhibits and supplemental filings by the MEK in support of the Petition, as well as information from a variety of sources, including the U.S. Intelligence Community." She wrote that "in considering the evidence as a whole, the MEK...continues to be a foreign organization that engages in terrorist activity...or terrorism...or retains the capability and intent to" do so....

The PMOI filed a timely petition for review on February 11, 2009 under 8 U.S.C. §1189(c). It asks us to vacate the Secretary's decision and remand with instructions to revoke its FTO designation based on a lack of substantial support in the record. Alternatively, the PMOI asks us to vacate its designation on the ground that the Secretary did not comply with the due process requirements set forth in our earlier decisions by failing to provide it with advance notice of her proposed action and the unclassified record on which she intended to rely, as well as by failing to provide it with any access to the classified record.

State submitted its classified administrative record on March 30, 2009 for ex parte and in camera review under 8 U.S.C. §1189(c)(2); it subsequently filed a redacted, unclassified version in August 2009. In filing the latter document, State noted that it intended to file additional documents as soon as its declassification review was finished. It later supplemented the record with newly declassified material ....[3]

II.

Ordinarily, we would be required to decide whether to set aside the Secretary's denial of the PMOI's revocation petition on the ground that her conclusion that the PMOI "engages in terrorist activity...or terrorism...or retains the capability and intent to engage in terrorist activity or terrorism,"..."lack[s] substantial support in the administrative record taken as a whole or in classified information submitted to the court." 8 U.S.C. §1189(c)(3)(D).

Here, however, we need not determine the adequacy of the record because, as the PMOI argues, our review "is not sufficient to supply the otherwise absent due process protection" of notice to the designated organization and an opportunity for a meaningful hearing. *NCRI I,* 251 F.3d at 208 (designated organization entitled to "opportunity to be heard 'at a meaningful time and in a meaningful manner'" (quoting *Mathews v. Eldridge,* 424 U.S. 319, 333 (1976))). In other words, even were we to agree with State that the record is sufficient, we cannot uphold the designation absent the procedural safeguards required by our precedent. Specifically, our cases require the Secretary to notify the PMOI of the unclassified material "upon which [s]he propose[d] to rely" and to allow "the PMOI the opportunity to present, at least in written form, such evidence as [it] may be able to produce to rebut the administrative record or otherwise negate the proposition that" it is an FTO. *NCRI I,* 251 F.3d at 209.

This did not happen here. The PMOI was notified of the Secretary's decision and permitted access to the unclassified portion of the record only *after* the decision was

---

3. Among the disclosures in the declassified material: "the MEK trained females at Camp Ashraf in Iraq to perform suicide attacks in Karbala"; "the MEK solicits money under the false pretext of humanitarian aid to the Iranian population"; "an August 2008 U.S. Intelligence Community Terrorist Threat Assessment, clearly states that the MEK retains a limited capability to engage in terrorist activity or terrorism"; "[t]he MEK publicly renounced violence in 2001, but limited intelligence reporting indicates that the group has not ended military operations, repudiated violence, or completely or voluntarily disarmed ....

final.[4] And even though the PMOI was given the opportunity to include in the record its own evidence supporting delisting, it had no opportunity to rebut the unclassified portion of the record the Secretary was compiling — an omission, the PMOI argues, that deprived it of the due process protections detailed in our previous decisions.

State does not deny that the Secretary failed to provide the type of notice specified in *NCRI I*. But it argues that she complied with our precedent well enough in light of the statutory scheme as altered by the 2004 AEDPA amendments and the "flexible" nature of due process. Within that framework, State argues, the Secretary provided the PMOI with all of the process constitutionally due by informally meeting with the PMOI in October 2008 (at the PMOI's request), by allowing the PMOI to supplement the administrative record with evidence of its own and by sharing unclassified material with the PMOI (but not before her denial of the revocation petition). State also urges that, even if the Secretary should have turned over the unclassified portion of the record before its January 2009 decision, her failure to do so was harmless.

We disagree on both counts. Nothing in the 2004 amendments provides a basis for relaxing the due process requirements.... [D]ue process requires that the PMOI be notified of the unclassified material on which the Secretary proposes to rely and an opportunity to respond to that material *before* its redesignation; nothing in the amended statute suggests that this protection is any less necessary in the revocation context.

Nor do we find the Secretary's failure to provide the required notice and unclassified material in advance of her decision harmless because the information at the "heart" of the Secretary's decision is classified and could not have been shared in any event. State's characterization notwithstanding, at argument it acknowledged that the Secretary's decision was based not on "just the classified information" but rather "on the record as a whole." Hence, State asks us to assume that nothing the PMOI would have offered — not even evidence refuting whatever *unclassified* material the Secretary may have relied on — could have changed her mind. We explicitly rejected this argument in *NCRI I. See* 251 F.3d at 209 ("We have no reason to presume that the petitioners in this particular case could have offered evidence which might have either changed the Secretary's mind or affected the adequacy of the record[, but] ... without the due process protections which we have outlined, we cannot presume the contrary either."). Far from *assuming* that the classified record obviated further review, we held that our limited role "is not sufficient to supply the otherwise absent due process protection." *Id.* at 209.

To illustrate, during the briefing in this case, the Secretary twice supplemented the unclassified record with formerly classified materials. These disclosures include the statement that PMOI members planned suicide attacks in Karbala. Because it learned of this information only after it petitioned for judicial review, the PMOI attempts to distinguish and discredit it for the first time before us.... State argues that the Secretary may consider "sources named and unnamed, the accuracy of which we have no way of evaluating," and that we cannot make any "judgment whatsoever regarding whether the material before the Secretary is or is not true." Nevertheless, to the extent we defer to the Secretary's fact-finding process, we have done so with the understanding that the Secretary has adhered to the procedural

---

4. Although we do not require advance notification of the Secretary's decision upon an adequate showing that "earlier notification would impinge upon the security and other foreign policy goals of the United States," *NCRI I*, 251 F.3d at 208, State does not suggest the Secretary had this concern.

safeguards of the due process clause, *see NCRI I*, 251 F.3d at 209, and afforded the designated organization a fair opportunity to respond to the unclassified record. . . .

Our reluctance to accept State's "no harm, no foul" theory is greater in light of the fact that we are unsure what material the Secretary in fact relied on or to what portion of 8 U.S.C. §1189(a)(1)(B) she found it relevant. While "it is emphatically not our province to second-guess the Secretary's judgment as to which affidavits to credit and upon whose conclusions to rely," the Congress has required us to determine "whether the 'support' marshaled for the Secretary's designation was 'substantial.'" [*National Council of Resistance of Iran v. Department of State*, 373 F.3d 152 (D.C. Cir. 2004) (*NCRI II*)], at 159 (quoting 8 U.S.C. §1189(b)(3)(D)). Some of the reports included in the Secretary's analysis on their face express reservations about the accuracy of the information contained therein. Similarly, while including reports about the Karbala suicide attack plot described above, the Secretary did not indicate whether she accepted or discredited the reports and we do not know whether the PMOI can rebut the reports.

In other instances, the Secretary cited a source that [she] seemed to regard as credible but did not indicate to what part of the statute the source's information was relevant. For example, her analysis described a federal grand jury indictment alleging that MEK has engaged in fraud in fundraising operations and she faulted the PMOI for failing to discuss its finances in its submission to the Secretary. It is unclear, however, whether the Secretary believes that fundraising under false pretenses is direct evidence of terrorist activity or instead bears on the PMOI's "capability" to engage in terrorist activity in the future or its "intent" to do so. 8 U.S.C. §1189(a)(1)(B). While we will not substitute our judgement for that of the Secretary in deciding which sources are credible, we must determine whether the record before her provides "a sufficient basis for a reasonable person to conclude" that the statutory requirements have been met. Without knowing whether, or how, the Secretary evaluated the record material, we are unable to do so.

III.

As we noted in *NCRI I*, "[w]e recognize that a strict and immediate application of the principles of law which we have set forth herein could be taken to require a revocation of the designation[ ] before us[, but] . . . we also recognize the realities of the foreign policy and national security concerns asserted by the Secretary in support of th[e] designation." 251 F.3d at 209. We thus leave the designation in place but remand with instructions to the Secretary to provide the PMOI the opportunity to review and rebut the unclassified portions of the record on which she relied. In so doing, we emphasize two things:

First, as earlier explained, the Secretary should indicate in her administrative summary which sources she regards as sufficiently credible that she relies on them; and she should explain to which part of section 1189(a)(1)(B) the information she relies on relates. Second, although the Secretary must give the PMOI an opportunity to rebut the unclassified material on which she relies, AEDPA does not allow access to the classified record as it makes clear that classified material "shall not be subject to disclosure for such time as it remains classified, except that such information may be disclosed to a court ex parte and in camera for purposes of judicial review." 8 U.S.C. §1189(a)(4)(B)(iv)(II). Our cases under AEDPA have suggested that this procedure can satisfy due process requirements, at least where the Secretary has not relied critically on classified material and the unclassified material provided to the FTO is sufficient to justify the designation. *See NCRI II*, 373 F.3d at 159-60. We note, however, that none of the AEDPA cases decides whether an administrative decision relying critically on undisclosed classified material would comport with due process because in none was the classified record essential to uphold an FTO designation. But they do indicate that, for the purpose of today's remand, affording PMOI an opportunity to review and rebut the unclassified portions of the record, coupled with the Secretary's assurance that she has evaluated the material — and the sources therefor — that she relied on to make her decision, may be sufficient to provide the requisite due process.

For the reasons set forth above, the Secretary's denial of the People's Mojahedin of Iran's petition for revocation of its 2003 designation as a foreign terrorist organization is remanded to the Secretary for further proceedings consistent with this opinion.

So ordered.

KAREN LECRAFT HENDERSON, Circuit Judge, concurring [omitted].

NOTES AND QUESTIONS

1. *Constitutional Rights for FTOs?* The Secretary of State's designation of an FTO must be set aside if a court finds the designation "contrary to constitutional right." 8 U.S.C. §1189(c)(3)(B). Such a right would have to be vindicated, of course, even if the statute did not require it. But do all FTOs have constitutional rights? The Supreme Court has suggested that aliens without a substantial connection to the United States have no right to due process. *See United States v. Verdugo-Urquidez*, 494 U.S. 259, 269 (1990) (citing *Johnson v. Eisentrager*, 339 U.S. 763 (1950), in asserting that "our rejection of extraterritorial application of the Fifth Amendment was emphatic") (*supra* p. 327). In *PMOI I* the D.C. Circuit Court declared, "A foreign entity without property or presence in this country has no constitutional rights, under the due process clause or otherwise." *PMOI v. United States Dep't of State*, 182 F.3d at 22. It was only because the PMOI had some U.S. members that it could assert a Fifth Amendment right to due process.

2. *The Practical Effects of FTO Designations.* As of mid-2011, 48 organizations were on the Secretary of State's list of designated FTOs. *See* Office of the Coordinator for Counterterrorism, U.S. Dep't of State, *Foreign Terrorist Organizations* (May 19, 2011), *at* http://www.state.gov/s/ct/rls/other/des/123085.htm. In passing the AEDPA, Congress intended to shut down the domestic operation of FTOs by cutting off financial support and barring members from entering the United States, and to make their operations abroad more difficult. Related criminal sanctions for material support of a designated FTO are reviewed in Chapter 20. These measures help to satisfy U.S. obligations under U.N. Security Council Resolution 1333 and the International Convention for the Suppression of the Financing of Terrorism, both set out above.

One practical effect of FTO designation — or the threat of such designation — is to make some organizations and their members much more careful about what they say and do. Can you outline the implications of this effect for First Amendment freedoms of speech and association? *See Holder v. Humanitarian Law Project*, 130 S. Ct. 2705 (2010), *supra* p. 604. Possible First Amendment issues in labeling "specially designated global terrorists" under different statutory authority are analyzed in

Humanitarian Law Project v. United States Treasury Department, 578 F.3d 1133 (9th Cir. 2009), set out below.

3. *Basis for Designation.* In designating an FTO, the Secretary must determine that the organization "engages in 'terrorist activity' or 'terrorism'" that "threatens the security of the United States or its nationals." 8 U.S.C. §1189(a)(1). The meaning of these criteria has been the subject of much litigation and academic analysis. *See, e.g.,* Wadie E. Said, *The Material Support Prosecution and Foreign Policy,* 86 Ind. L.J. 543, 558-593 (2011) (criticizing indeterminacy of criteria).

Considering the variety and unpredictability of threats to national security, is there any practical alternative to broad statutory language that gives the Secretary wide latitude in designating FTOs? To what extent should we expect courts to curb any possible abuses of the Secretary's discretion?

4. *Timing.* The court in the principal case describes due process protections for an FTO designee as including the right to receive, at a minimum, unclassified material upon which the Secretary proposes to base her decision and to be given a meaningful opportunity to contest its designation. Absent a showing that "earlier notification would impinge upon the security and other foreign policy goals of the United States," *NCRI I,* 251 F.3d at 208, the notice, information, and opportunity for hearing must be provided *before* the designation is finalized, not after. Why is the sequence of events so important?

Under what circumstances, if any, could a designee challenge the Secretary's claim that a delay was justified by "security and other foreign policy goals"? Can you articulate such goals that might justify a delay? Could a court?

5. *Access to Classified Information.* In the principal case, the government acknowledged that the Secretary's designation decision was made on "the record as a whole" — that is, both classified and unclassified material. 613 F.3d at 228. The court required the Secretary to "provide the PMOI the opportunity to review and rebut the unclassified portions of the record on which she relied." *Id.* at 230. But the Secretary need not divulge any classified information that has informed her decision.

The court directed the Secretary to identify to the court the sources — both classified and unclassified — on which she relied in deciding, and show how each one related to the statutory criteria for designation. The court noted that none of the AEDPA cases so far had involved a Secretary's reliance "critically on undisclosed classified material." *Id.* Should the court have tried to determine how relatively influential each source of information was? Could it properly test the Secretary's compliance with either AEDPA or due process requirements without doing so? Can you guess how a court might establish what is "critical"?

In other settings, Congress and the courts have developed elaborate procedures for balancing the protection of sensitive information against the needs of criminal defendants and civil litigants. For example, the Classified Information Procedures Act controls access to government secrets in criminal prosecutions. *See supra* pp. 632-640. In civil cases the government may invoke the state secrets privilege in discovery and at trial. *See, e.g., Mohamed v. Jeppesen Dataplan, Inc.,* 614 F.3d 1070 (9th Cir. 2010), *cert. denied,* 131 S. Ct. 2442 (2011).

In each instance, courts may review secret information in camera, or summaries of it may be furnished to parties. The court in the principal case indicates that it may review classified information ex parte and in camera. Why will this procedure satisfy due process? Should a court determine whether information withheld from an FTO designee is properly classified?

6. *Remedy for Improper Designation.* In allowing the FTO designation of the PMOI to stand while the case is reviewed on remand, the court noted "the realities of the foreign policy and national security concerns asserted by the Secretary in support of th[e] designation." 613 F.3d at 230. Will an FTO designee ever be in a position to contest the Secretary's assertion of such realities? How deferential should a court be to that assertion?

2. International Emergency Economic Powers Act (IEEPA)

Another powerful economic weapon in the U.S. counterterrorism arsenal is the 1977 International Emergency Economic Powers Act (IEEPA). 50 U.S.C. §§1701-1707 (2006 & Supp. IV 2010). The IEEPA authorizes the President to address "any unusual or extraordinary threat, which has its source in whole or substantial part outside the United States, to the national security, foreign policy, or economy of the United States" by declaring a national emergency and regulating "any property in which any foreign country or a national thereof has any interest." *Id.* §§1701(a), 1702(a)(1)(B). It was first used by President Carter to block Iranian assets worth about $12 billion when state-sponsored terrorists took 52 Americans hostage in the U.S. embassy in Tehran in 1979. *See Dames & Moore v. Regan*, 453 U.S. 654 (1981).

President Clinton invoked the IEEPA in 1995 and again in 1998 to prohibit transactions with "terrorists who threaten to disrupt the Middle East peace process." Exec. Order No. 12,947, 60 Fed. Reg. 5079 (1995); Exec. Order No. 13,099, 63 Fed. Reg. 45,167 (1998). On July 4, 1999, he issued Exec. Order No. 13,129, 64 Fed. Reg. 36,759, declaring a national emergency, freezing all Taliban assets in the United States, and banning all commerce, except for humanitarian assistance, with that part of Afghanistan controlled by the Taliban. The order preceded by several months U.N. Security Council Resolution 1267, noted above, which directed all member states to freeze Taliban financial resources. *See generally* Robert M. Chesney, *The Sleeper Scenario: Terrorism-Support Laws and the Demands of Prevention*, 42 Harv. J. on Legis. 1, 4-21 (2005) (describing the use of IEEPA and the development of related material-support laws).

Almost two weeks after the terrorist attacks on September 11, 2001, President Bush invoked the IEEPA in the following order.

Executive Order No. 13,224, Blocking Property and Prohibiting Transactions With Persons Who Commit, Threaten to Commit, or Support Terrorism

66 Fed. Reg. 49,079 (Sept. 23, 2001)

By the authority vested in me as President by the Constitution and the laws of the United States of America, including the International Emergency Economic Powers Act (50 U.S.C. 1701 et seq.) (IEEPA), the National Emergencies Act (50 U.S.C. 1601 et seq.), [and] section 5 of the United Nations Participation Act of 1945, as amended (22 U.S.C. 287c) (UNPA), . . . and in view of United Nations Security Council Resolution (UNSCR) 1214 of December 8, 1998, UNSCR 1267 of

October 15, 1999, UNSCR 1333 of December 19, 2000, and the multilateral sanctions contained therein...

I, GEORGE W. BUSH, President of the United States of America, find that grave acts of terrorism and threats of terrorism committed by foreign terrorists, including the terrorist attacks in New York, Pennsylvania, and the Pentagon committed on September 11, 2001, acts recognized and condemned in UNSCR 1368 of September 12, 2001, and UNSCR 1269 of October 19, 1999, and the continuing and immediate threat of further attacks on United States nationals or the United States constitute an unusual and extraordinary threat to the national security, foreign policy, and economy of the United States, and in furtherance of my proclamation of September 14, 2001, Declaration of National Emergency by Reason of Certain Terrorist Attacks, hereby declare a national emergency to deal with that threat. I also find that because of the pervasiveness and expansiveness of the financial foundation of foreign terrorists, financial sanctions may be appropriate for those foreign persons that support or otherwise associate with these foreign terrorists. I also find that a need exists for further consultation and cooperation with, and sharing of information by, United States and foreign financial institutions as an additional tool to enable the United States to combat the financing of terrorism.

I hereby order:

Sec. 1.... [A]ll property and interests in property of the following persons that are in the United States or that hereafter come within the United States, or that hereafter come within the possession or control of United States persons are blocked:

(a) foreign persons listed in the Annex to this order;

(b) foreign persons determined by the Secretary of State, in consultation with the Secretary of the Treasury and the Attorney General, to have committed, or to pose a significant risk of committing, acts of terrorism that threaten the security of U.S. nationals or the national security, foreign policy, or economy of the United States;

(c) persons determined by the Secretary of the Treasury, in consultation with the Secretary of State and the Attorney General, to be owned or controlled by, or to act for or on behalf of those persons listed in the Annex to this order...

(d) ...persons determined by the Secretary of the Treasury, in consultation with the Secretary of State and the Attorney General:

(i) to assist in, sponsor, or provide financial, material, or technological support for, or financial or other services to or in support of, such acts of terrorism or those persons listed in the Annex to this order or determined to be subject to this order; or

(ii) to be otherwise associated with those persons listed in the Annex to this order or those persons determined to be subject to subsection 1(b), 1(c), or 1(d)(i) of this order.

Sec. 2.... (a) any transaction or dealing by United States persons or within the United States in property or interests in property blocked pursuant to this order is prohibited, including but not limited to the making or receiving of any contribution of funds, goods, or services to or for the benefit of those persons listed in the Annex to this order or determined to be subject to this order....

Sec. 4. I hereby determine that the making of donations [of articles, such as food, clothing, and medicine, intended to be used to relieve human suffering] by United States persons to persons determined to be subject to this order would seriously impair my ability to deal with the national emergency declared in this order ... and hereby prohibit such donations as provided by section 1 of this order. . . .

Sec. 6. The Secretary of State, the Secretary of the Treasury, and other appropriate agencies shall make all relevant efforts to cooperate and coordinate with other countries, including through technical assistance, as well as bilateral and multilateral agreements and arrangements, to achieve the objectives of this order, including the prevention and suppression of acts of terrorism, the denial of financing and financial services to terrorists and terrorist organizations, and the sharing of intelligence about funding activities in support of terrorism. . . .

Executive Order No. 13,224 expanded the coverage of earlier orders to include persons "associated with" designated terrorist groups, and to allow the United States to deny access to its markets for foreign banks that refuse to freeze terrorist assets. *See generally* Nina J. Crimm, *High Alert: The Government's War on the Financing of Terrorism and Its Implications for Donors, Domestic Charitable Organizations, and Global Philanthropy*, 45 Wm. & Mary L. Rev. 1341, 1355-1304 (2004). Within a year, the annex referred to in Section 1 of the order contained the names of 219 individuals and organizations, from Osama bin Laden and Al Qaeda to the Al-Hamati Sweets Bakeries, with an address in Yemen. *See* Office of the Coordinator for Counterterrorism, U.S. Dep't of State, *Comprehensive List of Terrorists and Groups Identified Under Executive Order 13224*, Oct. 11, 2002, http://www.fas.org/irp/news/2002/10/dos101102.html. A current list, updated regularly, containing hundreds of additional names, may be found at U.S. Dep't of the Treasury, *Specially Designated Nationals List (SDN)*, http://www.treasury.gov/resource-center/sanctions/SDN-List/Pages/default.aspx. At the end of 2010, some $22 billion in assets of designated persons and groups was frozen.

The IEEPA was amended by the USA Patriot Act, to allow the President to confiscate the property of "any foreign person, foreign organization, or foreign country that he determines has planned, authorized, aided, or engaged in . . . hostilities or attacks against the United States." Pub. L. No. 107-56, §106, 115 Stat. 272, 278 (2001) (adding 50 U.S.C. §1702(a)(1)(C)). *See* Bethany Kohl Hipp, Comment, *Defending Expanded Presidential Authority to Regulate Foreign Assets and Transactions*, 17 Emory Int'l L. Rev. 1311 (2003).

The effectiveness of economic restrictions using the IEEPA is uncertain, because

> much of the flow of terrorist funds takes place outside of formal banking channels (in elusive "hawala" chains of money brokers). Alternatively, a wide variety of international banks in the Persian Gulf is used to manipulate and transfer funds through business fronts owned by Osama bin Laden. Furthermore, much of Al Qaeda's money is believed to be held not in banks but in untraceable assets such as gold and diamonds. Also, some observers have noted that lethal terrorist operations are relatively inexpensive. Current estimates of the cost of carrying out the September 11 attacks range from $300,000 to $500,000. [Perl, *supra* p. 805, at 9.]

Still, those restrictions sometimes hit home. For example, Chiquita Brands International, Inc. paid a $25 million fine to settle charges that it violated an IEEPA ban on transactions with a right-wing paramilitary organization called the United Self-Defense Forces of Colombia (AUC), listed as an FTO in 2001. Chiquita reportedly paid the AUC some $1.7 million in protection money. *See* Dep't of Justice, *Chiquita Brands International Pleads Guilty* (Mar. 19, 2007). Consider also the following case.

Humanitarian Law Project v. United States Treasury Department

United States Court of Appeals, Ninth Circuit, 2009
578 F.3d 1133

RYMER, Circuit Judge: . . . In the wake of September 11, 2001, President George W. Bush declared a national emergency and, invoking the powers vested in him by the International [Emergency] Economic Powers Act (IEEPA), 50 U.S.C. §1701, *et seq.*, and the United Nations Participation Act (UNPA), 22 U.S.C. §287c, signed Executive Order 13224. The Executive Order blocks property of twenty-seven designated terrorists, and authorizes the Secretary of the Treasury to designate others whom the Secretary determines to be acting for, providing support or services to, or are otherwise associated with, designated persons.

The Humanitarian Law Project (HLP) wants to support lawful activities of two organizations that are designated as foreign terrorist organizations — the Kurdistan Worker's Party (PKK) in Turkey, and the Liberation Tigers of Tamil Elam (LTTE) in Sri Lanka. It claims to have been deterred from doing so out of fear that HLP, too, will be designated as a terrorist organization pursuant to Executive Order 13224 and its implementing regulations, if HLP provides services of any sort to the PKK and the LTTE. Consequently, HLP brought this action to challenge, on First and Fifth Amendment grounds, the President's authority to designate organizations as terrorists under IEEPA and UNPA; the Secretary of the Treasury's designation authority from the President under Executive Order 13224; the Executive Order's ban on providing services to designated terrorist organizations; and the regulatory licensing scheme under which organizations may apply for permission to engage in activities that are otherwise prohibited. . . .

I

This is not the first time that HLP and the government have collided over the government's power to regulate non-terrorist activities in aid of terrorist organizations. HLP previously took on the ban against providing material support and resources to foreign terrorist organizations in the Antiterrorism and Effective Death Penalty Act of 1996 (AEDPA), Pub. L. No. 104-132, 110 Stat. 1214, and its 2004 amendment, the Intelligence Reform and Terrorism Prevention Act (IRTPA), *see* 18 U.S.C. §2339B. That history is recounted in *Humanitarian Law Project v. Mukasey*, 552 F.3d 916, 920-24 (9th Cir. 2009) (*HLP III*) (amending opinion filed December 10, 2007). Though involving a different statute with different text, *HLP III* and *Humanitarian Law Project v. Reno*, 205 F.3d 1130 (9th Cir. 2000) (*HLP I*), inform some of the issues in this case and both parties draw succor from what we have held. [The Ninth Circuit panel's ruling in *HLP III* was affirmed in part and reversed in part in *Holder v. Humanitarian Law Project*, 130 S. Ct. 2705 (2010) (excerpted *supra* p. 604).] . . .

IEEPA, which was enacted in 1977, was not at issue in the earlier litigation. It vests the President with authority to deal with any "unusual and extraordinary threat" to the national security whose source in whole or substantial part is outside of the United States, if the President declares a national emergency. 50 U.S.C. §1701(a). IEEPA mandates that the President must consult Congress "in every possible instance" before exercising his authority, *id.* §1703(a), and the President's actions are to be reviewed periodically by Congress, *id.* §1622(b). When such a national emergency is declared, IEEPA provides that the President may issue regulations to "block" any transaction "with respect to . . . any property in which any foreign country or a national thereof has any interest[.]" *Id.* §1702(a)(1)(B). However, the President's authority does not extend to regulating or prohibiting donations of food, clothing, and medicine, intended to be used to relieve human suffering, unless the President determines that such donations would "seriously impair his ability to deal with any national emergency." *Id.* §1702(b)(2). Section 1704 provides that "[t]he President may issue such regulations, including regulations prescribing definitions, as may be necessary for the exercise of the authorities granted...." *Id.* §1704. The Act provides for a civil penalty ($250,000, or twice the amount of the culpable transaction), *id.* §1705(b), and a criminal penalty for willful violations (a fine of not more than $1,000,000 or imprisonment for not more than 20 years, or both), *id.* §1705(c).

On September 23, 2001, President George W. Bush [promulgated Executive Order No. 13,244, as noted above]....

By regulation, any person or group whose property is blocked by reason of the Executive Order is known as a "specially designated global terrorist," or SDGT. 31 C.F.R. §594.310. Treasury regulations give examples of "services" that are forbidden, 31 C.F.R. §594.406(b),[3] and define the term "to be otherwise associated with," 31 C.F.R. §594.316.[4] Other regulations provide that a person or group that is designated as an SDGT may seek administrative reconsideration, 31 C.F.R. §594.201(a) n.3, *available at* 72 Fed. Reg. 4206 (Jan. 30, 2007); 31 C.F.R. §501.807, and allow the Department to grant licenses on a case-by-case basis to permit transactions that would otherwise be prohibited under the Executive Order, 31 C.F.R. §§594.501, 501.801-02.

PKK and the LTTE are designated SDGTs.[5] HLP wishes to support the nonviolent activities of these groups by providing money, humanitarian aid, engineering and technological support, as well as psychological counseling in areas of Sri Lanka affected by the tsunami, training in human rights alternatives, assistance with peacemaking negotiations, legal help, and assistance in appearing before international lawmaking bodies. HLP asserts that it has been inhibited from doing so by Executive Order [13224] and the regulations implementing it. This action attacks provisions in both....

II

HLP maintains that it has standing to challenge the President's designation authority under IEEPA because it credibly fears that if it engages in any activities that might be deemed to benefit or be associated with the PKK or the LTTE, it

---

3. The regulation states: "U.S. persons may not, except as authorized by or pursuant to this part, provide legal, accounting, financial, brokering, freight forwarding, transportation, public relations, educational, or other services to a person whose property or interests in property are blocked pursuant to §594.201(a)." 31 C.F.R. §594.406(b). Section 594.201(a) is the foundational regulation that basically tracks the blocking provisions of the Executive Order.

4. Section 594.316 provides:

The term "to be otherwise associated with," as used in §594.201(a)(4)(ii), means:
   (a)To own or control; or
   (b)To attempt, or to conspire with one or more persons, to act for or on behalf of or to provide financial, material, or technological support, or financial or other services to.

5. They were so designated by the Secretary of State after he determined that both met the criteria in §1(b) of Executive Order 13224. 67 Fed. Reg. 12633, 12633-34 (Office of the Coordinator For Counterterrorism, Dep't of State, March 19, 2002). The Secretary of State acted pursuant to an essentially parallel scheme under which the assets of foreign terrorist organizations are blocked and U.S. persons are prohibited from rendering them material support. *See* 8 U.S.C. §1189; 18 U.S.C. §2339B.

risks being designated itself.... HLP submits [that] it may pursue a facial vagueness challenge as IEEPA grants sweeping discretion to the President that allows him to censor, or shut down, disfavored political groups....

... HLP has never been designated as an SDGT. Nor does it point to any specific warning or threat of being designated. There is no evidence that HLP is similar to the organizations or individuals who have been designated by the President, or that it engages in conduct similar to those organizations. The President designated twenty-seven groups and individuals just after September 11, and added two more in July 2002, but no further designations have been made in the years since. In these circumstances, we cannot say that the threat of designation is "credible," instead of "imaginary or speculative." *Thomas* [*v. Anchorage Equal Rights Comm'n*, 220 F.3d 1134 (9th Cir. 2000)], at 1140....

... IEEPA is not aimed at expression. Nothing on the face of IEEPA implicates First Amendment rights. It simply allows the President, during peacetime national emergencies, to block transactions "with respect to... any property in which any foreign country or a national thereof has any interest." 50 U.S.C. §1702(a)(1)(B).[8] Further... to the extent HLP has any injury as a result of IEEPA, it is indirect. That is, because IEEPA is not directly aimed at HLP's expression, injury-in-fact does not come from IEEPA or from IEEPA's designation authority to the President, but from the *President's* designation authority to the *Secretary*. There is no suggestion that HLP lacks standing to pursue *this* designation .... But neither self-censorship nor subjective chill is the functional equivalent of a well-founded fear of enforcement when the statute on its face does not regulate expressive activity....

In sum,... IEEPA does not on its face implicate First Amendment rights. The harm of self-censorship is not present here. HLP has not been designated, nor threatened with imminent prosecution or designation. For these reasons, we conclude that HLP cannot establish injury-in-fact, and lacks standing to challenge the President's designation authority.

III

HLP argues that the Executive Order unconstitutionally gives the Secretary [of the Treasury] discretion to penalize and shut down individuals and groups on the basis of constitutionally protected activities, without any type of scienter, and leaves uncertain what it can do in conjunction with, or on behalf of, the LTTE and PKK.

---

8. Nor is the UNPA, under which the President also acted, aimed at HLP's speech. That Act simply authorizes the President to implement U.N. Security Council measures by taking certain actions, including prohibiting economic relations between any foreign country or national and persons subject to United States jurisdiction. *See* 22 U.S.C. §287c. The statute provides:

> [W]henever the United States is called upon by the [United Nations] Security Council to apply measures which said Council has decided... the President may,... under such orders, rules, and regulations as may be prescribed by him,... prohibit, in whole or in part, economic relations... between any foreign country or any national thereof or any person therein and the United States or any person subject to the jurisdiction thereof, or involving any property subject to the jurisdiction of the United States.

22 U.S.C. §287c(a).

A

HLP makes the overarching submission that the Secretary's authority to designate groups that have never engaged in terrorist activity is unconstitutionally vague and overbroad. . . .

. . . [T]he Executive Order does constrain the exercise of discretion. It requires the Secretary to find that the person or organization is "owned or controlled by," or "act[s] for or on behalf of," SDGTs, or else "provide[s] financial, material, or technological support for, or financial or other services to or in support of," acts of terrorism or acts of SDGTs, or is "otherwise associated with" SDGTs. Exec. Order 13224, §1(c)-(d). These are sufficient checks on the Secretary's discretion to allay constitutional concerns. They are reasonable in light of the fact that the Executive Order is a conduct regulation, not a speech restriction. As we explained in *HLP I*, there is no "right to provide resources with which terrorists can buy weapons and explosives." 205 F.3d at 1133. The restrictions in the Executive Order are aimed at stopping aid to terrorists. Therefore, the order "serves purposes unrelated to the content of the expression." *Id.* at 1135 (internal citation and quotation omitted). Moreover, the Secretary's designations are subject to reconsideration, after which a written decision must be furnished, 31 C.F.R. §501.807(d), and are subject to judicial review, *see, e.g., Islamic Am. Relief Agency v. Gonzales*, 477 F.3d 728 (D.C. Cir. 2007); *Holy Land Found. for Relief & Dev. v. Ashcroft*, 333 F.3d 156 (D.C. Cir. 2003). Thus, the Secretary's designation authority is not unconstitutionally vague.

Nor is the designation authority unconstitutionally overbroad. To prevail on a facial overbreadth challenge to a law aimed at regulating conduct, HLP must show that the Executive Order "punishes a 'substantial' amount of protected free speech, 'judged in relation to the statute's plainly legitimate sweep.'" *Virginia v. Hicks*, 539 U.S. 113, 118-19 (2003) (quoting *Broadrick v. Oklahoma*, 413 U.S. 601, 615 (1973)). HLP does not suggest how designation of U.S. groups or individuals under the Executive Order can be unconstitutional if the groups or individuals are aiding or supporting terrorists. . . .

B

HLP mounts facial and as-applied challenges to the ban imposed by the Executive Order on "services." Section 1(d)(i) of the Executive Order permits the Secretary to designate individuals and entities who "provide . . . financial or other services to or in support of" acts of terrorism and SDGTs. And §2(a) prohibits transactions by U.S. persons or within the United States, "including but not limited to . . . services to or for the benefit of" an SDGT.

i

"A statute must be sufficiently clear so as to allow persons of ordinary intelligence a reasonable opportunity to know what is prohibited." *Foti v. City of Menlo Park*, 146 F.3d 629, 638 (9th Cir. 1998) (quoting *Grayned v. City of Rockford*, 408 U.S. 104, 108 (1972)). Statutes that are insufficiently clear are void for three reasons: "(1) to avoid punishing people for behavior that they could not have known was illegal; (2) to avoid subjective enforcement of the laws based on arbitrary and discriminatory enforcement by government officers; and (3) to avoid any chilling effect on the exercise of First Amendment freedoms." *Id.*

... When a statute "clearly implicates free speech rights," it will survive a facial challenge so long as "it is clear what the statute proscribes 'in the vast majority of its intended applications.'" *Cal. Teachers Ass'n v. State Bd. of Educ.*, 271 F.3d 1141, 1149, 1151 (9th Cir. 2001) (quoting *Hill v. Colorado*, 530 U.S. 703, 733 (2000))....

... [T]he regulations clarify the term "services" by offering examples of what is contemplated. 31 C.F.R. §594.406(b) (citing "legal, accounting, financial, brokering, freight forwarding, transportation, public relations, educational, or other services").... They make clear that legal and educational services are prohibited. They also indicate that one should not perform a useful professional or business task for a terrorist organization. For these reasons, even if the term "services" standing alone would be ambiguous, the examples alert a person of ordinary intelligence to the services that should not be provided to or for the benefit of SDGTs. In these circumstances, it is clear what the term "services" proscribes in the vast majority of intended applications.

HLP is concerned that the term could ensnare independent advocacy undertaken for the benefit of the PKK and LTTE. It would undoubtedly offend the First Amendment if the regulations were to prohibit independent advocacy. However, they don't. And we see no basis for supposing that they might.

The Secretary has explicitly recognized that the "designation criteria [under the Executive Order] will be applied in a manner consistent with pertinent Federal law, including, where applicable, the First Amendment to the United States Constitution." 72 Fed. Reg. 4206 (January 30, 2007). This reflects the Treasury Department's intent to interpret its own regulations, including the ban on "services," to exclude independent advocacy because independent advocacy is always protected under the First Amendment. HLP points to no instance in the years since the Executive Order has been in force where the Secretary has designated an organization or individual for engaging in independent advocacy or whose "overwhelming function was political advocacy." Similarly, it points to no instance where any person engaged in independent advocacy has been subject to civil or criminal penalties under IEEPA for engaging in such conduct. The government's position is that the term "services" in Executive Order 13224 does not reach independent advocacy. Both because the ban cannot extend to independent advocacy, and because of the government's representation that it does not, we decline to void the order on this ground.

HLP also contends that it is unclear whether the ban on "services" covers activities such as teaching human rights advocacy, writing a human rights report, or engaging in public relations advocacy. However, we see no unconstitutional guesswork; as the district court observed, in the vast majority of cases a given individual can distinguish performing a service to an SDGT from independent activity. Should uncertainty lurk that is not purely hypothetical, however, administrative vehicles are available for clarification.[13]

"Condemned to the use of words, we can never expect mathematical certainty from our language." *Grayned*, 408 U.S. at 110. But it is clear what the Executive Order proscribes "in the vast majority of its intended applications." This being so, HLP's facial challenge fails.

---

13. Individuals or institutions in doubt about the propriety of proposed activities may call the Department of Treasury's compliance hotline; e-mail the Treasury's e-hotline mailbox; call Treasury's licensing division, or apply for a license; and consult an attorney in the Chief Counsel's Office, or submit a request for a written interpretation of whether the proposed activity would constitute a violation.

ii

The ban on "services" is not unconstitutionally vague as-applied to HLP's intended activities, either. The heart of HLP's position is that activities in which it proposes to engage for the benefit of the PKK and LTTE are not linked to the carrying out of terrorist activity. However, this is not so much a quarrel over vagueness, as it is about substance. As the district court explained, the proposed activities clearly constitute prohibited services, and for this reason an as applied challenge for vagueness does not lie.

iii

... [T]he ban on "services" is... [not] "specifically addressed to speech or to conduct necessarily associated with speech," and "[r]arely, if ever, will an over-breadth challenge succeed" in these circumstances. [*Virginia v. Hicks*, 539 U.S. 113 (2003)], at 124. The ban imposed by Executive Order 13224 ... is not aimed at the expressive component of HLP's conduct but at stopping aid to terrorist groups. It has obvious, legitimate applications. Providing legal, financial, accounting, educational, business, and like services to designated terrorist groups saves them money, which in turn increases the means at their disposal for terrorist acts.[14] Inhibiting this provision of services is for this reason a legitimate government regulation of constitutionally unprotected conduct. That some particular instances of protected speech may fall within the Executive Order does not make those instances substantial when compared to its legitimate scope. *HLP III*, 552 F.3d at 932. In sum, as the Executive Order is not aimed at speech and does not cover a substantial amount of it, the ban on "services" to SDGTs is not facially overbroad.

C

HLP faults IEEPA for imposing the penalties of designation, civil fines, and criminal sanctions without sufficient mens rea.[15] It claims that designation and

14. As the Seventh Circuit recently explained:

If you provide material support to a terrorist organization, you are engaged in terrorist activity even if your support is confined to the nonterrorist activities of the organization. Organizations that the statute, and indeed in this instance common parlance, describes as terrorist organizations, such as Hamas in Gaza and Hezbollah in Lebanon, often operate on two tracks: a violent one and a peaceful one (electioneering, charity, provision of social services). If you give money (or raise money to be given) for the teaching of arithmetic to children in an elementary school run by Hamas, you are providing material support to a terrorist organization even though you are not providing direct support to any terrorist acts.

Hussain v. Mukasey, 518 F.3d 534, 538 (7th Cir. 2008).

15. IEEPA's penalties section, 50 U.S.C. §1705, provides:

(a) Unlawful acts. It shall be unlawful for a person to violate, attempt to violate, conspire to violate, or cause a violation of any license, order, regulation, or prohibition issued under this chapter.

(b) Civil penalty. A civil penalty may be imposed on any person who commits an unlawful act described in subsection (a) of this section in an amount not to exceed the greater of—

(1) $250,000; or

(2) an amount that is twice the amount of the transaction that is the basis of the violation with respect to which the penalty is imposed.

(c) Criminal penalty. A person who willfully commits, willfully attempts to commit, or willfully conspires to commit, or aids or abets in the commission of, an unlawful act described in subsection (a) of this section shall, upon conviction, be fined not more than $1,000,000, or if a natural person, may be imprisoned for not more than 20 years, or both.

civil penalties, which in HLP's view are "quasi-criminal," run afoul of the First and Fifth Amendments because they do not require knowledge that the recipient of forbidden support is designated. And it maintains that both civil and criminal penalties must require specific intent.

i

We determine whether civil penalties are so severe that they should carry the same due process guarantees as criminal offenses by following the guideposts set out in *Hudson v. United States*, 522 U.S. 93 (1997). . . .

Congress clearly intended the civil penalties under IEEPA to be civil, not criminal. It said so in so many words, describing a "civil penalty" in §1705(b), and distinguishing a "civil penalty" from a "criminal penalty" that is separately provided for in §1705(c). *See Hudson*, 522 U.S. at 103. The nature of the penalty — $250,000 or double the amount of the transaction — is also civil, rather than criminal, in nature. Correspondingly, it is evident that the President meant for designation to be civil as he conferred authority to make further designations on the Treasury Department. *Id.*

The *Hudson* factors do not indicate that the civil penalties are really criminal. IEEPA's civil penalties are monetary, with no other "affirmative disability or restraint." *Reiserer* [*v. United States*, 479 F.3d 1160 (9th Cir. 2007)], at 1163 (quoting *Hudson*, 522 U.S. at 104). Such monetary penalties have not "historically been regarded as punishment." *Id.* (citation omitted). Designation carries more than monetary bite for U.S. entities, but exceptions are available on a case-by-case basis. Neither the civil penalty provision nor designation has a mens rea requirement, weighing against finding that these are criminal penalties. While civil fines and designation have a deterrent effect, "'the mere presence of this purpose is insufficient to render a sanction criminal.'" *Id.* at 1164 (quoting *Hudson*, 522 U.S. at 102). Finally, the same conduct may be punished both civilly and criminally, but this alone does not render all the penalties criminally punitive. *Hudson*, 522 U.S. at 105.

On balance, we conclude that HLP has not shown by "clearest proof" that either the civil penalty or designation is so punitive as to be criminal. *Id.* at 100. Although designation presents a closer call than the civil penalty, at the end of the day we are influenced by the fact that designation, at the core, is a function of national security and foreign policy[17] and thus serves an alternative function other than punishment. As such, we accord deference to the executive branch's decision that designation is necessary for the national interest. As a penalty, designation is not excessive in relation to that purpose.

Therefore, neither the civil penalty nor designation offends the First and Fifth Amendments for lack of sufficient *mens rea*.

ii

For the same reasons, IEEPA's civil penalties do not violate the First and Fifth Amendments because they do not require proof of specific intent to further a

---

17. *See, e.g., Islamic Am. Relief Agency*, 477 F.3d at 734 (reviewing designation under Executive Order 13224 deferentially); *Holy Land*, 333 F.3d at 166 (noting that review of SDGT designation "involv[es] sensitive issues of national security and foreign policy"); *see also, HLP I*, 205 F.3d at 1137 (AEDPA designations "involve[ ] the conduct of foreign affairs" so "we owe the executive branch even more latitude than in the domestic context").

designated entity's terrorist activities. HLP's principal argument [is] that both the civil and criminal penalties violate the First and Fifth Amendments' prohibition on guilt by association . . . . [T]o the extent IEEPA punishes "services," it does not punish association . . . . IEEPA's requirement that a person act "willfully" likewise "satisfies the requirement of 'personal guilt' and eliminates any due process concerns." [*HLP III*, 552 F.3d at 926.]

Thus, IEEPA's penalties do not violate the First and Fifth Amendments.

IV

HLP argues that the licensing scheme in 31 C.F.R. §§501.801-02 violates the First and Fifth Amendments by giving the Director of the Office of Foreign Assets Control (OFAC) unregulated discretion to grant or deny exemptions from IEEPA prohibitions. HLP lacks standing to pursue this issue, however . . . . HLP has not been denied a license under the licensing provision or even applied for one; the licensing provision is not the cause of HLP's asserted injury; and invalidation of the licensing provision would not redress any injury that HLP has suffered. . . .

Affirmed.

[The opinion of PREGERSON, Circuit Judge, dissenting in part, is omitted.]

NOTES AND QUESTIONS

1. *Challenging the President's Designation Authority.* Why did the *Humanitarian Law Project* (*HLP*) court rule that the organizational plaintiff lacked standing to challenge the President's designation authority under IEEPA? Do you agree that IEEPA, in delegating designation authority to the President, "does not on its face implicate First Amendment rights"? If such rights are implicated, is any injury suffered by HLP less acute in a constitutional sense because it is, in part, "indirect"?

2. *Challenging the Executive Order Facially.* The *HLP* plaintiffs asserted that the executive order ban on "services" was unconstitutionally vague. Are you satisfied that the Treasury Department regulations cited by the court make the meaning of the term clear "in the vast majority of cases"? Is it clear to you? The Supreme Court reached the same conclusion in a factually similar case based on AEDPA in *Holder v. Humanitarian Law Project*, 130 S. Ct. 2705 (2010), set forth *supra* p. 604.

Even if the meaning of "services" is most often clear, the regulation would be struck down if it prohibited "independent advocacy." The court offers three reasons for ruling that it does not: (1) the Secretary has not yet designated an individual or group for engaging in independent advocacy, (2) the regulatory ban "cannot" extend to such advocacy, and (3) the government insists that the regulation does not do so. Can you formulate a response to each of these reasons?

3. *Challenging the Executive Order as Applied.* The court concludes that HLP's proposed activities "clearly constitute prohibited services," thus barring an as-applied challenge for vagueness. Referring to the Treasury Department regulations, can you see how this is so?

Responding to the charge that the ban on HLP's proposed activities violates the organization's right of free expression, the court concluded that the ban is aimed not at speech but at conduct, namely, "stopping aid to terrorist groups." The *HLP* court concluded that contributions to terrorist groups for otherwise legitimate charitable purposes would simply permit those groups to use other resources to carry out acts of terrorism.

In *Holder v. Humanitarian Law Project, supra,* the Supreme Court ruled that while a similar ban on material support for foreign terrorist organizations under AEDPA implicates speech, as well as conduct, the resulting infringement was justified. It placed "significant weight" on "the considered judgment of Congress and the Executive that providing material support to a designated foreign terrorist organization — even seemingly benign support — bolsters the terrorist activities of that organization." 130 S. Ct. at 2728. See *supra* p. 620, Note 5. One critic offers this response:

> [T]he "money is fungible" theory should be subjected to a more extensive review. While the theory seems to make sense on an abstract level, the prosecution should have to make a specific showing that humanitarian support to a given organization does in fact facilitate violence. [Said, *supra* p. 812, 86 Ind. L.J. at 546.]

The Supreme Court called such a suggestion "dangerous." 130 S. Ct. at 2728.

As counsel to an organization like HLP, how would you advise your client which expressive activities might justify SDGT designation — or worse, criminal liability?

4. *Criminal Liability?* HLP claimed that the civil penalty for a violation of IEEPA is in fact a criminal penalty, and that, because it requires no showing of willfulness, it violates the First and Fifth Amendments. Upon what grounds, precisely, does the court reject that claim? How do you suppose HLP sought to refute each of the court's reasons?

Are you convinced that the term "willfully" in the statute's criminal penalty provision satisfies the requirement of "personal guilt" and "eliminates any due process concerns"? *See* Dru Stevenson, *Effect of the National Security Paradigm on Criminal Law,* 22 Stan. L. & Pol'y Rev. 129, 138 (2011) ("the scienter requirement in these modern [anti-terrorism] statutes is being . . . interpreted differently, to reflect a more risk-based concept of 'knowingly' or 'should have known.'"). If such a trend exists, is it justified?

The court concluded that HLP had not shown by "clearest proof" that designation as an SDGT is "so punitive as to be criminal," saying that "at the end of the day we are influenced by the fact that designation, at its core, is a function of national security and foreign policy and thus serves an alternative function other than punishment." Yet one critic argues that "[f]or an American organization, IEEPA designation is a death sentence. For an American individual, it amounts to house arrest," violating "the Fifth and Sixth Amendments by imposing punishment without providing the required procedural protections." Eric Sandberg-Zakian, *Counterterrorism, the Constitution, and the Civil-Criminal Divide: Evaluating the Designation of U.S. Persons under the International Emergency Economic Powers Act,* 48 Harv. J. on Legis. 95, 95 (2011). Can the practical consequences of designation — civil, criminal, or otherwise — be justified by calling them "a function of national security and foreign policy"? Extending the court's reasoning, is there any limit to the sacrifices one should expect to have to make in the name of "national security and foreign policy"?

3. Other Domestic Economic Sanctions Against State Supporters of Terrorism

One provision of the Antiterrorism and Effective Death Penalty Act of 1996, Pub. L. No. 104-132, §321(a), 110 Stat. 1214, 1254 (codified at 18 U.S.C. §2332d (2006)), makes it a crime for U.S. persons, except in accordance with Treasury Department regulations, to engage in financial transactions with the governments of states designated by the Secretary of State under §6(j) of the Export Administration Act of 1979, 50 U.S.C. app. §2405(j) (2006), as supporting international terrorism. As of mid-2011, four states were so designated: Cuba, Iran, Sudan, and Syria. *See* U.S. Dep't of State, *State Sponsors of Terrorism* (n.d.), *available at* http://www.state.gov/s/ct/c14151.htm.

The Secretary of State's designation also allows the President to restrict or prohibit exports of sensitive technology, including some computers, to such states. 50 U.S.C. app. §2405(j). Such a restriction could be especially painful for a developing nation. The Defense Department is barred from providing financial assistance to designated states, to states identified in the Secretary of State's annual *Country Reports on Terrorism, supra* p. 794, as "providing significant support for international terrorism," or to states that the President determines grant "sanctuary from prosecution to any individual or group that has committed an act of international terrorism; or otherwise supports international terrorism." 10 U.S.C. §2249a (2006). In addition, the Arms Export Control Act bars government exports, and provides civil and criminal penalties for transfers by U.S. persons, of munitions to states that the Secretary of State determines have "repeatedly provided support for acts of international terrorism." 22 U.S.C. §2780 (2006 & Supp. IV 2010). The Foreign Assistance Act employs the same language to bar certain other kinds of U.S. government aid. 22 U.S.C. §2371 (2006 & Supp. IV 2010). More narrowly, the Comprehensive Iran Sanctions, Accountability, and Divestment Act of 2010, Pub. L. No. 111-195, 124 Stat. 1312, citing Iran's support for international terrorism, requires the President to impose sanctions for certain activities that would, *inter alia*, enhance Iran's ability to develop its petroleum resources or weapons of mass destruction. And currency transfers that could be helpful to terrorists are targeted by provisions of the USA Patriot Act that address money laundering. Pub. L. No. 107-56, §§301-377, 115 Stat. 272, 296-342 (2001). *See* Michael Shapiro, *The USA Patriot Act and Money Laundering*, 123 Banking L.J. 629 (2006).

There is considerable redundancy among the various statutory sanctions, of which only some are mentioned here, and several of them provide for waiver by the President if, for example, he determines that it is "in the national security interests of the United States to do so." *See, e.g.*, 10 U.S.C. §2249a(b)(1)(A) (2006).

NOTES AND QUESTIONS

1. *Unilateral Executive Power to Impose Sanctions?* All of the economic sanctions we have examined have been based on statutory authority, or at least upon authority delegated to the President by Congress. (We include the suspension of claims in *Dames & Moore v. Regan*, 453 U.S. 654 (1981), as resting on Congress's acquiescence

or upon the "general tenor" of legislation in the area.) But could the President impose some new sanction without congressional approval? Professor Carter, recalling Justice Jackson's concurring opinion in *Youngstown Sheet & Tube Co. v. Sawyer*, 343 U.S. 579, 634 (1952), points out that statutory authorities for such sanctions "are both comprehensive and specific.... If the President were to act contrary to one of the limits on his discretion or if he were to operate outside the statutory procedures, his power would be at 'its lowest ebb,' and a court might refuse to uphold his act." Carter, *supra* p. 806, at 1245-1246. What arguments could the President make to support such a unilateral initiative?

2. *Unintended Consequences?* A number of observers have cautioned that wide-ranging U.S. economic sanctions designed to combat terrorism may actually have the opposite effect.

> [T]he government's approach may actually have the effect of undermining U.S. security interests by inadvertently chilling the flow of charitable dollars overseas to address serious problems, including those associated with the root causes of terrorism, such as extreme poverty, inadequate access to health care, stalled economic development, and poor education systems. [Garry W. Jenkins, *Soft Power, Strategic Security, and International Philanthropy*, 85 N.C. L. Rev. 773, 773 (2007).]

See also Peter Margulies, *Laws of Unintended Consequences: Terrorist Financing Restrictions and Transitions to Democracy*, 20 N.Y. Int'l L. Rev. 65, 67 (2007) ("an inflexible regime of restrictions on aid to governments, as opposed to terrorist groups, may have the unintended consequences of promoting terrorism and defeating democratic transitions"). How could the risks of such consequences be minimized?

26

Suing Terrorists and Their Supporters

In this concluding chapter we consider the use of a familiar legal device — the tort suit — to counter terrorism. Successful suits in tort may produce some measure of justice for victims of terrorism in the form of judgments for damages. Even if those judgments do not eventually provide economic relief for the plaintiffs, they condemn the terrorists or their supporters as outlaws, and they may make it much more difficult for terrorists to finance their activities by exposing their assets or the assets of their supporters to attachment.

The intersection of relevant domestic and international laws figures prominently in this study. In Part A we examine several domestic statutes, one of them incorporating international law, that have been invoked to bring actions for damages and to assert jurisdiction in federal courts. In Part B we take up the issue of sovereign immunity in suits against state supporters of terrorism. Finally, in Part C we review briefly the frustrations successful plaintiffs have experienced in trying to collect their judgments.

A. SUING TERRORISTS AND THEIR NON-STATE SUPPORTERS

Civil damages suits for terrorist acts are authorized by the Antiterrorism Act (ATA), 18 U.S.C. §2333 (2006), the Alien Tort Statute (ATS) (also known as the Alien Tort Claims Act), 28 U.S.C. §1350 (2006), and the Torture Victim Protection Act (TVPA), 28 U.S.C. §1350 note (2006). Application of the ATA is illustrated in the following case, and of the other statutes in the Notes and Questions that follow it.

Boim v. Holy Land Foundation for Relief and Development (*Boim III*)

United States Court of Appeals for the Seventh Circuit (en banc), 2008
549 F.3d 685

POSNER, Circuit Judge. In 1996 David Boim, a Jewish teenager who was both an Israeli citizen and an American citizen, living in Israel, was shot to death by two men at a bus stop near Jerusalem. His parents filed this suit four years later, alleging that his killers had been Hamas gunmen and naming as defendants Muhammad Salah plus three organizations: the Holy Land Foundation for Relief and Development, the American Muslim Society, and the Quranic Literacy Institute.... The complaint accused the defendants of having provided financial support to Hamas before David Boim's death and by doing so of having violated 18 U.S.C. §2333(a), which provides that "any national of the United States injured in his or her person, property, or business by reason of an act of international terrorism, or his or her estate, survivors, or heirs, may sue therefor in any appropriate district court of the United States and shall recover threefold the damages he or she sustains and the cost of the suit, including attorney's fees." ...

[Following a jury verdict, the district court awarded treble damages to the plaintiffs totaling $156 million, plus attorneys' fees, against all the defendants, jointly and severally.]

Section 2333 does not say that someone who assists in an act of international terrorism is liable; that is, it does not mention "secondary" liability, the kind that 18 U.S.C. §2 creates by imposing criminal liability on "whoever commits an offense against the United States or aids, abets, counsels, commands, induces or procures its commission," or "willfully causes an act to be done which if directly performed by him or another would be an offense against the United States." *See also* 18 U.S.C. §3 (accessory after the fact)....

... [S]tatutory silence on the subject of secondary liability means there is none; and section 2333(a) authorizes awards of damages to private parties but does not mention aiders and abettors or other secondary actors.... [The majority therefore declined to read into the statute a common law claim for aiding and abetting an act of international terrorism.]

The first panel opinion [*Boim v. Quranic Literacy Institute* (*Boim I*), 291 F.3d 1000 (7th Cir. 2002)] discussed approvingly an alternative and more promising ground for bringing donors to terrorist organizations within the grasp of section 2333. The ground involves a chain of explicit statutory incorporations by reference. The first link in the chain is the statutory definition of "international terrorism" as "activities that ... involve violent acts or acts dangerous to human life that are a violation of the criminal laws of the United States," that "appear to be intended ... to intimidate or coerce a civilian population" or "affect the conduct of a government by ... assassination," and that "transcend national boundaries in terms of the means by which they are accomplished" or "the persons they appear intended to intimidate or coerce." 18 U.S.C. §2331(1).... [T]he two sections are part of the same statutory scheme and are to be read together.

Section 2331(1)'s definition of international terrorism ... includes not only violent acts but also "acts dangerous to human life that are a violation of the criminal laws of the United States." Giving money to Hamas, like giving a loaded gun to a child (which also is not a violent act), is an "act dangerous to human life." And it violates a federal criminal statute enacted in 1994 and thus before the murder of David Boim, 18 U.S.C. §2339A(a) [*supra* p. 603], which provides that "whoever provides material support or resources ... knowing or intending that they are to be used in preparation for, or in carrying out, a violation of [18 U.S.C. §2332]," shall be guilty of a federal crime. So we go to 18 U.S.C. §2332 and discover that it criminalizes the killing (whether classified as homicide, voluntary manslaughter, or involuntary manslaughter), conspiring to kill, or inflicting bodily injury on, any American citizen outside the United States.

By this chain of incorporations by reference (section 2333(a) to section 2331(1) to section 2339A to section 2332), we see that a donation to a terrorist group that targets Americans outside the United States may violate section 2333. Which makes good sense as a counterterrorism measure. Damages are a less effective remedy against terrorists and their organizations than against their financial angels. Terrorist organizations have been sued under section 2333, e.g., *Ungar v. Palestine Liberation Organization*, 402 F.3d 274 (1st Cir. 2005); *Biton v. Palestinian Interim Self-Government Authority*, 252 F.R.D. 1 (D.D.C. 2008); *Knox v. Palestine Liberation Organization*, 248 F.R.D. 420 (S.D.N.Y. 2008), but to *collect* a damages judgment against such an organization, let alone a judgment against the terrorists themselves (if they can even be identified and thus sued), is, as the first panel opinion pointed out, 291 F.3d at 1021, well-nigh impossible. These are foreign organizations and individuals, operating abroad and often covertly, and they are often impecunious as well. So difficult is it to obtain monetary relief against covert foreign organizations like these that Congress has taken to passing legislation authorizing the payment of judgments against them from U.S. Treasury funds. *E.g.*, Victims of Trafficking and Violence Protection Act of 2000, Pub. L. No. 106-386, §2002, 114 Stat. 1464. But that can have no deterrent or incapacitative effect, whereas suits against financiers of terrorism can cut the terrorists' lifeline.

And whether it makes good sense or not, the imposition of civil liability through the chain of incorporations is compelled by the statutory texts—as the panel determined in its first opinion. 291 F.3d at 1012-16. . . .

In addition to providing material support after the effective date of section 2339A, a donor to terrorism, to be liable under section 2333, must have known that the money would be used in preparation for or in carrying out the killing or attempted killing of, conspiring to kill, or inflicting bodily injury on, an American citizen abroad. We know that Hamas kills Israeli Jews; and Boim was an Israeli citizen, Jewish, living in Israel, and therefore a natural target for Hamas. But we must consider the knowledge that the donor to a terrorist organization must be shown to possess in order to be liable under section 2333 and the proof required to link the donor's act to the injury sustained by the victim. The parties have discussed both issues mainly under the rubrics of "conspiracy" and "aiding and abetting." Although those labels are significant primarily in criminal cases, they can be used to establish tort liability, *see, e.g., Halberstam v. Welch*, 705 F.2d 472 (D.C. Cir. 1983); *Restatement (Second) of Torts* §§876(a), (b) (1979), and there is no impropriety in discussing them in reference to the liability of donors to terrorism under section 2333 just because that liability is primary. Primary liability in the form of material support to terrorism has the character of secondary liability. Through a chain of incorporations by reference, Congress has expressly imposed liability on a class of aiders and abettors.

When a federal tort statute does not create secondary liability, so that the only defendants are primary violators, the ordinary tort requirements relating to fault, state of mind, causation, and foreseeability must be satisfied for the plaintiff to obtain a judgment. *See, e.g., Bridge v. Phoenix Bond & Indemnity Co.*, __ U.S. __, 128 S. Ct. 2131, 2141-44 (2008). But when the primary liability is that of someone who aids someone else, so that functionally the primary violator is an aider and abettor or other secondary actor, a different set of principles comes into play. Those principles are most fully developed in the criminal context, but we must be careful in borrowing from criminal law because the state-of-mind and causation requirements in criminal cases often differ from those in civil cases. For example, because the criminal law focuses on the dangerousness of a defendant's conduct, the requirement of proving that a criminal act caused an injury is often attenuated and sometimes dispensed with altogether, as in the statutes that impose criminal liability on providers of material support to terrorism (18 U.S.C. §§2339A, B, and C), which do not require proof that the material support resulted in an actual terrorist act, or that punish an attempt (e.g., 18 U.S.C. §1113) that the intended victim may not even have noticed, so that there is no injury. The law of attempt has no counterpart in tort law, *United States v. Gladish*, 536 F.3d 646, 648 (7th Cir. 2008), because there is no tort without an injury.

So prudence counsels us not to halt our analysis with aiding and abetting but to go on and analyze the tort liability of providers of material support to terrorism under general principles of tort law. We begin by noting that knowledge and intent have lesser roles in tort law than in criminal law. A volitional act that causes an injury gives rise to tort liability for negligence if the injurer failed to exercise due care, period. But more is required in the case of intentional torts, and we can assume that since section 2333 provides for an automatic trebling of damages it would require proof of intentional misconduct even if the plaintiffs in this case did not have to satisfy the state-of-mind requirements of sections 2339A and 2332 (but they do).

Punitive damages are rarely if ever imposed unless the defendant is found to have engaged in deliberate wrongdoing. "Something more than the mere commission of a tort is always required for punitive damages. There must be circumstances of aggravation or outrage, such as spite or 'malice,' or a fraudulent or evil motive on the part of the defendant, or such a conscious and deliberate disregard of the interests of others that the conduct may be called wilful or wanton." W. Page Keeton et al., *Prosser and Keeton on the Law of Torts* §2, pp. 9-10 (5th ed. 1984). Treble damages too, not being compensatory, tend to have a punitive aim. "The very idea of treble damages reveals an intent to punish past, and to deter future, unlawful conduct." *Texas Industries, Inc. v. Radcliff Materials, Inc.*, 451 U.S. 630, 639 (1981).

To give money to an organization that commits terrorist acts is not intentional misconduct unless one either knows that the organization engages in such acts or is deliberately indifferent to whether it does or not, meaning that one knows there is a substantial probability that the organization engages in terrorism but one does not care. "When the facts known to a person place him on notice of a risk, he cannot ignore the facts and plead ignorance of the risk." *Makor Issues & Rights, Ltd. v. Tellabs Inc.*, 513 F.3d 702, 704 (7th Cir. 2008). That is recklessness and equivalent to recklessness is "wantonness," which "has been defined as the conscious doing of some act or omission of some duty under knowledge of existing conditions and conscious that from the doing of such act or omission of such duty injury will likely or probably result." *Graves v. Wildsmith*, 278 Ala. 228, 177 So. 2d 448, 451 (1965)....

So it would not be enough to impose liability on a donor for violating section 2333, even if there were no state-of-mind requirements in sections 2339A and 2332, that the average person or a reasonable person would realize that the organization he was supporting was a terrorist organization, if the actual defendant did not realize it. That would just be negligence. But if you give a gun you know is loaded to a child, you know you are creating a substantial risk of injury and therefore your doing so is reckless and if the child shoots someone you will be liable to the victim.... To give a small child a loaded gun would be a case of *criminal* recklessness and therefore satisfy the state of mind requirement for liability under section 2333 and the statutes that it incorporates by reference. For the giver would know he was doing something extremely dangerous and without justification. "If the actor knows that the consequences are certain, or substantially certain, to result from his act, and still goes ahead, he is treated by the law as if he had in fact desired to produce the result." *Restatement, supra,* §8A, comment b. That you did not desire the child to shoot anyone would thus be irrelevant, not only in a tort case, see *EEOC v. Illinois,* 69 F.3d 167, 170 (7th Cir. 1995), but in a criminal case. *United States v. Fountain,* 768 F.2d 790, 798 (7th Cir. 1985).

A knowing donor to Hamas — that is, a donor who knew the aims and activities of the organization — would know that Hamas was gunning for Israelis (unlike some other terrorist groups, Hamas's terrorism is limited to the territory of Palestine, including Israel, that Americans are frequent visitors to and sojourners in Israel, that many U.S. citizens live in Israel, and that donations to Hamas, by augmenting Hamas's resources, would enable Hamas to kill or wound, or try to kill, or conspire to kill more people in Israel. And given such foreseeable consequences, such donations would "appear to be intended . . . to intimidate or coerce a civilian population" or to "affect the conduct of a government by . . . assassination," as required by section 2331(1) in order to distinguish terrorist acts from other violent crimes, though it is not a state-of-mind requirement; it is a matter of external appearance rather than subjective intent, which is internal to the intender. . . .

So if you give a person rocks who has told you he would like to kill drivers by dropping them on cars from an overpass, and he succeeds against the odds in killing someone by this means, you are guilty of providing material support to a murderer, or equivalently of aiding and abetting — for remember that when the primary violator of a statute is someone who provides assistance to another he is functionally an aider and abettor. The mental element required to fix liability on a donor to Hamas is therefore present if the donor knows the character of that organization.

. . . That brings us to our next question — the standard of causation in a suit under section 2333.

It is "black letter" law that tort liability requires proof of causation. But like much legal shorthand, the black letter is inaccurate if treated as exceptionless. We made that point explicitly, with the aid of an example, in *Maxwell v. KPMG LLP,* 520 F.3d 713, 716 (7th Cir. 2008): "when two fires join and destroy the plaintiff's property and each one would have destroyed it by itself *and so was not a necessary condition* . . . each of the firemakers (if negligent) is [nevertheless] liable to the plaintiff for having 'caused' the injury." . . .

In [such] cases the requirement of proving causation is relaxed because otherwise there would be a wrong and an injury but no remedy because the court would be unable to determine which wrongdoer inflicted the injury. If "each [defendant] bears a like relationship to the event" and "each seeks to escape liability for a reason that, if recognized, would likewise protect each other defendant in the group, thus leaving the plaintiff without a remedy," the attempt at escape fails; each is liable. [Keeton et al., *supra,*] §41, p. 268.

But we must consider the situation in which there is uncertainty about the causal connection between the wrongful conduct of all potential tortfeasors and the injury. Suppose in our first case that there was a third fire, of natural origin (the result of a lightning strike, perhaps), and it alone might have sufficed to destroy the plaintiff's house. One might think the law would require the plaintiff to prove that it was more likely than not that had it not been for the defendants' negligence, his house would not have burned down — the fire of natural origin would have petered out before reaching it. Instead the law requires proof only that there was a substantial probability that the defendants' fires (or rather either of them) were the cause. *See, e.g., Restatement, supra,*

§432(2) ("if two forces are actively operating, one because of the actor's negligence, the other not because of any misconduct on his part, and each of itself is sufficient to bring about harm to another, the actor's negligence may be found to be a substantial factor in bringing it about"); *see also id.*, illustration 3. . . .

The cases that we have discussed do not involve monetary contributions to a wrongdoer. But then criminals and other intentional tortfeasors do not usually solicit voluntary contributions. Terrorist organizations do. But this is just to say that terrorism is *sui generis*. So consider an organization solely involved in committing terrorist acts and a hundred people all of whom know the character of the organization and each of whom contributes $1,000 to it, for a total of $100,000. The organization has additional resources from other, unknown contributors of $200,000 and it uses its total resources of $300,000 to recruit, train, equip, and deploy terrorists who commit a variety of terrorist acts one of which kills an American citizen. His estate brings a suit under section 2333 against one of the knowing contributors of $1,000. The tort principles that we have reviewed would make the defendant jointly and severally liable with all those other contributors. The fact that the death could not be traced to any of the contributors . . . and that some of them may have been ignorant of the mission of the organization (and therefore not liable under a statute requiring proof of intentional or reckless misconduct) would be irrelevant. The knowing contributors as a whole would have significantly enhanced the risk of terrorist acts and thus the probability that the plaintiff's decedent would be a victim, and this would be true even if Hamas had incurred a cost of more than $1,000 to kill the American, so that no defendant's contribution was a sufficient condition of his death.

This case is only a little more difficult because Hamas is (and was at the time of David Boim's death) engaged not only in terrorism but also in providing health, educational, and other social welfare services. The defendants other than Salah directed their support exclusively to those services. But if you give money to an organization that you know to be engaged in terrorism, the fact that you earmark it for the organization's nonterrorist activities does not get you off the liability hook. . . . The reasons are twofold. The first is the fungibility of money. If Hamas budgets $2 million for terrorism and $2 million for social services and receives a donation of $100,000 for those services, there is nothing to prevent its using that money for them while at the same time taking $100,000 out of its social services "account" and depositing it in its terrorism account.

Second, Hamas's social welfare activities reinforce its terrorist activities both directly by providing economic assistance to the families of killed, wounded, and captured Hamas fighters and making it more costly for them to defect (they would lose the material benefits that Hamas provides them), and indirectly by enhancing Hamas's popularity among the Palestinian population and providing funds for indoctrinating schoolchildren. Anyone who knowingly contributes to the nonviolent wing of an organization that he knows to engage in terrorism is knowingly contributing to the organization's terrorist activities. And that is the only knowledge that can reasonably be required as a premise for liability. To require proof that the donor *intended* that his contribution be used for terrorism — to make a benign intent a defense — would as a practical matter eliminate donor liability except in cases in which the donor was foolish enough to admit his true intent. It would also create a First Amendment Catch-22, as the only basis for inferring intent would in the usual case be a defendant's public declarations of support for the use of violence to achieve political ends.

Although liability under section 2333 is broad, to maintain perspective we note two cases that fall on the other side of the liability line. One is the easy case of a donation to an Islamic charity by an individual who does not know (and is not reckless, in the sense of strongly suspecting the truth but not caring about it) that the charity gives money to Hamas or some other terrorist organization.

The other case is that of medical (or other innocent) assistance by nongovernmental organizations such as the Red Cross and Doctors Without Borders that provide such assistance without regard to the circumstances giving rise to the need for it. Suppose an Israeli retaliatory strike at Hamas causes so many casualties that the local medical services cannot treat all of them, and Doctors Without Borders offers to assist. And suppose that many of the casualties that the doctors treat are Hamas fighters, so that Doctors Without Borders might know in advance that it would be providing medical assistance to terrorists.

However, section 2339A(b)(1) excludes "medicine" from the definition of "material resources." And even if the word should be limited (an issue on which we take no position) to drugs and other medicines, an organization like Doctors Without Borders would not be in violation of section 2333. It would be helping not a terrorist group but individual patients, and, consistent with the Hippocratic Oath, with no questions asked about the patients' moral virtue. It would be like a doctor who treats a person with a gunshot wound whom he knows to be a criminal. If doctors refused to treat criminals, there would be less crime. But the doctor is not himself a criminal unless, besides treating the criminal, he conceals him from the police (like Dr. Samuel Mudd, sentenced to prison for trying to help John Wilkes Booth, Lincoln's assassin, elude capture) or violates a law requiring doctors to report wounded criminals. The same thing would be true if a hospital unaffiliated with Hamas but located in Gaza City solicited donations.

Nor would the rendering of medical assistance by the Red Cross or Doctors Without Borders to individual terrorists "appear to be intended ... to intimidate or coerce a civilian population" or "affect the conduct of a government by ... assassination," and without such appearance there is no international terrorist act within the meaning of section 2331(1) and hence no violation of section 2333. . . .

An issue to which the first panel opinion gave much attention (see 291 F.3d at 1021-27), but which received little attention from the parties afterward, is brought into focus by our analysis of the elements of a section 2333 violation. That is whether the First Amendment insulates financiers of terrorism from liability if they do not intend to further the illegal goals of an organization like Hamas that engages in political advocacy as well as in violence. If the financier knew that the organization to which it was giving money engaged in terrorism, penalizing him would not violate the First Amendment. Otherwise someone who during World War II gave money to the government of Nazi Germany solely in order to support its anti-smoking campaign could not have been punished for supporting a foreign enemy.

But it is true that "an organization is not a terrorist organization just because one of its members commits an act of armed violence without direct or indirect authorization, even if his objective was to advance the organization's goals, though the organization might be held liable to the victim of his violent act." *Hussain v. Mukasey,* [518 F.3d 534, 538 (7th Cir. 2008)]. That is the principle of *NAACP v. Claiborne Hardware Co.*, 458 U.S. 886, 920 (1982). The defendants in the present case could not be held liable for acts of violence by members of Hamas that were not authorized by Hamas. Nor would persons be liable who gave moral rather than material support, short of incitement, to violent organizations that have political aims. As intimated earlier in this opinion, a person who gives a speech in praise of Hamas for firing rockets at Israel is exercising his freedom of speech, protected by the First Amendment. *See, e.g., Communist Party of Indiana v. Whitcomb*, 414 U.S. 441, 447-49 (1974); *Brandenburg v. Ohio*, 395 U.S. 444, 447-48 (1969) (per curiam). But as Hamas engages in violence as a declared goal of the organization, anyone who provides *material* support to it, knowing the organization's character, is punishable (provided he is enchained by the chain of statutory incorporations necessary to impose liability under section 2333) whether or not he approves of violence.

Enough about the liability standard. We have now to consider its application to the facts.... [For reasons not relevant here, the court reverses and remands as to the Holy Land Foundation and reverses as to Salah.]

...Regarding...the American Muslim Society and the Quranic Literacy Institute, the judgment of the district court was in our view correct. The activities of the American Muslim Society are discussed at length in the district court's second opinion. *See* [*Boim v. Quranic Literacy Institute*, 340 F. Supp. 2d 885 (N.D. Illinois 2004),] at 906-13. There we learn that while its activities included donating money to the Holy Land Foundation, there was much else besides. Moreover, the fact that the Foundation may not have known that Hamas was a terrorist organization (implausible as that is) would not exonerate the American Muslim Society, which *did* know and in giving money to the Foundation was deliberately funneling money to Hamas. The funnel doesn't have to know what it's doing to be an effective funnel.

Nor should donors to terrorism be able to escape liability because terrorists and their supporters launder donations through a chain of intermediate organizations. Donor *A* gives to innocent-appearing organization *B* which gives to innocent-appearing organization *C* which gives to Hamas. As long as *A* either knows or is reckless in failing to discover that donations to *B* end up with Hamas, *A* is liable. Equally important, however, if this knowledge requirement is not satisfied, the donor is not liable. And as the temporal chain lengthens, the likelihood that a donor has or should know of the donee's connection to terrorism shrinks. But to set the knowledge and causal requirement higher than we have done in this opinion would be to invite money laundering, the proliferation of affiliated organizations, and two-track terrorism (killing plus welfare). Donor liability would be eviscerated, and the statute would be a dead letter....

Affirmed in Part, Reversed in Part, and Remanded.

ROVNER, Circuit Judge, with whom WILLIAMS, Circuit Judge, joins, concurring in part and dissenting in part.... For the reasons outlined in the *Boim I* opinion, I continue to believe that Congress when it enacted section 2333(a) subjected to civil liability not only those who engage in terrorism but also those who aid or abet terrorism. The government as an amicus curiae has expressed agreement with that view. The secondary liability framework is a much more natural fit for what the defendants here are alleged to have done and ... the elements of aiding and abetting serve a useful function in distinguishing between those who intend to aid terrorism and those who do not....

[The opinion of WOOD, Circuit Judge, concurring in part and dissenting in part, is omitted.]

NOTES AND QUESTIONS

1. *Common Law Secondary Liability.* As the *Boim III* court notes, §2333 creates civil liability without identifying who might be liable. Clearly the liability includes primary violators of the ATA—terrorists themselves who commit an "act of international terrorism." But if these are the only eligible defendants, the ATA civil remedy will be a cruel joke when the terrorists either die in the attack or flee beyond the reach of U.S. courts (as will usually be the case).

Does liability under the ATA extend beyond these primary defendants? If so, how far? The answer suggested by the United States in amicus briefs in *Boim* drew on the common law of torts. According to the *Restatement (Second) of Torts* §876, the common law recognizes secondary tort liability:

> For harm resulting to a third person from the tortious conduct of another, one is subject to liability if he
> (a) does a tortious act in concert with the other or pursuant to a common design with him, or
> (b) knows that the other's conduct constitutes a breach of duty and gives substantial assistance or encouragement to the other so to conduct himself, or
> (c) gives substantial assistance to the other in accomplishing a tortious result and his own conduct, separately considered, constitutes a breach of duty to the third person.

Section §876(a) describes common law secondary tort liability for conspiracy, §876(b) describes common law secondary tort liability for aiding and abetting, and §876(c) describes common law secondary tort liability for committing an independent breach of duty that substantially assists another in accomplishing a tortious act. Arguably, violation of any of the material support statutes, *supra* pp. 603-604, could constitute such an independent breach.

The Boims originally relied on common law secondary liability, as the prior *Boim* opinions also apparently did. In *Boim III*, however, a divided *en banc* court concluded that the ATA's silence about secondary liability precluded common law secondary liability. The majority relied upon a Supreme Court decision in *Central Bank of Denver, N.A. v. First Interstate Bank of Denver, N.A.*, 511 U.S. 164 (1994), which rejected secondary liability under the Securities and Exchange Act of 1934. That Act, however, unlike the ATA, established no express civil remedy at all, and it explicitly created some duties for identified secondary actors, giving rise to the inference that liability would not run to omitted secondary actors. The ATA, in contrast, expressly creates a civil remedy, names no category of defendants, and, in fact, only identifies persons and entities that *cannot* be sued. 18 U.S.C. §2337 (agencies and officers of the United States or a foreign state).

Other federal courts have construed the ATA to include common law secondary liability for aiding and abetting, and for conspiracy to commit, an act of international terrorism, as did some of the concurring judges in *Boim III*, on the theory that the ATA's legislative history reflects a clear intent to reach up the "chain of causation." *See Wultz v. Islamic Republic of Iran*, 755 F. Supp. 2d 1, 54-57 (D.D.C. 2010) ("based on the structure of the ATA, the legislative history, and the persuasive authority of every court to have considered the question aside from *Boim III*, plaintiffs [the estate and family members of a U.S. citizen killed by a suicide attack in Tel Aviv] have convinced the Court to rebut the presumption [that Congress did not create a cause of action for aiding and abetting under the ATA]"); *In re Chiquita Brands Int'l, Inc. Alien Tort Statute & S'holder Deriv. Litig.*, 690 F. Supp. 2d 1296, 1309-1310 (S.D. Fla. 2010); *Linde v. Arab Bank, PLC*, 384 F. Supp. 2d 571, 583 (E.D.N.Y. 2005).

2. *"Statutory Secondary Liability."* Instead of adopting common law secondary liability, the *Boim III* majority adopts a novel theory of "primary liability... [with] the character of secondary liability." Such liability is based on a "chain of incorporations by reference" that connects §2333 to criminal statutes that provide sanctions for the sort of donations involved in this case. (Note that the chain did not include §2339B, which had not yet been enacted at the time of the events in *Boim*. Hamas was first designated a foreign terrorist organization in 1997.) Can you describe how each link in this chain is connected to the next? Is Judge Posner's theory of what could be termed "statutory secondary liability" significantly different from common law secondary liability? If so, how? Why does Judge Rovner say that the latter is a "much more natural fit"?

The court says its reading of §2333 "makes good sense as a counterterrorism measure." Did the court step out of role to set policy where Congress failed to do so? Consider the statute's legislative history, asserting that one purpose of the ATA was "the imposition of liability *at any point* along the causal chain of terrorism, [so as to] interrupt, or at least imperil, the flow of money [to terrorist organizations]." S. Rep. No. 102-342, at 22 (1992) (emphasis added).

3. *Criminal vs. Civil Liability.* The principal case involves a suit for damages. Why does the court discuss criminal law? If such law is relevant at all, how is its relevance limited?

4. *Knowledge and Intent.* The court finds that liability requires "proof of intentional misconduct." But §2333 itself makes no explicit reference to either knowledge or intent. Where does the court find these requirements? What are the *scienter* requirements for secondary liability?

The court goes on to determine that the intentional misconduct may be shown by "deliberate indifference" equivalent to recklessness and wantonness, when an actor is conscious that "injury will likely or probably occur." Is this a fair reading of the statutory scheme? How does the court find "recklessness and wantonness" in the donations to Hamas?

If any of the material support statutes, 18 U.S.C. §§2339A-2339C, is incorporated on the *Boim III* theory or on a *Restatement* §876 common law theory, how would that affect the *scienter* requirement? Does any of them require specific intent? Does the Fifth Amendment's requirement of "personal guilt," see *supra* pp. 618-619, have any relevance in a *civil* case?

5. *Causation.* The court notes that there can be no tort liability without a causal link between the defendant's act and the plaintiff's injury. (A court might, of course, grant injunctive relief for a threatened injury.) But a particular dollar contributed to or by one of the defendant organizations could never be directly traced to the murder of David Boim. Why not? How does the court establish the requisite causal link? And how is causation linked to the knowledge requirement? Does Judge Posner's approach make the knowing (or reckless) provision of material support to a foreign terrorist organization a prima facie violation of §2333, as long as the organization is

responsible for the death of a U.S. national at *any point* thereafter? Under what facts would such knowing support *not* be deemed to have proximately caused the death?

6. *Tracing Responsibility.* The court in the principal case clearly would hold individual donors to Hamas liable under §2333 if they were aware of the organization's terrorist activities. In *Linde v. Arab Bank, PLC*, 384 F. Supp. 2d 571 (E.D.N.Y. 2005), the court refused to dismiss a suit under the ATA by U.S. nationals injured by terrorist attacks in Israel. There the plaintiffs claimed that Arab Bank knowingly provided banking services for Hamas and other terrorist organizations (*see also Goldberg v. UBS AG*, 660 F. Supp. 2d 410 (E.D.N.Y. 2009)), and knowingly disbursed funds to terrorists and the families of "martyrs."

Will the person who delivers pizza to Hamas headquarters be liable if she knows of the organization's goals? The lawyer who provides advice about the legality of the organization's activities? How, if at all, would the common law of aiding and abetting under *Restatement* §876(b) distinguish these hypotheticals? The reach of criminal liability under the material support statutes is explored *supra* pp. 617-620.

7. *Medical Assistance.* The court concludes that "medical (or other innocent) assistance [to terrorists] by nongovernmental organizations such as the Red Cross and Doctors Without Borders" would not make such organizations or donors to them liable under the ATA. How is such assistance different, in providing practical support for terrorist acts, from financial donations to Hamas?

8. *First Amendment.* If someone gives a speech at a Hamas fund-raising event that advocates the organization's terrorist goals, any resulting contributions may help Hamas achieve those goals. Why does such a speech not give rise to liability under §2333, when a contribution inspired by the speech does? *See Holder v. Humanitarian Law Project*, 130 S. Ct. 2705 (2010), *supra* p. 604.

9. *Alien Tort Statute.* Aliens injured by acts of terrorism are not entitled to sue under the Antiterrorism Act invoked in *Boim III* unless they are heirs or survivors of an American victim, since that statute provides relief only for a "national of the United States . . . or his or her estate, survivor, or heirs." But they may seek recovery under the ATS, 28 U.S.C. §1350 (2006). The ATS establishes original jurisdiction in federal courts for "any civil action by an alien for a tort only, committed in violation of the law of nations or a treaty of the United States." In *Sosa v. Alvarez-Machain*, 542 U.S. 692 (2004), the Supreme Court held that the ATS only creates subject matter jurisdiction, not a cause of action, for violations of international law. The Court then read "tort . . . committed in violation of the law of nations" narrowly to include only those few torts that were recognized at the time of the Act's passage in 1789 (violation of safe conducts, infringement of the rights of ambassadors, and piracy), as well as any newer claim that "rest[s] on a norm of international character accepted by the civilized world and defined with a specificity comparable to the features of [these three] 18th-century paradigms. . . ." *Id.* at 725.

Does a claim of injury from terrorism meet this demanding test? In two cases excerpted *supra* pp. 10-23, the courts reached differing answers. *Compare Almog v. Arab Bank, PLC*, 471 F. Supp. 2d 257, 285 (E.D.N.Y. 2007) ("organized, systematic suicide bombings and other murderous attacks against innocent civilians for the purpose of intimidating a civilian population are a violation of the law of nations for which this court can and does recognize a cause of action under the ATS"), *with Saperstein v. Palestinian Auth.*, 2006 WL 3804718, at *7 (S.D. Fla. Dec. 22, 2006) ("politically motivated terrorism has not reached the status of a violation of the law of nations").

More recent ATS decisions have raised further questions as to which claims satisfy the high bar set by the Court in *Sosa*. In *Kiobel v. Royal Dutch Petroleum Co.*, 621 F.3d 111 (2d Cir. 2010), *cert. granted*, 2011 WL 4905479 (U.S. Oct. 17, 2011), the Second Circuit held that corporate defendants were not subject to liability under customary international law. Since *Kiobel*, other circuits have reached a contrary conclusion. *See Flomo v. Firestone Natural Rubber Co., LLC*, 643 F.3d 1013, 1025 (7th Cir. 2011) (finding international law precedent for corporate liability); *Doe v. Exxon Mobil Corp.*, 654 F.3d 11, 41 (D.C. Cir. 2011) (rejecting *Kiobel*'s reasoning in part because international law generally leaves aspects of the issue of civil liability to national law). The circuits have also split on the question of whether aiding and abetting principles under customary international law require purposeful conduct or merely knowing conduct. *Compare Presbyterian Church of Sudan v. Talisman Energy, Inc.*, 582 F.3d 244, 263 (2d Cir. 2009) (holding that, to be found liable under the ATS for aiding and abetting, one must purposefully violate international law and share the same purpose as the primary violator), *with Doe v. Exxon Mobil Corp.*, *supra*, 2011 WL 2652384, at *19 (holding that aiding and abetting liability under the ATS requires a showing that a defendant simply had "knowledge" of the primary violator's conduct).

10. *Torture Victim Protection Act.* The Torture Victim Protection Act (TVPA), 28 U.S.C. §1350 note (2006), creates a cause of action for an individual (or her successor) who, *inter alia*, is the victim of an extra-judicial killing by "an individual [acting] under actual or apparent authority, or color of law, of any foreign nation." In *In re Terrorist Attacks on September 11, 2001*, 392 F. Supp. 2d 539, 565-566 (S.D.N.Y. 2005), *aff'd*, 538 F.3d 71 (2d Cir. 2008), the court dismissed TVPA claims against several organizations that were potentially liable under the ATA because they were not "individuals" and against several individuals because they were not acting under "color of state law."

Interestingly, the D.C. Circuit has held that the TVPA does not create corporate liability, *Mohamad v. Rajoub*, 634 F.3d 604 (D.C. Cir.), *cert. granted*, 2011 WL 3055314 (U.S. Oct. 17, 2011), leading to "the incongruous result that an alien (who can sue corporations under the ATS) has broader rights than an American citizen (who cannot sue under the ATS and cannot sue a corporation under the TVPA)." Frank C. Razzano, Jeremy D. Frey & John C. Snodgrass, *More on the Alien Tort Statute: John Doe VIII and Flomo Rulings Add to the Chaos*, 80 U.S.L.W. 285 (Aug. 30, 2011).

11. *Extraterritorial and Personal Jurisdiction and Forum Non Conveniens.* More often than not, the defendants in a claim arising from an act of international terrorism will be foreign, and the act itself will have occurred abroad. *See* 18 U.S.C. §2331(1)(C) (2006) (defining international terrorism, in relevant part, as activities that "occur primarily outside the territorial jurisdiction of the United States. . . ."). In *Morrison v. National Australia Bank Ltd.*, 130 S. Ct. 2869, 2881 (2010), however, the Supreme Court noted a well-settled presumption against extraterritorial application of a statute absent a clear contrary indication. *See supra* pp. 621-622. Can such an indication be found in statutes providing for claims against terrorists and their supporters?

One of the first cases to address the *Morrison* decision, *Doe v. Exxon Mobil Corp.*, *supra*, suggests that courts may examine legal, legislative, and historical precedents when deciding whether to permit extraterritorial claims under existing statutes.

Regarding claims brought under the ATS, it found that, "[g]iven Congress's ratification of ATS lawsuits involving foreign conduct and the Supreme Court's failure to disapprove of such lawsuits in *Sosa*, . . . the extraterritoriality canon does not bar appellants from seeking relief. . . ." 2011 WL 2652384, at *9.

When Congress has conferred prescriptive jurisdiction, a court still must have personal jurisdiction over the defendant. If an act is conducted entirely abroad, upon what basis could a U.S. court exercise personal jurisdiction over the defendants? (Hint: the Quranic Literacy Institute and Holy Land Foundation, defendants in *Boim III*, were both based in and operated within the United States.)

The law of *forum non conveniens* establishes that if a plaintiff has an adequate alternative foreign forum that would be more convenient in light of the location of evidence and witnesses, forum interest, and other practical factors, then a U.S. court can dismiss the suit. *See* Gene R. Shreve & Peter Raven-Hansen, *Understanding Civil Procedure* §6.02[1] (4th ed. 2009). Why wouldn't application of this doctrine result in dismissal of most ATA or ATS claims? The answer for ATA claims lies in part in 18 U.S.C. §2334, which prohibits a *forum non conveniens* dismissal of a §2333 claim unless the "foreign court is *significantly* more convenient and appropriate" and "that foreign court offers a remedy which is *substantially the same* as the one available in the courts of the United States." 18 U.S.C. §2334(d)(2)-(3) (emphasis added).

B. SUITS AGAINST STATE SUPPORTERS OF TERRORISM

Until fairly recently the long-recognized general immunity of foreign states from suit in U.S. courts presented an insurmountable obstacle to recovery from a state supporter of terrorism. That immunity has been codified, yet limited by certain exceptions, in the Foreign Sovereign Immunities Act (FSIA), 28 U.S.C. §§1330, 1602-1611 (2006 & Supp. IV 2010). *See generally* Jennifer K. Elsea, *Suits Against Terrorist States by Victims of Terrorism* (Cong. Res. Serv. RL31258), Aug. 8, 2008. One exception, intended to provide relief for terrorists' victims, is addressed in the following case.

Gates v. Syrian Arab Republic

United States District Court, District of Columbia, 2008
580 F. Supp. 2d 53

ROSEMARY M. COLLYER, District Judge. It was a sunny day somewhere in Iraq and a light wind blew the long curtains into the room through the open door. A group of men clad in total black, faces covered, stood on a Persian rug facing a camera. Before them, a single man knelt. Dressed in an orange jumpsuit, hands bound behind his back, feet similarly bound, with eyes covered and mouth gagged, he rarely moved. One of the standing men began to read a proclamation in Arabic. It continued at length. Suddenly he stopped. The man in the orange jumpsuit tensed. Another of the men in black stepped forward and knocked the kneeling man over onto his side. Brandishing a knife, the man in black began to slice at the neck of the victim lying on the floor. The dying man audibly moaned and gurgled, as it took some time to cut all around his neck and through his bones before the head could be lifted in seeming triumph.

There is no doubt that al-Tawhid wal-Jihad ("al-Qaeda in Iraq") beheaded U.S. civilian contractors Jack Armstrong and Jack Hensley in the manner described, which it videotaped and played on the Internet for all the world, and ultimately this Court, to see. The question raised by this lawsuit is whether the Syrian Arab Republic can be held liable for money damages to the families of the two men pursuant to the Foreign Sovereign Immunities Act (the "FSIA"), 28 U.S.C. §1602 *et seq.*

I. PROCEDURAL POSTURE

Plaintiffs are Francis Gates and Jan Smith, the mother and sister of Jack Armstrong, and Pati and Sara Hensley, the widow and minor daughter of Jack Hensley. Plaintiffs filed this action on August 25, 2006, against Defendants who include: the Syrian Arab Republic ("Syria"); the president of Syria, Bashar al-Assad; the Syrian Military Intelligence, known as the al-Mukhabarat al-Askariya; and the Director of Military Intelligence, General Asif Shawkat. Plaintiffs allege that, acting through these principals, Syria provided material support and resources to the al-Tawhid wal-Jihad (al-Qaeda in Iraq) and its leader, Abu Mus'ab al-Zarqawi ("Zarqawi"). Plaintiffs assert a cause of action under the FSIA, 28 U.S.C. §1605A. . . .

None of the Defendants filed an answer or otherwise appeared. The Court proceeded to a default setting as provided by 28 U.S.C. §1608(e), which requires a court to enter a default judgment against a non-responding foreign state only where "the claimant establishes his claim or right to relief by evidence satisfactory to the court." *Id.* The Court held a three-day hearing on liability and damages beginning on January 7, 2008. Plaintiffs presented evidence in the form of live testimony, videotaped testimony, affidavit, and original documentary and videographic evidence. . . .

II. FINDINGS OF FACT

A. The Murders of Jack Armstrong and Jack Hensley . . .

16. The horrific sights and sounds of the videos have but one clear purpose — to glorify acts of terrorism, mayhem, and murder and to frighten the viewer. There is no doubt that Zarqawi and his organization, al-Qaeda in Iraq, killed Messrs. Armstrong and Hensley. . . .

B. Syria's Role in Assisting Zarqawi and Al-Qaeda in Iraq

17. Plaintiffs presented expert witness testimony and testimony from an Iraqi countryman concerning Syria's assistance to Zarqawi and al-Qaeda in Iraq. From this evidence, certain conclusions are clear. Syria was the critical geographic entry point for Zarqawi's fighters into Iraq, and served as a "logistical hub" for Zarqawi. Syria supported Zarqawi and his organization by: (1) facilitating the recruitment and training of Zarqawi's followers and their transportation into Iraq; (2) harboring and providing sanctuary to terrorists and their operational and logistical supply network; and (3) financing Zarqawi and his terrorist network in Iraq. . . . [T]he depth of [Zarqawi's] inhumanity was obvious but Syria did not withdraw its support. . . .

18. Syria and the Syrian Military Intelligence provided active assistance to Zarqawi and his followers in Iraq by allowing and helping their operatives to move through Syria and across the border. . . .

19. A militant Islamic cleric on the payroll of the Syrian government, Abu Qaqa, actively recruited terrorists for the Zarqawi network in 2003. . . .

27. Syria provided Zarqawi, a Jordanian national, with a Syrian passport, which it regularly gives to leading terrorists....

31. Syria offered safe haven and a logistical support network in Syria for Zarqawi and al-Qaeda in Iraq. Syria not only helped foreign fighters move through its country into Iraq but also provided funding for them....

32. The Zarqawi network conducted terrorist attacks from inside Syria....

45. Because Syria is a centrally-controlled police state, the Syrian government has knowingly acquiesced in, and approved of, the aid and support to al-Qaeda in Iraq....

III. CONCLUSIONS OF LAW

A. Burden of Proof

The FSIA specifies that a court cannot enter a default judgment against a foreign state "unless the claimant establishes his claim or right to relief by evidence satisfactory to the court." 28 U.S.C. §1608(e). Section 1608(e) provides protection to foreign States from unfounded default judgments rendered solely upon a procedural default.

For a plaintiff to prevail in a FSIA default proceeding, the plaintiff must present a legally sufficient prima facie case, *i.e.*, "a legally sufficient evidentiary basis for a reasonable jury to find for plaintiff." *Ungar v. Islamic Republic of Iran*, 211 F. Supp. 2d 91, 98 (D.D.C. 2002). Although a court receives evidence from only the plaintiff when a foreign sovereign defendant has defaulted, 28 U.S.C. §1608(e) does not require a court to demand more or different evidence than it would ordinarily receive in order to render a decision. In evaluating the plaintiff's proofs, a court may "accept as true the plaintiffs' uncontroverted evidence," *Estate of Botvin v. Islamic Republic of Iran*, 510 F. Supp. 2d 101, 103 (D.D.C. 2007), and a plaintiff may establish proof by affidavit. While a plaintiff needs to demonstrate a prima facie case to obtain a judgment of liability in a FSIA case, a plaintiff must show entitlement to punitive damages by clear and convincing evidence. *Peterson v. Islamic Republic of Iran*, 264 F. Supp. 2d 46, 48 (D.D.C. 2003).

... By its failure to appear and defend itself, Syria put itself at risk that the Plaintiffs' uncontroverted evidence would be satisfactory to prove its points. The Court finds that the Plaintiffs have presented satisfactory evidence to prove liability and damages, including punitive damages....

C. Jurisdiction and Liability under the State-Sponsored Terrorism Exception to the FSIA

The FSIA provides "the sole basis for obtaining jurisdiction over a foreign state in the courts of this country." *Argentine Republic v. Amerada Hess Shipping Corp.*, 488 U.S. 428, 443 (1989). Accordingly, this Court lacks jurisdiction over Syria unless one of the FSIA's enumerated exceptions applies. Here, the state-sponsored terrorism exception to sovereign immunity applies. 28 U.S.C. §1605A(a). Moreover, the FSIA was recently amended to provide a private cause of action by which a foreign state that sponsors terrorism can be held liable for certain enumerated damages arising from terrorist activities: economic damages, solatium, pain and suffering, and punitive damages. *Id.* §1605A(c).

Section 1605A(a) provides that a foreign state shall not be immune from the jurisdiction of U.S. courts in cases where plaintiffs seek money damages for personal injury or death caused by hostage taking, torture, or extrajudicial killing, if the damages were caused by:

> (1) the provision of "material support or resources" for hostage taking, torture, and extrajudicial killing;
> (2) if the provision of material support was engaged in by an official while acting within the scope of his office;
> (3) the defendant was a state-sponsor of terrorism at the time the act complained of occurred; and
> (4) the claimant or the victim was a "U.S. national" at the time of the act of terrorism.

28 U.S.C. §1605A(a)(1), (a)(2). Section 1605A(c) provides a private right of action to recover damages for state-sponsored terrorism:

> (c) Private Right of Action — A foreign state that is or was a state sponsor of terrorism . . . shall be liable to — (1) a national of the United States . . . or (4) the legal representative of [such] a person, for personal injury or death caused by acts described in subsection (a)(1) [i.e., the provision of material support or resources for hostage taking, torture, or extrajudicial killing]. . . . In any such action, damages may include economic damages, solatium, pain and suffering, and punitive damages. In any such action, a foreign state shall be vicariously liable for the acts of its officials, employees, or agents.

28 U.S.C. §1605A(c). . . .

Plaintiffs have presented evidence satisfactory to the Court in support [of] all elements of a claim under §1605A. Syria was a state-sponsor of terrorism,[10] and the Plaintiffs are and decedents were U.S. Citizens. The critical issue in this case is whether Syria, and its officials acting within the scope of their employment, provided material support and resources to Zarqawi and to al-Qaeda in Iraq.

Syria in fact did provide material support and resources to Zarqawi and al-Qaeda in Iraq which contributed to hostage taking, torture, and extrajudicial killings. Section 1605A(h)(3) defines "material support or resources" to have the meaning given that term in section 2339A of title 18. Section 2339A provides:

> "material support or resources" means any property, tangible or intangible, or service, including currency or monetary instruments or financial securities, financial services, lodging, training, expert advice or assistance, safehouses, false documentation or identification, communications equipment, facilities, weapons, lethal substances, explosives, personnel . . . and transportation, except medicine or religious materials.

---

10. The term "state sponsor of terrorism" is defined in §1605A as:

a country the government of which the Secretary of State has determined, for purposes of section 6(j) of the Export Administration Act of 1979 (50 U.S.C. App. [§]2405(j)), section 620A of the Foreign Assistance Act of 1961 (22 U.S.C. [§]2371), section 40 of the Arms Export Control Act (22 U.S.C. [§]2780), or any other provision of law, is a government that has repeatedly provided support for acts of international terrorism.

28 U.S.C. §1605A(h)(6). Syria has been designated by the U.S. Department of State as a state sponsor of terrorism continuously since December 29, 1979, see http://www.state.gov/s/ct/c14151.htm (last visited Sept. 17, 2008), and its continued designation as such was noted in 2004, 69 Fed. Reg. 28,098-28,100 (2004), and again in 2005, 31 C.F.R. §596.201 (2005).

18 U.S.C. §2339A(b). To determine whether a defendant country has provided material support to terrorism, courts consider first, whether a particular terrorist group committed the terrorist act and second, whether the defendant foreign state generally provided material support or resources to the terrorist organization which contributed to its ability to carry out the terrorist act. The types of support that have been identified as "material" have included, for example, financing and running camps that provided military and other training to terrorist operatives, *see, e.g., Sisso v. Islamic Republic of Iran*, No. 05-0394, 2007 WL 2007582, at *4-6 (D.D.C. July 5, 2007); allowing terrorist groups to use its banking institutions to launder money, *see, e.g., Rux v. Republic of Sudan*, 495 F. Supp. 2d 541, 549-550 (E.D. Va. 2007); and allowing terrorist groups to use its territory as a meeting place and safe haven, *see, e.g., id.* Such support has been found to have contributed to the actual terrorist act that resulted in a plaintiff's damages when experts testify that the terrorist acts could not have occurred without such support, *see, e.g., Ben-Rafael* [*v. Islamic Republic of Iran*, 540 F. Supp. 2d 39 (D.D.C. 2008),] at 47; or that a particular act exhibited a level of sophistication in planning and execution that was consistent with the advanced training that had been supplied by the defendant state, *see, e.g., Sisso*, 2007 WL 2007582, at *6; or when the support facilitated the terrorist group's development of the expertise, networks, military training, munitions, and financial resources necessary to plan and carry out the attack, *see, e.g., Rux*, 495 F. Supp. 2d at 553 (expert testimony that the "attack might have been possible, but would not have been as easy" without defendant's support). . . .

[Here the court provides additional details about Syria's support of Zarqawi and al-Qaeda in Iraq.]

In sum, jurisdiction over Syria is consistent with §1605A(a), the state-sponsored terrorism exception to sovereign immunity, and Plaintiffs have provided evidence satisfactory to the Court in support of their private cause of action for damages under §1605A(c).

D. Damages

Damages for a private action for proven acts of terrorism by foreign states under the FSIA §1605A(c) may include economic damages, solatium, pain and suffering, and punitive damages. 28 U.S.C. §1605A(c).

1. Economic Damages

Federal law allows the estates of Messrs. Armstrong and Hensley to seek economic damages arising from their deaths. Such damages constitute the present value of each man's anticipated earnings over the remainder of his lifetime. . . .

[Here the court bases its calculation of lost future earnings on each man's earnings history.]

2. Solatium

The legal term "solatium" is a Latin word for "solace" and is defined as "[c]ompensation; esp. damages for hurt feelings or grief, as distinguished from damages for physical injury." Black's Law Dictionary 1426 (8th ed. 2004). "Solatium is traditionally a compensatory damage which belongs to the individual heir personally for injury to the feelings and loss of decedent's comfort and society." *Flatow* [*v.*

Islamic Republic of Iran, 999 F. Supp. 1 (D.D.C. 1998),] at 29. Damages for solatium are awarded to close family members. *Id.* at 30-31. . . .

[The court goes on to describe the unconsolable, continuing anguish experienced by surviving members of the victims' families, and to find compensatory damages for solatium totaling $9,500,000.00.]

3. Pain and Suffering

The claims for the conscious pain and suffering of Jack Armstrong and Jack Hensley before their deaths are actionable through their estates. . . .

During their decapitations, each man suffered unimaginable mental and physical agony. . . .

. . . There is no existing metric to assess pain and suffering for the unbridled and intentional cruelty of the deaths of Mr. Armstrong and Mr. Hensley, after days of captivity in unknown circumstances. . . .

[The court awarded compensatory damages for pain and suffering in the amount of $50,000,000.00 to the estate of each man.]

4. Punitive Damages

As amended, the FSIA now specifically allows an award of punitive damages for personal injury or death resulting from an act of state-sponsored terrorism. 28 U.S.C. §1605A(c). Several factors are considered in the analysis of whether to award punitive damages and how substantial an award should be. Those factors include the character of the defendant's acts; the nature and extent of harm to the Plaintiffs that the Defendant caused or intended to cause; the need for deterrence; and the wealth of the Defendant. Restatement (Second) Torts §908(1)-(2) (1977). The purpose of punitive damages is two-fold: to punish those who engage in outrageous conduct and to deter others from similar conduct in the future. . . .

Al-Qaeda in Iraq wanted the world at large to know that Jack Armstrong and Jack Hensley died in conscious pain and terror. Syria was a willing and substantial supporter of Zarqawi and his terrorist organization and knew, full well, that they were capable of this kind of barbarism. . . . Through the Internet, Zarqawi and his fellow terrorists transformed heinous acts into infamous and indelible propaganda that served the Syrian political ends. The world at large must shout these actions down in infamy. . . .

. . . The evidence shows that Syria supported, protected, harbored, and subsidized a terrorist group whose *modus operandi* was the targeting, brutalization, and murder of American and Iraqi civilians. Premeditated violence against civilian targets is not a legitimate action by any government. Civilized society cannot tolerate states whose partnership with terrorist surrogates, like Zarqawi's terrorist network, is formed for the purpose of achieving political victory through heinous acts of barbarism.

In deciding the amount of punitive damages necessary, the Court undertakes the difficult task of quantifying in financial terms each act of such repugnance, premeditation, and cruelty as to earn the opprobrium of all civilized persons. . . .

In hopes that substantial awards will deter further Syrian sponsorship of terrorists, the Court will award to the estate of Jack Armstrong punitive damages in the amount of $150,000,000.00, and to the estate of Jack Hensley punitive damages in the amount of $150,000,000.00.

IV. CONCLUSION

Money judgments cannot compensate Jack Armstrong or Jack Hensley for their torture and deaths or compensate their family members for their losses. The law, however, cannot let depraved lawlessness go unremarked and without consequence. . . .

NOTES AND QUESTIONS

1. *The FSIA Exception for Terrorist Acts.* As we noted above, the customary international law principle that affords sovereign states complete immunity from suit in the courts of other states was codified, with certain exceptions, in the Foreign Sovereign Immunities Act of 1976, 28 U.S.C. §§1330, 1602-1611 (2006 & Supp. IV 2010). It was not until 1996, with the enactment of the so-called terrorism exception to FSIA, 28 U.S.C. §1605(a)(7), that U.S. courts were given jurisdiction to hear civil damage suits against state sponsors of terrorism and their officials acting in their official capacities on behalf of such states. In the same year, the Flatow Amendment, Pub. L. No. 104-208, §589, 110 Stat. 3009-172 (1996) (so-named for the victim of a terrorist attack in *Flatow v. Islamic Republic of Iran,* 999 F. Supp. 1 (D.D.C. 1998)), expressly created a cause of action against officials, employees, and agents of states whose sovereign immunity was waived by §1605(a)(7). Until 2004 most courts either held or assumed that §1605(a)(7) and the Flatow Amendment provided a cause of action against state supporters of terrorism, as well. *See, e.g., Flatow,* 999 F. Supp. at 26 (relying on the doctrine of "*respondeat superior:* an employer is liable in some cases for damages 'proximately resulting from acts of employee done within scope of his employment in the employer's service.'"); *Smith v. Islamic Emirate of Afghanistan,* 262 F. Supp. 2d 217, 228 (S.D.N.Y. 2003) ("While not free from doubt, the better view in my opinion is that the Flatow Amendment likely provides a cause of action against a foreign state.").

In *Cicippio-Puleo v. Islamic Republic of Iran,* 353 F.3d 1024 (D.C. Cir. 2004), however, the court ruled that while §1605(a)(7) waived the immunity of foreign governments that support terrorism, it did not create a federal statutory cause of action against them; the Flatow Amendment provided a right of action against foreign state officials, but not against the state itself. A different D.C. Circuit panel added that a FSIA plaintiff could not proceed under "generic common law," but must "instead identify a particular cause of action arising out of a specific source of law." *Acree v. Republic of Iraq,* 370 F.3d 41, 59 (D.C. Cir. 2004), *cert. denied,* 544 U.S. 1010 (2005). These two decisions led plaintiffs to seek recovery under the tort laws of U.S. states where the victims were domiciled. *See, e.g., Peterson v. Islamic Republic of Iran,* 515 F. Supp. 2d 25 (D.D.C. 2007) (applying the laws of North Carolina and other states).

Congress responded to *Cicippio-Puleo* in 2008 by replacing §1605(a)(7) and the Flatow Amendment with §1605A, Pub. L. No. 110-181, §1083, 122 Stat. 3, 338-344, continuing the waiver of sovereign immunity, but also expressly creating a federal statutory cause of action against state sponsors of terrorism, as well as their officials, employees, and agents acting in an official capacity. These changes are analyzed in Debra M. Strauss, *Reaching Out to the International Community: Civil Lawsuits as the Common Ground in the Battle Against Terrorism,* 19 Duke J. Comp. & Int'l L. 307 (2009).

2. *Content of a Cause of Action?* In a portion of the *Gates* decision omitted here, the court ruled that with the enactment of §1605A, "state law no longer controls the nature of the liability and damages that may be sought when it is a foreign government that is sued: Congress has provided the 'specific source of law' for recovery.... State-law claims for damages are not available against a foreign state that has engaged in state-sponsored terrorism." 580 F. Supp. 2d at 66. Moreover, said the court, "federal courts should look to the Restatement (Second) of Torts, and not state law, to provide content to Congress's express intentions." *Id.* at 66 n.9.

Does §1605A now embrace the full breadth of common law secondary liability, as described by the *Restatement*, as well as all other aspects of the *Restatement*'s account of the common law, or is it narrower? *Cf. Boim III, supra* (rejecting common law secondary liability under the ATA).

3. *Who May Sue?* Section 1605A(a)(2)(A)(ii) provides that a court may hear a suit in which the plaintiff is either "(I) a national of the United States; (II) a member of the armed forces; or (III) otherwise an employee of the Government of the United States, or of an individual performing a contract awarded by the United States Government, acting within the scope of the employee's employment." Does this leave any recourse in U.S. courts for injured aliens, other than government contractors, against state supporters of terrorism?

4. *Who May Be Sued?* A state's support for terrorism is expressed through the actions of its agencies and officials, as noted by the *Gates* court in considerable detail (mostly omitted here). Indeed, the suspension of sovereign immunity is dependent upon the commission of an "act or provision of material support or resources . . . by an official, employee, or agent of such foreign state while acting within the scope of his or her office, employment, or agency." 28 U.S.C. §1605A(a)(1).

But liability under §1605A extends not only to states but also to "any official, employee, or agent of that foreign state while acting within the scope of his or her office, employment, or agency." *Id.* §1605A(c). Over the years judgments against such officials have mounted up. A state is also vicariously liable for the acts of its officials, employees, or agents. *Id.*

Each element of the FSIA exception must be satisfied, however. In one recent decision, the court dismissed civil claims for damages against four Saudi princes and a Saudi government agency arising from the 9/11 terrorist attacks. *In re Terrorist Attacks on September 11, 2001,* 538 F.3d 71 (2d Cir. 2008). While the four princes and the government agency were found to be acting in their official government capacity, the claims did not come within the §1605A terrorism exception to sovereign immunity because Saudi Arabia was not designated as a state sponsor of terrorism.

However, §1605A's extension of the FSIA's terrorism exception to foreign state officials may now have been rendered superfluous by the U.S. Supreme Court's decision in *Samantar v. Yousuf,* 130 S. Ct. 2278 (2010), holding that foreign officials — even when acting in their official capacity — are not equivalent to "foreign states" and are therefore not entitled to immunity under the FSIA. *See id.* at 2289 ("Reading the FSIA as a whole, there is nothing to suggest we should read 'foreign state' in §1603(a) to include an official acting on behalf of the foreign state, and much to indicate that this meaning was not what Congress enacted."). The Court left open the possibility that such officials may be "entitled to immunity under the common law," *id.* at 2292-2293, and it remanded the case on that basis.

5. *Whose Policy?* The government strongly opposed the passage of §1605(a)(7) in 1996. *See, e.g., Price v. Socialist People's Libyan Arab Jamahiriya,* 294 F.3d 82, 89 (D.C. Cir. 2002) ("such legislation . . . had been consistently resisted by the executive branch."). In an amicus brief in *Cicippio, supra,* the government expressed the same opposition, arguing that "the imposition of liability for acts of state sponsored terrorism is an area of law with serious ramifications for the United States Government's conduct of foreign affairs." Brief for the United States as amicus curiae, at 4. Can you identify some of those ramifications?

In the Emergency Wartime Supplemental Appropriations Act (EWSAA), Pub. L. No. 108-11, 117 Stat. 559 (2003), Congress partly yielded, providing that:

> The President may suspend the application of any provision of the Iraq Sanctions Act of 1990: . . . *Provided further,* That the President may make inapplicable with respect to Iraq section 620A of the Foreign Assistance Act of 1961 *or any other provision of law that applies to countries that have supported terrorism.* . . . [117 Stat. 579 (emphasis added).]

The President promptly used this authority to suspend the terrorism exception to the FSIA with respect to Iraq. In *Republic of Iraq v. Beaty,* 129 S. Ct. 2183 (2009), the Supreme Court turned back a challenge to this waiver, explaining:

> To a layperson, the notion of the President's suspending the operation of a valid law might seem strange. But the practice is well established, at least in the sphere of foreign affairs. *See United States v. Curtiss-Wright Export Corp.,* 299 U.S. 304, 322-324 (1936) (canvassing precedents from as early as the "inception of the national government"). The granting of Presidential waiver authority is particularly apt with respect to congressional elimination of foreign sovereign immunity, since the granting or denial of that immunity was historically the case-by-case prerogative of the Executive Branch. *See, e.g., Ex parte Peru,* 318 U.S. 578, 586-590 (1943). It is entirely unremarkable that Congress, having taken upon itself in the FSIA to "free the Government" from the diplomatic pressures engendered by the case-by-case approach, *Verlinden* [*B.V. v. Central Bank of Nigeria,* 461 U.S. 480 (1983)], at 488, would nonetheless think it prudent to afford the President some flexibility in unique circumstances such as these. [*Id.* at 2189.]

Based on the statutory language we italicized in the excerpt from the EWSAA above, could ESWAA be read to permit the President to, say, suspend limits on funding for the ongoing war in Iraq, in order to afford him "some flexibility in unique circumstances such as these"? What is the significance of the Court's declaration, citing *Curtiss-Wright Export Corp.,* that "courts ought to be especially wary of overriding apparent statutory text supported by executive interpretation in favor of speculation about a law's true purpose"? *Id.* at 2191.

An earlier case presenting serious separation of powers issues, *Roeder v. Islamic Republic of Iran,* 333 F.3d 228 (D.C. Cir. 2003), involved a suit by hostages seized by Iran at the U.S. embassy in Tehran in 1979. The United States was allowed to intervene as a matter of right. The government argued, successfully, that §1605(a)(7) did not abrogate an existing executive agreement that barred claims against Iran arising out of the hostage taking. (The executive agreement was upheld in *Dames & Moore v. Regan,* 453 U.S. 654 (1981).)

These cases raise difficult questions about the wisdom of private tort litigation against international terrorism and its relation to an effective counterterrorism policy. Which branch of government should resolve such questions?

6. *Personal Jurisdiction over State Sponsors.* Private suits against state sponsors of terrorism have resulted in large, mostly default judgments against the defendant states and their officials. By 2008, awards in such cases totaled more than $19 billion, an amount far in excess of defendant states' assets within the jurisdiction of U.S. courts. *See* Elsea, *supra* p. 839, at 2. The financial stakes, in other words, are very high, as are the diplomatic ones.

If you represented the government of a defendant state in such a suit, what objections might you raise to the court's assertion of personal jurisdiction over your client?

Does a foreign government have Due Process rights under the U.S. Constitution? The *Flatow* court, comparing immunity from suit to the liberty interests protected by the Fifth Amendment, declared, "Foreign sovereign immunity, both under the common law and now under the FSIA, has always been a matter of grace and comity rather than a matter of right under United States law." 999 F. Supp. at 21. The court went on the suggest that "even if a foreign state is accorded the status of a 'person' for the purposes of Constitutional Due Process analysis, a foreign state that sponsors terrorist activities which causes the death or personal injury of a United States national will invariably have sufficient contacts with the United States to satisfy Due Process." *Id.* at 23. The issues are explored in Lee M. Caplan, *The Constitution and Jurisdiction Over Foreign States: The 1996 Amendment to the Foreign Sovereign Immunities Act in Perspective*, 41 Va. J. Int'l L. 369 (2001); Joseph W. Glannon & Jeffrey Atik, *Politics and Personal Jurisdiction: Suing State Sponsors of Terrorism Under the 1996 Amendments to the Foreign Sovereign Immunities Act*, 87 Geo. L.J. 675 (1999).

7. *Goosey Gander: Suits Against the United States for Its Alleged Sponsorship of Terrorism.* Before passage of the terrorism exception to FSIA in 1996, "Executive branch officials feared that the proposed amendment to FSIA might cause other nations to respond in kind, thus potentially subjecting the American government to suits in foreign countries for actions taken in the United States." *Price, supra*, 294 F.3d at 89. Their fears may have been justified.

> At least two of the states affected by the FSIA exception appear to have enacted legislation allowing their citizens to file suit against the United States for violations of human rights or interference in their countries' internal affairs. Cuba reportedly allows such suits for violations of human rights; and at least two judgments assessing billions of dollars in damages against the U.S. have apparently been handed down.
>
> Iran reportedly has authorized suit against foreign States for intervention in the internal affairs of the country and for terrorist activities resulting in the death, injury, or financial loss of Iranian nationals; and at least one judgment for half a billion dollars has been handed down against the United States. [Elsea, *supra*, at 66.]

Should the prospect of such retaliation influence courts' interpretation of domestic law?

C. COLLECTING THE JUDGMENT

Getting a judicial award for damages resulting from a terrorist act is one thing. Getting paid may be quite another. If assets belonging to a terrorist or his supporter can be located, of course, those assets are in principle subject to attachment to satisfy a judgment. *See generally* Jack D. Smith & Gregory J. Cooper, *Disrupting Terrorist Financing with Civil Litigation*, 41 Case W. Res. J. Intl'l L. 65, 68-72 (2009).

But successful plaintiffs have been frustrated in efforts to collect on their judgements when defendants' assets were blocked or even confiscated by the U.S. government. Recall that various resolutions of the U.N. Security Council, *supra* pp. 793-797, as well as the International Convention for the Suppression of the Financing of Terrorism, *supra* p. 800, require the freezing or seizure of terrorists' assets. The President has blocked or seized such assets under authority provided by the International Economic Emergency Powers Act (IEEPA), *supra* p. 813, and the Trading With the Enemy Act, 50 U.S.C. App. §§1-39, 41-44 (2006).

Suits against Iran and Cuba, for example, have resulted in very large judgments against both states. Both Iran and Cuba had substantial assets in the United States, yet those assets were either blocked by the Treasury Department or otherwise held by the U.S. government. With one modest exception the President refused to release them. Not surprisingly, the President's actions have been extremely controversial.

Congress acted in 1998 to make the blocked assets available to satisfy the judgments, but it also authorized the President to continue blocking in the interest of "national security," and the President immediately did so. *See* Presidential Determination No. 99-1, *Determination to Waive Requirements Relating to Blocked Property of Terrorist-List States*, 63 Fed. Reg. 59201 (Oct. 21, 1998). Two years later, Congress passed the Victims of Trafficking and Violence Protection Act of 2000, Pub. L. No. 106-386, §§2002-2003, 114 Stat. 1464, 1541-1546 (2000), directing the Treasury Secretary to pay compensatory damage awards in certain final and pending suits against Iran and Cuba out of blocked assets and other funds held by the government. The President then released Iranian and Cuban assets worth more than $476 million to make those payments. 65 Fed. Reg. 70,382 (Nov. 22, 2000) and 65 Fed. Reg. 78,533 (Dec. 15, 2000). In 2002, Congress acted yet again to add to the list of cases for which compensatory damage awards could be paid out of blocked assets. Pub. L. No. 107-228, §686, 116 Stat. 1350, 1411 (2002).

Subsequently, in late 2002, Congress passed and President Bush signed into law the Terrorism Risk Insurance Act, Pub. L. No. 107-297, 116 Stat. 2322. That Act includes the following provision:

> Notwithstanding any other provision of law, and except as provided in subsection (b), in every case in which a person has obtained a judgment against a terrorist party on a claim based upon an act of terrorism, or for which a terrorist party is not immune under section 1605(a)(7) of title 28, United States Code, the blocked assets of that terrorist party (including the blocked assets of any agency or instrumentality of that terrorist party) shall be subject to execution or attachment in aid of execution in order to satisfy such judgment to the extent of any compensatory damages for which such terrorist party has been adjudged liable. [*Id.* §201(a), 116 Stat. 2337.]

Subsection (b) states that the President may waive this provision "in the national security interest" to prevent the attachment of embassies and other properties subject to the Vienna Convention on Diplomatic Relations or the Vienna Convention on Consular Relations.

Nevertheless, immediately after the invasion of Iraq in 2003 President Bush confiscated and vested title in the United States to frozen Iraqi assets worth some $1.73 billion, changing them from "blocked" assets to U.S. assets, and preventing their attachment to satisfy judgments for Iraq's earlier support of terrorism. The confiscated assets were to be used, according to the President, in the postwar reconstruction of Iraq. Exec. Order No. 13,290, 68 Fed. Reg. 14,307 (Mar. 20, 2003). Congress then passed yet another measure allowing the President to bar attachments of Iraqi property. Pub. L. No. 108-11, §1503, 117 Stat. 559, 579 (2003).

The 2008 National Defense Authorization Act (NDAA) extensively amended 28 U.S.C. §1610, the FSIA provision for exceptions to immunity from attachment or execution. New §1610(g)(1) exposes to attachment most property in which a foreign state has an interest, when that state has a judgment entered against it under §1605A. Moreover, such property may be attached even though it is "regulated" under the IEEPA or the Trading with the Enemy Act. 28 U.S.C. §1610(g)(2). On the other hand, NDAA §1083(d)(1) gives the President authority to "waive any provision of this section with respect to Iraq" if the President determines that:

(A) the waiver is in the national security interest of the United States;
(B) the waiver will promote the reconstruction of, the consolidation of democracy in, and the relations of the United States with, Iraq; and
(C) Iraq continues to be a reliable ally of the United States and partner in combating acts of international terrorism.

Thus, the President's ability to bar the attachment of Iraqi assets was preserved. When a suit is filed under the new law, §1605A(g) automatically creates a *lis pendens* lien covering all of the defendant's real and personal property subject to attachment that is within the jurisdiction of the court. *See* Elsea, *supra*, at 50-54.

This dizzying political back-and-forth parallels efforts by the executive branch to dissuade courts from awarding judgments against state supporters of terrorism, as noted above. The history of competing efforts by the two political branches, often played out in the courts, is traced in Elsea, *supra*.

NOTES AND QUESTIONS

1. *A Disagreement About Tactics.* Does it strike you as odd that Congress has sought compensation for victims of terrorists from their state supporters, while the President has persistently thwarted the victims' efforts to collect on their judgments? In the case of Iraqi assets, the Administration wanted to use those resources to help rebuild the war-torn state, as noted above. Concerning other states' blocked assets, Presidents Clinton and Bush indicated that persons other than the successful litigants also had meritorious claims that needed to be satisfied (for example, exiled Cubans whose property was confiscated by Fidel Castro), and that the blocked assets served as a powerful diplomatic tool in negotiations with the state owners. How should these concerns be weighed against the need to bring some measure of justice to terrorists' victims, or against a broader counterterrorism policy? Who should decide national priorities in allocating such assets? Can you describe a program that would accommodate the concerns of both political branches?

2. *Which Property Is Subject to Attachment?* The FSIA provides that assets of a foreign state "used for a commercial activity in the United States" may be attached if "the judgment relates to a claim for which the foreign state is not immune under section 1605A, regardless of whether the property is or was involved with the act upon which the claim is based," 28 U.S.C. §1610(a)(7), and that "any property in the United

States of an agency or instrumentality of a foreign state engaged in commercial activity in the United States" may be attached to satisfy such a judgment. *Id.* §1610(b). New §1610(g)(1) broadened the universe of exposed assets to include most property in which the foreign state has any interest, as noted above.

In *Ministry of Defense & Support for the Armed Forces of the Islamic Republic of Iran v. Elahi,* 556 U.S. 366 (2009), a successful plaintiff in a suit against Iran under 28 U.S.C. §1605(a)(7) and the Flatow Amendment sought to attach an arbitration award obtained by Iran's Ministry of Defense against a third party in separate litigation. The Iranian Ministry of Defense claimed that it was not an "agency or instrumentality" of the state, whose property would be subject to attachment if the "state engaged in commercial activity in the United States," 28 U.S.C. §1610(b), but was instead an integral part of the state, whose property could be attached only if that property sought to be attached were "used for a commercial activity in the United States." *Id.* §1610(a). Avoiding the dispute over which part of §1610 applied, the Supreme Court ruled that the arbitration award was not (based on facts set out in the opinion) a "blocked asset" under the Terrorism Risk Insurance Act, *supra,* but that the plaintiff waived his right to attach that award when he earlier accepted a pro rata payment under the Victims of Trafficking and Violence Protection Act of 2000, *supra.*

Constitution of the United States

Appendix

We the People of the United States, in Order to form a more perfect Union, establish Justice, insure domestic Tranquility, provide for the common defence, promote the general Welfare, and secure the Blessings of Liberty to ourselves and our Posterity, do ordain and establish this Constitution for the United States of America.

Article I

Section 1. All legislative Powers herein granted shall be vested in a Congress of the United States, which shall consist of a Senate and House of Representatives.

Section 2. The House of Representatives shall be composed of Members chosen every second Year by the People of the several States, and the Electors in each State shall have the Qualifications requisite for Electors of the most numerous Branch of the State Legislature. . . .

The House of Representatives shall chuse their Speaker and other Officers; and shall have the sole Power of Impeachment.

Section 3. The Senate of the United States shall be composed of two Senators from each State, [chosen by the Legislature thereof,][1] for six Years; and each Senator shall have one Vote. . . .

The Senate shall have the sole Power to try all Impeachments. When sitting for that Purpose, they shall be on Oath or Affirmation. When the President of the United States is tried, the Chief Justice shall preside: And no Person shall be convicted without the Concurrence of two thirds of the Members present.

Judgment in Cases of Impeachment shall not extend further than to removal from Office, and disqualification to hold and enjoy any Office of honor, Trust or Profit under the United States: but the Party convicted shall nevertheless be liable and subject to Indictment, Trial, Judgment and Punishment, according to Law.

Section 4. The Times, Places and Manner of holding Elections for Senators and Representatives, shall be prescribed in each State by the Legislature thereof; but the

---

1. Changed by the Seventeenth Amendment to read "elected by the people thereof."

Congress may at any time by Law make or alter such Regulations, except as to the Places of chusing Senators.

The Congress shall assemble at least once in every Year, and such Meeting shall [be on the first Monday in December,][2] unless they shall by Law appoint a different Day.

Section 5. . . . Each House shall keep a Journal of its Proceedings, and from time to time publish the same, excepting such Parts as may in their Judgment require Secrecy; and the Yeas and Nays of the Members of either House on any question shall, at the Desire of one fifth of those Present, be entered on the Journal. . . .

Section 6. The Senators and Representatives shall receive a Compensation for their Services, to be ascertained by Law, and paid out of the Treasury of the United States. They shall in all Cases, except Treason, Felony and Breach of the Peace, be privileged from Arrest during their Attendance at the Session of their respective Houses, and in going to and returning from the same; and for any Speech or Debate in either House, they shall not be questioned in any other Place.

. . . [N]o Person holding any Office under the United States, shall be a Member of either House during his Continuance in Office.

Section 7. All Bills for raising Revenue shall originate in the House of Representatives; but the Senate may propose or concur with amendments as on other Bills.

Every Bill which shall have passed the House of Representatives and the Senate, shall, before it becomes a Law, be presented to the President of the United States; If he approve he shall sign it, but if not he shall return it, with his Objections to that House in which it shall have originated, who shall enter the Objections at large on their Journal, and proceed to reconsider it. If after such Reconsideration two thirds of that House shall agree to pass the Bill, it shall be sent, together with the Objections, to the other House, by which it shall likewise be reconsidered, and if approved by two thirds of that House, it shall become a Law. . . . If any Bill shall not be returned by the President within ten Days (Sundays excepted) after it shall have been presented to him, the Same shall be a Law, in like Manner as if he had signed it, unless the Congress by their Adjournment prevent its Return, in which Case it shall not be a Law.

Every Order, Resolution, or Vote to which the Concurrence of the Senate and House of Representatives may be necessary (except on a question of Adjournment) shall be presented to the President of the United States; and before the Same shall take Effect, shall be approved by him, or being disapproved by him, shall be repassed by two thirds of the Senate and House of Representatives, according to the Rules and Limitations prescribed in the Case of a Bill.

Section 8. [1] The Congress shall have Power To lay and collect Taxes, Duties, Imposts and Excises, to pay the Debts and provide for the common Defence and general Welfare of the United States; but all Duties, Imposts and Excises shall be uniform throughout the United States;

---

2. Changed by section 2 of the Twentieth Amendment to read "begin at noon on the 3d day of January."

[2] To borrow Money on the credit of the United States;

[3] To regulate Commerce with foreign Nations, and among the several States, and with the Indian Tribes;

[4] To establish an uniform Rule of Naturalization . . . ;

[9] To constitute Tribunals inferior to the supreme Court;

[10] To define and punish Piracies and Felonies committed on the high Seas, and Offences against the Law of Nations;

[11] To declare War, grant Letters of Marque and Reprisal, and make Rules concerning Captures on Land and Water;

[12] To raise and support Armies, but no Appropriation of Money to that Use shall be for a longer Term than two Years;

[13] To provide and maintain a Navy;

[14] To make Rules for the Government and Regulation of the land and naval Forces;

[15] To provide for calling forth the Militia to execute the Laws of the Union, suppress Insurrections and repel Invasions;

[16] To provide for organizing, arming, and disciplining, the Militia, and for governing such Part of them as may be employed in the Service of the United States, reserving to the States respectively, the Appointment of the Officers, and the Authority of training the Militia according to the discipline prescribed by Congress; . . .

[18] To make all Laws which shall be necessary and proper for carrying into Execution the foregoing Powers, and all other Powers vested by this Constitution in the Government of the United States, or in any Department or Officer thereof.

Section 9. . . . [2] The Privilege of the Writ of Habeas Corpus shall not be suspended, unless when in Cases of Rebellion or Invasion the public Safety may require it.

[3] No Bill of Attainder or ex post facto Law shall be passed. . . .

[7] No Money shall be drawn from the Treasury, but in Consequence of Appropriations made by Law; and a regular Statement and Account of the Receipts and Expenditures of all public Money shall be published from time to time.

[8] No Title of Nobility shall be granted by the United States: And no Person holding any Office of Profit or Trust under them, shall, without the Consent of the Congress, accept of any present, Emolument, Office, or Title, of any kind whatever, from any King, Prince, or foreign State.

Section 10. [1] No State shall enter into any Treaty, Alliance, or Confederation; grant Letters of Marque and Reprisal; coin Money; emit Bills of Credit; make any Thing but gold and silver Coin a Tender in Payment of Debts; pass any Bill of Attainder, ex post facto Law, or Law impairing the Obligation of Contracts, or grant any Title of Nobility. . . .

[3] No State shall, without the Consent of Congress, lay any Duty of Tonnage, keep Troops, or Ships of War in time of Peace, enter into any Agreement or Compact with another State, or with a foreign Power, or engage in War, unless actually invaded, or in such imminent Danger as will not admit of delay.

Article II

Section 1. The executive Power shall be vested in a President of the United States of America. He shall hold his Office during the Term of four Years, and, together with the Vice President, chosen for the same Term, be elected, as follows . . .

Before he enter on the Execution of his Office, he shall take the following Oath or Affirmation: — "I do solemnly swear (or affirm) that I will faithfully execute the Office of President of the United States, and will to the best of my Ability, preserve, protect and defend the Constitution of the United States."

Section 2. The President shall be Commander in Chief of the Army and Navy of the United States, and of the Militia of the several States, when called into the actual Service of the United States; he may require the Opinion, in writing, of the principal Officer in each of the executive Departments, upon any Subject relating to the Duties of their respective Offices, and he shall have Power to grant Reprieves and Pardons for Offences against the United States, except in Cases of Impeachment.

He shall have Power, by and with the Advice and Consent of the Senate, to make Treaties, provided two thirds of the Senators present concur; and he shall nominate, and by and with the Advice and Consent of the Senate, shall appoint Ambassadors, other public Ministers and Consuls, Judges of the supreme Court, and all other Officers of the United States, whose Appointments are not herein otherwise provided for, and which shall be established by Law: but the Congress may by Law vest the Appointment of such inferior Officers, as they think proper, in the President alone, in the Courts of Law, or in the Heads of Departments. . . .

Section 3. He shall from time to time give to the Congress Information of the State of the Union, and recommend to their Consideration such Measures as he shall judge necessary and expedient; he may, on extraordinary Occasions, convene both Houses, or either of them, and in Case of Disagreement between them, with Respect to the Time of Adjournment, he may adjourn them to such Time as he shall think proper; he shall receive Ambassadors and other public Ministers; he shall take Care that the Laws be faithfully executed, and shall Commission all the Officers of the United States.

Section 4. The President, Vice President and all civil Officers of the United States, shall be removed from Office on Impeachment for, and Conviction of, Treason, Bribery, or other high Crimes and Misdemeanors.

Article III

Section 1. The judicial Power of the United States, shall be vested in one supreme Court, and in such inferior Courts as the Congress may from time to time ordain and establish. The Judges, both of the supreme and inferior Courts, shall hold their Offices during good Behaviour, and shall, at stated Times, receive for their Services, a Compensation, which shall not be diminished during their Continuance in Office.

Section 2. The judicial Power shall extend to all Cases, in Law and Equity, arising under this Constitution, the Laws of the United States, and Treaties made, or which shall be made, under their Authority; — to all Cases affecting Ambassadors, other public Ministers and Consuls; — to all Cases of admiralty and maritime Jurisdiction; — to Controversies to which the United States shall be a Party; — to Controversies between two or more States; — [between a State and Citizens of another State; —] between Citizens of different States, — between Citizens of the same State claiming Lands under Grants of different States, [and between a State, or the Citizens thereof, and foreign States, Citizens or Subjects.]³

In all Cases affecting Ambassadors, other public Ministers and Consuls, and those in which a State shall be Party, the supreme Court shall have original Jurisdiction. In all the other Cases before mentioned, the supreme Court shall have appellate Jurisdiction, both as to Law and Fact, with such Exceptions, and under such Regulations as the Congress shall make. . . .

Section 3. Treason against the United States, shall consist only in levying War against them, or in adhering to their Enemies, giving them Aid and Comfort. No Person shall be convicted of Treason unless on the Testimony of two Witnesses to the same overt Act, or on Confession in open Court.

The Congress shall have Power to declare the Punishment of Treason, but no Attainder of Treason shall work Corruption of Blood, or Forfeiture except during the Life of the Person attainted.

Article IV . . .

Section 4. The United States shall guarantee to every State in this Union a Republican Form of Government, and shall protect each of them against Invasion; and on Application of the Legislature, or of the Executive (when the Legislature cannot be convened) against domestic Violence. . . .

Article VI . . .

This Constitution, and the Laws of the United States which shall be made in Pursuance thereof; and all Treaties made, or which shall be made, under the Authority of the United States, shall be the supreme Law of the Land; and the Judges in every State shall be bound thereby, any Thing in the Constitution or Laws of any State to the Contrary notwithstanding.

The Senators and Representatives before mentioned, and the Members of the several State Legislatures, and all executive and judicial Officers, both of the United States and of the several States, shall be bound by Oath or Affirmation, to support this Constitution; . . . .

---

3. The bracketed material in this section is changed by the Eleventh Amendment.

AMENDMENTS TO THE CONSTITUTION OF THE UNITED STATES OF AMERICA

Amendment I

Congress shall make no law respecting an establishment of religion, or prohibiting the free exercise thereof; or abridging the freedom of speech, or of the press, or the right of the people peaceably to assemble, and to petition the Government for a redress of grievances.

Amendment II

A well regulated Militia, being necessary to the security of a free State, the right of the people to keep and bear Arms, shall not be infringed.

Amendment III

No Soldier shall, in time of peace be quartered in any house, without the consent of the Owner, nor in time of war, but in a manner to be prescribed by law.

Amendment IV

The right of the people to be secure in their persons, houses, papers, and effects, against unreasonable searches and seizures, shall not be violated, and no Warrants shall issue, but upon probable cause, supported by Oath or affirmation, and particularly describing the place to be searched, and the persons or things to be seized.

Amendment V

No person shall be held to answer for a capital, or otherwise infamous crime, unless on a presentment or indictment of a Grand Jury, except in cases arising in the land or naval forces, or in the Militia, when in actual service in time of War or public danger; nor shall any person be subject for the same offence to be twice put in jeopardy of life or limb, nor shall be compelled in any criminal case to be a witness against himself, nor be deprived of life, liberty, or property, without due process of law; nor shall private property be taken for public use without just compensation.

Amendment VI

In all criminal prosecutions, the accused shall enjoy the right to a speedy and public trial, by an impartial jury of the State and district wherein the crime shall have been committed; which district shall have been previously ascertained by law, and to be informed of the nature and cause of the accusation; to be confronted with the witnesses against him; to have compulsory process for obtaining witnesses in his favor, and to have the assistance of counsel for his defence....

Amendment VIII

Excessive bail shall not be required, nor excessive fines imposed, nor cruel and unusual punishments inflicted.

Amendment IX

The enumeration in the Constitution of certain rights shall not be construed to deny or disparage others retained by the people.

Amendment X

The powers not delegated to the United States by the Constitution, nor prohibited by it to the States, are reserved to the States respectively, or to the people....

Amendment XIV

Section 1. All persons born or naturalized in the United States and subject to the jurisdiction thereof, are citizens of the United States and of the State wherein they reside. No State shall make or enforce any law which shall abridge the privileges or immunities of citizens of the United States; nor shall any State deprive any person of life, liberty, or property, without due process of law; nor deny to any person within its jurisdiction the equal protection of the laws....

Table of Cases

Index